macquarie
budget
dictionary

macquarie
budget
dictionary

Published by Macquarie Dictionary Publishers, an imprint of
Pan Macmillan Australia Pty Ltd
1 Market Street, Sydney, New South Wales, Australia 2000

Copyright © Macquarie Dictionary Publishers, 2024

First published 1985
This edition published 2024

ISBN: 9781761562754

Cover design: Natalie Bowra
Typeset by Macmillan Publishing Solutions, Bangalore-25

Printed by IVE

A Cataloguing-in-Publication entry is available from the
National Library of Australia

http://catalogue.nla.gov.au

contents

explanatory notes

The entry

All information within one complete entry has been arranged for the convenience of the user. In general, information about spelling and pronunciation comes first, meanings next, then run-on headwords, and usage notes last.

Headword

The headword is the word or words which are being defined in a particular entry; it appears in large bold-face type at the left, slightly farther into the left margin than the usual line of text.

Separate entries are made for all words which, although spelt identically, are of quite distinct derivation; in such cases, each headword is followed by a small superscript number, as in, for example, **gum**[1] and **gum**[2]. Entries are arranged under headwords in strict alphabetical order. A particular headword can be located by taking each successive letter of the headword in alphabetical order, ignoring hyphens, apostrophes and word spaces.

Variant spellings

Definitions always appear under the most common spelling of a word. Less common variants cross-refer to the main headword. For example, the word **cipher** has a variant **cypher** which appears as a headword followed by → **cipher** to show that the entry is at the main spelling **cipher**.

Pronunciation

The pronunciation, where given, follows the headword within slant brackets. It is given in the International Phonetic Alphabet, for which a guide may be found on pages viii and ix.

Parts of speech

The pronunciation is usually followed by an abbreviation in italics which indicates the part of speech of the headword, such as *n.* (noun) and *adj.* (adjective).

If the headword is used in more than one grammatical form, the part-of-speech label precedes each set of definitions to which it applies.

Inflected forms

If a headword has irregularly inflected forms (any form not made by the simple addition of the suffix to the main entry), the summary of these forms is given immediately after the relevant part of speech. Regularly inflected forms, not generally shown, include:

1. Nouns forming a plural merely by the addition of *-s* or *-es*, such as **dog** (**dogs**) or **class** (**classes**);
2. Verbs forming the past tense by adding *-ed*, such as **halt** (**halted**);
3. Verbs forming the present tense by adding *-s* or *-es*, such as **talk** (**talks**) or **smash** (**smashes**);
4. Verbs forming the present participle by adding *-ing*, such as **walk** (**walking**);
5. Verbs which drop *-e* before an inflection is added, such as **save** (**saved**, **saving**);

6. Adjectives forming the comparative and superlative by adding *-er*, *-est*, such as **black** (**blacker**, **blackest**).

Regular forms are given, however, when necessary for clarity or the avoidance of confusion.

The past tense, past participle and present participle are given as the inflected forms of verbs; where, as commonly happens, the past tense and past participle are the same in form, this form is shown once. For example, the inflected forms indicated for **put** are **put**, **putting**, where **put** is both the past tense and past participle.

Restrictive labels

Entries that are limited in usage as to the level of style, region, time or subject, are marked with such labels as *Informal*, *US*, *Law*, etc.

If the restrictive label applies to the entire entry, it appears before the definition(s) at the beginning of the entry. If however the restrictive label applies to only one grammatical form, it appears after that part-of-speech label to which it applies and before the definition(s). If the restrictive label applies to only one definition, it appears before that definition, after the definition number.

Some headwords are marked with the restrictive label *taboo*. This indicates that the word itself may give offence essentially because of its taboo nature. This label is also used if there is a particularly crass and offensive meaning given to a usually neutral word. Taboo words are to be differentiated from words which are intended to denigrate another person, which are labelled *derog.* (for *derogatory*). Some words can attract a combination of these restrictive labels.

Definitions

Definitions are individually numbered; numbers appear in a single sequence which does not begin afresh with each grammatical form. In some cases in which two definitions are very closely related, usually within the same field of information, they are marked with letters of the alphabet under the same definition number.

Secondary headwords

Idiomatic phrases, prepositional phrases, etc., are placed at the entry for the key word, and are listed, in bold-face type, alphabetically at the end of the entry following the label *phr.* (for *phrase*).

Cross-referencing

There are several forms of cross-referencing in this dictionary. The arrow → indicates that the headword which precedes it is not defined in this place but that a suitable definition is to be found under the headword which follows the arrow.

The word 'See' directs the reader to information relevant to the current definition but to be found within a different part of the dictionary.

The word 'Compare' is similar in function but limited to those cases where the information is in some way complementary or matching.

Run-on headwords

Words which are derivatives of the headword and which are simple extensions of the meaning are run on after the last definition in the entry. Such headwords appear in bold-face type followed by an indication of their part of speech.

pronunciation guide

Vowels

i	as in 'peat'	/pit/
ɪ	as in 'pit'	/pɪt/
ɛ	as in 'pet'	/pɛt/
æ	as in 'pat'	/pæt/
a	as in 'part'	/pat/
ɒ	as in 'pot'	/pɒt/
ʌ	as in 'putt'	/pʌt/
ɔ	as in 'port'	/pɔt/
ʊ	as in 'put'	/pʊt/
u	as in 'pool'	/pul/
ɜ	as in 'pert'	/pɜt/
ə	as in 'apart'	/ə'pat/
ɒ̃	as in 'bon voyage'	/bɒ̃ vwa'jaʒ/

Diphthongs

aɪ	as in 'buy'	/baɪ/
eɪ	as in 'bay'	/beɪ/
ɔɪ	as in 'boy'	/bɔɪ/
aʊ	as in 'how'	/haʊ/
oʊ	as in 'hoe'	/hoʊ/
ɪə	as in 'here'	/hɪə/
ɛə	as in 'hair'	/hɛə/
ʊə	as in 'tour'	/tʊə/

Stress

Primary stress:	'	as in 'clatter'	/'klætə/
Secondary stress:	ˌ	as in 'encyclopedia'	/ɛnˌsaɪklə'pidɪə/

Consonants	*Plosives*		
	p	as in 'pet'	/pɛt/
	b	as in 'bet'	/bɛt/
	t	as in 'tale'	/teɪl/
	d	as in 'dale'	/deɪl/
	k	as in 'came'	/keɪm/
	g	as in 'game'	/geɪm/

Fricatives

f	as in 'fine'	/faɪn/
v	as in 'vine'	/vaɪn/
θ	as in 'thin'	/θɪn/
ð	as in 'then'	/ðɛn/
s	as in 'seal'	/sil/
z	as in 'zeal'	/zil/
ʃ	as in 'show'	/ʃoʊ/
ʒ	as in 'pleasure'	/ˈplɛʒə/
h	as in 'heal'	/hil/
r	as in 'real'	/ril/

Affricates

tʃ	as in 'choke'	/tʃoʊk/
dʒ	as in 'joke'	/dʒoʊk/

Nasals

m	as in 'mail'	/meɪl/
n	as in 'nail'	/neɪl/
ŋ	as in 'sing'	/sɪŋ/

Semi-vowels

j	as in 'you'	/ju/
w	as in 'woo'	/wu/

Laterals

l	as in 'love'	/lʌv/

abbreviations used in the dictionary

abbrev.	abbreviation		*Mil.*	Military
ACT	Australian Capital Territory		*Mineral.*	Mineralogy
adj.	adjective		*Myth.*	Mythology
adv.	adverb			
Agric.	Agriculture		N	North, Northern
Anat.	Anatomy		*n.*	noun
Archit.	Architecture		*Naut.*	Nautical
Astron.	Astronomy		*Navig.*	Navigation
Aust.	Australia, Australian		NSW	New South Wales
aux.	auxiliary		NT	Northern Territory
			NZ	New Zealand
Biochem.	Biochemistry			
Biol.	Biology		*Obs.*	Obsolete
Bot.	Botany		*Obsolesc.*	Obsolescent
Brit.	British		*oft.*	often
			orig.	originally
Chem.	Chemistry		*Ornith.*	Ornithology
Colloq.	Colloquial			
conj.	conjunction		*Pathol.*	Pathology
			Pharm.	Pharmacy
def.	definition		*Philos.*	Philosophy
derog.	derogatory		*phr.*	phrase
det.	determiner		*Physiol.*	Physiology
			pl.	plural
E	East, Eastern		*prep.*	preposition
Eccles.	Ecclesiastical		*Psychol.*	Psychology
Ecol.	Ecology			
Econ.	Economics		Qld	Queensland
Educ.	Education			
Elect.	Electricity		S	South, Southern
Eng.	Engineering		SA	South Australia
esp.	especially		*Scot.*	Scottish
			sing.	singular
fol.	followed		*sthn*	southern
			Surg.	Surgery
Geog.	Geography			
Geol.	Geology		US	United States of America
Geom.	Geometry		*usu.*	usually
Govt	Government			
Gram.	Grammar		*v.*	verb
			Vet.	Veterinary
Hist.	History		*v.i.*	intransitive verb
			v.t.	transitive verb
interj.	interjection			
			W	West, Western
Ling.	Linguistics		WA	Western Australia
Lit.	Literature			
			Zool.	Zoology
Maths	Mathematics			
Meteorol.	Meteorology			

A, a

A, a /eɪ/ *n.* **1.** the first letter of the English alphabet. **2.** the first in any series.

a[1] /ə/, *emphatic* /eɪ/ *indefinite article* used especially before nouns beginning with a consonant sound to mean: **1.** some (indefinite singular referring to one individual of a class). **2.** another. **3.** one. **4.** any (a single). **5.** indefinite plural. Also, (*before a vowel sound*), **an.**

a[2] /eɪ/, *weak form* /ə/ *indefinite article* each; every.

a-[1] a prefix, meaning 'on', 'in', 'into', 'to', 'towards', as in *aside*, etc.

a-[2] a prefix, a reduced form of Old English *of*, as in *akin*, *afresh*, *anew*.

a-[3] a prefix indicating: **1.** up, out, or away, as in *arise*, *awake*. **2.** intensified action, as in *abide*, *amaze*.

a-[4] variant of **ab-** before *m*, *p*, and *v*, as in *avert*.

a-[5] variant of **ad-**, used: **1.** before *sc*, *sp*, *st*, as in *ascend*. **2.** in words of French derivation (often with the sense of increase, addition), as in *amass*.

a-[6] a prefix meaning 'not', 'without', 'lacking', used before consonants, as in *amoral*. Also, (*before a vowel or h*), **an-.**

aardvark /ˈɑdvɑk/ *n.* a large, nocturnal, burrowing mammal of Africa.

ab- a prefix meaning 'off', 'away', 'from', as in *abduct*, *abjure*.

aback /əˈbæk/ *phr.* **taken aback**, suddenly disconcerted.

abacus /ˈæbəkəs/ *n.* (*pl.* **-ci** /-sɪ/ *or* **-cuses**) a contrivance for calculating, consisting of beads or balls strung on wires or rods set in a frame.

abalone /æbəˈloʊni/ *n.* (*pl.* **-lone** *or* **-lones**) a type of shellfish, the flesh of which is used for food and the shell for ornaments.

abandon[1] /əˈbændən/ *v.t.* **1.** to leave completely and finally; forsake utterly; desert. **2.** to give up (something begun) without finishing.

abandon[2] /əˈbændən/ *n.* a giving up to natural impulses; freedom from constraint or conventionality.

abase /əˈbeɪs/ *v.t.* to reduce or lower, as in rank, office, estimation; humble; degrade.

abashed /əˈbæʃt/ *adj.* embarrassed; mortified.

abate /əˈbeɪt/ *v.t.* **1.** to reduce in amount, intensity, etc.; lessen. **2.** *Law* to put an end to or suppress (a nuisance); suspend or extinguish (an action); annul (a writ). –*v.i.* **3.** to decrease or become less in strength or violence.

abattoir /ˈæbətwɑ, -tɔ/ *n.* a building or place where animals are slaughtered for food. Also, **abattoirs.**

abbess /ˈæbɛs/ *n.* the female superior of a convent.

abbey /ˈæbi/ *n.* (*pl.* **-beys**) the religious body or establishment under an abbot or abbess; a monastery or convent.

abbot /ˈæbət/ *n.* the head or superior of a monastery.

abbreviate /əˈbrivieɪt/ *v.t.* to make brief; make shorter by contraction or omission. –**abbreviator**, *n.* –**abbreviation**, *n.*

abdicate /ˈæbdəkeɪt/ *v.i.* to renounce a throne or some claim; relinquish a right, power, or trust. –**abdication**, *n.*

abdomen /ˈæbdəmən, əbˈdoʊmən/ *n.* that part of the body of a mammal between the thorax and the pelvis; the belly. –**abdominal**, *adj.*

abduct /əbˈdʌkt, æb-/ *v.t.* to carry off surreptitiously or by force, especially to kidnap. –**abduction**, *n.*

aberrant /ˈæbərənt, əˈbɛrənt/ *adj.* **1.** straying from the right or usual course. **2.** deviating from the ordinary or normal type.

aberration /æbəˈreɪʃən/ *n.* **1.** a lapse from a sound mental state. **2.** a momentary departure from a usual practice. **3.** deviation from truth or moral rectitude.

abet /əˈbɛt/ *v.t.* (**abetted, abetting**) to encourage or countenance by aid or approval (used chiefly in a bad sense). –**abetment**, *n.* –**abetter**; *Law*, **abettor**, *n.*

abeyance /əˈbeɪəns/ *n.* temporary inactivity or suspension.

abhor /əbˈhɔ/ *v.t.* (**-horred, -horring**) to regard with repugnance; loathe or abominate.

abhorrent /əbˈhɒrənt/ *adj.* **1.** (fol. by *to*) utterly opposed. **2.** exciting horror; detestable. –**abhorrence**, *n.*

abide /əˈbaɪd/ *v.* (**abided** *or*, *Archaic*, **abode** /əˈboʊd/, **abiding**) –*v.t.* **1.** to put up with; tolerate. –*v.i.* **2.** *Archaic or Poetic* to remain; continue; stay. –*phr.* **3. abide by, a.** to accept and continue to observe (an undertaking, promise, agreement, rule, law, etc.) **b.** to stand by: *to abide by a friend.* **c.** to await or accept the consequences of: *to abide by the decision.*

ability /əˈbɪləti/ *n.* (*pl.* **-ties**) power or capacity to do or act in any relation.

abiotic /eɪbaɪˈɒtɪk/ *adj.* of or relating to the non-living parts of an ecosystem.

abject /ˈæbdʒɛkt/ *adj.* **1.** utterly humiliating or disheartening. **2.** contemptible; despicable. **3.** humble; servile.

ablation /əˈbleɪʃən/ *n.* **1.** *Med.* removal of organs, growths, etc., from the body, as by surgery. **2.** the melting or wearing away of a solid body.

ablaze /əˈbleɪz/ *adj.* (*used after the noun or pronoun*) **1.** on fire. **2.** excited.

able /ˈeɪbəl/ *adj.* **1.** having sufficient power, strength, or qualifications; qualified. **2.** showing talent or knowledge. –**ably**, *adv.*

-able a suffix used to form adjectives to denote ability, liability, tendency, worthiness, or likelihood, as in *teachable, perishable, obtainable.*

able-bodied seaman /ˈeɪbəl-bɒdid/ *n.* an experienced seaman who has passed certain tests in the practice of seamanship. Also, **able seaman.**

ablution /əˈbluʃən/ *n.* **1.** a cleansing with water or other liquid, as in ceremonial purification. **2.** (*pl.*) the act of washing oneself.

ABN /eɪ bi ˈɛn/ *n.* Australian Business Number; a number allocated by the government to a business, which must be displayed on invoices, receipts, letterhead, etc.

abnegate /ˈæbnəgeɪt/ *v.t.* to refuse or deny to oneself; reject; renounce.

abnormal /æb'nɔməl/ *adj.* not conforming to rule; deviating from the type or standard. **–abnormality**, *n.*

aboard /ə'bɔd/ *adv.* **1.** on board; on or in a ship, train, bus, etc. **2.** alongside.

abode /ə'boud/ *n.* **1.** a dwelling place. **2.** continuance in a place; sojourn; stay. *–v.* **3.** past tense and past participle of **abide.**

abolish /ə'bɒlɪʃ/ *v.t.* to put an end to; annul; destroy.

abolition /æbə'lɪʃən/ *n.* utter destruction; annulment. **–abolitionary**, *adj.*

abominable /ə'bɒmənəbəl, ə'bɒmnəbəl/ *adj.* detestable; loathsome.

abominate /ə'bɒməneɪt/ *v.t.* to dislike strongly; abhor.

abomination /əbɒmə'neɪʃən/ *n.* **1.** an object greatly disliked or abhorred. **2.** intense aversion. **3.** a detestable action; shameful vice.

aboriginal /æbə'rɪdʒənəl/ *adj.* of or relating to the first inhabitants of a country; indigenous.

Aboriginal /æbə'rɪdʒənəl/ *adj.* **1.** of or relating to the Australian Aborigines. *–n.* **2.** an Australian Aborigine.

Aboriginal customary law *n.* the traditional law of the Aboriginal people varying from region to region, but strongly influenced by claims of kinship. Also, **Aboriginal law.**

aborigine /æbə'rɪdʒəni/ *n.* (generally) one of a people living in a country or place from the earliest known times.

Aborigine /æbə'rɪdʒəni/ *n.* a member of a tribal people, the earliest known to live in Australia.

abort /ə'bɔt/ *v.i.* **1.** to be or become infertile; miscarry before the fetus is viable. **2.** to come to nothing; fail. *–v.t.* **3.** to cause to abort. **–abortive**, *adj.*

abortion /ə'bɔʃən/ *n.* **1. a.** the removal of a fetus from the mother's womb before it is viable. **b.** Also, **spontaneous abortion.** the involuntary expulsion of a fetus before it is viable. **2.** anything which fails in its progress before it is matured or perfected. **–abortionist**, *n.*

abound /ə'baʊnd/ *v.i.* **1.** to be in great plenty. **2.** (fol. by *in*) to be rich. **3.** (fol. by *with*) to be filled; teem. **–abounding**, *adj.*

about /ə'baʊt/ *prep.* **1.** of; concerning; in regard to. **2.** near; close to. **3.** on every side of; around. **4.** on the point of (followed by an infinitive). **5.** concerned with; engaged in doing. *–adv.* **6.** near in time, number, degree, etc.; approximately. **7.** on every side in every direction. **8.** half round; in the reverse direction. **9.** to and fro; here and there. **10.** in rotation or succession; alternately. *–phr.* **11. up and about**, active (after sleep).

about-face *n.* **1. → about-turn** (def. 1). *–v.i.* (**-faced, -facing**) **2. → about-turn** (def. 2).

about-turn *n.* **1.** a complete sudden change in position, principle, attitude, etc. *–v.i.* **2.** to turn in the opposite direction. Also, **about-face.**

above /ə'bʌv/ *adv.* **1.** in or to a higher place; overhead. **2.** higher in rank or power. **3.** before in order, especially in a book or writing. *–prep.* **4.** in or to a higher place than. **5.** more in quantity or number than. **6.** superior to, in rank or authority. **7.** not capable of (an undesirable thought, action, etc.). *–adj.* **8.** said, mentioned, or written above.

aboveboard /əbʌv'bɔd/ *adv., adj.* openly; without tricks, deceit or disguise.

abrade /ə'breɪd/ *v.t.* **1.** to scrape off. *–v.i.* **2.** to wear down by friction.

abrasion /ə'breɪʒən/ *n.* **1.** the result of rubbing or abrading; an abraded spot or place. **2.** the act or process of abrading.

abrasive /ə'breɪsɪv, -zɪv/ *n.* **1.** any material or substance used for grinding, polishing, lapping, etc., as emery or sand. *–adj.* **2.** tending to produce abrasion.

abreast /ə'brɛst/ *adv.* **1.** side by side. **2.** (fol. by *of* or *with*) up to date in knowledge of; conversant with.

abridge /ə'brɪdʒ/ *v.t.* (**abridged, abridging**) to shorten by condensation or omission; rewrite or reconstruct on a smaller scale.

abroad /ə'brɔd/ *adv.* **1.** in or to a foreign country or countries. **2.** at large; in circulation.

abrogate /'æbrəgeɪt/ *v.t.* to abolish summarily; annul by an authoritative act; repeal.

abrupt /ə'brʌpt/ *adj.* **1.** terminating or changing suddenly. **2.** sudden; unceremonious. **–abruptly**, *adv.*

abs- variant of **ab-** before *c, q, t,* as in *abscond.*

abscess /'æbsəs/ *n.* a localised collection of pus in a cavity. **–abscessed**, *adj.*

abscind /æb'sɪnd/ *v.t.* to cut off; sever.

abscission /æb'sɪʒən/ *n.* the act of cutting off; sudden termination.

abscond /æb'skɒnd, əb-/ *v.i.* to depart in a sudden and secret manner, especially to avoid legal process.

abseil /'æbseɪl/ *v.i.* to go down a cliff or wall using a rope attached to a harness and a device to control downward movement **–abseiling**, *n.* **–abseiler**, *n.*

absent *adj.* /'æbsənt/ **1.** not in a certain place at a given time; away (opposed to *present*). **2.** lacking. **3.** absent-minded. *–v.t.* /əb'sɛnt/ **4.** to take or keep (oneself) away. **–absence**, *n.*

absentee /æbsən'ti/ *n.* someone who is absent.

absenteeism /æbsən'tiɪzəm/ *n.* the practice of absenting oneself from duties, studies, employment, etc., often for inadequate reasons.

absentee vote *n.* a vote lodged by a voter who, on election day, is outside the division in which they are enrolled but still within their state or territory. Also, **absent vote.**

absent-minded /æbsənt-'maɪndəd/ *adj.* forgetful of one's immediate surroundings; preoccupied.

absolute /'æbsəlut/ *adj.* **1.** free from imperfection; complete; perfect. **2.** free from restriction or limitation; unqualified. **3.** arbitrary or despotic. **4.** viewed independently; not comparative or relative. **5.** positive. **6.** *Physics* **a.** as nearly independent as possible of arbitrary standards or of properties of special substances or systems. **b.** relating to a system of units based on some primary units, especially units of length, mass, and time. **–absolutely**, *adv.*

absolute zero *n.* the lowest possible temperature at which the particles whose motion constitutes heat would be at rest, being defined as **zero kelvin** or -273.15 degrees Celsius (or -459.67 degrees Fahrenheit).

absolution /æbsə'luʃən/ n. **1.** release from consequences, obligations, or penalties. **2.** the state of being absolved.

absolve /əb'zɒlv/ v.t. **1.** (fol. by *from*) to free from the consequences or penalties of actions. **2.** (fol. by *from*) to set free or release, as from some duty, obligation, or responsibility.

absorb /əb'sɔb, -'zɔb/ v.t. **1.** to swallow up the identity or individuality of. **2.** to engross wholly. **3.** to suck up or drink in (liquids). **4.** to assimilate (ideas, knowledge, etc.). **–absorbent,** adj.

absorption /əb'sɔpʃən, -'zɔp-/ n. **1.** assimilation. **2.** a taking in or reception by molecular or chemical action. **3.** preoccupation.

abstain /əb'stein/ v.i. (fol. by *from*) to refrain voluntarily, especially from doing or enjoying something. **–abstention,** n.

abstemious /əb'stimiəs/ adj. sparing in diet; moderate in the use of food and drink; temperate.

abstinence /'æbstənəns/ n. forbearance from any indulgence of appetite, especially from the drinking of alcohol. **–abstinent,** adj. **–abstinently,** adv.

abstract adj. /'æbstrækt/ **1.** theoretical; not applied. **2.** difficult to understand; abstruse. –n. /'æbstrækt/ **3.** a summary of a statement, document, speech, etc. **4.** an idea or term considered apart from some material basis or object. –v.t. /əb'strækt/ **5.** to draw or take away; remove. **6.** /əb'strækt/ to consider as a general object apart from special circumstances. **7.** /'æbstrækt/ to summarise.

abstracted /əb'stræktəd/ adj. lost in thought; preoccupied.

abstraction /əb'strækʃən/ n. **1.** an abstract or general idea or term. **2.** the act of taking away or separating; withdrawal. **3.** absent-mindedness; reverie.

abstruse /əb'strus/ adj. difficult to understand; esoteric.

absurd /əb'sɜd, -'zɜd/ adj. contrary to reason or commonsense; ridiculous. **–absurdity,** n.

abundant /ə'bʌndənt/ adj. **1.** present in great quantity; fully sufficient. **2.** (fol. by *in*) possessing in great quantity; abounding. **–abundance,** n.

abuse v.t. /ə'bjuz/ **1.** to use wrongly or improperly; misuse. **2.** to revile; malign. **3.** to inflict a sexual act on (a person), especially one whose relationship or proximity makes them vulnerable. –n. /ə'bjus/ **4.** wrong or improper use; misuse. **5.** insulting language. **6.** sexual violation as rape or sexual assault, especially of a child. **–abuser,** n. **–abusive,** adj.

abut /ə'bʌt/ v.i. (**abutted, abutting**) (oft. fol. by *on, upon,* or *against*) to be adjacent to. **–abuttal,** n.

abysmal /ə'bɪzməl/ adj. **1.** immeasurable. **2.** immeasurably bad.

abyss /ə'bɪs/ n. **1.** a very deep chasm. **2.** any deep, immeasurable space. **3.** anything profound and unfathomable. **–abyssal,** adj.

ac- variant of **ad-** (by assimilation) before *c* and *qu,* as in *accede, acquire,* etc.

-ac an adjective suffix meaning 'pertaining to', as in *cardiac.*

acacia /ə'keiʃə, ə'keisiə/ n. a tree or shrub, native in warm regions; usually known as wattle in Australia.

academic /ækə'dɛmɪk/ adj. **1.** relating to an advanced institution of learning; relating to higher education. **2.** relating to those university subjects which are concerned with the refinement of the mind rather than the learning of skills (opposed to *technical*). **3.** theoretical; not practical. –n. **4.** a teacher or researcher in a university or college.

academy /ə'kædəmi/ n. (pl. **-mies**) **1.** an association or institution for the promotion of literature, science, or art. **2.** a school for instruction in a particular art or science.

acai berry /ə'saii/ n. a small, purplish berry; valued for its high nutritional content and as an aid to weight loss.

accede /æk'sid/ v.i. **1.** to give consent; agree; yield. **2.** (fol. by *to*) to attain, as an office or dignity; arrive at.

accelerate /ək'sɛləreit, æk-/ v.t. **1.** to cause to move or advance faster. **2.** *Physics* to change the magnitude and/or direction of the velocity of a body. –v.i. **3.** to become faster; increase in speed. **–acceleration,** n.

accelerator /ək'sɛləreitə, æk-/ n. *Motor Vehicles* a device which increases the speed of a vehicle by opening and closing the throttle, especially one operated by the foot.

accent n. /'æksɛnt/ **1.** the distinctive character of a vowel or syllable determined by its degree or pattern of stress or musical tone. **2.** a mark indicating stress, musical tone, or vowel quality. **3.** *Prosody* regularly recurring stress. **4.** characteristic style of pronunciation as of a dialect. **5.** *Music* stress or emphasis given to certain notes. –v.t. /æk'sɛnt/ **6.** to pronounce (a vowel, syllable, or word) with one of the distinctive accents of the language, especially with a stress accent. **7.** to mark with a written accent or accents.

accentuate /ək'sɛntʃueit/ v.t. to emphasise.

accept /ək'sɛpt/ v.t. **1.** to take or receive (something offered); receive with approval or favour. **2.** to admit and agree to. **3.** to accommodate oneself to. **4.** to understand. **5.** *Commerce* to acknowledge, by signature, as calling for payment, and thus to agree to pay, as a draft. **–acceptance,** n. **–acceptor, accepter,** n.

acceptable /ək'sɛptəbəl/ adj. capable or worthy of being accepted. **–acceptability,** n.

accepted /ək'sɛptəd/ adj. customary; established; approved.

access /'æksɛs/ n. **1.** (fol. by *to*) the act or privilege of coming; admittance; approach. **2.** way, means, or opportunity of approach. **3.** a parent's right to see a child. –v.t. **4.** to gain admittance to: *you can access the foyer through this door.* **5.** *Computers* to locate and provide means of getting (information) out of or into a computer storage. –adj. **6.** *Radio, TV, etc.* run by special-interest or minority groups who wish to transmit their own programs.

accessible /ək'sɛsəbəl/ adj. **1.** easy of access; approachable. **2.** attainable. –phr. **3. accessible to,** open to being influenced by: *accessible to bribery.* **4. accessible to** (or **for**), affording easy entry to: *a building accessible to the disabled.*

accession /əkˈsɛʃən/ *n.* **1.** the act of coming into the possession of a right, dignity, office, etc. **2.** an increase by something added. **3.** consent. **4.** *International Law* formal acceptance of an agreement between states.

accessory /əkˈsɛsəri/ *n.* (*pl.* **-ries**) **1.** something added or attached for convenience, attractiveness, etc. **2.** Also, **accessary.** *Law* the person who is not the chief actor at a felony, nor present at its perpetration, but yet is in some way concerned therein (either before or after the fact committed). **3.** an item such as a bag, belt, piece of jewellery, etc., chosen to go with a particular outfit.

accident /ˈæksədənt/ *n.* **1.** an undesirable or unfortunate happening; mishap. **2.** anything that happens unexpectedly, without design, or by chance. –**accidental**, *adj.* –**accidentally**, *adv.*

acclaim /əˈkleɪm/ *v.t.* **1.** to salute with words or sounds of joy or approval; applaud. **2.** to announce or proclaim by acclamation. –*n.* **3.** strong approval or applause.

acclamation /ækləˈmeɪʃən/ *n.* **1.** a shout or other demonstration of welcome, goodwill, or applause. **2.** the act of acclaiming. –**acclamatory**, *adj.*

acclimatise /əˈklaɪmətaɪz/ *v.t.* **1.** to habituate to a new climate or environment. –*v.i.* **2.** to become habituated to a new climate or environment. Also, **acclimatize**.

accolade /ˈækəleɪd/ *n.* **1.** a ceremony used in conferring knighthood. **2.** any award; honour.

accommodate /əˈkɒmədeɪt/ *v.t.* **1.** to do a kindness or a favour to. **2.** to provide suitably. **3.** to make suitable or consistent; adapt. **4.** to bring into harmony; adjust; reconcile. **5.** to find or provide space for (something). –**accommodating**, *adj.*

accommodation /əkɒməˈdeɪʃən/ *n.* **1.** the act or result of accommodating. **2.** lodging, or food and lodging.

accompaniment /əˈkʌmpnimənt, əˈkʌmpənimənt/ *n.* **1.** something incidental or added for ornament, symmetry, etc. **2.** *Music* that part of a composition which provides the harmonic and rhythmic backing to a melodic line, especially a song.

accompany /əˈkʌmpəni, əˈkʌmpni/ *v.t.* (**-nied**, **-nying**) **1.** to go or be in company with. **2.** *Music* to play or sing an accompaniment to. –**accompanist**, *n.*

accomplice /əˈkʌmpləs, -ˈkɒm-/ *n.* an associate in a crime; partner in wrongdoing.

accomplish /əˈkʌmplɪʃ, -ˈkɒm-/ *v.t.* to bring to pass; carry out; finish.

accomplished /əˈkʌmplɪʃt, -ˈkɒm-/ *adj.* **1.** completed; effected. **2.** perfected; expert. **3.** perfected in the graces and attainments of polite society.

accomplishment /əˈkʌmplɪʃmənt, -ˈkɒm-/ *n.* **1.** the act of carrying into effect; fulfilment. **2.** anything accomplished; achievement. **3.** (*oft. pl.*) an acquired art or grace; polite attainment.

accord /əˈkɔd/ *v.i.* **1.** to be in correspondence or harmony; agree. –*v.t.* **2.** to grant; concede. –*n.* **3.** just correspondence of things; harmony of relation. **4.** consent or concurrence of opinions or wills; agreement. –*phr.* **5. of one's own accord**, voluntarily. **6. with one accord**, with spontaneous agreement. –**accordance**, *n.*

according /əˈkɔdɪŋ/ *adj.* **1.** agreeing. –*phr.* **2. according as**, conformably or proportionately as. **3. according to**, **a.** in the way described. **b.** proportionately. **c.** on the authority of; as stated by.

accordion /əˈkɔdiən/ *n.* **1.** a portable wind instrument with bellows and button-like keys sounded by means of metallic reeds. –*adj.* **2.** having folds like the bellows of an accordion.

accost /əˈkɒst/ *v.t.* to approach, especially with a greeting or remark.

accouchement /əˈkuʃmənt, -ˈkuʃ-/ *n.* period of confinement in childbirth; labour.

account /əˈkaʊnt/ *n.* **1.** a verbal or written recital of particular transactions and events; narrative. **2.** a statement of reasons, causes, etc., explaining some event. **3.** a statement of pecuniary transactions. **4.** *Bookkeeping* **a.** a formal record of debits and credits. **b.** a balance of a specified period's receipts and expenditures. **5.** access to computing resources obtained by identification and authorisation of the user. –*v.i.* **6.** to render an account, especially of money. –*v.t.* **7.** to count; consider as. –*phr.* **8. account for**, **a.** to give an explanation of. **b.** to take responsibility for. **c.** to cause the death, defeat, etc., of. **9. bring** (or **call**) **to account**, to demand explanation or justification of actions. **10. in account with**, having a credit arrangement with. **11. on** (or **to**) **account**, as an interim payment. **12. on account of**, **a.** because of; by reason of. **b.** for the sake of.

accountable /əˈkaʊntəbəl/ *adj.* liable to be called to account; responsible (*to* a person, *for* an act, etc.).

accountant /əˈkaʊntənt/ *n.* a person whose profession is analysing and communicating financial information and maintaining financial records for an organisation. –**accountancy**, *n.*

accounting /əˈkaʊntɪŋ/ *n.* the art of analysing the financial position and operating results of a business firm from a study of its sales, purchases, overheads, etc.

accoutrements /əˈkutrəmənts/ *pl. n.* articles of equipment or dress, especially of an ornamental character; trappings.

accredit /əˈkrɛdət/ *v.t.* **1.** (fol. by *with*) to ascribe or attribute to. **2.** to furnish (an officially recognised agent) with credentials. **3.** to certify as meeting official requirements. **4.** to believe.

accretion /əˈkriʃən/ *n.* **1.** an increase by natural growth or by gradual external addition. **2.** an extraneous addition. **3.** the growing together of separate parts into a single whole.

accrue /əˈkru/ *v.* (**-crued**, **-cruing**) –*v.i.* **1.** to accumulate in the course of time. –*v.t.* **2.** to collect over a period of time: *to accrue points.* –**accrual**, **accruement**, *n.*

acculturation /əkʌltʃəˈreɪʃən/ *n.* the process of borrowing between cultures, resulting in new and blended patterns.

accumulate /əˈkjumjəleɪt/ *v.t.* **1.** to gather or collect, as into a mass. –*v.i.* **2.** to grow into a heap or mass; form an increasing quantity. –**accumulation**, n. –**accumulative**, adj.

accurate /ˈækjərət/ adj. **1.** in exact conformity to truth, to a standard or rule, or to a model; free from error or defect. **2.** showing precision; meticulous: *an accurate typist*. –**accuracy**, **accurateness**, n. –**accurately**, adv.

accursed /əˈkɜsəd, əˈkɜst/ adj. **1.** subject to a curse; ruined. **2.** worthy of curses; detestable.

accusation /ˌækjuˈzeɪʃən/ n. **1.** a charge of wrongdoing; imputation of guilt or blame. **2.** the specific offence charged.

accusatory /əˈkjuzətəri, -tri/ adj. containing an accusation; accusing.

accuse /əˈkjuz/ v.t. **1.** to bring a charge against; charge with the fault or crime (*of*). **2.** to blame.

accustom /əˈkʌstəm/ v.t. to familiarise by custom or use; habituate.

accustomed /əˈkʌstəmd/ adj. customary; habitual.

ace /eɪs/ n. **1.** a single spot or mark on a card or die. **2.** (in tennis, badminton, etc.) a serve which the opponent fails to touch. **3.** a highly skilled person. –adj. **4.** *Colloq.* excellent.

-aceous a suffix of adjectives used in scientific terminology, indicating: **1.** of or relating to. **2.** of the nature of, or similar to. **3.** belonging to a scientific grouping, especially a botanic family.

acerbity /əˈsɜbəti/ n. **1.** sourness, with roughness or astringency of taste. **2.** harshness or severity, as of temper or expression. –**acerbic**, adj.

acetate /ˈæsəteɪt/ n. a salt or ester of acetic acid. –**acetated**, adj.

acetic acid /əˈsitɪk, əˈsɛtɪk/ n. a sour colourless acid, with a sharp smell, being the main constituent of vinegar, used to make certain artificial fibres, etc.

acetone /ˈæsətoʊn/ n. a colourless, volatile, flammable liquid, used as a solvent and in varnishes, etc.

acetylene /əˈsɛtəlin, -lən/ n. a colourless gas, used in metal welding, as an illuminant, and in organic synthesis.

ache /eɪk/ v.i. (**ached, aching**) **1.** to have or be in continuous pain. –n. **2.** pain of some duration, in opposition to sudden twinges or spasmodic pain.

achieve /əˈtʃiv/ v.t. to bring to a successful end; accomplish.

achievement /əˈtʃivmənt/ n. **1.** something accomplished; a great or heroic deed. **2.** the act of achieving; accomplishment.

acid[1] /ˈæsəd/ n. **1.** *Chem.* a compound which reacts with an alkali to form a salt. **2.** a substance with a sour taste. –adj. **3.** sharp or sour. –**acidic**, adj. –**acidity**, n.

acid[2] /ˈæsəd/ n. *Colloq.* LSD.

acidophilus /æsəˈdɒfələs/ n. See **lactobacillus**.

acid rain n. highly acidic rain, caused by pollution in the atmosphere.

acidulous /əˈsɪdʒələs/ adj. slightly acid.

-acious an adjective suffix made by adding **-ous** to nouns ending in **-acity** (the *-ty* being dropped), indicating a tendency towards or abundance of something, as *audacious*.

-acity a suffix of nouns denoting quality or a state of being, and the like.

acknowledge /əkˈnɒlɪdʒ/ v.t. (**-edged, -edging**) **1.** to admit to be real or true; recognise the existence, truth, or fact of. **2.** to express recognition or awareness of. **3.** to recognise the authority or claims of. **4.** to indicate appreciation or gratitude for. **5.** to admit or certify the receipt of. –**acknowledgement**, **acknowledgment**, n. –**acknowledgeable**, **acknowledgable**, adj.

acknowledgement of country n. the official recognition of the Indigenous traditional custodians of a locality, given in the preamble to a public event, meeting, etc.

acme /ˈækmi/ n. the highest point; culmination.

ACN /eɪ si ˈɛn/ n. Australian Company Number; a unique nine-digit number which is allotted to each Australian company as identification or official registration.

acne /ˈækni/ n. an inflammatory disease of the sebaceous glands, characterised by an eruption (often pustular) of the skin, especially of the face. –**acned**, adj.

acolyte /ˈækəlaɪt/ n. an attendant; an assistant.

acorn /ˈeɪkɔn/ n. the fruit of the oak, a nut in a hardened scaly cup.

acoustic /əˈkustɪk/ adj. **1.** Also, **acoustical**. relating to the sense or organs of hearing, or to the science of sound. **2.** *Music* of or relating to instruments whose sound is not electronically amplified.

acoustics /əˈkustɪks/ n. **1.** *Physics* the science of sound. **2.** (*construed as pl.*) acoustic properties, as of an auditorium.

acquaint /əˈkweɪnt/ v.t. (fol. by *with*) to make more or less familiar or conversant.

acquaintance /əˈkweɪntəns/ n. **1.** a person (or persons) known to one, especially a person with whom one is not on terms of great intimacy. **2.** the state of being acquainted; personal knowledge.

acquiesce /ˌækwiˈɛs/ v.i. (**-esced, -escing**) (oft. fol. by *in*) to assent tacitly; comply quietly; agree; consent. –**acquiescent**, adj. –**acquiescence**, n.

acquire /əˈkwaɪə/ v.t. to come into possession of; get as one's own. –**acquisition**, n.

acquired immune deficiency syndrome n. → **AIDS**.

acquisitive /əˈkwɪzətɪv/ adj. fond of acquiring possessions.

acquit /əˈkwɪt/ v.t. (**-quitted, -quitting**) **1.** to relieve from a charge of fault or crime. **2.** to release or discharge (a person) from an obligation. –**acquittal**, n.

acre /ˈeɪkə/ n. a large area of land in the imperial system, equal to almost half a hectare. –**acreage**, n.

acrid /ˈækrəd/ adj. sharp or biting.

acrimony /ˈækrəməni/ n. sharpness or severity of temper; bitterness of expression proceeding from anger or ill nature. –**acrimonious**, adj.

acro- a word element meaning 'tip', 'top', 'apex', or 'edge'.

acrobat /ˈækrəbæt/ n. a skilled performer who can walk on a tightrope, perform on a trapeze, or do other similar feats. –**acrobatic**, adj. –**acrobatically**, adv.

acronym /ˈækrənɪm/ n. a word formed from the initial letters of a sequence of words, as *radar* (from *radio detection and ranging*) or *ANZAC* (from *Australian and New Zealand Army Corps*).

acropolis /əˈkrɒpələs/ n. the citadel of an ancient Greek city.

across /əˈkrɒs/ prep. **1.** from side to side of. **2.** on the other side of. **3.** so as to meet or fall in with. *–adv.* **4.** from one side to another. **5.** on the other side. **6.** crosswise. *–phr.* **7. be across,** to have a thorough understanding of: *to be across the complexities of the design.*

acrostic /əˈkrɒstɪk/ n. a series of lines or verses in which the first, last, or other particular letters form a word, phrase, the alphabet, etc.

acrylic /əˈkrɪlɪk/ adj. **1.** of or relating to fibres formed by the polymerisation of acrylonitrile. **2.** of or relating to fabrics woven from such fibres. **3.** of or relating to items such as pieces of furniture, tableware, etc., made from such fibres.

acrylonitrile /əˌkrɪloʊˈnaɪtraɪl/ n. a colourless toxic organic chemical used in the manufacture of acrylic fibres, synthetic rubber, etc.

act /ækt/ n. **1.** anything done or performed; a doing; deed. **2.** the process of doing. **3.** (*oft. upper case*) a decree, edict, law, statute, judgement, resolve, or award, especially a decree passed by a legislature. **4.** one of the main divisions of a play or opera. **5.** an individual performance forming part of a variety show, radio program, etc. **6.** behaviour which is contrived and artificial, somewhat in the manner of a theatrical performance. *–v.i.* **7.** to do something; exert energy or force; be employed or operative. **8.** to behave. **9.** to pretend. **10.** to perform as an actor. *–v.t.* **11.** to represent (an imaginary or historical character) with one's person. **12.** to feign; counterfeit. **13.** to behave as. *–phr.* **14. act for,** to serve or substitute for. **15. act up,** *Colloq.* **a.** to play up; take advantage. **b.** (of a car, etc.) to malfunction.

actinium /ækˈtɪniəm/ n. a radioactive chemical element occurring in pitchblende. *Symbol:* Ac

action /ˈækʃən/ n. **1.** the process or state of acting or of being active. **2.** something done; an act; deed. **3.** way or manner of moving. **4.** military and naval combat. **5.** the main subject or story, as distinguished from an incidental episode. **6.** *Law* **a.** a proceeding instituted by one party against another. **b. take action,** to commence legal proceedings.

actionable /ˈækʃənəbəl/ adj. furnishing ground for a law suit. **–actionably,** adv.

action verb n. Gram. → **dynamic verb.**

activate /ˈæktəveɪt/ v.t. **1.** to make active. **2.** *Physics* to render radioactive. **3.** to aerate (sewage) as a purification measure. **–activation,** n.

activated carbon n. a granulated charcoal which absorbs gases and vapours. Also, **activated charcoal.**

active /ˈæktɪv/ adj. **1.** in a state of action; in actual progress or motion. **2.** constantly engaged in action; busy. **3.** nimble. **4.** capable of exerting influence. **5.** *Gram.* denoting a voice of verb inflection, in which the subject performs the action expressed by the verb, as *hit*

in the sentence *I hit him.* **6.** (of a volcano) erupting. **7.** (of a communications satellite) able to retransmit signals.

activist /ˈæktəvəst/ n. a zealous worker for a cause, especially a political cause.

activity /ækˈtɪvəti/ n. (*pl.* **-ties**) **1.** the state of action; doing. **2.** a specific deed or action; sphere of action. *–adj.* **3.** liveliness; agility.

act of God n. (*pl.* **acts of God**) a direct, sudden, and irresistible action of natural forces, such as could not humanly have been foreseen or prevented, for example, tornado, tidal wave, high water, flood, and earth movements.

actor /ˈæktə/ n. someone who plays the part of a character in a dramatic performance.

actress /ˈæktrəs/ n. a female actor.

actual /ˈæktʃuəl/ adj. **1.** existing in act or fact; real. **2.** now existing; present.

actuality /æktʃuˈæləti/ n. (*pl.* **-ties**) **1.** actual existence; reality. **2.** (*pl.*) actual conditions or circumstances; facts.

actually /ˈæktʃuəli, ˈæktʃəli/ adv. as an actual or existing fact; really.

actuary /ˈæktʃuəri/, *Orig. US* /ˈæktʃuɛri/ n. (*pl.* **-ries**) a statistician who computes risks, rates, etc., according to probabilities indicated by recorded facts. **–actuarial,** adj. **–actuarially,** adv.

actuate /ˈæktʃueɪt/ v.t. **1.** to incite to action. **2.** to put into action.

acuity /əˈkjuəti/ n. sharpness; acuteness.

acumen /ˈækjəmən/ n. quickness of perception; mental acuteness; keen insight.

acupressure /ˈækjəprɛʃə, ˈækə-/ n. the massage of muscles and application of pressure to acupuncture points to promote wellbeing or to cure illness; shiatsu.

acupuncture /ˈækjəpʌŋktʃə, ˈækə-/ n. a Chinese medical practice to treat disease, establish diagnosis or relieve pain, by puncturing specific areas of skin with long sharp needles. **–acupuncturist,** n.

acute /əˈkjut/ adj. **1.** sharp at the end; ending in a point (opposed to *blunt* or *obtuse*). **2.** sharp in effect; intense; poignant. **3.** severe; crucial. **4.** brief and severe, as disease (opposed to *chronic*). **5.** sharp or penetrating in intellect, insight, or perception. **6.** having quick sensibility. **7.** *Geom., etc.* (of an angle) less than 90°.

-acy a suffix of nouns of quality, state, office, etc., many of which accompany adjectives in *-acious* or nouns or adjectives in *-ate*, as in *efficacy*, etc., *advocacy*, etc., *accuracy*, etc.

ad /æd/ n. an advertisement.

ad- a prefix of direction, tendency, and addition, attached chiefly to stems not found as words themselves, as in *advert, advent.*

adage /ˈædɪdʒ/ n. a proverb.

adamant /ˈædəmənt/ adj. firm in purpose or opinion; unyielding. **–adamantly,** adv.

Adam's apple /ˈædəmz ˈæpəl/ n. a projection of the thyroid cartilage at the front of the throat, usually more prominent in men than in women.

adapt /əˈdæpt/ v.t. **1.** to make suitable to requirements; adjust or modify fittingly. *–v.i.* **2.** to adjust oneself. **–adaptive,** adj. **–adaptation,** n.

adaptable /ə'dæptəbəl/ *adj.* **1.** capable of being adapted. **2.** able to adapt oneself easily to new conditions.

adaptor /ə'dæptə/ *n.* **1.** a device for fitting together parts having different sizes or designs. **2.** an accessory to convert a machine, tool, etc., to a new or modified use. Also, **adapter**.

add /æd/ *v.t.* **1.** to unite or join so as to increase the number, quantity, size, or importance. **2.** Also, **add up.** to find the sum of. **3.** to say or write further. *–v.i.* **4.** to perform the arithmetical operation of addition. *–phr.* **5. add in**, to include. **6. add to**, to be or serve as an addition to: *to add to someone's grief.* **7. add up, a.** to accumulate. **b.** to make the desired or expected total. **c.** *Colloq.* to make sense, be logically consistent.

ADD /eɪ di 'di/ *n.* → **attention deficit disorder**.

added value *n.* something added to a product or process which increases its value.

addendum /ə'dɛndəm/ *n.* (*pl.* **-da** /-də/) a thing to be added; an addition.

adder /'ædə/ *n.* the common viper.

addict /'ædɪkt/ *n.* someone who is addicted to a practice or habit. **–addiction**, *n.* **–addictive**, *adj.*

addicted /ə'dɪktəd/ *adj.* (fol. by *to*) devoted or given up (to a practice, habit, or substance).

addition /ə'dɪʃən/ *n.* **1.** the act or process of adding or uniting. **2.** the process of uniting two or more numbers into one sum, denoted by the symbol +. **3.** anything added. **–additional**, *adj.*

additive /'ædətɪv/ *n.* something added.

addle /'ædl/ *v.t.* **1.** to muddle or confuse. *adj.* **2.** mentally confused; muddled, as in the combinations *addlebrained*, *addlepated*. **–addled**, *adj.*

address *n.* /ə'drɛs, 'ædrɛs/ **1.** a formal speech or writing directed to a person or a group of persons. **2.** a direction as to name and residence inscribed on a letter, etc. **3.** a place where a person lives or may be reached. **4.** *Computers* a number or symbol which identifies a particular register in the memory of a digital computer. **5.** manner of speaking to persons; personal bearing in conversation. **6.** skilful management; adroitness. *–v.t.* /ə'drɛs/ **7.** to speak to a person in an official position, such as a judge, governor-general, etc., using their formal title. **8.** to direct for delivery; put a direction on. **9.** to direct to the ear or attention. **10.** to deal with (a problem, question, etc.). **11.** to direct the energy or force of (used reflexively, followed by *to*). **–addresser**, **addressor**, *n.* **–addressee**, *n.*

adduce /ə'djus/ *v.t.* (**-duced**, **-ducing**) to bring forward in argument; cite as pertinent or conclusive.

-ade[1] **1.** a suffix found in nouns denoting action or process, product or result of action, person or persons acting, often irregularly attached, as in *blockade*, *escapade*, *masquerade*. **2.** a noun suffix indicating a drink made of a particular fruit, as in *lemonade*.

-ade[2] a collective suffix, as in *decade*.

adeno- a word element meaning 'gland'. Also, (*before vowels*), **aden-**.

adenoids /'ædənɔɪdz/ *pl. n.* the mass of lymphoid tissue in the upper pharynx; enlargement can prevent nasal breathing, especially in young children.

adept /ə'dɛpt/ *adj.* highly skilled; proficient; expert.

adequate /'ædəkwət/ *adj.* (oft. fol. by *to* or *for*) fully sufficient, suitable, or fit. **–adequacy**, *n.*

ADHD /eɪ di eɪtʃ 'di/ *n.* → **attention deficit hyperactivity disorder**.

adhere /əd'hɪə/ *v.i.* **1.** (fol. by *to*) to stick fast; cleave; cling. **2.** (fol. by *to*) to be devoted; be attached as a follower or upholder. **–adhesion**, *n.*

adherent /əd'hɪərənt, -'hɛrənt/ *n.* **1.** (fol. by *of*) someone who follows or upholds a leader, cause, etc.; supporter; follower. *–adj.* **2.** sticking; clinging; adhering. **–adherence**, *n.*

adhesive /əd'hisɪv, -'hizɪv/ *adj.* **1.** clinging; tenacious; sticking fast. *–n.* **2.** a substance for sticking things together.

ad hoc /æd 'hɒk/ *adj.* **1.** for this (special purpose); an **ad hoc committee** is one set up to deal with one subject only. **2.** impromptu; an **ad hoc decision** is one made with regard to the exigencies of the moment. *–adv.* **3.** with respect to this (subject or thing).

ad infinitum /ˌæd ɪnfə'naɪtəm/ *adv.* to infinity; endlessly; without limit.

adipose /'ædəpoʊs/ *adj.* fatty.

adjacent /ə'dʒeɪsənt/ *adj.* lying near, close, or contiguous; adjoining; neighbouring. **–adjacency**, *n.*

adjective /'ædʒəktɪv/ *n. Gram.* one of the major parts of speech of many languages, comprising words used to modify or limit a noun. **–adjectival**, *adj.*

adjoin /ə'dʒɔɪn/ *v.t.* **1.** to be in connection or contact with; abut on. *–v.i.* **2.** to lie or be next, or in contact. **–adjoining**, *adj.*

adjourn /ə'dʒɜn/ *v.t.* **1.** to suspend the meeting of (a public or private body) to a future time or to another place. *–v.i.* **2.** to postpone, suspend, or transfer proceedings. **–adjournment**, *n.*

adjudge /ə'dʒʌdʒ/ *v.t.* (**-judged**, **-judging**) **1.** to pronounce formally; decree. **2.** to award judicially; assign.

adjudicate /ə'dʒudəkeɪt/ *v.i.* to act as judge. **–adjudication**, *n.* **–adjudicator**, *n.*

adjunct /'ædʒʌŋkt/ *n.* **1.** something added to another thing but not essentially a part of it. **2.** a person joined to another in some duty or service. *–adj.* **3.** joined to a thing or person, especially subordinately; associated; auxiliary.

adjure /ə'dʒuə/ *v.t.* **1.** to charge, bind, or command, earnestly and solemnly, often under oath or the threat of a curse. **2.** to entreat or request earnestly.

adjust /ə'dʒʌst/ *v.t.* **1.** to make correspondent or conformable; adapt. **2.** to put in working order; bring to a proper state or position. **3.** to settle or bring to a satisfactory state, so that parties are agreed in the result. **4.** *Insurance* to fix (the sum to be paid on a claim); settle (a claim). *–v.i.* **5.** to adapt oneself; become adapted. **–adjustable**, *adj.* **–adjustment**, *n.*

adjutant /'ædʒətənt/ *n.* **1.** *Mil.* a staff officer who assists the commanding officer. **2.** an assistant. **–adjutancy**, *n.*

ad lib /æd 'lɪb/ *adv.* in an impromptu manner. **–ad-lib,** *adj., v.*

administer /æd'mɪnəstə, əd-/ *v.t.* **1.** to manage (affairs, a government, etc.). **2.** to bring into use or operation; dispense. **3.** to supervise or impose the taking of (an oath, etc.) –*v.i.* **4.** to contribute assistance. **5.** to perform the duties of an administrator.

administration /ədmɪnəs'treɪʃən/ *n.* **1.** the management or direction of any office or employment. **2.** the function of a political state in exercising its governmental duties. **3.** any body of people entrusted with administrative powers.

administrative /əd'mɪnəstrətɪv/ *adj.* relating to administration; executive.

administrator /əd'mɪnəstreɪtə/ *n.* **1.** someone who directs or manages affairs of any kind. **2.** *Law* a person appointed by a court to take charge of the estate of a person who died without appointing an executor.

admirable /'ædmərəbəl/ *adj.* worthy of admiration, exciting approval, reverence or affection. **–admirably,** *adv.*

admiral /'ædmərəl, 'ædmrəl/ *n.* a naval officer of high rank. **–admiralty,** *n.*

admire /əd'maɪə/ *v.t.* to regard with wonder, pleasure, and approbation. **–admiration,** *n.* **–admirer,** *n.*

admissible /əd'mɪsəbəl/ *adj.* **1.** that may be allowed or conceded; allowable. **2.** *Law* allowable as evidence.

admission /əd'mɪʃən/ *n.* **1.** the act of allowing to enter. **2.** the price paid for entrance, as to a theatre, etc. **3.** the act or condition of being received or accepted in a position or office; appointment. **4.** a point or statement admitted; concession.

admit /əd'mɪt/ *v.t.* (**-mitted, -mitting**) **1.** to allow to enter; grant or afford entrance to. **2.** to permit; allow. **3.** to permit to exercise a certain function or privilege. **4.** to allow as valid. **5.** to have capacity for the admission of at one time. **6.** to acknowledge; confess. **–admittance,** *n.*

admittedly /əd'mɪtədli/ *adv.* by acknowledgement.

admonish /əd'mɒnɪʃ/ *v.t.* **1.** to counsel against something; caution or advise. **2.** to notify of or reprove for a fault, especially mildly. **3.** to recall or incite to duty; remind. **–admonition,** *n.*

ad nauseam /æd 'nɔziəm, -si-/ *adv.* to a sickening or disgusting extent.

ado /ə'du/ *n.* activity; fuss.

adobe /ə'doubi/ *n.* a yellow silt or clay, deposited by rivers, used to make bricks.

adolescence /ædə'lesəns/ *n.* the transition period between puberty and adult stages of development; youth. **–adolescent,** *adj., n.*

adopt /ə'dɒpt/ *v.t.* **1.** to choose for or take to oneself; make one's own by selection or assent. **2.** to take (a child born to someone else) to be legally your own child, specifically by a formal legal act. **3.** to vote to accept. **–adoptable,** *adj.* **–adopter,** *n.* **–adoption,** *n.*

adoptive /ə'dɒptɪv/ *adj.* **1.** related by adoption. **2.** tending to adopt. **3.** (of children) for adoption. **–adoptively,** *adv.*

adorable /ə'dɔrəbəl/ *adj.* worthy of being adored.

adore /ə'dɔ/ *v.t.* **1.** to regard with the utmost esteem, love, and respect. **2.** to honour as divine; worship. **–adoration,** *n.*

adorn /ə'dɔn/ *v.t.* **1.** to make pleasing or more attractive. **2.** to increase or lend beauty to, as by dress or ornaments; decorate.

adrenal /ə'drinəl/ *adj.* **1.** situated near or on the kidneys. **2.** of or produced by the adrenal glands.

adrenaline /ə'drenələn, -lin/ *n.* a hormone produced in the body especially in response to stress, increasing heart rate, blood pressure, rate of breathing, as well as levels of glucose and lipids in the blood. Also, **adrenalin.**

adrift /ə'drɪft/ *adj.* not fastened by any kind of moorings; at the mercy of winds and currents.

adroit /ə'drɔɪt/ *adj.* expert in the use of the hand or mind.

adsorb /əd'sɔb/ *v.t.* to gather (a gas, liquid, or dissolved substance) on a surface in a condensed layer, as is the case when charcoal adsorbs gases.

adulate /'ædʒəleɪt/ *v.t.* to show pretended or undiscriminating devotion to; flatter servilely. **–adulation,** *n.* **–adulator,** *n.* **–adulatory,** *adj.*

adult /ə'dʌlt, 'ædʌlt/ *adj.* **1.** having attained full size and strength; mature. **2.** relating to or designed for adults. –*n.* **3.** a person who has reached the age at which an individual is considered legally responsible and able to perform certain civic duties, such as voting. **4.** a full-grown person, animal or plant.

adulterate /ə'dʌltəreɪt/ *v.t.* to make impure by the addition of inferior materials or substances. **–adulterator,** *n.* **–adulterant,** *n.* **–adulteration,** *n.*

adultery /ə'dʌltəri/ *n.* voluntary sexual intercourse between a married person and any other than the lawful spouse. **–adulterous,** *adj.*

adult stem cell *n.* a form of cell (def. 3), which, while rudimentary in form, is already specialised in certain ways so that it can develop only in certain parts of the body.

ad valorem /æd və'lɔrəm/ *adj.* in proportion to the value. An *ad valorem* duty charged on goods entering a country is fixed at a percentage of the customs value as stated on the invoice.

advance /əd'væns, -'vɑns/ *v.* (**-vanced, -vancing**) –*v.t.* **1.** to move or bring forwards in place. **2.** to bring to view or notice; propose. **3.** to improve; further. **4.** to raise in rate. **5.** to bring forwards in time; accelerate. **6.** to supply beforehand; furnish on credit, or before goods are delivered or work is done. **7.** to supply or pay in expectation of reimbursement. –*v.i.* **8.** to move or go forwards; proceed. **9.** to improve or make progress; grow. **10.** to increase in quantity, value, price, etc. –*n.* **11.** a moving forwards; progress in space. **12.** (*usu. pl.*) an effort to bring about acquaintance, accord, understanding, etc. **13.** addition to price; rise in price. **14.** *Commerce* **a.** a giving beforehand; a furnishing of something before an equivalent is received. **b.** a loan against securities, or in advance of payment due.

advantage /əd'væntɪdʒ, -'vɑn-/ *n.* **1.** any state, circumstance, opportunity, or means specially favourable to success, interest, or any desired end. **2.** benefit; gain; profit. **3.** *Tennis* the first point scored after deuce, or the resulting state of the score. *-v.t.* (**-taged, -taging**) **4.** to be of service to; yield profit or gain to; benefit. *-phr.* **5. take advantage of**, to make use of. **-advantageous** /ædvæn'teɪdʒəs/, *adj.*

advent /'ædvɛnt/ *n.* a coming into place, view, or being; arrival.

adventitious /ædvɛn'tɪʃəs/ *adj.* accidentally or casually acquired; added extrinsically; foreign.

adventure /əd'vɛntʃə/ *n.* **1.** an undertaking of uncertain outcome; a hazardous enterprise. **2.** an exciting experience. **3.** participation in exciting undertakings or enterprises. **4.** a commercial or financial speculation of any kind; a venture. *-v.i.* **5.** to venture. **-adventurous**, *adj.*

adverb /'ædvɜb/ *n.* a part of speech comprising words used to limit a verb, adjective, or another adverb, by expressing time, manner, place, cause, degree, etc. **-adverbial**, *adj.*

ad verbum /æd 'vɜbəm/ *adv.* exact in wording according to an original.

adversary /'ædvəsəri, -səri, əd'vɜsəri/, *Orig. US* /'ædvəsɛri/ *n.* (*pl.* **-ries**) an opponent in a contest.

adverse /'ædvɜs, əd'vɜs/ *adj.* **1.** antagonistic in purpose or effect. **2.** opposing one's interests or desire. **-adversity**, *n.*

advert[1] /əd'vɜt/ *v.i.* (fol. by *to*) to make a remark or remarks (about or in relation to); refer.

advert[2] /'ædvɜt/ *n. Colloq.* an advertisement.

advertise /'ædvətaɪz/ *v.t.* **1.** to give information to the public about (something). **2.** to praise the good qualities of, by advertisement, to induce the public to buy. *-v.i.* **3.** to ask (*for*) by placing an advertisement in a newspaper, magazine, etc.

advertisement /əd'vɜtəsmənt/ *n.* any device or public announcement designed to attract public attention, bring in custom, etc.

advertorial /ædvə'tɔriəl/ *n.* a media piece that looks like a news or feature article but which is written and paid for by an advertiser.

advice /əd'vaɪs/ *n.* **1.** an opinion recommended, or offered, as worthy to be followed. **2.** a communication, especially from a distance, containing information. **3.** a formal or professional opinion given, especially by a barrister.

advisable /əd'vaɪzəbəl/ *adj.* proper to be advised or to be recommended.

advise /əd'vaɪz/ *v.t.* **1.** to give counsel to; offer an opinion to, as worthy or expedient to be followed. **2.** to recommend as wise, prudent, etc. *-v.i.* **3.** to offer counsel; give advice. *-phr.* **4. advise someone of something**, to give someone information or notice about something. **-adviser**, *n.*

advisory /əd'vaɪzəri/ *adj.* **1.** of, or giving, advice; having power to advise. *-n.* (*pl.* **-sories**) **2.** a statement of advice.

advocate *v.t.* /'ædvəkeɪt/ **1.** to plead in favour of; support or urge by argument; recommend publicly. *-n.* /'ædvəkət, -keɪt/ **2.** (fol. by *of*) someone who defends, vindicates, or espouses a cause by argument; an upholder; a defender. **-advocacy**, *n.* **-advocator**, *n.* **-advocatory**, *adj.*

adze /ædz/ *n.* **1.** a heavy chisel-like tool fastened at right angles to a wooden handle, used to dress timber, etc. *-v.t.* **2.** to carve out using an adze. Also, *US*, **adz**.

ae- For words beginning in **ae-**, see also spellings under **e-**.

aegis /'idʒəs/ *n.* protection; sponsorship.

-aemia /'imiə/ *a* suffix referring to the state of the blood. Also, **-emia, -haemia, -hemia**.

aeon /'iən/ *n.* an indefinitely long period of time; an age. Also, **eon**.

aerate /'ɛəreɪt/ *v.t.* to charge or treat with air or a gas, especially with carbon dioxide.

aerial /'ɛəriəl/ *n.* **1.** that part of a radio or television system which radiates or receives electromagnetic or microwave signals into or from free space and which may consist of a simple wire, a single metal rod, or a complex metal framework; an antenna. *-adj.* **2.** of, in, or produced by the air. **3.** inhabiting or frequenting the air. **4.** unsubstantial; visionary. **5.** having a light and graceful beauty; ethereal. **6.** relating to or used for, against, or in aircraft. **-aerially**, *adv.*

aero- a word element indicating: **1.** air; atmosphere. **2.** gas. **3.** aeroplane.

aerobatics /ɛərə'bætɪks/ *pl. n.* stunts carried out by aircraft. **-aerobatic**, *adj.*

aerobic /ɛə'roubɪk/ *adj.* (of organisms or tissues) living or active only in the presence of free oxygen (opposed to *anaerobic*).

aerobic exercise *n.* physical exercise during which energy is derived from glucose produced by the reaction of oxygen in the blood with stored glycogen, and which typically involves moderate activity over a relatively long period of time.

aerobics /ɛə'roubɪks/ *pl. n.* physical exercises which stimulate the respiratory and circulatory systems to improve and maintain physical fitness.

aerobic threshold *n.* the physiological state of the body induced by a level of physical exercise just short of that required to cross the anaerobic threshold. *Abbrev.*: AeT

aerobridge /'ɛəroubrɪdʒ/ *n.* a covered portable walkway for the transfer of passengers from a departure terminal to an aeroplane. Also, **airbridge**.

aerodrome /'ɛərədroum/ *n.* a landing field for aeroplanes, especially private aeroplanes, usually smaller than an airport.

aerodynamic /ˌɛəroudaɪ'næmɪk/ *adj.* **1.** of or relating to aerodynamics. **2.** able to travel through the air; designed for air travel. **3.** of or relating to a shape that reduces drag (def. 9): *an aerodynamic spoiler.* **-aerodynamically**, *adv.*

aerodynamics /ˌɛəroudaɪ'næmɪks/ *n.* **1.** the study of air in motion and of the forces acting on solids in motion relative to the air through which they move. **2.** the properties of a solid object in relation to these forces acting on it: *the aerodynamics of the new-model car.*

aerogenerator /ɛərou'dʒɛnəreɪtə/ *n.* → **wind turbine**.

aerogram /'ɛərəgræm/ *n.* a sheet of lightweight paper which serves both as the envelope and the writing paper for an airmail letter. Also, **aerogramme**.

aeronautics /ɛərə'nɔtɪks/ *n.* the science or art of flight. **-aeronautical, aeronautic**, *adj.*

aeroplane /'ɛərəpleɪn/ *n.* an aircraft, heavier than air, kept aloft by the upward thrust exerted by the passing air on its fixed wings, and driven by propellers, jet propulsion, etc.

aerosol /'ɛərəsɒl/ n. a metal container for storing a substance under pressure and subsequently dispensing it as a spray; spray can.

aesthetic /əs'θɛtɪk, is-/ adj. relating to the sense of the beautiful or the science of aesthetics. Also, **esthetic**.

aesthetics /əs'θɛtɪks, is-/ n. Philos. the science which deduces from nature and taste the rules and principles of art; the theory of the fine arts. Also, **esthetics**. –**aesthetical**, adj. –**aesthetically**, adv.

aetiology /iti'ɒlədʒi/ n. the study of the causes of anything, especially of diseases. Also, **etiology**.

af- variant of **ad-** (by assimilation) before f, as in affect.

afar /ə'fa/ adv. (usu. preceded by from) from a distance.

affable /'æfəbəl/ adj. easy to talk to or to approach; polite; friendly.

affair /ə'fɛə/ n. **1.** anything done or to be done; that which requires action or effort; business; concern. **2.** (pl.) matters of interest or concern; particular doings or interests. **3.** an event or a performance; a particular action, operation, or proceeding. **4.** a sexual relationship.

affect[1] /ə'fɛkt/ v.t. **1.** to act on; produce an effect or a change in. **2.** to impress; move (in mind or feelings).

affect[2] /ə'fɛkt/ v.t. **1.** to make a show of; feign. **2.** to use or adopt by preference.

affectation /ˌæfɛk'teɪʃən/ n. **1.** pretence. **2.** artificiality of manner or conduct; effort to attract notice by pretence, assumption, or any assumed peculiarity.

affected[1] /ə'fɛktəd/ adj. **1.** acted upon; influenced. **2.** influenced injuriously; impaired; attacked, as by climate or disease. **3.** moved; touched.

affected[2] /ə'fɛktəd/ adj. **1.** assumed artificially. **2.** assuming or pretending to possess characteristics which are not natural.

affection /ə'fɛkʃən/ n. **1.** a settled goodwill, love, or attachment. **2.** the act or result of affecting.

affectionate /ə'fɛkʃənət/ adj. characterised by or manifesting affection; possessing or indicating love; tender.

affective /ə'fɛktɪv/ adj. of or relating to the feelings; emotional.

affiance /æfi'ɒns, ə'faɪəns/ v.t. to bind by promise of marriage; betroth.

affidavit /æfə'deɪvət/ n. a written statement on oath, sworn to before an authorised official, often used as evidence in court proceedings.

affiliate v.t. /ə'filieɪt/ **1.** (fol. by with) to attach as a branch or part; unite; associate. **2.** to bring into association or close connection. –v.i. /ə'filieɪt/ **3.** to associate oneself; be intimately united in action or interest. –n. /ə'filiət/ **4.** someone or that which is affiliated; associate or auxiliary. –**affiliation**, n.

affinity /ə'finəti/ n. (pl. **-ties**) **1.** a natural liking for, or attraction to, a person or thing. **2.** close resemblance or connection.

affirm /ə'fɜm/ v.t. **1.** to state or assert positively; maintain as true. **2.** to establish, confirm, or ratify. –v.i. **3.** to declare positively; assert

solemnly. **4.** Law to declare solemnly before a court or magistrate, but without oath (a practice allowed where the affirmant has scruples, usually religious, against taking an oath). –**affirmation**, n.

affirmative /ə'fɜmətɪv/ adj. **1.** giving affirmation or assent; not negative. –n. **2.** an affirmative word or phrase, as yes or I do.

affirmative action n. action designed to provide increased employment opportunities for groups who have previously suffered discrimination, especially women and minority racial groups.

affix v.t. /ə'fɪks/ **1.** (oft. fol. by to) to fix; fasten; join, or attach. –n. /'æfɪks/ **2.** that which is joined or attached. **3.** Gram. any meaningful element (prefix, infix, or suffix) added to a stem or base, as -ed added to want to form wanted. –**affixation**, n.

afflict /ə'flɪkt/ v.t. to distress with mental or bodily pain; trouble greatly or grievously. –**affliction**, n.

affluent /'æfluənt/ adj. rich. –**affluence**, n.

afford /ə'fɔd/ v.t. **1.** (oft. preceded by can or may and fol. by an infinitive) to have the means. **2.** (oft. preceded by can or may) to be able to meet the expense of; spare the price of. **3.** (oft. preceded by can or may) to be able to give or spare. **4.** to give or confer upon. –**affordable**, adj. –**affordability**, n.

affront /ə'frʌnt/ n. **1.** a personally offensive act or word; an intentional slight. –v.t. **2.** to offend by an open manifestation of disrespect or insolence. **3.** to put out of countenance.

aficionado /əfiʃiə'nadou/ n. (pl. **-dos**) **1.** an ardent devotee. **2.** a person who is very knowledgeable about something. Also, **afficionado**.

afield /ə'fild/ adv. **1.** abroad; away from home. **2.** off the beaten path; far and wide.

aflatoxin /æflə'tɒksən/ n. a naturally occurring carcinogenic toxin produced by a fungus; found in grains, peanuts, etc., before harvesting or in storage.

afloat /ə'flout/ adj., adv. **1.** borne on the water; in a floating condition. **2.** flooded. **3.** passing from place to place; in circulation. –phr. **4.** stay afloat, to survive financially.

afoot /ə'fut/ adj. in progress.

aforesaid /ə'fɔsɛd/ adj. said or mentioned previously.

afraid /ə'freɪd/ adj. **1.** feeling fear. **2.** reluctantly or regretfully of the opinion.

afresh /ə'frɛʃ/ adv. anew; again.

aft /aft/ adv. Naut. at, in, or towards the stern.

after /'aftə/ prep. **1.** behind in place or time. **2.** in pursuit of; in search of; with or in desire for. **3.** concerning. **4.** subsequent to and in consequence of. **5.** below in rank or excellence; next to. **6.** in imitation of, or in imitation of the style of. **7.** with name of. **8.** in proportion to; in accordance with. **9.** according to the nature of; in agreement or unison with; in conformity to. –adv. **10.** behind. –adj. **11.** later in time; next; subsequent; succeeding. **12.** Naut. farther aft, or towards the stern of the ship. –conj. **13.** subsequent to the time that.

afterbirth /'aftəbɜθ/ n. the placenta and fetal membranes expelled from the uterus after parturition.

afterlife /'aftəlaıf/ *n.* life after death.

aftermath /'aftəmæθ, -maθ/ *n.* resultant conditions, especially of a catastrophe.

afternoon /aftə'nun/ *n.* the time from noon until evening.

afterwards /'aftəwədz/ *adv.* in later or subsequent time; subsequently. Also, **afterward**.

ag- variant of **ad-** (by assimilation) before *g*, as in *agglutinate*.

again /ə'gɛn/ *adv.* **1.** once more; in addition; another time; anew. **2.** in an additional case or instance; moreover; besides; furthermore. **3.** on the other hand. **4.** in the opposite direction; to the same place or person.

against /ə'gɛnst, ə'geɪnst/ *prep.* **1.** in an opposite direction to, so as to meet; towards; upon. **2.** in contact with, or in pressure upon. **3.** in opposition to; adverse or hostile to. **4.** in resistance to or defence from. **5.** in preparation for; in provision for. **6.** in contrast with; having as background. **7.** in exchange for; in return for; as a balance to. **8.** (sometimes preceded by *as*) instead of, as an alternative to, in contrast with.

agape /ə'geɪp/ *adv.* **1.** in an attitude of wonder or eagerness; with the mouth wide open. *–adj.* **2.** wide open.

agate /'ægət/ *n.* a variegated variety of quartz showing coloured bands or other markings.

age /eɪdʒ/ *n.* **1.** the length of time during which a being or thing has existed. **2.** the lifetime of an individual, or of the individuals of a class or species on an average. **3.** one of the periods or stages of human life. **4.** old age. **5.** a particular period of history, as distinguished from others; a historical epoch. **6.** a generation or a succession of generations. **7.** *Colloq.* a great length of time. **8.** *Geol.* a long or short part of the world's history distinguished by special features. *–v.t., v.i.* (**aged, ageing** *or* **aging**) **9.** to make or become old or mature. *–phr.* **10. of age**, being in possession of full adult rights and responsibilities.

-age a noun suffix, forming: **1.** collective nouns as in *leafage*. **2.** nouns denoting condition, rank, service, fee, etc., as in *bondage, parsonage*. **3.** nouns expressing various relations, from verbs, as in *breakage, cleavage*. **4.** nouns denoting an amount or charge as in *postage, corkage*.

aged /eɪdʒd, 'eɪdʒed/ *for defs 1 and 7,* /eɪdʒd/ *for defs 2–6 –adj.* **1.** having lived or existed long: *an aged woman; an aged tree.* **2.** relating to old age: *the aged sector.* **3.** of the age of: *a woman aged 40 years.* **4.** (of horses) more than six (or sometimes eight) years old. **5.** (of a sheep) usually five years of age or older, and past the stage of its greatest economic usefulness. **6.** (of a product, as wine, cheese, etc.) having been subjected to an ageing process; matured. *–n.* **7. the aged**, aged people. **–agedly** /'eɪdʒədli/, *adv.* **–agedness** /'eɪdʒədnəs/, *n.*

ageism /'eɪdʒɪzəm/ *n.* an attitude which stereotypes a person, especially an elderly person, according to age.

agency /'eɪdʒənsi/ *n.* (*pl.* **-cies**) **1.** a commercial or other organisation furnishing some form of service for the public. **2.** the office of agent; the business of an agent entrusted with the concerns of another. **3.** the state of being in action or of exerting power; action; operation. **4.** a mode of exerting power; a means of producing effects.

agenda /ə'dʒɛndə/ *n.* **1.** a program or list of things to be done, discussed, etc. **2.** a set of motivating factors: *to be acting on a personal agenda.*

agender /eɪ'dʒɛndə/ *adj.* identifying as having no gender.

agent /'eɪdʒənt/ *n.* **1.** a person acting on behalf of another. **2.** someone who or that which acts or has the power to act. **3.** someone who acts for a buyer or seller of stock or wool, etc., and who usually represents a firm supplying manufactured rural requirements for the farmer. **4.** a representative of a business firm, especially a commercial traveller; a canvasser.

agent provocateur /ˌaʒõ prəvokə'tɜ/ *n.* (*pl.* **agents provocateurs** /ˌaʒõ prəvokə'tɜz/) any person who tries to incite dissatisfaction or unrest, especially someone who incites to an illegal action.

age spot *n.* → **liver spot**.

agglomerate *v.t.* /ə'glɒməreɪt/ **1.** to collect or gather into a mass. *–n.* /ə'glɒmərət/ **2.** a rock formation composed of large angular volcanic fragments. **–agglomeration**, *n.*

agglutinate /ə'glutəneɪt/ *v.t.* to unite or cause to adhere, as with glue. **–agglutination**, *n.*

aggrandise /ə'grændaɪz/ *v.t.* **1.** to make great or greater in power, wealth, rank, or honour. **2.** to make (something) appear greater. Also, **aggrandize**. **–aggrandisement**, *n.* **–aggrandiser**, *n.*

aggravate /'ægrəveɪt/ *v.t.* **1.** to make worse or more severe; intensify, as anything evil, disorderly, or troublesome. **2.** *Colloq.* to provoke; irritate; exasperate.

aggregate *adj.* /'ægrəgət/ **1.** formed by the conjunction or collection of particulars into a whole mass or sum; total; combined. *–n.* /'ægrəgət/ **2.** a sum, or assemblage of particulars; a total or gross amount. **3.** any hard material added to cement to make concrete. *–v.t.* /'ægrəgeɪt/ **4.** to bring together; collect into one sum, mass, or body. **5.** to amount to (the number of). **–aggregation**, *n.*

aggression /ə'grɛʃən/ *n.* **1.** any offensive action or procedure; an inroad or encroachment. **2.** *Psychol.* the emotional drive to attack; an offensive mental attitude (rather than defensive). **–aggressive**, *adj.* **–aggressor**, *n.*

aggrieve /ə'griv/ *v.t.* (*now used chiefly in the passive*) to oppress or wrong grievously; injure by injustice. **–aggrieved**, *adj.*

aggro /'ægroʊ/ *adj. Colloq.* aggressive; dominating.

aghast /ə'gast/ *adj.* struck with amazement; stupefied with fright or horror.

agile /'ædʒaɪl/ *adj.* **1.** quick and light in movement. **2.** active; lively. **–agility**, *n.*

agist /ə'dʒɪst/ *v.t.* to take in and feed or pasture (livestock) for payment.

agitate /'ædʒəteɪt/ *v.t.* **1.** to move or force into violent irregular action; shake or move briskly. **2.** to disturb, or excite into tumult; perturb. *–v.i.* **3.** to arouse or attempt to arouse public feeling as in some political or social question. **–agitation**, *n.* **–agitator**, *n.*

agnostic /æg'nɒstɪk/ n. **1.** someone who holds that the ultimate cause (God) and the essential nature of things are unknown or unknowable, or that human knowledge is limited to experience. –adj. **2.** relating to agnostics or their doctrines.

ago /ə'goʊ/ adv. in past time.

agog /ə'gɒg/ adj. highly excited by eagerness or curiosity.

-agogue a word element meaning 'leading' or 'guiding', found in a few agent nouns (often with pejorative value), as in demagogue, pedagogue.

agonist /'ægənəst/ n. an actively contracting muscle considered in relation to its opposing muscle (the antagonist).

agony /'ægəni/ n. (pl. **-nies**) **1.** extreme, and generally prolonged, pain; intense suffering. **2.** the struggle preceding natural death. –**agonise**, **agonize**, v.

agoraphobia /ægərə'foʊbiə/ n. a morbid fear of being in open or public spaces. –**agoraphobic**, adj., n.

agrarian /ə'grɛəriən/ adj. **1.** relating to land, land tenure, or the division of landed property. **2.** rural; agricultural.

agree /ə'gri/ v. (**agreed**, **agreeing**) –v.i. **1.** (oft. fol. by to, esp. with reference to things and acts) to yield assent; consent. **2.** (oft. fol. by with, esp. with reference to persons) to be of one mind; harmonise in opinion or feeling. **3.** (sometimes fol. by upon) to come to one opinion or mind; come to an arrangement or understanding; arrive at a settlement. –v.t. **4.** to concede; grant: I agree that she is the ablest of us. **5.** to determine; settle: to agree a price. –phr. **6. agree** with, to be accommodated or adapted to; suit. –**agreed**, adj.

agreeable /ə'griəbəl/ adj. **1.** to one's liking; pleasing. **2.** willing or ready to agree or consent.

agreement /ə'grimənt/ n. **1.** (the act of coming to) a mutual arrangement. **2.** the state of being in accord; concord; harmony; conformity.

agribusiness /'ægrɪbɪznəs/ n. the businesses, collectively, which are involved in the production, distribution and sale of agricultural produce. Also, **agri-business**.

agriculture /'ægrəkʌltʃə/ n. the cultivation of land, including crop-raising, forestry, stock-raising, etc.; farming. –**agricultural**, adj.

agro- a word element meaning 'soil', 'field'.

agronomy /ə'grɒnəmi/ n. the applied aspects of both soil science and the several plant sciences, often limited to applied plant sciences dealing with crops.

ahead /ə'hɛd/ adv. **1.** in or to the front; in advance; before. **2.** forward; onward.

ahoy /ə'hɔɪ/ interj. a call used in hailing, especially on ships.

AI /eɪ 'aɪ/ n. artificial intelligence.

aid /eɪd/ v.t. **1.** to afford support or relief to; help. –n. **2.** help; support; assistance.

aide-de-camp /eɪd-də-'kɒ̃/ n. (pl. **aides-de-camp**) a military or naval officer acting as a confidential assistant to a superior, especially a general, governor, etc.

AIDS /eɪdz/ n. acquired immune deficiency syndrome; a disease caused by a virus (HIV) which destroys the body's white cells, resulting in reduced immunity, and therefore severe infections, tumours, and ultimately death.

aikido /aɪ'kidoʊ, ˌaɪkɪdoʊ/ n. a Japanese martial art in which the attacker's energy or force is deflected and used against them.

ail /eɪl/ v.t. **1.** to affect with pain or uneasiness; trouble. –v.i. **2.** to feel pain; be ill (usually in a slight degree); be unwell. –**ailing**, adj. –**ailment**, n.

aileron /'eɪlərɒn/ n. a hinged, movable flap of an aeroplane wing, used primarily to maintain balance.

aim /eɪm/ v.t. **1.** to direct or point (something) at something. –v.i. **2.** to level a gun; give direction to a blow, missile, etc. **3.** to direct efforts towards an object. –n. **4.** the act of aiming or directing anything at or towards a particular point or object. **5.** something intended or desired to be attained by one's efforts; purpose. –**aimless**, adj.

air /ɛə/ n. **1.** a mixture of oxygen, nitrogen and other gases, which surrounds the earth and forms its atmosphere. **2.** the general character or complexion of anything; appearance. **3.** (pl.) Also, **airs and graces**. an affected manner; manifestation of pride or vanity; assumed haughtiness. **4.** Music a tune; a melody. –v.t. **5.** to expose to the air; give access to the open air; ventilate. **6.** to expose ostentatiously; bring into public notice; display. **7.** Communications to broadcast or telecast. –phr. **8. off (the) air**, no longer being broadcast; not on the air. **9. on (the) air**, in the act of broadcasting; being broadcast.

airbag /'ɛəbæg/ n. a safety device in a motor vehicle consisting of a bag which inflates instantly before the driver or front-seat passenger on collision.

air conditioning n. a system of treating air in buildings or vehicles to assure temperature, humidity, dustlessness, and movement at levels most conducive to personal comfort, manufacturing processes, or preservation of items stored. Also, **air-conditioning**. –**air-conditioned**, adj.

air corridor n. an air route established by international agreement or government regulation.

air cover n. **1.** the protection of ground forces by an air force. **2.** the aircraft so used.

aircraft /'ɛəkrɑft/ n. (pl. **-craft**) any machine supported for flight in the air by buoyancy (such as balloons and other lighter-than-air craft) or by dynamic action of air on its surfaces (such as aeroplanes, helicopters, gliders, and other heavier-than-air craft).

aircraft carrier n. a large naval ship, designed to serve as an air base at sea, with a long strip of deck for the taking off and landing of aircraft.

air crane n. (from trademark) a heavy-lifting helicopter as for aerial firefighting, agriculture and aerial construction.

airfare /'ɛəfɛə/ n. the price of a flight in a commercial aircraft.

air force n. the branch of the armed forces of any country concerned with military aircraft.

air guitar *n.* an imaginary guitar which someone pretends to hold and play, usually to rock music.

air gun *n.* a gun in which the projectile is discharged by the release of compressed air. Also, **airgun**.

airhead /ˈɛəhɛd/ *n. Colloq.* an absent-minded or forgetful person.

air kiss *n. Colloq.* a formalised kiss of greeting or farewell in which one's lips do not make contact with the other person.

airlift /ˈɛəlɪft/ *n.* a system of transporting people, supplies, equipment, etc., by aircraft when surface routes are blocked, as during a military blockade, or at a time of national emergency.

airline /ˈɛəlaɪn/ *n.* **1.** a system furnishing scheduled air transport between specified points. **2.** a company that owns or operates such a system.

airlock /ˈɛəlɒk/ *n. Eng.* an obstruction to or stoppage of a flow of liquid in a pipe caused by an air bubble.

airmail /ˈɛəmeɪl/ *n.* the system of transmitting mail by aircraft.

air marshal *n.* → **sky marshal**.

air pistol *n.* a pistol which has an air gun mechanism.

airplay /ˈɛəpleɪ/ *n.* the amount of public exposure a recording receives on radio or television.

air pocket *n. Aeronautics* a downward current of air, usually causing a sudden loss of altitude.

air pollution *n.* the contamination of the air by substances such as chemical fumes, particulate matter, gases, etc.

airport /ˈɛəpɔt/ *n.* a large area where aircraft land and take off, usually equipped with a control tower, hangars, and accommodation for the receiving and discharging of passengers and cargo.

air quotes *pl. n.* the representation of quotation marks during speech, made by a movement of the fingers in the air, and used to indicate that an expression is a quotation, is intended ironically, or is one that the speaker would not normally use.

air rage *n.* uncontrolled aggressive behaviour in an aeroplane, resulting from the tensions of air travel.

air raid *n.* a raid by hostile aircraft, especially for dropping bombs or other missiles. **–air-raider**, *n.*

airspace /ˈɛəspeɪs/ *n.* **1.** the space directly above a building which can be sold for the construction of another building on or over the first. **2.** the part or region of the atmosphere above the territory of a nation or other political division which is considered under its jurisdiction.

airtight /ˈɛətaɪt/ *adj.* so tight or close as to be impermeable to air.

airtime /ˈɛətaɪm/ *n.* **1.** the amount of television or radio broadcasting time dedicated to a particular subject, person, recording, etc. **2.** the amount of time a mobile phone is able to be used, especially as that allocated under a mobile phone service provision contract: *unlimited airtime.*

airy /ˈɛəri/ *adj.* (**airier**, **airiest**) **1.** open to a free current of air. **2.** light in appearance; thin. **3.** light in manner; sprightly; lively.

4. visionary; speculative. **5.** casual, off-hand; superficial, flippant.

aisle /aɪl/ *n.* a passageway between seats in a church, hall, etc., between seats in bus, train, aeroplane, etc., or between shelves in a supermarket, etc.

aitch (*sometimes considered non-standard*) /heɪtʃ/ *n.* the letter H, h.

ajar /əˈdʒɑ/ *adv.* **1.** neither quite open nor shut; partly opened. **–***adj.* **2.** partly open.

aka /ˈæka, eɪ keɪ ˈeɪ/ *adv.* also known as: *Smith aka Jones.*

akimbo /əˈkɪmboʊ/ *adv.* with hands on hips and elbows bent outwards.

akin /əˈkɪn/ *adj.* **1.** of kin; related by blood. **2.** allied by nature; partaking of the same properties.

al- variant of **ad-** before *l*, as in *allure.*

-al¹ an adjective suffix meaning 'relating to', 'connected with', 'being', 'like', 'befitting', etc., occurring in numerous adjectives and in many nouns of adjectival origin, as *annual*, *choral*, *equal*, *regal.*

-al² a suffix forming nouns of action from verbs, as in *refusal*, *denial*, *recital*, *trial.*

-al³ a suffix indicating that a compound includes an alcohol.

alabaster /ˈæləbæstə/ *n.* a finely granular variety of gypsum, often white and translucent, used for ornamental objects or work, such as lamp bases, figurines, etc.

alacrity /əˈlækrəti/ *n.* **1.** liveliness; briskness; sprightliness. **2.** cheerful readiness or willingness.

alarm /əˈlam/ *n.* **1.** a sudden fear or painful suspense excited by an apprehension of danger; apprehension; fright. **2.** any sound, outcry, or information intended to give notice of approaching danger. **3.** a self-acting contrivance of any kind used to call attention, rouse from sleep, warn of danger, etc. **–***v.t.* **4.** to surprise with apprehension of danger; disturb with sudden fear. **5.** to fit (a house, motor vehicle, etc.) with an alarm system.

alarmist /əˈlaməst/ *n.* somehow who raises an alarm, especially making the danger seem greater than it really is.

alas /əˈlæs, əˈlas/ *interj.* (an exclamation expressing sorrow, grief, pity, concern, or apprehension of evil).

albatross /ˈælbətrɒs/ *n.* any of various large web-footed seabirds related to the petrels.

albeit /ɔlˈbiət, æl-/ *conj.* although; notwithstanding that.

albino /ælˈbinoʊ, -ˈbaɪnoʊ/ *n.* (*pl.* **-nos**) a person with a pale, milky skin, light hair, and pink eyes, resulting from a congenital absence of pigmentation.

album /ˈælbəm/ *n.* **1.** a book consisting of blank leaves for the insertion or preservation of photographs, stamps, autographs, etc. **2.** a long-playing recording on which there is a collection of songs or pieces.

alchemy /ˈælkəmi/ *n.* the medieval form of chemistry which tried to find ways of changing all metals into gold. **–alchemist**, *n.*

alcheringa /æltʃəˈrɪŋgə/ *n.* → **Dreaming** (def. 1). Also, **alchera** /ˈæltʃərə/.

alcohol /ˈælkəhɒl/ *n.* **1.** a colourless, flammable liquid (**ethyl alcohol**), the intoxicating principle of fermented liquors. **2.** any intoxicating liquor containing this spirit. **3.** *Chem.* any of a class of compounds derived from the hydrocarbon by replacement of a hydrogen atom by the hydroxyl radical, OH.

alcoholic /ˈælkəˈhɒlɪk/ *adj.* **1.** of or relating to alcohol. *−n.* **2.** a person suffering from alcoholism. **3.** one addicted to intoxicating drinks.

alcoholism /ˈælkəhɒlɪzəm/ *n.* an addiction to alcohol which is detrimental to one's health or social functioning.

alcopop /ˈælkoʊpɒp/ *n.* a commercially-sold alcoholic drink based on a soft drink, such as lemonade, etc., to which alcohol has been added.

alcove /ˈælkoʊv/ *n.* a recess opening out of a room.

alderman /ˈɔldəmən/ *n.* (*pl.* **-men**) (in various countries, as Australia and the US) an elected local government representative having powers varying according to locality.

ale /eɪl/ *n.* beer.

aleatory /ˈæliˈentəri/ *adj.* **1.** dependent on chance. *−phr.* **2. aleatory contract**, a contract or agreement of which the effects with respect both to the advantages and the losses depend on uncertain events; a wagering contract.

alert /əˈlɜt/ *adj.* **1.** vigilantly attentive. *−n.* **2.** an attitude of vigilance, wariness or caution. *−v.t.* **3.** to prepare (troops, etc.) for action.

alfalfa /ælˈfælfə/ *n.* **1.** → **lucerne**. **2.** → **alfalfa sprouts**.

alfalfa sprouts *pl. n.* the sprouts of alfalfa seeds, used in salads. Also, **alfalfa**.

alfresco /ælˈfrɛskoʊ/ *adv.* **1.** in the open air; out-of-doors: *to dine alfresco.* *−adj.* **2.** open-air: *an alfresco cafe.* Also, **al fresco**.

algae /ˈældʒi, ˈælgi/ *pl. n.* (*sing.* **alga**) one or many-celled chlorophyll-containing plants, such as seaweed.

algebra /ˈældʒəbrə/ *n.* the mathematical art of reasoning about (quantitative) relations by means of a systematised notation including letters and other symbols. **−algebraic**, *adj.*

-algia a noun suffix meaning 'pain'.

algo- a word element meaning 'pain'.

ALGOL /ˈælgɒl/ *n.* an internationally accepted language in which computer programs are written.

algorithm /ˈælgərɪðəm/ *n.* an effective procedure for solving a particular mathematical problem in a finite number of steps. Also, **algorism**.

alias /ˈeɪliəs/ *adv.* **1.** known sometimes as: *Simpson alias Smith.* *−n.* **2.** an assumed name; another name: *living under an alias.*

alibi /ˈæləbaɪ/ *n.* (**-bis**) *Law* a defence by an accused person that they were elsewhere at the time the offence with which they are charged was committed.

alien /ˈeɪliən/ *n.* one born in or belonging to another country who has not acquired citizenship by naturalisation and is not entitled to the privileges of a citizen.

alienate /ˈeɪliəneɪt/ *v.t.* **1.** to make indifferent or averse; estrange. **2.** to turn away.

alight[1] /əˈlaɪt/ *v.i.* (**alighted** *or* **alit** /əˈlɪt/, **alighting**) to get down from a horse or out of a vehicle.

alight[2] /əˈlaɪt/ *adj.* burning.

align /əˈlaɪn/ *v.t.* **1.** to adjust to a line; lay out or regulate by line; form in line. **2.** to adjust (mechanical items such as car wheels) so that as a group they are in positions favouring optimum performance. *−v.i.* **3.** to fall or come into line; be in line.

alike /əˈlaɪk/ *adv.* **1.** in the same manner, form, or degree; in common; equally. *−adj.* **2.** having resemblance or similarity; having or exhibiting no marked or essential difference (used regularly after a plural noun or pronoun): *The sisters are alike.*

alimentary canal /æləˈmɛntri/ *n.* the digestive passage in any animal from mouth to anus. Also, **alimentary tract**.

alimony /ˈæləməni/, *Orig. US* /-moʊni/ *n.* *US* → **maintenance** (def. 2).

A-list /ˈeɪ-lɪst/ *n.* *Colloq.* a list, often unwritten, of the most desirable celebrities or other public figures sought for prestigious or spectacular social events, etc. Also, **A list**. **−A-lister**, *n.*

alive /əˈlaɪv/ *adj.* (*rarely preceding the noun or pronoun*) **1.** in life or existence; living. **2.** in a state of action; in force or operation. **3.** full of life; lively.

alkali /ˈælkəlaɪ/ *n.* (*pl.* **-lis** *or* **-lies**) *Chem.* any of various bases which neutralise acids to form salts and turn red litmus paper blue. **−alkaline**, *adj.* **−alkalinity**, *n.*

all /ɔl/ *adj.* **1.** the whole of (with reference to quantity, extent, duration, amount, or degree). **2.** the whole number of (with reference to individuals or particulars, taken collectively). *−pron.* **3.** the whole quantity or amount. *−n.* **4.** a whole; a totality of things or qualities. **5.** one's whole interest, concern, or property. *−adv.* **6.** wholly; entirely; quite. **7.** only; exclusively. **8.** each; apiece. **9.** (fol. by *the* and a comparative adjective) by so much; to that extent.

allay /əˈleɪ/ *v.t.* (**-layed**, **-laying**) **1.** to put at rest; quiet (tumult, fear, suspicion, etc.); appease (wrath). **2.** to mitigate; relieve or alleviate.

allege /əˈlɛdʒ/ *v.t.* (**-leged**, **-leging**) **1.** to assert without proof. **2.** to declare before a court, or elsewhere as if upon oath. **3.** to declare with positiveness; affirm; assert. **−allegation**, *n.* **−allegedly**, *adv.*

allegiance /əˈlidʒəns/ *n.* **1.** the obligation of a subject or citizen to their sovereign or government; duty owed to a sovereign or state. **2.** observance of obligation; faithfulness to any person or thing.

allegory /ˈæləgəri, -gri/ *n.* (*pl.* **-ries**) figurative treatment of one subject under the guise of another; a presentation of an abstract or spiritual meaning under concrete or material forms. **−allegorical**, *adj.*

allergen /ˈælədʒən/ *n.* any substance which might induce an allergy. **−allergenic** /æləˈdʒɛnɪk/, *adj.*

allergy /ˈælədʒi/ *n.* (*pl.* **-gies**) a state of physical hypersensitivity to certain things, as pollens, food, fruits, etc., which are normally harmless. **−allergic**, *adj.*

alleviate /əˈliviert/ *v.t.* to make easier to be endured; lessen; mitigate.

alley /ˈæli/ *n.* (*pl.* **-leys**) a narrow lane.

alliance /ə'laɪəns/ n. **1.** the state of being allied or connected; relation between parties allied or connected. **2.** any joining of efforts or interests by persons, families, states, or organisations.

alligator /'æləgeɪtə/ n. the broad-snouted representative of the crocodile group.

alliteration /əlɪtə'reɪʃən/ n. the commencement of two or more words of a word group with the same sound.

allo- a word element indicating difference, alternation, or divergence.

allocate /'æləkeɪt/ v.t. to set apart for a particular purpose; assign or allot. –**allocation**, n.

allot /ə'lɒt/ v.t. (-**lotted**, -**lotting**) to divide or distribute as by lot; distribute or parcel out; apportion.

allotment /ə'lɒtmənt/ n. **1.** a portion, share, or thing allotted. **2.** a block of land.

allotrope /'ælətroup/ n. one of two or more existing forms of a chemical element.

allow /ə'lau/ v.t. **1.** to grant permission to or for; permit. **2.** to admit; acknowledge; concede. –phr. **3. allow for**, to make concession, allowance, or provision for.

allowance /ə'lauəns/ n. **1.** a definite amount or share allotted; a ration. **2.** an addition, as to a wage, etc., on account of some extenuating or qualifying circumstance. **3.** sanction; tolerance. –phr. **4. make allowance(s)**, (sometimes fol. by for) **a.** to take special circumstances into account in mitigating a judgement. **b.** to include relevant factors in reaching a conclusion.

alloy /'ælɔɪ/ n. a substance composed of two or more metals (or, sometimes, a metal and a nonmetal).

all right adj. **1.** safe and sound: *Are you all right?* **2.** satisfactory; acceptable: *His work is sometimes all right.* –adv. **3.** satisfactorily; acceptably; correctly: *He did his job all right.* Also, **alright**.

allspice /'ɔlspaɪs/ n. **1.** the berry of a tropical American tree. **2.** a mildly sharp and fragrant spice made from it.

allude /ə'lud/ phr. **allude to**, to make an allusion to, refer casually or indirectly to.

all-up adj. total; inclusive.

allure /ə'luə, ə'ljuə/ v.t. **1.** to attract by the offer of some real or apparent good; tempt by something flattering or acceptable. –n. **2.** fascination; charm.

allusion /ə'luʒən/ n. a passing or casual reference; an incidental mention of something, either directly or by implication.

alluvial /ə'luviəl/ adj. **1.** of or relating to alluvium. **2.** of or relating to a mine, claim, diggings, etc., on alluvial soil.

alluvium /ə'luviəm/ n. (pl. **-via** /-viə/ or **-viums**) **1.** a deposit of sand, mud, etc., formed by flowing water. **2.** the sedimentary matter deposited thus within recent times, especially in the valleys of large rivers.

all-wheel drive n. **1.** a motor vehicle drive system which gives a constant connection of all four wheels to the source of power. **2.** a motor vehicle which has such a system. *Abbrev.*: AWD

ally v.t. /ə'laɪ/ (-**lied**, -**lying**) **1.** (fol. by to or with) to unite by marriage, treaty, league, or confederacy; connect by formal agreement. –n. /'ælaɪ/ (pl. -**lies**) **2.** one united or associated

with another, especially by treaty or league; an allied nation, sovereign, etc. **3.** someone who cooperates with another; supporter; associate.

almanac /'ɔlmənæk, 'æl-/ n. a calendar of the days of the year, in weeks and months, indicating the time of various events or phenomena during the period, as anniversaries, sunrise and sunset, changes of the moon and tides, etc.

almighty /ɔl'maɪti/ adj. possessing all power; omnipotent.

almond /'amənd/ n. a kind of nut, grown in warm temperate regions.

almost /'ɔlmoust/ adv. very nearly; all but.

alms /amz/ n. (construed as sing. or pl.) that which is given to the poor or needy; anything given as charity.

aloe vera /æloʊ 'vɪərə/ n. a plant with fleshy leaves whose sap is used in skin lotions, etc.

aloft /ə'lɒft/ adv., adj. high up; in or into the air; above the ground.

alone /ə'loun/ adj. (used after the noun or pronoun) **1.** apart from another or others. **2.** without friendly or familiar company. **3.** to the exclusion of all others or all else. –adv. **4.** solitarily. **5.** only; merely.

along /ə'lɒŋ/ prep. **1.** by the length of; parallel to or in a line with the length of. –adv. **2.** in a line, or with a progressive motion; onwards. **3.** by the length; lengthways. –phr. **4. along with**, in addition to.

alongside /əlɒŋ'saɪd/ adv. **1.** along or by the side; at or to the side of anything. –prep. **2.** beside; by the side of.

aloof /ə'luf/ adv. **1.** at a distance; not participating. –adj. **2.** reserved; unsympathetic; disinterested.

alopecia /ælə'piʃə/ n. loss of hair; baldness.

aloud /ə'laud/ adv. **1.** with the natural tone of the voice as distinguished from in a whisper or silently. **2.** with a loud voice; loudly.

alp /ælp/ n. **1.** a high mountain. **2.** (pl.) a high mountain system, usually with snowy peaks, as the Australian Alps, the Swiss Alps, etc. –**alpine**, adj.

alpaca /æl'pækə/ n. a domesticated camel-like South American ruminant allied to the llama, having long, soft, silky hair or wool.

alpha /'ælfə/ n. **1.** the first letter in the Greek alphabet, often used to designate the first in a series, especially in scientific classifications. –adj. **2.** Zool. holding the dominant position in a group of social animals: *alpha male.*

alphabet /'ælfəbet/ n. **1.** the letters of a language in their customary order. **2.** any system of characters or signs for representing sounds or ideas. –**alphabetical**, adj. –**alphabetise**, **alphabetize**, v.

alpha male n. **1.** Zool. the dominant male in a group of social animals. **2.** Colloq. an assertive or dominant man.

alphanumeric /ˌælfənju'merɪk/ adj. (of a set of characters) conveying information by using both letters and numbers. Also, **alphanumerical**.

already /ɔl'redi/ adv. by this (or that) time; previously to or at some specified time.

alright /ɔl'raɪt, ɔ'raɪt/ adj. **1.** safe and sound: *Are you alright?* **2.** satisfactory; acceptable: *His work is sometimes alright.* –adv.

3. satisfactorily; acceptably; correctly: *He did his job alright.* Also, **all right**.

Alsatian /æl'seɪʃən/ *n.* → **German shepherd**.

also /'ɔlsoʊ/ *adv.* in addition; too; further.

alt- variant of **alto-** before vowels.

altar /'ɔltə, 'ɒl-/ *n.* an elevated place or structure, on which sacrifices are offered or at which religious rites are performed.

alter /'ɔltə, 'ɒl-/ *v.t.* to make different in some particular; modify. **–alteration**, *n.*

altercation /ɔltə'keɪʃən, ɒl-/ *n.* a heated or angry dispute; a noisy wrangle.

alternate *v.i.* /'ɔltəneɪt, 'ɒl-/ **1.** (usu. fol. by *with*) to follow one another in time or place reciprocally. **2.** to change about by turns between points, states, actions, etc. *–v.t.* /'ɔltəneɪt, 'ɒl-/ **3.** to perform by turns, or one after another. *–adj.* /ɔl'tɜnət, ɒl-/ **4.** arranged or following each after the other, in succession. **5.** every other one of a series.

alternating current *n.* *Elect.* a current that reverses direction in regular cycles. *Abbrev.*: AC, a.c. Compare **direct current**.

alternative /ɔl'tɜnətɪv, ɒl-/ *n.* **1.** a possibility of one out of two (or, less strictly, more) things. *–adj.* **2.** affording a choice between two things, or a possibility of one thing out of two. **3.** of or relating to a minority group opposed to an established tradition: *alternative medicine.*

alternative energy *n.* energy which is not derived from fossil fuels, such as wind energy, solar energy, geothermal energy, etc.; usually not including nuclear power.

alternative medicine *n.* the range of practices and treatments, often based on traditional remedies, which fall outside the scope of mainstream medicine.

alternative technology *n.* technology which is environmentally friendly, such as that involved in fuel cells, solar panels, wind turbines, etc.

alternator /'ɔltəneɪtə, 'ɒl-/ *n.* a generator of alternating current.

although /ɔl'ðoʊ/ *conj.* even though (practically equivalent to *though,* but often preferred to it in stating fact). Also, *Poetic,* **altho'**.

altimeter /'æltəmitə/ *n.* an instrument for measuring height.

altitude /'æltətʃud/ *n.* **1.** the height above sea level of any point on the earth's surface or in the atmosphere. **2.** extent or distance upwards.

alto /'æltoʊ/ *n.* (*pl.* **-tos**) *Music* **1.** the lowest female voice or voice part; contralto. **2.** the highest male voice or voice part.

alto- a word element meaning 'high'. Also, **alt-**, **alti-**.

altogether /ɔltə'gɛðə/ *adv.* **1.** wholly; entirely; completely; quite. **2.** in all. **3.** on the whole. *–n.* **4.** a whole.

altruism /'æltru,ɪzəm/ *n.* the principle or practice of seeking the welfare of others (opposed to *egoism*). **–altruistic**, *adj.*

aluminium /ˌæljə'mɪniəm/ *n.* a silver-white, ductile, malleable, metallic element, which is not readily oxidised. *Symbol*: Al

always /'ɔlweɪz, -wəz/ *adv.* **1.** all the time. **2.** every time; on every occasion (opposed to *sometimes* or *occasionally*).

Alzheimer's disease /'æltshaɪməz/ *n.* a brain disease which usually appears in old age and

which results in confusion, memory failure, disorientation, etc.

am /æm/, *weak forms* /əm, m/ *v.* 1st person singular present indicative of **be**.

amalgam /ə'mælgəm/ *n.* **1.** a mixture or combination. **2.** an alloy of mercury with another metal or metals.

amalgamate /ə'mælgəmeɪt/ *v.t.* **1.** to mix so as to make a combination; blend; unite; combine. **2.** *Metallurgy* to mix or alloy (a metal) with mercury. **–amalgamation**, *n.*

amanuensis /əˌmænju'ɛnsəs/ *n.* (*pl.* **-enses** /-ɛnsiz/) a person employed to write or type what another dictates or to copy what has been written by another.

amass /ə'mæs/ *v.t.* to collect into a mass or pile; bring together.

amateur /'æmətə, 'æmətʃə/ *n.* **1.** someone who cultivates any study or art or other activity for personal pleasure rather than professionally or for gain. **2.** a sportsperson who does not earn money from playing sport. **3.** an athlete who has never competed for money.

amatory /'æmətri/ *adj.* relating to lovers or lovemaking; expressive of love.

amaze /ə'meɪz/ *v.t.* to overwhelm with surprise; astonish greatly.

amazon /'æməzən, 'æməzɒn/ *n.* a tall, physically strong woman.

ambassador /æm'bæsədə/ *n.* a diplomatic agent of the highest rank who represents his or her country's interests in another country.

amber /'æmbə/ *n.* **1.** a pale yellow, sometimes reddish or brownish, fossil resin of vegetable origin, translucent, brittle, and capable of gaining a negative electrical charge by friction. *–adj.* **2.** resembling amber.

ambergris /'æmbəgris, -gris/ *n.* an opaque, ash-coloured substance, a secretion of the sperm whale, fragrant when heated, usually found floating on the ocean or cast ashore, used chiefly in perfumery.

ambi- a word element meaning 'both', 'around', 'on both sides'.

ambidextrous /æmbi'dɛkstrəs/ *adj.* able to use both hands equally well. **–ambidexter**, *n.*

ambience /'æmbiəns/ *n.* environment; surrounding atmosphere.

ambient /'æmbiənt/ *adj.* **1.** completely surrounding. **2.** circulating.

ambiguous /æm'bɪgjuəs/ *adj.* open to various interpretations; having a double meaning; equivocal. **–ambiguity** /æmbə'gjuəti/, *n.*

ambit /'æmbət/ *n.* **1.** boundary; limits; sphere. **2.** scope; extent.

ambition /æm'bɪʃən/ *n.* **1.** an eager desire for distinction, preferment, power, or fame. **2.** the object desired or sought after. **–ambitious**, *adj.*

ambivalence /æm'bɪvələns/ *n.* **1.** the coexistence in one person of opposite and conflicting feelings towards someone or something. **2.** uncertainty or ambiguity, especially due to inability to make up one's mind. Also, **ambivalency**. **–ambivalent**, *adj.*

amble /'æmbəl/ *v.i.* **1.** to move with the gait of a horse, when it lifts first the two legs on one side and then the two on the other. **2.** to go at an easy pace. *–n.* **3.** an ambling gait.

ambulance /ˈæmbjələns/ n. a vehicle specially equipped for carrying sick or wounded persons.

ambush /ˈæmbʊʃ/ n. **1.** the act of attacking unexpectedly from a concealed position. –v.t. **2.** to attack from ambush.

ameliorate /əˈmiliəreɪt, əˈmiljəreɪt/ v.t., v.i. to make or become better; improve.

amen /eɪˈmɛn, a-/ interj. it is so; so be it (used after a prayer, creed, or other formal statement).

amenable /əˈmɛnəbəl, əˈmin-/ adj. **1.** disposed or ready to answer, yield, or submit; submissive; tractable. **2.** liable to be called to account; answerable; legally responsible. **3.** liable or exposed (to charge, claim, etc.).

amend /əˈmɛnd/ v.t. **1.** to alter (a motion, bill, constitution, etc.) by due formal procedure. **2.** to change for the better; improve. **3.** to remove or correct faults in; rectify. **–amendment**, n.

amends /əˈmɛndz/ phr. **make amends**, to compensate or make up for some offence, damage, loss, etc., caused: *He made amends for his rude behaviour by ringing to apologise.*

amenities /əˈmɛnətiz, əˈmin-/ pl. n. **1.** agreeable features, circumstances, ways, etc. **2.** public toilets.

amethyst /ˈæməθəst/ n. *Mineral.* a crystallised purple or violet quartz used in jewellery.

amiable /ˈeɪmiəbəl/ adj. having or showing agreeable personal qualities, as sweetness of temper, kind-heartedness, etc.

amicable /ˈæmɪkəbəl/ adj. characterised by or exhibiting friendliness; friendly; peaceable.

amid /əˈmɪd/ prep. in the midst of or surrounded by; among; amidst.

amidst /əˈmɪdst/ prep. amid.

amino acid /əˈminoʊ, ˈæmənoʊ/ n. an organic compound from which proteins are formed.

amiss /əˈmɪs/ adv. out of the proper course or order; in a faulty manner; wrongly.

amity /ˈæməti/ n. friendship; harmony; good understanding, especially between nations.

ammeter /ˈæmitə/ n. an instrument for measuring the strength of electric currents in amperes.

ammonia /əˈmoʊniə, -jə/ n. **1.** a colourless, pungent, suffocating gas, NH_3, a compound of nitrogen and hydrogen, very soluble in water. **2.** Also, **ammonia water**, **aqueous ammonia**. this gas dissolved in water, the common commercial form.

ammunition /ˌæmjəˈnɪʃən/ n. **1.** projectiles that can be discharged from firearms, etc., as bullets, shrapnel, etc. **2.** evidence used to support an argument.

amnesia /æmˈniʒə, -ziə/ n. loss of memory.

amnesty /ˈæmnəsti/ n. (pl. **-ties**) a general pardon for offences against a government.

amniocentesis /ˌæmniousɛnˈtisəs/ n. (pl. **-teses** /ˌæmniousɛnˈtisiz/) the removal of some amniotic fluid, especially to diagnose chromosomal abnormality in a fetus.

amnion /ˈæmniən/ n. (pl. **amnia** /ˈæmniə/) the innermost membrane containing the embryo of insects, reptiles, birds, and mammals. **–amniotic**, adj.

amoeba /əˈmibə/ n. (pl. **-bas** or **-bae** /-bi/) an extremely small, irregularly shaped, single-celled organism which changes shape as it moves and absorbs food. Also, **ameba**. **–amoebic**, adj.

amok /əˈmʌk/ phr. **run amok**, to rush about wildly. Also, **amuck**.

among /əˈmʌŋ/ prep. **1.** in or into the midst of; in association or connection with; surrounded by. **2.** to each of; by or for distribution to. **3.** each with the other; mutually.

amongst /əˈmʌŋst/ prep. among.

amoral /eɪˈmɒrəl, æ-/ adj. without moral quality; neither moral nor immoral.

amorous /ˈæmərəs/ adj. **1.** inclined or disposed to love. **2.** in love; enamoured.

amorphous /əˈmɔfəs/ adj. lacking definite form; having no specific shape.

amortise /əˈmɔtaɪz, ˈæmətaɪz/ v.t. to liquidate or extinguish (an indebtedness or charge) usually by periodic payments (or by entries) made to a sinking fund, to a creditor, or to an account. Also, **amortize**.

amount /əˈmaʊnt/ n. **1.** quantity or extent. **2.** the sum of the principal and interest of a loan. –v.i. **3.** (fol. by *to*) to reach, extend, or be equal in number, quantity, effect, etc.

ampere /ˈæmpɛə/ n. the unit of electric current. *Symbol*: A

ampersand /ˈæmpəsænd/ n. the character &, meaning *and*.

amphetamine /æmˈfɛtəmin, -mən/ n. any of a class of drugs which have stimulant and vasoconstrictor activity.

amphi- a word element meaning 'on both sides', 'on all sides', 'around', 'round about'.

amphibian /æmˈfɪbiən/ n. **1.** a vertebrate animal that lives on land but breeds in water, as a frog, salamander, etc. **2.** a vehicle which can be used on both land and water, as a tank. **–amphibious**, adj.

amphitheatre /ˈæmfɪθɪətə/ n. **1.** a level area of oval or circular shape surrounded by rising ground. **2.** any place for public contests or games; an arena. **3.** a semicircular sloping gallery in a modern theatre.

amphora /ˈæmfərə/ n. (pl. **-rae** /-ri/) a two-handled, narrow-necked vessel, used by the ancient Greeks and Romans for holding wine, oil, etc.

ample /ˈæmpəl/ adj. **1.** in full or abundant measure; copious; liberal. **2.** rather bulky or full in form or figure.

amplify /ˈæmpləfaɪ/ v.t. (**-fied**, **-fying**) **1.** to make larger or greater; enlarge; extend. **2.** to expand in stating or describing, as by details, illustration, etc. **3.** *Elect.* to increase the amplitude of (impulses or waves). **4.** to make louder; magnify (the sound of). **–amplifier**, n. **–amplification**, n.

amplitude /ˈæmpləˌtjud/ n. **1.** extension in space, especially breadth or width; largeness; extent. **2.** large or full measure; abundance; copiousness. **3.** *Physics* the distance or range from one extremity of an oscillation to the middle point or neutral value.

amputate /ˈæmpjəteɪt/ v.t. to cut off (a limb, arm, etc.) by a surgical operation.

amulet /ˈæmjələt/ n. an object superstitiously worn to ward off evil; a protecting charm.

amuse /əˈmjuz/ v.t. **1.** to hold the attention of agreeably; entertain; divert. **2.** to excite mirth in. **–amusement**, n.

an /æn/, *weak form* /ən/ *indefinite article* the form of **a** before an initial vowel sound. See **a**[1].

an-[1] variant of **a-**[6], used before vowels, as in *anorexia*.

an-[2] variant of **ad-**, before *n*, as in *announce*.

an-[3] variant of **ana-**, used before vowels.

-an a suffix meaning: **1.** 'belonging to', 'relating to', 'adhering to', as in *Australian*, *Christian*. **2.** *Zool.* 'relating to a certain class of organisms'.

ana- a prefix meaning 'up', 'throughout', 'again', 'back'.

-ana a noun suffix denoting a collection of material relating to a given subject, as in *Australiana*. Also, **-iana**.

anabranch /ˈænəbræntʃ/ *n.* a branch of a river which leaves the main stream and enters it again further on.

anachronism /əˈnækrənɪzəm/ *n.* something placed or occurring out of its proper time. **–anachronistic**, *adj.*

anaconda /ænəˈkɒndə/ *n.* a large South American snake of the boa family.

anaemia /əˈnimiə/ *n.* a reduced number of red blood cells, causing pallor, weakness, and breathlessness. Also, **anemia. –anaemic**, *adj.*

anaerobic /ænəˈroʊbɪk/ *adj.* (of organisms or tissues) needing the absence of free oxygen or not needing its presence (opposed to *aerobic*).

anaerobic exercise *n.* physical exercise of sufficient intensity to trigger anaerobic metabolism; typically involves a short burst of intense muscular activity, as in weightlifting, sprinting, etc. See **aerobic exercise**.

anaerobic threshold *n.* the point at which the body begins to accumulate unmetabolised lactic acid in the bloodstream, in response to the demands of intense physical exercise. *Abbrev.*: AT

anaesthesia /ænəsˈθiʒə, -ziə/ *n. Med.* general or local insensibility, as to pain and other sensation, induced by certain drugs. Also, **anesthesia**.

anaesthetic /ænəsˈθɛtɪk/ *n.* a substance such as ether, chloroform, cocaine, etc., that produces anaesthesia. See **general anaesthetic**, **local anaesthetic**. Also, **anesthetic. –anaesthetise**, **anaesthetize** /əˈnɪsθətaɪz/, *v.* **–anaesthetist** /əˈnɪsθətəst/, *n.*

anagram /ˈænəgræm/ *n.* a transposition of the letters of a word or sentence to form a new word or sentence, as *caned* is an anagram of *dance*.

anal /ˈeɪnəl/ *adj.* **1.** of, relating to, or near the anus. **2.** *Colloq.* obsessive; finicky; fussy. **–anally**, *adv.*

analgesic /ænəlˈdʒɪzɪk, -sɪk/ *n.* a remedy that relieves or removes pain.

analog /ˈænəlɒg/ *adj.* **1.** *Electronics*, *Broadcasting*, *etc.* relating to any device or procedure which encodes physical properties such as those of sound, sight, etc., in terms of frequencies and their amplitudes. **2.** of or relating to any device which represents a variable by a continuously moving or varying entity, such as a clock, the hands of which move to represent time. Compare **digital** (def. 3). Also, **analogue**.

analog broadcasting *n.* broadcasting by the use of an analog system (opposed to *digital broadcasting*).

analog computer *n.* a type of computer in which information is represented by directly measurable, continuously varying quantities. Also, **analogue computer**.

analogous /əˈnæləgəs, -dʒəs/ *adj.* having analogy; corresponding in some particular.

analog-to-digital converter *n.* a device which converts an analog signal to a digital equivalent. Also, **analog-digital converter**.

analogue /ˈænəlɒg/ *n.* **1.** something having analogy to something else. *–adj.* **2. → analog**.

analogy /əˈnælədʒi/ *n.* (*pl.* **-gies**) an agreement, likeness, or correspondence between the relations of things to one another; a partial similarity in particular circumstances on which a comparison may be based.

analyse /ˈænəlaɪz/ *v.t.* **1.** to resolve into elements or constituent parts; determine the elements or essential features of. **2.** to examine critically, so as to bring out the essential elements or give the essence of.

analysis /əˈnæləsəs/ *n.* (*pl.* **-lyses** /-ləsiz/) **1.** separation of a whole, whether a material substance or any matter of thought, into its constituent elements (opposed to *synthesis*). **2.** this process as a method of studying the nature of a thing or of determining its essential features. **3.** a brief presentation of essential features; an outline or summary, as of a book; a synopsis. **–analyst**, *n.* **–analytic**, **analytical**, *adj.*

anaphylactic shock /ænəfəˈlæktɪk/ *n.* an acute systemic reaction produced by an allergen to which the victim has become sensitised.

anarchy /ˈænəki/ *n.* **1.** a state of society without government or law. **2.** confusion in general; disorder. **–anarchic**, *adj.* **–anarchist**, *n.* **–anarchism**, *n.*

anathema /əˈnæθəmə/ *n.* (*pl.* **-mas**) a detested person or thing.

anatomy /əˈnætəmi/ *n.* **1.** the structure of an animal or plant, or of any of its parts. **2.** the science of the structure of animals and plants. **3.** any analysis or minute examination. **–anatomical**, *adj.*

-ance a suffix of nouns denoting action, state, or quality, as in *brilliance*, *distance*.

ancestor /ˈænsɛstə/ *n.* someone from whom a person is descended, usually distantly; a forefather; a progenitor. **–ancestral**, *adj.*

ancestry /ˈænsəstri, -sɛs-/ *n.* ancestral descent.

anchor /ˈæŋkə/ *n.* **1.** a device for holding boats, vessels, floating bridges, etc., in place. **2.** a means of stability. **3.** a key person; mainstay. **4.** *TV* the host or main presenter of a program. *–v.t.* **5.** to hold fast by an anchor. **6.** to fix or fasten; affix firmly. *–v.i.* **7.** to drop anchor. *–phr.* **8. weigh anchor**, to take up the anchor. **–anchorage**, *n.*

anchorite /ˈæŋkəraɪt/ *n.* someone who has retired to a solitary place for a life of religious seclusion; a hermit; a recluse.

anchovy /ˈæntʃəvi, ænˈtʃoʊvi/ *n.* (*pl.* **-vies** or **-vy**) any of a number of small, herring-like fishes, much used pickled and in the form of a salt paste.

ancient /ˈeɪnʃənt, ˈeɪntʃənt/ *adj.* **1.** of or in time long past, especially before the end of the Western Roman Empire, AD 476. **2.** dating from a remote period; of great age. **3.** *Law* having been in existence for a statutory period of time, often 20 years. **-n. 4.** a person who lived in ancient times, especially one of the ancient Greeks, Romans, Hebrews, etc.

ancillary /ˈænˈsɪləri/ *adj.* accessory; auxiliary.

-ancy an equivalent of **-ance**, used chiefly in nouns denoting state or quality, as in *buoyancy.*

and /ænd/, *weak forms* /ənd, ən, n/ *conj.* **1.** with; along with; together with; besides; also; moreover (used to connect grammatically co-ordinate words, phrases, or clauses). **2.** as well as. **3.** to (used between verbs): *to go and play.*

andro- a word element meaning 'man', 'male', as contrasted with 'female'. Also, **andr-.**

androgynous /ænˈdrɒdʒənəs/ *adj.* **1.** being both male and female. **2.** not conforming to a male or a female stereotype in appearance or behaviour. **-androgyny,** *n.*

android /ˈændrɔɪd/ *n.* (especially in science fiction) a robot made to resemble a human being.

-androus a word element meaning 'male'.

-ane 1. a noun suffix used in chemical terms, especially names of hydrocarbons of the methane or paraffin series. **2.** an adjective suffix used when a similar form (with a different meaning) exists in **-an**, as *human, humane.*

anecdote /ˈænɪkdoʊt/ *n.* a short narrative of a particular incident or occurrence of an interesting nature. **-anecdotal,** *adj.*

anemo- a word element meaning 'wind'.

anemometer /ænəˈmɒmətə/ *n.* an instrument for indicating wind velocity. **-anemometric** /ænəməˈmetrɪk/, **anemometrical** /ænəməˈmetrɪkəl/, *adj.*

anemone /əˈnɛməni/ *n.* **1.** a plant with mostly red and blue flowers. **2. → sea anemone.**

aneurysm /ˈænjərɪzəm/ *n.* a permanent cardiac or arterial dilatation usually caused by weakening of the vessel wall by diseases such as syphilis or arteriosclerosis. Also, **aneurism.**

anew /əˈnju/ *adv.* **1.** over again; once more. **2.** in a new form or manner.

angel /ˈeɪndʒəl/ *n.* **1.** *Theology* one of a class of spiritual beings, attendants of God. **2.** a messenger, especially of God. **3.** a person who resembles an angel in beauty, kindliness, etc. **-angelic,** *adj.*

anger /ˈæŋgə/ *n.* **1.** a strongly felt displeasure aroused by real or supposed wrongs, often accompanied by an impulse to retaliate; wrath; ire. **-v.t. 2.** to excite to anger or wrath.

angina /ænˈdʒaɪnə/ *n.* a pain in the chest caused by lack of blood to the heart, usually due to coronary artery disease.

angio- a word element meaning 'vessel', or 'container'.

angiosperm /ˈændʒiəˌspɜm/ *n.* a plant having its seeds enclosed in an ovary.

angle¹ /ˈæŋgəl/ *n.* **1.** *Maths* the space within two lines or three planes diverging from a common point, or within two planes diverging from a common line. **2.** an angular projection or recess. **3.** a point of view; standpoint. **4.** *Colloq.* a devious, artful scheme, method, etc. **-v.t. 5.** to move, direct, bend or present at an angle or in an angular course.

angle² /ˈæŋgəl/ *v.i.* to fish with hook and line. **-angler,** *n.*

Anglo /ˈæŋgloʊ/ *n.* **1.** a person of Anglo-Celtic ancestry. **2.** a person of English ancestry. **3.** a person who is a native speaker of English and who appears to be of Anglo-Celtic ancestry.

Anglo- a word element meaning 'relating to England or the English'.

Angora /æŋˈgɔrə/ *n.* (yarn or fabric made from) the long, silky hair of certain goats and rabbits. Also, **angora.**

angry /ˈæŋgri/ *adj.* (**-grier, -griest**) **1.** feeling or showing anger or resentment (*with* or *at* a person, *at* or *about* a thing). **2.** *Med.* inflamed; exhibiting inflammation. **-angrily,** *adv.*

angst /æŋst/ *n.* a feeling or outlook of dread, fear, etc.

anguish /ˈæŋgwɪʃ/ *n.* **1.** excruciating or agonising pain of either body or mind; acute suffering or distress. **-v.t., v.i. 2.** to affect with or suffer anguish.

angular /ˈæŋgjələ/ *adj.* **1.** having an angle or angles. **2.** consisting of, situated at, or forming an angle. **3.** bony; gaunt. **4.** stiff in manner; unbending. **-angularity,** *n.*

animadvert /ænəmædˈvɜt/ *v.i.* (fol. by *on* or *upon*) to comment critically; make remarks by way of criticism or censure.

animal /ˈænəməl/ *n.* **1.** any living thing that is not a plant, generally capable of voluntary motion, sensation, etc. **2.** any animal other than a human. **3.** a brutish or beast-like person. **-adj. 4.** of, relating to, or derived from animals. **5.** relating to the physical or carnal nature of humans, rather than their spiritual or intellectual nature.

animate *v.t.* /ˈænəmeɪt/ **1.** to give life to; make alive. **2.** to make lively, vivacious, or vigorous. **3.** to cause to appear or move as if alive, as in an animated film. **-adj.** /ˈænəmət/ **4.** alive; possessing life. **-animation,** *n.*

animated /ˈænəmeɪtəd/ *adj.* **1.** full of life, action, or spirit; lively. **2.** of or relating to a film which consists of a series of drawings, each slightly different from the ones before and after it, run through a projector to create the illusion of movement. **-animatedly,** *adv.*

anime /ˈænɪmeɪ/ *n.* **1. → manga movie. 2.** the genre of Japanese animation.

animism /ˈænəmɪzəm/ *n.* the belief that all natural objects and the universe itself possess a soul. **-animist,** *n.*, *adj.* **-animistic** /ænəˈmɪstɪk/, *adj.*

animosity /ænəˈmɒsəti/ *n.* (fol. by *between* or *towards*) a feeling of ill will or enmity animating the conduct, or tending to display itself in action.

anion /ˈænaɪən/ *n.* a negatively charged ion which is attracted to the anode in electrolysis.

aniseed /ˈænəsid/ *n.* an aromatic seed used in medicine, cookery, etc.

aniso- a word element meaning 'unlike' or 'unequal'.

ankle /ˈæŋkəl/ *n.* **1.** the aggregate joint connecting the foot with the leg. **2.** the slender part of the leg above the foot.

anklebiter /ˈæŋkəlbaɪtə/ *n. Colloq.* a child.

annals /ˈænəlz/ *pl. n.* history or relation of events recorded year by year.

anneal /əˈnil/ *v.t.* to heat (glass, metals, etc.) to remove or prevent internal stress.

annex *v.t.* /ˈænɛks, əˈnɛks/ **1.** to attach, join, or add, especially to something larger or more important; unite; append. **2.** to take possession of, to take to one's own use permanently. **3.** to invade and take possession of (a neighbouring country, territory, etc.). –*n.* /ˈænɛks/ **4.** something annexed or added, especially a supplement to a document. –**annexation**, *n.*

annexe /ˈænɛks/ *n.* a subsidiary building or an addition to a building.

annihilate /əˈnaɪəleɪt/ *v.t.* to reduce to nothing; destroy utterly.

anniversary /ænəˈvɜːsəri/ *n.* (*pl.* **-ries**) the yearly recurrence of the date of a past event.

annotate /ˈænoteɪt/ *v.t.* to supply with notes; remark upon in notes. –**annotator**, *n.* –**annotation**, *n.*

announce /əˈnaʊns/ *v.t.* (**-nounced, -nouncing**) **1.** to make known publicly; give notice of. **2.** to state the approach or presence of. –**announcement**, *n.* –**announcer**, *n.*

annoy /əˈnɔɪ/ *v.t.* to disturb (a person) in a way that is displeasing, troubling, or slightly irritating. –**annoyance**, *n.* –**annoying**, *adj.*

annual /ˈænjuəl/ *adj.* **1.** of, for, or relating to a year; yearly. –*n.* **2.** a plant living only one year or season.

annuity /əˈnjuəti/ *n.* (*pl.* **-ties**) **1.** a specified income payable at stated intervals for a fixed or a contingent period, often for the recipient's life, in consideration of a stipulated premium paid either in prior instalment payments or in a single payment. **2.** the right to receive such an income, or the duty to make such a payment or payments. –**annuitant**, *n.*

annul /əˈnʌl/ *v.t.* (**annulled, annulling**) to make void or null; abolish (used especially of laws or other established rules, usages, and the like). –**annulment**, *n.*

annular /ˈænjələ/ *adj.* having the form of a ring.

annunciate /əˈnʌnsieɪt/ *v.t.* to announce.

anode /ˈænoʊd/ *n.* the positive pole of a battery or other source of current. Compare **cathode**.

anoint /əˈnɔɪnt/ *v.t.* **1.** to put oil on; apply an unguent or oily liquid to. **2.** to consecrate by applying oil.

anomaly /əˈnɒməli/ *n.* (*pl.* **-lies**) deviation from the common rule or analogy. –**anomalous**, *adj.*

anonymous /əˈnɒnəməs/ *adj.* **1.** without any name acknowledged, as that of author, contributor, or the like. **2.** lacking individuality; without distinguishing features; without identity. –**anonymity, anonymousness**, *n.* –**anonymously**, *adv.*

anorak /ˈænəræk/ *n.* → **parka**.

anorexia /ænəˈrɛksiə/ *n.* a mental disorder, most common in adolescent girls, causing an aversion to food, which may lead to serious malnutrition. Also, **anorexia nervosa**. –**anorexic**, *adj.*

another /əˈnʌðə/ *adj.* **1.** a second; a further; an additional. **2.** a different; a distinct; of a different kind. –*pron.* **3.** one more; an additional one.

answer /ˈænsə, ˈɑn-/ *n.* **1.** a reply to a question, request, letter, etc., or to an accusation. **2.** a solution to a doubt or problem, especially in mathematics. –*v.i.* **3.** to make answer; reply. –*v.t.* **4.** to make answer to; to reply or respond

to. **5.** to give as an answer. **6.** to make a defence against (a charge); meet or refute (an argument). –*phr.* **7. answer for, a.** to be or declare oneself responsible or accountable for. **b.** to act or suffer in consequence of. **8. answer to, a.** to respond to (a stimulus, direction, command, etc.); obey; acknowledge. **b.** to correspond to; conform to. **c.** to be directly inferior to in a chain of command.

answerable /ˈænsərəbəl/ *adj.* **1.** accountable, responsible (*for* a person, act, etc.). **2.** liable to be called to account or asked to defend one's actions (*to* a person).

ant /ænt/ *n.* any of certain small, usually wingless, insects, very widely distributed in thousands of species, all of which have some degree of social organisation.

ant- variant of **anti-**, especially before a vowel or *h*, as in *antacid*.

-ant 1. adjective suffix, originally participial, as in *ascendant, pleasant*. **2.** noun suffix used in words of participial origin, denoting agency or instrumentality, as in *servant, irritant*.

antacid /æntˈæsəd/ *n.* a medicine which counteracts acidity, especially of the stomach.

antagonise /ænˈtægənaɪz/ *v.t.* to make hostile. Also, **antagonize**.

antagonism /ænˈtægənɪzəm/ *n.* **1.** the activity or the relation of contending parties or conflicting forces; active opposition. **2.** an opposing force, principle, or tendency. –**antagonistic**, *adj.* –**antagonist**, *n.*

antagonist /ænˈtægənəst/ *n.* **1.** someone who is opposed to or strives with another in any kind of contest; opponent; adversary. **2.** *Physiol.* a muscle which acts in opposition to another (the *agonist*). –**antagonistic** /ænˌtægəˈnɪstɪk/, *adj.*

antarctic /ænˈtaktɪk/ *adj.* of, at, or near the South Pole.

ante /ˈænti/ *n.* (especially in poker) a stake put into the pool by each player after seeing their hand but before drawing new cards.

ante- a prefix meaning 'before in space or time'.

anteater /ˈæntitə/ *n.* any of the echidnas or spiny anteaters of Australia and New Guinea.

antecedent /æntəˈsidnt/ *adj.* **1.** (oft. fol. by *to*) going or being before; preceding; prior. –*n.* **2.** (*pl.*) **a.** ancestry. **b.** one's personal history, especially in the early stages of one's life. **3.** a preceding circumstance, event, etc. **4.** *Gram.* the word or phrase, usually a noun, which is replaced by a pronoun later in the sentence.

antechinus /æntəˈkaɪnəs/ *n.* (*pl.* **-nuses**) a type of Australian marsupial mouse, having a grey head, orange-brown rump and feet, and a black tip on the tail.

antedate /ˈæntideɪt, æntiˈdeɪt/ *v.t.* **1.** to be of older date than; precede in time. **2.** to affix a date earlier than the true one to (a document, etc.).

antelope /ˈæntəloʊp/ *n.* (*pl.* **-lopes** *or*, *especially collectively*, **-lope**) a slenderly built, hollow-horned ruminant allied to cattle, sheep, and goats, found chiefly in Africa and Asia.

ante meridiem /ˈænti məˈrɪdiəm/ **1.** before noon. **2.** the time between 12 midnight and 12 noon. *Abbrev.*: A.M., a.m. –**antemeridian**, *adj.*

antenatal /æntiˈneɪtl/ *adj.* → **prenatal**.

antenna /æn'tɛnə/ n. (pl. **-tennae** /-'tɛni/ for def. 1, **-tennas** for def. 2) **1.** Zool. one of the jointed appendages occurring in pairs on the heads of insects, crustaceans, etc., often called feelers. **2.** an electrical device that receives, and sometimes sends, radio and television signals.

antepenultimate /ˌæntipə'nʌltəmət/ adj. last but two.

anterior /æn'tɪəriə/ adj. **1.** placed before; situated more to the front (opposed to posterior). **2.** going before in time; preceding; earlier.

anthem /'ænθəm/ n. a hymn, as of praise, devotion, or patriotism.

anther /'ænθə/ n. Bot. the pollen-bearing part of a stamen.

antho- a word element meaning 'flower'.

anthology /æn'θɒlədʒi/ n. (pl. **-gies**) a collection of literary pieces, especially poems, of varied authorship.

anthrax /'ænθræks/ n. an infectious disease of cattle, sheep, and other animals and of humans.

anthropo- a word element meaning 'human being'. Also, **anthrop-**.

anthropogenic /ˌænθrəpə'dʒɛnɪk/ adj. caused by human beings: anthropogenic climate change.

anthropoid /'ænθrəpɔɪd/ adj. resembling a human being.

anthropology /ænθrə'pɒlədʒi/ n. the systematic study that deals with the origin, development (physical, intellectual, cultural, moral, etc.) and varieties of humanity. **-anthropologist**, n. **-anthropological**, adj.

anthropomorphic /ænθrəpə'mɔfɪk/ adj. ascribing human form or attributes to beings or things not human. **-anthropomorphism**, n.

anti- a prefix meaning 'against', 'opposed to'. Also, **ant-**.

antibacterial /æntibæk'tɪəriəl/ adj. **1.** of or relating to a substance that kills or inhibits the growth of bacteria. **-n. 2.** such a substance.

antibiotic /ˌæntibaɪ'ɒtɪk/ n. a chemical substance used in the treatment of bacterial infections.

antibody /'æntibɒdi/ n. (pl. **-dies**) any of various substances existing in the blood or developed in immunisation which counteract bacterial or viral poisons or destroy bacteria in the system.

anticipate /æn'tɪsəpeɪt/ v.t. **1.** to realise beforehand; foretaste or foresee. **2.** to consider or mention before the proper time. **-anticipation** /æntɪsə'peɪʃən/, n.

anticlimax /ænti'klaɪmæks/ n. **1.** Theatre a noticeable or ludicrous descent in discourse from lofty ideas or expressions to what is much less impressive. **2.** an unexpected and disappointing conclusion.

anticlockwise /ænti'klɒkwaɪz/ adv., adj. in a direction opposite to that of the rotation of the hands of a clock.

antics /'æntɪks/ pl. n. odd or silly behaviour.

anticyclone /ænti'saɪkloʊn/ n. Meteorol. an extensive horizontal movement of the atmosphere spirally around and away from a gradually progressing central region of high barometric pressure, the spiral motion being clockwise in the Northern Hemisphere, anticlockwise in the Southern. **-anticyclonic** /ˌæntisaɪ'klɒnɪk/, adj.

antidepressant /ˌæntidə'prɛsənt/ n. **1.** any of a class of drugs used in treating mental depression. **-adj. 2.** of, relating to, or denoting, this class of drugs.

antidote /'æntidoʊt/ n. a medicine or other remedy for counteracting the effects of poison, disease, etc.

antigen /'æntidʒən, 'æntə-/ n. any substance which when injected into animal tissues will stimulate the production of antibodies. **-antigenic** /ænti'dʒɛnɪk/, adj.

antihistamine /ænti'hɪstəmɪn, -maɪn/ n. any of certain drugs which decrease the effect of the histamine released in allergic conditions of the body, as in hay fever, etc.

antilogy /æn'tɪlədʒi/ n. (pl. **-gies**) a contradiction in terms or ideas.

antinomy /æn'tɪnəmi/ n. (pl. **-mies**) opposition between laws and principles; contradiction in law.

antioxidant /ænti'ɒksədənt/ n. **1.** a substance which inhibits deterioration from oxidisation in certain materials, including many foods. **2.** such a substance in the body, which neutralises free radicals formed when body cells burn oxygen for energy, keeping the immune system healthy and reducing the risk of cancer and other diseases. Also, **anti-oxidant**.

antipasto /ænti'pæstoʊ/ n. (pl. **-pasti** or **-pastos**) in Italian cooking, a first course of a meal comprising an assortment of meats, cheeses, olives, etc.; hors d'oeuvres.

antipathy /æn'tɪpəθi/ n. **1.** a natural or settled dislike; repugnance; aversion. **2.** an instinctive contrariety or opposition in feeling. **-antipathetic** /ˌæntipə'θɛtɪk/, adj.

antiperspirant /ænti'pɜspərənt/ n. any preparation for decreasing or preventing perspiration.

antipodes /æn'tɪpədiz/ pl. n. points diametrically opposite to each other on the earth or any globe. **-antipodean**, adj., n.

antiquary /'æntəkwəri/ n. (pl. **-ries**) an expert on ancient things; a student or collector of antiquities. **-antiquarian**, adj.

antiquated /'æntəkweɪtəd/ adj. old-fashioned or out-of-date.

antique /æn'tik/ n. **1.** an object of art or a furniture piece of a former period. **-adj. 2.** belonging to former times as contrasted with modern.

antiquity /æn'tɪkwəti/ n. (pl. **-ties**) **1.** the quality of being ancient; great age. **2.** (usu. pl.) something belonging to or remaining from ancient times.

antiseptic /æntə'sɛptɪk/ n. an agent which destroys the micro-organisms that produce septic disease.

antisocial /ænti'soʊʃəl/ adj. **1.** unwilling or unable to associate normally with one's fellows. **2.** opposed, damaging, or motivated by antagonism to social order, or to the principles on which society is constituted.

anti-terrorism /ænti-'tɛrərɪzəm/ adj. of or relating to measures taken by a government, etc., to prevent or control terrorism. Also, **anti-terrorist**.

antithesis /æn'tɪθəsəs/ n. (pl. **-theses** /-'θisiz/) **1.** opposition; contrast. **2.** (fol. by of or to) the direct opposite.

antitoxin /ˌænti'tɒksən/ n. a substance which counteracts a specific toxin. –**antitoxic**, adj.

antivenene /ˌæntivə'niːn/ n. **1.** an antitoxin produced in the blood by repeated injections of venom, as of snakes. **2.** the antitoxic serum obtained from such blood. Also, **antivenin**, **antivenom**.

antler /'æntlə/ n. one of the solid deciduous horns, usually branched, of an animal of the deer family.

antonym /'æntənɪm/ n. a word opposed in meaning to another (opposed to synonym).

antsy /'æntsi/ adj. Colloq. **1.** agitated; irritable. **2.** restless; impatient.

anus /'eɪnəs/ n. the opening at the lower end of the alimentary canal, through which the solid refuse of digestion is excreted.

anvil /'ænvəl/ n. a heavy iron block with a smooth face, frequently of steel, on which metals, usually red-hot or white-hot, are hammered into desired shapes.

anxiety /æŋ'zaɪəti/ n. distress or uneasiness of mind caused by apprehension of danger or misfortune.

anxious /'æŋʃəs, 'æŋk-/ adj. **1.** full of anxiety or solicitude; greatly troubled or solicitous. **2.** earnestly desirous (followed by infinitive or for).

any /'ɛni/ adj. **1.** one, a, an, or (with plural noun) some; whatever or whichever it may be. **2.** in whatever quantity or number, great or small. **3.** every. **4.** a great or unlimited (amount). –pron. **5. a.** (construed as sing.) any person; anybody. **b.** (construed as pl.) any persons. **6.** any single one or any one's; anything or things; any quantity or number. –adv. **7.** in any degree; to any extent; at all.

anybody /'ɛnibɒdi, -bədi/ pron. **1.** any person. –n. (pl. **-bodies**) **2.** a person of little importance.

anyhow /'ɛnihaʊ/ adv. **1.** in any case; at all events. **2.** in a careless manner. **3.** in any way whatever.

anyone /'ɛniwʌn/ pron. any person; anybody.

anything /'ɛniθɪŋ/ pron. **1.** any thing whatever; something, no matter what. –n. **2.** a thing of any kind. –adv. **3.** in any degree; to any extent.

any way adv. **1.** in any way or manner. **2.** carelessly; haphazardly; anyhow.

anyway /'ɛniweɪ/ adv. in any case; anyhow.

anywhere /'ɛniwɛə/ adv. in, at, or to any place.

anywise /'ɛniwaɪz/ adv. in any way or respect.

Anzac biscuit n. a biscuit made from wheat flour, rolled oats, desiccated coconut, and golden syrup. Also, **anzac biscuit**.

A-1 /eɪ-'wʌn/ adj. **1.** registered as a first-class vessel in a shipping register, as Lloyd's Register. **2.** Colloq. first-class; excellent. Also, **A1**.

aorta /eɪ'ɔːtə/ n. Anat. the main trunk of the arterial system, conveying blood from the left ventricle of the heart to all of the body except the lungs.

ap- variant of **ad-**, before p as in appear.

apart /ə'pɑːt/ adv. **1.** in pieces, or to pieces. **2.** separately or aside in motion, place, or position. **3.** to or at one side, with respect to purpose or function. **4.** separately or individually in consideration. **5.** aside (used with a noun or gerund). –adj. **6.** separate; independent.

apartheid /ə'pɑːtaɪd, -eɪt/ n. (especially as applied to the former policy in South Africa) racial segregation.

apartment /ə'pɑːtmənt/ n. a flat or unit.

apathy /'æpəθi/ n. lack of feeling; absence or suppression of passion, emotion, or excitement. –**apathetic** /æpə'θɛtɪk/, adj.

apatosaurus /ə'pætəsɔːrəs/ n. a very large, herbivorous dinosaur (popularly known as a brontosaurus), having a long neck and tail and a relatively small head.

ape /eɪp/ n. **1.** a tailless monkey or a monkey with a very short tail. –v.t. (**aped**, **aping**) **2.** to imitate servilely; mimic.

aperitif /ə'pɛrətɪf/ n. a small alcoholic drink, often taken as an appetiser.

aperture /'æpətʃə/ n. a hole, slit, crack, gap, or other opening.

apex /'eɪpɛks/ n. (pl. **apexes** or **apices** /'eɪpəsiːz/) the tip, point, or vertex of anything; the summit.

aphasia /ə'feɪʒə, -ziə/ n. loss or impairment of symbolic formulation and speech ability due to a lesion in the central nervous system. –**aphasic**, adj.

aphid /'eɪfəd/ n. a plant-sucking insect.

aphorism /'æfərɪzəm/ n. a terse saying embodying a general truth.

aphrodisiac /æfrə'dɪziæk/ n. a drug or food that arouses sexual desire.

apiary /'eɪpiəri/ n. (pl. **-ries**) a place in which bees are kept; a stand or shed containing a number of hives. –**apiarist**, n.

apical /'æpɪkəl, 'eɪ-/ adj. of, at, or forming the apex.

apices /'eɪpəsiːz/ n. a plural of **apex**.

apiece /ə'piːs/ adv. for each piece, thing, or person; for each one; each.

aplomb /ə'plɒm/ n. **1.** imperturbable self-possession, poise, or assurance. **2.** a perpendicular position.

apnoea /'æpniə/ n. suspension of respiration. Also, **apnea**.

apocalypse /ə'pɒkəlɪps/ n. revelation; discovery; disclosure. –**apocalyptic**, adj.

apocryphal /ə'pɒkrəfəl/ adj. **1.** of doubtful authorship or authenticity. **2.** false; spurious. **3.** fabled; fictitious; mythical.

apolitical /eɪpə'lɪtɪkəl/ adj. **1.** having no interest in political issues. **2.** not involving obligations to a particular political party.

apologia /æpə'loʊdʒiə/ n. a formal defence or justification in speech or writing, as of a cause or doctrine.

apologise /ə'pɒlədʒaɪz/ v.i. **1.** to offer excuses or regrets for some fault, insult, failure, or injury. **2.** to make a formal defence in speech or writing. Also, **apologize**. –**apologetic**, adj.

apology /ə'pɒlədʒi/ n. (pl. **-gies**) **1.** an expression of regret offered for some fault, failure, insult, or injury. **2.** a poor specimen or substitute; a makeshift.

apoplexy /'æpəplɛksi/ n. **1.** marked loss of bodily function due to cerebral haemorrhage. **2.** extreme anger; rage. –**apoplectic**, adj.

apostasy /ə'pɒstəsi/ n. a total desertion of, or departure from, one's religion, principles, party, cause, etc.

apostle /ə'pɒsəl/ n. a vigorous and zealous upholder (of a principle, cause, etc.). –**apostolic**, adj.

apostrophe /ə'pɒstrəfi/ n. the sign (') used to indicate: **1.** the omission of one or more letters in a word, as in o'er for over, halo'd for haloed. **2.** the possessive case, as in lion's, lions'. **3.** certain plurals, as in several MD's. –**apostrophic**, adj.

apothecary /ə'pɒθəkri, -kəri/ n. (pl. **-ries**) Archaic a chemist; a pharmacist.

app /æp/ n. Computers **1.** an application (def. 6). **2.** a digital product which can be downloaded onto a smartphone, tablet, etc.

appal /ə'pɒl/ v.t. (**-palled**, **-palling**) **1.** to overcome with fear; fill with consternation and horror. **2.** to shock; dismay; displease.

apparatchik /æpə'rætʃik/ n. (pl. **-chiki** /-tʃiki/) **1.** an official in a communist bureaucracy, usually depicted as being mindlessly devoted to its beliefs and procedures. **2.** a person, usually in a position of influence, such as a technical specialist, journalist, etc., who acts so strongly to support a particular political body or system as to be considered part of its effective apparatus.

apparatus /æpə'ratəs, -'reɪtəs/ n. (pl. **-tus** or **-tuses**) an assemblage of instruments, machinery, appliances, materials, etc., for a particular use.

apparel /ə'pærəl/ n. a person's outer clothing; raiment.

apparent /ə'pærənt/ adj. **1.** capable of being clearly perceived or understood; plain or clear. **2.** seeming; ostensible. **3.** exposed to the sight; open to view. –**apparently**, adv.

apparition /æpə'rɪʃən/ n. **1.** a ghostly appearance; a spectre or phantom. **2.** anything that appears, especially something remarkable or phenomenal.

appeal /ə'pil/ n. **1.** a call for aid, support, mercy, etc.; an earnest request or entreaty. **2.** application or reference to some person or authority for corroboration, vindication, decision, etc. **3.** power to attract or to move the feelings. –v.i. **4.** to make an appeal. **5.** to resort for proof, decision, or settlement. –phr. **6. appeal to**, to offer a peculiar attraction, interest, enjoyment, etc., to: this colour appeals to me.

appear /ə'pɪə/ v.i. **1.** to come into sight; become visible. **2.** to have an appearance; seem; look. **3.** to be obvious; be clear or made clear by evidence. **4.** to come or be placed before the public. **5.** Law to come formally before a tribunal, authority, etc. –**appearance**, n.

appease /ə'piz/ v.t. **1.** to bring to a state of peace, quiet, ease, or content. **2.** to satisfy. –**appeasement**, n. –**appeasing**, adj. –**appeasingly**, adv.

appellant /ə'pelənt/ n. someone who appeals.

appellate /ə'pelət/ adj. Law relating to appeals.

appellation /æpə'leɪʃən/ n. **1.** a name, title, or designation. **2.** the act of naming.

append /ə'pend/ v.t. to add, as an accessory; annex. –**appendage**, n. –**appendant**, adj.

appendicitis /əpendə'saɪtəs/ n. inflammation of the appendix.

appendix /ə'pendiks/ n. (pl. **-dixes** or **-dices** /-dəsiz/) **1.** matter which supplements the main

text of a book, generally explanatory, statistical, or reference material. **2.** Anat. a narrow, blind tube at the beginning of the large intestine.

appertain /æpə'teɪn/ v.i. (fol. by to) to belong as a part, member, possession, attribute, etc.; pertain.

appetising /'æpətaɪzɪŋ/ adj. exciting or appealing to the appetite. Also, **appetizing**. –**appetiser**, n.

appetite /'æpətaɪt/ n. **1.** a desire for food or drink. **2.** a desire to supply any want or craving.

applaud /ə'plɔd/ v.i. **1.** to express approval by clapping the hands, shouting, etc. **2.** to give praise; express approval. –**applause**, n.

apple /'æpəl/ n. an edible fruit, usually round and with red, yellow or green skin.

applet /'æplət/ n. a small computer program which can be transferred over the internet and which runs on the client machine rather than the server.

appliance /ə'plaɪəns/ n. **1.** an instrument, apparatus, or device, especially one operated by electricity and designed for household use. **2.** a vehicle designed primarily for firefighting, as a water tanker, a pumper, a rescue vehicle, etc.

applicable /ə'plɪkəbəl, 'æp-/ adj. capable of being applied; fit; suitable; relevant.

applicant /'æplɪkənt/ n. someone who applies; a candidate.

application /æplə'keɪʃən/ n. **1.** the act of putting to a special use or purpose. **2.** the quality of being usable for a particular purpose or in a special way; relevance. **3.** something applied, as a salve. **4.** a written or spoken request or appeal. **5.** close attention; persistent effort. **6.** Also, **application program**. Computers a program which is written specifically to perform a specialised task.

appliqué /'æplikeɪ/ n. decorative needlework.

apply /ə'plaɪ/ v. (**-plied**, **-plying**) –v.t. **1.** to lay on; bring into physical proximity or contact. **2.** to put into practical operation, as a principle, law, rule, etc. **3.** to put to use; employ. **4.** to give with earnestness or assiduity. –v.i. **5.** to have a bearing or reference; be pertinent. **6.** to make application or request; ask.

appoint /ə'pɔɪnt/ v.t. **1.** to nominate or assign to a position, or to perform a function. **2.** to determine by authority or agreement; fix; settle. **3.** to provide with what is requisite; equip.

appointment /ə'pɔɪntmənt/ n. **1.** the act of appointing, designating, or placing in office. **2.** an office held by a person appointed. **3.** the act of fixing by mutual agreement.

apportion /ə'pɔʃən/ v.t. to distribute or allocate proportionally.

apposite /'æpəzət/ adj. suitable; well-adapted; pertinent.

apposition /æpə'zɪʃən/ n. the act of adding to or together; a placing together; juxtaposition.

appraise /ə'preɪz/ v.t. **1.** to estimate generally, as to quality, size, weight, etc. **2.** to value in current money; estimate the value of. –**appraisal**, n.

appreciable /ə'priʃəbəl/ adj. **1.** capable of being perceived or estimated; noticeable. **2.** fairly large.

appreciate /ə'priʃieit, ə'prisi-/ v.t. **1.** to place a sufficiently high estimate on. **2.** to be fully conscious of; be aware of; detect. **3.** to be pleased with or grateful for. **4.** to raise in value. –v.i. **5.** to increase in value. –**appreciation**, n. –**appreciative**, adj.

apprehend /æprə'hend/ v.t. **1.** to take into custody; arrest by legal warrant or authority. **2.** to grasp the meaning of; understand; conceive.

apprehension /æprə'henʃən/ n. **1.** anticipation of adversity; dread or fear of coming evil. **2.** the faculty of apprehending; understanding. **3.** a view, opinion, or idea on any subject. **4.** the act of arresting; seizure. –**apprehensible**, adj.

apprehensive /æprə'hensɪv/ adj. afraid or uneasy about something that may happen. –**apprehensively**, adv.

apprentice /ə'prentəs/ n. someone who works for another with obligations to learn a trade. **2.** a learner; a novice.

apprise /ə'praɪz/ v.t. (oft. fol. by of) to give notice to; inform; advise.

approach /ə'proutʃ/ v.t. **1.** to come nearer or near to. **2.** to make advances or a proposal to. –v.i. **3.** to come nearer; draw near. –n. **4.** the act of drawing near. **5.** any means of access. **6.** the method used or steps taken in setting about a task, problem, etc.

approachable /ə'proutʃəbəl/ adj. **1.** capable of being approached; accessible. **2.** (of a person) easy to approach.

approbation /æprə'beɪʃən/ n. approval; commendation. –**approbatory**, adj.

appropriate adj. /ə'proupriət/ **1.** suitable or fitting for a particular purpose, person, occasion, etc. –v.t. /ə'proupriert/ **2.** to set apart for some specific purpose or use. **3.** to take to or for oneself; take possession of. –**appropriation** /əproupri'eɪʃən/, n.

approval /ə'pruvəl/ n. **1.** the act of approving; approbation. **2.** sanction; official permission. –phr. **3. on approval**, for examination, without obligation to buy.

approve /ə'pruv/ v.t. **1.** to confirm or sanction officially; ratify. –v.i. **2.** (usu. fol. by of) to speak or think favourably.

approximate adj. /ə'prɒksəmət/ **1.** nearly exact, equal, or perfect. **2.** inaccurate; rough. –v.t. /ə'prɒksəmeɪt/ **3.** to come near to; approach closely to. –**approximately**, adv.

appurtenance /ə'pɜtənəns/ n. something accessory to another and more important thing; an adjunct. –**appurtenant**, adj.

apricot /'eɪprɪkɒt, -prə-/ n. **1.** a downy yellow fruit, somewhat resembling a small peach. **2.** a pinkish yellow or yellowish pink.

apron /'eɪprən/ n. a piece of clothing made in various ways for covering, and usually also protecting, the front of the person more or less completely.

apropos /æprə'pou/ adv. **1.** to the purpose; opportunely. **2.** with reference or regard. –adj. **3.** opportune; pertinent.

apse /æps/ n. a vaulted recess in a building, especially a church.

apt /æpt/ adj. **1.** unusually intelligent; quick to learn. **2.** suited to the purpose or occasion. –phr. **3. apt to**, inclined or disposed to.

aptitude /'æptətʃud/ n. **1.** a natural tendency or acquired inclination. **2.** readiness in learning; intelligence; talent. **3.** the state or quality of being apt; special fitness.

aptronym /'æptrɒnɪm/ n. a name that aptly reflects the job, hobby, etc., of the person so named, as Mr Green for a gardener. Also, **aptonym**.

aqua /'ækwə/ n. light blue-green or greenish blue.

aquaculture /'ækwəkʌltʃə/ n. **1.** cultivation of the food resources of the sea or of inland waters. **2.** the cultivation of fish in tank or pond systems. Also, **aquiculture**.

aqualung /'ækwəlʌŋ/ n. (from trademark) an apparatus enabling a diver to breathe underwater.

aquamarine /ækwəmə'rin/ n., adj. light blue-green or greenish blue.

aquarium /ə'kweəriəm/ n. (pl. **-riums** or **-ria** /-riə/) a pond, tank, or establishment in which living aquatic animals or plants are kept, as for exhibition.

aquatic /ə'kwɒtɪk/ adj. **1.** of or relating to water. **2.** living or growing in water.

aqueduct /'ækwədʌkt/ n. Civil Eng. a conduit or artificial channel for conducting water from a distance, the water usually flowing by gravity.

aqueous /'ækwiəs, 'eɪkwi-/ adj. of, like, or containing water; watery.

aquiculture /'ækwəkʌltʃə, 'eɪkwɪ-/ n. → **aquaculture**.

aquifer /'ækwəfə/ n. a geological formation which holds water and allows water to percolate through it.

aquiline /'ækwəlaɪn/ adj. **1.** of or like the eagle. **2.** (of the nose) curved like an eagle's beak; hooked.

ar- variant of **ad-** before r.

-ar[1] **1.** an adjective suffix meaning 'of or relating to', 'of the nature of', 'like'. **2.** a suffix forming adjectives not directly related to nouns.

-ar[2] a noun suffix, as in vicar, scholar, collar.

-ar[3] a noun suffix denoting an agent (replacing regular **-er[1]**), as in beggar, liar.

arabesque /ærə'besk/ n. **1.** a position in ballet in which one leg is stretched behind and the body lowered forward. **2.** a kind of ornament with a fanciful pattern of flowers, leaves, vases, animals, etc.

Arabic numerals /'ærəbɪk/ pl. n. the characters 0, 1, 2, 3, 4, 5, 6, 7, 8, 9, in general Western use since the 12th century.

arable /'ærəbəl/ adj. capable, without much modification, of producing crops by means of tillage.

arachnid /ə'ræknɪd/ n. any arthropod of the class which includes the spiders, scorpions, mites, etc.

arbiter /'ɑbətə/ n. **1.** a person empowered to decide points at issue. **2.** someone who has the sole or absolute power of judging or determining.

arbitrage /'ɑbətraʒ/ n. the simultaneous purchase and sale of the same securities, commodities, or moneys in different markets to profit from unequal prices. –**arbitrageur**, **arbitrager**, n.

arbitrary /ˈɑːbətrəri, ˈabətri/, *Orig. US* /ˈɑːbətrɛri/ *adj.* **1.** subject to individual will or judgement. **2.** not attributable to any rule or law; accidental. **3.** capricious; uncertain; unreasonable. **4.** selected at random or by convention. **–arbitrarily,** *adv.*

arbitrate /ˈɑːbətreɪt/ *v.t.* **1.** to submit to arbitration; settle by arbitration. **2.** *Obs.* to decide as arbiter or arbitrator; determine. **–arbitrator,** *n.*

arbitration /ˌɑːbəˈtreɪʃən/ *n.* **1.** *Law* the hearing or determining of a dispute between parties by a person or persons chosen, agreed between them, or appointed by virtue of a statutory obligation. **2.** *Industrial Law* the presentation of legal argument by parties (for whom conciliation has failed), before a government-appointed arbitrator who is empowered to make a binding decision.

arboreal /ɑːˈbɔriəl/ *adj.* **1.** of or relating to trees. **2.** *Zool.* adapted for living in trees.

arbour /ˈɑːbə/ *n.* a bower formed by trees, shrubs, or vines, often on a trellis. Also, **arbor.**

arc /ɑːk/ *n.* **1.** any part of a circle or other curved line. **2.** *Elect.* the luminous bridge formed by the passage of a current across a gap between two conductors or terminals. **3.** anything bow-shaped.

arcade /ɑːˈkeɪd/ *n.* a pedestrian way with shops on one side or both sides.

arcane /ɑːˈkeɪn/ *adj.* mysterious; secret; obscure.

arch¹ /ɑːtʃ/ *n.* **1.** a curved structure resting on supports at both extremities. *–v.t.* **2.** to cover with a vault, or span with an arch. **3.** to throw or make into the shape of an arch or vault; curve.

arch² /ɑːtʃ/ *adj.* **1.** chief; most important; principal. **2.** cunning; sly; roguish.

arch- a prefix meaning 'first', 'chief'.

-arch a suffix meaning 'chief'.

archaeo- a word element meaning 'primeval', 'primitive', 'ancient'. Also, (*especially before a vowel*), **archeo-, archae-, arche-.**

archaeology /ˌɑːkiˈɒlədʒi/ *n.* the systematic study of any culture, especially a prehistoric one, by excavation and description of its remains. Also, **archeology. –archaeologist,** *n.* **–archaeological,** *adj.*

archaic /ɑːˈkeɪɪk/ *adj.* **1.** marked by the characteristics of an earlier period; old-fashioned. **2.** no longer used in ordinary speech or writing; borrowed from older usage (distinguished from *obsolete*).

archaism /ˈɑːkeɪˌɪzəm/ *n.* something archaic, as a word or expression.

archangel /ˈɑːkeɪndʒəl/ *n.* a chief or principal angel.

archbishop /ɑːtʃˈbɪʃəp/ *n.* a bishop of the highest rank.

archenemy /ɑːtʃˈɛnəmi/ *n.* (*pl.* **-mies**) a chief enemy.

archer /ˈɑːtʃə/ *n.* someone who shoots with a bow and arrow. **–archery,** *n.*

archetype /ˈɑːkətaɪp/ *n.* **1.** the original pattern or model after which a thing is made. **2.** someone or something adhering closely to the model or first form. **–archetypal, archetypical,** *adj.*

archipelago /ˌɑːkəˈpɛləgoʊ/ *n.* (*pl.* **-gos** or **-goes**) any large body of water with many islands.

architect /ˈɑːkətɛkt/ *n.* one whose profession it is to design buildings and superintend their construction.

architecture /ˈɑːkətɛktʃə/ *n.* **1.** the art or science of building, including plan, design, construction, and decorative treatment. **2.** the style of building. **3.** the structure or design of something, as a computer, a novel, etc. **–architectural,** *adj.*

architrave /ˈɑːkətreɪv/ *n.* a band of mouldings or other ornamentation about a rectangular door or other opening or a panel.

archive /ˈɑːkaɪv/ *n.* (*oft. pl.*) **1.** the non-current documents or records relating to the activities, rights, claims, treaties, constitutions, etc., of a family, corporation, community, or nation. **2.** a place where public records or other historical documents are kept.

-archy a word element meaning 'rule', 'government'.

arctic /ˈɑːktɪk/ *adj.* **1.** of, at, or near the North Pole. **2.** extremely cold.

-ard a noun suffix, often depreciative, as in *coward, drunkard, wizard.* Also, **-art.**

ardent /ˈɑːdnt/ *adj.* **1.** glowing with feeling, earnestness, or zeal; passionate; fervent. **2.** burning, fiery, or hot.

ardour /ˈɑːdə/ *n.* warmth of feeling; fervour; eagerness; zeal. Also, **ardor.**

arduous /ˈɑːdʒuəs/ *adj.* requiring great exertion; laborious; strenuous.

are¹ /ɑː/, *weak form* /ə/ *v.* present indicative plural of the verb **be.**

are² /ɛə/ *n.* one hundredth of a hectare.

area /ˈɛəriə/ *n.* **1.** any particular extent of surface; region; tract. **2.** a piece of unoccupied ground; an open space. **3.** extent, range, or scope. **4.** a field of study, interest, or knowledge. **5.** *Maths* two dimensional extent. **–areal,** *adj.*

area code *n.* a sequence of numbers or letters preceding a telephone subscriber's number, indicating the area or exchange. Also, **STD code.**

arena /əˈrinə/ *n.* **1.** an enclosure for sports contests, shows, etc. **2.** a field of conflict or endeavour.

areola /əˈriələ/ *n.* (*pl.* **-lae** /-li/) a small ring of colour, as around a pustule or the human nipple.

argon /ˈɑːgɒn/ *n.* a colourless, odourless, chemically inactive, gaseous element. *Symbol:* Ar

argot /ˈɑːgoʊ/ *n.* the peculiar language or jargon of any class or group.

arguable /ˈɑːgjuəbəl/ *adj.* **1.** capable of being maintained; plausible. **2.** open to dispute or argument. **3.** capable of being argued. **–arguably,** *adv.*

argue /ˈɑːgju/ *v.* (**-gued, -guing**) *–v.i.* **1.** to present reasons for or against a thing. **2.** to contend in argument; dispute. *–v.t.* **3.** to state the reasons for or against. **4.** to argue in favour of; support by argument.

argument /ˈɑːgjəmənt/ *n.* **1.** an argumentation; debate. **2.** a matter of contention. **3.** a statement or fact tending to support a point. **4.** *Computers* a datum or value used while transferring information from part to part of a program.

argumentation /agjəmən'teɪʃən/ *n.* **1.** debate; discussion; reasoning. **2.** the setting forth of reasons together with the conclusion drawn from them; formal or logical reasoning.

argumentative /agjə'mɛntətɪv/ *adj.* **1.** given to argument. **2.** controversial.

aria /'arɪə/ *n.* an elaborate melody for a single voice, with accompaniment, in an opera, etc.

-arian a compound suffix of adjectives and nouns, often referring to pursuits, doctrines, etc.

arid /'ærɪd/ *adj.* dry; without moisture; parched with heat.

arise /ə'raɪz/ *v.i.* (**arose**, **arisen**, **arising**) **1.** to come into being or action; originate; appear. **2.** to move upwards. **3.** to rise; get up from sitting, lying, or kneeling.

aristo- a word element meaning 'best', 'superior'.

aristocracy /ærə'stɒkrəsi/ *n.* (*pl.* **-cies**) a class of hereditary nobility.

aristocrat /'ærəstəkræt, ə'rɪstəkræt/ *n.* **1.** someone who has the tastes, manners, etc., of the members of a superior group or class. **2.** (one of) the best of its kind. **–aristocratic**, *adj.*

arithmetic /ə'rɪθmətɪk/ **1.** the art or skill of computation with figures (the most elementary branch of mathematics). *–adj.* /ærəθ'mɛtɪk/ **2.** of or relating to arithmetic. **–arithmetical**, *adj.*

arithmetic unit *n.* the section of a computer which does arithmetical processes.

ark /ak/ *n.* **1.** a wooden chest or coffer. **2.** a large, floating vessel resembling this, as Noah's Ark.

arm¹ /am/ *n.* **1.** the upper limb of the human body from the shoulder to the hand. **2.** this limb, exclusive of the hand. **3.** the forelimb of any four-legged vertebrate. **4.** any arm-like part. **5.** a covering for the arm, as the sleeve of a garment.

arm² /am/ *n.* **1.** (*usu. pl.*) a weapon. *–v.t.* **2.** to equip with arms. **3.** to fit or prepare (a thing) for any specific purpose or effective use.

armada /a'madə/ *n.* **1.** a fleet of warships. **2.** a large number of boats or ships.

armadillo /amə'dɪloʊ/ *n.* (*pl.* **-los**) an armoured, burrowing mammal of Central and South America.

armament /'aməmənt/ *n.* the weapons with which a military unit, especially an aeroplane, vehicle, or warship, is equipped.

armature /'amətʃə/ *n.* protective covering.

armchair /'amtʃeə/ *n.* a chair with arms to support the forearms or elbows.

armistice /'aməstəs/ *n.* a truce.

armorial /a'mɔriəl/ *adj.* belonging to heraldry or to heraldic bearing.

armour /'amə/ *n.* **1.** defensive equipment; any covering worn as a protection against offensive weapons. **2.** that which serves as a protection or safeguard. Also, **armor. –armoured**, *adj.*

armoury /'aməri/ *n.* (*pl.* **-ries**) a storage place for weapons and other war equipment. Also, **armory.**

armpit /'ampɪt/ *n.* the hollow under the arm at the shoulder.

arms /amz/ *pl. n.* **1.** → **arm²** (def. 1). **2.** *Mil.* small arms. **3.** heraldic bearings.

army /'ami/ *n.* (*pl.* **-mies**) **1.** (*upper case or lower case*) the military forces of a nation. **2.** a large body of people trained and armed for war.

army reserve *n.* the part of a country's fighting force not in active service, but used as a further means of defence in case of necessity.

aroma /ə'roʊmə/ *n.* a smell, especially an agreeable smell; fragrance. **–aromatic**, *adj.*

aromatherapy /əroʊmə'θerəpi/ *n.* a type of therapy using scented oils. **–aromatherapist**, *n.*

arose /ə'roʊz/ *v.* past tense of **arise.**

around /ə'raʊnd/ *adv.* **1.** in a circle or sphere; round about; on every side. **2.** here and there; about. *–prep.* **3.** about; on all sides; encircling; encompassing. **4.** approximately; near in time, amount, etc.

arouse /ə'raʊz/ *v.t.* **1.** to excite into action; stir or put in motion; call into being. **2.** to wake from sleep. **–arousal**, *n.*

arpeggio /a'pedʒioʊ/ *n.* (*pl.* **-gios**) *Music* the sounding of the notes of a chord one after the other instead of together.

arraign /ə'reɪn/ *v.t. Law* to call or bring before a court to answer to a charge or accusation.

arrange /ə'reɪndʒ/ *v.t.* (**arranged**, **arranging**) **1.** to place in proper, desired, or convenient order; adjust properly. **2.** to come to an agreement or understanding regarding. **3.** to prepare or plan. **–arrangement**, *n.*

arrant /'ærənt/ *adj.* downright; thorough.

array /ə'reɪ/ *v.t.* **1.** to place in proper or desired order, as troops for battle. **2.** to clothe with garments, especially of an ornamental kind; deck. *–n.* **3.** regular order or arrangement. **4.** attire; dress.

arrear /ə'rɪə/ *n.* **1.** (*usu. pl.*) that which is behind in payment; a debt which remains unpaid, though due. *–phr.* **2. in arrear** or **in arrears**, behind in payments.

arrest /ə'rɛst/ *v.t.* **1.** to seize (a person) by legal authority or warrant. **2.** to capture; seize. **3.** to bring to a standstill; stop; check. *–n.* **4.** the taking of a person into custody in connection with a legal proceeding.

arresting /ə'rɛstɪŋ/ *adj.* catching the attention; striking.

arrhythmia /eɪ'rɪðmɪə/ *n.* any disturbance in the rhythm of the heartbeat.

arrive /ə'raɪv/ *v.i.* **1.** to come to a certain point in the course of travel; reach one's destination. **2.** (fol. by *at*) to reach in any course or process; attain. **–arrival**, *n.*

arrogant /'ærəgənt/ *adj.* making unwarrantable claims or pretensions to superior importance or rights. **–arrogance, arrogancy**, *n.*

arrow /'æroʊ/ *n.* **1.** a slender, straight, generally pointed, missile weapon made to be shot from a bow. **2.** a figure of an arrow used to indicate direction.

arrowroot /'ærərut/ *n.* a tropical American plant whose rhizomes yield a nutritious starch.

arse /as/ *n. Colloq.* (*taboo*) rump; bottom; buttocks; posterior.

arsenal /'asənəl/ *n.* a repository or magazine of arms and military stores.

arsenic /'asənɪk/ *n.* a greyish-white element having a metallic lustre, and forming poisonous compounds. *Symbol*: As

arson /'asən/ n. the act of maliciously setting fire to property.

art /at/ n. **1.** the production or expression of what is beautiful (especially visually), appealing, or of more than ordinary significance. **2.** (pl.) a branch of learning or university study. **3.** a skill or knack; a skilled method of doing something, especially something difficult. **4.** craft; cunning. **5.** studied action; artificiality in behaviour. **6.** learning or science.

-art variant of **-ard**, as in braggart.

artefact /'atəfækt/ n. any object made by humans, especially one used in daily life. Also, **artifact**.

arterial /a'tɪərɪəl/ adj. **1.** Anat. of, relating to, or resembling the arteries. **2.** having a main channel and many branches. **3.** carrying the main flow of traffic between large towns.

arteriosclerosis /a,tɪərɪousklə'rousəs/ n. a disease of the arteries characterised by inelasticity and thickening of the vessel walls, with lessened blood flow.

artery /'atəri/ n. (pl. **-ries**) **1.** Anat. a blood vessel which conveys blood from the heart to any part of the body. **2.** a main channel, as in drainage or roads.

artesian bore /a'tiʒən/ n. a bore in which the water level, under pressure, rises above ground. Also, **artesian well**.

artful /'atfəl/ adj. **1.** crafty; cunning; tricky: artful schemes. **2.** skilful in adapting means to ends; ingenious.

arthritis /a'θraɪtəs/ n. inflammation of a joint, as in gout or rheumatism. **–arthritic**, adj., n.

arthro- Anat. a word element meaning 'joint', as in arthropod. Also, **arthr-**.

arthropod /'aθrəpɒd/ n. any of the phylum of segmented invertebrates, having jointed legs, as the insects, arachnids, and crustaceans.

arthroscope /'aθrəskoup/ n. a thin, tubular instrument which is inserted into the cavity between bones to examine a joint and perform surgical procedures. **–arthroscopic**, adj.

arthroscopy /a'θrɒskəpi/ n. (pl. **-pies**) Med. **1.** the examination of a joint using an arthroscope. **2.** the use of this technique to remove damaged tissue or foreign matter in a joint.

artichoke /'atətʃouk, 'atɪtʃouk/ n. a herbaceous, thistlelike plant with an edible flower head.

article /'atɪkəl/ n. **1.** a piece of writing on a specific topic. **2.** an individual piece or thing of a class; an item or particular. **3.** a thing, indefinitely. **4.** in English, the words a, an and the. **5.** a clause, item, point, or particular in a contract, treaty, etc. **6.** a separate clause or provision of a statute. **7.** (pl.) a document drawn up in articles; an agreement or code. **–v.t. 8.** to set forth in articles; charge or accuse specifically. **9.** to bind by articles of covenant or stipulation. **10.** to bind by articles of agreement.

articled clerk n. a person under articles of agreement to serve a solicitor in return for training.

articulate v.t. /a'tɪkjəlaɪt/ **1.** to utter articulately. **2.** Phonetics to make the movements and adjustments of the speech organs necessary to utter (a speech sound). **3.** to unite by a joint or joints. **–v.i.** /a'tɪkjələt/ **4.** to utter distinct syllables or words. **5.** Phonetics to articulate a speech sound. **–adj.** /a'tɪkjələt/ **6.** clear; distinct. **7.** uttered clearly in distinct syllables. **8.** capable of speech; eloquent. **9.** Also, **articulated**. having joints; composed of segments. **–articulation**, n.

articulated /a'tɪkjəleɪtəd/ adj. **1.** connected by a joint or joints. **2.** (of a road vehicle) consisting of sections connected by a flexible joint.

artifice /'atəfəs/ n. **1.** a crafty device or expedient; a clever trick or stratagem. **2.** craft; trickery.

artificial /atə'fɪʃəl/ adj. **1.** made by human skill and labour (opposed to natural). **2.** made in imitation of or as a substitute; not genuine. **3.** feigned; fictitious; assumed.

artificial intelligence n. the ability of a computer or other machine to function as if possessing human intelligence.

artificial respiration n. any of various methods for restarting the breathing of a person whose breathing has stopped, as by mouth-to-mouth resuscitation or by the application of rhythmic pressure to the rib cage.

artillery /a'tɪləri/ n. mounted guns, movable or stationary, light or heavy, as distinguished from small arms.

artisan /'atəzən/ n. **1.** one skilled in an industrial or applied art. **–adj. 2.** made by traditional methods: artisan food. **–artisanal**, adj.

artist /'atəst/ n. **1.** a person who practises one of the fine arts, especially a painter or sculptor. **2.** a person who practises one of the performing arts, as an actor or singer.

artistic /a'tɪstɪk/ adj. **1.** conformable to the standards of art; aesthetically excellent or admirable. **2.** naturally gifted to be an artist. **3.** stormy, emotional, and capricious, as temperament or behaviour popularly ascribed to artists. **–artistically**, adv.

artistry /'atəstri/ n. **1.** artistic workmanship, effect, or quality. **2.** artistic pursuits.

artless /'atləs/ adj. free from pretence; natural; simple: an artless manner, artless beauty.

art union n. a lottery.

-ary¹ 1. an adjective suffix meaning 'relating to', attached chiefly to nouns (honorary) and to stems appearing in other words (voluntary). **2.** a suffix forming nouns from other nouns or adjectives indicating location or repository (dictionary, granary, apiary), officers (functionary, secretary), or other relations (adversary). **3.** a suffix forming collective numeral nouns, especially in time units (centenary).

-ary² variant of **-ar¹**, as in exemplary, military.

as /æz/, weak form /əz/ adv. **1.** to such a degree or extent. **–conj. 2.** the consequent in the correlations as (or so) ... as, same ... as, etc., denoting degree, extent, manner, etc. (as good as gold, in the same way as before), or in the correlations so as, such as, denoting purpose or result (followed by infinitive). **3.** (without antecedent) in the degree, manner, etc., of or that. **4.** though. **5.** as if; as though. **6.** when or while. **7.** since; because. **8.** for instance. **–prep. 9.** in the role, function, status, or manner of. **–phr. 10. as for** or **as to**, with regard or respect to; for the matter of. **11. as if** or **as though**, as it would be if. **12. as it were**, in some sort; so to speak. **13. as well**, **a.** equally; also; too. **b.** as well as not; equally well; better;

advisable. **14. as well as**, as much or as truly as; just as; equally as; as also; in addition to. **15. as yet, a.** up to now; even yet. **b.** for the moment; in the near future; just yet.

as- variant of **ad-** before *s*, as in *assert*.

asbestos /æsˈbɛstəs, æs-, -tɒs/ *n.* a fibrous mineral, formerly used for making fireproof articles and as a building material; now banned in many countries as known to cause mesothelioma and asbestosis.

asbestosis /æsbɛsˈtoʊsəs/ *n.* inflammation of the lungs caused by the inhalation of asbestos particles.

ascend /əˈsɛnd/ *v.i.* **1.** to climb or go upwards; mount; rise. –*v.t.* **2.** to go or move upwards upon or along; climb; mount. –**ascension**, *n.*

ascendancy /əˈsɛndənsi/ *n.* the state of being in the ascendant; governing or controlling influence; domination. Also, **ascendency**, **ascendance**, **ascendence**.

ascendant /əˈsɛndənt/ *n.* **1.** a position of dominance or controlling influence; superiority; predominance. –*adj.* **2.** superior; predominant.

ascent /əˈsɛnt/ *n.* **1.** the act of ascending; upward movement; rise. **2.** the act of climbing or travelling up. **3.** gradient.

ascertain /æsəˈteɪn/ *v.t.* to find out by trial, examination, or experiment, so as to know as certain; determine.

ascetic /əˈsɛtɪk/ *n.* **1.** a person who leads an austere life. –*adj.* **2.** rigorously abstinent; austere.

ASCII /ˈæski/ *n.* a standard computer code for representing alphabetical and numerical characters.

asco- a word element meaning 'bag'.

ascorbic acid /əsˈkɔbɪk/ *n.* a water-soluble vitamin, vitamin C, which has a major role in the formation of bones, blood vessels and connective tissues; occurring naturally in citrus fruits, tomatoes, capsicum, and green vegetables, but also produced synthetically.

ascribe /əˈskraɪb/ *v.t.* to attribute, impute, or refer, as to a cause or source; assign.

-ase a noun suffix used in names of enzymes.

aseptic /eɪˈsɛptɪk/ *adj.* free from the living germs of disease, fermentation, or putrefaction.

asexual /eɪˈsɛkʃuəl/ *adj.* **1.** not sexual. **2.** having no sex or no sexual organs. **3.** independent of sexual processes. –**asexuality**, *n.*

ash¹ /æʃ/ *n.* **1.** (*usu. pl., used as sing. chiefly in scientific and commercial language*) the powdery residue of matter that remains after burning. –*v.t.* **2.** to cause the ash collected on the tip of (a cigar or cigarette) to fall, usually by giving a light tap: *don't ash your cigarette on the carpet!*

ash² /æʃ/ *n.* **1.** a tree of the Northern Hemisphere. **2.** any of many Southern Hemisphere trees whose timber or foliage resembles that of the ash.

ashamed /əˈʃeɪmd/ *adj.* **1.** feeling shame; abashed by guilt. **2.** unwilling or restrained through fear of shame. **3.** (fol. by *of*) loath to acknowledge.

ashen /ˈæʃən/ *adj.* **1.** ash-coloured; grey. **2.** consisting of ashes.

ashore /əˈʃɔ/ *adv.* **1.** to shore; on or to the land. –*adj.* **2.** on land (opposed to *aboard* or *afloat*).

aside /əˈsaɪd/ *adv.* **1.** on or to one side; to or at a short distance; apart; away from some position or direction. **2.** away from one's thoughts or consideration. –*n.* **3.** words spoken in an undertone, so as not to be heard by some of the people present. **4.** a remark or comment which is incidental to the main subject.

asinine /ˈæsənaɪn/ *adj.* stupid; obstinate.

ask /ask/ *v.t.* **1.** to put a question to. **2.** to seek to be informed about. **3.** to seek by words to obtain; request. **4.** to call for; require. **5.** to invite. –*v.i.* **6.** to make inquiry; inquire. **7.** (fol. by *for*) to request or petition.

askance /əsˈkæns/ *adv.* **1.** with suspicion, mistrust, or disapproval. **2.** with a side glance; sideways.

askew /əsˈkju/ *adv.* **1.** to one side; out of line; obliquely; awry. –*adj.* **2.** oblique.

asleep /əˈslip/ *adv.* **1.** in or into a state of sleep. –*adj.* **2.** sleeping. **3.** (of the foot, hand, leg, etc.) numb.

asp /æsp/ *n.* **1.** any of several poisonous snakes. **2.** the common European viper or adder.

asparagus /əˈspærəgəs/ *n.* a plant cultivated for its edible shoots.

aspect /ˈæspɛkt/ *n.* **1.** appearance to the eye or mind; look. **2.** a way in which a thing may be viewed or regarded. **3.** view commanded; exposure. **4.** *Gram.* (in some languages) a category of verb inflection denoting various relations of the action or state of the verb to the passage of time, as duration, repetition, or completion.

aspen /ˈæspən/ *n.* any of various species of poplar.

Asperger's syndrome /ˈæspɜgəz, ˈæspɜdʒəz/ *n.* a form of autism characterised by a tendency to social isolation and eccentric behaviour.

asperity /æsˈpɛrəti, əs-/ *n.* **1.** roughness or sharpness of temper; severity; acrimony. **2.** hardship; difficulty; rigour. **3.** roughness of surface; unevenness.

aspersion /əˈspɜʒən, -spɜʃən/ *n.* a damaging imputation; a derogatory criticism.

asphalt /ˈæffɛlt, ˈæsfɛlt/ *n.* any of various dark-coloured, solid substances containing bitumen, composed mostly of mixtures of hydrocarbons, occurring native in various parts of the earth.

asphyxia /əsˈfɪksiə/ *n.* the extreme condition caused by lack of oxygen and excess of carbon dioxide in the blood, caused by sufficient interference with respiration, as in choking. –**asphyxiate**, *v.* –**asphyxiation**, *n.*

aspic /ˈæspɪk/ *n.* **1.** a cold dish of meat, fish, etc., served set in a jellied mould. **2.** the jellied garnish, made from fish or meat stock, sometimes with added gelatine.

aspirate /ˈæspəreɪt/ *v.t.* **1.** *Phonetics* **a.** to release (a stop) in such a way that the breath escapes with audible friction, as in *title* where the first *t* is aspirated, the second is not. **b.** to begin (a word or syllable) with an *h* sound, as in *when* (pronounced *hwen*), *howl*, opposed to *wen*, *owl*. **2.** *Med.* to remove (fluids) from body cavities by use of an aspirator. **3.** *Med.* to inhale (foreign matter) into the lungs.

aspiration /æspəˈreɪʃən/ *n.* **1.** something aspired to; an ambition. **2.** a breath.

aspirator /ˈæspəreɪtə/ *n.* **1.** an apparatus or device using suction. **2.** *Med.* an instrument for removing fluids from the body by suction.

aspire /əˈspaɪə/ *phr.* **aspire to**, to aim at (something, usually something great or lofty): *aspiring to greatness*.

aspirin /ˈæsprən/ *n.* (*from trademark*) a white crystalline substance, often in the form of a tablet, used to relieve pain.

ass /æs/ *n.* **1.** a long-eared, usually ash-coloured mammal related to the horse; the donkey. **2.** a fool.

assail /əˈseɪl/ *v.t.* **1.** to set upon with violence; assault. **2.** to set upon vigorously with arguments, entreaties, abuse, etc. **–assailant**, *n.*, *adj.*

assassin /əˈsæsən/ *n.* someone who undertakes to murder, especially from fanaticism or for a reward.

assassinate /əˈsæsəneɪt/ **1.** to kill by sudden or secret, premeditated assault, especially for political or religious motives. **2.** to blight or destroy treacherously. **–assassination**, *n.* **–assassinator**, *n.*

assault /əˈsɔlt, -ˈsɒlt/ *n.* **1.** the act of assailing; an attack; onslaught. **2.** *Law* an unlawful physical attack upon another; an attempt or offer to do violence to another, with or without a battery, as by holding a weapon in a threatening manner. **–v.t. 3.** to make an assault upon; attack. **–assaulter**, *n.*

assay /əˈseɪ/ *v.t.* **1.** to examine by trial; put to test or trial. **2.** to judge the quality of; evaluate.

assemblage /əˈsɛmblɪdʒ/ *n.* a number of persons or things assembled; an assembly.

assemble /əˈsɛmbəl/ *v.t.* **1.** to bring together; gather into one place, company, body or whole. **2.** to put or fit (parts) together; put together the parts of (a mechanism, etc.). **–v.i. 3.** to come together; gather; meet.

assembly /əˈsɛmbli/ *n.* (*pl.* **-lies**) **1.** a company of persons gathered together, usually for the same purpose, whether religious, political, educational, or social. **2.** (*upper case*) *Govt* a legislative body, especially a lower house of a legislature. **3.** the putting together of complex machinery, as aeroplanes, from interchangeable parts of standard dimensions.

assent /əˈsɛnt/ *v.i.* **1.** (oft. fol. by *to*) to express agreement or concurrence. **–n. 2.** agreement, as to a proposal; acquiescence; concurrence. **–assenter**, *n.*

assert /əˈsɜt/ *v.t.* **1.** to state as true; affirm; declare. **2.** to maintain or defend (claims, rights, etc.). **3.** to put (oneself) forward boldly and insistently. **–assertion**, *n.* **–assertive**, *adj.* **–assertable**, *adj.*

assess /əˈsɛs/ *v.t.* **1.** to measure or evaluate. **2.** to estimate officially the value of (property, income, etc.) as a basis for taxation. **3.** to fix or determine the amount of (damages, a tax, a fine, etc.). **–assessment**, *n.*

assessor /əˈsɛsə/ *n.* **1.** someone who makes assessments, as of damage for insurance purposes, or of property, etc., for taxation purposes. **2.** an advisory associate or assistant.

asset /ˈæsɛt/ *n.* **1.** a useful thing or quality. **2.** See **assets**.

assets /ˈæsɛts/ *pl. n.* **1.** *Commerce* resources of a person or business consisting of such items

as real property, machinery, inventories, notes, securities, cash, etc. **2.** property or effects (opposed to *liabilities*). **3.** any property available for paying debts, etc. **4.** *Accounting* the detailed listing of property owned by a firm and money owing to it.

asseverate /əˈsɛvəreɪt/ *v.t.* to declare earnestly or solemnly; affirm positively.

assiduous /əˈsɪdʒuəs/ *adj.* **1.** constant; unremitting. **2.** constant in application; attentive; devoted. **–assiduity**, *n.*

assign /əˈsaɪn/ *v.t.* **1.** to make over or give, as in distribution; allot. **2.** to appoint, as to a post or duty. **3.** (formerly) to allocate (a convict) for employment by an officer or settler. **4.** to designate; specify. **5.** to ascribe; attribute; refer.

assignation /æsɪgˈneɪʃən/ *n.* **1.** an appointment for a meeting, especially one made by lovers. **2.** the act of assigning; assignment.

assignee /əsaɪˈni/ *n.* **1.** *Law* someone to whom some right or interest is transferred, either for their own enjoyment or in trust. **2.** (formerly) a convict assigned as a servant.

assignment /əˈsaɪnmənt/ *n.* something assigned, as a particular task or duty.

assimilate /əˈsɪmələt/ *v.t.* **1.** to take in and incorporate as one's own; absorb: *to assimilate a migrant community*; *to assimilate information*. **2.** *Physiol.* to convert (food, etc.) into a substance suitable for absorption into the system. **–v.i. 3.** to be or become absorbed. **4.** (usu. fol. by *into* or *with*) to become or be like; blend into: *to assimilate with the rest of the community*. **–assimilable**, *adj.* **–assimilation**, *n.*

assist /əˈsɪst/ *v.t.* **1.** to give support, help, or aid to in some undertaking or effort, or in time of distress. **2.** to be associated with as an assistant. **–v.i. 3.** to give aid or help. **–assister** *Law*, **assistor**, *n.* **–assistance**, *n.*

assistance dog *n.* a dog trained to perform a number of functions for their disabled owner, such as opening and closing doors, turning light switches on and off, pressing pedestrian crossing buttons, retrieving objects, etc.

assistant /əˈsɪstənt/ *n.* **1.** someone who assists a superior in some office or work; helper. **–adj. 2.** assisting; helpful. **3.** associated with a superior in some office or work.

associate /əˈsoʊʃieɪt, -sieɪt/ *for defs 1–5*, /əˈsoʊʃiət, -siət/ *for defs 6 and 7* *–v.t.* **1.** to connect by some relation, as in thought. **2.** to join as a companion, partner, or ally. **3.** to unite; combine. **–v.i. 4.** to enter into a league or union; unite. **5.** to keep company, as a friend or intimate. **–n. 6.** a partner in interest, as in business or in an enterprise or action. **–adj. 7.** having subordinate membership; without full rights and privileges.

association /əsoʊsiˈeɪʃən/ *n.* **1.** an organisation of people with a common purpose and having a formal structure. **2.** companionship or intimacy. **3.** connection or combination. **4.** the connection of ideas in thought, or an idea connected with or suggested by a subject of thought.

assonance /ˈæsənəns/ *n.* **1.** resemblance of sounds. **2.** partial agreement.

assort /əˈsɔt/ *v.t.* **1.** to distribute according to sort or kind; classify. **2.** to furnish with a suitable assortment or variety of goods; make up of articles likely to suit a demand.

assortment /əˈsɔːtmənt/ n. **1.** the act of assorting; distribution; classification. **2.** an assorted collection.

assuage /əˈsweɪdʒ/ v.t. (**-suaged, -suaging**) **1.** to make milder or less severe; mitigate; ease. **2.** to appease; satisfy.

assume /əˈsjuːm/ v.t. **1.** to take for granted or without proof; suppose as a fact. **2.** to take upon oneself; undertake. **3.** to pretend to have or be; feign. **4.** to appropriate. –**assumption** /əˈsʌmʃən/, n.

assuming /əˈsjuːmɪŋ/ adj. arrogant; presuming. –**assumingly**, adv.

assurance /əˈʃɔːrəns, -ˈʃʊə-/ n. **1.** a positive declaration intended to give confidence. **2.** pledge; guarantee; surety. **3.** full confidence or trust; freedom from doubt; certainty. **4.** freedom from timidity; self-reliance; courage. **5.** insurance (now usually restricted to life insurance).

assure /əˈʃɔ/ v.t. **1.** to declare earnestly to; inform or tell positively. **2.** to make (one) sure or certain; convince, as by a promise or declaration. **3.** to make (a future event) sure; ensure. **4.** to secure or confirm; render safe or stable. **5.** to give confidence to; encourage. **6.** to insure, especially against death.

-aster a suffix used to form nouns denoting something that imperfectly resembles or merely apes the true thing, or an inferior or petty instance of something.

asterisk /ˈæstərɪsk/ n. **1.** the figure of a star (*), used in writing and printing as a reference mark or to indicate omission, doubtful matter, etc. **2.** something in the shape of a star or asterisk. –v.t. **3.** to identify or mark by means of this sign.

asteroid /ˈæstərɔɪd/ n. Astron. one of several hundred small celestial bodies with orbits lying mostly between those of Mars and Jupiter.

asthma /ˈæsmə/ n. a paroxysmal disorder of respiration with laboured breathing, a feeling of constriction in the chest, and coughing. –**asthmatic**, adj., n.

astigmatism /əˈstɪɡmətɪzəm/ n. a defect of the eye or of a lens whereby rays of light from an external point converge unequally in different meridians, thus causing imperfect vision or images.

astonish /əˈstɒnɪʃ/ v.t. to strike with sudden and overpowering wonder; surprise greatly; amaze.

astound /əˈstaʊnd/ v.t. to overwhelm with amazement; astonish greatly.

astral /ˈæstrəl/ adj. relating to or proceeding from the stars; consisting of or resembling stars; starry; stellar.

astray /əˈstreɪ/ adv. out of the right way or away from the right; straying; wandering.

astride /əˈstraɪd/ adv. **1.** in the posture of striding or straddling. –prep. **2.** with a leg on each side of.

astringent /əˈstrɪndʒənt/ adj. **1.** (as affecting the skin) refreshing, tightening, drying. **2.** severe, sharp, austere. –n. **3.** an astringent agent (especially cosmetic).

astro- a word element meaning 'star', as in astrology.

astrology /əsˈtrɒlədʒi/ n. **1.** a study which assumes, and professes to interpret, the influence of the heavenly bodies on human affairs. **2.** (formerly) practical astronomy, the earliest form of the science. –**astrologer**, n. –**astrological, astrologic**, adj.

astronaut /ˈæstrənɔt/ n. a person trained as a pilot, navigator, etc., to take part in the flight of a spacecraft; cosmonaut.

astronomical /æstrəˈnɒmɪkəl/ adj. **1.** of, relating to, or connected with astronomy. **2.** very large, like the numbers used in astronomical calculations. Also, **astronomic**.

astronomy /əsˈtrɒnəmi/ n. the science of the celestial bodies, their motions, positions, distances, magnitudes, etc. –**astronomer**, n.

astute /əsˈtjut/ adj. of keen penetration or discernment; sagacious; shrewd; cunning.

asunder /əˈsʌndə/ adv. into separate parts; in or into pieces.

asylum /əˈsaɪləm/ n. **1.** an institution for the maintenance and care of the insane, the blind, orphans or the like. **2.** an inviolable refuge, as formerly for criminals and debtors; a sanctuary. **3.** International Law protection, usually right of residence, granted by the government of a country to one or more refugees who have left their own country because of war or because of political or other persecution.

asylum seeker n. a person who has applied for asylum (def. 3) in a country not their own and who is awaiting the determination of his or her status as a refugee.

asymmetric /eɪsəˈmɛtrɪk/ adj. lacking symmetry. Also, **asymmetrical**. –**asymmetry**, n.

asystole /eɪˈsɪstəli/ n. Med. a state of the heart in which there is an absence of systole, and hence no contraction of the heart muscle and no blood flow, leading to death. –**asystolic** /eɪsɪs-ˈtɒlɪk/, adj.

at /æt/, weak form /ət/ prep. a particle specifying a point occupied, attained, sought, or otherwise concerned, as in place, time, order, experience, etc., and hence used in many idiomatic phrases expressing circumstantial or relative position, degree or rate, action, manner: at noon, at home, at length.

at- variant of **ad-** before t, as in attend.

atavism /ˈætəvɪzəm/ n. reversion to an earlier type. –**atavistic**, adj.

ate /eɪt, ɛt/ v. past tense of eat.

-ate¹ a suffix forming: **1.** adjectives equivalent to **-ed²** (in participial and other adjectives), as in accumulate, separate. **2.** nouns denoting especially persons charged with some duty or function, or invested with some dignity, right, or special character, as in advocate, candidate, curate, legate, prelate. **3.** nouns denoting some product or result of action, as in mandate (literally, a thing commanded). **4.** verbs, originally taken from Latin past participles but now formed from any Latin or other stem, as in actuate, agitate, calibrate.

-ate² a suffix forming nouns denoting a salt formed by action of an acid on a base, especially where the name of the acid ends in -ic, as in acetate.

-ate³ a suffix forming nouns denoting condition, estate, office, officials, or an official, etc., as in consulate, senate.

atheism /'eɪθi,ɪzəm/ n. **1.** the doctrine that there is no god. **2.** disbelief in the existence of a god (or gods) (opposed to *theism*). –**atheist**, n.

atherosclerosis /,æθərousklə'rousəs/ n. a form of the disease arteriosclerosis in which fatty substances deposit in the arteries and harden to form plaque, thus immobilising the artery.

athlete /'æθliːt/ n. **1.** anyone trained to perform exercises of physical agility and strength. **2.** someone trained for track and field events only.

athletic /æθ'lɛtɪk/ adj. **1.** physically active and strong. **2.** of, like, or befitting an athlete.

athletics /æθ'lɛtɪks/ n. **1.** (*usu. construed as pl.*) athletic sports, as running, hurdling, etc. **2.** (*usu. construed as sing.*) track and field events only.

-ation a suffix forming nouns denoting action or process, state or condition, a product or result, or something producing a result. See **-ion, -tion**.

-ative an adjective suffix expressing tendency, disposition, function, bearing, connection, etc., as in *affirmative, demonstrative, talkative*.

atlas /'ætləs/ n. **1.** a bound collection of maps. **2.** a volume of plates or tables illustrating any subject.

ATM /eɪ ti 'ɛm/ n. → **automatic teller machine**.

atmosphere /'ætməsfɪə/ n. **1.** the gaseous fluid surrounding the earth; the air. **2.** a feeling or mood. –**atmospheric**, adj.

atmospheric pressure n. the pressure exerted on an object by the atmosphere; at sea level a column of air 1 square metre across weighs 100 kilonewtons.

atoll /'ætɒl/ n. a ringlike coral island enclosing a lagoon.

atom /'ætəm/ n. *Chem., Physics* the smallest unit of an element that can take part in chemical reactions; consists of protons, neutrons and electrons, whose number and arrangement determine the element and its properties.

atomic /ə'tɒmɪk/ adj. **1.** relating to atoms. **2.** propelled or driven by atomic energy. **3.** using or having developed atomic weapons.

atomic energy n. **1.** the energy obtained from changes within the atomic nucleus, chiefly from nuclear fission, or fusion. **2.** this energy regarded as a source of power, as for industrial usage.

atomic mass n. the mass of an isotope of an element.

atomic number n. the number of protons in the nucleus of an atom of a given element. *Abbrev.*: at. no.

atomic power n. energy released in nuclear reactions.

atomic weapon n. any weapon (especially a bomb, shell, or missile) in which the destructive power is derived from atomic energy.

atomic weight n. → **relative atomic mass**.

atomiser /'ætəmaɪzə/ n. an apparatus for reducing liquids to a fine spray, as for medicinal application. Also, **atomizer**.

atone /ə'toʊn/ v.i. (fol. by *for*) to make amends or reparation, as for an offence or a crime, or for an offender. –**atonement**, n.

atrium /'eɪtriəm, 'eɪ-/ n. (*pl.* **-tria** /-triə/) **1.** *Archit.* **a.** the central main room of an ancient Roman private house. **b.** an open area which is central to the design of a building. **2.** *Zool.* an internal cavity or space; applied variously to different cavities in different organisms.

atrocious /ə'troʊʃəs/ adj. **1.** extremely or shockingly wicked or cruel; heinous. **2.** shockingly bad or lacking in taste; execrable.

atrocity /ə'trɒsəti/ n. (*pl.* **-ties**) **1.** the quality of being atrocious. **2.** an atrocious deed or thing.

atrophy /'ætrəfi/ n. **1.** wasting away of the body or of an organ or part, as from defective nutrition or other cause. **2.** degeneration; reduction in size and functional power through lack of use.–v. (**-phied, -phying**) –v.t. **3.** to affect with atrophy. –v.i. **4.** to undergo atrophy.

attach /ə'tætʃ/ v.t. **1.** to fasten to; affix; join; connect. **2.** to join in action or function. **3.** to connect as an adjunct; associate. **4.** to assign or attribute. **5.** to bind by ties of affection or regard. –**attachment**, n.

attaché /ə'tæʃeɪ/ n. one attached to an official staff, especially that of an embassy or legation.

attaché case n. a small rectangular case with a hinged lid, for documents, etc.

attack /ə'tæk/ v.t. **1.** to set upon with force or weapons; begin hostilities against. **2.** to direct unfavourable criticism, argument, etc., against; blame or abuse violently. **3.** to set about (a task) or go to work on (a thing) vigorously. **4.** (of disease, destructive agencies, etc.) to begin to affect. –n. **5.** the act of attacking; onslaught; assault. **6.** criticism; abuse; calumny.

attain /ə'teɪn/ v.t. **1.** to reach, achieve, or accomplish by continued effort. **2.** to come to or arrive at in due course. –phr. **3. attain to**, to arrive at; succeed in reaching or obtaining.

attempt /ə'tɛmpt, ə'tɛmt/ v.t. **1.** to make an effort at; try; undertake; seek. **2.** to attack; make an effort against. –n. **3.** effort put forth to accomplish something. **4.** an attack or assault.

attend /ə'tɛnd/ v.t. **1.** to be present at. **2.** to go with as a concomitant or result; accompany. **3.** to minister to; devote one's services to. –v.i. **4.** to give attention; pay regard or heed. **5.** to apply oneself. **6.** to take care or charge of. **7.** to be consequent (*on*). **8.** to wait (*on*) with service. –**attendee**, n.

attendance /ə'tɛndəns/ n. **1.** the act of attending. **2.** the (number of) persons present.

attendant /ə'tɛndənt/ n. **1.** someone who attends another, as for service or company. **2.** someone employed to take care or charge of someone or something, especially when this involves directing or assisting the public. –adj. **3.** concomitant; consequent.

attention /ə'tɛnʃən/ n. **1.** observant care; consideration; notice. **2.** civility or courtesy. **3.** (*pl.*) acts of courtesy indicating regard, as in courtship.

attention deficit disorder n. *Obs.* → **attention deficit hyperactivity disorder**. Also, **ADD**.

attention deficit hyperactivity disorder n. a genetic disorder resulting in biochemical imbalances in the brain which cause symptoms which may include inattentiveness, hyperactivity, and impulsivity. Also, **ADHD**, **attention-deficit/hyperactivity disorder**; *Obs.*, **attention deficit disorder**.

attentive /ə'tɛntɪv/ *adj.* **1.** characterised by or giving attention; observant. **2.** assiduous in service or courtesy; polite; courteous. –**attentiveness**, *n.*

attenuate /ə'tɛnjueɪt/ *v.t.* **1.** to make thin; make slender or fine; rarefy. –*v.i.* **2.** to grow less; weaken.

attest /ə'tɛst/ *v.t.* **1.** to bear witness to; certify; declare the truth of, in words or writing; especially, affirm in an official capacity. **2.** to give proof or evidence of; manifest. –*v.i.* **3.** to certify to the genuineness of a document by signing as witness. –**attestor**, **attester**, *n.* –**attestation**, *n.*

attic /'ætɪk/ *n.* that part of a building, especially a house, directly under a roof; garret.

attire /ə'taɪə/ *v.t.* **1.** to dress, array, or adorn, especially for special occasions, ceremonials, etc. –*n.* **2.** clothes or apparel, especially rich or splendid garments.

attitude /'ætətjud/ *n.* **1.** position, disposition, or manner with regard to a person or thing. **2.** position of the body appropriate to an action, emotion, etc.

attorney /ə'tɜni/ *n.* (*pl.* **-neys**) **1.** a person duly appointed or empowered by another to transact any business for him or her (**attorney in fact**). –*phr.* Also, **letter of attorney**, **warrant of attorney**. **2. power of attorney**, a formal document by which one person authorises another to act for him or her.

attorney-general /ətɜni-'dʒɛnrəl/ *n.* (*pl.* **attorneys-general** *or* **attorney-generals**) (*oft.* *upper case*) the chief law officer of a government and the minister responsible for the administration of justice.

attract /ə'trækt/ *v.t.* **1.** to act upon by a physical force causing or tending to cause approach or union (opposed to *repel*). **2.** to draw by other than physical influence; invite or allure; win. –*v.i.* **3.** to possess or exert the power of attraction. –**attraction**, *n.*

attractive /ə'træktɪv/ *adj.* appealing to one's liking or admiration; engaging; alluring; pleasing.

attribute *v.t.* /ə'trɪbjut/ **1.** (oft. fol. by *to*) to consider as belonging; regard as owing, as an effect to a cause. –*n.* /'ætrəbjut/ **2.** something attributed as belonging; a quality, character, characteristic, or property. –**attributive**, *adj.*

attrition /ə'trɪʃən/ *n.* **1.** a rubbing against; friction. **2.** a wearing down or away by friction; abrasion. **3.** a natural, gradual reduction in membership or personnel, as by retirement, resignation or death.

attune /ə'tjun/ *v.t.* **1.** to adjust to tune or harmony; bring into accord. **2.** (*usu. in the passive*) to adjust (a person) to accept their surroundings, situation, environment, etc.: *attuned to the office politics.*

atypical /eɪ'tɪpɪkəl/ *adj.* not typical; not conforming to the type; irregular; abnormal. Also, **atypic**. –**atypically**, *adv.*

aubergine /'oubəʒin, -dʒin/ *n.* → **eggplant**.

auburn /'ɔbən/ *n.* a reddish-brown or golden-brown colour.

auction /'ɒkʃən/ *n.* a public sale at which property or goods are sold to the highest bidder. –**auctioneer**, *n.*

audacious /ɔ'deɪʃəs/ *adj.* **1.** bold or daring; adventurous. **2.** reckless or bold in wrong-doing; impudent and presumptuous. –**audacity** /ɔ'dæsəti/, *n.*

audible /'ɔdəbəl/ *adj.* capable of being heard; actually heard.

audience /'ɔdiəns/ *n.* **1.** an assembly of hearers or spectators. **2.** *Govt* admission of a diplomatic representative to a sovereign or high officer of government; formal interview. **3.** the act of hearing or attending to words or sounds.

audio /'ɔdioʊ/ *adj.* relating to, recording, or reproducing sound.

audio- a word element meaning 'hear', 'of or for hearing', as in *audiology*.

audiology /ɔdi'ɒlədʒi/ *n.* the study of hearing mechanism, especially the diagnosis and measurement of impaired function. –**audiologist**, *n.*

audit /'ɔdət/ *n.* **1.** an official examination and verification of accounts and records, especially of financial accounts. –*v.t.* **2.** to make audit of; examine (accounts, etc.) officially.

audition /ɔ'dɪʃən/ *n.* **1.** the act, sense, or power of hearing. **2.** a hearing given to a musician, actor, etc., to test voice qualities, performance, etc.

auditor /'ɔdətə/ *n.* **1.** a hearer; listener. **2.** a person appointed and authorised to examine accounts and accounting records, compare the charges with the vouchers, verify balance sheet and income items, and state the result.

auditorium /ɔdə'tɔriəm/ *n.* (*pl.* **-toriums** *or* **-toria** /-'tɔriə/) **1.** the space for the audience in a concert hall, theatre, school, or other building. **2.** a large building or room for meetings, assemblies, theatrical performances, etc.

auditory /'ɔdətri, -təri/ *adj.* relating to hearing, to the sense of hearing, or to the organs of hearing. –**auditorily**, *adv.*

auger /'ɔgə/ *n.* a carpenter's tool for boring holes in wood.

aught /ɔt/ *n.* anything whatever; any part.

augment /ɔg'mɛnt/ *v.t.* to make larger; enlarge in size or extent; increase.

augur /'ɔgə/ *n.* **1.** a prophet. –*v.t.* **2.** to divine or predict, as from omens; prognosticate.

august /ɔ'gʌst/ *adj.* **1.** inspiring reverence or admiration; of supreme dignity or grandeur; majestic. **2.** venerable.

aunt /ant/ *n.* **1.** the sister of one's father or mother. **2.** the wife of one's uncle or aunt. Also, **aunty**.

aunty /'anti/ *n.* (*pl.* **-ties**) **1.** a familiar or diminutive form of **aunt**. **2.** *Aboriginal English* **a.** a female relative of an older generation. **b.** a closely-connected non-Aboriginal woman. **3.** (*capital*) a title of respect for a female elder of an Aboriginal community. Also, **auntie**.

aura /'ɔrə/ *n.* **1.** a distinctive air, atmosphere, character, etc. **2.** a subtle emanation proceeding from a body and surrounding it as an atmosphere. **3.** *Pathol.* a sensation, as of a current of cold air, or other sensory experience, preceding an attack of epilepsy, hysteria, etc.

aural /'ɔrəl/ adj. of, or perceived by, the organs of hearing. –**aurally**, adv.

aureole /'ɒrioʊl, 'ɔ-/ n. a radiance surrounding the head or the whole figure in the representation of a sacred personage.

auric /'ɒrɪk/ adj. of or containing gold, especially in the trivalent state.

auricle /'ɒrɪkəl, 'ɒr-/ n. 1. Anat. a. the projecting outer portion of the ear; the pinna. b. a chamber of the heart. 2. Bot., Zool. a part like or likened to an ear.

auriferous /ɔ'rɪfərəs/ adj. yielding or containing gold.

aurora /ə'rɔrə/ n. a display in the skies of moving bands of light, visible at high latitudes.

auspice /'ɔspəs/ n. 1. (usu. pl.) favouring influence; patronage. 2. a propitious circumstance.

auspicious /ɔ'spɪʃəs, ə-/ adj. showing signs of success; favourable.

austere /ɒs'tɪə, ɔs-/ adj. 1. harsh in manner; stern in appearance. 2. severe in disciplining or restraining oneself; morally strict. 3. severely simple; without ornament. –**austerity**, n.

Australian Business Number n. → **ABN**.

Australian Company Number n. → **ACN**.

Australian crawl n. → **freestyle**.

Australian Rules pl. n. a code of football requiring two teams of 18 players, which originated in Australia in 1859; influenced by the various forms of football played at the time, as association football, Gaelic football, Rugby football, etc., and also possibly by marngrook. Also, **Australian National Football**, **Australian Football**, **Aussie Rules**.

Australian salute n. Colloq. (humorous) the movement of hand and arm to brush away flies from one's face.

Australian terrier n. a small, sturdy, low-set and rather elongated dog with erect ears.

aut- variant of **auto-**[1] before most vowels.

autarchy /'ɔtaki/ n. (pl. **-chies**) 1. absolute sovereignty. 2. self-government.

autarky /'ɔtaki/ n. (pl. **-kies**) the condition of self-sufficiency, especially economic, as applied to a state.

authentic /ɔ'θɛntɪk/ adj. 1. entitled to acceptance or belief; reliable; trustworthy. 2. of the authorship or origin reputed; of genuine origin. 3. Law executed with all due formalities. –**authenticity**, n.

authenticate /ɔ'θɛntəkeɪt/ v.t. 1. to make authoritative or valid. 2. to establish as genuine.

author /'ɔθə/ n. a person who writes a novel, poem, essay, etc.; the composer of a literary work, as distinguished from a compiler, translator, editor, or copyist.

authorise /'ɔθəraɪz/ v.t. 1. to give authority or legal power to; empower (to do something). 2. to establish by authority or usage. 3. to afford a ground for; warrant; justify. Also, **authorize**. –**authorisation**, n.

authoritarian /ɔ,θɒrɪ'tɛəriən, ə-/ adj. favouring the principle of subjection to authority as opposed to that of individual freedom.

authority /ɔ'θɒrɪti, ə-/ n. (pl. **-ties**) 1. the right to determine, adjudicate, or otherwise settle issues or disputes; the right to control, command, or determine. 2. a person or body

with such rights. 3. an accepted source of information, advice, etc. 4. a statute, court rule, or judicial decision which establishes a rule or principle of law; a ruling. 5. title to respect or acceptance; commanding influence. 6. a warrant for action; justification. –**authoritative**, adj.

autism /'ɔtɪzəm/ n. Psychiatry a syndrome of unknown aetiology, chiefly characterised by some degree of inability to comprehend or communicate, failure to relate affectively, and inappropriate or obsessive behaviour. –**autistic**, adj.

autism spectrum disorder n. a disorder encompassing a wide range of symptoms including those identified as autism, Asperger's syndrome, etc. Abbrev.: ASD

auto-[1] a word element meaning 'self', 'same', as in autograph. Also, **aut-**.

auto-[2] a combining form of **automobile**.

autobiography /,ɔtəbaɪ'ɒɡrəfi/ n. (pl. **-phies**) an account of a person's life written by himself or herself. –**autobiographical**, adj.

autocracy /ɔ'tɒkrəsi/ n. (pl. **-cies**) 1. uncontrolled or unlimited authority over others, invested in a single person; the government or power of an absolute monarch. 2. independent or self-derived power. –**autocrat**, n. –**autocratic**, adj.

auto-electrician /,ɔtoʊ-ɛlɛk'trɪʃən/ n. someone who specialises in the repair and servicing of the electrical circuits of cars.

autograph /'ɔtəɡræf, -ɡraf/ n. 1. a person's own signature. –v.t. 2. to write one's name on or in.

autoimmune system /ɔtoʊɪm'jun/ n. the system within the body which produces antibodies.

automate /'ɔtəmeɪt/ v.t. to apply the principles of automation to (a mechanical process).

automatic /,ɔtə'mætɪk/ adj. 1. having the power of self-motion; self-moving or self-acting; mechanical. 2. Physiol. occurring independently of volition, as certain muscular actions. 3. done unconsciously or from force of habit; mechanical (opposed to voluntary). –n. 4. a machine which operates automatically, as a car with automatic gear shift. –**automatically**, adv.

automatic teller machine n. computerised equipment located outside banks and building societies, in shopping areas, etc., offering basic banking facilities and operated by inserting a plastic card with a magnetised strip and keying in a personal identification number. Also, **ATM**, **automated teller machine**.

automation /ɔtə'meɪʃən/ n. 1. the science of applying automatic control to industrial processes; the replacement of manpower by sophisticated machinery. 2. the process or act of automating a mechanical process. 3. the degree to which a mechanical process is automatically controlled.

automaton /ɔ'tɒmətən/ n. (pl. **-tons** or **-ta** /-tə/) 1. a mechanical figure or contrivance constructed to act as if spontaneously through concealed motive power. 2. a person who acts in a monotonous routine manner, without active intelligence.

automobile /'ɔtəməbil/ n. Chiefly US a car.

automotive /ɔtə'moʊtɪv/ adj. **1.** propelled by a self-contained power plant. **2.** of or relating to motor vehicles.

autonomic nervous system n. Physiol., Anat. the part of the peripheral nervous system which controls the involuntary functions of the glands, blood vessels, the viscera, and the heart and smooth muscles. Compare **somatic nervous system.**

autonomous /ɔ'tɒnəməs/ adj. self-governing; independent. **–autonomy,** n.

autopilot /'ɔtoʊˌpaɪlət/ n. **1.** a device in an aircraft that can be engaged to keep it flying on a preset course. –phr. **2. on autopilot, a.** (of an aircraft) flying under the control of the autopilot. **b.** (of a person) acting in a reasonably competent way but without giving full attention. Also, **automatic pilot.**

autopsy /'ɔtɒpsi/ n. (pl. **-sies**) inspection and dissection of a body after death, as for determination of the cause of death; a post-mortem examination.

autumn /'ɔtəm/ n. the season of the year between summer and winter. **–autumnal** /ɔ'tʌmnəl/, adj.

auxiliary /ɒg'zɪljəri, ɔg-/ adj. **1.** giving support; helping; aiding; assisting. **2.** subsidiary; additional. –n. (pl. **-ries**) **3.** person or thing that gives aid of any kind; helper. **4.** a group or organisation which assists or is supplementary to a larger one. **5.** (pl.) foreign troops in the service of a nation at war.

auxiliary verb n. a verb customarily preceding certain forms of other verbs, used to express distinctions of time, aspect, mood, etc., as do, am, etc., in I do think; I am going; we have spoken; may we go?; can they see?; we shall walk.

avail /ə'veɪl/ v.i. **1.** to have force or efficacy; be of use; serve. **2.** to be of value or profit. –v.t. **3.** to be of use or value to; profit; advantage. –n. **4.** efficacy for a purpose; advantage to an object or end. –phr. **5. avail oneself of,** to give oneself the advantage of; make use of.

available /ə'veɪləbəl/ adj. suitable or ready for use; at hand; of use or service. **–availability,** n.

avalanche /'ævəlæntʃ, -lɑnʃ/ n. a large mass of snow, ice, etc., detached from a mountain slope and sliding or falling suddenly downwards.

avant-garde /ˌævɒnt-'gad/ n. **1.** the leaders in progress in any field, especially the arts. –adj. **2.** modern; experimental; (affectedly) ultramodern.

avarice /'ævərəs/ n. insatiable greed for riches; inordinate, miserly desire to gain and hoard wealth. **–avaricious,** adj.

avatar /'ævətɑ/ n. Internet the representation of a person in virtual reality.

avenge /ə'vɛndʒ/ v.t. (**avenged, avenging**) to take vengeance or exact satisfaction for.

avenue /'ævənju/ n. **1.** a street or road, especially one lined with a double row of trees. **2.** means of access or attainment.

aver /ə'vɜ/ v.t. (**averred, averring**) to affirm with confidence; declare in a positive or peremptory manner.

average /'ævərɪdʒ, -vrɪdʒ/ n. **1.** an arithmetical mean. **2.** the ordinary, normal, or typical amount, rate, quality, kind, etc.; the common run. –adj. **3.** of or relating to an average;

estimated by average; forming an average. –v.t. (**-raged, -raging**) **4.** to find an average value for; reduce to a mean.

averse /ə'vɜs/ adj. having strong feelings of antipathy; opposed.

aversion /ə'vɜʒən, -vɜʃən/ n. **1.** (usu. fol. by to) an averted state of the mind or feelings; repugnance, antipathy, or rooted dislike. **2.** a cause of dislike; an object of repugnance.

avert /ə'vɜt/ v.t. **1.** to turn away or aside. **2.** to ward off; prevent.

avi- a word element meaning 'bird'.

avian /'eɪviən/ adj. of or relating to birds.

avian flu n. → avian influenza.

avian influenza n. any of a wide range of influenza viruses affecting birds, some strains of which, such as the H5N1 virus, are transmittable from birds to humans. Also, **avian flu, bird flu.**

aviary /'eɪvjəri, 'eɪvəri/ n. (pl. **-ries**) a large cage or enclosure in which birds are kept.

aviation /ˌeɪvi'eɪʃən/ n. the act, art, or science of flying by mechanical means, especially with heavier-than-air craft.

aviator /'eɪvieɪtə/ n. a pilot of an aeroplane or other heavier-than-air craft.

avid /'ævəd/ adj. keenly desirous; eager; greedy.

AVO /eɪ vi 'oʊ/ n. Law apprehended violence order; an injunction issued by a local court, which protects a person fearing molestation, etc., by forbidding the named party to approach or contact the protected person.

avocado /ævə'kadoʊ/ n. (pl. **-dos**) **1.** a tropical American fruit, green to black in colour and commonly pear-shaped, eaten raw, especially as a salad fruit. **2.** the tree. Also, **avocado pear.**

avocation /ævə'keɪʃən/ n. **1.** minor or occasional occupation; hobby. **2.** (also pl.) one's regular occupation, calling, or vocation. **3.** diversion or distraction.

avoid /ə'vɔɪd/ v.t. to keep away from; keep clear of; shun; evade. **–avoidance,** n.

avoirdupois /ævwadju'pwa/ adj. of or relating to a system of weights formerly used for goods other than gems, precious metals, and drugs.

avow /ə'vaʊ/ v.t. to admit or acknowledge frankly or openly; own; confess. **–avowal,** n.

avuncular /ə'vʌŋkjələ/ adj. like or characteristic of an uncle.

await /ə'weɪt/ v.t. **1.** to wait for; look for or expect. **2.** to be in store for; be ready for. –v.i. **3.** to wait, as in expectation.

awake /ə'weɪk/ v. (**awoke, awoken, awaking**) –v.t. **1.** to rouse from sleep; wake up. **2.** to stir the interest of; excite. **3.** to stir, disturb (the memories, fears, etc.). –v.i. **4.** to wake up. **5.** to come to a realisation of the truth; to rouse to action, attention, etc. –adj. **6.** waking, not sleeping. **7.** vigilant; alert.

awakening /ə'weɪkənɪŋ/ adj. **1.** rousing; alarming. –n. **2.** the act of awaking from sleep. **3.** an arousal or revival of interest or attention; a waking up, as from indifference, ignorance, etc.

award /ə'wɔd/ v.t. **1.** to adjudge to be due or merited; assign or bestow. **2.** to bestow by judicial decree; assign or appoint by deliberate judgement, as in arbitration. –n. **3.** something awarded, as a medal, rate of pay, particular working conditions, etc. –**awardee**, *n*.

award wage *n*. (in Australia and New Zealand) a wage arrived at by mutual consent or arbitration and fixed by an industrial court, payable by law to all employees in a particular occupation.

aware /ə'wɛə/ *adj*. **1.** cognisant or conscious. **2.** informed and up-to-date. –**awareness**, *n*.

away /ə'weɪ/ *adv*. **1.** from this or that place; off. **2.** apart; at a distance. **3.** aside. **4.** out of possession, notice, use, or existence. **5.** continuously; on. **6.** without hesitation. **7.** immediately; forthwith. *–adj*. **8.** absent. **9.** distant. **10.** *Sport* of or relating to a game not played on one's home ground: *an away match*. **11.** *Colloq*. on the move; having started; in full flight.

awe /ɔ/ *n*. **1.** respectful or reverential fear, inspired by what is grand or sublime. *–v.t.* (**awed**, **awing**) **2.** to inspire with awe. **3.** to influence or restrain by awe.

awesome /'ɔsəm/ *adj*. inspiring awe.

awful /'ɔfəl/ *adj*. **1.** extremely bad; unpleasant; ugly. **2.** inspiring fear; dreadful; terrible. –**awfulness**, *n*.

awfully /'ɔfəli/ *adv*. **1.** very badly. **2.** an intensifier: *awfully good*; *an awfully long way*.

awhile /ə'waɪl/ *adv*. for a short time or period.

awkward /'ɔkwəd/ *adj*. **1.** lacking dexterity or skill; clumsy; bungling. **2.** ungraceful; ungainly; uncouth. **3.** ill-adapted for use or handling. **4.** requiring caution; somewhat hazardous. **5.** difficult to handle; dangerous. **6.** embarrassing or trying. **7.** deliberately obstructive, difficult, or perverse.

awl /ɔl/ *n*. a pointed instrument for piercing small holes in leather, wood, etc.

awning /'ɔnɪŋ/ *n*. **1.** a roof-like shelter of canvas, etc., before a window or door, over a deck, etc., as for protection from the weather. **2.** a shelter.

awoke /ə'woʊk/ *v*. past tense of **awake**.

awry /ə'raɪ/ *adv*. **1.** with a turn or twist to one side; askew. **2.** away from reason or the truth. **3.** amiss; wrong.

axe /æks/ *n*. **1.** an instrument with a bladed head on a handle used for chopping, etc. *–v.t.* (**axed**, **axing**) **2.** to shape or trim with an axe. **3.** *Colloq*. to cut down or reduce (expenditure, prices, etc.) sharply. **4.** *Colloq*. to dismiss from a position. *–phr*. **5. have an axe to grind**, to have a private purpose or selfish end to attain. **6. the axe**, *Colloq*. **a.** a drastic cutting down (of expenses, etc.). **b.** dismissal from a job, etc.

axes[1] /'æksɪz/ *n*. plural of **axis**.

axes[2] /'æksəz/ *n*. plural of **axe**.

axial /'æksiəl/ *adj*. **1.** of, relating to, or forming an axis. **2.** situated in an axis or on the axis.

axilla /æk'sɪlə/ *n*. (*pl*. **axillae** /æk'sɪli/) *Anat*. the armpit.

axiom /'æksiəm/ *n*. **1.** a recognised truth. **2.** an established and universally accepted principle or rule. –**axiomatic**, *adj*.

axis /'æksəs/ *n*. (*pl*. **axes** /'æksiz/) **1.** the line about which a rotating body, such as the earth, turns. **2.** a fixed line adopted for reference, as in plotting a curve on a graph, in crystallography, etc.

axle /'æksəl/ *n*. *Machinery* the pin, bar, shaft, or the like, on which or with which a wheel or pair of wheels rotate.

axolotl /æksə'lɒtl, 'æksəlɒtl/ *n*. any of several Mexican salamanders that breed in the larval stage.

ayatollah /aɪə'tɒlə/ *n*. a high-ranking religious leader in the Shiite division of Islam, the official religion of Iran.

aye /aɪ/ *adv*. **1.** yes. *–n*. (*pl*. **ayes**) **2.** an affirmative vote or voter. Also, **ay**.

azalea /ə'zeɪljə/ *n*. any of various plants with handsome, variously coloured flowers.

azo- a prefix indicating the presence of a divalent nitrogen group.

azure /'eɪʒə, æ'zjʊə/ *adj*. of a sky blue colour.

B, b

B, b /biː/ n. the second letter of the English alphabet.

babaco /bəˈbakoʊ/ n. a seedless, five-sided fruit similar to the pawpaw.

baba ganoush /babə gəˈnʊʃ/ n. a paste of cooked eggplant seasoned with herbs and garlic. Also, **baba ghanoush, babaganoush, baba ghannouj.**

babble /ˈbæbəl/ v.i. **1.** to utter words imperfectly or indistinctly. **2.** to make a continuous murmuring sound. –n. **3.** inarticulate speech. **4.** a murmuring sound. –**babbler**, n.

babe /beɪb/ n. **1.** a baby. **2.** Colloq. a form of address to a close friend. **3.** Colloq. a very attractive woman or man.

baboon /bæˈbun, bə-/ n. a large, terrestrial monkey.

baby /ˈbeɪbi/ n. (pl. **-bies**) **1.** an infant; young child of either sex. **2.** Colloq. an invention or creation of which one is particularly proud.

baby boomer n. a person born in the period following World War II when a sudden and marked increase in the number of babies born occurred.

baby capsule n. a plastic container for carrying a baby, which slots into a base, the whole structure being anchored into a motor vehicle and incorporating various safety design features.

babysit /ˈbeɪbɪsɪt/ v.t. (**-sat**, **-sitting**) to mind (a child).

bachelor /ˈbætʃələ/ n. **1.** an unmarried man of any age. **2.** a person who has taken the first degree at a university (used only in titles and certain other expressions referring to such a degree).

bacillus /bəˈsɪləs/ n. (pl. **-cilli** /-ˈsɪli/) any of the group of rod-shaped bacteria which produce spores in the presence of free oxygen.

back¹ /bæk/ n. **1.** the hinder part of the human body, extending from the neck to the end of the spine. **2.** the part of the body of animals corresponding to the human back. **3.** the part opposite to or farthest from the face or front; the hinder side; the rear part. **4.** Football, etc. one of the defending players behind the forwards. –v.t. **5.** (oft. fol. by up) to support, as with authority, influence, or money. **6.** to cause to move backwards; reverse the action of. **7.** to bet in favour of. –adj. **8.** lying or being behind. **9.** away from the front position or rank; remote. –phr. **10. back up, a.** to go backwards. **b.** to cause to move backwards. **c.** to encourage; support. **d.** to give corroboration or credence to. **e.** (of water) to cease to flow freely. **f.** Computers to copy (data) on to a tape, disk, etc., as a safety measure. **g.** Computers to back up data. –**backer**, n.

back² /bæk/ adv. **1.** at, to, or towards the rear; backwards. **2.** towards the past. **3.** towards the original starting point, place, or condition. **4.** in reply; in return.

backbench /ˈbækbentʃ/ n. the non-office-holding parliamentary membership of a political party. –**backbencher**, n.

backbone /ˈbækboʊn/ n. **1.** the spinal or vertebral column; the spine. **2.** strength of character; resolution.

back-burn /ˈbæk-bɜn/ v. (**-burnt** or **-burned**, **-burning**) –v.t. **1.** to clear (land, grass or scrub) by burning into or against the wind. –v.i. **2.** to control a fire by burning off an area in advance of it, often into or against the wind. –n. **3.** the action or result of back-burning. –**back-burning**, n.

backburner /ˈbækbɜnə/ n. **1.** the rear burner of a stove, often used to keep food warm. –phr. **2. put on the backburner**, to take no further action on for the time being; postpone.

backdate /ˈbækdeɪt/ v.t. to date (something) earlier; apply retrospectively.

backdrop /ˈbækdrɒp/ n. the painted curtain or hanging at the back of a theatrical set.

backfire /bækˈfaɪə/ v.i. **1.** (of an internal-combustion engine) to have a premature explosion in the cylinder or in the admission or exhaust passages. **2.** to bring results opposite to those planned.

back foot n. **1.** the foot which moves backwards in stepping back. –phr. **2. on the back foot**, at a disadvantage.

backfoot /ˈbækfʊt/ v.t. to put at a disadvantage. –**backfooted**, adj.

backgammon /ˈbækgæmən, bækˈgæmən/ n. a game played by two persons at a board with pieces moved in accordance with throws of dice.

background /ˈbækgraʊnd/ n. **1.** the portions of a picture represented as in the distance. **2.** the social, historical and other antecedents which explain an event or condition. –adj. **3.** of or relating to the background; in the background. **4.** Computers of or relating to background processing.

backhand /ˈbækhænd/ n. a stroke, as in tennis, by a right-handed player from the left of the body (or the reverse for a left-handed player).

backing /ˈbækɪŋ/ n. **1.** aid or support of any kind. **2.** something that forms the back or is placed at or attached to the back of something else, as to support or strengthen it. **3.** musical accompaniment for a singer.

backlash /ˈbæklæʃ/ n. any sudden, violent, or unexpected reaction.

backload /ˈbækloʊd/ v.t. **1.** to transport (cargo, passengers, etc.) on a return trip from a major destination. –adj. **2.** of or relating to such cargo, passengers, etc. –**backloading**, n.

backlog /ˈbæklɒg/ n. **1.** an accumulation of business resources, stock, etc., acting as a reserve. **2.** an accumulation of work, correspondence, etc., awaiting attention.

backpack /ˈbækpæk/ n. **1.** a light, strong bag designed to be carried on the back. **2.** portable equipment carried on the back, as television or film cameras, or fire-fighting, hiking, camping equipment, etc.

backpacker /ˈbækpækə/ n. a traveller who carries their personal belongings in a backpack, and usually stays in lower priced accommodation.

back-seat driver *n.* **1.** a passenger in a car who offers unsolicited advice to the driver. **2.** someone who gives advice or orders in matters which are not their responsibility.

backside /ˈbækˈsaɪd/ *n.* the buttocks.

backslash /ˈbækslæʃ/ *n.* a short diagonal line (\), either printed or on a computer screen.

backspace /ˈbækspeɪs/ *v.i.* (in keyboarding) to move back in the text one space at a time, by depressing a particular key.

backstage /ˈbækˈsteɪdʒ/ *adv.* out of the view of the audience in a theatre; in the wings or dressing rooms, or behind the curtain on the stage.

backstop /ˈbækstɒp/ *n.* **1.** *Sport* a person, screen, or fence placed to prevent a ball going too far. **2.** a person who or a thing which is relied on for assistance when all else fails.

backstory /ˈbækstɔːri/ *n.* the background to a film, play, or computer game, which gives insight into the plot or characterisation.

backstroke /ˈbækstroʊk/ *n.* a swimming stroke in which the swimmer is on his or her back.

back-to-back *adj.* **1.** consecutive. *–adv.* **2.** consecutively.

backtrack /ˈbæktræk/ *v.i.* **1.** to return over the same course or route. **2.** to withdraw from an undertaking, position, etc.; pursue a reverse policy.

backup /ˈbækʌp/ *n.* **1.** a pent-up accumulation, especially of a liquid. **2.** a reserve supply or resource; a second means of support. **3.** *Computers* **a.** the process of copying data to a tape, CD-ROM, etc., so that a version is available if the original data is lost, corrupted, etc. **b.** the data so copied.

backward /ˈbækwəd/ *adj.* **1.** turned or moving towards the back. **2.** behind in growth, progress or development. *–adv.* **3.** → **backwards**.

backwards /ˈbækwədz/ *adv.* **1.** towards the back or rear. **2.** with the back foremost. **3.** towards the past. **4.** towards a worse or less advanced condition. Also, **backward**.

backwater /ˈbækwɔːtə/ *n.* **1.** a body of stagnant water connected to a river. **2.** a place or state considered to be stagnant or backward.

backwoods /ˈbækwʊdz/ *pl. n.* any unfamiliar or unfrequented area.

backyard /bækˈjɑːd/ *n.* **1.** an area, often of some size with gardens and lawn, at the back of a building, usually a house. **2.** *Colloq.* one's own neighbourhood, community, or society. *–adj.* **3.** illegal, illicit, improper or unqualified.

bacon /ˈbeɪkən/ *n.* meat from the back and sides of the pig, salted and dried or smoked.

bacteri- a word element meaning 'bacteria' or 'bacterial'. Also, **bacter-, bacterio-, bactero-**.

bacteria /bækˈtɪəriə/ *pl. n.* (*sing.* **bacterium**) microscopic organisms, various species of which produce disease. **–bacterial**, *adj.*

bad /bæd/ *adj.* (**worse, worst**) **1.** not good. **2.** unsatisfactory; poor; below standard; inadequate. **3.** regretful; contrite; sorry; upset. **4.** severe. **5.** rotten; decayed. *–phr.* **6. not bad**, quite good; fair. **7. too bad**, *Colloq.* **a.** an expression indicating a lack of sympathy. **b.** an expression of sympathy. **–badly**, *adv.*

bad cholesterol *n.* a naturally occurring substance which can clog blood vessels and cause heart disease. Compare **good cholesterol**.

bade /bæd/ *v.* past tense of **bid**.

badge /bædʒ/ *n.* a mark, token or device worn as a sign of allegiance, membership, authority, achievement. **–badging**, *n.*

badger /ˈbædʒə/ *n.* **1.** a burrowing carnivorous mammal. *–v.t.* **2.** to harass; torment.

badminton /ˈbædmɪntən/ *n.* a game, similar to tennis, but played with a high net and shuttlecock.

bad-tempered /bæd-ˈtɛmpəd/ *adj.* easily annoyed; often angry.

bae /beɪ/ *n. Colloq.* a girlfriend or boyfriend.

baffle /ˈbæfəl/ *v.t.* **1.** to thwart or frustrate disconcertingly; baulk; confuse. **2.** to puzzle or mystify.

bag /bæg/ *n.* **1.** a receptacle of leather, cloth, paper, etc. **2.** (*pl.*) *Colloq.* a lot; an abundance (of). **3.** a sac, as in the body of an animal or insect. *–v.* (**bagged, bagging**) *–v.i.* **4.** to swell or bulge. **5.** to hang loosely like an empty bag. *–v.t.* **6.** to put into a bag. **7.** to kill or catch, as in hunting.

bagel /ˈbeɪgəl/ *n.* a small ring-shaped, hard roll, made of dough.

baggage /ˈbægɪdʒ/ *n.* **1.** bags, suitcases, etc., used when travelling; luggage. **2.** emotions, beliefs, etc., retained from previous experience, especially as influencing one's behaviour.

baggy /ˈbægi/ *adj.* (**-gier, -giest**) bag-like; hanging loosely.

bagpipes /ˈbægpaɪps/ *n.* a reed instrument consisting of a melody pipe and one or more accompanying drone pipes protruding from a windbag into which the air is blown by the mouth or a bellows.

bail[1] /beɪl/ *n.* **1.** (in criminal proceedings) the release of a prisoner from legal custody into the custody of someone who undertakes to produce the prisoner to the court at a later date or forfeit the security deposited as a condition of the release. **2.** property given as security that a person released on bail will appear in court at the appointed time. Also, **bail out**. **3. a.** to help someone get their freedom by giving bail. **b.** to help someone out of trouble.

bail[2] /beɪl/ *v.t.* **1.** to remove (water) especially from a boat, as with a bucket or a can. *–v.i.* **2.** to bail water. *–n.* **3.** a bucket or other vessel for bailing. *–phr.* **4. bail out, a.** to empty (a boat) of water by dipping: *to bail out a boat.* **b.** to make a parachute-jump from a plane. **c.** *Colloq.* to abandon a dangerous position or course. Also, **bale**. **–bailer**, *n.*

bail[3] /beɪl/ *n.* **1.** *Cricket* either of the two small bars or sticks laid across the tops of the stumps which form the wicket. **2.** Also, **bails**. a framework for securing a cow's head during milking. **3.** Also, **bail rod, paper bail**. (in a typewriter) the rod which holds paper in place. *–phr.* **4. bail up**, to hold up.

bailiff /ˈbeɪlɪf/ *n.* an officer employed to deliver court orders, collect debts, etc.

bails /beɪlz/ *pl. n.* **1.** → **bail**[3] (def. 2). **2. the bails**, the milking shed.

bait /beɪt/ *n.* **1.** food or some substitute used as a lure in fishing, trapping, etc. **2.** food containing a harmful additive such as poison or razor blades used to lure and kill animals considered pests. *–v.t.* **3.** to prepare (a hook or trap) with bait. **4.** to add harmful substances to (food) to kill or drug animals. **5.** to goad to anger; torment (someone) for amusement.

bake /beɪk/ *v.i.* **1.** to cook by dry heat in an oven, under coals, or on heated metals or stones. **2.** to harden by heat.

baker /'beɪkə/ *n.* someone who bakes; someone who makes and sells bread, cake, etc. –**bakery**, *n.*

baking powder *n.* any of various powders used as a leavening agent in baking.

baking soda *n.* → **sodium bicarbonate.**

baklava /'bækləvə, 'ba-/ *n.* a Middle Eastern dessert made from filo pastry layered with chopped walnuts, and soaked in a honey and sugar syrup.

balaclava /bælə'klavə/ *n.* a knitted woollen hood that covers the whole head except for the face. Also, **balaclava helmet.**

balance /'bæləns/ *n.* **1.** an instrument for weighing, typically a bar poised or swaying on a central support according to the weights borne in scales (pans) suspended at the ends. **2.** a state of equilibrium; equal distribution of weight, amount, etc. **3.** mental steadiness; habit of calm behaviour, judgement, etc. **4.** harmonious arrangement or adjustment, especially in the arts of design. **5.** something used to produce equilibrium. **6.** the act of balancing; comparison as to weight, amount, importance, etc.; estimate. **7.** the remainder or rest. **8.** *Commerce* **a.** equality between the totals of the two sides of an account. **b.** the difference between the debit total and the credit total of an account. **c.** unpaid difference represented by the excess of debits over credits. **9.** an adjustment of accounts. *–v.* (**-anced, -ancing**) *–v.t.* **10.** to weigh in a balance. **11.** to estimate the relative weight or importance of; compare. **12.** to arrange, adjust, or proportion the parts of symmetrically. **13.** to be equal or proportionate to. **14.** *Commerce* **a.** to add up the two sides of (an account) and determine the difference. **b.** to make the necessary entries in (an account) so that the sums of the two sides will be equal. **c.** to settle by paying what remains due on an account. *–v.i.* **15.** *Commerce* to reckon or adjust accounts.

balanced /'bælənst/ *adj.* **1.** having a balance; having weight evenly distributed or being in good proportion. **2.** (of a discussion, opinion, etc.) taking everything into account in a fair, well-judged way; not biased. **3.** (of a diet) having different kinds of food in the correct proportion to maintain health.

balance of payments *n.* an account of a nation's total payments to foreign countries (debits) and its total receipts from foreign sources (credits).

balance of trade *n.* the difference between the value of the exports and imports of a country, said to be favourable or unfavourable as exports are greater or less than imports.

balance sheet *n.* the analysis at a given date of an enterprise's financial position, in accordance with which the total equities listed on

one side are balanced by the assets listed on the other.

balcony /'bælkəni/ *n.* (*pl.* **-nies**) a raised and railed platform projecting from the wall of a building.

bald /bɔld/ *adj.* **1.** lacking hair on some part of the scalp. **2.** (of pneumatic tyres) having the rubber tread worn off. **3.** bare; plain; unadorned.

bale¹ /beɪl/ *n.* a large bundle or package prepared for storage or transportation, especially one closely compressed and secured by cords, wires, hoops or the like, sometimes with a wrapping.

bale² /beɪl/ *v.t., v.i.* (**baled, baling**) → **bail².** –**baler**, *n.*

baleful /'beɪlfəl/ *adj.* full of menacing or malign influences; pernicious.

ball¹ /bɔl/ *n.* **1.** a spherical or approximately spherical body; a sphere. **2.** a round or roundish body, of different materials and sizes, hollow or solid, for use in various games, as cricket, football, tennis, or golf. **3.** *Colloq.* (*taboo*) a testicle. *–phr.* **4. on the ball**, alert; sharp.

ball² /bɔl/ *n.* **1.** a social gathering (usually formal) at which people dance. **2.** an enjoyable occasion.

ballad /'bæləd/ *n.* **1.** a simple narrative poem, often of popular origin, composed in short stanzas, especially one of romantic character and adapted for singing. **2.** a romantic or sentimental pop song, often in narrative form and sung at a slow tempo.

ballast /'bæləst/ *n.* **1.** any heavy material carried by a ship or boat for ensuring proper stability, so as to avoid capsizing and to secure the greatest effectiveness of the propelling power. **2.** anything that gives mental, moral, or political stability or steadiness.

ball bearing *n.* **1.** a bearing (def. 2) in which a number of steel balls run in a ring-shaped track which reduces friction. **2.** any of the steel balls so used.

ball boy /'bɔl bɔɪ/ *n. Tennis* a boy who retrieves balls and supplies them to the server.

ballerina /bælə'rinə/ *n.* **1.** the principal female dancer in a ballet company. **2.** any female ballet dancer.

ballet /'bæleɪ/ *n.* (performance of) an intricate style of dance using a formal technique and marked by grace and precision of movement.

ball girl /'bɔl gɜl/ *n. Tennis* a girl who retrieves balls and supplies them to the server.

ballistic /bə'lɪstɪk/ *adj.* **1.** relating to projectiles. *–phr.* **2. go ballistic**, *Colloq.* to become extremely angry.

ballistics /bə'lɪstɪks/ *n.* the science or study of the motion of projectiles, such as bullets, shells, bombs, rockets, etc., proceeding under no power and acted upon only by gravitational forces and the resistance of the medium through which they pass.

balloon /bə'lun/ *n.* **1.** a usually spherical bag made of some material impermeable to gas and filled with some gas lighter than air. *–v.i.* **2.** to swell like a balloon.

ballot /'bælət/ *n.* **1.** a ticket or paper used in voting. **2.** Also, **secret ballot.** the system or practice of secret voting by means of printed or written ballots or voting machines.

ballpark /'bɔlpak/ –n. **1.** US a park in which games, especially baseball, are played. –adj. **2.** Colloq. broadly estimated: a ballpark figure. –phr. Colloq. **3. in the ballpark**, within acceptable limits; relatively close to a desired target. **4. off the ballpark**, unofficially; at a guess.

ballpoint pen /'bɔlpɔɪnt/ n. a pen whose point contains a small rolling ball which distributes ink.

ballsy /'bɔlzi/ adj. Colloq. courageous.

balm /bam/ n. **1.** any aromatic or fragrant ointment. **2.** anything which heals, soothes, or mitigates pain.

Balmain bug /bæl'meɪn/ n. an edible flattened crustacean; first discovered in Sydney Harbour.

balmy /'bami/ adj. (-mier, -miest) mild and refreshing; soft; soothing.

baloney /bə'louni/ n. Colloq. nonsense; insincere or idle talk.

balsa /'bɔlsə/ n. an extremely light wood, formerly used in life-preservers, rafts, etc., now much used in crafts. Also, **balsawood**.

balsam /'bɔlsəm, 'bɒl-/ n. **1.** any of various fragrant exudations from certain trees. **2.** a common garden plant often with red, pink or white flowers. **3.** any aromatic ointment. **4.** any healing or soothing agent or agency.

balustrade /bælə'streɪd/ n. a railing with a row of short pillars holding it up, usually part of a balcony or staircase. –**balustraded**, adj.

bamboo /bæm'bu/ n. **1.** any of various woody or treelike tropical and semitropical grasses. **2.** the hollow woody stem of such a plant, used for building purposes and for making furniture, poles, etc. –adj. **3.** made with bamboo: bamboo ladder.

bamboozle /bæm'buzəl/ v.t. **1.** to deceive by trickery; impose upon. **2.** to perplex; mystify.

ban¹ /bæn/ v.t. (**banned, banning**) **1.** to prohibit; interdict. –n. **2.** a prohibition by law or decree.

ban² /bæn/ n. a public proclamation or edict.

banal /bə'nal, 'beɪnəl/ adj. hackneyed; trite. –**banality**, n.

banana /bə'nanə/ n. the pulpy, yellow-skinned, elongated fruit of a tropical plant.

banana kick n. Football a punt kick in which the ball is dropped at a diagonal angle across the boot, and swerves sharply in flight; used mainly in shooting for goal from difficult angles. Also, Chiefly SA Aust. Rules, **checkside kick**.

band¹ /bænd/ n. **1.** a group of people or animals. **2.** a company of musicians constituted according to the kind of music played, usually playing for performance or as an accompaniment to dancing. –v.i. **3.** (usu. fol. by together) to unite; form a group; confederate.

band² /bænd/ n. **1.** any strip that contrasts with its surroundings in colour, texture or material. **2.** Radio a range of frequencies lying between any two well-defined limits.

band³ /bænd/ n. (usu. pl.) anything which binds.

bandage /'bændɪdʒ/ n. a strip of cloth or other material used to bind up a wound, hold a dressing in place, etc.

bandaid /'bændeɪd/ n. (from trademark) a light adhesive dressing for covering superficial wounds.

bandaid solution n. an answer to a problem which is superficial by nature and does not address fundamental issues. Also, **bandaid remedy**.

bandana /bæn'dænə/ n. a large coloured handkerchief or scarf with spots or figures, usually white on a red or blue background. Also, **bandanna**.

bandicoot /'bændikut/ n. any of various small, omnivorous, somewhat rat-like Australian marsupials.

bandit /'bændət/ n. **1.** a robber, especially one who robs by violence. **2.** an outlaw.

bandwidth /'bændwɪdθ/ n. **1.** the difference between the upper and lower frequencies of a band (**band²** def. 2) . **2.** Telecommunications the volume of information per unit time that a transmission medium such as a cable is capable of carrying, usually measured in bits per second.

bandy /'bændi/ v.t. (-died, -dying) **1.** to pass from one to another, or back and forth; give and take. –adj. **2.** (of legs) having a bend or crook outward.

bane /beɪn/ n. a person or thing that ruins or destroys.

bang /bæŋ/ n. **1.** a loud, sudden explosive noise, as the discharge of a gun. **2.** a knock; a bump. –v.t. **3.** to strike or beat resoundingly. **4.** to slam. **5.** to knock or bump. –v.i. **6.** to strike violently or noisily. –adv. **7.** exactly; precisely; just.

bangle /'bæŋgəl/ n. a bracelet in the form of a ring, without a clasp.

banish /'bænɪʃ/ v.t. to condemn to exile; expel from or relegate to a country or place by authoritative decree.

banister /'bænəstə/ n. one of the supports of a stair rail, either plain or resembling a pillar. Also, **bannister**.

banjo /'bændʒou/ n. (pl. **-jos**) a musical instrument of the guitar family, having a circular body.

bank¹ /bæŋk/ n. **1.** a long pile or mass. **2.** a slope or incline. **3.** Physical Geog. the slope immediately bordering the course of a river along which the water normally runs. **4.** a lateral inclination during a curve. –v.i. **5.** to rise in or form banks, as clouds or snow. **6.** to tip or incline laterally, as an aircraft, road, cycle racing track, etc.

bank² /bæŋk/ n. **1.** an institution for receiving and lending money (in some cases, issuing notes or holding current accounts that serve as money) and transacting other financial business. **2.** any store or reserve. –v.i. **3.** to exercise the functions of a bank or banker. **4.** to keep money in, or have an account with, a bank. –v.t. **5.** to deposit in a bank. –phr. **6. bank on**, to rely or count on. **7. bank up**, to accumulate.

bank³ /bæŋk/ n. **1.** an arrangement of objects in line. **2.** a row or tier of oars.

bankbook /'bæŋkbuk/ n. a small book showing a record of a person's bank account; passbook.

bank cheque *n.* a cheque issued by a bank in its own name.

bank draft *n.* a draft drawn by one bank on another, payable on demand or at a specified future date.

banker /'bæŋkə/ *n.* **1.** someone who manages a bank or is in the banking business. **2.** someone who holds or supplies money for another.

banknote /'bæŋknoʊt/ *n.* a promissory note, payable on demand, issued by a central bank and intended to circulate as money.

bankroll /'bæŋkroʊl/ *n.* **1.** a roll of money notes. –*v.t.* **2.** to provide funds for; act as backer for.

bankrupt /'bæŋkrʌpt/ *n.* **1.** *Law* a person who upon his or her own petition or that of his or her creditors is adjudged insolvent by a court, and whose property is therefore to be administered by a trustee for the benefit of the creditors in accordance with bankruptcy legislation. **2.** any insolvent debtor; one unable to satisfy any just claims made upon him or her. **3.** a person completely depleted of some human quality or resource. –*adj.* **4.** *Law* subject to having (one's) property administered by a trustee in accordance with bankruptcy legislation. **5.** completely depleted of some human quality or resource. **6.** relating to bankrupts. –*v.t.* **7.** to make bankrupt. –**bankruptcy**, *n.*

banksia /'bæŋksiə/ *n.* any of various shrubs and trees with leathery leaves and dense cylindrical heads of flowers, sometimes called a bottlebrush.

banner /'bænə/ *n.* **1.** the flag of a country, army, troop, etc. **2.** a headline which extends across the width of the newspaper. **3.** Also, **web banner.** *Internet* a large rectangular section on a web page, often for branding or advertising purposes.

banquet /'bæŋkwət/ *n.* a formal and ceremonious meal, often one given to celebrate an event or to honour a person.

bantam /'bæntəm/ *n.* (*oft. upper case*) a domestic fowl of any of certain varieties or breeds characterised by very small size.

banter /'bæntə/ *n.* **1.** playfully teasing language; good-humoured raillery. –*v.i.* **2.** to use banter.

baobab /'beɪoʊbæb/ *n.* → **boab.**

baptism /'bæptɪzəm/ *n.* **1.** a ceremonial immersion in water, or application of water, as an initiatory rite or sacrament of the Christian church. **2.** any similar ceremony or action of initiation, dedication, etc. –**baptise, baptize,** *v.*

bar¹ /ba/ *n.* **1.** a relatively long and evenly shaped piece of some solid substance. **2.** a band or stripe. **3.** a ridge of sand or gravel in coastal waters. **4.** anything which obstructs, hinders, or impedes; an obstacle; a barrier. **5.** Also, **bar-line.** *Music* the vertical line drawn across the stave to mark the metrical accent. **6.** a counter or a room where alcoholic drinks, etc., are served to customers. **7.** *Law* **a.** (in a law court) an imaginary barrier isolating the bench and front row of counsel's seats from the rest of the court. **b.** practising barristers collectively. –*v.t.* (**barred, barring**) **8.** to provide or fasten with a bar or bars. **9.** to

block (a way, etc.) as with a barrier; prevent or hinder, as access. **10.** to forbid; preclude. –*prep.* **11.** except; omitting; but.

bar² /ba/ *n.* a unit for measuring pressure in the metric system, equal to 10 units a square metre.

barb /bab/ *n.* **1.** a point or pointed part projecting backwards from a main point, as of a fishhook, an arrow, or a fence wire. **2.** a sharp or unkind implication in a remark; cutting comment.

barbarian /ba'bɛəriən/ *n.* an ignorant, uncouth and cruel person. –**barbaric, barbarous,** *adj.*

barbecue /'babəkju/ *n.* **1.** a metal frame for cooking meat, etc., above an open fire of coals, wood, etc. **2.** a social occasion, usually outdoors, where barbecued food is served. –*v.t.* (**-cued, -cuing**) **3.** to cook on a barbecue. Also, **barbeque, bar-b-q.**

barbed wire *n.* steel wire to which barbs are attached at short intervals, used largely for fencing in livestock, protecting a defensive military position, etc. Also, **barbwire.**

barber /'babə/ *n.* one whose occupation it is to cut and dress the hair of customers and to shave or trim the beard.

barbie /'babi/ *n.* *Colloq.* a barbecue. Also, **barby.**

barbiturate /ba'bɪtʃərət, -eɪt/ *n.* a drug used as an anaesthetic or a sedative.

barcode /'bakoʊd/ *n.* Also, **bar code.** **1.** a product code containing information about prices, etc., in the form of a series of bars of varying thickness, designed to be read by an optical scanner. –*v.t.* **2.** to identify by means of a barcode.

bard /bad/ *n.* *Archaic* a poet.

bare /bɛə/ *adj.* (**barer, barest**) **1.** without covering or clothing; naked or nude. **2.** without the usual furnishings, contents, etc. **3.** open to view; unconcealed; undisguised. **4.** unadorned; bald; plain. **5.** scarcely or just sufficient. –*v.t.* (**bared, baring**) **6.** to make bare.

barefaced /'bɛəfeɪst/ *adj.* shameless; impudent; undisguised: *a barefaced lie.*

barely /'bɛəli/ *adv.* only; no more than.

bargain /'bagən/ *n.* **1.** an agreement between parties settling what each shall give and take, or perform and receive, in a transaction. **2.** *Stock Exchange* an agreement to sell or to purchase; a sale or purchase. **3.** an advantageous purchase. –*v.i.* **4.** to discuss the terms of a bargain; haggle over terms.

barge /badʒ/ *n.* **1.** a large flat-bottomed vessel, usually moved by towing, used for transporting freight. –*v.i.* (**barged, barging**) **2.** to move aggressively or with undue energy often knocking others out of the way.

bariatrics /bæri'ætrɪks/ *n.* the branch of medical science concerned with the causes and treatment of obesity. –**bariatric,** *adj.*

barista /ba'rɪstə/ *n.* (*pl.* **-ristas** *or* **-risti**) a person skilled in making espresso coffee in a cafe or restaurant.

baritone /'bærətoʊn/ *n.* a male voice or voice part intermediate between tenor and bass.

barium /'bɛəriəm/ *n.* a whitish, malleable, active, divalent, metallic element. *Symbol:* Ba

bark¹ /bak/ *n.* **1.** the abrupt, explosive cry of a dog. –*v.i.* **2.** to utter an abrupt, explosive cry or a series of such cries, as a dog. **3.** to speak or cry out sharply or gruffly.

bark² /bak/ *n.* the external covering of the woody stems, branches, and roots of plants, as distinct and separable from the wood itself.

barley /'bali/ *n.* a cereal plant whose grain is used as food and in the making of whisky.

bar mitzvah /ba 'mitsvə/ *n.* (in Judaism) **1.** a boy at the age of thirteen, when he acquires religious obligations. **2.** the ceremony and feast marking this. Also, **bar mizvah**.

barn /ban/ *n.* a building for storing hay, grain, etc., and often for stabling livestock.

barnacle /'banəkəl/ *n.* any of certain crustaceans which attach themselves to marine rocks.

barney /'bani/ *n. Colloq.* an argument; fight.

baro- a word element meaning 'weight', 'pressure'.

barometer /bə'rɒmətə/ *n.* **1.** an instrument for measuring atmospheric pressure, thus determining height, weather changes, etc. **2.** anything that indicates changes. –**barometric**, *adj.*

baron /'bærən/ *n.* **1.** a man holding a peerage of the lowest titular rank. **2.** a rich and powerful man; magnate.

baronet /'bærənət, -nɛt/ *n.* a member of a British hereditary order of honour, ranking below the barons.

baroque /bə'rɒk, bə'roʊk/ *adj.* **1.** *Music* of or relating to the ornate style of composition of the 17th and early 18th centuries. **2.** extravagantly ornamented.

barrack¹ /'bærək/ *n.* (*usu. pl.*) a building or range of buildings for lodging soldiers, especially in garrison.

barrack² /'bærɪk/ *v.i.* (fol. by *for*) to support; shout encouragement and approval.

barracouta /bærə'kutə/ *n.* (*pl.* **-couta** *or* **-coutas**) an elongated, cold water, sport and food fish.

barracuda /bærə'kudə/ *n.* (*pl.* **-cuda** *or* **-cudas**) any of various species of elongated, predatory, tropical and subtropical marine fishes.

barrage /'bæraʒ, -adʒ/ *n.* **1.** *Mil.* a barrier of artillery fire. **2.** a sustained attack.

barramundi /bærə'mʌndi/ *n.* (*pl.* **-di** *or* **-dis**) a large, silvery-grey food fish found in coastal rivers and estuaries of tropical northern Australia.

barrel /'bærəl/ *n.* **1.** a wooden cylindrical vessel having slightly bulging sides and flat parallel ends. **2.** the tube of a gun.

barren /'bærən/ *adj.* **1.** incapable of producing, or not producing, offspring; sterile. **2.** unproductive; unfruitful.

barrette /bə'rɛt/ *n.* a metal or plastic clasp for fastening hair in position, usually comprising two parts joined with a hinge.

barricade /'bærəkeɪd, bærə'keɪd/ *n.* a defensive barrier hastily constructed, as in a street, to stop an enemy. –*v.t.* **2.** to obstruct or block with a barricade. **3.** to shut in and defend with or as with a barricade.

barrier /'bæriə/ *n.* anything that bars passage or access.

barrister /'bærəstə/ *n.* a lawyer allowed to plead cases in any court.

barrow /'bæroʊ/ *n.* a cart for selling goods, especially fruit and vegetables, in the street.

barter /'batə/ *v.i.* to trade by exchange of commodities rather than by the use of money.

BAS /bæz, bæs/ *n.* → **business activity statement**.

basalt /'bæsɒlt, 'bæsəlt/ *n.* a dark, dense igneous rock.

base¹ /beɪs/ *n.* **1.** the bottom of anything, considered as its support; that on which a thing stands or rests. **2.** the principal element or ingredient of anything, considered as its fundamental part. **3.** *Mil.* a fortified or protected area or place used by any of the armed services. **4.** *Maths* **a.** the number which serves as a starting point for a logarithmic or other numerical system. **b.** the side or face of a geometric figure to which an altitude is thought to be drawn. **5.** *Chem.* any of numerous compounds which react with an acid to form a salt. –*v.t.* (**based, basing**) **6.** to make or form a base or foundation for. **7.** to place or establish on a base or basis; ground; found; establish. **8.** to locate the main part of (a business, enterprise, etc.). –*phr.* **9. base on** (or **upon**), **a.** to arrive at as a result of. **b.** to create after the pattern of. –**baseless**, *adj.*

base² /beɪs/ *adj.* **1.** morally low; without dignity of sentiment; mean-spirited; selfish; cowardly. **2.** debased or counterfeit.

baseball /'beɪsbɔl/ *n.* a game played with a wooden bat and a hard ball. –**baseballer**, *n.*

BASE-jump *n.* a parachute jump from a tall structure, as opposed to a jump from an aeroplane. –**BASE-jumper**, *n.* –**BASE-jumping**, *n.*

baseline /'beɪslaɪn/ *n.* a basic standard or level, usually regarded as a reference point for comparison.

baseline-and-credit *adj.* of or relating to an emissions trading scheme in which polluters earn credits for emissions below agreed baselines, such credits being available to be sold to other polluters. See **cap-and-trade**.

basement /'beɪsmənt/ *n.* a storey of a building partly or wholly underground.

bash /bæʃ/ *v.t.* to strike with a crushing or smashing blow.

bashful /'bæʃfəl/ *adj.* uncomfortably diffident or shy; timid and easily embarrassed.

basic /'beɪsɪk/ *adj.* **1.** of, relating to, or forming a base; fundamental. –*n.* **2.** something that is basic or essential. –**basically**, *adv.*

basic wage *n.* the minimum wage payable to an adult employee under an award or agreement.

basil /'bæzəl/ *n.* any of various herbs having aromatic leaves used in cookery.

basilica /bə'sɪlɪkə, -'zɪl-/ *n.* **1.** an oblong building, especially a church with a nave higher than its aisles. **2.** one of the seven main churches of Rome or another Roman Catholic church accorded certain religious privileges.

basin /'beɪsən/ *n.* **1.** a usually circular container of greater width than depth, contracting towards the bottom, used chiefly to hold water or other liquid, especially for washing. **2.** a small circular container of approximately equal width and depth, used chiefly for mixing, cooking, etc. **3.** *Physical Geog.* a hollow or depression in the earth's surface, wholly or partly surrounded by higher land.

basis /'beɪsəs/ n. (pl. **bases** /'beɪsiːz/) **1.** the bottom or base of anything, or that on which it stands or rests. **2.** a groundwork or fundamental principle. **3.** the principal constituent; a fundamental ingredient.

basis point n. a measure used in financial markets, equal to one hundredth of one percentage point.

bask /bask/ v.i. to lie in or be exposed to a pleasant warmth.

basket /'baskət/ n. **1.** a receptacle made of twigs, rushes, thin strips of wood, or other flexible material, woven together. **2.** Econ. a list of retail goods from which the consumer price index is calculated.

basketball /'baskətbɔl/ n. a ball game, the object of which is to throw the ball through an elevated basket. —**basketballer**, n.

basmati rice /'bæz'mati, bas'mati/ n. an Indian long-grain rice variety which, when cooked, produces light dry grains which separate easily.

bas mitzvah /bas 'mɪtsvə/ n. → **bat mitzvah**.

bas-relief /ba-rə'lif/ n. sculpture in which the figures project only slightly from the background.

bass¹ /beɪs/ adj. low in pitch; of the lowest pitch or range.

bass² /bæs/ n. an Australian freshwater fish.

basset /'bæsət/ n. a long-bodied, short-legged dog resembling a dachshund but larger and heavier. Also, **basset hound**.

bassinet /bæsə'nɛt/ n. a basket in which a baby sleeps. Also, **bassinette**.

bassoon /bə'sun/ n. a double-reed woodwind instrument.

bastard /'bastəd/ n. **1.** an illegitimate child. **2.** something irregular, inferior, spurious, or unusual. **3.** Colloq. an unpleasant or despicable person or thing.

baste¹ /beɪst/ v.t. to sew with temporary stitches, as a garment in the first stages of making; tack.

baste² /beɪst/ v.t. to moisten (meat, etc.) while cooking, with dripping, butter, etc.

bastion /'bæstiən/ n. **1.** a fortified place. **2.** any person or object which affords support or defence.

bat¹ /bæt/ n. **1.** Sport **a.** the club used in certain games, as cricket and baseball, to strike the ball. **b.** a racquet, especially one used in table tennis. **2.** Colloq. rate of motion. —v.t. (**batted, batting**) **3.** to strike or hit with or as with a bat or club.

bat² /bæt/ n. **1.** a nocturnal or flying mammal characterised by modified forelimbs which serve as wings and are covered with a membranous skin extending to the hind limbs. —phr. **2. old bat**, Colloq. an unpleasant or eccentric woman, usually old.

bat³ /bæt/ v.t. (**batted, batting**) to wink or flutter (one's eyelids).

batch /bætʃ/ n. **1.** a quantity or a number taken together; a group. **2.** the quantity of material prepared or required for one operation or that quantity produced by one operation.

bate /beɪt/ v.t. to moderate or restrain (the breath).

bath /baθ/ n. **1.** the washing, especially of a body, in water, other liquid, steam, etc. **2.** the water or other liquid used for a bath. **3.** a vessel for containing this. —v.t. **4.** to put or wash in a bath. —phr. **5. take a bath**, Colloq. to suffer a defeat or misfortune, especially a financial loss.

bathe /beɪð/ v.t. **1.** to immerse in water or other liquid for cleansing, refreshment, etc. **2.** to apply water or other liquid to, with a sponge, cloth, etc.

bathers /'beɪðəz/ pl. n. → **swimming costume**.

batho- a word element meaning 'deep'.

bathroom /'baθrum/ n. **1.** a room fitted with a bath or a shower (or both), and sometimes with a toilet and a basin. **2.** a room fitted with a toilet.

baths /baðz/ pl. n. **1.** Obsolesc. a public swimming pool. **2.** a building containing apartments for washing or bathing, or fitted up for bathing.

batik /'batik, 'bætɪk/ n. a method of printing cloth using a wax deposit to achieve the desired pattern.

bat mitzvah /bat 'mɪtsvə/ n. (in Judaism) **1.** a girl at the age of twelve, when she acquires religious obligations. **2.** the ceremony and feast marking this. Also, **bas mitzvah**.

baton /'bætn/ n. **1.** a staff, club, or truncheon, especially as a mark of office or authority. **2.** Music the wand used by a conductor. **3.** Athletics (in relay racing) a metal or wooden tube, handed on by one relay runner to the next.

battalion /bə'tæljən/ n. Mil. a ground-force unit composed of three or more companies or similar units.

batten /'bætn/ n. **1.** a light strip of wood usually having an oblong cross-section and used to fasten main members of a structure together. —v.t. **2.** Naut. (usu. fol. by down) to fasten (as hatches) with battens and tarpaulins.

batter¹ /'bætə/ v.t. **1.** to beat persistently or hard; pound. **2.** to damage by beating or hard usage.

batter² /'bætə/ n. a mixture of flour, milk or water, eggs, etc., beaten together for use in cookery.

batter³ /'bætə/ n. Cricket, Baseball, etc. a player whose role is to strike the ball with the bat or whose turn it is to do this.

battery /'bætəri/ n. (pl. **-ries**) **1.** Elect. either of two chemical cells or groups of cells: **a.** one which produces electrical energy. **b.** one which stores electrical energy. **2.** a group of similar items used together. **3.** a large number of cages in which chickens etc., are reared for intensive productivity. **4.** Law unlawful and intentional interference with the person of another.

battle /'bætl/ n. **1.** a hostile encounter or engagement between opposing forces. **2.** any extended or intense fight, struggle or contest. —v.i. **3.** to engage in battle. **4.** to fight.

battleaxe block /'bætəlæks/ n. a block or section of land, behind those with street frontages and accessible through a drive or lane.

battlefield /'bætlfild/ n. **1.** the field or ground on which a battle is fought. **2.** any sphere in which conflict occurs: *the political battlefield.* Also, **battleground** /'bætlgraʊnd/.

battlement /'bætlmənt/ *n.* a wall or parapet with indentations or openings, originally for shooting through.

bauble /'bɔbl/ *n.* a cheap ornament; trinket.

baud /bɔd/ *n.* a unit for measuring the speed with which electronic data is transmitted, especially in computers.

baulk /bɔk/ *v.i.* **1.** to stop, as at an obstacle. **2.** *Sport* to make an incomplete or misleading move, especially an illegal one.

bauxite /'bɔksaɪt/ *n.* a rock, the principal ore of aluminium.

bawdy /'bɔdi/ *adj.* rollickingly vulgar; lewd.

bawl /bɔl/ *v.i.* to cry loudly and vigorously.

bay[1] /beɪ/ *n.* a recess or inlet in the shore of a sea or lake between two capes or headlands, not as large as a gulf but larger than a cove.

bay[2] /beɪ/ *n.* **1.** a recessed space projecting outwards from the line of a wall, as to contain a window. **2.** the aisle between parallel shelvings as in a library.

bay[3] /beɪ/ *n.* a deep, prolonged bark, as of a hound or hounds in hunting.

bay[4] /beɪ/ *n.* a reddish brown colour.

bayonet /'beɪnət, 'beɪənət, beɪə'net/ *n.* a stabbing or slashing instrument of steel, made to be attached to the muzzle of a rifle.

bazaar /bə'zɑ/ *n.* a marketplace.

bazooka /bə'zukə/ *n.* an individual infantry weapon that fires a rocket.

be /bi/ *substantive* **1.** to exist; have reality; live; take place; occur; remain as before. **2.** (*used in the perfect and pluperfect*) to pay a visit; go: *I have been to Spain; have you been to the shops today?* –*v.* (*copular*) **3.** a link connecting a subject with predicate or qualifying words in assertive, interrogative, and imperative sentences, or serving to form infinitive and participial phrases. –*v.* (*aux.*) **4.** used with the present participle of a verb to form the progressive (*I am waiting*), or with a past participle in passive forms of transitive verbs (*the date was fixed; it must be done*).
The different forms of the verb **be** are:
Present tense: I **am**, you **are**, he/she/it **is**, we **are**, they **are**
Past tense: I **was**, you **were**, he/she/it **was**, we **were**, they **were**
Past participle: **been**
Present participle: **being**

be- a prefix meaning 'about', 'around', 'all over', as in *besiege.*

beach /bitʃ/ *n.* **1.** the sand or loose water-worn pebbles of the seashore. **2.** that part of the shore of the sea, or of a large river or lake, washed by the tide or waves. **3.** the seaside as a place of recreation. –*v.t. Naut.* to run or haul up (a ship or boat) on the beach.

beacon /'bikən/ *n.* a guiding or warning signal, such as a lighthouse, fire, etc.

bead /bid/ *n.* **1.** a small ball of glass, pearl, wood, etc., with a hole through it, strung with others like it, and used as an ornament or in a rosary. **2.** a drop of liquid.

beagle /'bigəl/ *n.* one of a breed of small hounds with short legs and drooping ears, used especially in hunting.

beak /bik/ *n.* the horny bill of a bird.

beaker /'bikə/ *n.* a large drinking vessel with a wide mouth.

beam /bim/ *n.* **1.** a thick, long piece of timber, shaped for structural use. **2.** *Naut.* the side of a vessel, or the direction at right angles to the keel, with reference to the wind, sea, etc. **3.** the widest part. **4.** the transverse bar of a balance from the ends of which the scales or pans are suspended. **5.** a ray, or bundle of parallel rays, of light or other radiation. **6.** a gleam; suggestion. **7.** *Radio, Aeronautics* a signal transmitted along a narrow course, used to guide pilots through darkness, bad weather, etc. –*v.i.* **8.** to emit beams, as of light. **9.** to look or smile radiantly.

bean /bin/ *n.* **1.** the edible fruit or seed of various plants. **2.** any of various other bean-like seeds or plants, as the coffee bean.

bean curd *n.* → **tofu.** Also, **beancurd.**

beanie /'bini/ *n.* a small close-fitting knitted cap.

bean sprout *n.* the very young shoot of any of certain beans, used in Asian cookery and as a salad vegetable. Also, **beansprout, bean shoot.**

bear[1] /beə/ *v.* (**bore, borne** *or* **born, bearing**) –*v.t.* **1.** to hold up; support. **2.** to carry. **3.** to render; afford; give. **4.** to undergo; suffer. **5.** to be fit for or worthy of. **6.** to possess as a quality, characteristic, etc.; have in or on. **7.** to manage (oneself, one's body, head, etc.). **8.** to give birth to. **9.** to produce by natural growth. –*v.i.* **10.** to tend in course or direction; move; go. **11.** to be located or situated. **12.** to bring forth young, fruit, etc. –*phr.* **13. bear on,** to have an effect, reference, or bearing on. **14. bear out,** to confirm; prove right. **15. bear up, a.** to hold or remain firm, as under pressure. **b.** to remain strong in a time of difficulty. **16. bear with,** to be patient with.

bear[2] /beə/ *n.* **1.** a carnivorous or omnivorous mammal, having a massive body, coarse, heavy fur, relatively short limbs, and an almost rudimentary tail. **2.** (in general business) someone who believes that conditions are or will be unfavourable. –*adj.* **3.** *Stock Exchange* of, relating to, or caused by declining prices in stocks, etc. –*v.i.* (**beared, bearing**) **4.** *Stock Exchange* to operate in stocks for a decline in price.

beard /bɪəd/ *n.* the growth of hair on the face of an adult male, sometimes exclusive of the moustache. –**bearded,** *adj.*

bearing /'beərɪŋ/ *n.* **1.** the manner in which one bears or carries oneself, including posture, gestures, etc. **2.** *Machinery* a part in which a journal, pivot, or the like, turns or moves. **3.** (*oft. pl.*) direction or relative position. **4.** *Geog.* a horizontal angle measured from 0° to 90° fixing the direction of a line with respect to either the north or south direction. –*phr.* **5. get one's bearings,** to establish one's position in or as in relation to. **6. have a bearing on,** to have an effect on or relevance to one's environment, circumstances, etc. **7. lose one's bearings,** to become lost, especially by losing one's sense of relative position in or as in a particular environment, set of circumstances, etc.

bear market *n. Stock Exchange* a gloomy period of trading during and after a decline in share prices when traders consider there is little prospect of immediate recovery.

beast /bist/ *n.* **1.** any animal except a human being, especially a large four-footed one. **2.** a coarse, filthy, or otherwise beast-like human.

beastly /'bistli/ *adj.* (**-lier, -liest**) **1.** of or like a beast; bestial. **2.** nasty; disagreeable.

beat /bit/ *v.* (**beat, beaten** or **beat, beating**) *−v.t.* **1.** to strike repeatedly and usually violently, especially as a punishment. **2.** to whisk; stir, as in order to thicken or aerate. **3.** to flutter or flap. **4.** to sound as on a drum. **5.** (usu. fol. by *out*) to hammer (metal) thin; flatten. **6.** to make (a path) by repeated treading. **7.** *Music* to mark (time) by strokes, as with the hand or a metronome. **8.** to overcome in a contest; defeat. **9.** to be superior to. *−v.i.* **10.** to strike repeated blows; pound. **11.** to throb or pulsate. **12.** to radiate intense light or heat; glare. **13.** to resound under blows, as a drum. *−n.* **14.** a stroke or blow. **15.** a throb or pulsation. **16.** a beaten path or habitual round, as of a police officer. **17.** *Music* **a.** the audible, visual, or mental marking of the metrical divisions of music. **b.** a stroke of the hand, baton, etc., marking time division or accent for music during performance. *−adj.* **18.** *Colloq.* exhausted; worn out.

beatbox /'bitbɒks/ *n.* a music synthesiser which produces a rhythmic beat. Also, **beat box**.

beatboxing /'bitbɒksɪŋ/ *n.* a style of vocalisation which imitates the sounds and rhythms produced by a beatbox. **−beatboxer**, *n.*

beatific /biə'tɪfɪk/ *adj.* **1.** making blessed. **2.** blissful.

beatify /bi'ætɪfaɪ/ *v.t.* (**-fied, -fying**) **1.** to make blissfully happy. **2.** *Roman Catholic Church* to declare (a deceased person) to be among the blessed, and thus entitled to specific religious honour.

beatnik /'bitnɪk/ *n. Colloq.* someone who avoids traditional conventions of behaviour, dress, etc.

beau /bou/ *n.* (*pl.* **beaus** /bouz/ or **beaux** /bou, bouz/) a boyfriend or lover of a girl or woman.

Beaufort scale /'boufət skeɪl/ *n.* a scale for indicating the force or velocity of the wind, ranging from 0 for calm to 12 for hurricane.

beaut /bjut/ *Colloq. −adj.* **1.** fine; good. *−interj.* Also, **you beaut!. 2.** an exclamation of approval, delight, enthusiasm, etc.

beauteous /'bjutiəs/ *adj.* beautiful.

beautician /bju'tɪʃən/ *n.* a person skilled in cosmetic treatment and beauty aids.

beautiful /'bjutəfʊl/ *adj.* **1.** having or exhibiting beauty. **2.** very pleasant.

beautify /'bjutəfaɪ/ *v.t.* (**-fied, -fying**) to decorate, adorn or make more beautiful.

beauty /'bjuti/ *n.* **1.** that quality or characteristic which excites an admiring pleasure, or delights the eye or the aesthetic sense. **2.** something or someone beautiful. **3.** *Colloq.* an excellent or remarkable example of its kind. **4.** *Colloq.* a particular advantage. *−interj.* **5.** an exclamation of approval, delight, etc.

beaver /'bivə/ *n.* an amphibious rodent noted for its ingenuity in damming streams with branches, mud, etc.

bebop /'bibɒp/ *n.* a style of jazz composition and performance characterised by dissonant

harmony, complex rhythmic devices, and experimental, often bizarre, instrumental effects. Also, **bop, rebop**. **−bebopper**, *n.*

became /bə'keɪm/ *v.* past tense of **become**.

because /bi'kɒz, -'kʌz, bə-/ *conj.* **1.** for the reason that; due to the fact that. *−adv.* **2.** (fol. by *of*) by reason; on account.

beck /bɛk/ *phr.* **at someone's beck and call**, ready to obey someone immediately; subject to someone's slightest wish.

beckon /'bɛkən/ *v.t.* **1.** to signal, summon, or direct by a gesture of the head or hand. **2.** to lure; entice.

become /bə'kʌm, bi-/ *v.* (**-came, -come, -coming**) *−v.i.* **1.** to come into being; come or grow to be (as stated). **2.** to be the fate (of). *−v.t.* **3.** to befit; suit.

becoming /bə'kʌmɪŋ, bi-/ *adj.* **1.** attractive. **2.** suitable; proper.

bed /bɛd/ *n.* **1.** a piece of furniture upon which or within which a person sleeps. **2.** a piece of ground (in a garden) in which plants are grown. **3.** a piece or part forming a foundation or base.

bed and breakfast *n.* **1.** (in a motel or the like) the provision of sleeping accommodation and breakfast. **2.** an establishment providing sleeping accommodation and breakfast to paying guests. *Abbrev.*: B & B

bedlam /'bɛdləm/ *n.* a scene of wild uproar and confusion.

bedraggled /bə'drægəld, bi-/ *adj.* wet and dishevelled.

bedridden /'bɛdrɪdn/ *adj.* confined to bed.

bedrock /'bɛdrɒk/ *n.* **1.** *Geol.* unbroken solid rock, overlaid in most places by soil or rock fragments. **2.** any firm foundation.

bedroom /'bɛdrum/ *n.* a room set aside to sleep in.

bee¹ /bi/ *n.* a four-winged, usually stinging insect which gathers pollen.

bee² /bi/ *n.* a local gathering for work, entertainment, contests, etc.

beech /bitʃ/ *n.* a type of tree growing in temperate regions.

beef /bif/ *n.* **1.** the meat from a bull or cow. *−v.i.* **2.** *Chiefly US Colloq.* to complain; grumble.

beefy /'bifi/ *adj.* (**-fier, -fiest**) fleshy; brawny; solid; heavy.

beeline /'bilaɪn/ *n.* a direct line, like the course of bees returning to a hive.

been /bin/ *v.* past participle of **be**.

beer /bɪə/ *n.* an alcoholic beverage made by brewing and fermentation from cereals, usually malted barley and flavoured with hops, etc., to give a bitter taste.

beet /bit/ *n.* any of various biennial plants including the red beet, which has a fleshy edible root, and the sugar beet, which yields sugar.

beetle /'bitl/ *n.* any insect characterised by having forewings modified as hard, horny structures, not vibrated in flight.

beetroot /'bitrut/ *n.* the edible root of the red beet.

befall /bə'fɔl, bi-/ *v.* (**-fell, -fallen, -falling**) *−v.i.* **1.** to happen or occur. *−v.t.* **2.** to happen to.

befit /bə'fɪt, bi-/ v.t. (**-fitted, -fitting**) to be fitting or appropriate for; be suited to.

before /bə'fɔ, bi-/ adv. **1.** in front; in advance; ahead. **2.** earlier or sooner. –prep. **3.** in front of; ahead of; in advance of. **4.** previously to; earlier than. **5.** in preference to; rather than. **6.** in precedence of, as in order or rank. **7.** in the presence or sight of. **8.** under the jurisdiction or consideration of. –conj. **9.** previously to the time when. **10.** sooner than; rather than.

beforehand /bə'fɔhænd, bi-/ adv. in anticipation; in advance; ahead of time.

befriend /bə'frɛnd, bi-/ v.t. to act as a friend to; aid.

befuddle /bə'fʌdl, bi-/ **1.** to make stupidly drunk. **2.** to confuse, as with glib argument.

beg /bɛg/ v. (**begged, begging**) –v.t. **1.** to ask for in charity; ask as alms. **2.** to ask for, or of, with humility or earnestness, or as a favour. –v.i. **3.** to ask alms or charity; live by asking alms. **4.** to ask humbly or earnestly.

began /bə'gæn, bi-/ v. past tense of **begin**.

beget /bə'gɛt, bi-/ v.t. (**-got, -gotten** or **-got, -getting**) to procreate or generate (used chiefly of the male parent).

beggar /'bɛgə/ n. **1.** someone who begs alms, or lives by begging. **2.** a penniless person. **3.** (in playful use) a wretch or rogue.

begin /bə'gɪn/ v. (**began, begun, beginning**) –v.i. **1.** to enter upon an action; take the first step; commence; start. **2.** to come into existence; arise; originate. –v.t. **3.** to take the first step in; set about; start; commence. **4.** to originate; be the originator of. –**beginning**, n.

beginner /bə'gɪnə/ n. someone who has recently begun to learn a skill; a novice.

begrudge /bə'grʌdʒ, bi-/ v.t. to be discontented at seeing (a person) have (something).

beguile /bə'gaɪl, bi-/ v.t. **1.** to influence by guile; mislead; delude. **2.** to charm or divert. –**beguiling**, adj. –**beguilingly**, adv.

begun /bə'gʌn, bi-/ v. past participle of **begin**.

behalf /bə'haf, bi-/ n. (preceded by on) side, interest, or aid.

behave /bə'heɪv, bi-/ v.i. **1.** to conduct oneself or itself; act. **2.** to act in a socially acceptable manner. –**behaviour**, n.

behead /bə'hɛd, bi-/ v.t. to cut off the head of; kill or execute by decapitation.

behest /bə'hɛst, bi-/ n. bidding or injunction; mandate or command.

behind /bə'haɪnd, bi-/ prep. **1.** at the back of; at the rear of. **2.** after; later than. **3.** less advanced than; inferior to. **4.** on the farther side of; beyond. **5.** supporting; promoting. **6.** hidden or unrevealed by. –adv. **7.** at or towards the back; in the rear. **8.** in arrears; behindhand. –n. **9.** the buttocks.

behindhand /bə'haɪndhænd, bi-/ adj. **1.** late. **2.** behind in progress; backward.

behold /bə'hoʊld, bi-/ v.t. (**-held, -holding**) to observe; look at; see.

behove /bə'hoʊv, bi-/ v.t. to be needful or proper for or incumbent on (now only in impersonal use).

beige /beɪʒ/ n., adj. very light brown.

being /'biɪŋ/ n. **1.** existence, as opposed to non-existence. **2.** conscious existence; life. **3.** substance or nature. **4.** a living thing.

belated /bə'leɪtəd, bi-/ adj. coming or being late or too late.

belch /bɛltʃ/ v.i. **1.** to eject wind spasmodically and noisily from the stomach through the mouth; burp. **2.** to emit contents violently, as a gun, geyser, or volcano. –v.t. **3.** to eject spasmodically or violently; give forth. –n. **4.** a belching.

beleaguer /bə'ligə, bi-/ v.t. **1.** to surround with an army. **2.** to surround: to beleaguer the city. **3.** to beset with troubles and annoyances. –**beleaguered**, adj.

belfry /'bɛlfri/ n. (pl. **-ries**) a tower housing a bell, either attached to a church or other building or standing apart.

belie /bə'laɪ, bi-/ v.t. (**-lied, -lying**) **1.** to misrepresent. **2.** to show to be false.

belief /bə'lif, bi-/ n. **1.** that which is believed; an accepted opinion. **2.** conviction of the truth or reality of a thing, based upon grounds insufficient to afford positive knowledge. **3.** confidence; faith; trust.

believable /bə'livəbəl/ adj. able to be believed in or likely to be true.

believe /bə'liv, bi-/ v.t. **1.** to have belief in: to believe a person. **2.** to think: I believe she has left the city. **3.** to credit; accept as true: to believe a story. –phr. **4.** **believe in, a.** to have confidence in; trust; rely through faith on: I believe in you implicitly. **b.** to be persuaded of the truth, existence, etc., of: he still believes in Santa Claus. **c.** to accept or agree with (a doctrine, principle, system, etc.): I don't believe in private education. –**believer**, n.

belittle /bə'lɪtl, bi-/ v.t. to make little or less important; depreciate; disparage.

bell /bɛl/ n. **1.** a sounding instrument, usually of metal, cup-shaped with a flaring mouth, rung by the strokes of a clapper, tongue, or hammer suspended within it. **2.** any instrument emitting a ringing signal, especially an electrical device as a doorbell. **3.** Naut. the half-hourly subdivisions of a watch of four hours, each being marked by single or double strokes of a bell. –phr. **4.** **ring a bell**, to remind one; jog the memory.

bellbird /'bɛlbɜd/ n. a yellowish-green honeyeater with a distinctive, tinkling, bell-like call.

bellicose /'bɛləkoʊs/ adj. inclined to war; warlike; pugnacious.

belligerent /bə'lɪdʒərənt/ adj. **1.** warlike; given to waging war. **2.** relating to war, or to those engaged in war. –n. **3.** a state or nation at war, or a member of the military forces of such a state.

bellow /'bɛloʊ/ v.i. **1.** to make a hollow, loud, animal cry, as a bull or cow. **2.** to roar; bawl.

bellows /'bɛloʊz/ n. (sing. and pl.) an instrument which produces a strong current of air when the air-chamber inside is contracted.

belly /'bɛli/ n. (pl. **bellies**) **1.** the front or underpart of a vertebrate body from the breastbone to the pelvis, containing the abdominal viscera; the abdomen. –phr. **2.** **go belly up**, Colloq. to fail.

belong /bə'lɒŋ, bi-/ v.i. **1.** to have one's rightful place; to bear relation as a member, adherent, inhabitant, etc. **2.** to be proper or due.

belongings /bə'lɒŋɪŋz, bi-/ pl. n. possessions.

beloved /bə'lʌvəd, -'lʌvd, bi-/ *adj.* **1.** greatly loved; dear to the heart. *–n.* **2.** someone who is greatly loved.

below /bə'lou, bi-/ *adv.* **1.** in or to a lower place; lower down; beneath. **2.** at a later point on a page or in writing. **3.** in a lower rank or grade. *–prep.* **4.** lower down than. **5.** too low or base to be worthy of.

belt /bɛlt/ *n.* **1.** a band of flexible material, as leather, worn around the waist to support clothing, for decoration, etc. **2.** any encircling or transverse band, strip, or strips. **3.** *Machinery* a flexible band or cord connecting and pulling about each of two or more wheels, pulleys or the like, to transmit or change the direction of motion. **4.** *Boxing* an imaginary line round the body at the level of the navel below which the boxer must not strike. *–v.t.* **5.** to gird or furnish with a belt. **6.** *Colloq.* to give a thwack or blow to. **7.** (fol. by *out*) to sing very loudly and often raucously. *–v.i.* **8.** *Colloq.* to move quickly or expeditiously. *–phr.* **9. belt up**, *Colloq.* be quiet; shut up.

bemused /bə'mjuzd, bi-/ *adj.* **1.** confused; muddled; stupefied. **2.** lost in thought; preoccupied.

bench /bɛntʃ/ *n.* **1.** a long seat with or without a back to accommodate several people. **2.** a seat on which members sit in a house of parliament. **3.** the strong work-table of a carpenter or other mechanic. *–phr.* **4. the bench, a.** the position or office of a judge: *appointed to the bench.* **b.** the body of persons sitting as judges.

benchmark /'bɛntʃmak/ *n.* **1.** a point of reference from which quality or excellence is measured. *–v.t.* **2.** to set a benchmark for: *this case will benchmark all future judgements in the wages area.*

bend /bɛnd/ *v.* (**bent, bending**) *–v.t.* **1.** to force into a different or particular, especially curved, shape, as by pressure. **2.** to cause to submit. **3.** to turn in a particular direction. **4.** (fol. by *to* or *towards*) to incline mentally. *–v.i.* **5.** to become curved, crooked, or bent. **6.** to move one's body forward or down in order to reach something, etc. **7.** to bow in submission or reverence; yield; submit. **8.** to turn or incline in a particular direction; be directed. *–n.* **9.** the act of bending. **10.** the state of being bent. **11.** a bent thing or part; curve; crook.

bends /bɛndz/ *pl. n.* **the**, a dangerous disorder where nitrogen bubbles form in the blood because of a too rapid decrease in surrounding pressure, found especially in divers who have surfaced too quickly.

bene- a word element meaning 'well'.

beneath /bə'niθ, bi-/ *adv.* **1.** below; in a lower place, position, state, etc. *–prep.* **2.** below; under. **3.** unworthy of; below the level or dignity of.

benediction /bɛnə'dɪkʃən/ *n.* the act of uttering a blessing.

benefactor /'bɛnəfæktə/ *n.* **1.** someone who confers a benefit; kindly helper. **2.** someone who makes a bequest or endowment.

beneficent /bə'nɛfəsənt/ *adj.* doing good or causing good to be done; conferring benefits; kindly in action or purpose.

beneficial /bɛnə'fɪʃəl/ *adj.* **1.** conferring benefit; advantageous; helpful. **2.** *Law* helpful in the meeting of needs.

beneficiary /bɛnə'fɪʃəri/ *n.* (*pl.* **-aries**) **1.** someone who receives benefits, profits, or advantages. **2.** *Law* a person designated as the recipient of funds or other property under a trust, will, insurance policy, etc.

benefit /'bɛnəfət/ *n.* **1.** an act of kindness. **2.** anything that is for the good of a person or thing. **3.** a payment or other assistance given by an insurance company, mutual benefit society, or public agency. *–v.* (**-fited** *or* **-fitted, -fiting** *or* **-fitting**) *–v.t.* **4.** to do good to; be of service to. *–v.i.* **5.** to gain advantage; make improvement.

benevolent /bə'nɛvələnt/ *adj.* **1.** desiring to do good for others. **2.** intended for benefits rather than profit.

benighted /bə'naɪtəd/ *adj.* intellectually or morally ignorant; unenlightened.

benign /bə'naɪn/ *adj.* **1.** of a kind disposition; kind. **2.** (of a tumour, etc.) not malignant.

bent /bɛnt/ *adj.* **1.** curved; crooked. **2.** *Colloq.* diverging from what is considered to be normal or conservative behaviour. *–n.* **3.** direction taken; inclination; bias. *–phr.* **4. bent on** (*or* **upon**), set on: *bent on having fun.*

bento box /'bɛntoʊ/ *n.* a selection of Japanese foods served in a compartmentalised container, traditionally an elaborately decorated lacquered box.

bequeath /bə'kwɪð, -'kwɪθ/ *v.t. Law* to dispose by last will of (personal property, especially money). *–***bequest***, n.*

berate /bə'reɪt/ *v.t.* to scold.

bereave /bə'riv, bi-/ *v.t.* (**-reaved** *or* **-reft, -reaving**) to make desolate through loss (*of*), especially by death.

bereft /bə'rɛft/ *adj.* **1.** suffering loss; deprived of possession. **2.** lacking.

beret /'bɛreɪ, bə'reɪ/ *n.* a soft, round, peakless cap that fits closely.

berley /'bɜli/ *n.* any bait, as chopped fish or broken bread or chopped green weed mixed with sand, thrown into the water by fishermen to attract fish. Also, **burley, birley.**

berry /'bɛri/ *n.* (*pl.* **-ries**) **1.** any small, (usually) stoneless and juicy fruit, as the gooseberry, strawberry, holly berry, rose hip, etc. **2.** a dry seed or kernel, as of wheat.

berserk /bə'zɜk/ *adj.* violently and destructively frenzied.

berth /bɜθ/ *n.* a shelf-like space, bunk, or whole room allotted to a traveller on a vessel or a train as a sleeping space.

beseech /bə'sitʃ, bi-/ *v.t.* (**besought** *or* **beseeched, beseeching**) **1.** to implore urgently. **2.** to beg eagerly for; solicit.

beset /bə'sɛt, bi-/ *v.t.* (**-set, -setting**) to attack on all sides; assail; harass.

beside /bə'saɪd, bi-/ *prep.* **1.** by or at the side of; near. **2.** compared with.

besides /bə'saɪdz, bi-/ *adv.* **1.** moreover. **2.** in addition. **3.** otherwise; else. *–prep.* **4.** over and above; in addition to. **5.** other than; except.

besiege /bə'sidʒ, bi-/ *v.t.* **1.** to lay siege to. **2.** to assail or ply, as with requests, etc.

besotted /bə'sɒtəd, bi-/ *adj.* **1.** filled with foolish love: *He was besotted with her.* **2.** made stupid, or drunk.

bespoke /bə'spoʊk, bi-/ *adj.* made to order.

best /bɛst/ *adj. (superlative of* **good)** **1.** of the highest quality, excellence, or standing. **2.** most advantageous, suitable, or desirable. **3.** favourite. *–adv. (superlative of* **well) 4.** most excellently or suitably; with most advantage or success. **5.** in or to the highest degree; most fully. *–n.* **6.** the best thing, state, or part. **7.** utmost or best quality. *–v.t.* **8.** to defeat; beat. **9.** to outdo; surpass.

bestial /'bɛstiəl/ *adj.* **1.** of or belonging to a beast. **2.** brutal; inhuman; irrational.

bestiality /bɛsti'æləti/ *n.* sexual relations of a human with an animal.

best man *n.* the chief attendant of the bridegroom at a wedding.

bestow /bə'stoʊ, bi-/ *v.t.* to present as a gift; give; confer. **–bestowal,** *n.*

bet /bɛt/ *v.* (**bet** *or* **betted, betting)** *–v.t.* **1.** to pledge as a forfeit to another who makes a similar pledge in return, in support of an opinion; stake; wager. **2.** to predict (a certain outcome): *I bet it rains on the weekend. –v.i.* **3.** to lay a wager. **4.** to make a practice of betting. *–n.* **5.** a pledge of something to be forfeited, in case one is wrong, to another who has the opposite opinion.

betacarotene /bitə'kærətin/ *n.* a form of carotene found in fruit and vegetables, popularly believed to help prevent cancer and heart disease.

beta test /'bitə/ *n.* a final test of a newly developed product, especially a piece of computer software, prior to its official release, carried out in the environment for which it was designed and by users other than its creators.

betide /bə'taɪd, bi-/ *v.t. Archaic* to happen; befall; come to.

betray /bə'treɪ, bi-/ *v.t.* **1.** to deliver or expose to an enemy by treachery or disloyalty. **2.** to be unfaithful in keeping or upholding. **3.** to reveal or disclose in violation of confidence. **4.** to show; exhibit. **5.** to deceive; mislead. **–betrayal,** *n.*

betrothed /bə'troʊðd, bi-/ *adj.* **1.** engaged to be married. *–n.* **2.** an engaged person.

better /'bɛtə/ *adj. (comparative of* **good) 1.** of superior quality or excellence. **2.** of superior value, use, fitness, desirability, acceptability, etc. **3.** larger; greater. *–adv. (comparative of* **well) 4.** in a more excellent way or manner. **5.** to a superior degree. *–v.t.* **6.** to make better; improve; increase the good qualities of. *–n.* **7.** that which has superior excellence, etc. **8.** (*usu. pl.*) one's superior in wisdom, wealth, etc. *–phr.* **9. better off**, in better circumstances. **10. had better**, would be wiser, safer, etc., to.

bettong /'bɛtɒŋ/ *n.* any of various small nocturnal marsupials which resemble a small wallaby with brown-grey fur above and white below.

between /bə'twin, bi-/ *prep.* **1.** in the space separating (two or more points, objects, etc.). **2.** intermediate to, in time, quantity, or degree. **3.** connecting. **4.** distinguishing one thing from another. *–adv.* **5.** in the intervening space or time; in an intermediate position or relation.

bevel /'bɛvəl/ *n.* the inclination that one line or surface makes with another when not at right angles.

beverage /'bɛvrɪdʒ, 'bɛvərɪdʒ/ *n.* a drink of any kind.

bevy /'bɛvi/ *n.* (*pl.* **-vies)** a flock.

beware /bə'wɛə, bi-/ *v.i.* **1.** (fol. by *of* or a clause) to be wary, cautious, or careful. *–v.t.* **2.** *Archaic* be wary of.

bewilder /bə'wɪldə, bi-/ *v.t.* to confuse or puzzle completely; perplex.

bewitch /bə'wɪtʃ, bi-/ *v.t.* to affect by witchcraft or magic; put a spell on.

beyond /bi'jɒnd/ *prep.* **1.** on or to the farther side of. **2.** farther on than; more distant than. **3.** outside the understanding, limits, or reach of; past. **4.** more than; in excess of; over and above. *–adv.* **5.** farther on or away.

bi- a prefix meaning 'twice, doubly, two', as in *bilateral, binocular, biweekly.* Also, **bin-.**

biannual /baɪ'ænjuəl/ *adj.* occurring twice a year.

bias /'baɪəs/ *n.* **1.** an oblique or diagonal line of direction, especially across a woven fabric. **2.** a particular tendency or inclination, especially one which prevents unprejudiced consideration of a question. *–v.t.* (**biased, biasing) 3.** to influence, usually unfairly; prejudice; warp.

biased /'baɪəst/ *adj.* having or showing an opinion based on personal prejudice.

bib /bɪb/ *n.* an article of clothing worn under the chin by a child, especially while eating, to protect the clothes.

bible /'baɪbəl/ *n.* any book accepted as an authority or essential text on a subject: *the home renovator's bible.*

biblio- a word element meaning 'book'.

bibliography /bɪbli'ɒgrəfi/ *n.* (*pl.* **-phies) 1.** a complete or selective list of literature on a particular subject. **2.** a list of works by a given author. **3.** a list of source materials used or consulted in the preparation of a work. **–bibliographical,** *adj.*

bicameral /baɪ'kæmərəl/ *adj.* having two branches, chambers, or houses, as a legislative body. Compare **unicameral.**

bicentenary /baɪsən'tinari, -'tɛnəri/ *n.* a 200th anniversary.

bicentennial /baɪsən'tɛniəl/ *adj.* **1.** consisting of or lasting 200 years. **2.** recurring every 200 years.

biceps /'baɪsɛps, -sɛps/ *n.* a muscle having two heads or origins, especially the muscle on the front of the upper arm, which bends the forearm.

bicker /'bɪkə/ *v.i.* to engage in petulant argument; wrangle.

bicuspid /baɪ'kʌspəd/ *n.* one of eight teeth in humans, each having two cusps.

bicycle /'baɪsɪkəl/ *n.* a vehicle with two wheels, one in front of the other, and having a saddle-like seat for the rider.

bid /bɪd/ *v.t.* (**bade** /bæd/, **bad** /bæd/ *for defs 1 and 2, or* **bid,** *for defs 3 and 4;* **bidden** *or* **bid; bidding)** **1.** to command; order; direct. **2.** to say as a greeting or benediction. **3.** *Commerce* to offer, as a price at an auction or as terms in a competition to secure a contract. **4.** *Cards* to enter a bid of a given quantity or suit; call: *to bid two no-trumps.* –*n.* **5.** the act of someone who bids. **6.** an offer, as at an auction. **7.** an attempt to attain some goal or purpose.

biddy /'bɪdi/ *n.* (*pl.* **-dies**) *Colloq.* an old woman.

bide /baɪd/ *phr.* (**bided, biding**) **bide one's time,** to wait for a favourable opportunity.

bidet /'bideɪ/ *n.* a small low bath, straddled by the user, for washing the genitals.

biennial /baɪ'ɛniəl/ *adj.* happening every two years.

bier /bɪə/ *n.* a frame or stand on which a corpse, or the coffin containing it, is laid before burial.

bifocal /baɪ'foʊkəl/ *adj.* **1.** *Chiefly Optics* having two foci. **2.** (of spectacle lenses) having two portions, one for near and the other for far vision.

bifocals /baɪ'foʊkəlz/ *pl. n.* spectacles with bifocal lenses.

bi-fold /'baɪ-foʊld/ *adj.* of or relating to narrow doors which are hinged together and open by folding sideways. Also, **bifold.**

big /bɪg/ *adj. n.* (**bigger, biggest**) **1.** large in size, height, width, amount, etc. **2.** large in compass or conception; magnanimous; generous; liberal.

bigamy /'bɪgəmi/ *n.* the offence of purporting to marry while already legally married to another. –**bigamist,** *n.* –**bigamous,** *adj.*

bight /baɪt/ *n.* **1.** the loop or bent part of a rope, as distinguished from the ends. **2.** a bend or curve in the shore of a sea or a river.

bigot /'bɪgət/ *n.* a person who is intolerantly convinced of the rightness of a particular creed, opinion, practice, etc.

big time *n.* **the,** *Colloq.* the top level, especially in business or society.

big-time /'bɪg-taɪm/ *Colloq.* –*adj.* **1.** at the top level in any business or pursuit. –*adv.* **2.** (used after the verb) wholly; completely: *she loves you big-time.*

big top *n.* **1.** the main tent in a circus. **2.** the circus.

bigwig /'bɪgwɪg/ *n. Colloq.* a very important person.

bike /baɪk/ *n.* a bicycle, tricycle, or motorcycle.

bikini /bə'kini/ *n.* a very brief, two-piece swimming costume.

bilateral /baɪ'lætrəl/ *adj.* **1.** relating to, involving, or affecting two sides or parties. **2.** *Law, etc.* (of a contract) binding the parties to reciprocal obligations.

bilby /'bɪlbi/ *n.* (*pl.* **bilbies**) a small bandicoot with big rabbit-like ears.

bile /baɪl/ *n.* **1.** a bitter yellow or greenish liquid secreted by the liver and helping in digestion. **2.** ill nature; peevishness.

bilge /bɪldʒ/ *n. Naut.* **1.** the lowest portion of a ship's interior. **2.** foul water that collects there.

bilingual /baɪ'lɪŋgwəl/ *adj.* able to speak two languages with approximately equal facility.

bilious /'bɪljəs/ *adj.* **1.** *Physiol.* relating to bile or to an excess secretion of bile. **2.** peevish; testy; cross. **3.** sick; nauseated. **4.** sickly; nauseating.

-bility a suffix forming nouns from adjectives in *-ble*, as in *nobility.*

bill¹ /bɪl/ *n.* **1.** an account of money owed for goods or services supplied. **2.** a slip or ticket showing the amount owed for goods consumed or purchased, especially in a restaurant. **3.** *Govt* a form or draft of a proposed statute presented to a legislature, but not yet enacted or passed and made law. **4.** a written or printed public notice or advertisement. **5.** a bill of exchange. **6.** program; entertainment. –*v.t.* **7.** to announce by bill or public notice. **8.** to schedule as part of a program. **9.** to render an account of money owed.

bill² /bɪl/ *n.* that part of the jaws of a bird covered with a horny sheath; a beak.

billabong /'bɪləbɒŋ/ *n.* a waterhole, originally part of a river, formed when the channel connecting it to the river dries up.

billboard /'bɪlbɔd/ *n.* → **hoarding** (def. 2).

billet /'bɪlət/ *n.* **1.** lodging for a soldier, especially lodging in private or non-military public buildings. **2.** private, usually unpaid, temporary lodgings arranged for members of a group or team.

billiards /'bɪljədz/ *n.* a game played by two or more persons on a rectangular table, with balls driven by means of cues.

billing /'bɪlɪŋ/ *n.* **1.** the relative position in which a performer or act is listed on handbills, posters, etc. **2.** the total business of an advertising agency during a given period.

billion /'bɪljən/ *n.* (*pl.* **-lions,** *as after a numeral,* **-lion**) **1.** a cardinal number, a thousand times a million, or 10⁹. **2.** *Obsolesc.* a million times a million, or 10¹². –*adj.* **3.** amounting to one billion in number. –**billionth,** *adj., n.*

billionaire /bɪljə'nɛə/ *n.* the owner of a billion dollars, pounds, euros, etc.

bill of exchange *n.* a written authorisation or order to pay a specified sum of money to a specified person.

bill of lading *n.* a document recording particulars of a contract for the carriage of goods by sea, serving also as a document of title to the goods.

bill of sale *n.* a document transferring title in personal property from one person to another, either temporarily as security against a loan or debt (**conditional bill of sale**), or permanently (**absolute bill of sale**).

billow /'bɪloʊ/ *n.* **1.** a great wave or surge of the sea. –*v.i.* **2.** to rise or roll in or like billows; surge.

billposter /'bɪlpoʊstə/ *n.* someone who pastes up bills and advertisements.

billy /'bɪli/ *n.* (*pl.* **-lies**) a cylindrical container for liquids, sometimes enamelled, usually having a close-fitting lid.

billycart /'bɪlikat/ *n.* a small four-wheeled cart.

billy goat *n.* a male goat.

bimbo /'bɪmboʊ/ *n. Colloq.* an attractive but unintelligent young woman.

bimensal /baɪ'mɛnsəl/ *adj.* occurring once in two months; bimonthly.

bimonthly /baɪ'mʌnθli/ *adj., adv.* **1.** every two months. **2.** twice a month.

bin /bɪn/ *n.* **1.** a box or enclosed space used for storing grain, wool as it is shorn, coal, refuse, etc. **2.** a container for rubbish or waste material. **3.** a partitioned stand used by a winemaker for storing wine in bottles. *–v.t.* (**binned, binning**) **4.** to throw into a rubbish bin: *you should bin stale food.*

binary /'baɪnəri/ *adj.* **1.** consisting of, indicating, or involving two. **2.** using, involving, or expressed in the binary number system. **3.** *Maths* having two variables.

binary code *n.* any means of representing information by a sequence of the digits 1 and 0.

binary digit *n.* a single digit in a binary number.

binary number system *n.* a number system which uses only the digits 1 and 0, based on the rules $1+0=1$, $1+1=10$. Also, **binary system**.

bind /baɪnd/ *v.* (**bound, binding**) *–v.t.* **1.** to make fast with a band or bond. **2.** (oft. fol. by *up*) to wrap a bandage around. **3.** to unite by any legal or moral tie. **4.** to hold to a particular state, place, employment, etc. **5.** (*usu. passive*) to place under obligation or compulsion. **6.** *Law* (fol. by *over*) to put under legal obligation. **7.** (oft. fol. by *out*) to indenture as an apprentice. **8.** to fasten or secure within a cover, as a book. *–v.i.* **9.** to become compact or solid; cohere. **10.** to have power to oblige. *–n.* **11.** something that binds. **12.** something regarded as a nuisance or inconvenience. **–binder**, *n.*

bindi-eye /'bɪndi-aɪ/ *n.* any of a number of plants with small, burr-like fruits. Also, **bindi, bindy-eye, bindy.**

binge /bɪndʒ/ *n.* **1.** a spree; a period of excessive indulgence, as in eating or drinking. *–v.i.* (**binged, binging**) **2.** to engage in such a binge.

binge drinking *n.* a pattern of alcohol consumption in which a person punctuates periods of total abstinence with sessions in which alcohol is consumed to the point of intoxication. **–binge drinker**, *n.*

bingo /'bɪŋgoʊ/ *n.* a gambling game in which players put markers on a card of numbered squares according to the numbers drawn and announced by a caller.

binocular /bə'nɒkjələ/ *adj.* **1.** involving (the use of) two eyes. *–n.* **2.** (*pl.*) a double telescope used by both eyes at once; field-glasses.

binomial /baɪ'noumiəl/ *n. Maths* an expression which is a sum or difference of two terms, as $3x + 2y$ and $x^2 - 4x$.

bio- a word element meaning 'life', 'living things'.

bioaccumulate /baɪoʊə'kjumjəleɪt/ *v.i.* (of a substance, especially a toxin) to remain within an organism, increasing in concentration with repeated doses, as mercury, PCBs, some pesticides, etc. **–bioaccumulation**, *n.*

bioavailable /baɪoʊə'veɪləbəl/ *adj. Pharmacology* of or relating to that portion of a medication which is taken up by the body when not administered intravenously. **–bioavailability**, *n.*

biochar /'baɪoʊtʃɑ/ *n.* charcoal produced from the imperfect burning of biomass; able to store carbon dioxide and fertilise the soil.

biochemistry /baɪoʊ'kɛməstri/ *n.* the branch of chemistry concerned with living matter. **–biochemical**, *adj.* **–biochemist**, *n.*

biodegradable /,baɪoʊdə'greɪdəbəl/ *adj.* capable of being decomposed by the action of living organisms, especially of bacteria.

biodiesel /'baɪoʊdizəl/ *n.* a biodegradable fuel, being a methyl ester produced from field crop oils, especially from recycled cooking oil. Compare **petrodiesel**.

biodiversity /baɪoʊdaɪ'vɜsəti/ *n.* variety in the types of organisms living within an area. **–biodiverse**, *adj.*

biodynamic /baɪoʊdaɪ'næmɪk/ *adj.* of or relating to agricultural or horticultural techniques and management which aim to improve the soil and vegetation without chemical fertilisers and in a way that is environmentally sound and sustainable.

bioenergy /'baɪoʊɛnədʒi/ *n.* the energy produced in the burning of biomass.

bioethanol /baɪoʊ'ɛθənɒl/ *n.* ethanol produced from the starch or sugar in various crops, such as corn, for use as a biofuel.

biofuel /'baɪoʊfjuəl/ *n.* a fuel derived from renewable sources such as biological matter.

biography /baɪ'ɒgrəfi/ *n.* (*pl.* **-phies**) a written account of a person's life. **–biographer**, *n.* **–biographical**, *adj.*

biohazard /'baɪoʊhæzəd/ *n.* a biological agent considered likely to cause human disease or environmental contamination. **–biohazardous**, *adj.*

biological clock *n.* a hypothetical mechanism controlling the timing of the development of an organism through the various stages of its life span.

biological warfare *n.* warfare which makes use of biologically produced poisons that affect humans, domestic animals, or food crops, especially bacteria or viruses.

biological weapon *n.* a weapon used in biological warfare.

biology /baɪ'ɒlədʒi/ *n.* the science of life or living matter in all its forms and phenomena, especially with reference to origin, growth, reproduction, structure, etc. **–biologist**, *n.* **–biological**, *adj.*

biomarker /'baɪoʊmɑkə/ *n. Med.* a molecule specifically associated with a particular disease, the detection of which provides an early indication of the onset and status of the disease.

biomass /'baɪoʊmæs/ *n.* organic matter used as a source of energy.

biome /'baɪoʊm/ *n.* a large community of plants and animals adapted to a particular climate or environment, as coral reef, tropical rainforest, etc.

bionic /baɪ'ɒnɪk/ *adj.* of or relating to body parts or functions replaced or improved by electronic equipment: *a bionic hand.*

biopsy /'baɪɒpsi/ *n.* (*pl.* **-sies**) *Med.* the excision and diagnostic study of a piece of tissue from a living body.

bioremediation /,baɪoʊrəmidi'eɪʃən/ *n.* a process that uses microorganisms, enzymes, fungi, green plants, etc., to decontaminate the environment.

biorhythms /'baɪoʊrɪðəmz/ *pl. n.* the three internal cycles, the physiological, emotional, and intellectual, that theoretically affect our well-being.

biosecurity /ˌbaɪoʊsə'kjʊərəti/ n. **1.** security measures against the transmission of disease to the plants or animals of a particular region. **2.** security measures taken against bioterrorism.

-biosis a word element meaning 'way of life'.

biosphere /'baɪəsfɪə/ n. the part of the earth where living organisms are to be found.

biotech /'baɪoʊtɛk/ n. **1.** biotechnology. –adj. **2.** of or relating to biotechnology.

biotechnology /ˌbaɪoʊtɛk'nɒlədʒi/ n. the use of micro-organisms to produce desirable products (as drugs) and services (as waste recycling). –**biotechnological**, adj. –**biotechnologically**, adv. –**biotechnologist**, n.

bioterrorism /ˌbaɪoʊ'tɛrərɪzəm/ n. terrorism involving the use of biological agents such as bacteria, viruses, etc., that affect humans, domestic animals or food crops. –**bioterrorist**, n.

biotic /baɪ'ɒtɪk/ adj. relating to life, especially to the animal and plant life of a region or period. Also, **biotical**.

bioweapon /ˌbaɪoʊ'wɛpn/ n. a weapon which uses a living organism or a toxin produced by it to cause the death of humans or the destruction of crops.

bip /bɪp/ n. **1.** a small sharp noise, usually emitted by an electronic device as a signal that its functioning has terminated or reached some significant stage. –v.i. (**bipped, bipping**) **2.** to emit such a noise.

bipartisan /baɪ'pɑːtəzən, -zæn/ adj. representing, supported, or characterised by two parties, especially political parties.

bipartite /baɪ'pɑːtaɪt/ adj. Law being in two corresponding parts.

bipolar disorder /baɪ'poʊlə/ n. a mental disorder marked by alternating periods of excitation and depression; manic depression. Also, **bipolar affective disorder**, **bipolar mood disorder**.

birch /bɜːtʃ/ n. a tree or shrub with a smooth, outer bark and close-grained wood.

bird /bɜːd/ n. **1.** any of the class of warm-blooded vertebrates having a body more or less completely covered with feathers, and the forelimbs so modified as to form wings by means of which most species fly. **2.** Colloq. a girl; a girlfriend.

bird flu n. → **avian influenza**.

birdie /'bɜːdi/ n. Golf a score of one stroke under par on a hole.

bird of paradise n. **1.** a bird of Australia and New Guinea, noted for its magnificent plumage. **2.** a perennial plant with showy purple and orange flowers.

bird of prey n. any flesh-eating bird such as the eagle, hawk, vulture, owl, etc., usually with a strong beak and claws for catching, killing or eating animals or other birds.

bird's-eye /'bɜːdz-aɪ/ adj. seen from above.

biro /'baɪroʊ/ n. (from trademark) a ballpoint pen.

birth /bɜːθ/ n. **1.** the fact of being born. **2.** the act of bearing or bringing forth. **3.** lineage; extraction; descent. **4.** supposedly natural heritage. **5.** any coming into existence; origin.

birth certificate n. a certificate issued by a registrar upon the birth of each person, recording sex and parentage.

birth control n. the regulation of birth through the deliberate control or prevention of conception.

birthday /'bɜːθdeɪ/ n. **1.** the day of one's birth. **2.** the anniversary of one's birth or the origin of something.

birthmark /'bɜːθmɑːk/ n. a congenital mark on the body.

birthplace /'bɜːθpleɪs/ n. place of birth or origin.

birthright /'bɜːθraɪt/ n. any right or privilege to which a person is entitled by birth.

birthstone /'bɜːθstoʊn/ n. a precious stone associated with a person's month of birth and worn as a lucky charm.

biscuit /'bɪskət/ n. a mixture of flour, liquid, shortening, etc., baked in small pieces.

bisect /baɪ'sɛkt/ v.t. to cut or divide into two parts.

bisexual /baɪ'sɛkʃuəl/ adj. **1.** of both sexes. –n. **2.** a person sexually attracted to either sex.

bishop /'bɪʃəp/ n. **1.** a member of the clergy consecrated for the spiritual direction of a diocese. **2.** a chess piece.

bison /'baɪsən/ n. (pl. **bison**) Zool. a large North American bovine ruminant.

bisque /bɪsk/ n. **1.** any smooth, creamy soup. **2.** a thick soup made of shellfish or game stewed long and slowly. Also, **bisk**.

bistro /'bɪstroʊ/ n. (pl. **-tros**) **1.** a wine bar. **2.** a small restaurant.

bit¹ /bɪt/ n. **1.** the metal mouthpiece of a bridle, with the adjacent parts to which the reins are fastened. **2.** anything that curbs or restrains. **3.** Machinery the cutting or penetrating part of various tools.

bit² /bɪt/ n. **1.** a small piece or quantity of anything. **2.** share or part of a duty, task, etc.

bit³ /bɪt/ n. a single, basic unit of information stored by a computer, being the smallest possible unit, and having one of only two possible values, 0 or 1.

bit⁴ /bɪt/ v. past tense of **bite**.

bitch /bɪtʃ/ n. **1.** a female dog. **2.** Colloq. (taboo) a woman, especially a disagreeable or malicious one. **3.** Colloq. a complaint. **4.** Colloq. something which is giving rise to difficulties and dissatisfaction. –v.i. **5.** Colloq. to complain. –**bitchy**, adj.

bite /baɪt/ v. (**bit, bitten** or **bit, biting**) –v.t. **1.** to cut into or wound, or cut (off, out, etc.) with the teeth. **2.** to sting, as an insect. **3.** Colloq. to trouble; worry; disturb. **4.** to cheat; deceive. –v.i. **5.** to press the teeth (into, on, etc.); snap. **6.** Angling (of fish) to take the bait. **7.** to accept a deceptive offer or suggestion. –n. **8.** the act of biting. **9.** a wound made by biting. **10.** Dentistry the angle at which the upper and lower teeth meet. **11.** pungency; sharpness.

bitmap /'bɪtmæp/ n. a computer graphics image consisting of rows and columns of dots stored as bits. –**bitmapped**, adj. –**bitmapping**, n.

bitter /'bɪtə/ adj. **1.** having a harsh, disagreeable taste, like that of quinine. **2.** hard to bear; grievous; distressful. **3.** characterised by intense animosity.

bittersweet /bɪtə'swiːt/ adj. **1.** both bitter and sweet to the taste. **2.** both pleasant and painful.

bitumen /'bɪtʃəmən/ n. **1.** any of various natural substances, as asphalt, etc., consisting mainly of hydrocarbons, and used in surfacing roads, roofing, etc. –*phr.* **2. the bitumen,** a tarred or sealed road.

bitzer /'bɪtsə/ *n. Colloq.* a dog, etc., of mixed breed; mongrel. Also, **bitser.**

bivalve /'baɪvælv/ *n.* a mollusc having two shells hinged together.

bivouac /'bɪvɑwæk/ *n.* a temporary camp, especially a military one, made out in the open with little or no equipment.

biweekly /baɪ'wikli/ *adj., adv.* **1.** every two weeks. **2.** twice a week.

bizarre /bə'za/ *adj.* singular in appearance, style, or general character; whimsically strange; odd.

blab /blæb/ *v.t.* (**blabbed, blabbing**) to reveal indiscreetly and thoughtlessly.

black /blæk/ *adj.* **1.** without brightness or colour; absorbing all or nearly all the rays emitted by a light source. **2.** relating or belonging to an ethnic group characterised by dark skin pigmentation. **3.** soiled or stained with dirt. **4.** gloomy; dismal. **5.** indicating censure, disgrace, or liability to punishment. **6.** illicit. **7.** prohibited or banned by a trade union. –*n.* **8.** a colour without hue at one extreme end of the scale of greys, opposite to white. A black surface absorbs light of all hues equally. **9.** (*sometimes upper case*) a person belonging to an ethnic group characterised by dark skin pigmentation. –*v.t.* **10.** to make black; put black on. **11.** (of a trade union) to ban or prevent normal industrial working in (a factory, industry, or the like.). –*v.i.* **12.** to become black; take on a black colour. –*phr.* **13. black out, a.** to obscure by concealing all light in defence against air raids. **b.** to lose consciousness. **14. in the black,** financially solvent.

black armband *n.* **1.** a band of black material worn around one's left sleeve or upper arm as a sign of mourning. –*adj.* Also, **black-armband. 2.** (*derog.*) of or relating to an interpretation of Australian history highlighting past injustices and wrongs, especially those committed against Indigenous Australians: *a black armband view of history.* Compare **white blindfold.**

blackball /'blækbɔl/ *v.t.* **1.** to ostracise. **2.** to vote against.

black ban *n.* a refusal by a group, as of producers, trade unions, consumers, etc., to supply or purchase goods or services, in an attempt to force a particular change or action. –**black-ban,** *v.*

blackberry /'blækbəri, -bri/ *n.* (*pl.* **-ries**) a black or very dark purple fruit.

blackbird /'blækbɜd/ *n.* a European songbird of the thrush family, introduced into Australia.

blackboard /'blækbɔd/ *n.* a smooth dark board, used in schools, etc., for writing or drawing on with chalk.

black box *n.* → **flight recorder.**

blackcurrant /blæk'kʌrənt/ *n.* **1.** a small, black edible fruit. **2.** the shrub itself.

black economy *n.* the part of a country's economy in which payment for goods and services is made in cash without receipts, usually as a means of tax evasion. Also, **cash economy.**

black eye *n.* bruising round the eye, resulting from a blow, etc.

blackguard /'blægad/ *n.* a coarse, despicable person; a scoundrel.

blackhead /'blækhɛd/ *n.* a small, black-tipped, fatty mass in a follicle, especially of the face.

black hole *n.* a region postulated as arising from the collapse of a star under its own gravitational forces and from which no radiation or matter can escape.

black ice *n.* a thin, barely visible coating of newly formed ice, as on a road, etc.

blackleg /'blækleg/ *n.* **1.** → **scab** (def. 2). **2.** a swindler especially in racing or gambling.

black light *n.* ultraviolet light.

blacklist /'blæklɪst/ *n.* Also, **black list. 1.** a list of persons under suspicion, disfavour, censure, etc., or a list of fraudulent or unreliable customers or firms. –*v.t.* Also, **black-list. 2.** to put on a blacklist. –**blacklisted,** *adj.*

black magic *n.* magic used for evil purposes.

blackmail /'blækmeɪl/ *n.* **1.** *Law* **a.** any payment extorted by intimidation, as by threats of injurious revelations or accusations. **b.** the extortion of such payment. –*v.t.* **2.** to extort blackmail from.

black maria /mə'raɪə/ *n. Colloq.* a closed police vehicle used for conveying prisoners to and from jail. Also, **Black Maria.**

black market *n.* an illegal market violating price controls, rationing, etc.

blackout /'blækaʊt/ *n.* **1.** the extinguishing of all visible lights in a city, etc., as a wartime protection. **2.** the extinguishing or failure of light as in a power failure. **3.** temporary loss of consciousness or vision, especially in aviation due to high acceleration.

black pepper *n.* a hot, sharp condiment prepared from the dried berries of a tropical vine.

black pudding *n.* a dark sausage made from pig's blood, finely minced pork fat, herbs and other ingredients.

black sheep *n.* a person regarded as a disappointment or failure in comparison to the other members of their family or group.

blacksmith /'blæksmɪθ/ *n.* **1.** a person who makes horseshoes and shoes horses. **2.** someone who works in or with iron or, in the modern era, steel.

black spot *n.* any of various fungal infections causing black spots on plant foliage.

blackspot /'blækspɒt/ *n.* any dangerous or difficult place where accidents frequently occur, especially on a road.

black swan *n.* a large, stately swimming bird, with black plumage and a red bill.

black tie *n.* a formal style of evening dress for men, with a dinner suit and, usually, a black bow tie.

blackwater /'blækwɔtə/ *n.* **1.** water in rivers, waterholes, etc., which is dark-coloured. **2.** underground water as in underground lakes or rivers. **3.** raw sewage (opposed to *greywater*).

bladder /'blædə/ *n.* **1.** *Anat., Zool.* a pelvic sac with membranous and muscular walls, for storage and expulsion of urine excreted by the kidneys. **2.** any similar sac or receptacle, as the inflatable inner bag of a football.

blade /bleɪd/ *n.* **1.** the flat cutting part of a sword, knife, etc. **2.** a sword. **3.** the leaf of a plant, especially of a grass or cereal. **4.** a thin, flat part of something, as of a bone, an oar, a propeller, a bat, etc. **5.** a dashing, swaggering, or rakish young fellow. **6.** a blade-shaped prosthetic leg, adapted for running.

blame /bleɪm/ *v.t.* **1.** to lay the responsibility of (a fault, error, etc.) on a person. *–n.* **2.** imputation of fault; censure. **3.** responsibility for a fault, error, etc. *–phr.* **4. to blame**, responsible for a fault or error; blamable; culpable.

blanch /blænʃ, blanʃ/ *v.i.* to become white; turn pale.

blancmange /blə'mɒnʒ, -'mɒndʒ/ *n.* a jelly-like preparation of milk thickened with cornflour, gelatine, or the like, and flavoured.

bland /blænd/ *adj.* **1.** (of a person's manner) suave; deliberately agreeable or pleasant but often without real feeling. **2.** soothing or balmy, as air. **3.** mild, as food or medicines.

blandish /'blændɪʃ/ *v.t.* to treat flatteringly; coax; cajole.

blank /blæŋk/ *adj.* **1.** (of paper, etc.) free from marks; not written or printed on. **2.** not filled in. **3.** unrelieved or unbroken by ornament or opening. **4.** lacking some usual or completing feature; empty. **5.** complete, utter, or unmitigated. *–n.* **6.** a place where something is lacking. **7.** a void; emptiness. **8.** a space left (to be filled in) in written or printed matter. **9.** *Machinery* a piece of metal prepared to be stamped or cut into a finished object, such as a coin or key. *–phr.* **10. draw a blank, a.** to draw from a lottery an unmarked counter, one not associated with any prize. **b.** to be unsuccessful, especially when looking for someone or something, or trying to find out about something. **11. in blank**, (of a document) with spaces left to be filled in.

blank cheque *n.* a cheque bearing a signature but no stated amount.

blanket /'blæŋkət/ *n.* **1.** a large rectangular piece of soft, loosely woven fabric, usually wool, used especially as a bed covering. **2.** any heavy concealing layer or covering. *–adj.* **3.** covering or intended to cover a group or class of things, conditions, etc.

blare /blɛə/ *v.i.* to emit a loud raucous sound.

blasé /bla'zeɪ, 'blazeɪ/ *adj.* indifferent to and bored by pleasures of life.

blaspheme /blæs'fim/ *v.* (-**phemed, -pheming**) *–v.t.* **1.** to speak irreverently of (God or sacred things). *–v.i.* **2.** to utter irreverent words. –**blasphemy**, *n.* –**blasphemous**, *adj.*

blast /blast/ *n.* **1.** a sudden blowing or gust of wind. **2.** the blowing of a trumpet, whistle, etc. **3.** a forcible stream of air from the mouth, from bellows, or the like. **4.** the act of exploding; explosion. **5.** severe criticism. *–v.t.* **6.** to blow (a trumpet, etc.). **7.** to affect with any pernicious influence; ruin; destroy. **8.** to tear (rock, etc.) to pieces with an explosive. **9.** to criticise (someone) abusively. *–interj.* **10.** an exclamation of anger or irritation.

-blast a combining form meaning 'embryo', 'sprout', 'germ'.

blast furnace *n.* a vertical, steel cylindrical furnace using a forced blast to produce molten iron for conversion into steel, etc.

blatant /'bleɪtnt/ *adj.* (of actions, etc.) flagrantly obvious or undisguised.

blaze¹ /bleɪz/ *n.* **1.** a bright flame or fire. **2.** a sudden, intense outburst, as of fire, passion, fury. *–v.i.* **3.** to burn brightly.

blaze² /bleɪz/ *n.* **1.** a spot or mark made on a tree, as by removing a piece of the bark, to indicate a boundary or a path in a forest. **2.** a white spot on the face of a horse, cow, etc.

blazer /'bleɪzə/ *n.* a jacket.

blazon /'bleɪzən/ *v.t.* to set forth conspicuously or publicly; display; proclaim.

-ble variant of **-able**, as in *noble*.

bleach /blitʃ/ *v.t.* **1.** to make white, pale, or colourless. *–n.* **2.** a bleaching agent.

bleak /blik/ *adj.* **1.** bare, desolate, and windswept. **2.** cold and piercing.

bleary /'blɪəri/ *adj.* (-**rier, -riest**) (of the eyes) dim from a watery discharge, or from tiredness.

bleat /blit/ *v.i.* **1.** to cry as a sheep, goat, or calf. **2.** to complain; moan.

bleed /blid/ *v.* (**bled** /blɛd/, **bleeding**) *–v.i.* **1.** to lose blood, from the body or internally from the vascular system. **2.** to exude sap, juice, etc. *–v.t.* **3.** to cause to lose blood, especially surgically. **4.** *Colloq.* to obtain, as in excessive amount, or extort money from. *–n.* **5.** a bleeding from part of the body.

blemish /'blemɪʃ/ *v.t.* **1.** to destroy the perfection of. *–n.* **2.** a defect; a disfigurement; stain.

blench /blentʃ/ *v.i.* to shrink; flinch; quail.

blend /blend/ *v.t.* **1.** to mix smoothly and inseparably together. **2.** to mix (various sorts or grades) in order to obtain a particular kind or quality. *–n.* **3.** a mixture or kind produced by blending. –**blender**, *n.*

blended family *n.* a family formed from the members of separate families, usually as a result of the parents' remarriage.

bless /blɛs/ *v.t.* **1.** to consecrate by a religious rite; make or pronounce holy. **2.** to request of God the bestowal of divine favour on. **3.** to bestow good of any kind upon. –**blessed** /'blɛsəd, blɛst/, *adj.* –**blessing**, *n.*

blew /blu/ *n.* past tense of **blow²**.

blight /blaɪt/ *n.* **1.** any cause of destruction, ruin, or frustration. *–v.t.* **2.** to destroy; ruin; frustrate.

blind /blaɪnd/ *adj.* **1.** lacking the sense of sight. **2.** unwilling or unable to try to understand. **3.** lacking all awareness. **4.** having no outlets. **5.** made without knowledge in advance. *–v.t.* **6.** to make blind, as by injuring, dazzling, or covering the eyes. *–n.* **7.** something that obstructs vision or keeps out light. **8.** a shade for a window, as a strip of cloth on a roller, or a venetian blind. **9.** a cover for masking action or purpose; decoy. *–adv.* **10.** without being able to see one's way. **11.** without assessment or prior consideration.

blind-bake *v.t.* to bake (a pastry case) before it is filled.

blindfold /'blaɪndfoʊld/ *v.t.* to prevent sight by covering (the eyes); cover the eyes of.

blindside /'blaɪndsaɪd/ *v.t.* to catch unawares with an unforeseen decision or strategy.

blindsided /'blaɪndsaɪdəd/ *adj.* caught off guard.

bling /blɪŋ/ *n.* showy jewellery, especially when worn in large quantity.

blink /blɪŋk/ *v.i.* **1.** to wink, especially rapidly and repeatedly. –*n.* **2.** a glance or glimpse. –*phr.* **3. on the blink**, *Colloq.* not working properly.

blinker /'blɪŋkə/ *n.* **1.** a flashing indicator light on a car. **2.** either of two flaps on a bridle, to prevent a horse from seeing sideways or backwards.

bliss /blɪs/ *n.* **1.** lightness of heart; blitheness; gladness. **2.** supreme happiness or delight.

blister /'blɪstə/ *n.* **1.** a thin vesicle on the skin, containing watery matter or serum, as from a burn or other injury. **2.** any similar swelling, as an air bubble in a casting or a paint blister. –*v.i.* **3.** to rise in blisters; become blistered.

blithe /blaɪð/ *adj.* joyous or merry in disposition; cheerful.

blithering /'blɪðərɪŋ/ *adj.* nonsensical; jabbering.

blitz /blɪts/ *n.* **1.** *Mil.* war waged by surprise, swiftly and violently, as by the use of aircraft. **2.** *Colloq.* any swift, vigorous attack.

blizzard /'blɪzəd/ *n.* a violent windstorm with dry, driving snow and intense cold.

bloat /bloʊt/ *v.t.* **1.** to make distended, as with air, water, etc.; cause to swell. **2.** to puff up; make vain or conceited. –*v.i.* **3.** to become swollen; be puffed out or dilated.

bloated /'bloʊtəd/ *adj.* **1.** swollen: *bloated features.* **2.** suffering from flatulence. **3.** suffering from excessive size: *a bloated bureaucracy.*

blob /blɒb/ *n.* a small lump, drop or splotch.

bloc /blɒk/ *n.* a group of states or territories united by some common factor.

block /blɒk/ *n.* **1.** a solid mass of wood, stone, etc., usually with one or more plane or approximately plane faces. **2.** a mould or piece on which something is shaped or kept in shape, as a hat block. **3.** a piece of wood prepared for cutting, or as cut, for wood engraving. **4.** *Printing* a letter-press printing plate mounted on a base to make it type-high. **5.** *Mechanics* **a.** a device consisting of one or more grooved pulleys mounted in a casing or shell, to which a hook or the like is attached, used for transmitting power, changing direction of motion, etc. **b.** the casing or shell holding the pulley. **6.** a blocking or obstructing, or blocked or obstructed state or condition. **7.** *Computers* a set of data or instructions. **8. a.** a fairly large area of land, especially for settlement, mining, farming, etc. **b.** a section of land, frequently suburban, as for building a house, etc. **9.** one large building, divided into offices, apartments, etc.: *an office block, a block of flats.* **10.** a portion of a city, town, etc., enclosed by (usually four) neighbouring and intersecting streets. **11.** a large number of shares taken together, as on the stock exchange. **12.** a writing or sketching pad. –*v.t.* **13.** to fit with blocks; mount on a block. **14.** to shape or prepare on or with a block. **15.** (fol. by *out* or *in*) to sketch or outline roughly or in a general plan, without details. **16.** to obstruct

(a space, progress, etc.); check or hinder (a person, etc.) by placing obstacles in the way.

blockade /blɒ'keɪd/ *n.* any obstruction of passage or progress.

blockage /'blɒkɪdʒ/ *n.* an obstruction.

blockbuster /'blɒkbʌstə/ *n.* anything large and spectacular, as a lavish theatrical production.

block letter *n.* a plain capital letter. Also, **block capital**.

blockout /'blɒkaʊt/ *n.* (*from trademark*) → **sunscreen** (def. 2).

blog /blɒg/ *n.* **1.** a record of items of interest found on the internet, published as a website in edited form with comments and links. **2.** a personal diary published on the internet. –*v.i.* (**blogged**, **blogging**) **3.** to post entries on a blog. –**blogger**, *n.*

blogosphere /'blɒgəsfɪə/ *n.* blogs, viewed collectively, as creating a world which bloggers inhabit.

bloke /bloʊk/ *n. Colloq.* a man; fellow; guy. –**blokeish**, **blokish**, *adj.*

blokey /'bloʊki/ *adj. Colloq.* stereotypically masculine.

blond /blɒnd/ *adj.* **1.** (of a person or a people) having light-coloured hair and skin. **2.** light-coloured. –*n.* **3.** a blond person.

blonde /blɒnd/ *n.* **1.** a female with light-coloured hair. –*adj.* **2.** (of a female) having light-coloured hair and skin.

blood /blʌd/ *n.* **1.** the fluid that circulates in the arteries and veins or principal vascular system of animals, in humans being of a red colour and consisting of a pale yellow plasma containing semisolid corpuscles. **2.** physical and cultural extraction. **3.** descent from a common ancestor. –*phr.* **4. in cold blood**, calmly, coolly, and deliberately.

blood bank *n.* a place where blood is stored for later use.

bloodbath /'blʌdbɑθ/ *n.* a massacre.

blood count *n.* the count of the number of red or white blood cells in a specific volume of blood.

bloodcurdling /'blʌd,kɜdlɪŋ/ *adj.* frightening; terrifyingly horrible.

blood group *n.* one of several classifications into which the blood may be grouped according to its clotting reactions. Also, **blood type**.

bloodhound /'blʌdhaʊnd/ *n.* one of a breed of large, powerful dogs with a very acute sense of smell, used for tracking game, human fugitives, etc.

blood pressure *n.* the pressure of the blood against the inner walls of the blood vessels.

blood rule *n.* a ruling which exists in many sports that a person who is bleeding must leave the field of play immediately until such time as the blood flow is staunched.

bloodshed /'blʌdʃɛd/ *n.* destruction of life; slaughter.

bloodshot /'blʌdʃɒt/ *adj.* (of the eyes) red from dilated blood vessels.

bloodstream /'blʌdstrim/ *n.* the blood flowing through a circulatory system.

blood sugar *n.* glucose in the blood. Also, **blood glucose**.

bloodthirsty /'blʌdθɜsti/ *adj.* eager to shed blood; murderous.

blood type *n.* → **blood group**.

blood vessel *n.* any of the vessels (arteries, veins, capillaries) through which the blood circulates.

bloody /'blʌdi/ *adj.* (**-dier, -diest**) **1.** stained with blood. **2.** attended with bloodshed. **3.** *Colloq.* an intensifier signifying approval, as in *bloody beauty*, or disapproval, as in *bloody bastard*. **4.** *Colloq.* difficult; obstinate; cruel. *–v.t.* (**-died, -dying**) **5.** to stain with blood. *–adv.* **6.** *Colloq.* very; extremely.

bloom /blum/ *n.* **1.** the flower of a plant. **2.** a flourishing, healthy condition. **3.** a whitish, powdery surface coating or appearance. *–v.i.* **4.** to produce or yield blossoms. **5.** to flourish.

bloomers /'blumez/ *n.* **1.** loose trousers gathered at the knee, formerly worn by women for gymnastics, riding, or other active exercise. **2.** a woman's undergarment of similar design.

blossom /'blɒsəm/ *n.* **1.** *Bot.* the flower of a plant, especially of one producing an edible fruit. *–v.i.* **2.** to flourish; develop.

blot /blɒt/ *n.* **1.** a spot or stain, especially of ink on paper. *–v.* (**blotted, blotting**) *–v.t.* **2.** to spot, stain, or spatter. **3.** (fol. by *out*) to make indistinguishable. **4.** to dry with absorbent paper or the like. *–v.i.* **5.** (of ink, etc.) to spread in a stain. **6.** to become blotted or stained.

blotch /blɒtʃ/ *n.* a large irregular spot or blot.

blouse /blauz/ *n.* **1.** a light, loosely fitting bodice or shirt, especially one that is gathered or held in at the waist. *–v.i.* **2.** to hang loose and full.

blow[1] /blou/ *n.* **1.** a sudden stroke with hand, fist, or weapon. **2.** a sudden shock, or a calamity or reverse.

blow[2] /blou/ *v.* (**blew** /blu/, **blown, blowing**) *–v.i.* **1.** (of the wind or air) to be in motion. **2.** to produce or emit a current of air, as with the mouth, a bellows, etc. **3.** *Music* (of horn, trumpet, etc.) to give out sound. **4.** (oft. fol. by *out*) (of a fuse, gasket, light bulb, radio valve, tyre, etc.) to burn out or perish; become unusable. **5.** (fol. by *out*) to be extinguished, as by the wind. *–v.t.* **6.** to drive by means of a current of air. **7.** (fol. by *out*) to extinguish (a flame, etc.) with a puff of air. **8.** to shape (glass, etc.) with a current of air. **9.** to cause to sound, especially by a current of air. **10.** (fol. by *up, to bits,* etc.) to cause to explode. **11.** *Colloq.* to waste; squander. **12.** *Colloq.* to fail in. *–phr.* **13. blow up, a.** to explode. **b.** *Photography* to reproduce by enlargement. **c.** *Colloq.* to lose one's temper.

blow-dry *v.t.* (**-dried, -drying**) **1.** to style hair by brushing it into shape while drying it with a blow dryer. *–n.* (*pl.* **-dries**) **2.** an instance of blow-drying: *a wash and blow-dry.* Also, **blowdry**.

blow dryer *n.* a handheld machine which blows out warm air and is used to dry the hair. Also, **blow drier**.

blowfly /'bloflaɪ/ *n.* (*pl.* **-flies**) any of various flies which deposit their eggs or larvae on carcasses or meat, or in sores, wounds, etc.

blowhole /'blouhoul/ *n.* **1.** a nostril at the top of the head of a whale, dolphin, etc., through which they breathe. **2.** a hole in a coastal rock formation through which sea water is forced through.

blowlamp /'bloulæmp/ *n.* a small portable apparatus which gives a hot flame by forcing kerosene under pressure through a small nozzle and burning it in air.

blowout /'blouaut/ *n.* a rupture of a motor vehicle tyre. Also, **blow-out**.

blowtorch /'bloutɔtʃ/ *n.* a portable apparatus which gives an extremely hot flame.

blowzy /'blauzi/ *adj.* (**-zier, -ziest**) dishevelled; unkempt.

blubber /'blʌbə/ *n.* **1.** *Zool.* the fat found between the skin and muscle of whales and other cetaceans, from which oil is made. *–v.i.* **2.** to weep, usually noisily and with contorted face.

bludge /blʌdʒ/ *Colloq.* *–v.* (**bludged, bludging**) *–v.i.* **1.** to evade responsibilities. **2.** (fol. by *on*) to impose on others. *–v.t.* **3.** to cadge. *–n.* **4.** a job which entails next to no work. *–***bludger**, *n.*

bludgeon /'blʌdʒən/ *n.* **1.** a short, heavy club with one end loaded, or thicker and heavier than the other. *–v.t.* **2.** to strike or fell with a bludgeon. **3.** to force (someone) into something; bully.

blue /blu/ *n.* **1.** the pure hue of clear sky (between green and violet in the spectrum). **2.** *Colloq.* a fight; dispute. **3.** *Colloq.* a mistake. **4.** *Colloq.* a nickname for a red-headed person. *–adj.* (**bluer, bluest**) **5.** of the colour blue. **6.** depressed in spirits. **7.** obscene, or relating to obscenity.

blueberry /'blubəri/ *n.* (*pl.* **-ries**) a small bluish berry.

blue blood *n.* aristocratic descent.

bluebottle /'blubɒtl/ *n.* a coelenterate found in warm seas and having an elongated, deep blue, gas-filled bladder, from which trail numerous stinging tentacles.

blue chip *n.* **1.** *Stock Exchange* a stock in which investment is secure. **2.** a valuable asset.

blue-collar /'blu-kɒlə/ *adj.* belonging or relating to workers involved in some sort of manual labour, as distinct from clerical or professional workers.

bluegrass /'blugrɑs/ *n.* **1.** any of various grasses, as the Kentucky bluegrass, etc. **2.** music of the south-eastern US characterised by instruments such as steel-string acoustic guitar, bottleneck guitar, and fiddle, with emphasis on the solo banjo. Also, **blue grass**.

blue-green algae *pl. n.* a poisonous blue-green growth resembling algae occurring in stagnant fresh water in hot weather. See **cyanobacteria**.

blue heeler *n.* a purebred dog with black or red face and ears and dark blue body speckled with lighter blues, developed in Australia for work with cattle.

blueprint /'bluprint/ *n.* a process of photographic printing in which the prints are white on a blue ground.

blue-ribbon /'blu-ribən/ *adj.* **1.** (of an electorate) sure to be held by a particular party or candidate; safe; certain. **2.** of or relating to a prize-winner.

blue-ringed octopus *n.* a small octopus of eastern Australia, with a highly venomous bite and blue to purple bands on the tentacles appearing when the octopus is disturbed.

blues /bluz/ *pl. n.* **1.** *Colloq.* despondency; melancholy. **2.** a style of popular music, of African American origin, predominantly melancholy in character and usually performed in slow tempo.

blue screen /blu 'skrin/ *n.* a large blue background for a film or video shot which is then filled in with an image of the desired background.

blue-sky /'blu-skai/ *adj.* **1.** engaged in research that has no immediate practical application or moneymaking potential: *a blue-sky company.* **2.** fanciful; impractical. –*v.i.* (**-skied** *or* **-skyed**, **-skying**) **3.** to give an excessively optimistic view, especially of business prospects.

blue swimmer *n.* an edible Australian crab of blue-green colour and capable of powerful sustained swimming.

blue-tongue *n.* **1.** Also, **blue-tongue lizard.** any of several large, stout-bodied Australian skinks which are harmless but display their broad blue tongues in a threatening manner when disturbed. **2.** → **rouseabout**.

bluetooth /'blutuθ/ *adj.* of or relating to a wireless technology that provides connectivity between mobile phones, mobile computers, portable handheld devices and the internet.

bluff[1] /blʌf/ *adj.* **1.** somewhat abrupt and unconventional in manner; hearty; frank. –*n.* **2.** a cliff, headland, or hill with a broad, steep face.

bluff[2] /blʌf/ *v.t.* to mislead by presenting a bold front.

blunder /'blʌndə/ *n.* **1.** a gross or stupid mistake. –*v.i.* **2.** to move or act blindly, stupidly, or without direction or steady guidance.

blunt /blʌnt/ *adj.* **1.** having an obtuse, thick, or dull edge or tip; rounded; not sharp. **2.** abrupt in address or manner; forthright; plain-spoken.

blur /blɜ/ *v.* (**blurred**, **blurring**) –*v.t.* **1.** to obscure by making confused in form or outline; make indistinct. –*v.i.* **2.** to become indistinct. –*n.* **3.** a blurred condition; indistinctness.

blurb /blɜb/ *n.* an announcement or advertisement, usually an effusively laudatory one, especially on the jacket flap of a book or the cover of a record.

blurt /blɜt/ *v.t.* (usu. fol. by *out*) to utter suddenly or inadvertently; divulge unadvisedly.

blush /blʌʃ/ *v.i.* **1.** to redden as from embarrassment, shame, or modesty. –*n.* **2.** a rosy or pinkish tinge.

bluster /'blʌstə/ *v.i.* **1.** to roar and be tumultuous, as wind. –*n.* **2.** noisy, empty menaces or protests; inflated talk.

BMX *adj.* **1.** of or relating to the racing of small sturdily-built bicycles on circuits presenting a variety of surfaces and terrain. –*n.* **2.** a bicycle designed for such a use.

BO /bi 'oʊ/ *n. Colloq.* body odour, especially due to excessive perspiration.

boa /'boʊə/ *n.* (*pl.* **boas**) **1.** any of various non-venomous snakes notable for their vestiges of hind limbs, as the **boa constrictor** of the American tropics. **2.** a long, snake-shaped wrap of silk, feathers, or other material.

boab /'boʊæb/ *n.* a large tree with a very thick trunk, native to northern Australia and tropical Africa. Also, **baobab**.

boar /bɔ/ *n.* an uncastrated male pig.

board /bɔd/ *n.* **1.** a piece of timber sawn thin, and of considerable length and breadth compared with the thickness. **2.** daily meals, especially as provided for pay. **3.** an official body of persons who direct or supervise some activity, as a business. **4.** the border or edge of anything, as in *seaboard*. –*v.t.* **5.** to cover or close with boards. **6.** to go on board of or enter (a ship, train, etc.). –*v.i.* **7.** to take one's meals, or be supplied with food and lodging at a fixed price. –*phr.* **8. on board**, on or in a ship, aeroplane, or vehicle.

boarder /'bɔdə/ *n.* **1.** someone who pays for meals and a room to sleep in. **2.** a pupil who resides at a boarding school during term.

boardercross /'bɔdəkrɒs/ *n.* a winter-sports competition in which snowboarders race down a cross-country track, being required to go over banks, jumps and other obstacles. –**boardercrosser**, *n.*

boardies /'bɔdiz/ *pl. n. Colloq.* board shorts.

boardroom /'bɔdrum/ *n.* a room in which a board (def. 3) meets to carry out business.

board shorts *pl. n.* shorts with an extended leg, often made of quick-drying fabric, originally designed to protect surfers against waxed surfboards.

boast /boʊst/ *v.i.* **1.** to speak exaggeratedly and objectionably, especially about oneself. **2.** (fol. by *of*) to speak with pride. –*v.t.* **3.** to be proud in the possession of.

boat /boʊt/ *n.* a vessel for transport by water, constructed to provide buoyancy by excluding water and shaped to give stability and permit propulsion.

boater /'boʊtə/ *n.* a straw hat with a flat hard brim.

boat people *pl. n.* refugees who leave their own country and arrive in another country by sea, usually in small boats.

boatswain /'boʊsən/ *n.* a warrant officer on a warship, or a petty officer on a merchant vessel, in charge of rigging, anchors, cables, etc. Also, **bo's'n, bosun.**

bob[1] /bɒb/ *n.* **1.** a short jerky motion. **2.** a quick curtsy. –*v.i.* (**bobbed, bobbing**) **3.** to move up and down with a bouncing motion.

bob[2] /bɒb/ *n.* **1.** a style of short haircut. **2.** a small dangling object, as the weight on a pendulum or plumbline.

bobbin /'bɒbən/ *n.* a reel, cylinder, or spool upon which yarn or thread is wound, as used in spinning, machine sewing, etc.

bobble /'bɒbəl/ *n.* any small ball which dangles or bobs.

bobsleigh /'bɒbsleɪ/ *n.* a racing sledge with two sets of runners, one behind the other.

bocconcini /bɒkən'tʃini/ *n.* a soft white cheese which is about the shape and size of a golf ball.

bode /boʊd/ *v.t.* to be an omen of; portend.

bodice /'bɒdəs/ *n.* the fitted upper part of or body of a woman's dress.

bodkin /'bɒdkən/ *n.* a blunt needle-like instrument for drawing tape, cord, etc., through a loop, hem, or the like.

body /'bɒdi/ *n.* (*pl.* **-dies**) **1.** the physical structure of an animal (and sometimes, of a plant) living or dead. **2.** a corpse; carcass. **3.** the trunk or main mass of a thing. **4.** a number of things or people taken together. **5.** consistency or density; substance; strength as opposed to thinness. **6.** matter or physical substance (as opposed to *spirit* or *soul*). –**bodily**, *adj.*, *adv.*

body art *n.* the decorative modification of the body by piercing, tattooing, etc.

bodyboard /'bɒdibɔd/ *n.* a short surfboard, usually ridden lying down. –**bodyboarder**, *n.* –**bodyboarding**, *n.*

body corporate *n.* the governing body of a block of units (def. 3) consisting of the unit owners or their representatives.

bodyguard /'bɒdigad/ *n.* a personal or private guard, as for a high official.

body image *n.* the perception that a person has of their own body, particularly in relation to whether they see themselves as fat or thin, good-looking or not.

body language *n.* the non-linguistic communication of attitudes or feelings by movements or postures of the body, usually unintentional.

body mass index *n.* a measure of body mass that is calculated as weight divided by height squared; used to define nutritional status in relation to health risk. *Abbrev.:* BMI

body-search /'bɒdi-sɜtʃ/ *n.* a searching of the body, as at airports, seaports, etc., for concealed weapons or other forbidden matter.

body shop *n. Colloq.* an agency for computer programmers.

bodysurfing /'bɒdi,sɜfɪŋ/ *n.* the sport of swimming in the surf, and especially of riding waves, by holding the body stiff, usually with the arms outstretched, and allowing oneself to be carried along by the force of the water. Also, **surfing**. –**bodysurfer**, *n.*

bog /bɒg/ *n.* **1.** wet, spongy ground, with soil composed mainly of decayed vegetable matter. –*v.t.*, *v.i.* (**bogged**, **bogging**) **2.** (oft. fol. by *down*) to sink in or as in a bog.

bogan /'bɒugən/ *n. Colloq.* (*mildly derog.*) a person, generally from an outer suburb of a city or town and from a lower socio-economic background, viewed as uncultured.

bogey[1] /'bougi/ *Golf* –*n.* (*pl.* -**geys**) **1.** a score of one over par. –*v.t.* (-**geyed**, -**geying**) **2.** to score a bogey on (a certain hole).

bogey[2] /'bougi/ *n. Colloq.* **1.** a bath or shower; a wash. **2.** a swim. **3.** a swimming hole. Also, **bogie**.

bogeyman /'bougimæn, 'bugimæn, 'bugimæn/ *n.* (*pl.* -**men**) **1.** an evil spirit in the guise of a man. **2.** anything that is persistently frightening. Also, **bogyman**, **boogieman**.

boggle /'bɒgəl/ *v.i.* to take alarm; start with fright.

bogie[1] /'bougi/ *n.* a low truck or trolley.

bogie[2] /'bougi/ *n.* → **bogey**[2].

bog-standard /'bɒg-stændəd/ *adj.* ordinary or basic; run-of-the-mill.

bogus /'bougəs/ *adj.* counterfeit; spurious; sham.

bogy /'bougi/ *n.* (*pl.* -**gies**) **1.** a hobgoblin; evil spirit. **2.** anything that haunts, frightens or annoys one.

bohemian /bou'himiən/ *n.* **1.** a person with artistic or intellectual tendencies or pretensions who lives and acts without regard for conventional rules of behaviour. –*adj.* **2.** relating to or characteristic of bohemians.

boil[1] /bɔil/ *v.i.* **1.** to change from liquid to gaseous state, producing bubbles of gas that rise to the surface of the liquid, agitating it as they rise. **2.** to be agitated by angry feeling. **3.** *Colloq.* to feel very hot. –*v.t.* **4.** to cause to boil. **5.** to cook by boiling.

boil[2] /bɔil/ *n.* a painful, suppurating, inflammatory sore forming a central core.

boiler /'bɔilə/ *n.* **1.** a closed vessel together with its furnace, in which steam or other vapour is generated for heating or for driving engines. **2.** a vessel for boiling or heating, especially a copper one.

boisterous /'bɔistrəs/ *adj.* rough and noisy; clamorous; unrestrained.

bok choy /bɒk 'tʃɔi/ *n.* a vegetable with white stalks and dark green leaves. Also, **buk choy**.

bold /bould/ *adj.* **1.** not hesitating in the face of actual or possible danger or rebuff. **2.** not hesitating to breach the rules of propriety; forward. **3.** *Printing* (of type, etc.) with heavy lines.

bolero /bə'lɛərou, bə'liərou/ *n.* (*pl.* -**ros**) **1.** a lively Spanish dance. **2.** the music for it. **3.** a short jacket ending above or at the waistline.

bolognaise /bɒlə'neɪz/ *adj.* of or relating to a sauce for pasta, made with minced meat, onions, garlic, tomato paste and seasonings. Also, **bolognese**.

bolster /'boulstə/ *n.* **1.** a long ornamental pillow for a bed, sofa, etc. **2.** a support, as one for a bridge truss. –*v.t.* **3.** to support with or as with a pillow. **4.** (oft. fol. by *up*) to prop, support, or uphold (something weak, unworthy, etc.).

bolt /boult/ *n.* **1.** a movable bar which when slid into a socket fastens a door, gate, etc. **2.** a strong metal pin, often with a head at one end and with a screw thread at the other to receive a nut. **3.** a woven length of cloth. **4.** any sudden dash, run, flight, etc. –*v.t.* **5.** to fasten with or as with bolts. **6.** to swallow (one's food) hurriedly or without chewing. –*v.i.* **7.** to run away in alarm and uncontrollably, especially of horses and rabbits. –*adv.* **8.** suddenly; with sudden meeting or collision. –*phr.* **9. bolt upright**, stiffly upright.

bomb /bɒm/ *n.* **1.** a hollow projectile filled with an explosive charge. **2.** *Colloq.* an old car. **3.** *Colloq.* a failure, as in an examination. –*v.t.* **4.** to hurl bombs at; drop bombs upon, as from an aeroplane; bombard. **5.** to jump onto (someone) in water. **6.** to fail; perform badly at. –*v.i.* **7.** to explode a bomb or bombs. **8.** to hurl or drop bombs. **9.** (oft. fol. by *out*) to err; to fail. –**bomber**, *n.*

bombard /bɒm'bad/ *v.t.* to assail vigorously.

bombardier /bɒmbə'dɪə/ *n. Mil.* the member of a bomber crew who operates the bomb release mechanism.

bombast /'bɒmbæst/ *n.* high-sounding and often insincere words; verbiage. –**bombastic**, *adj.*

bombora /bɒmˈbɔrə/ *n.* **1.** a submerged reef of rocks. **2.** a dangerous current over a reef.

bombshell /ˈbɒmʃel/ *n.* **1.** a bomb. **2.** a sudden or devastating action or effect. **3.** *Colloq.* a very attractive woman.

bona fide /ˌboʊnə ˈfaɪdi/ *adj.* **1.** genuine; real. **2.** undertaken in good faith; without fraud. Also, **bona-fide**.

bond /bɒnd/ *n.* **1.** something that binds, fastens, confines, or holds together. **2.** something that unites individual people into a group. **3.** a sealed document under which a person or corporation guarantees to pay a stated sum of money on or before a specified day. **4.** any written obligation under seal. **5.** a written undertaking to work for a specified period, or to pay back an agreed sum of money in default, as a condition for accepting certain scholarships, awards or privileges from an employer. **6.** *Law* **a.** a contract under seal to pay a debt, or to pay a sum of money in default of fulfilling some condition. **b.** an undertaking by an offender to be of good behaviour for a certain period. **7.** the state of dutiable goods on which the duties are unpaid (especially in phrase *in bond*). **8.** *Finance* a fixed-term security, esp. one issued by government or semi-government authorities, that pays a fixed rate of interest during its life and repays the principal at maturity. Compare **debenture**. **9.** *Insurance* **a.** a surety agreement. **b.** the money deposited, or the promissory arrangement entered into, under any such agreement. **10.** → **bond money**. **11.** a substance that causes particles to adhere; a binder. **12.** *Chem.* any linkage between atoms in a compound. –*v.t.* **13.** to put (goods, an employee, official, etc.) in or under bond. **14.** *Finance* to place a bonded debt on; mortgage. **15.** *Building Trades* to cause (bricks or other building materials) to hold together firmly by laying them in some overlapping pattern. **16.** to unite (members of a group, etc.). –*v.i.* **17.** to hold together by being bonded, as bricks in a wall. **18.** to establish a close interpersonal relationship with another or others.

bondage /ˈbɒndɪdʒ/ *n.* the state of being bound by or subjected to external control.

bond money *n.* money additional to any rent which a new tenant pays as surety against damages to the premises rented.

bond store *n.* a warehouse licensed under the Customs Act for the storage of goods on which duty has not yet been paid.

bone /boʊn/ *n.* **1.** *Anat., Zool.* any of the separate pieces of which the skeleton of a vertebrate is composed. **2.** any of various similar substances, such as ivory, whalebone, etc. **3.** an off-white colour. –*v.t.* (**boned**, **boning**) **4.** to remove the the bones from: *to bone a fish.* –*phr.* **5. bone of contention**, a matter which causes disagreement. **6. bone up**, *Colloq.* (fol. by *on*) to study hard; acquire information.

bone marrow *n.* → **marrow** (def. 1).

bonfire /ˈbɒnfaɪə/ *n.* a large fire in an open place, for entertainment, celebration, or as a signal.

bongo /ˈbɒŋɡoʊ/ *n.* (*pl.* **-gos** *or* **-goes**) one of a pair of small drums, played by beating with the fingers.

bonito /bəˈnitoʊ/ *n.* (*pl.* **bonito** *or* **bonitos**) any of several fishes belonging to the tuna family, as *Sarda chiliensis australis* found along the eastern Aust. coast.

bonkers /ˈbɒŋkəz/ *adj. Colloq.* crazy.

bonnet /ˈbɒnət/ *n.* **1.** a woman's or child's outdoor head covering, commonly fitting down over the hair, and often tied under the chin. **2.** any of various hoods, covers, or protective devices, such as the metal cover over the engine of a car.

bonny /ˈbɒni/ *adj.* (**-nier**, **-niest**) radiant with health; handsome; pretty.

bonobo /ˈbɒnəboʊ, bəˈnoʊboʊ/ *n.* a chimpanzee found in humid forests of the Congo region, and forming communities which are female-centred.

bonsai /ˈbɒnsaɪ/ *n.* **1.** the art of keeping trees and shrubs very small and shaping them in particular ways by cutting their roots and branches. **2.** a tree or shrub grown this way.

bonus /ˈboʊnəs/ *n.* **1.** something given or paid over and above what is due. **2.** *Insurance* **a.** dividend. **b.** free additions to the sum assured.

bonus issue *n.* a free issue of shares to shareholders of a company. Also, **bonus**.

bony /ˈboʊni/ *adj.* (**-nier**, **-niest**) **1.** of or like bone. **2.** emaciated.

bonzer /ˈbɒnzə/ *adj. Colloq.* excellent, attractive, pleasing. Also, **bonza**.

boob¹ /bub/ *n. Colloq.* a fool; a dunce.

boob² /bub/ *n. Colloq.* a woman's breast.

booby prize /ˈbubi/ *n.* a prize given in consolation or good-natured ridicule to the worst player in a game or contest.

booby trap *n.* an object so placed as to fall on or trip up an unsuspecting person.

boofy /ˈbufi/ *adj. Colloq.* **1.** dull-witted; stupid. **2.** having a muscular or large physique but considered to be lacking in intelligence or personality: *boofy boys.* **3.** large, inflated or distended: *boofy hair.*

boogie board /ˈbugi, ˈbʊgi/ *n.* (*from trademark*) a small surfboard, usually ridden lying down.

book /bʊk/ *n.* **1.** a text of some length, comprising a whole work as a treatise or other literary composition. **2.** such a text in printed form on consecutive sheets fastened or bound together. **3.** such a text in digital form; ebook. **4.** a number of sheets of writing paper bound together and used for making entries, as of commercial transactions. **5.** a set of tickets, cheques, stamps, etc., bound together like a book. **6.** a number of mares, bitches, etc., to be mated with the one sire. **7.** anything that serves for the recording of facts or events. –*v.t.* **8.** to enter in a book or list; record; register. **9.** to engage (a place, passage, etc.) beforehand. **10.** to put (somebody, something) down for a place, passage, etc. **11.** to engage (a person or company) for a performance or performances. **12.** to record the name of, with a view to possible prosecution for a minor offence. –*v.i.* **13.** (fol. by *in*) to register one's name. **14.** to engage a place, services, etc. –*phr.* **15. the books**, a record of commercial transactions.

bookcase /ˈbʊkkeɪs/ *n.* a set of shelves for books.

bookend /'bʊkɛnd/ n. **1.** a support placed at the end of a row of books to hold them upright. –v.t. **2.** to act as a marker at the beginning and end of a process, activity, etc.: *a concert bookended by Beethoven sonatas.*

bookish /'bʊkɪʃ/ adj. given to reading or study.

bookkeeping /'bʊkkipɪŋ/ n. the work or skill of keeping account books or systematic records of money transactions. –**bookkeeper**, n.

booklet /'bʊklət/ n. a little book, especially one with paper covers; pamphlet.

bookmaker /'bʊkmeɪkə/ n. a professional betting person, who accepts the bets of others, as on horses in racing.

bookmark /'bʊkmak/ n. **1.** a strip of cardboard, ribbon, or the like placed between the pages of a book to mark a place. **2.** *Internet* a URL reference stored in a file by a browser for future reference. –v.t. **3.** *Internet* to store (a URL) in a file for future reference by a browser.

book value n. *Econ.* the amount which a trader shows in his or her accounts as the value of an item.

bookworm /'bʊkwɜm/ n. a person fond of reading or study.

Boolean operator /'bulian/ n. an operator (def. 4), as 'and', 'or', or 'not', used in computer programming and to phrase queries in database searches.

Boolean search n. a search of a computer database in which Boolean operators may be used.

boom[1] /bum/ v.i. **1.** to make a deep, prolonged, resonant sound; make a rumbling, humming, or droning noise. **2.** to progress or flourish vigorously, as a business, a city, etc. –n. **3.** a deep, hollow, continued sound. **4.** a period of high economic growth and general prosperity.

boom[2] /bum/ n. **1.** *Naut.* a long pole or spar used to extend the foot of certain sails. **2.** (in a television or film studio) a movable arm supporting a camera, microphone or floodlight above the actors.

boomer /'bumə/ n. **1.** *Colloq.* something large, as a surfing wave. **2.** *Colloq.* something successful or popular, as a party or song. **3.** a large male kangaroo.

boomerang /'buməræŋ/ n. **1.** a bent or curved piece of hard wood traditionally used by Aboriginal people as a missile, one form of which can be thrown so as to return to the thrower. **2.** *Colloq.* that which is expected to be returned by a borrower. –v.i. **3.** to return to, or recoil upon, the originator.

boon /bun/ n. a benefit enjoyed; a thing to be thankful for; a blessing.

boor /bɔ, bʊə/ n. a rude or bad-mannered person.

boost /bust/ v.t. **1.** to lift or raise by pushing from behind or below. **2.** to increase; push up. –n. **3.** an upward shove or push. **4.** an aid or encouragement to success.

booster /'bustə/ n. **1.** someone who or that which boosts. **2.** *Elect.* a device connected in series with a current for increasing or decreasing the nominal circuit voltage. **3.** *Pharmaceutical* a substance, usually injected, for prolonging a person's immunity to a specific infection.

boot[1] /but/ n. **1.** a heavy shoe, especially one reaching above the ankle. **2.** a place for baggage, usually at the rear of a vehicle. **3.** a kick. –phr. **4. get the boot**, to be discharged.

boot[2] /but/ phr. **to boot**, into the bargain; in addition.

boot[3] /but/ v.t. Also, **boot up. 1.** to start (a computer) as by activating the operating system. –phr. **2. boot up**, (of a computer) to become operational.

boot camp n. **1.** *US Mil.* a training camp for recruits. **2.** a prison camp for young offenders which places emphasis on military-style discipline. **3.** *Sport* a training camp of high physical intensity, involving strenuous outdoor activities.

booth /buð, buθ/ n. a small compartment for a telephone, film projector, etc.

bootleg /'butlɛg/ v.t. (**-legged, -legging**) to deal in (spirits or other goods) illicitly.

bootscoot /'butskut/ v.i. to dance in a line-dance. –**bootscooting**, n.

bootstrap /'butstræp/ n. *Computers* a program or procedure by which a computer can be made to translate progressively more complex programs.

booty /'buti/ n. spoils taken from an enemy in war; plunder; pillage.

bootylicious /buti'lɪfəs/ adj. *Colloq.* (of a woman) physically attractive.

booze /buz/ n. *Colloq.* alcoholic drink.

booze bus n. *Colloq.* a bus used by a mobile police unit engaged in breath analysis.

bop /bɒp/ n. **1.** → **bebop**. –v.i. (**bopped, bopping**) **2.** to dance or move rhythmically to pop or rock music.

boracic acid /bə'ræsɪk/ n. boric acid, especially when used domestically as an antiseptic or insecticide.

bordello /bɔ'dɛloʊ/ n. a brothel.

border /'bɔdə/ n. **1.** a side, edge, or margin. **2.** the line that separates one country, state, or province from another; frontier line. –phr. **3. border on** (or **upon**), **a.** to touch or abut at the border. **b.** to approach closely in character; verge.

borderline /'bɔdəlaɪn/ adj. **1.** on or near a border or boundary. **2.** (in examinations, etc.) qualifying or failing to qualify by a narrow margin.

bore[1] /bɔ/ v.t. (**bored, boring**) **1.** to pierce (a solid substance) or make (a round hole, etc.) with an auger, drill, or other rotated instrument. **2.** to force by persistent forward thrusting. –n. **3.** a deep hole of small diameter through which water is obtained from beneath the ground. **4.** the inside diameter of a hollow cylindrical object or device, such as a bush or bearing, or the barrel of a gun.

bore[2] /bɔ/ v.t. (**bored, boring**) **1.** to weary by tedious repetition, dullness, unwelcome attentions, etc. –n. **2.** a dull, tiresome, or uncongenial person. –**boredom**, n.

bore[3] /bɔ/ v. past tense of **bear**[1].

borer /'bɔrə/ n. *Entomology* any insect that burrows in trees, fruits, etc., especially any beetle of certain groups.

boric acid /'bɒrɪk/ n. any of a group of acids used as an antiseptic, preservative, and in fireproofing compounds, cosmetics, cements and enamel.

boring /'bɔːrɪŋ/ *adj.* causing boredom; tiresome; dull. –**boringly**, *adv.*

born /bɔːn/ *adj.* **1.** brought forth into independent being or life. **2.** possessing from birth the quality or character stated: *a born leader.*

borne /bɔːn/ *v.* a past participle of **bear**[1].

boron /'bɔːrɒn/ *n.* a non-metallic element. *Symbol:* B

boronia /bə'rəʊniə/ *n.* any of a number of Australian shrubs with small flowers.

borough /'bʌrə/ *n. Victoria* an area of land corresponding to a municipality in the other states of Australia.

borrow /'bɒrəʊ/ *v.t.* **1.** to take or obtain (a thing) on the promise to return it or its equivalent; obtain the temporary use of. **2.** to get from another or from a foreign source; appropriate or adopt. **3.** *Arithmetic* (in subtraction) to take from one column to add to the next lower.

bosom /'bʊzəm/ *n.* **1.** the breast of a human being, especially a woman. **2.** the breast, conceived of as the seat of thought or emotion. –*adj.* **3.** intimate or confidential.

boss /bɒs/ *n. Colloq.* **1.** someone who employs or superintends workers; a foreperson or manager. **2.** anyone who asserts mastery, especially someone who controls an organisation: *a mafia boss.* –*v.i.* **3.** to be domineering.

bot /bɒt/ *v.i., v.t.* (**botted, botting**) *Colloq.* to cadge.

botany /'bɒtəni/ *n.* the science of plants; the branch of biology that deals with plant life. –**botanist**, *n.* –**botanical, botanic,** *adj.*

botch /bɒtʃ/ *v.t.* to spoil by poor work; bungle.

both /bəʊθ/ *adj.* **1.** two together: *Both children were sick.* –*pron.* **2.** the one and the other: *They were both sick.* –*adv.* **3.** alike; equally.

bother /'bɒðə/ *v.t.* **1.** to give trouble to; annoy; pester; worry. –*v.i.* **2.** to trouble oneself. –*n.* **3.** an annoying disturbance. **4.** worried or perplexed state. **5.** someone who bothers. –**bothersome,** *adj.*

botox /'bəʊtɒks/ (*from trademark*) –*n.* **1.** a preparation which causes muscle relaxation and paralysis, used for medical and cosmetic purposes. –*v.t.* **2.** to apply botox to (a part of the face or body).

bottle /'bɒtl/ *n.* **1.** a portable vessel with a neck or mouth, now commonly made of glass, used for holding liquids. –*v.t.* **2.** to put into or seal in a bottle; to preserve (fruit or vegetables) in bottles.

bottlebrush /'bɒtlbrʌʃ/ *n.* an Australian plant whose flower spikes resemble a cylindrical brush.

bottleneck /'bɒtlnɛk/ *n.* **1.** a place, or stage in a process, where progress is retarded. **2. a.** a narrow part of a road between two wide stretches. **b.** a congested junction, road, town, etc., fed by several roads, where traffic is likely to be held up.

bottom /'bɒtəm/ *n.* **1.** the lowest or deepest part of anything, as distinguished from the top. **2.** the underside. **3.** the place of least honour, achievement, etc.: *the bottom of the class.* **4.** the ground under any body of water. **5.** the buttocks. **6.** the fundamental part; basic aspect.

–*v.i.* **7.** to be based; rest. **8.** to strike against the bottom or end; reach the bottom. –*adj.* **9.** lowest. –*phr.* **10. bottom out**, to reach the lowest level of economic activity thought likely.

bottom feeder *n.* **1.** a freshwater or saltwater animal, especially a fish, which feeds on plants and animals living on the bottom of a river, lake, bay, etc. **2.** a person who takes advantage of what others provide while making no contribution themselves.

bottom line *n.* the last line of a financial statement where overall cost, profit, loss, etc., is likely to be found.

botulism /'bɒtʃəlɪzəm/ *n.* a serious form of food poisoning.

bouclé /'buːkleɪ/ *n.* yarn with loops, which produces a woven or knitted fabric with rough appearance.

bougainvillea /ˌbuːgən'vɪliə/ *n.* a shrub or spiny climber with brightly coloured bracts.

bough /baʊ/ *n.* a branch of a tree, especially one of the larger of the main branches.

bought /bɔːt/ *v.* past tense and past participle of **buy**.

boulder /'bəʊldə/ *n.* a detached and rounded or worn rock, especially a large one.

boulevard /'buːləvɑːd/ *n.* **1.** a broad avenue of a city, often having trees and used as a promenade. **2.** a street. Also, **boulevarde.**

bounce /baʊns/ *v.* (**bounced, bouncing**) –*v.i.* **1.** to move with a bound, and rebound, as a ball. **2.** to burst ebulliently (*into* or *out of*). **3.** *Colloq.* (of cheques) to be dishonoured; to be returned unpaid. –*v.t.* **4.** to cause to bound or rebound. **5.** *Colloq.* to eject or discharge summarily. **6.** *Colloq.* to arrest. –*n.* **7.** a rebound or bound. **8.** ability to bounce; resilience.

bound[1] /baʊnd/ *adj.* **1.** tied; in bonds: *a bound prisoner.* **2.** made fast as by a band or bond. **3.** secured within a cover, as a book. **4.** under obligation, legally or morally. **5.** destined or sure.

bound[2] /baʊnd/ *v.i.* **1.** to move by leaps; leap; jump; spring. –*n.* **2.** a leap onwards or upwards; a jump.

bound[3] /baʊnd/ *n.* **1.** (*usu. pl.*) a limiting line, or boundary. –*v.t.* **2.** to form the boundary or limit of. –*phr.* **3. out of bounds,** not to be entered or accessed; forbidden.

bound[4] /baʊnd/ *adj.* going or intending to go; on the way (*to*); destined (*for*).

boundary /'baʊndri/ *n.* (*pl.* **-ries**) something that indicates bounds or limits; a limiting or bounding line.

bounteous /'baʊntiəs/ *adj.* **1.** giving or disposed to give freely; generously liberal. **2.** freely bestowed; plentiful; abundant.

bountiful /'baʊntəfəl/ *adj.* **1.** liberal in bestowing gifts, favours, or bounties; munificent; generous. **2.** abundant; ample.

bounty /'baʊnti/ *n.* (*pl.* **-ties**) **1.** generosity in giving. **2.** whatever is given bounteously; a benevolent, generous gift. **3.** a premium or reward, especially one offered by a government. **4.** an amount paid by a government to a person or company in the private sector to encourage them to produce particular goods that they would not otherwise produce.

bouquet /buːˈkeɪ, booˈkeɪ/ *n.* **1.** a bunch of flowers. **2.** the characteristic aroma of wine, liqueurs, etc.

bourbon /ˈbɜːbən/ *n.* a kind of whisky distilled from a mash containing 51 per cent or more maize. Also, **bourbon whisky**.

bourgeois /ˈbʊəʒwɑ, buˈ-/ *n.* (*pl.* **-geois**) **1.** a member of the middle class. **2.** one whose outlook is said to be determined by a concern for property values; a capitalist, as opposed to a member of the wage-earning class. *–adj.* **3.** lacking in refinement or elegance; conventional. **–bourgeoisie**, *n.*

bout /baʊt/ *n.* **1.** a contest, especially a boxing or wrestling match; a trial of strength. **2.** period; spell.

boutique /buːˈtiːk/ *n.* a small shop selling fashionable or luxury articles.

bovine /ˈbəʊvaɪn/ *n.* **1.** an animal of the ox family. *–adj.* **2.** oxlike. **3.** stolid; dull.

bow¹ /baʊ/ *v.i.* **1.** to bend or curve downwards; stoop. **2.** to yield; submit. **3.** to bend the body or head in worship, reverence, salutation, respect, or submission. *–v.t.* **4.** to bend or incline in worship, submission, respect, civility, or agreement. **5.** to cause to submit; subdue; crush. *–n.* **6.** an inclination of the head or body in salutation, assent, thanks, reverence, respect, or submission.

bow² /bəʊ/ *n.* **1.** a strip of flexible wood or other material bent by a string stretched between its ends, used for shooting arrows. **2.** something curved or arc-shaped. **3.** a looped knot, as of ribbon, composed of one or two loops and two ends. **4.** *Music* an implement, originally curved, but now almost always straight, with horsehairs stretched upon it, designed for playing any stringed instrument. *–adj.* **5.** curved; bent like a bow. *–v.t.* **6.** to bend into the form of a bow; curve.

bow³ /baʊ/ *n.* (*sometimes pl.*) the front or forward part or end of a ship, boat, etc.

bowdlerise /ˈbaʊdləraɪz/ *v.t.* to expurgate prudishly. Also, **bowdlerize**.

bowel /ˈbaʊəl/ *n.* **1.** *Anat.* **a.** an intestine. **b.** (*usu. pl.*) the parts of the alimentary canal below the stomach; the intestines or entrails. **2.** the inward or interior parts.

bower /ˈbaʊə/ *n.* a leafy shelter or recess; an arbour.

bowerbird /ˈbaʊəbɜːd/ *n.* **1.** any of various birds which build bowerlike structures, used, not as nests, but as places of resort to attract the females. **2.** someone who collects useless objects.

bowl¹ /bəʊl/ *n.* **1.** a rather deep, round dish or basin, used chiefly for holding liquids, food, etc. **2.** any bowl-shaped depression or cavity.

bowl² /bəʊl/ *n.* **1.** one of the biased or weighted balls used in the game of bowls; wood. **2.** a cast or delivery of the ball in bowling. *–v.i.* **3.** to play with bowls, or at bowling. *–v.t.* **4.** to roll or trundle, as a ball, hoop, etc. **5.** *Cricket* to dismiss (the person batting) by delivering a ball which breaks their wicket. *–phr.* **6. bowl over**, to knock over or strike, as by the ball in bowling. **7. bowl someone over**, **a.** to disconcert; upset. **b.** to impress greatly.

bowler /ˈbəʊlə/ *n.* a hard felt hat with a rounded crown and narrow brim.

bowls /bəʊlz/ *n.* **1.** → **lawn bowls**. **2.** a similar game (**carpet bowls**) played indoors.

bowser /ˈbaʊzə/ *n.* (*from trademark*) a pump at a service station for putting fuel into motor vehicles.

bow tie *n.* a man's tie, made into a bow at the front of the collar, usually worn on very formal occasions

box¹ /bɒks/ *n.* **1.** a case or receptacle, usually rectangular, of wood, metal, cardboard, etc., with a lid or removable cover. **2.** a compartment or place shut or railed off for the accommodation of a small number of people in a public place, especially in theatres, opera houses, sporting venues, etc. **3.** (in a court of law) a stand or pew reserved for witnesses, the accused or the jury. **4.** part of a page of a periodical set off by lines, border, or white space. **5.** *Cricket, etc.* a lightweight padded shield worn to protect the genitals. *–v.t.* **6.** to put into a box. **7.** (oft. fol. by *up* or *in*) to enclose or confine as in a box.

box² /bɒks/ *n.* **1.** a blow as with the hand or fist. *–v.t.* **2.** to strike with the hand or fist, especially on the ear. **3.** to fight in a boxing match.

boxer /ˈbɒksə/ *n.* **1.** someone who boxes. **2.** the person who looks after the bets in a two-up game. **3.** a smooth-coated, brown dog of medium size, related to the bulldog and terrier.

boxer shorts *pl. n.* loose-fitting men's underpants with an elasticised waist, resembling shorts.

boxing /ˈbɒksɪŋ/ *n.* the act or art of fighting with the fists.

box jellyfish *n.* a highly venomous jellyfish with long tentacles.

box office *n.* the office in which tickets are sold at a theatre or other place of public entertainment.

box seat *n. Colloq.* any position of vantage.

boy /bɔɪ/ *n.* **1.** a male child or young person. **2.** a young male servant. *–interj.* **3.** an exclamation of surprise, delight, etc.

boycott /ˈbɔɪkɒt/ *v.t.* **1.** to combine in abstaining from, or preventing dealings with, as a means of intimidation or coercion. **2.** to abstain from buying or using. *–n.* **3.** the practice or an instance of boycotting.

boyfriend /ˈbɔɪfrɛnd/ *n.* **1.** a man with whom one has a steady romantic relationship. **2.** any young male friend.

boysenberry /ˈbɔɪzənbɛri, -bri/ *n.* (*pl.* **-ries**) a blackberry-like fruit with a flavour similar to raspberries.

bra /brɑ/ *n.* a woman's undergarment which supports the breasts. Also, **brassiere**.

brace /breɪs/ *n.* **1.** something that holds parts together or in place, as a clasp or clamp. **2.** anything that imparts rigidity or steadiness. **3.** *Machinery* a device for holding and turning tools for boring or drilling. **4.** *Building Trades* a piece of timber, metal, etc., used to support or position another piece or portion of a framework. **5.** (*oft. pl.*) *Dentistry* a round or flat metal wire placed against surfaces of the teeth, and used to straighten irregularly arranged teeth. **6.** *Med.* an appliance for supporting a weak joint or joints. **7.** (*pl.*) straps or bands worn over the shoulders for holding up the trousers. **8.** a pair; a couple. **9. a.** Also, **curly bracket**. one of a pair of marks, { }, used in writing or printing to enclose parenthetical matter, etc. **b.** (pl.) Maths → **bracket** (def. 3). −v.t. (**braced**, **bracing**) **10.** to furnish, fasten, or strengthen with or as with a brace. **11.** to fix firmly; make steady. **12.** to make tight; increase the tension of. **13.** to act as a stimulant to.

bracelet /'breislət/ n. **1.** an ornamental band or circlet for the wrist. **2.** Colloq. a handcuff.

bracken /'brækən/ n. a large, coarse fern.

bracket /'brækət/ n. **1.** a wooden, metal, etc., support of triangular outline placed under a shelf or the like. **2.** one of two marks used in writing or printing to enclose parenthetical matter, interpolations, etc., as [or], or { or }, or (or), or < or > . **3.** (pl.) Maths parentheses of various forms indicating that the enclosed quantity is to be treated as a unit. **4.** a grouping of persons, especially as based on the amount of their taxable income. **5.** a small group of musical items in a performance. −v.t. **6.** to furnish with or support by a bracket or brackets. **7.** to associate or mention together, implying equality of some kind.

bracket creep n. the gradual shift as a result of inflation of an income subject to a progressive income tax from one tax bracket to another where more tax is paid despite the real level of the income (its purchasing power) remaining unchanged.

brackish /'brækɪʃ/ adj. slightly salt; having a salty or briny flavour.

bract /brækt/ n. a specialised leaf-like part, usually situated at the base of a flower.

brag /bræg/ v.i. (**bragged**, **bragging**) to use boastful language; boast. −**braggart**, n.

braid /breɪd/ v.t. to weave together strips or strands of; plait.

braille /breɪl/ n. a system of writing or printing for the blind, in which combinations of tangible points are used to represent letters, etc.

brain /breɪn/ n. **1.** (sometimes pl.) the soft mass of greyish and whitish nerve substance which fills the cranium of humans and other vertebrates; centre of sensation, body coordination, thought, emotion, etc. **2.** (usu. pl.) understanding; intellectual power; intelligence. **3.** Colloq. a highly intelligent or well-informed person.

brain death n. the irreversible loss of function in the upper brain as a result of severe damage caused by trauma, stroke, haemorrhage or lack of oxygen.

brainiac /'breɪniæk/ n. Colloq. a very intelligent person.

brain stem n. the area connecting the brain to the spinal cord; responsible for the regulation of heart rate, blood pressure and breathing.

brainstorm /'breɪnstɔm/ n. **1.** a sudden, violent attack of mental disturbance. **2.** a sudden inspiration, idea, etc. −v.t. **3.** to use brainstorming as a means to address or solve (a problem, etc.).

brainstorming /'breɪnstɔmɪŋ/ n. a technique in which a group meets in order to stimulate creative thinking, develop new ideas, devise a solution to a problem, etc.

brainteaser /'breɪntizə/ n. Colloq. a mental puzzle.

brainwashing /'breɪnwɒʃɪŋ/ n. systematic indoctrination that changes or undermines one's convictions, especially political.

brainwave /'breɪnweɪv/ n. a sudden idea or inspiration.

brainy /'breɪni/ adj. (**-nier**, **-niest**) having brains; intelligent; clever.

braise /breɪz/ v.t. (**braised**, **braising**) to cook (meat or vegetables) by sautéing in fat and then cooking slowly in very little moisture.

brake[1] /breɪk/ n. **1.** any mechanical device for arresting the motion of a wheel, a motor, or a vehicle, chiefly by means of friction or pressure. −v.i. **2.** to use or apply a brake.

brake[2] /breɪk/ n. a place overgrown with bushes, shrubs, brambles, or cane; a thicket.

bramble /'bræmbəl/ n. **1.** the common blackberry. **2.** any rough prickly shrub.

bran /bræn/ n. the ground husk of wheat or other grain, separated from flour or meal by bolting.

branch /brɑntʃ, bræntʃ/ n. **1.** Bot. a division or subdivision of the stem or axis of a tree, shrub, or other plant. **2.** a limb, offshoot, or ramification. **3.** any member or part of a body or system; a section or subdivision. **4.** Geog. a tributary stream. −v.i. **5.** to put forth branches; spread in branches. **6.** to divide into separate parts or subdivisions; diverge.

brand /brænd/ n. **1.** a trademark or trade name to identify a product, as that of a distributor, or a manufacturer or other producer. **2.** a mark made by burning or otherwise, to indicate kind, grade, make, ownership, etc. **3.** any mark of infamy; a stigma.

brandish /'brændɪʃ/ v.t. **1.** to shake or wave, as a weapon; flourish. −n. **2.** a wave or flourish, as of a weapon.

brandy /'brændi/ n. (pl. **-dies**) the spirit distilled from the fermented juice of grapes or, sometimes, of apples, peaches, plums, etc.

brash /bræʃ/ adj. impertinent; impudent; forward. −**brashly**, adv. −**brashness**, n.

brass /brɑs/ n. **1.** a durable, malleable, and ductile yellow alloy, consisting essentially of copper and zinc. **2.** a collective term for musical instruments of the trumpet and horn families (brass instruments), usually made of brass and having a funnel-shaped mouthpiece without a reed. Also, **top brass**. Colloq. high-ranking people. **3.** Colloq. excessive assurance; impudence; effrontery. **5.** Colloq. money.

brasserie /'brasəri/ n. a restaurant, especially one for informal dining.

brassiere /'bræziə, -siə/ n. → **bra**.

brat /bræt/ n. (derog.) a badly-behaved child.

bravado /brə'vadoʊ/ n. boasting; swaggering pretence.

brave /breɪv/ adj. **1.** possessing or exhibiting courage or courageous endurance. −v.t. **2.** to meet or face courageously. **3.** to defy; challenge; dare. −**bravery**, n.

bravo /bra'voʊ/ interj. well done! good!

bravura /brə'vʊrə, -'vju-/ n. a display of daring.

brawl /brɔl/ n. **1.** a noisy quarrel; a squabble. **2.** a rough, noisy fight, often involving more than two people: a drunken brawl outside the pub.

brawn /brɔn/ n. 1. well-developed muscles. 2. meat, especially pork, boiled, pickled, and pressed into a mould.

bray /breɪ/ n. a harsh, breathy cry, as of the donkey.

brazen /ˈbreɪzən/ adj. 1. made of brass. 2. like brass, as in sound, colour, strength, etc. 3. shameless or impudent.

brazier[1] /ˈbreɪziə/ n. a person who works in brass.

brazier[2] /ˈbreɪziə/ n. a metal receptacle for holding burning charcoal or other fuel.

brazil nut /brəˈzɪl/ n. a triangular edible nut.

breach /briːtʃ/ n. 1. the act or result of breaking; a break or rupture. 2. a gap made in a wall, dyke, fortification, etc.; rift; fissure. 3. an infraction or violation, as of law, trust, faith, promise, etc. 4. a severance of friendly relations. -v.t. 5. to make a breach or opening in. 6. to violate (trust, a law, etc.): to breach someone's trust; to breach the rules. -v.i. 7. (of a whale) to thrust itself above the water.

breach of contract n. the breaking, by action or omission, of an obligation imposed by a contract.

breach of privilege n. an abuse of any of the privileges accorded to members of parliament.

bread /bred/ n. 1. a food made of flour or meal, milk or water, etc., made into a dough or batter, with or without yeast or the like, and baked. 2. food or sustenance; livelihood. 3. Colloq. money; earnings.

breadcrumb trail n. the information which visitors to a website leave about who they are and their patterns of behaviour, in particular their buying patterns.

breadline /ˈbredlaɪn/ phr. **on the breadline**, living at subsistence level.

breadth /bredθ/ n. 1. Maths the measure of the second principal diameter of a surface or solid, the first being length, and the third (in the case of a solid) thickness; width. 2. freedom from narrowness or restraint. 3. size in general; extent.

breadwinner /ˈbredwɪnə/ n. someone who earns a livelihood for a family or household.

break /breɪk/ v. (**broke**, **broken**, **breaking**) -v.t. 1. to divide into parts violently; reduce to pieces or fragments. 2. to separate into parts or pieces: to break bread. 3. to detach from a larger object: to break a leaf from a plant. 4. to fracture a bone of. 5. to lacerate; wound: to break the skin. 6. to cause to stop functioning properly. 7. to violate: to break one's word. 8. (oft. fol. by off) to dissolve or annul. 9. to separate into components: to break a difficult job into manageable steps. 10. to destroy the regularity of. 11. to put an end to; overcome. 12. to exchange for a smaller amount or smaller units. 13. to make one's way through; penetrate. 14. Law to open or force one's way into (a dwelling, store, etc.). 15. to disable or destroy by or as by shattering or crushing. 16. to ruin financially, or make bankrupt. 17. to impair or weaken in strength, spirit, force, or effect. 18. to publish (a news item). 19. to defeat the purpose of (a strike). 20. (oft. fol. by in) to train to obedience; tame.

21. Elect. to render (a circuit) incomplete; stop the flow of (a current). -v.i. 22. to become broken; separate into parts or fragments, especially suddenly and violently. 23. to stop functioning properly. 24. (fol. by off, etc.) to become suddenly discontinuous or interrupted; leave off abruptly. 25. (fol. by up or with) to sever relations. 26. (of a wave) to topple forward after developing a crest through the opposing pull of an undertow in shallow water. 27. (oft. fol. by away) to free oneself or escape suddenly, as from restraint. 28. (fol. by in, through, out, etc.) to force a way. 29. (fol. by in, forth, from, etc.) to burst. 30. (fol. by into) to change state or activity. 31. to dawn, as the day. 32. (of the heart) to be crushed or overwhelmed, especially by grief. 33. (of stock-exchange prices) to drop quickly and considerably. 34. (of the voice) to vary between two registers, especially in emotion or during adolescence. 35. (in a race) to start before the signal to do so has been given. -n. 36. a forcible disruption or separation of parts; a breaking; a fracture, rupture, or shattering. 37. an opening made by breaking; a gap. 38. a rush away from a place; an attempt to escape. 39. an interruption of continuity; suspension, stoppage. 40. an abrupt or marked change, as in sound or direction. 41. an opportunity; chance. 42. a brief rest, as from work, especially a midmorning pause, usually of fifteen minutes, between school classes. 43. Stock Exchange a sudden drop in prices. 44. any continuous run, especially of good fortune. 45. Billiards the shot that breaks or scatters the balls at the beginning of the game. 46. a premature start in racing. -phr. 47. **break down**, a. to take down or destroy by breaking. b. to overcome. c. to analyse. d. to collapse. e. to cease to function. 48. **break in**, a. to interrupt. b. to adapt to one's convenience by use. c. to accustom a horse to harness and use. d. to enter (a house or the like) forcibly, as a burglar. 49. **break out**, a. to issue forth; arise. b. (of certain diseases) to appear in eruptions. c. to have a sudden appearance of various eruptions on the skin. 50. **break up**, a. to separate; disband (especially of a school at end of term). b. (of a marriage) to cease. c. to put an end to; discontinue. d. to dissolve and separate: the ice on the lake started to break up. e. to cut up (fowl, etc.). f. Colloq. to collapse with laughter.

breakage /ˈbreɪkɪdʒ/ n. 1. an act of breaking; a break. 2. the amount or quantity of things broken. 3. an allowance or compensation for loss or damage of articles broken in transit or in use.

breakaway /ˈbreɪkəweɪ/ n. 1. the formation of a splinter group in a political party, or similar group. 2. a panic rush of or among a mob of cattle, horses, etc.

breakdance /ˈbreɪkdæns/ n. 1. a style of acrobatic dancing performed to rap music, and involving spectacular movements such as spinning the body on the ground. -v.i. 2. to dance in this style. -**breakdancer**, n.

breakdancing /ˈbreɪkdænsɪŋ/ n. a form of street dancing which involves spectacular movements such as spinning the body on the ground.

breakdown /'breɪkdaʊn/ *n.* **1.** a ceasing to function, as of a machine. **2.** a collapse of physical or mental health.

breakfast /'brɛkfəst/ *n.* the first meal of the day; a morning meal.

breakneck /'breɪknɛk/ *adj.* dangerous; hazardous.

breakpoint /'breɪkpoɪnt/ *n.* **1.** an instruction inserted by a debug program. **2.** the point in a program at which such an instruction operates.

breakthrough /'breɪkθru/ *n.* any development, as in science, technology, or diplomacy, which removes a barrier to progress.

breakwater /'breɪkwɔtə/ *n.* a barrier, either artificial or natural, which breaks the force of waves.

bream /brim/ *n.* a marine food and sport fish.

breast /brɛst/ *n.* **1.** *Anat., Zool.* the outer front part of the thorax, or the front part of the body from neck to belly; the chest. **2.** *Anat., Zool.* a mammary or milk gland, especially of a woman, or of female animals whose milk glands are similarly formed. **3.** the bosom regarded as the seat of thoughts and feelings.

breastbone /'brɛstboʊn/ *n.* the long bone extending vertically down the centre of the chest; sternum.

breastfeed /'brɛstfid/ *v.* **(-fed, -feeding)** –*v.t.* **1.** to feed (a child) from the breast (opposed to *bottle-feed*). –*v.i.* **2.** to feed a child in this manner. **3.** (of a baby) to feed from the breast.

breaststroke /'brɛststroʊk/ *n.* a swimming stroke made in the prone position in which both hands move simultaneously forwards, outwards and rearwards in front of the chest, and the legs move in a frog-like manner.

breath /brɛθ/ *n.* **1.** the air inhaled and exhaled in respiration. **2.** ability to breathe, especially freely. **3.** the brief time required for it; an instant. **4.** a light current of air. –**breathless**, *adj.*

breathalyser /'brɛθəlaɪzə/ *n.* a breath-analysing device which contains chemicals which react with alcohol and which change colour in proportion to the amount of alcohol in the breath. –**breathalyse**, *v.*

breathe /brið/ *v.* **(breathed** /briðd/, **breathing)** –*v.i.* **1.** to inhale and exhale air. **2.** to blow lightly, as air. **3.** to live; exist. **4.** to be redolent (*of*). –*v.t.* **5.** to inhale and exhale in respiration. **6.** to give utterance to; whisper.

breathtaking /'brɛθteɪkɪŋ/ *adj.* causing amazement. –**breathtakingly**, *adv.*

breathy /'brɛθi/ *adj.* (of the voice) characterised by excessive emission of breath.

bred /brɛd/ *v.* past tense and past participle of **breed**.

breech /britʃ/ *n.* **1.** the lower part of the trunk of the body behind; the posterior or buttocks. **2.** the hinder or lower part of anything.

breeches /'brɪtʃəz/ *pl. n.* **1.** a garment worn by men (and by women for riding, etc.), covering the hips and thighs. **2.** trousers.

breed /brid/ *v.* **(bred, breeding)** –*v.t.* **1.** to produce (offspring). **2.** to procure by the mating of parents; propagate. **3.** *Hort.* to cause to reproduce by controlled pollination. **4.** to cause; occasion; produce. –*v.i.* **5.** to produce offspring. –*n.* **6.** *Genetics* a relatively

homogeneous group of animals within a species, developed and maintained by humans. **7.** lineage; strain.

breeding /'bridɪŋ/ *n.* **1.** the rearing of livestock to improve their quality or merit. **2.** the results of training as shown in behaviour and manners; good manners.

breeze /briz/ *n.* **1.** a wind or current of air, especially a light or moderate one. **2.** *Colloq.* an easy task. –*v.i.* **3.** *Colloq.* (oft. fol. by *along, in*) to move or proceed in a casual, quick, carefree manner. –*phr.* **4. breeze through**, *Colloq.* to perform without effort. –**breezy**, *adj.*

brethren /'brɛðrən/ *n.* **1.** *Archaic* plural of **brother**. **2.** fellow members.

breve /briv/ *n. Music* a note equal in length to two semibreves.

brevi- a word element meaning 'short'.

brevity /'brɛvəti/ *n.* shortness of time or duration; briefness.

brew /bru/ *v.t.* **1.** to make (beer, ale, etc.) from malt, etc., by steeping, boiling, and fermentation. **2.** (oft. fol. by *up*) to make (tea). **3.** to concoct or contrive; bring about. –*v.i.* **4.** (oft. fol. by *up*) to be in preparation; be forming or gathering. –*n.* **5.** a quantity brewed in a single process. –**brewery**, *n.*

briar /'braɪə/ *n.* a prickly shrub or plant.

bribe /braɪb/ *n.* **1.** anything of value, as money or preferential treatment, privilege, etc., given or promised for corrupt behaviour in the performance of official or public duty. –*v.t.* **2.** to influence or corrupt by a bribe. –**bribery**, *n.*

bric-a-brac /'brɪk-ə-bræk/ *n.* miscellaneous articles of old-fashioned, ornamental, or other interest. Also, **bric-à-brac**.

brick /brɪk/ *n.* **1.** a block of clay, usually rectangular, hardened by drying in the sun or burning in a kiln, and used for building, paving, etc. **2.** *Colloq.* a person who has gained one's special admiration. –*phr.* **3. like a ton of bricks**, heavily.

brick veneer *n.* a building whose external walls each consist of a timber framework faced with a single skin of bricks, the brickwork being non-structural.

bridal shower *n.* a party for a bride-to-be to which the guests, usually other women, bring a present for her future home; shower tea; kitchen tea.

bride /braɪd/ *n.* a woman newly married, or about to be married. –**bridal**, *adj.*

bridegroom /'braɪdgrum/ *n.* a man newly married, or about to be married.

bridesmaid /'braɪdzmeɪd/ *n.* a woman who attends the bride at a wedding.

bridge[1] /brɪdʒ/ *n.* **1.** a structure spanning a river, chasm, road, or the like, and affording passage. **2.** *Anat.* the ridge or upper line of the nose. –*v.t.* **(bridged, bridging)** **3.** to make a bridge over; span.

bridge[2] /brɪdʒ/ *n. Cards* a game for four players, derived from whist, in which the trump suit is decided by bidding amongst players and in which one partnership plays to fulfil a certain declaration against the other partnership which tries to prevent this.

bridging finance *n.* a temporary loan at high interest, usually to someone who has disposed of one asset, as a house, but who has not yet been paid for it, and who is obliged to pay for another.

bridle /'braɪdl/ *n.* **1.** the part of the harness of a horse, etc., around the head, used to restrain and guide the animal. *–v.i.* **2.** (oft. fol. by *at*) to draw up the head and draw in the chin, as in disdain or resentment; to be resentful or annoyed.

brie /bri/ *n.* a kind of salted, white, soft cheese, ripened through bacterial action, waxy to semiliquid, as made in Brie, a district in northern France.

brief /brif/ *adj.* **1.** of little duration. **2.** using few words; concise; succinct. **3.** abrupt or curt. *–n.* **4.** an outline, the form of which is determined by set rules, of all the possible arguments and information on one side of a controversy. **5.** *Law* a summary prepared by a solicitor for a barrister, containing all the information and documents relevant to the presentation of a case in court. *–v.t.* **6.** to give instructions to for a particular task.

briefcase /'brifkeɪs/ *n.* a flat, rectangular leather case used for carrying documents, books, manuscripts, etc. Also, **dispatch case**.

briefing /'brifɪŋ/ *n.* a short, accurate summary of the details of a plan or operation, as one given to a military unit, crew of an aeroplane, etc., before it undertakes the operation.

briefs /brifs/ *n.* close-fitting, legless underpants.

brig /brɪg/ *n.* **1.** a two-masted ship with square sails on both masts. **2.** the compartment of a ship where prisoners are confined.

brigade /brə'geɪd/ *n.* **1.** a large body of troops. **2.** a body of individuals organised for a special purpose.

brigadier /brɪgə'dɪə/ *n.* an army rank above colonel.

brigand /'brɪgənd/ *n.* a bandit.

bright /braɪt/ *adj.* **1.** radiating or reflecting light; luminous; shining. **2.** vivid or brilliant, as colour. **3.** quick-witted or intelligent. **4.** animated; lively; cheerful, as a person. *–adv.* **5.** in a bright manner. *–***brighten**, *v.*

brilliant /'brɪljənt/ *adj.* **1.** shining brightly; sparkling; glittering; lustrous. **2.** distinguished; illustrious. **3.** having or showing great intelligence or mental ability. *–***brilliance**, *n.*

brim /brɪm/ *n.* **1.** the upper edge of anything hollow; rim. **2.** a projecting edge. *–v.i.* (**brimmed**, **brimming**) **3.** to be full to the brim; to be full to overflowing.

brindled /'brɪndld/ *adj.* grey or tawny with darker streaks or spots. Also, **brinded** /'brɪndəd/.

brine /braɪn/ *n.* water saturated or strongly impregnated with salt.

bring /brɪŋ/ *v.t.* (**brought** /brɔt/, **bringing**) **1.** to cause to come with oneself; conduct or convey. **2.** to lead or induce. **3.** *Law* to put forward before a tribunal; declare in or as if in court. *–phr.* **4. bring about,** to cause; accomplish. **5. bring down, a.** to shoot down or cause to fall (a plane, animal, footballer, etc.) **b.** to reduce (a price); lower in price. **c.** to humble or subdue. **d.** introduce proposed legislation. **6. bring forward, a.** to produce to view. **b.** *Accounting* to transfer (a figure) to the top of the next column. **7. bring in,**

a. to introduce. **b.** to pronounce (a verdict). **8. bring off,** to bring to a successful conclusion; achieve. **9. bring out, a.** to expose; show; reveal. **b.** to encourage (a timid or diffident person) **c.** to induce (workers, etc.) to leave work and go on strike. **10. bring up, a.** to care for during childhood; rear. **b.** to introduce to notice or consideration. **c.** to vomit.

brink /brɪŋk/ *n.* any extreme edge; verge.

brinkmanship /'brɪŋkmənʃɪp/ *n.* the practice of courting disaster, especially nuclear war, to gain one's ends.

briny /'braɪni/ *adj.* (**-nier**, **-niest**) of or like brine; salty.

brisk /brɪsk/ *adj.* quick and active; lively.

bristle /'brɪsəl/ *n.* **1.** one of the short, stiff, coarse hairs of certain animals, especially swine, used in making brushes, etc. *–v.i.* (**-tled**, **-tling**) **2.** to stand or rise stiffly, like bristles. **3.** to erect the bristles, as an irritated animal. **4.** to be visibly roused to anger, hostility, or resistance.

brittle /'brɪtl/ *adj.* breaking readily with a comparatively smooth fracture, as glass.

broach /broʊtʃ/ *v.t.* to mention or suggest for the first time.

broad /brɔd/ *adj.* **1.** of great breadth. **2.** of great extent; large. **3.** widely diffused; open; full. **4.** not limited or narrow; liberal. **5.** of extensive range or scope. **6.** main or general. **7.** (of pronunciation) strongly dialectal. *–adv.* **8.** fully. *–n.* **9.** *Colloq.* a woman.

broadband /'brɔdbænd/ *n.* **1.** high-speed internet access having a bandwidth sufficient to carry multiple voice, video and data channels simultaneously. *–v.t.* **2.** to link to a broadband network: *to broadband the office.*

broad-based *adj.* taking into account a wide range of factors. Also, **broadbased**.

broadbrush /'brɔdbrʌʃ/ *adj.* wide-ranging and general in treatment.

broadcast /'brɔdkast/ *v.t.* (**-cast** *or* **-casted**, **-casting**) **1.** to send (sound and images) by radio or television. **2.** to spread or disseminate widely. *–n.* **3.** that which is broadcast.

broadleaf /'brɔdlif/ *n.* **1.** any of various trees or shrubs having broad leaves. *–adj.* **2.** having broad leaves.

broad-minded /brɔd-'maɪndəd/ *adj.* easily able to accept other people's ideas and ways of life; not prejudiced. *–***broad-mindedly**, *adv.* *–***broad-mindedness**, *n.*

broadsheet /'brɔdʃit/ *n.* **1.** a sheet of paper, especially of large size, printed on one side only, as for distribution or posting. **2.** a newspaper printed on the standard sheet size of paper, usually giving greater depth of reporting than a tabloid.

broadside /'brɔdsaɪd/ *n.* **1.** *Naut.* the whole side of a ship above the waterline, from the bow to the quarter. **2.** an attack, as of criticism.

broad-spectrum /'brɔd-spɛktrəm/ *adj.* **1.** of or relating to drugs which can deal with a wide range of bacterial diseases. **2.** (of a sunscreen) effective against a range of harmful wavelengths of ultraviolet light.

brocade /brə'keɪd/ n. fabric woven with an elaborate design, with one side having a raised effect.

broccoli /'brɒkəli, -lai/ n. a plant of the mustard family, resembling the cauliflower.

brochure /'brəʊʃə, brə'ʃʊə/ n. a booklet, or piece of folded paper, containing printed advertising or information.

brogue¹ /brəʊg/ n. a broad accent, especially Irish, in the pronunciation of English.

brogue² /brəʊg/ n. a strongly made, comfortable type of ordinary shoe.

broil /brɔɪl/ v.t. to cook by direct radiant heat, as on a griller, or under an electric coil, gas grill or the like; grill.

broke /brəʊk/ v. **1.** past tense of **break**. –phr. **2. flat broke,** Colloq. completely out of money.

broken /'brəʊkən/ v. **1.** past participle of **break**. –adj. **2.** having undergone breaking. **3.** (of a machine, etc.) not working properly. **4.** (of a surface) rough or uneven. **5.** interrupted: broken sleep. **6.** weakened in strength, spirit, etc. **7.** imperfectly spoken, as language.

broker /'brəʊkə/ n. **1.** an agent who buys or sells (property, shares, etc.) for another person. –v.t. **2.** to negotiate (a deal, etc.). –**brokerage,** n.

brolga /'brɒlgə/ n. a large, pale grey crane of northern and eastern Australia.

brolly /'brɒli/ n. Colloq. an umbrella.

bromance /'brəʊmæns/ n. Colloq. a non-sexual but intense friendship between two males.

bromine /'brəʊmiːn, -aɪn/ n. an element, a darkreddish fuming liquid, resembling chlorine and iodine in chemical properties. Symbol: Br

bronchitis /brɒŋ'kaɪtəs/ n. a inflammation of the membrane lining of the bronchial tubes.

bronchus /'brɒŋkəs/ n. (pl. **-chi** /-ki/) either of the two main branches of the trachea. –**bronchial,** adj.

brontosaurus /brɒntə'sɔrəs/ n. → **apatosaurus**.

bronze /brɒnz/ n. Metallurgy a durable brown alloy, consisting essentially of copper and tin.

brooch /brəʊtʃ/ n. a clasp or ornament for the dress, having a pin at the back for passing through the clothing and a catch for securing the pin.

brood /bruːd/ n. **1.** a number of young creatures produced or hatched at one time; a family of offspring or young. –v.i. **2.** to sit on eggs to hatch them. **3.** to think too much about a particular subject. –**broody,** adj.

brook¹ /brʊk/ n. a small, natural stream of fresh water; creek.

brook² /brʊk/ v.t. (usu. in a negative sentence) to bear; suffer; tolerate.

broom /bruːm/ n. a sweeping implement consisting of a flat brush of bristles, nylon, etc., on a long handle.

broth /brɒθ/ n. thin soup of concentrated meat or fish stock.

brothel /'brɒθəl/ n. a house of prostitution.

brother /'brʌðə/ n. **1.** a male child of the same parents as another. **2.** a male member of the same kinship group, nationality, profession, etc.; an associate; a fellow countryman, fellow man, etc. **3.** Eccles. a male lay member of a

religious organisation which has a priesthood. –**brotherly,** adj., adv. –**brotherhood,** n.

brother-in-law /'brʌðər-ɪn-lɔ/ n. (pl. **brothers-in-law**) **1.** one's husband's or wife's brother. **2.** one's sibling's husband. **3.** the husband of one's wife's or husband's sibling.

brought /brɔt/ v. past tense and past participle of **bring**.

brouhaha /'bruːhaha/ n. an uproar; turmoil.

brow /braʊ/ n. the ridge over the eye.

browbeat /'braʊbit/ v.t. (**-beat, -beaten, -beating**) to intimidate by overbearing looks or words; bully.

brown /braʊn/ n. **1.** a dark shade with yellowish or reddish hue. –adj. **2.** of the colour brown. **3.** having skin of that colour. **4.** sunburned or tanned. –v.t. **5.** to make brown.

brownfield /'braʊnfild/ adj. of or relating to an urban site which has been previously developed or used.

brown goods /'braʊn gʊdz/ pl. n. electronic goods such as televisions, sound systems, videos, etc. Also, **browngoods**.

brownout /'braʊnaʊt/ n. a partial blackout, resulting in a dimming of lights, sometimes imposed deliberately to conserve electricity or, as in World War II, to reduce the glare in the sky of big industrial cities.

browse /braʊz/ v.i. **1.** to glance though merchandise in a shop. **2.** to glance at random through a book or books.

browser /'braʊzə/ n. **1.** someone who browses. **2.** Also, **web browser**. Computers computer software designed to facilitate searches on the World Wide Web by viewing the contents of web pages.

bruise /bruːz/ v. (**bruised, bruising**) –v.t. **1.** to injure by striking or pressing, without breaking the skin or drawing blood. **2.** to damage (fruit, etc.) by applying pressure, without breaking the skin. **3.** to injure or hurt superficially. –v.i. **4.** to develop a discoloured spot on the skin as the result of a blow, fall, etc. –n. **5.** an injury due to bruising; a contusion. **6.** a damaged area on a piece of fruit, etc., due to bruising.

brumby /'brʌmbi/ n. a wild horse, especially one descended from runaway stock.

brunch /brʌntʃ/ n. a midmorning meal that serves as both breakfast and lunch.

brunette /bru'net/ adj. (of a person) having dark or brown hair.

brunt /brʌnt/ n. the shock or force of an attack, etc.; the main stress, force, or violence.

bruschetta /brʊs'ketə, bru'ʃetə/ n. grilled slices of bread brushed with olive oil and fresh garlic, often served with various toppings.

brush¹ /brʌʃ/ n. **1.** an instrument consisting of bristles, hair, or the like, set in or attached to a handle, used for painting, cleaning, polishing, rubbing, etc. **2.** an act of brushing; an application of a brush. **3.** the bushy tail of an animal, especially of a fox. **4.** a slight skimming touch or contact. **5.** a brief hostile encounter; argument; skirmish. –v.t. **6.** to sweep, rub, clean, polish, etc., with a brush. **7.** to touch lightly in passing; pass lightly over. **8.** (usu. fol. by aside) to remove by brushing or by lightly passing over. **9.** to dress (the hair) using a brush.

brush² /brʌʃ/ n. a dense growth of bushes, shrubs, etc.; scrub; a thicket.

brush-tailed possum n. any of various strongly-built, medium-sized possums.

brush turkey n. a large mound-building bird of the wooded regions of eastern Australia. Also, **bush turkey**, **scrub turkey**.

brusque /brʌsk, brʊsk/ adj. abrupt in manner; blunt; rough.

brussels sprout n. a plant with small edible heads or sprouts along the stalk, which resemble miniature cabbage heads.

brutal /'brutl/ adj. **1.** savage; cruel; inhuman. **2.** crude; coarse; harsh. –**brutality**, n.

brute /brut/ n. **1.** a non-human animal; beast. **2.** a brutal person.

bubble /'bʌbəl/ n. **1.** a small globule of gas in a liquid or solid. **2.** a small globule of gas in a thin liquid envelope. –v.i. **3.** to send up bubbles; effervesce. –**bubbly**, adj.

bubblegum /'bʌbəlgʌm/ n. a type of chewing gum which can be blown into bubbles.

bubbler /'bʌblə/ n. Chiefly NSW a drinking fountain.

bubble wrap n. a plastic wrapping material consisting of innumerable small, sealed air pockets, used for protecting delicate items during transport or storage.

buccaneer /ˌbʌkəˈnɪə/ n. a pirate.

buck¹ /bʌk/ n. the male of certain animals, as the deer, antelope, rabbit, or hare.

buck² /bʌk/ v.i. **1.** (of a saddle or pack animal) to leap with arched back and come down with head low and forelegs stiff, in order to dislodge rider or pack. **2.** Colloq. to resist obstinately; object strongly: to buck at improvements. **3.** Colloq. (fol. by up) to become more cheerful, vigorous, etc.

buck³ /bʌk/ phr. **pass the buck**, Colloq. to shift the responsibility or blame to another person.

buck⁴ /bʌk/ n. Colloq. a dollar.

bucket /'bʌkət/ n. **1.** a vessel, usually round with flat bottom and a semicircular handle, for carrying water, sand, etc. –v.t. (**-eted, -eting**) **2.** Colloq. to criticise strongly. –phr. **3. kick the bucket**, Colloq. to die.

bucket list n. Colloq. a list of activities or experiences which a person feels they must undertake before they die.

bucket seat n. (in a car, etc.) a seat with a rounded or moulded back, to hold one person. Also, **bucket**.

bucket shop n. a stockbroking firm, usually small, which offers to transact its clients' orders at reduced commission rates.

buckle /'bʌkl/ n. **1.** a clasp consisting of a rectangular or curved rim with one or more movable tongues, used for fastening together two loose ends, as of a belt or strap. **2.** a bend, bulge, or kink, as in a saw blade. –v.t. **3.** to fasten with a buckle or buckles. **4.** to bend and shrivel, by applying heat or pressure; warp; curl. –v.i. **5.** (fol. by to or down to) to set to work with vigour. **6.** to bend, warp, or give way suddenly, as with heat or pressure.

Buckley's /'bʌkliz/ n. Colloq. a very slim chance; forlorn hope. Also, **Buckley's chance**.

bucks party n. a party in which only the bridegroom and his male associates participate,

held as part of the preliminaries to a wedding. Also, **bucks night**.

bucktooth /bʌk'tuθ/ n. (pl. **buckteeth** /-'tiθ/) a projecting tooth. –**bucktoothed**, adj.

bucolic /bju'kɒlɪk/ adj. rustic; rural.

bud /bʌd/ n. Bot. a small shoot or growth on the stem of a plant containing the first stages of a leaf, flower, or both.

buddy /'bʌdi/ n. (pl. **-dies**) Colloq. **1.** comrade; mate. **2.** someone who acts as either a mentor or partner to another, as to provide emotional, physical or practical support with a particular task or experience.

budge /bʌdʒ/ v. (**budged, budging**) –v.i. **1.** (usu. with negative) to move slightly; give way. –v.t. **2.** (usu. with negative) to cause to budge.

budgerigar /'bʌdʒəri,ga/ n. a small endemic Australian parrot of arid and semi-arid grasslands and woodlands; green and yellow with a blue tail in the wild, it has been widely domesticated and bred in many coloured varieties.

budget /'bʌdʒət/ n. **1.** an estimate, often itemised, of expected income and expenditure, or operating results, for a given period in the future. –v.t. (**-eted, -eting**) **2.** to plan allotment of (funds, time, etc.). –**budgetary**, adj.

buff¹ /bʌf/ n. **1.** a kind of thick leather. **2.** yellowish brown; medium or light tan. **3.** Colloq. the bare skin. **4.** Colloq. an enthusiast; an expert (sometimes self-proclaimed). –v.t. **5.** to polish (metal) or to give a grainless finish of high lustre to (plated surfaces).

buff² /bʌf/ v.t. to reduce or deaden the force of, as a buffer.

buffalo /'bʌfəloʊ/ n. (pl. **-loes** or **-los** or, especially collectively, **-lo**) any of several species of bovine mammals native to parts of Asia and Africa, especially those valued as draught animals.

buffer¹ /'bʌfə/ n. **1.** anything serving to neutralise the shock of opposing forces. **2.** Computers an area of temporary storage where data is held during computer operations.

buffer² /'bʌfə/ n. a device for polishing.

buffet¹ /'bʌfət/ n. **1.** a blow, as with the hand or fist. –v.t. (**-feted, -feting**) **2.** to strike, as with the hand or fist.

buffet² /'bʌfeɪ, 'bʊfeɪ/ n. **1.** a counter, bar, or the like, for lunch or refreshments. **2.** a sideboard or cabinet for holding china, plate, etc. –adj. **3.** (of a meal) spread on tables or buffets from which the guests serve themselves.

buffoon /bə'fun/ n. someone who amuses others by tricks, odd gestures and postures, jokes, etc.

bug /bʌg/ n. **1.** any insect. **2.** Colloq. an illness caused by bacteria or a virus. **3.** Computers an error in a program or the machine itself, often undetected by the most stringent tests. **4.** Colloq. an idea or belief with which one is obsessed. **5.** Colloq. a microphone hidden in a room to tap conversation. –v.t. (**bugged, bugging**) Colloq. **6.** to install a hidden microphone in (a room, etc.). **7.** to cause annoyance or distress to (a person).

bugbear /'bʌgbeə/ n. any source, real or imaginary, of needless fright or fear.

bugger /'bʌgə/ n. **1.** (taboo) someone who practises bestiality or sodomy. **2.** Colloq. a contemptible person. –v.t. **3.** Colloq. (fol. by *up*) to cause damage, frustration or inconvenience to. –*interj.* **4.** a strong exclamation of annoyance, disgust, etc. –*phr.* **5. bugger all**, *Colloq.* nothing. **–buggery,** *n.*

buggy /'bʌgi/ *n.* (*pl.* **-gies**) a two-wheeled horse-drawn carriage with or without a hood.

bugle /'bjugəl/ *n.* a cornet-like military wind instrument, usually metal, used for sounding signals and sometimes fitted with keys or valves.

build /bɪld/ *v.* (**built, building**) –*v.t.* **1.** to construct (something relatively complex) by assembling and combining parts. **2.** (oft. fol. by *up*) to establish, increase, and strengthen. **3.** to base; form; construct. **4.** (fol. by *out*) to obstruct the view from (a building) by erecting another building close to it. –*v.i.* **5.** to engage in the art or business of building. **6.** (fol. by *on* or *upon*) to form or construct a plan, system of thought, etc. –*n.* **7.** manner or style of construction or formation: *a yacht with a sleek build; a person with a heavy build.*

building /'bɪldɪŋ/ *n.* **1.** a structure built for people to live or work in. **2.** the act or business of constructing houses, etc.

building society *n.* an organisation which uses money subscribed by its members as a fund for lending money to members, as for the purchase of homes.

built-up area *n.* an area of dense habitation within which speed-limits apply to traffic.

buk choy /bʌk 'tʃɔɪ/ *n.* → **bok choy**.

bulb /bʌlb/ *n.* **1.** *Bot.* a storage organ, having fleshy leaves and usually subterranean, in which the stem is reduced to a flat disc, rooting from the underside, as in the onion, lily, etc. **2.** → **light globe. –bulbous,** *adj.*

bulge /bʌldʒ/ *n.* **1.** a rounded projecting or protruding part; protuberance; hump. –*v.i.* (**bulged, bulging**) **2.** to swell out; be protuberant.

bulimia /bə'limiə/ *n.* a compulsive eating disorder marked by bouts of overeating followed by induced vomiting. Also, **bulimia nervosa**. **–bulimic,** *adj., n.*

bulk /bʌlk/ *n.* **1.** magnitude in three dimensions. **2.** the greater part; the main mass or body. –*phr.* **3. in bulk, a.** unpackaged. **b.** in large quantities. **–bulky,** *adj.*

bulkhead /'bʌlkhɛd/ *n.* **1.** *Naut.* one of the upright partitions dividing a ship into compartments. **2.** a similar partition in an aircraft, vehicle, etc.

bull[1] /bʊl/ *n.* **1.** the male of a bovine animal, with sexual organs intact and capable of reproduction. **2.** the male of various other large animals, as the elephant, whale, etc. –*adj.* **3.** *Stock Exchange* of, relating to, or caused by rising prices in stocks, etc.: *a bull market*.

bull[2] /bʊl/ *n.* *Roman Catholic Church* **1.** a formal and solemn papal document dealing with an important matter and usually having a bulla attached. **2.** the bulla itself.

bull[3] /bʊl/ *n.* *Colloq.* nonsense.

bulla /'bʊlə, 'bʌlə/ *n.* (*pl.* **bullae** /'bʊli, 'bʌli/) a seal attached to an official document.

bull ant *n.* a large, aggressive ant with powerful jaws and a painful sting.

bull bar *n.* a metal grid placed in front of a motor vehicle to protect it from collision

damage, especially with kangaroos, stray cattle, etc. Also, **bullbar**.

bulldog /'bʊldɒg/ *n.* a large-headed, short-haired, heavily built variety of dog, of comparatively small size but very muscular and vigorous.

bulldozer /'bʊldoʊzə/ *n.* a large tractor moving on tracks (def. 7) or wheels, having a vertical blade at the front end for moving earth, tree stumps, rocks, etc.

bullet /'bʊlət/ *n.* **1.** a small metal projectile, part of a cartridge, for firing from small arms. **2.** a heavy dot used in a document to make a particular passage of text more prominent.

bulletin /'bʊlətən/ *n.* **1.** a brief account or statement, as of news or events, issued for the information of the public. **2.** a periodical publication, as of a learned society.

bulletin board *n.* **1.** *US* → **noticeboard**. **2.** an electronic message directory accessible on a computer.

bullfight /'bʊlfaɪt/ *n.* a form of entertainment in which a person fights with and usually kills a bull. **–bullfighter,** *n.*

bull-headed /bʊl-'hɛdəd/ *adj.* obstinate; blunderingly stubborn; stupid.

bullion /'bʊljən/ *n.* **1.** gold or silver in the mass. **2.** gold or silver in the form of bars or ingots.

bull market *n.* *Stock Exchange* a buoyant period of trading during and immediately after a rise in share prices when traders consider that there are strong prospects of further price rises.

bullock /'bʊlək/ *n.* **1.** a castrated male of a bovine animal, not having been used for reproduction; ox; steer. –*v.t.* **2.** to force.

bullroarer /'bʊlrɔrə/ *n.* a thin piece of wood on a string, which it is whirled in the air to make a roaring noise.

bullseye /'bʊlzaɪ/ *n.* the central spot, usually black, of a target.

bullshit /'bʊlʃɪt/ *n.* *Colloq.* (*taboo*) nonsense.

bull-terrier *n.* one of a breed of dogs produced by crossing the bulldog and the terrier.

bully /'bʊli/ *n.* (*pl.* **-lies**) **1.** a blustering, quarrelsome, overbearing person who brow-beats smaller or weaker people. **2.** someone who intimidates or demeans another, especially as by repeated threats to their person, career, or social standing, or by harassment in person, on social networks, etc. –*v.i.* (**-lied, -lying**) **3.** to be loudly arrogant and overbearing.

bum /bʌm/ *Colloq.* –*n.* **1.** the rump; buttocks. **2.** a habitual loafer and tramp. –*v.t.* (**bummed, bumming**) **3.** to get for nothing; borrow without expectation of returning: *to bum a cigarette*.

bumble /'bʌmbəl/ *v.i.* to proceed clumsily or inefficiently.

bumblebee /'bʌmbəlbi/ *n.* any of various large, hairy social bees. Also, **humblebee**.

bummer /'bʌmə/ *n.* *Colloq.* something which causes disappointment.

bump /bʌmp/ *v.t.* **1.** to come more or less heavily in contact with; strike; collide with. **2.** *Colloq.* (fol. by *up*) to increase (in extent, etc.). –*v.i.* **3. a.** (oft. fol. by *against, into*) to come in contact with; collide. **b.** (fol. by *into*) to meet by chance. –*n.* **4.** the act of bumping; a blow. **5.** a dull thud; the noise of collision. **6.** a small area raised above the level of the surrounding surface, as on the skull or on a road.

bumper bar *n.* a horizontal bar affixed to the front or rear of a vehicle to give some protection in collisions.

bumpkin /ˈbʌmpkən/ *n.* an awkward, clumsy yokel.

bumptious /ˈbʌmpʃəs/ *adj.* offensively self-assertive.

bun /bʌn/ *n.* **1.** a kind of bread roll, usually slightly sweetened and round-shaped, and sometimes containing spice, dried currants, etc. **2.** hair arranged on the head in a bun shape.

bunch /bʌntʃ/ *n.* **1.** a connected group; cluster. –*v.t.* **2.** to group together; make a bunch of.

bundle /ˈbʌndl/ *n.* **1.** a group loosely held together. **2.** something wrapped for carrying; package. –*v.t.* **3.** (fol. by *up*) to dress snugly. **4.** (fol. by *off, out*, etc.) to send away hurriedly or unceremoniously.

bundling /ˈbʌndlɪŋ/ *n. Computers* the practice of including some software with a hardware purchase for the same price.

bundy /ˈbʌndi/ *n. Colloq. (from trademark)* a clock which marks the time on a card inserted in it, used to record arrival and departure times of employees; time clock.

bung¹ /bʌŋ/ *n.* **1.** a stopper, as for the hole of a cask. –*v.t.* **2.** *Colloq.* to put. –*phr.* **3. bung it on, a.** to behave temperamentally. **b.** to act in a pretentious or ostentatious manner.

bung² /bʌŋ/ *adj. Colloq.* not in good working order; impaired; injured.

bungalow /ˈbʌŋɡəloʊ/ *n.* a house or cottage of one storey.

bungee jumping *n.* a sport in which one throws oneself from a high place such as a bridge to which one is attached by an elasticised cord (**bungee**). Also, **bungy jumping**. –**bungee jumper**, *n.*

bungle /ˈbʌŋɡəl/ **1.** to do clumsily and awkwardly; botch. –*n.* **2.** something badly done.

bunion /ˈbʌnjən/ *n.* a swelling on the foot.

bunk /bʌŋk/ *n.* **1.** a built-in platform bed, as on a ship. **2.** one of a pair of beds built one above the other.

bunker /ˈbʌŋkə/ *n.* **1.** a chest or box; a large bin or receptacle. **2.** a fortified shelter, often underground. **3.** *Golf* a shallow excavation, usually at the side of a green, which has been nearly filled with sand.

bunker buster *n.* a laser-guided bomb designed to penetrate underground bunkers before exploding.

bunkum /ˈbʌŋkəm/ *n.* insincere talk; humbug.

bunny /ˈbʌni/ *n. (pl.* **-nies**) *Colloq.* **1.** Also, **bunny rabbit.** a rabbit. **2.** someone who accepts the responsibility for a situation, sometimes willingly.

bunny boiler *n. Colloq.* a woman who is violent or vengeful to the point of insanity.

Bunsen burner /bʌnsən ˈbɜnə/ *n.* a type of gas burner with a very hot, blue flame, used widely in laboratories.

bunting /ˈbʌntɪŋ/ *n.* **1.** a coarse open fabric of worsted or cotton used for flags, signals. **2.** festive decorations made from bunting, paper, etc., usually in the form of draperies, wide streamers, etc.

bunyip /ˈbʌnjəp/ *n.* an imaginary creature of Aboriginal legend, said to haunt swamps and billabongs.

buoy /bɔɪ/ *n.* **1.** *Naut.* a distinctively marked and shaped anchored float, sometimes carrying a light, whistle, or bell, marking a channel or obstruction. –*v.t.* **2.** to support by or as by a buoy; keep afloat in a fluid. **3.** to bear up or sustain, as hope or courage does.

buoyant /ˈbɔɪənt/ *adj.* **1.** tending to float or rise in a fluid. **2.** not easily depressed; cheerful. **3.** (of production levels, prices, etc.) having the capacity of recovering from a reverse. –**buoyancy**, *n.*

burble /ˈbɜbəl/ *v.i.* to make a bubbling sound; bubble.

burden /ˈbɜdn/ *n.* **1.** that which is carried; a load. **2.** that which is borne with difficulty. **3.** *Commerce* the duty to discharge an obligation or responsibility. –*v.t.* **4.** to load heavily. –**burdensome**, *adj.*

bureau /ˈbjʊroʊ, bjuˈroʊ/ *n. (pl.* **-reaus** *or* **-reaux** /-roʊz/) **1.** a desk or writing table with drawers for papers. **2.** a division of a government department or independent administrative unit.

bureaucracy /bjuˈrɒkrəsi/ *n. (pl.* **-cies**) **1.** government by administrative officials organised into departments, bureaus, etc. **2.** the body of such officials. **3.** excessive governmental red tape and routine. –**bureaucrat**, *n.* –**bureaucratic**, *adj.*

burgeon /ˈbɜdʒən/ *v.i.* (oft. fol. by *out, forth*) to begin to grow, as a bud; to put forth buds, shoots, as a plant.

burger /ˈbɜɡə/ *n.* **1.** → **hamburger**. **2.** any of various adaptations of the hamburger which have different main contents in the bun: *fish burger; chicken burger.*

burghul /ˈbɜɡəl/ *n.* crushed wheat that has been hulled, parboiled, dried, and then ground, used especially in Lebanese cookery. Also, **bourghul, bur'ghul, bulgar**.

burglary /ˈbɜɡləri/ *n. (pl.* **-ries**) the offence of breaking into and entering the house of another with intent to commit a felony therein. –**burglar**, *n.*

burgundy /ˈbɜɡəndi/ *n. (pl.* **-dies**) **1.** (*sometimes upper case*) wine of many varieties, red and white, mostly still, full, and dry, produced in the Burgundy region of France. **2.** a purplish red.

burial /ˈbɛriəl/ *n.* the act of burying.

burka /ˈbɜkə/ *n.* → **burqa**.

burkini /bɜˈkini/ *n. (from trademark)* a swimsuit designed for Muslim women, comprising leggings and a tunic top with a hood. Also, **burqini**.

burl /bɜl/ *n. Colloq.* an attempt.

burlesque /bɜˈlɛsk/ *n.* a theatrical or cabaret entertainment featuring coarse, crude, often vulgar comedy and dancing.

burly /ˈbɜli/ *adj.* (**-lier, -liest**) **1.** great in bodily size; stout; sturdy. **2.** bluff; brusque.

burn /bɜn/ *v.* (**burnt** *or* **burned, burning**) –*v.i.* **1.** to be on fire. **2.** to feel heat or a physiologically identical sensation. **3.** to give light. **4.** to feel strong passion. **5.** to become discoloured, tanned, or charred through heat. –*v.t.* **6.** to consume, partly or wholly, with fire. **7.** to injure, discolour, char, or treat with heat. **8.** to produce with fire. **9.** (fol. by *up*) to pass through or over quickly and easily. **10.** (oft. fol. by *off*) to clear or improve (land) by burning the cover. –*n.* **11.** an injury produced by heat or by abnormal cold, chemicals, poison gas, electricity, or lightning.

burnish /'bɜnɪʃ/ *v.t.* to polish (a surface) by friction.

burnout /'bɜnaʊt/ *n.* **1.** the point in time or in the trajectory of a missile or rocket when combustion of fuels in the rocket engine is terminated by other than programmed cut-off. **2.** *Colloq.* a nervous breakdown brought on by exhaustion and stress: *executive burnout.* **3.** *Colloq.* a car stunt in which the back tyres are made to spin on the spot at very high speed and thus cause as much smoke as possible.

burnt /bɜnt/ *v.* a past tense and past participle of **burn.**

burp /bɜp/ *v.i.*, *n.* → **belch** (defs 1 and 4).

burqa /'bɜkə/ *n.* a traditional garment for Muslim women, giving full body covering with a mesh-covered opening for the eyes. Also, **burka.**

burr[1] /bɜ/ *n. Bot.* the rough, prickly case around the seeds of certain plants.

burr[2] /bɜ/ *n.* **1.** any of various tools and appliances for cutting or drilling. **2.** to form a rough point or edge on. Also, **bur.**

burrito /bə'ritoʊ/ *n.* in Mexican cooking, a tortilla folded over a filling of meat, cheese or beans.

burrow /'bʌroʊ/ *n.* **1.** a hole in the ground made by a rabbit, fox, or similar small animal, for refuge and habitation. –*v.i.* **2.** to make a hole or passage (*in*, *into*, or *under* something).

bursar /'bɜsə/ *n.* **1.** a treasurer or business officer, especially of a college or university. **2.** a student holding a bursary.

bursary /'bɜsəri/ *n.* (*pl.* **-ries**) a scholarship.

burst /bɜst/ *v.* (**burst**, **bursting**) –*v.i.* **1.** to fly apart or break open with sudden violence; explode. **2.** to issue forth suddenly and forcibly from or as from confinement. **3.** to break or give way from violent pain or emotion. **4.** to be extremely full, as if ready to break open. –*v.t.* **5.** to cause to burst; break suddenly and violently. –*n.* **6.** the act of bursting. **7.** a sudden display of activity or energy. **8.** a sudden expression or manifestation of emotion, etc.

bury /'bɛri/ *v.t.* (**-ried**, **-rying**) **1.** to put in the ground and cover with earth. **2.** to cover in order to conceal from sight. **3.** to occupy (oneself) completely.

bus /bʌs/ *n.* (*pl.* **buses** *or* **busses**) **1.** a vehicle with a long body equipped with seats or benches for passengers, usually operating as part of a scheduled service. **2.** *Computers* → **busbar** (def. 2).

busbar /'bʌsbɑ/ *n.* **1.** an electrical conductor having low resistance connecting several like points in an electrical system, frequently used to supply power to various points. **2.** *Computers* a group of such electrical conductors providing a communication path within a computer or between two or more computerised devices.

bush /bʊʃ/ *n.* **1.** a woody plant, especially a low one, with many branches which usually arise from or near the ground. **2.** something resembling or suggesting this, as a thick, shaggy head of hair. **3.** terrain covered with bushy vegetation or trees. –*v.t.* **4.** to cover with bushes; protect with bushes set round about; support with bushes. –*adj.* **5.** found in or typical of the bush: *a bush nurse; a bush pub; bush hospitality.* **6.** uncivilised; rough; makeshift: *a bush bed; bush carpentry.* –*phr.* **7. go bush, a.** (of animals) to stray and live in the bush. **b.** (of people) to reject civilisation and live an isolated life in the bush. **c.** to adopt a way of life which is without the comforts and attractions of the big city, especially one which is close to nature. **8. take to the bush,** to go to live in the bush, especially to turn one's back on civilisation and adopt a way of life close to nature. **9. the bush,** any rural area, when contrasted with the city. –**bushy,** *adj.*

bush band *n.* a band which performs Australian folk music, usually with such instruments as the accordion, tea-chest bass, guitar, etc.

bushcare /'bʊʃkɛə/ *n.* the maintenance of remnant bush or the revegetation of land with native trees, as by landowners and community groups. –**bushcarer,** *n.*

bushcraft /'bʊʃkrɑft/ *n.* the ability to live in and travel through the bush with a minimum of equipment and assistance.

bushed /bʊʃt/ *adj. Colloq.* **1.** lost. **2.** exhausted. **3.** confused.

bushel /'bʊʃəl/ *n.* a unit of dry measure in the imperial system equal to 36.36872×10^{-3} m^3 (8 gal).

bushfire /'bʊʃfaɪə/ *n.* a fire that has broken out in forest, scrub or grassland; often caused by lightning strike.

bushland /'bʊʃlænd/ *n.* natural, uncultivated land.

bushman /'bʊʃmən/ *n.* someone skilled in bushcraft.

bushranger /'bʊʃreɪndʒə/ *n.* (formerly) a bandit or criminal who hid in the bush and stole from settlers and travellers at gunpoint.

bush regeneration *n.* the regeneration of areas of bush in which the native flora has been supplanted by exotic species, or destroyed.

bush telegraph *n. Colloq.* an unofficial chain of communication by which information is conveyed and rumour spread, as by word of mouth. Also, **bush wireless.**

bush tucker *n.* **1.** simple fare, as eaten by one living in or off the bush. **2.** food from Australian indigenous plants and trees. **3.** traditional Aboriginal food, especially food caught or collected using traditional Aboriginal methods.

bush turkey *n.* → **brush turkey.**

bushwalk /'bʊʃwɔk/ *v.i.* **1.** to hike through the bush for pleasure. –*n.* **2.** such an excursion. **3.** an established route for a bushwalk. –**bushwalker,** *n.* –**bushwalking,** *n.*

bushwhacker /'bʊʃwækə/ *n. Colloq.* an unsophisticated person who lives in the bush. Also, **bushwacker.**

business /'bɪznəs/ *n.* **1.** one's occupation, profession, or trade. **2.** *Econ.* the purchase and sale of goods in an attempt to make a profit.

3. *Commerce* a person, partnership, or corporation engaged in this; an established or going enterprise or concern. **4.** volume of trade; patronage. **5.** that with which one is principally and seriously concerned. **6.** that with which one is rightfully concerned. **7.** affair; matter. *–phr.* **8. mean business**, to be in earnest. **9. mind one's own business**, *Colloq.* to refrain from attempting to learn about or becoming involved in someone else's affairs. **10. (secret) men's business → men's business. 11. (secret) women's business → women's business.**

business activity statement *n.* a statement which a business is required to submit to the government agency on a regular basis, containing an account of transactions and allowing the calculation of tax, especially GST, payable. Also, **BAS.**

businesslike /'bɪznəslaɪk/ *adj.* conforming to the methods of business or trade; methodical; systematic.

businessperson /'bɪznəspɜsən/ *n.* (*pl.* **-people**) a person engaged in business or commerce. **–businessman**, *masc. n.* **–businesswoman**, *fem. n.*

busker /'bʌskə/ *n.* an entertainer who gives performances in streets, parks, markets, etc., usually collecting donations from the audience.

bust[1] /bʌst/ *n.* **1.** the head and shoulders of a person done in sculpture, either in the round or in relief. **2.** the chest or breast; the bosom.

bust[2] /bʌst/ *Colloq.* *–v.i.* **1.** to burst. **2.** (oft. fol. by *up*) to go bankrupt. **3.** (fol. by *up*) to part finally; quarrel and part. *–v.t.* **4.** (oft. fol. by *in*) to burst. **5.** (fol. by *up*) to smash. **6.** (oft. fol. by *up*) to bankrupt; ruin. **7.** (fol. by *up*) to interrupt violently a political meeting or other gathering. **8.** to reduce in rank or grade; demote. *–n.* **9.** a complete failure; bankruptcy. **10.** a police raid, often in search of an illegal substance. *–adj.* **11.** Also, **busted.** broken; ruined. **12.** bankrupt.

bustard /'bʌstəd/ *n.* a large, heavy bird inhabiting grassy plains and open scrub country of Australia and New Guinea; plain turkey.

bustle[1] /'bʌsəl/ *v.i.* (**-tled, -tling**) (oft. fol. by *about*) to move or act with a great show of energy.

bustle[2] /'bʌsəl/ *n.* (formerly) a pad, cushion, or wire framework worn by women on the back part of the body below the waist, to expand and support the skirt.

busy /'bɪzi/ *adj.* (**busier, busiest**) **1.** actively and attentively engaged. **2.** having a lot of things to do. **3.** full of or characterised by activity. **4.** (of a telephone, etc.) already in use. *–v.t.* (**busied, busying**) **5.** to keep occupied; make or keep busy.

busybody /'bɪzibɒdi/ *n.* (*pl.* **-dies**) a person who pries into and meddles in the affairs of others.

but /bʌt/, *weak form* /bət/ *conj.* **1.** on the contrary; yet. **2.** except, rather than, or save. **3.** except that (followed by a clause, often with *that* expressed). **4.** without the circumstance that, or that not. **5.** otherwise than. **6.** that (especially after *doubt, deny*, etc., with a negative). **7.** who or which not. *–prep.* **8.** with

the exception of; except; save. *–adv.* **9.** only; just. *–n.* **10.** a restriction or objection.

butane /'bjuteɪn, bju'teɪn/ *n.* a hydrocarbon used as a fuel.

butch /bʊtʃ/ *adj. Colloq.* (of a man or woman) exhibiting masculine characteristics.

butcher /'bʊtʃə/ *n.* **1.** a retail dealer in meat. **2.** a person guilty of cruel or indiscriminate slaughter. *–v.t.* **3.** to murder indiscriminately or brutally. **–butchery**, *n.*

butcherbird /'bʊtʃəbɜd/ *n.* any of several birds so called because they impale their prey of small birds, etc., on spikes or thorns or wedge it in the forks of trees.

butler /'bʌtlə/ *n.* the head male servant of a household.

butt[1] /bʌt/ *n.* **1.** the end or extremity of anything, especially the thicker, larger, or blunt end, as of a rifle, fishing rod, whip handle, arrow, log, etc. **2.** an end which is not used up. **3.** *Colloq.* the buttocks; bottom.

butt[2] /bʌt/ *n.* **1.** a person or thing that is an object of wit, ridicule, sarcasm, etc., or contempt. **2.** the target for archery practice. *–v.i.* **3.** to have an end or projection (*on*); be adjacent (*to*).

butt[3] /bʌt/ *v.t.* **1.** to strike with the head or horns. **2.** to project. *–phr. Colloq.* **3. butt in**, to interrupt; interfere; intrude. **4. butt out**, to mind one's own business and not interfere in something which is not one's proper concern.

butter /'bʌtə/ *n.* **1.** the fatty portion of milk, separating as a soft whitish or yellowish solid when milk or cream is agitated or churned. *–v.t.* **2.** to put butter on or in. *–phr.* **3. butter up**, to flatter grossly.

butterfly /'bʌtəflaɪ/ *n.* (*pl.* **-flies**) **1.** an insect with large, broad wings often conspicuously coloured and marked. **2.** (*pl.*) nervousness. **3.** Also, **butterfly stroke**. a swimming stroke in prone position, with both arms flung forward simultaneously.

butterfly knife *n.* a folding knife with two handles so that, when closed, the blade is concealed within the handles.

buttermilk /'bʌtəmɪlk/ *n.* the liquid remaining after the butter has been separated from milk or cream.

butterscotch /'bʌtəskɒtʃ/ *n.* a kind of toffee made with butter.

buttock /'bʌtək/ *n. Anat.* either of the two protuberances which form the rump.

button /'bʌtn/ *n.* **1.** a disc or knob on a piece of cloth which, when passed through a slit or loop either in the same piece or another, serves as a fastening. **2.** anything resembling a button. **3.** a disc pressed to close an electric circuit, as in ringing a bell. **4.** *Computers* a small outlined area on a screen which, when selected, performs some function. *–v.t.* **5.** to fasten with a button or buttons.

buttonhole /'bʌtnhoʊl/ *n.* **1.** the hole, slit, or loop through which a button is passed. **2.** a small flower or nosegay worn in the buttonhole in the lapel of a jacket.

buttress /'bʌtrəs/ *n.* **1.** *Archit.* a structure built against a wall or building for the purpose of giving it stability. **2.** any prop or support.

buxom /'bʌksəm/ *adj.* (of a woman) full-bosomed, plump, and attractive because of radiant health.

buy /baɪ/ *v.* (**bought, buying**) –*v.t.* **1.** to acquire the possession of, or the right to, by paying an equivalent, especially in money. **2.** (fol. by *off*) to get rid of (a claim, opposition, etc.) by payment; purchase the non-intervention of; bribe. **3.** (fol. by *out*) to secure all of (an owner's or partner's) share or interest in an enterprise. **4.** (fol. by *up*) to buy as much as one can of. **5.** (fol. by *in, into*) to acquire shares; become involved in. **6.** *Colloq.* to accept. –*v.i.* **7.** to be or become a purchaser. –*n.* **8.** *Colloq.* a purchase, esp. a good purchase. –*phr.* **9. buy in, a.** *Stock Exchange* (of a broker) to obtain a share scrip from another broker to cover his or her position after another broker fails to deliver shares. **b.** to join in; become involved. **10. buy into,** to choose to become involved in.

buyback /'baɪbæk/ *n.* **1.** an act or instance of buying back something previously sold. **2.** an agreement between two parties, whereby the first party sells securities to the second party and at the same time undertakes to buy them back at a specified price at some agreed time in the future. Also, **buy-back.**

buyer /'baɪə/ *n.* **1.** someone who buys; a purchaser. **2.** a purchasing agent, as for a chain-store.

buyers' market *n.* a situation where, at current prices, supply exceeds demand so that buyers tend to determine price and the terms and/or conditions by which sales are effected.

buzz /bʌz/ *n.* **1.** a low, vibrating, humming sound, as of bees. **2.** *Colloq.* a telephone call. **3.** *Colloq.* **a.** a feeling of exhilaration or pleasure, especially as induced by drugs. **b.** a similar experience of pleasure, delight, etc.: *I get a real buzz out of going sailing.* –*v.i.* **4.** to make a low, vibrating, humming sound. **5.** (usu. fol. by *about*) to move busily from place to place. **6.** *Colloq.* (usu. fol. by *off* or *along*) to go; leave. –*v.t.* **7.** to make a buzzing sound with. **8.** *Aeronautics Colloq.* **a.** to fly an aeroplane very low over. **b.** to signal or greet (someone) by flying an aeroplane low and slowing the motor spasmodically.

buzzard /'bʌzəd/ *n.* any of various birds of prey related to but smaller than eagles.

buzzkill /'bʌzkɪl/ *n. Colloq.* someone or something that has the effect of dampening excitement or enthusiasm. Also, **buzzkiller.**

buzzword /'bʌzwɜd/ *n. Colloq.* a word used for its emotive value or its ability to impress the listener.

by /baɪ/ *prep.* **1.** near to. **2.** using as a route. **3.** through or on as a means of conveyance. **4.** not later than. **5.** to the extent of. **6.** through evidence or authority of. **7.** in conformity with. **8.** before; in the presence of. **9.** through the agency or efficacy of. **10.** after; in serial order. **11.** combined with in multiplication or relative dimension. **12.** involving as unit of measure. –*adv.* **13.** near to something. **14.** to and past a point near something. **15.** aside. **16.** over; past. –*n.* **17. → bye¹.** –*phr.* **18. by and by,** at some time in the future; before

long; presently. **19. by and large,** in general; on the whole.

by- a prefix meaning: **1.** secondary; incidental, as in *by-product.* **2.** out of the way; removed, as in *byway.* **3.** near, as in *bystander.* Also, **bye-.**

bycatch /'baɪkætʃ/ *n.* the unwanted fish, sea creatures, etc., caught in nets along with the targeted fish.

bye¹ /baɪ/ *n. Sport* the state of having no competitor in a contest where several competitors are engaged in pairs, conferring the right to compete in the next round in a competition. Also, **by.**

bye² /baɪ/ *interj.* goodbye.

by-election /'baɪ-əlekʃən/ *n.* a parliamentary election held between general elections, to fill a vacancy caused by the death or resignation of a member of parliament. Also, **bye-election.**

bygone /'baɪgɒn/ *adj.* **1.** past; gone by; out of date. –*n.* **2.** that which is past.

by-law /'baɪ-lɔ/ *n.* **1.** an ordinance of an authority having legal effect only within the boundaries of that authority's jurisdiction. **2.** subordinate legislation, generally at the level of local government. **3.** a standing rule, as of a company or society, not in its constitution. Also, **bye-law.**

by-line /'baɪ-laɪn/ *n. Journalism* a line under the heading of a newspaper or magazine article giving the writer's name.

byname /'baɪneɪm/ *n.* **1.** a secondary name. **2.** a nickname.

BYO /bi waɪ 'oʊ/ an abbreviation used to indicate that guests, restaurant patrons, etc., should bring their own supply of liquor. Also, **BYOG.**

bypass /'baɪpas/ *n.* **1.** a road enabling motorists to avoid towns and other heavy traffic points or any obstruction to easy travel on a main road. **2.** *Med.* **a.** a channel inserted by surgery in order to avoid the normal passage of fluids in the circulatory or digestive systems. **b. → bypass operation.** –*v.t.* **3.** to avoid (obstructions, etc.) by following a bypass. **4.** to go over the head of (one's immediate supervisor, etc.).

bypass operation *n. Med.* an operation in which a diseased or obstructed segment of the circulatory or digestive systems of the body is circumvented; particularly used to circumvent diseased blood vessels in the heart.

by-product /'baɪ-prɒdʌkt/ *n.* a secondary or incidental product, as in a process of manufacture.

byre /'baɪə/ *n.* a cattle pen.

bystander /'baɪstændə/ *n.* a person present but not involved; a chance looker-on.

byte /baɪt/ *n.* a unit of information, usually eight bits, stored by a computer. See **bit².**

byway /'baɪweɪ/ *n.* **1.** a secluded, or obscure road. **2.** a subsidiary or obscure field of research, endeavour, etc.

byword /'baɪwɜd/ *n.* **1.** the name of a quality or concept which characterises some person or group; the epitome (of). **2.** a word or phrase used proverbially; a common saying; a proverb.

C, c

C, c /si/ *n.* the third letter of the English alphabet.

C /si/ *n. Computers* a computer language which combines the sophistication and flexibility of a high-level computer language with the ability to directly address hardware.

cab /kæb/ *n.* **1.** → **taxi**. **2.** the covered part of a truck, etc., where the driver sits.

cabal /kə'bal, kə'bæl/ *n.* the secret schemes of a small group of plotters.

cabanossi /kæbə'nɒsi/ *n.* a thin, pre-cooked, mildly seasoned beef or pork sausage. Also, **kabanossi**.

cabaret /'kæbəreɪ/ *n.* a form of musical entertainment at a restaurant, nightclub, etc.

cabbage /'kæbɪdʒ/ *n.* a vegetable with a short stem and leaves formed into a compact, edible head.

caber /'keɪbə/ *n.* a pole or beam, especially one thrown as a trial of strength in the Scottish Highland game of **tossing the caber**.

cabernet sauvignon /ˌkæbəneɪ 'souvɪnjɒn/ *n.* (*sometimes upper case*) **1.** a highly regarded grape variety widely used in the making of claret-style wines. **2.** a dry red wine made from this variety. Also, *Colloq.,* **cab sav**.

cabin /'kæbən/ *n.* **1.** a small temporary house. **2.** an apartment or room in a ship, as for passengers. **3.** the enclosed place in an aircraft for the pilot, passengers, or cargo.

cabinet /'kæbənət, 'kæbnət/ *n.* **1.** a piece of furniture with shelves, drawers, etc. **2.** (*also upper case*) a council advising a sovereign or chief executive; the group of ministers responsible for the government of a nation.

cabin fever *n.* an emotional state fluctuating between torpor and aggression, brought on by being confined to a small space for a length of time with few or no companions.

cable /'keɪbəl/ *n.* **1.** a thick, strong rope. **2.** (formerly) a message sent by electric signals, especially along submarine cable. **3.** → **cable TV**.

cable TV *n.* a system of broadcasting television programs by sending them directly from the distribution centre to the receiving set by means of a cable. Also, **cable television**, **cable**.

caboodle /kə'budl/ *phr.* **the whole (kit and) caboodle**, *Colloq.* the whole lot, pack, or crowd.

cabotage /'kæbətaʒ/ *n.* trade or navigation in coastal waters.

cabriolet /'kæbrɪəleɪ/ *n.* a type of car resembling a coupé, with a folding top.

cacao /kə'keɪoʊ, -'kaoʊ/ *n.* (*pl.* **-caos**) a small evergreen tree, cultivated for its seeds, the source of cocoa, etc.

cache /kæʃ/ *for defs 1 and 2,* /keɪʃ/ *for def. 3 –*n. **1.** a store of provisions, treasure, etc., especially one hidden in the ground. **2.** a hiding place. **3.** → **cache memory**.

cache memory *n.* a section of computer memory which can be accessed at high speed and in which information is stored for fast retrieval.

cackle /'kækəl/ *v.i.* to utter a shrill, broken sound or cry, as a hen after laying an egg.

cacophony /kə'kɒfəni/ *n.* a harsh sound.

cactus /'kæktəs/ *n.* (*pl.* **-tuses** *or* **-ti** /-taɪ, -ti/) a spiky plant which stores water in its thick skin and grows in hot dry places.

cad /kæd/ *n.* a contemptible person.

cadastre /kə'dæstə/ *n.* an official register of property, with details of boundaries, ownership, etc.

cadaver /kə'dævə, -'davə/ *n.* a corpse.

caddie /'kædi/ *n. Golf* an attendant hired to carry the player's clubs, find the ball, etc.

caddy /'kædi/ *n.* (*pl.* **-dies**) a small box, tin, or chest, especially one for holding tea.

cadence /'keɪdns/ *n.* **1.** rhythmic flow, as of verses; rhythm. **2.** the general modulation of the voice.

cadet /kə'dɛt/ *n.* a person undergoing training, especially in the armed services.

cadge /kædʒ/ *v.t.* (**cadged, cadging**) to borrow without intent to repay.

cadmium /'kædmiəm/ *n.* a white, ductile, divalent metallic element, like tin in appearance, used in plating and in making certain alloys. *Symbol:* Cd

cadre /'kadə, 'keɪdə/ *n.* a unit within an organisational framework, especially personnel.

caesarean section /sə'zɛəriən/ *n.* the operation by which a fetus is taken from the womb by cutting through the walls of the abdomen and womb. Also, **caesarian section**, **cesarean section**, **cesarian section**.

caesar salad /'sizə/ *n.* a salad containing lettuce, bread croutons, parmesan cheese and sometimes anchovies, seasoned and dressed with egg, oil and vinegar.

caesium /'siziəm/ *n.* a rare, extremely active, soft, monovalent metallic element. *Symbol:* Cs

cafe /'kæfeɪ, kæ'feɪ/ *n.* a room or building where coffee and light refreshments are served. Also, **café**.

cafe latte /'latei/ *n.* an Italian style of coffee in which espresso coffee is poured into a large glass of hot milk. Also, **caffe latte**, **latte**.

cafeteria /kæfə'tɪəriə/ *n.* an inexpensive restaurant or snack-bar, usually self-service.

caffeine /'kæfin/ *n.* a bitter substance obtained from coffee, tea, etc., used as a stimulant.

caffe latte /kæfeɪ 'lateɪ/ *n.* → **cafe latte**.

caftan /'kæftæn/ *n.* a long, loose garment. Also, **kaftan**.

cage /keɪdʒ/ *n.* **1.** a box-shaped receptacle or enclosure for confining birds or other animals. –*v.t.* (**caged, caging**) **2.** to put or confine in or as in a cage.

cage fight *n.* a martial arts event in which the contestants fight inside a cage. –**cage fighter**, *n.* –**cage fighting**, *n.*

cagey /'keɪdʒi/ *adj.* (**cagier, cagiest**) *Colloq.* cautious; secretive. Also, **cagy**.

cahoots /kə'huts/ *phr.* **in cahoots**, in partnership; in league.

caiman /'keɪmən/ *n.* a tropical American reptile resembling and related to the alligators, but with overlapping abdominal plates.

caino- a word element meaning 'new', 'recent'. Also, **ceno-**, **caeno-**.

cairn /keən/ n. a heap of stones set up as a landmark, monument, tombstone, etc.

cajole /kə'dʒoʊl/ v.t. to persuade by flattery or promises. **–cajolery, cajolement, cajoler,** n.

cake /keɪk/ n. a sweet baked food in loaf or layer form.

cakeage /'keɪkɪdʒ/ n. a charge levied by a restaurant for serving cake, such as a birthday cake, brought in from outside the premises.

calamari /kælə'mari/ n. squid used as food.

calamine /'kæləmaɪn/ n. a liquid soothing to the skin. Also, **calamine lotion.**

calamity /kə'læməti/ n. (pl. **-ties**) a disaster. **–calamitous,** adj.

calcareous /kal'keəriəs/ adj. chalk-like.

calcify /'kælsəfaɪ/ v.i. (-**fied, -fying**) Physiol. to become chalky or bony.

calcium /'kælsiəm/ n. a silver-white divalent metal. Symbol: Ca

calculate /'kælkjəleɪt/ v.t. to ascertain by mathematical methods. **–calculation,** n. **–calculable,** adj. **–calculated,** adj. **–calculatedly,** adv.

calculating /'kælkjəleɪtɪŋ/ adj. shrewd.

calculator /'kælkjəleɪtə/ n. a machine that performs mathematical operations.

calculus /'kælkjələs/ n. (pl. **-luses** for def. 1, **-li** /-laɪ/ for def. 2) **1.** a method of calculation. **2.** a hard stone-like mass which has formed in the body.

calendar /'kæləndə/ n. any of various systems of reckoning time, especially with reference to the beginning, length, and divisions of the year.

calf¹ /kaf/ n. (pl. **calves**) the young of the cow or certain other animals.

calf² /kaf/ n. (pl. **calves**) the fleshy part of the back of the human leg below the knee.

calibrate /'kæləbreɪt/ v.t. to determine, check, or rectify the graduation or accuracy of.

calibre /'kæləbə/ n. **1.** the diameter of something of circular section, especially that of the inside of a tube, as the bore of a gun. **2.** personal character.

calico /'kælɪkoʊ/ n. white cotton cloth.

caliper /'kæləpə/ n. **1.** (usu. pl.) a tool for measuring diameters. **2.** Med. a limb brace. Also, **calliper.**

caliph /'keɪləf/ n. the head of a Muslim state. **–caliphate** /'kæləfət/, n.

call /kɔl/ v.t. **1.** to cry out in a loud voice. **2.** (of a bird or other animal) to utter (its characteristic cry). **3.** to command or request to come. **4.** to give a name to. **5.** to telephone. **6.** Econ. to ask for payment of (all or part of the unpaid part of a company's share capital). –v.i. **7.** to speak loudly, as to attract attention; shout. **8.** (of a bird or animal) to utter its characteristic cry. **9.** to make a short visit; stop at a place on some errand or business. –n. **10.** a cry or shout. **11.** the cry of a bird or other animal. **12.** a short visit. **13.** a telephone conversation. **14.** a summons; invitation. **15.** a demand or claim. **16.** a demand for payment of an obligation, especially where payment is at the option of the creditor. **17.** Stock Exchange the option of claiming stock at or before a given date. –adj. **18.** Commerce repayable on demand. –phr. **19. call in, a.** to collect. **b.** to

withdraw from circulation. **20. on call, a.** Also, **at call.** Commerce payable or subject to return without advance notice. **b.** (of doctors, etc.) available for duty at short notice.

call centre n. a location at which operators make phone calls for client organisations, as for marketing, information services, etc.

callgirl /'kɔlgɜl/ n. a prostitute who makes herself available for appointments by telephone.

calli- a word element meaning 'beauty'.

calligraphy /kə'lɪgrəfi/ n. the art of doing beautiful handwriting.

calling /'kɔlɪŋ/ n. a vocation, profession, or trade.

calliper /'kæləpə/ n., v.t. → **caliper.**

callisthenics /kæləs'θɛnɪks/ pl. n. light gymnastic exercises.

call option n. Stock Exchange the right to buy a specified parcel of shares at an agreed price within a specified period of time.

callous /'kæləs/ adj. showing no concern for the feelings of others.

callow /'kæloʊ/ adj. immature or inexperienced.

callus /'kæləs/ n. (pl. **-luses**) a hardened or thickened part of the skin.

calm /kam/ adj. **1.** without rough motion; still. **2.** free from excitement or passion; tranquil. –n. **3.** freedom from movement, excitement, etc. –v.t. **4.** to make calm.

calorie /'kæləri/ n. **1.** a non-SI unit equal to the large calorie, used to express the heat output of an organism or the energy value of a food. The recommended SI unit is the kilojoule; 1 calorie is equivalent to 4.1868 kJ. –phr. **2. count calories,** to be watchful of the amount of food consumed in order to control one's weight.

calumny /'kæləmni/ n. slander. **–calumniate,** v.

calve /kav/ v.i. to give birth to a calf.

calves /kavz/ n. plural of **calf.**

calyx /'keɪlɪks, 'kæl-/ n. (pl. **calyces** /'keɪləsiz, 'kæ-/ or **calyxes**) the outermost parts of a flower, usually green.

cam /kæm/ n. a webcam.

camaraderie /kæmə'radəri/ n. comradeship; close friendship.

cambist /'kæmbəst/ n. **1.** a dealer in the foreign exchange market. **2.** a manual giving the moneys, weights, and measures of different countries with their equivalents.

came /keɪm/ v. past tense of **come.**

camel /'kæməl/ n. **1.** a large humped ruminant quadruped. **2.** a brown colour somewhat lighter than fawn.

camellia /kə'miljə/ n. a glossy leaved shrub with white, pink, or red, waxy, rose-like flowers.

camembert /'kæməmbeə/ n. a rich, cream-coloured variety of soft, ripened cheese, usually made in small, flat, round loaves, covered with a thin greyish-white rind.

cameo /'kæmioʊ/ n. (pl. **-meos**) **1.** an engraving in relief upon a gem, stone, etc. **2.** a short performance or appearance in a play or film by a celebrity.

camera¹ /'kæmrə, 'kæmərə/ n. a photographic apparatus in which sensitive plates or film are exposed, the image being formed by means of a lens.

camera² /'kæmrə, 'kæmərə/ *phr.* **in camera**, **1.** *Law* in the privacy of a judge's chambers, with the public excluded. **2.** in private; in secret.

camisole /'kæməsoʊl/ *n.* a woman's simple top with narrow shoulder straps, now usually worn as an undergarment.

camomile /'kæməmaɪl/ *n.* → **chamomile**.

camouflage /'kæməflaʒ, -fladʒ/ *n.* the means by which any object or creature renders itself indistinguishable from its background.

camp¹ /kæmp/ *n.* **1.** a group of tents, caravans, or other temporary shelters in one place. **2.** a group of people favouring the same ideals, doctrines, etc. –*v.i.* **3.** to establish or pitch a camp. **4.** (oft. fol. by *out*) to live temporarily in a tent or similar shelter. –**camper**, *n.*

camp² /kæmp/ *adj.* **1.** exaggeratedly theatrical and flashy in style. **2.** of a male, homosexual.

campaign /kæm'peɪn/ *n.* any course of aggressive activities for some special purpose.

camphor /'kæmfə/ *n.* **1.** a whitish, translucent, crystalline substance used in medicine, etc. **2.** any of various similar substances, for household use as an insect deterrent.

campus /'kæmpəs/ *n.* **1.** the grounds of a university or other educational institution. **2.** the grounds of an institution such as a hospital, museum, or large business organisation.

can¹ /kæn/, *weak form* /kən/ (*or, if followed by k or g* /kəŋ/ *v.* (*aux.*) (**could**) **1.** to know how to; be able to; have the ability, power, right, qualifications, or means to. **2.** may; have permission.

can² /kæn/ *n.* **1.** a container made of aluminium or sheet iron coated with tin or other metal. **2.** *Colloq.* the blame for something. –*v.t.* (**canned, canning**) **3.** to put in a container, usually sealed for preservation.

canal /kə'næl/ *n.* an artificial waterway.

canapé /'kænəpeɪ/ *n.* a thin piece of bread, toast, etc., spread or topped with cheese, caviar, anchovies, or other appetising foods.

canary /kə'neəri/ *n.* (*pl.* **-ries**) a cage bird, usually yellow.

canasta /kə'næstə/ *n.* a card game.

cancel /'kænsəl/ *v.* (**-celled, -celling**) –*v.t.* **1.** to decide not to proceed with (an appointment, a meeting, an event, etc.). **2.** to cross out (writing, etc.) by drawing a line or lines over. **3.** to make void. –*v.i.* **4.** to withdraw support for (a person, especially a public figure), in response to a socially unacceptable action or comment. **5.** to decide not to proceed with a previously arranged appointment, meeting, event.: *to cancel at the last minute.*

cancer /'kænsə/ *n.* a malignant and invasive growth or tumour. –**cancerous**, *adj.*

candela /kæn'dilə, -'deɪlə/ *n.* the SI base unit of luminous intensity. *Symbol:* cd

candelabrum /kændə'labrəm/ *n.* (*pl.* **-bra** /-brə/) an ornamental branched candlestick.

candid /'kændəd/ *adj.* frank; outspoken; open and sincere.

candidate /'kændədeɪt, -dət/ *n.* someone who seeks an office, an honour, etc.

candle /'kændl/ *n.* a long, usually slender, piece of tallow, wax, etc., with an embedded wick, burnt to give light.

candour /'kændə/ *n.* frankness; sincerity; honesty. Also, **candor**.

candy /'kændi/ *n.* (*pl.* **-dies**) **1.** a sweet made of sugar crystallised by boiling. –*v.t.* (**-died, -dying**) **2.** to cook in heavy syrup until transparent, as fruit, fruit peel, or ginger.

cane /keɪn/ *n.* **1.** a long, hollow or pithy, jointed woody stem, as that of bamboo, rattan, sugar cane, certain palms, etc. **2.** the stem of a bamboo, etc., used as a rod for punishing school children. **3.** a walking stick. –*v.* (**caned, caning**) –*v.t.* **4.** to beat with a cane. **5.** *Colloq.* to beat severely in a competition. **6.** *Colloq.* to hurt: *my leg is caning me.* –*v.i.* **7.** *Colloq.* to hurt: *my leg is really caning.*

cane toad *n.* a large toad, native to South America and introduced into north-eastern Australia in an unsuccessful attempt to control sugarcane insect pests, now itself a pest.

canine /'keɪnaɪn/ *adj.* **1.** relating to or characteristic of dogs. –*n.* **2.** any animal belonging to the dog family. **3.** a pointed tooth on each side of each jaw.

canister /'kænəstə/ *n.* a small box, usually of metal, for holding tea, coffee, etc.

canker /'kæŋkə/ *n.* **1.** a gangrenous or ulcerous sore, especially in the mouth. **2.** anything that corrodes, corrupts, destroys, or irritates.

cannabis /'kænəbəs/ *n.* hashish.

cannelloni /kænə'loʊni/ *pl. n.* tubular or rolled pieces of pasta usually filled with a mixture of meat or cheese and served with a tomato or cream sauce.

cannibal /'kænəbəl/ *n.* any animal that eats its own kind.

cannon /'kænən/ *n.* **1.** a large ancient gun for firing heavy projectiles, mounted on a carriage. **2.** any strike and rebound, as a ball striking a wall and glancing off.

cannot /'kænɒt, kæ'nɒt/ *v.* a form of **can not**.

cannula /'kænjələ/ *n.* a metal tube for insertion into the body, used to keep a passage open, to draw off fluid, or to introduce medication.

canny /'kæni/ *adj.* (**-nier, -niest**) careful; cautious; wary. –**cannily**, *adv.*

canoe /kə'nu/ *n.* any light and narrow boat that is propelled by paddles. –**canoeist**, *n.*

canola /kə'noʊlə/ *n.* a plant with a seed from which is produced an oil extract for human consumption and a meal for livestock feed.

canon¹ /'kænən/ *n.* **1.** an ecclesiastical rule or law. **2.** the body of ecclesiastical law. **3.** a fundamental principle. **4.** any officially recognised set of representative writings. –**canonical**, *adj.*

canon² /'kænən/ *n.* a member of the chapter of a cathedral or collegiate church.

canonise /'kænənaɪz/ *v.t.* to acknowledge as a saint. Also, **canonize**. –**canonisation**, *n.*

canoodle /kə'nudl/ *v.i.* *Colloq.* to indulge in fondling and petting.

canopy /'kænəpi/ *n.* (*pl.* **-pies**) a covering suspended or supported over a throne, bed, etc.

cant¹ /kænt/ *n.* **1.** insincere statements. **2.** the words, phrases, etc., peculiar to a particular class, party, profession, etc.

cant² /kænt/ n. **1.** a salient angle. **2.** a sudden movement that tilts or overturns a thing. **3.** an oblique or slanting face of anything.

can't /kant/ v. contraction of **cannot**.

cantaloupe /'kæntəloup, 'kæntəlup/ n. a type of melon with orange-coloured flesh; rockmelon. Also, **cantaloup**.

cantankerous /kæn'tæŋkərəs/ adj. ill-natured; quarrelsome.

canteen /kæn'tin/ n. **1.** a restaurant or cafeteria attached to a factory, office, etc. **2.** Also, **tuckshop, kiosk.** a similar food outlet in a school, sportsground, etc., usually staffed by volunteer parents. **3.** a box containing a set of cutlery. **4.** a small container used by soldiers and others for carrying water or other liquids.

canter /'kæntə/ n. **1.** an easy gallop. –v.i. **2.** to go or ride at a canter.

cantilever /'kæntəlivə/ n. **1.** Machinery a free part of any horizontal member projecting beyond a support. **2.** Civil Eng. either of two bracket-like arms projecting towards each other from opposite banks or piers, serving to form the span of a bridge (**cantilever bridge**) when united.

canton /'kænton, kæn'ton/ n. a small territorial district, especially in Switzerland.

canvas /'kænvəs/ n. **1.** a closely woven, heavy cloth used for tents, sails, etc. **2.** a piece of this material on which an oil painting is made. **3.** a tent, or tents collectively. **4.** sails collectively.

canvass /'kænvəs/ v.t. to solicit votes, subscriptions, opinions, etc., from (a district, group of people, etc.).

canyon /'kænjən/ n. a deep valley with steep sides.

canyoning /'kænjənɪŋ/ n. the sport of following a river down a canyon, usually involving whitewater rafting, rock climbing, abseiling, etc.

cap /kæp/ n. **1.** a covering for the head, especially one fitting closely and made of softer material than a hat, and having little or no brim, but often having a peak. **2.** a close-fitting waterproof head covering worn when swimming, etc. **3.** the detachable protective top of a fountain pen, jar, etc. **4.** a noisemaking device for toy pistols. **5.** an upper limit on a price, salary, etc. –v.t. (**capped, capping**) **6.** to provide or cover with or as with a cap. **7.** to surpass. **8.** to place an upper limit on (a price, salary, etc.).

capable /'keipəbəl/ adj. **1.** having much intelligence or ability; competent; efficient; able. –phr. **2. capable of, a.** having the ability to: capable of running a kilometre. **b.** likely to: capable of murder. –**capability**, n.

capacious /kə'peiʃəs/ adj. capable of holding much.

capacitance /kə'pæsətəns/ n. Elect. the property of a system which enables it to store electrical charge, usually measured in farads.

capacitor /kə'pæsətə/ n. a device for storing an electric charge.

capacity /kə'pæsəti/ n. (pl. **-ties**) **1.** cubic contents; volume. **2.** power, ability, or possibility of doing something. **3.** position; function; relation.

cap-and-trade adj. of or relating to an emissions trading scheme in which a cap is set for allowable emissions in a particular area, and individual emitters are given their allocation of emission permits which they can use or sell provided the overall cap is not breached. See **baseline-and-credit**.

cape¹ /keip/ n. a sleeveless garment fastened round the neck and falling loosely over the shoulders.

cape² /keip/ n. a piece of land jutting into the sea or some other body of water.

Cape Barren goose n. a large goose endemic to southern Australia.

caper¹ /'keipə/ v.i. **1.** to leap or skip about in a sprightly manner. –n. **2.** a prank; capricious action.

caper² /'keipə/ n. the pickled flower bud of a shrub, used in cookery.

capillary /kə'pɪləri/ n. (pl. **-laries**) **1.** Anat. one of the minute blood vessels between the terminations of the arteries and the beginnings of the veins. –adj. **2.** relating to or occurring in or as in a tube of fine bore. **3.** Physics of or relating to the property of surface tension.

capillary action n. the elevation or depression of liquids in fine tubes, etc., due to the relative strengths of the intermolecular forces within the liquid, as by surface tension, and the attraction between the molecules of the liquid and the tube; it accounts for the seeping up of water through the interstices of rock, the rising of sap in trees, the soaking up of water in paper towel, etc.

capital /'kæpətl/ n. **1.** the city or town which is the official seat of government in a country, state, etc. **2.** any form of wealth employed or capable of being employed in the production of more wealth. **3.** Commerce the ownership interest in a business. **4.** any source of profit, advantage, power, etc. –adj. **5.** relating to capital. **6.** principal; highly important. **7.** (of letters) of the large size. **8.** punishable by death.

capital gains tax n. a tax on the profits arising from the disposal of an asset. Abbrev.: CGT

capital goods pl. n. goods used in the production of other goods.

capital-intensive /'kæpətl-ɪn,tɛnsɪv/ adj. of or relating to an industry which, while requiring relatively little labour, requires a high capital investment in plant, etc. (opposed to labourintensive).

capitalise /'kæpətəlaiz/ v.t. **1.** to write or print in capital letters, or with an initial capital. **2.** to authorise a certain amount of stocks and bonds in the corporate charter. **3.** to convert (floating debt) into stock or shares. **4.** Accounting to set up (expenditures) as business assets in the books of account instead of treating as expense. **5.** to supply with capital. **6.** to estimate the value of (a stock or an enterprise). **7.** (oft. fol. by on) to take advantage of; turn to one's advantage. Also, **capitalize**. –**capitalisation**, n.

capitalism /'kæpətəlɪzəm/ n. **1.** a system under which the means of production, distribution, and exchange are in large measure privately owned and directed. **2.** the concentration of capital in the hands of a few, or the resulting power or influence. **3.** a system favouring such concentration of wealth.

capitalist /'kæpətələst/ n. 1. someone who has capital, especially extensive capital, in business enterprises. –adj. 2. founded on or believing in capitalism.

capital punishment n. death as punishment for a crime; the death penalty.

capitation /kæpə'teɪʃən/ n. 1. a numbering or assessing by the head. 2. a poll tax. 3. a fee or payment of a uniform amount for each person.

capitulate /kə'pɪtʃəleɪt/ v.i. to surrender unconditionally or on stipulated terms. –**capitulation**, n.

cappuccino /kæp'tʃinou/ n. espresso coffee topped with hot milk which has been frothed up by passing steam through it.

caprice /kə'pris/ n. a sudden change of mind without apparent or adequate reason; whim. –**capricious**, adj.

capsicum /'kæpsəkəm, 'kæpsɪkəm/ n. the common pepper of the garden, with mild to hot, pungent seeds enclosed in a bell-shaped fruit.

capsicum spray n. → **pepper spray**.

capsize /kæp'saɪz/ v.i., v.t. to overturn.

capsule /'kæpsjul, 'kæpful, -fəl/ n. 1. a gelatinous case enclosing a dose of medicine; the dose itself. 2. the compartment of a spacecraft containing the crew or instruments.

captain /'kæptn/ n. 1. someone who is in authority over others; a chief; leader. 2. an officer in the army.

captcha /'kæptʃə/ n. Computers (from trademark) an application that enables the identification of a human response, as opposed to a computer response, by setting a task, such as reading distorted letters, that only a human being can do.

caption /'kæpʃən/ n. 1. Printing an inscription for a picture or illustration. 2. Film the title of a scene, the text of a speech, etc., shown on the screen.

captivate /'kæptəveɪt/ v.t. to enthral by beauty or excellence.

captive /'kæptɪv/ n. 1. a prisoner. –adj. 2. made or held prisoner, especially in war. –**captivity**, n.

captor /'kæptə/ n. a person who captures.

capture /'kæptʃə/ v.t. 1. to take prisoner; seize. –n. 2. the act of capturing. 3. the thing or person captured.

car /ka/ n. 1. a vehicle, especially one for passengers, carrying its own power-generating and propelling mechanism, usually an internal-combustion engine, for travel on ordinary roads. 2. a vehicle of various kinds running on rails, as a restaurant car, tramcar, etc.

carabiner /kærə'binə/ n. (in mountaineering) a spring-loaded metal clip designed for joining ropes together. Also, **karabiner**.

carafe /kə'raf, -'ræf, 'kærəf/ n. a glass bottle for water, wine, etc.

caramel /'kærəməl/ n. burnt sugar, used for colouring and flavouring food, etc.

carat /'kærət/ n. 1. Also, **metric carat**. a unit of weight for measuring gems, equal to 200 milligrams. Symbol: CM 2. a twenty-fourth part (used in expressing the fineness of gold, pure gold being 24 carats fine).

caravan /'kærəvæn/ n. 1. a vehicle in which people may live, usually having two wheels and designed to be drawn by a car. 2. a group

of merchants or others travelling together, especially over deserts, etc.

caraway /'kærəweɪ/ n. a herb bearing aromatic seedlike fruit used in cookery and medicine.

carb /kab/ n. Colloq. a carbohydrate.

carbine /'kabam, 'kabən/ n. (formerly) a short rifle for cavalry use.

carbo- a word element meaning 'carbon'. Also, **carb-**.

carbohydrate /kabə'haɪdreɪt, kabou-/ n. any of a class of organic compounds including sugars, starch, and cellulose, which are important food for animals.

carbohydrate loading n. a strategy, employed especially by long-distance runners, which involves having a large intake of carbohydrates to maximise the storage of glycogen in the muscles on the evening before a race.

carbon /'kabən/ n. Chem. a widely distributed element which forms organic compounds in combination with hydrogen, oxygen, etc., and which occurs in a pure state as charcoal. Symbol: C

carbonate /'kabəneɪt/ v.t. to charge or impregnate with carbon dioxide. –**carbonated**, adj. –**carbonation**, n.

carbon cap n. an upper limit, set by a government or international body, of permissible production of carbon dioxide as part of a strategy to limit global production and reduce the risk of climate change.

carbon capture n. the process of removing carbon dioxide from a point where it is normally released in large quantities, as from a power plant, so that it can then be prevented from entering the atmosphere. See **carbon sequestration**.

carbon credit n. a credit earned within the carbon tax system for decreasing carbon dioxide in the atmosphere, as by planting forests, etc.

carbon dioxide n. a colourless, odourless, incombustible gas, CO_2, used extensively in industry as dry ice, and in fizzy drinks, fire extinguishers, etc.

carbon emission n. an amount of carbon dioxide released into the atmosphere when coal is used as fuel for transport or to generate electricity, or during forest burning or some processes used in agriculture.

carbon footprint n. the carbon dioxide emissions for which an individual or organisation can be held responsible, as by their travel, fuel consumption, diet, energy requirements, etc.

carbon gas n. carbon dioxide, the principal greenhouse gas.

carbon monoxide n. a colourless, odourless, poisonous gas.

carbon-neutral adj. having achieved carbon neutrality.

carbon paper n. paper faced with a preparation of carbon or other material, used between two sheets of plain paper in order to reproduce upon the lower sheet that which is written or typed on the upper.

carbon sequestration n. the process by which carbon dioxide is removed from the atmosphere, naturally by plants in their growth but artificially by various means, and then prevented from returning to the atmosphere by the creation of products with long-term use, as timber from forests, or by storing it in sealed reservoirs, as by injecting it into underground geological formations.

carbon sink *n.* a large vegetated area which absorbs carbon dioxide from the atmosphere, thus reducing the level of greenhouse gases.

carbon tax *n.* a tax on the consumption of fossil fuels, designed to recoup some or all the costs of managing and repairing the environmental damage caused by such fuels.

carb soda *n. Colloq.* sodium bicarbonate.

carbuncle /'kabaŋkəl/ *n.* a painful circumscribed inflammation of the subcutaneous tissue.

carburettor /'kabjəreta, kabjə'retə/ *n.* a device in an internal-combustion engine for mixing a volatile fuel with the correct proportion of air in order to form an explosive gas. Also, **carburetter**.

carcass /'kakəs/ *n.* the dead body of an animal. Also, **carcase**.

carcinogen /ka'sınədʒən/ *n.* any substance which tends to produce a cancer in a body. –**carcinogenic**, *adj.*

carcinoma /kasə'noumə/ *n.* (pl. **-mas** or **-mata** /-mətə/) a malignant and invasive tumour that spreads and often recurs after excision; a cancer.

card¹ /kad/ *n.* **1.** a piece of stiff paper, usually rectangular, for various uses. **2.** one of a set of small pieces of cardboard with spots or figures, used in playing various games. **3.** *Computers* a circuit board: *a video card; a sound card.* **4.** *Colloq.* a likeable, amusing, or facetious person.

card² /kad/ *n.* a toothed implement or wire brush used in disentangling and combing out fibres of wool, flax, etc., preparatory to spinning.

cardamom /'kadəməm/ *n.* the aromatic seed of various Asian plants, used as a spice.

cardboard /'kadbɔd/ *n.* a thick, stiff, paper-like material.

cardi- variant of **cardio-** before vowels.

cardiac /'kadiæk/ *adj.* relating to the heart.

cardigan /'kadigən/ *n.* a knitted jacket.

cardinal /'kadənəl/ *adj.* **1.** of prime importance; chief; principal; fundamental. –*n.* **2.** one of the members of the Sacred College of the Roman Catholic Church, ranking next to the pope.

cardinal number *n. Maths* a number such as *one, two, three,* etc., which indicates how many things are in a given set, and not the order in which those things occur (the latter is indicated by the ordinal numbers, *first, second, third,* etc.).

cardio- a word element meaning 'heart'. Also, **cardi-**.

cardiogram /'kadiəgræm/ *n. Med.* **1.** → **electrocardiogram**. **2.** any of various other records of the activity of the heart, as an echocardiogram.

cardiology /kadi'ɒlədʒi/ *n.* the branch of medical science that deals with the heart and its functions. –**cardiologist**, *n.*

cardiopulmonary resuscitation /,kadiou-'pʌlmənri/ *n.* → **CPR**.

cardiovascular /,kadiou'væskjələ/ *adj.* relating to the heart and blood vessels.

card reader *n. Computers* a device which reads data on a card by sensing or analysing the information coded on it and converting it into electronic messages.

care /kɛə/ *n.* **1.** worry; anxiety; concern. **2.** serious attention; heed; caution. **3.** protection; charge. –*v.i.* (**cared, caring**) **4.** to be troubled; to be affected emotionally. **5.** to be concerned or solicitous; have thought or regard. **6.** (fol. by *for*) to have a fondness or affection. **7.** (fol. by *for*) to look after; make provision. –*phr.* Also, **c/o**. **8. care of**, at the address of.

careen /kə'rin/ *v.i.* to lean, sway, or tip to one side, as a ship.

career /kə'rɪə/ *n.* **1.** general course of action or progress of a person through life. **2.** an occupation, profession, etc., followed as one's lifework. **3.** speed; full speed. –*adj.* **4.** relating to someone in a profession who regards their role as a career (def. 2): *a career politician.*

careful /'kɛəfəl/ *adj.* **1.** taking care to avoid risks. **2.** paying close attention to detail, or carried out with close attention to detail. –**carefully**, *adv.*

careless /'kɛələs/ *adj.* **1.** done without paying enough attention. **2.** done or said without thinking. –**carelessly**, *adv.* –**carelessness**, *n.*

caress /kə'rɛs/ *n.* **1.** an act or gesture expressing affection. –*v.t.* **2.** to touch or pat gently to show affection.

caret /'kærət/ *n.* **1.** a mark (^) made in written or printed matter to show the place where something is to be inserted. **2.** *Computers* the symbol ^.

caretaker /'kɛəteɪkə/ *n.* **1.** a person who takes care of a thing or place, especially one whose job is to maintain and protect a building or group of buildings. –*adj.* **2.** holding office temporarily until a new appointment, election, etc., can be made, as an administration.

cargo /'kagoʊ/ *n.* (pl. **-goes**) **1.** the goods carried on a ship, aircraft, truck, etc. **2.** any load.

cargo pants *pl. n.* trousers or shorts with pockets sewn onto the outside of the legs, usually at mid-thigh level.

caribou /'kærəbu/ *n.* (pl. **-bou** or **-bous**) any of several North American subspecies of reindeer, especially those living wild as opposed to domesticated.

caricature /'kærəkətʃʊə/ *n.* a picture, description, etc., ludicrously exaggerating the peculiarities or defects of persons or things.

caries /'kɛəriz/ *n.* decay, as of bone or teeth, or of plant tissue.

carillon /kə'rɪljən/ *n.* a set of stationary bells hung in a tower and sounded by manual or pedal action, or by machinery.

carjack /'kadʒæk/ *v.t.* to steal (a car) by forcing the driver to vacate it, or by forcing the driver to drive to a chosen destination. Also, **car-jack**. –**carjacker**, *n.* –**carjacking**, *n.*

cark /kak/ *v.i. Colloq.* to collapse; die.

car kit *n.* a hands-free mobile phone system installed in a vehicle.

carmine /'kamaɪn/ *n.* crimson.

carnage /'kanɪdʒ/ *n.* the slaughter of a great number, as in battle.

carnal /'kanəl/ *adj.* **1.** relating to the flesh or the body, its passions and appetites; sensual. **2.** sexual.

carnal knowledge n. sexual intercourse especially with one under the age of consent.

carnation /ka'neɪʃən/ n. any of numerous cultivated plants with fragrant flowers of various colours.

carnival /'kɑːnəvəl/ n. **1.** a festive procession. **2.** a fair or amusement show, especially one erected temporarily. **3.** a series of sporting events as a racing carnival, etc.

carnivorous /kɑː'nɪvərəs/ adj. Zool. flesh-eating. **–carnivore,** n.

carob /'kærəb/ n. the fruit of a tree used as animal fodder, and in cookery as a substitute for chocolate.

carol /'kærəl/ n. a song, especially of joy.

carotene /'kærətiːn/ n. any of three isomeric red hydrocarbons, $C_{40}H_{56}$, found in many plants, especially carrots, and transformed to vitamin A in the liver.

carotid /kə'rɒtəd/ n. either of the two great arteries, one on each side of the neck, which carry blood to the head.

carouse /kə'raʊz/ n. **1.** a noisy or drunken feast; jovial revelry. –v.i. **2.** to engage in a carouse. **–carousal,** n.

carousel /kærə'sɛl/ n. **1.** → **merry-go-round. 2.** a revolving device by which luggage is returned to travellers after a journey by plane, ship, bus, etc. **3.** a revolving tray in a microwave oven, on which the food is placed to ensure even cooking.

carp¹ /kɑːp/ v.i. to find fault.

carp² /kɑːp/ n. (pl. **carp** or **carps**) a large, coarse, freshwater food fish.

-carp a noun termination meaning 'fruit', used in botanical terms.

carpenter /'kɑːpəntə/ n. someone who erects and fixes the wooden parts, etc., in the building of houses and other structures. **–carpentry,** n.

carpet /'kɑːpət/ n. a heavy fabric, commonly of wool, for covering floors.

-carpic a word element related to **-carp.**

carpo- a word element meaning 'fruit'.

car pool n. **1.** an arrangement whereby a group of people travel together in one car on a regular basis, taking turns to drive their own car. –v.i. **2.** → **carpool.**

carpool /'kɑːpuːl/ v.i. to take part in a car pool. Also, **car pool. –carpooling,** n.

-carpous a combining form related to **-carp.**

carrel /'kɑːrɛl, 'kærəl/ n. (in a library) a small area or cubicle used by students and others for individual study; a stall.

carriage /'kærɪdʒ/ n. **1.** a wheeled vehicle for conveying persons. **2.** manner of carrying the head and body; bearing. **3.** a part of a machine, etc., designed for carrying something.

carriage return n. **1.** (on a typewriter) a key or lever which causes the next character typed to be positioned at the left margin and down a line. **2.** (on a computer) a key or character which performs a similar function.

carrier pigeon /'kærɪə/ n. a pigeon trained to fly home from great distances and thus transport written messages.

carrion /'kærɪən/ n. dead and putrefying flesh.

carrot /'kærət/ n. a plant valued for its reddish edible root.

carry /'kæri/ v. (**-ried, -rying**) –v.t. **1.** to convey from one place to another. **2.** to bear the weight, burden, etc., of; sustain. **3.** to hold (the body, head, etc.) in a certain manner. **4.** to secure the election of (a candidate) or the adoption of (a motion or bill). **5.** to support or give validity to (a related claim, etc.). **6.** Commerce **a.** to keep on hand or in stock. **b.** to keep on one's account books, etc. –v.i. **7.** to be transmitted, propelled, or sustained. –phr. **8. carry away,** to influence greatly or beyond reason. **9. carry forward,** Bookkeeping to transfer (an amount, etc.) to the next column, page, etc. **10. carry off,** to face consequences boldly. **11. carry on, a.** to manage; conduct. **b.** to behave in an excited, foolish, or improper manner; flirt. **12. carry out,** to accomplish or complete (a plan, scheme, etc.). **13. carry over, a.** to postpone; hold off until later. **b.** Stock Exchange to defer completion of (a contract) so that it falls under a different account. **–carrier,** n.

cart /kɑːt/ n. a heavy horse-drawn vehicle.

carte blanche /kɑːt 'blɒntʃ/ n. unconditional authority; full power.

cartel /kɑː'tɛl/ n. an international syndicate formed to regulate prices and output in some field of business.

cartilage /'kɑːtəlɪdʒ, 'kɑːtlɪdʒ/ n. Zool., Anat. a firm, elastic, flexible substance of a translucent whitish or yellowish colour, consisting of a connective tissue.

cartography /kɑː'tɒgrəfi/ n. the production of maps.

carton /'kɑːtən/ n. a cardboard box, especially one in which food is packaged and sold.

cartoon /kɑː'tuːn/ n. **1.** a humorous or satirical sketch of some subject or person of current interest, as in a newspaper, etc. **2.** a film consisting of a series of drawings, each slightly different from the ones before and after it, run through a projector. **–cartoonist,** n.

cartridge /'kɑːtrɪdʒ/ n. **1.** Also, **cartridge case.** a cylindrical case for holding a complete charge of powder, and often also the bullet or the shot, for a rifle, etc. **2.** anything resembling a cartridge, as the disposable container of ink for some types of fountain pen. **3.** (in a tape recorder) a plastic container enclosing recording tape usually in the form of an endless loop.

carve /kɑːv/ v.t. **1.** to fashion by cutting. **2.** to cut into slices or pieces, as meat.

cascade /kæs'keɪd/ n. **1.** a waterfall over steep rocks. –v.i. **2.** to fall in or like a cascade.

case¹ /keɪs/ n. **1.** an instance of the occurrence, existence, etc., of something. **2.** the actual state of things. **3.** a statement of facts, reasons, etc. **4.** Law a suit or action at law. **5.** Gram. a category in the inflection of nouns, pronouns, and adjectives, denoting the syntactic relation of these words to other words in the sentence, indicated by the form or the position of the words. –phr. **6. (just) in case, a.** if; if it should happen that: just in case there is an emergency; insurance in case civil action is brought. **b.** as a precaution: I'll take an umbrella, just in case.

case² /keɪs/ n. **1.** a receptacle. **2.** a sheath or outer covering. **3.** a suitcase. –v.t. **4.** to put or enclose in a case. **5.** Colloq. to examine or survey (a house, bank, etc.) in planning a crime.

case law *n.* law established by judicial decisions in particular cases, instead of by legislation.

casement /ˈkeɪsmənt/ *n.* a window sash opening on hinges.

cash /kæʃ/ *n.* **1.** money, especially money on hand, as opposed to a money equivalent (as a cheque). *–v.t.* **2.** to give or obtain cash for (a cheque, etc.). *–phr.* **3. cash up**, (of shopkeepers, etc.) to add up the takings.

cash account *n.* **1.** current account. **2.** *Bookkeeping* a record kept of cash transactions.

cash crop *n.* a crop which, when harvested, offers a quick return of money.

cash economy *n.* → **black economy**.

cashew /ˈkæʃu/ *n.* (a tropical tree yielding) a small, edible kidney-shaped nut (**cashew nut**).

cash flow *n.* (of a company) the amount of cash generated by a company in a given period. It equals the net profit after tax, less dividends paid out, plus depreciation in that period.

cashier /kæˈʃɪə/ *n.* someone who has charge of cash or money, especially someone who superintends monetary transactions.

cashmere /ˈkæʃmɪə/ *n.* the fine downy wool at the roots of the hair of Kashmir goats of India.

cash register *n.* a till with a mechanism for indicating amounts of sales, etc.

casino /kəˈsinoʊ/ *n.* (*pl.* **-nos**) a building or large room used for gambling, etc.

cask /kask/ *n.* **1.** a barrel-like container for holding liquids, etc. **2.** a lightweight container, usually cardboard with a plastic lining and small tap, used for holding and serving wine for domestic use.

casket /ˈkaskət/ *n.* **1.** a small chest or box, as for jewels. **2.** a coffin.

cassava /kəˈsavə/ *n.* any of several tropical plants cultivated for their tuberous roots.

casserole /ˈkæsəroʊl/ *n.* **1.** a baking dish of glass, pottery, etc., usually with a cover. **2.** any food, usually a mixture, baked in such a dish.

cassette /kəˈsɛt, kæˈsɛt/ *n.* **1.** (in a tape recorder) a plastic container enclosing both a recording tape and two hubs about which it winds. **2.** (in a video recorder, computer, etc.) a device of similar principle with wider tape.

cassia /ˈkæsiə/ *n.* an ornamental tropical tree with clusters of bright yellow flowers and long pods whose pulp is a mild laxative.

cassock /ˈkæsək/ *n.* a long, close-fitting garment worn by ecclesiastics.

cassowary /ˈkæsəwəri, ˈkæsəwɛri/ *n.* (*pl.* **-ries**) a large, three-toed, flightless bird of Australia, New Guinea and nearby islands, superficially resembling the ostrich.

cast /kast/ *v.* (**cast, casting**) *–v.t.* **1.** (oft. fol. by *away, off, out*, etc.) to throw; fling; hurl. **2.** to direct (the eye, a glance, etc.) **3.** to shed or drop (hair, fruit, etc.), especially prematurely. **4.** to deposit (a vote, etc.) **5.** to compute or calculate astrologically, as a horoscope; forecast. **6.** *Naut.* (fol. by *loose, off*, etc.) to let go or let loose, as a vessel from a mooring. *–v.i.* **7.** (oft. fol. by *out*) to throw a fishing line or the like. **8.** (oft. fol. by *about*) to consider; plan or scheme. *–n.* **9.** the act of casting or throwing. **10.** the form in which something is

made or written; arrangement. **11.** *Theatre* the actors to whom the parts in a play are assigned. **12.** something shaped in a mould while in a fluid or plastic state; a casting. **13.** any impression or mould made from an object. **14.** *Med.* a rigid surgical dressing usually made of plaster-of-Paris bandage. **15.** a permanent twist or turn, especially a squint. **16.** a conjecture; forecast. *–phr.* **17. cast off**, **a.** to discard or reject. **b.** *Knitting* to make the final row of stitches. **18. cast on**, to make the initial row of stitches.

castanet /kæstəˈnɛt/ *n.* a pair or one of a pair of shells held in the palm of the hand and struck together as an accompaniment to music and dancing.

castaway /ˈkastəweɪ/ *n.* **1.** a ship-wrecked person. **2.** an outcast.

caste /kast/ *n.* **1.** *Sociology* a social group. **2.** one of the divisions or social classes into which the Hindus are separated and by which privileges or social handicaps are inherited.

castigate /ˈkæstəgeɪt/ *v.t.* to punish in order to correct.

casting vote *n.* the deciding vote of the presiding officer when votes are equally divided.

cast iron *n.* an alloy of iron, carbon, and other elements.

castle /ˈkasəl, ˈkæsəl/ *n.* **1.** a fortified residence. **2.** → **rook²**.

castor /ˈkastə/ *n.* a small wheel on a swivel, set under a piece of furniture, etc. Also, **caster**.

castor oil *n.* a viscid oil used as a cathartic, lubricant, etc.

castrate /ˈkæstreɪt, ˈkas-/ *v.t.* to deprive of the testicles; emasculate.

casual /ˈkæʒuəl/ *adj.* **1.** happening by chance. **2.** unpremeditated; offhand. **3.** careless; negligent; unconcerned. **4.** irregular; occasional. **5.** informal. **6.** employed only irregularly.

casualty /ˈkæʒuəlti/ *n.* (*pl.* **-ties**) **1.** an unfortunate accident, especially one involving bodily injury or death. **2.** *Mil.* a soldier who is missing in action, or who has been killed, wounded, or captured. **3.** someone who is injured or killed in an accident. **4.** Also, **casualty ward**. the section of a hospital to which accident or emergency cases are taken.

casuarina /kæʒjəˈrinə/ *n.* a group of trees and shrubs characterised by jointed stems with leaves reduced to whorls of teeth at the joints.

cat /kæt/ *n.* any of the carnivorous feline mammals, as the domesticated cat, or the lion, tiger, etc.

cata- a prefix meaning 'down', 'against', 'back'.

cataclysm /ˈkætəklɪzəm/ *n.* any violent upheaval. *–***cataclysmic**, *adj.*

catacomb /ˈkætəkoʊm, -kum/ *n.* a series of underground tunnels and caves, especially for burial.

catalogue /ˈkætəlɒg/ *n.* **1.** a list, usually in alphabetical order, with brief notes on the names, articles, etc., listed. *–v.t.* (**-logued, -loguing**) **2.** to enter in a catalogue.

catalyst /ˈkætəlɒst/ *n.* **1.** *Chem.* a substance which causes or accelerates a chemical change without being itself permanently affected by the reaction. **2.** the manipulating agent of any event, unaffected by the completion of the event or by its consequences.

catamaran /'kætəməræn/ n. Naut. any craft with twin parallel hulls.

catapult /'kætəpʌlt/ n. **1.** an ancient military engine for hurling darts, stones, etc. **2.** a Y-shaped stick with an elastic strip between the prongs for propelling stones, etc.

cataract /'kætərækt/ n. **1.** a waterfall, especially one of considerable size. **2.** an abnormality of the eye, characterised by opacity of the lens.

catarrh /kə'ta/ n. inflammation of a mucous membrane, especially of the respiratory tract, accompanied by excessive secretions.

catastrophe /kə'tæstrəfi/ n. **1.** a sudden and widespread disaster. **2.** a final event or conclusion, usually an unfortunate one. —**catastrophic** /kætəs'trɒfik/, adj. —**catastrophically** /kætəs'trɒfikli/, adv.

catatonia /kætə'tounia/ n. Psychol. abnormal behaviour showing unusual limitations of movement and speech, as well as resistance to suggestions from others. —**catatonic** /kætə'tɒnɪk/, adj.

catch /kætʃ/ v. (**caught, catching**) —v.t. **1.** to capture, especially after pursuit; take captive. **2.** to ensnare, entrap, or deceive. **3.** to be in time to reach (a train, boat, etc.). **4.** to come upon suddenly; surprise or detect, as in some action. **5.** to strike; hit. **6.** to intercept and seize (a ball, etc.). **7.** to get, receive, incur, or contract (often used figuratively). —v.i. **8.** to become fastened or entangled. **9.** to take hold. **10.** to become lit, take fire, ignite. **11.** to spread or be communicated, as a disease. —n. **12.** the act of catching. **13.** anything that catches; a device for checking motion. **14.** that which is caught, as a quantity of fish. **15.** anything worth getting.

catchcry /'kætʃkraɪ/ n. an ear-catching expression or group of words, voicing a popular sentiment.

catchment area n. Geog. a drainage area, especially of a reservoir or river. Also, **catchment basin**.

catchphrase /'kætʃfreɪz/ n. a phrase caught up and repeated because it is fashionable.

catch 22 /,kætʃ twɛnti 'tu/ n. a rule or condition which prevents the completion of a sequence of operations and which may establish a futile, self-perpetuating cycle.

catch-up adj. of or relating to a price rise, award increase, etc., which is an attempt to compensate for related increases elsewhere in the economy.

catch-up TV n. a facility offered by a television station where pre-telecasted programs are made available for viewing online.

catechism /'kætəkɪzəm/ n. an elementary book containing a summary of the principles of the Christian religion in the form of questions and answers.

categorical /kætə'gɒrɪkəl/ adj. not involving a condition, qualification, etc.

category /'kætəgɒri, -təgri/, Orig. US /-gɒri/ n. (pl. **-ries**) **1.** a classificatory division in any field of knowledge. **2.** any general or comprehensive division; a class.

cater /'keɪtə/ v.i. **1.** (fol. by for) to provide food and service, means of amusement, or the like at

functions. **2.** (fol. by to) to go out of one's way to placate or provide for.

caterpillar /'kætəpɪlə/ n. **1.** the wormlike larva of a butterfly or a moth. **2.** (from trademark) a tractor having the driving wheels moving inside endless tracks on either side.

caterwaul /'kætəwɔl/ v.i. to cry as cats on heat.

cath- variant of **cata-**.

catharsis /kə'θasəs/ n. **1.** Psychol. an emotional discharge with symptomatic relief. **2.** Med. a purging. —**cathartic**, adj.

cathedral /kə'θidrəl/ n. the principal church of a diocese.

catheter /'kæθətə/ n. Med. a flexible or rigid hollow tube employed to drain fluids from body cavities or to distend body passages.

cathode /'kæθoud/ n. the negative pole of a battery or other source of current. Compare **anode**.

catholic /'kæθlɪk, -əlɪk/ adj. universal in extent.

cation /'kætaɪən/ n. Physical Chem. a positively charged ion.

cat-o'-nine-tails /,kæt-ə-'nam-,teɪlz/ n. (pl. **cat-o'-nine-tails**) (formerly) a whip, usually having nine knotted lines or cords fastened to a handle, used to flog offenders.

CAT scan /kæt/ n. Med. an examination of part of the body using a **CAT scanner**, which produces a series of X-rays.

cattle /'kætl/ n. ruminants of the bovine kind, of any age, breed, or sex.

cattle dog n. one of several breeds of dog bred and trained to watch and tend cattle.

catwalk /'kætwɔk/ n. **1.** any narrow walking space. **2.** a long narrow platform on which fashion models parade clothes.

caucus /'kɔkəs/ n. **1.** the parliamentary members of a political party or faction of a political party. **2.** a private meeting of the parliamentary members of a political party or faction to discuss policy or tactics.

caught /kɔt/ v. past tense and past participle of **catch**.

caul /kɔl/ n. a part of the amnion sometimes covering the head of a child at birth.

cauldron /'kɔldrən/ n. a large kettle or boiler.

cauliflower /'kɒliflaʊə/ n. a cultivated plant with a compact, fleshy head, which is used as a vegetable.

caulk /kɔk/ v.t. to fill or close (a seam, joint, etc.), as in a boat.

causal /'kɔzəl/ adj. of, constituting, or implying a cause.

causality /kɔ'zæləti/ n. **1.** the relation of cause and effect. **2.** causal quality or agency.

causation /kɔ'zeɪʃən/ n. **1.** the action of causing or producing. **2.** the relation of cause to effect. **3.** anything that produces an effect. —**causative**, adj.

cause /kɔz/ n. **1.** that which produces an effect; the thing, person, etc., from which something results. **2.** the ground of any action or result; reason; motive. **3.** any subject of discussion or debate. **4.** that side of a question which a person or party supports; the aim, purpose, etc., of a group. —v.t. **5.** to be the cause of; bring about.

causeway /'kɔzweɪ/ n. a raised road or path, as across low or wet ground.

caustic /'kɒstɪk, 'kɔ-/ *adj.* **1.** capable of burning, corroding, or destroying living tissue. **2.** severely critical or sarcastic.

cauterise /'kɔtəraɪz/ *v.t.* to burn, especially for curative purposes. Also, **cauterize.**

caution /'kɔʃən/ *n.* **1.** prudence in regard to danger or evil; carefulness. **2.** a warning. *-v.t.* **3.** to give warning to. –**cautionary**, *adj.*

cautious /'kɔʃəs/ *adj.* taking great care to avoid danger or risk.

cavalcade /'kævəlkeɪd, kævəl'keɪd/ *n.* any procession.

cavalier /kævə'lɪə/ *n.* **1.** a soldier or knight on horseback. *–adj.* **2.** haughty, disdainful, or supercilious. **3.** offhand; casual. **4.** reckless.

cavalry /'kævəlri/ *n.* (*pl.* **-ries**) *Mil.* part of an army, formerly mounted on horseback, and now equipped with armoured vehicles.

cave /keɪv/ *n.* **1.** a hollow in the earth, especially one opening more or less horizontally into a hill, mountain, etc. *–v.i.* **2.** (fol. by *in*) to fall or sink, as ground.

caveat /'keɪviæt/ *n.* **1.** *Law* a notice to suspend a proceeding until the notifier is given a hearing. **2.** any warning or caution.

caveat emptor /keɪviæt 'ɛmptɔ/ let the buyer beware (since he or she buys without recourse).

cavern /'kævən/ *n.* a cave, especially a large, deep cave. –**cavernous,** *adj.*

caviar /'kævia, kævi'a/ *n.* the salted eggs of certain fish, considered a great delicacy.

cavil /'kævəl/ *v.i.* (**-illed, -illing**) to raise irritating and trivial objections.

cavity /'kævəti/ *n.* (*pl.* **-ties**) any hollow place.

cavort /kə'vɔt/ *v.i. Colloq.* to prance or caper about.

cay /keɪ, ki/ *n.* a small island; key.

cayenne /keɪ'ɛn/ *n.* a hot, biting spice consisting of the ground pods and seeds of any of several varieties of capsicum. Also, **cayenne pepper.**

CBD /si bi 'di/ *n.* the central business district of a city.

CB radio /si 'bi/ *n.* citizen band radio. Also, **CB.**

CCV number /si si 'vi/ *n.* credit card verification number; the three-digit number printed on the back of a credit card to provide added protection against fraud.

CD /si 'di/ *n.* → **compact disc.**

CD burner *n.* a device which copies digitally encoded data onto a CD.

CDMA /si di ɛm 'eɪ/ *n.* a technology for cellular telephone communication that uses the full available spectrum rather than a specific frequency to transmit signals.

CD-ROM /si di 'rɒm/ *n.* a laser disc designed for storing digitised text and graphics which can be displayed on a visual display unit.

cease /sis/ *v.i.* **1.** to stop. *–v.t.* **2.** to put a stop or end to. –**ceaseless,** *adj.*

ceasefire /sis'faɪə/ *n.* a cessation of active hostilities; truce.

cedar /'sidə/ *n.* any of several coniferous trees.

cede /sid/ *v.i.* (**ceded, ceding**) to yield or formally resign and surrender to another.

ceiling /'silɪŋ/ *n.* **1.** the overhead interior lining of a room. **2.** top limit.

-cele¹ a word element meaning 'tumour'.

-cele² variant of **-coele.**

celebrant /'sɛləbrənt/ *n.* **1. a.** the priest who officiates at the performance of a religious rite. **b.** an official who conducts civil marriages, funerals, etc. **2.** a participant in any celebration. –**celebrancy,** *n.*

celebrate /'sɛləbreɪt/ *v.t.* **1.** to observe (a day) or commemorate (an event) with ceremonies or festivities. **2.** to make known publicly. **3.** to sound the praises of. *–v.i.* **4.** to observe a day or commemorate an event with ceremonies or festivities. –**celebration,** *n.*

celebrated /'sɛləbreɪtəd/ *adj.* famous; renowned; well known.

celebrity /sə'lɛbrəti/ *n.* (*pl.* **-ties**) **1.** a famous or well-known person. **2.** fame; renown.

celerity /sə'lɛrəti/ *n.* swiftness; speed.

celery /'sɛləri/ *n.* a plant whose leafstalks are used raw for salad, and cooked as a vegetable.

celestial /sə'lɛstiəl/ *adj.* **1.** relating to the spiritual or invisible heaven; divine. **2.** relating to the sky or visible heaven.

celibate /'sɛləbət/ *adj.* **1.** abstaining from sexual relations: *he has been celibate for ten years.* **2.** unmarried. *–n.* **3.** someone who remains unmarried and abstains from sexual relations, especially for religious reasons. –**celibacy,** *n.*

cell /sɛl/ *n.* **1.** a small room in a convent, prison, etc. **2.** a small group acting as a unit within a larger organisation. **3.** *Biol.* the structural unit of plant and animal life. **4.** *Elect.* a device which generates electricity. **5.** *Physical Chem.* a device for producing electrolysis. **6.** the area covered by a radio transmitter for cellular telephones. –**cellular,** *adj.*

cellar /'sɛlə/ *n.* an underground room or store; basement.

cello /'tʃɛloʊ/ *n.* (*pl.* **-los** *or* **-li**) a four-stringed instrument of the violin family. Also, **'cello, violoncello.** –**cellist,** *n.*

cellophane /'sɛləfeɪn/ *n.* (*from trademark*) a transparent, paper-like product used to wrap sweets, gifts, etc.

cell phone *n.* → **cellular telephone.**

cellular telephone *n.* a type of telephone, usually portable or for use in a car, which sends and receives signals by a radio transmitter, each transmitter covering a specific area (**cell**) but linked to other such areas by a computer network. Also, **cellular phone.**

cellulite /'sɛljəlaɪt/ *n.* deposits of fat and fibrous tissue, resulting in a dimply appearance of the overlying skin.

celluloid /'sɛljəlɔɪd/ (*from trademark*) *n.* **1.** *Chem.* a type of plastic. **2.** films; the cinema.

cellulose /'sɛljəloʊs/ *n. Chem.* the chief constituent of the cell walls of plants.

Celsius /'sɛlsiəs/ *adj.* denoting or relating to a scale of temperature on which the boiling point of water under a pressure of 101.325 kPa is approximately 100°C. *Symbol:* C

cement /sə'mɛnt/ *n.* **1.** a mixture of clay and limestone, used for making concrete. **2.** any substance which is soft when first prepared but later becomes hard. *–v.t.* **3.** to fix firmly: *to cement a friendship.*

cemetery /'sɛmətri/, *Orig. US* /'sɛmətɛri/ *n.* (*pl.* **-ries**) a burial ground.

-cene a word element meaning 'recent', 'new'.

ceno-¹ variant of **caino-.**

ceno-² variant of **coeno-**. Also, (*before vowels*), **cen-**.

cenotaph /'sɛnətaf/ *n.* a municipal, civic or national memorial to those killed in war.

censor /'sɛnsə/ *n.* **1.** an official who examines books, plays, news reports, films, radio programs, etc., for the purpose of suppressing parts deemed objectionable on moral, political, military, or other grounds. *–v.t.* **2.** to examine and act upon as a censor does.

censorious /sɛn'sɔriəs/ *adj.* fault-finding; carping.

censure /'sɛnʃə/ *n.* **1.** an expression of disapproval. *–v.t.* **2.** to criticise adversely.

census /'sɛnsəs/ *n.* an official enumeration of inhabitants, with details as to age, sex, pursuits, etc.

cent /sɛnt/ *n.* **1.** the hundredth part of the dollar. **2.** (formerly, in Australia) a coin of the value of a cent.

cent- /sɛnt-/ → **centi-**.

centenary /sɛn'tinəri, -'tɛn-/ *adj.* **1.** of or relating to a 100th anniversary. *–n.* (*pl.* **-ries**) **2.** a 100th anniversary. **3.** a period of 100 years; a century.

centennial /sɛn'tɛniəl/ *adj.* consisting of, or marking the completion of, 100 years.

centi- a prefix denoting 10^{-2} of a given unit, as in *centigram*. *Symbol*: c Also, (*before vowels*), **cent-**.

Centigrade /'sɛntəɡreɪd/ *n.* **1.** (*lower case*) a non-SI unit of plane angle, equal to 10^{-4} of a right angle. *–adj.* **2.** *Obs.* → **Celsius**. *Symbol*: C

centigram /'sɛntəɡræm/ *n.* a unit of mass equal to 0.01 gram. *Symbol*: cg

centimetre /'sɛntəmitə/ *n.* a unit of length in the metric system, equal to 0.01 metre. *Symbol*: cm

centipede /'sɛntəpid/ *n.* a small, segmented arthropod with a pair of legs attached to each segment.

centr- variant of **centro-** before vowels.

central /'sɛntrəl/ *adj.* **1.** of or forming the centre. **2.** in, at, or near the centre. **3.** principal; chief; dominant.

centralise /'sɛntrəlaɪz/ *v.t.* **1.** to draw to or towards a centre. **2.** to bring under one control, especially in government. *–v.i.* **3.** to come together at a centre. Also, **centralize**.

centralism /'sɛntrəlɪzəm/ *n.* **1.** centralisation, or a centralising system. **2.** the principle of centralisation, especially in government. **3.** (in a federal system of government) the policy of redistributing legislative power so that the states or regions have less and the central government has more. **–centralist**, *n.*, *adj.*

central locking *n.* a system in which all car doors (and sometimes the boot lid) are automatically locked by operating a single control.

central nervous system *n.* *Physiol.*, *Anat.* the brain and spinal cord considered together. Compare **peripheral nervous system**.

central processing unit *n.* → **CPU**.

centre /'sɛntə/ *n.* **1.** *Geom.* the middle point. **2.** a point, pivot, axis, etc., round which anything rotates or revolves. **3.** the middle or most important part of something, around which things are grouped or to which things are attracted: *the centre of activity; the centre of attention.* **4.** a building or building complex

which houses a number of related specified services: *shopping centre; sports centre; medical centre.* *–v.t.* (**-tred, -tring**) **5.** to place in or on a centre.

centrefold /'sɛntəfoʊld/ *n.* the folded pages in the centre of a magazine, designed to be lifted out and unfolded.

centre of gravity *n.* that point of a body (or system of bodies) from which it could be suspended or on which it could be supported and be in equilibrium in any position in a uniform gravitational field.

centre party *n.* a political party or group which describes its policies as occupying the middle ground between existing major parties, or between left and right attitudes.

centri- variant of **centro-**, as in *centrifugal*.

centrifugal force /sɛn'trɪfəɡəl/ *n.* an effect of inertia, in that the natural tendency of a moving object is to travel in a straight line, which is mistakenly perceived to be a force pulling an object outwards when it is travelling around a central point. Also, **centrifugal action**.

centripetal force /sɛn'trɪpətl/ *n.* a force, directed towards the centre of a circle or curve, which causes a body to move in a circular or curved path. Also, **centripetal action**.

-centrism a word part indicating a bias towards whatever is specified, as in *Eurocentrism*.

centrist /'sɛntrɪst/ *n.* *Politics* a person who favours the concentration of power and responsibility in a central government. **–centrism**, *n.*

centro- a word element meaning 'centre'. Also, **centr-**, **centri-**.

century /'sɛntʃəri/ *n.* (*pl.* **-ries**) **1.** a period of one hundred years. **2.** any group or collection of 100.

cephalic /sə'fælɪk/ *adj.* of or relating to the head.

-cephalic a word element meaning 'head'.

cephalo- a word element denoting the 'head'.

cephalopod /'sɛfələpɒd/ *n.* a type of mollusc with tentacles attached to the head, as the octopus.

-cephalous a word element related to **cephalo-**.

-ceptor a word element meaning 'taker', 'receiver'.

cer- variant of **cero-**, used before vowels.

ceramic /sə'ræmɪk/ *adj.* **1.** relating to products made from clay and similar materials, such as pottery, brick, etc., or to their manufacture. *–n.* **2.** such a product. **–ceramics**, *n.*

cereal /'sɪəriəl/ *n.* **1.** any grass-like plant yielding an edible farinaceous grain, as wheat, rye, oats, rice, maize, etc. **2.** some edible preparation of it, especially a breakfast food made from some grain.

cerebellum /sɛrə'bɛləm/ *n.* (*pl.* **-bella** /-'bɛlə/) the back part of the brain, controlling voluntary movements, posture, and balance.

cerebral /'sɛrəbrəl, sə'ribrəl/ *adj.* **1.** of or relating to the brain. **2.** intellectual.

cerebral palsy *n.* a form of paralysis caused by brain damage.

cerebrovascular /ˌsɛrəbroʊ'væskjələ/ *adj.* of or relating to blood vessels and the supply of blood to the brain.

ceremony /'sɛrəməni/, *Orig. US* /-mouni/ *n.* (*pl.* **-nies**) **1.** the formalities observed on some solemn or important public or state occasion. **2.** a solemn rite. **3.** any formal act or observance, especially a meaningless one. **–ceremonious**, *adj.* **–ceremonial**, *adj.*, *n.*

cerise /sə'ris, -riz/ *adj.*, *n.* mauve-tinged cherry red.

cero- a word element meaning 'wax'.

certain /'sɜtn/ *adj.* **1.** having no doubt; confident; assured. **2.** sure; inevitable. **3.** unquestionable; indisputable. **4.** definite or particular, but not named or specified. **5.** some though not much. **–certainty,** *n.*

certainly /'sɜtnli/ *adv.* **1.** with certainty; without doubt; assuredly. *–interj.* **2.** yes! of course!

certificate /sə'tıfəkət/ *n.* a writing on paper certifying to the truth of something or to status, qualifications, privileges, etc.

certify /'sɜtəfaɪ/ *v.t.* (**-fied, -fying**) **1.** to guarantee as certain; give reliable information of. **2.** to declare insane.

certitude /'sɜtətjud, -tʃud/ *n.* sense of absolute conviction; certainty.

cervic- a combining form of **cervical**. Also, **cervico-**.

cervical /'sɜvɪkəl, sə'vaɪkəl/ *adj.* **1.** of or relating to the neck: *cervical vertebrae*. **2.** of or relating to the cervix (def. 2): *cervical cancer*.

cervix /'sɜvɪks/ *n.* (*pl.* **cervixes** or **cervices** /sə'vaɪsiz/) *Anat.* **1.** the neck. **2.** the neck of the uterus, which dilates just before giving birth.

cessation /sɛ'seɪʃən/ *n.* a ceasing; pause.

cession /'sɛʃən/ *n.* **1.** the act of ceding, as by treaty. **2.** the voluntary surrender by a debtor of his or her effects to creditors.

cesspool /'sɛspul/ *n.* **1.** a cistern, well, or pit for retaining the sediment of a drain, or for receiving waste from a sewerage system, etc. **2.** any filthy receptacle or place.

cetacean /sə'teɪʃən/ *n.* one of the order of aquatic mammals including the whales, dolphins, porpoises, etc. **–cetaceous,** *adj.*

chablis /'ʃæbli/ *n.* a very dry white table wine.

chador /'tʃadə/ *n.* an outer piece of clothing worn by some Muslim women, consisting of a loose, dark cloak which covers the whole body but leaves the face uncovered.

chafe /tʃeɪf/ *v.t.* **1.** to warm by rubbing. **2.** to wear or abrade by rubbing. **3.** to irritate; annoy.

chaff[1] /tʃaf/ *n.* the husks of grains and grasses separated from the seed.

chaff[2] /tʃaf/ *v.t.* to ridicule or tease goodnaturedly.

chagrin /'ʃægrən, ʃə'grɪn/ *n.* a feeling of vexation and disappointment or humiliation.

chai /tʃaɪ/ *n.* a sweet milky tea beverage flavoured with spices such as cardamom, cinnamon, cloves, vanilla, etc.

chai latte /tʃaɪ/ *n.* spiced tea with hot frothed milk.

chain /tʃeɪn/ *n.* **1.** a connected series of metal or other links. **2.** something that binds or restrains. **3.** a series of things connected or following in succession. **4.** a number of similar establishments, as banks, theatres, hotels, etc., under one ownership and management. **5.** a surveying measure. *–v.t.* **6.** to fasten or secure with or as with a chain.

chain reaction *n.* a series of reactions provoked by one event.

chain store *n.* one of a group of retail stores under the same ownership and management and stocked from a common supply point or points.

chair /tʃeə/ *n.* **1.** a seat with a back and legs or other support, usually for one person. **2.** a seat of office or authority. **3.** the person occupying a seat of office, especially the chairperson of a meeting. *–v.t.* **4.** to preside over. *–phr.* **5. take the chair,** to assume the position of chair (def. 3) of a meeting; begin or open a meeting.

chairlift /'tʃeəlɪft/ *n.* a series of chairs suspended from an endless cable driven by a motor, for conveying people up or down mountains.

chairman /'tʃeəmən/ *n.* (*pl.* **-men**) **1. → chairperson. 2.** a male chairperson.

chairperson /'tʃeəpɜsən/ *n.* the presiding officer of a meeting, committee, board, etc.

chairwoman /'tʃeəwʊmən/ *n.* (*pl.* **-women**) a female chairperson.

chakra /'tʃʌkrə/ *n.* (in yoga) one of the centres of spiritual power in the body.

chalet /'ʃæleɪ/ *n.* a kind of cottage, low and with wide eaves, common in alpine regions.

chalice /'tʃæləs/ *n. Eccles.* a cup for the wine of the Eucharist or mass.

chalk /tʃɔk/ *n.* **1.** *Geol.* a soft, white, pure limestone. **2.** a prepared piece of chalk or chalk-like substance for marking. *–v.t.* **3.** to mark or write with chalk. *–phr.* **4. chalk up,** to score. **5. chalk up to, a.** to ascribe to. **b.** to regard as having contributed towards the gain of.

chalkie /'tʃɔki/ *n. Colloq.* a teacher. Also, **chalky.**

challenge /'tʃæləndʒ/ *n.* **1.** a call to engage in a contest of skill, strength, etc. **2.** something that makes demands upon one's abilities, endurance, etc. **3.** a calling to account or into question. *–v.t.* (**-lenged, -lenging**) **4.** to summon to a contest. **5.** to make demands, especially stimulating demands, upon. **6.** to call in question.

chamber /'tʃeɪmbə/ *n.* **1.** a room or apartment, usually a private room, and especially a bedroom. **2.** the meeting hall of a legislative or other assembly. **3.** (*pl.*) a place where a judge hears matters not requiring action in court. **4.** (*pl.*) a suite of rooms of barristers and others. **5.** a legislative, judicial, or other like body. **6.** a compartment or enclosed space.

chambermaid /'tʃeɪmbəmeɪd/ *n.* a female servant who takes care of bedrooms.

chamber music *n.* music suited for performance in a room or a small concert hall, especially using a small number of instruments.

chamber of commerce *n.* an association, primarily of businesspeople, to protect and promote the business activities of a city, etc.

chamber-pot *n.* a portable vessel used chiefly in bedrooms as a toilet.

chameleon /kə'miliən, ʃə-/ *n.* a slow-moving lizard noted for its power of changing skin colour and its projectile tongue.

chamois /'ʃæmwa/ *for def. 1,* /'ʃæmi/ *for defs 2 and 3 –n.* (*pl.* **chamois** /'ʃæmwa/ *for def. 1,* /'ʃæmiz/ *for defs 2 and 3*) **1.** an agile goat-like antelope. **2.** Also, **shammy.** a soft, pliable leather. **3.** Also, **shammy. a.** a piece of chamois used for drying glass, motor vehicles, etc., after washing. **b.** an absorbent cloth made of synthetic material, similarly used.

chamomile /'kæməmaɪl/ n. a herb with strongly scented foliage and flowers which are used medicinally. Also, **camomile**.

champ¹ /tʃæmp/ v.t. to bite upon, especially impatiently.

champ² /tʃæmp/ n. Colloq. a champion.

champagne /ʃæm'peɪn/ n. a sparkling white wine.

champignon /'ʃæmpɪnjõ/ n. a very small mushroom.

champion /'tʃæmpiən/ n. **1.** someone who holds first place in any sport, etc., having defeated all opponents. **2.** someone who fights for or defends any person or cause. –v.t. **3.** to act as champion of; defend; support. –**championship**, n.

chance /tʃæns, tʃɑns/ n. **1.** the absence of any known reason why an event should turn out one way rather than another, spoken of as if it were a real agency. **2.** fortune; fate; luck. **3.** a possibility or probability of anything happening. **4.** an opportunity. **5.** a risk or hazard. –v. (**chanced, chancing**) –v.i. **6.** (fol. by on or upon) to come by chance. –v.t. **7.** Colloq. to take the chances or risks of; risk (usually followed by impersonal it). –adj. **8.** due to chance.

chancellor /'tʃænsələ, 'tʃɑnsələ/ n. **1.** the title of various important judges and other high officials. **2.** the titular, honorary head of a university.

chandelier /ʃændə'lɪə/ n. a branched support for a number of lights, especially one suspended from a ceiling.

change /tʃeɪndʒ/ v. (**changed, changing**) –v.t. **1.** to alter in condition, appearance, etc. **2.** to substitute another or others for; exchange for something else. **3.** to remove and replace the coverings of. –v.i. **4.** (sometimes fol. by to or into) to become different; alter. **5.** to change trains or other conveyances. **6.** to change one's clothes. –n. **7.** variation; alteration. **8.** the substitution of one thing for another. **9.** variety or novelty. **10.** the passing from one place, state, form, or phase to another. **11.** a balance of money that is returned when the sum tendered is larger than the sum due. **12.** coins of low denomination. **13.** (oft. upper case) Commerce a place where merchants meet for business transactions; an exchange.

channel /'tʃænəl/ n. **1.** the bed and banks of a stream or waterway. **2.** the deeper part of a waterway. **3.** a route through which anything passes or progresses, such as a means of communication. **4.** a frequency band for one-way communication (as telephone, radio, television, etc.). **5.** a television station. **6.** Computers a connection from a data source, as the participants in a chat room, to the device that receives and controls the flow of data. –v.t. (**-nelled, -nelling**) **7.** to convey through a channel. **8.** to direct towards or into some particular course.

channel-surf v.i. Colloq. to switch rapidly from one television channel to another, usually with the aid of a remote control, in order to assess the range of program. –**channel-surfing**, n. –**channel-surfer**, n.

chant /tʃænt, tʃɑnt/ n. **1.** a short, simple melody. –v.t. **2.** to sing to a chant, or in the manner of a chant.

chaos /'keɪɒs/ n. utter confusion or disorder. –**chaotic**, adj.

chap¹ /tʃæp/ v. (**chapped, chapping**) –v.t. **1.** (of cold or exposure) to crack, roughen, and redden (the skin). –v.i. **2.** to become chapped.

chap² /tʃæp/ n. Colloq. a man.

chapel /'tʃæpəl/ n. a separately dedicated part of a church, or a small, independent, churchlike edifice, devoted to special services.

chaperone /'ʃæpəroʊn/ n. **1.** an adult who accompanies one or more children or young people on a public outing, as to ensure their safety, to ensure that they behave appropriately, etc. **2.** an older person who, for propriety, attends a young unmarried woman in public or accompanies a group of young people on public outings, etc. –v.t. **3.** to attend or accompany as chaperone. Also, **chaperon**.

chaplain /'tʃæplən/ n. an ecclesiastic attached to the chapel of a royal court, or to a college, school, etc.

chapter /'tʃæptə/ n. **1.** a main division, usually numbered, of a book, treatise, or the like. **2.** a branch, usually localised, of a society or fraternity.

char¹ /tʃɑ/ v.t. (**charred, charring**) **1.** to burn or reduce to charcoal. **2.** to burn slightly; scorch.

char² /tʃɑ/ n. Brit. Colloq. a woman paid to do housework.

char³ /tʃɑ/ n. tea.

character /'kærəktə/ n. **1.** the aggregate of qualities that distinguishes one person or thing from others. **2.** good moral constitution or status. **3.** a formal statement from an employer concerning the qualities and habits of a former employee. **4.** a person. **5.** Colloq. an odd or interesting person. **6.** a person represented in a drama, story, etc. **7.** a symbol as used in a writing system, as a letter of the alphabet. **8.** Computers a group of bits representing such a symbol or a numeral.

characterise /'kærəktəraɪz/ v.t. **1.** to mark or distinguish as a characteristic; be a characteristic of. **2.** to describe the characteristic or peculiar quality of. Also, **characterize**.

characteristic /kærəktə'rɪstɪk/ adj. **1.** typical; distinctive. –n. **2.** a distinguishing feature or quality.

charade /ʃə'rɑd/ n. **1.** a game in which a player or players act out in pantomime a word or phrase which the others try to guess. **2.** a ridiculous or pointless act or series of acts.

charcoal /'tʃɑkoʊl/ n. a form of carbon obtained by the incomplete combustion of wood, etc.

chardonnay /'ʃɑdəneɪ/ n. (sometimes upper case) a dry white wine.

charge /tʃɑdʒ/ v. (**charged, charging**) –v.t. **1.** to put a load or burden on or in. **2.** to fill or furnish (something) with the appropriate quantity of that which it is designed to receive. **3.** to supply a quantity of electricity to (a battery) usually sufficient to make it fully operational again. **4.** to lay a command or injunction upon. **5.** (usu. fol. by with) to lay blame upon; blame; accuse. **6.** to hold liable for payment. **7.** to postpone payment on (a service or purchase) by having it recorded on one's charge account. **8.** to impose or ask as a price. **9.** to attack by rushing violently against. −*v.i.* **10.** to rush, as to an attack. −*n.* **11.** a load or burden. **12.** the quantity of anything which an apparatus is fitted to hold, or holds, at one time. **13.** *Elect.* an electric charge. **14.** care, custody, or superintendence. **15.** anything or anybody committed to one's care or management. **16.** a command or injunction. **17.** an accusation or imputation of guilt. **18.** a sum or price charged. **19.** an impetuous onset or attack, as of soldiers. **20.** the quantity of stored energy. −*phr.* **21. in charge**, having supervisory powers. **22. take charge**, to put oneself in control of people or events.

chargé d'affaires /ˌʃaʒeɪ dəˈfɛə/ *n.* (*pl.* **chargés d'affaires**) **1.** an official placed in charge of diplomatic business during the temporary absence of the ambassador or minister. **2.** an envoy to a state to which a diplomat of higher grade is not sent.

chariot /ˈtʃæriət/ *n.* a two-wheeled vehicle.

charisma /kəˈrɪzmə/ *n.* those special personal qualities that give an individual influence or authority over large numbers of people. −**charismatic**, *adj.*, *n.*

charitable /ˈtʃærətəbəl/ *adj.* **1.** generous in gifts to relieve the needs of others. **2.** kindly or lenient in judging others.

charity /ˈtʃærəti/ *n.* (*pl.* **-ties**) **1.** the private or public relief of unfortunate or needy people. **2.** a charitable fund, foundation, or institution. **3.** benevolent feeling, especially towards those in need.

charlatan /ˈʃalətən/ *n.* someone who pretends to more knowledge or skill than they possesses; a quack.

charm /tʃam/ *n.* **1.** a power to please and attract. **2.** a trinket to be worn on a chain, bracelet, etc. **3.** a verse or formula credited with magical power. −*v.t.* **4.** to attract powerfully by beauty, etc.; please greatly. **5.** to act upon with or as with a charm; enchant.

chart /tʃat/ *n.* **1.** a sheet exhibiting information in tabulated or methodical form. **2.** a map, especially a marine map. −*v.t.* **3.** to make a chart of. **4.** to plan.

charter /ˈtʃatə/ *n.* **1.** a written instrument or contract, especially relating to land transfers. **2.** a written instrument, granted by a sovereign or legislature giving privileges, rights, the benefit of a new invention, a peerage, etc. **3.** Also, **charter party**. a contract by which part or all of a ship is leased for a voyage or a stated time, and safe delivery of the cargo is agreed. −*v.t.* **4.** to establish by charter. **5.** to hire a vehicle, etc. −*adj.* **6.** founded, granted, or protected by a charter. **7.** hired for a particular purpose or journey.

chartered accountant *n.* an accountant who is a full member of one of the institutes of accountants granted a royal charter which have branches in Australia.

charter member *n.* one of the original members.

chary /ˈtʃɛəri/ *adj.* (**-rier**, **-riest**) **1.** careful; wary. **2.** shy.

chase[1] /tʃeɪs/ *v.t.* **1.** to pursue in order to seize, overtake, etc. −*v.i.* **2.** to follow in pursuit. −*n.* **3.** the act of chasing. **4.** a flora and fauna reserve.

chase[2] /tʃeɪs/ *v.t.* to ornament (metal) by engraving or embossing.

chasm /ˈkæzəm/ *n.* a deep cleft in the earth's surface.

chassis /ˈʃæzi/ *n.* (*pl.* **chassis** /ˈʃæziz/) the frame, wheels, and machinery of a motor vehicle, on which the body is supported.

chaste /tʃeɪst/ *adj.* **1.** virgin, especially when considered as being virtuous. **2.** pure in style; simple. −**chastity**, *n.*

chasten /ˈtʃeɪsən/ *v.t.* to chastise.

chastise /tʃæsˈtaɪz/ *v.t.* **1.** to punish, especially physically. **2.** to scold or rebuke.

chat /tʃæt/ *v.* (**chatted**, **chatting**) −*v.i.* **1.** to converse in a familiar or informal manner. **2.** *Internet* to take part in real-time communication using internet relay chat. −*v.t.* **3.** *Colloq.* (fol. by *up*) to talk persuasively to or flirt with. −*n.* **4.** informal conversation. **5.** *Internet* a session of real-time communication using internet relay chat. −**chatty**, *adj.*

chatbot /ˈtʃætbɒt/ *n.* a piece of computer software which uses auditory or textual prompts to mimic the conversational responses of a human being. Also, **chat bot**.

chat line *n.* *Computers* a real-time connection to a chat room.

chat room *n.* *Internet* a virtual venue on the internet for conversation, discussion, etc., using internet relay chat.

chattels /ˈtʃætlz/ *pl. n.* movable articles of property.

chatter /ˈtʃætə/ *v.i.* **1.** to utter a succession of quick, inarticulate, speech-like sounds. **2.** to talk rapidly and to little purpose; jabber.

chatterbox /ˈtʃætəbɒks/ *n.* a very talkative person.

chauffeur /ˈʃoʊfə, ʃoʊˈfɜ/ *n.* **1.** a person employed as a driver for a private car. −*v.t.* **2.** to act as chauffeur to.

chauvinism /ˈʃoʊvənɪzəm/ *n.* narrow-minded belief in the superiority of one's own gender, group, ideology, etc. −**chauvinist**, *n.*, *adj.*

cheap /tʃip/ *adj.* **1.** of a relatively low price; at a bargain. **2.** of poor quality. **3.** *Colloq.* (of a person) not willing to spend money unless absolutely necessary; mean; stingy. −**cheapen**, *v.* −**cheaply**, *adv.*

cheat /tʃit/ *v.i.* **1.** to behave deceitfully or dishonestly. −*v.t.* **2.** to defraud; swindle. −*n.* **3.** a person who cheats or defrauds. **4.** a fraud; swindle; deception. −**cheating**, *n.*

check /tʃek/ *v.t.* **1.** to stop or arrest the motion of suddenly or forcibly. **2.** to restrain; hold in restraint or control. **3.** to investigate or verify as to correctness. **4.** (fol. by *in*) to leave in temporary custody. **5.** to mark in a pattern of checks or squares. **6.** *Chess* to place (an opponent's king) under direct attack. −*v.i.* **7.** to prove to be right; to correspond accurately. **8.** (usu. fol. by *up* or *on*) to make an inquiry or investigation for verification, etc. −*n.* **9.** a person or thing that checks or restrains. **10.** a sudden arrest or stoppage; repulse; rebuff. **11.** control with a view to ascertaining performance or preventing error. **12.** a means or standard to insure against error, fraud, etc. **13.** a pattern formed of squares. **14.** *US* → **cheque**. **15.** *US* → **bill**[1] (def. 2). *–phr.* **16. check in**, to register one's arrival. **17. check out**, to register one's departure.

checkmate /ˈtʃɛkmeɪt/ *n. Chess* the act of putting the opponent's king into an inextricable check, thus winning the game.

check-up *n.* **1.** an examination or close scrutiny for purposes of verification as to accuracy, comparison, etc. **2.** a comprehensive physical examination.

cheddar /ˈtʃɛdə/ *n.* a firm white or yellow cheese.

cheek /tʃik/ *n.* **1.** either side of the face below eye level. **2.** the side wall of the mouth between the upper and lower jaws. **3.** a buttock. **4.** *Colloq.* impudence or effrontery.

cheeky /ˈtʃiki/ *adj.* (**-kier, -kiest**) impudent; insolent.

cheep /tʃip/ *v.i.* to chirp; peep.

cheer /tʃɪə/ *n.* **1.** a shout of encouragement, approval, congratulation, etc. **2.** gladness, gaiety, or animation. *–v.t.* **3.** to salute with shouts of approval, congratulation, etc. **4.** (oft. fol. by *up*) to inspire with cheer; gladden. **5.** (fol. by *on*) to encourage or incite. *–cheerful, adj.*

cheer squad *n.* **1.** a group of dancers who perform at a sporting match, to lead the crowd in support of a particular team. **2.** a group of people who support someone's ideas, proposals, ambitions, etc. Also, **cheersquad**.

cheese /tʃiz/ *n.* **1.** the curd of milk separated from the whey and prepared in many ways as a food. *–phr.* **2. hard** (or **stiff**) **cheese**, *Colloq.* bad luck.

cheetah /ˈtʃitə/ *n.* an animal of the cat family, having a pale yellow coat covered with small black spots; reputed to be the fastest four-legged animal.

chef /ʃɛf/ *n.* a cook, especially a head cook.

cheiro- variant of **chiro-**.

cheli- a word element meaning 'claws'.

chem- a word element representing **chemical** used before vowels. Also, (*especially before a consonant*), **chemo-**.

chemical /ˈkɛmɪkəl/ *adj.* **1.** of or concerned with the science or the operations or processes of chemistry. *–n.* **2.** a substance produced by or used in a chemical process.

chemical warfare *n.* warfare with asphyxiating, poisonous, and corrosive gases, oil flames, etc.

chemical weapon *n.* a weapon which uses chemicals other than explosives to attack an enemy, as asphyxiating or poisonous gases, gases which blister skin, etc.

chemise /ʃəˈmiz/ *n.* a woman's loose-fitting shirt-like undergarment.

chemist /ˈkɛməst/ *n.* **1.** someone who studies or is professionally qualified in the science of chemistry. **2.** a retailer of medicinal drugs and toilet preparations.

chemistry /ˈkɛməstri/ *n.* **1.** the science concerned with the composition of substances, the various elementary forms of matter, and the interactions between them. **2.** chemical properties, reactions, etc.

chemotherapy /kimoʊˈθɛrəpi/ *n. Med.* treatment of disease by means of chemicals which have a specific toxic effect upon the disease-producing micro-organisms. *–chemotherapist, n.*

chenille /ʃəˈnil/ *n.* cotton fabric with a design of tufted threads.

cheongsam /tʃɒŋˈsæm/ *n.* a Chinese-style dress, tight-fitting with a high collar and long straight openings up the sides of the skirt.

cheque /tʃɛk/ *n.* **1.** *Banking* a written order, usually on a standard printed form, directing a bank to pay a specified sum of money to, or to the order of, some particular person or the bearer, either *crossed* (payable only through a bank account), or *uncrossed* (payable on demand). **2.** wages, pay.

cheque account *n.* a bank account from which money may be withdrawn by cheque at any time by the customer.

chequered /ˈtʃɛkəd/ *adj.* **1.** marked with squares: *a chequered board.* **2.** marked by changes in good or bad: *a chequered career.*

chequered flag *n. Car Racing* a flag with a pattern of alternating black and white squares which is waved to signal the end of a race, practice session, or qualifying session.

cherish /ˈtʃɛrɪʃ/ *v.t.* to hold or treat as dear.

cheroot /ʃəˈrut/ *n.* a cigar having open, unpointed ends.

cherry /ˈtʃɛri/ *n.* (*pl.* **-ries**) the fruit of any of various trees, consisting of a red-coloured, pulpy, globular drupe enclosing a one-seeded smooth stone.

cherry picker *n. Colloq.* a crane, especially one mounted on a truck, with an enclosed platform on the end, designed to lift people to a height where they can perform a function, such as changing streetlights, checking stores, etc.

cherub /ˈtʃɛrəb/ *n.* (*pl.* **cherubim** *for def. 1,* **cherubs** *for def. 2*) **1.** *Bible* a kind of celestial being. **2.** a beautiful or innocent person, especially a child.

chess /tʃɛs/ *n.* a game played by two persons, each with sixteen pieces, on a chequered board.

chest /tʃɛst/ *n.* **1.** the trunk of the body from the neck to the belly. **2.** a box, usually a large, strong one, for the safekeeping of valuables.

chest cold *n.* a form of the common cold that mainly involves inflammation or infection of the respiratory tract. Compare **head cold**.

chestnut /ˈtʃɛsnʌt/ *n.* **1.** the edible nut of trees, of the beech family. **2.** reddish brown.

chevre /ˈʃɛvrə/ *n.* cheese made from goat's milk. Also, **chèvre**.

chevron /ˈʃɛvrən/ *n.* a badge with V-shaped stripes, worn on the sleeve of a police or armed forces uniform, etc., to show rank, etc.

chew /tʃu/ *v.t.* **1.** to crush or grind with the teeth; masticate. **2.** (fol. by *up*) to damage or destroy by or as if by chewing. **3.** (fol. by *over*) to meditate on; consider deliberately.

chewing gum *n.* a preparation for chewing, usually made of sweetened and flavoured gum.

chewy /ˈtʃui/ *adj.* requiring chewing; tough.

chia /ˈtʃiə/ *n.* a plant of the mint family with seeds high in antioxidants and dietary fibre.

chianti /kiˈænti/ *n.* (*sometimes upper case*) a red or white wine, usually bottled in a colourful straw-covered bottle.

chic /ʃik/ *adj.* stylish.

chicanery /ʃəˈkeɪnəri/ *n.* the use of legal tricks or misleading arguments, usually to take advantage of someone.

chick /tʃɪk/ *n.* **1.** a young chicken or other bird. **2.** *Colloq.* a young woman.

chicken /ˈtʃɪkən/ *n.* **1.** a common domesticated gallinaceous bird having a prominent comb and wattles and farmed for its eggs and flesh; bred into numerous breeds and varieties. **2.** the young of the domestic fowl; chick. **3.** a slaughtered and dressed chicken, either raw or cooked. **4.** the flesh of this bird used as food. **5.** *Colloq.* a coward. *–phr.* **6. chicken out,** to withdraw because of cowardice, tiredness, etc.

chickenpox /ˈtʃɪkənpɒks/ *n.* a mild, contagious eruptive disease, commonly of children, caused by a virus.

chick flick *n. Colloq.* a film seen as appealing more to female than to male viewers, especially a romance.

chick lit *n. Colloq.* a genre of popular fiction appealing typically to young women, often set in a stylish urban business environment and usually featuring romance.

chickpea /ˈtʃɪkpi/ *n.* a leguminous plant bearing edible pea-like seeds, much used for food.

chicory /ˈtʃɪkəri/ *n.* a blue-flowered herb, the leaves of which may be used in salads, while the roasted, powdered roots are added to coffee.

chide /tʃaɪd/ *v.* (**chided, chiding**) *–v.i.* **1.** to scold; find fault. *–v.t.* **2.** to drive, impel, etc., by chiding.

chief /tʃif/ *n.* **1.** the head or ruler of a clan or tribe. **2.** *Colloq.* boss. *–adj.* **3.** highest in rank or authority. **4.** most important. *–chiefly, adv.*

chief minister *n.* (in Australia) the leader of the government of a self-governing territory.

chieftain /ˈtʃiftən/ *n.* the chief of a clan or a tribe.

chiffon /ʃəˈfɒn, ˈʃɪfɒn/ *n.* sheer fabric of silk, nylon, or rayon in plain weave.

chignon /ˈʃinjɒn/ *n.* a large coil of hair, worn at the back of the head by women.

Chihuahua /tʃəˈwauwə, tʃəˈwawə/ *n.* a Mexican breed of very small dog. Also, **chihuahua.**

chil- variant of **chilo-,** used before vowels.

chilblain /ˈtʃɪlbleɪn/ *n.* (*usu. pl.*) an inflammation on the hands and feet caused by exposure to cold and moisture.

child /tʃaɪld/ *n.* (*pl.* **children**) **1.** a baby or infant. **2.** a boy or girl. **3.** any descendant.

child care *n.* professional superintendence of children.

childcare centre *n.* a place where children, especially young children, may be minded while their parents work or are otherwise occupied.

childcare worker *n.* a person who is professionally employed in child care.

childish /ˈtʃaɪldɪʃ/ *adj.* like a child; weak or foolish.

children /ˈtʃɪldrən/ *n.* plural of **child.**

child restraint *n.* any of various devices, as a seatbelt, baby capsule, etc., which may be fitted to a motor vehicle to secure a child against injury in the event of collision or sudden braking.

chill /tʃɪl/ *n.* **1.** coldness, especially a moderate but penetrating coldness. **2.** a sensation of cold, usually with shivering. **3.** a cold stage, as a first symptom of illness. **4.** a depressing influence or sensation. **5.** a coldness of manner, lack of friendliness. *–adj.* **6.** cold; tending to cause shivering. **7.** shivering with cold. **8.** depressing or discouraging. *–v.i.* **9.** to become cold. *–v.t.* **10.** to affect with cold; make chilly. **11.** to make cool, but not freeze. *–chilly, adj.*

chilli /ˈtʃɪli/ *n.* (*pl.* **-lies**) the pungent fruit of some species of capsicum, usually small but hot to the taste.

chilo- a word element meaning 'lip', 'labial'. Also, **chil-.**

chime /tʃaɪm/ *n.* **1.** an arrangement for striking a bell or bells so as to produce a musical sound. **2.** a set of vertical metal tubes struck with a hammer, as used in the modern orchestra. **3.** harmonious relation; accord. *–v.i.* **4.** to sound harmoniously or in chimes, as a set of bells. **5.** to harmonise; agree. *–v.t.* **6.** to give forth (music, etc.), as a bell or bells.

chimney /ˈtʃɪmni/ *n.* (*pl.* **-neys**) a structure, usually vertical, containing a passage or flue by which the smoke, gases, etc., of a fire or furnace are carried off.

chimpanzee /tʃɪmpænˈzi/ *n.* an anthropoid ape, smaller, with larger ears, and more arboreal than the gorilla.

chin /tʃɪn/ *n.* the lower extremity of the face, below the mouth.

china /ˈtʃaɪnə/ *n.* **1.** a vitreous, translucent earthenware, originally produced in China. **2.** plates, cups, etc., collectively.

Chinese gooseberry /tʃaɪˈniz/ *n.* → **kiwifruit.**

chink[1] /tʃɪŋk/ *n.* a crack, cleft, or fissure.

chink[2] /tʃɪŋk/ *v.i.* to make a short, sharp, ringing sound, as of coins or glasses striking together.

chintz /tʃɪnts/ *n.* a printed cotton fabric, glazed or unglazed, used especially for draperies.

chip /tʃɪp/ *n.* **1.** a small piece, as of wood, separated by chopping, cutting, or breaking. **2.** a very thin slice or piece of food, etc. **3. a.** a deep-fried finger of potato. **b.** a wafer of potato fried, dried, and usually served cold; crisp. **4.** *Games* a counter or disc used to represent money in certain gambling games. **5.** *Electronics* a minute square of semiconductor material, processed in various ways to have certain electrical characteristics. *–v.* (**chipped, chipping**) *–v.t.* **6.** to hew or cut with an axe, chisel, etc. *–v.i.* **7.** to break off in small pieces; to become chipped. *–phr. Colloq.* **8. chip in,** to contribute money, help, etc. **9. chip on the shoulder,** a long-standing resentment; grievance.

chipboard /ˈtʃɪpbɔd/ *n.* a resin-bonded artificial wood made from wood chips, sawdust, etc., used in sheets for light structural work.

chipmunk /ˈtʃɪpmʌŋk/ *n.* any of various small striped terrestrial squirrels.

chiro- a word element meaning 'hand', as in *chiropractic.*

chiropody /kəˈrɒpədi, ʃəˈrɒpədi/ *n.* the treatment of minor foot ailments, such as corns, bunions, etc. *–chiropodist, n.*

chiropractic /kaɪroˈpræktɪk/ *n.* a therapeutic system based upon the premise that disease is caused by interference with nerve function, the method being to restore normal condition by adjusting the segments of the spinal column. –**chiropractor**, *n*.

chirp /tʃɜp/ *v.i.* to make a short, sharp sound, as small birds and certain insects.

chirpy /'tʃɜpi/ *adj. Colloq.* cheerful.

chirrup /'tʃɪrəp/ *v.i.* (**-ruped**, **-ruping**) to chirp.

chisel /'tʃɪzəl/ *n.* **1.** a tool, as of steel, with a cutting edge for cutting or shaping wood, stone, etc. –*v.i.* (**-elled**, **-elling**) **2.** to work with a chisel.

chit¹ /tʃɪt/ *n.* a voucher.

chit² /tʃɪt/ *n.* a young, silly girl.

chivalry /'ʃɪvəlri/ *n.* **1.** the rules and customs of medieval knighthood. **2.** good manners. –**chivalrous**, *adj.*

chives /tʃaɪvz/ *pl. n.* a small bulbous plant related to the leek and onion.

chlamydia /klə'mɪdiə/ *n.* **1.** a sexually transmitted disease which is responsible for infections of the eye and the urogenital system. **2.** a disease which can occur in animals and to which koalas are particularly prone.

chlor-¹ a word element meaning 'green'.

chlor-² a combining form denoting 'chlorine'.

chloride /'klɔraɪd/ *n.* **1.** a compound usually of two elements only, one of which is chlorine. **2.** a salt of hydrochloric acid.

chlorine /'klɔrin/ *n.* a greenish yellow gaseous element used as a powerful bleaching agent and in various industrial processes. *Symbol*: Cl

chloro-¹ variant of **chlor-¹**, used before consonants, as in *chlorophyll*.

chloro-² variant of **chlor-²**, used before consonants, as in *chloroform*.

chlorofluorocarbon /ˌklɔrou,fluərou'kabən/ *n.* any of several compounds of carbon, fluorine, chlorine and hydrogen, formerly used in aerosols.

chloroform /'klɔrəfɔm/ *n.* a colourless volatile liquid, used as an anaesthetic and solvent.

chlorophyll /'klɔrəfɪl/ *n.* the green colouring substances of leaves and plants, associated with the production of carbohydrates by photosynthesis.

chock /tʃɒk/ *n.* **1.** a block or wedge of wood, etc., for filling in a space, especially for preventing movement, as of a wheel or a cask. –*adv.* **2.** as close or tight as possible; quite.

chocolate /'tʃɒklət, 'tʃɒkələt/ *n.* a preparation of the seeds of cacao, often sweetened and flavoured, as with vanilla.

choice /tʃɔɪs/ *n.* **1.** the act of choosing; selection. **2.** power of choosing; option. **3.** the person or thing chosen. **4.** an abundance and variety from which to choose. –*adj.* (**choicer**, **choicest**) **5.** worthy of being chosen; excellent; superior. **6.** carefully selected.

choir /'kwaɪə/ *n.* a company of singers.

choke /tʃoʊk/ *v.t.* **1.** to stop the breath of, by squeezing or obstructing the windpipe; strangle; stifle; suffocate. **2.** to obstruct; clog; congest. –*v.i.* **3.** to suffer strangling or suffocation. **4.** to be obstructed or clogged. **5.** to be temporarily overcome, as with emotion. –*n.* **6.** the act or sound of choking. **7.** (in internal-combustion engines) the mechanism by which the air supply to a carburettor is diminished or stopped.

choko /'tʃoʊkou/ *n.* (*pl.* **-kos** *or* **-koes**) a pear-shaped green fruit used as a vegetable. Also, **chayote**.

chol- a word element meaning 'gall' or 'bile'. Also, **chole-**, **cholo-**.

choler /'kɒlə/ *n.* anger; wrath; irritability.

cholera /'kɒlərə/ *n.* an acute, infectious disease marked by diarrhoea, vomiting, cramp, etc.

cholesterol /kə'lestərɒl/ *n.* an organic compound found in bile and gallstones, and in the blood and brain, the yolk of eggs, etc. See **bad cholesterol**, **good cholesterol**.

cholo- variant of **chol-** before consonants.

chook /tʃʊk/ *n.* a domestic chicken.

choose /tʃuz/ *v.t.* (**chose**, **chosen**, **choosing**) **1.** to select from a number, or in preference to another or other things or persons. **2.** to prefer and decide (to do something).

choosy /'tʃuzi/ *adj. Colloq.* hard to please. Also, **choosey**.

chop¹ /tʃɒp/ *v.* (**chopped**, **chopping**) –*v.t.* **1.** to cut with a quick, heavy blow or series of blows, using an axe, etc. –*v.i.* **2.** to make a quick heavy stroke or a series of strokes, as with an axe. **3.** to go, come, or move suddenly or violently. –*n.* **4.** the act of chopping. **5.** a cutting blow. **6.** a slice of lamb, veal, pork, mutton, etc., containing some bone. **7.** *Colloq.* the sack; dismissal.

chop² /tʃɒp/ *v.i.* (**chopped**, **chopping**) to turn, shift, or change suddenly, as the wind.

chopper /'tʃɒpə/ *n. Colloq.* **1.** a helicopter. **2.** a modified motorcycle with the front wheel moved forward and high handlebars.

choppy /'tʃɒpi/ *adj.* (**-pier**, **-piest**) (of the sea, etc.) forming short, irregular, broken waves.

chopstick /'tʃɒpstɪk/ *n.* one of a pair of thin sticks used to raise food to the mouth.

chord¹ /kɔd/ *n.* **1.** a string of a musical instrument. **2.** a feeling or emotion. **3.** *Geom.* that part of a straight line between two of its intersections with a curve.

chord² /kɔd/ *n. Music* a combination of three or more tones, mostly in harmonic relation, sounded either simultaneously or in quick succession.

chore /tʃɔ/ *n.* a small or odd job; a piece of minor domestic work.

choreography /kɒri'ɒɡrəfi/ *n.* the art of composing ballets, etc., and arranging separate dances. –**choreographer**, *n.* –**choreographic**, *adj.* –**choreograph**, *v.*

chorister /'kɒrəstə/ *n.* a singer in a choir.

chortle /'tʃɔtl/ *v.i.* to chuckle with glee.

chorus /'kɔrəs/ *n.* (*pl.* **-ruses**) **1. a.** a group of persons singing in concert. **b.** a part of a song in which others join the principal singer or singers. **c.** any recurring refrain. **2.** simultaneous utterance in singing, speaking, etc. **3.** (in musical shows) the company of dancers and singers. –**choral**, *adj.*

chose /tʃoʊz/ *v.* past tense of **choose**.

chowder /'tʃaʊdə/ *n.* a kind of soup or stew made of clams, fish, or vegetables.

choy sum /tʃɔɪ 'sʊm/ *n.* a cabbage with flat green leaves and small heads of yellow flowers. Also, **choi sum**.

christen /ˈkrɪsən/ v.t. to give a name to, especially at baptism.

Christian name /ˈkrɪstʃən/ n. the name given to a person at baptism or at birth, as distinguished from the family name; given name; forename; first name.

Christmas bell /ˈkrɪsməs/ n. a plant of eastern Australia with hanging red and yellow flowers.

-chroic an adjectival word element indicating colour (of skin, plants, etc.).

chrom- 1. a word element referring to colour. 2. a word element referring to chromium.

chromatic /krəˈmætɪk/ adj. 1. relating to colour or colours. 2. Music relating to a scale which progresses by semitones.

chromato- a word element referring to colour.

chrome /kroʊm/ n. chromium, especially as a source of various pigments.

-chrome a word element meaning 'colour', as in *monochrome*.

chroming /ˈkroʊmɪŋ/ n. the practice of inhaling the vapour from chrome-based spray paint, as a form of drug abuse.

chromium /ˈkroʊmiəm/ n. a lustrous, hard, brittle metallic element used for making pigments in photography, to harden gelatine, as a mordant, etc.; also used in corrosion-resisting chromium plating. *Symbol*: Cr

chromosome /ˈkroʊməsoʊm, -zoʊm/ n. any of several threadlike, rodlike, or beadlike bodies in the cell nucleus which carry the genes.

chron- a word element meaning 'time'.

chronic /ˈkrɒnɪk/ adj. 1. inveterate; constant. 2. continuing a long time.

chronic fatigue syndrome n. a severe, systemic illness acquired after an apparently mild viral infection, and characterised chiefly by incapacitating fatigue. Also, **myalgic encephalomyelitis (ME)**.

chronicle /ˈkrɒnɪkəl/ n. 1. a record or account of events in the order of time; a history. –v.t. (**-cled**, **-cling**) 2. to record in or as in a chronicle.

chrono- variant of **chron-**.

chronograph /ˈkrɒnəgræf, -grɑf/ n. a clock-driven instrument for recording the exact instant of occurrences, or for measuring small intervals of time.

chronological /krɒnəˈlɒdʒɪkəl/ adj. arranged in the order of time.

chronology /krəˈnɒlədʒi/ n. (pl. **-gies**) a particular statement of the supposed or accepted order of past events.

chronometer /krəˈnɒmətə/ n. a timekeeper with special mechanism for ensuring accuracy.

-chroous → **-chroic**.

chrysalis /ˈkrɪsələs/ n. (pl. **chrysalises** or **chrysalids** or **chrysalides** /krəˈsælədiz/) the hard-shelled pupa of a moth or butterfly.

chrysanthemum /krəˈsænθəməm, krəˈzænθ-/ n. a garden plant with flowers notable for the diversity of colour and size.

chubby /ˈtʃʌbi/ adj. (**-bier**, **-biest**) round and plump.

chuck /tʃʌk/ v.t. 1. to pat or tap lightly, as under the chin. 2. to throw with a quick motion, usually a short distance. 3. *Colloq.* to vomit. –n. *Colloq.* 4. an act of vomiting. 5. the vomit itself.

chuckle /ˈtʃʌkəl/ v.i. 1. to laugh in a soft, amused manner, usually with satisfaction. –n. 2. a soft, amused laugh.

chum /tʃʌm/ n. 1. an intimate friend or companion. –phr. (**chummed**, **chumming**) 2. **chum up with**, to become friendly with.

chump /tʃʌmp/ n. 1. *Colloq.* a fool. 2. the section of lamb, between the leg and the loin, which is cut into chops.

chunder /ˈtʃʌndə/ v.i., v.t. *Colloq.* to vomit.

chunk /tʃʌŋk/ n. a thick mass or lump of anything.

church /tʃɜtʃ/ n. 1. an edifice for public worship, especially Christian worship. 2. (*upper case*) the whole body of Christian believers. 3. (*upper case*) any division of this body professing the same creed and acknowledging the same ecclesiastical authority; a Christian denomination.

churl /tʃɜl/ n. a rude, boorish, or surly person. –**churlish**, adj.

churn /tʃɜn/ n. 1. a vessel or machine in which cream or milk is agitated to make butter. –v.t. 2. to shake or agitate with violence or continued motion.

chute /ʃut/ n. 1. a channel, trough, tube, shaft, etc., for conveying water, grain, coal, etc., to a lower level. 2. a waterfall; a steep descent, as in a river; a rapid. 3. an inclined board, with sides, down which a swimmer may slide into the water. 4. *Agric.* a narrow passage through which animals are moved for branding, drenching, or loading, often having a very steep incline.

chutney /ˈtʃʌtni/ n. a fruit or vegetable relish.

ciabatta /tʃəˈbatə/ n. a type of open-textured Italian bread with a thick crust.

cicada /səˈkadə, -ˈkeɪdə/ n. any of several large insects noted for the shrill sound produced by the male by means of vibrating membranes or drums on the underside of the abdomen.

cicatrice /ˈsɪkətrəs/ n. (pl. **cicatrices** /sɪkəˈtraɪsiz/ or **cicatrixes**) the new tissue which forms over a wound or the like, and later contracts into a scar. Also, **cicatrix** /ˈsɪkətrɪks/. –**cicatricial** /sɪkəˈtrɪʃəl/, adj. –**cicatricose** /ˈsɪkətrəkoʊs/, adj.

-cidal adjective form of **-cide**.

-cide a word element meaning 'killer' or 'act of killing'.

cider /ˈsaɪdə/ n. the expressed juice of apples.

cigar /səˈgɑ/ n. a small, shaped roll of tobacco leaves prepared for smoking.

cigarette /sɪgəˈrɛt/ n. a roll of finely cut tobacco for smoking, usually enclosed in thin paper.

cinch /sɪntʃ/ n. *Colloq.* something certain or easy.

cinders /ˈsɪndəz/ pl. n. any residue of combustion; ashes.

cine- a word element meaning 'motion', used of films, etc.

cinema /ˈsɪnəmə/ n. 1. a theatre where films are shown. 2. films in general. 3. the art of making films. –**cinematic**, adj. –**cinematically**, adv.

cinematography /sɪnəməˈtɒgrəfi/ n. the art or practice of film photography. –**cinematographer**, n. –**cinematographic**, adj.

cineraria /sɪnəˈrɛəriə/ n. a plant with heart-shaped leaves and clusters of flowers with white, blue, purple, red, or variegated rays.

cinnamon /ˈsɪnəmən/ n. a spice from the inner bark of certain trees.

-cion a suffix having the same function as **-tion**, as in *suspicion*.

cipher /ˈsaɪfə/ n. **1.** an arithmetical symbol (0) which denotes nought, or no quantity or magnitude. **2.** any of the Arabic numerals or figures. **3.** something of no value or importance. **4.** a secret method of writing, as by a specially formed code of symbols. **5.** the key to a secret method of writing. Also, **cypher**.

circa /ˈsɜkə, ˈsɜsə/ prep. about (used especially in approximate dates). *Abbrev.*: c., c, ca

circadian rhythm /sɜˈkeɪdiən/ n. the roughly 24-hour cycle in which physiological processes occur, some being affected by external factors such as sunlight and temperature.

circle /ˈsɜkəl/ n. **1.** a closed plane curve which is at all points equidistant from a fixed point within it, called the centre. **2.** any circular object, formation, or arrangement. **3.** an upper section of seats in a theatre. **4.** the area within which something acts, exerts influence, etc. **5.** a complete series forming a connected whole; cycle. **6.** a number of persons bound by a common tie; a coterie. *-v.t.* **7.** to enclose in a circle; surround. **8.** to move in a circle or circuit round. *-v.i.* **9.** to move in a circle.

circuit /ˈsɜkət/ n. **1.** the act of going or moving round. **2.** any circular or roundabout journey; a round. **3.** a number of venues or events at which an entertainer, etc., performs in turn. **4.** a course regularly travelled. **5.** *Elect.* the complete path of an electric current.

circuit board n. *Electronics* **1.** an insulated board on which circuits are mounted or printed, which can be inserted into a piece of electronic equipment such as a computer. **2.** → **power board**.

circuit breaker n. a device for interrupting an electric circuit. Also, **circuit-breaker**.

circuitous /səˈkjuətəs/ adj. roundabout; not direct.

circular /ˈsɜkjələ/ adj. **1.** having the form of a circle. *-n.* **2.** a letter, notice, advertisement, or statement for circulation among the general public or within an organisation. **-circularise**, **circularize**, v.

circular breathing n. a technique employed by players of some wind instruments, as the didgeridoo, to produce an almost continuous sound by breathing in through the nose while blowing out through the lips.

circulate /ˈsɜkjəleɪt/ v.i. **1.** to move in a circle or circuit. **2.** to move amongst the guests at a social function.

circulation /sɜkjəˈleɪʃən/ n. **1.** the act of circulating. **2.** *Physiol.* the recurrent movement of the blood through the various vessels of the body. **3.** the distribution of copies of a publication among readers. **4.** coin, notes, bills, etc., in use as currency; currency. **-circulatory**, adj.

circum- a prefix referring to movement round or about motion on all sides, as in *circumvent*, *circumnavigate*, *circumference*.

circumcise /ˈsɜkəmsaɪz/ v.t. to remove the foreskin of (males) sometimes as a religious rite. **-circumcision**, n.

circumference /səˈkʌmfərəns/ n. the outer boundary, especially of a circular area.

circumlocution /sɜkəmləˈkjuʃən/ n. a roundabout way of speaking.

circumnavigate /sɜkəmˈnævəgeɪt/ v.t. to sail round.

circumscribe /ˈsɜkəmskraɪb, sɜkəmˈskraɪb/ v.t. **1.** to draw a line round; encircle. **2.** to enclose within bounds; limit or confine, especially narrowly.

circumspect /ˈsɜkəmspɛkt/ adj. watchful on all sides; cautious; prudent.

circumstance /ˈsɜkəmstæns/ n. **1.** a condition, with respect to time, place, manner, agent, etc., which accompanies, determines, or modifies a fact or event. **2.** ceremonious accompaniment or display. **-circumstantial**, adj.

circumstantiate /sɜkəmˈstænʃieɪt/ v.t. to set forth or support with circumstances or particulars.

circumvent /sɜkəmˈvɛnt, ˈsɜkəmvɛnt/ v.t. **1.** to get around or avoid: *to circumvent a problem*. **2.** to gain advantage over by artfulness or deception; outwit; overreach.

circus /ˈsɜkəs/ n. a company of performers, animals, etc., especially a travelling company.

cirrhosis /sɪˈrəʊsəs, sə-/ n. a disease of the liver.

cirro- a combining form of **cirrus**.

cirrus /ˈsɪrəs/ n. *Meteorol.* a high, thin, thread-like cloud.

cisgender /ˈsɪsdʒɛndə/ adj. relating to or designating a person whose gender identity matches their gender as designated at birth.

cistern /ˈsɪstən/ n. a reservoir, tank, or vessel for holding water or other liquid.

citadel /ˈsɪtədɛl/ n. any strongly fortified place; a stronghold.

cite /saɪt/ v.t. **1.** to quote (a passage, book, author, etc.), especially as an authority. **2.** to mention in support, proof, or confirmation; refer to as an example. **-citation**, n.

citizen /ˈsɪtəzən/ n. **1.** a member, native or naturalised, of a state or nation (as distinguished from *alien*). **2.** an inhabitant of a city or town, especially one entitled to its privileges or franchises. **-citizenry**, n.

citronella /sɪtrəˈnɛlə/ n. a fragrant grass of southern Asia, the source of an oil used especially as an insect repellent.

citrus /ˈsɪtrəs/ n. any tree or shrub of the group which includes the lemon, lime, orange, grapefruit, etc.

city /ˈsɪti/ n. (pl. **-ties**) **1.** a large or important town. **2.** the central business area of a city.

city council n. the local administrative body which serves a capital city or large country town. Compare **municipal council**, **shire council**.

civet /ˈsɪvət/ n. **1.** a yellow, oily substance with a strong musk-like smell, obtained from civet cats and used in perfumery. **2.** Also, **civet cat**. a cat-like, carnivorous mammal of southern Asia and Africa that has glands in the genital area that secrete civet.

civic /ˈsɪvɪk/ adj. **1.** of or relating to a city; municipal. **2.** of or relating to citizenship; civil. **3.** of citizens.

civil /'sɪvəl/ *adj.* **1.** of or consisting of citizens. **2.** of or relating to the state or state authorities, as opposed to religious or other authorities. **3.** of the ordinary life and affairs of citizens (distinguished from *military, ecclesiastical,* etc.). **4.** polite; courteous.

civilian /sə'vɪljən/ *n.* someone engaged in civil pursuits, distinguished from a soldier, etc.

civilisation /sɪvəlaɪ'zeɪʃən/ *n.* **1.** an advanced state of human society, in which a high level of art, science, religion, and government has been reached. **2.** those people or nations that have reached such a state. **3.** the type of culture, society, etc., of a specific group. **4.** the act or process of civilising. Also, **civilization**.

civilise /'sɪvəlaɪz/ *v.t.* to make civilised. Also, **civilize**.

civilised /'sɪvəlaɪzd/ *adj.* **1.** having an advanced culture, society, etc. **2.** polite; well-bred; refined. Also, **civilized**.

civility /sə'vɪləti/ *n.* courtesy; politeness.

civil marriage *n.* a marriage performed by a government official rather than a member of the clergy.

civil war *n.* a war between parties, regions, etc., within their own country.

civvies /'sɪviz/ *pl. n. Colloq.* civilian clothes, as opposed to military dress.

clack /klæk/ *v.i.* to make a quick, sharp sound, or a succession of such sounds, as by striking or cracking.

clad /klæd/ *v.* a past tense and past participle of **clothe**.

clado- a word element meaning 'sprout', 'branch'. Also, *(before vowels)*, **clad-**.

claim /kleɪm/ *v.t.* **1.** to demand as a right or as due. **2.** to assert or maintain as a fact. *–n.* **3.** a demand for something as due. **4.** a just title to something. **5.** that which is claimed; a piece of public land to which formal claim is made for mining or other purposes. **6.** a payment demanded in accordance with an insurance policy, etc.

claimant /'kleɪmənt/ *n.* someone who makes a claim.

clairvoyant /kleə'vɔɪənt/ *adj.* **1.** having the power of seeing objects or actions beyond the natural range of the senses. *–n.* **2.** a clairvoyant person.

clam /klæm/ *n.* **1.** a type of mollusc. *–phr.* **(clammed, clamming) 2. clam up**, *Colloq.* to be silent.

clamber /'klæmbə/ *v.i.* to climb, using both feet and hands.

clammy /'klæmi/ *adj.* **(-mier, -miest)** covered with a cold, sticky moisture.

clamour /'klæmə/ *n.* **1.** a loud outcry. **2.** popular outcry. *–v.i.* **3.** to make a clamour; raise an outcry. Also, **clamor**.

clamp /klæmp/ *n.* **1.** a device, usually of some rigid material, for strengthening or supporting objects or fastening them together. *–v.t.* **2.** to fasten with or fix in a clamp. *–phr.* **3. clamp down**, to become more strict.

clan /klæn/ *n.* a group of people tracing their descent from a common ancestor. **–clannish**, *adj.*

clandestine /klæn'dɛstən/ *adj.* secret; private.

clang /klæŋ/ *v.i.* to give out a loud, resonant sound, as metal when struck.

clangour /'klæŋə, 'klæŋgə/ *n.* a loud, resonant sound, as of pieces of metal struck together or of a trumpet. Also, **clangor**.

clap¹ /klæp/ *v.* **(clapped, clapping)** *–v.t.* **1.** to strike with a quick, smart blow, producing an abrupt, sharp sound; slap; pat. **2.** to strike together resoundingly, as the hands to express applause. *–v.i.* **3.** to make an abrupt, sharp sound, as of bodies in collision. **4.** to move or strike with such a sound. **5.** to clap the hands, as in applause. *–n.* **6.** the act or sound of clapping. **7.** a resounding blow; a slap. **8.** a loud and abrupt or explosive noise, as of thunder.

clap² /klæp/ *n. Colloq.* (usu. preceded by *the*) gonorrhoea, or any other venereal disease.

claret /'klærət/ *n.* a red (originally light red or yellowish) table wine.

clarify /'klærəfaɪ/ *v.t.* **(-fied, -fying) 1.** to make clear, pure, or intelligible. **2.** to make (a liquid) clear by removing sediment, often by heating gently. **–clarification**, *n.* **–clarifier**, *n.*

clarinet /klærə'nɛt/ *n.* a wind instrument in the form of a cylindrical tube with a single reed attached to its mouthpiece.

clarion /'klæriən/ *adj.* **1.** clear and shrill. **2.** inspiring; rousing.

clarity /'klærəti/ *n.* clearness.

clash /klæʃ/ *v.i.* **1.** to make a loud, harsh noise. **2.** to collide, especially noisily. **3.** to conflict; disagree, as of temperaments, colours, etc. **4.** to coincide unfortunately (especially of events). *–n.* **5.** the noise of, or as of, a collision. **6.** a collision, especially a noisy one.

clasp /klæsp, klasp/ *n.* **1.** a device, usually of metal, for fastening things or parts together. **2.** a grasp; an embrace. *–v.t.* **3.** to take hold of.

class /klas/ *n.* **1.** a number of persons, things, animals, etc., regarded as forming one group through the possession of similar qualities; a kind; sort. **2.** any division of persons or things according to rank or grade. **3. a.** a group of pupils taught together. **b.** a period during which they are taught. **4.** a section of society sharing essential economic, political or cultural characteristics, and having the same social position: *middle class.* **5.** high quality in style, dress or manner. **6.** a grade of accommodation in aeroplanes, ships, etc. **7.** *Biol.* the usual major subdivision of a phylum or subphylum *–v.t.* **8.** to arrange, place, or rate as to class.

class action *n.* a legal proceeding brought on by a group of people all with the same grievance or claim.

classic /'klæsɪk/ *adj.* **1.** of the first or highest class or rank. **2.** serving as a standard, model, or guide. **3.** of literary or historical renown. *–n.* **4.** an author or a literary production of the first rank, especially in Greek or Latin. **5.** *(pl.)* the literature of ancient Greece and Rome; the Greek and Latin languages. **6.** something considered to be a perfect example of its type. **–classical**, *adj.*

classical /'klæsɪkəl/ *adj.* **1.** of or relating to the culture, language and literature of the ancient world. **2.** conforming to established taste or critical standards; adhering to traditional forms. **3.** (of music) deemed to be exalted in tone, often taking traditional forms, as a sonata, symphony, etc., and distinguished from more popular music, as jazz, pop, folk, rock, etc.

classified ad *n. Colloq.* a newspaper advertisement, usually single-column, placed in an appropriately headed set, as for job vacancies, objects for sale, etc.

classify /'klæsəfaɪ/ *v.t.* (**-fied**, **-fying**) **1.** to arrange or distribute in classes; place according to class. **2.** to mark or otherwise declare (a document, paper, etc.) of value to an enemy, and limit and safeguard its handling and use. **–classification**, *n.*

classmate /'klasmeɪt/ *n.* a member of the same class, as at school.

classroom /'klasrum/ *n.* a room in a school, etc., in which classes meet.

clatter /'klætə/ *v.i.* **1.** to make a rattling sound, as of hard bodies striking rapidly together. *–n.* **2.** a clattering noise; disturbance.

clause /klɔz/ *n.* **1.** *Gram.* a group of words containing a subject and a predicate. **2.** part of a written composition containing complete sense in itself, as a sentence or paragraph (in modern use commonly limited to such parts of legal documents, as of statutes, contracts, wills, etc.).

claustrophobia /klɒstrə'foubiə, klɔs-/ *n.* an extreme fear of confined places. **–claustrophobic**, *adj.*

claves /kleɪvz, 'klaveɪz/ *pl. n.* a musical instrument consisting of two resonant wooden sticks which are struck together.

clavicle /'klævɪkəl/ *n.* the collarbone.

claw /klɔ/ *n.* **1.** a sharp, usually curved, nail on the foot of an animal. **2.** any part or thing resembling a claw. *–v.t.* **3.** to tear, scratch, seize, pull, etc., with or as with claws.

clay /kleɪ/ *n.* **1.** a natural earthy material used for making bricks, pottery, etc. **2.** earth; mud.

claymation /kleɪ'meɪʃən/ *n. (from trademark)* an animation technique using clay figures as the basis for the film rather than drawn figures.

-cle variant of **-cule**.

clean /klin/ *adj.* **1.** free from dirt or filth; unsoiled; unstained. **2.** free from defect or blemish. **3.** free from disease, bacteria or infection. **4.** free from encumbrances or obstructions. **5.** free from any form of defilement. **6.** neatly or evenly made or proportioned; shapely; trim. **7.** *Colloq.* carrying no weapons, stolen goods, drugs, etc. *–adv.* **8.** in a clean manner. **9.** wholly; completely; quite. *–v.t.* **10.** to make clean. *–phr.* **11. come clean,** to make a full confession. **–cleanly**, *adv.* **–cleaner**, *n.*

clean coal *n.* coal which has been processed to make it environmentally less damaging. See **clean-coal technology**.

clean-coal technology *n.* any of various processes which aim to reduce the amount of carbon dioxide or pollutants produced in the burning of coal as a fuel, as coal washing, coal gasification, carbon sequestration, etc.

clean-cut *adj.* **1.** distinctly outlined. **2.** definite. **3.** well groomed and neatly dressed.

clean fuel *n.* a fuel which produces minimal greenhouse gas emissions.

cleanliness /'klɛnlinəs/ *n.* the condition or quality of being clean or being kept clean.

cleanse /klɛnz/ *v.t.* (**cleansed**, **cleansing**) to make clean.

cleanskin /'klinskɪn/ *n.* **1.** an unbranded animal. **2.** someone who is free from blame, or has no record of police conviction. **3.** a bottle of wine labelled as a generic wine type from a particular region but with no brand name.

clean sweep *n.* (in a series of competitions, lotteries, etc.) a complete set of wins.

clear /klɪə/ *adj.* **1.** free from darkness, obscurity, or cloudiness; light. **2.** bright; shining. **3.** transparent; pellucid. **4.** distinctly perceptible to the eye, ear, or mind. **5.** free from guilt or blame; innocent. **6.** free from obstructions or obstacles; open. **7.** (fol. by *of*) unentangled or disengaged; free; quit or rid. **8.** without limitation or qualification. **9.** without obligation or liability; free from debt. **10.** without deduction or diminution. *–v.t.* **11.** to make clear. **12.** to pass or get over without entanglement or collision. **13.** to pass (cheques, etc.) through a clearing house. **14.** to gain as clear profit. **15.** to approve or authorise, or to obtain approval or authorisation for, a thing or person. **16.** to remove trees, undergrowth, etc., from (an area of land). *–v.i.* **17.** to become clear.

clearance /'klɪərəns/ *n.* **1.** the act of clearing. **2.** a clear space; a clearing. **3.** distance or extent of an object to be passed over or under. **4.** official approval or consent.

clearing /'klɪərɪŋ/ *n.* a tract of cleared land, as in a forest.

clearing house *n.* a central office for receiving and distributing information.

clearway /'klɪəweɪ/ *n.* a stretch of road, especially in a built-up area, on which, between stated times, motorists may stop only in emergencies.

cleat /klit/ *n.* a small wedge-shaped block.

cleavage /'klividʒ/ *n.* **1.** the state of being cleft or split; division. **2.** *Colloq.* the cleft between a woman's breasts.

cleave[1] /kliv/ *v.i.* (**cleaved**, **cleaving**) (fol. by *to*) to stick or adhere; cling or hold fast.

cleave[2] /kliv/ *v.i.* (**cleft** *or* **cleaved** *or* **clove**, **cleft** *or* **cleaved** *or* **cloven**, **cleaving**) to part or split, especially along a natural line of division.

cleaver /'klivə/ *n.* a heavy knife or hatchet with a long blade used by butchers for cutting up carcasses.

clef /klɛf/ *n.* a symbol in music notation placed upon a stave to indicate the name and pitch of the notes corresponding to its lines and spaces.

cleft[1] /klɛft/ *n.* a space or opening made by cleavage; a split.

cleft[2] /klɛft/ *adj.* cloven; split; divided.

cleft palate *n.* a congenital defect of the palate in which a longitudinal fissure exists in the roof of the mouth.

clement /'klɛmənt/ *adj.* **1.** lenient; compassionate. **2.** (of the weather, etc.) mild or pleasant.

clench /klɛntʃ/ *v.t.* to close (the hands, teeth, etc.) tightly.

clergy /'klɜdʒi/ n. (pl. **-gies**) the body of ministers of religion in the Christian church, as distinct from the laity. **–clergyman**, n.

cleric /'klɛrɪk/ n. a member of the clergy.

clerical /'klɛrɪkəl/ adj. **1.** relating to a clerk or to clerks. **2.** of, relating to, or characteristic of the clergy.

clerk /klak/ n. **1.** one employed in an office, shop, etc., to keep records or accounts, attend to correspondence, etc. **2.** the administrative officer, and chief executive of a town or borough council.

clerk of the peace n. an officer of a court who acts both as a clerk and as the attorney of the Crown.

clerk of works n. the representative of the owner of the building during day to day supervision of construction works.

clever /'klɛvə/ adj. **1.** bright mentally; having quick intelligence; able. **2.** dexterous or nimble with the hands or body.

cliché /'klifeɪ/ n. (pl. **clichés** /-feɪz/) a trite, stereotyped expression, idea, practice, etc.

click /klɪk/ n. **1.** a slight, sharp sound. –v.i. **2.** to emit or make a click or clicks. **3.** Colloq. to fall into place or be understood. **4.** Colloq. to understand. **5.** Computers to operate the mouse button.

clickbait /'klɪkbeɪt/ n. an attention-grabbing link on a website which turns out to be of spurious value or interest.

click fraud n. the practice of artificially increasing the number of clicks on an advertisement on a website, as by paying people to click on it repeatedly, so as to satisfy the requirements of the advertiser. **–click fraudster**, n.

click-through n. a link from one website to another which can be activated by clicking an advertisement on the first site.

client /'klaɪənt/ n. **1.** someone who employs or seeks advice from a professional adviser. **2.** a customer. **3.** a computer which accesses the resources of another computer (the server) via a network.

clientele /kliən'tɛl/ n. the customers, clients, etc. (of a solicitor, businessperson, etc.) as a whole.

cliff /klɪf/ n. the high, steep face of a rocky mass; precipice.

climate /'klaɪmət/ n. the composite or generalisation of weather conditions of a region.

climate canary n. a significant change in the state of a geographical feature, a plant or animal species, or a human habitat, which provides an early warning of a climate change which will have more far-reaching effects.

climate change n. a significant change in the usual climatic conditions, especially that thought to be caused by global warming.

climax /'klaɪmæks/ n. **1.** the highest point of anything; the culmination. –v.i. **2.** to reach the climax. **–climactic**, adj.

climb /klaɪm/ v.i. **1.** to move up something, especially by using both hands and feet. **2.** to move upwards slowly by, or as by, continued effort. **3.** to slope upward. –v.t. **4.** to move up (something).

clinch /klɪntʃ/ v.t. **1.** to secure (a driven nail, etc.) by beating down the point. **2.** to settle (a matter) decisively. –n. **3.** Boxing, etc. the act or an instance of one or both contestants

holding the other in such a way as to hinder the other's punches. **4.** Colloq. an embrace or passionate kiss.

cling /klɪŋ/ v.i. (**clung**, **clinging**) to adhere closely; stick.

cling wrap n. thin, clear plastic wrapping, usually for packaging food. Also, **cling film**.

clinic /'klɪnɪk/ n. **1.** any medical centre used for such treatments as X-rays, child care, vaccinations, etc. **2.** an organised session of instruction in a particular activity or subject: a maths clinic; a basketball clinic.

clinical /'klɪnɪkəl/ adj. **1.** relating to a clinic. **2.** scientific; involving professional knowledge and not affected by the emotions.

clinical pathology n. → **pathology** (def. 2).

clinical psychology n. that branch of psychology which is put to clinical use in diagnosing and treating psychologically-based dysfunction and in the promotion of mental health and wellbeing.

clink /klɪŋk/ v.i. to make a light, sharp, ringing sound.

clip¹ /klɪp/ v. (**clipped**, **clipping**) –v.t. **1.** to cut, or cut off or out, as with shears; trim by cutting. **2.** to punch a hole in (a ticket). **3.** to omit sounds of (a word) in pronouncing. **4.** Colloq. to hit with a quick, sharp blow. **5.** Colloq. to defraud. –v.i. **6.** to clip or cut something; make the motion of clipping something. **7.** to move swiftly. –n. **8.** the act of clipping. **9.** anything clipped off. **10.** a short video recording or extract.

clip² /klɪp/ n. a device for gripping and holding tightly; a metal clasp, especially one for papers, letters, etc.

clip art n. Computers a collection of graphical images designed to be copied and inserted into other applications.

clipper /'klɪpə/ n. **1.** (oft. pl.) a cutting tool, especially shears. **2.** a sailing vessel built and rigged for speed.

clique /klik/ n. a small set or coterie, especially one that is snobbishly exclusive.

clitoris /'klɪtərəs/ n. the part of a female's genitals at the upper end of the vulva.

cloak /kloʊk/ n. a loose outer garment.

clobber¹ /'klɒbə/ v.t. Colloq. to batter severely; maul.

clobber² /'klɒbə/ n. Colloq. clothes or gear.

clock /klɒk/ n. **1.** an instrument for measuring and indicating time. **2.** Colloq. a piece of measuring equipment having a dial, as an odometer, taxi-meter, etc. –v.t. **3.** to time, test, or ascertain by the clock.

clockwise /'klɒkwaɪz/ adv., adj. in the direction of rotation of the hands of a clock.

clockwork /'klɒkwɜk/ n. **1.** the mechanism of a clock. –phr. **2. like clockwork**, with perfect regularity or precision.

clod /klɒd/ n. **1.** a lump or mass, especially of earth or clay. **2.** a stupid person; dolt.

clodhoppers /'klɒdhɒpəz/ pl. n. strong, heavy shoes.

clog /klɒg/ v.t. (**clogged**, **clogging**) **1.** to hinder or obstruct, especially by sticky matter; choke up. –n. **2.** a kind of shoe with a thick sole usually of wood.

cloister /ˈklɔɪstə/ n. **1.** a covered walk. **2.** any quiet, secluded place. −v.t. **3.** to confine in retirement; seclude.

clone /kloʊn/ v.t. **1.** to bring about the asexual reproduction of (an individual), the resulting individual being identical with the donor. −n. **2.** an asexually produced descendant.

clop /klɒp/ n. the sound made by a horse's hoofs.

close /kloʊz/ v., /kloʊs/ adj., /kloʊz/ for defs 21 and 22, /kloʊs/ for def. 23 n. −v. (**closed**, **closing**) −v.t. **1.** to stop or obstruct (a gap, entrance, aperture, etc.). **2.** to stop or obstruct the entrances, apertures, or gaps in. **3.** to refuse access to or passage across. **4.** to bring together the parts of; join; unite. **5.** to bring to an end; to shut down, either temporarily or permanently. −v.i. **6.** to become closed; shut. **7.** to come together; unite. **8.** to come close. **9.** to come to an end; terminate. **10.** Stock Exchange to be worth at the end of a trading period. −adj. (**closer**, **closest**) **11.** shut; shut tight; not open. **12.** shut in; enclosed. **13.** confined; narrow. **14.** lacking fresh or freely circulating air. **15.** practising secrecy; reticent. **16.** stingy. **17.** near, or near together, in space, time, or relation. **18.** intimate; confidential. **19.** not deviating from a model or original. **20.** nearly even or equal. −n. **21.** the act of closing. **22.** the end or conclusion. **23.** a narrow entry or alley, or a courtyard to which it leads; a cul-de-sac.

closed-circuit television n. a television system in which cameras and receivers are linked by wire, used to watch what is happening in another part of a building for security, monitoring production operations, etc. Abbrev.: CCTV

closed shop n. a workshop, factory, or the like, in which all employees must belong to a particular trade union.

closet /ˈklɒzət/ n. **1.** a small room, enclosed recess, or cabinet for clothing, food, utensils, etc. −adj. **2.** secret.

closure /ˈkloʊʒə/ n. **1.** the act of closing or shutting. **2.** a bringing to an end; conclusion. **3.** a sense of completion or finality experienced upon the resolution of a conflict, acceptance of a loss, etc.

clot /klɒt/ n. **1.** a mass or lump. **2.** a semisolid mass, as of coagulated blood. **3.** Colloq. a stupid person.

cloth /klɒθ/ n. (pl. **cloths** /klɒθs/) **1.** a fabric formed by weaving, etc., used for garments, upholstery, and many other purposes. **2.** a particular profession, especially that of the clergy.

clothe /kloʊð/ v.t. (**clothed** or **clad**, **clothing**) to dress; attire.

clothes /kloʊðz/ pl. n. garments for the body; articles of dress; wearing apparel.

cloud /klaʊd/ n. **1.** a visible collection of particles of water or ice suspended in the air. **2.** any similar mass, especially of smoke or dust. **3.** anything that obscures, darkens, or causes gloom, trouble, etc. **4. the cloud**, Computers the software resources and other services, particularly storage, made available through the internet or other network. See **cloud computing**. −v.t. **5.** to overspread or cover with, or as with, a cloud or clouds. −**cloudy**, adj.

cloud computing n. the provision of computer applications over the internet as a service to users of a particular site.

cloud server n. a server which handles the applications provided and managed by cloud computing.

clout /klaʊt/ n. **1.** a blow, especially with the hand; a cuff. **2.** effectiveness; force.

clove¹ /kloʊv/ n. the dried flower bud of a tropical tree used whole or ground as a spice.

clove² /kloʊv/ n. one of the small bulbs making up a larger bulb, as in garlic.

clove³ /kloʊv/ v. past tense of **cleave²**.

cloven /ˈkloʊvən/ adj. divided.

clover /ˈkloʊvə/ n. any of various herbs with leaves with three leaflets and dense flower heads.

clown /klaʊn/ n. **1.** a jester or buffoon in a circus, pantomime, etc. −v.i. **2.** to act like a clown.

cloy /klɔɪ/ v.t. to weary by an excess of food, sweetness, pleasure, etc.

cloying /ˈklɔɪɪŋ/ adj. **1.** sickeningly sweet. **2.** excessively emotional; sentimental. −**cloyingly**, adv. −**cloyingness**, n.

club /klʌb/ n. **1.** a heavy stick, usually thicker at one end than at the other, suitable for a weapon; a cudgel. **2.** a stick or bat used to drive a ball, etc., in various games. **3.** a group of persons organised for a social, literary, sporting, political, or other purpose, regulated by rules agreed by its members. **4.** the building or rooms owned by or associated with such a group. **5.** a black three-leafed figure on a playing card. −v.t. (**clubbed**, **clubbing**) **6.** to beat with, or as with, a club. **7.** to unite; combine; join together.

clubbing /ˈklʌbɪŋ/ phr. **go clubbing**, to visit nightclubs. −**clubber**, n.

club foot n. a deformed or distorted foot.

cluck /klʌk/ v.i. to utter the cry of a hen brooding or calling her chicks.

clucky /ˈklʌki/ adj. (of a hen) broody.

clue /klu/ n. anything that serves to guide or direct in the solution of a problem, mystery, etc.

cluey /ˈklui/ adj. Colloq. **1.** well-informed. **2.** showing good sense and keen awareness.

clump /klʌmp/ n. **1.** a cluster, especially of trees, or other plants. −v.i. **2.** to walk heavily and clumsily.

clumsy /ˈklʌmzi/ adj. (**-sier**, **-siest**) awkward in movement or action.

clung /klʌŋ/ v. past tense and past participle of **cling**.

cluster /ˈklʌstə/ n. a number of things of the same kind, growing or held together; a bunch.

clutch¹ /klʌtʃ/ v.t. **1.** to seize with, or as with, the hands or claws; snatch. **2.** to grip or hold tightly or firmly. −n. **3.** (usu. pl.) power of disposal or control; mastery: in the clutches of an enemy. **4.** a device for gripping something. **5.** (especially in a motor vehicle) the device which engages and disengages the engine from the transmission, or the pedal, etc., which operates the device. **6.** → **clutch bag**.

clutch² /klʌtʃ/ n. a hatch of eggs.

clutch bag *n.* a woman's handbag with no handles.

clutch-start *v.t.* **1.** to start (the engine of a motor vehicle) by having it in gear with the clutch disengaged while it is rolled forward, and then suddenly engaging the clutch. *–n.* **2.** the result of such a procedure.

clutter /ˈklʌtə/ *v.t.* **1.** to heap, litter, or strew in a disorderly manner. *–n.* **2.** a disorderly heap or assemblage; litter.

CMS /si ɛm ˈɛs/ *n. Internet* content management system; a software application which assists in the creation, control, and management of content on a website.

co- **1.** a prefix signifying association and accompanying action. **2.** a prefix signifying partnership, joint responsibility or ownership, as in *co-producer*, *co-writer*.

coach /koʊtʃ/ *n.* **1.** a large, enclosed, four-wheeled carriage. **2.** a bus, especially a single-decker, used for long distances or for sightseeing. **3.** a person who trains athletes for games, a contest, etc. **4.** a private tutor, especially one who prepares a student for an examination. *–v.t.* **5.** to give instruction or advice to in the capacity of a coach.

coagulate /koʊˈægjəleɪt/ *v.i.* to change from a fluid into a thickened mass; curdle; congeal.

coal /koʊl/ *n.* a black or brown coloured compact and earthy organic rock formed by the accumulation and decomposition of plant material and used as a fuel.

coalesce /koʊəˈlɛs/ *v.i.* (**-lesced**, **-lescing**) to unite so as to form one mass, community, etc.

coalface /ˈkoʊlfeɪs/ *n.* **1.** the part of the coal seam from which the coal is cut. *–phr.* **2. at the coalface**, at the place where the real work is done, as opposed to administration, theorising, etc.

coal gasification *n.* the process of gasifying coal before it is burned, making it possible to trap pollutants and emissions linked to global warming before burning.

coalition /koʊəˈlɪʃən/ *n.* a combination or alliance between persons, political parties, states, etc.

coal seam gas *n.* gas, mostly methane, coming from fractures in coal seams and released when pressure on the coal seam is reduced, usually by the removal of water; mined as a source of energy. *Abbrev.*: CSG Also, **coal bed methane.**

coal washing *n.* a process in which coal is washed to reduce a type of sulphur, reducing sulphur dioxide pollution as the coal is burned.

coarse /kɔs/ *adj.* **1.** of inferior or faulty quality. **2.** composed of relatively large parts or particles. **3.** lacking in fineness or delicacy of texture, structure, etc.

coast /koʊst/ *n.* **1.** the land next to the sea; the seashore. *–v.i.* **2.** to move along after effort has ceased; keep going on acquired momentum. **–coastal**, *adj.*

coastguard /ˈkoʊstgad/ *n.* a coastal police force responsible for preventing smuggling, watching for ships in distress or danger, etc.

coat /koʊt/ *n.* **1.** an outer garment with sleeves. **2.** a natural covering, as the hair of an animal, the bark of a tree, or the skin of a fruit.

3. anything that covers or conceals. *–v.t.* **4.** to cover with a layer or coating.

coathanger /ˈkoʊthæŋə/ *n.* a curved piece of wood, plastic, etc., with a hook attached, on which clothes are hung.

coating /ˈkoʊtɪŋ/ *n.* a thin covering of a substance spread over a surface.

coat of arms *n.* the heraldic bearings of a person, corporation, city, etc.

coax /koʊks/ *v.t.* **1.** to influence by gentle persuasion, flattery, etc. **2.** to get or win by coaxing. *–v.i.* **3.** to use gentle persuasion, etc.

cob /kɒb/ *n.* **1.** a corncob. **2.** a male swan. **3.** a short-legged, thickset horse.

cobalt /ˈkoʊbɒlt, -bɒlt/ *n.* **1.** *Chem.* a silver-white metallic element which, when occurring as the silicate, gives important blue colouring substances for ceramics; also used in alloys, particularly in cobalt steel. *Symbol*: Co **2.** a blue pigment containing cobalt.

cobber /ˈkɒbə/ *n. Colloq.* mate; friend.

cobbler /ˈkɒblə/ *n.* **1.** someone who mends shoes. **2.** a clumsy worker.

cobblestone /ˈkɒbəlstoʊn/ *n.* a rounded brick used in paving. **–cobblestoned**, *adj.*

COBOL /ˈkoʊbɒl/ *n.* a language for writing computer programs for general commercial use, as opposed to the more complex languages used in the sciences. Also, **Cobol.**

cobra /ˈkɒbrə, ˈkoʊbrə/ *n.* any of several extremely venomous snakes with the ability to dilate the neck to a hood-like form.

cobweb /ˈkɒbwɛb/ *n.* a web or net spun by a spider to catch its prey.

cocaine /koʊˈkeɪn/ *n.* a bitter substance obtained from the leaves of a South American plant, used illegally as a recreational drug and formerly in medicine as a local anaesthetic.

coccyx /ˈkɒksɪks, ˈkɒkɪks/ *n.* (*pl.* **coccyges** /kɒkˈsaɪdʒiz/) a small triangular bone forming the lower extremity of the human spinal column. **–coccygeal**, *adj.*

cochineal /kɒtʃəˈnil, ˈkɒtʃənil/ *n.* a red dye.

cochlea /ˈkɒkliə/ *n.* (*pl.* **-leae** /-lii/) *Anat.* a division, spiral in form, of the internal ear, in humans and most other mammals. **–cochlear**, *adj.*

cock¹ /kɒk/ *n.* **1.** the male of any bird, especially of the gallinaceous kind. **2.** a device for permitting or arresting the flow of a liquid or gas from a receptacle or through a pipe. **3.** *Colloq.* (*taboo*) the penis. *–v.t.* **4.** to pull back and set the hammer of (a firearm) preparatory to firing.

cock² /kɒk/ *v.t.* to set or turn up or to one side, often in an assertive, jaunty, or significant manner.

cockatiel /kɒkəˈtiəl/ *n.* a small, crested, long-tailed cockatoo, common in inland areas of Australia.

cockatoo /kɒkəˈtu/ *n.* any of several large crested parrots, having powerful hooked bills and loud screeching calls.

cockerel /ˈkɒkərəl, ˈkɒkrəl/ *n.* a young domestic cock.

cocker spaniel /ˈkɒkə/ *n.* one of a breed of small spaniels trained for use in hunting or kept as pets.

cockeyed /ˈkɒkaɪd/ *adj.* having a squinting eye; cross-eyed.

cockle /'kɒkəl/ n. a type of mollusc.

cockpit /'kɒkpɪt/ n. **1.** (in some aeroplanes) an enclosed space containing seats for the pilot and copilot. **2.** the driver's seat in a racing car.

cockroach /'kɒkroʊtʃ/ n. an insect, usually active at night, with a flattened body and long feelers, which is a common household pest.

cockscomb /'kɒkskoʊm/ n. the comb of a cock.

cocksure /'kɒkʃʊə/ adj. overconfident.

cocktail /'kɒkteɪl/ n. **1.** any of various short mixed drinks. **2.** a small piece of chicken, fish, etc., served as a savoury.

cocky[1] /'kɒki/ adj. (**-kier, -kiest**) Colloq. arrogantly smart; conceited.

cocky[2] /'kɒki/ n. (pl. **-kies**) Colloq. **1.** a cockatoo, or other parrot. **2.** a farmer, especially one who farms in a small way.

cocoa /'koʊkoʊ/ n. **1.** the roasted, husked, and ground seeds of the cacao. **2.** a beverage made from cocoa powder.

coconut /'koʊkənʌt/ n. the seed of the coconut palm, large, hard-shelled, lined with a white edible meat, and containing a milky liquid.

cocoon /kə'kun/ n. the silky envelope spun by the larvae of many insects, as silkworms, serving as a covering while they are in the chrysalis or pupal state.

cod /kɒd/ n. any of a number of often unrelated fishes both freshwater and marine.

coda /'koʊdə/ n. a more or less independent passage, at the end of a musical composition, introduced to bring it to a satisfactory close.

coddle /'kɒdl/ v.t. **1.** to cook (eggs, fruit, etc.) slowly in water just below boiling point. **2.** to treat tenderly or indulgently; pamper.

code /koʊd/ n. **1.** any system or collection of rules and regulations. **2.** a system of symbols for use in communication by telegraph, etc., as Morse code. **3.** a system of arbitrarily chosen symbols, words etc., used for secrecy. **4.** a system of symbols for conveying information or instructions to a computer. –v.t. **5.** to arrange in a code; enter in a code. –**coder**, n.

codeine /'koʊdin/ n. a drug obtained from opium, used in medicine as an analgesic.

codger /'kɒdʒə/ n. Colloq. a man, especially elderly and slightly odd.

codicil /'kɒdəsɪl/ n. **1.** a supplement to a will, containing an addition, explanation, modification, etc. **2.** a similar supplement.

codify /'koʊdəfaɪ, 'kɒdə-/ v.t. (**-fied, -fying**) **1.** to reduce (laws, etc.) to a code. **2.** to digest; arrange in a systematic collection.

cod-liver oil n. a fixed oil, extracted from the liver of the common cod or of allied species, extensively used in medicine as a source of vitamins A and D.

co-education /ˌkoʊ-ɛdʒə'keɪʃən/ n. joint education, especially of both sexes in the same institution and classes.

coefficient /koʊə'fɪʃənt/ n. Maths a number or quantity placed (generally) before and multiplying another quantity.

-coele a word element referring to some small cavity of the body. Also, **-cele, -coel.**

coelenterate /sə'lɛntərət, -tərət/ n. one of the phylum of invertebrate animals that includes the jellyfishes, corals, etc.

coeliac /'siliæk/ adj. **1.** of or relating to the cavity of the abdomen. **2.** of or relating to coeliac disease. –n. **3.** a person suffering from coeliac disease. Also, **celiac.**

coeliac disease n. a congenital disorder characterised by diarrhoea due to intolerance of the bowels to gluten. Also, **celiac disease.**

coemption /koʊ'ɛmpʃən, -'ɛmʃən/ n. the buying up of the whole of a particular commodity, especially in order to acquire a monopoly.

coeno- a word element meaning 'common'. Also, **ceno-**; (before a vowel), **coen-.**

coerce /koʊ'ɜs/ v.t. (**-erced, -ercing**) to compel by forcible action. –**coercion,** n. –**coercive,** adj.

coffee /'kɒfi/ n. a beverage made from the roasted and ground **coffee beans** of various tropical trees and shrubs.

coffer /'kɒfə/ n. **1.** a box or chest, especially one for valuables. **2.** (pl.) a treasury; funds.

coffin /'kɒfən/ n. the box or case in which a corpse is placed for burial.

cog /kɒg/ n. a tooth or projection (usually one of a series) on a wheel, etc., for transmitting motion to, or receiving motion from, a corresponding tooth or part with which it engages.

cogent /'koʊdʒənt/ adj. compelling assent or belief; convincing. –**cogency,** n.

cogitate /'kɒdʒəteɪt/ v.i. to think hard; ponder; meditate.

cognac /'kɒnjæk/ n. French brandy.

cognate /'kɒgneɪt/ adj. related by birth or origin.

cognisance /'kɒgnəzəns, 'kɒnə-/ n. **1.** knowledge; notice; perception. **2.** the right of taking judicial notice, as possessed by a court. Also, **cognizance.** –**cognisant,** adj.

cognition /kɒg'nɪʃən/ n. the act or process of knowing; perception. –**cognitive,** adj.

cohabit /koʊ'hæbət/ v.i. to live together in a sexual relationship.

cohere /koʊ'hɪə/ v.i. (**-hered, -hering**) **1.** to hold fast, as parts of the same mass. **2.** to agree; be congruous.

coherent /koʊ'hɪərənt/ adj. **1.** able to express oneself in a clear and logical way. **2.** clear and logical. –**coherence,** n. –**coherently,** adv.

cohesion /koʊ'hiʒən/ n. the act or state of cohering, uniting, or sticking together. –**cohesive,** adj.

cohort /'koʊhɔt/ n. **1.** any group or company. **2.** a crony; ally; supporter: the mayor and his cohorts. **3.** a group of people at the same level, as in education, skill development, etc.

coiffure /kwʌ'fjʊə/ n. a style of arranging or combing the hair.

coil /kɔɪl/ v.t. **1.** to wind into rings one above another; twist or wind spirally. –n. **2.** a connected series of spirals or rings. **3.** a single such ring.

coin /kɔɪn/ n. **1.** a piece of metal stamped and issued by the authority of the government for use as money. **2.** such pieces collectively. –v.t. **3.** to make; invent; fabricate.

coincide /koʊən'saɪd/ v.i. to occupy the same place in space, the same point or period in time, or the same relative position.

coincidence /koʊ'ɪnsədəns/ n. **1.** the condition or fact of coinciding. **2.** a striking occurrence of two or more events at one time apparently by mere chance. **3.** exact agreement in nature, character, etc. –**coincidental**, *adj.*

coir /'kɔɪə/ *n.* the prepared fibre of the coconut, used in making rope, matting, etc.

coitus /'kouətəs, 'kɔɪtəs/ *n.* sexual intercourse. Also, **coition** /kou'ɪʃən/. –**coital**, *adj.*

coke[1] /kouk/ *n.* the solid product resulting from imperfect combustion, used as a fuel, in metallurgy, etc.

coke[2] /kouk/ *n. Colloq.* cocaine.

col-[1] variant of **com-**, by assimilation before *l*, as in *collateral*.

col-[2] variant of **colo-** before vowels.

cola /'koulə/ *n.* **1.** the cola nut. **2.** an extract prepared from it. **3.** a carbonated soft drink containing such an extract. **4.** the tree producing it. Also, **kola**.

colander /'kʌləndə, 'kɒl-/ *n.* a strainer for draining off liquids, especially in cookery. Also, **cullender**.

cold /kould/ *adj.* **1.** having a relatively low temperature; having little or no warmth. **2.** producing or feeling, especially in a high degree, a lack of warmth. **3.** *Colloq.* unconscious because of a severe blow, shock, etc. **4.** not affectionate, cordial, or friendly; unresponsive. –*n.* **5.** the relative absence of heat. **6.** the sensation produced by loss of heat from the body. **7.** Also, **the common cold**. an indisposition caused by a virus, characterised by catarrh, hoarseness, coughing, etc.

cold-blooded /'kould-blʌdəd/ *adj.* **1.** without feeling; unsympathetic; cruel. **2.** designating or relating to animals, as fishes and reptiles, whose body temperature approximates to that of the surrounding medium.

cold-call *v.t.* to attempt to sell a product or service by making an unsolicited call to (a prospective customer), usually by telephone. –**cold-calling**, *n.*

cold case *n.* a criminal investigation which has proved impossible to bring to a conclusion, usually for lack of evidence.

cold front *n.* the contact surface between two air-masses where the cooler mass is advancing against and under the warmer mass.

cold-pressed /'kould-prɛst/ *adj.* of or relating to an unrefined high-grade oil produced from the first pressing of fruit, seeds, etc., such as olives, almonds, canola, etc., which are then heated to produce the next output.

cold-shoulder *v.t.* to ignore; show indifference to.

cold sore *n.* a vesicular eruption on the face often accompanying a cold or a febrile condition; herpes simplex.

cold turkey *Colloq.* –*n.* **1.** the sudden and complete withdrawal of narcotics as a treatment of drug addiction. –*adv.* **2.** without the aid of other drugs. **3.** without warning, rehearsal, preliminaries, or cushioning of any kind.

cold war *n.* intense economic and political rivalry just short of military conflict.

coleslaw /'koulslɔ/ *n.* a dressed salad of finely sliced white cabbage. Also, **slaw**.

colic /'kɒlɪk/ *n.* paroxysmal pain in the abdomen or bowels. –**colicky**, *adj.*

collaborate /kə'læbəreɪt/ *v.i.* **1.** to work, one with another. **2.** to cooperate treacherously. –**collaboration**, *n.* –**collaborator**, *n.* –**collaborative**, *adj.*

collage /kə'lɑʒ, kɒ'lɑʒ, 'kɒlɑʒ/ *n.* a pictorial composition made from any or a combination of various materials.

collagen /'kɒlədʒən/ *n.* a protein contained in connective tissue and bones which gives gelatine when boiled.

collapse /kə'læps/ *v.i.* **1.** to fall or cave in; crumble suddenly. **2.** to break down; come to nothing; fail. –*n.* **3.** a sudden, complete failure; a breakdown.

collapsible /kə'læpsəbəl/ *adj.* designed to fold into a more compact or manageable size, as a pram, bicycle, etc.

collar /'kɒlə/ *n.* **1.** anything worn or placed round the neck. **2.** the part of a shirt, blouse, coat, etc., round the neck, usually folded over. **3.** *Machinery* an enlargement encircling a rod or shaft, and serving usually as a holding or bearing piece. –*v.t.* **4.** to put a collar on; furnish with a collar. **5.** to seize by the collar or neck.

collarbone /'kɒləboun/ *n.* either of two slender bones each connecting the breastbone with the shoulderblade, and forming the front part of the shoulder.

collate /kə'leɪt, kɒ-/ *v.t.* to put together (a document) by sorting its pages into the correct order. –**collator**, *n.* –**collation**, *n.*

collateral /kə'lætərəl/ *adj.* **1.** situated at the side. **2.** accompanying; attendant; auxiliary. –*n.* **3.** security pledged for the payment of a loan.

collateral damage *n.* unintended destruction or injury, especially unintended civilian casualties in a military operation.

colleague /'kɒlig/ *n.* an associate in office, professional work, etc.

collect /kə'lɛkt/ *v.t.* **1.** to gather together; assemble. **2.** to accumulate; make a collection of. **3.** to regain control of (one's thoughts, faculties, etc., or oneself). **4.** to fetch; call for and remove. **5.** to run into or collide with, especially in a motor vehicle. –*v.i.* **6.** to gather together; assemble. **7.** to accumulate. –*adj.*, *adv.* **8.** to be paid for by the receiver. –**collection**, *n.* –**collector**, *n.*

collectable /kə'lɛktəbəl/ *n.* **1.** an object of great antiquarian value, such as a rare coin, often collected as an investment. **2.** an object of no intrinsic value, such as a matchbox or beer can, collected as a hobby or as a memento. Also, **collectible**.

collective /kə'lɛktɪv/ *adj.* **1.** forming a collection or aggregate; aggregate; combined. **2.** relating to a group of individuals taken together. –*n.* **3.** a collective body; aggregate. **4.** a communal enterprise or system. –**collectively**, *adv.*

collective bargaining *n.* a non-institutionalised system of negotiation between employers and employees on matters such as pay and working conditions.

collective noun *n.* a noun that under the singular form expresses a grouping of individual objects or persons, as *herd*, *jury*, and *clergy*.

college /ˈkɒlɪdʒ/ *n.* **1.** a (usually) post-secondary, diploma-awarding, technical or professional school, as a teachers' college or technical college. **2.** an institution for special or professional instruction, as in medicine, pharmacy, agriculture, music, etc., often part of a university. **3.** an endowed, self-governing association of scholars incorporated within a university, as the church colleges within the University of Sydney. **4.** any of certain large private schools, or sometimes public schools. **5.** an organised association of persons having certain powers and rights, and performing certain duties or engaged in a particular pursuit. **–collegian**, *n.* **–collegiate**, *adj.*

collegial /kəˈlidʒiəl, kəˈlidʒəl/ *adj.* **1.** belonging or relating to a college. **2.** involving shared responsibility, as among a group of people working together.

collide /kəˈlaɪd/ *v.i.* to come together with force; come into violent contact; crash. **–collision**, *n.*

collie /ˈkɒli/ *n.* a dog of any of certain intelligent varieties much used for tending sheep.

colliery /ˈkɒljəri/ *n.* (*pl.* **-ries**) a coal mine, including all buildings and equipment.

collocate /ˈkɒləkeɪt/ *v.t.* to set or place together. **–collocation**, *n.*

colloquial /kəˈloʊkwiəl/ *adj.* appropriate to or characteristic of conversational or informal speech or writing.

colloquium /kəˈloʊkwiəm/ *n.* (*pl.* **-quia** *or* **-quiums**) an informal conference or group discussion.

collude /kəˈlud/ *v.i.* **1.** to act together through a secret understanding. **2.** to conspire in a fraud. **–colluder**, *n.*

collusion /kəˈluʒən/ *n.* secret agreement for a fraudulent purpose; conspiracy.

colo- a combining form of **colon²**.

cologne /kəˈloʊn/ *n.* a perfumed toilet water.

colon¹ /ˈkoʊlən/ *n.* a point of punctuation (:) marking off a main portion of a sentence (intermediate in force between the semicolon and the full stop).

colon² /ˈkoʊlən/ *n.* the portion of the bowel which comprises most of the large intestine.

colonel /ˈkɜnəl/ *n.* a senior officer in the army.

colonnade /ˌkɒləˈneɪd, kɒləˈneɪd/ *n.* **1.** a series of columns set at regular intervals. **2.** a long row of trees.

colony /ˈkɒləni/ *n.* (*pl.* **-nies**) **1.** a group of people who leave their native country to form in a new land a settlement subject to, or connected with, the parent state. **2.** the country or district settled or colonised. **3.** any people or territory separated from but subject to a ruling power. **4.** a group of animals or plants of the same kind, living together. **–colonial**, *adj.* **–colonise, colonize**, *v.* **–colonist**, *n.*

colophon /ˈkɒləfɒn, -fən/ *n.* a publisher's distinctive emblem.

color /ˈkʌlə/ *n., v.t., v.i.* → **colour**. **–colored**, *adj.* **–colorer**, *n.* **–colorist**, *n.* **–colorless**, *adj.*

colossal /kəˈlɒsəl/ *adj.* gigantic; vast.

colostomy /kəˈlɒstəmi/ *n.* (*pl.* **-tomies**) the surgical formation of an artificial anus.

colour /ˈkʌlə/ *n.* **1.** that quality of light (reflected or transmitted by a substance) which is basically determined by its spectral composition. **2.** skin pigmentation as an indication of ethnicity or race. **3.** vivid or distinctive quality, as of literary work. **4.** that which is used for colouring; pigment; paint; dye. **5.** (*pl.*) a flag, ensign, etc., as of a military body or ship. **6.** outward appearance or aspect; guise or show. **7.** an apparent or prima-facie right or ground (especially in legal sense). *–v.t.* **8.** to give or apply colour to; tinge; paint; dye. **9.** to cause to appear different from the reality. *–v.i.* **10.** to take on or change colour. **11.** to blush. Also, **color**.

colourblind /ˈkʌləblaɪnd/ *adj.* having a congenital inability to detect or distinguish between certain colours (usually red and green). Also, **colorblind**. **–colour blindness**, *n.*

colourfast /ˈkʌləfast/ *adj.* (of fabric dyes) lasting. Also, **colorfast**.

colourful /ˈkʌləfəl/ *adj.* **1.** brightly coloured or having many colours. **2.** interesting and exciting: *a colourful story.* Also, **colorful**. **–colourfully**, *adv.*

-colous a word element indicating habitat.

colt /koʊlt/ *n.* a male horse not past its fourth birthday.

column /ˈkɒləm/ *n.* **1.** *Archit.* an upright shaft or body of greater length than thickness, usually serving as a support; a pillar. **2.** any column-like object, mass, or formation. **3.** one of the two or more vertical rows of lines of type or printed matter of a page. **4.** a regular contribution to a newspaper, usually signed, and consisting of comment, news, etc.

com- a prefix meaning 'with', 'jointly', 'in combination' and (with intensive force) 'completely'.

coma /ˈkoʊmə/ *n.* (*pl.* **comas**) a state of prolonged unconsciousness. **–comatose**, *adj.*

comb /koʊm/ *n.* **1.** a toothed piece of bone, metal, etc., for arranging or cleaning the hair, or for keeping it in place. **2.** any comb-like instrument, object, or formation. **3.** the fleshy, more or less serrated excrescence or growth on the head of the domestic fowl. *–v.t.* **4.** to dress (the hair, etc.) with, or as with, a comb. **5.** to search everywhere and with great thoroughness.

combat *v.t.* /ˈkɒmbæt, kəmˈbæt/ **1.** to fight or contend against; oppose vigorously. *–n.* /ˈkɒmbæt/ **2.** a fight between two people, armies, etc. **–combatant**, *n.*

combine *v.t.* /kəmˈbaɪn/ **1.** to bring or join into a close union or whole; unite; associate; coalesce. *–n.* /ˈkɒmbaɪn/ **2.** a combination of persons or groups for the furtherance of their political, commercial, or other interests. **–combination**, *n.*

combustible /kəmˈbʌstəbəl/ *adj.* capable of catching fire and burning.

combustion /kəmˈbʌstʃən/ *n.* the act or process of burning.

come /kʌm/ *v.i.* (**came, come, coming**) **1.** to move towards the speaker or towards a particular place; approach. **2.** to arrive by movement or in course of progress. **3.** to extend; reach. **4.** to issue; emanate; be derived. **5.** (fol. by *from*) to be born in or live in. **6.** to arrive or appear as a result. **7.** to turn out to be. **8.** *Colloq.* to have an orgasm. *–phr.* **9. come about**, to arrive in due course; come to pass.

10. come across, to meet with, especially by chance. **11. come (a)round, a.** to relent. **b.** to recover consciousness; revive. **c.** to change direction, point of view, etc. **12. come down with,** to become afflicted with, especially with a disease. **13. come good,** *Colloq.* to improve after an unpromising beginning. **14. come in, a.** to enter. **b.** to become useful, fashionable, etc. **15. come into, a.** to get. **b.** to inherit. **16. come out, a.** to appear; be published. **b.** to be revealed; show itself. **c.** to declare one's homosexuality. **17. come the raw prawn,** *Colloq.* (fol. by *with*) to try to deceive. **18. come to, a.** to recover consciousness. **b.** to amount to; equal.

comedian /kə'midiən/ *n.* an actor or writer of comedy. **–comedienne,** *fem. n.*

comedown /'kʌmdaʊn/ *n.* **1.** an unexpected or humiliating descent from dignity, importance, or prosperity. **2.** a let-down; disappointment. **3.** a flash flooding of a dry creek.

comedy /'kɒmədi/ *n.* (*pl.* **-dies**) **1.** a play, film, etc., of light and humorous character. **2.** the comic element of drama, of literature generally, or of life.

comely /'kʌmli/ *adj.* (**-lier, -liest**) pleasing in appearance; fair.

come-on *n. Colloq.* **1.** an instance of behaviour which indicates a desire to engage in sexual activity with someone. **2.** an inducement; lure.

comet /'kɒmət/ *n.* a celestial body moving about the sun in an elongated orbit.

comeuppance /kʌm'ʌpəns/ *n. Colloq.* a well-deserved punishment or retribution. Also, **comeupance.**

comfort /'kʌmfət/ *v.t.* **1.** to soothe when in grief; console; cheer. *–n.* **2.** relief in affliction; consolation; solace. **3.** a person or thing that affords consolation. **4.** a state of ease, with freedom from pain and anxiety, and satisfaction of bodily wants.

comfortable /'kʌmftəbəl, 'kʌmfətəbəl/ *adj.* **1.** producing or attended with comfort or ease of mind or body. **2.** being in a state of comfort or ease; easy and undisturbed. **3.** having adequate income or wealth. **4.** easily achieved, as a victory.

comfort zone *n.* the set of conditions within which someone feels comfortable in their ability to handle a situation, giving them a sense of being in control.

comic /'kɒmɪk/ *adj.* **1.** of, relating to, or of the nature of comedy, as distinct from tragedy. **2.** provoking laughter; humorous. *–n.* **3.** a comic actor. **4.** a magazine containing one or more stories in comic strip form. **5.** (*pl.*) comic strips.

comical /'kɒmɪkəl/ *adj.* provoking laughter, or amusing; funny.

comic strip *n.* a series of cartoon drawings, relating a comic incident, an adventure story, etc.

comma /'kɒmə/ *n.* a mark of punctuation (,) used to indicate the smallest interruptions in continuity of thought or grammatical construction.

command /kə'mænd, -'mand/ *v.t.* **1.** to order or direct with authority. **2.** to require with authority; demand. **3.** to have or exercise authority over. *–n.* **4.** the act of commanding or ordering. **5.** control; mastery; disposal. **6.** *Computers* an expression in part of a program that defines an operation, or results in the performance of an operation. **–commanding,** *adj.*

commandant /'kɒmənˌdænt, -dant/ *n.* the commanding officer of a place, group, etc.; commander.

commandeer /kɒmən'dɪə/ *v.t.* to seize (private property) for military or other public use.

commander /kə'mændə, -'mand-/ *n.* someone who exercises authority; a leader; a chief officer.

commandment /kə'mændmənt, kə'mand-/ *n.* a command or edict.

commando /kə'mændoʊ, -'man-/ *n.* (*pl.* **-dos** or **-does**) **1.** a member of a small specially trained fighting force used for making quick, destructive raids against enemy-held areas. **2.** such a force.

commemorate /kə'mɛmərent/ *v.t.* **1.** to serve as a memento of. **2.** to honour the memory of by some solemnity or celebration.

commence /kə'mɛns/ *v.i.* (**-menced, -mencing**) to begin; start.

commend /kə'mɛnd/ *v.t.* **1.** to present or mention as worthy of confidence, notice, kindness, etc.; recommend. **2.** to entrust; give in charge; deliver with confidence. **–commendation,** *n.*

commensurate /kə'mɛnʃərət/ *adj.* **1.** of equal extent or duration. **2.** proportionate.

comment /'kɒmɛnt/ *n.* **1.** a short note or statement. *–v.i.* **2.** to make such a note or statement.

commentary /'kɒmɛntəri, -tri/ *n.* (*pl.* **-ries**) **1.** a series of comments or annotations. **2.** a description of a public event, as a state occasion, sporting match, etc., broadcast or televised as it happens.

commentate /'kɒmɛnteɪt/ *v.i.* to act as a commentator.

commentator /'kɒmənteɪtə/ *n.* a writer or broadcaster who makes critical or explanatory remarks about news, events, or describes sporting events, etc.

commerce /'kɒmɜs/ *n.* **1.** interchange of goods or commodities, especially on a large scale between different countries (**foreign commerce**) or between different parts of the same country (**domestic commerce** or **internal commerce**); trade; business. **2.** social relations.

commercial /kə'mɜʃəl/ *adj.* **1.** of, or of the nature of, commerce. **2.** engaged in commerce. **3.** capable of being sold in great numbers. **4.** setting possible commercial return above artistic considerations. **5.** not entirely or chemically pure. **6.** *Radio, TV* financially dependent on revenue from advertising. **7.** *Music* created specifically to appeal to the widest market. *–n.* **8.** *Radio, TV* an advertisement.

commercial artist *n.* an artist who makes a living from creating artwork for commercial use, as for advertising, publishing, etc.

commercial law *n.* the principles and rules drawn chiefly from custom, determining the rights and obligations of commercial transactions.

commiserate /kəˈmɪzəreɪt/ v.i. (fol. by *with*) to sympathise.

commission /kəˈmɪʃən/ n. **1.** the act of committing or giving in charge. **2.** an authoritative order, charge, or direction. **3.** a body of persons authoritatively charged with particular functions. **4.** the condition of anything in active service or use. **5.** a task or matter committed to one's charge. **6.** authority to act as agent for another or others in commercial transactions. **7.** a sum or percentage allowed to an agent, salesperson, etc., for services. **8.** the position or rank of an officer in the army or navy. –v.t. **9.** to give a commission to. **10.** to authorise; send on a mission.

commissioner /kəˈmɪʃənə/ n. **1.** a person commissioned to act officially; a member of a commission. **2.** a government official in charge of a department.

commit /kəˈmɪt/ v.t. (**-mitted, -mitting**) **1.** to give in trust or charge; entrust; consign. **2.** to consign to custody in an institution, as a jail, mental hospital, etc. **3.** to hand over for treatment, disposal, etc. **4.** to do; perform; perpetrate. **5.** to bind by pledge or assurance; pledge. –**commitment**, n.

committee /kəˈmɪti/ n. a person or a group of persons elected or appointed from a larger body to investigate, report, or act in special cases.

commode /kəˈmoʊd/ n. **1.** a piece of furniture containing drawers or shelves. **2.** a stand or cupboard containing a chamber-pot or washbasin.

commodious /kəˈmoʊdiəs/ adj. convenient and roomy; spacious.

commodities market n. a market in which commodities are bought and sold, either immediately (the **spot market**) or more commonly for delivery at a future date (the **futures market**).

commodity /kəˈmɒdəti/ n. (pl. **-ties**) an article of trade or commerce.

commodore /ˈkɒmədɔ/ n. the senior captain of a line of merchant vessels.

common /ˈkɒmən/ adj. **1.** belonging equally to, or shared alike by, two or more or all in question. **2.** of frequent occurrence; familiar; usual. **3.** of mediocre or inferior quality; mean; low. –n. Also, **town common**. **4.** (*also pl.*) an area of public land.

common denominator n. Maths an integer, usually the least, divisible by all the denominators of a set of fractions.

commoner /ˈkɒmənə/ n. one of the common people.

common gateway interface n. Computers a standard piece of communications software linking a web server to a program on a host machine. Also, **CGI**.

common law n. **1.** the system of law originating in England, as distinct from the civil or Roman law and the canon or ecclesiastical law. **2.** the unwritten law, especially of England, Australia, and other countries with a similar legal system, based on custom or court decision, as distinct from statute law. **3.** the law administered through the system of writs, as distinct from equity, etc.

common-law adj. **1.** based on or relating to the common law. **2. a.** relating to a marriage that is deemed in law to exist because the partners have cohabited for a certain period of time, though not having taken part in a formal marriage. **b.** relating to one of the partners in such a marriage: *a common-law wife*.

common market n. a group of countries which agree to trade with one another without tariffs, and to impose common tariffs on countries outside the group.

common noun n. Gram. a noun that can be preceded by an article or other limiting modifier, in meaning applicable to any one or all the members of a class, as *man, men, city, cities*, in contrast to *Shakespeare, Hobart*. Compare **proper noun**.

commonplace /ˈkɒmənpleɪs/ adj. ordinary; without individuality.

common room n. (in schools, universities, etc.) a sitting room for the use of the teaching staff, or, in some cases, of the students.

commons /ˈkɒmənz/ pl. n. **1.** the body of people not of noble birth. **2.** Internet a website where material is freely available: *information commons; software commons*.

common sense n. sound, practical perception or understanding. Also, **commonsense**.

commonwealth /ˈkɒmənwɛlθ/ n. **1.** the whole body of people of a nation or state; the body politic. **2.** (*upper case*) a federation of states and territories with powers and responsibilities divided between a central government and a number of smaller governments, each controlling certain responsibilities in a defined area, as *the Commonwealth of Australia*.

commotion /kəˈmoʊʃən/ n. violent or tumultuous motion; agitation.

communal /kəˈmjunəl, ˈkɒmjənəl/ adj. relating to a commune or a community.

commune¹ /kəˈmjun/ v.i. to converse; talk together; interchange thoughts or feelings.

commune² /ˈkɒmjun/ n. any community of like-minded people choosing to live independently of the state.

communicate /kəˈmjunəkeɪt/ v.t. **1.** to give to another as a partaker; impart; transmit. **2.** to impart knowledge of; make known. –v.i. **3.** to have interchange of thoughts.

communication /kəmjunəˈkeɪʃən/ n. **1.** the act or fact of communicating; transmission. **2.** a document or message imparting views, information, etc. **3.** (*pl.*) the means of transmitting information by telephone, radio, television, etc.

communicative /kəˈmjunəkətɪv/ adj. inclined to communicate or impart.

communion /kəˈmjunjən/ n. **1.** the act of sharing, or holding in common; participation. **2.** interchange of thoughts or interests; communication; intimate talk. **3.** (*sometimes upper case*) Eccles. the celebration of the Lord's Supper; the Eucharist.

communiqué /kəˈmjunəkeɪ/ n. an official bulletin or communication as of war news, events at a conference, etc., usually to the press or public.

communism /ˈkɒmjənɪzəm/ n. a theory or system of social organisation based on the holding of all property in common. –**communist**, n. –**communistic**, adj.

community /kə'mjunəti/ n. (pl. **-ties**) **1.** all the people of a specific locality or country: *for the benefit of the whole community.* **2.** a particular locality, considered together with its inhabitants: *a rural community.*

community bank n. (*from trademark*) a bank which is owned and managed locally and which serves the needs of the local community.

community correction order n. an order issued by a judge and encompassing a range of provisions such as home detention, drug treatment, community service, etc., carried out by the person sentenced who is released into the community rather than sent to jail.

community title n. *Law* a form of title which allows for common areas in the subdivision of land, as for community groups, retirement villages, etc.

commute /kə'mjut/ v.t. **1.** to change (a penalty, etc.) for one less burdensome or severe. –v.i. **2.** to serve as a substitute. **3.** to make a collective payment, especially of a reduced amount, as an equivalent for a number of payments. **4.** to travel some distance regularly between home and work, as from an outer suburb to the city. –n. **5.** a trip undertaken as a commuter: *a long commute to work.*

commuter /kə'mjutə/ n. **1.** someone who regularly travels some distance between home and work, as from an outer suburb to the city. –adj. **2.** of, relating to, or designed for commuters: *commuter bus; commuter car park.*

compact[1] adj. /kɒm'pækt, 'kɒmpækt/ **1.** joined or packed together; closely and firmly united; dense; solid. **2.** arranged within a relatively small space. **3.** expressed concisely. –v.t. /kɒm-'pækt/ **4.** to join or pack closely together; consolidate; condense. –n. /'kɒmpækt/ **5.** a small case containing a mirror, face powder, a puff, and (sometimes) rouge.

compact[2] /'kɒmpækt/ n. an agreement between parties; covenant; contract.

compact disc n. a digitally-encoded disc, used for the reproduction of high-fidelity sound and low-resolution video information, and decoded by a laser beam. Also, **CD**.

compact fluorescent light bulb n. a small fluorescent light with its tube shaped in various compact ways, so as to fit into most standard light fittings; using less energy and having a longer life than a traditional light bulb. *Abbrev.*: CFL

companion /kəm'pænjən/ n. **1.** someone who accompanies or associates with another. **2.** a handbook; guide.

companionable /kəm'pænjənəbəl/ adj. fitted to be a companion; sociable.

company /'kʌmpəni/ n. (pl. **-nies**) **1.** a number of individuals assembled or associated together; a group of people. **2.** a guest or guests. **3.** a number of persons united or incorporated for joint action, especially for business. **4.** the member or members of a firm not specifically named in the firm's title.

company tax n. a tax imposed on the profits of limited companies, intended to separate the taxation of companies from that of individuals.

company title n. *Law* a form of interest in property, particularly multi-storey buildings,

where the whole of the building is owned by a company, shares in which are held by tenants.

comparative /kəm'pærətɪv/ adj. **1.** of or relating to comparison. **2.** estimated by comparison; not positive or absolute; relative. **3.** *Gram.* denoting the intermediate degree of the comparison of adjectives and adverbs.

compare /kəm'pεə/ v. (**-pared, -paring**) –v.t. **1.** (fol. by *to*) to represent as similar or analogous; liken. **2.** (fol. by *with*) to note the similarities and differences of. –v.i. **3.** to bear comparison; be held equal. –**comparable**, adj.

comparison /kəm'pærəsən/ n. **1.** the act of comparing. **2.** the state of being compared. **3.** a likening; an illustration by similitude; a comparative estimate or statement.

compartment /kəm'patmənt/ n. **1.** a part or space marked or partitioned off. **2.** a separate room, section, etc.

compass /'kʌmpəs/ n. **1.** an instrument for determining directions. **2.** space within limits; area; extent; range; scope. **3.** (*usu. pl.*) an instrument for describing circles, measuring distances, etc., consisting generally of two movable legs hinged at one end. –v.t. **4.** to extend or stretch around; hem in; encircle.

compassion /kəm'pæʃən/ n. a feeling of sorrow or pity for the sufferings or misfortunes of another; sympathy. –**compassionate**, adj.

compatible /kəm'pætəbəl/ adj. **1.** capable of existing together in harmony. **2.** (of a computer device) able to work in conjunction with another specified device.

-compatible a combining element meaning 'able to work in conjunction with another specified computer device', as in *IBM-compatible.*

compatriot /kəm'peɪtriət/ n. another person of one's own country.

compel /kəm'pεl/ v.t. (**-pelled, -pelling**) to force or drive, especially to a course of action.

compelling /kəm'pεlɪŋ/ adj. (of a person, writer, actor, etc.) demanding attention, respect.

compendium /kəm'pεndiəm/ n. (pl. **-diums** or **-dia** /-diə/) a comprehensive summary of a subject.

compensate /'kɒmpənseɪt/ v.t. **1.** to offset; make up for. –v.i. **2.** to provide or be an equivalent. **3.** (fol. by *for*) make up; make amends. –**compensation**, n.

compere /'kɒmpεə/ n. someone who introduces and links the acts in an entertainment.

compete /kəm'pit/ v.i. to contend with another for a prize, profit, etc.; engage in a contest; vie.

competent /'kɒmpətənt/ adj. properly qualified, capable. –**competence**, n.

competition /kɒmpə'tɪʃən/ n. **1.** a contest for some prize or advantage. **2.** the rivalry between competing people, teams, businesses, etc. **3.** a competitor or competitors.

competitive /kəm'pεtɪtɪv/ adj. **1.** of, relating to, involving, or decided by competition. **2.** having a feature comparable or superior to that of a commercial rival: *competitive prices.* **3.** having the urge to compete against or succeed over others.

competitor /kəm'pεtətə/ n. someone who competes; a rival.

compile /kəm'paɪl/ v.t. to put together (literary materials) in one book or work. **–compilation**, n.

compiler /kəm'paɪlə/ n. Computers a computer program which converts higher level programming languages into a form that can be executed by the computer.

complacent /kəm'pleɪsənt/ adj. pleased, especially with oneself or one's own merits, advantages, etc. **–complacency**, n.

complain /kəm'pleɪn/ v.i. to express grief, pain, uneasiness, censure, resentment, or dissatisfaction; find fault. **–complaint**, n.

complainant /kəm'pleɪnənt/ n. someone who makes a complaint, as in a legal action.

complaisant /kəm'pleɪsənt, -zənt/ adj. tending to please; obliging; agreeable; gracious; compliant. **–complaisantly**, adv.

complement n. /'kɒmpləmənt/ 1. that which completes or makes perfect. 2. either of two parts or things needed to complete the whole. 3. full quantity or amount; complete allowance. –v.t. /'kɒmplə,ment/ 4. to complete; form a complement to. **–complementary**, adj.

complementary medicine n. the range of treatments and procedures of an alternative nature which are considered, on scientific evidence, to assist mainstream medical treatments and procedures.

complete /kəm'plit/ adj. 1. having all its parts or elements; whole; entire; full. 2. finished; ended; concluded. –v.t. 3. to make complete. **–completion**, n.

complex /'kɒmplɛks/ adj. 1. composed of interconnected parts; compound; composite. 2. complicated; intricate. –n. 3. a complex whole or system; a complicated assembly of particulars. 4. the buildings and ancillary equipment required for a specified purpose: a shopping complex; a launch complex. **–complexity**, n.

complex carbohydrate n. any polysaccharide present in grains, vegetables, fruits, legumes and dairy products, broken down by the body into simple sugars and used as a source of energy.

complexion /kəm'plɛkʃən/ n. 1. the natural colour and appearance of the skin, especially of the face. 2. appearance; aspect; character.

compliance /kəm'plaɪəns/ n. the act of complying; an acquiescing or yielding.

complicate /'kɒmpləkeɪt/ v.t. to make complex, intricate, or involved. **–complication**, n.

complicated /'kɒmpləkeɪtəd/ adj. difficult to use or understand because there are many parts.

complicit /kəm'plɪsət/ adj. involved with a degree of guilt.

complicity /kəm'plɪsəti/ n. the state of being an accomplice; partnership in wrongdoing. **–complicitous**, adj.

compliment n. /'kɒmpləmənt/ 1. an expression of praise, commendation, or admiration. 2. a formal act or expression of civility, respect, or regard. –v.t. /'kɒmplə,ment/ 3. to pay a compliment to.

complimentary /kɒmplə'mentri/ adj. 1. of the nature of, conveying, or addressing a compliment. 2. politely flattering. 3. free: a complimentary ticket. **–complimentarily**, adv.

comply /kəm'plaɪ/ v.i. (-plied, -plying) (fol. by with) to act in accordance with wishes, requests, commands, requirements, conditions, etc.

compo /'kɒmpoʊ/ n. Colloq. compensation for injury at or in connection with a person's work; workers' compensation.

component /kəm'poʊnənt/ adj. 1. composing; constituent. –n. 2. a constituent part.

comport /kəm'pɔt/ v.t. 1. to bear or conduct (oneself); behave. –v.i. 2. (fol. by with) to agree or accord; suit. **–comportment**, n.

compose /kəm'poʊz/ v.t. 1. to make or form by uniting parts or elements. 2. to devise and make (a literary or musical production). 3. to bring (the body or mind) to a condition of repose, calmness, etc.; calm; quiet. **–composer**, n.

composite /'kɒmpəzət/ adj. made up of various parts or elements; compound.

composite number n. Maths an integer greater than 1 which is exactly divisible by some integer other than itself and 1.

composite rating n. a property rating system based on both unimproved capital value and the commercial value.

composition /kɒmpə'zɪʃən/ n. 1. the act of combining parts or elements to form a whole. 2. the resulting state or product. 3. a compound or composite substance. 4. a short essay written as a school exercise. 5. an agreement or compromise, especially one by which a creditor (or group of creditors) accepts partial payment from a debtor. 6. a sum of money so paid.

compositor /kəm'pɒzətə/ n. Printing a person who assembles the type for a printed page.

compos mentis /kɒmpəs 'mɛntəs/ adj. sane.

compost /'kɒmpɒst/ n. a mixture of various kinds of organic matter used for fertilising land.

composure /kəm'poʊʒə/ n. serene state of mind; calmness; tranquillity.

compote /'kɒmpɒt/ n. a preparation or dish of fruit stewed in a syrup.

compound¹ adj. /'kɒmpaʊnd/ 1. composed of two or more parts, elements, or ingredients, or involving two or more actions, functions, etc.; composite. –n. /'kɒmpaʊnd/ 2. something formed by compounding or combining parts, elements, etc. –v.t. /kəm'paʊnd/ 3. to put together into a whole; combine. 4. to settle or adjust by agreement, especially for a reduced amount, as a debt. 5. to pay (interest) on the accrued interest as well as the principal. 6. to increase or make worse: the rain compounded their problems.

compound² /'kɒmpaʊnd/ n. an enclosed area containing buildings, houses, etc., not normally accessed other than by the residents.

compound interest n. interest paid, not only on the principal, but on the interest after it has periodically come due and, remaining unpaid, been added to the principal.

comprehend /kɒmprə'hɛnd/ v.t. 1. to understand the meaning or nature of; conceive; know. 2. to take in or embrace; include; comprise. **–comprehension**, n.

comprehensive /kɒmprə'hɛnsɪv/ adj. comprehending; inclusive; comprehending much; of large scope.

comprehensive insurance *n.* a form of insurance covering a wide range of instances in which the insured asset or property may be lost or damaged.

compress *v.t.* **1.** to press together; force into less space. **2.** *Computers* to convert (data) into a form that uses less storage; zip. –*n.* /'kɒmprɛs/ **3.** *Med.* a soft pad held in place by a bandage, used as a means of pressure or to supply moisture, cold, heat, or medication. –**compression**, *n.*

comprise /kəm'praɪz/ *v.t.* **1.** to comprehend; include; contain: *an analysis comprising all the data to hand.* **2.** to consist of; be composed of: *a house comprising seven rooms.* **3.** (*sometimes considered non-standard*) to combine to make up: *the book is comprised of ten chapters.*

compromise /'kɒmprəmaɪz/ *n.* **1.** a settlement of differences by mutual concessions. **2.** something intermediate between different things. **3.** an endangering, especially of reputation; exposure to danger, suspicion, etc. –*v.t.* **4.** to settle by a compromise. **5.** to make liable to danger, suspicion, scandal, etc.; endanger the reputation.

compulsion /kəm'pʌlʃən/ *n.* **1.** the act of compelling; coercion. **2.** *Psychol.* a strong irrational impulse to carry out a given act. –**compulsive**, *adj.*

compulsory /kəm'pʌlsəri/ *adj.* **1.** using compulsion; compelling. **2.** compelled; forced; obligatory.

compulsory conference *n.* a meeting to which parties to an industrial dispute and, on occasion, other interested parties, are summoned by an industrial tribunal.

compulsory unionism *n.* the requirement that people become and remain financial members of the union covering their calling as a pre-condition of employment.

compunction /kəm'pʌŋkʃən, -'pʌnʃən/ *n.* regret for wrongdoing or giving pain to another.

compute /kəm'pjut/ *v.t.* to determine by calculation; reckon; calculate. –**computation**, *n.*

computer /kəm'pjutə/ *n.* an apparatus for performing mathematical computations electronically according to a series of stored instructions called a program; an **analog computer** represents information in the form of continuously varying voltages; a **digital computer** represents information by patterns of on-off states of voltages.

computer-aided design *n.* the use of computers in design allowing the designer greater flexibility in formulating projects on screen. *Abbrev.:* CAD

computer-aided manufacturing *n.* the use of computers in the manufacturing process for networking machines and computerised devices such as robots. *Abbrev.:* CAM

computer crime *n.* crime, usually fraud, involving illegal access to a computer system for personal gain, as in transferring funds or gaining unauthorised access to data.

computer geek *n.* → **geek** (def. 2).

computerise /kəm'pjutəraɪz/ *v.t.* **1.** to process or store (data) in a computer. **2.** to furnish or provide with a computer system. Also, **computerize**. –**computerisation**, *n.*

computer language *n.* any artificial language coded in text or graphics that can be interpreted by a machine, particularly a computer. Also, **programming language**.

computer program *n.* → **program** (def. 5). –**computer programming**, *n.* –**computer programmer**, *n.*

computer terminal *n.* an input or output device connected to a computer but at a distance from it.

computing /kəm'pjutɪŋ/ *n.* **1.** the science or study of the principles and uses of computers. **2.** the field of computer technology: *to have a job in computing.* –*adj.* **3.** relating to computers: *computing skills.*

comrade /'kɒmreɪd, 'kɒmrəd/ *n.* an associate in occupation or friendship.

con¹ /kɒn/ *adv.* **1.** against a proposition, opinion, etc. (opposed to *pro*). –*n.* **2.** the argument, arguer, or voter against (something) (opposed to *pro*).

con² /kɒn/ *n.* **1.** a confidence trick; swindle. –*v.t.* (**conned**, **conning**) **2.** to swindle; defraud.

con- variant of **com-**.

con artist *n.* a person who swindles a victim out of their money or property, or persuades them to do something they would not otherwise have done, by initially gaining their trust.

concave /'kɒnkeɪv/ *adj.* curved like the interior of a circle or hollow sphere.

conceal /kən'sil/ *v.t.* to hide.

concede /kən'sid/ *v.* (**-ceded**, **-ceding**) –*v.t.* **1.** to admit as true, just, or proper; admit. **2.** to grant as a right or privilege; yield. –*v.i.* **3.** to admit defeat in an election.

conceit /kən'sit/ *n.* **1.** an exaggerated estimate of one's own ability, importance, wit, etc. **2.** a fanciful thought, idea, or expression, especially of a strained or far-fetched nature.

conceited /kən'sitəd/ *adj.* too proud of oneself, one's own abilities, etc. –**conceitedly**, *adv.*

conceivable /kən'sivəbəl/ *adj.* imaginable.

conceive /kən'siv/ *v.* (**-ceived**, **-ceiving**) –*v.t.* **1.** to form (a notion, opinion, purpose, etc.). **2.** to apprehend in the mind; understand. –*v.i.* **3.** to become pregnant with. **4.** (fol. by *of*) to form an idea; think. **5.** to become pregnant.

concentrate /'kɒnsəntreɪt/ *v.t.* **1.** to bring or draw to a common centre or point of union. **2.** make more intense, stronger, or purer by removing or reducing the proportion of what is foreign or inessential. –*v.i.* **3.** to converge to a centre. **4.** to become more intense, stronger, or purer. **5.** to direct one's thoughts or actions towards one subject. –*n.* **6.** a concentrated form of something; a product of concentration. –**concentration**, *n.*

concentrated /'kɒnsəntreɪtəd/ *adj.* **1.** applied with great energy and intensity; focused: *concentrated attention.* **2.** reduced to the essential ingredient, as by removing water: *concentrated juice.* **3.** clustered densely together: *concentrated population.*

concentration camp *n.* a prison camp for prisoners of war or enemies of a country.

concentric /kən'sɛntrɪk/ *adj.* having a common centre, as circles or spheres. Also, **concentrical**.

concept /'kɒnsɛpt/ n. **1.** a thought, idea, or notion, often one deriving from a generalising mental operation. **2.** an idea that includes all that is associated with a word or other symbol. –**conceptual**, adj.

conception /kən'sɛpʃən/ n. **1.** the act of conceiving. **2.** the state of being conceived. **3.** fertilisation; inception of pregnancy. **4.** that which is conceived. **5.** beginning; origin.

concern /kən'sɜn/ v.t. **1.** to relate to; be connected with; be of interest or importance to; affect. **2.** to interest, engage, or involve. **3.** to disquiet or trouble. –n. **4.** that which relates or pertains to one; business; affair. **5.** a matter that engages one's attention, interest, or care, or that affects one's welfare or happiness. **6.** solicitude or anxiety. **7.** important relation or bearing. **8.** a commercial or manufacturing firm or establishment.

concert /'kɒnsət/ n. **1.** a public performance, usually by two or more musicians. **2.** agreement of two or more in a design or plan.

concerted /kən'sɜtəd/ adj. contrived or arranged by agreement.

concerto /kən'ʃɛtou, kən'tʃɛtou/ n. (pl. **-tos** or **-ti**) a musical composition for one or more solo instruments with an orchestral accompaniment.

concession /kən'sɛʃən/ n. **1.** the act of conceding or yielding, as a right or privilege, or as a point or fact in an argument. **2.** the thing or point yielded. **3.** something conceded by a government or a controlling authority, as a grant of land, a privilege, or a franchise. **4.** an outlet, especially a food outlet, at a sporting or entertainment venue, etc.

conch /kɒntʃ, kɒŋk/ n. (pl. **conches** /'kɒntʃəz/ or **conchs** /kɒŋks/) the spiral shell of a gastropod.

concierge /kɒnsi'ɛəʒ, -'ʒʒ/ n. a hotel employee whose job is to assist guests with their travel arrangements, theatre and restaurant reservations, etc.

conciliate /kən'sɪli,eɪt/ v.t. **1.** to overcome the distrust or hostility of, by soothing or pacifying means; placate; win over. **2.** to render compatible; reconcile.

conciliation /kənsɪli'eɪʃən/ n. **1.** the act of conciliating. **2.** a procedure for the resolution of a dispute. **3.** a system of resolving industrial disputes between employees and employers by official talks in the presence of a government-appointed third party. See **arbitration** (def. 2).

concise /kən'saɪs/ adj. expressing much in few words.

conclave /'kɒnkleɪv, 'kɒŋ-/ n. any private meeting.

conclude /kən'klud, kəŋ-/ v.t. **1.** to bring to an end; finish; terminate. **2.** to determine by reasoning; deduce; infer. –v.i. **3.** to come to an end; finish. **4.** to arrive at an opinion or judgement; come to a decision; decide. –**conclusion**, n.

conclusive /kən'klusɪv, kəŋ-/ adj. serving to settle or decide a question; decisive; convincing.

concoct /kən'kɒkt, kəŋ-/ v.t. to prepare; make up; contrive. –**concoction**, n.

concomitant /kən'kɒmətənt, kəŋ-/ adj. accompanying; concurrent.

concord /'kɒnkɔd, 'kɒŋ-/ n. agreement.

concourse /'kɒnkɔs, 'kɒŋ-/ n. **1.** an assembly. **2.** an open space or main hall in a public building, especially a railway station.

concrete /'kɒnkrit, 'kɒŋ-/ adj. **1.** constituting an actual thing or instance; real. **2.** representing or applied to an actual substance or thing as opposed to an abstract quality. –n. **3.** a concrete idea or term; a concrete object or thing. **4.** an artificial stone-like material used for foundations, etc. –v.t. **5.** to treat or lay with concrete. –v.i. **6.** to coalesce into a mass; become solid; harden. –**concretion**, n.

concubine /'kɒŋkjubaɪn/ n. (among polygamous peoples) a secondary wife.

concur /kən'kɜ, kəŋ-/ v.i. (**-curred, -curring**) **1.** to accord in opinion; agree. **2.** to cooperate; combine; be associated. **3.** to coincide. **4.** to come together, as lines; unite. –**concurrent**, adj. –**concurrently**, adv. –**concurrence**, n.

concussion /kən'kʌʃən, kəŋ-/ n. **1.** the act of shaking or shocking, as by a blow. **2.** shock occasioned by a blow or collision.

condemn /kən'dɛm/ v.t. **1.** to pronounce adverse judgement on; express strong disapproval of. **2.** to pronounce to be guilty. **3.** to judge or pronounce to be unfit for use or service. –**condemnation**, n. –**condemnatory**, adj.

condense /kən'dɛns/ v.t. **1.** to make more dense or compact; reduce the volume or compass of. **2.** to reduce to another and denser form, as a gas or vapour to a liquid or solid state. **3.** to compress into fewer words; abridge. –**condensation**, n.

condescend /kɒndə'sɛnd/ v.i. **1.** to stoop or deign (to do something). **2.** to behave as if one is conscious of descending from a superior position, rank, or dignity.

condiment /'kɒndəmənt/ n. something used to give a special or additional flavour to food, as a sauce or seasoning.

condition /kən'dɪʃən/ n. **1.** particular mode of being of a person or thing; situation with respect to circumstances; existing state or case. **2.** fit or requisite state. **3.** a circumstance indispensable to some result; a prerequisite; that on which something else is contingent. **4.** something demanded as an essential part of an agreement. –v.t. **5.** to put in fit or proper state. **6.** to subject to particular conditions or circumstances.

conditional /kən'dɪʃənəl/ adj. **1.** imposing, containing, or depending on a condition or conditions. –n. **2.** Computers an instruction which is acted upon only when a certain condition pertains.

condole /kən'doul/ v.i. to express sympathy with one in affliction. –**condolence**, n.

condom /'kɒndɒm/ n. a contraceptive device worn over the penis during intercourse.

condominium /kɒndə'mɪniəm/ n. Chiefly US **1.** a block of apartments. **2.** an apartment. Also, **condo**.

condone /kən'doun/ v.t. **1.** to pardon or overlook (an offence). **2.** to atone for; make up for.

conducive /kən'djusɪv/ adj. (sometimes fol. by to) contributive or helpful. –**conduciveness**, n.

conduct n. /'kɒndʌkt/ **1.** personal behaviour; way of acting; deportment. **2.** direction or management; execution. —*v.t.* /kənˈdʌkt/ **3.** to behave (oneself). **4.** to direct in action or course; manage; carry on. **5.** to lead or guide; escort. **6.** to serve as a channel or medium for (heat, electricity, sound, etc.). —**conduction**, *n.*

conductivity /ˌkɒndʌkˈtɪvəti/ *n.* the property or power of conducting heat, electricity, or sound.

conductor /kənˈdʌktə/ *n.* **1.** someone who conducts; a leader, guide, director, or manager. **2.** the person on a public transport vehicle, who collects fares, issues tickets, etc. **3.** a substance, body, or device that readily conducts heat, electricity, sound, etc.

conduit /ˈkɒndʒuət, ˈkɒndjuət, ˈkɒndɪt/ *n.* a pipe, tube, or the like, for conveying water or other fluid.

cone /koʊn/ *n.* **1.** *Geom.* a solid which tapers to a point from a circular base. **2.** *Bot.* the more or less conical multiple fruit of the pine, fir, etc. **3.** anything cone-shaped.

confabulate /kənˈfæbjuleɪt/ *v.i.* to talk together; converse.

confection /kənˈfɛkʃən/ *n.* a piece of confectionery.

confectionery /kənˈfɛkʃənri/ *n.* lollies, candies or sweets.

confederacy /kənˈfɛdərəsi, -ˈfɛdrəsi/ *n.* (*pl.* **-cies**) an alliance of persons, parties, or states for some common purpose.

confederate *adj.* /kənˈfɛdərət/ **1.** united in a league or alliance, or a conspiracy. —*n.* /kənˈfɛdərət/ **2.** an accomplice. —*v.i.* /kənˈfɛdəreɪt/ **3.** to unite in a league or alliance, or a conspiracy. —**confederation**, *n.*

confer /kənˈfɜ/ *v.t.* (**-ferred, -ferring**) (fol. by *on* or *upon*) to bestow as a gift, favour, honour, etc.

conference /ˈkɒnfərəns/ *n.* **1.** a meeting for consultation or discussion. **2.** a cartel of shipping interests.

confess /kənˈfɛs/ *v.t.* **1.** to acknowledge or avow. **2.** to own or admit; admit the truth or validity of. **3.** to acknowledge one's belief in; declare adherence to. —**confession**, *n.*

confessor /kənˈfɛsə/ *n.* a priest authorised to hear confessions.

confetti /kənˈfɛti/ *pl. n.* (*sing.* **-fetto** /-ˈfɛtoʊ/) small bits of coloured paper, thrown at carnivals, weddings, etc.

confidant /kɒnfəˈdænt, ˈkɒnfədænt/ *n.* one to whom secrets are confided. —**confidante**, *fem. n.*

confide /kənˈfaɪd/ *v.* (**-fided, -fiding**) —*v.i.* **1.** (fol. by *in*) to show trust by imparting secrets. —*v.t.* **2.** to tell in assurance of secrecy.

confidence /ˈkɒnfədəns/ *n.* **1.** full trust; belief in the trustworthiness or reliability of a person or thing. **2.** *Politics* the wish to retain the incumbent government in office, as shown by a vote on a particular issue. **3.** self-reliance, assurance, or boldness. **4.** assured expectation. **5.** a confidential communication; a secret. —*phr.* **6. in confidence**, as a secret or private matter, not to be divulged to others.

confidence trick *n.* a swindle in which the victim's confidence is gained in order to induce them to part with money or property. Also, *US*, **confidence game**.

confident /ˈkɒnfədənt/ *adj.* **1.** having strong belief or full assurance; sure. **2.** sure of oneself; bold.

confidential /kɒnfəˈdɛnʃəl/ *adj.* **1.** spoken or written in confidence; secret. **2.** enjoying another's confidence.

configuration /kənfɪgəˈreɪʃən, -fɪgju-/ *n.* the relative disposition of the parts or elements of a thing.

configure /kənˈfɪgə/ *v.t.* (**-gured, -guring**) **1.** to design or adapt to form a desired configuration. **2. a.** to set (a computer) so that it can run a particular application. **b.** to design (a computer system) with a particular arrangement of computer and peripherals, such as printer, monitor, disk drive, etc. —**configurable**, *adj.*

confine *v.t.* /kənˈfaɪn/ **1.** to enclose within bounds; limit or restrict. —*n.* /ˈkɒnfaɪn/ **2.** (*usu. pl.*) a boundary or bound; a border or frontier. —**confiner**, *n.* —**confinement**, *n.*

confirm /kənˈfɜm/ *v.t.* **1.** to make certain or sure; corroborate; verify. **2.** to make valid or binding by some formal or legal act; sanction; ratify. **3.** to reaffirm (a booking, ticket reservation, appointment, etc). **4.** to strengthen (a person) in habit, resolution, opinion, etc. —**confirmation**, *n.*

confiscate /ˈkɒnfəskeɪt/ *v.t.* **1.** to seize as forfeited to the public treasury; appropriate, by way of penalty, to public use. **2.** to seize as if by authority; appropriate summarily.

conflagration /kɒnfləˈgreɪʃən/ *n.* a large and destructive fire.

conflict *v.i.* /kənˈflɪkt/ **1.** to come into collision; clash, or be in opposition or at variance; disagree. —*n.* /ˈkɒnflɪkt/ **2.** a battle or struggle, especially a prolonged struggle; strife.

conflicted /kənˈflɪktəd/ *adj.* experiencing mental conflict; torn.

conflicting /kənˈflɪktɪŋ/ *adj.* **1.** in disagreement: *conflicting opinions.* **2.** generating conflict: *a conflicting issue.*

conform /kənˈfɔm/ *v.i.* (fol. by *to*) to act in accord or harmony; comply. —**conformist**, *n.* —**conformity**, *n.*

confound /kənˈfaʊnd/ *v.t.* **1.** to throw into confusion or disorder. **2.** to refute in argument; contradict.

confront /kənˈfrʌnt/ *v.t.* stand and meet facing.

confuse /kənˈfjuz/ *v.t.* **1.** to combine without order or clearness; jumble; render indistinct. **2.** to throw into disorder. **3.** to fail to distinguish between; associate by mistake; confound. **4.** to perplex or bewilder. —**confusion**, *n.*

confute /kənˈfjut/ *v.t.* to prove to be false or defective: *to confute an argument.*

congeal /kənˈdʒil/ *v.i.* to change from a fluid or soft to a solid or rigid state.

congenial /kənˈdʒiniəl/ *adj.* agreeing or suited in nature or character.

congenital /kənˈdʒɛnətl/ *adj.* existing at or from one's birth.

congest /kənˈdʒɛst/ *v.t.* to fill to excess. —**congestion**, *n.*

conglomerate *n.* /kənˈglɒmərət, kən-/ **1.** anything composed of heterogeneous materials or elements. **2.** a company which controls or undertakes a widely diversified range of activities. *–adj.* /kənˈglɒmərət, kən-/ **3.** gathered into a rounded mass. *–v.i.* /kənˈglɒməreɪt, kən-/ **4.** to collect or cluster together.

congratulate /kənˈgrætʃəleɪt, kən-/ *v.t.* to express sympathetic joy to (a person), as on a happy occasion. **–congratulation**, *n.* **–congratulatory**, *adj.*

congregate /ˈkɒŋgrəgeɪt/ *v.t.* to come or bring together; assemble, especially in large numbers. **–congregation**, *n.*

congress /ˈkɒŋgrɛs/ *n.* a formal meeting or assembly of representatives for the discussion, arrangements, or promotion of some matter of common interest. **–congressional**, *adj.*

congruent /ˈkɒŋgruənt/ *adj.* agreeing; corresponding; congruous.

congruous /ˈkɒŋgruəs/ *adj.* agreeing or harmonious in character. **–congruity**, *n.*

conifer /ˈkɒnəfə, ˈkoʊ-/ *n.* any of the cone-bearing (mostly evergreen) trees and shrubs, such as pine, fir, and spruce. **–coniferous**, *adj.*

conjecture /kənˈdʒɛktʃə/ *n.* **1.** the formation or expression of an opinion without sufficient evidence for proof. *–v.t.* **2.** to conclude or suppose from grounds or evidence insufficient to ensure reliability.

conjoined twins /kənˈdʒɔɪnd/ *pl. n.* any twins who are born joined together in any manner.

conjugal /ˈkɒndʒəgəl, -dʒu-/ *adj.* marital.

conjugate *v.t.* /ˈkɒndʒəgeɪt/ **1.** *Gram.* to recite or display all, or some subset of, the inflected forms of (a verb), in a fixed order. *–adj.* /ˈkɒndʒəgət/ **2.** joined together, especially in a pair or pairs; coupled. **–conjugation**, *n.*

conjunction /kənˈdʒʌŋkʃən/ *n.* **1.** the act or result of joining together; combination; union. **2.** *Gram.* something that joins, especially a word joining sentences, clauses, etc.

conjunctiva /ˌkɒndʒʌŋkˈtaɪvə/ *n.* the mucous membrane which lines the inner surface of the eyelids.

conjunctivitis /kəndʒʌŋktəˈvaɪtəs/ *n. Pathol.* inflammation of the conjunctiva.

conjure /ˈkʌndʒə, ˈkɒndʒə/ *v.t.* **1.** to effect, produce, bring, etc., by, or as by, magic. *–v.i.* **2.** to practise conjuring or magic. **–conjurer**, **conjuror**, *n.* **–conjuration**, *n.*

conk /kɒŋk/ *v.t. Colloq.* **1.** to hit or strike, especially on the head. **2.** to faint; collapse.

connect /kəˈnɛkt/ *v.t.* **1.** to bind or fasten together. **2.** to establish communication between. **3.** to associate or attach. *–v.i.* **4.** to become connected; join or unite. **–connective**, *adj.*

connection /kəˈnɛkʃən/ *n.* **1.** the act of connecting. **2.** the state of being connected. **3.** anything that connects; a connecting part. **4.** (*usu.* pl.) influential friends, associates, relatives, etc.

connive /kəˈnaɪv/ *v.i.* **1.** to give aid to wrongdoing, etc., by forbearing to act or speak. **2.** (fol. by *with*) to cooperate secretly.

connoisseur /kɒnəˈsɜ/ *n.* someone competent to pass critical judgements in an art, especially one of the fine arts, or in matters of taste.

connote /kəˈnoʊt/ *v.t.* to denote secondarily; signify in addition to the primary meaning; imply. **–connotation**, *n.*

conquer /ˈkɒŋkə/ *v.t.* **1.** to overcome by force; subdue. **2.** to gain the victory over; surmount. **–conqueror**, *n.* **–conquest**, *n.*

consanguineous /kɒnsæŋˈgwɪniəs/ *adj.* related by birth. **–consanguinity**, *n.*

conscience /ˈkɒnʃəns/ *n.* the internal recognition of right and wrong as regards one's actions and motives.

conscience clause *n.* a clause or article in an act or law or the like, which relieves persons whose conscientious or religious scruples forbid their compliance with it.

conscientious /kɒnʃiˈɛnʃəs/ *adj.* controlled by or done according to conscience; scrupulous.

conscionable /ˈkɒnʃənəbəl/ *adj.* conformable to conscience; just.

conscious /ˈkɒnʃəs/ *adj.* **1.** aware of one's own existence, sensations, cognitions, etc.; endowed with consciousness. **2.** having the mental faculties awake.

conscript *v.t.* /kənˈskrɪpt/ **1.** to enrol compulsorily for service in the armed forces. *–n.* /ˈkɒnskrɪpt/ **2.** someone who has been enlisted compulsorily in the armed forces. **–conscription**, *n.*

consecrate /ˈkɒnsəkreɪt/ *v.t.* to make or declare sacred. **–consecration**, *n.*

consecutive /kənˈsɛkjətɪv/ *adj.* following one another in uninterrupted succession.

consensus /kənˈsɛnsəs/ *n.* general agreement or concord.

consent /kənˈsɛnt/ *v.i.* **1.** (fol. by *to* or infinitive) to give assent; agree; comply or yield. *–n.* **2.** assent; acquiescence; permission; compliance. **–consenting**, *adj.*

consent award *n.* an award made by an industrial tribunal where the parties have already reached agreement on the terms of a settlement but want it to have the force of an arbitrated award and hence submit it to a tribunal for ratification. Also, **consent agreement**.

consequence /ˈkɒnsəkwəns/ *n.* **1.** the act or fact of following as an effect or result upon something antecedent. **2.** that which so follows; an effect or result. **3.** importance or significance. **–consequent**, *adj.* **–consequential**, *adj.* **–consequently**, *adv.*

conservation /kɒnsəˈveɪʃən/ *n.* the preservation or conserving of natural resources or areas or objects of cultural significance. **–conservationist**, *n.*

conservative /kənˈsɜvətɪv/ *adj.* **1.** disposed to preserve existing conditions, institutions, etc. **2.** having the power or tendency to conserve; preservative. *–n.* **3.** a person of conservative principles. **–conservatism**, *n.*

conservatorium /kənsɜvəˈtɔriəm/ *n.* a school of music. Also, **conservatoire**.

conservatory /kənˈsɜvətri/, *Orig. US* /kənˈsɜvətɔri/ *n.* (*pl.* **-ries**) a glass-covered house or room into which plants in bloom are brought from the greenhouse.

conserve *v.t.* /kənˈsɜv/ **1.** to keep in a safe or sound state. *–n.* /ˈkɒnsɜv, kənˈsɜv/ **2.** (*oft. pl.*) a mixture of several fruits, cooked, with sugar, to a jam-like consistency. **–conserver**, *n.*

consider /kənˈsɪdə/ *v.t.* **1.** to contemplate mentally; meditate or reflect on. **2.** to regard as or deem to be. **3.** to make allowance for. **4.** to regard with consideration or respect; hold in honour; respect.

considerable /kənˈsɪdrəbəl/ *adj.* worthy of consideration.

considerate /kən'sıdərət/ *adj.* showing consideration or regard for another's circumstances, feelings, etc.

consideration /kənsıdə'reıʃən/ *n.* **1.** the act of considering; meditation or deliberation. **2.** regard or account; something taken, or to be taken, into account. **3.** a recompense for service rendered, etc.; a compensation. **4.** thoughtful or sympathetic regard or respect; thoughtfulness for others. **5.** estimation; esteem.

consign /kən'saın/ *v.t.* **1.** (sometimes fol. by *to*) to hand over or deliver formally; commit. **2.** (sometimes fol. by *to*) to transfer to another's custody or charge; entrust. **–consignor**, *n.* **–consignee**, *n.*

consignment /kən'saınmənt/ *n.* property sent to an agent for sale, storage, or shipment.

consist /kən'sıst/ *v.i.* **1.** (fol. by *of*) to be made up or composed. **2.** (fol. by *in*) to be included or contained.

consistency /kən'sıstənsi/ *n.* (*pl.* **-cies**) **1.** agreement among themselves of the parts of a complex thing. **2.** degree of density or viscosity. **3.** constant adherence to the same principles, course, etc. Also, **consistence**. **–consistent**, *adj.*

console[1] /kən'soul/ *v.t.* to alleviate the grief or sorrow of; comfort; solace; cheer. **–consolation**, *n.*

console[2] /'kɒnsoul/ *n.* **1.** a desk on which are mounted the controls of an electrical or electronic system. **2.** *Computers* a computer operator's control panel or terminal.

consolidate /kən'sɒlədeıt/ *v.t.* to bring together compactly in one mass or connected whole; unite; combine. **–consolidation**, *n.*

consolidated revenue *n.* the funds which a government treasury receives by way of taxes, duties, etc.

consommé /'kɒnsɒmeı, kən'sɒmeı/ *n.* a clear soup made from a concentrated clarified meat or vegetable stock. Also, **consomme**.

consonant /'kɒnsənənt/ *n.* **1.** a sound made with more or less obstruction of the breath stream in its passage outwards, as the *l, s,* and *t* of *list*. **–adj.** **2.** (fol. by *to* or *with*) in agreement; consistent.

consort *n.* /'kɒnsɔt/ **1.** a spouse, especially of a reigning monarch. **2.** one vessel or ship accompanying another. **–v.i.** /kən'sɔt/ **3.** to associate; keep company.

consortium /kən'sɔtiəm, -ʃiəm/ *n.* (*pl.* **-tiums** *or* **-tia** /-tiə, -ʃə/) a combination of financial institutions, capitalists, etc., for carrying into effect some financial operation requiring large resources of capital.

conspicuous /kən'spıkjuəs/ *adj.* **1.** easy to be seen. **2.** readily attracting the attention.

conspiracy /kən'spırəsi/ *n.* (*pl.* **-cies**) **1.** the act of conspiring. **2.** a combination of persons for an evil or unlawful purpose; a plot.

conspiracy theory *n.* (*pejorative*) any theory which proposes that some damaging event or situation which lacks an obvious explanation has been brought about by the unseen and evil machinations of government or covert organisations. **–conspiracy theorist**, *n.*

conspirator /kən'spırətə/ *n.* someone who is part of a conspiracy. **–conspiratorial**, *adj.* **–conspiratorially**, *adv.*

conspire /kən'spaıə/ *v.i.* to agree together, especially secretly, to do something reprehensible or illegal; combine for an evil or unlawful purpose.

constable /'kʌnstəbəl, 'kɒn-/ *n.* a police officer ranking below sergeant, the lowest in rank in a police force.

constant /'kɒnstənt/ *adj.* **1.** invariable; uniform; always present. **2.** continuing without intermission. **3.** standing firm in mind or purpose; resolute. **–n.** **4.** something constant, invariable, or unchanging.

constellation /kɒnstə'leıʃən/ *n.* *Astron.* any of various groups of stars to which definite names have been given.

consternation /kɒnstə'neıʃən/ *n.* amazement and dread tending to confound the faculties.

constipation /kɒnstə'peıʃən/ *n.* a condition of the bowels marked by defective or difficult evacuation.

constituency /kən'stıtʃuənsi/ *n.* (*pl.* **-cies**) any body of supporters; a clientele.

constituent /kən'stıtʃuənt/ *adj.* **1.** serving to make up a thing; component; elementary. **2.** having power to frame or alter a political constitution or fundamental law (as distinguished from law-making power). **–n.** **3.** a constituent element, material, etc.; a component. **4.** a voter, or (loosely) a resident, in a district represented by an elected official.

constitute /'kɒnstətjut/ *v.t.* **1.** (of elements, etc.) to compose; form. **2.** to appoint to an office or function; make or create. **3.** to give legal form to (an assembly, court, etc.).

constitution /kɒnstə'tjuʃən/ *n.* **1.** the way in which anything is constituted; make-up or composition. **2.** the physical character of the body as to strength, health, etc. **3.** the act of constituting; establishment. **4.** any established arrangement or custom. **5.** the system of fundamental principles according to which a nation, state or body politic is governed. **–constitutional**, *adj.*

constitutional monarchy *n.* a form of monarchy in which the power of the sovereign is limited by a constitution, whether written (as in Australia) or unwritten (as in Britain).

constrain /kən'streın/ *v.t.* **1.** to force, compel, or oblige; bring about by compulsion. **2.** to confine forcibly, as by bonds. **3.** to repress or restrain. **–constraint**, *n.*

constrict /kən'strıkt/ *v.t.* **1.** to draw together; compress. **2.** to restrict. **–constriction**, *n.* **–constrictive**, *adj.*

construct *v.t.* /kən'strʌkt/ **1.** to form by putting together parts; build; frame; devise. **–n.** /'kɒnstrʌkt/ **2.** a complex image or idea resulting from a synthesis by the mind.

construction /kən'strʌkʃən/ *n.* **1.** the act or art of constructing. **2.** the way in which a thing is constructed; structure. **3.** that which is constructed; a structure. **4.** explanation or interpretation, as of a law or a text, or of conduct or the like.

constructive /kən'strʌktıv/ *adj.* constructing, or tending to construct.

construe /kən'stru/ v.t. (-strued, -struing) **1.** to show the meaning or intention of. **2.** to deduce by construction or interpretation; infer.

consul /'kɒnsəl/ n. an agent appointed by an independent state to reside in a foreign state and discharge certain administrative duties. —**consular**, adj. —**consulate**, n.

consult /kən'sʌlt/ v.t. **1.** to refer to for information or advice. —v.i. **2.** to consider or deliberate.

consultant /kən'sʌltənt/ n. someone who gives professional or expert advice.

consultation /kɒnsəl'teɪʃən/ n. **1.** the act of consulting; conference. **2.** a meeting for deliberation. **3.** an application for advice to one engaged in a profession, especially to a medical practitioner, etc.

consumable /kən'sjuməbəl/ adj. **1.** able to be consumed. **2.** (of an item of equipment or supply) normally consumed in use: consumable fuel; consumable paper products. —n. **3.** a consumable product or supply. —**consumability**, n.

consume /kən'sjum/ v.t. **1.** to destroy or expend by use; use up. **2.** to eat or drink up; devour. **3.** to absorb; engross.

consumer /kən'sjumə/ n. someone who uses a commodity or service (opposed to producer).

consumer goods pl. n. goods ready for consumption in satisfaction of human wants, as clothing, food, etc., and which are not utilised in any further production.

consumerism /kən'sjumərɪzəm/ n. **1.** a movement which aims at educating consumers to an awareness of their rights and at protecting their interests, as from illegal or dishonest trading practices. **2.** a theory that the economy of a Western capitalist society requires an ever increasing consumption of goods.

consumer price index n. an index which provides a measure of the change in the average cost of a standard basket of retail goods by relating the cost in the current period to that of a base period; used as a measure of inflation.

consummate v.t. /'kɒnsəmeɪt, 'kɒnsjumeɪt/ **1.** to bring to completion or perfection. **2.** to fulfil (a marriage) by having sexual intercourse. —adj. /'kɒnsjumət, 'kɒnsəmət/ **3.** complete or perfect.

consumption /kən'sʌmpʃən/ n. **1.** the act of consuming; destruction or decay. **2.** the amount consumed. **3.** Econ. the using up of goods and services having an exchangeable value. **4.** a wasting disease, especially tuberculosis of the lungs. —**consumptive**, adj., n.

contact n. /'kɒntækt/ **1.** the state or fact of touching; a touching or meeting of bodies. **2.** immediate proximity or association. **3.** a person through whom contact is established, often a business acquaintance. **4.** Hist. the point at which two different peoples are brought into contact with each other, as by colonisation. —v.t. /kən'tækt/ **5.** to put or bring into contact. **6.** to get in touch with (a person). —**contactable**, adj.

contact lens n. a small lens usually of plastic which covers the eye and is held in place by eye fluid, used to aid defective vision inconspicuously.

contact sport n. a sport, such as Rugby football, in which bodies regularly come into contact, creating the possibility of injury.

contagious /kən'teɪdʒəs/ adj. **1.** communicable to other individuals by physical contact, as a disease. **2.** tending to spread from one to another: panic is contagious.

contain /kən'teɪn/ v.t. **1.** to have within itself; hold within fixed limits. **2.** to have as contents or constituent parts; comprise; include. **3.** to keep within proper bounds; restrain.

container /kən'teɪnə/ n. **1.** anything that contains or can contain, as a carton, box, crate, tin, etc. **2.** a box-shaped unit for carrying goods; its standardised size facilitates easy transference from one form of transport to another.

contaminate /kən'tæməneɪt/ v.t. to render impure by contact or mixture. —**contamination**, n. —**contaminant**, n.

contango /kən'tæŋgoʊ/ n. the position in a futures market where the more distantly traded contracts are selling at a premium over the nearer dated contracts.

contemplate /'kɒntəmpleɪt/ v.t. **1.** to look at or view with continued attention; observe thoughtfully. **2.** to have as a purpose; intend. —v.i. **3.** to think studiously; meditate; consider deliberately. —**contemplation**, n.

contemplative /'kɒntəm.pleɪtɪv, kən'templətɪv/ adj. given to or characterised by contemplation.

contemporaneous /kəntempə'reɪniəs/ adj. contemporary.

contemporary /kən'tɒmpəri, -pri/, Orig. US /kən'tempəreri/ adj. **1.** belonging to the same time; existing or occurring at the same time. **2.** of the present time. —n. (pl. **-ries**) **3.** one belonging to the same time or period with another or others.

contempt /kən'tempt/ n. **1.** the feeling with which one regards anything considered mean, vile, or worthless. **2.** the state of being despised; dishonour; disgrace. **3.** Law disobedience to, or open disrespect of, the rules or orders of a court or legislature.

contemptible /kən'temptəbəl/ adj. deserving of or held in contempt; despicable.

contemptuous /kən'temptʃuəs/ adj. manifesting or expressing contempt or disdain.

contend /kən'tend/ v.i. **1.** to struggle in opposition. —v.t. **2.** to assert or maintain earnestly.

content[1] /'kɒntent/ n. **1.** (usu. pl.) that which is contained. **2.** (usu. pl.) the chapters or chief topics of a book or document; a list of such chapters or topics. **3.** substance or purport, as of a document. **4.** the information which is in a communication, as opposed to the format, design, etc.: the content of a web page.

content[2] /kən'tent/ adj. **1.** having the desires limited to what one has; satisfied. **2.** willing or resigned; assenting.

contention /kən'tenʃən/ n. **1.** a struggling together in opposition; strife. **2.** strife in debate; a dispute; a controversy. —**contentious**, adj.

conterminous /kɒn'tɜmənəs/ adj. having a common boundary.

contest n. /'kɒntest/ **1.** struggle for victory or superiority. —v.t. /kən'test/ **2.** to struggle or fight for, as in battle. **3.** to argue against; dispute.

contestant /kən'testənt/ n. someone who takes part in a contest or competition.

context /'kɒntɛkst/ n. 1. the parts of a discourse or writing which precede or follow, and are directly connected with, a given passage or word. 2. the circumstances or facts that surround a particular situation, event, etc. –**contextual**, adj.

contiguous /kən'tɪgjuəs/ adj. 1. touching; in contact. 2. in close proximity without actually touching; near.

continence /'kɒntənəns/ n. ability to exercise voluntary control over natural functions, especially urination and defecation. Also, **continency**.

continent /'kɒntənənt/ n. 1. one of the main land masses of the globe. –adj. 2. Pathol. able to control urination and defecation. –**continental**, adj.

continental climate n. a type of climate characterised by extremely hot, sunny summers, bitterly cold winters, and little rainfall occurring mainly in early summer.

continental crust n. Geol. that portion of the lithosphere which comprises the earth's continents and the shallow seabeds surrounding the continents. Compare **oceanic crust**.

continental drift n. the movement of continents away from the original single landmass to their present position.

continental quilt n. → doona.

continental shelf n. that portion of a continent found under a shallow sea, in contrast with the deep open ocean.

contingent /kən'tɪndʒənt/ adj. 1. (oft. fol. by on or upon) dependent for existence, occurrence, character, etc., on something not yet certain; conditional. 2. liable to happen or not; uncertain; possible. –n. 3. the proportion that falls to one as a share to be contributed or furnished. 4. any one of the representative groups composing an assemblage. –**contingency**, n.

continual /kən'tɪnjuəl/ adj. 1. proceeding without interruption or cessation; continuous in time. 2. of regular or frequent recurrence; often repeated; very frequent.

continue /kən'tɪnju/ v. (-ued, -uing) –v.i. 1. to go forwards or onwards in any course or action; keep on. 2. to go on after suspension or interruption. 3. to remain in a particular state or capacity. –v.t. 4. to go on with or persist in. 5. to extend from one point to another in space; prolong. 6. to carry on from the point of suspension or interruption. –**continuation**, n.

continuity /kɒntə'njuəti/ n. the state or quality of being continuous.

continuous /kən'tɪnjuəs/ adj. 1. having the parts in immediate connection, unbroken. 2. uninterrupted in time; without cessation.

continuum /kən'tɪnjuəm/ n. (pl. **-tinuums** or **-tinua** /-'tɪnjuə/) a continuous extent, series, or whole.

contort /kən'tɔt/ v.t. to twist; bend or draw out of shape; distort. –**contortion**, n.

contortionist /kən'tɔʃənəst/ n. someone who performs gymnastic feats involving contorted postures.

contour /'kɒntʊə, -tɔ/ n. the outline of a figure or body; the line that defines or bounds anything.

contour line n. a line joining points of equal elevation on a surface.

contra- a prefix meaning 'against', 'opposite', or 'opposing'.

contraband /'kɒntrəbænd/ n. anything prohibited by law from being imported or exported.

contraception /kɒntrə'sɛpʃən/ n. the prevention of conception by deliberate measures; birth control. –**contraceptive**, adj., n.

contract n. /'kɒntrækt/ 1. an agreement between two or more parties for the doing or not doing of some definite thing. 2. an agreement enforceable by law. –v.t. /kən'trækt/ 3. to draw together or into smaller compass; draw the parts of together. 4. to shorten (a word, etc.) by combining or omitting some of its elements. 5. to acquire or incur. 6. to settle or establish by agreement. –**contraction**, n. –**contractor**, n. –**contractual**, adj. –**contractile**, adj.

contra deal /'kɒntrə/ n. an agreement involving an exchange of goods or services, rather than money.

contradict /kɒntrə'dɪkt/ v.t. to assert the contrary or opposite of. –**contradiction**, n. –**contradictory**, adj.

contralto /kən'træltoʊ, -'trɑl-/ n. (pl. **-tos** or **-ti**) the lowest female voice.

contraption /kən'træpʃən/ n. a device.

contrary /'kɒntrəri/ for defs 1, 2 and 4, /kən'trɛəri/ for def. 3 adj. 1. opposite in nature or character. 2. opposite in direction or position. 3. perverse; self-willed. –n. 4. that which is contrary or opposite. –**contrariety**, n.

contrast v.t. /kən'trast/ 1. to compare by observing differences. 2. to afford or form a contrast to; set off. –v.i. /kən'trast/ 3. to exhibit unlikeness on comparison; form a contrast. 4. the state of being contrasted. –n. /'kɒntrast/ 5. something strikingly unlike. 6. opposition or juxtaposition of different forms, lines, or colours in a work of art to intensify each other's properties and produce a more dynamic expression. –**contrasting**, adj.

contravene /kɒntrə'vin/ v.t. to violate, infringe, or transgress. –**contravention**, n.

contribute /kən'trɪbjut, 'kɒntrəbjut/ v.t. to give to a common stock or for a common purpose. –**contribution**, n. –**contributor**, n. –**contributory**, adj.

contrite /kən'traɪt, 'kɒntraɪt/ adj. feeling a strong sense of guilt; penitent. –**contrition** /kən'trɪʃən/, **contriteness**, n.

contrive /kən'traɪv/ v.t. 1. to plan with ingenuity; devise; invent. 2. to bring about or effect by a device, stratagem, plan, or scheme; manage (to do something). –**contrivance**, n.

control /kən'troʊl/ v.t. (-trolled, -trolling) 1. to exercise restraint or direction over; dominate; command. –n. 2. the act or power of controlling; regulation; domination or command. 3. check or restraint. 4. something that serves to control; a check; a standard of comparison in scientific experimentation. 5. (pl.) a co-ordinated arrangement of devices for regulating and guiding a machine.

control order n. an order issued by a court which restricts a person's movements and associations, and may also require home detention, the wearing of a tracking device, reporting to police stations at specified times, etc.

control panel *n.* **1.** a panel in which the controls of a device, vehicle, etc., are fitted. **2.** *Computers* an interface (def. 2) for setting system parameters on a computer, made to resemble a control panel (def. 1) on the screen.

controversy /ˈkɒntrəvɜsi, kənˈtrɒvəsi/ *n.* (*pl.* **-sies**) dispute, debate, or contention; dispute concerning a matter of opinion. **—controversial**, *adj.*

contumely /ˈkɒntʃuməli, kənˈtjuməli/ *n.* contemptuous or humiliating treatment. **—contumelious**, *adj.*

contuse /kənˈtjuz/ *v.t.* to bruise. **—contusion**, *n.* **—contusive**, *adj.*

conundrum /kəˈnʌndrəm/ *n.* a riddle.

convalesce /kɒnvəˈlɛs/ *v.i.* to grow stronger after illness. **—convalescence**, *n.* **—convalescent**, *adj., n.*

convection /kənˈvɛkʃən/ *n. Physics* the transference of heat by the circulation or movement of the heated parts of a liquid or gas.

convene /kənˈvin/ *v.i.* **1.** to come together; assemble, usually for some public purpose. **—v.t. 2.** to cause to assemble; convoke. **—convener**, *n.*

convenient /kənˈviniənt/ *adj.* **1.** agreeable to the needs or purpose. **2.** at hand; easily accessible. **—convenience**, *n.*

convent /ˈkɒnvənt/ *n.* **1.** a community of persons, especially nuns, devoted to religious life under a superior. **2.** a Roman Catholic or other school where children are taught by nuns.

convention /kənˈvɛnʃən/ *n.* **1.** a meeting or assembly, especially a formal assembly. **2.** general agreement or consent; accepted usage, especially as a standard of procedure. **—conventional**, *adj.*

converge /kənˈvɜdʒ/ *v.i.* **1.** to tend to meet in a point or line; incline towards each other, as lines which are not parallel. **2.** to tend to a common result, conclusion, etc. **—convergence**, *n.* **—convergent**, *adj.*

conversant /kənˈvɜsənt, ˈkɒnvəsənt/ *adj.* (fol. by *with*) familiar by use or study.

conversation /kɒnvəˈseɪʃən/ *n.* informal interchange of thoughts by spoken words; a talk.

converse /kənˈvɜs/ *v.i.* to talk informally with another.

converse² /ˈkɒnvɜs/ *adj.* **1.** turned about; opposite or contrary in direction or action. **—n. 2.** a thing which is the opposite or contrary of another.

convert *v.t.* /kənˈvɜt/ **1.** to change into something of different form or properties; transmute; transform. **2.** to cause to adopt a different religion, party, opinion, etc., especially one regarded as better. **—n.** /ˈkɒnvɜt/ **3.** someone who has been converted, as to a religion or an opinion. **—conversion**, *n.*

convertible /kənˈvɜtəbəl/ *adj.* **1.** capable of being converted. **2.** (of a car) having a removable top.

convex /ˈkɒnvɛks/ *adj.* bulging and curved.

convey /kənˈveɪ/ *v.t.* **1.** to carry or transport from one place to another. **2.** to communicate; impart; make known. **3.** *Law* to transfer; pass the title to.

conveyance /kənˈveɪəns/ *n.* **1.** the act of conveying; transmission; communication. **2.** a means of conveyance, especially a vehicle. **3.** *Law* **a.** the transfer of property from one person to another. **b.** the instrument or document by which this is effected.

conveyancing /kənˈveɪənsɪŋ/ *n.* that branch of legal practice consisting of examining titles, giving opinions as to their validity, and preparing of deeds, etc., for the conveyance of property from one person to another.

conveyor belt /kənˈveɪə/ *n.* a flexible band passing about two or more wheels, etc., used to transport objects from one place to another, especially in a factory. Also, **conveyer belt**.

convict *v.t.* /kənˈvɪkt/ **1.** to prove or declare guilty of an offence, especially after a legal trial. **—n.** /ˈkɒnvɪkt/ **2.** a person proved or declared guilty of an offence. **3.** a person serving a prison sentence.

conviction /kənˈvɪkʃən/ *n.* **1.** the fact or state of being convicted. **2.** the state of being convinced. **3.** a fixed or firm belief.

convince /kənˈvɪns/ *v.t.* (**-vinced, -vincing**) to persuade by argument or proof.

convivial /kənˈvɪviəl/ *adj.* agreeable; sociable; merry.

convoke /kənˈvoʊk/ *v.t.* to call together. **—convocation**, *n.*

convolution /kɒnvəˈluʃən/ *n.* a rolled up or coiled condition.

convoy /ˈkɒnvɔɪ/ *n.* any group of vehicles travelling together.

convulse /kənˈvʌls/ *v.i.* **1.** to shake violently; agitate. **2.** to cause to laugh violently. **3.** to cause to suffer violent muscular spasms. **—convulsion**, *n.* **—convulsive**, *adj.*

coo /ku/ *v.i.* to utter the soft, murmuring sound characteristic of pigeons or doves, or a similar sound.

cooee /ˈkui, kuˈi/ *n.* a prolonged clear call, the second syllable of which rises rapidly in pitch, used most frequently in the bush as a signal to attract attention.

cook /kʊk/ *v.t.* **1.** to prepare (food) by the action of heat, as by boiling, baking, roasting, etc. **—v.i. 2.** (of food) to undergo cooking. **—n.** **3.** someone who cooks. **—cookery**, *n.*

cookie /ˈkʊki/ *n.* (*pl.* **-kies**) **1.** *Chiefly US* a biscuit. **2.** *Colloq.* a person: *a smart cookie; a tough cookie.* **3.** *Internet* a small data file sent by a web server to a browser for use by the web server when being accessed in the future. Also, **cooky**.

cooktop /ˈkʊktɒp/ *n.* an assemblage of electric hotplates or gas burners for cooking, designed to be fitted into a benchtop.

cool /kul/ *adj.* **1.** moderately cold; neither warm nor very cold. **2.** imparting or permitting a sensation of moderate coldness. **3.** not excited; calm; unmoved; not hasty; deliberate; aloof. **4.** deficient in ardour or enthusiasm. **5.** *Colloq.* in fashion or stylish. **6.** *Colloq.* okay: *Don't worry, it's cool.* **—n. 7.** that which is cool; the cool part, place, time, etc. **—v.t. 8.** to make cool; impart a sensation of coolness to.

coolamon /ˈkuləmɒn/ *n.* a basin-shaped wooden dish traditionally made and used by some Aboriginal peoples.

coolant /ˈkulənt/ n. **1.** a substance, usually a liquid or gas, used to reduce heat in an engine, etc. **2.** lubricant used to reduce heat caused by friction.

coolibah /ˈkuləba/ n. a species of eucalypt common in the Australian inland. Also, **coolabah**.

cooling-off period n. a period in which a person may legally back out of a financial agreement.

co-op /ˈkoʊ-ɒp/ n. a cooperative shop, store, or society.

coop /kup/ n. **1.** an enclosure, cage, or pen, usually with bars or wires on one side or more, in which fowls, etc., are confined. –v.t. **2.** (oft. fol. by *up* or *in*) to place in, or as in, a coop; confine narrowly.

cooperate /koʊˈɒpəreɪt/ v.i. to work or act together or jointly. Also, **co-operate**. –**cooperation**, n.

cooperative /koʊˈɒpərətɪv, -ˈɒprətɪv/ adj. **1.** cooperating. **2.** showing a willingness to cooperate; helpful. –n. **3.** a cooperative society or shop. Also, **co-operative**.

cooperative society n. a business undertaking owned and controlled by its members, and formed to provide them with work or with goods at advantageous prices. Also, **co-operative society**.

coopt /koʊˈɒpt/ v.t. to elect into a body by the votes of the existing members. Also, **co-opt**.

coordinate /koʊˈɔdəneɪt/ *for defs 1–4*, /koʊˈɔdənət/ *for defs 5–7* –v.t. **1.** to place or class in the same order, rank, division, etc. **2.** to place or arrange in due order or proper relative position. –v.i. **3.** to become coordinate. **4.** to act in harmonious combination. –adj. **5.** of the same order or degree; equal in rank or importance. –n. **6.** someone who or that which is equal in rank or importance; an equal. **7.** *Maths* any of the magnitudes which define the position of a point, line, or the like, by reference to a fixed figure, system of lines, etc. Also, **co-ordinate**. –**coordination**, n.

cop /kɒp/ *Colloq.* –n. **1.** a police officer. –v.t. (**copped**, **copping**) **2.** to accept resignedly; put up with.

cope /koʊp/ v.i. (fol. by *with*) to struggle or contend, especially on fairly even terms or with a degree of success.

copha /ˈkoʊfa/ n. (*from trademark*) a white waxy solid derived from coconut flesh, used as shortening. Also, **copha butter**.

copious /ˈkoʊpiəs/ adj. large in quantity or number; abundant.

cop-out /ˈkɒp-aʊt/ n. *Colloq.* an easy way out of a situation of embarrassment or responsibility.

copper¹ /ˈkɒpə/ n. **1.** *Chem.* a malleable, ductile metallic element having a characteristic reddish brown colour. *Symbol:* Cu **2.** a large vessel (formerly of copper) for boiling clothes.

copper² /ˈkɒpə/ n. *Colloq.* a police officer.

copperplate /ˈkɒpəpleɪt/ n. an ornate, rounded style of handwriting, formerly much used in engravings.

coppice /ˈkɒpəs/ n. a wood, thicket, or plantation of small trees or bushes. Also, **copse**.

copra /ˈkɒprə/ n. the dried kernel or meat of he coconut, from which coconut oil is pressed.

copro- a prefix meaning 'dung'.

copula /ˈkɒpjələ/ n. (*pl.* **-lae** /-li/) **1.** something that connects or links together. **2.** *Gram.* a word, as the verb *be*, which acts as a connecting link between subject and predicate. –**copular**, adj.

copulate /ˈkɒpjuleɪt/ v.i. to unite in sexual intercourse.

copy /ˈkɒpi/ n. (*pl.* **-pies**) **1.** a transcript, reproduction, or imitation of an original. **2.** written, typed or printed matter, or images, intended to be reproduced in print. –v.t. (**-pied**, **-pying**) **3.** to make a copy of; transcribe; reproduce. **4.** to follow as a pattern or model; imitate. **5.** to add (a secondary recipient) to an email address list.

copyedit /ˈkɒpi,ɛdət/ v.t. to correct, style and mark up copy (def. 2) to make it ready for printing. –**copyediting**, n.

copyright /ˈkɒpiraɪt/ n. the exclusive right, granted by law for a certain term of years, to make and dispose of copies of, and otherwise to control, a literary, musical, dramatic, or artistic work. *Symbol:* ©

cor- variant of **com-** before *r*, as in *corrupt*.

coral /ˈkɒrəl/ n. **1.** the hard, chalky skeleton of any of various marine animals. **2.** such skeletons collectively, as forming reefs, islands, etc.

coral bleaching n. the whitening of coral brought about when the coral host expels the algae which gives the coral much of its colour and most of its food, such expulsion most commonly occurring because of an increase in ocean temperature under which conditions the algae becomes toxic; bleaching is reversible if the stress-inducing circumstances do not persist and the algae grows again, otherwise the starved coral eventually dies.

cord /kɔd/ n. **1.** a string or small rope composed of several strands twisted or woven together. **2.** a ribbed fabric, especially corduroy.

cord blood n. blood which contains many different types of cells, including stem cells, taken from the umbilical cord.

cordial /ˈkɔdiəl/ adj. **1.** hearty; warmly friendly. –n. **2.** a sweet, flavoured, concentrated syrup to be mixed with water as a drink.

corduroy /ˈkɔdərɔɪ, ˌkɔdʒərɔɪ/ n. a cotton pile fabric with lengthwise cords or ridges.

core /kɔ/ n. **1.** the central part of a fleshy fruit, containing the seeds. **2.** the central, innermost, or most essential part of anything. **3.** the primary memory of a computer. –v.t. **4.** to remove the core of (fruit).

corella /kəˈrɛlə/ n. any of three Australian cockatoos having predominantly white plumage tinged with pink or red.

core memory n. a formerly used read-write random access memory in a computer which retains data in storage on cores.

co-respondent /koʊ-rəˈspɒndənt/ n. the person alleged to have committed adultery with the respondent in a suit for divorce (no longer legally relevant in Australia).

core strength n. strength in the muscles of the torso that stabilise the spine, pelvis and shoulders.

core time n. that part of the working day during which one must be at one's place of work. See **flexitime**.

corgi /'kɔgi/ n. a short-legged Welsh dog with a squat body, and erect ears.

coriander /ˌkɒri'ændə/ n. herb used in cooking and medicine.

cork /kɔk/ n. 1. the outer bark of the cork oak, used for making stoppers of bottles, floats, etc. 2. a piece of cork, or other material (as rubber), used as a stopper for a bottle, etc.

corkage /'kɔkɪdʒ/ n. a charge made by a restaurant, etc., for serving liquor brought in by the customers.

cork hat n. a hat with corks dangling from strings attached to the brim; traditionally worn in the bush to keep insects away from one's face.

corkscrew /'kɔkskru/ n. an instrument used to draw corks from bottles.

cormorant /'kɔmərənt/ n. any of several large, voracious, waterbirds with a long neck and a pouch under the beak in which captured fish are held; shag.

corn[1] /kɔn/ n. 1. a widely cultivated cereal plant bearing grain in large ears or spikes. −v.t. 2. to preserve in brine, as meat.

corn[2] /kɔn/ n. a hard growth of skin, usually with a central core, caused by undue pressure or friction, especially on the toes or feet.

corn chip n. a chip (def. 3) made from processed corn instead of potato.

corncob /'kɔnkɒb/ n. the elongated woody core in which the grains of an ear of corn are embedded.

cornea /'kɔniə/ n. (pl. **-neas** or **-neae** /-nii/) the transparent anterior part of the external coat of the eye, covering the iris and the pupil.

corned beef n. a cut of beef that is cured in brine. Also, **corn beef**.

corner /'kɔnə/ n. 1. the meeting place of two converging lines or surfaces. 2. the space between two converging lines or surfaces near their intersection; angle. 3. the place where two streets meet. 4. an end; margin; edge. 5. any situation from which escape is impossible. 6. Finance a monopolising or a monopoly of the available supply of a stock or commodity, to a point permitting control of price. 7. a region; quarter. 8. Soccer, Hockey, etc. a free kick or hit from the corner of the field taken by the attacking side when the ball has crossed the goal line after last being touched by a member of the defending side. −v.t. 9. to place in or drive into a corner. 10. to form a corner in (a stock, etc.). −v.i. 11. to form a corner in a stock or commodity. 12. in a motor vehicle, to turn a corner, especially at speed. −adj. 13. situated at a junction of two roads. 14. made to be fitted or used in a corner. −phr. 15. **cut corners**, **a.** to take short cuts habitually. **b.** to bypass an official procedure, or the like.

cornet /'kɔnət/ n. a brass wind instrument of the trumpet class, with valves or pistons.

cornflour /'kɔnflaʊə/ n. a starchy flour made from maize, rice, or other grain, used as a thickening agent in cookery.

cornice /'kɔnəs/ n. the moulding or mouldings between the walls and ceiling of a room.

cornucopia /ˌkɔnjə'koupiə/ n. an overflowing supply of anything.

corny /'kɔni/ adj. (**-nier**, **-niest**) Colloq. 1. lacking subtlety: a corny joke. 2. sentimental; mawkish and of poor quality.

corollary /kə'rɒləri/ n. (pl. **-ries**) a natural consequence or result.

corona /kə'roʊnə/ n. (pl. **-nas** or **-nae** /-ni/) a white or coloured circle of light seen round a luminous body. −**coronal**, adj.

coronary /'kɒrənri/ adj. 1. relating to the arteries which supply the heart tissues. −n. 2. a heart attack.

coronation /ˌkɒrə'neɪʃən/ n. the act or ceremony of investing a king, etc., with a crown.

coronavirus /kə'roʊnəvaɪrəs/ n. 1. a virus affecting mammals, the cause in humans of the common cold, but, in other animals, of respiratory and intestinal disorders which can be fatal. 2. → **COVID-19**.

coroner /'kɒrənə/ n. an officer, as of a county or municipality, whose chief function is to investigate by inquest (often before a **coroner's jury**) any death not clearly due to natural causes. −**coronial**, adj.

coronet /'kɒrənət, kɒrə'nɛt/ n. a small or inferior crown.

corpora /'kɔpərə/ n. a plural of **corpus**.

corporal[1] /'kɔpərəl/ adj. of the human body; bodily; physical.

corporal[2] /'kɔprəl/ n. a junior officer in the army or air force.

corporal punishment n. any punishment that causes pain or injury to the body, such as caning or smacking.

corporate /'kɔpərət, -prət/ adj. 1. forming a corporation. 2. of a corporation. 3. relating to a united body, as of persons.

corporate raider n. someone who purchases large blocks of a company's shares, hoping to profit by their increase in value when the company reacts by attempting to secure control.

corporation /ˌkɔpə'reɪʃən/ n. a type of organisation, created by law or under authority of law, having a continuous existence irrespective of that of its members, and powers and liabilities distinct from those of its members.

corporeal /kə'pɔriəl/ adj. of the nature of the physical body; bodily.

corps /kɔ/ n. (pl. **corps** /kɔz/) a group of persons associated or acting together.

corpse /'kɔps/ n. a dead body, usually of a human being.

corpulent /'kɔpjələnt/ adj. stout; fat.

corpus /'kɔpəs/ n. (pl. **-puses** or **-pora** /-pərə/) 1. the body of a human or animal. 2. a large or complete collection of writings, laws, etc.

corpuscle /'kɔpəsəl/ n. Physiol. one of the minute bodies which form a constituent of the blood.

corpus delicti /ˌkɔpəs də'lɪktaɪ/ n. the body of essential facts constituting a criminal offence.

corral /kɒ'ral/ n. 1. a pen or enclosure for horses, cattle, etc. −v.t. (**-ralled**, **-ralling**) 2. to confine in, or as in, a corral.

correct /kə'rɛkt/ v.t. 1. to set right; remove the errors or faults of. 2. to point out or mark the errors in. 3. to counteract the operation or effect of (something hurtful). −adj. 4. conforming to fact or truth; free from error; accurate. **5.** in accordance with an acknowledged or accepted standard; proper. –**correction**, n. –**corrective**, adj.

correctional centre n. a prison, usually classified as minimum, medium or maximum security.

correlation /kɒrəˈleiʃən/ n. **1.** mutual relation of two or more things, parts, etc. **2.** *Statistics* the degree of relationship of two attributes or measurements on the same group of elements. –**correlate**, v. –**correlative**, adj.

correspond /kɒrəˈspɒnd/ v.i. **1.** (oft. fol. by *with* or *to*) to be in agreement or conformity. **2.** to be similar or analogous. **3.** to communicate by exchange of letters.

correspondence /kɒrəˈspɒndəns/ n. **1.** the act or fact of corresponding. **2.** letters that pass between correspondents.

correspondent /kɒrəˈspɒndənt/ n. **1.** someone who communicates by letters. **2.** someone employed to contribute news, etc., regularly from a distant place. **3.** a thing that corresponds to something else. –adj. **4.** corresponding; having a relation of correspondence.

corridor /ˈkɒrədɔː/ n. a gallery or passage connecting parts of a building.

corrigendum /kɒrəˈdʒɛndəm/ n. (pl. -**genda** /-dʒɛndə/) an error to be corrected, especially an error in print.

corroborate /kəˈrɒbəreit/ v.t. to make more certain; confirm. –**corroboration**, n. –**corroborative**, adj.

corroboree /kəˈrɒbəri/ n. an Aboriginal assembly of sacred, festive, or warlike character.

corrode /kəˈroʊd/ to eat away gradually as by chemical action. –**corrosion**, n. –**corrosive**, n., adj.

corrugate /ˈkɒrəgeit/ v.t. to draw or bend into folds or alternate furrows and ridges. –**corrugation**, n.

corrupt /kəˈrʌpt/ adj. **1.** guilty of dishonesty, especially involving bribery. **2.** made bad by errors or alterations, as a text. **3.** *Computers* (of data or programs) damaged by errors or electrical interference. –v.t. **4.** to destroy the integrity of. **5.** to lower morally; pervert. –**corruption**, n.

corsage /kɔˈsaʒ/ n. a small bouquet worn on the clothes.

corset /ˈkɔːsət/ n. (oft. pl.) a shaped, close-fitting undergarment worn to give shape and support to the body; stays.

cortege /kɔˈteʒ, -ˈteɪʒ/ n. a train of attendants; retinue.

cortex /ˈkɔːtɛks/ n. (pl. **cortices** /ˈkɔːtəsiz/) the layer of grey matter around the brain. –**cortical**, adj.

cortisone /ˈkɔːtəzoʊn/ n. a hormone used in treating shock, inflammation, arthritic disease, etc.

corvette /kɔˈvɛt/ n. a small, lightly armed, fast ship.

cosh /kɒʃ/ n. any instrument, usually flexible, used as a bludgeon.

cosmeceutical /kɒzməˈsjutɪkəl/ n. a pharmaceutical product which has cosmetic benefits.

cosmetic /kɒzˈmɛtɪk/ n. **1.** a preparation for beautifying the complexion, skin, etc. –adj. **2.** serving to beautify. **3.** designed to effect a superficial alteration while keeping the basis unchanged.

cosmo- a word element representing **cosmos**.

cosmonaut /ˈkɒzmənɔːt/ n. → **astronaut**.

cosmopolitan /kɒzməˈpɒlətn/ adj. **1.** belonging to all parts of the world. **2.** free from local, provincial, or national ideas, prejudices, or attachments.

cosmos /ˈkɒzmɒs/ n. **1.** the physical universe. **2.** a complete and harmonious system. –**cosmic**, adj.

cosset /ˈkɒsət/ v.t. to pamper; coddle.

cossie /ˈkɒzi/ n. *Colloq.* → **swimming costume**. Also, **cozzie**.

cost /kɒst/ n. **1.** the price paid to acquire, produce, accomplish, or maintain anything. **2.** outlay or expenditure of money, time, labour, trouble, etc. **3.** (pl.) *Law* the sums which the successful party is usually entitled to recover for reimbursement of particular expenses incurred in the litigation. –v.t. (**cost** or, for def. 5 **costed**, **costing**) **4.** to require the expenditure of (money, time, labour, etc.). **5.** to estimate or determine the cost of.

costal /ˈkɒstl/ adj. relating to the ribs or the side of the body.

cost-benefit analysis n. the study of a project's financial viability by comparing its cost to its actual or expected returns or benefits.

cost-effective /ˈkɒst-əˌfɛktɪv/ adj. offering profits deemed to be satisfactory in view of the costs involved. –**cost-effectively**, adv. –**cost-effectiveness**, n.

costly /ˈkɒstli/ adj. (**-lier, -liest**) costing much; of great price or value.

costo- a word element meaning 'rib'.

cost of living n. the average retail prices of food, clothing, and other necessities paid by a person, family, etc., in order to live at their usual standard.

cost-plus /kɒst-ˈplʌs/ n. the cost of production plus an agreed rate of profit (often used as a basis of payment in government contracts).

cost price n. **1.** the price at which a merchant buys goods for resale. **2.** the cost of production.

costume /ˈkɒstʃum/ n. the style of dress, especially that peculiar to a nation, class, or period.

cosy /ˈkoʊzi/ adj. (**-sier, -siest**) snug; comfortable. Also, *US*, **cozy**.

cot /kɒt/ n. a child's bed with enclosed sides.

cot death n. the sudden and apparently inexplicable death of a child while sleeping. See **sudden infant death syndrome**.

cote /koʊt/ n. a shelter for doves, pigeons, sheep, etc.

coterie /ˈkoʊtəri/ n. a clique.

cottage /ˈkɒtɪdʒ/ n. a small bungalow.

cottage cheese n. a kind of soft unripened white cheese.

cotton /ˈkɒtn/ n. **1.** the soft, white, downy fibres of a certain plant, used in making fabrics, thread, etc. **2.** a plant yielding cotton. **3.** cloth, thread, etc., made of cotton. –phr. **4. cotton on (to)**, *Colloq.* to understand.

cottonwool /ˈkɒtnˈwʊl/ n. raw cotton for surgical dressings and toilet purposes.

couch[1] /kaʊtʃ/ n. **1.** a seat for two to four people, with a back and sometimes armrests.

2. a similar piece of upholstered furniture, without a back but with a headrest, as used by doctors for their patients. *–v.t.* **3.** to arrange or frame (words, a sentence, etc.); put into words; express.

couch² /kutʃ/ *n.* any of various grasses popular as lawn grass.

couch surfing *n.* → **sofa surfing**.

cougar /'kugə/ *n.* → **puma**.

cough /kɒf/ *v.i.* **1.** to expel the air from the lungs suddenly and with a characteristic noise. *–n.* **2.** the act or sound of coughing.

could /kʊd/ *v.* past tense of **can¹**.

coulomb /'kulɒm/ *n.* the derived SI unit of electric charge. *Symbol:* C

council /'kaʊnsəl/ *n.* **1.** an assembly of persons convened or appointed for consultation, deliberation, or advice. **2.** the local administrative body of a city, municipality, or shire. **–councillor**, *n.*

counsel /'kaʊnsəl/ *n.* **1.** advice. **2.** interchange of opinions as to future procedure; consultation; deliberation. **3.** the barrister or barristers engaged in the direction of a cause in court; a legal adviser. *–v.t.* (**-selled, -selling**) **4.** to give counsel to; advise. **–counsellor**, *n.*

count¹ /kaʊnt/ *v.t.* **1.** to check over one by one (the individuals of a collection) in order to ascertain their total number; enumerate. **2.** to include in a reckoning; take into account. **3.** to reckon to the credit of another; ascribe; impute. **4.** to esteem; consider. *–v.i.* **5.** to count the items of a collection one by one in order to know the total. **6.** (fol. by *on* or *upon*) to depend or rely. **7.** to be accounted or worth. **8.** to enter into consideration. *–n.* **9.** the act of counting. **10.** the number representing the result of a process of counting; the total number. **11.** *Law.* a distinct charge or cause of action in a declaration or indictment. **12.** regard; notice.

count² /kaʊnt/ *n.* (in some European countries) a nobleman corresponding in rank to the English earl. **–countess**, *fem. n.*

countenance /'kaʊntənəns/ *n.* **1.** aspect; appearance, especially the look or expression of the face. **2.** appearance of favour; encouragement; moral support. *–v.t.* (**-anced, -ancing**) **3.** to give countenance or show favour to; encourage; support. **4.** to tolerate; permit.

counter¹ /'kaʊntə/ *n.* **1.** a table or board on which money is counted, business is transacted, or goods are laid for examination. **2.** (in a cafe, restaurant or hotel) a long, narrow table, shelf, bar, etc., at which customers eat. **3.** anything used in keeping account.

counter² /'kaʊntə/ *adv.* **1.** in the wrong way; contrary to the right course; in the reverse direction. *–adj.* **2.** opposite; opposed; contrary. *–n.* **3.** that which is opposite or contrary to something else. *–v.t.* **4.** to go counter to; oppose. **5.** to meet or answer (a move, blow, etc.) by another in return. *–v.i.* **6.** to make a counter or opposing move.

counteract /kaʊntər'ækt/ *v.t.* to act in opposition to.

counterclaim /'kaʊntəkleɪm/ *n.* a claim set up against another claim.

counterfeit /'kaʊntəfət, -fɪt/ *adj.* **1.** not genuine. *–n.* **2.** an imitation designed to pass as an original; a forgery.

counterintuitive /kaʊntərɪn'tjuətɪv/ *adj.* contrary to what one would normally think or expect. Also, **counter-intuitive**. **–counterintuitively**, *adv.* **–counterintuitiveness**, *n.*

countermand /kaʊntə'mænd, -'mand/ *v.t.* to revoke (a command, order, etc.).

counterpart /'kaʊntəpat/ *n.* **1.** a copy; duplicate. **2.** a part that answers to another, as each part of a document executed in duplicate. **3.** one of two parts which fit each other; a thing that complements something else.

countersign /'kaʊntəsaɪn/ *v.t.* to sign (a document) in addition to another signature, especially in confirmation or authentication.

counterterrorism /kaʊntə'terərɪzəm/ *n.* **1.** measures taken by a government, etc., to prevent or control terrorism. **2.** an act of reprisal by a government, etc., against terrorism. **–counterterrorist**, *adj., n.*

countertop /'kaʊntətɒp/ *n.* the top of kitchen waist-high cupboards serving as a counter, usually surfaced with laminate, stone, stainless steel, etc., to provide a non-staining durable surface.

countless /'kaʊntləs/ *adj.* too many to count.

country /'kʌntri/ *n.* (pl. **-tries**) **1. a.** a relatively large area of land occupied by a group of people organised under a single, usually independent, government; nation; state; land: *the countries of Asia*; *to visit a foreign country*. **b.** the people forming such a group: *the whole country rebelled*. **2.** the rural districts (as opposed to towns or cities). **3.** land, especially with reference to its character, quality, or use, or its association with a person or people: *good grazing country*; *Shakespeare country*.

country and western *n.* a type of music consisting mainly of rural songs accompanied by a stringed instrument. Also, **country music**.

county /'kaʊnti/ *n.* (pl. **-ties**) **1.** (in NSW) an area of land delineated for administrative convenience or some specific purpose such as development planning or the supply of electricity. **2.** (in some countries) a larger division, as for purposes of local administration.

coup /ku/ *n.* (pl. **coups** /kuz/) **1.** an unexpected and successfully executed stratagem; masterstroke. **2.** → **coup d'état**.

coup d'état /ku deɪ'ta/ *n.* (pl. **coups d'état** /ku deɪ'ta/) a sudden and decisive measure in politics, especially one effecting a change of government illegally or by force.

coupe¹ /kup, 'kupeɪ/ *n.* **1.** a chilled dessert consisting of fruit and ice cream. **2.** a stemmed glass in which such a dessert may be served. **3.** a shallow, bowl-shaped dish.

coupe² /kup/ *n.* a single defined area of forest, usually less than 50 hectares, from which trees are, or will be, harvested for logs or woodchips.

coupé /'kupeɪ/ *n.* an enclosed two-door car. Also, *Chiefly US,* **coupe**.

couple /'kʌpəl/ *n.* **1.** a combination of two; a pair. **2.** two of the same sort connected or considered together. **3.** a small number; a few: *a couple of things to do.*

coupon /'kupɒn/ *n.* **1.** a separable part of a certificate, ticket, advertisement, etc., entitling the holder to something. **2.** one of a number of such parts calling for periodical payments on a bond. **3.** a separate ticket or the like, for a similar purpose. **4.** a printed entry form for football pools, newspaper competitions, etc.

courage /'kʌrɪdʒ/ n. bravery. **–courageous**, adj. **–courageously**, adv.

courgette /kɔ'ʒɛt/ n. → **zucchini**.

courier /'kʊriə/ n. a messenger.

course /kɔs/ n. **1.** onward movement. **2.** the path, route or channel along which anything moves. **3.** customary manner of procedure. **4.** a particular manner of proceeding. **5.** a systematised or prescribed series. **6.** a part of a meal served at one time. –v.t. **7.** to run; move swiftly; race. –phr. **8. of course**, certainly; obviously.

court /kɔt/ n. **1.** an open space wholly or partly enclosed by a wall, buildings, etc. **2.** a smooth, level area on which to play tennis, netball, etc. **3.** the residence of a sovereign or other high dignitary; palace. **4.** the collective body of persons forming a sovereign's retinue. **5.** assiduous attention directed to gain favour, affection, etc. **6.** Law **a.** a place where justice is administered. **b.** a judicial tribunal duly constituted for the hearing and determination of cases. **c.** the judge or judges who sit in a court. **7.** the body of qualified members of a corporation, council, board, etc. –v.t. **8.** to endeavour to win the favour of: *the politician was courting the media.*

courteous /'kɜtiəs/ adj. having or showing good manners; polite.

courtesan /'kɔtəzæn/ n. **1.** a court mistress. **2.** any female prostitute.

courtesy /'kɜtəsi/ n. (pl. **-sies**) **1.** excellence of manners or behaviour; politeness. **2.** a courteous act or expression.

courtly /'kɔtli/ adj. (**-lier, -liest**) polite; elegant; refined.

court martial n. (pl. **courts martial** or **court martials**) a court consisting of naval, army, or air force officers appointed by a commander to try charges of offence against martial law. **–court-martial**, v.

courtroom /'kɔtrum/ n. a room in which the sessions of a law court are held.

courtship /'kɔtʃɪp/ n. **1.** the seeking of a person's affections, especially with a view to marriage. **2.** solicitation, especially of favours. **3.** distinctive animal behaviour seen before and during mating.

courtyard /'kɔtjad/ n. a space enclosed by walls.

couscous /'kʊskʊs/ n. small grains consisting largely of semolina but with some flour and salt added.

cousin /'kʌzən/ n. the son or daughter of an uncle or aunt.

couturier /ku'turiə/ n. a person who designs, makes, and sells fashionable clothes for women.

cove /koʊv/ n. a small indentation or recess in the shoreline of a sea, lake, or river.

coven /'kʌvən/ n. a gathering of witches.

covenant /'kʌvənənt/ n. **1.** an agreement; a contract. –v.i. **2.** to enter into a covenant.

cover /'kʌvə/ v.t. **1.** to put something over or upon as for protection or concealment. **2.** to extend over; occupy the surface of. **3.** to shelter; protect; serve as a defence to. **4.** to hide from view; screen. **5.** to spread thickly the surface of. **6.** to include; comprise; provide for; take in. **7.** to suffice to meet (a charge, expense, etc.). **8.** to act as reporter of (occurrences, performances, etc.), as for a newspaper, etc. **9.** to pass or travel over. –v.i. **10.** to serve as substitute for someone who is absent. –n. **11.** that which covers. **12.** protection; shelter; concealment. **13.** adequate insurance against risk as loss, damage, etc. **14.** Finance funds to cover liability or secure against risk of loss.

covering /'kʌvərɪŋ/ n. Commerce the operation of buying securities, etc., that one has sold short, in order to return them to the person from whom they were borrowed.

cover note n. a document given by an insurance company or agent to the insured to provide temporary cover until a policy is issued.

covert /'kʌvət, 'koʊvət/ adj. **1.** covered; sheltered. **2.** concealed; secret; disguised.

covet /'kʌvət/ v.t. to desire (another's possessions) inordinately.

COVID-19 /koʊvəd-naɪn'tin, kɒvəd-/ n. a highly contagious respiratory disease caused by the coronavirus, SARS-CoV-2. Also, **COVID**, **coronavirus**.

cow¹ /kaʊ/ n. **1.** a large domesticated bovine kept for dairy and beef farming. **2.** the female of a bovine animal. **3.** the female of various other large animals, as the elephant, whale, etc. **4.** Colloq. an ugly or bad-tempered woman.

cow² /kaʊ/ v.t. to intimidate.

coward /'kaʊəd/ n. someone who lacks courage to meet danger or difficulty. **–cowardice**, n. **–cowardly**, adj.

cowboy /'kaʊbɔɪ/ n. a person employed, especially in the US, to herd cattle, usually on horseback.

cower /'kaʊə/ v.i. to crouch in fear or shame.

cowlick /'kaʊlɪk/ n. a tuft of hair turned up, usually over the forehead.

cowry /'kaʊri/ n. (pl. **-ries**) a glossy, tropical shell. Also, **cowrie**.

coxswain /'kɒksən, -sweɪn/ n. the person at the helm who steers a boat. Also, **cox**.

coy /kɔɪ/ adj. affectedly shy or reserved.

coyote /kɔɪ'oʊti, kaɪ'oʊti/ n. a wild dog of North and Central America.

cozen /'kʌzən/ v.t. to cheat; deceive.

C++ /si plʌs 'plʌs/ n. a computer language based on C, with features enabling object-oriented software development.

CPR /si pi 'a/ n. cardiopulmonary resuscitation; an emergency life-support procedure using a combination of expired air resuscitation and external heart massage.

CPU /si pi 'ju/ n. that section of a computer which controls arithmetic, logical and control functions. Also, **central processor unit**.

crab¹ /kræb/ n. a crustacean having a short, broad, more or less flattened body.

crab² /kræb/ n. an ill-tempered or grouchy person.

crabapple /'kræbæpəl/ n. **1.** a small, sour wild apple. **2.** any of various cultivated species and varieties of apple, small, sour, and astringent or slightly bitter, used for making jelly and preserves. **3.** any tree bearing such fruit.

crack /kræk/ v.i. **1.** to make a sudden, sharp sound in, or as in, breaking; snap, as a whip.

2. to break with a sudden, sharp sound. **3.** to break without complete separation of parts; become fissured. *–v.t.* **4.** to break with a sudden sharp sound. **5.** *Colloq.* to break into (a safe, vault, etc.). **6.** to utter or tell, as a joke. *–n.* **7.** a sudden, sharp noise, as of something breaking. **8.** a break without complete separation of parts; a fissure; a flaw. **9.** a slight opening, as one between door and doorpost. **10. → crack cocaine. 11.** *Colloq.* a try; an opportunity or chance. *–phr.* **12. crack down on,** *Colloq.* to take severe measures, especially in enforcing discipline. **13. crack up,** to suffer a physical, mental or moral breakdown.

crack cocaine *n.* a very pure form of cocaine sold in pellet-sized crystalline pieces and prepared with other ingredients for smoking. Also, **crack.**

cracker /ˈkrækə/ *n.* **1.** a thin, crisp biscuit. **2.** a kind of firework which explodes with a loud report.

crackle /ˈkrækəl/ *v.i.* **1.** to make slight, sudden, sharp noises, rapidly repeated. *–v.t.* **2.** to cause to crackle. *–n.* **3.** a crackling noise.

crackling /ˈkræklɪŋ/ *n.* **1.** the making of slight cracking sounds rapidly repeated. **2.** the crisp browned skin or rind of roast pork.

-cracy a noun termination meaning 'rule', 'government', 'governing body'.

cradle /ˈkreɪdl/ *n.* **1.** a little bed or cot for an infant, usually built on rockers. **2.** the place where anything is nurtured during its early existence. **3.** any of various contrivances similar to a child's cradle. *–v.t.* **4.** to place or rock in or as in a cradle; hold tenderly.

craft /kraft/ *n.* **1.** skill; ingenuity; dexterity. **2.** cunning; deceit; guile. **3.** an art, trade, or occupation requiring special skill, especially manual skill; a handicraft. **4.** (*construed as pl.*) boats, ships, and vessels collectively. **–craftsman,** *n.*

crafty /ˈkrafti/ *adj.* (**-tier, -tiest**) cunning, deceitful; sly.

crag /kræg/ *n.* a steep, rugged rock.

craggy /ˈkrægi/ *adj.* (**-gier, -giest**) rugged; rough.

cram /kræm/ *v.t.* (**crammed, cramming**) **1.** to fill (something) by force with more than it can conveniently hold. **2.** *Colloq.* to get a knowledge of (a subject) by memorising information quickly.

cramp¹ /kræmp/ *n.* **1.** a sudden involuntary, persistent contraction of a muscle. *–v.t.* **2.** to affect with, or as with, a cramp.

cramp² /kræmp/ *n.* **1.** a small metal bar with bent ends, for holding together planks, masonry, etc. *–v.t.* **2.** to confine narrowly; restrict; restrain; hamper.

cramped /kræmpt/ *adj.* contracted; narrow.

cranberry /ˈkrænberi, -bri/ *n.* (*pl.* **-ries**) a sour red berry used for a sauce, jelly, etc.

crane /kreɪn/ *n.* **1.** any of a group of large wading birds. **2.** a device with a hoisting tackle, for lifting and moving heavy weights. *–v.t.* **3.** to hoist, lower, or move by or as by a crane. **4.** to stretch (the neck) as a crane does.

cranio- a combining form of **cranium.** Also, **crani-.**

cranium /ˈkreɪniəm/ *n.* (*pl.* **-nia** /-niə/) the skull of a vertebrate.

crank¹ /kræŋk/ *n.* **1.** *Machinery* a device for communicating motion, or for changing rotary motion into reciprocating motion, or vice versa. *–v.t.* **2.** to cause (a shaft) to revolve by applying force to a crank. *–phr.* **3. crank up, a.** to get (something) started or operating smoothly. **b.** to increase; take to a higher or more intense level.

crank² /kræŋk/ *Colloq. –n.* **1.** an eccentric person. *–adj.* **2.** odd, false or phoney.

crankshaft /ˈkræŋkʃaft/ *n.* a shaft driving or driven by a crank.

cranky /ˈkræŋki/ *adj.* (**-kier, -kiest**) ill-tempered; cross.

cranny /ˈkræni/ *n.* (*pl.* **-nies**) a small, narrow opening (in a wall, rock, etc.).

crap /kræp/ *n. Colloq.* **1.** excrement. **2.** nonsense; rubbish. *–adj.* **3.** of poor quality: *a crap movie.* **4.** unpleasant: *a crap day.*

craps /kræps/ *n.* a gambling game played with two dice.

crash /kræʃ/ *v.t.* **1.** to force or impel with violence and noise. **2.** to damage (a car, aircraft, etc.) in a collision. **3.** to break (something) into pieces violently and noisily; shatter. *–v.i.* **4.** to break or fall to pieces with noise. **5.** to make a loud, clattering noise as of something dashed to pieces. **6.** to collapse or fail suddenly, as a financial enterprise. **7.** of an aircraft, to fall to the ground. **8.** of a computer system, to shut down because of a fault. *–n.* **9.** a breaking or falling to pieces with loud noise. **10.** the shock of collision and breaking. **11.** the shutting down of a computer system because of a fault. **12.** a sudden collapse of a financial enterprise or the like. **13.** a sudden loud noise. **14.** the act of crashing.

crash tackle *n.* **1.** *Rugby Football* a tactic in which the player with the ball runs directly at the opposition line, attempting to draw the tackle from the opposing players before offloading the ball to a teammate who can run through the gaps created in the line. **2.** any forceful direct tackle which fells the person tackled.

crash-tackle *v.t.* to bring (someone) down by tackling them forcefully.

crass /kræs/ *adj.* gross; stupid.

-crat a noun termination meaning 'ruler', 'member of a ruling body', 'advocate of a particular form of rule'. Compare **-cracy.**

crate /kreɪt/ *n.* a box or framework, usually of wooden slats, for packing and transporting fruit, furniture, etc.

crater /ˈkreɪtə/ *n.* the cup-shaped depression or cavity marking the orifice of a volcano.

cravat /krəˈvæt/ *n.* a scarf worn round the neck as a tie.

crave /kreɪv/ *v.t.* **1.** to long for or desire eagerly. **2.** to need greatly; require. **3.** to ask earnestly for (something); beg for.

craven /ˈkreɪvən/ *adj.* cowardly.

craw /krɔ/ *n.* **1.** the crop of a bird or insect. **2.** the stomach of an animal.

crawl /krɔl/ *v.i.* **1.** to move by dragging the body along the ground, as a worm, or on the hands and knees, as a young child. **2.** to progress slowly, laboriously, or timorously. **3.** to behave abjectly and obsequiously. **4.** to be, or feel as if, overrun with crawling things. *–n.*

5. the act of crawling; a slow, crawling motion. **6.** → **freestyle**.

crayfish /'kreɪfɪʃ/ n. (pl. **-fish** or **-fishes**) any of various freshwater crustaceans.

crayon /'kreɪɒn/ n. **1.** a pointed stick or pencil of coloured wax, chalk, etc., used for drawing. **2.** a drawing in crayons.

craze /kreɪz/ v.t. **1.** to make small cracks on the surface of (pottery, etc.). –n. **2.** a mania; a popular fashion, etc., usually short-lived; a rage. **3.** insanity; an insane condition.

crazy /'kreɪzi/ adj. (**-zier, -ziest**) **1.** demented; mad. **2.** eccentric; bizarre; unusual. **3.** unrealistic; impractical.

creak /krik/ v.i. **1.** to make a sharp, harsh, grating, or squeaking sound. **2.** to move with creaking. –n. **3.** a creaking sound.

cream /krim/ n. **1.** the fatty part of milk, which rises to the surface when the liquid is allowed to stand. **2.** any creamlike substance, especially various cosmetics. **3.** the best part of anything. **4.** yellowish white; light tint of yellow or buff. –v.t. **5.** to work (butter and sugar, etc.) to a smooth, creamy mass. **6.** to add cream to (coffee, or the like).

crease /kris/ n. **1.** a line or mark produced in anything by folding. **2.** Cricket one of three lines near the wicket marking the limits of movement of the bowler or the person batting. –v.t. **3.** to make a crease or creases in or on; wrinkle.

create /kri'eɪt/ v.t. **1.** to bring into being; cause to exist; produce. **2.** to evolve from one's own thought or imagination. **3.** to make by investing with new character or functions; constitute; appoint. **–creator**, n.

creation /kri'eɪʃən/ n. **1.** the act of creating. **2.** that which is created. **3.** the world; universe. **4.** an original work, especially of the imaginative faculty.

creative /kri'eɪtɪv/ adj. **1.** having the quality or power of creating. **2.** resulting from originality of thought or expression.

creative commons pl. n. a website where the owners of copyright material make such material available to the public with partial or no restrictions, thus enabling greater general access to information.

creature /'kritʃə/ n. anything created, especially an animate being.

creche /kreɪʃ, krɛʃ/ n. an establishment for the minding of babies or young children.

credence /'kridns/ n. **1.** belief. **2.** something giving a claim to belief or confidence.

credential /krə'dɛnʃəl/ n. **1.** anything which is the basis for the belief or trust of others in a person's abilities, authority, etc. **2.** (usu. pl.) a letter or other testimonial attesting the bearer's right to confidence or authority.

credible /'krɛdəbəl/ adj. **1.** capable of being believed; believable. **2.** worthy of belief or confidence; trustworthy.

credit /'krɛdɪt/ n. **1.** commendation or honour given for some action, quality, etc. **2.** influence or authority resulting from the confidence of others or from one's reputation. **3.** trustworthiness; credibility. **4.** (pl.) a list, appearing at the beginning or end of a film or television program, which shows the names of those who have been associated with its production.

5. the practice of allowing time for payment for goods, etc., obtained on trust. **6.** anything valuable standing on the credit side of an account. **7.** the balance in one's favour in an account. **8.** Bookkeeping **a.** the acknowledgement of payment or value received, in an account by an entry on the right-hand side. **b.** the side (right-hand) of an account on which such entries are made (opposed to debit). **c.** an entry, or the total shown, on the credit side. **9.** any deposit or sum against which one may draw. –v.t. **10.** to believe; put confidence in. **11.** to give reputation or honour to. **12.** to ascribe (something) to a person, etc. **13. a.** Bookkeeping to enter upon the credit side of an account; give credit for or to. **b.** to give the benefit of such an entry to (a person, etc.). –phr. **14. give credit to**, to believe. **15. on credit**, by deferred payment.

creditable /'krɛdətəbəl/ adj. bringing credit, honour, reputation, or esteem.

credit agency n. an organisation that investigates on behalf of a client the credit worthiness of the client's prospective customers.

credit card n. a card which identifies the holder as entitled to obtain without payment of cash, goods, food, services, etc., which are then charged to the holder's account.

creditor /'krɛdətə/ n. one to whom money is due (opposed to debtor).

credit rating n. an estimation of the extent to which a customer can be granted credit.

credit squeeze n. **1.** restriction by a government of the amount of credit available to borrowers. **2.** the period during which the restrictions are in operation.

credit union n. a financial organisation for receiving and lending money, usually formed by workers in some industry or at some place of employment.

credulous /'krɛdʒələs/ adj. ready or disposed to believe, especially on weak or insufficient evidence. **–credulity**, n.

creed /krid/ n. **1.** any system of belief or of opinion. **2.** any formula of religious belief, as of a denomination.

creek /krik/ n. **1.** a small stream. –phr. **2. up the creek** (**without a paddle**), Colloq. in a predicament; in trouble.

creep /krip/ v.i. (**crept, creeping**) **1.** to move with the body close to the ground, as a reptile or an insect. **2.** to move slowly, imperceptibly, or stealthily. **3.** to have a sensation as of something creeping over the skin. –n. **4.** the act of creeping. **5.** Colloq. an unpleasant, obnoxious, or insignificant person. –phr. **6. the creeps**, Colloq. a sensation as of something creeping over the skin, usually as a result of feelings of fear or horror.

creeper /'kripə/ n. Bot. a plant which grows upon or just beneath the surface of the ground, or other surface.

cremate /krə'meɪt/ v.t. to reduce (a corpse) to ashes by fire. **–cremation**, n.

crematorium /krɛmə'tɔriəm/ n. an establishment for cremating dead bodies.

crenellated /'krɛnəleɪtəd/ adj. having battlements. **–crenellation**, n.

creole /'krioʊl/ n. a language which has changed from a pidgin to a community's first language.

crepe /kreɪp/ n. **1.** a thin, light fabric with a finely crinkled or ridged surface. **2.** Also, **crepe paper**. thin paper wrinkled to resemble crepe. **3.** a thin pancake.

crept /krept/ v. past tense and past participle of **creep**.

crescendo /krə'ʃendoʊ/ n. (pl. **-dos** /-doʊz/) a gradual increase in force or loudness.

crescent /'kresənt, 'krezənt/ n. the shape of the moon in its first or last quarter.

cress /kres/ n. any of various plants used for salad and as a garnish.

crest /krest/ n. **1.** a tuft or other natural growth of the top of an animal's head, as the comb of a cock. **2.** anything resembling or suggesting such a tuft. **3.** the head or top of anything. **4.** Heraldry a figure or design used as a family emblem.

crestfallen /'krestfɔlən/ adj. dejected; depressed.

cretin /'kretn/ n. a fool; a stupid person. **–cretinous**, adj.

crevasse /krə'væs/ n. a fissure or deep cleft in the ice of a glacier.

crevice /'krevəs/ n. a crack forming an opening.

crew[1] /kru/ n. a group of persons engaged upon a particular work; a gang.

crew[2] /kru/ v. past tense of **crow**[2].

crew cut n. a very closely cropped haircut.

crib /krɪb/ n. **1.** a child's bed, usually decorated. **2. a.** a book which gives a summary of information, sometimes used as a study aid: *she bought a crib on Jane Eyre the day before the literature exam.* **b.** a translation or other illicit aid used by students. –v.t. (**cribbed, cribbing**) **3.** to confine in, or as in, a crib. **4.** Colloq. to steal or plagiarise (a piece of writing, etc.).

cribbage /'krɪbɪdʒ/ n. a card game.

crick /krɪk/ n. a sharp, painful spasm of the muscles, as of the neck or back, making it difficult to move the part.

cricket[1] /'krɪkət/ n. any of the insects noted for the ability of the males to produce shrill sounds by friction of their leathery forewings.

cricket[2] /'krɪkət/ n. **1.** an outdoor game played with ball, bats, and wickets, by two sides of eleven players each. **2.** Colloq. fair play.

crime /kraɪm/ n. an act committed or an omission of duty, injurious to the public welfare, for which punishment is prescribed by law.

criminal /'krɪmənəl/ adj. **1.** of or relating to crime or its punishment. **2.** of the nature of or involving crime. –n. **3.** a person guilty or convicted of a crime.

criminalise /'krɪmənəlaɪz/ v.t. to make into a criminal offence. Also, **criminalize**. **–criminalisation**, n.

criminology /ˌkrɪmə'nɒlədʒi/ n. the science dealing with the causes and treatment of crimes and criminals. **–criminologist**, n.

crimp /krɪmp/ v.t. to press into small regular folds.

crimson /'krɪmzən/ adj. deep purplish red.

cringe /krɪndʒ/ v.i. (**cringed, cringing**) **1.** to shrink, bend, or crouch, especially from fear or servility; cower. **2.** to feel embarrassment or discomfort, as when confronted by inappropriate or distasteful social behaviour.

crinkle /'krɪŋkəl/ v.i. to wrinkle; ripple.

crinoline /'krɪnələn/ n. a petticoat made of stiff material, formerly worn by women under a full skirt.

cripple /'krɪpəl/ n. **1.** someone who is partially or wholly deprived of the use of one or more limbs; a lame person. –v.t. **2.** to disable; impair. **–crippled**, adj. **–crippling**, adj.

crisis /'kraɪsəs/ n. (pl. **crises** /'kraɪsiz/) a critical time or occasion.

crisp /krɪsp/ adj. **1.** hard but easily breakable; brittle. **2.** firm and fresh. –n. **3.** → **chip** (def. 3b).

criteria /kraɪ'tɪəriə/ n. the plural of **criterion**.

criterion /kraɪ'tɪəriən/ n. (pl. **-teria** /-'tɪəriə/) an established rule or principle for testing something.

critic /'krɪtɪk/ n. **1.** a person skilled in judging the qualities or merits of some class of things, especially of literary or artistic work. **2.** someone who censures or finds fault.

critical /'krɪtɪkəl/ adj. **1.** of or relating to critics or criticism. **2.** relating to, or of the nature of, a crisis; crucial.

criticise /'krɪtəsaɪz/ v.i. **1.** to make judgements as to merits and faults. **2.** to find fault. –v.t. **3.** to judge or discuss the merits and faults of. **4.** to find fault with. Also, **criticize**. **–criticism**, n.

critique /krə'tik, krɪ-/ n. **1.** an article or essay criticising a literary or other work; a review. –v.t. (**-tiqued, -tiquing**) **2.** to review critically; evaluate.

croak /kroʊk/ v.i. **1.** to utter a low, hoarse, dismal cry, as a frog or a raven. **2.** to speak with a low, hollow voice. **3.** Colloq. to die.

crochet /'kroʊʃə, 'kroʊʃeɪ/ n. **1.** a kind of needlework done with a needle having at one end a small hook for drawing the thread or yarn into intertwined loops. –v.t., v.i. (**-cheted** /-ʃəd, -ʃeɪd/, **-cheting** /-ʃərɪŋ, -ʃeɪɪŋ/) **2.** to form by crochet.

crock /krɒk/ n. an earthen pot, jar, or other vessel.

crockery /'krɒkəri/ n. china in general, especially as for domestic use.

crocodile /'krɒkədaɪl/ n. any of several large, thick-skinned, lizard-like reptiles.

crocodile tears pl. n. a hypocritical show of sorrow.

croissant /krwʌ'sɒ/ n. a roll of leavened dough or puff pastry, shaped into a crescent and baked.

crone /kroʊn/ n. an old woman, especially one who is withered in appearance and disagreeable in manner.

crony /'kroʊni/ n. (pl. **-nies**) an intimate friend or companion.

cronyism /'kroʊniːɪzəm/ n. unfair partiality shown for one's friends, especially in political or business appointments.

crook /krʊk/ n. **1.** a bent or curved implement, piece, appendage, etc. **2.** any bend, turn, or curve. **3.** a dishonest person, especially a swindler, or thief. –adj. Colloq. **4.** sick; disabled. **5.** bad; inferior.

crooked /'krʊkəd/ adj. **1.** bent; not straight; curved. **2.** dishonest.

croon /krun/ v.i. to sing softly, especially with exaggerated feeling.

crop /krɒp/ n. **1.** the cultivated produce of the ground, as grain or fruit, while growing or when gathered. **2.** the stock or handle of a whip. **3.** a style of wearing the hair cut short. **4.** a special pouch-like enlargement of the gullet of many birds. **5.** to cut off the ends or a part of. **6.** to cut short. −v.i. (**cropped, cropping**) **7.** to bear or yield a crop or crops. **8.** (fol. by *up* or *out*) to appear unintentionally or unexpectedly.

cropper /'krɒpə/ phr. **come a cropper**, *Colloq.* to fall heavily.

croquembouche /'krɒkəmbuʃ, -buʃ/ n. an elaborate pastry in which small puff balls, usually with a vanilla cream filling, are arranged in a pyramid shape, and then covered with a thin crisp toffee crust topped with threads of spun sugar.

croquet /'krəʊkeɪ/ n. an outdoor game played by knocking wooden balls through a series of iron arches by means of mallets.

croquette /krəʊ'kɛt/ n. a small mass of minced meat, fish, etc., fried in deep fat.

cross /krɒs/ n. **1.** a structure consisting essentially of an upright and a transverse piece, upon which persons were formerly put to death. **2.** the cross as the symbol of Christianity. **3.** any burden, affliction, responsibility, etc., that one has to bear. **4.** any object, figure, or mark resembling a cross, as two intersecting lines. **5.** an opposing; thwarting. **6.** a mixing of breeds. **7.** something intermediate in character between two things. −v.t. **8.** to move, pass, or extend from one side to the other side of (a street, river, etc.). **9.** to lie or pass across; intersect. **10.** to meet and pass. **11.** to oppose openly; thwart. **12.** to mark with a cross. **13.** to put or draw (a line, etc.) across. **14.** to mark (the face of a cheque) with two vertical parallel lines with or without the words *not negotiable* written between them. **15.** to make the sign of the cross upon or over, as in devotion. −v.i. **16.** to lie or be across; intersect. **17.** to move, pass, extend from one side or place to another. **18.** to meet and pass. **19.** to interbreed. −adj. **20.** lying or passing crosswise or across each other; transverse. **21.** involving interchange; reciprocal. **22.** contrary; opposite. **23.** adverse; unfavourable. **24.** ill-humoured. −phr. **25. cross the floor**, in parliament, to vote with an opposing party.

cross- a first element of compounds, modifying the second part, meaning: **1.** going across. **2.** counter. **3.** cross-shaped.

crossbench /'krɒsbentʃ/ n. **1.** one of a set of seats, as at the houses of parliament, for those who belong neither to the government nor to opposition parties. −adj. **2.** independent. −**crossbencher**, n.

cross-country adj. **1.** directed across fields or open country; not following the main roads. −n. **2.** a running race which is routed across the country, often on difficult terrain, as opposed to one held on a prepared track. −adv. **3.** across open country.

cross-dress v.i. to adopt a manner of dress typical of the opposite sex. −**cross-dressing**, n., adj. −**cross-dresser**, n.

cross-examine v.t. to examine by questions intended to check a previous examination; examine closely or minutely.

cross-eye n. a disorder in which both eyes turn towards the nose. −**cross-eyed**, adj.

crossholding /'krɒshəʊldɪŋ/ n. among a group of allied commercial companies, the holding of shares in companies within the group, as a mutually protective device.

crossing /'krɒsɪŋ/ n. **1.** the act of someone who or that which crosses. **2.** a place where lines, tracks, etc., cross each other. **3.** a place at which a road, river, etc., may be crossed.

cross rate n. the exchange rate between two currencies, calculated by reference to a third currency, usually the US dollar.

cross-reference n. a reference from one part of a book, etc., to a word, item, etc., in another part.

cross-section n. **1.** a section made by a plane cutting anything transversely, especially at right angles to the longest axis. **2.** a typical selection.

crossword /'krɒswɜd/ n. a puzzle in which the answers to various clues must be fitted into a grid-like figure.

crotch /krɒtʃ/ n. **1.** a forked piece, part, support, etc. **2.** a forking or place of forking, as of the human body between the legs.

crotchet /'krɒtʃət/ n. *Music* a note having half the value of a minim.

crotchety /'krɒtʃəti/ adj. *Colloq.* irritable, difficult, or cross.

crouch /kraʊtʃ/ v.i. **1.** (of people) to lower the body with one or both knees bent, in any position which inclines the trunk forward. **2.** (of animals) to lie close to or on the ground with legs bent as in the position taken when about to spring.

croup /krup/ n. inflammation of the larynx, especially in children, marked by a hoarse cough and difficulty in breathing.

croupier /'krupiə/ n. an attendant who collects and pays the money at a gambling table.

crouton /'krutɒn/ n. a small piece of fried or toasted bread served in soup, etc.

crow[1] /krəʊ/ n. **1.** any of several large lustrous black birds having a harsh call. −phr. **2. as the crow flies**, in a straight line.

crow[2] /krəʊ/ v.i. (**crowed** or, *for def. 1,* **crew, crowed, crowing**) **1.** to utter the characteristic cry of a cock. **2.** to utter an inarticulate cry of pleasure, as an infant does. **3.** to exult loudly; boast.

crowbar /'krəʊba/ n. a bar of iron, for use as a lever, etc.

crowd /kraʊd/ n. **1.** a large number of persons gathered closely together; a throng. **2.** a large number of things gathered or considered together. −v.i. **3.** to gather in large numbers; throng; swarm. **4.** to press forward; advance by pushing. −v.t. **5.** to press closely together; force into a confined space. **6.** to fill to excess; fill by crowding or pressing into.

crowdfunding /'kraʊdfʌndɪŋ/ n. the obtaining of small donations from individuals contacted through social networks, as to fund a project, support a cause, etc. Also, **crowd source funding**. −**crowdfunded**, adj.

crowdsource /'kraʊdsɔs/ v. (**-sourced, -sourcing**) –v.t. **1.** to develop (software, products, etc.) by utilising the expertise and creativity of the general public via the internet. –v.i. **2.** to operate in this way. **–crowdsourcing**, n.

crowd-surfing n. an activity at a rock concert or party in which someone is held up by the main group and moved about over their heads. **–crowd-surf**, v.

crown /kraʊn/ n. **1.** a decorative covering for the head, worn as a symbol of sovereignty. **2.** the top or highest part of anything. –adj. **3.** of or relating to that which belongs to the crown (def. 7c) or acts on its behalf: *crown lease*; *crown prosecutor*. –v.t. **4.** to invest with a regal crown, or with regal dignity and power. **5.** to honour as with a crown. **6.** to surmount as with a crown; surmount as a crown does. –phr. **7. the crown**, (oft. upper case) **a.** the sovereign as head of the state. **b.** the imperial or regal power; sovereignty. **c.** the government, or governments above local government level, of a country with a constitutional monarch.

Crown land n. (sometimes lower case) land belonging to the government.

crown-of-thorns starfish n. a starfish with sharp, stinging spines, found widely in tropical waters, especially on the Great Barrier Reef, where it destroys coral.

crow's-foot /'kraʊz-fʊt/ n. (pl. **-feet**) (usu. pl.) a wrinkle at the outer corner of the eye.

crucial /'kruʃəl/ adj. involving a final and supreme decision; decisive; critical.

cruciate ligament /'kruʃiət/ n. one of two major ligaments of the knee which connect the femur to the tibia and give stability to the knee.

crucible /'krusəbəl/ n. a vessel for heating substances to high temperatures.

crucifix /'krusəfɪks/ n. a cross, especially one with the figure of Jesus crucified upon it.

crucify /'krusəfaɪ/ v.t. (**-fied, -fying**) to put to death by nailing or binding the body to a cross. **–crucifixion**, n.

crude /krud/ adj. **1.** in a raw or unprepared state; unrefined. **2.** lacking culture, refinement, tact, etc. **–crudity**, n.

crude oil n. oil as it is found in nature, usually brown or black, and often in association with natural gas which forms a cap above it and saline water which collects underneath it. Also, **crude**.

cruel /'kruəl/ adj. **1.** (of a person) liking or likely to cause pain; hard-hearted; pitiless. **2.** causing, or marked by, great pain or distress. **–cruelty**, n.

cruet /'kruət/ n. a set, on a stand, of containers for salt, pepper, etc.

cruise /kruz/ v. (**cruised, cruising**) –v.i. **1.** to sail to and fro, or from place to place. **2.** (of a car, aeroplane, etc.) to move along easily at a moderate speed. –v.t. **3.** to cruise over. –n. **4.** a voyage made by cruising.

cruise missile n. a self-propelled, air-breathing guided missile which carries a conventional or a nuclear warhead.

cruisy /'kruzi/ adj. Colloq. easy; not taxing: *a cruisy job*.

crumb /krʌm/ n. **1.** a small particle of bread, cake, etc. **2.** a small particle or portion of anything. –v.t. **3.** to dress or prepare with breadcrumbs. **4.** to break into crumbs or small fragments.

crumble /'krʌmbəl/ v.t., v.i. to break into small fragments or crumbs.

crummy /'krʌmi/ adj. (**-mier, -miest**) Colloq. very inferior, mean, or shabby.

crumpet /'krʌmpət/ n. a kind of flat round bread with small holes, usually served toasted and buttered.

crumple /'krʌmpəl/ v. –v.t. **1.** to draw or press into irregular folds; rumple; wrinkle. –v.i. **2.** to collapse; give way.

crunch /krʌntʃ/ v.t. **1.** to crush with the teeth; chew with a crushing noise. –phr. **2. the crunch**, a moment of crisis.

crunch time n. Colloq. the time when a decision or action is required.

crusade /kru'seɪd/ n. any vigorous, aggressive movement for the defence or advancement of an idea, cause, etc.

crush /krʌʃ/ v.t. **1.** to press and bruise between two hard bodies. **2.** to break into small fragments or particles, as ore, stone, etc. **3.** to force out by pressing or squeezing. **4.** to put down, overpower, or subdue completely; overwhelm. **5.** to oppress harshly. –v.i. **6.** to become crushed. **7.** to advance with crushing; press or crowd forcibly. –n. **8.** the act of crushing. **9.** the state of being crushed. **10.** a great crowd. **11.** Colloq. an infatuation.

crust /krʌst/ n. **1.** the hard outer portion of a loaf of bread, a pie, etc. **2.** any more or less hard external covering or coating.

crustacean /krʌs'teɪʃən/ n. any of a class of (chiefly marine) animals with a hard shell, as the lobsters, crabs, barnacles, etc.

crusty /'krʌsti/ adj. (**-tier, -tiest**) **1.** of the nature of or resembling a crust; having a crust. **2.** harsh; surly.

crutch /krʌtʃ/ n. **1.** a staff or support to assist a lame or infirm person in walking. **2.** the crotch of the human body. **3.** anything relied on as a comfort or support in adversity.

crux /krʌks/ n. a vital, basic, or decisive point.

cry /kraɪ/ v. (**cried, crying**) –v.i. **1.** to utter inarticulate sounds, especially of lamentation, grief, or suffering, usually with tears. **2.** to weep; shed tears, with or without sound. **3.** to call loudly; shout. –v.t. **4.** to utter or pronounce loudly; call out. –n. (pl. **cries**) **5.** the act or sound of crying. **6.** a political or party slogan. **7.** the utterance or call of an animal. –phr. **8. cry down**, to disparage; belittle. **9. cry off**, to break a promise, agreement, etc. **10. cry up**, to praise; extol.

cryo- a word element meaning 'icy cold', 'frost', 'low temperature'.

cryogenics /kraɪə'dʒɛnɪks/ n. that branch of physics concerned with the properties of materials at very low temperatures.

crypt /krɪpt/ n. a subterranean chamber or vault used as a burial place, etc.

cryptic /'krɪptɪk/ adj. hidden; secret.

crypto- a word element meaning 'hidden'.

cryptosporidium /krɪptoʊspə'rɪdiəm/ n. a protozoan which is a parasite in humans and animals, causing diarrhoea.

crystal /'krɪstl/ *n.* **1.** a clear, transparent mineral or glass resembling ice. **2.** *Chem., Mineral.* a solid body having a characteristic internal structure. **3.** Also, **crystal meth**. *Colloq.* a powdered narcotic, especially methamphetamine. –**crystalline**, *adj.*

crystallise /'krɪstəlaɪz/ *v.i., v.t.* **1.** to form into crystals. **2.** to assume or cause to assume definite or concrete form. Also, **crystallize**.

crystallo– a word element meaning 'crystal'.

crystal meth *n.* → **crystal** (def. 3).

CTP insurance /si ti 'pi/ *n.* a form of third-party insurance for drivers of motor vehicles which provides compensation for other people injured in an accident when the person insured or any other person driving the vehicle is the driver at fault.

cub /kʌb/ *n.* **1.** the young of certain animals, as the fox, bear, etc. **2.** a novice or apprentice, especially a reporter.

cubbyhouse /'kʌbihaʊs/ *n.* a children's playhouse.

cube /kjub/ *n.* **1.** solid bounded by six equal squares, the angle between any two adjacent faces being a right angle. **2.** the third power of a quantity. –*v.t.* (**cubed, cubing**) **3.** to make into a cube or cubes. **4.** to raise to the third power; find the cube of. –**cubic**, *adj.*

cube root *n.* the quantity of which a given quantity is the cube.

cubicle /'kjubɪkəl/ *n.* any small space or compartment partitioned off.

cuckold /'kʌkəld/ *n.* the husband of an unfaithful wife.

cuckoo /'kʊku/ *n.* **1.** any of a number of widespread birds noted for their habit of laying eggs in the nests of other birds. **2.** a fool; simpleton.

cucumber /'kjukʌmbə/ *n.* a long fleshy fruit which is commonly eaten green as a salad and used for pickling.

cud /kʌd/ *n.* the portion of food which a ruminating animal returns from the first stomach to the mouth to chew a second time.

cuddle /'kʌdl/ *v.t.* **1.** to draw or hold close in an affectionate manner. –*n.* **2.** the act of cuddling; a hug; an embrace. –**cuddly**, *adj.*

cudgel /'kʌdʒəl/ *n.* a short, thick stick used as a weapon; a club.

cue¹ /kju/ *n.* **1.** anything said or done on or behind the stage that is followed by a specific line or action. **2.** a hint; an intimation; a guiding suggestion.

cue² /kju/ *n.* a long tapering rod, tipped with a soft leather pad, used to strike the ball in billiards, etc.

cuff¹ /kʌf/ *n.* **1.** a fold, band, or variously shaped piece serving as a trimming or finish for the bottom of a sleeve or trouser leg. –*phr.* **2. off the cuff**, impromptu.

cuff² /kʌf/ *v.t.* to strike with the open hand.

cufflink /'kʌflɪŋk/ *n.* a link which fastens a shirt cuff.

cuisine /kwə'zin/ *n.* style of cooking; cookery.

cul-de-sac /'kʌl-də-sæk/ *n.* a street, lane, etc., closed at one end; blind alley.

–cule a diminutive suffix of nouns. Also, **–cle**.

culinary /'kʌlənri, -ənəri/, *Orig. US* /'kʌləneri/ *adj.* relating to the kitchen or to cookery.

cull /kʌl/ *v.t.* **1.** to pick out the best from: *to cull the main points from the long report.* **2.** to remove animals of inferior quality from (a herd or flock). **3.** to kill (animals, such as deer, kangaroos, etc.), with a view to controlling numbers. –*n.* **4.** the killing of animals in order to reduce their numbers: *a kangaroo cull.*

culminate /'kʌlməneɪt/ *v.t.* to reach the highest point. –**culmination**, *n.*

culottes /kə'lɒts/ *pl. n.* trousers cut wide to look like a skirt.

culpable /'kʌlpəbəl/ *adj.* deserving blame or censure.

culprit /'kʌlprət/ *n.* one guilty of or responsible for a specified offence or fault.

cult /kʌlt/ *n.* **1.** a particular system of religious worship, especially with reference to its rites and ceremonies. **2.** (*derog.*) a religious or pseudo-religious movement, characterised by the extreme devotion of its members, who usually form a relatively small, tightly controlled group under an authoritarian and charismatic leader. **3.** an instance of an almost religious veneration for a person or thing.

cultivate /'kʌltəveɪt/ *v.t.* **1.** to bestow labour upon (land) in raising crops. **2.** to develop or improve by education or training; train; refine. **3.** to promote the growth or development of. **4.** to seek the acquaintance or friendship of (a person).

cultural /'kʌltʃərəl/ *adj.* of or relating to culture or cultivation.

culture /'kʌltʃə/ *n.* **1.** skills, arts, customs, etc., of a people passed from generation to generation. **2.** development or improvement by education or training. **3.** the action or practice of cultivating the soil.

culvert /'kʌlvət/ *n.* a drain or channel crossing under a road, etc.; sewer; conduit.

cum /kʌm, kʊm/ *prep.* **1.** with; together with; including (used sometimes in financial phrases as *cum dividend, cum rights,* etc., which are often abbreviated simply *cum*). **2.** (in combination) serving a dual function as, the functions being indicated by the preceding and following elements.

cumbersome /'kʌmbəsəm/ *adj.* burdensome; troublesome.

cumin /'kjumən, 'ku-, 'kʌ-/ *n.* a small plant, bearing aromatic seedlike fruit used in cookery.

cumquat /'kʌmkwɒt/ *n.* a small, round, or oblong citrus fruit with a sweet rind and acid pulp. Also, **kumquat**.

cumulative /'kjumjələtɪv/ *adj.* increasing or growing by accumulation or successive additions.

cumulus /'kjumjələs/ *n.* (*pl.* **-uli** /-jəlaɪ/) *Meteorol.* a cloud made up of rounded heaps, and with flat base.

cunning /'kʌnɪŋ/ *adj.* **1.** exhibiting or done with ingenuity. **2.** artfully subtle or shrewd; crafty; sly. –*n.* **3.** skill employed in a crafty manner; guile.

cup /kʌp/ *n.* **1.** a small, open container, especially of porcelain or metal, used mainly to drink from. **2.** (*oft. upper case*) an ornamental cup or other article, especially of precious metal, offered as a prize for a contest: *Melbourne Cup; Davis Cup.* **3.** a unit of volume, measuring 250 ml. **4.** any of various beverages, as a mixture of wine and various ingredients. **5.** any cuplike utensil, organ, part, cavity, etc. –*v.t.* (**cupped, cupping**) **6.** to take or place in or as in a cup.

cupboard /'kʌbəd/ *n.* a place or article of furniture used for storage.

cupr- a word element referring to copper. Also, (*before consonants*) **cupri-, cupro-**.

cur /kɜ/ *n.* **1.** a snarling, worthless, or outcast dog. **2.** a low, despicable person.

curate[1] /'kjurət/ *n.* a member of the clergy employed as assistant or deputy of a rector or vicar.

curate[2] /kju'reɪt/ *v.t.* to supervise and maintain (an art collection, museum, etc.). –**curation**, *n.*

curator /kju'reɪtə/ *n.* the person in charge of a museum, art collection, etc.

curb /kɜb/ *n.* **1.** anything that restrains or controls; a restraint; a check. –*v.t.* **2.** to control as with a curb; restrain; check.

curd /kɜd/ *n.* (*oft. pl.*) a substance obtained from milk by coagulation, used for making into cheese or eaten as food.

curdle /'kɜdl/ *v.t.* to change into curd.

cure /'kjuə, 'kjʊə/ *n.* **1.** a method or course of remedial treatment, as for disease. **2.** successful remedial treatment; restoration to health. –*v.t.* **3.** to relieve or rid of something troublesome or detrimental, as an illness, a bad habit, etc. **4.** to prepare (meat, fish, etc.) for preservation, by salting, drying, etc. –**curable**, *adj.* –**curative**, *n., adj.*

curfew /'kɜfju/ *n.* a regulation, as enforced during civil disturbances, which establishes strict controls on movement after nightfall.

curious /'kjuriəs/ *adj.* **1.** desirous of learning or knowing; inquisitive. **2.** exciting attention or interest because of strangeness or novelty. **3.** odd; eccentric. –**curiosity**, *n.*

curl /kɜl/ *v.t.* **1.** to form into ringlets, as the hair. **2.** to form into a spiral or curved shape; coil. –*n.* **3.** a ringlet of hair. **4.** anything of a spiral or curved shape.

curlicue /'kɜlikju/ *n.* a fantastic curl or twist.

curly bracket *n.* → **brace** (def. 9a).

currajong /'kʌrədʒɒŋ/ *n.* → **kurrajong**.

currant /'kʌrənt/ *n.* a small seedless raisin.

currawong[1] /'kʌrəwɒŋ/ *n.* any of several large black and white or greyish Australian birds.

currawong[2] /'kʌrəwɒŋ/ *n.* a small tree found in inland eastern Australia.

currency /'kʌrənsi/ *n.* (*pl.* **-cies**) **1.** that which is current as a medium of exchange; the money in actual use. **2.** the fact or quality of being passed on, as from person to person. **3.** general acceptance; prevalence; vogue.

current /'kʌrənt/ *adj.* **1.** passing in time, or belonging to the time actually passing. **2.** passing from one to another; circulating, as coin. **3.** prevalent. –*n.* **4.** a flowing; flow, as of a river. **5.** a movement or flow of electric charges.

curriculum /kə'rɪkjələm/ *n.* (*pl.* **-lums** or **-la** /-lə/) the aggregate of courses of study given in a school, college, university, etc. –**curricular**, *adj.*

curriculum vitae /kə,rɪkjələm 'vitaɪ, 'vitɛɪ/ *n.* (*pl.* **curricula vitae** or **curriculum vitaes**) → **CV**.

curry[1] /'kʌri/ *n.* (*pl.* **-ries**) any of several hot sauces or dishes originating in India.

curry[2] /'kʌri/ *v.t.* (**-ried, -rying**) to rub and clean (a horse, etc.) with a comb.

curse /kɜs/ *n.* **1.** the expression of a wish that evil, etc., befall another. **2.** a profane oath. –*v.t.* **3.** to wish or invoke evil, calamity, injury, or destruction upon. –*v.i.* **4.** to utter curses; swear profanely.

cursive /'kɜsɪv/ *adj.* (of writing or printing type) in flowing strokes, with the letters joined together.

cursor /'kɜsə/ *n.* an indicator on a video display unit screen, usually a small rectangle of light, which shows where the next character will form.

cursory /'kɜsəri/ *adj.* going rapidly over something, without noticing details; hasty; superficial.

curt /kɜt/ *adj.* rudely brief in speech, manner, etc.

curtail /kɜ'teɪl/ *v.t.* to cut short; abridge; reduce.

curtain /'kɜtn/ *n.* **1.** a hanging piece of fabric used to shut out the light from a window, adorn a room, etc. **2.** anything that shuts off, covers, or conceals.

curtain call *n.* the appearance of performers at the conclusion of a performance in response to the applause of the audience.

curtsey /'kɜtsi/ *n.* (*pl.* **-seys**) **1.** a bow by women in recognition or respect, consisting of bending the knees and lowering the body. –*v.i.* (**-seyed, -seying**) **2.** to make a curtsey. Also, **curtsy**.

curvaceous /kɜ'veɪʃəs/ *adj.* (of a woman) having a full and shapely figure.

curvature /'kɜvətʃə/ *n.* curved condition, often abnormal.

curve /kɜv/ *n.* **1.** a continuously bending line, usually without angles. **2.** a line on a graph, diagram, etc., representing a continuous variation in force, quantity, etc. –*v.i.* **3.** to bend in a curve.

cushion /'kuʃən/ *n.* **1.** a soft bag filled with feathers, air, etc., used to sit, kneel, or lie on. **2.** anything similar in appearance or use. **3.** something to absorb or counteract a shock, jar, or jolt, as a body of air or steam. –*v.t.* **4.** to lessen or soften the effects of.

cusp /kʌsp/ *n.* **1.** a point; pointed end. **2.** *Astrology* the transitional first or last part of a sign or house.

cuspid /'kʌspəd/ *n.* a tooth with a single point.

custard /'kʌstəd/ *n.* a sauce made from milk, eggs and sugar.

custard apple *n.* a tropical fruit with a soft pulp.

custody /'kʌstədi/ *n.* **1.** keeping; guardianship; care. **2.** the keeping or charge of officers of the law. –**custodian**, *n.* –**custodial**, *adj.*

custom /'kʌstəm/ *n.* **1.** a habitual practice; the usual way of acting in given circumstances. **2.** habits or usages collectively; convention. **3.** (*pl.*) customs duties. **4.** habitual patronage of a particular shop, etc.; business patronage. –**customary**, *adj.*

customer /'kʌstəmə/ *n.* someone who purchases goods from another; buyer; patron.

custom-made /'kʌstəm-meɪd/ *adj.* made to individual order.

customs duty *n.* a duty imposed by law on imported or, less commonly, exported goods.

cut /kʌt/ *v.* (**cut, cutting**) −*v.t.* **1.** to penetrate, with or as with a sharp-edged instrument. **2.** to divide, with or as with a sharp-edged instrument; sever; carve. **3.** to reap; mow; harvest. **4.** to stop; halt the running of. **5.** to reduce. **6.** to make or fashion by cutting. **7.** *Colloq.* to absent oneself from. −*v.i.* **8.** to penetrate or divide something as with a sharp-edged instrument; make an incision. **9.** to allow incision or severing. **10.** to pass, go, or come, especially in the most direct way. **11.** *Radio, TV* to stop filming or recording. **12.** *Film, TV, etc.* to edit (filmed material) by cutting and rearranging pieces of film. **13.** to produce (a CD, record, etc.) by recording: *they cut two CDs last year.* −*n.* **14.** the act of cutting. **15.** *Colloq.* share. **16.** the result of cutting. **17.** manner or fashion in which anything is cut. **18.** a passage or course straight across: *a short cut.* **19.** a reduction in price, salary, etc. −*phr.* **20. cut and paste,** *Computers* to move (data) from one application or document to another, or from one location in a document to another. **21. cut back,** to shorten or reduce. **22. cut down, a.** to bring down by cutting. **b.** to reduce, especially expenses, costs, etc. **23. cut in, a.** to interrupt. **b.** (in traffic) to pull in dangerously soon after overtaking. **c.** to allow (oneself or someone else) a share: *he cut his brother in on the deal.* **24. cut it,** *Colloq.* to make the grade; be competent: *she couldn't cut it in her new job.* **25. cut off, a.** to separate from the main body or part. **b.** to intercept. **c.** to interrupt. **26. cut one's losses,** to abandon a project in which one has already invested some part of one's capital, so as not to incur more losses. **27. cut out, a.** to omit; delete; excise. **b.** to stop; cease; come to an end: *the shearing cut out; the electricity cut out.* **28. cut up,** to cut into pieces. **29. make the cut,** (in sports where players or competitors are selected from a large field during preliminary trials) to qualify for the actual game or competition.

cutaneous /kjuˈteɪniəs/ *adj.* of, relating to, or affecting the skin. −**cutaneously,** *adv.*

cute /kjut/ *adj.* appealing in manner or appearance, especially of someone or something which is small or which is pretty in a childlike way.

cuticle /ˈkjutɪkəl/ *n.* the non-living epidermis which surrounds the edges of the fingernail or toenail.

cutlass /ˈkʌtləs/ *n.* a short, heavy, slightly curved sword.

cutlery /ˈkʌtləri/ *n.* knives, forks, and spoons collectively, as used for eating.

cutlet /ˈkʌtlət/ *n.* a cut of meat, usually lamb or veal, containing a rib.

cuttlefish /ˈkʌtlfɪʃ/ *n.* (*pl.* **-fish** *or* **-fishes**) any of various marine animals which eject a black, ink-like fluid when pursued.

CV /si ˈvi/ *n.* curriculum vitae; a short written summary of one's education and previous employment; résumé.

-cy a suffix of abstract nouns, as in *accuracy, lunacy, magistracy.*

cyanide /ˈsaɪənaɪd/ *n.* a highly poisonous chemical.

cyanobacteria /ˌsaɪænoʊbækˈtɪəriə/ *pl. n.* (*sing.* **-terium**) photosynthetic organisms containing chlorophyll; they thrive in marine or fresh water and contribute to bluish-green scum in late summer. −**cyanobacterial,** *adj.*

cyber /ˈsaɪbə/ *adj.* **1.** of, relating to, or typified by an internet culture: *the cyber age.* **2.** in the style associated with the visuals of computer games: *a cyber goth.*

cyber- a prefix popularly used to indicate a connection with computers, in particular with the internet and virtual reality: *cyberspace.*

cyber attack *n.* an infiltration of the internet communications system of a country, organisation, etc., with the intent to damage or disrupt the system. Also, **cyberattack.**

cyberbully /ˈsaɪbəbuli/ *n.* (*pl.* **-bullies**) **1.** a person who bullies another using email, social network sites, online forums, etc. −*v.t.* (**-bullied, -bullying**) **2.** to bully (another) in this way. Also, **cyber bully, cyber-bully.** −**cyberbullying,** *n.*

cyber cafe *n.* → **internet cafe.**

cyber hacking *n.* the gaining of unauthorised access to a computer network. −**cyber hacker,** *n.*

cybernetics /saɪbəˈnɛtɪks/ *n.* the scientific study of those methods of control and communication which are common to living organisms and machines, especially as applied to the analysis of the operations of machines such as computers.

cyber safety *n.* safety in an online environment achieved by taking precautions in one's dealings online, as by not providing personal information, etc.

cybersecurity /saɪbəsəˈkjurəti/ *n.* protection provided for an information system, such as computer and telecommunications networks, against attacks over the internet.

cyberspace /ˈsaɪbəspeɪs/ *n.* **1.** a communication network, conceived of as a separate world, access to which is gained through the use of computers. **2.** a world created in virtual reality. **3.** the internet.

cyberstalking /ˈsaɪbəstɔkɪŋ/ *n.* sustained harassment or threatening behaviour directed at someone through the use of the internet, email, chat rooms, or other digital communications devices. Also, **internet stalking.**

cyberterrorism /saɪbəˈtɛrərɪzm/ *n.* a type of terrorism in which computer networks, data, etc., are damaged or altered to harm a targeted group or country. −**cyberterrorist,** *n.*

cycl- a word element meaning 'cycle'. Also, **cyclo-.**

cyclamate /ˈsaɪkləmeɪt, -mət/ *n.* any of a group of artificial sweeteners, sometimes used as food additives.

cyclamen /ˈsaɪkləmən, ˈsɪk-/ *n.* any of various plants with white, purple, pink or red flowers whose petals fold backwards.

cycle /ˈsaɪkəl/ *n.* **1.** a recurring period of time, especially one in which certain events or phenomena repeat themselves in the same order and at the same intervals. **2.** any round of operations or events. **3.** a bicycle, tricycle, etc. −*v.i.* **4.** to ride or travel by a bicycle, etc. **5.** to

move or revolve in cycles; pass through cycles.
–**cyclic**, *adj.* –**cyclist**, *n.*

cyclone /'saɪkloʊn/ *n.* a tropical hurricane, especially in the Indian Ocean. –**cyclonic** /saɪ-'klɒnɪk/, *adj.*

cyder /'saɪdə/ *n.* → **cider**.

cygnet /'sɪgnət/ *n.* a young swan.

cylinder /'sɪləndə/ *n.* **1.** *Geom.* a tube-like figure. **2.** any cylinder-like object or part, whether solid or hollow. –**cylindrical**, *adj.*

cymbal /'sɪmbəl/ *n.* a brass or bronze concave plate giving a metallic sound when struck.

cymo- a word element meaning 'wave'.

cynic /'sɪnɪk/ *n.* someone who doubts or denies the goodness of human motives, and who often displays this attitude by sneers, sarcasm, etc. –**cynical**, *adj.*

cypher /'saɪfə/ *n.* → **cipher**.

cypress /'saɪprəs/ *n.* any of several coniferous evergreen trees.

cyrto- a word element meaning 'curved.'

cyst /sɪst/ *n.* a closed bladder-like sac formed in animal tissues, containing fluid or semifluid matter.

cyst- a combining form representing **cyst**. Also, **cysti-**, **cysto-**.

cystic fibrosis /ˌsɪstɪk faɪ'broʊsəs/ *n.* a hereditary, chronic disease of the pancreas, lungs, etc., beginning in infancy, in which there is difficulty in breathing and an inability to digest.

cystitis /sɪs'taɪtəs/ *n.* inflammation of the urinary bladder.

-cyte a word element referring to cells or corpuscles.

cytotoxic /saɪtoʊ'tɒksɪk/ *adj.* of or relating to the destruction of cells.

czar /zɑ/ *n.* → **tsar**. –**czardom**, *n.*

D, d

D, d /diː/ n. the fourth letter of the English alphabet.

'd contraction of: **1.** had. **2.** would.

dab /dæb/ v.t. (**dabbed, dabbing**) to tap lightly, as with the hand.

dabble /ˈdæbəl/ v.i. **1.** to play in water, as with the hands or feet. **2.** to do anything in a slight or superficial manner.

dachshund /ˈdæksənd, ˈdækshʊnd/ n. one of a German breed of small dogs with a long body and very short legs.

D-A converter /diː-ˈeɪ/ n. digital to analog converter. Also, **D to A converter**.

dad /dæd/ n. Colloq. father.

daddy /ˈdædi/ n. (pl. **-dies**) (with children) dad; father.

daddy-long-legs n. (pl. **daddy-long-legs**) a small web-spinning spider with long, thin legs, frequently found indoors.

dado /ˈdeɪdoʊ/ n. (pl. **-dos** or **-does**) the lower broad part of an interior wall finished in wallpaper, a fabric, paint, or the like.

daffodil /ˈdæfədɪl/ n. a plant with single or double yellow nodding flowers.

daft /dɑːft/ adj. simple or foolish.

dag¹ /dæg/ n. Colloq. **1.** someone who dresses or behaves in an unfashionable or unstylish manner. **2.** an odd, eccentric, or amusing person. **–daggy**, adj.

dag² /dæg/ n. wool on a sheep's rear quarters which is dirty with mud and excreta.

dagger /ˈdægə/ n. a short-edged and pointed weapon, like a small sword, used for thrusting and stabbing.

dahlia /ˈdeɪljə/ n. a plant native to Mexico and Central America, widely cultivated for its showy, variously coloured flowers.

daikon /ˈdaɪkɒn/ n. a Japanese variety of radish with white flesh and a mild flavour.

daily /ˈdeɪli/ adj. **1.** of, done, occurring, or issued each day or each weekday. –adv. **2.** every day.

dainty /ˈdeɪnti/ adj. (**-tier, -tiest**) of delicate beauty or charm; exquisite.

dairy /ˈdɛəri/ n. (pl. **-ries**) a place where milk and cream are kept and made into butter and cheese.

dais /ˈdeɪəs/ n. a raised platform, as at the end of a room, for a throne, seats of honour, a lecturer's desk, etc.

daisy /ˈdeɪzi/ n. (pl. **-sies**) a plant whose flower heads have a yellow disc and white rays.

dak /dæk/ v.t. (**dakked, dakking**) Colloq. to forcibly pull down the trousers, and sometimes the underpants, of: *he dakked me in front of everyone.* Also, **dack**.

daks /dæks/ pl. n. Colloq. (from trademark) trousers.

dal /dɑːl/ n. in Indian cooking, lentils or pulses. Also, **dhal**.

dale /deɪl/ n. a vale; valley.

dally /ˈdæli/ v.i. (**-lied, -lying**) to waste time; loiter; delay. **–dalliance**, n.

Dalmatian /dælˈmeɪʃən/ n. one of a breed of dogs of a white colour profusely marked with small black or liver-coloured spots.

dam¹ /dæm/ n. **1.** a barrier to obstruct the flow of water, especially one of earth, masonry, etc., built across a river. **2.** a body of water confined by such a barrier. –v.t. (**dammed, damming**) **3.** to stop up; block up.

dam² /dæm/ n. a female parent (used especially of quadrupeds).

damage /ˈdæmɪdʒ/ n. **1.** injury or harm that impairs value or usefulness. **2.** (pl.) Law the estimated money equivalent for detriment or injury sustained. –v.t. (**-aged, -aging**) **3.** to cause damage to; injure or harm; impair the usefulness of.

damage control n. **1.** measures to limit damage, as during or after a disaster **2.** attempts to mitigate the unpleasant consequence of an event, action, etc. Also, **damage limitation**.

damask /ˈdæməsk/ n. a reversible fabric of linen, silk, cotton, or wool, woven with patterns.

dame /deɪm/ n. **1.** (upper case) the title of a woman who holds a particular honour, as a Dame of the Order of Australia. **2.** Chiefly US Colloq. a woman.

damn /dæm/ v.t. **1.** to declare (something) to be bad, unfit, invalid, or illegal. **2.** to bring condemnation upon; ruin. –n. **3.** a negligible amount. –interj. **4.** an intensifier expressing anger, annoyance, or emphasis. **–damnation**, n. **–damnable**, adj.

damp /dæmp/ adj. **1.** moderately wet; moist. –v.t. **2.** to stifle or suffocate; extinguish.

dampen /ˈdæmpən/ v.t. **1.** to make damp; moisten. **2.** to dull or deaden; depress.

damper /ˈdæmpə/ n. bread made from a simple flour and water dough, traditionally cooked in the coals of an open fire.

dance /dæns, dɑːns/ v.i. (**danced, dancing**) **1.** to move with the feet or body rhythmically, especially to music. **2.** to bob up and down. –n. **3.** a successive group of rhythmical steps, generally executed to music. **4.** an act or round of dancing. **5.** a social gathering for dancing; ball. **–dancer**, n.

dance music n. any of various genres of pop music with a strong beat, designed to be danced to.

dandelion /ˈdændəlaɪən, -dɪ-/ n. a common weed, with golden yellow flowers.

dandruff /ˈdændrəf, -rʌf/ n. dry skin which forms on the scalp and comes off in small scales.

dandy /ˈdændi/ n. (pl. **-dies**) **1.** a man who is excessively concerned about clothes and appearance; a fop. **2.** Colloq. something very fine or first rate.

danger /ˈdeɪndʒə/ n. liability or exposure to harm or injury; risk; peril. **–dangerous**, adj.

dangerous driving n. Law the statutory offence of driving on a road or road-related area at a speed that is furious, negligent or reckless and in a manner that is dangerous to the public.

dangle /ˈdæŋgəl/ v.i. to hang loosely with a swaying motion.

dank /dæŋk/ *adj.* unpleasantly moist or humid; damp.

dapper /'dæpəl/ *adj.* neat; trim; smart.

dapple /'dæpəl/ *n.* mottled marking, as of an animal's skin or coat.

dare /deə/ *v.* (**dared**, **daring**) –*v.i.* **1.** to have the necessary courage or boldness for something; be bold enough. –*v.t.* **2.** to meet defiantly. **3.** to challenge or provoke to action, especially by doubting one's courage; defy. –*phr.* **4. dare say**, to assume as probable; have no doubt. –**daring**, *n.*, *adj.*

daredevil /'deədevəl/ *n.* **1.** a recklessly daring person. –*adj.* **2.** recklessly daring.

dark /dak/ *adj.* **1.** without light; with very little light. **2.** not pale or fair. **3.** gloomy; cheerless; dismal. **4.** evil; wicked. –*n.* **5.** absence of light; darkness. **6.** ignorance. –*phr.* **7. dark side**, the less agreeable aspect of the nature or personality of someone or something. –**darkness**, *n.*

dark matter *n.* theoretically postulated matter of unknown nature that comprises ninety per cent or more of the total mass of the universe and that accounts for the fact that the density of the universe appears to exceed the value that would have been accorded it on the basis of visible matter.

darkroom /'dakrum/ *n.* a room from which light has been excluded, used in making, handling, and developing photographic film, etc.

darling /'dalɪŋ/ *n.* a term of address for a beloved person.

darn¹ /dan/ *v.t.* to mend (clothes, etc., or a tear or hole) with rows of stitches, sometimes with crossing and interwoven rows to fill up a gap.

darn² /dan/ *v.t. Colloq.* to curse.

dart /dat/ *n.* **1.** a long, slender, pointed, missile weapon propelled by the hand or otherwise. –*v.i.* **2.** to move swiftly; spring or start suddenly and run swiftly.

dash /dæʃ/ *v.t.* **1.** to strike violently, especially so as to break to pieces. **2.** to throw or thrust violently or suddenly. **3.** to ruin or frustrate (hopes, plans, etc.). **4.** (usu. fol. by *off* or *down*) to write, make, sketch, etc., hastily. –*v.i.* **5.** to strike with violence. **6.** to move with violence; rush. –*n.* **7.** a violent and rapid blow or stroke. **8.** a small quantity of anything thrown into or mixed with something else. **9.** a hasty stroke, especially of a pen. **10.** a horizontal line of varying length (– or —) used in writing and printing as a mark of punctuation to indicate an abrupt break or pause in a sentence, to begin and end a parenthetic clause, as an indication of omission of letters, words, etc., as a dividing line between distinct portions of matter, and for other purposes. **11.** an impetuous movement; a rush; a sudden onset. **12.** *Athletics* a short race or sprint decided in one attempt, not in heats. –*interj.* **13.** a mild expletive. –*phr.* **14. do one's dash**, to exhaust one's energies or opportunities.

dashboard /'dæʃbod/ *n.* the instrument board of a motor vehicle, aeroplane or boat.

dashing /'dæʃɪŋ/ *adj.* **1.** impetuous; spirited; lively. **2.** brilliant; showy; stylish.

dastardly /'dæstədli/ *adj.* cowardly; meanly base; sneaking.

data /'deɪtə, 'datə/ *n.* **1.** plural of **datum**. **2.** (*construed as sing. or pl.*) figures, statistics, etc., known or available; information collected for analysis or reference. **3.** *Computers* digital information.

database /'deɪtəbeɪs, 'datə-/ *n.* **1.** a large volume of information stored in a computer and organised in categories to facilitate retrieval. **2.** any large collection of information or reference material. Also, **databank**.

data bus *n.* a main connecting channel or path for transferring data between sections of a computer system.

datacast /'deɪtəkast/ *v.i.* (**-cast** or **-casted**, **-casting**) to broadcast digital information. –**datacaster**, *n.* –**datacasting**, *n.*

data haven *n.* a digital data storage device, offering complete privacy, especially from government regulation, by means of data encryption and location in a state which does not have laws allowing legal access.

data packet *n.* → **packet** (def. 2).

date¹ /deɪt/ *n.* **1.** a particular day, as denoted by some system for marking the passage of time. **2.** *Colloq.* an appointment made for a particular time, especially for a social meeting between two people. **3.** *Colloq.* a person with whom one has a social appointment, especially someone in whom one has a romantic interest. –*v.i.* **4.** to have a date. **5.** to belong to a particular period; have its origin. –*v.t.* **6.** to mark or furnish with a date. **7.** to ascertain or fix the date or time of; assign a date or time to. **8.** to show to be of a certain age, old-fashioned, or out of date. **9.** *Colloq.* to go out with (a person in whom one has a romantic interest) on social engagements. –*phr.* **10. to date**, to the present time.

date² /deɪt/ *n.* the oblong, fleshy fruit of the date palm, a staple food in northern Africa, the Middle East, etc.

dative /'deɪtɪv/ *adj. Gram.* denoting a case, in some inflected languages, having as one function indication of the indirect object of a verb.

datum /'deɪtəm, 'datəm/ *n.* (*pl.* **-ta** /-tə/) **1.** any proposition assumed or given, from which conclusions may be drawn. **2.** (*oft. pl.*) any fact assumed to be a matter of direct observation.

daub /dɔb/ *v.t.* to cover or coat with soft, adhesive matter, such as plaster, mud, etc.

daughter /'dɔtə/ *n.* **1.** a female child or person in relation to her parents. **2.** any female descendant. **3.** one related as if by the ties binding daughter to parent. –**daughterly**, *adj.*

daughter-in-law *n.* (*pl.* **daughters-in-law**) the wife of one's son or daughter.

daunt /dɔnt/ *v.t.* **1.** to overcome with fear; intimidate. **2.** to lessen the courage of; dishearten. –**daunting**, *adj.* –**dauntingly**, *adv.*

dauntless /'dɔntləs/ *adj.* not to be daunted; fearless; intrepid; bold.

dawdle /'dɔdəl/ *v.i.* **1.** to waste time; idle. **2.** to walk slowly or lag behind others.

dawn /dɔn/ *n.* **1.** the first appearance of daylight in the morning. **2.** the beginning or rise of anything; advent. –*v.i.* **3.** to begin to open or develop. **4.** (fol. by *on* or *upon*) to begin to be perceived.

day /deɪ/ *n.* **1.** the interval of light between two successive nights; the time between sunrise and sunset. **2.** the light of day. **3.** a day as a point or unit of time, or on which something occurs. **4.** a day of contest, or the contest itself. **5.** (*oft. pl.*) a particular time or period. **6.** period of power or influence. –*phr.* **7. call it a day,** to bring an activity to a close, either temporarily or permanently. **8. make someone's day,** *Colloq.* to bring happiness to someone.

day care *n.* care and supervision of young children or elderly people given daily by trained staff.

daydream /'deidrīm/ *n.* **1.** a visionary fancy indulged in while awake; reverie. –*v.i.* (**-dreamed** *or* **-dreamt, -dreaming**) **2.** to indulge in daydreams.

daylight robbery *n.* a shameless attempt to rob, overcharge or cheat someone.

daylight saving *n.* a system of reckoning time one or more hours later than the standard time for a country or community, usually used during summer months to give more hours of daylight to the working day.

daze /deiz/ *v.t.* **1.** to stun or stupefy with a blow, a shock, etc. **2.** to confuse; bewilder; dazzle.

dazzle /'dæzəl/ *v.t.* **1.** to overpower or dim the vision of by intense light. **2.** to bewilder by brilliance of execution or display of any kind.

D-day /'di-dei/ *n.* the day, usually unspecified, set for the beginning of a previously planned undertaking.

DDT /di di 'ti/ *n.* a very powerful insecticide, dichlorodiphenyltrichloroethane.

de- a prefix meaning: **1.** privation and separation, as in *debar*. **2.** negation, as in *demerit, deranged*. **3.** descent, as in *degrade, deduce*. **4.** reversal, as in *decontaminate*.

deacon /'dikən/ *n.* **1.** (in the Roman Catholic and Anglican Churches) a member of the clergy, ranked below a priest. **2.** a church official with variously defined duties. **–deaconess,** *fem. n.*

dead /dɛd/ *adj.* **1.** no longer living; deprived of life. **2.** not endowed with life; inanimate. **3.** bereft of sensation; insensible; numb: *my foot is dead.* **4.** no longer in existence or use. **5.** *Law* deprived of civil rights so that one is in the state of civil death, especially deprived of the rights of property. **6.** *Colloq.* very tired; exhausted. **7. a.** without resonance. **b.** without resilience or bounce. **8.** not glossy, bright, or brilliant. **9.** complete; absolute. **10.** *Sport* out of play. –*adv.* **11.** absolutely; completely. **12.** with abrupt and complete stoppage of motion, etc.

deaden /'dɛdən/ *v.t.* **1.** to make less sensitive, active, energetic, or forcible; dull; weaken. **2.** to make impervious to sound, as a floor.

dead letter *n.* **1.** a law, ordinance, etc., which has lost its force, though not formally repealed or abolished. **2.** a letter which lies unclaimed for a certain time at a post office, or which, because of faulty address, etc., cannot be delivered.

deadline /'dɛdlaɪn/ *n.* the latest time for finishing something.

deadlock¹ /'dɛdlɒk/ *n.* **1.** a state of affairs in which progress is impossible; complete standstill. **2.** *Parliamentary Procedure* **a.** a situation in which the two houses of parliament are in disagreement. **b.** a tied vote on a motion

with no chance or opportunity for a change in the allocation of votes that would break the tie.

deadlock² /'dɛdlɒk/ *n.* a type of lock which can only be opened from inside and outside with a key. Also, **dead latch.**

deadly /'dɛdli/ *adj.* (**-lier, -liest**) **1.** causing or tending to cause death; fatal. **2.** excessive.

deadpan /'dɛdpæn/ *adj.* (of a person or their face) completely lacking expression or reaction.

deadweight tonnage *n.* the mass of the cargo, fuel, ballast, stores, crew, gear, etc., on a ship.

deaf /dɛf/ *adj.* lacking or deprived of the sense of hearing, wholly or partially; unable to hear. **–deafen,** *v.* **–deafness,** *n.*

deal /dil/ *v.* (**dealt, dealing**) –*v.i.* **1.** (fol. by *with* or *in*) to occupy oneself or itself. **2.** (usu. fol. by *with*) to take action with respect to a thing or person. **3.** to trade or do business. **4.** to distribute, especially the cards required in a game. –*v.t.* **5.** (oft. fol. by *out*) to give to someone as their share; apportion. **6.** to distribute among a number of recipients, as the cards required in a game. **7.** to deliver (blows, etc.). –*n.* **8.** a business transaction. **9.** an indefinite but large amount or extent. **10.** *Cards* **a.** the distribution to the players of the cards in a game. **b.** the turn of a player to deal. **11.** any undertaking, organisation, etc.; affair.

dealer /'dilə/ *n.* **1.** someone who buys and sells articles without altering their condition; trader or merchant. **2.** someone who buys and sells drugs, as marijuana, heroin, etc., in large quantities. **3.** *Cards* the player distributing the cards.

dealt /dɛlt/ *v.* past tense and past participle of **deal.**

dean /din/ *n.* **1.** *Educ.* the head of a medical school, university faculty, or the like. **2.** any of various ecclesiastical dignitaries, as the head of a division of a diocese.

dear /dɪə/ *adj.* **1.** beloved or loved. **2.** (in the salutation of a letter) highly esteemed. **3.** precious in one's regard. **4.** high-priced; expensive. –*n.* **5.** a term of address for a beloved person.

dearth /dɜθ/ *n.* scarcity or scanty supply; lack.

death /dɛθ/ *n.* **1.** the act of dying; the end of life; the total and permanent cessation of the vital functions of an animal or plant. **2.** the state of being dead. **3.** extinction; destruction. –*phr.* **4. like grim death,** tenaciously, firmly. **5. put to death,** to kill; execute.

death adder *n.* a venomous snake of Aust. and New Guinea with thick body and broad head.

death duty *n.* (*usu. pl.*) a tax paid upon the inheritance of property.

death march *n.* a forced march, as of prisoners, in which many people die from illness and deprivation.

debacle /dei'bakəl, də-/ *n.* a general break-up or rout; sudden overthrow or collapse; overwhelming disaster.

debar /di'ba, də-/ *v.t.* (**-barred, -barring**) **1.** to exclude from a place or condition. **2.** to prevent or prohibit (an action, etc.).

debase /dəˈbeɪs/ *v.t.* **1.** to reduce in quality or value; adulterate. **2.** to lower in rank or dignity.

debate /dəˈbeɪt/ *n.* **1.** a discussion, especially of a public question in an assembly. **2.** deliberation; consideration. **3.** a systematic contest of speakers in which two opposing points of view of a proposition are advanced. –*v.i.* **4.** to engage in discussion, especially in a legislative or public assembly. –*v.t.* **5.** to dispute about. –**debater**, *n.* –**debatable**, *adj.*

debauch /dəˈbɔtʃ/ *v.t.* to corrupt by sensuality, intemperance, etc.; seduce. –**debauchery**, *n.*

debenture /dəˈbɛntʃə/ *n.* **1.** a note or certificate acknowledging a debt, as given by an incorporated company or other private organisation; the corporate equivalent of a government bond (def. 8). **2.** a deed conferring a charge or mortgage on a company's assets; a mortgage debenture.

debilitate /dəˈbɪləteɪt/ *v.t.* to make weak or feeble; weaken. –**debility**, *n.*

debit /ˈdɛbət/ *n.* **1.** the recording of an entry of debt in an account. **2.** the side (left side) of an account on which such entries are made (opposed to *credit*). –*v.t.* **3.** to charge with a debt. **4.** to charge as a debt. **5.** to enter upon the debit side of an account.

debit card *n.* a plastic card, issued by a bank or other financial institution, which allows the holder to obtain cash and purchase goods and services, the cost of which is then withdrawn directly from the holder's bank account. Compare **credit card.**

debonair /dɛbəˈnɛə/ *adj.* **1.** suave; stylish. **2.** of pleasant manners; courteous.

debouch /dəˈbuʃ, dəˈbautʃ/ *v.i.* to issue or emerge from a narrow opening.

debrief /diˈbrif/ *v.t.* to interrogate (a soldier, astronaut, diplomat, etc.) on return from a mission in order to assess the conduct and results of the mission. –**debriefing**, *n.*

debris /ˈdɛbri, ˈdeɪbri, dəˈbri/ *n.* the remains of anything broken down or destroyed; ruins; fragments; rubbish.

debt /dɛt/ *n.* **1.** that which is owed; that which one person is bound to pay to or perform for another. **2.** the condition of being under such an obligation. –*phr.* **3. bad debt**, a debt of which there is no prospect of payment.

debtor /ˈdɛtə/ *n.* someone who is in debt or under obligations to another (opposed to *creditor*).

debug /diˈbʌg/ *v.t.* (**-bugged, -bugging**) *Computers* to remove errors or incompatible logical conditions from (a program).

debunk /diˈbʌŋk/ *v.t. Colloq.* to challenge or destroy the good standing of.

debut /ˈdeɪbju, -bu, deɪˈbu/ *n.* **1.** a first public appearance. –*v.i.* (**debuted** /ˈdeɪbjud/, **debuting** /ˈdeɪbjuŋ/) **2.** to make a first appearance.

debutant /ˈdɛbjətɑnt, -tɒnt/ *n. Sport* a young player making their first appearance at a particular level.

debutante /ˈdɛbjətɒnt/ *n.* **1.** a young woman making a debut, especially into society. **2.** *Sport* a young player making her first appearance at a particular level.

dec- → **deca-**.

deca- **1.** a word element meaning 'ten'. **2.** (in the metric system) → **deka-**. Also, **dec-**.

decade /ˈdɛkeɪd, dəˈkeɪd/ *n.* **1.** a period of ten years. **2.** a group, set, or series of ten.

decadence /ˈdɛkədəns/ *n.* **1.** the act or process of falling into an inferior condition or state, especially moral; decay; deterioration. **2.** luxurious self-indulgence. –**decadent**, *adj.*

decaffeinated /diˈkæfəneɪtəd/ *adj.* having had the caffeine removed.

decagon /ˈdɛkəgɒn, -gən/ *n.* a polygon having ten angles and ten sides.

decahedron /dɛkəˈhidrən/ *n.* (*pl.* **-drons** or **-dra** /-drə/) a solid figure having ten faces.

decant /dəˈkænt/ *v.t.* **1.** to pour off gently, as liquor, without disturbing the sediment. **2.** to pour from one container into another.

decanter /dəˈkæntə/ *n.* **1.** a bottle used for decanting. **2.** a vessel, usually an ornamental bottle, from which wine, water, etc., are served at table.

decapitate /dəˈkæpəteɪt, di-/ *v.t.* to cut off the head of; behead; kill by beheading.

decathlon /dəˈkæθlɒn, -lən/ *n.* an athletic contest comprising ten different events. –**decathlete**, *n.*

decay /dəˈkeɪ/ *v.i.* **1.** to fall away from a state of excellence, prosperity, health, etc.; deteriorate; decline. **2.** to become decomposed; rot. –*n.* **3.** a gradual falling into an inferior condition; progressive decline. **4.** decomposition; rotting.

decease /dəˈsis/ *n.* **1.** departure from life; death. –*v.i.* (**-ceased, -ceasing**) **2.** to depart from life; die.

deceased /dəˈsist/ *adj.* **1.** dead. –*phr.* **2. the deceased**, the dead person or persons.

deceive /dəˈsiv/ *v.t.* to mislead by a false appearance or statement; delude. –**deceit**, *n.* –**deceitful**, *adj.*

decent /ˈdisənt/ *adj.* **1.** fitting; appropriate. **2.** conforming to recognised standards of propriety, good taste, modesty, etc. **3.** *Colloq.* kind; obliging. –**decency**, *n.*

decentralise /diˈsɛntrəlaɪz/ *v.t.* **1.** to disperse (industry, population, etc.) from an area of concentration or density, especially from large cities to relatively undeveloped rural areas. **2.** to undo the centralisation of administrative powers (of an organisation, government, etc.). Also, **decentralize.** –**decentralisation**, *n.*

deception /dəˈsɛpʃən/ *n.* **1.** the act of deceiving. **2.** the state of being deceived. **3.** something that deceives or is intended to deceive; an artifice; a sham; a cheat. –**deceptive**, *adj.*

deci- /ˈdɛsi-/ a prefix denoting 10^{-1} of a given unit, as in *decibel*. *Symbol:* d

decibel /ˈdesəbɛl/ *n.* a unit expressing difference in power, usually between electric or acoustic signals, or between some particular signal and a reference level understood. *Symbol:* dB

decide /dəˈsaɪd/ *v.* (**-cided, -ciding**) –*v.t.* **1.** to determine or settle (a question, controversy, struggle, etc.) by giving victory to one side. **2.** to bring (a person) to a decision. –*v.i.* **3.** to settle something in dispute or doubt. **4.** to pronounce a judgement; come to a conclusion.

decided /dəˈsaɪdəd/ *adj.* resolute; determined.

deciduous /dəˈsɪdʒuəs/ *adj.* shedding the leaves annually, as trees, shrubs, etc.

decile /ˈdɛsaɪl/ n. Statistics one of the values of a variable which divides its distribution into ten groups having equal frequencies.

decimal /ˈdɛsəməl/ adj. **1.** relating to tenths, or to the number ten. **2.** proceeding by tens. –n. **3.** a decimal fraction. **4.** a decimal number.

decimal currency n. currency in which units are graded in multiples of ten.

decimal fraction n. a fraction whose denominator is some power of ten, usually indicated by a dot (the **decimal point**) written before the numerator, as $0.4 = {}^4/_{10}$.

decimal number n. Maths any finite or infinite string of digits containing a decimal point: 1.0, 5.23, 3.14159... are decimal numbers.

decimal place n. **1.** the position of a digit to the right of a decimal point. In 9.623, 3 is in the third decimal place. **2.** the number of digits to the right of a decimal point. 9.623 is a number in three decimal places.

decimal point n. (in the decimal system) a dot preceding the fractional part of a number.

decimate /ˈdɛsəmeɪt/ v.t. to destroy a great number or proportion of.

decipher /dəˈsaɪfə/ v.t. **1.** to make out or discover the meaning of. **2.** to interpret by the use of a key, as something written in cipher. –**decipherable**, adj.

decision /dəˈsɪʒən/ n. **1.** the act of deciding; determination (of a question or doubt). **2.** a judgement, as one formally pronounced by a court.

decisive /dəˈsaɪsɪv/ adj. **1.** having the power or quality of determining; putting an end to controversy. **2.** decided; determined.

deck /dɛk/ n. **1.** a horizontal platform extending from side to side of a ship or of part of a ship, forming a covering for the space below and itself serving as a floor. **2.** a floor, platform or tier. **3.** a pack of playing cards. –v.t. **4.** to clothe or attire in something ornamental; array.

declaim /dəˈkleɪm/ v.i. **1.** to speak aloud rhetorically; make a formal speech. **2.** (fol. by against) to inveigh. –**declamatory**, adj.

declare /dəˈklɛə/ v.t. **1.** to make known, especially in explicit or formal terms. **2.** to state emphatically; affirm. **3.** to manifest; reveal. **4.** to make due statement of (dutiable goods, etc.). **5.** to make (a dividend) payable. –**declaration**, n. –**declaratory**, adj.

declension /dəˈklɛnʃən/ n. **1.** Gram. the inflection of nouns, etc., for categories such as case and number. **2.** a bending, sloping, or moving downward.

decline v.t. /dəˈklaɪn/ **1.** to withhold consent to do, enter upon, or accept; refuse. **2.** to cause to slope or incline downward. **3.** Gram. to inflect (a noun, pronoun, or adjective). –v.i. /dəˈklaɪn/ **4.** to express courteous refusal; refuse. **5.** to bend or slant down; slope or trend downward; descend. **6.** to fail in strength, vigour, character, value, etc.; deteriorate. –n. /dəˈklaɪn, ˈdiklaɪn/ **7.** a downward incline or slope. **8.** a failing or gradual loss, as in strength, character, value, etc.; deterioration.

decoction /dəˈkɒkʃən/ n. the act of boiling in water, in order to extract the peculiar properties or virtues.

decode /diˈkoʊd, dəˈkoʊd/ v.t. to translate from code into the original language or form.

decommission /dikəˈmɪʃən/ v.t. **1.** to remove from service, as a naval vessel, army officer, etc. **2.** to close down (a facility, as a power station, sewerage plant, etc.).

decompose /dikəmˈpoʊz/ v.t. **1.** to separate or resolve into constituent parts or elements. –v.i. **2.** to rot; putrefy. –**decomposition**, n.

decompress /dikəmˈprɛs/ v.t. **1.** to cause to undergo decompression. **2.** Computers to decode (data) from a compressed storage format into its original format; unzip. –v.i. **3.** to undergo decompression.

decompression /dikəmˈprɛʃən/ n. **1.** the act or process of relieving pressure. **2.** the gradual return of persons, as divers or construction workers, to normal atmospheric pressure after working in deep water or in air under compression.

decongestant /dikənˈdʒɛstənt/ n. a substance used to relieve congestion especially in the upper respiratory tract.

deconsolidate /dikənˈsɒlədeɪt/ v.t. to remove goods from a shipping container and place in a store awaiting acceptance or delivery.

decontaminate /dikənˈtæməneɪt/ v.t. to make (any object or area) safe for unprotected personnel by absorbing, making harmless, or destroying chemicals with which they have been in contact.

decor /ˈdeɪkɔ, ˈdɛkɔ/ n. **1.** the interior decoration, especially of a home or office. **2.** a style of decoration.

decorate /ˈdɛkəreɪt/ v.t. **1.** to furnish or deck with something becoming or ornamental; embellish. **2.** to plan and execute the design, wallpaper, etc., and sometimes the furnishings of (a house, room, or the like). **3.** to confer distinction upon by a badge, a medal of honour, etc. –**decoration**, n. –**decorator**, n. –**decorative**, adj.

decorum /dəˈkɔrəm/ n. propriety of behaviour, speech, dress, etc. –**decorous**, adj.

decoupage /ˌdeɪkuˈpɑʒ/ n. the art or process of decorating something with an arrangement of cut-out paper, cardboard, etc. Also, **découpage**.

decoy /ˈdikɔɪ/ n. someone who entices or allures, as into a trap, danger, etc.

decrease v.i. /dəˈkris/ **1.** to diminish gradually in extent, quantity, strength, power, etc. –v.t. /dəˈkris/ **2.** to make less; cause to diminish. –n. /ˈdikris, dəˈkris/ **3.** a process of growing less, or the resulting condition; gradual diminution. **4.** the amount by which a thing is lessened.

decree /dəˈkri/ n. **1.** an ordinance or edict promulgated by civil or other authority. **2.** Law a judicial decision or order. –v.t. (**-creed**, **-creeing**) **3.** to ordain or decide by decree.

decrement /ˈdɛkrəmənt/ n. **1.** the process or fact of decreasing; gradual diminution. **2.** the amount lost by diminution. –v.t. **3.** Computers to reduce the numerical contents of (a counter).

decrepit /dəˈkrɛpət/ adj. broken down or weakened by old age; feeble; infirm. –**decrepitude**, n.

decriminalise /diˈkrɪmənəlaɪz/ v.t. to remove legal restrictions against (an activity, such as smoking marijuana), and thus eliminate the legal penalties previously associated with it. Also, **decriminalize**.

decry /dəˈkraɪ/ v.t. (**-cried**, **-crying**) to speak disparagingly of; censure as faulty or worthless.

dedicate /ˈdedəkeɪt/ v.t. **1.** to set apart and consecrate to a deity or to a sacred purpose. **2.** to give up wholly or earnestly, as to some person or end; set apart or appropriate. **–dedication**, n. **–dedicatory**, adj.

dedicated /ˈdedəkeɪtəd/ adj. **1.** wholly committed to something. **2.** (of a computer) limited to one purpose or set of operations.

deduce /dəˈdjus/ v.t. (**-duced**, **-ducing**) to derive as a conclusion from something known or assumed; infer.

deduct /dəˈdʌkt/ v.t. to take away, as from a sum or amount. **–deductible**, adj.

deduction /dəˈdʌkʃən/ n. **1.** the act of deducting; subtraction. **2.** that which is deducted. **3.** the process of drawing a conclusion from something known or assumed. **–deductive**, adj.

deed /did/ n. **1.** that which is done, performed, or accomplished; an act. **2.** Law a signed agreement, usually about ownership of land.

deed poll n. a deed in the form of a declaration to all the world of the grantor's act and intention, as, for example, to change his or her name.

deejay /ˈdidʒeɪ/ n. → DJ.

deem /dim/ v.i. to form or have an opinion; judge; think.

deep /dip/ adj. **1.** extending far downwards, inwards, or backwards. **2.** having a specified dimension downwards, inwards, or backwards. **3.** situated far or a certain distance down, in, or back. **4.** difficult to penetrate or understand; abstruse. **5.** not superficial; profound. **6.** great in measure; intense. **7.** (of colours) intense; dark and vivid. **8.** low in pitch, as sound. **9.** absorbed. **–n. 10.** the deep part of the sea, a river, etc. **–adv. 11.** to or at a considerable or specified depth.

deepfake /ˈdipˌfeɪk/ n. a video of a computer-generated likeness of an individual, created without their knowledge, often out of malice or to spread misleading information. Also, **deep fake**.

deep freeze n. (from trademark) a locker or compartment in a refrigerator in which food can be quickly frozen and stored at a very low temperature.

deep-fry /dip-ˈfraɪ/ v.t. (**-fried**, **-frying**) to fry in a sufficient quantity of fat or oil to cover the food being cooked.

deep vein thrombosis n. Med. a thrombosis occurring in a non-superficial vein, usually in the thigh or calf, which can dislodge from the vein wall and travel to the lungs, causing a life-threatening pulmonary embolism. Also, **deep venous thrombosis, DVT**.

deer /dɪə/ n. (pl. **deer**) a type of ruminant with solid antlers (usually the male only).

deface /dəˈfeɪs/ v.t. **1.** to mar the face or appearance of; disfigure. **2.** to blot out; obliterate; efface.

de facto /di ˈfæktoʊ, də, deɪ/ adj. **1.** in fact; in reality. **2.** actually existing, whether with or without right. **3.** of or relating to a situation in which two people live together in a marriage-like relationship, although not legally married: a de facto relationship. **–n. 4.** a person who lives with someone as their husband or wife without actually being married to them.

defalcation /difælˈkeɪʃən/ n. Law **1.** misappropriation of money, etc., held by a trustee or other fiduciary. **2.** the sum misappropriated.

defame /dɪˈfeɪm, də-/ v.t. to attack the good name or reputation of, as by uttering or publishing maliciously anything injurious; slander; libel. **–defamation**, n. **–defamatory**, adj.

default /dəˈfɒlt/ n. **1.** failure to act; neglect. **2.** Law failure to perform an act or obligation legally required, especially to appear in court or to plead at a time assigned. **3.** failure to participate in or complete anything, as a scheduled match. **4.** a procedure which has preset parameters which operate unless changed by the user. **–v.t. 5.** to fail to perform or pay.

defeasance /dəˈfizəns/ n. Law a rendering null and void.

defeat /dəˈfit/ v.t. **1.** to overcome in a contest, battle, etc.; vanquish; win or achieve victory over. **2.** to frustrate; thwart. **–n. 3.** the act or result of defeating.

defecate /ˈdefəkeɪt/ v.i. to void excrement. **–defecation**, n.

defect n. /ˈdifekt, dəˈfekt/ **1.** a falling short; a fault or imperfection. **–v.i.** /dəˈfekt/ **2.** to desert a country, cause, etc. **–defection**, n. **–defector**, n. **–defective**, adj.

defence /dəˈfens/ n. **1.** resistance against attack; protection. **2.** the defending of a cause or the like by speech, argument, etc. **3.** Law the denial or pleading of the defendant in answer to the claim or charge against him or her.

defend /dəˈfend/ v.t. **1.** (oft. fol. by from or against) to ward off attack from; guard against assault or injury. **2.** to maintain by argument, evidence, etc.; uphold. **3.** to contest (a legal charge, claim, etc.). **4.** to act as counsel for (an accused person). **–defendable**, adj. **–defender**, n.

defendant /dəˈfendənt/ n. Law the party against whom a claim or charge is brought in a proceeding.

defensible /dəˈfensəbəl/ adj. capable of being defended.

defensive /dəˈfensɪv/ adj. **1.** serving to defend; protective. **2.** made or carried on for the purpose of resisting attack.

defer¹ /dəˈfɜ/ v.t. (**-ferred**, **-ferring**) to put off (action, etc.) to a future time. **–deferment**, **deferral**, n.

defer² /dəˈfɜ/ v.i. (**-ferred**, **-ferring**) (fol. by to) to yield in judgement or opinion.

deference /ˈdefərəns/ n. **1.** submission or yielding to the judgement, opinion, will, etc., of another. **2.** respectful or courteous regard. **–deferential**, adj.

defiance /dəˈfaɪəns/ n. **1.** a daring or bold resistance to authority or to any opposing force. **2.** open disregard. **3.** a challenge to meet in combat or contest. **–defiant**, adj.

deficient /dəˈfɪʃənt/ adj. **1.** lacking some element or characteristic; defective. **2.** insufficient; inadequate. **–deficiency**, n.

deficit /ˈdefəsət/ n. the amount by which a sum of money falls short of the required amount.

defile /dəˈfaɪl/ v.t. **1.** to make foul, dirty, or unclean. **2.** to violate the chastity of.

define /dəˈfaɪn/ v.t. **1.** to state or set forth the meaning of (a word, phrase, etc.). **2.** to explain the nature or essential qualities of; describe. **3.** to fix or lay down definitely; specify distinctly. **–definition**, n.

definite /ˈdɛfənət/ adj. **1.** clearly defined or determined; not vague or general; fixed; precise; exact. **2.** certain; sure.

definitive /dəˈfɪnətɪv/ adj. **1.** having the function of deciding or settling; determining; conclusive; final. **2.** having its fixed and final form.

deflate /dəˈfleɪt/ v.t. **1.** to release the air or gas from (something inflated, as a tyre). **2.** to reduce (currency, prices, etc.) from an inflated condition. **3.** to reduce in esteem, especially self-esteem (a person or a person's ego).

deflation /dəˈfleɪʃən/ n. **1.** the act of deflating. **2.** an abnormal decline in the level of commodity prices, especially one not accompanied by an equal reduction in the costs of production.

deflect /dəˈflɛkt/ v.i. **1.** to bend or turn aside; swerve. **–v.t. 2.** to cause to turn from a true course or right line. **–deflection**, n.

defoliate /dəˈfoʊlieɪt/ v.t. to strip or deprive (a tree, etc.) of leaves. **–defoliant**, n.

deforest /diˈfɒrəst/ v.t. to strip (land) of forests or trees.

deforestation /diˌfɒrəstˈeɪʃən/ n. the permanent removal of forests or trees from a large area, usually for commercial purposes.

deform /dəˈfɔm/ v.t. **1.** to mar the natural form or shape of; put out of shape; disfigure. **2.** to make ugly, ungraceful, or displeasing; mar the beauty of; spoil. **–deformity**, n. **deformed**, adj.

defrag Computers Colloq. **–v.t.** /diˈfræg/ **1.** → defragment. **–n.** /ˈdifræg/ **2.** the process of defragmenting a disk.

defragment /difrægˈmɛnt/ v.t. Computers to reorganise the data stored on (a disk) so that whole files are stored in the same place. Also, Colloq., **defrag**. **–defragmentation**, n.

defraud /dəˈfrɔd/ v.t. to deprive of a right or property by fraud; cheat.

defray /dəˈfreɪ/ v.t. to bear or pay (the costs, expenses, etc.).

defriend /diˈfrɛnd/ v.t. → unfriend. **–defriended**, adj. **–defriending**, n.

defrost /diˈfrɒst, də-/ v.t. **1.** to remove the frost or ice from. **2.** to cause (food, etc.) to thaw, as by removing from a freezer.

deft /dɛft/ adj. dexterous; nimble; skilful; clever.

defunct /dəˈfʌŋkt/ adj. **1.** deceased; dead; extinct. **2.** no longer operative; not in use.

defuse /diˈfjuz/ v.t. **1.** to remove the fuse from (a bomb). **2.** to calm (a situation or action).

defy /dəˈfaɪ/ v.t. **(-fied, -fying) 1.** to challenge the power of; resist boldly or openly. **2.** to challenge (one) to do something deemed impossible.

degenerate v.i. /dəˈdʒɛnəreɪt/ **1.** to decline in physical, mental, or moral qualities; deteriorate. **–adj.** /dəˈdʒɛnərət/ **2.** having declined in physical or moral qualities; degraded. **–n.** /dəˈdʒɛnərət/ **3.** someone who has retrogressed from a normal type or standard, as in morals, or character. **–degenerative**, adj. **–degeneracy**, n. **–degeneration**, n.

degrade /dəˈgreɪd/ v.t. **1.** to reduce from a higher to a lower rank, degree, etc.; deprive of office, rank, or title as a punishment. **2.** to lower in character or quality; debase. **3.** to lower in dignity or estimation; bring into contempt. **–degradation**, n.

degree /dəˈgri/ n. **1.** a step or stage in an ascending or descending scale, or in a course or process. **2.** the angle between two radii of a circle which cut off on the circumference an arc equal to $^{1}/_{360}$ of that circumference (often indicated by the sign °). **3.** a unit in the measurement of temperature. **4.** Geog. the unit of measurement of latitude or longitude, usually employed to indicate position on the earth's surface. **5.** a qualification conferred by a university for successful work, as judged by examination, or as an honorary recognition of achievement.

degustation /deɪgʊsˈteɪʃən/ n. a sampling of a variety of different food dishes, as in a restaurant, etc.

dehydrate /ˈdihaɪdreɪt/ v.t. **1.** to deprive of water. **2.** to free (vegetables, etc.) of moisture, for preservation. **–v.i. 3.** to lose water or moisture. **–dehydration**, n.

deify /ˈdiəfaɪ, ˈdeɪə-/ v.t. **(-fied, -fying) 1.** to make a god of; exalt to the rank of a deity. **2.** to adore or regard as a deity.

deign /deɪn/ v.i. to think fit or in accordance with one's dignity; condescend.

deity /ˈdiəti, ˈdeɪ-/ n. (pl. **-ties) 1.** a god or goddess. **2.** divine character or nature.

deja vu /deɪʒa ˈvu/ n. the sense or illusion of having previously experienced something actually being encountered for the first time. Also, **déjà vu**.

dejected /dəˈdʒɛktəd/ adj. depressed in spirits; disheartened; low-spirited.

deka- (in the metric system) a prefix denoting 10 times a given unit, as in dekametre. Symbol: da Also, **deca-**; (before vowels), **dec-, dek-**.

delay /dəˈleɪ, di-/ v.t. **1.** to put off to a later time; defer; postpone. **2.** to impede the progress of; retard; hinder. **–v.i. 3.** to put off action; linger; loiter. **–n. 4.** the act of delaying; procrastination; loitering. **5.** an instance of being delayed.

delectable /dəˈlɛktəbəl/ adj. delightful; highly pleasing; enjoyable.

delectation /ˌdilɛkˈteɪʃən/ n. a high degree of enjoyment or pleasure; delight.

delegate n. /ˈdɛləgət/ **1.** a person delegated to act for or represent another or others; a deputy; a representative, as at a conference, or the like. **–v.t.** /ˈdɛləgeɪt/ **2.** to send or appoint (a person) as deputy or representative. **3.** to commit (powers, functions, etc.) to another as agent or deputy.

delegation /dɛləˈgeɪʃən/ n. a group of delegates.

delete /dəˈlit/ v.t. to strike out or take out (anything written or printed). **–deletion**, n.

deleterious /dɛləˈtɪəriəs/ adj. **1.** injurious to health. **2.** hurtful; harmful; injurious.

deliberate adj. /dəˈlɪbərət/ **1.** carefully weighed or considered; intentional. **2.** characterised by deliberation; careful or slow in deciding. **–v.i.** /dəˈlɪbəreɪt/ **3.** to think carefully or attentively; reflect. **–deliberation**, n.

deliberative /dəˈlibərətɪv, -ˌlibrə-/ adj. having the function of deliberating, as a legislative assembly.

delicacy /ˈdelɪkəsi/ n. (pl. -cies) 1. quality of being delicate. 2. something delightful or pleasing, especially to the palate.

delicate /ˈdelɪkət/ adj. 1. fine in texture, quality, construction, etc. 2. so fine or slight as to be scarcely perceptible; subtle. 3. easily damaged; fragile. 4. requiring great care, caution, or tact. 5. distinguishing subtle differences. 6. fastidious.

delicatessen /ˌdelɪkəˈtresən/ n. a shop selling cooked or prepared foods ready for serving, such as cold meats.

delicious /dəˈlɪʃəs/ adj. highly pleasing to the senses, especially to taste or smell.

delight /dəˈlaɪt/ n. a high degree of pleasure or enjoyment; joy; rapture.

delightful /dəˈlaɪtfəl/ adj. affording delight; highly pleasing.

delineate /dəˈlɪnieɪt/ v.t. to trace the outline of; sketch or trace in outline; represent pictorially. –**delineation**, n.

delinquent /dəˈlɪŋkwənt/ adj. 1. guilty of a misdeed or offence. –n. 2. someone who is delinquent, especially a young person. –**delinquency**, n.

delirious /dəˈlɪəriəs/ adj. 1. affected with delirium. 2. characteristic of delirium. 3. wild with excitement, enthusiasm, etc.

delirium /dəˈlɪəriəm/ n. (pl. -riums or -ria /-riə/) a temporary mental disorder marked by excitement, hallucinations, etc.

deliver /dəˈlɪvə/ v.t. 1. to give up or surrender; give into another's possession or keeping. 2. to strike (a blow). 3. to assist at the birth of. 4. to give or declare (a verdict, etc.). 5. to set free; liberate. –**deliverance**, n.

delivery /dəˈlɪvəri/ n. (pl. -ries) 1. the act of delivering. 2. something delivered.

delta /ˈdeltə/ n. a nearly flat plain of alluvial deposit between diverging branches of the mouth of a river.

delude /dəˈlud, -ˈljud/ v.t. to mislead the mind or judgement of; deceive. –**delusion**, n.

deluge /ˈdeljudʒ/ n. a flood.

deluxe /dəˈlʌks/ adj. of special elegance, sumptuousness, or fineness. Also, **de luxe**.

delve /delv/ v.i. to carry on intensive or thorough research for information, etc.

demagogue /ˈdeməgɒg/ n. an unprincipled popular orator or agitator.

demand /dəˈmænd, -ˈmand/ v.t. 1. to ask for with authority; claim as a right. –n. 2. the act of demanding. 3. an urgent or pressing requirement. 4. the state of being in request for purchase or use. 5. Econ. a. the desire to purchase and possess, coupled with the power of purchasing. b. the quantity of any goods which buyers will take at a particular price. See **supply** (def. 6). –phr. 6. **on demand**, a. subject to payment upon presentation and demand. b. as required.

demand economy n. an economy in which a sellers' market prevails.

demand-side economics n. management of the national economy which seeks to overcome recession by stimulating demand for goods and services.

demarcation /ˌdimaˈkeɪʃən/ n. 1. the marking off of the boundaries of something. 2. a division between things, especially the division between types of work carried out by members of different trade unions.

demean /dəˈmin/ v.t. to lower in dignity or standing; debase.

demeanour /dəˈminə/ n. conduct; behaviour; bearing. Also, **demeanor**.

demented /dəˈmentəd/ adj. out of one's mind; insane.

dementia /dəˈmenʃiə, -ʃə/ n. a state of mental disorder characterised by impairment or loss of the mental powers.

demerit /diˈmerət/ n. 1. a punishable quality; fault. 2. a mark against a person for misconduct or deficiency.

demesne /dəˈmein/ n. 1. possession (of land) as one's own. 2. an estate possessed, or in the actual possession or use of the owner. 3. a district; region.

demi- a prefix meaning: 1. half. 2. inferior.

demise /dəˈmaɪz/ n. death or decease.

demo- a word element meaning 'people', 'population', 'common people'.

democracy /dəˈmɒkrəsi/ n. (pl. -cies) 1. government by the people; a form of government in which the supreme power is vested in the people and exercised by them or by their elected agents under a free electoral system. 2. a nation, etc., having such a form of government. –**democrat**, n. –**democratic**, adj.

demography /dəˈmɒgrəfi/ n. the science of population statistics, as of births, deaths, diseases, marriages, etc. –**demographer**, n. –**demographic**, adj. –**demographics**, n.

demolish /dəˈmɒlɪʃ/ v.t. to throw or pull down (a building, etc.); reduce to ruins. –**demolition**, n.

demon /ˈdimən/ n. an evil spirit; a devil. –**demonic**, **demoniac**, adj.

demonstrate /ˈdemənstreɪt/ v.t. 1. to make evident by arguments or reasoning; prove. 2. to describe and explain with the help of specimens or by experiment. 3. to manifest or exhibit.

demonstration /ˌdemənˈstreɪʃən/ n. 1. the act or result of demonstrating. 2. a public exhibition of sympathy, opposition, etc., as a parade or mass meeting.

demonstrative /dəˈmɒnstrətɪv/ adj. 1. characterised by or given to open exhibition or expression of the feelings, etc. 2. serving to demonstrate; explanatory or illustrative. 3. serving to prove the truth of anything; indubitably conclusive. 4. Gram. indicating or specifying the thing referred to. –n. 5. Gram. a demonstrative word, as this or these. –**demonstratively**, adv. –**demonstrativeness**, n.

demoralise /dɪˈmɒrəlaɪz/ v.t. to deprive of spirit, courage, etc. Also, **demoralize**.

demote /dəˈmoʊt, di-/ to reduce to a lower grade or class (opposed to promote). –**demotion**, n.

demur /dəˈmɜ/ v.i. (-murred, -murring) 1. to make objection; take exception; object. 2. Law to interpose a demurrer. –n. 3. an objection raised. –**demurral**, n. –**demurrer**, n.

demure /dəˈmjʊə, -ˈmjuə/ adj. affectedly or unnaturally modest, decorous, or prim.

demurrage /dəˈmʌrɪdʒ/ n. Commerce **1.** the detention of a vessel, as in loading or unloading, beyond the time agreed upon. **2.** a charge for this.

den /dɛn/ n. **1.** a secluded place, as a cave, serving as the habitation of a wild beast. **2.** a cosy or secluded room for personal use. **3.** a place devoted to an illicit activity: a gambling den.

denature /diˈneɪtʃə/ v.t. to alter the natural state of.

dendro- a word element meaning 'tree'. Also, (before vowels), **dendr-**.

-dendron a word element meaning 'tree'.

denial /dəˈnaɪəl/ n. **1.** a contradiction of a statement, etc. refusal. –phr. **3. in denial**, closing one's mind to an unpleasant fact or experience.

denigrate /ˈdɛnəɡreɪt/ v.t. to sully; defame.

denim /ˈdɛnəm/ n. a heavy cotton for overalls, trousers, etc.

denizen /ˈdɛnəzən/ n. an inhabitant.

denomination /dənɒməˈneɪʃən/ n. **1.** a class or kind of persons or things distinguished by a specific name. **2.** a religious group.

denominator /dəˈnɒmɪneɪtə/ n. Maths that term of a fraction (usually under the line) which shows the number of equal parts into which the unit is divided. Compare **numerator**.

denotation /dɪnoʊˈteɪʃən/ n. the meaning of a term when it identifies something by naming it (distinguished from connotation).

denote /dəˈnoʊt/ v.t. to be a mark or sign of; indicate.

denounce /dəˈnaʊns/ v.t. to condemn openly; assail with censure.

dense /dɛns/ adj. **1.** having the component parts closely compacted together; compact. **2.** thickheaded; obtuse; stupid. –**density**, n.

dent /dɛnt/ n. a hollow or depression in a surface, as from a blow.

dental /ˈdɛntl/ adj. **1.** of or relating to the teeth. **2.** of or relating to dentistry.

dental floss n. soft, waxed thread used for cleaning between the teeth. Also, **floss**.

denti- a word element meaning 'tooth'. Also, (before vowels), **dent-**.

dentistry /ˈdɛntəstri/ n. the science or art dealing with the prevention and treatment of oral disease. –**dentist**, n.

dentition /dɛnˈtɪʃən/ n. the arrangement of teeth.

denture /ˈdɛntʃə/ n. an artificial restoration of teeth.

denude /dəˈnjud/ v.t. to make naked or bare; strip.

denunciation /dənʌnsiˈeɪʃən/ n. a denouncing.

deny /dəˈnaɪ/ v.t. (**-nied, -nying**) **1.** to assert the negative of; declare not to be true. **2.** to refuse to grant (a claim, request, etc.). **3.** to refuse to recognise or acknowledge; repudiate.

deodorant /diˈoʊdərənt/ n. an agent for destroying odours.

depart /dəˈpat/ v.i. **1.** to go away. **2.** (fol. by from) to turn aside. –**departure**, n.

department /dəˈpatmənt/ n. a distinct part of anything arranged in divisions; a division of a complex whole or organised system.

department store n. a large shop selling a wide range of goods in different departments.

depend /dəˈpɛnd/ v.i. **1.** to rely; trust. **2.** to be conditioned or contingent. –**dependable**, adj.

dependant /dəˈpɛndənt/ n. someone who depends on or looks to another for support, favour, etc.

dependent /dəˈpɛndənt/ adj. depending on something or someone else. –**dependence**, n.

depict /dəˈpɪkt/ v.t. to represent by or as by painting; portray; delineate.

depilatory /dəˈpɪlətri/ adj. **1.** capable of removing hair. –n. (pl. **-ries**) **2.** a depilatory agent.

deplete /dəˈplit/ v.t. to deprive of that which fills; decrease the fullness of; reduce the stock or amount of.

deplorable /dəˈplɔrəbəl/ adj. **1.** causing grief; lamentable. **2.** causing censure; bad; wretched. –**deplore**, v.

deploy /dəˈplɔɪ/ v.t. **1.** to spread out (troops or military units) and form an extended front. **2.** to make careful utilisation of (mineral resources). –**deployment**, n. –**deployable**, adj.

deport /dəˈpɔt/ v.t. to expel (an illegal immigrant, etc.) from a country; banish.

deportment /dəˈpɔtmənt/ n. manner of bearing; carriage.

depose /dəˈpoʊz/ v.t. **1.** to remove from office or position. –v.i. **2.** to bear witness. –**deposal**, n.

deposit /dəˈpɒzət/ v.t. **1.** to put or lay down. **2.** to place for safekeeping or in trust. –n. **3.** anything laid or thrown down, as matter precipitated from a fluid; sediment. **4.** an accumulation. **5.** money placed in a financial institution. **6.** anything given as security or in part payment.

depot /ˈdepoʊ/ n. **1.** a storehouse. **2.** a place where buses, trams, trucks, etc., are kept when they are not in service.

depraved /dəˈpreɪvd/ adj. corrupt or perverted, especially morally; wicked. –**depravity**, n.

deprecate /ˈdɛprəkeɪt/ v.t. to express earnest disapproval of. –**deprecatory**, adj.

depreciation /dəprɪʃiˈeɪʃən, -prisi-/ n. **1.** a decrease in value due to wear and tear, decay, decline in price, etc. **2.** a decrease in the purchasing or exchange value of money. –**depreciate**, v.

depredate /ˈdɛprədeɪt/ v.t. to prey upon; plunder.

depress /dəˈprɛs/ v.t. **1.** to lower in spirits. **2.** to press down.

depressed /dəˈprɛst/ adj. **1.** feeling sad and as if there is no hope. **2.** in a situation where prices and values are held down.

depression /dəˈprɛʃən/ n. **1.** unhappiness and a feeling that there is no hope. **2.** a mental illness where one feels in a low mood for a long time without there being an apparent cause of unhappiness. **3.** a period when there is a lot of unemployment and businesses are not making profits. **4.** a part of a surface which is lower than the rest, forming a slight hole.

deprive /dəˈpraɪv/ v.t. to divest of something; dispossess. –**deprivation**, n.

depth /dɛpθ/ n. **1.** measure or distance downwards, inwards, or backwards. **2.** intensity, as of silence, colour, etc. **3.** lowness of pitch. **4.** extent of intellectual penetration, sagacity, or profundity.

deputation /dɛpjuˈteɪʃən/ n. **1.** appointment to represent or act for another or others. **2.** the person(s) so appointed.

deputy /ˈdɛpjəti/ n. (pl. **-ties**) **1.** a person appointed or authorised to act for another or others. **2.** a person appointed or elected as assistant to a public official.

derail /diˈreɪl/ v.t. **1.** to cause (a train, etc.) to run off the rails. —v.i. **2.** (of a train, etc.) to run off the rails of a track. —**derailment**, n.

deranged /dəˈreɪndʒd/ adj. insane.

derby /ˈdɑbi, ˈdɜːbi/ n. (pl. **-bies**) an important race, especially of horses.

deregulation /diːrɛɡjəˈleɪʃən/ n. the removal of government regulations, restrictions and controls to allow greater efficiency through improved competition. —**deregulate**, v.

derelict /ˈdɛrəlɪkt/ adj. **1.** left or abandoned, as by the owner or guardian (said especially of a ship abandoned at sea). **2.** guilty of lack of care for one's obligations; remiss: *derelict in one's duty.* —n. **3.** a person forsaken or abandoned, especially by society.

dereliction /dɛrəˈlɪkʃən/ n. culpable neglect, as of duty; delinquency; fault.

deride /dəˈraɪd/ v.t. to laugh at in contempt; scoff or jeer. —**derision**, n. —**derisive**, adj.

derivative /dəˈrɪvətɪv/ adj. **1.** imitative of others. **2.** derived. **3.** not original or primitive; secondary. —n. **4.** *Stock Exchange* a financial instrument or asset, the value of which is derived from a link to some other investment or asset, such as a future contract, option contract, etc.

derive /dəˈraɪv/ v.t. **1.** (fol. by *from*) to receive or obtain from a source or origin. **2.** to trace, as from a source or origin. **3.** to obtain by reasoning; deduce. —v.i. **4.** to come from a source; originate. —**derivation**, n.

dermatitis /dɜːməˈtaɪtəs/ n. inflammation of the skin.

dermatology /dɜːməˈtɒlədʒi/ n. the science of the skin and its diseases. —**dermatologist**, n.

derogatory /dəˈrɒɡətri, -ətəri/ adj. disparaging.

desalination /ˌdiːsæləˈneɪʃən/ n. the removal of salt from sea water so that it becomes suitable for drinking or for irrigation. Also, **desalinisation.** —**desalinate**, v.

descant /ˈdɛskænt/ n. *Music* a melody accompanying a simple theme and usually written above it.

descend /dəˈsɛnd/ v.i. **1.** to move or pass from a higher to a lower place; go or come down; fall; sink. **2.** to be derived by birth or extraction. **3.** (usu. fol. by *on*) to approach in a hostile or intimidating manner, especially as a large group: *the gang descended on him after school; the relatives all descended on us at Christmas time.* —**descent**, n. —**descendent**, adj.

descendant /dəˈsɛndənt/ n. someone descended from an ancestor; offspring, near or remote.

describe /dəˈskraɪb/ v.t. **1.** to set forth in written or spoken words; give an account of. **2.** *Geom.* to draw or trace, as an arc. —**description**, n. —**descriptive**, adj.

desecrate /ˈdɛsəkreɪt/ v.t. to divest of sacred or hallowed character.

deselect /disəˈlɛkt/ v.t. *Computers* to cancel the selection of (an item, a set of items, highlighted

text, etc.) by clicking the mouse outside or inside (depending on the program operating) the target to have its selection cancelled.

desert[1] /ˈdɛzət/ n. **1.** an area so deficient in moisture as to support only a sparse, widely spaced vegetation, or none at all. —adj. **2.** of, relating to, or like a desert. **3.** uninhabited: *a desert island.*

desert[2] /dəˈzɜːt/ v.t. **1.** to abandon. —v.i. **2.** (especially of a soldier or sailor) to forsake one's duty, etc. —**desertion**, n.

desert[3] /dəˈzɜːt/ n. that which is deserved; a due reward or punishment.

deserve /dəˈzɜːv/ v.t. to merit (reward, punishment, esteem, etc.) in return for actions, qualities, etc.

desiccate /ˈdɛsəkeɪt/ v.t. to dry thoroughly; dry up.

desiccated /ˈdɛsəkeɪtəd/ adj. **1.** dehydrated or powdered: *desiccated coconut.* **2.** completely dried out.

design /dəˈzaɪn/ v.t. **1.** to prepare the preliminary sketch or the plans for (a work to be executed). **2.** to plan or fashion artistically or skilfully. **3.** to intend for a definite purpose. **4.** to form or conceive in the mind; contrive; plan. —n. **5.** an outline, sketch, or plan. **6.** the combination of details or features of a picture, building, etc.; the pattern or device of artistic work. **7.** the end in view; intention; purpose. —**designer**, n.

designate v.t. /ˈdɛzɪɡneɪt/ **1.** to nominate or select for a duty, purpose, etc.; appoint; assign. —adj. /ˈdɛzɪɡnət, -neɪt/ **2.** appointed to an office but not yet in possession of it.

designated driver n. a member of a group of people attending a social event at which alcohol will be drunk, who agrees to drink little or no alcohol and to be responsible for driving the other members home safely.

designer drug n. a synthetically-produced drug, designed to imitate an illegal drug (especially cocaine or heroin), the new substance being not specifically proscribed by law.

designer gene n. a gene created or modified by genetic engineering.

desirable /dəˈzaɪrəbəl/ adj. **1.** worthy to be desired; pleasing, excellent, or fine. **2.** advisable.

desire /dəˈzaɪə/ v.t. **1.** to wish or long for; crave; want. —n. **2.** a longing or craving. **3.** an expressed wish; request.

desirous /dəˈzaɪrəs/ phr. **desirous of**, having or experiencing a wish or hope for.

desist /dəˈzɪst, dəˈsɪst/ v.i. to cease, as from some action or proceeding; stop.

desk /dɛsk/ n. a table specially adapted for convenience in writing or reading.

de-skilling /diːˈskɪlɪŋ/ n. the process whereby an individual is left without appropriate skills and therefore made unemployable because of changes in work practices, such as the introduction of new technology. Also, **deskilling.**

desktop /ˈdɛsktɒp/ n. **1.** the background image displayed on a computer screen by some computer programs, which includes icons representing programs, documents, etc. —adj. **2.** (of a computer, office equipment, etc.) small enough in design to be used at a desk.

desktop publishing n. the production of printed material by means of a computer system comprising a personal computer, software, and a laser printer.

desolate /ˈdɛsələt, ˈdɛz-/ adj. **1.** devastated. **2.** deserted. **3.** left alone; lonely. –v.t. /ˈdɛsəleɪt, ˈdɛz-/ **4.** to devastate. **5.** to forsake or abandon. –**desolation**, n.

despair /dəˈspɛə/ n. hopelessness.

desperate /ˈdɛsprət, -pərət/ adj. **1.** reckless from despair. **2.** very serious or dangerous. –**desperation**, n.

despicable /dəˈspɪkəbəl/ adj. that is to be despised; contemptible.

despise /dəˈspaɪz/ v.t. to look down upon, as in contempt.

despite /dəˈspaɪt/ prep. in spite of.

despondent /dəˈspɒndənt/ adj. depressed or dejected. –**despondency**, n.

despot /ˈdɛspɒt/ n. an ruler who exercises power arbitrarily and without restraint; tyrant.

dessert /dəˈzɜt/ n. the final course of a meal including puddings, fruit.

destabilise /diˈsteɪbəlaɪz/ v.t. **1.** to make unstable. **2.** Politics to deliberately create uncertainty about: to destabilise the leadership. Also, **destabilize**. –**destabilising**, adj. –**destabilisation**, n.

destination /dɛstəˈneɪʃən/ n. the predetermined end of a journey or voyage.

destine /ˈdɛstən/ v.t. to appoint or ordain beforehand, as by divine decree; predetermine.

destined /ˈdɛstənd/ adj. **1.** bound for a certain destination. **2.** predetermined.

destiny /ˈdɛstəni/ n. (pl. **-nies**) **1.** a predetermined course of events. **2.** the power or agency which determines the course of events.

destitute /ˈdɛstətjut/ adj. bereft of means or resources.

destroy /dəˈstrɔɪ/ v.t. **1.** to ruin; spoil; demolish. **2.** to put an end to. –**destruction**, n. –**destructive**, adj.

desultory /ˈdɛsəltri, -təri, ˈdɛz-/ adj. lacking purpose, method, or enthusiasm.

detach /dəˈtætʃ/ v.t. to unfasten and separate; disengage; disunite.

detail /ˈditeɪl/ n. **1.** an individual or minute part; an item or particular. **2.** fine, intricate decoration.

detain /dəˈteɪn/ v.t. **1.** to keep from proceeding; keep waiting; delay. **2.** to keep under restraint or in custody. –**detention**, n.

detect /dəˈtɛkt/ v.t. to discover or notice a fact, a process, or an action. –**detection**, n.

detective /dəˈtɛktɪv/ n. a person, usually a member of the police force, who investigates crimes.

detention centre /dəˈtɛnʃən/ n. an institution for holding people in custody, as one used to confine illegal immigrants, or certain categories of criminal offenders.

deter /dəˈtɜ/ v.t. (**-terred, -terring**) to discourage or restrain (one) from acting or proceeding, through fear, doubt, etc. –**deterrent**, adj., n.

detergent /dəˈtɜdʒənt/ n. any cleaning agent, including soap.

deteriorate /dəˈtɪəriəreɪt/ v.i. to become worse.

determinate /dəˈtɜmənət/ adj. fixed.

determination /dətɜməˈneɪʃən/ n. **1.** the quality of being determined or resolute. **2.** the act or result of determining.

determine /dəˈtɜmən/ v.t. **1.** to settle or decide (a dispute, question, etc.) by an authoritative decision. **2.** to conclude or ascertain, as after reasoning, observation, etc. **3.** to fix or decide causally; condition.

determined /dəˈtɜmənd/ adj. resolute; unflinching; firm.

detest /dəˈtɛst/ v.t. to feel abhorrence of; hate; dislike intensely.

detonate /ˈdɛtəneɪt/ v.t. to cause to explode. –**detonation**, n. –**detonator**, n.

detour /ˈdituə, -tuə, -tɔ/ n. a roundabout or circuitous way or course, especially one used temporarily instead of the main route.

detox /ˈditɒks/ n. **1.** the process of detoxification. –v.i. **2.** to go through the process of detoxification.

detoxification /ˌditɒksəfəˈkeɪʃən/ n. the process of withdrawing from physical or psychological dependency on a substance of abuse, such as drugs, alcohol, etc.

detract /dəˈtrækt/ v.i. to take away a part, as from quality, value, or reputation.

detriment /ˈdɛtrəmənt/ n. loss, damage, or injury. –**detrimental**, adj.

detritus /dəˈtraɪtəs/ n. any disintegrated material; debris.

deuce /djus/ n. **1.** a card, or the side of a dice, having two pips. **2.** Tennis, etc. a juncture in a game at which the scores are level at forty all.

devalue /diˈvælju/ v.t. (**-ued, -uing**) **1.** to lower the legal value of (a currency); devaluate. **2.** to diminish the worth or value of.

devastate /ˈdɛvəsteɪt/ v.t. to lay waste; ravage; render desolate.

develop /dəˈvɛləp/ v.t. **1.** to bring out the capabilities or possibilities of; bring to a more advanced or effective state. **2.** to cause to grow or expand. **3.** to bring into being or activity; generate; evolve. **4.** to build on (land). **5.** to treat (a photographic plate, etc.) with chemical agents so as to bring out the latent image. –v.i. **6.** to grow into a more mature or advanced state; advance; expand. **7.** to come gradually into existence or operation; be evolved. –**development**, n.

developed /dəˈvɛləpt/ adj. **1.** having undergone development. **2.** (of a country or economy) industrialised.

developing /dəˈvɛləpɪŋ/ adj. **1.** undergoing development. **2.** (of a country) in the early stages of becoming industrialised.

deviant /ˈdiviənt/ adj. **1.** deviating from an accepted norm, especially in sexual behaviour. –n. **2.** a person or thing that is deviant.

deviate /ˈdivieɪt/ v.i. **1.** to turn aside (from a way or course). **2.** to depart or swerve, as from a procedure, course of action, or acceptable standard.

deviation /diviˈeɪʃən/ n. **1.** the act of deviating; divergence. **2.** Statistics the difference between one of a set of values and the mean of the set.

device /dəˈvaɪs/ n. **1.** an invention or contrivance. **2.** a plan or scheme for effecting a purpose. **3.** (pl.) will; desire; ingenuity; inclination. **4.** a figure or design used as an emblem, badge, trademark, etc. **5.** Computers → peripheral device.

device driver n. Computers a program that enables the operating system of a computer to recognise peripheral devices, such as modems, printers, mouses, etc. Also, **driver**.

devil /'dɛvəl/ n. 1. (*sometimes upper case*) *Theology* the supreme spirit of evil. 2. (in many religions) an evil spirit; demon. 3. an atrociously wicked, cruel, or ill-tempered person.

devious /'diviəs/ adj. 1. departing from the accepted way; roundabout. 2. not straightforward; tricky; deceptive; deceitful.

devise /də'vaɪz/ v.t. 1. to order or arrange the plan of; think out; plan; contrive; invent. 2. *Law* to assign or transmit (property, especially real property) by will.

devoid /də'vɔɪd/ adj. (fol. by *of*) empty, not possessing, free from, void, or destitute.

devolve /də'vɒlv/ v.t. 1. to transfer or delegate (a duty, responsibility, etc.) to or upon another; pass on. –v.i. 2. to fall as a duty or responsibility on a person.

devon /'dɛvən/ n. a large, smooth sausage, usually sliced and eaten cold.

devote /də'voʊt/ v.t. to give up or appropriate to or concentrate on a particular pursuit, occupation, purpose, cause, person, etc. –**devotion**, n. –**devotee**, n.

devour /də'vaʊə/ v.t. to swallow or eat up voraciously or ravenously.

devout /də'vaʊt/ adj. devoted to divine worship or service; pious; religious.

dew /dju/ n. moisture condensed from the atmosphere, especially at night, and deposited in the form of small drops upon any cool surface.

dexterity /dɛks'tɛrəti/ n. adroitness or skill in using the hands or the mind. –**dexterous**, adj.

dhal /dal/ n. → **dal**.

di-[1] a prefix meaning 'twice', 'doubly', 'two'. Also, **dis-**.

di-[2] variant of **dis-**[1], before *b, d, l, m, n, r, s,* and *v,* and sometimes *g* and *j,* as in *divide*.

diabetes /daɪə'bitiz/ n. a disease in which the ability of the body to produce or process insulin is impaired; in **type 1 diabetes** the body does not produce insulin properly; in **type 2 diabetes** the body is not able to use the insulin produced properly. –**diabetic**, n., adj.

diabetic /daɪə'bɛtɪk/ adj. 1. of or relating to diabetes. 2. having diabetes. –n. 3. a person who has diabetes.

diabolical /daɪə'bɒlɪk/ adj. having the qualities of a devil; fiendish; outrageously wicked. Also, **diabolic**.

diagnosis /daɪəg'noʊsəs/ n. (pl. -**noses** /-'noʊsiz/) *Med.* the process of determining by examination the nature and circumstances of a diseased condition. –**diagnose**, v. –**diagnostic**, adj.

diagonal /daɪ'ægənəl/ adj. *Maths* connecting, as a straight line, two non-adjacent angles, as between opposite corners of a square.

diagram /'daɪəgræm/ n. a drawing or plan that outlines and explains, the parts, operation, etc., of something.

dial /'daɪəl/ n. 1. a face upon which time is indicated by hands, pointers, or shadows. 2. a plate or disc with graduations or figures, as for measuring, or on a telephone, etc. –v.t. (**dialled** *or, Chiefly US,* **dialed**, **dialling** *or, Chiefly US,* **dialing**) 3. to measure, select,

show or tune in by means of a dial. 4. to call (a number or person) on a telephone.

dialect /'daɪəlɛkt/ n. the language of a particular district or class. –**dialectal**, adj.

dialogue /'daɪəlɒg/ n. 1. conversation between two or more persons. 2. an exchange of ideas or opinions on a particular issue.

dialysis /daɪ'æləsəs/ n. (pl. -**alyses** /-'æləsiz/) *Med.* (in cases of defective kidney function) the removal of waste products from the blood by causing them to diffuse through a semipermeable membrane. –**dialyse**, v.

diameter /daɪ'æmətə/ n. *Geom.* a straight line passing through the centre of a circle or sphere and terminated at each end by the circumference or surface.

diametric /daɪə'mɛtrɪk/ adj. 1. relating to a diameter; along a diameter. 2. direct; complete; absolute. Also, **diametrical**.

diamond /'daɪəmənd, 'daɪmənd/ n. 1. an extremely hard, pure or nearly pure form of carbon, which, when used as a precious stone, has great brilliance. 2. an equilateral quadrilateral, especially as placed with its diagonals vertical and horizontal.

diaphanous /daɪ'æfənəs/ adj. transparent; translucent.

diaphragm /'daɪəfræm/ n. 1. *Anat.* the partition separating the thoracic cavity from the abdominal cavity in mammals. 2. a contraceptive membrane covering the cervix.

diarrhoea /daɪə'riə/ n. an intestinal disorder marked by frequency and fluidity of bowel movements. Also, **diarrhea**.

diary /'daɪəri/ n. (pl. -**ries**) a daily record, especially of the writer's own experiences or observations. –**diarist**, n. –**diarise**, **diarize**, v.

diastole /daɪ'æstəli/ n. *Physiol., etc.* the normal rhythmical relaxation and dilatation of the heart, especially that of the ventricles. Compare **systole**. –**diastolic** /daɪə'stɒlɪk/, adj.

diatribe /'daɪətraɪb/ n. a bitter and violent denunciation, attack, or criticism.

dice /daɪs/ pl. n. (sing. **die**) 1. small cubes of plastic, ivory, bone, or wood, marked on each side with a different number of spots (1 to 6), usually used in pairs in games of chance or in gambling. –v.t. (**diced**, **dicing**) 2. to cut into small cubes.

dicey /'daɪsi/ adj. *Colloq.* dangerous; risky; tricky.

dichotomy /daɪ'kɒtəmi/ n. (pl. -**mies**) division into two parts or into twos; subdivision into halves or pairs.

dick /dɪk/ n. *Colloq.* (taboo) the penis.

dicky[1] /'dɪki/ n. (pl. -**kies**) a detachable shirt front.

dicky[2] /'dɪki/ adj. *Colloq.* unsteady, shaky; in bad health: *a dicky heart*.

dictaphone /'dɪktəfoʊn/ n. (*from trademark*) an instrument that records and reproduces dictation.

dictate /dɪk'teɪt/ v.t. 1. to say or read aloud (something) to be taken down in writing or recorded mechanically. 2. to prescribe positively; command with authority. 3. to influence or control (a decision, action, etc.). –**dictation**, n.

dictator /dɪk'teɪtə, 'dɪkteɪtə/ n. a person exercising absolute power. –**dictatorial**, adj.

diction /'dɪkʃən/ n. style of speaking or writing as dependent upon choice of words.

dictionary /'dɪkʃənri, 'dɪkʃənəri/, *Orig. US* /'dɪkʃənɛri/ n. (pl. **-ries**) a reference work containing a selection of the words of a language, usually arranged alphabetically, with explanations of their meanings, pronunciations, and other information concerning them.

did /dɪd/ v. past tense of **do**.

didactic /daɪ'dæktɪk, də-/ adj. **1.** intended for instruction; instructive. **2.** inclined to teach or lecture others too much.

diddle /'dɪdl/ v.t. *Colloq.* to cheat; swindle; victimise. **–diddler**, n.

didgeridoo /ˌdɪdʒəri'duː/ n. an Aboriginal wind instrument. Also, **didjeridu**.

didj /dɪdʒ/ n. *Colloq.* a didgeridoo. Also, **didge**, **didg**.

didn't /'dɪdnt, 'dɪdn/ v. contraction of *did not*.

die[1] /daɪ/ v.i. (**died**, **dying**) **1.** to cease to live; undergo the complete and permanent cessation of all vital functions. **2.** (usu. fol. by *away*, *out*, or *down*) to pass gradually; fade or subside gradually. –*phr. Colloq.* **3. be dying for**, to desire or want keenly or greatly: *I'm dying for a drink.* **4. be dying to**, to desire or want keenly to: *I'm dying to see Venice.*

die[2] /daɪ/ n. (pl. **dies** for def. 1, **dice** for def. 2) **1.** any of various devices for cutting or forming material in a press or a stamping or forging machine. **2.** singular of **dice**.

diehard /'daɪhɑd/ n. someone who resists vigorously to the last.

diesel /'dizəl/ n. the oil left after petrol and kerosene have been taken from crude petroleum; used in diesel engines.

diesel engine n. a type of internal-combustion engine in which an oil is used as fuel.

diet /'daɪət/ n. **1.** a particular selection of food, especially as prescribed to improve the physical condition, regulate weight, or cure a disease. **2.** the usual or regular food or foods a person eats most frequently. –v.i. (**-eted**, **-eting**) **3.** to select or limit the food one eats to improve one's physical condition or lose weight. **–dietitian**, n. **–dietary**, adj.

differ /'dɪfə/ v.i. **1.** (oft. fol. by *from*) to be unlike, dissimilar, or distinct in nature or qualities. **2.** (oft. fol. by *with* or *from*) to disagree in opinion, belief, etc.; be at variance.

difference /'dɪfrəns/ n. **1.** the state or relation of being different; dissimilarity. **2.** a significant change in or effect upon a situation. **3.** a disagreement in opinion; dispute; quarrel. **4.** *Maths* the amount by which one quantity is greater or less than another.

different /'dɪfrənt/ adj. **1.** not the same or similar; not having qualities alike. **2.** separate or distinct: *a different country.* **3.** various or several: *it comes in different colours.* **4.** striking or not ordinary: *now that's different!*

differential /dɪfə'rɛnʃəl/ adj. **1.** constituting a difference; distinctive. –n. **2.** *Machinery* a set of gears in a car which permit the driving wheels to revolve at different speeds when the car is turning.

differentiate /dɪfə'rɛnʃieɪt/ v.t. **1.** to mark off by differences; distinguish; alter; change. **2.** *Maths* to obtain the derivative of. –v.i. **3.** to make a distinction; discriminate.

difficult /'dɪfəkəlt/ adj. **1.** hard to do, perform, or accomplish; not easy; requiring much effort. **2.** hard to deal with or get on with. **–difficulty**, n.

diffident /'dɪfədənt/ adj. lacking confidence; timid. **–diffidence**, n.

diffraction /də'frækʃən/ n. the breaking up of light. **–diffract**, v.

diffuse v.t. /də'fjuz/ **1.** to spread or scatter widely or thinly; disseminate. –adj. /də'fjus/ **2.** widely spread or scattered; dispersed. **–diffusion**, n.

dig /dɪg/ v. (**dug**, **digging**) –v.i. **1.** to break up, turn over, or remove earth, etc. –v.t. **2.** to break up and turn over, or penetrate and loosen (the ground). **3.** to make (a hole, tunnel, etc.) by removing material. **4.** (oft. fol. by *up* or *out*) to obtain or remove by digging. –n. **5.** thrust; poke. **6.** a cutting, sarcastic remark. **7.** an archaeological site undergoing excavation. **8.** (pl.) lodgings.

digest v.t. /də'dʒɛst, daɪ-/ **1.** to prepare (food) in the alimentary canal for assimilation into the system. **2.** to assimilate mentally. –n. /'daɪdʒɛst/ **3.** a collection or summary, especially of literary, historical, legal, or scientific matter, often classified or condensed. **–digestion**, n. **–digestive**, adj.

digger /'dɪgə/ n. **1.** a miner, especially a gold-miner. **2.** *Colloq.* an Australian soldier.

diggings /'dɪgɪŋz/ pl. n. a mining operation or locality.

digit /'dɪdʒət/ n. **1.** a finger or toe. **2.** any of the figures 0, 1, …9.

digital /'dɪdʒətəl/ adj. **1.** of or relating to a digit. **2.** *Electronics* of or relating to information represented by patterns made up from qualities existing in two states only, on and off, as pulses (opposed to *analog*). **3.** of or relating to a device which represents a variable as a series of digits, as a digital watch which shows passing time by a series of changing numbers, or a digital tuner which similarly shows the frequencies to which it is being tuned. Compare **analog** (def. 2). **–digitally**, adv.

digital broadcasting n. broadcasting by the use of digitally compressed signals which are decoded by a specifically designed receiver (opposed to *analog broadcasting*).

digital camera n. a camera which stores pictures as digital files.

digital display n. a display in which information is represented in digital rather than analog form; readout.

digital native n. a person who grows up using digital media and communications systems, and thus has complete familiarity with them.

digital signature n. a unique code, in the form of a series of characters, used to verify the identity of the creator or sender of an electronic document, and to ensure that the document has not been altered before reaching the receiver.

digital tattoo n. the information which is traceable online about an individual's interests, purchasing patterns, etc.

digital-to-analog converter n. an electronic device for converting digital signals to analog signals.

digital TV n. the technology of sending and receiving television images and sound as binary data. Also, **digital television**, **DTV**.

digitise /ˈdɪdʒətaɪz/ v.t. to express (analog information) in digital form so that it can be processed by a computer. Also, **digitize**.

dignitary /ˈdɪgnətri, -nətəri/ n. (pl. **-ries**) someone who holds a high rank or office, especially in government or the church.

dignity /ˈdɪgnəti/ n. **1.** nobility of manner or style; stateliness; gravity. **2.** nobleness or elevation of mind. **–dignify**, v.

digress /daɪˈgrɛs/ v.i. to deviate or wander away from the main purpose. **–digression**, n.

dike¹ /daɪk/ n. → **dyke¹**.

dike² /daɪk/ n. → **dyke²**.

dilapidated /dəˈlæpədeɪtəd/ adj. reduced to, or fallen into, ruin or decay.

dilate /daɪˈleɪt, də-/ v.t. to make wider or larger; cause to expand. **–dilation**, n.

dilatory /ˈdɪlətri, -təri/ adj. inclined to delay or procrastinate; slow; tardy.

dilemma /dəˈlɛmə, daɪ-/ n. a situation requiring a choice between equally undesirable alternatives.

diligent /ˈdɪlədʒənt/ adj. constant and persistent in an effort to accomplish something. **–diligence**, n.

dill¹ /dɪl/ n. a herb of the parsley family, with aromatic seeds and finely divided leaves used as a flavouring in cooking.

dill² /dɪl/ n. Colloq. a fool.

dillybag /ˈdɪlibæg/ n. a small bag.

dillydally /ˈdɪlidæli/ v.i. (**-dallied, -dallying**) to waste time, especially by indecision.

dilute /daɪˈlut, -ˈljut/ v.t. **1.** to make thinner or weaker by the addition of water or the like. **2.** to reduce the strength of. **3.** to increase the proportion (in a labour force) of unskilled to skilled. **–adj. 4.** reduced in strength. **–dilution**, n.

dim /dɪm/ adj. (**dimmer, dimmest**) **1.** not bright or strong. **–v.t., v.i. (dimmed, dimming) 2.** to make or become dim.

dimension /dəˈmɛnʃən/ n. **1.** magnitude measured in a particular direction, or along a diameter or principal axis. **2.** an aspect; appearance.

diminish /dəˈmɪnɪʃ/ v.t. **1.** to make, or cause to seem, smaller; lessen; reduce. **–v.i. 2.** to lessen; decrease. **–diminution**, n.

diminishing returns pl. n. the fact, often stated as a law or principle, that as any factor in production (as labour, capital, etc.) is increased, the output per unit factor will eventually decrease.

diminutive /dəˈmɪnjətɪv/ adj. small; little; tiny.

dimple /ˈdɪmpəl/ n. a small natural hollow, especially in the cheek.

dim sim /dɪm ˈsɪm/ n. a dish of Chinese origin, made of seasoned meat wrapped in thin dough and steamed or fried.

dim sum /dɪm ˈsʊm, ˈsʌm/ n. **1.** in Chinese cooking, individual servings of food, as offered during yum cha. See **yum cha**. **2.** → **dim sim**.

din /dɪn/ n. a loud, confused noise.

dine /daɪn/ v.i. to eat the principal meal of the day; have dinner.

ding /dɪŋ/ v.i. **1.** to sound, as a bell; ring, especially with wearisome continuance. **–n. 2.** a blow or stroke. **3.** the sound of a bell or the like. **4.** Colloq. a minor accident involving a car, bike, surfboard, etc.

dinghy /ˈdɪŋgi, ˈdɪŋi/ n. (pl. **-ghies**) a small rowing or sailing boat.

dingo /ˈdɪŋgoʊ/ n. (pl. **-goes** or **-gos**) a wild dog, often tawny-yellow in colour, with erect ears, a bushy tail and distinctive gait, and with a call resembling a howl or yelp rather than a bark, found throughout mainland Australia.

dingy /ˈdɪndʒi/ adj. (**-gier, -giest**) of a dark, dull, or dirty colour or aspect; lacking brightness or freshness; shabby.

dinkum /ˈdɪŋkəm/ Colloq. –adj. Also, **dinky-di**. **1.** true; honest; genuine. **–adv. 2.** truly. See **fair dinkum**.

dinky-di /ˈdɪŋki-daɪ/ adj. → **dinkum**.

dinner /ˈdɪnə/ n. the main meal of the day, usually taken in the evening.

dinner suit n. a man's suit for formal evening wear, usually black and often worn with a bow tie.

dinosaur /ˈdaɪnəsɔː/ n. **1.** an extinct reptile, mostly of gigantic size. **2.** something completely outdated.

dint /dɪnt/ phr. **by dint of**, by means of: by dint of argument.

diocese /ˈdaɪəsəs/ n. (pl. **dioceses** /ˈdaɪəsəsəz, ˈdaɪəsiːz/) the district, with its population, falling under the care of a bishop.

diode /ˈdaɪoʊd/ n. a valve or device that allows electric current to flow in only one direction through it.

diorama /daɪəˈrɑːmə/ n. a miniature scene reproduced in three dimensions with the aid of lights, colours, etc.

dioxin /daɪˈɒksən/ n. any of a group of chemical compounds present as contaminants in certain herbicides.

dip /dɪp/ v. (**dipped, dipping**) **–v.t. 1.** to plunge temporarily into a liquid, as to wet or to take up some of the liquid. **2.** to lower and raise. **–v.i. 3.** to plunge into water or other liquid and emerge quickly. **4.** to sink or drop down, as if plunging into water. **5.** to incline or slope downwards. **–n. 6.** the act of dipping; a plunge into water, etc. **7.** a liquid into which something is dipped. **8.** a lowering momentarily; a sinking down. **9.** a soft savoury mixture into which biscuits, etc., are dipped before being eaten. **10.** downward extension, inclination, or slope. **11.** a hollow or depression in the land.

diphtheria /dɪfˈθɪəriə/ n. an infectious disease marked by the growth of a false membrane in the air passages.

diphthong /ˈdɪfθɒŋ/ n. a combination of two vowel sounds with only one syllabic peak, as ei in vein.

diplodocus /dəˈplɒdəkəs, dɪpləˈdoʊkəs/ n. a huge herbivorous dinosaur with a long neck and tail.

diploma /dəˈploʊmə/ n. a document stating one's success in an examination, etc.

diplomacy /dəˈploʊməsi/ n. **1.** the conduct by government officials of negotiations and other relations between states. **2.** skill in managing any negotiations; artful management.

–**diplomat** /'dɪpləmæt/, n. –**diplomatic** /dɪplə-'mætɪk/, adj.

diplomatic immunity n. the immunity from local jurisdiction, taxation, etc., which is the privilege of official representatives of a foreign state.

dipsomaniac /dɪpsə'meɪniæk/ n. someone who suffers from an irresistible and insatiable craving for intoxicants.

dire /'daɪə/ adj. causing or attended with great fear or suffering; dreadful; awful.

direct /də'rɛkt, daɪ-/ v.t. **1.** to guide. **2.** to give authoritative instructions to; command. **3.** to organise and supervise the artistic production of (a play or film). –adj. **4.** proceeding in a straight line or by the shortest course. **5.** without intervening agency; immediate; personal. **6.** going straight to the point; straightforward; downright. –adv. **7.** in a direct manner; directly; straight. –**director**, n.

direct current n. Elect. a relatively steady current in one direction in a circuit; a continuous stream of electrons through a conductor. Abbrev.: DC, d.c. Compare **alternating current**.

direction /də'rɛkʃən, daɪ-/ n. **1.** the act of directing, pointing, aiming, etc. **2.** the line along which anything lies, faces, moves, etc., with reference to the point or region towards which it is directed. **3.** management; control.

directive /də'rɛktɪv, daɪ-/ n. an authoritative instruction or direction.

directly /də'rɛktli, daɪ-/ adv. **1.** in a direct line, way, or manner; straight. **2.** without delay; immediately. **3.** presently; soon.

direct marketing n. a marketing technique in which the producer sells directly to the customer by such means as door-to-door selling, home parties, etc. Also, **direct selling**.

direct memory access n. a data path to a computer memory in which the central processing unit does not intervene.

directorate /də'rɛktərət, -trət, daɪ-/ n. **1.** the office of a director. **2.** a body of directors.

directory /də'rɛktəri, -tri/ n. (pl. **-ries**) **1.** a book or the like containing names, addresses, telephone numbers, etc. **2.** Also, (in some operating systems), **folder**. Computers a defined area on a computer disk used to store files.

dirge /dɜdʒ/ n. a funeral song or tune.

dirigible /'dɪrədʒəbəl, də'rɪdʒəbəl/ n. an early self-propelled, lighter-than-air craft.

dirt /dɜt/ n. **1.** earth or soil, especially when loose. **2.** any foul or filthy substance, as excrement, mud, etc. **3.** unsavoury or malicious gossip.

dirt bike n. a motorbike designed for cross-country conditions, built with a high engine and exhaust system, often of especially light construction. Also, **dirtbike**, **trail bike**.

dirty /'dɜti/ adj. (**dirtier**, **dirtiest**) **1.** soiled with dirt; foul; unclean. **2.** morally unclean; indecent. **3.** stormy; squally, as the weather. **4.** Colloq. angry. –v.t., v.i. (**dirtied**, **dirtying**) **5.** to make or become dirty.

dis-1 (a prefix meaning 'apart', 'asunder', 'away', 'utterly', or having a privative, negative, or reversing force). See **de-**, **un-2**. Also, **di-**.

dis-2 variant of **di-1**.

disability /dɪsə'bɪləti/ n. (pl. **-ties**) a condition which restricts a person's mental or sensory processes, or their mobility.

disable /dɪs'eɪbəl/ v.t. **1.** to make unable; weaken or destroy the capability of; incapacitate. **2.** to make inoperative: to disable an alarm.

disabled /dɪs'eɪbəld/ adj. incapacitated in some way, especially by permanent injury or disease.

disaccharide /daɪ'sækəraɪd/ n. any of a group of carbohydrates whose molecules consist of two bonded monosaccharides.

disadvantage /dɪsəd'væntɪdʒ/ n. **1.** an unfavourable circumstance or condition. –v.t. **2.** to subject to disadvantage.

disagree /dɪsə'gri/ v.i. **1.** (fol. by with) to fail to agree; differ. **2.** to differ in opinion; dissent. –**disagreement**, n.

disagreeable /dɪsə'griəbəl/ adj. unpleasant.

disallow /dɪsə'laʊ/ v.t. to refuse to admit the truth or validity of.

disappear /dɪsə'pɪə/ v.i. **1.** to cease to appear or be seen; vanish from sight. **2.** to cease to exist or be known; pass away; end gradually. –v.t. **3.** to abduct, and usually subsequently murder or imprison (a political opponent, dissident, etc.), without making their fate known. –**disappearance**, n.

disappoint /dɪsə'pɔɪnt/ v.t. **1.** to fail to fulfil the expectations or wishes of (a person). **2.** to defeat the fulfilment of (hopes, plans, etc.); thwart; frustrate.

disappointment /dɪsə'pɔɪntmənt/ n. **1.** a feeling of being disappointed. **2.** something that disappoints.

disapprove /dɪsə'pruv/ v.i. (fol. by of) to have an unfavourable opinion. –**disapproval**, n.

disarm /dɪs'am/ v.t. **1.** to deprive of weapons. **2.** to divest of hostility, suspicion, etc.; make friendly. **3.** to take out of a state of readiness for any specific purpose or effective use: to disarm a land mine. –**disarming**, adj. –**disarmingly**, adv.

disarray /dɪsə'reɪ/ n. disorder; confusion.

disassociate /dɪsə'soʊʃieɪt, -sieɪt/ v.t. → **dissociate**. –**disassociation**, n. –**disassociative**, adj.

disaster /də'zastə/ n. any unfortunate event, especially a sudden or great misfortune. –**disastrous**, adj.

disavow /dɪsə'vaʊ/ v.t. to disclaim knowledge of, connection with, or responsibility for; disown; repudiate.

disband /dɪs'bænd/ v.t. to break up or disorganise (a band or company).

disbelieve /dɪsbə'liv/ v.t. **1.** to reject as false. –v.i. **2.** (fol. by in) to have no faith in. –**disbelief**, n.

disburse /dɪs'bɜs/ v.t. to pay out (money); expend.

disc /dɪsk/ n. **1.** any thin, flat, circular plate or object. **2.** a round, flat area. **3.** Computers → **disk**. **4. a.** a record. **b.** a CD or DVD.

discard v.t. /dɪs'kad/ **1.** to cast aside; reject; dismiss, especially from use. **2.** Cards to throw out (a card or cards) from one's hand. –n. /'dɪskad/ **3.** someone who or that which is cast out or rejected.

discern /dəˈsɜn/ v.t. to perceive by the sight or some other sense or by the intellect; see, recognise, or apprehend clearly.

discernment /dəˈsɜnmənt/ n. faculty of discerning; discrimination.

discharge v.t. /dɪsˈtʃadʒ/ (-charged, -charging) 1. to relieve of a charge or load. 2. to fulfil or perform. 3. to dismiss from service. −n. /ˈdɪstʃadʒ/ 4. the act of discharging a ship, load, etc. 5. a sending or coming forth; ejection; emission. 6. a relieving or ridding, or a getting rid, of something of the nature of a charge.

disciple /dəˈsaɪpəl/ n. an adherent of the doctrines of another; a follower.

discipline /ˈdɪsəplən/ n. 1. training to act in accordance with rules; drill. 2. punishment inflicted by way of correction and training. 3. the training effect of experience, adversity, etc. 4. a branch of instruction or learning. −v.t. (-plined, -plining) 5. to bring to a state of order and obedience by training and control. −**disciplinary**, adj. −**disciplinarian**, n.

disc jockey n. → DJ.

disclaim /dɪsˈkleɪm/ v.t. to repudiate or deny interest in or connection with; disavow; disown. −**disclaimer**, n.

disclose /dəsˈkloʊz/ v.t. 1. to cause to appear; allow to be seen; make known; reveal. 2. to uncover; lay open to view.

disco /ˈdɪskoʊ/ n. (pl. -cos) a place of public entertainment or a club in which patrons may dance, especially to recorded music.

discolour /dɪsˈkʌlə/ v.t. to change the colour of; spoil the colour of; stain. Also, **discolor**.

discomfiture /dɪsˈkʌmfətʃə/ n. 1. frustration of hopes or plans. 2. confusion.

discomfort /dɪsˈkʌmfət/ n. absence of comfort or pleasure; uneasiness; disturbance of peace; pain.

disconcert /dɪskənˈsɜt/ v.t. to disturb the self-possession of; confuse; perturb.

disconnect /dɪskəˈnɛkt/ v.t. to separate or to break the connection of or between: to disconnect a hose; to disconnect the telephone. −**disconnected**, adj. −**disconnection**, n.

disconsolate /dɪsˈkɒnsələt/ adj. without consolation or solace; unhappy.

discontinue /dɪskənˈtɪnju/ v.t. to cause to finish or to come to an end. −**discontinuation**, n.

discord /ˈdɪskɔd/ n. lack of harmony. −**discordant**, adj.

discotheque /ˈdɪskətɛk/ n. → disco.

discount /ˈdɪskaʊnt/ for defs 1–3 and 5–7, /dɪsˈkaʊnt/ for def. 4 −v.t. 1. to deduct. 2. to advance money with deduction of interest on (not immediately payable). 3. to purchase or sell (a bill or note) before maturity at a reduction based on the interest for the time it still has to run. 4. to leave out of account; disregard. −n. 5. the act of discounting. 6. amount deducted. −phr. 7. **at a discount**, a. Commerce below par. b. not in demand.

discourage /dɪsˈkʌrɪdʒ/ v.t. 1. to cause to lose spirit or courage; dishearten. 2. to dissuade.

discourse /ˈdɪskɔs/ n. communication of thought by words; talk; conversation.

discover /dəsˈkʌvə/ v.t. to get knowledge of, learn of, or find out; gain sight or knowledge of

(something previously unseen or unknown). −**discovery**, n.

discredit /dɪsˈkrɛdət/ v.t. to injure the credit or reputation of.

discreet /dəsˈkrit, dɪsˈkrit/ adj. wise or judicious in avoiding mistakes or faults; prudent; circumspect; cautious; not rash.

discrepancy /dɪsˈkrɛpənsi/ n. (pl. -cies) an instance of difference or inconsistency.

discrete /dəsˈkrit, dɪsˈkrit/ adj. detached from others; separate; distinct.

discretion /dɪsˈkrɛʃən/ n. 1. freedom of judgement or choice. 2. the quality of being discreet. −**discretionary**, adj.

discretionary income n. income which is above that needed for subsistence and which may be spent at the earner's discretion.

discriminate /dəsˈkrɪmɪneɪt/ v.i. 1. to make a distinction, in favour of or against a person or thing. 2. to note or observe a difference; distinguish accurately. −v.t. 3. to differentiate. −**discrimination**, n.

discursive /dɪsˈkɜsɪv/ adj. passing freely from one subject to another; wide-ranging.

discus /ˈdɪskəs/ n. (pl. **discuses** or **disci** /ˈdɪskaɪ/) a disc, usually made of wood rimmed with metal, thrown by athletes.

discuss /dəsˈkʌs/ v.t. to examine by argument; sift the considerations for and against; debate; talk over.

discussion /dəsˈkʌʃən/ n. 1. the act of discussing; critical examination by argument; debate. 2. a written or spoken text type or form which offers a balanced presentation of different points of view on an issue.

disdain /dɪsˈdeɪn/ n. a feeling of contempt for anything regarded as unworthy; haughty contempt; scorn.

disease /dəˈziz/ n. a sickness which can affect a part or all of any living thing. −**diseased**, adj.

diseconomy /dɪsəˈkɒnəmi/ n. 1. the lack of economy; a faulty economy. −phr. 2. **diseconomies of scale**, a situation where a manufacturer finds that any increase in capital outlay in plant and machinery results in higher costs per unit of production.

disembark /dɪsəmˈbak/ v.i. to leave a ship, plane, etc., as after a journey; land.

disembowel /dɪsəmˈbaʊəl/ v.t. (-elled or, Chiefly US, -eled, -elling or, Chiefly US, -eling) to remove the bowels or entrails from.

disenfranchise /dɪsənˈfræntʃaɪz/ v.t. to take certain rights from (persons), especially the right to vote. Also, **disfranchise**. −**disenfranchisement**, n.

disfavour /dɪsˈfeɪvə/ n. lack of favour; state of being regarded unfavourably. Also, **disfavor**.

disfigure /dɪsˈfɪɡə/ v.t. to mar the figure, appearance, or beauty of.

disgrace /dəsˈɡreɪs/ n. 1. the state of being in dishonour; ignominy; shame. 2. the state of being out of favour. −v.t. (-graced, -gracing) 3. to bring or reflect shame or reproach upon. −**disgraceful**, adj.

disgruntled /dɪsˈɡrʌntld/ adj. mildly upset; discontented.

disguise /dəsˈɡaɪz/ v.t. 1. to conceal the identity of. −n. 2. that which disguises. 3. the make-up, mask or costume of an entertainer.

disgust /dəs'gʌst/ v.t. **1.** to cause nausea or loathing in. –n. **2.** strong distaste; loathing.

disgusting /dɪs'gʌstɪŋ/ adj. **1.** causing feelings of strong dislike or disapproval. **2.** extremely unpleasant, often in a way that makes one feel sick. –**disgustingly**, adv.

dish /dɪʃ/ n. **1.** an open more or less shallow container of pottery, glass, metal, wood, etc., used for various purposes, especially for holding or serving food. **2.** a particular article or preparation of food. **3.** anything like a dish in form or use, as a concave antenna for satellite television reception, the larger receptors of radio telescopes, etc.

dishevelled /dɪ'ʃevəld/ adj. untidy.

dishonest /dɪs'ɒnəst/ adj. not honest; disposed to lie, cheat, or steal. –**dishonesty**, n.

dishonour /dɪs'ɒnə/ n. **1.** lack of honour; dishonourable character or conduct. **2.** disgrace; ignominy; shame. **3.** failure or refusal of the drawee or acceptor of a bill of exchange or cheque to accept it, or, if it is accepted, to pay it. –v.t. **4.** to deprive of honour; disgrace; bring reproach or shame on. Also, **dishonor**. –**dishonourable**, adj.

dishwasher /'dɪʃwɒʃə/ n. an electric machine which automatically washes and sometimes dries dishes, plates, etc.

disillusion /dɪsə'luʒən/ v.t. to free from illusion.

disinfectant /dɪsən'fektənt/ n. any chemical agent that destroys bacteria. –**disinfect**, v.

disinflation /ˌdɪsɪn'fleɪʃən/ n. a reduction of prices generally with attendant increase in the purchasing power of money.

disinformation /dɪsɪnfə'meɪʃən/ n. misleading information supplied intentionally.

disinherit /ˌdɪsɪn'herət/ v.t. to deprive of the right to inherit.

disintegrate /dɪs'ɪntəgreɪt/ v.i. to fall apart; break up.

disinterested /dɪs'ɪntrəstəd/ adj. **1.** unbiased by personal involvement or advantage. **2.** (sometimes considered non-standard) uninterested.

disjointed /dɪs'dʒɔɪntəd/ adj. disconnected; incoherent.

disk /dɪsk/ n. a memory unit for computers consisting of a rapidly spinning magnetic disc on which information is recorded by magnetising the surface. Also, **disc**.

diskette /dɪs'ket/ n. → **floppy disk**.

dislike /dɪs'laɪk/ v.t. **1.** to regard with displeasure or aversion. –n. **2.** displeasure or aversion felt towards someone or something.

dislocate /'dɪsləkeɪt/ v.t. **1.** to displace. **2.** to put out of joint.

dislodge /dɪs'lɒdʒ/ v.t. (-**lodged**, -**lodging**) to remove or drive from a place of rest or lodgement.

disloyal /dɪs'lɔɪəl/ adj. not loyal.

dismal /'dɪzməl/ adj. **1.** gloomy; dreary. **2.** terrible; dreadful.

dismantle /dɪs'mæntl/ v.t. to pull down; take apart; take to pieces.

dismay /dɪs'meɪ/ v.t. **1.** to dishearten utterly; daunt. –n. **2.** consternation.

dismember /dɪs'membə/ v.t. **1.** to deprive of members or limbs; divide limb from limb. **2.** to

separate into parts; divide and distribute the parts of (a kingdom, etc.).

dismiss /dɪs'mɪs/ v.t. **1.** to bid or allow (a person) to go; give permission to depart. **2.** to discharge or remove, as from office or service. **3.** to put off or away; lay aside, especially to put aside from consideration. **4.** Law to put out of court, as a complaint or appeal. –**dismissal**, n.

disobedient /dɪsə'bidiənt/ adj. neglecting or refusing to obey; refractory. –**disobedience**, n.

disobey /dɪsə'beɪ/ v.t. to neglect or refuse to obey (an order, person, etc.).

disorder /dɪs'ɔdə/ n. **1.** lack of order or regular arrangement; confusion. **2.** a derangement of physical or mental health or functions. –**disorderly**, adj.

disorganise /dɪs'ɔgənaɪz/ v.t. to destroy the organisation of. Also, **disorganize**.

disorganised /dɪs'ɔgənaɪzd/ adj. **1.** in a state of confusion or disorder. **2.** prone to disorder: a disorganised person. Also, **disorganized**.

disorientate /dɪs'ɔriənteɪt/ v.t. **1.** to confuse as to direction. **2.** to perplex; to confuse. Also, **disorient**.

disown /dɪs'oʊn/ v.t. to deny the ownership of or responsibility for; renounce.

disparage /dəs'pærɪdʒ, dɪs-/ v.t. (-**raged**, -**raging**) to speak of or treat slightingly; belittle.

disparate /'dɪspərət/ adj. essentially different; dissimilar. –**disparity**, n.

dispassionate /dɪs'pæʃənət/ adj. free from or unaffected by passion; devoid of personal feeling or bias; impartial; calm.

dispatch /dəs'pætʃ/ v.t. **1.** to send off; put under way. –n. **2.** the sending off of a messenger, letter, etc., to a destination. **3.** prompt or speedy transaction, as of business. **4.** a written message sent in haste.

dispel /dɪs'pel/ v.t. (-**pelled**, -**pelling**) to drive off in various directions; scatter; disperse; dissipate.

dispensable /dɪs'pensəbəl/ adj. able or liable to be dispensed with or done without; unimportant.

dispensary /dɪs'pensəri, -sri/ n. (pl. -**ries**) a place where something is dispensed, especially medicines.

dispensation /ˌdɪspen'seɪʃən/ n. **1.** the act of dispensing. **2.** Roman Catholic Church the relaxation of a law in a specific case.

dispense /dɪs'pens/ v.t. **1.** to deal out; distribute. **2.** to administer (laws, etc.). –phr. **3. dispense with**, **a.** to do without; forgo. **b.** to grant exemption from (a law, promise, etc.).

disperse /dəs'pɜs/ v.t. **1.** to scatter. –v.i. **2.** to move apart in different directions without order or regularity: the crowd dispersed.

displace /dɪs'pleɪs/ v.t. to put out of the usual or proper place. –**displacement**, n.

display /dɪs'pleɪ/ v.t. **1.** to show; exhibit; make visible. **2.** to reveal; betray. **3.** to show ostentatiously. –n. **4.** the act of displaying; exhibition; show. **5.** an electronic system capable of representing information visually.

displease /dɪs'pliz/ v.t. (-**pleased**, -**pleasing**) to annoy.

disposable /dəsˈpouzəbəl/ adj. designed or intended to be discarded after one use: *disposable nappy*.

disposable income n. that part of a person's income which remains after the deduction of income tax, etc.

dispose /dəsˈpouz/ v.t. 1. to put in a particular or the proper order or arrangement. 2. to incline. –*phr.* 3. **dispose of**, to deal with definitely; get rid of.

disposition /dıspəˈzıʃən/ n. mental or moral constitution; turn of mind.

dispossess /dıspəˈzɛs/ v.t. to put (a person) out of possession, especially of real property; oust.

disprove /ˈdıspruːv/ v.t. to prove to be false or wrong. –**disproval**, n.

dispute /dəsˈpjut/ v.i. 1. to engage in argument or discussion. –v.t. 2. to argue or debate about; discuss. –n. 3. argumentation; a debate or controversy; a quarrel.

disqualify /dısˈkwoləfaı/ v.t. (**-fied, -fying**) to deprive of qualification or fitness; render unfit or ineligible.

disquiet /dısˈkwaıət/ v.t. 1. to disturb; make uneasy. –n. 2. unrest; uneasiness.

disregard /dısrəˈgad/ v.t. 1. to pay no attention to; leave out of consideration. –n. 2. lack of regard or attention; neglect.

disrepair /dısrəˈpɛə/ n. the state of being out of repair; impaired condition.

disrepute /dısrəˈpjut/ n. ill repute. –**disreputable**, adj.

disrespect /dısrəˈspɛkt/ n. lack of respect.

disrupt /dısˈrʌpt/ v.t. to break or rend asunder. –**disruption**, n. –**disruptive**, adj.

dissatisfied /dısˈsætəsfaıd/ adj. not satisfied. –**dissatisfaction**, n.

dissect /daıˈsɛkt, də-/ v.t. 1. to cut apart (an animal body, plant, etc.) to examine it. 2. to examine minutely part by part.

dissemble /dəˈsɛmbəl/ v.t. 1. to conceal the real nature of. 2. to feign. –v.i. 3. to speak or act hypocritically.

disseminate /dəˈsɛmɪneɪt/ v.t. to scatter; spread. –**dissemination**, n.

dissent /dəˈsɛnt/ v.i. 1. to disagree. –n. 2. difference in sentiment or opinion. –**dissension**, n.

dissertation /dısəˈteıʃən/ n. a written essay, treatise, or thesis.

disservice /dısˈsɜvəs/ n. harm; injury; an ill turn.

dissident /ˈdısədənt/ n. someone who differs; a dissenter, especially against a particular political system.

dissimilar /dıˈsımələ/ adj. not similar; unlike; different. –**dissimilarly**, adv.

dissipate /ˈdısəpeıt/ v.t. 1. to scatter in various directions; disperse; disintegrate. 2. to scatter wastefully or extravagantly; squander. –v.i. 3. to become scattered or dispersed; be dispelled; disintegrate. 4. to indulge in extravagant, intemperate, or dissolute pleasure.

dissipated /ˈdısəpeıtəd/ adj. 1. indulging in or characterised by excessive devotion to pleasure; intemperate; dissolute. 2. dispersed; scattered; dispelled.

dissociate /dıˈsouʃıeıt, -ˈsousıeıt/ v.t. to sever the association of; separate. Also, **disassociate**. –**dissociation**, n.

dissolute /ˈdısəlut/ adj. licentious.

dissolution /dısəˈluʃən/ n. 1. the undoing or breaking up of a tie, bond, union, etc. 2. *Govt* an order issued by the head of the state terminating a parliament and necessitating a new election. 3. death or destruction. 4. the legal termination of business activity, including the distribution of assets and the fixing of liabilities.

dissolve /dəˈzolv/ v.t. 1. to make a solution of in a solvent. 2. to break up (an assembly or organisation); dismiss; disperse. 3. to bring to an end; destroy; dispel. 4. *Law* to deprive of force; annul. –v.i. 5. to become dissolved, as in a solvent. 6. to break up or disperse. 7. to disappear gradually; fade from sight or apprehension.

dissonance /ˈdısənəns/ n. 1. discord. 2. disagreement.

dissuade /dıˈsweıd/ v.t. to persuade not to do something.

distance /ˈdıstns, ˈdıstəns/ n. 1. the extent of space intervening between things or points. 2. remoteness. 3. reserve or aloofness.

distant /ˈdıstənt/ adj. 1. far off or apart in space; not near at hand; remote. 2. far apart in any respect. 3. reserved; not familiar or cordial.

distaste /dısˈteıst/ n. dislike.

distemper[1] /dısˈtɛmpə/ n. an infectious disease of animals, especially young dogs.

distemper[2] /dısˈtɛmpə/ n. a water paint used for the decoration of interior walls and ceilings.

distend /dısˈtɛnd/ v.i. to swell.

distil /dəsˈtıl/ v. (**-tilled, -tilling**) –v.t. 1. to subject to a process of vaporisation and subsequent condensation, as for purification or concentration. –v.i. 2. to fall in drops; trickle; exude. Also, **distill**. –**distillery**, n. –**distillation**, n.

distinct /dəsˈtıŋkt/ adj. 1. (fol. by *from* or used absolutely) distinguished as not being the same; not identical; separate. 2. clear to the senses or intellect; plain; definite; unmistakable.

distinction /dəsˈtıŋkʃən/ n. 1. a marking off or distinguishing as different. 2. a discrimination made between things as different. 3. a distinguishing characteristic. 4. a mark of special favour. 5. marked superiority; note; eminence. –**distinctive**, adj.

distinguish /dəsˈtıŋgwıʃ/ v.t. 1. (fol. by *from*) to mark off as different. 2. to recognise as distinct or different; discriminate. 3. to perceive clearly by sight or other sense; discern; recognise. 4. to serve to separate as different; be a distinctive characteristic of; characterise. 5. to make prominent, conspicuous, or eminent. –v.i. 6. (fol. by *between*) to indicate or show a difference. 7. to recognise or note differences; discriminate.

distort /dəsˈtɔt/ v.t. 1. to twist awry or out of shape; make crooked or deformed. 2. to pervert; misrepresent. –**distortion**, n.

distract /dəsˈtrækt/ v.t. 1. to draw away or divert, as the mind or attention. 2. to entertain; amuse; divert. –**distraction**, n.

distraught /dəs'trɔt/ adj. **1.** distracted; bewildered; deeply agitated. **2.** crazed.

distress /dəs'trɛs/ n. great pain, anxiety, or sorrow; acute suffering; affliction; trouble.

distressed /dəs'trɛst/ adj. **1.** in a troubled emotional state; upset. **2.** (of wood) artificially weathered so as to create an aged appearance. **3.** (of furniture) built using distressed wood.

distribute /dəs'trɪbjut, 'dɪstrəbjut/ v.t. **1.** to give out: to distribute pamphlets. **2.** to divide and give out in shares: to distribute the profits among the staff. **3.** to scatter or spread: to distribute manure evenly over the garden. –**distribution**, n. –**distributor**, n.

district /'dɪstrɪkt/ n. a region or locality.

disturb /də'stɜb/ v.t. **1.** to interfere with; interrupt; hinder. **2.** to throw into commotion or disorder; agitate; disorder; disarrange; unsettle. **3.** to perplex; trouble. –**disturbance**, n.

disuse /dɪs'jus/ n. discontinuance of use.

ditch /dɪtʃ/ n. **1.** a long, narrow hollow made in the earth by digging, as one for draining or irrigating land; a trench. **2.** any open passage or trench, as a natural channel or waterway. –v.t. **3.** Colloq. to get rid of; get away from.

dither /'dɪðə/ v.i. to be vacillating; uncertain.

ditto /'dɪtoʊ/ n. (pl. **-tos**) the same (used in accounts, lists, etc., to avoid repetition). Symbol: " Abbrev.: do

ditty /'dɪti/ n. (pl. **-ties**) a simple song.

ditzy /'dɪtsi/ adj. Colloq. flighty; empty-headed; scatterbrained. Also, **ditsy**.

diurnal /daɪ'ɜnəl/ adj. **1.** daily. **2.** of or belonging to the daytime.

divan /də'væn/ n. a low bed.

dive /daɪv/ v.i. (**dived**, **diving**) **1.** to plunge, especially head first, as into water. **2.** to go below the surface of the water, as a submarine, scuba diver, etc. **3.** to dart. –n. **4.** the act of diving. **5.** an instance of diving. **6.** Colloq. a disreputable place, as for drinking, gambling, etc., especially a cellar or basement. –**diver**, n.

diverge /daɪ'vɜdʒ/ v.i. to move or lie in different directions from a common point; branch off. –**divergence**, n. –**divergent**, adj.

diverse /daɪ'vɜs, 'daɪvɜs, də'vɜs/ adj. different; varied. –**diversity**, n.

diversify /daɪ'vɜsəfaɪ, də-/ v. (**-fied**, **-fying**) –v.t. **1.** to make diverse. **2.** to vary (investments). –v.i. **3.** to extend one's activities, especially in business, over more than one field. –**diversification**, n.

divert /də'vɜt, daɪ-/ v.t. **1.** to turn aside or from a path or course; deflect. **2.** to draw off to a different object, purpose, etc. **3.** to distract from serious occupation; entertain or amuse. –**diversion**, n.

divest /daɪ'vɛst/ v.t. **1.** to strip of clothing, etc. **2.** to strip or deprive of anything; dispossess.

divide /də'vaɪd/ v.t. **1.** to separate. **2.** to deal out in parts; apportion; share. **3.** Maths to separate into equal parts by the process of division. –v.i. **4.** to become divided or separated. **5.** to share something with others. –**divisible**, adj.

dividend /'dɪvədɛnd/ n. **1.** Maths a number to be divided by another number (the divisor). **2.** Finance **a.** a pro-rata share in an amount to be distributed. **b.** a sum of money paid to shareholders of a company or trading concern out of earnings. **c.** interest payable on public funds. **3.** a payment to creditors and shareholders in a liquidated company. **4.** a share of anything divided.

divine /də'vaɪn/ adj. **1.** of or relating to a god. –v.t. **2.** to discover (water, metal, etc.), by a divining rod. **3.** to prophesy.

divining rod n. a rod, especially a forked stick, said to tremble when held over a spot where water, metal, etc., is underground.

divinity /də'vɪnəti/ n. **1.** the quality of being divine. **2.** the science of divine things; theology.

division /də'vɪʒən/ n. **1.** the act of dividing; partition. **2.** the state of being divided. **3.** Maths the operation inverse to multiplication; the finding of a quantity (the quotient) which, when multiplied by a given quantity (the divisor), gives another given quantity (the dividend). Symbol: ÷ **4.** one of the parts into which a thing is divided; a section.

divisive /də'vaɪsɪv, -'vɪzɪv/ adj. creating division or discord.

divisor /də'vaɪzə/ n. Maths a number by which another number (the dividend) is divided.

divorce /də'vɔs/ n. **1.** the dissolution of the marriage contract. –v.t. **2.** to separate by legal dissolving of marriage. –**divorcee**, n.

divulge /də'vʌldʒ, daɪ-/ v.t. (**-vulged**, **-vulging**) to disclose or reveal.

dizzy /'dɪzi/ adj. (**-zier**, **-ziest**) **1.** affected with a sensation of whirling, with tendency to fall; giddy. **2.** Colloq. foolish or stupid.

DJ /'dɪdʒeɪ, di'dʒeɪ/ n. a person who plays and announces recorded music, as on a radio program, at a dance, etc. Also, **disc jockey**, **deejay**.

DNA /di ɛn 'eɪ/ n. **1.** deoxyribonucleic acid; one of a class of large molecules which are found in the nuclei of cells and in viruses and which are responsible for the transference of genetic characteristics. **2.** fundamental nature or structure: Lying is not in his DNA.

DNA fingerprinting n. → **genetic fingerprinting**.

do /du/ v.t. **1.** to perform (acts, duty, penance, a part, etc.). **2.** to be the cause of (good, harm, credit, etc.); bring about; effect. **3.** to render (homage, justice, etc.). **4.** to solve or find the answer to: to do a maths problem. **5.** to serve (a period of time) in a prison. **6.** to make; create; form. **7.** to study. **8.** Colloq. to serve; suffice for. **9.** Colloq. to cheat or swindle. **10.** Colloq. to use up; expend. –v.i. **11.** to act, especially effectively; be in action. **12.** to get along or fare (well or ill); manage (with; without, etc.). **13.** to suffice; be enough. **14.** (fol. by by) to deal; treat. –v. (aux.) **15.** (used without special meaning in interrogative, negative, and inverted constructions). **16.** (used to lend emphasis to a principal verb). –n. **17.** Colloq. a festivity or treat. **18.** (pl.) rules; customs, etc.
The different forms of the verb **do** are:
Present tense: I **do**, you **do**, he/she/it **does**, we **do**, they **do**
Past tense: I **did**, you **did**, he/she/it **did**, we **did**, they **did**
Past participle: **done**
Present participle: **doing**

dob /dɒb/ v. (**dobbed**, **dobbing**) Colloq. –v.t. **1.** (fol. by in) to betray, report (someone), as for a misdemeanour. —*v.i.* **2.** to report another's misdemeanour.

docile /ˈdousail/ *adj.* easily managed or handled; tractable.

dock[1] /dɒk/ *n.* **1.** a wharf. **2.** the space or waterway between two piers or wharves, as for receiving a ship while in port. **3.** a semi-enclosed structure which a plane, truck, etc., can enter for the purpose of loading, repair, maintenance, etc.

dock[2] /dɒk/ *n.* **1.** the solid or fleshy part of an animal's tail. **2.** the part of a tail left after cutting or clipping. —*v.t.* **3.** to cut off the end of (a tail, etc.). **4.** to deduct a part from (wages, etc.).

dock[3] /dɒk/ *n.* an enclosed place in a courtroom where the accused is placed during trial.

docket /ˈdɒkət/ *n.* a receipt.

doctor /ˈdɒktə/ *n.* **1.** a person licensed to practise medicine. **2.** a person who has received a doctorate.

doctorate /ˈdɒktərət/ *n.* the highest academic degree awarded in any branch of knowledge. —**doctoral**, *adj.*

doctrine /ˈdɒktrən/ *n.* a body or system of teachings relating to a particular subject.

document *n.* /ˈdɒkjəmənt/ **1.** a written or printed paper furnishing information or evidence; a legal or official paper. **2.** *Computers* a file produced by an application, especially a text-based file produced by word processing software. —*v.t.* /ˈdɒkjuˌment/ **3.** to furnish with documents, evidence, or the like. **4.** to record, give an account of: *an attempt to document the period.* —**documentation**, *n.*

documentary /dɒkjuˈmentəri, -tri/ *adj.* **1.** relating to, consisting of, or derived from documents. —*n.* (*pl.* **-ries**) **2.** a factual television or radio program, film, etc.

dodder /ˈdɒdə/ *v.i.* to shake; tremble.

dodge /dɒdʒ/ *v.* (**dodged, dodging**) —*v.i.* **1.** to move aside or change position suddenly, as to avoid a blow or to get behind something. **2.** to use evasive methods; prevaricate. —*v.t.* **3.** to elude by a sudden shift of position or by strategy.

dodo /ˈdoudou/ *n.* (*pl.* **-does** or **-dos**) **1.** an extinct, large, ground-dwelling bird related to the pigeon family. —*phr.* **2. dead as a dodo**, *Colloq.* completely lifeless or inactive.

doe /dou/ *n.* the female of the deer, antelope, and certain other animals.

does /dʌz/, *weak form* /dəz/ *v.* 3rd person singular present indicative of **do**.

doesn't /ˈdʌzənt/ *v.* contraction of *does not.*

doff /dɒf/ *v.t.* to remove (the hat) in salutation.

dog /dɒg/ *n.* **1.** a domesticated carnivore, bred in a great many varieties. **2.** any animal belonging to the same family, including the wolves, jackals, foxes, etc. —*v.t.* (**dogged, dogging**) **3.** to follow or track constantly like a dog; hound; worry; plague. —*phr.* **4. the black dog**, (in figurative use) clinical depression.

dogbox /ˈdɒgbɒks/ *n. Colloq.* a compartment in a passenger train or tram to which there is no access by corridor from other compartments within the carriage.

dog-ear *n.* the corner of a page in a book folded over like a dog's ear, as by careless use or to mark a place.

dogged /ˈdɒgəd/ *adj.* not giving in easily; determined; obstinate. —**doggedly**, *adv.*

doggerel /ˈdɒgərəl/ *adj.* **1.** (of verse) comic or burlesque, and usually loose or irregular in measure. —*n.* **2.** doggerel verse.

dogma /ˈdɒgmə/ *n.* (*pl.* **-mas** or **-mata** /-mətə/) **1.** a system of principles or tenets, as of a church. **2.** prescribed doctrine.

dogmatic /dɒgˈmætɪk/ *adj.* **1.** of, relating to, or of the nature of a dogma or dogmas. **2.** asserting opinions in an authoritative, positive, or arrogant manner; positive; opinionated. Also, **dogmatical**.

dog sled *n.* a sled drawn by dogs. Also, **dog sledge**.

dog sledding *n.* **1.** travelling across the snow on a sled pulled by dogs. **2.** this form of travel as a competitive sport.

dog whistling *n.* **1.** the summoning of a dog using a dog whistle. **2.** *Politics* the making of a public statement designed to appeal to a particular group of voters while drawing no response from the rest of the electorate.

doily /ˈdɔɪli/ *n.* (*pl.* **-lies**) a small ornamental mat, as of embroidery or lace.

doldrums /ˈdɒldrəmz/ *pl. n.* **the, 1.** the region of relatively calm winds near the equator. **2. a.** a period of dullness, gloominess, etc. **b.** a period of stagnation or inactivity.

dole /doul/ *n.* **1.** a payment by a government to an unemployed person. —*v.t.* (**doled, doling**) **2.** (fol. by *out*) to give out sparingly or in small quantities.

doleful /ˈdoulfəl/ *adj.* full of grief; sorrowful; gloomy.

doll /dɒl/ *n.* Also, **dolly**. **1.** a toy representing a child or other human being. —*v.t.* **2.** (fol. by *up*) to dress (oneself) up rather too smartly or too much.

dollar /ˈdɒlə/ *n.* **1.** the monetary unit of Australia, equal to 100 cents. *Symbol:* $ **2.** any of various units elsewhere, as in the US, Hong Kong, etc.

dollop /ˈdɒləp/ *n. Colloq.* a lump; a mass.

dolly /ˈdɒli/ *n.* (*pl.* **-lies**) **1.** (*with children*) a doll. **2.** a low truck with small wheels for moving loads too heavy to be carried by hand.

dolorous /ˈdɒlərəs/ *adj.* expressing pain or sorrow.

dolphin /ˈdɒlfən/ *n.* any of various cetaceans, some of which are commonly called porpoises.

dolt /doult/ *n.* a dull, stupid person.

-dom a noun suffix meaning: **1.** domain, as in *kingdom*. **2.** collection of persons, as in *officialdom*. **3.** rank or station, as in *earldom*. **4.** general condition, as in *freedom*.

domain /dəˈmeɪn/ *n.* **1.** an estate; any land held in possession. **2.** a field of action, thought, etc. **3.** a region with specific characteristics, types of growth, animal life, etc.

domain name *n. Computers* the name of a server connected to the internet comprising the name of the host, followed by the domain, such as commercial, academic, news, etc., followed by the country of origin with the exception of the US.

Domain Name System *n.* a system for naming servers on the internet and translating them into IP addresses. *Abbrev.:* DNS

dome /doum/ *n.* a large, hemispherical roof.

domestic /dəˈmɛstɪk/ *adj.* **1.** of or relating to the home, the household, or household affairs. **2.** living with humans; tame. **3.** of or relating to one's own or a particular country as apart from other countries. –**domestically**, *v.* –**domesticity**, *n.*

domesticate /dəˈmɛstəkeɪt/ *v.t.* **1.** to convert to domestic uses; tame. **2.** to attach to home life or affairs. **3.** to cause to be or feel at home; naturalise. –**domestication**, *n.*

domesticity /ˌdɒmɛsˈtɪsəti/ *n.* **1.** the state of being domesticated; domestic or home life. **2.** (*pl.*) domestic affairs; home conditions and arrangements.

domestic violence *n.* violence committed or threatened by one member of a household against another.

domicile /ˈdɒməsaɪl/ *n.* **1.** a place of residence; an abode; a house or home. **2.** *Commerce* a place at which a bill of exchange is made payable other than the acceptor's private or business address.

dominate /ˈdɒməneɪt/ *v.t.* **1.** to rule over; govern; control. **2.** to tower above; overshadow. –*v.i.* **3.** to rule; exercise control; predominate. –**dominant**, *adj.* –**domination**, *n.*

domineer /dɒməˈnɪə/ *v.i.* to govern arbitrarily; tyrannise.

dominion /dəˈmɪnjən/ *n.* **1.** the power or right of governing and controlling; sovereign authority. **2.** a territory, usually of considerable size, in which a single rulership holds sway.

domino /ˈdɒmənoʊ/ *n.* (*pl.* **-noes**) **1.** (*pl. construed as sing.*) any of various games played with flat, oblong pieces, the face of which is divided into two parts, each left blank or marked with pips, usually from one to six. **2.** one of these pieces.

domino effect *n.* an effect whereby one event or action triggers a chain reaction of consequential or similar events or actions.

don /dɒn/ *v.t.* (**donned, donning**) to put on (clothing, etc.).

donate /doʊˈneɪt/ *v.t.* **1.** to present as a gift to a fund or cause. **2.** to provide, as a donor (def. 2) (an organ, sperm, etc.) to another person. –**donation**, *n.*

done /dʌn/ *v.* past participle of **do**.

doner kebab /ˈdoʊnə kəˌbæb/ *n.* a dish consisting of slices of lamb cut from a vertical spit, and served with onion, tomato, etc., rolled up in a piece of flat bread. Also, **kebab**.

dongle /ˈdɒŋgəl/ *n.* *Computers* a hardware device which, when plugged into a computer, can provide software copying protection, as well as wireless connectivity, such as to audio and video sources, printers, mobile phones, GPS devices, etc.

donkey /ˈdɒŋki/ *n.* a domesticated ass used as a beast of burden.

donkey vote *n.* (in a compulsory preferential system of voting) a vote in which the voter's preferences are marked in the order in which the candidates appear on the ballot paper.

donor /ˈdoʊnə/ *n.* **1.** someone who gives or donates. **2.** *Med.* **a.** a person or animal furnishing blood for transfusion. **b.** a person from whose body an organ, bone marrow, body part, etc., is transplanted to a recipient. **c.** a person or animal furnishing sperm, ova or an embryo

as part of assisted reproduction. –*adj.* **3.** *Med.* of or relating to the blood, organ, sperm, etc., furnished by a donor (def. 2).

don't /doʊnt/ *v.* contraction of *do not*.

donut /ˈdoʊnʌt/ *n.* → **doughnut**.

doodle /ˈdudl/ *v.i.* to scribble idly.

doof /duf/ *n.* **1.** a type of popular electronic dance music characterised by a heavy beat. –*adj.* **2.** of or relating to doof.

doom /dum/ *n.* **1.** fate or destiny, especially adverse fate. –*v.t.* **2.** to condemn to unhappiness, ruin or a difficult situation.

doona /ˈdunə/ *n.* (*from trademark*) a quilted bedcover, filled with down, or synthetic padding, and often used instead of top sheets and blankets; continental quilt.

door /dɔ/ *n.* **1.** a movable barrier of wood or other material, commonly turning on hinges or sliding in a groove, for closing and opening a passage or opening into a building, room, cupboard, etc. –*v.t.* **2.** to open the door of a vehicle in the path of (an oncoming bicyclist).

dopamine /ˈdoʊpəmin/ *n.* a hormone-like substance, present in the brain where it functions as a neurotransmitter; an imbalance in dopamine activity can cause central nervous system disorders such as Parkinson's disease and schizophrenia.

dope /doʊp/ *n.* **1.** any drug, especially marijuana. **2.** information or data. **3.** a stupid person. –*v.t.* **4.** *Colloq.* to affect with dope or drugs. –*v.i.* **5.** to take performance-enhancing drugs.

doppelganger /ˈdɒpəlgæŋə/ *n.* an apparitional double or counterpart of a living person. Also, **doppelgänger** /ˈdɒpəlgɛŋə/, **doubleganger**.

dormant /ˈdɔmənt/ *adj.* lying asleep or as if asleep; inactive as in sleep; torpid.

dormitory /ˈdɔmətri/ *n.* (*pl.* **-ries**) a room for sleeping, usually large, for the inmates of a school or other institution.

Dorothy Dixer /ˌdɒrəθi ˈdɪksə/ *n.* *Colloq.* a question asked in parliament specifically to allow a minister to reply with political propaganda.

dorsal /ˈdɔsəl/ *adj.* *Zool.* of, relating to, or situated on the back.

dosage /ˈdoʊsɪdʒ/ *n.* **1.** the administration of medicine in doses. **2.** the amount of a medicine to be given.

dose /doʊs/ *n.* a quantity of medicine prescribed to be taken at one time.

doss /dɒs/ *v.i.* *Colloq.* (oft. fol. by *down*) to make a temporary sleeping place for oneself.

dossier /ˈdɒsiə/ *n.* a bundle of documents on the same subject, especially information about a particular person.

dot /dɒt/ *n.* **1.** a minute or small spot on a surface; a speck. **2.** a small, roundish mark made with or as with a pen. **3.** anything relatively small or speck-like. **4. a.** a full stop. **b.** a decimal point. **c.** the keyboard symbol (.), especially as used in domain names. –*v.t.* (**dotted, dotting**) **5.** to mark with or as with a dot or dots.

dot art *n.* a style of Aboriginal art in which ochre or other pigment is applied as a series of dots to build up a composite picture.

dotcom /ˈdɒtˌkɒm/ *n.* **1.** a company trading over the internet. **2.** a company involved in the information technology industry. –*adj.* **3.** of or relating to a dotcom. **4.** (of a company) trading over the internet. Also, **dot com, dot-com, dot.com.**

dote /doʊt/ v.i. **1.** (fol. by *on* or *upon*) to bestow excessive love or fondness. **2.** to be weak-minded, especially from old age. –**dotage**, *n.*

dotty /ˈdɒti/ adj. (**-tier, -tiest**) *Colloq.* crazy; eccentric.

double /ˈdʌbəl/ adj. **1.** twice as great, heavy, strong, etc. **2.** twofold in form, size, amount, extent, etc. **3.** composed of two like parts or members; paired. **4.** twofold in character, meaning, or conduct; ambiguous. **5.** a twofold size or amount; twice as much. **6.** a duplicate; a counterpart. **7.** *Film, etc.* a substitute actor who takes another's place, as in difficult or dangerous scenes. **8.** (*pl.*) a game in which there are two players on each side. –v.t. **9.** to make double or twice as great. **10.** (oft. fol. by *over, up, back,* etc.) to bend or fold with one part upon another. **11.** to convey as a second person on a horse, bicycle or motorcycle. –v.i. **12.** to become double. **13.** (oft. fol. by *back*) to turn back on a course. **14.** (fol. by *up*) to share quarters, etc. **15.** to serve in two capacities. –adv. **16.** twofold; doubly.

double bass *n.* the largest instrument of the violin family.

double bond *n.* *Chem.* two covalent bonds linking two atoms of a molecule together, characteristic of unsaturated organic compounds.

double-brick adj. of a building in which each apparently single brick walls with a small cavity between them, providing additional strength, insulation, etc.

doublecross /dʌbəlˈkrɒs/ *Colloq.* –v.t. **1.** to prove treacherous to; betray. –n. **2.** such a betrayal.

double date *n.* a date (**date**[1] def. 2) involving two groups of two people.

double dip v.i. **1.** to draw income from two sources, sometimes illegally, in Australia especially to receive two types of retirement benefit from public funds as by receiving tax concessions on superannuation savings and then disposing of the superannuation proceeds in such as way as to be eligible for a whole or part age pension. **2.** to use the same implement or food item with which one has already taken and eaten food from a dish for general consumption to dip into the food again. Also, **double-dip.** –**double dipping**, *n.* –**double dipper**, *n.*

double dissolution *n.* *Govt* (in Australia) the simultaneous dissolving by the governor or governor-general of both houses of parliament prior to the calling of a general election, used as a means of solving the deadlock situation when the upper house consistently rejects legislation passed by the lower house.

doubleganger /ˈdʌbl̩gæŋə/ *n.* → **doppelganger.**

double take *n.* a second look, either literal or figurative, given to a person, event, etc., whose significance is suddenly understood.

double-take v.i. to be surprised into reconsidering one's judgement.

doubt /daʊt/ v.t. **1.** to be uncertain in opinion about; hold questionable. **2.** to distrust. –v.i. **3.** to feel uncertainty as to something; be undecided in opinion or belief. –n. **4.** undecidedness of opinion or belief; a feeling of uncertainty. **5.** distrust; suspicion.

doubtful /ˈdaʊtfəl/ adj. **1.** admitting of or causing doubt; uncertain; ambiguous. **2.** undecided in opinion or belief; hesitating.

douche /duʃ/ *n.* a jet or current of water applied to a body part, organ, or cavity for medicinal, hygienic, or contraceptive purposes.

douchebag /ˈduʃbæg/ *n.* **1.** a piece of equipment used for douching, consisting of a bag for water or fluid and a nozzle for insertion. **2.** *Colloq.* (*derog.*) a person with an inflated opinion of their own worth. Also, **douche bag.**

dough /doʊ/ *n.* **1.** flour or meal combined with water, milk, etc., in a mass for baking into bread, cake, etc. **2.** *Colloq.* money.

doughnut /ˈdoʊnʌt/ *n.* a small, usually ring-shaped cake of dough, deep-fried in fat and often coated in sugar and cinnamon. Also, **donut.**

doula /ˈdulə/ *n.* a woman experienced in childbirth, who provides physical, emotional and informational support to a new mother, before, during and following childbirth.

dour /ˈdaʊə, dʊə/ adj. hard; severe; stern.

douse /daʊs/ v.t. **1.** to plunge into water or the like; drench. **2.** *Colloq.* to put out or extinguish (a light).

dove /dʌv/ *n.* a bird of the pigeon family.

dowager /ˈdaʊədʒə/ *n.* a woman who holds some title or property from her deceased husband, especially the widow of a king, duke, or the like.

dowdy /ˈdaʊdi/ adj. (**-dier, -diest**) ill-dressed; not smart, or stylish.

dowel /ˈdaʊəl/ *n.* *Carpentry* a pin, usually round, fitting into corresponding holes in two adjacent pieces to prevent slipping or to align the two pieces.

down[1] /daʊn/ adv. **1.** from higher to lower; in descending direction or order; into or in a lower position or condition. **2.** on or to the ground. **3.** to a point of submission, inactivity, etc. **4.** to or in a position spoken of as lower, as the south, the country, a business district, etc. **5.** from a greater to a less bulk, degree of consistency, strength, etc. **6.** in due position or state. **7.** on paper or in a book. **8.** in cash; at once. –prep. **9.** to, towards, or at a lower place on or in. **10.** to, towards, near, or at a lower station, condition, or rank in. –adj. **11.** downwards; going or directed downwards. **12.** (of a computer or a computerised system) not operational, usually because of a malfunction. **13.** *Games* losing or behind an opponent by a specified number of points, holes, etc. **14.** depressed; unhappy. –n. **15.** a downward movement; a descent. **16.** *Colloq.* a grudge; a feeling of hostility. –v.t. **17.** to put or throw down; subdue. **18.** to drink down. –phr. **19. down to earth,** practical; realistic.

down[2] /daʊn/ *n.* **1.** the first feathering of young birds. **2.** a soft hairy growth.

down[3] /daʊn/ *n.* (*usu. pl.*) open, rolling, upland country with fairly smooth slopes.

downcast /ˈdaʊnkast/ adj. **1.** directed downwards, as the eyes. **2.** dejected in spirit; depressed.

downfall /'daʊnfɔl/ n. 1. descent to a lower position or standing; overthrow; ruin. 2. a fall, as of rain or snow.

download Computers –v.t. /daʊn'loʊd/ 1. to transfer or copy (data) from one computer to another, or from a computer to a disk or peripheral device. –n. /'daʊnloʊd/ 2. the act or process of downloading data. 3. the data downloaded in such an operation. –**downloadable**, adj.

down-market adj. inferior in style or production. Compare **up-market**.

down payment n. the initial deposit on a purchase made on an instalment plan or mortgage.

downpour /'daʊnpɔ/ n. a heavy, continuous fall of water, rain, etc.

downright /'daʊnraɪt/ adj. 1. thorough; absolute; out-and-out. 2. direct; straightforward.

downsize /'daʊnsaɪz/ v.t. to reduce (a work force, space requirements, financial commitment, etc.).

downstairs adv. /daʊn'stɛəz/ 1. down the stairs; to or on a lower floor. –adj. /'daʊnstɛəz/ 2. on or relating to a lower floor.

Down syndrome n. a genetic condition resulting from a third chromosome on the 21st chromosomal pairing, characterised by varying degrees of intellectual and physical impairment. Also, **Down's syndrome**.

downtime /'daʊntaɪm/ n. 1. time during which a machine is not operational. 2. time during which a machine, etc., is not operational. 3. a period of relaxation. Also, **down time**.

downward /'daʊnwəd/ adj. 1. moving or going towards a lower place or condition. –adv. 2. → **downwards**.

downwards /'daʊnwədz/ adv. from a higher to a lower place or condition. Also, **downward**.

downwind /daʊn'wɪnd/ adv. in the direction of the wind; with the wind.

dowry /'daʊəri, 'daʊri/ n. (pl. **-ries**) the money, goods, or estate which a woman brings to her husband at marriage.

doyen /'dɔɪən/ n. the senior member of a body, class, profession, etc. –**doyenne**, fem. n.

doze /doʊz/ v.i. to sleep lightly or fitfully.

dozen /'dʌzən/ n. (pl. **-zen** or **-zens**) 1. a group of twelve units or things. –determiner 2. amounting to a dozen in number: a dozen eggs.

drab /dræb/ adj. (**drabber, drabbest**) dull or uninteresting.

draft /draft/ n. 1. Also, **draught**. a drawing, sketch, or design. 2. Also, **draught**. a first or preliminary form of any writing, subject to revision and copying. 3. military conscription. 4. an animal or animals selected and separated from the herd or flock. –v.t. 5. Also, **draught**. to draw the outlines or plan of, or sketch. 6. Also, **draught**. to draw up in written form, as a first draft. 7. to conscript.

draftsman /'draftsmən/ n. (pl. **-men**) someone who draws sketches, plans, or designs. Also, **draughtsman**.

drag /dræg/ v. (**dragged, dragging**) –v.t. 1. to draw with force, effort, or difficulty; pull heavily or slowly along; haul; trail. 2. Computers to move (text, a file, etc.) across a computer screen by selecting with the mouse and moving the cursor to another part of the screen. 3. (fol.

by in) to introduce, as an irrelevant matter. 4. (oft. fol. by out or on) to protract or pass tediously. –v.i. 5. to be drawn or hauled along. 6. to trail on the ground. 7. to proceed or pass with tedious slowness. –n. 8. something used by or for dragging. 9. the force due to the relative airflow exerted on an aeroplane or other body tending to reduce its forward motion. 10. Colloq. somebody or something that is extremely boring. 11. Colloq. a puff or a pull on a cigarette. 12. Colloq. the clothes and accessories typically worn by one sex, when worn by the other.

dragnet /'drægnɛt/ n. a net to be drawn along the bottom of a river, pond, etc., or along the ground, to catch something.

dragon /'drægən/ n. 1. a mythical monster variously represented, generally as a huge winged reptile with crested head and terrible claws, and often spouting fire, but in the Eastern tradition as powerful but beneficent. 2. a fierce, violent person. 3. any of various lizards, as the frillneck lizard of Australia.

dragonfly /'drægənflaɪ/ n. (pl. **-flies**) a large, harmless insect which feeds on mosquitoes and other insects.

dragon's teeth /'drægənz/ pl. n. NSW a road marking comprising a row of small triangular shapes, indicating a school zone where vehicles must slow to 40 km/h at specified times.

drain /dreɪn/ v.t. 1. to draw off gradually, as a liquid; remove by degrees, as by filtration. 2. to draw off or take away completely. –n. 3. that by which anything is drained, as a pipe or conduit. 4. gradual or continuous outflow, withdrawal, or expenditure.

drainage /'dreɪnɪdʒ/ n. 1. the act or process of draining. 2. a system of drains, artificial or natural.

drake /dreɪk/ n. a male duck.

dram /dræm/ n. 1. a unit of measurement in the imperial system. 2. a small quantity of anything.

DRAM /'di ræm/ n. → **dynamic random access memory**. Also, **Dram**.

drama /'dramə/ n. 1. a composition in prose or verse presenting in dialogue or pantomime a story involving conflict or contrast of character, especially one intended to be acted on the stage; a play. 2. any series of events having dramatic interest or results. –**dramatise, dramatize**, v. –**dramatisation, dramatization**, n. –**dramatist**, n.

dramatic /drə'mætɪk/ adj. 1. of or relating to the drama. 2. characteristic of or appropriate to the drama; involving conflict or contrast. 3. sudden and marked: a dramatic rise in unemployment.

drank /dræŋk/ v. past tense and former past participle of **drink**.

drape /dreɪp/ v.t. to cover or hang with cloth or some fabric.

draper /'dreɪpə/ n. a dealer in textiles and cloth goods, etc. –**drapery**, n.

drastic /'dræstɪk/ adj. acting with force or violence; violent.

draught /draft/ n. 1. a current of air, especially in a room, chimney, stove, or any enclosed space. 2. an act of drawing or pulling, or that which is drawn; a pull; haul. 3. the drawing of a liquid from its receptacle, as of ale from a cask. **4.** an amount drunk as a continuous act. **5.** *Naut.* the depth of water needed by a ship to float: *a draught of 30 metres.* **6.** (*pl. construed as sing.*) a game played by two people each with twelve pieces on a chequered board. **7.** → **draft** (defs 1 and 2). *–adj.* **8.** being on draught; drawn as required. **9.** used or suited for drawing loads. *–v.t.* **10.** → **draft** (defs 5 and 6).

draughtsman /'dra:ftsmən/ *n.* (*pl.* **-men**) → **draftsman**.

draw /drɔ:/ *v.* (**drew** /dru:/, **drawn, drawing**) *–v.t.* **1.** (oft. fol. by *along, away, in, out, off,* etc.) to cause to come in a particular direction as by a pulling force; pull; drag; lead. **2.** to bring towards oneself or itself, as by inherent force or influence; attract. **3.** to pick or choose at random. **4.** to sketch in lines or words; delineate; depict. **5.** to frame or formulate as a distinction. **6.** to pull out to full or greater length; stretch; make by attenuating, as wire. **7.** to wrinkle or shrink by contraction. **8.** to write or sign (an order, draft, or bill of exchange). *–v.i.* **9.** to exert a pulling, moving, or attracting force. **10.** to use or practise the art of tracing figures; practise drawing. **11.** *Games* to leave a contest undecided. *–n.* **12.** the act of drawing. **13.** that which is drawn, as a lot. **14.** *Sport* a drawn or undecided contest.

drawback /'drɔ:bæk/ *n.* **1.** a hindrance or disadvantage. **2.** *Commerce* an amount paid back from a charge made. **3.** *Govt* refund of excise or import duty, as when imported goods are re-exported. See **rebate**.

drawbridge /'drɔ:brɪdʒ/ *n.* a bridge of which the whole or a part may be drawn up or aside to prevent access or to leave a passage open for boats, etc.

drawee /drɔ:'i:/ *n.* a person on whom an order, draft, or bill of exchange is drawn.

drawer *n.* **1.** /drɔ:/ a sliding compartment, as in a piece of furniture, that may be drawn out in order to get access to it. **2.** /drɔ:/ (*pl.*) a garment for the lower part of the body, with a separate portion for each leg; underpants. **3.** /'drɔ:ə/ *Finance* someone who draws an order, draft, or bill of exchange.

drawing /'drɔ:ɪŋ, 'drɔ:rɪŋ/ *n.* **1.** the act of a person or thing that draws. **2.** representation by lines; delineation of form without reference to colour. **3.** a sketch, plan, or design, especially one made with pen, pencil, or crayon. **4.** the art of making these.

drawing-pin *n.* a short broad-headed tack designed to be pushed in by the thumb. Also, **thumbtack**.

drawing room *n.* a room for the reception and entertainment of visitors; a living room.

drawl /drɔ:l/ *v.t., v.i.* **1.** to say or speak with slow, lingering utterance. *–n.* **2.** the act or utterance of someone who drawls.

drawn /drɔ:n/ *v.* **1.** past participle of **draw**. *–adj.* **2.** haggard; tired; tense.

dray /dreɪ/ *n.* a low, strong cart.

dread /drɛd/ *v.t.* **1.** to fear greatly. *–n.* **2.** terror or apprehension. **3.** deep awe. *–adj.* **4.** greatly feared.

dreadful /'drɛdfəl/ *adj.* **1.** extremely bad, unpleasant, ugly, etc. **2.** causing great dread, fear, or terror; terrible.

dream /dri:m/ *n.* **1.** a succession of images or ideas present in the mind during sleep. **2.** a vision voluntarily indulged in while awake; daydream. **3.** something or somebody of an unreal beauty or charm. **4.** a hope that gives one inspiration; an aim. *–v.* (**dreamed** *or* **dreamt** /drɛmt/, **dreaming**) *–v.i.* **5.** to have a dream or dreams. *–v.t.* **6.** to see or imagine in sleep or in a vision. *–phr.* **7. in your dreams,** *Colloq.* an exclamation indicating that the person addressed is indulging in wishful thinking or unrealistic fantasy.

dreamcatcher /'dri:mkætʃə/ *n.* an artefact comprising a net stretched on a ring with feathers hanging from it; believed in some American Indian traditions to catch bad dreams.

Dreaming /'dri:mɪŋ/ *n.* (*also lower case*) **1. the,** Also, **the Dreamtime.** (in Aboriginal mythology) the time in which the earth received its present form and in which the patterns and cycles of life and nature were initiated; alcheringa. **2.** a division of an Aboriginal people, based on allegiance to a totemic ancestor: *honey ant Dreaming.*

Dreaming track *n.* (*also lower case*) (among Aboriginal people) a trail with religious significance.

dreary /'drɪəri/ *adj.* (**-rier, -riest**) dull or depressing.

dredge¹ /drɛdʒ/ *n.* **1.** a contrivance for gathering material or objects from the bed of a river, etc. *–v.* (**dredged, dredging**) *–v.t.* **2.** to clear out with a dredge; remove sand, silt, mud, etc., from the bottom of. *–v.i.* **3.** to use a dredge. **4.** (fol. by *up*) to find, usually with some difficulty.

dredge² /drɛdʒ/ *v.t.* (**dredged, dredging**) to sprinkle or coat with flour, etc.

dreg /drɛg/ *n.* a small remnant or quantity.

dregs /drɛgz/ *pl. n.* **1.** sediment of wine or other drink; lees; grounds. **2.** any waste or worthless residue. *–phr.* **3. the dregs (of society),** a person or class of people considered to be low or despicable, especially immoral.

drench /drɛntʃ/ *v.t.* **1.** to wet thoroughly; steep; soak. **2.** *Vet. Science* to administer medicine to (an animal), especially by force.

dress /drɛs/ *n.* **1.** a one-piece outer garment worn by women and girls, comprising a skirt and bodice, with or without sleeves. **2.** clothing; apparel; garb. *–adj.* **3.** of or for a dress or dresses. **4.** of or for a formal occasion. *–v.t.* **5.** to put clothes on; deck; attire. **6.** to arrange a display in; ornament or adorn. **7.** to prepare (fowl, game, skins, fabrics, timber, stone, ore, etc.) by special processes. **8.** to treat (wounds or sores). **9.** *Colloq.* (fol. by *down*) to scold severely; upbraid and rebuke. *–v.i.* **10.** to clothe or attire oneself, especially in formal or evening clothes.

dressage /'drɛsɑ:ʒ/ *n.* the art and training of a horse in obedience, deportment, and responses.

dress circle *n.* the first gallery above the floor in a theatre, etc.

dresser /'drɛsə/ *n.* a kitchen sideboard.

dressing /'drɛsɪŋ/ *n.* **1.** a sauce for food: *salad dressing.* **2.** an application for a wound.

dressing-gown n. a loose gown or robe generally worn over night attire.

dressing table n. a table or stand, usually surmounted by a mirror.

drew /druː/ v. past tense of **draw**.

dribble /'drɪbəl/ v. (**-bled, -bling**) –v.i. **1.** to fall or flow in drops or small quantities; trickle. **2.** to drivel; slaver. **3.** Soccer, Hockey, etc. to advance a ball by a series of short kicks or pushes. –v.t. **4.** to let fall in drops.

dried /draɪd/ v. past tense and past participle of **dry**.

drift /drɪft/ n. **1.** a driving movement or force; impulse; impetus; pressure. **2.** Navig. movement or course under the impulse of water currents, wind, etc. **3.** Physical Geog. a broad and shallow current. **4.** the course of anything; tendency; aim. **5.** something driven, or formed by driving. –v.i. **6.** to be carried along by currents of water or air, or by the force of circumstances. **7.** to wander aimlessly.

driftwood /'drɪftwʊd/ n. wood floating on, or cast ashore by, the water.

drill[1] /drɪl/ n. **1.** a tool or machine for making cylindrical holes, especially by rotation. **2.** Mil. training in formal marching or other precise military or naval movements. **3.** any strict, methodical training, instrument, or exercise. –v.t. **4.** to pierce or bore a hole in (anything). **5.** to impart (knowledge) by strict training or discipline.

drill[2] /drɪl/ n. strong cotton fabric.

drink /drɪŋk/ v. (**drank, drunk, drinking**) –v.i. **1.** to swallow water or other liquid; imbibe. **2.** to imbibe alcoholic beverages, especially habitually or to excess; tipple. –v.t. **3.** to take in (a liquid) in any manner; absorb. **4.** to take through the senses, especially with eagerness and pleasure. –n. **5.** any liquid which is swallowed to quench thirst, for nourishment, etc.; a beverage. **6.** an alcoholic drink. –**drinking**, n.

drip /drɪp/ v.i. **1.** to fall in drops, as a liquid. –n. **2.** the liquid that drips. **3.** Med. the continuous slow infusion of fluid containing nutrients or drugs to a patient, especially after surgery. **4.** Colloq. a dull or boring person.

dripping /'drɪpɪŋ/ n. fat exuded from meat in cooking.

drive /draɪv/ v. (**drove, driven, driving**) –v.t. **1.** to send along, away, off, in, out, back, etc., by compulsion; force along. **2.** to overwork. **3.** to cause and guide the movement of (an animal, vehicle, etc.). **4.** to convey in a vehicle. –v.i. **5.** to go along before an impelling force; be impelled. **6.** to rush or dash violently. **7.** (fol. by at) to make an effort to reach or obtain; aim. **8.** to go or travel in a driven vehicle. –n. **9.** the act of driving. **10.** an impelling along, as of game, cattle, or floating logs, in a particular direction. **11.** Psychol. a source of motivation. **12.** a vigorous onset or onward course. **13.** a united effort to accomplish some purpose, especially to raise money for a government loan or for some charity. **14.** energy and initiative. **15.** a trip in a driven vehicle. **16.** Computers a controlling mechanism for moving magnetic tapes,

floppy disks, etc., thus enabling data to be accessed.

drive-in n. **1.** a cinema so designed that patrons drive in to a large area in front of an outdoor screen and view the film while seated in their cars. –adj. **2.** (of any shop, food outlet, etc.) catering for customers in cars.

drivel /'drɪvəl/ v.i. (**-elled, -elling**) **1.** to let saliva flow from the mouth; slaver. –n. **2.** idiotic or silly talk.

driven /'drɪvən/ adj. pursuing a goal with relentless determination.

driver /'draɪvə/ n. **1.** someone who drives a vehicle. **2.** Machinery a part that transmits force or motion. **3.** Computers → **device driver**. **4.** a golf club with a long shaft, used for making long shots, as from the tee.

drizzle /'drɪzəl/ v.t. **1.** to rain gently and steadily in fine drops. –n. **2.** a very light rain; mist.

droll /drəʊl/ adj. amusingly odd.

-drome 1. a word element meaning 'running', 'course', 'racecourse'. **2.** a word element referring to a large structure or area for a specific use, as in aerodrome.

drone[1] /drəʊn/ n. **1.** the male of the honey bee and other bees, stingless and making no honey. **2.** an unmanned aerial vehicle, used for various purposes: film drone.

drone[2] /drəʊn/ v.i. **1.** to make a dull, continued, monotonous sound; hum; buzz. **2.** to speak in a monotonous tone.

drool /druːl/ v.i. **1.** to let saliva spill from the mouth. –phr. **2. drool over**, to have a greedy interest in: she drooled over her friend's new car.

droop /druːp/ v.i. to sink, bend, or hang down, as from weakness or exhaustion.

drop /drɒp/ n. **1.** a small quantity of liquid which falls or is produced in a more or less spherical mass; a liquid globule. **2.** a minute quantity of anything. **3.** something like or likened to a drop. **4.** the distance or depth to which anything drops or falls. **5.** a steep slope. **6.** a fall in degree, amount, value, etc. –v. (**dropped, dropping**) –v.i. **7.** to fall in globules or small portions, as water or other liquid. **8.** to fall vertically like a drop; have an abrupt descent. **9.** (fol. by out) to withdraw; disappear. **10.** to fall lower in condition, degree, etc.; sink. **11.** to fall or move (back, behind, to the rear, etc.). **12.** (fol. by in, by, across, etc.) to come or go casually or unexpectedly into a place; to visit informally. –v.t. **13.** to let fall in drops or small portions. **14.** to let fall; allow to sink to a lower position; lower. **15.** to utter or express casually or incidentally, as a hint. **16.** to send or post (a note, etc.). **17.** (fol. by off) to set down, as from a ship, car, etc. **18.** to omit (a letter or syllable) in pronunciation or writing. **19.** to cease to keep up or have to do with.

drop-down menu n. → **pull-down menu**.

drop-in n. **1.** Skating a manoeuvre in which the rider enters a ramp from the top. **2.** Colloq. a person who arrives to visit unexpectedly.

dropout /'drɒpaʊt/ n. someone who decides to opt out of conventional society, a given social group or an educational institution.

droppings /'drɒpɪŋz/ pl. n. animal dung.

drop zone *n.* **1.** the place where skydivers, parachutists, etc., are intended to land. **2.** *Golf* the designated place on a golf course where play must be resumed after the ball has been lost for any of various reasons. Also, **dropzone**.

dross /drɒs/ *n.* **1.** *Metallurgy* a waste product taken off molten metal during smelting, essentially metallic in character. **2.** waste matter; refuse. **–drossy**, *adj.* **–drossiness**, *n.*

drought /draʊt/ *n.* **1.** dry weather; lack of rain. **2.** scarcity.

droughtproof /ˈdraʊtpruf/ *v.t.* **1.** to ensure a supply of drinking water for. *–adj.* **2.** designed so as to be unaffected by drought. **–droughtproofing**, *n.*

drove¹ /droʊv/ *v.* past tense of **drive**.

drove² /droʊv/ *n.* **1.** a number of oxen, sheep, or swine driven in a group; herd; flock. **2.** (*usu. pl.*) a large crowd of human beings, especially in motion: *to come for tickets in droves. –v.t.* (**droved, droving**) **3.** to drive (cattle or sheep) over long distances, to market or to better pasture, etc. **–drover**, *n.* **–droving**, *n.*

drown /draʊn/ *v.i.* **1.** to be suffocated by immersion in water or other liquid. *–v.t.* **2.** to suffocate (a person, etc.) by immersion in water or other liquid. **3.** to make inaudible; muffle; obscure.

drowse /draʊz/ *v.i.* to be sleepy; be half asleep. **–drowsy**, *adj.*

drudge /drʌdʒ/ *n.* someone who labours at servile or uninteresting tasks; a hard toiler. **–drudgery**, *n.*

drug /drʌg/ *n.* **1.** a chemical substance given with the intention of preventing or curing disease or otherwise enhancing the physical or mental welfare of humans or animals. **2.** a chemical substance taken to bring about a change in behaviour, mood or perception. *–v.t.* (**drugged, drugging**) **3.** to stupefy or poison with a drug.

drug cheat *n.* a person who takes banned substances to improve their sporting performance.

drug mule *n.* → **mule¹** (def. 3).

drum /drʌm/ *n.* **1.** a musical instrument consisting of a hollow body, often covered at one or both ends with a tightly stretched membrane, or head, which is struck with the hand, a stick, or a pair of sticks. **2.** a natural organ by which an animal produces a loud or bass sound. **3.** something resembling a drum in shape or structure, or in the noise it produces. **4.** *Computers* (formerly) a magnetically coated cylinder revolving at high speed, used for data storage. *–v.* (**drummed, drumming**) *–v.i.* **5.** to beat or play a drum. **6.** to beat on anything rhythmically. *–v.t.* **7.** to beat rhythmically; perform (a tune) by drumming. **8.** to drive or force by persistent repetition. **9.** (*oft. fol. by up*) to solicit or obtain (trade, customers, etc.).

drunk /drʌŋk/ *v.* **1.** past participle of **drink**. *–adj.* **2.** (*used esp. after the noun or pronoun*) intoxicated with, or as with, alcoholic drink. *–n.* **3.** *Colloq.* a person intoxicated with alcoholic drink. **–drunkard**, *n.*

drunken /ˈdrʌŋkən/ *adj.* **1.** intoxicated; drunk. **2.** given to drunkenness. **3.** relating to, proceeding from, or marked by intoxication: *a drunken quarrel.* **–drunkenly**, *adv.* **–drunkenness**, *n.*

drupe /drup/ *n.* a fruit, as the peach, cherry, plum, etc., with soft, pulpy flesh and a single stone. **–drupaceous**, *adj.*

dry /draɪ/ *adj.* (**drier, driest**) **1.** free from moisture; not moist; not wet. **2.** having little or no rain. **3.** not under, in, or on water. **4.** not yielding water or other liquid. **5.** desiring drink; thirsty. **6.** dull; uninteresting. **7.** humorous or sarcastic in an unemotional or impersonal way. **8.** (of wines) not sweet. *–v.* (**dried, drying**) *–v.t.* **9.** to make dry; to free from moisture. *–v.i.* **10.** to become dry; lose moisture. *–n.* (*pl.* **dries**) **11.** a dry state, condition, or place. **12.** *Colloq.* dry ginger ale: *brandy and dry.*

dry-clean *v.t.* to clean (garments, etc.) with chemical solvents, etc., rather than water. **–drycleaner**

dry dock *n.* a basin-like structure from which the water can be removed after the entrance of a ship, used when making repairs on a ship's bottom, etc.

dry ice *n.* solid carbon dioxide.

dryland /ˈdraɪlænd/ *adj.* **1.** of or relating to land which is often dry, especially land having sandy soil. *–n.* Also, **drylands**. **2.** such a tract of land.

dryland salinity *n.* the presence of high levels of salt in soil, resulting in the death of plants and soil organisms, and caused by the rise in the watertable that follows land clearing.

dry measure *n.* the system of units of capacity formerly used in Britain, Australia and the US for measuring dry commodities, as grain, fruit, etc.

dry season *n.* the period of an annual cycle in the tropics when there is little rainfall and the days are hot and sunny, usually as a result of the change in the prevailing winds. Compare **wet season**.

dual /ˈdjuəl/ *adj.* **1.** of or relating to two. **2.** composed or consisting of two parts; double.

dub¹ /dʌb/ *v.t.* (**dubbed, dubbing**) **1.** to strike lightly with a sword in the ceremony of conferring knighthood; make, or designate as, a knight. **2.** to invest with any title; name; call.

dub² /dʌb/ *v.t.* (**dubbed, dubbing**) to change the soundtrack (of a film or videotape), as in substituting a dialogue in another language.

dubious /ˈdjubiəs/ *adj.* **1.** doubtful; marked by or occasioning doubt. **2.** wavering or hesitating in opinion; inclined to doubt.

duchess /ˈdʌtʃəs, ˈdʌtʃəs/ *n.* the wife or widow of a duke.

duchy /ˈdʌtʃi/ *n.* (*pl.* **-chies**) the territory ruled by a duke or duchess.

duck¹ /dʌk/ *n.* any of numerous wild or domesticated web-footed swimming birds.

duck² /dʌk/ *v.i.* **1.** to plunge the whole body or the head momentarily under water. **2.** to avoid a blow, unpleasant task, etc.

duck³ /dʌk/ *n.* *Cricket* an individual score of nought made when batting.

duckbill /ˈdʌkbɪl/ *n.* → **platypus**.

duckling /ˈdʌklɪŋ/ *n.* a young duck.

duct /dʌkt/ *n.* **1.** any tube, canal, or conduit by which fluid or other substances are conducted or conveyed. –v.t. **2.** to convey by means of a duct or ducts.

ductile /'dʌktail/ adj. **1.** capable of being hammered out thin, as certain metals; malleable. **2.** capable of being moulded or shaped; plastic.

dud /dʌd/ Colloq. –n. **1.** any thing or person that proves a failure. –adj. **2.** useless; defective.

dudgeon /'dʌdʒən/ phr. **in high dudgeon**, in a state of anger or indignation.

due /dju/ adj. **1.** immediately payable. **2.** owing, irrespective of whether the time of payment has arrived. **3.** rightful; proper; fitting. **4.** attributable, as to a cause. **5.** under engagement as to time; expected to be ready, be present, or arrive. –n. **6.** (usu. pl.) a payment due, as a charge, a fee, a membership subscription, etc.

due diligence n. the process of acquiring objective and reliable information on a person or a company as required, especially before a commercial acquisition.

duel /'djuəl/ n. a prearranged combat between two persons, fought with deadly weapons according to an accepted code of procedure, especially to settle a private quarrel.

due process n. the proper legal procedures which enshrine the rights of an individual, and which should not be tampered with, especially by governments. Also, **due process of law**.

duet /dju'et/ n. a musical composition for two voices or performers.

duffer /'dʌfə/ n. (humorous) a foolish person: you're a silly duffer!

dug /dʌg/ v. past tense and past participle of **dig**.

dugong /'djugɒŋ/ n. a large marine mammal of northern Australia, having flipper-like forelimbs.

duke /djuk/ n. **1.** a sovereign prince, the ruler of a small state. **2.** (in Britain) a nobleman of the highest rank after that of a prince.

dukkah /'dukə/ n. an Egyptian spice blend made from selected toasted nuts and seeds. Also, **dukka**.

dulcet /'dʌlsət/ adj. agreeable to the feelings, the eye, or, especially the ear; soothing.

dull /dʌl/ adj. **1.** slow of understanding; obtuse; stupid. **2.** not intense or acute. **3.** listless; spiritless. **4.** tedious; uninteresting. **5.** not bright, intense, or clear; dim. –v.t., v.i. **6.** to make or become dull.

duly /'djuli/ adv. **1.** in a due manner; properly. **2.** in due season; punctually. **3.** adequately.

dumb /dʌm/ adj. **1.** without the power of speech. **2.** made, done, etc., without speech. **3.** Colloq. stupid; dull-witted. –phr. **4. dumb down**, Colloq. **a.** to put (information) in simpler terms, as for a less informed audience. **b.** to cause (a group, country, etc.) to become less informed or less intelligent.

dumbbell /'dʌmbel/ n. a weight used for exercises, consisting of two balls joined by a bar-like handle.

dumbfound /'dʌmfaʊnd/ v.t. to strike dumb with amazement.

dumbstruck /'dʌmstrʌk/ adj. shocked into speechlessness.

dummy /'dʌmi/ n. (pl. **-mies**) **1.** an imitation or copy of something, as for display, to indicate appearance, exhibit clothing, etc. **2.** Colloq. a stupid person; dolt. **3.** (at an auction, etc.) someone ostensibly acting on their own behalf while actually acting as an agent for others. **4.** Cards **a.** (in bridge) the dealer's partner whose hand is exposed and played by the dealer. **b.** the cards so exposed. **5.** a rubber teat, etc., given to a baby to suck. –adj. **6.** counterfeit; sham; imitation.

dummy spit n. Colloq. a display of exasperation or bad temper, similar to a child's tantrum.

dump /dʌmp/ v.t. **1.** to throw down in a mass; fling down or drop heavily. **2.** to get rid of; hand over to somebody else. **3.** Computers to print out, with minimal editing, the content of computer memory, usually for diagnostic purposes in debugging. **4.** Commerce **a.** to put (goods) on the market in large quantities and at a low price, especially to a large or favoured buyer. **b.** to market (goods) thus in a foreign country, as at a price below that charged in the home country. –n. **5.** Also, **rubbish dump**. → **tip**[2] (def. 4). **6.** Mil. a collection of ammunition, stores, etc., to be distributed for use. **7.** Colloq. a place, house, or town that is poorly kept up, and generally of wretched appearance.

dumpling /'dʌmpliŋ/ n. a rounded mass of steamed dough.

dumps /dʌmps/ phr. **down in the dumps**, Colloq. in a dull or depressed state of mind.

dumpy /'dʌmpi/ adj. (**-pier, -piest**) short and stout; squat.

dun[1] /dʌn/ v.t. (**dunned, dunning**) to make repeated and insistent demands upon, especially for the payment of a debt.

dun[2] /dʌn/ adj. **1.** dull or greyish brown. **2.** dark; gloomy.

dunce /dʌns/ n. a dull-witted or stupid person.

dune /djun/ n. a sand hill or sand ridge formed by the wind, usually in desert regions or near lakes and oceans.

dung /dʌŋ/ n. manure; excrement, especially of animals.

dungeon /'dʌndʒən/ n. any strong, close cell, especially underground.

dunk /dʌŋk/ v.t. **1.** to immerse in water. **2.** to dip (biscuits, etc.) into coffee, milk, etc.

dunnart /'dʌnat/ n. any of various narrow-footed marsupial mice.

dunny /'dʌni/ n. (pl. **-nies**) Colloq. a toilet.

duo /'djuoʊ/ n. a pair of singers, entertainers, etc.

duo- a word element meaning 'two'.

duodenum /djuə'dinəm/ n. the first portion of the small intestine. –**duodenal**, adj.

dupe /djup/ n. a person who is imposed upon or deceived.

duple /'djupəl/ adj. double.

duplex /'djupleks/ adj. **1.** twofold; double. –n. **2.** a building consisting of two separate dwellings, arranged either on each storey of a two-storey building, or as a pair of semi-detached cottages.

duplicate adj. /'djupləkət/ **1.** exactly alike or corresponding to something else. **2.** double; consisting of or existing in two corresponding parts. –n. /'djupləkət/ **3.** a copy exactly like an original. –v.t. /'djupləkeɪt/ **4.** to make an exact copy of; repeat. –**duplication**, n. –**duplicator**, n.

duplicity /dju'plisəti/ n. deceitfulness in speech or conduct. –**duplicitous**, adj.

durable /ˈdjurəbəl/ *adj.* having the quality of lasting or enduring; not easily worn out, decayed, etc. **–durability,** *n.*

duration /djuˈreɪʃən/ *n.* **1.** continuance in time. **2.** the length of time anything continues.

duress /djuˈrɛs/ *n.* **1.** constraint; compulsion. **2.** forcible restraint of liberty; imprisonment.

during /ˈdjurɪŋ/ *prep.* **1.** throughout the continuance of. **2.** in the course of.

durum wheat /ˈdjurəm/ *n.* a species or variety of wheat, the flour from which is largely used for pasta. Also, **durum.**

dusk /dʌsk/ *n.* partial darkness; a state between light and darkness; twilight.

dusky /ˈdʌski/ *adj.* **(-kier, -kiest)** somewhat dark; dark-coloured.

dust /dʌst/ *n.* **1.** earth or other matter in fine, dry particles. **2.** any finely powdered substance, as sawdust. *–v.t.* **3.** to free from dust; wipe the dust from. **4.** to sprinkle with dust or powder. **–dusty,** *adj.*

dust jacket *n.* a jacket for a book. Also, **dust cover.**

duty /ˈdjuti/ *n.* **(pl. -ties) 1.** that which one is bound to do by moral or legal obligation. **2.** action required by one's position or occupation; office; function. **3.** a levy imposed by law on the import, export, sale, or manufacture of goods, the legal recognition of deeds and documents, etc. **–dutiful,** *adj.* **–dutiable,** *adj.*

dux /dʌks/ *n.* the top pupil at a school in terms of academic achievement.

DVD /di vi ˈdi/ *n.* **1.** a high-capacity disc with enough capacity to store the video and audio data for a full-length movie. **2.** the technology related to this storage. *–adj.* **3.** relating to or utilising this technology.

DVR /di vi ˈa/ *n.* an electronic device which records video in a digital format, allowing capture and playback to and from a disk.

dwarf /dwɔf/ *n.* **(pl. dwarfs or dwarves** /dwɔvz/**) 1.** a person suffering from a genetic condition resulting in short stature. **2.** an unusually small person or thing. **3.** of unusually small stature or size; diminutive. *–v.t.* **4.** to cause to appear or seem small in size, extent, character, etc.

dwarf star *n.* a star of relatively small volume and low luminosity, but often of high density.

dwell /dwɛl/ *v.i.* **(dwelt or dwelled, dwelling) 1.** to abide as a permanent resident. **2.** to continue for a time. **3.** (oft. fol. by *on* or *upon*) to linger over in thought, speech, or writing; to emphasise. **–dwelling,** *n.*

dwindle /ˈdwɪndl/ *v.i.* to become smaller and smaller; shrink.

dye /daɪ/ *n.* **1.** a colouring material or matter. *–v.t.* **(dyed, dyeing) 2.** to colour or stain.

dying /ˈdaɪɪŋ/ *adj.* **1.** ceasing to live; approaching death. **2.** given, uttered, or manifested just before death. **3.** drawing to a close.

dyke¹ /daɪk/ *n. Colloq.* a lesbian. Also, **dike.**

dyke² /daɪk/ *n.* **1.** an embankment for restraining the waters of the sea or a river. **2.** *Colloq.* a toilet. Also, **dike.**

dynamic /daɪˈnæmɪk/ *adj.* **1.** of or relating to force not in equilibrium (opposed to *static*) or to force in any state. **2.** relating to or characterised by energy or effective action; active; forceful. Also, **dynamical.**

dynamics /daɪˈnæmɪks/ *n.* **1.** *Physics* the branch of mechanics concerned with those forces which cause or affect the motion of bodies. **2.** the science or principles of forces acting in any field.

dynamic verb *n. Gram.* a verb which indicates an action or process, as *The child jumps*, or *The light fades.* Compare **stative verb.** Also, **action verb.**

dynamite /ˈdaɪnəmaɪt/ *n.* **1.** a high explosive. **2.** *Colloq.* anything or anyone potentially dangerous and liable to cause trouble. **3.** *Colloq.* anything or anyone exceptional.

dynamo /ˈdaɪnəmoʊ/ *n.* **(pl. -mos) 1.** any rotating machine in which mechanical energy is converted into electrical energy. **2.** *Colloq.* a forceful, energetic person.

dynasty /ˈdɪnəsti/, *Chiefly US* /ˈdaɪ-/ *n.* **(pl. -ties)** a sequence of rulers from the same family or stock. **–dynastic,** *adj.*

dyne /daɪn/ *n.* the unit of force in the centimetre-gram-second system, equal to 10×10^{-6} newtons. *Symbol:* dyn

dys- a prefix, especially medical, indicating difficulty, poor condition.

dysentery /ˈdɪsəntri/ *n.* an infectious disease marked by inflammation and ulceration of the lower part of the bowels, with diarrhoea.

dysfunctional /dɪsˈfʌŋkʃənəl/ *adj.* **1.** not functioning properly or normally: *a dysfunctional engine.* **2.** not functioning in a way that conforms behaviourally, socially, etc., to accepted norms: *a dysfunctional family*; *a dysfunctional relationship.* **–dysfunction,** *n.* **–dysfunctionality,** *n.*

dyslexia /dɪsˈlɛksiə/ *n.* impairment in reading ability, often associated with other disorders especially in writing and coordination. **–dyslexic, dyslectic,** *n.*, *adj.*

dyspepsia /dɪsˈpɛpsiə/ *n. Pathol.* unsettled or impaired digestion; indigestion.

E, e

E, e /i/ n. the fifth letter of the English alphabet.

e-[1] variant of **ex-**[1].

e-[2] **1.** a prefix used to indicate that the specified activity is associated with the internet in some way: *email; e-banking; ecommerce; e-activism*. **2.** a prefix which indicates that something operates electronically: *e-tag; e-ticket*.

each /itʃ/ adj. **1.** every, of two or more considered individually or one by one. *–pron.* **2.** each one. *–adv.* **3.** apiece.

each-way bet n. *Horseracing, etc.* a bet in which a racehorse, etc., is staked to win the place dividend for a place (def. 12b), or both the win and place dividends for a win.

eager /'igə/ adj. keen or ardent in desire or feeling.

eagle /'igəl/ n. **1.** any of certain large birds of prey. **2.** *Golf* a score two below par on any but par-three holes.

ear[1] /iə/ n. **1.** the organ of hearing. **2.** attention, especially favourable.

ear[2] /iə/ n. that part of a cereal plant which contains the grains and kernels.

earl /ɜl/ n. a British nobleman.

earlobe /'iəloʊb/ n. the soft pendulous lower part of the external ear.

early /'ɜli/ adv. **(-lier, -liest) 1.** in or during the first part of some division of time, or of some course or series. **2.** before the usual or appointed time; in good time. *–adj.* **(-lier, -liest) 3.** occurring in the first part of some division of time, or of some course or series. **4.** occurring before the usual or appointed time. **5.** belonging to a period far back in time.

earmark /'iəmak/ v.t. to set aside for a specific purpose or use.

earn /ɜn/ v.t. **(earnt** or **earned** /ɜnd/, **earning)** to gain by labour or service. **–earnings,** *pl. n.*

earnest /'ɜnəst/ adj. serious in intention, purpose, or effort.

earphone /'iəfoʊn/ n. a small device for converting electric signals into soundwaves, and designed that it is meant to fit into the ear or to be held close to it.

earring /'iə,rɪŋ/ n. a ring or other ornament worn in or on the lobe of the ear.

earshot /'iəʃɒt/ n. range of hearing: *within earshot*.

earth /ɜθ/ n. **1.** (*oft. upper case*) the planet which we inhabit. **2.** the softer part of the land, as distinguished from rock; soil. **3.** *Elect.* a conducting connection between an electric circuit or equipment and the ground. **4.** any of several metallic oxides.

earthen /'ɜθən/ adj. made of baked clay.

earthquake /'ɜθkweɪk/ n. tremors or earth movements in the earth's crust.

earthworm /'ɜθwɜm/ n. any one of many segmented worms that burrow in soil and feed on soil and decaying organic matter.

earthy /'ɜθi/ adj. **(-thier, -thiest) 1.** of the nature of soil. **2.** coarse or unrefined. **3.** direct; unaffected.

ease /iz/ n. **1.** freedom from labour, pain, or annoyance of any kind. **2.** freedom from stiffness, constraint, or formality. *–v.t.* **3.** to give rest or relief to. **4.** to mitigate, lighten, or lessen. **5.** to facilitate. **6.** to move slowly and with great care. *–v.i.* **7.** (oft. fol. by *off* or *up*) to reduce severity, pressure, pain, tension, etc. **8.** to move with great care.

easel /'izəl/ n. a frame for supporting an artist's canvas, etc.

easement /'izmənt/ n. *Law* a right held by one person to make use of the land of another.

easily /'izəli/ adv. **1.** in an easy manner; with ease; without trouble. **2.** beyond question: *easily the best*. **3.** probably; likely.

east /ist/ n. **1.** a cardinal point of the compass (90° to the right of north) corresponding to the point where the sun is seen to rise. *–adj.* **2.** lying or proceeding towards the east. **3.** coming from the east. *–adv.* **4.** in the direction of the sunrise; towards or in the east. **5.** from the east. **–easterly,** *adj.,* n. **–eastern,** *adj.*

easy /'izi/ adj. **(easier, easiest) 1.** not difficult; requiring no great labour or effort. **2.** free from pain, discomfort, worry, or care. **3.** *Colloq.* having no firm preferences in a particular matter. **4.** free from formality, constraint, or embarrassment. **5.** *Commerce* **a.** (of a commodity) not difficult to obtain; in plentiful supply and (often) weak in price. **b.** (of the market) not characterised by eager demand. *–adv.* **6.** *Colloq.* in an easy manner; comfortably. *–phr.* **7. take it easy,** *Colloq.* **a.** to proceed at a comfortable pace. **b.** to relax and rest.

easygoing /izi'goʊɪŋ/ adj. taking matters in an easy way.

eat /it/ v. **(ate** /eɪt, ɛt/, **eaten** /'itn/, **eating)** *–v.t.* **1.** to take into the mouth and swallow for nourishment, especially to masticate and swallow, as solid food. **2.** to consume by or as by devouring. *–v.i.* **3.** to consume food; take a meal. **4.** to make a way as by gnawing or corrosion.

eating disorder n. a pattern of eating which involves compulsive over-eating or abstinence to such an extent that it affects one's physical and mental health.

eaves /ivz/ pl. n. the overhanging lower edge of a roof.

eavesdrop /'ivzdrɒp/ v.i. **(-dropped, -dropping)** to listen secretly.

ebb /ɛb/ n. **1.** the falling of the tide (opposed to *flow*). *–v.i.* **2.** to flow back or away, as the water of a tide. **3.** to decline or decay.

Ebola /ə'boʊlə/ n. a virus causing high fever and internal haemorrhaging, often fatal. Also, **Ebola virus.**

ebony /'ɛbəni/ n. a hard, durable wood, usually black, from various tropical trees.

ebook /'ibʊk/ n. a book in an electronic format designed to be read in an ereader. Also, **e-book.**

ebullient /ə'bʊljənt, ə'bʌl-, ə'bjul-/ adj. **1.** seething or overflowing with fervour, enthusiasm, excitement, etc. **2.** bubbling like a boiling liquid.

ebusiness /i'bɪznəs/ n. **1.** → **ecommerce. 2.** a business run via the internet. Also, **e-business, eBusiness.**

ec- variant of **ex-¹**, before consonants.

eccentric /ək'sentrık/ *adj.* **1.** not conventional; odd. **2.** not concentric, as two circles or spheres. —*n.* **3.** an eccentric person. —**eccentricity**, *n.*

ecclesiastic /əklizi'æstık/ *n.* **1.** a member of the clergy, or person in orders. —*adj.* **2.** ecclesiastical.

ecclesiastical /əklizi'æstıkəl/ *adj.* of or relating to the church or the clergy.

echelon /'ɛʃəlɒn/ *n.* a level of command.

echidna /ə'kıdnə/ *n.* a spine-covered insectivorous egg-laying monotreme; spiny anteater.

echinacea /ɛkə'neıʃə/ *n.* a North American plant, extracts of which are used in herbal medicine as a cold remedy, antibiotic, and immune system stimulant.

echo /'ɛkoʊ/ *n.* (*pl.* **echoes**) **1.** a repetition of sound, produced by the reflection of soundwaves from an obstructing surface. —*v.* (**echoed**, **echoing**) —*v.i.* **2.** to emit an echo; resound with an echo. —*v.t.* **3.** to repeat by or as by an echo. —**echoic**, *adj.*

echocardiogram /ɛkoʊ'kadiəgræm/ *n. Med.* an ultrasound image of the heart.

eclair /eı'klɛə, ə-/ *n.* a light, finger-shaped cake made of pastry, filled with cream or custard, and coated with icing.

eclectic /ɛ'klɛktık, ə-/ *adj.* selecting; choosing from various sources.

eclipse /ə'klıps, i-/ *n.* **1.** *Astron.* the obscuration of the light of a satellite by the intervention of its primary planet between it and the sun. —*v.t.* (**eclipsed**, **eclipsing**) **2.** to make dim by comparison; surpass.

eco /'ıkoʊ/ *adj.* of, relating to, or employing environmentally friendly practices, materials, technology, etc.

eco- a prefix denoting **1.** 'ecology' or 'ecological', as in *ecosphere*. **2.** protective of or beneficial to the environment: *eco-agriculture*.

ecological footprint *n.* a measure of the demands put on the environment by humans, as in growing food, providing fuel, etc., taking into account the emissions produced in the production of food and in goods and services, as well as those produced in fuel consumption and household requirements such as heating, cooling, etc. Also, **footprint**.

ecological sustainability *n.* the capacity for development that can be sustained into the future without destroying the environment in the process.

ecology /ə'kɒlədʒi/ *n.* **1.** the branch of biology that deals with the relations between organisms and their environment. **2.** the balanced interrelationship of organisms and their environment. —**ecologist**, *n.* —**ecological**, *adj.*

ecommerce /i'kɒmɜs/ *n.* commerce transacted via the internet. Also, **e-commerce**, **eCommerce**, **ebusiness**

economic /ɛkə'nɒmık, ikə-/ *adj.* **1.** of or relating to the production, distribution, and use of income and wealth. **2.** of or relating to an economy, or system of organisation or operation, especially of the process of production. **3.** → **economical**.

economical /ɛkə'nɒmıkəl, ikə-/ *adj.* avoiding waste or extravagance; thrifty. Also, **economic**.

economics /ɛkə'nɒmıks, ikə-/ *n.* the science that deals with the production, distribution, and consumption of goods and services, or the material welfare of humankind. —**economist**, *n.*

economise /ə'kɒnəmaız/ *v.i.* to practise economy; avoid waste. Also, **economize**.

economy /ə'kɒnəmi/ *n.* (*pl.* **-mies**) **1.** thrifty management; frugality. **2.** *Econ.* the interrelationship between the factors of production and the means of production, distribution, and exchange. **3.** the management, or science of management, of the resources of a community, etc., with a view to productiveness and avoidance of waste.

ecosphere /'ıkoʊsfıə/ *n.* **1.** the global ecosystem of a planet. **2.** the part of the atmosphere of a planet or other heavenly body which can sustain life.

ecosystem /'ıkoʊ,sıstəm, 'ɛk-/ *n.* a community of organisms, interacting with one another, plus the environment in which they live and with which they also interact, such as a pond or a forest.

ecotourism /ikoʊ'tʊərızəm/ *n.* **1.** tourism so arranged that it involves no degradation of the environment. **2.** tourism which takes in places of ecological interest.

ecowarrior /'ıkoʊwɒriə/ *n.* an environmental activist, especially one who takes public action for a cause.

ecstasy /'ɛkstəsi/ *n.* (*pl.* **-sies**) **1.** overpowering emotion, especially delight. **2.** an instance of this. **3.** Also, **MDMA**. a synthetic drug, 3,4 methylenedioxymethamphetamine, used illicitly as a stimulant. —**ecstatic**, *adj.*

ecto- a prefix meaning 'outside', 'external'.

-ectomy a combining form attached to the name of a part of the body and producing a word meaning an operation for the excision of that part.

ecumenical /ɛkjə'mɛnıkəl, ik-/ *adj.* general; universal.

eczema /'ɛksəmə/ *n.* an inflammatory disease of the skin.

-ed¹ a suffix forming the past tense, as in *she crossed the river*. Compare **-t**.

-ed² a suffix forming: **1.** the past participle, as in *he had crossed the river*. Compare **-t**. **2.** participial adjectives indicating a condition or quality resulting from the action of the verb, as *inflated balloons*.

-ed³ a suffix serving to form adjectives from nouns, as *bearded*, *moneyed*.

edam /'idam, 'ɛdəm/ *n.* a hard, round, yellow cheese, with a red wax rind.

eddy /'ɛdi/ *n.* (*pl.* **eddies**) a current at variance with the main current in a stream of liquid or gas, especially one having a rotary or whirling motion.

edge /ɛdʒ/ *n.* **1.** a brim or margin. **2.** a brink or verge. **3.** one of the narrow surfaces of a thin, flat object. **4.** the line in which two surfaces of a solid object meet. **5.** sharpness or keenness. —*v.* (**edged**, **edging**) —*v.t.* **6.** to put an edge on; sharpen. **7.** to move edgeways; move or force gradually. —*v.i.* **8.** to move edgeways; advance gradually.

edgy /'ɛdʒi/ *adj.* (**edgier**, **edgiest**) **1.** impatient; irritable. **2.** *Colloq.* at the forefront or cutting edge: *edgy fashion designers*.

edible /ˈɛdəbəl/ *adj.* fit to be eaten.

edict /ˈidɪkt/ *n.* an authoritative proclamation or command.

edifice /ˈɛdəfəs/ *n.* a building, especially large.

edify /ˈɛdəfaɪ/ *v.t.* (**-fied, -fying**) to instruct or benefit, especially morally. —**edification**, *n.*

edit /ˈɛdət/ *v.t.* **1.** to supervise or direct the preparation of (a newspaper, magazine, etc.). **2.** to make (a film, sound recording, etc.) by cutting and arranging, etc. **3.** to revise and correct (written material). —**editor**, *n.*

edition /əˈdɪʃən/ *n.* one of a number of printings of the same book, newspaper, etc.

editorial /ɛdəˈtɔriəl/ *n.* **1.** an article, in a newspaper or the like, presenting the opinion or comment of an editor. —*adj.* **2.** of or relating to an editor.

educate /ˈɛdʒəkeɪt/ *v.t.* to develop the faculties and powers of (a person) by teaching, instruction, or schooling. —**education**, *n.*

-ee a suffix of nouns denoting someone who is the object of some action, or undergoes or receives something, as in *employee*.

eel /il/ *n.* a snake-like fish.

-eer a suffix of nouns denoting someone who is concerned with, or employed in connection with, something, as in *auctioneer*, *engineer*, *profiteer*. Also, **-ier**.

eerie /ˈɪəri/ *adj.* (**eerier, eeriest**) weird, strange, or uncanny.

ef- variant of **ex-**[1] before *f*.

efface /əˈfeɪs/ *v.t.* to wipe out; destroy; do away with.

effect /əˈfɛkt, i-/ *n.* **1.** a result; a consequence. **2.** power to produce results; efficacy. **3.** the state of being operative. **4.** a mental impression produced, as by a painting, speech, etc. **5.** *Film, Theatre* a sight, sound, etc., simulated by artificial means to give a particular impression. **6.** a scientific phenomenon: *the greenhouse effect.* **7.** (*pl.*) personal property. —*v.t.* **8.** to produce as an effect.

effective /əˈfɛktɪv, i-/ *adj.* **1.** producing the intended or expected result. **2.** actually in effect. **3.** producing a striking impression.

effectual /əˈfɛktʃuəl, i-/ *adj.* producing, or capable of producing, an intended effect.

effeminate /əˈfɛmənət, i-/ *adj.* (of a man) soft or delicate in a way considered more typical of a woman than of a man.

effervesce /ɛfəˈvɛs/ *v.i.* (**-vesced, -vescing**) to give off bubbles of gas, as fermenting liquors. —**effervescent**, *adj.* —**effervescence**, *n.*

effete /əˈfit/ *adj.* **1.** weak and ineffectual as a result of over-refinement: *an effete intellectual.* **2.** that has lost its vigour or energy.

efficacy /ˈɛfəkəsi/ *n.* capacity to produce effects; effectiveness. —**efficacious**, *adj.*

efficient /əˈfɪʃənt, i-/ *adj.* **1.** effective in the use of energy and resources. **2.** avoiding waste. —**efficiency**, *n.*

effigy /ˈɛfədʒi/ *n.* (*pl.* **-gies**) a representation or image.

efflorescence /ɛfləˈrɛsəns/ *n.* a rash or eruption.

effluent /ˈɛfluənt/ *adj.* **1.** flowing out. —*n.* **2.** that which flows out, such as outflow from sewage during purification. —**effluence**, *n.*

effort /ˈɛfət/ *n.* **1.** exertion of power, physical or mental. **2.** an attempt.

effrontery /əˈfrʌntəri, i-/ *n.* shameless or impudent boldness.

effusion /əˈfjuʒən, i-/ *n.* **1.** a pouring forth. **2.** unrestrained expression of feeling.

effusive /əˈfjusɪv, -zɪv, i-/ *adj.* unduly demonstrative; without reserve.

EFTPOS /ˈɛftpɒs/ *n.* a system of electronic funds transfer from a customer's account to a merchant's account, operated by the customer by means of a coded plastic card inserted into a special-purpose terminal and a PIN by which the transaction is authorised.

egalitarian /əgæləˈtɛəriən, i-/ *adj.* asserting the equality of all people.

egg[1] /ɛg/ *n.* **1.** the female reproductive cell and its envelopes. **2.** the egg produced by birds, especially the domestic hen. **3.** the contents of an egg, especially that of a domestic hen, used as food.

egg[2] /ɛg/ *v.t.* (fol. by *on*) to incite or urge; encourage.

eggplant /ˈɛgplænt/ *n.* a plant with purple egg-shaped fruit; aubergine.

ego /ˈigoʊ/ *n.* the 'I' or self of any person.

egotism /ˈɛgətɪzəm, ˈigə-/ *n.* self-conceit.

egregious /əˈgridʒəs/ *adj.* remarkably or extraordinarily bad; flagrant.

egress /ˈigrɛs/ *n.* a means or place of going out.

egret /ˈigrət/ *n.* any of various herons.

eiderdown /ˈaɪdədaʊn/ *n.* **1.** down or soft feathers from the eider duck. **2.** a quilt.

eight /eɪt/ *n.* **1.** a cardinal number, seven plus one. —*adj.* **2.** amounting to eight in number. —**eighth**, *adj., n.*

eighteen /eɪˈtin/ *n.* **1.** a cardinal number, ten plus eight. —*adj.* **2.** amounting to eighteen in number. —**eighteenth**, *adj., n.*

eighty /ˈeɪti/ *n.* (*pl.* **-ties**) **1.** a cardinal number, ten times eight. —*adj.* **2.** amounting to eighty in number. —**eightieth**, *adj., n.*

eisteddfod /aɪˈstɛdfəd/ *n.* (*pl.* **-fods** or **-fodau** /-fədaɪ/) a competitive music festival.

either /ˈaɪðə, ˈiðə/ *adj.* **1.** one or the other of two. **2.** each of the two; the one and the other. —*pron.* **3.** one or the other but not both. —*conj.* **4.** used as one of two coordinate alternatives. —*adv.* **5.** used after negative sentences coordinated by *and, or,* or *nor*.

ejaculate /əˈdʒækjəleɪt, i-/ *v.i.* **1.** to discharge semen. —*v.t.* **2.** to utter suddenly and briefly; exclaim. —**ejaculation**, *n.*

eject /əˈdʒɛkt, i-/ *v.t.* **1.** to drive or force out. —*v.i.* **2.** to propel oneself out of an aeroplane, etc., by means of a mechanical device. —**ejection**, *n.*

eke /ik/ *phr.* **eke out**, **1.** to use (resources) frugally. **2.** to contrive to make (a living).

elaborate *adj.* /əˈlæbərət/ **1.** worked out with great care and nicety of detail; complicated. —*v.i.* /əˈlæbəreɪt, i-/ **2.** (fol. by *on* or *upon*) to give additional or fuller treatment. —**elaboration**, *n.*

elapse /əˈlæps, i-/ *v.i.* (of time) to slip by or pass away.

elastic /əˈlæstɪk, i-/ *adj.* **1.** springing back or rebounding. **2.** flexible; yielding. —*n.* **3.** elastic material. —**elasticity**, *n.*

elate /ə'leɪt, ɪ-/ v.t. to put in high spirits. **–elated**, adj. **–elation**, n.

elbow /'elboʊ/ n. 1. the bend or joint of the arm between upper arm and forearm. –v.t. 2. to push with or as with the elbow; jostle.

elder[1] /'eldə/ adj. 1. older. –n. 2. a person who is older than oneself. 3. one of the older and more influential people of a tribe or community.

elder[2] /'eldə/ n. any of several flowering shrubs or trees.

elderly /'eldəli/ adj. in one's old age.

eldest /'eldəst/ adj. oldest.

elect /ə'lekt, ɪ-/ v.t. 1. to select by vote, as for an office. 2. to determine in favour of (a course of action, etc.). –adj. 3. selected for an office, but not yet inducted (usually after the noun). **–elector**, n.

election /ə'lekʃən, ɪ-/ n. the selection by vote of a person or persons for office.

elective /ə'lektɪv, ɪ-/ adj. 1. (of an office) filled by election. –n. 2. an optional course of study.

electoral /ə'lektərəl, -trəl, ɪ-/ adj. relating to electors or election.

electorate /ə'lektərət, -trət, ɪ-/ n. 1. the body of voters represented by an elected member. 2. such a body, especially as represented by a member of parliament.

electric /ə'lektrɪk, -ɪ/ adj. relating to, derived from, produced by, or involving electricity. Also, **electrical**.

electrician /ələk'trɪʃən, elɛk-, iɛk-/ n. someone who installs, operates, maintains, or repairs electrical devices.

electricity /ələk'trɪsəti, elɛk-, iɛk-/ n. an agency producing various physical phenomena, due to the presence and movements of electrons, protons, and other electrically charged particles.

electrify /ə'lektrəfaɪ, ɪ-/ v.t. (**-fied, -fying**) to charge with or subject to electricity.

electro- a word element meaning 'relating to or caused by electricity'.

electrocardiogram /ə,lektroʊ'kadiəgræm, ɪ-/ n. Med. the graphic record produced by an electrocardiograph. Abbrev.: ECG Also, **cardiogram**.

electrocardiograph /ə,lektroʊ'kadiəgræf, -graf, ɪ-/ n. a device which detects and records electrical activity of the heart. Abbrev.: ECG

electrocute /ə'lektrəkjut, ɪ-/ v.t. to kill by electricity. **–electrocution**, n.

electrode /ə'lektroʊd, ɪ-/ n. a conductor of electricity through which a current enters or leaves an electrolytic cell, etc.

electroencephalograph /ə,lektroʊen'sefələgræf, -graf, ɪ-/ n. a device which detects and records the electrical activity of the brain. Abbrev.: EEG

electrolysis /ələk'trɒləsəs, i-, ˌelək'trɒləsəs/ n. 1. the decomposition of a chemical compound by an electric current. 2. Surg. the destruction of tumours, hair roots, etc., by an electric current. **–electrolytic**, adj.

electrolyte /ə'lektrəlaɪt/ n. 1. a substance, such as an acid, base, or salt, which separates into ions when dissolved in water, etc., or when melted, thus becoming a conductor of electricity. 2. such a substance present in the blood and vital to body functions.

electromagnetic /ə,lektroʊmæg'netɪk, ɪ-/ adj. relating to the interaction of electricity and magnetism. **–electromagnetism**, n.

electron /ə'lektrɒn, ɪ-/ n. a negatively charged elementary particle which is a constituent of all atoms.

electronic /ələk'trɒnɪk, ələk-, ɪ-/ adj. of, relating to, or concerned with, electronics or any devices or systems based on electronics. **–electronically**, adv.

electronica /ələk'trɒnɪkə, ələk-, ɪ-/ n. the broad array of music created electronically.

electronic banking n. banking transactions conducted by means of electronic systems or networks, as by EFTPOS.

electronic funds transfer n. a computerised banking system for the transfer of funds from one account to another. Abbrev.: EFT

electronics /ələk'trɒnɪks, i-, ˌelək-/ n. the investigation and application of phenomena involving the movement of electrons in valves and semiconductors.

electronic tag n. → e-tag.

electronic whiteboard n. a whiteboard that has digital capability and can be connected to the internet, a printer, etc.

elegant /'eləgənt, 'elɪ-/ adj. tastefully fine or luxurious in dress, manner, etc. **–elegance**, n.

elegy /'elədʒi/ n. (pl. **-gies**) a mournful or plaintive poem, especially a lament for the dead. **–elegiac**, adj.

element /'eləmənt/ n. 1. a component or constituent part of a whole. 2. (pl.) the rudimentary principles of an art, science, etc. 3. (pl.) atmospheric agencies or forces. 4. Chem. one of a class of substances which consist entirely of atoms of the same atomic number. 5. Elect. the heating unit of an electric domestic appliance. **–elemental**, adj.

elementary /elə'mentri, -təri/ adj. relating to or dealing with elements, rudiments, or first principles.

elephant /'eləfənt/ n. 1. a very large, herbivorous mammal, having a long, prehensile trunk and curved tusks. –phr. 2. **the elephant in the room**, a topic that everyone knows about but no-one wants to discuss openly. **–elephantine**, adj.

elevate /'eləveɪt/ v.t. to move or raise to a higher place or position; lift up.

elevation /elə'veɪʃən/ n. 1. altitude above sea or ground level. 2. the act of elevating. 3. the state of being elevated. 4. Archit. a drawing or design of a face of a building.

elevator /'eləveɪtə/ n. → lift (def. 7).

eleven /ə'levən/ n. 1. a cardinal number, ten plus one. –adj. 2. amounting to eleven in number. **–eleventh**, adj., n.

elf /elf/ n. (pl. **elves** /elvz/) one of a class of imaginary beings, usually a diminutive human. **–elfin, elfish, elvish**, adj.

elicit /ə'lɪsət/ v.t. to draw or bring out or forth; evoke.

eligible /'elədʒəbəl/ adj. fit or proper to be chosen; worthy of choice.

eligible termination payment n. a lump-sum payment made by an employer to an employee on termination of employment. Also, ETP.

eliminate /ə'lɪməneɪt, i-/ v.t. to get rid of; expel; remove. **–elimination**, n.

elite /ə'lit, eɪ-, i-/ n. 1. (construed as pl.) persons of the highest class. 2. the most privileged or socially advantaged groups in a society, organisation, etc. **–elitism**, n. **–elitist**, n.

elixir /ə'lɪksə, ɛ-, i-/ n. a preparation formerly believed to prolong life.

elk /ɛlk/ n. (pl. **elks** or, especially collectively, **elk**) the largest existing European and Asiatic deer.

ellipse /ə'lɪps, i-/ n. a plane figure, oval in shape or outline. **–elliptical**, adj.

ellipsis /ə'lɪpsɪs, i-/ n. (pl. **-lipses** /-lɪpsiz/) the omission from a sentence or argument of something which would complete or clarify the construction. **–elliptical**, adj.

elm /ɛlm/ n. any of several large, deciduous trees.

elocution /ɛlə'kjuʃən/ n. manner of speaking or reading in public.

elongate /'iloŋgeɪt/ v.t. to draw out to greater length. **–elongation**, n.

elope /ə'loup, i-/ v.i. to run away with a lover, usually in order to marry without parental consent.

eloquent /'ɛləkwənt/ adj. characterised by fluent, persuasive expression.

else /ɛls/ adv. other than the person or the thing mentioned.

elsewhere /'ɛlswɛə, ɛls'wɛə/ adv. somewhere else.

elucidate /ə'lusədeɪt, i-/ v.t. to make lucid or clear; explain.

elude /ə'lud, i-/ v.t. to avoid or escape by dexterity or artifice.

em /ɛm/ n. Printing a unit of measurement.

em- variant of **en-**.

emaciated /ə'meɪsieɪtəd, i-/ adj. lean; wasted, as by disease. **–emaciation**, n.

email /'imeɪl/ n. 1. Also, **electronic mail**. the sending of messages over a computer network, especially the internet: most businesses use email these days. 2. messages sent this way: you've got email. 3. such a message: an email from my mother. –v.t. 4. to send (a message) by email: I'll email the information this afternoon. 5. to send such messages to (someone): he emailed me about the party. Also, **e-mail**.

emanate /'ɛməneɪt/ v.i. to flow out, issue, or proceed as from a source or origin. **–emanation**, n.

emancipate /ə'mænsəpeɪt, i-/ v.t. to free from restraint. **–emancipation**, n. **–emancipist**, n.

emasculate /ə'mæskjəleɪt, i-/ v.t. 1. to castrate. 2. to deprive of strength or vigour.

embalm /ɛm'bam/ v.t. to treat (a corpse) in order to preserve from decay.

embankment /ɛm'bæŋkmənt, ə-/ n. a bank, mound, dyke, or the like, raised to hold back water, carry a road, etc.

embargo /ɛm'bagou/ n. (pl. **-goes**) 1. an order of a government prohibiting the movement of merchant vessels from or into its ports. 2. any restriction imposed upon commerce by law, as when a government suspends trade with another country.

embark /ɛm'bak/ v.i. 1. to board a ship, plane, etc., as for a voyage. 2. (oft. fol. by on) to begin a journey, project, etc.

embarrass /ɛm'bærəs/ v.t. to disconcert; make uncomfortable, self-conscious, etc.

embassy /'ɛmbəsi/ n. (pl. **-sies**) the official headquarters of an ambassador.

embattled /ɛm'bætld/ adj. 1. involved in a battle or argument. 2. beleaguered; under attack.

embed /ɛm'bɛd/ v.t. (**-bedded, -bedding**) 1. to fix firmly in a surrounding mass. 2. Journalism to attach (a war correspondent) to a military unit, with the advantage of protection and access but with the risk of compromised objectivity.

embellish /ɛm'bɛlɪʃ/ v.t. to beautify by or as by ornamentation; enhance.

ember /'ɛmbə/ n. a small live coal.

embezzle /ɛm'bɛzəl/ v.t. to appropriate fraudulently to one's own use.

emblazon /ɛm'bleɪzən/ v.t. to portray or inscribe on or as on a heraldic shield.

emblem /'ɛmbləm/ n. a symbol.

embody /ɛm'bɒdi/ v.t. (**-bodied, -bodying**) to give a concrete form to.

embolism /'ɛmbəlɪzəm/ n. the obstruction of a blood vessel by any material such as tissue fragments, bacteria, etc., carried by the bloodstream.

emboss /ɛm'bɒs/ v.t. to raise designs on the surface of (leather, etc.).

embrace /ɛm'breɪs/ v.t. (**-braced, -bracing**) 1. to hug. 2. to accept (an idea, etc.) willingly. 3. to include or contain. –n. 4. a hug.

embroider /ɛm'brɔɪdə/ v.t. 1. to decorate with ornamental needlework. 2. to adorn or embellish rhetorically, especially with fictitious additions. **–embroidery**, n.

embroil /ɛm'brɔɪl, əm-/ v.t. 1. to involve in contention or strife. 2. to throw into confusion; complicate.

embryo /'ɛmbriou/ n. (pl. **-bryos**) an organism in the earlier stages of its development, as a mammal still in its mother's body. **–embryonic**, adj.

embryonic stem cell /ɛmbri'ɒnɪk/ n. Biol. an unspecialised form of cell (**cell** def. 3), capable of dividing and giving rise to various specialised cells. Also, **ES cell**.

emend /ə'mɛnd, i-/ v.t. to free from faults or errors; correct. **–emendation**, n.

emerald /'ɛmrəld, 'ɛmərəld/ n. a green gemstone.

emerge /ə'mɜdʒ, i-/ v.i. to rise or come forth, as from concealment or obscurity.

emergency /ə'mɜdʒənsi, i-/ n. (pl. **-cies**) a sudden and urgent occasion for action.

emergent /ə'mɜdʒənt/ adj. 1. (of a nation) recently independent or newly formed as a political entity. 2. emerging. **–emergence**, n.

emery /'ɛməri/ n. a granular mineral substance used for grinding and polishing.

emetic /ə'mɛtɪk/ adj. inducing vomiting, as a medicinal substance.

-emia variant of **-aemia**.

emigrate /'ɛməgreɪt/ v.i. to leave one country or region to settle in another. **–emigration**, n. **–emigrant**, n.

eminent /'ɛmənənt/ *adj.* **1.** high-ranking; distinguished. **2.** conspicuous. **–eminence**, *n.*

emir /e'mɪə, 'emɪə/ *n.* a Muslim or Arabian chieftain or prince. Also, **emeer**. **–emirate** /'ɛmərət/, *n.*

emissary /'ɛməsəri, -əsri/, *Orig. US* /'ɛməseri/ *n.* (*pl.* **-ries**) an agent sent on a mission.

emission /ə'mɪʃən, i-/ *n.* **1.** the act of emitting. **2.** something that is emitted; a discharge; an emanation. **3.** such a discharge, especially of pollutants such as greenhouse gases, into the environment.

emission control *n.* the control of polluting gases released into the atmosphere by motor vehicles, factories, etc.

emission permit *n.* a permit to release a certain quota of emissions of a pollutant such as carbon dioxide into the atmosphere, usually for a period of time to allow for a transition into a technology which does not produce such emissions.

emissions market *n.* a market in which emission permits are bought and sold.

emissions trading *n.* trading in emission permits under a system by which countries or organisations not using their quotas are able to sell their excess permits to others exceeding their quota. See **carbon cap**.

emission tax *n.* a tax set for every unit of pollution produced.

emit /ə'mɪt, i-/ *v.t.* (**emitted, emitting**) to give out or forth; discharge. **–emitter**, *n.*

emo /'iməʊ/ *n. Colloq.* a person who is overly pessimistic and emotional.

emoji /ə'məʊdʒi/ *n.* (*pl.* **emoji**) a small image used in digital communication to express an emotion, concept, etc.

emollient /ə'mɒliənt, -'məʊ-/ *adj.* soothing.

emolument /ə'mɒljəmənt/ *n.* profit arising from office or employment; salary or fees.

emoticon /ə'məʊtəkɒn/ *n. Computers* an image, created with keyboard characters, used in texts to indicate an emotion, such as :-) to denote happiness and :-(unhappiness.

emotion /ə'məʊʃən, i-/ *n.* **1.** any of the feelings of joy, sorrow, fear, hate, love, etc. **2.** a state of agitation of the feelings actuated by experiencing fear, joy, etc.

emotional /ə'məʊʃənəl, i-/ *adj.* **1.** easily affected by emotion. **2.** appealing to the emotions.

emotive /ə'məʊtɪv, i-/ *adj.* exciting emotion.

empanada /ɛmpə'nadə/ *n.* in Spanish cooking, a pastry turnover with a spicy savoury or sweet filling.

empathy /'ɛmpəθi/ *n.* an entering into the feeling or spirit of another; appreciative perception or understanding. **–empathetic** /ɛmpə-'θɛtɪk/, *adj.* **–empathise, empathize**, *v.*

emperor /'ɛmpərə/ *n.* the sovereign or supreme ruler of an empire. **–empress**, *fem. n.*

emphasis /'ɛmfəsəs/ *n.* (*pl.* **-phases** /-fəsiz/) **1.** stress laid upon, or importance or significance attached to anything. **2.** intensity or force of expression, action, etc. **3.** prominence, as of outline. **–emphatic**, *adj.*

emphasise /'ɛmfəsaɪz/ *v.t.* to give emphasis to or point out the importance of. Also, **emphasize**.

empire /'ɛmpaɪə/ *n.* an aggregate of nations or peoples ruled over by an emperor or other powerful sovereign or government.

empirical /ɛm'pɪrɪkəl/ *adj.* derived from or guided by experience or experiment.

employ /ɛm'plɔɪ/ *v.t.* **1.** to use the services of (a person). **2.** to make use of (an instrument, means, etc.). **3.** to occupy or devote (time, energies, etc.). **–n.** **4.** employment; service. **–employment**, *n.* **–employer**, *n.* **–employee**, *n.*

emporium /ɛm'pɔriəm/ *n.* (*pl.* **-poriums** or **-poria** /-'pɔriə/) a large store selling a great variety of articles.

empower /ɛm'paʊə/ *v.t.* **1.** to give power or authority to; authorise. **2.** to cause (a person or group of people) to feel confident and in control of their own life.

empty /'ɛmpti, 'ɛmti/ *adj.* (**-tier, -tiest**) **1.** containing nothing. **2.** vacant; unoccupied. **–v.t.** (**-tied, -tying**) **3.** to make empty.

emu /'imju/ *n.* (*pl.* **emu** or **emus**) a large, flightless, Australian bird.

emulate /'ɛmjuleɪt, -jə-/ *v.t.* to imitate with intent to equal or excel.

emulsion /ə'mʌlʃən/ *n.* a suspension of a liquid in another liquid.

en /ɛn/ *n.* (*pl.* **ens**) *Printing* a unit of measurement, half the width of an em.

en- a prefix meaning primarily 'in', 'into', often with the force of bringing the object into the specified condition, as in *endear*. Compare **in-**[1]. Also, **em-**.

-en[1] a suffix forming verbs from adjectives, as in *fasten*, or from nouns, as in *heighten*.

-en[2] a suffix of adjectives indicating 'material', 'appearance', as in *ashen*, *golden*.

-en[3] a suffix used to mark the past participle in some verbs, as in *taken*, *proven*.

-en[4] a suffix forming the plural of some nouns, as in *children*, *oxen*.

-en[5] a diminutive suffix, as in *maiden*, *kitten*, etc.

enable /ɛn'eɪbəl, ən-/ *v.t.* to make able; give power, means, or ability to.

enabling /ɛn'eɪblɪŋ, ən-/ *adj.* (of an act, statute, or bill) making it possible for a person or a company to do something that would otherwise be illegal.

enact /ɛn'ækt, ən-/ *v.t.* **1.** to make into an act or statute. **2.** to act the part of.

enamel /ə'næməl/ *n.* **1.** a glassy substance, usually opaque, applied by fusion to the surface of metal, pottery, etc., as an ornament or for protection. **2.** any of various enamel-like varnishes, paints, etc. **3.** *Anat., Zool.* the hard, glossy, calcareous outer structure of the crowns of the teeth.

enamoured /ɛn'æmɔd, ən-/ *adj.* (usu. fol. by *of*) filled with love; charmed; delighted: *to be enamoured of a lady*. Also, **enamored**.

encapsulate /ɛn'kæpsjəleɪt, ən-, -fə-/ *v.t.* to enclose in or as in a capsule. **–encapsulation**, *n.*

-ence a noun suffix equivalent to **-ance**, and corresponding to **-ent** in adjectives.

encephalo- a word element meaning 'brain'.

encephalogram /ɛn'sɛfələgræm, ɛnkɛf-/ *n.* an X-ray photograph of the brain.

enchant /ɛnˈtʃænt, ən-, -ˈtʃɑnt/ v.t. **1.** to cast a spell over; bewitch. **2.** to delight; charm.

enchilada /ˌɛntʃəˈlɑdə/ n. a Mexican dish of a rolled tortilla filled with meat and seasonings.

encircle /ɛnˈsɜkəl, ən-/ v.t. to form a circle round; surround.

enclave /ˈɛnkleɪv, ˈɒnkleɪv/ n. a portion of a country surrounded by the territory of another country.

enclose /ɛnˈkloʊz, ən-/ v.t. **1.** to shut in; close in on all sides. **2.** to insert in the same envelope, etc., with the main letter, etc. **–enclosure,** n.

encompass /ɛnˈkʌmpəs, ən-/ v.t. **1.** to encircle; surround. **2.** to enclose; contain.

encore /ˈɒnkɔ, ˈɒŋkɔ/ n. an extra piece of music performed in answer to continued clapping by the audience.

encounter /ɛnˈkaʊntə, ən-/ v.t. **1.** to come upon; meet with, especially unexpectedly. **2.** to meet (a person, military force, etc.) in conflict. –n. **3.** a meeting with a person or thing, especially casually or unexpectedly. **4.** a meeting in conflict or opposition; a battle; a combat.

encourage /ɛnˈkʌrɪdʒ, ən-/ v.t. (**-raged, -raging**) **1.** to inspire with courage, spirit, or confidence. **2.** to stimulate by assistance, approval, etc. **–encouragement,** n.

encroach /ɛnˈkroʊtʃ, ən-/ v.i. to trespass upon the property or rights of another.

encrust /ɛnˈkrʌst, ən-/ v.t. to cover or line with a crust or hard coating.

encumber /ɛnˈkʌmbə, ən-/ v.t. to impede or hamper. **–encumbrance,** n.

encyclopedia /ɛnˌsaɪkləˈpidiə, ən-/ n. a work treating separately various topics from one or all branches of knowledge, usually in alphabetical arrangement. Also, **encyclopaedia.**

end /ɛnd/ n. **1.** an extreme or farthermost part of anything extended in space. **2.** anything that bounds an object at one of its extremities; a limit. **3.** the act of coming to an end; termination. **4.** a purpose or aim. **5.** a remnant or fragment. –v.t. **6.** to bring to an end or natural conclusion. **7.** to form the end of. –v.i. **8.** to come to an end; terminate; cease. **9.** to issue or result. **10.** Colloq. (oft. fol. by up) to reach a final condition, circumstance, goal.

endanger /ɛnˈdeɪndʒə, ən-/ v.t. to expose to danger.

endear /ɛnˈdɪə, ən-/ v.t. to make dear, esteemed, or beloved.

endearment /ɛnˈdɪəmənt, ən-/ n. a caress or an affectionate term.

endeavour /ɛnˈdɛvə, ən-/ v.i. **1.** to make an effort; strive. –n. **2.** an attempt. Also, **endeavor.**

endemic /ɛnˈdɛmɪk/ adj. peculiar to a particular people or locality, as a disease.

endive /ˈɛndaɪv/ n. a herb, used in salads and as a cooked vegetable.

endo- a word element meaning 'internal'.

endocrine gland /ˈɛndəkrən/ n. a gland (as the thyroid gland) which secretes hormones directly to the blood or lymph.

endorse /ɛnˈdɔs, ən-/ v.t. **1.** to write (something) on the back of a document, etc. **2.** to sign one's name on (a commercial document or other instrument). **3.** to designate (another) as

payee by one's endorsement. **4.** to acknowledge (payment) by placing one's signature on a bill, draft, etc. **5.** to add a modifying statement to (a document). **6.** (of a branch of a political party) to select as a candidate for an election. **7.** to approve; give support to: *I don't endorse that sort of behaviour*. Also, **indorse.** **–endorsement,** n.

endoscope /ˈɛndoʊskoʊp/ n. a slender tubular medical instrument used to examine the interior of a body cavity or hollow organ. **–endoscopic,** adj.

endoscopy /ɛnˈdɒskəpi/ n. a medical examination by means of an endoscope. **–endoscopist,** n.

endow /ɛnˈdaʊ, ən-/ v.t. **1.** to provide with a permanent fund or source of income. **2.** to furnish as with some gift, faculty, or quality; equip. **–endowment,** n.

endue /ɛnˈdju, ən-/ v.t. to invest or endow with some gift, quality, or faculty.

endurance /ɛnˈdjurəns/ n. the ability to last or endure for a long time, particularly in difficult conditions.

endure /ɛnˈdjuə/ v.t. **1.** to sustain without impairment or yielding; undergo. **2.** to bear without resistance or with patience; tolerate.

-ene 1. a noun suffix used in chemistry, in names of hydrocarbons. **2.** a generalised suffix used in trademarks for substances, often implying synthetic manufacture.

enema /ˈɛnəmə/ n. a fluid injected into the rectum, as to evacuate the bowels.

enemy /ˈɛnəmi/ n. (pl. **-mies**) **1.** someone who cherishes hatred or harmful designs against another; an adversary or opponent. **2.** a hostile nation or state. **3.** a subject of such a state. **4.** something harmful or prejudicial.

energetic /ˌɛnəˈdʒɛtɪk/ adj. possessing or exhibiting energy; forcible; vigorous.

energy /ˈɛnədʒi/ n. (pl. **-gies**) **1.** capacity or habit of vigorous activity. **2.** ability to produce action or effect.

energy drink n. a drink designed to promote physical stamina, usually containing a stimulant such as caffeine.

energy efficiency rating n. an energy labelling approved by a regulatory authority and required for devices such as washing machines, dryers, refrigerators, dishwashers, etc., which indicates the performance level of the device with respect to energy efficiency. Abbrev.: EER

enervate /ˈɛnəveɪt/ v.t. to deprive of nerve, force, or strength; weaken.

enforce /ɛnˈfɔs, ən-/ v.t. **1.** to put or keep in force; compel obedience to. **2.** to obtain (payment, obedience, etc.) by force or compulsion.

enfranchise /ɛnˈfræntʃaɪz, ən-/ v.t. **1.** to admit to citizenship, especially to the right of voting. **2.** Law to invest with the right of being represented in Parliament. **3.** to set free; liberate, as from slavery.

engage /ɛnˈgeɪdʒ, ən-/ v.t. (**-gaged, -gaging**) **1.** to occupy the attention or efforts of (a person, etc.). **2.** to secure for aid, employment, use, etc.; hire. **3.** to reserve or secure. **4.** to attract or please. **5.** to bind as by pledge, promise, contract, or oath; make liable. **6.** to bring (troops) into conflict; enter into conflict with. **7.** *Mechanics* to cause to become interlocked; interlock with. –**engagement**, *n.*

engaged /ɛn'geɪdʒd, ən-/ *adj.* **1.** busy or occupied; involved. **2.** under agreement to marry. **3.** *Mechanics* **a.** interlocked. **b.** (of toothed wheels) in gear with each other. **4.** (of a telephone line) inaccessible because already in use.

engender /ɛn'dʒɛndə, ən-/ *v.t.* to produce, cause, or give rise to.

engine /'ɛndʒən/ *n.* **1.** any mechanism or machine designed to convert energy into mechanical work. **2.** any mechanical contrivance.

engineer /ɛndʒə'nɪə/ *n.* **1.** a person professionally qualified in the design, construction, and use of engines or machines. –*v.t.* **2.** to plan, construct, or manage as an engineer. **3.** to arrange, manage or carry through by skilful or artful contrivance. –**engineering**, *n.*

English muffin /'ɪŋglɪʃ/ *n.* a thick, flat yeast cake, made from a soft, risen dough, baked without browning, served cut open and usually toasted, with butter, etc.

English spinach /'ɪŋglɪʃ/ *n.* → **spinach** (def. 1).

engrain /ɛn'greɪn, ən-/ *v.t.* → **ingrain**.

engrave /ɛn'greɪv, ən-/ *v.t.* to cut (letters, designs, etc.) on a hard surface.

engross /ɛn'groʊs, ən-/ *v.t.* to occupy wholly, as the mind or attention; absorb.

engulf /ɛn'gʌlf, ən-/ *v.t.* to swallow up in or as in a chasm.

enhance /ɛn'hæns, -'hans, ən-/ *v.t.* (**-hanced, -hancing**) to raise to a higher degree.

enigma /ə'nɪgmə/ *n.* somebody or something puzzling or inexplicable. –**enigmatic**, *adj.*

enjoin /ɛn'dʒɔɪn, ən-/ *v.t.* to order or direct.

enjoy /ɛn'dʒɔɪ, ən-/ *v.t.* **1.** to experience with joy; take pleasure in. **2.** to have the benefit of. **3.** to find or experience pleasure for (oneself). –**enjoyment**, *n.*

enlarge /ɛn'ladʒ, ən-/ *v.* (**-larged, -larging**) –*v.t.* **1.** to make larger. –*v.i.* **2.** to speak or write at large. –**enlargement**, *n.*

enlighten /ɛn'laɪtn, ən-/ *v.t.* to give intellectual or spiritual light to; instruct.

enlist /ɛn'lɪst, ən-/ *v.t.* **1.** to secure (a person, services, etc.) for some cause, enterprise, etc. –*v.i.* **2.** to enter into some cause, enterprise, etc.

enliven /ɛn'laɪvən, ən-/ *v.t.* to make vigorous or active; invigorate.

en masse /ɒn 'mæs/ *adv.* in a mass or body; all together.

enmity /'ɛnməti/ *n.* a feeling or condition of hostility.

enormity /ə'nɒməti, i-/ *n.* **1.** enormousness; hugeness of size, scope, extent, etc. **2.** outrageous or heinous character; atrociousness: *the enormity of his offences.*

enormous /ə'nɔməs, i-/ *adj.* greatly exceeding the common size, extent, etc.; huge; immense. –**enormousness**, *n.* –**enormously**, *adv.*

enough /ə'nʌf, i-/ *adj.* **1.** adequate for the want or need; sufficient. –*n.* **2.** an adequate quantity or number. –*adv.* **3.** sufficiently.

enquire /ɪn'kwaɪə, ən-, ɛn-/ *v.i.* → **inquire**. –**enquiry**, *n.*

enrage /ɛn'reɪdʒ, ən-/ *v.t.* to put into a rage; infuriate.

enrapture /ɛn'ræptʃə, ən-/ *v.t.* to delight beyond measure.

enrich /ɛn'rɪtʃ, ən-/ *v.t.* **1.** to supply with riches. **2.** to enhance; make finer.

enrol /ɛn'roʊl, ən-/ *v.* (**-rolled, -rolling**) –*v.t.* **1.** to insert the name of (a person) in a roll or register. –*v.i.* **2.** to enrol oneself. –**enrolment**, *n.*

enrolled nurse *n.* a nurse with a non-degree qualification, as from a nursing college, TAFE college, etc. *Abbrev.*: EN Compare **registered nurse**.

ensconce /ɛn'skɒns, ən-/ *v.t.* to settle securely or snugly.

ensemble /ɒn'sɒmbəl/ *n.* **1.** all the parts of a thing taken together. **2.** the entire costume of an individual, especially when all the parts are in harmony.

enshrine /ɛn'ʃraɪn, ən-/ *v.t.* to enclose in or as in a shrine.

ensign /'ɛnsən, 'ɛnsaɪn/ *n.* **1.** a flag or banner, as of a nation. **2.** any sign, token, or emblem.

enslave /ɛn'sleɪv, ən-/ *v.t.* to make a slave of.

ensnare /ɛn'snɛə, ən-/ *v.t.* to trap.

ensue /ɛn'sju, ən-/ *v.i.* (**-sued, -suing**) to follow, especially in immediate succession.

ensuite /ɒn'swit, 'ɒnswit/ *n.* a small bathroom attached to a bedroom. Also, **en suite**.

ensure /ɛn'ʃɔ, ən-/ *v.t.* to make sure or certain to come, occur, etc.

-ent a suffix equivalent to **-ant**.

entail /ɛn'teɪl, ən-/ *v.t.* **1.** to bring on or involve by necessity or consequences. **2.** to cause (anything) to descend to a fixed series of possessors.

entangle /ɛn'tæŋgəl, ən-/ *v.t.* to involve in difficulties, etc.

entente /ɒn'tɒnt/ *n.* an understanding or agreement between parties.

enter /'ɛntə/ *v.i.* **1.** to come or go in. **2.** to be admitted. **3.** (oft. fol. by *on* or *upon*) to make a beginning. –*v.t.* **4.** to come or go into. **5.** to become a member of, or join. **6.** to make a record of, as in a register. **7.** to type (data, text, etc.) into a computer file. **8.** *Law* to place in regular form before a court, as a writ.

entero- a word element meaning 'intestine'.

enterococcus /ɛntərou'kɒkəs/ *n.* (*pl.* **-cocci** /-'kɒkaɪ, -'kɒki/) a type of lactic acid bacterium found in the human gut, which is difficult to distinguish from the streptococcus; can cause urinary tract infections, diverticulitis, meningitis, etc.

enterprise /'ɛntəpraɪz/ *n.* **1.** a project, especially one that requires boldness or energy. **2.** boldness or readiness in undertaking. **3.** a company organised for commercial purposes.

enterprise agreement *n.* an agreement between the employees and employers of an enterprise regarding pay and working conditions, which results from enterprise bargaining.

enterprise bargaining *n.* bargaining on wages and conditions conducted between the employer and employees of an enterprise.

enterprise information portal *n.* → **information portal**.

entertain /ɛntəˈteɪn/ v.t. **1.** to hold the attention of agreeably; divert; amuse. **2.** to receive as a guest. **3.** to admit into the mind; consider. –**entertainment**, n.

enthral /ɛnˈθrɔl, ən-/ v.t. (**-thralled, -thralling**) to captivate; charm.

enthusiasm /ɛnˈθuːziæzəm, -ˈθjuz-, ən-/ n. absorbing or controlling possession of the mind by any interest or pursuit; lively interest. –**enthusiast**, n. –**enthusiastic**, adj. –**enthuse**, v.

entice /ɛnˈtaɪs, ən-/ v.t. to draw on by exciting hope or desire.

entire /ɛnˈtaɪə, ən-/ adj. **1.** whole; complete. **2.** full or thorough. –**entirety**, n.

entitle /ɛnˈtaɪtl, ən-/ v.t. to give (a person or thing) a title, right, or claim to something. –**entitlement**, n.

entity /ˈɛntəti/ n. (pl. **-ties**) something that has a real existence; a thing, especially when considered as independent of other things.

ento- variant of **endo-**.

entomology /ɛntəˈmɒlədʒi/ n. the branch of zoology that deals with insects. –**entomologist**, n.

entourage /ˈɒnturadʒ, -raʒ/ n. any group of people accompanying or assisting someone.

entrails /ˈɛntreɪlz/ pl. n. the internal parts of the trunk of an animal body.

entrance¹ /ˈɛntrəns/ n. **1.** the act of entering. **2.** a point or place of entering.

entrance² /ɛnˈtræns, -ˈtrans, ən-/ v.t. (**-tranced, -trancing**) to fill with delight.

entrant /ˈɛntrənt/ n. a competitor in a contest.

entreat /ɛnˈtrit, ən-/ v.t. to make supplication to (a person); beseech; implore. –**entreaty**, n.

entree /ˈɒntreɪ/ n. a dish served at dinner before the main course. Also, **entrée**.

entrench /ɛnˈtrɛntʃ, ən-/ v.t. **1.** to dig trenches for defensive purposes around (oneself, a military position, etc.). **2.** to establish so strongly or securely as to make any change very difficult.

entrepreneur /ɒntrəprəˈnɜ/ n. (originally in theatrical use) someone who organises and manages any enterprise.

entrust /ɛnˈtrʌst, ən-/ v.t. **1.** to invest with a trust or responsibility. **2.** to commit (something) in trust (to).

entry /ˈɛntri/ n. (pl. **-ries**) **1.** an act of entering. **2.** a place of entrance.

entwine /ɛnˈtwaɪn, ən-/ v.t., v.i. (**-twined, -twining**) to twine with, about, or around.

enumerate /əˈnjuməreɪt, i-/ v.t. to name one by one.

enunciate /əˈnʌnsieɪt, i-/ v.t. to utter or pronounce (words, etc.), especially in a particular manner. –**enunciation**, n.

envelop /ɛnˈvɛləp, ən-/ v.t. to wrap up in or as in a covering.

envelope /ˈɛnvəloup, ˈɒn-/ n. a cover for a letter, etc., usually sealable.

enviable /ˈɛnviəbəl/ adj. that is to be envied; highly desirable.

envious /ˈɛnviəs/ adj. full of envy.

environment /ɛnˈvaɪrənmənt, ən-/ n. **1.** the aggregate of surrounding things, conditions, or influences. **2.** the totality of the surrounding conditions, physical and social, of a particular area. –phr. **3. the environment**, the broad natural surrounding conditions, such as the bush, the rivers, the air, the sea, in which human beings live: *the burning of fossil fuels harms the environment.* –**environmental**, adj. –**environmentally**, adv.

environmentalism /ɛnˌvaɪrənˈmɛntəlɪzəm, ən-/ n. the advocacy of the protection and conservation of the natural environment. –**environmentalist**, n.

environs /ɛnˈvaɪrənz, ən-/ pl. n. surrounding parts or districts.

envisage /ɛnˈvɪzədʒ, -zɪdʒ, ən-/ v.t. (**-aged, -aging**) to contemplate.

envoy /ˈɛnvɔɪ/ n. a diplomatic agent.

envy /ˈɛnvi/ n. **1.** a feeling of discontent at seeing another's superiority, advantages, or success. **2.** desire for some advantage possessed by another. –v.t. (**-vied, -vying**) **3.** to regard with envy.

enzyme /ˈɛnzaɪm/ n. any protein capable of causing a chemical reaction necessary to the cell.

eo- a word element meaning 'early'.

eon /ˈiɒn/ n. → **aeon**.

-eous variant of **-ous**.

epaulet /ˈɛpəlɛt, -lət/ n. an ornamental shoulder piece worn on uniforms. Also, **epaulette**.

ephemeral /əˈfɛmərəl, i-/ adj. short-lived; transitory.

epi- a prefix meaning 'on', 'to', 'against', 'above', 'near', 'after', 'in addition to'. Also, **ep-, eph-**.

epic /ˈɛpɪk/ adj. **1.** of or relating to poetry dealing with a series of heroic achievements or events, in a long narrative with elevated style. –n. **2.** an epic poem. **3.** any novel or film resembling an epic.

epicentre /ˈɛpisɛntə/ n. a point from which earthquake waves go out, directly above the true centre of disturbance. Also, US, **epicenter**.

epicure /ˈɛpəkjuə, ˈɛpi-, -kjuə/ n. someone who cultivates a refined taste, as in food, drink, art, music, etc. –**epicurean**, adj., n.

epidemic /ɛpəˈdɛmɪk/ adj. **1.** affecting at the same time a large number of people in a locality, as a disease. –n. **2.** a temporary prevalence of a disease.

epidermis /ɛpiˈdɜməs, ɛpə-, ˈɛpidɜməs/ n. Anat. the outer layer of the skin. –**epidermal**, adj.

epidural anaesthetic /ɛpiˈdjurəl/ n. **1.** an agent injected into a part of the spinal cord to produce regional anaesthesia, especially in childbirth. **2.** the procedure for doing this. Also, **epidural anesthetic**.

epiglottis /ɛpiˈglɒtəs/ n. Anat. a thin, valvelike structure that covers the glottis during swallowing, preventing the entrance of food and drink into the larynx. –**epiglottal, epiglottic**, adj.

epigram /ˈɛpigræm, ˈɛpə-/ n. any witty or pointed saying tersely expressed.

epigraph /ˈɛpigræf, -graf, ˈɛpə-/ n. an inscription, especially on a building, statue, etc.

epilepsy /ˈɛpəlɛpsi/ n. a nervous disease usually characterised by convulsions. –**epileptic**, adj., n.

epilogue /ˈɛpilɒg, ˈɛpə-/ n. a speech, usually in verse, by one of the actors after the conclusion of a play.

epiphany /ə'pɪfəni/ *n.* (*pl.* **-nies**) **1.** an appearance, revelation, or manifestation of a divine being. **2.** a revelation of the basic nature of something.

episcopal /ə'pɪskəpəl/ *adj.* relating to a bishop.

episode /'ɛpəsoʊd/ *n.* **1.** an incident in the course of a series of events. **2.** (in radio, television, etc.) any of the separate programs constituting a serial. **–episodic**, *adj.*

epistemology /əpɪstə'mɒlədʒi/ *n.* the branch of philosophy which investigates the origin, nature, methods, and limits of human knowledge.

epistle /ə'pɪsəl/ *n.* a letter, especially one of formal or didactic character.

epitaph /'ɛpitaf, 'ɛpə-/ *n.* a commemorative inscription on a tomb, etc.

epithet /'ɛpəθɛt, ɛpi-, -θət/ *n.* a term applied to a person or thing to express an attribute.

epitome /ə'pɪtəmi/ *n.* **1.** a summary or condensed account. **2.** a condensed representation or typical characteristic of something. **–epitomise, epitomize**, *v.*

epoch /'ipɒk, 'ɛpɒk/ *n.* a particular period of time as marked by distinctive character, events, etc.

EPROM /'iprɒm/ *n.* a computer memory chip whose contents can be erased and reprogrammed for other purposes.

equable /'ɛkwəbəl/ *adj.* **1.** uniform, as motion or temperature. **2.** tranquil, as the mind.

equal /'ikwəl/ *adj.* **1.** like or alike in quantity, degree, value, etc. **2.** evenly proportioned or balanced. **3.** having adequate powers, ability, or means. *–n.* **4.** someone who or that which is equal. *–v.t.* (**equalled, equalling**) **5.** to be or become equal to. **–equalise, equalize**, *v.* **–equality**, *n.*

equanimity /ɛkwə'nɪməti, ikwə-/ *n.* evenness of mind or temper.

equate /i'kweɪt, ə-/ *v.t.* **1.** to state the equality of or between. **2.** to make such correction or allowance in as will reduce to a common standard of comparison. **3.** to regard, treat, or represent as equivalent.

equation /i'kweɪʒən, ə-, -ʃən/ *n. Maths* an expression of, or a proposition asserting, the equality of two quantities, employing the sign = between them.

equator /ə'kweɪtə, i-/ *n.* the great circle of the earth, equidistant from the North and South Poles. **–equatorial**, *adj.*

equerry /'ɛkwəri/ *n.* **1.** an officer of a royal or similar household, charged with the care of the horses. **2.** an officer who attends on the British sovereign or on a representative of the sovereign, such as an Australian state governor.

equestrian /ə'kwɛstriən, i-/ *adj.* of or relating to horses and horseriding.

equi- a word element meaning 'equal'.

equilateral /ikwə'lætərəl/ *adj.* having all the sides equal.

equilibrium /ikwə'lɪbriəm, ɛ-/ *n.* a state of rest due to the action of forces that counteract each other.

equine /'ɛkwaɪn, i-/ *adj.* **1.** of or resembling a horse. *–n.* **2.** a horse.

equine influenza *n.* a viral respiratory disease which causes flu-like symptoms in horses; horse flu. *Abbrev.*: EI Also, **equine flu**.

equinox /'ikwənɒks, ɛ-/ *n.* the time when the sun crosses the plane of the earth's equator, making night and day all over the earth of equal length. **–equinoctial**, *adj.*

equip /ə'kwɪp, i-/ *v.t.* (**equipped, equipping**) to furnish or provide with whatever is needed.

equipment /ə'kwɪpmənt/ *n.* anything used to equip for a job, etc., especially a collection of tools, machines, resources, skills, etc.

equity /'ɛkwəti/ *n.* (*pl.* **-ties**) **1.** fairness; impartiality. **2.** the interest of a shareholder, of common stock in a company. **3.** (*pl.*) stocks and shares not bearing fixed interest. **4.** the amount by which the market value of a debtor's securities exceeds his or her indebtedness. **–equitable**, *adj.*

equivalent /ə'kwɪvələnt, i-/ *adj.* **1.** equal in value, measure, force, effect, significance, etc. **2.** corresponding in position, function, etc. *–n.* **3.** that which is equivalent.

equivocal /ə'kwɪvəkəl, i-/ *adj.* questionable; dubious; suspicious.

equivocate /ə'kwɪvəkeɪt, i-/ *v.i.* to use equivocal or ambiguous expressions, especially in order to mislead.

-er¹ a suffix serving as the regular English formative of agent nouns, as in *bearer, creeper, employer, harvester, teacher, theoriser.*

-er² a suffix of nouns denoting persons or things concerned or connected with something, as in *grocer, officer.*

-er³ a suffix forming the comparative degree of adjectives and adverbs, as in *harder, smaller, faster.*

-er⁴ a termination of certain nouns denoting action or process, as in *dinner, rejoinder, remainder.*

era /'ɪərə/ *n.* **1.** a period of time marked by distinctive character, events, etc. **2.** a system of chronological notation reckoned from a given date.

eradicate /ə'rædəkeɪt, i-/ *v.t.* to remove or destroy utterly.

erase /ə'reɪz, i-/ *v.t.* to rub or scrape out, as written letters, etc.

ereader /'iridə/ *n.* a handheld electronic device for reading publications in electronic form. Also, **e-reader**.

erect /ə'rɛkt, i-/ *adj.* **1.** upright in position or posture. *–v.t.* **2.** to build; construct; raise. **3.** to raise and set in an upright or perpendicular position. **–erector, erecter**, *n.*

erection /ə'rɛkʃən, i-/ *n.* **1.** the act of erecting. **2.** the state of being erected. **3.** something erected, as a building or other structure. **4.** *Physiol.* **a.** a distended and rigid state of an organ or part containing erectile tissue. **b.** an erect penis.

erg /3g/ *n.* a unit of work or energy in the centimetre-gram-second system.

ergo /'3goʊ/ *conj., adv.* therefore.

ergonomics /3gə'nɒmɪks, 3goʊ-/ *n.* the study of the relationship between workers and their working environment. **–ergomonic**, *adj.*

ermine /'3mən/ *n.* (*pl.* **-mines** *or, especially collectively,* **-mine**) a weasel of northern regions, which turns white in winter. See **stoat**.

-ern *n.* an adjectival suffix occurring in *northern*, etc.

erode /ə'roʊd, i-/ v.t. to wear away. **–erosion**, n. **–erosive**, adj.

erogenous /ə'rɒdʒənəs, ɛ-, i-/ adj. arousing or tending to arouse sexual desire. **–erogeneity**, n.

erotic /ə'rɒtɪk, ɛ-, i-/ adj. **1.** of or relating to sexual love. **2.** arousing or satisfying sexual desire. **–erotically**, adv.

err /ɜ/ v.i. to be mistaken or incorrect.

errand /'ɛrənd/ n. a short journey for a specific purpose.

errant /'ɛrənt/ adj. journeying or travelling. **–errantry**, n.

erratic /ə'rætɪk, i-/ adj. **1.** irregular in conduct or opinion. **2.** having no certain course; wandering.

erroneous /ə'roʊniəs/ adj. containing error; mistaken; incorrect.

error /'ɛrə/ n. **1.** deviation from accuracy or correctness. **2.** a mistake.

ersatz /'ɜzæts, 'ɛəz-, -zæts/ adj. serving as a substitute.

erstwhile /'ɜstwaɪl/ adj. former.

erudition /ɛrə'dɪʃən/ n. learning; scholarship. **–erudite**, adj.

erupt /ə'rʌpt, i-/ v.i. **1.** (of a volcano, geyser, etc.) to eject matter. **2.** to break out suddenly or violently, as if from restraint. **–eruption**, n.

-ery 1. an adoption of a French word ending in *-erie*, as in *bravery*, *nunnery*, *cutlery*. **2.** a suffix of nouns denoting **a.** a place of employment, as in *bakery*, *brewery*, *fishery*. **b.** a class of goods, as in *confectionery*, *pottery*. **c.** things collectively, as in *machinery*, *crockery*, *scenery*. **d.** a state or condition, as in *slavery*, *foolery*, *witchery*. **e.** a place where certain animals are kept, as in *piggery*, *rookery*. **f.** (*humorous*) a place where an article or service may be obtained, as in *eatery*, *fish and chippery*.

erythro- a word element meaning 'red'.

erythrocyte /ə'nθrəsaɪt, ə'nθroʊ-/ n. one of the red corpuscles of the blood; red blood cell.

-es a variant of **-s²** and **-s³** after *s*, *z*, *ch*, *sh*, and in those nouns ending in *-f* which have *-v-* in the plural. Compare **-ies**.

escalate /'ɛskəleɪt/ v.t., v.i. to intensify. **–escalation**, n.

escalator /'ɛskəleɪtə/ n. (*from trademark*) a continuously moving staircase.

escapade /'ɛskəpeɪd, ɛskə'peɪd/ n. a reckless proceeding; a wild prank.

escape /əs'keɪp/ v.i. **1.** to slip or get away, as from confinement or restraint. *–v.t.* **2.** to slip away from or elude (pursuers, captors, etc.). **3.** to fail to be noticed or recollected by (a person). *–n.* **4.** an act or instance of escaping. **–escapee, escaper**, n.

escapism /əs'keɪpɪzəm/ n. the avoidance of reality by absorption of the mind in entertainment, or in an imaginative situation, activity, etc. **–escapist**, adj., n.

escarpment /əs'kɑpmənt/ n. a long, cliff-like ridge of rock, or the like.

-esce a suffix of verbs meaning to begin to be or do something, as in *convalesce*.

ES cell /i 'ɛs/ n. **→ embryonic stem cell**.

-escence a suffix of nouns denoting action or process, change, state, or condition, etc., and corresponding to verbs ending in *-esce* or adjectives ending in *-escent*, as in *convalescence*.

eschew /ə'ʃu, ɛ'ʃu, əs'tʃu, ɛs-/ v.t. to abstain from.

escort n. /'ɛskɔt/ **1.** one or more people or things accompanying another or others for protection, guidance, or courtesy. *–v.t.* /əs'kɔt, ɛs-/ **2.** to attend or accompany as an escort.

escrow /'ɛskroʊ, əs'kroʊ, ɛs-/ n. a contract, deed, bond, or other written agreement deposited with a third person, by whom it is to be delivered to the grantee or promisee on the fulfilment of some condition.

escutcheon /əs'kʌtʃən/ n. an armorial shield.

-ese a noun and adjective suffix referring to locality, nationality, language, literary style, etc., as in *Japanese, journalese*.

e-signature /'i-sɪgnətʃə/ n. **→ digital signature**.

esky /'ɛski/ n. (*pl.* **eskies**) (*from trademark*) a portable container for keeping things cold. Also, **Esky**.

esoteric /ɛsə'tɛrɪk, isə-/ adj. understood by or meant for a select few.

ESP /i ɛs 'pi/ n. extrasensory perception; perception or communication outside of normal sensory activity, as in telepathy and clairvoyance. Also, **e.s.p.**

especial /əs'pɛʃəl/ adj. **1.** special; exceptional. **2.** of a particular kind.

especially /əs'pɛʃəli/ adv. **1.** particularly; unusually: *be especially watchful*. **2.** principally: *especially on Sundays*.

espionage /'ɛspiənaʒ, -nadʒ/ n. the practice of spying on others.

esplanade /'ɛsplənad, -neɪd/ n. any open level space serving for public walks, etc.

espouse /əs'paʊz, ɛs-/ v.t. to make one's own, adopt, or embrace, as a cause. **–espousal**, n.

espresso /ɛs'prɛsoʊ/ n. coffee made by forcing steam under pressure or boiling water through ground coffee beans.

espy /əs'paɪ, ɛs-/ v.t. (**-pied, -pying**) to see at a distance; catch sight of; detect.

-esque an adjective suffix indicating style, manner, or distinctive character.

esquire /əs'kwaɪə, 'ɛs-/ n. (*upper case*) a polite title, usually abbreviated to *Esq.*, after a man's last name; *Mr* or *Dr* is omitted when it is used.

-ess a suffix forming distinctively feminine nouns, as *countess, hostess, lioness*.

essay /'ɛseɪ/ *for def. 1*, /'ɛseɪ, ɛ'seɪ/ *for def. 2*, /ɛ'seɪ/ *for defs 3 and 4* –n. **1.** a short literary composition on a particular subject. **2.** an attempt. *–v.t.* **3.** to try; attempt. **4.** to put to the test; make trial of.

essence /'ɛsəns/ n. **1.** intrinsic nature; important elements or features of a thing. **2.** a concentrated extract.

essential /ə'sɛnʃəl/ adj. **1.** absolutely necessary. **2.** relating to or constituting the essence of a thing. *–n.* **3.** an indispensable element.

-est a suffix forming the superlative degree of adjectives and adverbs, as in *warmest, fastest, soonest*.

establish /əs'tæblɪʃ/ v.t. **1.** to set up on a firm or permanent basis; institute; found. **2.** to settle or install in a position, business, etc. **3.** to show to be valid or well grounded; prove.

establishment /əsˈtæblɪʃmənt, ɛs-/ n. **1.** a place of business or residence. **2.** an institution.

estate /əˈsteɪt, ɛs-/ n. **1.** a piece of landed property, especially one of large extent. **2.** *Law* **a.** property or possessions. **b.** the property of a deceased person, a bankrupt, etc., viewed as an aggregate. **3.** a housing development. **4.** condition or circumstances with reference to worldly prosperity, estimation, etc.; social status or rank.

estate agent n. → **real estate agent**.

esteem /əsˈtim/ v.t. **1.** to regard highly or favourably. **2.** to set a value on; value. –n. **3.** favourable opinion or judgement; respect or regard.

ester /ˈɛstə/ n. a compound formed by the reaction between an acid and an alcohol.

estimable /ˈɛstəməbəl/ adj. **1.** worthy of esteem. **2.** capable of being estimated.

estimate v.t. /ˈɛstəmeɪt/ **1.** to form an approximate judgement or opinion regarding the value, amount, size, weight, etc., of; calculate approximately. –n. /ˈɛstəmət/ **2.** an approximate judgement or calculation. –**estimation**, n.

estrange /əˈstreɪndʒ/ v.t. (**estranged**, **estranging**) to alienate the affections of.

estuary /ˈɛstʃʊri, ˈɛstʃuəri, *Orig. US* /ˈɛstʃuɛri/ n. (pl. **-ries**) **1.** that part of the mouth of a river in which its current meets the sea's tides. **2.** an arm or inlet of the sea. –**estuarine**, adj.

e-tag /ˈi-tæg/ n. an electronic device attached to a vehicle which, when it comes within range, activates an electronic reader, causing a toll to be debited from the customer's account. Also, **etag**, **electronic tag**.

etc. et cetera.

et cetera /ət ˈsɛtrə, ɛt-, -ərə/ and others; and so forth; and so on. *Abbrev.*: etc.

etch /ɛtʃ/ v.t. **1.** to engrave (metals, etc.) with an acid or the like. **2.** to fix in the memory. –**etching**, n.

E10 /i ˈtɛn/ n. a fuel consisting of ethanol and unleaded petrol, being 10 per cent ethanol and 90 per cent petrol.

eternity /əˈtɜnəti, i-/ n. (pl. **-ties**) infinite time; duration without beginning or end. –**eternal**, adj.

-eth variant of **-th²** after a vowel.

ethanol /ˈɛθənɒl, ˈiθ-/ n. an alcohol produced from crops and used as a biofuel.

ether /ˈiθə/ n. **1.** *Chem.* a volatile, flammable, colourless liquid used as an anaesthetic. **2.** the upper regions of space; the clear sky; the heavens.

ethereal /əˈθɪəriəl, i-/ adj. **1.** light, airy or tenuous. **2.** heavenly or celestial.

ethernet /ˈiθənɛt/ n. (*from trademark*) a system used to connect computers in a network, allowing them to communicate with each other in a regulated way. Also, **Ethernet**.

ethical /ˈɛθɪkəl/ adj. relating to or dealing with morals or the principles of morality.

ethics /ˈɛθɪks/ pl. n. a system of moral principles, by which human actions and proposals may be judged good or bad or right or wrong.

ethnic /ˈɛθnɪk/ adj. **1.** relating to or peculiar to a human population or group, especially one with a common ancestry, language, etc. **2.** of or relating to members of the community who

are migrants or the descendants of migrants and whose first language is not English.

ethno- a word element meaning 'race', 'nation'.

ethnography /ɛθˈnɒgrəfi/ n. the scientific description and classification of the various cultural and racial groups of humankind.

ethnology /ɛθˈnɒlədʒi/ n. the science that deals with the distinctive subdivisions of humankind, their origin, relations, speech, institutions, etc.

ethos /ˈiθɒs/ n. *Sociology* the fundamental spiritual characteristics of a culture.

etiquette /ˈɛtɪkət/ n. conventional requirements as to social behaviour.

-ette a noun suffix, occurring especially: **1.** with the original diminutive force, as in *cigarette*. **2.** in trademarks of imitations or substitutes, as in *leatherette*. **3.** as a distinctively feminine ending, as in *coquette*, *brunette*.

etymology /ɛtəˈmɒlədʒi/ n. (pl. **-gies**) **1.** the study of historical linguistic change, especially as applied to individual words. **2.** the derivation of a word.

eucalypt /ˈjukəlɪpt/ n. any eucalyptus.

eucalyptus /jukəˈlɪptəs/ n. (pl. **-tuses** or **-ti** /-taɪ/) any of many tall trees native to the Australian region.

eugenic /juˈdʒinɪk, -ˈdʒɛn-/ adj. of or bringing about improvement in the type of offspring produced.

eukaryote /juˈkærioʊt/ n. an organism which has cells with a distinct nucleus within which the DNA is contained. Compare **prokaryote**. Also, **eucaryote**. –**eukaryotic** /jukæriˈɒtɪk/, adj.

eulogy /ˈjulədʒi/ n. (pl. **-gies**) a speech or writing in praise of a person or thing. –**eulogise**, **eulogize**, v. –**eulogistic**, adj.

eunuch /ˈjunək/ n. a castrated man.

euphemism /ˈjufəmɪzəm/ n. **1.** the substitution of a mild, indirect, or vague expression for a harsh or blunt one. **2.** the expression so substituted. –**euphemistic**, adj.

euphonium /juˈfoʊniəm/ n. a tenor tuba mainly used in brass bands.

euphony /ˈjufəni/ n. agreeableness of sound. –**euphonic**, **euphonious**, adj.

euphoria /juˈfɔriə/ n. a feeling or state of wellbeing, especially one of unnatural elation. –**euphoric** /juˈfɒrɪk/, adj. –**euphorically** /juˈfɒrɪkli/, adv.

eureka /juˈrikə/ interj. an exclamation of triumph at a discovery.

euro¹ /ˈjuroʊ/ n. (pl. **euros**) → **wallaroo**.

euro² /ˈjuroʊ/ n. (pl. **euros**) the monetary unit of the European Union, introduced as legal tender in most of the member nations in 2002.

eury- a word element meaning 'broad'.

Eustachian tube /juˈsteɪʃən/ n. *Anat.* a canal extending from the middle ear to the pharynx; auditory canal.

euthanase /ˈjuθəneɪz/ v.t. to subject to euthanasia. Also, **euthanise**.

euthanasia /juθəˈneɪʒə/ n. the deliberate bringing about of the death of a person suffering from an incurable disease or condition, as by administering a lethal drug or by withdrawing existing life-supporting treatments.

evacuate /ə'vækjueɪt/ *v.t.* **1.** to leave empty; vacate. **2.** to move (persons or things) from a threatened place, disaster area, etc.

evade /ə'veɪd, i-/ *v.t.* **1.** to escape from by trickery or cleverness. **2.** to avoid answering directly. **3.** to elude.

evaluate /ə'væljueɪt, i-/ *v.t.* to ascertain the value of.

evangelist /i'vændʒələst/ *n.* someone who spreads the Christian gospel. –**evangelical**, *adj.*

evaporate /ə'væpəreɪt, i-/ *v.i.* to turn to vapour; pass off in vapour. –**evaporation**, *n.*

evasion /ə'veɪʒən, i-/ *n.* the act of escaping something by trickery or cleverness. –**evasive**, *adj.* –**evasively**, *adv.* –**evasiveness**, *n.*

eve /iv/ *n.* the evening, or often the day, before a particular date or event.

even /'ivən/ *adj.* **1.** level; flat; without irregularities; smooth. **2.** on the same level; in the same plane or line; parallel. **3.** uniform in action, character, or quality. **4.** equal in measure or quantity. **5.** divisible by 2 (opposed to *odd*). **6.** leaving no balance of debt on either side. **7.** equitable, impartial, or fair. –*adv.* **8.** evenly. **9.** still; yet (used to emphasise a comparative). **10.** indeed (used for stressing identity or truth of something). –*v.t.* **11.** to make even; level; smooth.

evening /'ivnɪŋ/ *n.* the latter part of the day and the early part of the night.

evening star *n.* a bright planet seen in the west after sunset, especially Venus.

event /ə'vɛnt, i-/ *n.* anything that happens; an occurrence, especially one of some importance.

eventful /ə'vɛntfəl, i-/ *adj.* full of events or incidents, especially striking ones.

event horizon *n.* the boundary of a black hole at which the escape velocity is equal to the speed of light, thus preventing radiation from reaching an external observer.

eventual /ə'vɛntʃuəl, -tʃəl/ *adj.* consequent; ultimate. –**eventually**, *adv.*

eventuality /əvɛntʃu'æləti/ *n.* (*pl.* **-ties**) a contingent event; a possible occurrence or circumstance.

eventuate /ə'vɛntʃueɪt/ *v.i.* to come about.

ever /'ɛvə/ *adv.* **1.** at all times. **2.** continuously. **3.** at any time.

evergreen /'ɛvəgrin/ *adj.* (of trees, shrubs, etc.) having living leaves all year long.

every /'ɛvri/ *adj.* **1.** each (referring one by one to all the members of an aggregate) **2.** all possible.

everybody /'ɛvribɒdi/ *pron.* every person.

everyday /'ɛvrideɪ/ *adj.* **1.** daily. **2.** ordinary; commonplace.

everyone /'ɛvriwʌn/ *pron.* every person.

everything /'ɛvriθɪŋ/ *pron.* every thing or particular of an aggregate or total; all.

everywhere /'ɛvriwɛə/ *adv.* in every place.

evict /ə'vɪkt, i-/ *v.t.* to expel (a person, especially a tenant) from land, a building, etc., by legal process. –**eviction**, *n.*

evidence /'ɛvədəns/ *n.* **1.** that which tends to prove or disprove something. **2.** something that makes evident; an indication or sign.

evident /'ɛvədənt/ *adj.* plain or clear to the sight or understanding. –**evidently**, *adv.*

evil /'ivəl/ *adj.* **1.** violating or inconsistent with the moral law; wicked. **2.** harmful; injurious. **3.** characterised by anger, irascibility, etc. –*n.* **4.** that which is evil.

evince /ə'vɪns, i-/ *v.t.* to show clearly; make evident.

evoke /ə'voʊk, i-/ *v.t.* **1.** to call up, or produce (memories, feelings, etc.). **2.** to provoke, or elicit. –**evocation**, *n.* –**evocative**, *adj.*

evolution /ɛvə'luʃən, ivə-/ *n.* **1.** any process of formation or growth; development. **2.** *Biol.* the continuous genetic adaptation of organisms or species to the environment.

evolve /ə'vɒlv, i-/ *v.t., v.i.* (**evolved, evolving**) to develop gradually.

ewe /ju/ *n.* a female sheep.

ewer /'juə/ *n.* a pitcher with a wide spout.

ex-[1] a prefix meaning 'out of', 'from', and hence 'utterly', 'thoroughly', and sometimes serving to impart a negative force or to indicate a former title, status, etc.

ex-[2] variant of **exo-**.

exacerbate /əg'zæsəbeɪt/ *v.t.* to increase the bitterness or violence of (disease, ill feeling, etc.).

exact /əg'zækt, ɛg-/ *adj.* **1.** strictly accurate or correct. **2.** admitting of no deviation, as laws, discipline, etc.; strict or rigorous. –*v.t.* **3.** to call for, demand, or require. **4.** to force or compel the payment, yielding, or performance of. –**exactitude, exactness**, *n.*

exaggerate /əg'zædʒəreɪt, ɛg-/ *v.t.* **1.** to magnify beyond the limits of truth. –*v.i.* **2.** to employ exaggeration, as in speech or writing. –**exaggeration**, *n.*

exalt /əg'zɔlt, ɛg-/ *v.t.* **1.** to elevate in rank, honour, power, character, quality, etc. **2.** to praise; extol. –**exaltation**, *n.*

exam /əg'zæm, ɛg-/ *n.* an examination.

examine /əg'zæmən, ɛg-/ *v.t.* **1.** to inspect or scrutinise carefully; inquire into or investigate. **2.** to test the knowledge, etc., of, as by questions. **3.** to interrogate. –**examination**, *n.*

example /əg'zæmpəl, -'zampəl, ɛg-/ *n.* **1.** one of a number of things, or a part of something, taken to show the character of the whole. **2.** something to be imitated; a pattern or model. **3.** an instance serving for illustration; a specimen.

exasperate /əg'zæspəreɪt, ɛg-/ *v.t.* to irritate to a high degree. –**exasperation**, *n.*

excavate /'ɛkskəveɪt/ *v.t.* to make a hole or cavity in, as by digging. –**excavation**, *n.*

exceed /ək'sid, ɛk-/ *v.t.* to go beyond in quantity, degree, rate, etc.

excel /ək'sɛl, ɛk-/ *v.t., v.i.* (**-celled, -celling**) to surpass others.

excellence /'ɛksələns/ *n.* the fact or state of excelling; superiority; eminence.

excellency /'ɛksələnsi/ *n.* (*pl.* **-cies**) (*usu. upper case*) a title of honour given to certain high officials, as governors, etc.

excellent /'ɛksələnt/ *adj.* very good, or of a very high quality. –**excellently**, *adv.*

except[1] /ək'sɛpt, ɛk-/ *prep.* **1.** with the exclusion of; excluding. –*conj.* **2.** with the exception (that).

except[2] /ək'sɛpt, ɛk-/ *v.t.* to exclude.

exception /ək'sɛpʃən, ɛk-/ n. **1.** something excepted; an instance or case not conforming to the general rule. **2.** opposition of opinion; objection; demurral.

exceptional /ək'sɛpʃənəl, ɛk-/ adj. **1.** unusual; extraordinary. **2.** extraordinarily good or clever.

excerpt /'ɛksɜpt/ n. a passage taken out of a book or the like.

excess /ək'sɛs, 'ɛk-/ n. **1.** the amount or degree by which one thing exceeds another. **2.** an extreme or excessive amount or degree. **3.** immoderate indulgence. –adj. **4.** more than necessary or usual: *excess baggage*. **–excessive**, adj.

exchange /əks'tʃeɪndʒ, ɛk-/ v.t. (**-changed, -changing**) **1.** to replace by another or something else; change for another. –n. **2.** the act or process of exchanging. **3.** a place for buying and selling commodities, securities, etc., typically open only to members. **4.** a central office or central station. **5.** the method or system by which debits and credits in different places are settled without the actual transference of money, by means of documents representing money values. **6.** the discharge of obligations in different places by the transfer of credits. **7.** the reciprocal transference of equivalent sums of money, as in the currencies of two different countries. **8.** the giving or receiving of a sum of money in one place for a bill ordering the payment of an equivalent sum in another. **9.** the varying rate or sum, in one currency, given for a fixed sum in another currency; exchange rate. **10.** the amount of the difference in value between two or more currencies, or between the values of the same currency at two or more places. **11.** the cheques, drafts, etc., exchanged at a clearing house. **12.** → stock exchange.

exchange rate n. the ratio at which the unit of currency of one country can be exchanged for the unit of currency of another country.

exchequer /əks'tʃɛkə, ɛks-/ n. a treasury, as of a state or nation.

excise¹ /'ɛksaɪz, 'ɛksaɪs/ n. **1.** a tax or duty on certain commodities, as spirits, tobacco, etc., levied on their manufacture, sale, or consumption within a country. **2.** a tax levied for a licence to carry on certain types of employment, pursue certain sports, etc. **3.** *Brit.* that branch of the public service which collects excise duties. **–excisable**, adj.

excise² /ɛk'saɪz/ v.t. to cut out or off. **–excision**, n.

excite /ək'saɪt, ɛk-/ v.t. **1.** to arouse or stir up the feelings of. **2.** to stir to action; stir up. **3.** *Physiol.* to stimulate. **–exciting**, adj. **–excitement**, n. **–excitation**, n.

exclaim /əks'kleɪm, ɛks-/ v.i. to cry out or speak suddenly and vehemently, as in surprise, strong emotion, protest, etc. **–exclamation**, n.

exclude /əks'klud, ɛks-/ v.t. to shut or keep out; prevent the entrance of. **–exclusion**, n.

exclusive /əks'klusɪv, ɛks-/ adj. **1.** excluding from consideration or account. **2.** shutting out all other activities. **3.** single or sole. **4.** available through only one channel of marketing. **5.** disposed to resist the admission of outsiders to association, intimacy, etc. **6.** fashionable.

excommunicate /ɛkskə'mjunəkeɪt/ v.t. to cut off from communion or membership, especially from the church.

excrement /'ɛkskrəmənt/ n. waste matter discharged from the body, especially the faeces.

excrescence /ɛks'krɛsəns/ n. abnormal growth or increase.

excrete /əks'krit, ɛks-/ to separate and eliminate from the blood or tissues, as waste matter. **–excreta**, pl. n. **–excretion**, n. **–excretory**, adj.

excruciating /əks'kruʃieɪtɪŋ, ɛks-/ adj. extremely painful; causing extreme suffering; torturing.

exculpate /'ɛkskʌlpeɪt, ɛks'kʌlpeɪt/ v.t. to free from blame.

excursion /ək'skʒən, ɛk-, -ʒən/ n. **1.** a short journey or trip for a special purpose. **2.** deviation or digression.

excuse v.t. /ək'skjuz, ɛk-/ (**-cused, -cusing**) **1.** to pardon or forgive. **2.** to apologise for; seek to remove the blame of. **3.** to serve as an apology or justification for; justify. **4.** to release from an obligation or duty. –n. /ək'skjus/ **5.** that which is offered as a reason for being excused. **6.** an inferior or inadequate example of something specified.

execrable /'ɛksəkrəbəl/ adj. abominable.

executable file n. *Computers* a version of an application (def. 6) that can be directly read by the computer.

execute /'ɛksəkjut/ v.t. **1.** to carry out; accomplish. **2.** to put to death according to law. **–execution**, n.

executive /əg'zɛkjətɪv, ɛg-/ adj. **1.** of the kind requisite for practical performance or direction. **2.** charged with or relating to execution of laws, or administration of affairs. –n. **3.** a person or body having administrative authority, as in a company. **4.** *Govt* the body of people, members of the governing party or parties, drawn from both houses of parliament, who devise policy and control the appropriate government departments and instrumentalities, and who are responsible to parliament for such administration. Compare **legislature**, **judiciary**.

executor /əg'zɛkjətə, ɛg-/ n. *Law* a person named by a testator in his or her will to carry out the provisions of the will. **–executrix**, fem. n.

exemplary /əg'zɛmpləri, ɛg-/ adj. **1.** worthy of imitation; commendable. **2.** serving as a model or pattern. **3.** serving as an example; typical.

exemplify /əg'zɛmpləfaɪ, ɛg-/ v.t. (**-fied, -fying**) **1.** to show or illustrate by example. **2.** to furnish, or serve as, an example of.

exempt /əg'zɛmpt, ɛg-/ v.t. to free from an obligation or liability to which others are subject; release. **–exemptible**, adj. **–exemption**, n.

exercise /'ɛksəsaɪz/ n. **1.** bodily or mental exertion, especially for the sake of training or improvement. **2.** something done or performed as a means of practice or training. **3.** a putting into action, use, operation, or effect. –v.t. **4.** to put through exercises, or forms of practice or exertion, designed to train, develop, condition, etc. **5.** to put (faculties, rights, etc.) into action, practice, or use. **6.** to discharge (a function);

perform. –*v.i.* **7.** to go through exercises; take bodily exercise.

exert /əg'zɜt, ɛg-/ *v.t.* to put forth, as power; exercise, as ability or influence.

exertion /əg'zɜʃən, ɛg-/ *n.* vigorous action or effort.

exfoliate /ɛks'fouliert/ *v.t.* **1.** to throw off in scales. **2.** to remove dirt, dead skin, etc., from the surface of (human skin). –**exfoliation**, *n.*

exhale /ɛks'heɪl/ *v.i.* to emit breath or vapour.

exhaust /əg'zɔst, ɛg-/ *v.t.* **1.** to empty by drawing out the contents. **2.** to use up or consume completely; expend the whole of. **3.** to drain of strength or energy. –*n.* **4.** *Machinery* the escape of gases from the cylinder of an engine. –**exhaustion**, *n.* –**exhaustive**, *adj.*

exhibit /əg'zɪbət, ɛg-/ *v.t.* **1.** to offer or expose to view; present for inspection. **2.** to manifest or display. **3.** to place on show. –*n.* **4.** that which is exhibited. –**exhibition**, *n.*

exhibitionism /ɛksə'bɪʃənɪzəm/ *n.* a tendency to behave in such a way as to attract attention. –**exhibitionist**, *n.*

exhilarate /əg'zɪləreɪt, ɛg-/ *v.t.* to enliven; stimulate; invigorate.

exhort /əg'zɔt, ɛg-/ *v.t.* to urge, advise, or caution earnestly; admonish urgently. –**exhortation**, *n.*

exhume /ɛks'hjum/ *v.t.* to dig (something buried, especially a corpse) out of the earth.

exigent /'ɛksədʒənt/ *adj.* requiring immediate action or aid; urgent; pressing. –**exigency**, **exigence**, *n.*

exile /'ɛgzaɪl, 'ɛksaɪl/ *n.* **1.** prolonged separation from one's country or home, as by stress of circumstances. **2.** expulsion from one's native land by authoritative decree. –*v.t.* (**-iled**, **-iling**) **3.** to separate from country, home, etc.

exist /əg'zɪst, ɛg-, ɪg-/ *v.i.* **1.** to have actual being; be. **2.** to have life or animation; live.

existence /əg'zɪstəns, ɛg-, ɪg-/ *n.* **1.** the state or fact of existing; being. **2.** continuance in being or life; life: *a struggle for existence.* **3.** mode of existing. **4.** all that exists. **5.** something that exists, an entity, or a being. –**existent**, *adj.*

existentialism /ɛgzɪs'tɛnʃəlɪzəm/ *n.* a modern philosophical doctrine which stresses the importance of existence, as such, and of the freedom and responsibility of the human individual. –**existentialist**, *adj.*, *n.*

exit /'ɛgzət, 'ɛksət/ *n.* **1.** a way or passage out. **2.** a going out or away; a departure. –*v.i.* **3.** to depart; go away. –*v.t.* **4.** to depart from: *she exited the stage to great applause.*

exit strategy *n.* a plan for the termination of a project, especially in a military or business context, which meets the objective of maintaining political or financial security.

exo- a prefix meaning 'external'. Also, **ex-**[2].

exodus /'ɛksədəs/ *n.* a going out; a departure or emigration, usually of a large number of people.

exonerate /əg'zɒnəreɪt, ɛg-/ *v.t.* to clear, as of a charge; free from blame; exculpate.

exorbitant /əg'zɔbətənt, ɛg-/ *adj.* exceeding the bounds of custom, propriety, or reason, especially in amount or extent.

exorcise /'ɛksɔsaɪz/ *v.t.* to seek to expel (an evil spirit) by religious or solemn ceremonies. Also, **exorcize**. –**exorcism**, *n.* –**exorcist**, *n.*

exoteric /ɛksoʊ'tɛrɪk/ *adj.* suitable for or communicated to the general public.

exotic /əg'zɒtɪk, ɛg-/ *adj.* **1.** of foreign origin or character. **2.** strikingly unusual or colourful in appearance or effect. **3.** rare: *an exotic item impossible to buy.* –**exotically**, *adv.*

expand /ək'spænd, ɛk-/ *v.t.* **1.** to increase in extent, size, volume, scope, etc. **2.** to express in fuller form or greater detail; develop. –*v.i.* **3.** to increase or grow in extent, bulk, scope, etc. –**expansion**, *n.*

expanse /ək'spæns, ɛk-/ *n.* an uninterrupted space or area; a wide extent of anything.

expatiate /əks'peɪʃieɪt, ɛk-/ *v.i.* to enlarge in discourse or writing.

expatriate *v.t.* /ɛks'pætrieɪt/ **1.** to banish (a person) from their native country. **2.** to withdraw (oneself) from residence in and/or allegiance to one's native country. –*adj.* /ɛks'pætriət/ **3.** expatriated; exiled. –*n.* /ɛks'pætriət/ **4.** an expatriated person.

expect /ək'spɛkt, ɛk-/ *v.t.* **1.** to regard as likely to happen. **2.** to look for with reason or justification. –**expectation**, *n.* –**expectancy**, *n.* –**expectant**, *adj.*

expectorate /ək'spɛktəreɪt, ɛk-/ *v.t.* to eject or expel (phlegm, etc.). –**expectorant**, *n.*

expedient /ək'spidiənt, ɛk-/ *adj.* **1.** tending to promote some proposed or desired object. **2.** conducive to advantage or interest, as opposed to right. –*n.* **3.** a means to an end. –**expediency**, *n.*

expedite /'ɛkspədaɪt/ *v.t.* to speed up the progress of; hasten. –**expeditious**, *adj.*

expedition /ɛkspə'dɪʃən/ *n.* **1.** an excursion, journey, or voyage made for some specific purpose. **2.** promptness or speed in accomplishing something.

expel /ək'spɛl, ɛk-/ *v.t.* (**-pelled**, **-pelling**) **1.** to drive or force out or away; discharge or eject. **2.** to cut off from membership or relations.

expend /ək'spɛnd, ɛk-/ *v.t.* to use up.

expendable /ək'spɛndəbəl, ɛk-/ *adj.* (of personnel, equipment, etc.) capable of being sacrificed to achieve an objective.

expenditure /ək'spɛndətʃə, ɛk-/ *n.* **1.** the act of expending. **2.** that which is expended; expense.

expense /ək'spɛns, ɛk-/ *n.* **1.** cost or charge. **2.** a cause or occasion of spending.

expense account *n.* a record of expenditure incurred by an employee in the course of business to be refunded by the employer or claimed against tax.

expensive /ək'spɛnsɪv, ɛk-/ *adj.* costly.

experience /ək'spɪəriəns, ɛk-/ *n.* **1.** a particular instance of personally encountering or undergoing something. **2.** the process or fact of personally observing, encountering, or undergoing something. **3.** knowledge or practical wisdom gained from what one has observed, encountered, or undergone. –*v.t.* (**-enced**, **-encing**) **4.** to have experience of; meet with; undergo; feel. –**experienced**, *adj.* –**experiential**, *adj.*

experiment *n.* /ək'spɛrəmənt, ɛk-/ **1.** an act or operation for the purpose of discovering something unknown or testing a principle, supposition, etc. –*v.i.* /ək'spɛrəmənt, ɛk-/ **2.** to try or test in order to find something out. –**experimental**, *adj.* –**experimentation**, *n.*

expert /'ɛkspɜt/ *n.* **1.** a person who has special skill or knowledge in some particular field. –*adj.* **2.** having or displaying such skill or knowledge: *expert advice.*

expertise /ɛksps'tiz/ *n.* expert skill or knowledge; expertness.

expiate /'ɛkspieɪt/ *v.t.* to atone for; make amends or reparation for.

expire /ək'spaɪə, ɛk-/ *v.i.* **1.** to come to an end; terminate. **2.** to emit the last breath; die. **3.** (of food products) to be beyond the use-by date: *this milk has expired.* –*v.t.* **4.** *Computers* to delete (a document) from an archive file after a specified date. –**expiration**, **expiry**, *n.*

explain /ək'spleɪn, ɛk-/ *v.t.* **1.** to make plain or clear; render intelligible. **2.** to make known in detail. **3.** to assign a meaning to; interpret. –**explanatory**, *adj.*

explanation /ɛksplə'neɪʃən/ *n.* **1.** the act or process of explaining. **2.** something that explains; a statement made to clarify something and make it understandable; an exposition. **3.** a meaning or interpretation: *to find an explanation of a mystery.* **4.** a written or spoken text type or form which describes how something operates or why something happens.

expletive /ək'splitɪv, ɛk-/ *n.* an interjectory word or expression, frequently profane; an exclamatory oath.

explicate /'ɛksplɪkeɪt/ *v.t.* **1.** to develop (a principle, etc.). **2.** to make plain or clear; explain; interpret. –**explication**, *n.* –**explicable**, *adj.*

explicit /ək'splɪsət, ɛk-/ *adj.* leaving nothing merely implied; clearly expressed; unequivocal.

explode /ək'sploʊd, ɛk-/ *v.i.* to expand with force and noise because of rapid chemical change or decomposition, as gunpowder, nitroglycerine, etc. –**explosion**, *n.* –**explosive**, *adj.*, *n.*

exploit¹ /'ɛksplɔɪt/ *n.* a striking or notable deed.

exploit² /ək'splɔɪt, ɛk-/ *v.t.* **1.** to turn to practical account; utilise for profit. **2.** to use selfishly for one's own ends. –**exploitation**, *n.*

explore /ək'splɔ, ɛk-/ *v.t.* **1.** to traverse or range over (a region, etc.) for the purpose of discovery. **2.** to look into closely; scrutinise; examine. –**exploration**, *n.* –**exploratory**, *adj.*

expo /'ɛkspoʊ/ *n.* a large exhibition of technology, arts and crafts, industrial products, etc.

exponent /ək'spoʊnənt, ɛk-/ *n.* **1.** someone who or that which expounds, explains, or interprets. **2.** *Maths* a symbol placed above and at the right of another symbol (the base), to denote to what power the latter is to be raised, as in x^3. –**exponential**, *adj.*

export *v.t.* /ək'spɔt, ɛk-, 'ɛkspɔt/ **1.** to send (commodities) to other countries or places for sale, exchange, etc. –*n.* /'ɛkspɔt/ **2.** the act of exporting; exportation. **3.** that which is exported; an article exported. –**exportation**, *n.*

expose /ək'spoʊz, ɛk-/ *v.t.* **1.** to lay open. **2.** to uncover. **3.** to display. **4.** to hold up to public reprehension or ridicule. **5.** *Photography* to subject (a plate, film or paper) to the action of light. –**exposure**, *n.*

exposé /ɛkspoʊ'zeɪ/ *n.* an exposing.

exposition /ɛkspə'zɪʃən/ *n.* **1.** an exhibition or show. **2.** an act of expounding, setting forth, or explaining. **3.** a written or spoken text type or form which represents a detailed statement or explanation; an explanatory treatise. **4.** *Lit.* the opening section of a text in which characters are introduced and the background of their situation presented.

expostulate /ək'spɒstʃuleɪt, ɛk-/ *v.i.* to reason earnestly.

expound /ək'spaʊnd, ɛk-/ *v.t.* **1.** to set forth or state in detail. **2.** to explain; interpret.

express /ək'sprɛs, ɛk-/ *v.t.* **1.** to put (thought) into words. **2.** to show, manifest, or reveal. **3.** to press or squeeze out. –*adj.* **4.** clearly indicated; distinctly stated. **5.** special; particular; definite. **6.** specially direct or fast, as a train, etc. –*n.* **7.** an express train, bus or coach. –**expressive**, *adj.*

expression /ək'sprɛʃən, ɛk-/ *n.* **1.** the act of expressing or setting forth in words. **2.** a particular word, phrase, or form of words. **3.** indication of feeling, spirit, character, etc.

expressway /ək'sprɛsweɪ/ *n.* a freeway.

expropriate /ɛks'proʊprieɪt/ *v.t.* to take, especially for public use.

expulsion /ək'spʌlʃən, ɛk-/ *n.* the act of driving out or expelling.

expunge /ək'spʌndʒ, ɛk-/ *v.t.* (**-punged, -punging**) to erase; obliterate. –**expunction**, *n.*

expurgate /'ɛksps3geɪt, -pɜgeɪt/ *v.t.* to amend by removing offensive or objectionable matter.

exquisite /ək'skwɪzət, ɛk-, 'ɛkskwəzət/ *adj.* **1.** of peculiar beauty or charm, or rare and appealing excellence. **2.** intense or keen, as pleasure, pain, etc.

extant /ɛk'stænt, 'ɛkstənt/ *adj.* in existence; still existing.

extempore /ək'stɛmpəri, ɛk-/ *adv.* without premeditation or preparation.

extend /ək'stɛnd, ɛk-/ *v.t.* **1.** to stretch out. **2.** to increase the length or duration of. **3.** to stretch out in various or all directions; expand. **4.** to hold forth as an offer or grant. **5.** *Commerce* to transfer (figures) from one column to another in bookkeeping, invoices, etc. –*v.i.* **6.** to be or become extended.

extension /ək'stɛnʃən, ɛk-/ *n.* **1.** the act of extending. **2.** that by which something is extended, as an addition to a house. **3.** an extra telephone connected to the same line as a main telephone. **4.** *Commerce* a written engagement on the part of a creditor, allowing a debtor further time to pay a debt.

extensive /ək'stɛnsɪv, ɛk-/ *adj.* of great extent.

extent /ək'stɛnt, ɛk-/ *n.* **1.** the space or degree to which something extends; length, area or volume. **2.** a particular extent.

extenuate /ək'stɛnjueɪt, ɛk-/ *v.t.* to represent (a fault, offence, etc.) as less serious.

exterior /ɛk'stɪəriə, ɛk-/ *adj.* **1.** outer; being on the outer side. –*n.* **2.** the outer surface or part; the outside; outward form or appearance.

exterminate /ək'stɜməneɪt, ɛk-/ *v.t.* to get rid of by destroying; destroy totally; extirpate.

external /ək'stɜnəl, ɛk-/ *adj.* **1.** of or relating to the outside or outer part; outer. **2.** relating to the outward or visible appearance or show. **3.** *Educ.* studying or studied outside the campus of a university or similar institution.

extinct /əks'tɪŋkt, ɛk-/ adj. 1. extinguished; quenched; having ceased eruption, as a volcano. 2. having come to an end; without a living representative, as a species. **–extinction,** n.

extinguish /ək'stɪŋwɪʃ, ɛk-/ v.t. 1. to put out (a fire, light, etc.). 2. to put an end to or bring to an end.

extirpate /'ɛkstɜpeɪt, -stə-/ v.t. to remove utterly; destroy totally.

extol /ək'stoʊl, ɛk-/ v.t. (-tolled, -tolling) to praise highly.

extort /ək'stɔt, ɛk-/ v.t. to obtain (money, information, etc.) by force, torture, threat, or the like. **–extortion,** n. **–extortionate,** adj. **–extortionist,** n.

extra /'ɛkstrə/ adj. 1. beyond or more than what is usual, expected, or necessary; additional. –n. 2. something extra or additional. –adv. 3. in excess of the usual or specified amount.

extra- a prefix meaning 'outside', 'beyond', 'besides'. Also, **extro-.**

extract v.t. /ək'strækt, ɛk-/ 1. to draw forth or get out by force. 2. to derive or obtain from a particular source. 3. to take or copy out (matter from a book, etc.). 4. to separate or obtain (a juice, ingredient, principle, etc.) from a mixture by pressure, distillation, treatment with solvents, or the like. –n. /'ɛkstrækt/ 5. something extracted.

extraction /ək'strækʃən, ɛk-/ n. 1. the act of extracting. 2. the state or fact of being extracted. 3. descent or lineage.

extracurricular /ɛkstrəkə'rɪkjələ/ adj. outside the regular course of study.

extradite /'ɛkstrədaɪt/ v.t. to give up (a fugitive or prisoner) to another nation, state, or authority. **–extradition,** n.

extraneous /ək'streɪniəs, ɛk-/ adj. not belonging or proper to a thing; foreign; not essential.

extraordinary /ək'strɔdənri, ɛk-/, Orig. US /-dənɛri, also for def. 3 /ɛkstrə'ɔdənri/, Orig. US /-dənɛri/ –adj. 1. beyond what is ordinary. 2. exceptional; unusual; remarkable. 3. (of a meeting) in addition to the usual scheduled meetings, usually to discuss an urgent item of business that has arisen: an extraordinary general meeting.

extrapolate /ɛk'stræpəleɪt/ v.t. to infer (what is not known) from that which is known; conjecture.

extrasensory /ɛkstrə'sɛnsəri/ adj. outside the normal sense perception.

extrasensory perception n. → ESP.

extraterrestrial /ɛkstrətə'rɛstriəl/ adj. 1. outside or originating outside the earth. –n. 2. a being not from the earth.

extravagant /ək'strævəgənt, ɛk-/ adj. 1. wasteful. 2. exceeding the bounds of reason. **–extravagance,** n.

extravaganza /əkstrævə'gænzə, ɛk-/ n. a lavish, elaborate opera or other entertainment.

extreme /ək'strim, ɛk-/ adj. 1. of a character or kind farthest removed from the ordinary or average. 2. utmost or exceedingly great in degree. 3. last or final. –n. 4. the utmost or highest degree, or a very high degree. 5. one of two things as remote or different from each other as possible. **–extremity,** n.

extreme sport n. a sport, such as bungee jumping, canyoning, etc., in which a person contends with the forces of nature, and in so doing incurs a high degree of physical risk.

extricate /'ɛkstrəkeɪt/ v.t. to disentangle; disengage; free.

extrinsic /ɛks'trɪnzɪk/ adj. extraneous.

extro- variant of **extra-.**

extrovert /'ɛkstrəvɜt/ n. a person with a lively and outgoing nature. **–extroversion,** n. **–extroverted,** adj.

extrude /ɛk'strud/ v.t. to force or press out.

exuberant /əg'zjubərənt, ɛg-/ adj. 1. lavish; effusive. 2. full of vigour and high spirits.

exude /əg'zjud, ɛg-/ v.i. to come out gradually in drops like sweat through pores or small openings; ooze out. **–exudation,** n.

exult /əg'zʌlt, ɛg-/ v.i. to show or feel a lively and triumphant joy.

-ey¹ variant of **-y¹.**

-ey² variant of **-y²,** used especially after y.

eye /aɪ/ n. (pl. **eyes**) 1. the organ of sight or vision. 2. this organ with respect to the colour of the iris. 3. the region surrounding the eye. 4. sight; vision. 5. power of seeing; appreciative or discriminating visual perception. 6. (oft. pl.) look, glance, or gaze. 7. regard, respect, view, aim, or intention. 8. (oft. pl.) estimation, or opinion. 9. mental view. 10. something resembling or suggesting the eye in appearance, shape, etc. 11. Meteorol. the central region of low pressure in a tropical hurricane, where calm conditions prevail. –v.t. (**eyed, eyeing** or **eying**) 12. to fix the eyes upon; view. 13. to observe or watch narrowly. –phr. 14. **catch someone's eye,** to attract someone's attention. 15. **keep an eye on,** to watch attentively; mind. 16. **see eye to eye,** to have the same opinion; agree.

eyeball /'aɪbɔl/ n. the ball or globe of the eye.

eyebrow /'aɪbraʊ/ n. 1. the arch or ridge forming the upper part of the orbit of the eye. 2. the fringe of hair growing upon it.

eye candy n. Colloq. 1. something that is visually appealing but not of intrinsic value. 2. a person considered as such.

eyelash /'aɪlæʃ/ n. one of the short, thick, curved hairs growing as a fringe on the edge of an eyelid.

eyelet /'aɪlət/ n. 1. a small, typically round hole, especially one finished at the edge, as in cloth or leather. 2. a metal ring for lining a small hole.

eyelid /'aɪlɪd/ n. the movable lid of skin which serves to cover and uncover the eyeball.

eyesore /'aɪsɔ/ n. something unpleasant to look at.

eyetooth /'aɪtuθ/ n. (pl. **eyeteeth** /-tiθ/) a canine tooth, especially of the upper jaw.

eyewitness /'aɪwɪtnəs/ n. someone who actually beholds some act or occurrence.

eyrie /'ɪəri, 'ɛəri/ n. 1. the nest of a bird of prey. 2. an elevated habitation or situation. Also, **aerie, aery, eyry.**

ezine /i'zin/ n. a magazine published on the internet. Also, **e-zine.**

F, f

F, f /ɛf/ the sixth letter of the English alphabet.

fable /ˈfeɪbəl/ n. a short tale to teach a moral.

fabric /ˈfæbrɪk/ n. **1.** cloth, especially woven. **2.** framework; structure.

fabricate /ˈfæbrɪkeɪt/ v.t. **1.** to construct. **2.** to assemble. **3.** to devise or invent (a legend, lie, etc.). **4.** to forge. –**fabrication**, n.

fabulous /ˈfæbjuləs/ adj. **1.** Colloq. wonderful; exceptionally pleasing. **2.** told about in fables; not true or real.

facade /fəˈsad, fæ-/ n. **1.** Archit. a face or front of a building. **2.** an appearance, especially a misleading one.

face /feɪs/ n. **1.** the front part of the head, from the forehead to the chin. **2.** a person, especially with regard to familiarity or some other quality: *it's time for some fresh faces on council*. **3.** a look or expression on the face, especially showing ridicule, disgust, etc. **4.** Colloq. boldness; impudence. **5.** outward appearance. **6.** the surface. **7.** any one of the surfaces of a solid figure. **8.** Printing the style or appearance of type; typeface. –v. (**faced**, **facing**) –v.t. **9.** to have the front towards or in the direction of. **10.** to meet face to face; confront. **11.** to cover or partly cover with a different material. –v.i. **12.** (oft. fol. by to, towards) to be turned. –phr. **13. in one's face**, Colloq. demanding attention. **14. lose face**, to suffer embarrassment and loss of prestige. **15. on the face of it**, to all appearances; seemingly.

face lift n. plastic surgery to eliminate wrinkles, etc. Also, **facelift**.

facet /ˈfæsət/ n. **1.** one of the polished surfaces of a cut gem. **2.** aspect; phase.

facetious /fəˈsiʃəs/ adj. **1.** intended to be amusing. **2.** trying to be amusing.

face value n. **1.** par value; the value stated on the face of a financial instrument or document. **2.** apparent value.

face washer n. a small piece of towelling or similar material used for washing the face or body; flannel. Also, **washer**.

facial /ˈfeɪʃəl/ adj. **1.** of the face. –n. **2.** a massage or treatment for the face.

-facient a suffix forming adjectives meaning 'that makes or causes (something)' and nouns meaning 'one that makes or causes (something)'.

facile /ˈfæsaɪl/ adj. **1.** moving, acting, working, proceeding, etc., with ease. **2.** agreeable or easily influenced. **3.** glib.

facilitate /fəˈsɪləteɪt/ v.t. to make easier or less difficult.

facility /fəˈsɪləti/ n. (pl. **-ties**) **1.** freedom from difficulty; ease. **2.** (usu. pl.) **a.** the equipment necessary to perform some particular activity: *sporting facilities; banking facilities*. **b.** bathroom and toilet: *a hotel room with facilities*.

facsimile /fækˈsɪməli/ n. **1.** an exact copy. **2.** → **fax** (defs 1–3).

fact /fækt/ n. **1.** what has really happened; truth; reality. **2.** something known to have happened. –**factual**, adj.

faction /ˈfækʃən/ n. a smaller group of people within a larger group.

factitious /fækˈtɪʃəs/ adj. artificial.

factor /ˈfæktə/ n. **1.** one of the elements that contribute to bringing about any given result. **2.** Maths one of two or more numbers, algebraic expressions, or the like, which when multiplied together produce a given product; a divisor.

factorial /fækˈtɔriəl/ n. Maths the product of an integer multiplied by all the lower integers.

factory /ˈfæktri, -təri/ n. (pl. **-ries**) a building or group of buildings, usually with equipment, where goods are manufactured.

faculty /ˈfækəlti/ n. (pl. **-ties**) **1.** one of the powers of the mind, as memory, reason, speech, etc. **2.** Educ. one of the branches of learning in a university.

fad /fæd/ n. a temporary pursuit, fashion, etc.

fade /feɪd/ v.i. **1.** to lose freshness, vigour, strength, or health. **2.** (oft. fol. by away or out) to disappear or die gradually.

faeces /ˈfisiz/ pl. n. excrement. Also, **feces**. –**faecal**, adj.

fag /fæg/ Colloq. –v.t. (**fagged**, **fagging**) **1.** (oft. fol. by out) to tire. –n. **2.** a cigarette.

faggot /ˈfægət/ n. a bundle of sticks.

Fahrenheit /ˈfærənhaɪt/ adj. denoting or relating to a thermometric scale in which the melting point of ice is 32 degrees above zero (32°F) and the boiling point of water is 212 degrees above zero (212°F).

fail /feɪl/ v.i. **1.** to come short or be wanting in action, detail, or result. **2.** to fall off; dwindle. –v.t. **3.** to neglect to perform or observe. **4.** to prove of no use or help to. **5.** to take (an examination, etc.) without passing. **6.** to declare (a person) unsuccessful in a test, course of study, etc. –**failing**, n.

failure /ˈfeɪljə/ n. **1.** an act of failing or being unsuccessful. **2.** something or someone that does not succeed.

faint /feɪnt/ adj. **1.** lacking brightness, loudness, strength, etc. **2.** feeling weak, dizzy, or exhausted. –v.i. **3.** to lose consciousness temporarily.

fair¹ /fɛə/ adj. **1.** free from bias, dishonesty, or injustice. **2.** proper under the rules. **3.** moderately good, large, or satisfactory. **4.** (of the weather) fine. **5.** free from imperfection. **6.** of a light hue; not dark. **7.** beautiful. –adv. **8.** in a fair manner.

fair² /fɛə/ n. **1.** a collection of amusements, such as merry-go-rounds, sideshows, etc., often travelling from place to place. **2.** an exhibition or display.

fair dinkum Colloq. –adj. **1.** true; genuine; dinkum. –interj. Also, **fair dink, dinkum. 2.** an assertion of truth or genuineness.

fairly /ˈfɛəli/ adv. **1.** in a fair manner; justly; impartially. **2.** moderately; tolerably. **3.** actually; completely: *the wheels fairly spun*. **4.** properly; legitimately.

fairway /ˈfɛəweɪ/ n. **1.** an unobstructed passage or way. **2.** Golf that part of the links between tees and putting greens where the grass is kept short.

fairy /ˈfeəri/ n. (pl. **-ries**) a small magical being.

fairy penguin n. a small penguin, steely blue on top and white underneath, found in the southern coastal regions of Australia and in NZ.

fairytale /ˈfeəriteɪl/ n. Also, **fairy story**. **1.** a tale, usually involving magical happenings, as told to children. **2.** a lie; fabrication. –adj. **3.** unreal.

faith /feɪθ/ n. **1.** confidence or trust in a person or thing. **2.** belief which is not based on proof. **3.** belief in the doctrines or teachings of religion. **4.** a system of religious belief.

faithful /ˈfeɪθfəl/ adj. **1.** strict or thorough in the performance of duty. **2.** full of or showing loyalty or fidelity. **3.** able to be relied upon, trusted, or believed. **4.** adhering or true to fact or an original.

fake /feɪk/ Colloq. –v.t., v.i. (**faked, faking**) **1.** to pretend. –n. **2.** something faked. **3.** someone who fakes. –adj. **4.** designed to deceive or cheat.

fake news pl. n. disinformation and hoaxes published on websites for political purposes or to drive web traffic, the incorrect information being passed along by social media.

falafel /fəˈlæfəl, -ˈlaf-/ n. (pl. **-fel** or **-fels**) fried balls of ground chickpeas and spices, often eaten with a sauce, pita bread and salad. Also, **felafel**.

falcon /ˈfælkən, ˈfɔlkən/ n. any of various birds of prey.

fall /fɔl/ v.i. (**fell, fallen, falling**) **1.** to descend from a higher to a lower place or position through loss or lack of support; drop. **2.** to come down suddenly from a standing or erect position. **3.** to become less or lower. **4.** to hang down; extend downwards. **5.** to succumb to temptation. **6.** to succumb to attack. **7.** to come to pass; occur; happen. **8.** (fol. by into) to be naturally divisible. **9.** to lose animation, as the face. **10.** to slope, as land. –n. **11.** the act of falling. **12.** (usu. pl.) a cataract or waterfall. **13.** Chiefly US autumn. –phr. **14. fall for,** Colloq. to be deceived by. **15. fall for someone** (**like a ton of bricks**), to fall in love with. **16. fall through**, to come to naught; fail; miscarry.

fallacy /ˈfæləsi/ n. (pl. **-cies**) a deceptive, misleading, or false notion, belief, etc. –**fallacious**, adj.

fallible /ˈfæləbəl/ adj. liable to be deceived or mistaken; liable to err.

falling star n. an incandescent meteor; a shooting star.

fallopian tubes /fəˈloʊpiən/ pl. n. Anat. the tubes leading from the ovaries to the uterus, for transport and fertilisation of ova. Also, **Fallopian tubes**.

fallout /ˈfɔlaʊt/ n. the descent of particles of radioactive materials released into the air by a nuclear explosion.

fallow /ˈfæloʊ/ adj. ploughed and left unseeded for a season or more; uncultivated.

false /fɔls, fɒls/ adj. **1.** not true or correct; erroneous. **2.** deceptive; used to deceive or mislead. **3.** not genuine.

falsehood /ˈfɔlshʊd/ n. a lie.

false pretences pl. n. the obtaining of money or property by the use of false representations, forged documents, or similar illegal device.

falsetto /fɔlˈsɛtoʊ/ n. (pl. **-tos**) an unnaturally or artificially high-pitched voice or register, especially in a man.

falsify /ˈfɔlsəfaɪ/ v.t. (**-fied, -fying**) **1.** to make false or incorrect, especially so as to deceive. **2.** to alter fraudulently.

falter /ˈfɔltə/ v.i. to hesitate or waver.

fame /feɪm/ n. widespread reputation.

familiar /fəˈmɪljə/ adj. **1.** commonly or generally known or seen. **2.** well-acquainted; thoroughly conversant. **3.** easy; informal; unceremonious; unconstrained. –**familiarity**, n. –**familiarise, familiarize**, v.

family /ˈfæmli, ˈfæməli/ n. (pl. **-lies**) **1.** parents and their children, whether dwelling together or not. **2.** all those persons descended from a common ancestor. **3.** Biol. the usual major subdivision of an order or suborder. **4.** any group of related things. –**familial**, adj.

family name n. **1.** the hereditary surname of a family. **2.** a given name frequently used in a family.

family room n. a room in a house which is devoted to the leisure pursuits of the members of a family, rather than entertaining visitors.

family tree n. a genealogical chart.

famine /ˈfæmən/ n. extreme and general scarcity of food.

famished /ˈfæmɪʃt/ adj. very hungry.

famous /ˈfeɪməs/ adj. celebrated in fame or public report; renowned; well-known.

fan[1] /fæn/ n. **1.** any device for causing a current of air. –v. (**fanned, fanning**) –v.t. **2.** to move or agitate (the air) with, or as with, a fan. **3.** to stir to activity with, or as with, a fan. **4.** to spread out like a fan. –v.i. **5.** (fol. by out) to spread out like a fan.

fan[2] /fæn/ n. an enthusiastic devotee or follower.

fanatic /fəˈnætɪk/ n. **1.** a person who is extremely enthusiastic about or devoted to an activity, practice, etc. **2.** a person with an extreme and unreasoning enthusiasm or zeal, especially in religious matters. –**fanatical**, adj. –**fanaticism**, n.

fanbelt /ˈfænbɛlt/ n. the belt which drives the cooling fan of a motor, especially a car motor.

fancy /ˈfænsi/ n. (pl. **-cies**) **1.** imagination. **2.** a mental image or conception. **3.** a caprice; whim; vagary. –adj. (**-cier, -ciest**) **4.** adapted to please the taste or fancy; of delicate or refined quality. –v.t. (**-cied, -cying**) **5.** to form a conception of; picture to oneself. **6.** to have a desire or appetite for: I fancy a cold drink just now. **7.** to be sexually attracted to: I think she fancies you, mate! **8.** to place one's hopes or expectations on. –**fanciful**, adj.

fanfare /ˈfænfeə/ n. a flourish or short air played on trumpets or the like.

fang /fæŋ/ n. **1.** one of the long, sharp, hollow or grooved teeth of a snake, by which venom is injected. **2.** a canine tooth.

fanlight /ˈfænlaɪt/ n. a fan-shaped or other window above a door or other opening.

fantastic /fænˈtæstɪk/ adj. **1.** odd, quaint, eccentric, or grotesque. **2.** extravagantly fanciful; irrational. **3.** Colloq. very good; fine; wonderful. Also (for defs 1 and 2), **fantastical**.

fantasy /ˈfæntəsi, -zi/ n. (pl. **-sies**) **1.** imagination, especially when unrestrained. **2.** an imaginative mental image. **3.** an imagined event that one hopes will happen in reality. **4.** *Colloq.* → **GHB. 5.** a genre of literature, film, computer games, etc., featuring magic and the supernatural, often set in an imaginary world and involving heroic quests and battles. *–adj.* **6.** of or relating to fantasy (def. 5): *fantasy fiction.* –**fantasise**, **fantasize**, *v.*

far /fa/ *adv.* **1.** (**further**, **furthest**) at or to a great distance; a long way off; to a remote point. **2.** to or at a remote time, etc. **3.** to a great degree; very much. *–adj.* (**further** *or* **farther**, **furthest** *or* **farthest**) **4.** distant. **5.** more distant of the two.

farad /ˈfærəd/ *n.* the derived SI unit of electric capacitance. *Symbol:* F

faraway /ˈfarəweɪ/ *adj.* **1.** distant; remote. **2.** abstracted or dreamy, as a look.

farce /fas/ *n.* **1.** a light, humorous play. **2.** foolish show; mockery; a ridiculous sham. –**farcical**, *adj.*

fare /feə/ *n.* **1.** the price of conveyance or passage. **2.** the person or persons who pay to be conveyed in a vehicle. **3.** food; provisions. *–v.i.* (**fared**, **faring**) **4.** to experience good or bad fortune, treatment, etc.; get on. **5.** to go; turn out; happen (used impersonally).

farewell /feəˈwɛl/ *interj.* goodbye; may you fare well.

farinaceous /færəˈneɪʃəs/ *adj.* of or relating to flour.

farm /fam/ *n.* **1.** a tract of land devoted to agriculture. **2.** a tract of land or water devoted to the raising of livestock, fish, etc.: *a chicken farm*; *an oyster farm. –v.t.* **3.** to cultivate (land). **4.** to raise (livestock, fish, etc.) on a farm. **5.** (usu. fol. by *out*) to distribute (responsibilities, duties, etc.). –**farming**, *n.*

farmer /ˈfamə/ *n.* someone who farms; someone who cultivates land or operates a farm.

farrier /ˈfæriə/ *n.* **1.** a blacksmith who shoes horses. **2.** a veterinary surgeon for horses.

fart /fat/ *Colloq. –n.* **1.** an emission of intestinal gas from the anus, especially an audible one. *–v.i.* **2.** to emit intestinal gas from the anus.

farther /ˈfaðə/ *adj.*, *adv.* comparative of **far**.

farthest /ˈfaðəst/ *adj.*, *adv.* superlative of **far**.

farthing /ˈfaðɪŋ/ *n.* a former British coin.

fascia /ˈfeɪʃə, ˈfeɪʃiə/ *for defs 1, 2 and 4*, /ˈfæʃiə/ *for def.* 3 *–n.* (*pl.* **fascias** *or* **fasciae** /-ʃii/) **1.** a band or fillet. **2.** *Archit.* **a.** a long, flat member or band. **b.** a long flat board covering the ends of rafters. **3.** *Anat.*, *Zool.* a band or sheath of connective tissue surrounding, supporting, or binding together internal organs or parts of the body. **4.** the plastic covering for the face of a mobile phone, often coloured, decorated or branded. Also, **facia**.

fascinate /ˈfæsəneɪt/ *v.t.* to attract and hold irresistibly by delightful qualities. –**fascination**, *n.*

fascism /ˈfæʃɪzəm, ˈfæsɪzəm/ *n.* (*oft. upper case*) a governmental system with strong centralised power, permitting no opposition or criticism, controlling all affairs of the nation (industrial, commercial, etc.), and emphasising an aggressive nationalism.

fashion /ˈfæʃən/ *n.* **1.** a prevailing custom or style of dress, etiquette, procedure, etc. **2.** styles of dress in general: *are you interested in fashion?* **3.** manner; way; mode. **4.** the make or form of anything. **5.** a kind; sort. *–v.t.* **6.** to give a particular shape or form to; make. –**fashionable**, *adj.*

fashion victim *n. Colloq.* (*humorous*) a person who slavishly follows the current clothing fashions.

fast¹ /fast/ *adj.* **1.** moving or able to move quickly; quick; swift; rapid. **2.** finished in comparatively little time. **3.** (of a clock) indicating a time in advance of the correct time. **4.** firmly fixed in place; not easily moved; securely attached. **5.** deep or sound, as sleep. **6.** deceptive, insincere, inconstant, or unreliable. *–adv.* **7.** tightly. **8.** soundly. **9.** quickly, swiftly, or rapidly.

fast² /fast/ *v.i.* **1.** to abstain from all food. **2.** to eat only sparingly or of certain kinds of food, especially as a religious observance. *–n.* **3.** a fasting.

-fast an adjective suffix meaning 'lasting', 'not fading', as in *colourfast*.

fasten /ˈfasən/ *v.t.* to fix securely.

fast forward *n.* the mode on a video or audio tape recorder which runs the tape forward quickly. –**fast-forward**, *v.*

fastidious /fæsˈtɪdiəs/ *adj.* **1.** hard to please; excessively critical. **2.** anxious to achieve the best result; particular.

fast-track *v.t.* **1.** to move (people, etc.) into or through a system with unusual speed. **2.** to bring (something) about with unusual speed.

fat /fæt/ *adj.* (**fatter**, **fattest**) **1.** having much flesh other than muscle; fleshy; corpulent; obese. *–n.* **2.** any of several white or yellowish substances, greasy to the touch, forming the chief part of the adipose tissue of animals and also found in plants. **3.** the richest or best part of anything. –**fatty**, *adj.*

fatal /ˈfeɪtl/ *adj.* **1.** causing death. **2.** causing destruction or ruin.

fatalism /ˈfeɪtlɪzəm/ *n.* **1.** the doctrine that all events are subject to fate. **2.** the acceptance of all things and events as inevitable. –**fatalist**, *n.* –**fatalistic**, *adj.*

fatality /fəˈtæləti, feɪ-/ *n.* (*pl.* **-ties**) **1.** a disaster resulting in death; a calamity or misfortune. **2.** someone who is killed in an accident or disaster.

fate /feɪt/ *n.* **1.** that which is to happen to a particular person or thing, or the power which predetermines this; fortune; lot; destiny. *–v.t.* (**fated**, **fating**) **2.** (*usu. in the passive*) to predetermine: *fated to win.*

fateful /ˈfeɪtfəl/ *adj.* decisively important.

father /ˈfaðə/ *n.* **1.** a male parent. **2.** any male ancestor, especially the founder of a people, family, or line. **3.** (*oft. upper case*) *Eccles.* a title of reverence. *–v.t.* **4.** to beget. –**fatherly**, *adj.* –**fatherhood**, *n.*

father-in-law /ˈfaðər-ɪn-lɔ/ *n.* (*pl.* **fathers-in-law**) the father of one's husband or wife.

fathom /ˈfæðəm/ *n.* (*pl.* **fathoms** *or, especially collectively,* **fathom**) **1.** a measure of the depth of water in the imperial system, equal to 6 feet, or nearly 2 metres in the metric system. *Symbol:* fm *–v.t.* **2.** to penetrate to or find the bottom or extent of.

fatigue /fə'tiɡ/ n. **1.** weariness from bodily or mental exertion. **2.** *Mechanics* the weakening of material subjected to stress. –*v.* (**-tigued, -tiguing**) –*v.t.* **3.** to weary with bodily or mental exertion. –*v.i.* **4.** to grow weary as a result of exertion.

fatuous /'fætʃuəs/ adj. foolish, especially in an unconscious, complacent manner; silly.

fatwa /'fætwə/ n. a religious decree issued by a Muslim scholar qualified to issue such decrees. Also, **fatwah**.

faucet /'fɔsət/ n. *Chiefly US* any device for controlling the flow of liquid from a pipe or similar by opening or closing it.

fault /fɔlt, fɒlt/ n. **1.** a defect or imperfection; a flaw; a failing. **2.** an error or mistake. **3.** culpability. **4.** *Geol., Mining* a break in the continuity of a body of rock. **5.** *Sport* an infringement of the rules which results in a warning or a penalty. –*v.t.* **6.** to find fault with, blame, or censure. –*phr.* **7. to a fault**, excessively. –**faulty**, adj.

fault line n. **1.** *Geol.* the line along which the movement in an earthquake is liable to occur. **2.** *Sociology* a difference which may become socially divisive, such as class, gender, race, etc. Also, **faultline**.

fauna /'fɔnə/ n. the animals of a given region or period.

faux /foʊ/ adj. imitation: *faux antiques; faux marble.*

faux pas /foʊ 'pa, 'foʊ pa/ n. (pl. **faux pas** /foʊ 'paz, foʊ 'pa/) a false step; a slip in manners; a breach of etiquette.

favour /'feɪvə/ n. **1.** a kind act; something done or granted out of goodwill, rather than from justice or for remuneration. **2.** a state of being approved, or held in regard. –*v.t.* **3.** to regard with favour. **4.** to have a preference for; treat with partiality. **5.** to aid or support. –*phr.* **6. in favour of**, **a.** in support of; on the side of. **b.** to the advantage of. **c.** (of a cheque, etc.) payable to. Also, **favor**. –**favourable**, adj.

favourite /'feɪvərət, -vrət/ n. **1.** a person or thing regarded with special favour or preference. **2.** *Sport* a competitor considered likely to win. –*adj.* **3.** regarded with particular favour or preference. Also, **favorite**.

favouritism /'feɪvərətɪzəm, -vrə-/ n. the favouring of one person or group over others having equal claims. Also, **favoritism**.

fawn[1] /fɔn/ n. **1.** a young deer. –*adj.* **2.** light yellowish brown.

fawn[2] /fɔn/ v.i. to seek notice or favour by servile demeanour.

fax /fæks/ n. Also, **facsimile**. **1.** a method of transmission of documents, pictures, etc., by wire or radio. **2.** a document, picture, etc., so transmitted. **3.** a machine which transmits and receives graphic data by wire or radio. –*v.t.* **4.** to send (a document, picture, etc.) by fax.

faze /feɪz/ v.t. *Colloq.* to disturb; discomfit; daunt.

fear /fɪə/ n. **1.** a painful feeling of impending danger, evil, trouble, etc.; the feeling or condition of being afraid. **2.** reverential awe, as towards a god. –*v.t.* **3.** to regard with fear; be afraid of. –**fearful**, adj. –**fearless**, adj.

fearsome /'fɪəsəm/ adj. causing fear.

feasible /'fizəbəl/ adj. **1.** capable of being done, effected, or accomplished. **2.** likely; probable. –**feasibility, feasibleness**, n. –**feasibly**, adv.

feast /fist/ n. **1.** a periodical celebration of religious or other character. **2.** a sumptuous entertainment or meal for many guests. **3.** any rich or abundant meal. –*v.i.* **4.** to have, or partake of, a feast; eat sumptuously.

feat /fit/ n. a noteworthy or extraordinary act or achievement, usually displaying boldness, skill, etc.

feather /'fɛðə/ n. **1.** one of the epidermal appendages which together constitute the plumage of birds. **2.** something like a feather. –*v.t.* **3.** to provide with feathers, as an arrow.

feature /'fitʃə/ n. **1.** any part of the face, as the nose, chin, etc. **2.** a prominent or conspicuous part or characteristic. **3.** the main film in a cinema program. **4.** a special article, column, cartoon, etc., in a newspaper or magazine. –*v.t.* **5.** to be a feature or distinctive mark of. **6.** to make a feature of, or give prominence to. –*v.i.* **7.** (sometimes fol. by *in*) to be a feature or distinctive mark: *fine details feature in her paintings.*

febri- a word element meaning 'fever'.

febrile /'fɛbraɪl, 'fi-/ adj. relating to, or marked by fevers.

feces /'fisiz/ pl. n. ⟶ **faeces**.

feckless /'fɛkləs/ adj. **1.** ineffective; feeble. **2.** spiritless; worthless.

fed /fɛd/ v. past tense and past participle of **feed**.

federal /'fɛdərəl, 'fɛdrəl/ adj. of or relating to a compact or a league, especially a league between nations or states.

federate /'fɛdəreɪt/ v.i. to unite in a federation.

federation /fɛdə'reɪʃən/ n. **1.** the formation of a political unity, with a central government, out of a number of separate states, etc., each of which retains control of its own internal affairs. **2.** the unity so formed.

fee /fi/ n. a payment for services.

feeble /'fibəl/ adj. **1.** physically weak, as from age, sickness, etc. **2.** weak intellectually or morally.

feed /fid/ v. (**fed, feeding**) –*v.t.* **1.** to give food to; supply with nourishment. **2.** to yield, or serve as, food for. **3.** to satisfy; minister to; gratify. –*v.i.* **4.** to take food; eat. –*n.* **5.** food, especially for cattle, etc.

feedback /'fidbæk/ n. the returning of a part of the output of any system as input, especially for correction or control purposes.

feel /fil/ v. (**felt, feeling**) –*v.t.* **1.** to perceive or examine by touch. **2.** to have a sensation (other than sight, hearing, taste, and smell) of. **3.** to be emotionally affected by. **4.** to experience the effects of. –*v.i.* **5.** to have perception by touch or by any nerves of sensation other than those of sight, hearing, taste, and smell. **6.** to be consciously, in emotion, opinion, etc. **7.** (fol. by *with* or *for*) to have sympathy or compassion. –*n.* **8.** a quality of an object that is perceived by feeling or touching. –*phr.* **9. feel like**, to have a desire or inclination for.

feeler /'filə/ n. *Zool.* an organ of touch, as an antenna or a tentacle.

feeling /'filɪŋ/ n. **1.** the function or the power of perceiving by touch. **2.** a consciousness or impression. **3.** an intuition or premonition. **4.** capacity for emotion; pity. **5.** (*pl.*) sensibilities; susceptibilities.

feet /fit/ *n.* plural of **foot**.

feign /fein/ *v.t., v.i.* to pretend.

feint¹ /feint/ *n.* a movement made with the object of deceiving an adversary.

feint² /feint/ *n.* the lightest weight of line used in printing ruled paper.

feisty /'faisti/ *adj.* (**-tier, -tiest**) **1.** excitable; quarrelsome. **2.** showing courage and independence; high-spirited. **–feistily**, *adv.* **–feistiness**, *n.*

felafel /fə'lʌfəl, -'læf-/ *n.* → falafel.

feldspar /'feldspa, 'felspa/ *n.* any of a group of minerals, characterised by two cleavages at nearly right angles. Also, **felspar**.

felicitate /fə'lɪsəteɪt/ *v.t.* to compliment upon a happy event; congratulate. **–felicitation**, *n.*

felicity /fə'lɪsəti/ *n.* **1.** the state of being happy, especially in a high degree. **2.** a source of happiness. **–felicitous**, *adj.*

feline /'filaɪn/ *adj.* **1.** belonging or relating to the cat family. **–n. 2.** a feline animal.

fell¹ /fel/ *v.* past tense of **fall**.

fell² /fel/ *v.t.* to cause to fall; knock, strike, or cut down.

fell³ /fel/ *adj. Archaic* fierce; cruel; dreadful.

fellow /'fɛloʊ, 'fɛlə/ *n.* **1.** *Colloq.* a man or boy. **2.** one belonging to the same class; an equal; peer. **3.** one of a pair; a mate or match. **4.** (*usu. upper case*) a member of any of certain learned or professional societies. **–adj. 5.** belonging to the same class or group. **–fellowship**, *n.*

felony /'fɛləni/ *n.* (*pl.* **-nies**) *Law* any of various indictable offences, as murder, burglary, etc., of graver character than those called misdemeanours. **–felon**, *n.* **–felonious**, *adj.*

felspar /'felspa/ *n.* → feldspar.

felt¹ /felt/ *v.* past tense and past participle of **feel**.

felt² /felt/ *n.* a non-woven fabric.

felt pen *n.* a pen with a thick nib made of felt, usually a bright colour, used for colouring in, etc. Also, **texta**.

female /'fimeɪl/ *n.* **1.** a human being of the sex which conceives and brings forth young; a woman or girl. **2.** any animal of corresponding sex. **–adj. 3.** relating to or characteristic of this sex. **4.** *Machinery* designating some part, etc., into which a corresponding part fits.

feminine /'fɛmənən/ *adj.* **1.** relating to the female sex. **2.** having qualities thought to be typical of women. **–femininity**, *n.*

feminism /'fɛmənɪzəm/ *n.* advocacy of equal rights and opportunities for women. **–feminist**, *n., adj.*

femur /'fimə/ *n.* (*pl.* **femurs** *or* **femora** /'fɛmərə/) *Anat.* the thigh bone.

fence /fɛns/ *n.* **1.** an enclosure or barrier. **2.** *Colloq.* a person who receives and disposes of stolen goods. **–v.** (**fenced, fencing**) **–v.t. 3.** to enclose by some barrier. **–v.i. 4.** to take part in fencing.

fencing /'fɛnsɪŋ/ *n.* the act, practice, or art of using a sword, foil, etc., for attack and defence.

fend /fɛnd/ *v.t.* **1.** (oft. fol. by *off*) to ward. **–v.i. 2.** (fol. by *for*) to provide.

fender /'fɛndə/ *n.* a metal guard.

feng shui /fɛŋ 'ʃweɪ, fʌŋ, 'ʃwi/ *n.* the balancing of Yin and Yang in one's physical surroundings in accordance with Chinese tradition, achieved by following rules in relation to the architecture and location of buildings, the position of objects and furniture in a room, etc. Also, **fung shui**.

fennel /'fɛnəl/ *n.* a plant bearing aromatic fruits used in cookery and medicine.

-fer a noun suffix meaning 'bearing', 'producing', 'yielding'.

feral /'fɛrəl, 'fɪərəl/ *adj.* **1.** wild, or existing in a state of nature. **2.** having reverted to the wild state, as from domestication. **3.** *Colloq.* living as or looking like a feral (def. 5). **–n. 4.** a domesticated animal which has reverted to the wild state. **5.** *Colloq.* a person who espouses environmentalism to the point of living close to nature in more or less primitive conditions and who deliberately shuns the normal code of society with regard to dress, habitat, hygiene, etc.

ferment *n.* /'fɜmɛnt/ **1.** any of various agents or substances which cause fermentation. *–v.t.* /fə'mɛnt, fɜ-/ **2.** to act upon as a ferment. *–v.i.* /fə'mɛnt, fɜ-/ **3.** to seethe with agitation or excitement.

fermentation /fɜmɛn'teɪʃən/ *n.* **1.** *Biochem.* the breakdown of complex molecules brought about by a ferment, as in the changing of grape sugar into ethyl alcohol by yeast enzymes. **2.** the act or process of undergoing such a change. **3.** agitation; excitement. **–fermentative**, *adj.*

fern /fɜn/ *n.* a leafy plant bearing spores.

ferocious /fə'roʊʃəs/ *adj.* savagely fierce; violently cruel. **–ferocity**, *n.*

-ferous an adjective suffix meaning 'bearing', 'producing', 'yielding'.

ferret /'fɛrət/ *n.* a domesticated form of the polecat, used for hunting rabbits and rats in their burrows.

ferri- a word element meaning 'iron'.

ferric /'fɛrɪk/ *adj.* of or containing iron, especially in the trivalent state.

ferro- a word element meaning 'iron'.

ferrous /'fɛrəs/ *adj.* of or containing iron, especially in the divalent state.

ferrule /'fɛrul, -rəl/ *n.* a metal ring or cap put round the end of a post, stick, handle, etc., for strength or protection.

ferry /'fɛri/ *n.* (*pl.* **-ries**) **1.** (a vessel used in) a service for transport across a body of water. *–v.t.* (**-ried, -rying**) **2.** to carry or convey over water in a boat or plane.

fertile /'fɜtaɪl/ *adj.* **1.** bearing or capable of bearing vegetation, crops, etc., abundantly, as land or soil. **2.** abundantly productive or inventive. **3.** able to produce offspring. **–fertility**, *n.*

fertilise /'fɜtəlaɪz/ *v.t.* **1.** *Biol.* to render (an egg, ovum, or female cell) capable of development by union with the male element, or sperm. **2.** to make fertile; enrich (soil, etc.) for crops, etc. Also, **fertilize**. **–fertilisation, fertilization**, *n.*

fervour /'fɜvə/ *n.* great warmth and earnestness of feeling. Also, **fervor**. **–fervent**, *adj.*

fester /'fɛstə/ *v.i.* **1.** to generate pus; suppurate. **2.** to rankle, as a feeling of resentment.

festival /ˈfɛstəvəl/ n. a public festivity, with performances of music, processions, exhibitions, etc.

festive /ˈfɛstɪv/ adj. joyful; merry.

festivity /fɛsˈtɪvəti/ n. (pl. **-ties**) a festive celebration or occasion.

festoon /fɛsˈtun/ v.t. to adorn with, or as with, a string or chain of flowers, foliage, ribbon, etc., suspended in a curve between two points.

fetch /fɛtʃ/ v.t. **1.** to go and return with, or bring to or from a particular place. **2.** to realise or bring in (a price, etc.).

fetching /ˈfɛtʃɪŋ/ adj. charming; captivating.

fete /feɪt/ n. **1.** a function to raise money for charity, church, school, etc., frequently outdoor and combining the activities of bazaar and fair. −v.t. (**feted, feting**) **2.** to give a hospitable public reception to (someone).

fetid /ˈfɛtəd, ˈfitəd/ adj. having a strong, offensive smell; stinking. Also, **foetid**.

fetish /ˈfɛtɪʃ, ˈfit-/ n. an obsession or fixation.

fetlock /ˈfɛtlɒk/ n. a part of a horse's leg bearing a tuft of hair.

fetta /ˈfɛtə/ n. a soft, ripened white cheese, originally from Greece, made originally from goats' or ewes' milk and now also from cows' milk, and cured in brine. Also, **feta**.

fetter /ˈfɛtə/ n. (usu. pl.) anything that confines or restrains.

fettle /ˈfɛtl/ phr. **in fine fettle, 1.** in good condition. **2.** in good health or spirits.

fettuccine /fɛtəˈtʃini/ n. pasta cut into long narrow strips. Also, **fettucine, fettucini**.

fetus /ˈfitəs/ n. the young of a mammal in the womb or in the egg, especially in its later stages. Also, **foetus**. −**fetal**, adj.

feud /fjud/ n. **1.** a bitter, continuous hostility, especially between two families, clans, etc. −v.i. **2.** to conduct a feud.

feudal /ˈfjudl/ adj. relating to a way of life in which ordinary people lived on and used the land of a noble person, giving military and other service in return: *a feudal lord.*

fever /ˈfivə/ n. an unusually high body temperature caused by illness.

few /fju/ adj. **1.** not many; a small number (of). −phr. **2. a few,** a small number.

fey /feɪ/ adj. aware of supernatural influences.

fiancée /fiˈɒnseɪ/ n. a woman engaged to be married. Also, **fiancee**. −**fiancé, fiance,** masc. n.

fiasco /fiˈæskoʊ/ n. (pl. **-cos**) an ignominious failure.

fiat /ˈfiæt, ˈfiət/ n. an authoritative decree, sanction, or order.

fib /fɪb/ Colloq. −n. **1.** a trivial falsehood. −v.i. (**fibbed, fibbing**) **2.** to tell a fib.

fibr- a word element meaning 'fibre'.

fibre /ˈfaɪbə/ n. **1.** a fine threadlike piece, as of cotton, jute, or asbestos. **2.** character. **3.** cellulose and other undigested material which add bulk to the contents of the large intestine. −**fibrous**, adj.

fibreglass /ˈfaɪbəɡlas/ n. (from trademark) a material consisting of extremely fine filaments of glass.

fibro /ˈfaɪbroʊ/ n. (from trademark) compressed asbestos and cement used for building materials.

fibromyalgia /faɪbroʊmaɪˈældʒə/ n. Med. a disorder of the muscles and bones, the cause of which is unknown, which has symptoms such as widespread pain and fatigue in the muscle ligaments and tendons. Abbrev.: FMS Also, **fibromyalgia syndrome**.

fibula /ˈfɪbjələ/ n. (pl. **-las** or **-lae** /-li/) Anat. the outer and thinner of the two bones of the lower leg, extending from the knee to the ankle. −**fibular**, adj.

-fic an adjective suffix meaning 'making', 'producing', 'causing'.

-fication a suffix of nouns of action or state corresponding to verbs ending in -fy.

fickle /ˈfɪkəl/ adj. likely to change, from caprice, irresolution, or instability.

fiction /ˈfɪkʃən/ n. **1.** the branch of literature comprising works of imaginative narration, especially in prose form. **2.** any story, idea, etc., which is not true. −**fictional**, adj.

fictitious /fɪkˈtɪʃəs/ adj. counterfeit; false; not genuine.

fictive /ˈfɪktɪv/ adj. invented or imagined; not real.

-fid an adjective suffix meaning 'divided'.

fiddle /ˈfɪdl/ v.i. **1.** to make aimless movements, as with the hands. **2.** to play on the fiddle. −n. **3.** a violin. **4.** Colloq. a manipulation of laws, rules etc., to execute an underhand transaction.

fiddly /ˈfɪdli/ adj. Colloq. difficult or exacting, as something small done with the hands.

fidelity /fəˈdɛləti/ n. **1.** loyalty; faithfulness. **2.** quality of sound reproduction.

fidget /ˈfɪdʒət/ v.i. to move about restlessly or impatiently; be uneasy.

fiduciary /fɪˈdjuʃəri/ adj. **1.** Law of or relating to the relation between a fiduciary and his or her principal. **2.** depending on public confidence for value or currency. −n. (pl. **-ries**) **3.** Law a trustee.

fiefdom /ˈfifdəm/ n. **1.** a feudal lord's estate. **2.** a powerful person's area of control.

field /fild/ n. **1.** a piece of open or cleared ground, especially one suitable for pasture or tillage. **2.** a piece of ground devoted to sports or contests. **3.** a sphere, or range of activity, interest, opportunity, study, etc. **4.** a place of investigation, work, etc., away from one's office, laboratory, study, etc., especially one where basic data and original material are gathered for later analysis. **5.** Computers a specified area of a record, considered as a unit of information. −v.t., v.i. **6.** Cricket, etc. to stop, or catch, and throw (the ball).

field glasses pl. n. binoculars.

fiend /find/ n. **1.** any evil spirit. **2.** a diabolically cruel or wicked person. **3.** Colloq. someone who is devoted or addicted to some game, sport, etc.

fierce /fɪəs/ adj. **1.** wild or vehement in temper, appearance, or action. **2.** violent in force, intensity, etc.

fiery /ˈfaɪəri/ adj. (**-rier, -riest**) **1.** consisting of, attended with, characterised by, or containing fire. **2.** flashing or glowing, as the eye. **3.** easily angered; irritable.

fiesta /fiˈɛstə/ n. a festival.

fife /faɪf/ n. a high-pitched flute.

fifteen /ˈfɪfˈtɪn/ n. **1.** a cardinal number, ten plus five. *–adj.* **2.** amounting to fifteen in number. **–fifteenth,** *adj., n.*

fifty /ˈfɪftɪ/ n. (pl. **-ties**) **1.** a cardinal number, ten times five. *–adj.* **2.** amounting to fifty in number. **–fiftieth,** *adj., n.*

fig /fɪg/ n. any of several trees or shrubs bearing a pear-shaped fruit.

fight /faɪt/ n. **1.** a battle or combat. **2.** any quarrel, contest, or struggle. **3.** ability or inclination to fight. *–v.* (**fought, fighting**) *–v.i.* **4.** to engage in battle or in single combat. **5.** to contend in any manner. *–v.t.* **6.** to contend with. **7.** to carry on (a battle, duel, etc.).

figment /ˈfɪgmənt/ n. a mere product of the imagination; a pure invention.

figurative /ˈfɪgjərətɪv, ˈfɪgə-/ adj. of the nature of or involving a figure of speech, especially a metaphor; metaphorical; not literal.

figure /ˈfɪgə/ n. **1.** a written symbol other than a letter. **2.** an amount or value expressed in numbers. **3.** form or shape. **4.** appearance or impression. **5.** a representation, pictorial or sculptured, of something, especially of the human form. **6.** a movement, pattern, or series of movements in skating. *–v.t.* **7.** to conclude, judge, reason, reflect. *–v.i.* **8.** to compute or work with numerical figures. **9.** to make a figure or appearance; be conspicuous. *–phr.* **10. figure out,** to solve; understand; make out. **11. go figure,** *Chiefly US* an expression used after a statement to indicate that the listener should try to make sense of it because the speaker cannot.

figurehead /ˈfɪgəhɛd/ n. a person who is nominally the head of a society, community, etc., but has no real authority or responsibility.

figure of speech n. a literary mode of expression, as a metaphor, simile, personification, antithesis, etc., in which words are used out of their literal sense.

figurine /ˈfɪgjurin/ n. a small ornamental figure of pottery, metalwork, etc.

filament /ˈfɪləmənt/ n. a very fine thread or threadlike structure.

filch /fɪltʃ/ v.t. to steal (especially something of small value).

file¹ /faɪl/ n. **1.** any device, as a cabinet or folder, in which papers, etc., are arranged or classified for convenient reference. **2.** *Computers* a collection of data with a unique name. **3.** a line of persons or things arranged one behind another. *–v.t.* (**filed, filing**) **4.** to place in a file. **5.** *Law* to bring (a suit) before a court of law.

file² /faɪl/ n. **1.** a tool for smoothing or cutting. *–v.t.* (**filed, filing**) **2.** to reduce, smooth, cut, or remove with or as with a file.

file extension n. *Computers* (in some operating systems) the final part of a filename, following a full stop or other separator and often identifying the file type.

file transfer protocol n. → FTP (def. 1).

filial /ˈfɪliəl, -jəl/ adj. relating to or befitting a son or daughter.

filibuster /ˈfɪləbʌstə/ n. the use of obstructive tactics to delay legislative action.

filigree /ˈfɪləgri/ n. ornamental work of fine wires.

fill /fɪl/ v.t. **1.** to make full; put as much as can be held into. **2.** to supply to fullness or

plentifully: *to fill a house with furniture.* **3.** to extend throughout; pervade completely. **4.** to occupy and perform the duties of (a position, post, etc.). **5.** to execute (a business order). *–v.i.* **6.** to become full. *–n.* **7.** a full supply; enough to satisfy want or desire. **8.** a mass of earth, stones, etc., used to fill a hollow, etc. *–phr.* **9. fill in, a.** to complete (a document, design, etc.) by filling blank spaces. **b.** to act as a substitute, replace. **10. fill out,** to complete the details of (a plan, form, etc.).

fillet /ˈfɪlət/ n. **1.** a narrow band. **2.** *Cookery* **a.** a boneless piece of fish or chicken. **b.** a cut of beef or pork.

filly /ˈfɪli/ n. (pl. **-lies**) a young mare.

film /fɪlm/ n. **1.** a thin layer or coating. **2.** a strip or roll of cellulose coated with a light-sensitive emulsion, used in photography. **3. a.** a series of pictures or photographs on a strip of film, which, when projected, give the illusion of movement. **b.** a story, event, etc., recorded in such a way and shown in a cinema, on television or video, etc. **c.** films in general or the art of making films. *–v.t.* **4.** to reproduce in the form of a film or films.

filmography /fɪlmˈɒgrəfi/ n. a listing of films selected on the basis of containing the work of a particular actor, director, etc., or of dealing with a particular subject. **–filmographic, filmographical,** adj.

filmy /ˈfɪlmi/ adj. (**-mier, -miest**) of the nature of, resembling, or covered with a thin layer or film.

filo pastry /ˈfiloʊ, ˈfaɪloʊ/ n. a paper-thin pastry made from flour and water, often used in Greek cookery. Also, **fillo pastry.**

filter /ˈfɪltə/ n. **1.** any device through which liquid is passed to remove suspended impurities or to recover solids. *–v.t.* **2.** to remove by the action of a filter.

filth /fɪlθ/ n. **1.** foul matter; offensive or disgusting dirt. **2.** foul condition. **3.** moral impurity, corruption, or obscenity. **4.** foul language. **–filthy,** adj.

fin /fɪn/ n. **1.** an organ of fishes and certain other aquatic animals, used for propulsion, steering, or balancing. **2.** any part, as of a mechanism, resembling a fin.

final /ˈfaɪnəl/ adj. **1.** relating to or coming at the end; last in place, order, or time. **2.** conclusive or decisive. *–n.* **3.** that which is last; that which forms an end or termination of a series. **–finalise, finalize,** v. **–finality,** n.

finale /fəˈnali, -ˈnaleɪ/ n. the concluding part of any performance, course of proceedings, etc.

finance /ˈfaɪnæns, fəˈnæns/ n. **1.** the conduct or transaction of money matters. **2.** (pl.) pecuniary resources. *–v.t.* (**-anced, -ancing**) **3.** to supply with means of payment; provide capital for. **–financial,** adj. **–financier,** n.

financial institution n. an organisation offering financial services, as a bank, building society, finance company, or credit union.

financial year n. any twelve-monthly period at the end of which a government, company, etc., balances its accounts and determines its financial condition. Also, **fiscal year.**

finch /fɪntʃ/ n. a type of small bird with a large beak for eating seeds.

find /faɪnd/ *v.t.* (**found**, **finding**) **1.** to come upon by chance; meet. **2.** to discover. **3.** to recover (something lost). **4.** *Law* to pronounce as an official act (an indictment, verdict, or judgement). –*n.* **5.** the act of finding; a discovery.

fine¹ /faɪn/ *adj.* **1.** of very high grade or quality. **2.** consisting of minute particles. **3.** very thin or slender. **4.** polished or refined. **5.** in good health; well.

fine² /faɪn/ *n.* **1.** a sum of money exacted as a penalty for an offence. –*v.t.* (**fined**, **fining**) **2.** to punish by a fine.

fine arts *pl. n.* those arts which seek expression through beautiful or significant modes, as architecture, sculpture, painting, music, and engraving.

fine motor skills *pl. n.* those physical skills required for coordinated small muscle movements, such as picking up small items between the thumb and a finger. Compare **gross motor skills**.

finery /faɪnəri/ *n.* fine or showy dress, ornaments, etc.

finesse /fəˈnɛs/ *n.* delicacy of execution.

finger /ˈfɪŋɡə/ *n.* **1.** any of the terminal members of the hand, especially one other than the thumb. **2.** something like or likened to a finger. –*v.t.* **3.** to touch with the fingers; handle; toy or meddle with.

fingerprint /ˈfɪŋɡəprɪnt/ *n.* an impression of the markings of the inner surface of the last joint of the thumb or a finger.

finicky /ˈfɪnɪki/ *adj.* fastidious; fussy.

finish /ˈfɪnɪʃ/ *v.t.* **1.** to bring to an end or to completion. **2.** to come to the end of (a course, period of time, etc.). **3.** (oft. fol. by *up* or *off*) to use up completely. **4.** to complete and perfect in detail; put the final touches on. –*v.i.* **5.** to come to an end. **6.** to complete a course, etc. –*n.* **7.** the end or conclusion; the last stage. **8.** the quality of being finished or completed with smoothness, elegance, etc. **9.** the surface coating or texture of wood, metal, etc.

finite /ˈfaɪnaɪt/ *adj.* **1.** having bounds or limits. **2.** *Gram.* (of a verb) limited by person, number, tense, etc.

fink /fɪŋk/ *n. Colloq.* a contemptible or undesirable person.

fiord /ˈfiɔd/ *n.* → **fjord**.

fir /fɜ/ *n.* a pyramidal coniferous tree.

fire /ˈfaɪə/ *n.* **1.** the active principle of burning or combustion, manifested by the evolution of light and heat. **2.** a burning mass of material, as on a hearth or in a furnace. **3.** the destructive burning of a building, town, forest, etc.; a conflagration. **4.** flashing light; luminous appearance. **5.** burning passion; ardour; enthusiasm. **6.** the discharge of firearms. –*v.* (**fired**, **firing**) –*v.t.* **7.** to set on fire. **8.** to apply heat to in a kiln, for glazing, etc. **9.** to discharge, as a gun. **10.** to project (a missile) by discharging from a gun, etc. **11.** to dismiss from a job. –*v.i.* **12.** to take fire; be kindled. **13.** to discharge a gun, etc. **14.** (of an internal-combustion engine) to cause ignition of the air-fuel mixture in the cylinder or cylinders.

fire ant *n.* a small red ant with a painful burning sting; native to South America.

firearm /ˈfaɪərɑm/ *n.* a small arms weapon from which a projectile is discharged by an explosion.

firebreak /ˈfaɪəbreɪk/ *n.* a strip of ploughed or cleared land made to check the spread of fire.

fire-engine *n.* a motor vehicle equipped for fire fighting.

firefighter /ˈfaɪəfaɪtə/ *n.* a person employed to extinguish or prevent fires.

firefly /ˈfaɪəflaɪ/ *n.* (*pl.* **-flies**) a beetle with abdominal light-producing organs.

fire front *n.* the part of a fire within which continuous flaming combustion is taking place.

fireplace /ˈfaɪəpleɪs/ *n.* that part of a chimney which opens into a room and in which fuel is burnt.

firestorm /ˈfaɪəstɔm/ *n.* **1.** an atmospheric phenomenon caused by a large fire, as after the mass bombing of a city, in which a rising column of air above the fire draws in strong winds creating an inferno. **2.** a huge and uncontrollable bushfire. Also, **fire storm**.

firewall /ˈfaɪəwɔl/ *n.* **1.** a wall made of fireproof material, designed to prevent the spread of a fire, as in buildings, aircraft, motor vehicles, etc. **2.** *Computers* a system designed for the protection of a network from unauthorised users.

fireworks /ˈfaɪəwɜks/ *pl. n.* combustible or explosive devices for producing a striking display of light, etc.

firey /ˈfaɪəri, ˈfaɪri/ *n. Colloq.* a firefighter.

firing squad *n.* a military detachment assigned to execute a condemned person by shooting.

firm¹ /fɜm/ *adj.* **1.** comparatively solid, hard, stiff or rigid. **2.** securely fixed in place. **3.** steady; not shaking or trembling.

firm² /fɜm/ *n.* **1.** a business organisation or partnership. **2.** the name or title under which associated parties transact business.

firmament /ˈfɜməmənt/ *n.* the vault of heaven; the sky.

first /fɜst/ *adj.* **1.** being before all others. –*adv.* **2.** before all others. **3.** for the first time. –*n.* **4.** that which is first in time, order, rank, etc.

first aid *n.* emergency aid or treatment given to persons suffering from accident, etc., until the services of a doctor can be obtained.

first-class *adj.* /ˈfɜst-klas/ **1.** of the highest or best class or quality. –*adv.* /fɜst-ˈklas/ **2.** by first-class conveyance.

firsthand /ˈfɜsthænd/ *adj.* direct from the original source.

first name *n.* a forename; given name.

First Nation *n.* (in Aust.) any of various Aboriginal or Torres Strait Islander peoples. Also, **First People**.

first-past-the-post *adj.* of or relating to an electoral system in which the candidate who gains the largest number of votes wins. Compare **preferential voting**.

first person *n.* See **person** (def. 3).

First World problem *n.* a problem that relates to the affluent lifestyle associated with the First World, that would never arise in the poverty-stricken circumstances of the Third World, as having to settle for plunger coffee when one's espresso machine is not functioning.

fiscal /'fɪskəl/ *adj.* **1.** of or relating to the public treasury or revenues. **2.** relating to financial matters in general.

fiscal year *n.* → **financial year**.

fish /fɪʃ/ *n.* (*pl.* **fish** *or* **fishes**) **1.** any of various cold-blooded, completely aquatic vertebrates, having gills, fins, and typically an elongated body usually covered with scales. **2.** any of various other aquatic animals. –*v.t.* **3.** (fol. by *up*, *out*, etc.) to draw as by fishing. –*v.i.* **4.** to catch or attempt to catch fish, as by angling or drawing a net. **5.** to seek to obtain something by artifice.

fisher /'fɪʃə/ *n.* someone who fishes.

fisherman /'fɪʃəmən/ *n.* (*pl.* **-men**) a man engaged in fishing. –**fisherwoman**, *n.* –**fisherperson**, *n.*

fishwife /'fɪʃwaɪf/ *n.* (*pl.* **-wives**) a coarse-mannered woman who uses abusive language.

fishy /'fɪʃi/ *adj.* (**-shier**, **-shiest**) **1.** fishlike. **2.** *Colloq.* of questionable character.

fissi- a word element meaning 'cleft'.

fissile /'fɪsaɪl/ *adj.* capable of being split or divided; cleavable.

fission /'fɪʃən/ *n.* the act of cleaving or splitting into parts.

fissure /'fɪʃə/ *n.* a narrow opening produced by cleavage or separation of parts; a cleft.

fist /fɪst/ *n.* the hand closed tightly, with the fingers doubled into the palm.

fisticuffs /'fɪstɪkʌfs/ *pl. n.* combat with the fists.

fistula /'fɪstʃələ/ *n.* (*pl.* **fistulas** *or* **fistulae** /-li/) a narrow passage or duct formed by congenital abnormality, disease or injury.

fit¹ /fɪt/ *adj.* (**fitter**, **fittest**) **1.** well adapted or suited. **2.** proper or becoming. **3.** in good health. –*v.* (**fitted**, **fitting**) –*v.t.* **4.** to be adapted to or suitable for (a purpose, object, occasion, etc.). **5.** to conform or adjust to something. **6.** (fol. by *in*, *into*, *on*, *over*, *together*, etc.) to put with precise adjustment. **7.** to provide; furnish; equip. –*v.i.* **8.** to be suitable or proper. **9.** to be of the right size or shape. –*n.* **10.** the manner in which a thing fits. –**fitness**, *n.*

fit² /fɪt/ *n.* **1.** a sudden, acute attack or manifestation of a disease. **2.** an access, spell or period of emotion or feeling, inclination, activity, idleness, etc. **3.** a convulsion. –*v.i.* (**fitted**, **fitting**) **4.** *Med.* to suffer a fit.

fitful /'fɪtfəl/ *adj.* irregularly intermittent.

fitspiration /fɪtspə'reɪʃən/ *n.* an exhortation, usually online, designed to push the reader or viewer to undertake more strenuous exercise in the pursuit of health and fitness, sometimes associated with the pursuit of an ideal body image.

five /faɪv/ *n.* **1.** a cardinal number, four plus one. –*adj.* **2.** amounting to five in number. –**fifth**, *adj.*, *n.*

fix /fɪks/ *v.t.* (**fixed**, **fixing**) **1.** to make fast, firm, or stable. **2.** to settle definitely; determine. **3.** to direct (the eyes, the attention, etc.) steadily. **4.** to put or place (responsibility, blame, etc.) on a person. **5.** to repair. **6.** to settle down. –*n.* **7.** *Colloq.* a predicament. **8.** the determining of a position, as of an aeroplane by mathematical, electronic, or other means.

fixation /fɪk'seɪʃən/ *n.* **1.** the state of being fixed. **2.** *Psychol.* an obsession.

fixed interest *n.* an interest rate which is payable on a loan and which is fixed for the entire period of the loan.

fixture /'fɪkstʃə/ *n.* **1.** something securely fixed in position. **2.** a sporting event.

fizz /fɪz/ *v.i.* **1.** to make a hissing or sputtering sound. –*n.* **2.** a hissing sound; effervescence.

fizzle /'fɪzəl/ *v.* (**-zled**, **-zling**) –*v.t.* **1.** to make a hissing or sputtering sound, especially one that dies out weakly. –*v.i.* **2.** *Colloq.* (oft. fol. by *out*) to fail ignominiously after a good start.

fjord /'fjɔd/ *n.* a long, relatively narrow arm of the sea, bordered by steep cliffs, as on the coast of Norway. Also, **fiord**.

flab /flæb/ *n. Colloq.* bodily fat. –**flabby**, *adj.*

flabbergast /'flæbəgæst, -gast/ *v.t.* to overcome with surprise and bewilderment; astound.

flaccid /'flæsəd/ *adj.* soft and drooping.

flag¹ /flæg/ *n.* **1.** a piece of cloth of varying size, shape, colour, and device, used as an ensign, standard, symbol, signal, decoration, display, etc. –*v.t.* (**flagged**, **flagging**) **2.** (sometimes fol. by *down*) to signal or warn (a person, motor vehicle, etc.) with, or as with a flag.

flag² /flæg/ *v.i.* (**flagged**, **flagging**) to fall off in vigour, energy, activity, interest, etc.

flag³ /flæg/ *n.* a flat slab of stone used for paving, etc.

flagellate /'flædʒəleɪt/ *v.t.* to whip; scourge; flog; lash.

flag fall *n.* an initial fee for hiring a taxi.

flagon /'flægən/ *n.* a large bottle.

flagrant /'fleɪgrənt/ *adj.* glaring; notorious; scandalous.

flagship /'flægʃɪp/ *n.* **1.** a ship which carries the admiral of a fleet, etc. **2.** the best example of a commercial item or enterprise. –*adj.* **3.** relating to the finest example of some commercial item or enterprise.

flail /fleɪl/ *v.t.*, *v.i.* to strike out wildly (at).

flair /flɛə/ *n.* talent; aptitude; keen perception.

flak /flæk/ *n.* anti-aircraft fire.

flake¹ /fleɪk/ *n.* **1.** a small, flat, thin piece of anything. –*v.i.* **2.** to peel off or separate in flakes. **3.** Also, **flake out**. *Colloq.* to collapse, faint, or fall asleep.

flake² /fleɪk/ *n.* the flesh of various sharks.

flambé /flom'beɪ/ *adj.* **1.** (of food) served with a flaming sauce. –*v.t.* (**-béed**, **-béing**) **2.** to dress or serve in flaming spirits.

flamboyant /flæm'bɔɪənt/ *adj.* **1.** extroverted and consciously theatrical. **2.** flaming; gorgeous. **3.** florid; ornate; showy.

flame /fleɪm/ *n.* **1.** burning gas or vapour, as from wood, etc., undergoing combustion. **2.** heat or ardour. **3.** *Colloq.* a sweetheart. –*v.i.* **4.** to burn with a flame or flames; burst into flames; blaze. **5.** *Internet* to express in emails, chat rooms, etc., one's strongly felt opinions, especially one's hostile reactions to others' opinions, with great intensity and frequency. –*v.t.* **6.** *Internet* to attack by flaming.

flamenco /flə'mɛŋkoʊ/ *n.* (*pl.* **-cos**) a type of Spanish music or dance.

flamingo /flə'mɪŋgoʊ/ *n.* (*pl.* **-gos** *or* **-goes**) an aquatic bird with very long neck and legs and pinkish plumage.

flammable /'flæməbəl/ *adj.* easily set on fire; combustible; inflammable. –**flammability**, *n.*

flan /flæn/ *n.* an open tart.

flange /flændʒ/ *n.* a projecting rim.

flank /flæŋk/ *n.* **1.** the side of an animal or a human being between the ribs and hip. **2.** the side of anything, as of a building. –*v.t.* **3.** to stand or be placed or posted at the flank or side of.

flannel /ˈflænəl/ *n.* **1.** a warm, soft fabric. **2.** → face washer.

flannelette /flænəˈlɛt/ *n.* a cotton fabric made to imitate flannel.

flannel flower *n.* an Australian plant with soft, felt-like leaves and daisy-like flowers.

flap /flæp/ *v.* (**flapped, flapping**) –*v.i.* **1.** to swing or sway about loosely, especially with noise. **2.** to move up and down, as wings. **3.** to flap the wings, or make similar movements. –*v.t.* **4.** to move (arms, wings, etc.) up and down. –*n.* **5.** a flapping motion. **6.** something broad and flexible, or flat and thin, that hangs loosely, attached at one side only. **7.** *Colloq.* a state of panic or nervous excitement.

flare /flɛə/ *v.i.* (**flared, flaring**) **1.** to burn with an unsteady, swaying flame. **2.** (oft. fol. by *up*) to blaze with a sudden burst of flame. **3.** to start up or burst out in sudden fierce activity. **4.** to spread gradually outwards as the end of a trumpet. –*n.* **5.** a sudden blaze of fire or light used as a signal or for illumination or guidance, etc. **6.** a sudden burst, as of zeal or of temper. **7.** a gradual spread outwards in form; outward curvature.

flash /flæʃ/ *n.* **1.** a sudden, transitory outburst of flame or light. **2.** a sudden, brief outburst or display of joy, wit, etc. **3.** the time occupied by a flash of light; an instant. **4.** ostentatious display. –*v.i.* **5.** to break forth into sudden flame or light, especially transiently or intermittently; to gleam. **6.** to move like a flash. –*v.t.* **7.** to emit or send forth (fire or light) in sudden flashes. –*adj.* **8.** *Colloq.* showy or ostentatious.

flashback /ˈflæʃbæk/ *n.* a representation, during the course of a novel, film, etc., of some event or scene which occurred at a previous time.

flash drive *n.* → USB drive.

flashforward /flæʃˈfɔwəd/ *n.* a representation, during the course of a film, etc., of an event or scene from some future time.

flash memory *n.* *Computers* a computer memory chip which can be erased and reprogrammed without the necessity of removing it from the computer.

flashpacker /ˈflæʃpækə/ *n.* *Colloq.* a backpacker who travels in relative luxury. –**flashpacking**, *n.*

flask /flask/ *n.* a bottle-shaped container.

flat¹ /flæt/ *adj.* (**flatter, flattest**) **1.** level, even, or without inequalities of surface, as land, etc. **2.** lying at full length, as a person. **3.** low and broad. **4.** (of feet) having little or no arch. **5.** spread out. **6.** collapsed; deflated. **7.** unqualified, downright, or positive. **8.** uninteresting, dull, or tedious. **9.** (of beer, etc.) having lost its effervescence. –*adv.* **10.** in a flat position; horizontally; levelly. **11.** *Music* below the true pitch. –*n.* **12.** something flat. **13.** a flat surface, side or part of anything. **14.** *Music* **a.** a note that is one semitone below a given note **b.** the music sign 'b' which lowers a note by a semitone when it is placed before it –*phr.*

15. flat out, *Colloq.* **a.** as fast as possible. **b.** very busy. –**flatness**, *n.* –**flatly**, *adv.*

flat² /flæt/ *n.* **1.** a suite of rooms, usually on one floor only, forming a complete residence, and usually rented. –*v.i.* (**flatted, flatting**) **2.** to live in a flat.

flatbread /ˈflætbrɛd/ *n.* any of various unleavened breads, baked in thin sheets.

flatfish /ˈflætfɪʃ/ *n.* (*pl.* **-fish** or **-fishes**) any of a group of flat-bodied fishes which swim on one side, having both eyes on the upper side.

flathead /ˈflæthɛd/ *n.* a food fish with a depressed, ridged head.

flat-leaf parsley *n.* a variety of parsley with a broad flat leaf and a stronger flavour than curly-leaf parsley. Also, **continental parsley, Italian parsley**.

flatline /ˈflætlaɪn/ *v.i.* *Colloq.* to die.

flat pack *n.* a product, especially an item of furniture, which is sold and delivered in its constituent pieces packed in a flat box for later assembly. Also, **flatpack**.

flatter /ˈflætə/ *v.t.* **1.** to seek to please by complimentary speech or attentions; compliment or praise, especially insincerely. **2.** to show to advantage. –**flattery**, *n.*

flatulent /ˈflætʃələnt/ *adj.* **1.** generating gas in the alimentary canal. **2.** pretentious; empty. –**flatulence**, *n.*

flaunt /flɔnt/ *v.i.* to parade or display oneself conspicuously or boldly.

flautist /ˈflɔtəst/ *n.* a flute player.

flavour /ˈfleɪvə/ *n.* **1.** taste, especially a characteristic taste, or a noticeable element in the taste, of a thing. **2.** the characteristic quality of a thing. Also, **flavor**.

flaw /flɔ/ *n.* a defect.

flax /flæks/ *n.* **1.** a plant cultivated for its fibre and seeds. **2.** the fibre of this plant, manufactured into linen yarn for thread or woven fabrics.

flaxen /ˈflæksən/ *adj.* **1.** made of flax. **2.** of a pale yellowish colour.

flay /fleɪ/ *v.t.* **1.** to strip off the skin or outer covering of. **2.** to criticise or reprove with scathing severity.

flea /fli/ *n.* any of numerous small, wingless, bloodsucking insects.

fleck /flɛk/ *n.* **1.** any spot or patch of colour, light, etc. –*v.t.* **2.** to mark with a fleck or flecks; spot; dapple.

fled /flɛd/ *v.* past tense and past participle of **flee**.

fledge /flɛdʒ/ *v.t.* (**fledged, fledging**) to bring up (a young bird) until it is able to fly.

fledgling /ˈflɛdʒlɪŋ/ *n.* **1.** a young bird just fledged. **2.** an inexperienced person. –*adj.* **3.** new or inexperienced. Also, **fledgeling**.

flee /fli/ *v.i.* (**fled, fleeing**) to run away (from).

fleece /flis/ *n.* **1.** the coat of wool that covers a sheep or some similar animal. –*v.t.* (**fleeced, fleecing**) **2.** to strip of money or belongings; plunder; swindle.

fleet¹ /flit/ *n.* **1.** the largest organised unit of naval ships. **2.** the vessels, aeroplanes or vehicles collectively of a single transport company or undertaking.

fleet² /flit/ *adj.* swift; rapid.

fleeting /ˈfliːtɪŋ/ *adj.* passing swiftly; transient; transitory.

flesh /fleʃ/ *n.* **1.** the soft substance of an animal body, consisting of muscle and fat. **2.** the body, especially as distinguished from the spirit or soul. **3.** the soft pulpy portion of a fruit, vegetable, etc.

flew /fluː/ *v.* past tense of **fly**[1].

flex /fleks/ *v.t.* **1.** to bend (something pliant or jointed). *–n.* **2.** a small, flexible insulated electric cable or wire.

flexible /ˈfleksəbəl/ *adj.* **1.** easily bent. **2.** adaptable. **–flexibility,** *n.*

flexiday /ˈfleksideɪ/ *n.* a day taken off from work under a flexitime scheme.

flexitime /ˈfleksitaɪm/ *n.* an arrangement of ordinary hours of work in which employees may elect to vary their commencing, ceasing, and meal-break times while still maintaining the total number of hours worked.

flick /flɪk/ *n.* **1.** a sudden light blow or stroke, as with a whip or the finger. *–v.t.* **2.** to remove with a flick. **3.** to turn on or off (a switch).

flicker /ˈflɪkə/ *v.i.* **1.** to burn unsteadily; shine with a wavering light. *–n.* **2.** an unsteady flame or light. **3.** a brief spark.

flight[1] /flaɪt/ *n.* **1.** the act, manner, or power of flying. **2.** the distance covered or the course pursued by a flying object. **3.** a journey by air, especially by aeroplane. **4.** swift movement in general. **5.** a soaring above or transcending ordinary bounds. **6.** a series of steps or stairs. **–flightless,** *adj.*

flight[2] /flaɪt/ *n.* the act of fleeing.

flight recorder *n.* a box containing recording equipment which collects information about an aircraft's flight, used especially to determine the cause of a crash; black box.

flighty /ˈflaɪti/ *adj.* (**-tier, -tiest**) often changing one's mind; frivolous.

flimsy /ˈflɪmzi/ *adj.* (**-sier, -siest**) without material strength or solidity.

flinch /flɪntʃ/ *v.i.* to draw back or shrink from what is dangerous, difficult, or unpleasant.

fling /flɪŋ/ *v.t.* (**flung, flinging**) **1.** to throw, cast, or hurl, especially with violence. **2.** to put suddenly or violently. *–n.* **3.** a spell of unrestrained indulgence of one's impulses.

flint /flɪnt/ *n.* a hard kind of stone.

flip /flɪp/ *v.t.* (**flipped, flipping**) **1.** to toss or put in motion with a snap of a finger and thumb; flick. *–n.* **2.** a smart tap or strike. **3.** a somersault.

flip-flop *n.* **1.** an electronic circuit which alternates polarity. **2.** *Computers* a simple electronic circuit that changes from one stable state to another as it receives a pulse and then back again; used in integrated circuits to build computers. **3.** → **thong** (def. 2). **4.** a complete reversal of position, policy, etc.

flippant /ˈflɪpənt/ *adj.* **1.** clever or pert in speech. **2.** characterised by a shallow or disrespectful levity.

flipper /ˈflɪpə/ *n.* **1.** a broad, flat limb, as of a seal, whale, etc., especially adapted for swimming. **2.** a device resembling in form an animal's flipper, usually made of rubber, used as an aid in swimming.

flirt /flɜːt/ *v.i.* **1.** to trifle in love. *–n.* **2.** a person given to flirting.

flit /flɪt/ *v.i.* (**flitted, flitting**) to move lightly and swiftly.

float /floʊt/ *v.i.* **1.** to rest on the surface of a liquid; be buoyant. **2.** to move or drift about free from attachment. **3.** *Commerce* to be in circulation, as an acceptance; be awaiting maturity. *–v.t.* **4.** to cause to float. **5.** to launch (a company, scheme, etc.). **6.** to allow the exchange rate of (a currency) to find its own level in a foreign exchange market. *–n.* **7.** something that floats, as a raft. **8.** a platform on wheels, bearing a display and drawn in a procession. **9.** an inflated bag to sustain a person in water; a life jacket. **10.** a quantity of money used by shopkeepers and others to provide change. **11.** the total value of cheques written but still not presented at one's bank.

flocculent /ˈflɒkjələnt/ *adj.* consisting of or containing loose woolly masses.

flock[1] /flɒk/ *n.* **1.** a number of animals of one kind now especially of sheep or goats, or of birds. *–v.i.* **2.** to gather or go in a flock, company, or crowd.

flock[2] /flɒk/ *n.* a lock or tuft of wool, hair, etc.

floe /floʊ/ *n.* a field of floating ice formed on the surface of the sea, etc.

flog /flɒg/ *v.t.* (**flogged, flogging**) **1.** to beat hard with a whip, stick, etc.; whip. **2.** *Colloq.* to sell or attempt to sell. **3.** *Colloq.* to steal.

flood /flʌd/ *n.* **1.** a great flowing or overflowing of water, especially over land not usually submerged. **2.** any great outpouring or stream. *–v.t.* **3.** to overflow in or cover with a flood; fill to overflowing. **4.** to overwhelm with an abundance of something. *–v.i.* **5.** to flow or pour in or as in a flood.

floodlight /ˈflʌdlaɪt/ *n.* **1.** an artificial light so directed or diffused as to give a comparatively uniform illumination over a given area. *–v.t.* (**-lit, -lighting**) **2.** to illuminate with or as with a floodlight.

flood-proof *v.t.* **1.** to protect from flooding, as by levees, walls, etc. *–adj.* **2.** of or relating to a location protected in such a way.

floor /flɔː/ *n.* **1.** that part of a room or the like which forms its lower enclosing surface, and upon which one walks. **2.** a storey of a building. **3.** the flat bottom of any more or less hollow place. **4.** any more or less flat extent or surface. **5.** the part of a legislative chamber, etc., where the members sit, and from which they speak. **6.** the right of one member to speak from such a place in preference to other members. **7.** the main part of a stock exchange or the like, as distinct from galleries, etc. **8.** the bottom, base, or minimum charged or paid. *–v.t.* **9.** to cover or furnish with a floor. **10.** *Colloq.* to confound or nonplus.

flop /flɒp/ *v.i.* (**flopped, flopping**) **1.** to drop or turn with a sudden bump or thud. **2.** *Colloq.* to yield or break down suddenly; fail. *–n.* **3.** *Colloq.* a failure. **–floppy,** *adj.*

floppy disk *n.* a flexible magnetically coated disk used for storing data; diskette.

flora /ˈflɔːrə/ *n.* the plants of a particular region.

floral /ˈflɔːrəl, ˈflɒrəl/ *adj.* relating to or consisting of flowers.

florid /ˈflɒrəd/ *adj.* **1.** highly coloured or ruddy, as complexion, cheeks, etc. **2.** flowery.

florin /'florən/ *n.* (formerly) a silver coin worth two shillings.

florist /'florəst/ *n.* a retailer of flowers. **–floristry**, *n.*

-florous an adjectival suffix meaning 'flower'.

floss /flos/ *n.* **1.** silky filamentous matter. **2.** → **dental floss**.

flotation /floʊ'teɪʃən/ *n.* **1.** the act or state of floating. **2.** the floating or launching of a commercial venture, a loan, etc.

flotilla /flə'tɪlə/ *n.* a number of small naval vessels.

flotsam /'flotsəm/ *n.* such part of the wreckage of a ship and its cargo as is found floating on the water. Compare **jetsam**.

flotsam and jetsam *n.* the wreckage of a ship and its cargo found either floating upon the sea or washed ashore.

flounce[1] /flaʊns/ *v.i.* to go with an impatient or angry fling of the body.

flounce[2] /flaʊns/ *n.* a gathered strip of material on a skirt, etc.

flounder[1] /'flaʊndə/ *v.i.* **1.** to struggle with stumbling or plunging movements, in or as in mud. **2.** to struggle clumsily or helplessly in embarrassment or confusion.

flounder[2] /'flaʊndə/ *n.* (*pl.* **-der** *or* **-ders**) any of numerous species of flat-bodied fishes.

flour /'flaʊə/ *n.* the finely ground meal of wheat or other grain.

flourish /'flʌrɪʃ/ *v.i.* **1.** to be in a vigorous state; thrive; prosper; be successful. *–v.t.* **2.** to brandish or wave (a sword, a stick, the limbs, etc.) about in the air. *–n.* **3.** a brandishing or waving, as of a sword, a stick, or the like. **4.** a parade or ostentatious display. **5.** a decoration or embellishment in writing. **6.** *Music* a trumpet call or fanfare.

flout /flaʊt/ *v.t.* to mock; scoff at.

flow /floʊ/ *v.i.* **1.** to move along in a stream, as a liquid; circulate, as the blood. **2.** to proceed continuously and smoothly, like a stream, as thought, speech, or verse. **3.** to fall or hang loosely at full length, as hair. *–n.* **4.** the act of flowing. **5.** movement in or as in a stream; any continuous movement, as of thought, speech, trade, etc., like that of a stream of water. **6.** the rise of the tide (opposed to *ebb*).

flow chart *n.* a diagram showing the step-by-step operation of a system. Also, **flow diagram, flow sheet**.

flowchart /'floʊtʃat/ *v.t.* to provide a flow chart for: *to flowchart the work processes.* **–flowcharting,** *n.*

flower /'flaʊə/ *n.* **1.** the blossom of a plant. **2.** the best or finest member or part of a number, body, or whole. *–v.i.* **3.** to produce flowers, or blossom, as a plant; to come to full bloom. **4.** to reach the stage of full development.

flower girl *n.* a very young girl attending a bride.

flowery /'flaʊəri/ *adj.* **1.** full of or covered with flowers. **2.** containing highly ornate language.

flown /floʊn/ *v.* past participle of **fly**[1].

flow-on *n.* the wider application of changes in wages, costs, etc., which have arisen in one part of the community.

flu /flu/ *n.* → **influenza**.

fluctuate /'flʌktʃueɪt/ *v.i.* to change continually, as by turns, from one course, position, condition, amount, etc., to another.

flue /flu/ *n.* any duct or passage for air, gases, or the like.

fluent /'fluənt/ *adj.* **1.** flowing smoothly and easily. **2.** able to speak or write readily. **3.** easy; graceful.

fluff /flʌf/ *n.* **1.** light, downy particles, as of cotton. **2.** *Colloq.* a blunder or error.

fluid /'fluəd/ *n.* a substance which is capable of flowing; a liquid or a gas.

fluke[1] /fluk/ *n.* any accidental advantage; a lucky chance. **–fluky**, *adj.*

fluke[2] /fluk/ *n.* **1.** a type of flounder (**flounder**[2]). **2.** a type of worm.

flummox /'flʌməks/ *v.t. Colloq.* to bewilder; confuse.

flung /flʌŋ/ *v.* past tense and past participle of **fling**.

flunk /flʌŋk/ *v.t., v.i. Colloq.* to fail, as a student in an examination.

flunkey /'flʌŋki/ *n.* (*pl.* **-keys**) **1.** a male servant in livery. **2.** a servile follower.

fluorescence /fluə'resəns, flɔ-/ *n.* the property possessed by certain substances of emitting light upon exposure to external radiation or bombardment by a stream of particles. **–fluorescent**, *adj.*

fluoride /'fluəraɪd, 'flu-/ *n.* an organic compound used to prevent tooth decay.

fluorine /'fluərin, 'flu-/ *n.* a pale yellow corrosive gas. *Symbol:* F

fluorspar /'fluəspa/ *n.* a common mineral, calcium fluoride.

flurry /'flʌri/ *n.* **1.** a sudden gust of wind. **2.** commotion.

flush[1] /flʌʃ/ *n.* **1.** a blush; a rosy glow. **2.** a rushing or overspreading flow, as of water. **3.** a rush of emotion; elation. **4.** waves of heat, as during fever, menopause, etc.

flush[2] /flʌʃ/ *adj.* **1.** even or level, as with a surface; in one plane. **2.** well-supplied, as with money; affluent; prosperous.

flush[3] /flʌʃ/ *v.t.* (oft. fol. by *out*) to cause (others) to reveal themselves.

flush[4] /flʌʃ/ *n. Cards* a hand consisting entirely of cards of one suit.

fluster /'flʌstə/ *v.t.* to confuse; make nervous.

flute /flut/ *n.* **1.** a musical wind instrument consisting of a tube with a series of finger holes or keys. **2.** a channel or furrow.

flutter /'flʌtə/ *v.i.* **1.** to flap or wave lightly in air, as a flag. **2.** to beat fast and irregularly, as the heart. *–n.* **3.** a fluttering movement. **4.** a state of nervous excitement or mental agitation. **5.** *Colloq.* a small wager or bet.

fluvial /'fluviəl/ *adj.* of, relating to, or produced by a river.

flux /flʌks/ *n.* a flowing or flow.

fly[1] /flaɪ/ *v.* (**flew, flown, flying**) *–v.i.* **1.** to move through the air on wings, as a bird. **2.** to be borne through the air. **3.** to move or pass swiftly; move with a start or rush. **4.** to flee. *–v.t.* **5.** to cause to fly. **6.** to avoid; flee from. *–n.* (*pl.* **flies**) **7.** a strip sewn along one edge of a garment, to aid in concealing the buttons or other fasteners. **8.** a flap forming the door of a tent. **9.** a piece of canvas extending over the ridgepole of a tent and forming an outer roof. **10.** a light tent. **11.** (*pl.*) *Theatre* the space and apparatus above the stage. **12.** *Colloq.* an attempt: *give it a fly.*

fly² /flaɪ/ *n.* (*pl.* **flies**) **1.** any of various two-winged insects, especially the common housefly. **2.** *Angling* a fishhook designed to resemble an insect.

flying fox *n.* **1.** any of various large bats having a foxlike head. **2.** a cable-operated carrier over watercourses or difficult terrain.

flying saucer *n.* any of various disc-shaped objects allegedly seen flying at high speeds and altitudes.

flyleaf /ˈflaɪliːf/ *n.* (*pl.* **-leaves** /-liːvz/) a blank leaf in the front or at the back of a book.

flystrike /ˈflaɪstraɪk/ *n.* an infestation of the flesh of a living sheep by the maggots of a blowfly. Also, **fly strike**.

foal /foʊl/ *n.* **1.** the young of a horse. *–v.i.* **2.** to bring forth a foal.

foam /foʊm/ *n.* **1.** an aggregation of minute bubbles formed on the surface of a liquid by agitation, fermentation, etc. **2.** the froth of perspiration or saliva. **3.** a light material, in either spongy or rigid form, used for packing, etc.

fob¹ /fɒb/ *n.* **1.** Also, **fob pocket.** a small pocket just below the waistline in trousers, to hold a watch, etc. **2.** a short chain for a watch.

fob² /fɒb/ *phr.* (**fobbed, fobbing**) **fob off, 1.** to rid oneself of (something) dishonestly: *she fobbed the stolen watch off on him; I fobbed the job off onto Bill.* **2.** to put off or appease (someone) dishonestly: *she asked where you were but I managed to fob her off.*

focaccia /fəˈkatʃə/ *n.* flat Italian bread which can be eaten with various fillings or toppings.

focus /ˈfoʊkəs/ *n.* (*pl.* **-cuses** or **-ci** /-kaɪ, -saɪ/) **1.** *Physics* a point at which rays of light, heat, or other radiation, meet after being refracted or reflected. **2.** clear and sharply defined condition of an image. **3.** a central point, as of attraction, attention, or activity. *–v.t.* (**-cused** or **-cussed, -cusing** or **-cussing**) **4.** to bring to a focus or into focus. **5.** to concentrate. *–focal, adj.*

fodder /ˈfɒdə/ *n.* food for livestock.

foe /foʊ/ *n.* an enemy or opponent.

fog /fɒg/ *n.* **1.** a cloudlike mass or layer of minute globules of water in the air near the earth's surface; thick mist. **2.** a state of mental confusion or obscurity.

fogey /ˈfoʊgi/ *n.* (*pl.* **-gies** or **-geys**) an old-fashioned or excessively conservative person. Also, **fogy.**

foghorn /ˈfɒghɔːn/ *n. Naut.* a horn for sounding warning signals, as to vessels, in foggy weather.

foible /ˈfɔɪbəl/ *n.* a weakness or failing of character.

foil¹ /fɔɪl/ *v.t.* to frustrate (a person, an attempt, a purpose); baffle; baulk.

foil² /fɔɪl/ *n.* **1.** a metallic substance formed into very thin sheets. **2.** anything that serves to set off another thing distinctly or to advantage by contrast.

foil³ /fɔɪl/ *n.* a flexible, thin sword with a protective knob at the end, for use in fencing.

foist /fɔɪst/ *v.t.* (fol. by *on* or *upon*) to impose dishonestly or unjustifiably.

fold¹ /foʊld/ *v.t.* **1.** to double or bend (cloth, paper, etc.) over upon itself. **2.** to cover or enclose (a person or thing) with something bent around them. **3.** (oft. fol. by *up*) to bring into a compact form, or shut, by bending and laying the parts together. **4.** *Cookery* to mix (*in*) gently. *–v.i.* **5.** to be folded or be capable of folding. **6.** to be closed or brought to an end, usually with financial loss, as a business enterprise or theatrical production. *–n.* **7.** a part that is folded; pleat; layer. **8.** a hollow place in undulating ground.

fold² /foʊld/ *n.* **1.** an enclosure for domestic animals, especially sheep. **2.** a church or congregation.

-fold a suffix denoting multiplication by or division into a certain number, as in *twofold, manifold.*

folder /ˈfoʊldə/ *n.* **1.** an outer cover, usually a folded sheet of light cardboard, for papers. **2.** Also, (*in some operating systems*), **directory.** *Computers* a defined area on a computer disk used to store files.

foliage /ˈfoʊliɪdʒ/ *n.* the leaves of a plant, collectively.

folio /ˈfoʊlioʊ/ *n.* **1.** a sheet of paper folded once to make two leaves (four pages) of a book. **2.** a paper size. **3.** *Printing* the page number of a book. **4.** *Bookkeeping* a page of an account book, or a left-hand page and a right-hand page facing each other and having the same serial number. **5.** *Law* a certain number of words, usually 72, taken as a unit for computing the length of a document. *–v.t.* **6.** to number the leaves of (a book) on one side only.

folk /foʊk/ *n.* (*pl.* **folk** or **folks**) people in general, especially the common people.

folk dance *n.* a traditional dance performed and passed down from generation to generation by the common people of a particular community, country, etc.

folklore /ˈfoʊklɔː/ *n.* the traditional beliefs, legends, customs, etc., of a people. *–folkloric, adj.*

folk music *n.* **1.** a traditional style of music, originating and handed down among the common people. **2.** music originating in America in the 1940s and 1950s, with traditional instruments and songs that concentrate on social issues. Also, **folk.**

follicle /ˈfɒlɪkəl/ *n.* **1.** *Bot.* a seed vessel. **2.** *Anat.* a small cavity, sac, or gland.

follow /ˈfɒloʊ/ *v.t.* **1.** to come after in natural sequence, order of time, etc.; succeed. **2.** to go or come after; move behind in the same direction. **3.** to accept as a guide or leader. **4.** to move forward along (a path, etc.). **5.** to watch the movements, progress, or course of. **6.** *Internet* to link oneself to (a site on a social network). *–v.i.* **7.** to come next after something else in natural sequence, order of time, etc. **8.** to result as an effect; occur as a consequence. *–phr.* **9. follow suit, a.** *Cards* to play a card of the same suit as that first played. **b.** to follow the example of another. **10. follow through,** to carry out completely. **11. follow up, a.** to pursue closely, or to a conclusion. **b.** to take further action, investigation, etc., after the elapse of an interval of time; reopen.

folly /'fɒli/ n. (pl. **-lies**) **1.** the state or quality of being foolish. **2.** a foolish action, practice, idea, etc.

foment /fə'mɛnt/ v.t. **1.** to promote the growth or development of; instigate or foster (discord, rebellion, etc.). **2.** to apply warm water or medicated liquid to (the surface of the body).

fond /fɒnd/ adj. **1.** (fol. by of) liking. **2.** loving. **3.** foolishly tender; over-affectionate; doting. **4.** cherished with strong or unreasoning affection. –**fondly**, adv.

fondle /'fɒndl/ v.t. to show fondness to, as by manner, words, or caresses.

fondue /'fɒndu, 'fɒndju/ n. a dish of melted cheese or other sauce into which pieces of bread, meat, etc., are dipped.

font[1] /fɒnt/ n. a receptacle for the water used in baptism.

font[2] /fɒnt/ n. a complete assortment of printing type of one style and size. Also, **fount**.

food /fud/ n. **1.** what is eaten, or taken into the body, for nourishment. **2.** more or less solid nourishment (as opposed to drink).

food chain n. a series of organisms dependent on each other in their feeding habits.

fool /ful/ n. **1.** someone who lacks sense; a silly or stupid person. **2.** a professional jester. **3.** someone who is made to appear a fool; someone who has been imposed on by others. –v.t. **4.** to make a fool of; impose on; trick; deceive. –v.i. **5.** to act like a fool; joke; play.

foolhardy /'fulhadi/ adj. bold without judgement.

foolish /'fulɪʃ/ adj. silly; without sense.

foolscap /'fulzkæp/ n. a printing paper size.

foot /fʊt/ n. (pl. **feet**) **1.** (in vertebrates) the terminal part of the leg, below the ankle joint, on which the body stands and moves. **2.** (in invertebrates) any part similar in position or function. **3.** a unit of length in the imperial system, equal to about 30 centimetres. **4.** any thing or part resembling a foot, as in function. **5.** the part of a stocking, etc., covering the foot. **6.** the part of anything opposite the top or head. –v.i. **7.** to walk; go on foot (always followed by indefinite it). –v.t. **8.** Colloq. to pay or settle (a bill).

footage /'fʊtɪdʒ/ n. **1.** length or extent in feet. **2. a.** material recorded on a film or video camera. **b.** a length of cinematographic film.

foot-and-mouth disease n. a contagious viral disease of cattle, etc.

football /'fʊtbɔl/ n. **1.** any game in which the kicking of a ball has a large part, as Australian Rules, Rugby Union, Rugby League, soccer, American football, etc. **2.** the ball used in such games.

foothill /'fʊthɪl/ n. a minor elevation at the base of a mountain or mountain range.

footing /'fʊtɪŋ/ n. **1.** a secure position. **2.** the basis or foundation on which anything is established. **3.** position or status assigned to a person, etc., in estimation or treatment.

footlights /'fʊtlaɪts/ pl. n. Theatre a row of lights at the front of the stage.

footloose /'fʊtlus/ adj. free to go or travel about; not confined by responsibilities, etc.

footman /'fʊtmən/ n. (pl. **-men**) a male servant, especially in livery.

footnote /'fʊtnoʊt/ n. a note or comment at the foot of a page, referring to a specific part of the text on the page.

footpath /'fʊtpaθ/ n. a path for pedestrians only, especially one at the side of a road or street.

footprint /'fʊtprɪnt/ n. **1.** a mark left by the foot. **2.** the area of the earth's surface covered by a satellite transmission. **3.** the amount of space taken up on a desk, etc., by a computer or other appliance. **4.** the area of land which is overshadowed by something else, as a building. **5.** → **ecological footprint**.

footstep /'fʊtstɛp/ n. a step or tread of the foot, or the sound produced by it.

fop /fɒp/ n. a man who is excessively concerned about his manners and appearance.

for /fɔ/, weak forms /fə, f/ prep. **1.** with the object or purpose of. **2.** intended to belong to, suit the purposes or needs of, or be used in connection with. **3.** in order to obtain. **4.** in consideration of, or in return for. **5.** appropriate or adapted to. **6.** with regard or respect to. **7.** during the continuance of. **8.** in favour of, or on the side of. **9.** in place of, or instead of. **10.** by reason of, or because of. –conj. **11.** seeing that; since. **12.** because.

for- a prefix meaning 'away', 'off', 'extremely', 'wrongly', or imparting a negative force.

forage /'fɒrɪdʒ/ n. **1.** food for horses and cattle. –v.i. (**-raged**, **-raging**) **2.** to hunt or search about.

foray /'fɒreɪ, 'fɔ-/ n. **1.** a raid for the purpose of taking plunder. **2.** a first attempt at a new activity.

forbade /fə'beɪd/ v. past tense of **forbid**. Also, **forbad** /fə'bæd/.

forbear /fɔ'bɛə/ v.t. (**-bore**, **-borne**, **-bearing**) to refrain from; desist from; cease.

forbearance /fɔ'bɛərəns/ n. **1.** patience. **2.** an abstaining from the enforcement of a right.

forbid /fə'bɪd/ v.t. (**-bade** or **-bad**, **-bidden** or **-bid**, **-bidding**) **1.** to command (a person, etc.) not to do, have, use, etc., something, or not to enter some place. **2.** to prohibit (something).

force /fɔs/ n. **1.** strength; power. **2.** Law violence offered to persons or things. **3.** (oft. pl.) a large body of armed personnel; an army. **4.** any body of persons combined for joint action. **5.** operation. **6.** Physics an influence which produces or tends to produce motion or change of motion. **7.** value; significance; meaning. –v.t. (**forced**, **forcing**) **8.** to compel to do something. **9.** to drive or propel against resistance. **10.** to break open (a door, lock, etc.).

forceps /'fɔsəps/ n. an instrument, as pincers or tongs, for seizing and holding objects, as in surgical operations.

forcible /'fɔsəbəl/ adj. **1.** effected by force. **2.** having force; producing a powerful effect; effective.

ford /fɔd/ n. **1.** a place where a river or other body of water may be crossed by wading. –v.t. **2.** to cross (a river, etc.) by a ford.

fore /fɔ/ adj. **1.** situated at or towards the front, as compared with something else. **2.** first in place, time, order, rank, etc.; forward; earlier. –n. **3.** the forepart of anything; the front. –adv. **4.** Naut. at or towards the bow of a ship.

fore- a prefix form of **before** meaning 'front' (*forehead*), 'ahead of time' (*forecast*), 'superior' (*foreman*), etc.

forearm /'fɔːrɑːm/ n. the part of the arm between the elbow and the wrist.

forebear /'fɔːbeə/ n. (*usu. pl.*) an ancestor; forefather.

forebode /fɔː'bəʊd/ v.t. to foretell or predict; portend. **–foreboding,** n.

forecast /'fɔːkɑːst/ v.t. (**-cast** *or* **-casted, -casting**) **1.** to conjecture beforehand; predict. **–**n. **2.** a prediction, especially as to the weather.

foreclose /fɔː'kləʊz/ v. (**-closed, -closing**) **–**v.t. **1.** *Law* **a.** to deprive (a mortgagor or pledgor) of the right to redeem his or her property. **b.** to take away the right to redeem (a mortgage or pledge). **–**v.i. **2.** to foreclose a mortgage or pledge.

forefather /'fɔːfɑːðə/ n. an ancestor.

forefinger /'fɔːfɪŋgə/ n. the first finger, next to the thumb; the index finger.

forego /fɔː'gəʊ/ v.t., v.i. (**forewent, foregone, foregoing**) to go before.

foreground /'fɔːgraʊnd/ n. the ground or parts situated, or represented as situated, in the front.

forehand /'fɔːhænd/ adj. *Sport* (of a stroke, etc.) made to the right side of the body (when the player is right-handed).

forehead /'fɔːrəd, 'fɔːhed/ n. the part of the face above the eyes; the brow.

foreign /'fɒrən/ adj. **1.** relating to, characteristic of, or derived from another country or nation; not native or domestic. **2.** not related to or connected with the thing under consideration. **–foreigner,** n.

foreign exchange n. **1.** the buying and selling of the money of other countries. **2.** the money of other countries.

forelock /'fɔːlɒk/ n. the lock of hair that grows from the front part of the head.

foremost /'fɔːməʊst/ adj., adv. first in place, order, rank, etc.

forename /'fɔːneɪm/ n. a name that precedes the family name or surname; a first name.

forensic /fə'rɛnzɪk, -sɪk/ adj. **1.** relating to, connected with, or used in courts of law or legal proceedings. **2.** applied to the process of collecting evidence for a legal case: *forensic linguistics*.

foreperson /'fɔːpɜːsən/ n. **1.** the supervisor of a group of workers. **2.** the spokesperson of a jury. **–foreman,** n. **–forewoman,** n.

foreplay /'fɔːpleɪ/ n. stimulation preceding sexual intercourse.

forerunner /'fɔːrʌnə/ n. **1.** a predecessor; ancestor. **2.** a herald.

foresee /fɔː'siː/ v.t. (**-saw, -seen, -seeing**) to see beforehand.

foreshore /'fɔːʃɔː/ n. **1.** the part of the shore between the ordinary high-water mark and low-water mark. **2.** the ground between the water's edge and the land cultivated or built upon.

foresight /'fɔːsaɪt/ n. care or provision for the future; provident care.

foreskin /'fɔːskɪn/ n. → **prepuce.**

forest /'fɒrəst/ n. a large tract of land covered with trees. **–forestry,** n.

forestall /fɔː'stɔːl/ v.t. to take measures concerning or deal with (a thing) in advance.

forever /far'evə/ adv. **1.** eternally; without ever ending. **2.** continually.

foreword /'fɔːwɜːd/ n. a preface or introductory statement in a book, etc.

forfeit /'fɔːfət/ n. **1.** a fine; a penalty. **2.** the act of forfeiting. **–**v.t. **3.** to lose as a forfeit. **4.** to lose, or become liable to lose, in consequence of crime, fault, breach of engagement, etc. **–forfeiture,** n.

forgave /fə'geɪv/ v. past tense of **forgive.**

forge¹ /fɔːdʒ/ n. **1.** the special fireplace, hearth, or furnace in which metal is heated before shaping. **–**v.t. (**forged, forging**) **2.** to form by heating and hammering. **3.** to form or make in any way. **4.** to imitate (a signature, etc.) fraudulently. **–forgery,** n.

forge² /fɔːdʒ/ v.i. (**forged, forging**) to move ahead slowly.

forget /fə'get/ v. (**-got, -gotten, -getting**) **–**v.t. **1.** to cease to remember; fail to remember; be unable to recall. **2.** to neglect or omit; overlook. **–**v.i. **3.** to cease or omit to think of something.

forgetful /fə'getfəl/ adj. apt to forget.

forgive /fə'gɪv/ v. (**-gave, -given, -giving**) **–**v.t. **1.** to pardon (an offence or offender); excuse. **2.** to cease to feel resentment against. **–**v.i. **3.** to pardon an offence or an offender.

forgo /fɔː'gəʊ/ v.t. (**-went, -gone, -going**) to abstain or refrain from; do without.

fork /fɔːk/ n. **1.** an instrument having two or more prongs for holding, lifting, etc. **2.** something resembling or suggesting this in form.

forlorn /fə'lɔːn/ adj. **1.** unhappy or miserable, as in feeling, condition, or appearance. **2.** desperate or hopeless.

form /fɔːm/ n. **1.** external shape or appearance considered apart from colour or material. **2.** a particular structural condition, character, or mode of being exhibited by a thing. **3.** any assemblage of similar things constituting a component of a group, especially of a zoological group. **4.** a document with blank spaces to be filled in with particulars before it is executed. **5.** procedure or conduct, as judged by social standards: *good form*; *bad form*. **6.** type or kind: *surfing as a form of sport*. **7.** condition, especially good condition, with reference to fitness for performing. **8.** a single division of a school containing pupils of about the same age or of the same level of scholastic progress. **9.** a bench or long seat. **10.** *Horseracing, etc.* the record of an entrant's past performance by which chances of success in a race are assessed. **–**v.t. **11.** to construct or frame. **12.** to make or produce; to serve to make up, or compose. **13.** to contract (habits, friendships, etc.). **14.** to give form or shape to; shape; fashion. **–**v.i. **15.** to take or assume form. **–phr. 16. have form,** *Colloq.* to have a criminal record. **17. in good form, a.** in good health. **b.** performing at one's peak: *a batsman in good form*. **c.** entertaining by being lively and amusing: *in good form at the party*.

-form a suffix meaning 'having the form of'.

formal /'fɔːməl/ adj. **1.** being in accordance with conventional requirements; conventional. **2.** marked by form or ceremony. **3.** made or done in accordance with forms ensuring validity. **–formalise**, **formalize**, *v.* **–formality**, *n.*

formaldehyde /fɔ'mældəhaɪd/ *n.* a disinfectant and preservative gas.

format /'fɔmæt/ *n.* **1.** the general physical appearance of a book, newspaper, or magazine, etc., such as the typeface, binding, quality of paper, margins, etc. **2.** the plan or style of something. **3.** *Computers* the arrangement of data for storage, display, etc.

formation /fɔ'meɪʃən/ *n.* **1.** the manner in which a thing is formed; disposition of parts. **2.** a group of things arranged according to a fixed plan.

formative /'fɔmətɪv/ *adj.* **1.** giving form or shape. **–n.** **2.** *Gram.* an affix, especially one which changes the part of speech of a word.

former /'fɔmə/ *adj.* **1.** earlier or past: *the former prime minister.* **2.** being the first one of two (opposed to *latter*). **–n.** **3. the former,** the first of two things mentioned. **–formerly**, *adv.*

formidable /'fɔmədəbəl, fɔ'mɪdəbəl/ *adj.* **1.** that is to be feared or dreaded. **2.** inspiring respect; powerful: *a formidable intellect.*

formula /'fɔmjələ/ *n.* (*pl.* **-las** or **-lae** /-li/) **1.** a set form of words. **2.** *Maths* a rule or principle, frequently expressed in algebraic symbols. **3.** a fixed and successful method of doing something. **4.** *Chem.* an expression of the constituents of a compound by symbols and figures. **5.** a recipe or prescription. **–formulaic**, *adj.*

formulate /'fɔmjəleɪt/ *v.t.* to express in precise form; state definitely or systematically.

fornication /fɔnə'keɪʃən/ *n.* voluntary sexual intercourse between unmarried persons. **–fornicate**, *v.*

forsake /fə'seɪk/ *v.t.* (**-sook**, **-saken**, **-saking**) **1.** to desert or abandon. **2.** to give up or renounce (a habit, way of life, etc.).

forswear /fɔ'sweə/ *v.t.* (**-swore**, **-sworn**, **-swearing**) **1.** to reject or renounce upon oath or with protestations. **2.** to perjure (oneself).

fort /fɔt/ *n.* a strong or fortified place.

forte /'fɔteɪ/ *n.* a strong point, as of a person; that in which one excels.

forth /fɔθ/ *adv.* **1.** forwards; onwards or outwards. **2.** out, as from concealment or inaction; into view or consideration.

forthcoming /'fɔθkʌmɪŋ/ *adj.* **1.** about to appear; approaching in time. **2.** ready or available when required or expected. **3.** ready to provide information; open.

forthright /'fɔθraɪt/ *adj.* going straight to the point; outspoken.

forthwith /fɔθ'wɪθ, -'wɪð/ *adv.* immediately; at once; without delay.

fortify /'fɔtəfaɪ/ *v.t.* (**-fied**, **-fying**) **1.** to strengthen against attack. **2.** to furnish with a means of resisting force or standing strain, wear, etc. **3.** to add alcohol to (wines, etc.) to increase the strength. **–fortification**, *n.*

fortitude /'fɔtətjud/ *n.* moral strength or endurance.

fortnight /'fɔtnaɪt/ *n.* the space of fourteen nights and days; two weeks.

fortress /'fɔtrəs/ *n.* a large fortified place.

fortuitous /fɔ'tjuətəs/ *adj.* happening or produced by chance; accidental.

fortunate /'fɔtʃənət/ *adj.* **1.** having good fortune; receiving good from uncertain or

unexpected sources; lucky. **2.** bringing or presaging good fortune.

fortune /'fɔtʃən/ *n.* **1.** position in life as determined by wealth. **2.** great wealth; ample stock of wealth. **3.** chance; luck. **4.** lot; destiny.

fortune teller *n.* someone who professes to tell people what will happen in the future. **–fortune-telling**, *adj.*, *n.*

forty /'fɔti/ *n.* (*pl.* **-ties**) **1.** a cardinal number, ten times four. **–adj.** **2.** amounting to forty in number. **–fortieth**, *adj.*, *n.*

forum /'fɔrəm/ *n.* (*pl.* **forums** or **fora** /'fɔrə/) **1.** an assembly for the discussion of questions of public interest. **2.** a vehicle for public discussion, as a publication, radio program, etc. **3.** *Internet* an online discussion website, essentially a message board devoted to a particular topic.

forward /'fɔwəd/ *adj.* **1.** directed towards a point in advance; moving ahead; onward. **2.** being in a condition of advancement; well-advanced. **3.** presumptuous, pert, or bold. **4.** situated in the front or forepart. **5.** of or relating to the future. **–n.** **6.** (in some team sports) a player placed in front of the rest of the team. **–adv.** **7. → forwards.** **–v.t.** **8.** to send forward, as mail to a new address. **9.** to advance or help onwards; hasten; promote.

forwards /'fɔwədz/ *adv.* **1.** towards or at a place, point, or time in advance; onwards; ahead. **2.** towards the front. **3.** into view or consideration. Also, **forward.**

forward slash *n.* → **slash** (def. 6).

fossick /'fɒsɪk/ *v.i.* to search unsystematically or in a small way.

fossil /'fɒsəl/ *n.* any remains, impression, or trace of an animal or plant of a former geological age, as a skeleton or a footprint.

fossil fuel *n.* the remains of organisms (or their products) embedded in the earth, with high carbon and/or hydrogen contents, which are used as fuels; especially coal, oil, and natural gas.

foster /'fɒstə/ *v.t.* **1.** to promote the growth or development of; further; encourage. **2.** to bring up or rear, as a foster-child.

foster-child /'fɒstə-tʃaɪld/ *n.* (*pl.* **-children**) a child brought up by someone who is not their natural or adoptive mother or father.

fought /fɔt/ *v.* past tense and past participle of **fight.**

foul /faʊl/ *adj.* **1.** grossly offensive to the senses; disgustingly loathsome; noisome. **2.** filthy or dirty, as places, vessels, or clothes. **3.** unfavourable or stormy, as weather. **4.** abominable, wicked, or vile, as deeds, crime, slander, etc. **5.** contrary to the rules or established usages, as of a sport or game; unfair. **6.** having many errors or marks of correction, as a printer's proof. **–adv.** **7.** in a foul manner; foully; unfairly. **–n.** **8.** that which is foul. **9.** a violation of the rules of a sport or game. **–v.t.** **10.** to make foul; defile; soil. **11.** to defile; dishonour; disgrace.

found[1] /faʊnd/ *v.* past tense and past participle of **find.**

found[2] /faʊnd/ *v.t.* **1.** to set up or establish on a firm basis or for enduring existence. **2.** to lay the lowest part of, fix, or build (a structure) on a firm base or ground. **3.** (fol. by *on* or *upon*) to base or ground.

found³ /faʊnd/ *v.t.* to melt and pour (metal, glass, etc.) into a mould. **–foundry**, *n.*

foundation /faʊnˈdeɪʃən/ *n.* **1.** that on which something is founded. **2.** the natural or prepared ground or base on which some structure rests. **3.** the act of founding, setting up, establishing, etc. **4.** an endowed institution. **5.** a cosmetic preparation, usually in the form of a cream or liquid, which is spread over the face to hide or minimise blemishes and to improve the colour and texture of the skin; make-up.

founder¹ /ˈfaʊndə/ *n.* someone who begins or establishes something.

founder² /ˈfaʊndə/ *v.i.* **1.** to fill with water and sink, as a ship. **2.** to suffer wreck, or fail utterly.

foundling /ˈfaʊndlɪŋ/ *n.* an infant found abandoned.

fount /faʊnt/ *n.* **1.** a spring of water; fountain. **2.** a source or origin.

fountain /ˈfaʊntn/ *n.* **1.** a spring or source of water. **2.** the source or origin of anything. **3.** a jet or stream of water (or other liquid) made by mechanical means to spout or rise from an opening or structure.

fountain pen *n.* a pen with a reservoir for supplying ink to the point of the nib.

four /fɔ/ *n.* **1.** a cardinal number, three plus one. *–adj.* **2.** amounting to four in number. **–fourth**, *adj., n.*

fourteen /fɔˈtin/ *n.* **1.** a cardinal number, ten plus four. *–adj.* **2.** amounting to fourteen in number. **–fourteenth**, *adj., n.*

four-wheel drive *n.* **1.** the system which connects all four wheels of a motor vehicle to the source of power. **2.** a motor vehicle which has such a system. *Abbrev.*: 4WD **–four-wheel driving**, *n.*

fowl /faʊl/ *n.* (*pl.* **fowls** *or, especially collectively,* **fowl**) **1.** → **chicken** (def. 1). **2.** any bird (now chiefly in combination).

fox /fɒks/ *n.* **1.** any of certain carnivores of the dog family. **2.** a cunning or crafty person. *–v.t.* **3.** *Colloq.* to deceive or trick.

foxtrot /ˈfɒkstrɒt/ *n.* a ballroom dance, in 4/4 time.

foyer /ˈfɔɪə, ˈfɔɪjə/ *n.* the large entrance hall in a theatre or hotel.

fracas /ˈfrækə, -kəs/ *n.* (*pl.* **fracas** /ˈfrækə, ˈfrækəz/ *or* **fracases** /ˈfrækəsəz/) an uproar.

fracking /ˈfrækɪŋ/ *n.* → **hydraulic fracturing**. Also, **fracing**, **fraccing**.

fractal /ˈfræktəl/ *n.* a geometric structure having an irregular or fragmented appearance which is of a similar character at all magnifications.

fraction /ˈfrækʃən/ *n.* **1.** *Maths* one or more parts of a unit or whole number. **2.** a part as distinct from the whole of anything. **–fractional**, *adj.*

fractious /ˈfrækʃəs/ *adj.* **1.** cross, fretful, or peevish. **2.** refractory or unruly.

fracto- a word element meaning 'broken'.

fracture /ˈfræktʃə/ *n.* **1.** a break, breach, or split, especially in a bone. *–v.* (**-tured**, **-turing**) *–v.t.* **2.** to break or crack. **3.** to cause or to suffer a fracture in (a bone, etc.). *–v.i.* **4.** to undergo fracture; break.

fragile /ˈfrædʒaɪl/ *adj.* easily broken, shattered, or damaged. **–fragility**, *n.*

fragment /ˈfrægmənt/ *n.* **1.** a part broken off or detached. **2.** an odd piece, bit, or scrap. **–fragmentary**, *adj.*

fragmentation /ˈfrægmənˈteɪʃən/ *n.* **1.** the act or process of fragmenting. **2.** *Computers* the process by which data is broken into parts and scattered throughout a disk, so as to be stored in spaces left vacant by previously deleted files. **3.** *Mil.* the fragments from an exploded bomb or hand grenade.

fragrant /ˈfreɪgrənt/ *adj.* having a pleasant odour. **–fragrance**, *n.*

frail /freɪl/ *adj.* **1.** weak; not robust; having delicate health. **2.** easily broken or destroyed; fragile. **–frailty**, *n.*

frame /freɪm/ *n.* **1.** an enclosing border or case, as for a picture. **2.** anything composed of parts fitted and joined together; a structure. **3.** the body, especially the human body, with reference to its make or build. **4.** a particular state, as of the mind. **5.** one of the successive small pictures on a strip of film. *–v.t.* (**framed**, **framing**) **6.** to form or make, as by fitting and uniting parts together; construct. **7.** *Colloq.* to incriminate unjustly by a plot, as a person.

framework /ˈfreɪmwɜk/ *n.* **1.** a structure composed of parts fitted and united together. **2.** a structure designed to support or enclose something.

franchise /ˈfræntʃaɪz/ *n.* **1.** the rights of a citizen, especially the right to vote. **2.** permission granted by a manufacturer to a distributor or retailer to sell the manufacturer's products. **–franchisor**, *n.* **–franchising**, *n.*

frangible /ˈfrændʒəbəl/ *adj.* capable of being broken; breakable.

frangipani /ˌfrændʒəˈpæni/ *n.* (*pl.* **-nis**) a shrub or tree cultivated for its strongly scented yellow and white, occasionally pink, flowers.

frank /fræŋk/ *adj.* **1.** open or unreserved in speech; candid or outspoken; sincere. **2.** undisguised; avowed; downright. *–v.t.* **3.** to mark (a letter, parcel, etc.) to indicate that postage has been paid or that it does not need to be paid.

franked /fræŋkt/ *adj.* **1.** (of a dividend) registered as having had tax paid at the corporate rate. **2. fully franked**, with tax paid at the corporate rate on the entire sum. **3. partly franked**, with tax paid at the corporate rate on some part, the rest being unfranked and therefore fully taxable.

frankfurt /ˈfræŋkfət/ *n.* a reddish pre-cooked sausage made of beef or pork, commonly re-heated by steaming or boiling; saveloy. Also, **frankfurter**, **frank**.

franking /ˈfræŋkɪŋ/ *n.* a system of giving taxation credits to shareholders in a company when the company has already paid corporate tax on the dividends being paid to the shareholders.

frantic /ˈfræntɪk/ *adj.* wild with excitement, passion, fear, pain, etc.

fraternal /frəˈtɜnəl/ *adj.* of or befitting a brother or brothers; brotherly.

fraternise /ˈfrætənaɪz/ *v.i.* to associate in a fraternal or friendly way. Also, **fraternize**.

fraternity /frəˈtɜnəti/ *n.* (*pl.* **-ties**) a body of persons associated as by ties of brotherhood.

fraud /frɔd/ n. **1.** deceit, trickery, sharp practice, or breach of confidence, by which it is sought to gain some unfair or dishonest advantage. **2.** someone who makes deceitful pretences; impostor. **–fraudulent,** adj.

fraught /frɔt/ adj. (fol. by *with*) involving; full of.

fray[1] /freɪ/ n. a fight, skirmish, or battle.

fray[2] /freɪ/ v.t. **1.** to wear (cloth, rope, etc.) to loose, ravelled threads or fibres at the edge or end; cause to unravel. **2.** to strain (a person's temper); exasperate; upset. –v.i. **3.** to become frayed, as cloth, etc.; ravel out.

frazzled /ˈfræzəld/ adj. weary; tired out.

freak /frik/ n. **1.** any abnormal product or curiously unusual object. –adj. **2.** unusual; odd; irregular.

freckle /ˈfrɛkəl/ n. a small brownish spot on the skin.

free /fri/ adj. (**freer, freest**) **1.** enjoying personal rights or liberty, as one not in slavery. **2.** not literal, as a translation. **3.** clear of obstructions or obstacles, as a corridor. **4.** available; unoccupied; not in use. **5.** exempt or released from something specified. **6.** that may be used by or open to all. **7.** unimpeded, as motion or movements; easy, firm, or swift in movement. **8.** loose, or not held fast or attached. **9.** ready in giving, liberal, or lavish. **10.** provided without, or not subject to, a charge or payment. –v.t. (**freed, freeing**) **11.** make free; set at liberty. **12.** (fol. by *from* or *of*) to disengage.

free alongside ship adj. a term of sale meaning that the seller agrees to deliver the merchandise alongside ship without extra charge to the buyer. *Abbrev.*: FAS, f.a.s.

freecycle /ˈfrisaɪkəl/ v.t. to give away (items) so that they can be used again by others. **–freecycling,** n.

freedom /ˈfridəm/ n. **1.** civil liberty, as opposed to subjection to an arbitrary or despotic government. **2.** exemption from external control, interference, regulation, etc. **3.** absence of or release from ties, obligations, etc. **4.** ease or facility of movement or action.

free enterprise n. an economic system in which private business enterprises compete with each other with a minimum amount of government control.

freefall /ˈfrifɔl/ n. **1.** the motion of any unpowered body travelling in a gravitational field. **2.** the part of a parachute descent before the parachute opens where acceleration is due to gravity. **3.** an unrestrained and uncontrollable fall in commodity prices, monetary units, etc.; a sharp reduction in prices. –adj. **4.** of or relating to a freefall. –v.i. (**-fell, -fallen, -falling**) **5.** to fall swiftly and without check, as or as if in a freefall. **6.** (of prices, monetary values, etc.) to fall sharply and unrestrainedly. Also, **free-fall. –freefalling,** n. **–freefalling,** adj.

freehand /ˈfrihænd/ adj. done by the hand without guiding instruments, measurements, or other aids.

freehold /ˈfrihoʊld/ n. **1.** a tenure of real property by which an estate of inheritance is held. **2.** an estate held by such tenure. Compare **leasehold.**

freelance /ˈfrilæns/ n. a journalist, commercial artist, editor, etc., who does not work on a regular salaried basis for any one employer.

freeload /ˈfriloʊd/ v.i. to contrive to take food, benefits, etc., without paying or contributing; cadge.

free market n. *Econ.* an economic system that allows unrestricted supply and demand, thus intended to be self-regulating in terms of prices, wages, etc., rather than government regulated. **–free marketeer,** n.

free port n. a port open under equal conditions to all traders.

free radical n. a molecule or ion with one or more unpaired electrons, which exists independently for short periods during the course of a chemical reaction, or for longer periods under special conditions.

free-range adj. of, relating to, or denoting chickens reared in an open or free environment rather than in a battery.

freesia /ˈfriʒə/ n. a type of plant cultivated for its fragrant tubular flowers.

freestyle /ˈfristaɪl/ n. **1.** Also, **crawl, Australian crawl.** a swimming stroke in prone position characterised by alternate overarm movements and a continuous up and down kick. **2.** a style of BMX or skateboard riding consisting of complicated tricks and manoeuvres. **3.** (in sports such as skiing, skating, gymnastics, etc.) a style which allows the performer scope to demonstrate skill, as by featuring unrestricted movement, aerobatics, etc.

free-to-air adj. (of television programs) supplied at no cost to the consumer.

free vote n. in a house of parliament, a vote on a motion in which members are free to vote according to their own judgement without being bound by any party policy or decision; conscience vote.

freeware /ˈfriwɛə/ n. computer software which is available online for free.

freeway /ˈfriweɪ/ n. a road designed for high-speed traffic. Also, **expressway, motorway.**

freeze /friz/ v. (**froze, frozen, freezing**) –v.i. **1.** to change from the liquid to the solid state by loss of heat. **2.** to be extremely cold. **3.** to suffer the effects of intense cold; have the sensation of extreme cold. **4.** to stop suddenly; become immobilised, as through fear, shock, etc. **5.** (of a computer) to stop producing or accepting data due to some fault. –v.t. **6.** to congeal by loss of heat. **7.** to subject (something) to a freezing temperature, as in a refrigerator. **8.** (fol. by *out*) to exclude, or compel to withdraw, from society, business, etc., as by chilling behaviour, severe competition, etc. **9.** *Finance* to render impossible of liquidation or collection. **10.** to fix (wages, prices, etc.) at a specific level, usually by government order. –n. **11.** the act of freezing. **12.** the state of being frozen. **13.** legislative action by a government to fix wages, prices, etc., at a specific level.

freeze-dry v.t. (**-dried, -drying**) to dry (food, blood, serum, etc.) while frozen and under high vacuum, as for prolonged storage. **–freeze-drying,** n.

freezer /'frizə/ n. a refrigerated cabinet held at or below 0°C.

freight /freɪt/ n. **1.** cargo or lading carried for pay either by land, water, or air. **2.** the charge made for transporting goods. –v.t. **3.** to transport as freight; send by freight.

French fries pl. n. thin strips of potatoes fried in deep fat; chips. Also, **French fried potatoes**.

French horn n. a mellow-toned brass wind instrument.

frenemy /'frɛnəmi/ n. (pl. **-mies**) a person who appears to be one's friend but acts in ways that are injurious to one's wellbeing or interests.

frenetic /frə'nɛtɪk/ adj. frantic.

frenzy /'frɛnzi/ n. (pl. **-zies**) **1.** violent mental agitation; wild excitement or enthusiasm. **2.** mental derangement; delirium. **–frenzied**, adj.

frequency /'frikwənsi/ n. (pl. **-cies**) **1.** the state or fact of being frequent; frequent occurrence. **2.** rate of recurrence. **3.** Physics the number of cycles, oscillations, or vibrations of a wave motion or oscillation in unit time. **4.** Statistics the number of items occurring in a given category.

frequent adj. /'frikwənt/ **1.** happening or occurring at short intervals. **2.** constant, habitual, or regular. –v.t. /frə'kwɛnt/ **3.** to visit often; go often to; be often in.

frequent flyer n. a person who is part of a scheme in which discounted or free flights are awarded by an airline after a certain distances have been travelled with a particular airline or group of airlines, or after a certain number of points have been collected by spending on a credit card which is linked to such a scheme.

fresco /'frɛskou/ n. (pl. **-coes** or **-cos**) **1.** the art of painting on fresh lime plaster, as on a wall or ceiling. **2.** a picture or design so painted.

fresh /frɛʃ/ adj. **1.** newly made or obtained, etc. **2.** newly arrived. **3.** new; not previously known, met with, etc.; novel. **4.** (of water) not salt. **5.** retaining the original properties unimpaired; not deteriorated. **6.** looking youthful and healthy. **7.** pure, cool, or refreshing, as air. **8.** forward or presumptuous; cheeky.

fret¹ /frɛt/ v.i. (**fretted, fretting**) to give oneself up to feelings of irritation, resentful discontent, regret, worry, or the like. **–fretful**, adj.

fret² /frɛt/ n. an interlaced, angular design; fretwork.

fret³ /frɛt/ n. any of the ridges set across the neck of a guitar, etc., which help the fingers to stop the strings at the correct points.

fretwork /'frɛtwɜk/ n. ornamental work consisting of interlacing parts.

friable /'fraɪəbəl/ adj. easily crumbled.

friand /'friɒnd/ n. a small cake containing almond meal, which is usually oval or round in shape and sometimes flavoured with fruit, chocolate chips, etc.

friar /'fraɪə/ n. a brother or member of one of certain Christian religious orders.

friction /'frɪkʃən/ n. **1.** clashing or conflict, as of opinions, etc. **2.** Mechanics, Physics the resistance to the relative motion (sliding or rolling) of surfaces of bodies in contact. **3.** the

rubbing of the surface of one body against that of another.

fridge /frɪdʒ/ n. Colloq. → **refrigerator**.

fried /fraɪd/ v. past tense and past participle of **fry¹**.

friend /frɛnd/ n. someone attached to another by feelings of affection or personal regard.

friendly /'frɛndli/ adj. (**-lier, -liest**) kind and ready to behave like a friend towards people.

fries /fraɪz/ pl. n. → **French fries**.

frieze /friz/ n. any decorative band or feature, as on a wall.

frigate /'frɪgət/ n. a general-purpose warship.

fright /fraɪt/ n. **1.** sudden and extreme fear; a sudden terror. **2.** a person or thing of shocking, grotesque, or ridiculous appearance.

frighten /'fraɪtn/ v.t. to make afraid. **–frightening**, adj. **–frightened**, adj.

frightful /'fraɪtfəl/ adj. such as to cause fright; dreadful, terrible, or alarming.

frigid /'frɪdʒəd/ adj. **1.** very cold in temperature. **2.** without warmth of feeling; without ardour or enthusiasm.

frill /frɪl/ n. a trimming consisting of a strip of material or lace, gathered at one edge and left loose at the other; a ruffle.

frillneck lizard n. a lizard of northern Australia possessing a large, ruff-like, erectable frill behind the head and using hind legs for propulsion.

fringe /frɪndʒ/ n. **1.** an ornamental bordering having projecting lengths of thread, cord, etc. **2.** anything resembling or suggesting this. **3.** hair falling over the brow. **4.** border; margin; outer part or extremity. –adj. **5.** accessory; supplementary. **6.** of or relating to a person or group living on the outskirts of social acceptability.

fringe benefit n. any remuneration received in addition to one's wage, as a car, travel allowance, etc.

fringe benefits tax n. a tax on fringe benefits. Abbrev.: FBT

frisbee /'frɪzbi/ n. (from trademark) a flat plastic disc with a rim, designed to stay aloft for some time when thrown with horizontal spin, usually as part of a game.

frisk /frɪsk/ v.i. **1.** to dance, leap, or skip. –v.t. **2.** Colloq. to search (a person) for concealed weapons, etc., by feeling their clothing. **–frisky**, adj.

frittata /frɪ'tatə/ n. an open omelette containing vegetables, cheese, seasonings, etc.

fritter¹ /'frɪtə/ v.t. (usu. fol. by away) to waste little by little.

fritter² /'frɪtə/ n. a small cake of batter, sometimes containing fruit, etc.

frivolous /'frɪvələs/ adj. **1.** not worthy of serious notice. **2.** given to trifling or levity, as persons.

frizz /frɪz/ v.t. (**frizzed, frizzing**) **1.** to make into small, crisp curls or little tufts. –n. (pl. **frizzes**) **2.** something frizzed; frizzed hair. Also, **friz**. **–frizzy**, adj.

frizzle /'frɪzəl/ v.t. **1.** to frizz. –n. **2.** a short, crisp curl.

fro /frou/ phr. **to and fro**, back and forth.

frock /frɒk/ n. a dress.

frog /frɒg/ n. **1.** a tailless amphibian having a smooth skin and long hind legs adapted for leaping. –*phr.* **2. a frog in one's throat,** a slight hoarseness due to mucus on the vocal cords.

frolic /ˈfrɒlɪk/ n. **1.** merry play; gaiety; fun. –*v.i.* (**-icked, -icking**) **2.** to play merrily; have fun.

from /frɒm/, *weak form* /frəm/ *prep.* a particle specifying a starting point, and hence used to express removal or separation in space, time, order, etc., discrimination or distinction, source or origin, instrumentality, and cause or reason.

frond /frɒnd/ n. a finely divided leaf, often large.

front /frʌnt/ n. **1.** the foremost part or surface of anything. **2.** someone or something that serves as a cover for another activity, especially an illegal or disreputable one. **3.** *Mil.* (during a war) the position of an army, etc., closest to territory held by the enemy. **4.** → **fire front**. **5.** outward impression of rank, position, or wealth. **6.** *Meteorol.* a surface of discontinuity separating two dissimilar air masses. –*adj.* **7.** of or relating to the front. –*v.t.* **8.** to have the front towards; face. –*v.i.* **9.** to have or turn the front in some specified direction. **10.** Also, **front up.** *Colloq.* to arrive; turn up. –**frontal,** *adj.*, n.

frontbencher /ˈfrʌntbentʃə, frʌntˈbentʃə/ n. a member of parliament who is a government minister or opposition spokesperson. –**frontbench,** *adj.*

frontier /frʌnˈtɪə/ n. that part of a country which borders another country; boundary; border; extreme limit.

frontispiece /ˈfrʌntəspis/ n. an illustrated leaf preceding the title page of a book.

frost /frɒst/ n. **1.** a covering of minute ice needles, formed from the atmosphere at night on cold surfaces. –*v.t.* **2.** to cover with frost. **3.** to give a frost-like surface to (glass, etc.). **4.** to ice (a cake, etc.).

frostbite /ˈfrɒstbaɪt/ n. the inflamed, sometimes gangrenous effect on a part of the body, especially the extremities, due to excessive exposure to extreme cold.

frosting /ˈfrɒstɪŋ/ n. a fluffy cake icing.

froth /frɒθ/ n. an aggregation of bubbles; foam.

frown /fraʊn/ v.i. to contract the brow as in displeasure or deep thought; scowl.

frowzy /ˈfraʊzi/ adj. (**-zier, -ziest**) dirty and untidy; slovenly.

frozen /ˈfroʊzən/ v. past participle of **freeze**.

fructose /ˈfrʌktoʊz, -toʊs, ˈfrʌk-/ n. a white, crystalline, very sweet sugar found in honey and fruit, $C_6H_{12}O_6$.

frugal /ˈfrugəl/ adj. economical in use or expenditure; prudently saving or sparing.

fruit /frut/ n. **1.** the edible part which grows from the flower of a plant. **2.** anything produced or accruing; product, result or effect; return or profit.

fruitful /ˈfrutfəl/ adj. **1.** bearing fruit abundantly, as trees or other plants. **2.** producing an abundant growth, as of fruit. **3.** productive of results; profitable: *fruitful investigations.* –**fruitfully,** *adv.* –**fruitfulness,** n.

fruition /fruˈɪʃən/ n. attainment of anything desired; attainment of maturity; realisation of results.

fruitless /ˈfrutləs/ adj. **1.** useless; unproductive; vain; without results. **2.** without fruit; barren. –**fruitlessly,** *adv.* –**fruitlessness,** n.

fruity /ˈfruti/ adj. (**-tier, -tiest**) **1.** resembling fruit; having the taste or flavour of fruit. **2.** (of wine) having body and fullness of flavour. **3.** *Colloq.* sexually suggestive; salacious.

frump /frʌmp/ n. a dowdy, drably dressed woman.

frustrate /frʌsˈtreɪt/ v.t. **1.** to make (plans, efforts, etc.) of no avail; defeat; baffle; nullify. **2.** to disappoint or thwart (a person). –**frustration,** n.

fry[1] /fraɪ/ v.t. (**fried, frying**) **1.** to cook in fat, oil, etc., usually over direct heat. –n. (pl. **fries**) **2.** a dish of something fried.

fry[2] /fraɪ/ n. (pl. **fry**) **1.** the young of fishes, or of some other animals, as frogs. –*phr.* **2. small fry, a.** unimportant or insignificant people. **b.** young children.

FTP /ef ti ˈpi/ n. **1.** file transfer protocol; a computer program which enables the transfer of data from one computer to another via a communications network. –*v.t.* (**FTPed, FTPing**) **2.** to transfer (data) by this means. Also, **ftp.**

fuchsia /ˈfjuʃə/ n. any of several plants cultivated for their handsome drooping flowers.

fuddle /ˈfʌdl/ v.t. **1.** to intoxicate. **2.** to muddle or confuse.

fuddy-duddy /ˈfʌdi-dʌdi/ n. (pl. **-duddies**) a fussy, stuffy, or old-fashioned person.

fudge[1] /fʌdʒ/ n. a kind of soft sweet composed of sugar, butter, cream, chocolate, or the like.

fudge[2] /fʌdʒ/ v. (**fudged, fudging**) –*v.t.* **1.** to put together in a makeshift, clumsy, or dishonest way; fake. –*v.i.* **2.** (in games and contests) to gain advantage improperly.

fuel /ˈfjuəl, fjul/ n. **1.** combustible matter used to maintain a fire or feed an engine, as wood, petrol, etc. **2.** something which nourishes or sustains.

fuel cell n. a continuously fed battery in which a chemical reaction is used directly to produce electricity.

-fuge a word element referring to 'flight'.

fugitive /ˈfjudʒətɪv, -əv/ n. a person who is fleeing; a runaway.

fugue /fjug/ n. *Music* a composition based upon one, two, or even more themes, which are enunciated by the several voices or parts in turn.

-ful a suffix meaning: **1.** full of or characterised by. **2.** tending or able to. **3.** as much as will fill.

fulcrum /ˈfʊlkrəm/ n. (pl. **-crums** or **-cra** /-krə/) the support, or point of rest, on which a lever turns in moving a body.

fulfil /fʊlˈfɪl/ v.t. (**-filled, -filling**) **1.** to carry out, or bring to consummation, as a prophecy, promise, etc. **2.** to satisfy (requirements, etc.)

full /fʊl/ adj. **1.** filled; containing all that can be held; filled to utmost capacity. **2.** complete; entire; maximum. **3.** (of garments, etc.) wide, ample, or having ample folds. **4.** *Colloq.* intoxicated. –*adv.* **5.** completely or entirely. **6.** exactly or directly.

fullback /ˈfʊlbæk/ n. **1.** *Aust. Rules* **a.** the central position on the back line nearest to the defenders' goal. **b.** someone who plays in this position. **2.** *Soccer, Rugby Football, Hockey,* *etc.* a player whose main purpose is to defend their own goal.

full monty /'mɒnti/ *n. Colloq.* everything; the full extent: *we don't want half the story – give us the full monty.*

full preferential voting *n.* a form of preferential voting in which voters must indicate their order of preference for all the candidates. Compare **optional preferential voting, preferential voting.**

full stop *n.* the point or character (.) used to mark the end of a sentence, indicate an abbreviation, etc.; a period. Also, **full point.**

full-time /'fʊl-taɪm/ *adj.* **1.** of, or relating to, or taking all the normal working hours (opposed to *part-time*). –*adv.* **2.** during all the normal working hours.

fully-paid /'fʊli-peɪd/ *adj.* of or relating to shares or stock on which the face value of the capital represented has been paid in full.

fulminate /'fʊlməneɪt, 'fʌl-/ *v.i.* **1.** (oft. fol. by *against*) to issue denunciations or the like. –*n.* **2.** *Chem.* an unstable explosive compound.

fulsome /'fʊlsəm/ *adj.* **1.** offensive to good taste, especially as being excessive. **2.** lavish.

fumble /'fʌmbəl/ *v.i.* to feel or grope about clumsily.

fume /fjum/ *n.* **1.** (*oft. pl.*) any smoke-like or vaporous exhalation from matter or substances. –*v.i.* (**fumed, fuming**) **2.** to show irritation or anger.

fumigate /'fjuməgeɪt/ *v.t.* to expose to smoke or fumes, as in disinfecting.

fun /fʌn/ *n.* **1.** enjoyment or amusement. –*phr.* **2. make fun of** or **poke fun at,** to ridicule.

function /'fʌŋkʃən, 'fʌŋʃən/ *n.* **1.** the kind of action or activity proper to a person, thing, or institution. **2.** any ceremonious public or social gathering or occasion. **3.** any basic computer operation. –*v.i.* **4.** to perform a function; serve; operate. **5.** to carry out normal work, activity, or processes. –**functional,** *adj.*

functionality /fʌŋkʃə'næləti/ *n.* **1.** the purpose designed to be fulfilled by a device, tool, machine, etc. **2.** *Computers* the range of functions which an application has.

function key *n.* any of a numbered set of keys (usually 10 or 12) on a computer keyboard, which can be programmed to perform certain functions.

fund /fʌnd/ *n.* **1.** a stock of money. **2.** a store or stock of something, now often of something immaterial: *a fund of knowledge.* **3.** an organisation which manages money invested for a particular purpose, such as superannuation. **4.** (*pl.*) money in hand; pecuniary resources. –*v.t.* **5.** to raise or provide money for: *to fund a child's education.*

fundamental /fʌndə'mɛntl/ *adj.* serving as, or being a component part of, a foundation or basis; basic; underlying.

funeral /'fjunrəl, 'fjunərəl/ *n.* a ceremony connected with the disposal of the body of a dead person. –**funereal,** *adj.*

fung shui /fʊŋ 'ʃweɪ, fʌŋ, 'ʃwi/ *n.* → **feng shui.**

fungus /'fʌŋgəs/ *n.* (*pl.* **fungi** /'fʌŋgi/ *or* **funguses**) a plant without chlorophyll, as mushrooms, moulds, or mildews.

funicular railway /fə'nɪkjələ/ *n.* a railway system operating up steep gradients, in which cable-linked cars or trains move up and down simultaneously.

funk¹ /fʌŋk/ *n. Colloq.* cowering fear; state of fright or terror.

funk² /fʌŋk/ *n.* an up-tempo style of soul music originating on the west coast of America and distinguished by much syncopation.

funky /'fʌŋki/ *adj.* (**-kier, -kiest**) **1.** exciting, satisfying, or pleasurable. **2.** (of an item of apparel) eye-catching for its quirkiness: *funky shoes.*

funnel /'fʌnəl/ *n.* **1.** a cone-shaped utensil with a tube at the apex, for conducting liquid, etc., through a small opening, as into a bottle. **2.** a metal chimney, especially of a ship or a steam-engine.

funnel-web *n.* either of two species of large, aggressive, venomous, eastern Australian spiders.

funny /'fʌni/ *adj.* (**-nier, -niest**) **1.** affording fun; amusing; comical. **2.** curious; strange; odd.

funny money *n. Colloq.* **1.** money which is nominally exchanged between different sections of the one organisation for bookkeeping purposes. **2.** foreign currency. **3.** counterfeit money.

fur /fɜ/ *n.* **1.** the skin of certain animals, covered with a thick, hairy coating. **2.** the cured and treated skin of some of these animals, used in garments, etc.

furbish /'fɜbɪʃ/ *v.t.* (oft. fol. by *up*) to restore to freshness of appearance or condition.

furious /'fjuriəs/ *adj.* **1.** full of fury, violent passion, or rage. **2.** intensely violent, as wind, storms, etc.

furl /fɜl/ *v.t.* to draw into a compact roll, as a sail, etc.

furlong /'fɜlɒŋ/ *n.* a unit of distance in the imperial system, just over 200 metres long. *Symbol:* **fur.**

furlough /'fɜloʊ/ *n.* leave of absence from official duty, usually for a longish period.

furnace /'fɜnəs/ *n.* **1.** a structure or apparatus in which to generate heat, as for heating buildings, smelting ores, producing steam, etc. **2.** a place of burning heat.

furnish /'fɜnɪʃ/ *v.t.* **1.** to provide or supply. **2.** to fit up (a house, room, etc.) with necessary appliances, especially furniture.

furniture /'fɜnɪtʃə/ *n.* the movable articles, as tables, chairs, beds, desks, cabinets, etc., required for use or ornament in a house, office, or the like.

furore /'fjurɔ/ *n.* a public reaction of anger, disapproval, etc. Also, **furor.**

furphy /'fɜfi/ *n.* (*pl.* **-phies**) a rumour; a false story.

furrow /'fʌroʊ/ *n.* a narrow trench or groove.

further /'fɜðə/ *adv.* (*comparative of* **far**) **1.** at or to a greater distance; farther. **2.** at or to a more advanced point; to a greater extent; farther. **3.** in addition; moreover. –*adj.* (*comparative of* **far**) **4.** more distant or remote; farther. **5.** more extended. **6.** additional; more. –*v.t.* **7.** to help forward (a work, undertaking, cause, etc.); promote; advance; forward.

furthermore /fɜðə'mɔ/ adv. moreover; in addition.

furtive /'fɜtɪv/ adj. 1. taken, done, used, etc., by stealth; secret. 2. sly; shifty.

fury /'fjuri/ n. frenzied or unrestrained violent passion, especially anger.

fuse¹ /fjuz/ n. 1. Elect. a device for preventing an excessive current from passing through a circuit. 2. a tube, ribbon, or the like, filled or saturated with combustible matter, for igniting an explosive.

fuse² /fjuz/ v.t. (**fused, fusing**) to combine or blend by melting together; melt.

fuselage /'fjuzəlaʒ, -lɪdʒ/ n. the body of an aircraft.

fusillade /'fjuzəleɪd, -lad/ n. 1. a simultaneous or continuous discharge of firearms. 2. a general discharge or outpouring of anything.

fusion /'fjuʒən/ n. 1. the act or process of fusing. 2. that which is fused. 3. Physics a thermonuclear reaction in which nuclei of light atoms join to form nuclei of heavier atoms, usually with the release of large amounts of energy.

fuss /fʌs/ n. 1. an excessive display of anxious activity; needless or useless bustle. 2. a commotion, argument, or dispute. –v.i. 3. to make a fuss; make much ado about trivial matters; to move fussily about. –**fussy**, adj.

fusty /'fʌsti/ adj. (**-tier, -tiest**) 1. mouldy; musty; having a stale smell; stuffy. 2. old-fashioned or conservative.

futile /'fjutaɪl/ adj. incapable of producing any result; ineffective; useless; not successful. –**futility**, n.

futon /'futɒn/ n. a Japanese-style bed consisting of an unsprung mattress on a support of wooden slats.

future /'fjutʃə/ n. 1. time that is to be or come hereafter. 2. what will exist or happen in future time. 3. (pl.) Stock Exchange futures contracts. –adj. 4. relating to or connected with time to come.

futures contract n. a purchase or sale of commodities for future receipt or delivery.

futuristic /fjutʃə'rɪstɪk/ adj. (of design in clothes, furniture, etc.) expressing elements of an imagined future.

fuzz /fʌz/ n. 1. loose, light, fibrous, or fluffy matter. 2. Colloq. a blur. 3. Colloq. the police. –**fuzzy**, adj.

-fy a suffix meaning: 1. to make; cause to be; render. 2. to become; be made. Also, **-ify**.

G, g

G, g /dʒiː/ n. the seventh letter of the English alphabet.

gab /gæb/ Colloq. –v.i. (**gabbed, gabbing**) **1.** to talk for the sake of talking; chatter. –n. **2.** purposeless talk; chatter. –phr. **3. the gift of the gab**, the ability to speak eloquently and persuasively.

gabble /ˈgæbəl/ v.i. to talk rapidly and unintelligibly; jabber.

gaberdine /ˈgæbəˈdin, ˈgæbədin/ n. a closely woven twill fabric of worsted, cotton or spun rayon. Also, **gabardine**.

gable /ˈgeɪbəl/ n. the triangular wall enclosed by the two slopes of a roof and a horizontal line across the eaves.

gad /gæd/ phr. **gad about** (or **around**), to move restlessly or idly from place to place, especially in search of pleasure.

gadget /ˈgædʒət/ n. a mechanical contrivance or device; any ingenious article.

gaff /gæf/ n. a strong hook with a handle, used for landing large fish.

gaffe /gæf/ n. a social blunder.

gaffer tape /ˈgæfə/ n. a strong adhesive cloth tape for electrical and other purposes.

gag[1] /gæg/ v. (**gagged, gagging**) –v.t. **1.** to stop up the mouth so as to prevent sound or speech. **2.** to restrain by force or authority from freedom of speech or expression. –v.i. **3.** to retch, as with nausea. –n. **4.** something thrust into or bound around the mouth to prevent speech.

gag[2] /gæg/ v.i. (**gagged, gagging**) **1.** to make jokes. –n. **2.** a joke.

gaga /ˈgagə/ adj. Colloq. **1.** senile. **2.** eccentric.

gage /geɪdʒ/ n., v.t. (**gaged, gaging**) → **gauge**.

gaggle /ˈgægəl/ n. a flock of geese.

gaiety /ˈgeɪəti/ n. the state of being happy or cheerful.

gain /geɪn/ v.t. **1.** to obtain; secure (something desired); acquire. **2.** to acquire as an increase or addition. **3.** to reach by effort; get to; arrive at. –v.i. **4.** to improve; make progress; advance. –n. **5.** profit; advantage. **6.** an increase or advance.

gainsay /ˈgeɪnˈseɪ/ v.t. (**-said, -saying**) **1.** to deny. **2.** to speak or act against.

gait /geɪt/ n. **1.** a particular manner of walking. **2.** the pace of a horse.

gaiter /ˈgeɪtə/ n. a covering for the ankle and instep.

gala /ˈgalə/ n. a festive occasion.

galah /gəˈla/ n. **1.** a common small cockatoo, pale grey above and deep pink below. **2.** Colloq. a fool.

galaxy /ˈgæləksi/ n. (pl. **-xies**) Astron. any large system of stars held together by mutual gravitation. –**galactic**, adj.

gale /geɪl/ n. a strong wind.

gall /gɔl/ n. **1.** bile. **2.** something very bitter or severe. **3.** bitterness of spirit. **4.** impudence; effrontery.

gallant /ˈgælənt, gəˈlænt/ adj. **1.** brave and dashing. **2.** (of a man) noticeably polite and attentive to women. **3.** generous or sporting.

gall bladder n. a vesicle attached to the liver containing bile.

galleon /ˈgæliən, ˈgæljən/ n. a kind of large sailing vessel.

gallery /ˈgæləri/ n. (pl. **-ries**) **1.** a long, narrow, covered walk, open at one or both sides. **2.** a platform projecting from the interior walls of a church, theatre, etc., to provide seats or room for a part of the audience. **3.** any audience. **4.** a room, series of rooms, or building devoted to the exhibition of works of art.

galley /ˈgæli/ n. (pl. **-leys**) **1.** an early seagoing vessel propelled by oars or by oars and sails. **2.** the kitchen of a ship or aeroplane.

gallinaceous /gæləˈneɪʃəs/ adj. relating to or resembling the domestic fowls.

gallivant /ˈgælɪvænt/ v.i. to go from place to place in a rollicking, frivolous or flirtatious manner. Also, **galavant**.

gallon /ˈgælən/ n. a measure of liquid in the imperial system, equal to about 4.5 litres.

gallop /ˈgæləp/ v.i. **1.** to ride a horse at a gallop; ride at full speed. **2.** to go fast, race, or hurry.

gallows /ˈgæloʊz/ n. (pl. **-lows** or **-lowses**) a wooden frame used for the hanging of condemned persons.

gallstone /ˈgɔlstoʊn/ n. a stone formed in the bile ducts or gall bladder.

gallup poll /ˈgæləp/ n. the questioning of a representative cross-section of the population in order to assess public opinion, as of voting intentions.

galore /gəˈlɔ/ adj. (used only after nouns) in abundance.

galoshes /gəˈlɒʃəz/ pl. n. a pair of rubber coverings for the shoes, for use in wet weather.

galvanise /ˈgælvənaɪz/ v.t. **1.** to startle into sudden activity. **2.** to coat (iron or steel) with zinc. Also, **galvanize**.

gambit /ˈgæmbət/ n. an opening in chess, in which the player seeks by sacrificing a pawn or other piece to obtain some advantage.

gamble /ˈgæmbəl/ v.i. **1.** to play at any game of chance for stakes. **2.** to act on favourable hopes or assessment. –n. **3.** any matter or thing involving risk or uncertainty.

gambol /ˈgæmbəl/ v.i. (**-bolled** or, Chiefly US, **-boled, -bolling** or, Chiefly US, **-boling**) to frolic.

game /geɪm/ n. **1.** an amusement or pastime. **2.** a contest for amusement according to set rules; a match. **3.** sport of any kind; joke. **4.** wild animals, including birds and fishes, such as are hunted or taken for sport, food, or profit. –adj. (**gamer, gamest**) **5.** relating to animals hunted or taken as game. **6.** with fighting spirit; plucky.

gameplay /ˈgeɪmpleɪ/ n. **1.** the action or process of playing a game, especially a computer game. **2.** the style in which this is done.

gamer /ˈgeɪmə/ n. a person who plays a game, especially a computer game.

games cafe n. commercial premises which offer for a fee a number of computers for the playing of computer games, sometimes also selling coffee and light refreshments.

gamete /'gæmit, gə'mit/ *n.* either of the two germ cells which unite to form a new organism; a mature reproductive cell.

gamin /'gæmən/ *adj.* (of a person's appearance, or hairstyle) elfin.

gammon¹ /'gæmən/ *n.* a smoked or cured ham.

gammon² /'gæmən/ *adj. Colloq.* **1.** not true. **2.** not real; fake.

gamo- a word element meaning 'sexual union'.

-gamous an adjectival word element corresponding to the noun element **-gamy**, as in *polygamous*.

gamut /'gæmət/ *n.* the whole scale or range.

-gamy 1. a word element meaning 'marriage', as in *polygamy*. **2.** *Biol.* a word element meaning 'sexual union'.

ganache /gə'naʃ/ *n.* a rich confection made from chocolate and cream, often used as a cake icing.

gander /'gændə/ *n.* **1.** the male of the goose. *–phr.* **2. take** (or **have**) **a gander at**, *Colloq.* to take a look at.

gang /gæŋ/ *n.* **1.** a band or group. **2.** a group of persons, usually considered disreputable, violent or criminal, associated for a particular purpose. **–gangster**, *n.*

gangly /'gæŋgli/ *adj.* awkwardly tall and spindly. Also, **gangling**.

gangplank /'gæŋplæŋk/ *n.* a plank used as a temporary bridge in passing into and out of a ship, etc.

gangrene /'gæŋgrin/ *n.* the dying of tissue, as from interruption of circulation. **–gangrenous**, *adj.*

gangway /'gæŋweɪ/ *n.* a passageway.

gannet /'gænət/ *n.* a large seabird.

gantry /'gæntri/ *n.* (*pl.* **-tries**) a spanning framework.

gaol /dʒeɪl/ *n.* → **jail**.

gap /gæp/ *n.* **1.** a break or opening. **2.** a vacant space or interval.

gape /geɪp/ *v.i.* **1.** to stare with open mouth, as in wonder. **2.** to open as a gap; split or become open wide.

gap year *n.* a period of one academic year taken off from study, usually before commencing tertiary studies.

garage /'gæraʒ, -radʒ, gə'raʒ, -'radʒ/ *n.* **1.** a building for sheltering a motor vehicle or vehicles. **2.** → **service station**.

garb /gab/ *n.* fashion or mode of dress.

garbage /'gabɪdʒ/ *n.* rubbish.

garble /'gabəl/ *v.t.* to make unfair or misleading selections from (facts, statements, writings, etc.).

garden /'gadn/ *n.* **1.** a plot of ground devoted to the cultivation of useful or ornamental plants. *–v.i.* **2.** to lay out or cultivate a garden. **–gardener**, *n.*

gardenia /ga'dinjə, -niə/ *n.* a plant cultivated for its fragrant, waxlike, white flowers.

garfish /'gafɪʃ/ *n.* (*pl.* **-fish** or **-fishes**) a fish having a slender body and the lower jaw produced as a needle-like point.

gargantuan /ga'gæntʃuən/ *adj.* gigantic; prodigious.

gargle /'gagəl/ *v.t.* to wash or rinse (the throat or mouth) with a liquid held in the throat and kept in motion by a stream of air from the lungs.

gargoyle /'gagɔɪl/ *n.* a spout, often terminating in a grotesque head.

garish /'gɛərɪʃ, 'gar-/ *adj.* glaring, or excessively bright.

garland /'galənd/ *n.* a wreath or string of flowers, leaves, or other material.

garlic /'galɪk/ *n.* a hardy plant, with a strong-scented pungent bulb used in cookery and medicine.

garment /'gamənt/ *n.* any article of clothing.

garnet /'ganət/ *n.* a deep red gemstone.

garnish /'ganɪʃ/ *v.t.* **1.** to fit out with something that adorns or decorates. **2.** *Law* to warn; give notice. *–n.* **3.** something that decorates, especially food.

garnishee /ganə'ʃi/ *v.t.* (**-sheed**, **-sheeing**) **1.** to attach (money or property) by garnishment. **2.** to make (a person) a garnishee. *–n.* **3.** a person served with a garnishment.

garnishment /'ganɪʃmənt/ *n.* a warning served on a person, at the suit of a creditor plaintiff, to hold, subject to the court's direction, money or property of the defendant in his or her possession.

garret /'gærət/ *n.* → **attic**.

garrison /'gærəsən/ *n.* a body of troops stationed in a fortified place.

garrotte /gə'rɒt/ *n.* a method of killing, originally with an instrument causing strangulation, later by one breaking the neck.

garrulous /'gærələs/ *adj.* given to much talking, especially about trivial matters.

garter /'gatə/ *n.* a fastening to keep up stockings or long socks.

gas¹ /gæs/ *n.* (*pl.* **gases**) **1.** *Physics* a substance consisting of atoms or molecules which are sufficiently mobile for it to occupy the whole of the space in which it is contained. *–v.t.* (**gassed**, **gassing**) **2.** to affect, overcome, or asphyxiate with gas or fumes. **–gaseous**, *adj.*

gas² /gæs/ *n.* **1.** *Chiefly US* petrol. *–phr.* **2. step on the gas**, to hurry.

gash /gæʃ/ *n.* a long, deep wound or cut.

gasify /'gæsəfaɪ/ *v.t.* (**-fied**, **-fying**) to convert into a gas. **–gasification**, *n.*

gasket /'gæskət/ *n.* anything used as a packing or jointing material for making joints fluid-tight.

gasp /gæsp, gasp/ *n.* **1.** a sudden, short breath. **2.** a short, convulsive utterance, especially as a result of fear or surprise. *–v.i.* **3.** to catch the breath, or struggle for breath, with open mouth, as from exhaustion; breathe convulsively.

gastric /'gæstrɪk/ *adj.* relating to the stomach.

gastric bypass *n.* a surgical procedure in which the stomach is stapled to make it smaller as a remedy for obesity.

gastro- a word element meaning 'stomach', as in *gastropod, gastronome*. Also, **gastero-, gastr-**.

gastroenteritis /ˌgæstrouɛntə'raɪtəs/ *n. Pathol.* inflammation of the stomach and intestines.

gastronomy /gæs'trɒnəmi/ *n.* the art or science of good eating. **–gastronomic**, *adj.*

gastropod /'gæstrəpɒd/ *n.* any of a class of molluscs including the snails.

gate /geɪt/ *n.* **1.** a movable barrier, as a swinging frame, in a fence or wall, or across a passageway. **2.** a device for regulating the passage of water, steam, or the like, as in a dam, pipe, etc.; valve. **3.** *Elect.* an electronic circuit which controls the passage of information signals.

gatecrash /ˈgeɪtkræʃ/ *v.t.* to attend (a party, etc.) uninvited.

gateway /ˈgeɪtweɪ/ *n.* **1.** a passage or entrance which is closed by a gate. **2.** a frame or arch in which a gate is hung; structure built at or over a gate. **3.** any means of entering or leaving a place. **4.** a location through which one has access to an area: *the harbour is the gateway to the city.* **5.** *Computers* **a.** a piece of software or hardware which acts as a translator between dissimilar networks or protocols. **b.** → **router**.

gather /ˈgæðə/ *v.t.* **1.** to bring (persons, animals, or things) together into one company or aggregate. **2.** to learn or infer from observation. **3.** to wrap or draw around or close to someone or something. **4.** to draw up (cloth) on a thread in fine folds or puckers by running a thread through. **5.** to increase (speed, etc.). *–v.i.* **6.** to come together or assemble.

gauche /gəʊʃ/ *adj.* awkward; clumsy. **–gaucheness,** *n.*

gaudy /ˈgɔːdi/ *adj.* (**-dier, -diest**) excessively showy without taste; vulgar; flashy.

gauge /geɪdʒ/ *v.t.* (**gauged, gauging**) **1.** to appraise, estimate, or judge. **2.** to determine the dimensions, capacity, quantity, or force of. *–n.* **3.** a standard of measure; standard dimension or quantity. **4.** a means of estimating or judging; criterion; test. **5.** any instrument for measuring pressure, volume, or dimensions. Also, **gage.**

gaunt /gɔnt/ *adj.* abnormally thin; emaciated; haggard.

gauntlet /ˈgɔntlət/ *n.* **1.** a medieval glove. *–phr.* **2. throw down the gauntlet,** to extend a challenge, originally to a duel.

gauss /gaʊs/ *n.* *Elect.* a unit of magnetic induction in the centimetre-gram-second system, equal to 0.1×10^{-3} teslas.

gauze /gɔz/ *n.* any thin transparent fabric.

gave /geɪv/ *v.* past tense of **give.**

gavel /ˈgævəl/ *n.* a small mallet used by a presiding officer to signal for attention or order.

gawk /gɔk/ *v.i.* *Colloq.* to stare stupidly.

gawky /ˈgɔki/ *adj.* (**-kier, -kiest**) awkward; ungainly; clumsy. **–gawkily,** *adv.*

gay /geɪ/ *adj.* (**gayer, gayest**) **1.** (especially of a male) homosexual. **2.** of, relating to, or for homosexuals: *gay rights; a gay bar.* **3.** *Colloq.* unfashionable; unstylish. **4.** having or showing a joyous mood. **5.** bright or showy. *–n.* **6.** a homosexual, especially a male.

gaze /geɪz/ *v.i.* **1.** to look steadily or intently. *–n.* **2.** a steady or intent look.

gazebo /gəˈziboʊ/ *n.* (*pl.* **-bos** *or* **-boes**) a structure offering an extensive view, as a pavilion.

gazelle /gəˈzɛl/ *n.* (*pl.* **-zelles** *or, especially collectively,* **-zelle**) a small antelope.

gazette /gəˈzɛt/ *n.* **1.** a newspaper (now common only in newspaper titles). **2.** an official government journal, containing lists of government appointments and promotions, bankruptcies, etc. *–v.t.* (**-zetted, -zetting**) **3.** to publish, announce, or list in a gazette.

gazump /gəˈzʌmp/ *v.t.* to bypass (a buyer of real estate with whom a price has been agreed) by selling at a higher price to another.

gear /gɪə/ *n.* **1.** *Machinery* **a.** a mechanism for transmitting or changing motion, as by toothed wheels. **b.** a toothed wheel which engages with another wheel or part. **2.** implements, tools, or apparatus, especially as used for a particular operation; harness; tackle.

gearing /ˈgɪərɪŋ/ *n.* the relationship of total invested capital to equity capital.

gearstick /ˈgɪəstɪk/ *n.* a device for selecting or connecting gears for transmitting power, especially in a motor vehicle. Also, **gearlever.**

gecko /ˈgɛkoʊ/ *n.* (*pl.* **-kos** *or* **-koes**) a small nocturnal lizard, often having adhesive pads on the toes.

gee¹ /dʒi/ *interj.* a mild exclamation of surprise.

gee² /dʒi/ *phr.* **gee up,** a command to horses, etc., directing them to go faster.

geek /gik/ *n.* *Colloq.* **1.** a social misfit, especially one who is overly preoccupied with some interest or pursuit that is seen as unfashionable. **2.** Also, **computer geek.** a person who is overly preoccupied with computers.

geese /gis/ *n.* plural of **goose.**

geezer /ˈgizə/ *n.* *Colloq.* an odd character.

Geiger counter /ˈgaɪgə/ *n.* an instrument for detecting radioactivity.

geisha /ˈgeɪʃə/ *n.* (*pl.* **-sha** *or* **-shas**) (in Japan) a woman trained to entertain men with singing, dancing, and conversation.

gel /dʒɛl/ *n.* **1.** a jelly-like substance. *–v.i.* (**gelled, gelling**) **2.** to form or become a gel. **3.** to unite to form a cohesive whole. **4.** (of an idea, etc.) to become clearer or more fixed.

gelatine /ˈdʒɛlətin, dʒɛləˈtin/ *n.* a brittle, nearly transparent organic substance, the basis of jellies, glues, and the like. **–gelatinous,** *adj.*

gelato /dʒəˈlatoʊ/ *n.* (*pl.* **-latos** *or* **-lati**) an iced confection made from cream, milk, or water.

geld /gɛld/ *v.t.* to castrate (an animal).

gelding /ˈgɛldɪŋ/ *n.* a castrated animal, especially a horse.

gelignite /ˈdʒɛləgnaɪt/ *n.* an explosive.

gem /dʒɛm/ *n.* **1.** a stone used in jewellery, fashioned to bring out its beauty. **2.** something likened to, or prized as, a gem because of its beauty or worth, especially something small.

-gen a suffix meaning: **1.** something produced, or growing. **2.** something that produces.

gender /ˈdʒɛndə/ *n.* **1.** *Gram.* (in many languages) a set of classes, such as masculine, feminine and neuter, which together include all nouns. **2.** a socially constructed sexual identity, such as male, female, genderqueer, etc., distinguished from physiological determination as to one's sex (def. 1). **3.** sex (def. 2).

genderqueer /ˈdʒɛndəkwɪə/ *adj.* of or relating to a person who identifies as neither, both, or a combination of the conventional genders of male and female.

gene /dʒin/ *n.* *Biol.* the unit of inheritance, situated on and transmitted by the chromosome, which develops into a hereditary character as it reacts with the environment and with the other genes.

genealogy /dʒiniˈælədʒi/ n. (pl. **-gies**) an account of the descent of a person or family through an ancestral line. **–genealogist**, n.

genera /ˈdʒɛnərə/ n. plural of **genus**.

general /ˈdʒɛnrəl/ adj. 1. relating to, affecting, including, or participated in by all members of a class or group; not partial or particular. 2. not specific or special. –n. 3. an army officer of very high rank. **–generally**, adv.

general anaesthesia n. 1. drug-induced insensibility to pain and other sensation throughout the whole body, involving a state of unconsciousness. 2. the administration of a drug to produce this effect. Also, **general anesthesia**.

general anaesthetic n. 1. a substance which anaesthetises the entire body and produces loss of consciousness. 2. the procedure for this. Also, **general anesthetic**.

general election n. a parliamentary election in which all seats in the house are thrown open, as a federal or state election for the lower house.

generalise /ˈdʒɛnrəlaɪz/ v.t. 1. to give a general (rather than specific or special) character to. 2. to infer (a general principle, etc.) from facts, etc. –v.i. 3. to form general notions. Also, **generalize**.

generality /dʒɛnəˈræləti/ n. (pl. **-ties**) 1. a general or vague statement. 2. general principle; general rule or law.

general practitioner n. a doctor who does not specialise in any particular branch of medicine. Abbrev.: GP

generate /ˈdʒɛnəreɪt/ v.t. to bring into existence; give rise to; produce; cause to be.

generation /dʒɛnəˈreɪʃən/ n. 1. the whole body of individuals born about the same time. 2. production by natural or artificial processes; evolution, as of heat or sound.

generation C n. the group of people who are versed in the creation of content, especially on the internet, using multimedia tools.

generation text n. the generation that has grown up using mobile phones, viewed as adept in texting.

generation X n. the generation born in the late 1960s and 1970s, portrayed as being cynical about traditional authority and open to new forms of communality and spirituality. Also, **X generation**.

generation Y n. the generation born in the 1980s and 1990s, portrayed as giving a high priority to personal satisfaction, being markedly visually-oriented and less deferential to authority.

generation Z n. the generation born in the early 2000s, characterised as being at ease with computer technology, online and mobile phone communication, and multitasking.

generator /ˈdʒɛnəreɪtə/ n. a machine which converts mechanical energy into electrical energy.

generic /dʒəˈnɛrɪk/ adj. 1. relating to a genus. 2. applicable or referring to all the members of a genus or class. 3. of or relating to a class of commodities marketed under the brand name of a retailing chain with the implication of greater cheapness than if they appeared under the brand name of the producer. 4. identified by the name of the product itself, not by a particular brand name. –n. 5. a generic commodity. Also, **generical**.

generous /ˈdʒɛnərəs, ˈdʒɛnrəs/ adj. 1. munificent or bountiful; unselfish. 2. free from meanness or smallness of mind or character. **–generosity**, n.

genesis /ˈdʒɛnəsəs/ n. (pl. **-neses** /-nəsiz/) origin; production; creation.

gene therapy n. Med. a procedure in which defective genes are replaced or mutated in order to correct a genetic defect.

genetically-modified /dʒə,nɛtɪkli-ˈmɒdəfaɪd/ adj. 1. (of an animal or plant) having had its genetic material altered by technological means, usually to change certain characteristics and thereby improve the organism in some specific way. 2. (of a food) containing such an ingredient. Abbrev.: GM

genetic code n. the code, based on the arrangement of the molecular elements of the chromosomes, by which hereditary characteristics are passed on.

genetic engineering n. the modification of an organism's genes through the transference of DNA material from one organism to another. **–genetically engineered**, adj.

genetic fingerprinting n. a process by which the genetic code of the DNA in human organic material such as skin, hair, blood, semen, etc., found at the scene of a crime is matched against the DNA of a suspect, thus, because of the uniqueness of each person's genetic code, establishing whether the suspect was or was not present. Also, **DNA fingerprinting**.

genetics /dʒəˈnɛtɪks/ n. the science of heredity, dealing with resemblances and differences of related organisms flowing from the interaction of their genes and the environment. **–geneticist**, n. **–genetic**, adj.

genial /ˈdʒiniəl/ adj. pleasantly warm and friendly.

genie /ˈdʒini/ n. a spirit in Arabian mythology.

genital /ˈdʒɛnətl/ adj. relating to reproduction or the organs of reproduction.

genital herpes n. a sexually transmitted form of herpes.

genitalia /dʒɛnəˈteɪliə/ pl. n. the genitals.

genitals /ˈdʒɛnətlz/ pl. n. the reproductive organs, especially the external organs.

genius /ˈdʒiniəs/ n. 1. exceptional natural capacity for creative and original conceptions; the highest level of mental ability. 2. a person having such capacity.

genocide /ˈdʒɛnəsaɪd/ n. extermination of a national or racial group as a planned move. **–genocidal**, adj.

genome /ˈdʒinoʊm/ n. the complete genetic material for any cell. **–genomic**, adj. **–genomically**, adv.

-genous an adjective suffix derived from nouns in **-gen** and **-geny**.

genre /ˈʒɒnrə/ n. 1. genus; kind; sort; style. 2. a conventional literary form, such as the novel, etc. 3. a type of text, such as exposition, report, narrative, recount, procedure, etc.

genteel /dʒɛnˈtil/ adj. belonging or suited to polite society.

gentile /ˈdʒɛntaɪl/ n. any person who is not Jewish, especially a Christian.

gentility /dʒɛn'tɪləti/ n. **1.** superior refinement or elegance, possessed or affected. **2.** gentle or noble birth.

gentle /'dʒɛntl/ adj. **1.** mild, kindly, or amiable. **2.** not severe, rough, or violent. **3.** moderate; gradual. **4.** of good birth or family; well-born.

gentleman /'dʒɛntlmən/ n. (pl. **-men**) **1.** a man of good breeding, education, and manners. **2.** (as a polite form of speech) any man.

gentry /'dʒɛntri/ n. Brit. the class below the nobility.

genuflect /'dʒɛnjəflɛkt/ v.i. to bend the knee or knees, especially in reverence.

genuine /'dʒɛnjuən/ adj. **1.** being truly such; real; authentic. **2.** sincere; free from pretence or affectation.

genus /'dʒiːnəs/ n. (pl. **genera** /'dʒɛnərə/) **1.** a kind; sort; class. **2.** Biol. the usual major subdivision of a family or subfamily.

-geny a suffix meaning 'origin'.

gen Z /dʒɛn 'zɛd/ n. → **generation Z**.

geo- a word element meaning 'the earth'.

geoengineering /ˌdʒiːoʊɛndʒə'nɪərɪŋ/ n. the manipulation of the earth's climate to produce specific effects, usually to counteract the effects of global warming. **–geoengineer**, n., v.

geography /dʒi'ɒgrəfi/ n. the study of the earth's surface, climate, vegetation, population, etc. **–geographer**, n. **–geographical**, adj.

geology /dʒi'ɒlədʒi/ n. the science that deals with the earth, the rocks of which it is composed, and the changes which it has undergone or is undergoing. **–geological**, adj. **–geologist**, n.

geometry /dʒi'ɒmətri/ n. that branch of mathematics which deduces the properties of figures in space. **–geometric**, **geometrical**, adj.

geophysics /dʒiːoʊ'fɪzɪks/ n. the physics of the earth, dealing especially with the study of inaccessible portions of the earth.

geothermal /dʒiːoʊ'θɜːməl/ adj. of or relating to heat emanating from the molten core of the earth. Also, **geothermic** /dʒiːoʊ'θɜːmɪk/.

geranium /dʒə'reɪniəm/ n. a plant cultivated for its showy flowers.

geriatric /dʒɛri'ætrɪk/ adj. **1.** of or relating to the medical field of geriatrics or to aged persons. **–n. 2.** an aged person, especially one incapacitated or invalided by old age.

geriatrics /dʒɛri'ætrɪks/ n. the science of the medical and hygienic care of, or the diseases of, aged persons. **–geriatrician** /dʒɛriə'trɪʃən/, n.

germ /dʒɜːm/ n. **1.** a microorganism, especially when disease-producing. **2.** that from which anything springs as if from a seed.

german /'dʒɜːmən/ adj. **1.** having the same father and mother (always placed after the noun). **2.** being the child of the brother or sister of one's father or mother, or from brothers or sisters.

germane /dʒɜː'meɪn/ adj. closely related; pertinent.

German measles n. → **rubella**.

German shepherd n. a highly intelligent wolf-like breed of dog; Alsatian.

germinate /'dʒɜːməneɪt/ v.i. to begin to grow or develop.

gerrymander /'dʒɛrimændə/ n. Politics an arbitrary arrangement of the political divisions of an electorate, etc., made so as to give one party an unfair advantage in elections.

gerund /'dʒɛrənd/ n. Gram. the -ing form of a verb when in nominal function, as walking in the sentence 'walking is good exercise'.

gestate /'dʒɛsteɪt/ v.t. to carry in the womb during the period from conception to delivery. **–gestation**, n.

gesticulate /dʒɛs'tɪkjəleɪt/ v.i. to make or use gestures, especially in an animated or excited manner with or instead of speech.

gesture /'dʒɛstʃə/ n. **1.** movement of the body, head, arms, hands, or face expressive of an idea or an emotion. **2.** any action or proceeding intended for effect or as a formality; demonstration. **–v.i. 3.** to make or use gestures.

get /gɛt/ v. (**got**, **getting**) **–v.t. 1.** to obtain, gain, or acquire by any means. **2.** to fetch or bring. **3.** to hear or understand. **4.** to be afflicted with (an illness, etc.). **5.** Colloq. to hit. **–v.i. 6.** to come to or arrive. **7.** to become; grow. **8.** (fol. by away, in, into, out, over, through, etc.) to succeed in coming or going. **–phr. 9. get across**, to be made understood. **10. get at**, **a.** to reach; make contact with. **b.** Colloq. to hint at or imply. **c.** Colloq. to tamper with, as by corruption or bribery. **11. get away with**, to avoid punishment or blame for. **12. get by**, to manage; carry on in spite of difficulties. **13. get down**, to depress; discourage. **14. get even with**, to square accounts with. **15. get his, hers**, etc., to get a just reward. **16. get on**, **a.** to age. **b.** to make progress; proceed; advance. **c.** to agree or be friendly (with). **17. get one's own back**, to be revenged. **18. get round**, **a.** to outwit. **b.** to cajole or ingratiate oneself with. **c.** to overcome (difficulties, etc.). **19. get (stuck) into**, Colloq. **a.** to attack (someone) vigorously either physically or verbally. **b.** to set about (a task) vigorously. **20. get to**, **a.** to arouse deep feeling in. **b.** to annoy or irritate. **21. get up**, **a.** to arise. **b.** to dress elaborately. **c.** to prepare, arrange, or organise. **d.** to win (an election, court case, contest, etc.) **22. get up to**, to be involved in (mischief, etc.). **23. get with child**, to make pregnant.

geyser /'giːzə, 'gaɪzə/ n. a hot spring which intermittently sends up fountain-like jets of water and steam into the air.

ghastly /'gɑːstli/ adj. (**-lier**, **-liest**) frightful; dreadful; horrible.

GHB /dʒi eɪtʃ 'bi/ n. an anaesthetic drug, gamma hydroxybutyric acid, used recreationally as a stimulant; fantasy.

ghee /gi/ n. clarified butter, used especially in Indian cookery.

gherkin /'gɜːkən/ n. the small, immature fruit of cucumber, used in pickling.

ghetto /'gɛtoʊ/ n. (pl. **-tos** or **-toes**) a quarter in a city in which any minority group lives.

ghetto-blaster /'gɛtoʊ-blɑːstə/ n. a large, powerful, portable stereo cassette or CD player. Also, **ghetto blaster**.

ghost /goʊst/ n. **1.** the spirit of a dead person imagined as wandering among or haunting living persons. **2.** Optics, Television a bright spot or secondary image, from a defect of the instrument. **–v.t. 3.** to write for someone else who is publicly known as the author.

ghoul /gul/ *n.* **1.** an evil demon. **2.** a grave robber. **3.** someone who revels in what is revolting. **–ghoulish,** *adj.*

giant /'dʒaɪənt/ *n.* **1.** an imaginary being of human form but superhuman size, strength, etc. **2.** a person or thing of unusually great size, endowments, importance, etc. *–adj.* **3.** gigantic; huge.

giardia /dʒi'adɪə, gɪ'adɪə/ *n.* any flagellate parasitic to the intestines of vertebrates.

gibber¹ /'dʒɪbə/ *v.i.* to speak inarticulately; chatter. **–gibberish,** *n.*

gibber² /'gɪbə/ *n.* a rounded stone, especially one found in the arid Australian inland.

gibbon /'gɪbən/ *n.* a small ape.

gibe /dʒaɪb/ *v.i.* (**gibed, gibing**) **1.** to utter mocking words; scoff; jeer. *–n.* **2.** a taunting or sarcastic remark. Also, **jibe.**

giblet /'dʒɪblət/ *n.* (*usu. pl.*) the heart, liver, or gizzard from a fowl.

giddy /'gɪdi/ *adj.* (**-dier, -diest**) **1.** frivolously light; impulsive; flighty. **2.** affected with vertigo; dizzy.

GIF /gɪf/ *n. Computers* **1.** a data format for image files. **2.** a file in this format. Also, **gif.**

gift /gɪft/ *n.* **1.** something given; a present. **2.** a quality, or special ability; natural endowment; talent.

gig¹ /gɪg/ *n.* a light, two-wheeled one-horse carriage.

gig² /gɪg/ *n. Colloq.* a booking for an entertainer or band to perform.

gig³ /gɪg/ *n. Computers Colloq.* → **gigabyte.**

gigabyte /'gɪgəbaɪt/ *n. Computers* a measure of computer memory equal to 2^{30} (approximately 10^9) bytes. *Symbol:* G, GB

gigajoule /'gɪgədʒul/ *n.* a metric unit of energy equal to 10^9 joules.

gigantic /dʒaɪ'gæntɪk/ *adj.* **1.** huge. **2.** of, like, or befitting a giant.

giggle /'gɪgəl/ *v.i.* **1.** to laugh in childish way; titter. *–n.* **2.** a silly, childish laugh; a titter. **3.** *Colloq.* an amusing occasion.

gigolo /'ʒɪgəloʊ/ *n.* (*pl.* **-los**) a man supported by a woman, especially a young man supported by an older woman in return for companionship.

gild /gɪld/ *v.t.* (**gilded** *or* **gilt, gilding**) to coat with gold, gold leaf, or gold-coloured substance.

gill¹ /gɪl/ *n.* an aquatic respiratory organ.

gill² /dʒɪl/ *n.* a unit of liquid measure in the imperial system, equal to ¼ pint.

gilt /gɪlt/ *v.* a past tense and past participle of **gild.**

gilt-edged /'gɪlt-ɛdʒd/ *adj.* **1.** having the edges gilded. **2.** of the highest order or quality.

gimlet /'gɪmlət/ *n.* a small tool for boring holes, consisting of a shaft with a pointed screw at one end and a handle at the other.

gimmick /'gɪmɪk/ *n. Colloq.* a pronounced eccentricity of dress, manner, voice, etc., or an eccentric action or device, especially one exploited to gain publicity.

gin¹ /dʒɪn/ *n.* an alcoholic beverage obtained by redistilling spirits with flavouring agents, especially juniper berries, orange peel, etc.

gin² /dʒɪn/ *n.* **1.** a machine for separating cotton from its seeds, as a cotton gin. **2.** a trap or snare for game, etc.

gin³ /dʒɪn/ *n.* a card game similar to rummy. Also, **gin rummy.**

ginger /'dʒɪndʒə/ *n.* **1.** the pungent, spicy rhizome of any of a reed-like plant, variously used in cookery and medicine. **2.** (of hair) red. *–v.t.* **3.** *Colloq.* to impart spiciness or piquancy to; make lively.

gingerly /'dʒɪndʒəli/ *adv.* with extreme care or caution; warily. **–gingerliness,** *n.*

gingham /'gɪŋəm/ *n.* yarn-dyed, plain-weave cotton fabric.

gingivitis /dʒɪndʒə'vaɪtəs/ *n.* inflammation of the gums.

ginkgo /'gɪŋkoʊ/ *n.* (*pl.* **-goes**) **1.** Also, **gingko biloba.** a large, ornamental tree; originally of China. **2.** an extract drawn from the leaves of this tree, used traditionally in Chinese herbal medicine as a general restorative. Also, **gingko.**

gipsy /'dʒɪpsi/ *n.* (*pl.* **-sies**) → **gypsy.**

giraffe /dʒə'raf/ *n.* a tall, long-necked, spotted ruminant of Africa.

gird /gɜd/ *v.t.* (**girt** *or* **girded, girding**) **1.** to encircle with a belt or girdle. *–phr.* **2. gird oneself (up) for,** to prepare oneself mentally for.

girder /'gɜdə/ *n.* (in structural work) any main horizontal supporting member or beam.

girdle /'gɜdl/ *n.* **1.** a belt, cord, or the like, worn about the waist. **2.** a lightweight undergarment which supports the abdominal region of the body. *–v.t.* **3.** to encompass; enclose; encircle.

girl /gɜl/ *n.* a female child or young person.

girlfriend /'gɜlfrɛnd/ *n.* **1.** a female companion with whom one has a steady romantic relationship. **2.** a female friend.

girth /gɜθ/ *n.* **1.** the measure around anything; circumference. **2.** a band passed under the belly of a horse, etc., to secure a saddle or pack on its back.

gist /dʒɪst/ *n.* the substance or pith of a matter; essential part.

give /gɪv/ *v.* (**gave, given, giving**) *–v.t.* **1.** to deliver freely; bestow; hand over. **2.** to deliver to another in exchange for something; pay. **3.** to grant permission or opportunity to; enable; assign; award. **4.** to present. **5.** to assign as a basis of calculation or reasoning; suppose; assume. **6.** to assign to someone as their right, lot, etc. **7.** *Colloq.* to tell; offer as explanation. **8.** to furnish or provide. **9.** to produce; present. *–v.i.* **10.** to make a gift or gifts. **11.** to yield, as to pressure or strain; draw back; relax. *–n.* **12.** the act or fact of yielding to pressure; elasticity. *–phr.* **13. give in, a.** to yield; acknowledge defeat. **b.** to hand in. **14. give up, a.** to lose all hope. **b.** to abandon as hopeless. **c.** to desist from; forsake. **d.** to surrender. **e.** to devote entirely. **f.** to inform against.

given name *n.* a name borne by an individual, often assigned by his or her parents shortly after birth, as opposed to the inherited surname; first name; forename. Compare **Christian name.**

gizzard /'gɪzəd/ *n.* the grinding or muscular stomach of birds.

glacier /ˈgleɪsɪə, ˈglæsɪə/ n. an extended mass of ice formed from falling snow and moving very slowly. **–glacial**, adj.

glad /glæd/ adj. (fol. by of, at, etc., or an infinitive or clause) delighted or pleased.

glade /gleɪd/ n. an open space in a forest.

gladiator /ˈglædɪeɪtə/ n. Roman Hist. a person, often a slave or captive, who fought in public with a sword or other weapon to entertain the people.

gladiolus /glædɪˈoʊləs/ n. (pl. **-lus** or **-li** /laɪ/ or **-luses**) a plant with erect leaves, and spikes of variously coloured flowers.

glamour /ˈglæmə/ n. alluring and often illusory charm; fascination. Also, **glamor**. **–glamorous**, adj.

glance /glæns, glɑns/ v.i. (**glanced, glancing**) 1. to look quickly or briefly. 2. to gleam or flash. 3. to go off in an oblique direction from an object struck. –n. 4. a quick or brief look.

gland /glænd/ n. Anat. an organ or tissue which elaborates and discharges a substance which is used elsewhere in the body (secretion), or eliminated (excretion). **–glandular**, adj.

glare /glɛə/ n. 1. a strong, dazzling light; brilliant lustre. –v.i. 2. to shine with a strong, dazzling light. 3. to be conspicuous. 4. to look with a fierce or piercing stare.

glass /glɑs/ n. 1. a hard, brittle, more or less transparent substance produced by fusion. 2. a glass container for drinking.

glasses /ˈglɑsəz/ pl. n. a device to aid defective vision, consisting usually of two glass lenses set in a frame which rests on the nose and is held in place by pieces passing over the ears.

glaucoma /glɔˈkoʊmə/ n. a disease of the eye, causing gradual loss of vision.

glaze /gleɪz/ v.t. 1. to furnish or fit with glass; cover with glass. 2. to produce a vitreous or glossy surface on (pottery, pastry, etc.). –n. 3. a smooth, glossy surface or coating.

glazier /ˈgleɪzɪə/ n. someone who fits windows, etc., with glass.

gleam /glim/ n. 1. a flash or beam of light. 2. dim or subdued light. –v.i. 3. to send forth a gleam or gleams. 4. to appear suddenly and clearly, like a flash of light.

glean /glin/ v.t. 1. to gather slowly and laboriously in bits. 2. to gather (grain, etc.) after the reapers or regular gatherers. 3. to discover or find out.

glee /gli/ n. demonstrative joy.

glen /glɛn/ n. a small, narrow, secluded valley.

glib /glɪb/ adj. (**glibber, glibbest**) ready and fluent, often thoughtlessly or insincerely so.

glide /glaɪd/ v.i. 1. to move smoothly along, as if without effort or difficulty, as a flying bird. 2. Aeronautics to move in the air, especially at an easy angle downwards, by the action of gravity or by virtue of momentum already acquired. –n. 3. a gliding movement, as in dancing.

glider /ˈglaɪdə/ n. Aeronautics a motorless aeroplane for gliding from a higher to a lower level by the action of gravity, or from a lower to a higher level by the action of air currents.

glimmer /ˈglɪmə/ n. a faint or unsteady light; gleam.

glimpse /glɪmps/ n. 1. a momentary sight or view. –v.t. 2. to catch a glimpse of.

glint /glɪnt/ n. 1. a gleam or glimmer; flash. 2. gleaming brightness; lustre. –v.i. 3. to gleam or flash.

glisten /ˈglɪsən/ v.i. 1. to shine with a sparkling light, especially as a result of being wet. –n. 2. a glistening; sparkle.

glitch /glɪtʃ/ n. a hitch; snag; malfunction.

glitter /ˈglɪtə/ v.i. to shine with a brilliant, sparkling light or lustre.

gloat /gloʊt/ v.i. to smile smugly or scornfully.

global /ˈgloʊbəl/ adj. 1. relating to or covering the whole world. 2. all-embracing; comprehensive. 3. (of a computer command) operating over an entire database, set of records, etc. –n. 4. a computer operation performed on an entire document, database, etc. **–globally**, adj.

globalisation /ˌgloʊbəlaɪˈzeɪʃən/ n. 1. the process of becoming international in scope, application or influence, as of an industry, etc. 2. the perceived development of a single worldwide economy and culture, brought about by the removal of restrictions to international trade, travel and mass communication. Also, **globalization**. **–globalise**, v.

globalism /ˈgloʊbəlɪzəm/ n. 1. the pursuit of globalisation. 2. the worldwide integration of economies. **–globalist**, n., adj.

global warming n. the significant rise in temperature of the whole of the earth's atmosphere.

globe /gloʊb/ n. 1. (usu. preceded by the) the earth. 2. a sphere on which is depicted a map of the earth. 3. anything more or less spherical. 4. → light globe.

globule /ˈglɒbjul/ n. a small spherical body. **–globular**, adj.

glockenspiel /ˈglɒkənspil, -kənʃpil/ n. a musical instrument comprising a set of steel bars mounted in a frame and struck with hammers.

gloom /glum/ n. 1. darkness or dimness. 2. a state of melancholy or depression; low spirits.

gloomy /ˈglumi/ adj. (**-mier, -miest**) 1. dark or dim, especially in a depressing way. 2. (of a person) unhappy and having no or little hope. 3. showing or causing gloom. **–gloomily**, adv.

glorious /ˈglɔrɪəs/ adj. 1. full of glory. 2. brilliantly beautiful.

glory /ˈglɔri/ n. (pl. **-ries**) 1. exalted praise, honour, or distinction, accorded by common consent. 2. resplendent beauty or magnificence. 3. the splendour and bliss of heaven; heaven. –v.i. (**-ried, -rying**) 4. (fol. by in) to be boastful; exult arrogantly. **–glorify**, v.

glory box n. a chest in which young women store clothes, linen, etc., in expectation of being married.

gloss¹ /glɒs/ n. a superficial lustre. **–glossy**, adj.

gloss² /glɒs/ n. 1. an explanation by means of a marginal or interlinear note, of a technical or unusual expression in a manuscript text. 2. (oft. fol. by over) to give a specious interpretation of; explain away.

glossary /ˈglɒsəri/ n. (pl. **-ries**) a list of technical, dialectal, and difficult terms in a subject or field, with definitions.

-glot a suffix indicating proficiency in language, as in polyglot.

glottis /ˈglɒtəs/ n. the opening at the upper part of the larynx, between the vocal cords. **–glottal**, adj.

glove /glʌv/ n. a covering for the hand.

glow /gloʊ/ n. **1.** light emitted by a substance heated to luminosity; incandescence. **2.** warmth of emotion or passion; ardour. **3.** to emit bright light and heat without flame; be incandescent. **4.** to be animated with emotion.

glower /ˈgloʊə, ˈglaʊə/ v.i. to stare with sullen dislike or discontent.

glow-worm n. a firefly.

glucosamine /gluˈkoʊsəmin/ n. a compound used in the treatment of osteoarthritis.

glucose /ˈglukoʊz, -oʊs/ n. Chem. a sugar occurring in many fruits, animal tissues and fluids, etc.

glue /glu/ n. **1.** any adhesive substance made from any natural or synthetic resin or material. –v.t. (**glued, gluing**) **2.** to join or fasten with glue.

gluggy /ˈglʌgi/ adj. Colloq. sticky.

glum /glʌm/ adj. (**glummer, glummest**) gloomily sullen or silent; dejected.

glut /glʌt/ v.t. (**glutted, glutting**) **1.** to feed or satisfy to the full. –n. **2.** a full supply. **3.** a surfeit. –phr. **4. glut the market**, to overstock the market.

gluten /ˈglutn/ n. the tough, viscid nitrogenous substance remaining when the flour of wheat or other grain is washed to remove the starch.

glutinous /ˈglutənəs/ adj. of the nature of glue; gluey; viscid; sticky.

glutton /ˈglʌtn/ n. **1.** someone who eats to excess. **2.** (fol. by for) someone who accepts an inordinate amount of unpleasantness or difficulty. –**gluttonous**, adj. –**gluttony**, n.

glycaemic /glaɪˈsimɪk/ adj. relating to the level of glucose in the blood. Also, **glycemic**.

glycerine /ˈglɪsəˈrin, ˈglɪsərən/ n. Chem. → **glycerol**. Also, **glycerin** /ˈglɪsərən/.

glycerol /ˈglɪsərɒl/ n. a colourless, odourless, liquid alcohol, of syrupy consistency and sweet taste, used as a solvent, in plastics, or as a sweetener.

glycogen /ˈglaɪkədʒən/ n. a form of sugar found in liver and muscle; readily converted into glucose, it provides the body with a carbohydrate store of energy. –**glycogenic**, adj.

gnarled /nald/ adj. **1.** (of trees) knotty. **2.** (of persons) having a rugged, weather-beaten appearance. Also, **gnarly**.

gnash /næʃ/ v.t. to grind (the teeth).

gnat /næt/ n. any of various small winged insects.

gnaw /nɔ/ v. (**gnawed, gnawed** or **gnawn, gnawing**) –v.t. **1.** to wear away little by little by persistent biting. **2.** to consume with passion; torment. –v.i. **3.** to bite persistently.

gneiss /naɪs/ n. a metamorphic rock. –**gneissic**, adj.

gnocchi /ˈnjɒki, ˈnɒki/ pl. n. small dumplings made from potato and flour or semolina.

gnome /noʊm/ n. **1.** one of a species of diminutive beings. **2.** a banker, involved in international currency and loan dealings, thought to exercise a mysterious and sinister effect on world economic affairs.

gnomic /ˈnoʊmɪk, ˈnɒm-/ adj. like or containing aphorisms.

gnu /nu/ n. (pl. **gnus** or, especially collectively, **gnu**) → **wildebeest**.

go /goʊ/ v. (**went, gone, going**) –v.i. **1.** to move or pass along; proceed. **2.** to move away or out; depart (opposed to come or arrive). **3.** to keep or be in motion; act, work, or run. **4.** to become; assume another state or condition. **5.** to belong; have a place. **6.** (of colours, etc.) to harmonise; be compatible; be suited. **7.** to develop, especially with reference to success, or failure. **8.** to fail; give way. **9.** to carry final authority. **10.** (fol. by into) to be contained: 4 goes into 12. **11.** to be about, intending, or destined (used in the present participle followed by an infinitive). –v.t. **12.** to proceed on. –n. (pl. **goes**) **13.** the act of going. **14.** Colloq. energy, spirit, or animation. **15.** Colloq. one's turn to play or to make an attempt at something. **16.** Colloq. something that goes well; a success. –phr. **17. fair go**, Colloq. adequate opportunity. **18. go at, a.** to undertake with vigour. **b.** to attack. **19. go down, a.** to descend; slope down. **b.** to be defeated. **c.** to be remembered by posterity. **20. go into**, to investigate or study thoroughly. **21. go off, a.** to discharge; explode. **b.** (of food, etc.) to become bad; deteriorate. **c.** to take place (in a specified manner). **d.** Colloq. to come to dislike. **22. go over, a.** to read or re-read. **b.** to repeat. **c.** to examine. **d.** to have an effect (as specified). **23. have a go**, Colloq. to make an attempt; try. **24. on the go**, Colloq. constantly going; very active.

goad /goʊd/ n. **1.** a stick with a pointed end, for driving cattle, etc. –v.t. **2.** to prick or drive with or as with a goad; incite.

goal /goʊl/ n. **1.** that towards which effort is directed; aim or end. **2.** (in ball games) an area, basket, cage, object or structure towards which the players strive to advance the ball, etc.

goanna /goʊˈænə/ n. any of various large Australian lizards.

goat /goʊt/ n. **1.** an agile hollow-horned ruminant closely related to the sheep. **2.** Colloq. a fool.

goatee /goʊˈti/ n. a man's beard trimmed to a tuft or a point on the chin.

gob¹ /gɒb/ n. a mass or lump.

gob² /gɒb/ n. Colloq. the mouth.

gobble¹ /ˈgɒbəl/ v.t. to swallow hastily in large pieces; gulp.

gobble² /ˈgɒbəl/ v.i. to make the characteristic throaty cry of a turkey cock.

gobbledegook /ˈgɒbldi,guk, -,guk/ n. Colloq. language characterised by circumlocution and jargon. Also, **gobbledygook**.

goblet /ˈgɒblət/ n. a drinking glass with a foot and stem.

goblin /ˈgɒblən/ n. a mischievous sprite or elf.

gobsmacked /ˈgɒbsmækt/ adj. Colloq. astonished; flabbergasted.

go-cart /ˈgoʊ-kat/ n. → **go-kart**.

god /gɒd/ n. **1.** a supernatural being who is believed to have power to control human affairs or the world of nature, and is worshipped according to particular religious beliefs. **2. God**, in religions that believe in only one god, the highest being who is the maker and ruler of the universe. **3.** someone or something which is given too much attention: money is his god. –interj. **4.** an exclamation of surprise, fear, etc.

godchild /'gɒdtʃaɪld/ n. (pl. **-children**) someone for whom a person (godparent) stands sponsor at baptism.

goddaughter /'gɒddɔtə/ n. a female godchild.

goddess /'gɒdəs, 'gɒdɛs/ n. a female god or deity.

godfather /'gɒdfaðə/ n. a man who sponsors a child at baptism.

godforsaken /'gɒdfəseɪkən/ adj. desolate; remote.

godly /'gɒdli/ adj. (**-lier**, **-liest**) pious.

godmother /'gɒdmʌðə/ n. a woman who sponsors a child at baptism.

godparent /'gɒdpɛərənt/ n. someone who takes responsibility for a child (their godchild) at baptism

godsend /'gɒdsɛnd/ n. something unexpected but particularly welcome and timely.

godson /'gɒdsʌn/ n. a male godchild.

godspeed /gɒd'spid/ interj. Archaic an expression of good wishes to someone taking a journey.

goggle /'gɒgəl/ v.i. 1. to stare with bulging eyes. 2. to roll the eyes.

goggles /'gɒgəlz/ pl. n. spectacles often with special rims, lenses, or sidepieces, so devised as to protect the eyes from wind, dust, water, or glare.

goitre /'gɔɪtə/ n. an enlargement of the thyroid gland, on the front and side of the neck.

go-kart /'gou-kat/ n. a small light vehicle with a low-powered engine, used for relatively safe racing. Also, **go-cart**, **kart**.

gold /gould/ n. 1. a precious yellow metal, highly malleable and ductile, and free from liability to rust. Symbol: Au 2. something likened to this metal in brightness, preciousness, etc. 3. bright metallic yellow, sometimes tending towards brown. –**golden**, adj.

golden goal n. (in soccer, hockey, etc.) a goal scored in extra time which wins the game for the team which scored it and ends the match.

golden handshake n. Colloq. a gratuity or benefit given to employees in recognition of their services on the occasion of their retirement.

golden mean n. the happy medium between extremes.

golden syrup n. a sweet viscous substance derived from sugar processing; used in cookery and as a sauce for porridge, desserts, etc.

goldfish /'gouldfɪʃ/ n. (pl. **-fish** or **-fishes**) a small fish of the carp family.

gold leaf n. gold beaten into a very thin sheet, used for gilding, etc.

goldmine /'gouldmaɪn/ n. 1. a mine yielding gold. 2. a source of great wealth. 3. a source of anything required.

golf /gɒlf/ n. an outdoor game, in which a small resilient ball is driven with special clubs into a series of holes, distributed at various distances over a course. –**golfer**, n.

golliwog /'gɒliwɒg/ n. a soft, black-faced doll. Also, **gollywog**.

-gon a suffix denoting geometrical figures having a certain number or kind of angles, as in polygon, pentagon.

gonad /'gɒunæd/ n. the sex gland, male or female, in which gametes develop and appropriate sex hormones are produced.

gondola /'gɒndələ/ n. a long, narrow boat used on the Venetian canals.

gone /gɒn/ adj. departed; left.

gong /gɒŋ/ n. Music a bronze disc with the rim turned up, to be struck with a soft-headed stick.

gonorrhoea /gɒnə'riə/ n. a sexually transmitted disease causing inflammation mainly of the urethra and cervix. Also, **gonorrhea**.

-gony a word element meaning 'production', 'genesis', 'origination'.

good /gʊd/ adj. (**better**, **best**) 1. morally excellent; righteous; pious. 2. satisfactory in quality, quantity, or degree; excellent. 3. right; proper; qualified; fit. 4. (of food) fresh and palatable; not tainted. 5. reliable; safe. 6. agreeable; pleasant. 7. (of clothes) best or newest. 8. competent or skilful; clever. 9. a. (oft. fol. by for) valid. b. (fol. by for) entitling (a person) to. c. (fol. by for) (of a person) willing to provide. –n. 10. profit; worth; advantage; benefit. 11. excellence or merit; righteousness; kindness; virtue. 12. (pl.) possessions, especially movable ones. 13. (pl.) articles of trade; wares; merchandise, especially that which is transported by land. –interj. 14. an expression of approval or satisfaction. –phr. 15. **all to the good**, generally advantageous, often used to justify an unpleasant event. 16. **be up to no good**, Colloq. to do wrong; break the law in some undisclosed way; behave in a suspicious manner. 17. **feel good**, Colloq. to be happy or in good health. 18. **for good (and all)**, finally and permanently; forever. 19. **good for you**, Colloq. (often patronising or ironic) an expression of approval, encouragement, etc. 20. **good luck**, an expression wishing a person well. 21. **good on you**, Colloq. an expression of approval, encouragement, etc. 22. **make good**, **a.** to make recompense for; pay for. **b.** to keep to an agreement; fulfil. **c.** to be successful. **d.** to prove the truth of; substantiate.

goodbye /gʊd'baɪ/ interj. farewell (a conventional expression used at parting).

good cholesterol n. a naturally occurring substance which unclogs blood vessels and reduces the risk of heart disease. Compare **bad cholesterol**.

good-looking /gʊd-'lʊkɪŋ/ adj. having a pleasing appearance.

goods and services tax n. an indirect tax, usually imposed on the consumption of goods and services and most often calculated on the value that is added at each stage of the manufacturing and distribution process. Abbrev.: GST

goodwill /gʊd'wɪl/ n. 1. friendly disposition; benevolence; favour. 2. Commerce an intangible, saleable asset arising from the reputation of a business and its relations with its customers.

goog /gʊg/ n. Colloq. an egg.

google /'gugəl/ (from trademark) –v. (**-gled**, **-gling**) –v.i. 1. to search for information on the internet, in particular using the Google search engine. –v.t. 2. to search the internet for information about, in particular using the Google search engine: *to google the research topic.* *–n.* **3.** an instance of such a search: *to have a little google.*

googol /'gugɒl/ *n.* the number 10^{100}.

goose /gus/ *n.* (*pl.* **geese**) **1.** any of numerous wild or domesticated web-footed birds, most of them larger and with a longer neck than the ducks. **2.** the female of this bird, as distinguished from the male (or gander). **3.** a silly or foolish person; simpleton.

gooseberry /'guzbəri, -bri/ *n.* (*pl.* **-ries**) the small fruit or berry of certain prevailingly prickly shrubs.

goosebumps /'gusbʌmps/ *pl. n.* a rough condition of the skin induced by cold or fear. Also, **goose pimples**.

gopher /'goufə/ *n.* a rodent of North America.

gore[1] /gɔ/ *n.* blood that is shed, especially when clotted.

gore[2] /gɔ/ *v.t.* (of an animal) to pierce with the horns or tusks.

gorge /gɔdʒ/ *n.* **1.** a narrow cleft with steep, rocky walls, especially one through which a stream runs. **2.** the throat; gullet. *–v.t.* (**gorged**, **gorging**) **3.** (*mainly reflexive and passive*) to stuff with food.

gorgeous /'gɔdʒəs/ *adj.* sumptuous; magnificent; splendid in appearance or colouring.

gorilla /gə'rɪlə/ *n.* the largest of the anthropoid apes.

gormless /'gɔmləs/ *adj. Colloq.* (of a person) dull; stupid; senseless.

gory /'gɔri/ *adj.* (**-rier**, **-riest**) **1.** covered or stained with gore; bloody. **2.** *Colloq.* distasteful or unpleasant.

goshawk /'gɒshɔk/ *n.* any of various powerful, short-winged hawks.

gosling /'gɒzlɪŋ/ *n.* a young goose.

go-slow /'goʊ-sloʊ/ *n. Colloq.* a deliberate curtailment of output by workers as an industrial sanction; work-to-rule.

gospel /'gɒspəl/ *n.* **1.** (*oft. upper case*) (in Christianity) the body of doctrine taught by Christ and the apostles. **2.** something regarded as true and implicitly believed.

gospel music *n.* a primarily vocal music based on hymns, a precursor of the blues.

gossamer /'gɒsəmə/ *n.* **1.** a fine filmy cobweb. **2.** a very fine fabric.

gossip /'gɒsəp/ *n.* **1.** idle talk, especially about the affairs of others. **2.** a person given to tattling or idle talk. *–v.i.* (**-siped** *or* **-sipped**, **-siping** *or* **-sipping**) **3.** to talk idly, especially about the affairs of others; go about tattling.

got /gɒt/ *v.* past tense and past participle of **get**.

goth /gɒθ/ *n.* (*sometimes upper case*) **1.** a type of pop music which typically features bleak imagery, and which is associated with a style of dress featuring black clothes, black hair, silver jewellery, and often dramatic black eye make-up and lipstick. **2.** a person who adopts this style of dress. **–gothic**, *adj.*, *n.*

gotten /'gɒtn/ *v.* a past participle of **get**.

gouda /'gaʊdə/ *n.* a smooth, mild-tasting cheese, often made in a large wheel shape.

gouge /gaʊdʒ/ *n.* **1.** a chisel whose blade is curved. *–v.t.* (**gouged**, **gouging**) **2.** to dig or force out with or as with a gouge.

goulash /'gulæʃ/ *n.* a meat stew containing onions and paprika.

gourd /gʊəd, gɔd/ *n.* a fruit whose dried shell is used for bottles, bowls, etc.

gourmand /gə'mɒnd, 'gɔmənd/ *n.* someone fond of good eating. Also, **gormand**.

gourmet /'gʊəmeɪ, 'gɔ-/ *n.* a connoisseur in the delicacies of the table; an epicure.

gout /gaʊt/ *n.* a disease characterised by painful inflammation of the joints.

govern /'gʌvən/ *v.t.* **1.** to rule by right of authority, as a sovereign does. **2.** to exercise a directing or restraining influence over; guide. **3.** *Gram.* to be accompanied by (a particular form) as in 'they helped *us*', not 'they helped *we*'; the verb 'helped' is said to govern the objective case of the pronoun.

governess /'gʌvənes/ *n.* a woman who directs the education of children, generally in their own homes.

government /'gʌvənmənt/ *n.* **1.** the authoritative direction and restraint exercised over the actions of people in communities, societies, and states. **2.** (*sometimes construed as pl.*) the governing body of persons in a state, community, etc.; the executive power; the administration.

governor /'gʌvənə, 'gʌvnə/ *n.* **1.** a person charged with the direction or control of an institution, society, etc. **2.** the principal representative of the sovereign in a state of the Commonwealth of Australia.

governor-general *n.* (*pl.* **governor-generals** *or* **governors-general**) the principal representative of the sovereign in certain independent Commonwealth countries.

gown /gaʊn/ *n.* **1.** a dress worn by women on formal occasions. **2.** a loose, flowing, outer garment.

gozleme /'gɜzləme/ *n.* (in Turkish cuisine) a dish comprising two layers of flatbread dough with a filling of spinach, fetta, etc., the whole being cooked on a griddle.

GPS /dʒi pi 'ɛs/ *n.* **1.** global positioning system; a navigational system which relies on information received from a network of satellites to provide the latitude and longitude of an object, as a ship at sea, etc. **2.** a device which uses this system to determine location.

grab /græb/ *v.t.* **1.** to take suddenly and eagerly; snatch. **2.** *Colloq.* to affect; impress: *the film was OK but it didn't really grab me.*

grace /greɪs/ *n.* **1.** elegance or beauty of form, manner, motion, or act. **2.** mercy; clemency; pardon. **3.** (*pl.*) affected manner; manifestation of pride or vanity. **4.** *Law* an allowance of time to a debtor before suit can be brought against him or her after the debt has by its terms become payable. **5.** a short prayer before or after a meal, in which a blessing is asked and thanks are given. **6.** (*usu. upper case*) (preceded by *your*, *her*, etc.) a formal title used in addressing or mentioning a duke, duchess, or archbishop, and formerly also a sovereign. *–v.t.* (**graced**, **gracing**) **7.** to lend or add grace to; adorn. **8.** to favour or honour. **–graceful**, *adj.*

gracious /'greɪʃəs/ *adj.* disposed to show grace or favour; kind; benevolent; courteous.

gradation /grə'deɪʃən/ n. any process or change taking place through a series of stages, by degrees, or gradually.

grade /greɪd/ n. **1.** a degree in a scale, as of rank, advancement, quality, value, intensity, etc. **2.** a step or stage in a course or process. **3.** inclination with the horizontal of a road, railway, etc. –v.t. **4.** to arrange in a series of grades; class; sort. **5.** to determine the grade of. **6.** to reduce to a level.

-grade a word element meaning 'walking', 'moving', 'going', as in *retrograde*.

grader /'greɪdə/ n. a motor-driven vehicle, with a blade for pushing earth, used for grading roads and for shallow excavation.

gradient /'greɪdiənt/ n. **1.** the degree of inclination, or the rate of ascent or descent, in a railway, etc. **2.** an inclined surface; grade; ramp.

gradual /'grædʒuəl/ adj. **1.** taking place, changing, moving, etc., by degrees or little by little. **2.** rising or descending at an even, moderate inclination.

graduate n. /'grædʒuət/ **1.** someone who has received a degree on completing a course of study, as at a university or college. –v.i. /'grædʒueɪt/ **2.** to receive a degree or diploma on completing a course of study. –v.t. /'grædʒueɪt/ **3.** to divide into or mark with degrees or divisions, as the scale of a thermometer. –**graduation**, n.

graffiti /grə'fiti/ pl. n. (sing. **graffito** /grə'fitou/) (usu. construed as sing.) drawings or words, sometimes obscene, sometimes political, etc., written on public walls.

graft¹ /graft/ n. **1.** Hort. a shoot or part of a plant (the scion) inserted in a groove, slit, or the like in another plant or tree (the stock) so as to become nourished by and united with it. **2.** Surg. a portion of living tissue surgically transplanted. –v.t. **3.** to cause (a plant) to reproduce through grafting. **4.** Surg. to transplant (a portion of living tissue) as a graft.

graft² /graft/ n. **1.** work, especially hard work. **2.** the acquisition of gain or advantage by dishonest, unfair, or shady means, especially through the abuse of one's position or influence in politics, business, etc.

grain /greɪn/ n. **1.** a small hard seed. **2.** any small, hard particle, as of sand, gold, pepper, etc. **3.** the arrangement or direction of fibres in wood. **4.** temper or natural character.

gram /græm/ n. a measure of weight in the metric system, one thousandth of a kilogram. Symbol: g

-gram¹ a word element meaning 'something drawn or written', as in *diagram*.

-gram² a word element meaning 'grams', 'of or relating to a gram', as in *kilogram*.

gramma /'græmə/ n. a type of pumpkin.

grammar /'græmə/ n. the features of a language (sounds, words, formation and arrangement of words, etc.) considered systematically as a whole, especially with reference to their mutual contrasts and relations. –**grammarian**, n. –**grammatical**, adj.

gramophone /'græməfoun/ n. a record-player.

grampus /'græmpəs/ n. a cetacean of the dolphin family.

granary /'grænəri/ n. (pl. **-ries**) a storehouse or repository for grain.

grand /grænd/ adj. **1.** imposing in size or appearance or general effect. **2.** magnificent or splendid. **3.** of great importance, distinction, or pretension. **4.** one degree more remote in ascent or descent (used in compounds), as in *grand-aunt, grandchild*, etc. –**grandeur**, n.

grandchild /'græntʃaɪld/ n. (pl. **-children**) a child of one's son or daughter.

granddaughter /'grændɔtə/ n. a daughter of one's son or daughter. Also, **grand-daughter**.

grandfather /'grænfaðə, 'grænd-/ n. the father of one's father or mother.

grandiloquent /græn'dɪləkwənt/ adj. speaking or expressed in a lofty or pompous style; bombastic.

grandiose /'grændious/ adj. grand in an imposing or impressive way.

grandmother /'grænmʌðə, 'grænd-/ n. the mother of one's father or mother.

grandparent /'grænpeərənt/ n. a parent of a parent.

grandson /'grænsʌn, 'grænd-/ n. a son of one's son or daughter.

grandstand /'grænstænd, 'grænd-/ n. **1.** the principal stand for spectators at a racecourse, athletic field, etc. –v.i. **2.** to behave ostentatiously in order to impress or win approval.

granite /'grænət/ n. a granular igneous rock composed chiefly of feldspar and quartz.

grant /grænt, grant/ v.t. **1.** to bestow or confer, especially by a formal act. **2.** to give or accord. **3.** to admit or concede; accept for the sake of argument. –n. **4.** that which is granted, as a privilege or right, a sum of money, as for a student's maintenance, or a tract of land. –phr. **5. take for granted**, to accept without appreciation. –**grantor**, n. –**grantee**, n.

granular /'grænjələ/ adj. **1.** of the nature of granules. **2.** composed of or bearing granules or grains. **3.** showing a granulated structure.

granulate /'grænjəleɪt/ v.t. **1.** to form into granules or grains. –v.i. **2.** to become granular. –**granulator**, n. –**granulation**, n.

granule /'grænjul/ n. a little grain, pellet, or particle.

grape /greɪp/ n. a small, round, smooth-skinned greenish or purplish fruit which grows in bunches on vines, used for eating or making wine.

grapefruit /'greɪpfrut/ n. a large roundish, yellow-skinned edible citrus fruit.

graph /græf, graf/ n. **1.** a diagram representing a system of connections or inter-relations among two or more things by a number of distinctive dots, lines, bars, etc. –v.t. **2.** to draw a graph of.

graph- variant of **grapho-** before vowels.

-graph a word element meaning: **1.** drawn or written, as in *autograph*. **2.** something drawn or written, as in *lithograph, monograph*. **3.** an apparatus for drawing, writing, recording, etc., as in *barograph*.

graphic /'græfɪk/ adj. **1.** relating to the use of diagrams, graphs, mathematical curves, or the like; diagrammatic. **2.** relating to writing. **3.** life-like; vivid: *graphic description*. **4.** shockingly explicit: *graphic images of the war*. –n.

5. a graphic image or icon: *computer graphics.* –**graphically,** *adv.*

graphical user interface *n. Computers* an interface which uses graphic displays, such as icons and pull-down menus. *Abbrev.:* GUI Also, **graphic interface.**

graphic designer *n.* a designer, as of advertisements, books, etc., who uses print styles, images, page layout, etc., as design elements. –**graphic design,** *n.*

graphite /ˈgræfaɪt/ *n.* a very common mineral, soft native carbon.

grapho- a word element meaning 'writing'. Also, **graph-.**

-graphy a combining form denoting some process or form of drawing, representing, writing, recording, describing, etc.

grapnel /ˈgræpnəl/ *n.* a device consisting essentially of one or more hooks or clamps, for grasping or holding something.

grapple /ˈgræpəl/ *n.* **1.** a hook or an iron instrument by which one thing, as a ship, fastens on another; a grapnel. –*v.i.* **2.** to hold or make fast to something as with a grapple. **3.** to seize another, or each other, in a firm grip, as in wrestling; clinch. **4.** (fol. by *with*) to try to overcome or deal.

grasp /græsp, grasp/ *v.t.* **1.** to seize and hold by or as by clasping with the fingers. **2.** to lay hold of with the mind; comprehend; understand. –*v.i.* **3.** to make the motion of seizing; seize something firmly or eagerly. –*n.* **4.** a grasping or gripping; grip of the hand. **5.** hold, possession, or mastery. **6.** broad or thorough comprehension.

grass /gras/ *n.* **1.** a low-growing green plant with thin leaves growing close together. **2.** *Colloq.* marijuana.

grasshopper /ˈgrashɒpə/ *n.* a terrestrial, herbivorous insect with long hind legs for leaping.

grassland /ˈgrasland/ *n.* an area in which the natural vegetation consists largely of perennial grasses, characteristic of subhumid and semi-arid climates.

grate¹ /greɪt/ *n.* a frame of metal bars for holding fuel when burning, as in a fireplace or furnace.

grate² /greɪt/ *v.t.* **1.** to reduce to small particles by rubbing against a rough surface or a surface with many sharp-edged openings. **2.** to rub together with a harsh, jarring sound. –*v.i.* **3.** to have an irritating or unpleasant effect on the feelings. **4.** to make a sound as of rough scraping. –**grater,** *n.*

grateful /ˈgreɪtfəl/ *adj.* warmly or deeply appreciative of kindness or benefits received; thankful. –**gratitude,** *n.*

gratify /ˈgrætəfaɪ/ *v.t.* (**-fied, -fying**) **1.** to give pleasure to (persons) by satisfying desires or humouring inclinations or feelings. **2.** to satisfy; indulge; humour. –**gratifier,** *n.* –**gratification,** *n.*

gratis /ˈgrætəs/ *adv.* **1.** for nothing. –*adj.* **2.** free of cost.

gratuitous /grəˈtjuːətəs/ *adj.* **1.** freely bestowed or obtained; free. **2.** being without reason, cause, or justification.

gratuity /grəˈtjuːəti/ *n.* (*pl.* **-ties**) a gift, usually of money, over and above payment due for service; tip.

grave¹ /greɪv/ *n.* an excavation made in the earth to receive a dead body in burial.

grave² /greɪv/ *adj.* **1.** dignified; sedate; serious; earnest; solemn. **2.** important or critical; involving serious issues.

gravel /ˈgrævəl/ *n.* small stones and pebbles, or a mixture of these with sand.

gravitate /ˈgrævəteɪt/ *v.i.* **1.** to move or tend to move under the influence of gravitational force. –*phr.* **2. gravitate to** (or **towards**), to have a natural tendency towards or be strongly attracted to.

gravitation /grævəˈteɪʃən/ *n. Physics* that force of attraction between all particles or bodies, or that acceleration of one towards another, of which the fall of bodies to the earth is an instance. –**gravitational,** *adj.* –**gravitationally,** *adv.*

gravity /ˈgrævəti/ *n.* **1.** *Physics* the force of attraction by which terrestrial bodies tend to fall towards the centre of the earth. **2.** seriousness; dignity; solemnity. **3.** serious or critical character.

gravy /ˈgreɪvi/ *n.* the fat and juices that drip from meat during cooking, often made into a sauce for meat, etc.

graze¹ /greɪz/ *v.i.* to feed on growing grass, etc., as cattle, sheep, etc.

graze² /greɪz/ *v.t.* **1.** to touch or rub lightly in passing. **2.** to scrape the skin from (the leg, arm, etc.); abrade. –*n.* **3.** a slight scratch in passing; abrasion.

grazier /ˈgreɪziə/ *n.* the owner of a rural property on which sheep or cattle are grazed.

grease *n.* /gris/ **1.** the melted or rendered fat of animals, especially when in a soft state. **2.** fatty or oily matter in general; lubricant. –*v.t.* /griz, gris/ **3.** to smear with grease. –**greasy,** *adj.*

great /greɪt/ *adj.* **1.** unusually or comparatively large in size or dimensions. **2.** notable or remarkable. **3.** of much consequence; important. **4.** being such in an extreme degree. **5.** *Colloq.* first-rate; very good; fine. **6.** one degree more remote in direct ascent or descent than a specified relationship.

greed /grid/ *n.* inordinate or rapacious desire, especially for food or wealth.

greedy /ˈgridi/ *adj.* (**-dier, -diest**) **1.** wanting a great or unreasonable amount of something, especially food, money or possessions. –*phr.* **2. greedy guts,** *Informal* someone who likes to eat too much, especially a child. –**greedily,** *adv.* –**greediness,** *n.*

green /grin/ *adj.* **1.** of the colour of growing foliage, between yellow and blue in the spectrum. **2.** covered with grass or foliage; verdant. **3.** characterised by, or relating to, a concern for environmental issues. **4.** not fully developed or perfected in growth or condition; unripe; not properly aged. **5.** immature in age or judgement; untrained; inexperienced. **6.** (of certain foods, such as prawns) uncooked, raw. –*n.* **7.** green colour. **8.** *Golf* the whole course or links on which golf is played. **9.** a level grassed playing field for the game of bowls; bowling green.

green ban *n.* **1.** a refusal by employees to work or to allow work to proceed on a building site that is situated in a green belt. **2.** a similar

green belt refusal with respect to any construction work which would necessitate destroying something of natural, historical or social significance.

green belt *n.* an area of parkland, rural or uncultivated land, or native bush, near a town or a city on which building is either strictly controlled or not permitted.

green energy *n.* energy derived from environmentally friendly sources, such as wind power, solar power, etc.

green-eyed /'grin-aid/ *adj.* **1.** having green eyes. **2.** jealous.

greenfield /'grinfild/ *adj.* **1.** of or relating to a location for a business where there has not previously been any building. **2.** of or relating to any enterprise which is becoming active in a market where there has been little or no previous activity. Also, **greenfields**.

greenfields /'grinfildz/ *pl. n.* **1.** parkland or agricultural land on the outskirts of a city. –*adj.* **2.** → **greenfield**.

green footprint *n.* an ecological footprint which is environmentally friendly. See **ecological footprint**.

greengrocer /'gringroosə/ *n.* a retailer of fresh vegetables and fruit.

greenhouse /'grinhaus/ *n.* a building, chiefly of glass, for the cultivation or protection of plants.

greenhouse effect *n.* the increase in the temperature of the earth caused by its atmosphere acting as the glass of a greenhouse does, possibly to be increased as pollution adds more and more carbon dioxide to the atmosphere.

greenhouse-friendly *adj.* either not producing or else actually reducing greenhouse gas emissions.

greenhouse gas *n.* one of a number of gases found in the atmosphere that contribute to the greenhouse effect.

greenie /'grini/ *n. Colloq.* a conservationist.

green lung *n.* an area in or near to a city which is covered with vegetation which acts to draw in carbon dioxide and produce oxygen.

greenmail /'grinmeil/ *n.* the purchase of a large block of a company's shares, threatening a takeover, but actually in order to have the shares purchased at a much higher price by a group friendly to the company. –**greenmailer**, *n.* –**greenmailing**, *n.*

green room *n.* a room set aside for use of artists in a theatre, opera house, television studio, etc., in which they can relax and entertain when they are not performing.

green screen *n.* an alternative to a blue screen where an actor is wearing something blue that would be misinterpreted by the computer as needing to have a replacement image. See **blue screen**.

greenstick /'grinstik/ *n.* a type of make-up with a slight green hue to it which covers up redness on the skin.

greenstick fracture *n.* a partial fracture of a bone of a young person or animal, in which only one side of a bone is broken.

greet /grit/ *v.t.* to address with some form of salutation; welcome.

greeting /'gritiŋ/ *n.* **1.** the act or words of someone who greets. **2.** (*usu. pl.*) a friendly message.

gregarious /grə'gɛəriəs/ *adj.* **1.** living in flocks or herds, as animals. **2.** *Bot.* growing in open clusters; not matted together. **3.** fond of company; sociable.

gremlin /'gremlən/ *n.* something that causes mischief or trouble.

grenade /grə'neid/ *n.* a small explosive shell thrown by hand or fired from a rifle.

grevillea /grə'viliə/ *n.* any shrub or tree of a very large, mainly Australian, genus.

grew /gru/ *v.* past tense of **grow**.

grey /grei/ *adj.* **1.** of a colour between white and black, having no definite hue. **2.** dark, overcast, dismal, gloomy. **3.** grey-haired. –*n.* **4.** any colour between white and black, having no definite hue. **5.** a grey horse.

greyhound /'greihaund/ *n.* one of a breed of tall, slender dogs, notable for keen sight and for fleetness.

greywater /'greiwɔtə/ *n.* untreated domestic or industrial waste water that can be used for watering lawns and gardens, or for other purposes, instead of being drained into the sewerage system.

grid /grid/ *n.* **1.** a grating of crossed bars. **2.** a network of cables, pipes, etc., for the distribution and supply of electricity, gas, water, etc. **3.** a network of horizontal and vertical lines designed to give fixed points of reference, as those superimposed on a map, etc.

griddle /'gridl/ *n.* a flat, heated surface on top of a stove.

grief /grif/ *n.* **1.** keen mental suffering or distress over affliction or loss; sharp sorrow; painful regret. –*phr.* **2. come to grief**, to come to a bad end; turn out badly.

grievance /'grivəns/ *n.* a wrong, real or fancied, considered as grounds for complaint.

grieve /griv/ *v.i.* **1.** to feel grief; sorrow. –*v.t.* **2.** to distress mentally; cause to feel grief or sorrow.

grievous /'grivəs/ *adj.* **1.** causing grief or sorrow. **2.** flagrant; atrocious.

grill /gril/ *n.* **1.** a griller. **2.** a meal in which the meat component is grilled. –*v.t.* **3.** to cook under a griller. **4.** *Colloq.* to subject to severe questioning.

grille /gril/ *n.* **1.** a lattice screen, as a window or gate, usually of metal and often of decorative design. **2.** an ornamental metal screen at the front of a car. –**grilled**, *adj.*

griller /'grilə/ *n.* a cooking device, or that part of a stove, in which meat, etc., is cooked by exposure to direct radiant heat.

grim /grim/ *adj.* (**grimmer**, **grimmest**) **1.** stern; unrelenting; uncompromising. **2.** of a fierce or forbidding aspect.

grimace /'griməs, grə'meis/ *n.* **1.** a wry face; facial contortion; ugly facial expression. –*v.i.* (**-maced**, **-macing**) **2.** to make grimaces. –**grimacer**, *n.*

grime /graim/ *n.* dirt or foul matter, especially on or ingrained in a surface.

grin /grin/ *v.i.* (**grinned**, **grinning**) **1.** to smile broadly. –*n.* **2.** a broad smile.

grind /graind/ *v.t.* (**ground**, **grinding**) **1.** to wear, smooth, or sharpen by friction; whet. **2.** to reduce to fine particles as by pounding or crushing. –*n.* **3.** the act of grinding. **4.** *Colloq.*

laborious or monotonous work; close or laborious study.

grip /grɪp/ n. **1.** the act of grasping; a seizing and holding fast; firm grasp. **2.** mental or intellectual hold; competence. **3.** a special mode of clasping hands. **4.** something which seizes and holds, as a clutching device on a cable car. **5.** a sudden, sharp pain; spasm of pain. –v.t. (**gripped, gripping**) **6.** to grasp or seize firmly; hold fast. **7.** to take hold on; hold the interest of.

gripe /graɪp/ v.i. (**griped, griping**) **1.** Colloq. to complain constantly; grumble. –n. **2.** an objection; complaint.

grisly /'grɪzli/ adj. (**-lier, -liest**) such as to cause a shuddering horror; gruesome.

grist /grɪst/ n. corn to be ground.

gristle /'grɪsəl/ n. → **cartilage**.

grit /grɪt/ n. **1.** fine, stony, or hard particles such as are deposited like dust from the air or occur as impurities in food, etc. **2.** firmness of character; indomitable spirit; pluck. –v.t. (**gritted, gritting**) **3.** to clench or grind.

grizzle /'grɪzəl/ v.i. to whimper; whine; complain fretfully. –**grizzly**, adj.

groan /groʊn/ n. **1.** a low, mournful sound uttered in pain or grief. **2.** a deep murmur uttered in derision, disapproval, etc. –v.i. **3.** to utter a moan.

grocer /'groʊsə/ n. a dealer in general supplies for the table, as flour, sugar, coffee, etc. –**grocery**, n.

grog /grɒg/ n. Colloq. alcohol.

groggy /'grɒgi/ adj. (**-gier, -giest**) **1.** staggering, as from exhaustion or blows. **2.** Colloq. drunk; intoxicated.

groin /grɔɪn/ n. Anat. the fold or hollow where the thigh joins the abdomen.

grolar bear /groʊlə 'beə/ n. a hybrid species, the offspring of a grizzly bear and a polar bear; occurring naturally in greater numbers as a result of climate change.

grommet[1] /'grɒmət/ n. **1.** a ring or eyelet of metal, rubber, etc. **2.** Med. a small, plastic tube inserted through the eardrum into the middle ear to assist in preventing infection. Also, **grummet**.

grommet[2] /'grɒmət/ n. Colloq. **1.** a young surfie. **2.** a young snowboarder.

groom /grum/ n. **1.** a person in charge of horses or the stable. **2.** a man newly married, or about to be married; bridegroom. –v.t. **3.** to tend carefully as to person and dress; make neat or tidy. **4.** to prepare for a position, election, etc.

groomsman /'grumzmən/ n. (pl. **-men**) a man who attends the bridegroom at a wedding.

groove /gruv/ n. **1.** a furrow or channel cut by a tool. **2.** a fixed routine.

groovy /'gruvi/ adj. (**-vier, -viest**) Colloq. **1.** exciting, satisfying, or pleasurable. **2.** fashionable.

grope /groʊp/ v.i. **1.** to feel about with the hands; feel one's way. **2.** to search blindly or uncertainly.

groper /'groʊpə/ n. (pl. **-per** or **-pers**) any of several species of large Australian or NZ marine fish.

gross /groʊs/ adj. **1.** whole, entire, or total, especially without having been subjected to deduction, as for charges, loss, etc. **2.** glaring or flagrant. **3.** morally coarse; lacking refinement; indelicate or indecent. **4.** large, big, or bulky. –n. (pl. **gross**) **5.** a unit consisting of twelve dozen, or 144. –v.t. **6.** to make a gross profit of; earn a total of.

gross domestic product n. an estimate of the total value of all legal goods and services produced in a country in a specified time, usually a year. Abbrev.: GDP

gross motor skills pl. n. the physical skills considered basic to human activity, such as locomotion, balance, spatial orientation, etc. Compare **fine motor skills**.

gross national product n. gross domestic product plus income earned by domestic residents from overseas investments, minus income earned in the domestic market accruing to overseas (foreign) residents. Abbrev.: GNP

gross tonnage n. a measure of the enclosed internal volume of a ship and its superstructure, with certain spaces exempted.

grotesque /groʊˈtesk/ adj. odd or unnatural in shape, appearance, or character; fantastically ugly or absurd; bizarre.

grotto /'grɒtoʊ/ n. (pl. **-toes** or **-tos**) a cave or cavern.

grotty /'grɒti/ adj. (**-tier, -tiest**) Colloq. **1.** dirty; filthy. **2.** useless; rubbishy.

grouch /graʊtʃ/ Colloq. –v.i. **1.** to be sulky or morose; show discontent; complain. –n. **2.** a sulky or morose person. –**grouchy**, adj.

ground[1] /graʊnd/ n. **1.** the earth's solid surface; firm or dry land. **2.** earth or soil. **3.** (oft. pl.) a tract of land occupied, or appropriated to a special use. **4.** (oft. pl.) the foundation or basis on which a theory or action rests; motive; reason. **5.** the underlying or main surface or background, in painting, decorative work, lace, etc. –adj. **6.** situated on or at, or adjacent to, the surface of the earth. **7.** relating to the ground. –v.t. **8.** to lay or set on the ground. **9.** to place on a foundation; found; fix firmly; settle or establish. **10.** Elect. to establish an earth for (a circuit, device, etc.). **11.** to prevent (an aircraft or a pilot) from flying. **12.** to restrict, or withdraw privileges from. –phr. **13.** **common ground**, matters on which agreement exists. **14.** **gain ground**, to advance; make progress. **15.** **hold** (or **stand**) **one's ground**, to maintain one's position. **16.** **lose ground**, to lose what one has gained; retreat; give way. **17.** **run to ground**, to hunt down; track down.

ground[2] /graʊnd/ v. past tense and past participle of **grind**.

ground plan n. the plan of a ground floor of a building.

ground rent n. the rent at which land is leased to a tenant for a specified term, usually ninety-nine years.

ground rule n. (usu. pl.) a basic rule of a game, meeting, procedure, etc.

groundsheet /'graʊndʃit/ n. a waterproof sheet spread on the ground to give protection against dampness.

groundwater /'graʊndwɔtə/ n. the water beneath the surface of the ground, consisting largely of surface water that has seeped down, and which eventually drains into rivers, lakes or wetlands. Also, **ground water**.

groundwork /'graʊndwɜk/ n. the foundation, base, or basis of anything.

ground zero n. **1.** the point on the surface of the earth directly below the point at which a nuclear weapon explodes, or the centre of the crater if the weapon is exploded on the ground. **2.** the target of a missile, bomb, etc. **3.** a starting point or base.

group /grup/ n. **1.** any assemblage of persons or things; cluster. **2.** a number of persons or things ranged or considered together as being related in some way. –v.t. **3.** to place in a group, as with others.

group certificate n. a certificate issued by an employer to an employee at the end of a financial year, detailing gross income, tax paid, etc.

grouper /'grupə/ n. (pl. **-per** or **-pers**) any of various often large fishes found in warm seas.

grouse[1] /graʊs/ n. a game bird of the Northern Hemisphere.

grouse[2] /graʊs/ v.i. Colloq. to grumble; complain.

grouse[3] /graʊs/ adj. **1.** Colloq. very good. –phr. **5.** extra grouse, excellent.

grout /graʊt/ n. a thin coarse mortar poured into the joints of masonry and brickwork.

grove /groʊv/ n. a small wood or plantation of trees.

grovel /'grɒvəl/ v.i. (**-elled** or, Chiefly US, **-eled, -elling** or, Chiefly US, **-eling**) to humble oneself or act in an abject manner, as in fear or in mean servility. –**groveller**, n.

grow /groʊ/ v. (**grew, grown, growing**) –v.i. **1.** to increase by natural development, as any living organism or part by assimilation of nutriment; increase in size or substance. **2.** to increase gradually; become greater. **3.** to come to be, or become, by degrees. –v.t. **4.** to cause to grow. –phr. **5. grow up**, to increase in growth; attain maturity.

growl /graʊl/ v.i. **1.** to utter a deep guttural sound of anger or hostility. –n. **2.** the act or sound of growling.

grown-up /'groʊn-ʌp/ adj. **1.** adult. –n. **2.** a grown-up person; an adult.

growth /groʊθ/ n. **1.** the act, process, or manner of growing; development; gradual increase. **2.** a diseased mass of tissue, as a tumour.

grub /grʌb/ n. **1.** the bulky larva of certain insects, especially of certain beetles. **2.** Colloq. food.

grubby /'grʌbi/ adj. (**-bier, -biest**) **1.** dirty; grimy. **2.** morally dubious; sleazy: a grubby little film.

grudge /grʌdʒ/ n. a feeling of ill will or resentment excited by some special cause, as a personal injury or insult, etc.

gruel /'gruəl/ n. a light, usually thin, cooked cereal made by boiling meal, especially oatmeal, in water or milk.

gruelling /'gruəlɪŋ/ adj. exhausting; very tiring; severe.

gruesome /'grusəm/ adj. inspiring horror; revolting.

gruff /grʌf/ adj. **1.** low and harsh; hoarse. **2.** rough; surly.

grumble /'grʌmbəl/ v.i. **1.** to murmur in discontent; complain ill-humouredly. –n. **2.** an ill-humoured complaining; murmur; growl.

grumpy /'grʌmpi/ adj. (**-pier, -piest**) Colloq. surly; ill-tempered. –**grump**, n.

grunge /grʌndʒ/ n. **1.** a substance of an unpleasant nature, especially a dirty scum or slime. **2.** a guitar-based form of heavy rock music using simple minor-chord progressions, on-the-beat rhythms and lyrics ranging from the frivolous to the unsavoury. **3.** a fashion in which clothes are worn which are normally considered shabby or unfashionable, as those bought in second-hand shops. –**grungy**, adj.

grunt /grʌnt/ v.i. to utter the deep guttural sound characteristic of a pig.

gruyere /'gruiə, gru'jɛə/ n. a firm pale yellow variety of Swiss cheese. Also, **Gruyère, Gruyere**.

guacamole /gwakə'moʊli, gwɒkə-/ n. a dip consisting of mashed avocado, seasonings, and lemon or lime juice, sometimes mixed with sour cream, mayonnaise, etc.

guano /'gwanoʊ/ n. (pl. **-nos**) **1.** a natural manure composed chiefly of the excrement of seabirds. **2.** Also, **bat guano**. the droppings of bats, used as a fertiliser.

guarantee /gærən'ti/ n. **1.** a warrant, pledge, or promise accepting responsibility for the discharging of another's liabilities, as the payment of a debt. **2.** a promise or assurance, especially one given in writing by a manufacturer, that something is of a specified quality, and generally including an undertaking to make good any defects under certain conditions. **3.** someone who gives a guarantee; guarantor. **4.** something that has the force or effect of a guarantee. –v.t. (**-teed, -teeing**) **5.** to secure, as by giving or taking security. **6.** to make oneself answerable for on behalf of one primarily responsible. **7.** to undertake to secure to another, as rights or possessions. **8.** to serve as a warrant or guarantee for. **9.** (fol. by from, against, or in) to engage to protect or indemnify. **10.** to promise.

guarantor /gærən'tɔ/ n. someone who makes or gives a guarantee.

guaranty /'gærənti/ n. (pl. **-ties, -tied, -tying**) → **guarantee**.

guard /gad/ v.t. **1.** to keep safe from harm; protect; watch over. **2.** to keep under close watch in order to prevent escape, outbreaks, etc. –v.i. **3.** (fol. by against) to take precautions. –n. **4.** someone who guards, protects, or keeps a protecting or restraining watch. **5.** something intended or serving to guard or protect; a safeguard. **6.** an official in general charge of a railway train.

guardian /'gadiən/ n. **1.** someone who guards, protects, or preserves. **2.** Law someone who is entrusted by law with the care of the person or property, or both, of another. –adj. **3.** guarding; protecting.

guava /'gwavə/ n. any of various trees and shrubs with an edible fruit.

guerilla /gə'rɪlə/ n. a member of an irregular, usually politically motivated armed force, which harasses the enemy, usually the regular army, by surprise raids, attacks on communication and supply lines, etc. Also, **guerrilla**.

guernsey /'gɜnzi/ n. (pl. **-seys**) **1.** a close-fitting knitted jumper. **2.** Sport a distinctively coloured or marked top worn by footballers.

guess /gɛs/ v.t. to form an opinion of at random or from evidence admittedly uncertain.

guest /gɛst/ n. a person entertained at the house or table of another.

guff /gʌf/ n. Colloq. empty or foolish talk.

guffaw /gʌ'fɔ, gə-/ n. **1.** a loud, coarse burst of laughter. –v.i. **2.** to laugh loudly.

guidance /'gaɪdns/ n. advice; instruction.

guide /gaɪd/ v.t. **1.** to lead or conduct on the way, as to a place or through a region; show the way to. **2.** to direct the movement or course of. –n. **3.** someone who guides.

guide dog n. a dog specially trained to lead or guide a vision-impaired person.

guild /gɪld/ n. an organisation of persons with common professional or cultural interests formed for mutual aid and protection.

guile /gaɪl/ n. insidious cunning.

guillotine /'gɪlətin/ n. **1.** a machine for beheading persons by means of a heavy blade falling in two grooved posts. **2.** a device incorporating a long blade for trimming paper. **3.** a time restriction imposed by resolution on a parliamentary debate.

guilt /gɪlt/ n. **1.** the fact or state of having committed an offence or crime. **2.** a feeling of responsibility or remorse for some crime, wrong, etc., either real or imagined. –**guilty**, adj.

guinea pig /'gɪni/ n. **1.** a short-eared, short-legged rodent. **2.** a person used as the subject of any type of experiment.

guise /gaɪz/ n. **1.** external appearance in general; aspect or semblance. **2.** assumed appearance or mere semblance.

guitar /gə'ta/ n. a musical stringed instrument with a long fretted neck and a flat, somewhat violin-like body.

gulf /gʌlf/ n. **1.** a portion of an ocean or sea partly enclosed by land. **2.** a deep hollow; chasm or abyss.

gull /gʌl/ n. a web-footed, aquatic bird.

gullet /'gʌlət/ n. the oesophagus, or tube by which food and drink swallowed pass to the stomach.

gullible /'gʌləbəl/ adj. easily deceived or cheated. –**gullibility**, n. –**gullibly**, adv.

gully /'gʌli/ n. a small valley cut by running water.

gulp /gʌlp/ v.t. **1.** to swallow eagerly, as when taking large draughts of liquids. –n. **2.** the act of gulping.

gum¹ /gʌm/ n. **1.** any of various viscid, amorphous exudations from plants. **2.** a preparation of such a substance, as for use in the arts, etc. **3.** → **gum tree** (def. 1). –v.t. (**gummed, gumming**) **4.** to smear, stiffen, or stick together with gum. **5.** (oft. fol. by up) to clog with or as with some gummy substance.

gum² /gʌm/ n. (oft. pl.) the firm, fleshy tissue covering the jaw and enveloping the bases of the teeth.

gumboot /'gʌmbut/ n. a rubber boot reaching to the knee or thigh; wellington boot.

gumption /'gʌmpʃən/ n. Colloq. **1.** initiative; resourcefulness. **2.** shrewd, practical common sense.

gum tree n. Also, **gum**. **1.** any tree or shrub of a mostly Australian genus of which some yield eucalyptus oil and some hardwood timber; eucalypt. –phr. **2. up a gum tree**, Colloq. **a.** in difficulties; in a predicament. **b.** completely baffled.

gun /gʌn/ n. **1.** a metallic tube, from which missiles are thrown by the force of an explosive. **2.** any similar device for projecting something. **3.** Colloq. a champion, especially in shearing. **4.** (oft. in the pl.) Colloq. a biceps, especially one developed, as in bodybuilding. –v.t. (**gunned, gunning**) **5.** (oft. fol. by down) to shoot with a gun. –adj. **6.** Colloq. of or relating to someone who is expert.

gunboat diplomacy n. diplomacy or foreign affairs in conjunction with the use or threat of military force.

gunnery /'gʌnəri/ n. **1.** the art and science of constructing and managing guns, especially large guns. **2.** the firing of guns. **3.** guns collectively.

gunny /'gʌni/ n. a strong, coarse material made commonly from jute, used for sacking, etc.

gunpowder /'gʌnpaʊdə/ n. an explosive mixture of saltpetre (potassium nitrate), sulphur, and charcoal, used especially in gunnery.

gunwale /'gʌnəl/ n. the upper edge of a vessel's or boat's side.

gunyah /'gʌnjə/ n. a hut traditionally made by Aboriginal people of boughs and bark. Also, **gunya**.

guppy /'gʌpi/ n. (pl. **-pies**) a small viviparous fish; common in home aquariums.

gurgle /'gɜgəl/ v.i. **1.** to flow in a broken, irregular, noisy current. **2.** to make a sound as of water doing this (often used of birds or of human beings).

guru /'guru, 'guru/ n. (in Hinduism) a spiritual guide.

gush /gʌʃ/ v.i. **1.** to issue with force, as a fluid escaping from confinement; flow suddenly and copiously. **2.** to express oneself extravagantly or emotionally; talk effusively.

gusset /'gʌsət/ n. an angular piece of material inserted in a garment to strengthen, enlarge or give freedom of movement to some part of it.

gust /gʌst/ n. a sudden, strong blast, as of wind. –**gusty**, adj.

gusto /'gʌstoʊ/ n. keen relish or hearty enjoyment, as in eating, drinking, or in action or speech generally.

gut /gʌt/ n. **1.** the alimentary canal between the stomach and the anus, or some portion of it. **2.** a preparation of the intestines of an animal used for various purposes, as for violin strings, tennis rackets, fishing lines, etc. –v.t. (**gutted, gutting**) **3.** to take out the guts or entrails of; disembowel. **4.** to destroy the interior of. –adj. **5.** of or relating to feelings, emotion, intuition. See **guts**.

guts /gʌts/ Colloq. –pl. n. (oft. construed as sing.) **1.** the bowels or entrails. **2.** the stomach or abdomen. **3.** courage; stamina; endurance: to have guts. **4.** essential information: the guts of the matter. **5.** essential parts or contents: let me get to the guts of the motor. **6.** Also, **greedy-guts**. someone greedy for food; a glutton. –v.t. **7.** to cram (oneself) with food. –phr. **8. hate someone's guts**, to loathe or detest someone. **9. have someone's guts for garters,** to exact revenge on someone. **10. rough as guts,** (of a person) coarse in manner and behaviour. **11. spill** (or **give**) **one's guts,** to give information, as to the police, without restraint: *they had broken him – he was about to spill his guts to them.* **12. the (good) guts,** (sometimes fol. by *on*) accurate information, especially when intended to be used against someone. **13. work one's guts out,** to work excessively hard. See **gut**. –**gutsy**, *adj.*

gutter /'gʌtə/ *n.* **1.** a channel at the side (or in the middle) of a road or street, for leading off surface water. **2.** a channel at the eaves or on the roof of a building, for carrying off rainwater.

guttural /'gʌtərəl/ *adj.* **1.** relating to the throat. **2.** harsh; throaty.

guy¹ /gaɪ/ *n. Colloq.* **1.** a man or boy. **2.** (*pl.*) people of either sex, regarded as members of a group: *Are you guys ready?*

guy² /gaɪ/ *n.* a rope, wire, etc., used to guide and steady something being hoisted or lowered, or to secure anything liable to shift its position.

guzzle /'gʌzəl/ *v.t.* to drink (or sometimes eat) frequently and greedily.

gym /dʒɪm/ *n.* **1.** a centre providing fitness equipment and classes. **2.** a gymnasium.

gymkhana /dʒɪm'kanə/ *n.* a horseriding event featuring games and novelty contests.

gymnasium /dʒɪm'neɪziəm/ *n.* (*pl.* **-siums** or **-sia** /-ziə/) a building or room equipped with facilities for gymnastics and sport.

gymnast /'dʒɪmnæst, -nəst/ *n.* someone trained and skilled in, or a teacher of, gymnastics.

gymnastic /dʒɪm'næstɪk/ *adj.* relating to exercises which develop flexibility, strength, and agility. –**gymnastics**, *n.*

gyn- variant of **gyno-**.

gynaecology /gaɪnə'kɒlədʒi/ *n.* the department of medical science which deals with the functions and diseases peculiar to women, especially those affecting the reproductive organs. Also, **gynecology**. –**gynaecological**, *adj.* –**gynaecologist**, *n.*

gyno- a word element meaning 'woman', 'female'. Also, **gyn-**.

-gynous 1. a word element forming an adjective termination referring to the female sex, as in *androgynous*. **2.** a suffix meaning 'woman'.

gyp /dʒɪp/ *Colloq.* –*v.t.* (**gypped, gypping**) **1.** to swindle; cheat; defraud or rob by some sharp practice. –*n.* **2.** a swindle.

gyprock /'dʒɪprɒk/ *n.* (*from trademark*) → **plasterboard**. –**gyprocker**, *n.*

gypsum /'dʒɪpsəm/ *n.* a very common mineral, used to make plaster as an ornamental material, as a fertiliser, etc.

gypsy /'dʒɪpsi/ *n.* (*pl.* **-sies**) someone who has an unconventional or nomadic lifestyle. Also, **gipsy**.

gyrate /dʒaɪ'reɪt/ *v.i.* to move in a circle or spiral, or round a fixed point; whirl. –**gyration**, *n.* –**gyratory**, *adj.*

gyre /'dʒaɪə/ *n.* a ring or circle.

gyro- a word element meaning: **1.** 'ring'; 'circle'. **2.** 'spiral'.

gyroscope /'dʒaɪrəskoʊp/ *n.* an apparatus consisting of a rotating wheel so mounted that its axis can turn freely in certain or all directions, and capable of maintaining the same absolute direction in space in spite of movements of the mountings and surroundings parts. –**gyroscopic**, *adj.*

H, h

H, h /eɪtʃ/, *sometimes considered non-standard* /heɪtʃ/ *n.* the 8th letter of the English alphabet.

habeas corpus /ˌheɪbɪəs ˈkɔːpəs/ *n.* a writ commanding that a prisoner appear in court.

haberdashery /ˈhæbəˈdæʃəri, ˈhæbə-/ *n.* (*pl.* **-ries**) **1.** a shop where goods such as buttons, needles, etc., are sold. **2.** the goods themselves. –**haberdasher,** *n.*

habit /ˈhæbət/ *n.* **1.** a disposition or tendency, constantly shown, to act in a certain way. **2.** garb of a particular rank, profession, religious order, etc. –**habitual,** *adj.*

habitable /ˈhæbətəbəl/ *adj.* able to be lived in.

habitat /ˈhæbətæt/ *n.* the native environment of an animal or plant.

habitation /hæbəˈteɪʃən/ *n.* a place of abode; dwelling.

habituate /həˈbɪtʃueɪt/ *v.t.* **1.** to accustom. **2.** to frequent.

háček /ˈhætʃek/ *n.* a mark (ˇ) over a letter used especially in the spelling of Slavic languages to represent particular phonetic qualities.

hack¹ /hæk/ *v.t.* **1.** to cut, notch, or chop irregularly, as with heavy blows. **2.** to damage by cutting harshly or ruthlessly. –*n.* **3.** a short, broken cough. **4.** *Computers* unauthorised access to a computer, a computer network, or a digital device. **5.** *Computers* a contrived method of achieving a programming goal that takes advantage of opportunities that are provided by software but were not intended by the original developer. **6.** an improvised solution to a problem, as in living one's life, improving one's health, etc. –*phr.* **7. hack into,** to gain unauthorised access, as to the information stored on an organisation's computer.

hack² /hæk/ *n.* **1.** a horse used for general work, especially ordinary riding. **2.** a horse kept for common hire. **3.** a person who for a living undertakes literary or other work of little or no originality. –*v.t.* **4.** *Colloq.* to put up with; endure.

hacker /ˈhækə/ *n.* **1.** someone or something that hacks. **2.** *Internet* a person who is adept at manipulating computer systems, especially someone who achieves unauthorised access to the computer system of a business organisation, government department, etc.

hackle /ˈhækəl/ *n.* **1.** a neck feather of certain birds, as the domestic cock. **2.** (*pl.*) the hair on a dog's neck.

hackneyed /ˈhæknid/ *adj.* trite.

hacksaw /ˈhæksɔ/ *n.* a saw used for cutting metal, consisting typically of a narrow, fine-toothed blade fixed in a frame.

hackwork /ˈhækwɜk/ *n.* the routine aspects of a creative or artistic occupation, considered as mundane, or of an inferior quality, especially in the literary field.

had /hæd/, *weak forms* /həd, əd, d/ *v.* past tense and past participle of **have**.

haddock /ˈhædək/ *n.* (*pl.* **-dock**) a food fish related to the cod.

hadj /hadʒ/ *n.* → **hajj.**

hadji /ˈhadʒi/ *n.* (*pl.* **-jis**) → **hajji.**

haematoma /himəˈtoumə, hem-/ *n.* (*pl.* **-mas** *or* **-mata** /-mətə/) a bruise or collection of blood in a tissue. Also, **hematoma.**

haemo- a word element meaning 'blood'. Also, **hemo-, haem-, haema-, haemat-, haemato-.**

haemoglobin /himəˈgloubən/ *n.* a protein responsible for the red colour of blood which carries oxygen to the tissues. Also, **hemoglobin.**

haemophilia /himəˈfɪliə, -ˈfil-, -jə/ *n.* a blood disorder of males in which clotting occurs abnormally slowly, resulting in excessive bleeding from even minor injuries. Also, **hemophilia.** –**haemophiliac,** *n.*

haemorrhage /ˈhemərɪdʒ/ *n.* a discharge of blood, as from a ruptured blood vessel. Also, **hemorrhage.**

haemorrhoid /ˈhemərɔɪd/ *n.* a swelling of a vein of the anus; pile. Also, **hemorrhoid.**

haft /haft/ *n.* a handle, as of a knife.

hag /hæg/ *n.* a repulsive old woman.

haggard /ˈhægəd/ *adj.* gaunt, as from prolonged suffering, anxiety, etc.

haggis /ˈhægəs/ *n.* a dish made of the heart, liver, etc., of a sheep, etc.

haggle /ˈhægəl/ *v.i.* to bargain in a petty and tedious manner.

haiku /ˈhaɪku/ *n.* a Japanese verse form, usually containing 17 syllables arranged in three lines of five, seven, and five syllables respectively.

hail¹ /heɪl/ *v.t.* **1.** to salute or greet; welcome. **2.** to acclaim; to approve with enthusiasm. **3.** to attract the attention of, by calling out, waving the hand, etc. –*phr.* **4. hail from,** to belong to as the place of residence, point of departure, etc.

hail² /heɪl/ *n.* **1.** pellets of ice falling from the clouds in a shower. –*v.i.* **2.** to pour down hail.

hair /heə/ *n.* **1.** the natural covering of the human head. **2.** the aggregate of hairs which grow on an animal. **3.** one of the numerous fine, usually cylindrical filaments growing from the skin and forming the coat of most mammals.

haircut /ˈheəkʌt/ *n.* **1.** a cutting of the hair. **2.** the style in which the hair is cut and worn. –**haircutting,** *n.*

hairdo /ˈheədu/ *n.* (*pl.* **-dos**) the style in which a person's hair is arranged, etc.

hairdresser /ˈheədresə/ *n.* someone who arranges or cuts hair.

hairline fracture *n.* a break or fault in a bone, metal casting, etc., which reveals itself as a very thin line on the surface.

hair-raising /ˈheə-reɪzɪŋ/ *adj.* terrifying.

hair-trigger /ˈheə-trɪɡə/ *n.* a trigger that allows the firing mechanism of a firearm to be operated by very slight pressure.

hairy /ˈheəri/ *adj.* (**-rier, -riest**) **1.** covered with hair. **2.** *Colloq.* difficult: *a hairy problem.* **3.** *Colloq.* frightening: *a hairy drive.*

hajj /hadʒ/ *n.* the pilgrimage to Mecca, which every Muslim is expected to make at least once in a lifetime. Also, **haj, hadj.**

hajji /'hadʒi/ *n.* (*pl.* **-jis**) a Muslim person who has made the pilgrimage to Mecca. Also, **hadji**, **haji**.

haka /'haka/ *n.* a Maori ceremonial posture dance with vocal accompaniment.

hake /heɪk/ *n.* (*pl.* **hake** *or* **hakes**) a fish related to the cod.

hakea /'heɪkiə/ *n.* a type of Australian shrub or tree that has a hard woody fruit with winged seeds.

halal /'hæ'læl/ *adj.* of meat from animals slaughtered in accordance with Muslim rites.

halcyon /'hælsiən/ *adj.* **1.** calm, tranquil, or peaceful. **2.** carefree; joyous.

hale /heɪl/ *adj.* free from disease or infirmity; robust; vigorous.

half /haf/ *n.* (*pl.* **halves** /havz/) **1.** one of the two equal parts into which anything is or may be divided. **2.** *Sport* either of the two periods of a game. **3.** one of a pair. *–adj.* **4.** being one of the two equal parts into which anything is or may be divided. **5.** being equal to only about half of the full measure. *–adv.* **6.** to the extent or measure of half. **7.** to some extent.

halfback /'hafbæk/ *n.* **1.** *Rugby Football* the player who puts the ball in the scrum, and tries to catch it as it emerges. **2.** *Aust. Rules* any of the three positions on the line between the centre-line and the full-back line. **3.** *Soccer* one of the three players in the next line behind the forward line.

half-brother /'haf-brʌðə/ *n.* a brother by one parent only.

half-caste /'haf-kast/ *n.* (*usually derog.*) a person of mixed ancestry, especially the off-spring of one dark-skinned and one fair-skinned parent.

half-hearted /'haf-hatəd/ *adj.* having or show-ing little enthusiasm.

half-life /'haf-laɪf/ *n.* the time required for one half of a sample of unstable material to undergo chemical change, as the disintegration of radioactive material, etc.

half-sister /'haf-sɪstə/ *n.* a sister by one parent only.

halfway *adv.* /haf'weɪ/ **1.** to or at half the dis-tance. *–adj.* /'hafweɪ/ **2.** midway, as between two places or points.

halibut /'hælɪbət/ *n.* (*pl.* **-but** *or* **-buts**) a large food fish of northern seas.

halitosis /hælə'tousəs/ *n.* bad breath.

hall /hɔl/ *n.* **1.** the entrance room or vestibule of a house or building. **2.** a corridor or passage-way in a building. **3.** a large building or room for public assembly and other community uses.

hallelujah /hælə'lujə/ *interj.* Praise ye the Lord!

hallmark /'holmak/ *n.* **1.** an official mark or stamp indicating a standard of purity, used in marking gold and silver articles. **2.** any outstanding feature or characteristic.

hallow /'hælou/ *v.t.* to make holy.

hallucination /həlusə'neɪʃən/ *n.* subjective sense perceptions for which there is no appropriate external source, as 'hearing voices'. *–hallucinate, v.*

hallucinogen /hə'lusənədʒən/ *n.* a drug or chemical capable of producing hallucinations. *–hallucinogenic, adj.*

halo /'heɪlou/ *n.* (*pl.* **-loes** *or* **-los**) **1.** a radiance surrounding the head in the representation of a sacred personage. **2.** a circle of light, appearing round the sun or moon.

haloumi /ha'lumi/ *n.* a soft cheese matured in brine, with a firm, putty-like texture and a slightly mint flavour. Also, **halloumi**.

halt /hɔlt, holt/ *v.i.* **1.** to make a temporary or permanent stop. *–n.* **2.** a temporary stop.

halter /'hɔltə, 'holtə/ *n.* a rope or strap for leading or fastening horses or cattle.

halve /hav/ *v.t.* **1.** to divide in halves; share equally. **2.** to reduce to half.

halves /havz/ *n.* plural of **half**.

halyard /'hæljəd/ *n.* a rope or tackle used to hoist or lower a sail, yard, flag, etc. Also, **hal-liard**.

ham¹ /hæm/ *n.* **1.** one of the rear quarters of a pig. **2.** the meat of this part.

ham² /hæm/ *n. Colloq.* **1.** an actor who over-acts. **2.** an amateur.

hamburger /'hæmbɜgə/ *n.* a cooked cake of minced beef, especially as in a bread roll with salad, etc.

hamlet /'hæmlət/ *n.* a small village.

hammer /'hæmə/ *n.* **1.** an instrument consisting of a solid head, usually of metal, set crosswise on a handle, used for beating metals, driving in nails, etc. **2.** any of various instruments or devices resembling a hammer in form, action, or use. **3.** *Athletics* a metal ball attached to a long, flexible handle, used in certain throwing contests. *–v.t.* **4.** to beat, drive or impel with or as with a hammer. **5.** to hit with some force; pound. *–phr.* **6.** **hammer and tongs**, *Colloq.* with great noise, vigour, or force.

hammerhead /'hæməhɛd/ *n.* a shark with a head resembling a double-headed hammer.

hammock /'hæmək/ *n.* a kind of hanging bed or couch made of canvas, etc.

hamper¹ /'hæmpə/ *v.t.* to impede; hinder.

hamper² /'hæmpə/ *n.* **1.** a large basket or receptacle made from cane, wickerwork, etc., usually with a cover. **2.** such a basket or other container filled with food or other items, and given as a gift, prize, etc.

hamster /'hæmstə/ *n.* a short-tailed, stout-bod-ied, burrowing rodent.

hamstring /'hæmstrɪŋ/ *n.* **1.** one of the tendons bounding the hollow of the knee. *–v.t.* (**-strung**, **-stringing**) **2.** to cripple; render useless; thwart.

hand /hænd/ *n.* **1.** the terminal, prehensile part of the arm, consisting of the palm and five digits. **2.** something resembling a hand in shape or function. **3.** a person employed in manual labour. **4.** (*oft. pl.*) possession or power; control, custody, or care. **5.** a side of a subject, question, etc. **6.** style of handwriting. **7.** a person, with reference to action, ability, or skill. **8.** a pledge of marriage. **9.** a unit of measurement, about 10 centimetres, used for measuring the height of horses. **10.** *Cards* **a.** the cards dealt to or held by each player at one time. **b.** a single part of a game, in which all the cards dealt at one time are played. **11.** a bundle or bunch of various fruit, leaves, etc. **12.** a round or outburst of applause for a per-former. *–v.t.* **13.** to deliver or pass with the hand. **14.** (fol. by *on*) to pass on; transmit. *–phr.* **15. at hand, a.** within reach. **b.** near in time. **c.** ready for use. **16. free hand,** freedom to act as desired. **17. give a hand**, to help; assist. **18. hand it to**, *Colloq.* to give due credit to. **19. in hand**, **a.** under control. **b.** in immediate possession. **c.** in process. **20. on hand**, **a.** in immediate possession. **b.** before one for attention. **c.** present.

handbag /'hændbæg/ *n.* a small bag, most commonly used by women, used for carrying money, personal articles, etc., held in the hand or worn over the shoulder by means of a strap.

handbook /'hændbʊk/ *n.* a small book or treatise serving for guidance, as in an occupation or study.

handcuff /'hændkʌf/ *n.* a ring-shaped shackle for the wrist, usually one of a pair connected by a short chain or linked bar.

handgun /'hændgʌn/ *n.* a firearm that can be held and operated in one hand, as a pistol, revolver, etc.

handheld /'hændheld/ *adj.* **1.** held in the hand; supported only by the unaided hand. **2.** of or relating to a device which is designed to be small enough to be held in the hand. —*n.* **3.** such a device. Also, **hand-held**.

handicap /'hændikæp/ *n.* **1.** a race or other contest in which certain disadvantages or advantages of weight, distance, time, past records, etc., are placed upon competitors to equalise their chances of winning. **2.** the disadvantage or advantage itself. **3.** any encumbrance or disadvantage that makes success more difficult. **4.** a physical or mental disability. —*v.t.* (**-capped, -capping**) **5.** to serve as a handicap or disadvantage to.

handicraft /'hændikraft/ *n.* **1.** manual skill. **2.** a manual art or occupation.

handiwork /'hændiwɜk/ *n.* work done or a thing or things made by the hands.

handkerchief /'hæŋkətʃif/ *n.* a small square piece of fabric, usually cotton, carried about the person for wiping the nose, face, etc. Also, **hanky, hankie**.

handle /'hændl/ *n.* **1.** a part of a thing which is intended to be grasped by the hand in using or moving it. —*v.t.* **2.** to touch or feel with the hand; use the hands on, as in picking up. **3.** to manage, direct, or control. **4.** to deal with or treat in a particular way. **5.** to deal or trade in (goods, etc.). —*v.i.* **6.** to respond to handling.

handlebar /'hændlbɑ/ *n.* (*usu. pl.*) the curved steering bar of a bicycle, motorcycle, etc., in front of the rider.

handshake /'hænʃeɪk, 'hænd-/ *n.* **1.** a clasping of another's right hand in salutation, congratulation, agreement, etc. **2.** *Computers* a signal sent from one device to another, indicating readiness to receive transferred information.

handsome /'hænsəm/ *adj.* **1.** of fine or admirable appearance; comely; tastefully or elegantly fine. **2.** considerable, ample, or liberal in amount.

handstand /'hænstænd, 'hænd-/ *n.* the act, or an instance of balancing upside down on one's hands.

handwriting /'hænd,raɪtɪŋ/ *n.* **1.** writing done with the hand. **2.** a kind or style of writing.

handy /'hændi/ *adj.* (**-dier, -diest**) **1.** ready to hand; conveniently accessible. **2.** ready or

skilful with the hands; deft; dexterous. **3.** convenient or useful.

hang /hæŋ/ *v.* (**hung** *or, esp. for capital punishment and suicide,* **hanged, hanging**) —*v.t.* **1.** to fasten or attach (a thing) so that it is supported only from above; suspend. **2.** to suspend by the neck until dead. **3.** to let droop or bend downwards. **4.** to fasten into position; fix at a proper angle. **5.** to attach (paper, etc.) to walls. —*v.i.* **6.** to be suspended; dangle. **7.** to be suspended from a cross or gallows. **8.** to bend forwards or downwards; lean over. **9.** to be conditioned or contingent; be dependent. **10.** (fol. by *on* or *upon*) to hold fast, cling, or adhere; rest for support. **11.** to be doubtful or undecided; remain unfinished. —*n.* **12.** the way in which a thing hangs. —*phr.* **13. hang about** (or **around**), to loiter. **14. hang on**, **a.** to persevere. **b.** to linger. **c.** to wait. **15. hang out**, *Colloq.* (sometimes fol. by *at* or *in*) to reside or regularly be found at (a particular place). **16. hang up**, **a.** to suspend on a hook or peg. **b.** to break off a telephone call by putting down the receiver.

hangar /'hæŋə/ *n.* **1.** a shed or shelter. **2.** a shed for aircraft.

hang-glider /'hæŋ-glaɪdə/ *n.* a simple kite-like glider without a fuselage but with a framework from which a person hangs feet downwards.

hangover /'hæŋoʊvə/ *n.* the after-effects of excessive indulgence in alcoholic drink.

hang-up /'hæŋ-ʌp/ *n. Colloq.* something which occasions unease, inhibition, or conflict in an individual.

hank /hæŋk/ *n.* a skein.

hanker /'hæŋkə/ *v.i.* (oft. fol. by *after, for,* or an infinitive) to have a restless or incessant longing.

hanky /'hæŋki/ *n. Colloq.* → **handkerchief.** Also, **hankie**.

hanky-panky /,hæŋki-'pæŋki/ *n. Colloq.* **1.** trickery; subterfuge or the like. **2.** sexual play.

Hansard /'hænsad/ *n.* the official printed reports of the debates and proceedings of parliament.

haphazard /hæp'hæzəd/ *adj.* determined by or dependent on mere chance.

hapless /'hæpləs/ *adj.* luckless.

happen /'hæpən/ *v.i.* **1.** to come to pass, take place, or occur. **2.** to befall, as to a person or thing. **3.** (fol. by *on* or *upon*) to come by chance.

happy /'hæpi/ *adj.* (**-pier, -piest**) **1.** characterised by or indicative of pleasure, content, or gladness. **2.** delighted, pleased, or glad, as over a particular thing. **3.** favoured by fortune; fortunate or lucky.

harakiri /hærə'kɪri/ *n.* suicide by ripping open the abdomen with a dagger or knife.

harangue /hə'ræŋ/ *n.* **1.** a passionate, vehement speech; noisy and intemperate address. —*v.t.* (**-rangued, -ranguing**) **2.** to address in a harangue.

harass /hə'ræs, 'hærəs/ *v.t.* to disturb persistently.

harbinger /'habɪndʒə/ *n.* **1.** someone who goes before and makes known the approach of another. **2.** something that foreshadows a future event; an omen.

harbour /'hɑbə/ n. **1.** a portion of a body of water along the shore deep enough for ships to anchor and offering either natural or artificial shelter. **2.** any place of shelter or refuge. –v.t. **3.** to conceal; give a place to hide. **4.** to entertain in the mind; indulge (usually unfavourable or evil feelings). Also, **harbor**.

hard /hɑd/ adj. **1.** solid and firm to the touch; not soft. **2.** firmly formed; tight. **3.** difficult to do or accomplish; troublesome. **4.** involving or performed with great exertion, energy, or persistence. **5.** carrying on work in this manner. **6.** vigorous or violent; harsh; severe. **7.** unfeeling; callous. **8.** confronting to the eye, ear, or aesthetic sense. **9.** severe or rigorous in terms. **10. a.** alcoholic or intoxicating. **b.** dangerously addictive. **11.** (of water) containing mineral salts which interfere with the action of the soap. –adv. **12.** with great exertion; with vigour or violence. **13.** harshly or severely; badly. **–harden**, v.

hardback /'hɑdbæk/ n. a book bound in stiff covers, usually of boards covered with cloth, leather, laminated paper, etc.

hardball /'hɑdbɔl/ phr. **play hardball**, Colloq. to use tough, uncompromising or ruthless tactics in business, politics, etc.

hard disk n. a rigid magnetic storage disk, usually built into the computer, with a higher recording density than a floppy disk, providing fast access to a greater amount of stored data.

hard-headed /'hɑd-hɛdəd/ adj. not easily moved or deceived; practical; shrewd.

hardline /'hɑdlaɪn/ adj. not deviating from a set doctrine, policy, etc.

hardly /'hɑdli/ adv. **1.** barely; almost not at all. **2.** not quite.

hard-nosed /'hɑd-nouzd/ adj. ruthless.

hard sell n. a method of selling or advertising which is direct, forceful, and insistent. Compare **soft sell**. **–hard-sell**, v.

hardship /'hɑdʃɪp/ n. a condition that bears hard upon one; severe toil, trial, oppression, or need.

hard-up /'hɑd-ʌp/ adj. in financial difficulties; poor.

hardware /'hɑdwɛə/ n. **1.** building materials, tools, etc. **2.** the physical components of a computer system (opposed to software).

hardwired /'hɑd'waɪəd/ adj. **1.** Computers **a.** (of a circuit) permanently wired into a computer. **b.** (of a function) determined by the hardware and therefore not programmable. **2.** (of people) inherently equipped to act in a certain way: humans are hardwired for language. **3.** not modifiable. Also, **hard-wired**.

hardworking /'hɑdwɜkɪŋ/ adj. prepared to work hard and in a careful way.

hardy /'hɑdi/ adj. (**-dier**, **-diest**) capable of enduring fatigue, hardship, exposure, etc.

hare /hɛə/ n. (pl. **hares** or, especially collectively, **hare**) a rabbit-like mammal.

harebrained /'hɛəbreɪnd/ adj. irrational; reckless. Also, **hairbrained**.

harelip /'hɛəlɪp/ n. a congenitally deformed lip, usually the upper one in which there is a vertical fissure causing it to resemble the cleft lip of a hare. **–hare-lipped**, adj.

harem /'hɛərəm, hɑ'rim/ n. (in some Muslim societies) the women of a household.

harem pants pl. n. long loose trousers gathered at the ankle, worn by women.

hark /hɑk/ v.i. **1.** (used chiefly in the imperative) to listen. –phr. **2. hark back**, to return to a previous point or subject.

harlot /'hɑlət/ n. a promiscuous woman; prostitute.

harm /hɑm/ n. **1.** injury; damage; hurt. –v.t. **2.** to do harm to; injure; damage; hurt.

harmonica /hɑ'mɒnɪkə/ n. a musical instrument having a set of small metallic reeds mounted in a case and played by the breath; a mouth organ.

harmony /'hɑməni/ n. (pl. **-nies**) **1.** agreement; accord. **2.** a consistent, orderly, or pleasing arrangement of parts; congruity. **3.** Music any simultaneous combination of notes. **–harmonise**, **harmonize**, v. **–harmonic**, **harmonious**, adj.

harness /'hɑnəs/ n. **1.** the combination of straps, bands, and other parts forming the working gear of a horse or other draught animal. **2.** a similar combination worn by persons for safety, protection, restraint, etc. –v.t. **3.** to put harness on (a horse, etc.); attach by a harness, as to a vehicle. **4.** to bring under conditions for working.

harp /hɑp/ n. **1.** a triangular stringed instrument, played with the hands. –v.i. **2.** (fol. by on or upon) to dwell persistently or tediously in speaking or writing.

harpoon /hɑ'pun/ n. a spear attached to a rope.

harpsichord /'hɑpsəkɔd/ n. a keyboard instrument, precursor of the piano.

harridan /'hærədən/ n. (derog.) a disreputable violent woman.

harrow /'hærou/ n. **1.** an implement for levelling soil, etc. –v.t. **2.** to disturb keenly or painfully; distress the mind, feelings, etc.

harry /'hæri/ v.t. (**-ried**, **-rying**) **1.** to torment; worry. **2.** to ravage, as in war; devastate.

harsh /hɑʃ/ adj. **1.** ungentle and unpleasant in action or effect. **2.** rough to the touch or to any of the senses.

hart /hɑt/ n. (pl. **harts** or, especially collectively, **hart**) a male deer.

harvest /'hɑvəst/ n. **1.** the gathering of crops. **2.** a crop or yield, as of grain. **3.** the product or result of any labour or process. –v.t. **4.** to gather, as a crop. **5.** to gather, as the product of a biological process, experiment, etc.: to harvest eggs for fertilisation. **6.** to collect electronically, as in the gathering of email addresses.

has /hæz/, weak forms /həz, əz/ v. 3rd person singular present indicative of **have**.

hash¹ /hæʃ/ n. **1.** a mess, jumble, or muddle. **2.** a dish of reheated food.

hash² /hæʃ/ n. the symbol (#) found on a computer keyboard, telephone keypad, etc.; hatch.

hashish /hæ'ʃiʃ, 'hæʃɪʃ/ n. a resin produced from the flowering tops, leaves, etc., of Indian hemp, smoked, chewed, or otherwise used as a narcotic and intoxicant.

hashtag /'hæʃtæg/ n. Internet a tag to a tweet (**tweet²** def. 3), which connects it to a common theme. **–hashtagging**, n.

hasp /hæsp, hɑsp/ n. a clasp for a door, lid, etc.

hassle /'hæsəl/ n. **1.** a quarrel; squabble. **2.** a struggle; period of unease. –v.t. **3.** worry; harass.

hassock /ˈhæsək/ *n.* a thick, firm cushion used as a footstool or for kneeling.

haste /heɪst/ *n.* **1.** energetic speed in motion or action. **2.** quickness without due reflection; thoughtless or rash speed. —**hasty**, *adj.*

hasten /ˈheɪsən/ *v.i.* to move or act with haste; proceed with haste; hurry.

hat /hæt/ *n.* a shaped covering for the head, usually with a crown and a brim.

hatch[1] /hætʃ/ *v.t.* **1.** to bring forth (young) from the egg. **2.** to contrive; devise; concoct.

hatch[2] /hætʃ/ *n.* a cover for an opening in a ship's deck, a floor, a roof, or the like.

hatch[3] /hætʃ/ *v.t.* to mark with lines, especially closely set parallel lines, as for shading in drawing or engraving.

hatchback /ˈhætʃbæk/ *n.* a type of car fitted with a door at the rear which includes the rear window, and which has hinges at the top.

hatchet /ˈhætʃət/ *n.* a small, short-handled axe for use with one hand.

hatchet man *n.* someone employed or delegated to perform unpleasant tasks, such as cutting costs, firing personnel, etc.

hate /heɪt/ *v.t.* to regard with a strong or passionate dislike; detest.

hate crime *n.* criminal violence enacted upon an individual or group perceived as belonging to a social or racial group hated by the attacker.

hateful /ˈheɪtfəl/ *adj.* odious.

hatred /ˈheɪtrəd/ *n.* intense dislike.

hat-trick *n.* **1.** *Cricket* the act by a bowler of taking three wickets with three successive balls. **2.** three goals, tries, etc., achieved by a player in a single game, etc. **3.** a feat involving a set of three successes.

haughty /ˈhɔːti/ *adj.* (**-tier**, **-tiest**) disdainfully proud; arrogant; supercilious.

haul /hɔːl/ *v.t.* **1.** to pull or draw with force; move or transport by drawing. —*v.i.* **2.** (oft. fol. by *round* or *to*) (of the wind) to change direction, shift, or veer. —*n.* **3.** the act of hauling; a strong pull or tug. **4.** the distance over which anything is hauled. **5.** the proceeds of a robbery: *the thieves made away with a haul of $25 000.* —*phr.* **6. in** (or **over**) **the long haul**, in the long term; in a long period of time.

haunch /hɔːntʃ/ *n.* the hip.

haunt /hɔːnt/ *v.t.* **1.** to visit habitually as a supposed spirit or ghost. **2.** to worry or disturb. **3.** to visit frequently. —*n.* **4.** (oft. pl.) a place of frequent resort.

have /hæv/ *v.t.* **1.** to hold or possess. **2.** to get, receive, or take. **3.** to be required, compelled, or under obligation (followed by an infinitive). **4.** to experience, enjoy or suffer. **5.** to require or cause (to do something, to be done, or as specified). **6.** to engage in or perform. **7.** to permit or allow. **8.** to give birth to. **9.** *Colloq.* to outwit, deceive, or cheat. —*v.* (*aux.*) **10.** (used with the past participle of a verb to form a compound or perfect tense). The different forms of the verb **have** are: *Present tense*: I **have**, you **have**, he/she/it **has**, we **have**, they **have** *Past tense*: I **had**, you **had**, he/she/it **had**, we **had**, they **had** *Past participle*: **had** *Present participle*: **having**

haven /ˈheɪvən/ *n.* **1.** a harbour or port. **2.** any place of shelter and safety.

haversack /ˈhævəsæk/ *n.* a bag carried on the back or shoulders, used for provisions, etc.

havoc /ˈhævək/ *n.* devastation.

hawk[1] /hɔːk/ *n.* any of numerous birds of prey.

hawk[2] /hɔːk/ *v.i.* to clear the throat noisily.

hawker /ˈhɔːkə/ *n.* someone who travels from place to place selling goods.

hawthorn /ˈhɔːθɔːn/ *n.* a thorny shrub.

hay /heɪ/ *n.* grass, clover, lucerne, etc., cut and dried for use as fodder.

hay fever *n.* inflammation of the mucous membranes of the eyes and respiratory tract, caused by pollen.

haywire /ˈheɪwaɪə/ *adj.* **1.** in disorder; out of order. **2.** out of control; crazy.

hazard /ˈhæzəd/ *n.* **1.** a risk; exposure to danger or harm. —*v.t.* **2.** to venture to offer (a statement, conjecture, etc.). **3.** to run the risk of (a misfortune, penalty, etc.). —**hazardous**, *adj.*

haze /heɪz/ *n.* a thin mist, caused by dust, heat, etc. —**hazy**, *adj.*

hazel /ˈheɪzəl/ *n.* **1.** a type of shrub or small tree which bears edible nuts. **2.** light yellowish-brown.

hazmat /ˈhæzmæt/ *n.* **1.** a hazardous material, such as a corrosive or poisonous chemical. —*adj.* **2.** of or relating to hazardous materials. Also, **Hazmat**, **HAZMAT**.

HDL /eɪtʃ di ˈɛl/ *n.* high-density lipoprotein; a substance which forms the lesser part of the cholesterol in the blood and which is thought to carry cholesterol from the artery wall to the liver. See **good cholesterol**. Compare **LDL**.

HDTV /eɪtʃ di ti ˈvi/ *n.* high definition TV; a type of digital TV that sends a greater volume of information than analog TV with the same amount of bandwidth, by digitising and compressing the signal, resulting in higher quality picture and sound. Compare **SDTV**.

he /hi/ *pron.* **1.** the personal pronoun used to refer to a particular male: *He married my sister yesterday.* **2.** anyone; that person: *If anyone comes to the door, he can just wait.*

head /hɛd/ *n.* **1.** the upper part of the body, joined to the trunk by the neck. **2.** the head considered as the seat of thought, memory, understanding, etc. **3.** the position of leadership. **4.** that part of anything which forms or is regarded as forming the top, summit, or upper end. **5.** the foremost part or end of anything; a projecting point. **6.** (*pl.* **head**) a person or animal considered merely as one of a number: *120 head of cattle; to charge $50 a head.* **7.** culmination or crisis; conclusion. **8.** something resembling a head in form. **9.** a projecting point of a coast. **10.** the side of a coin bearing a head or other principal figure (opposed to *tail*). **11.** the source of a river or stream. **12.** collar, froth or foam, as that formed on beer when poured. —*adj.* **13.** situated at the top or front. **14.** being in the position of leadership or superiority. —*v.t.* **15.** to go at the head of or in front of; lead; precede. **16.** to be the head or chief of. —*v.i.* **17.** (oft. fol. by *for*) to move forwards towards a point specified. —*phr.* **18. head off**, to intercept (something) and force it to change course.

headache /'hɛdeɪk/ n. **1.** a pain situated in the head. **2.** *Colloq.* a troublesome or worrying problem.

head cold n. a form of the common cold that mainly involves inflammation or infection of the nasal passages. Compare **chest cold**.

headfirst /hɛd'fɜst/ adv. **1.** with the head in front or bent forwards; headlong. **2.** too quickly; rashly; precipitately. Also, **headforemost**.

headhunt /'hɛdhʌnt/ v.t. **1.** to recruit (staff) by approaching people in existing jobs to offer them a new one. –v.i. **2.** (formerly) to collect the heads of slain enemies as trophies.

headhunting /'hɛdhʌntɪŋ/ n. *Colloq.* **1.** the eliminating of political enemies. **2.** (in a business or other organisation) the seeking of a scapegoat for a misfortune or setback. **3.** the search for new executives, usually senior, through personal contacts rather than advertisements.

heading /'hɛdɪŋ/ n. a title or caption of a page, chapter, etc.

headland /'hɛdlənd, -lænd/ n. a promontory extending into a large body of water.

headlight /'hɛdlaɪt/ n. a light equipped with a reflector, on the front of any vehicle.

headline /'hɛdlaɪn/ n. **1.** a display line over an article, etc., as in a newspaper. **2.** (pl.) the few most important items of news briefly stated: *here again are the headlines.* –adj. **3.** given as a summary or key item: *a headline indicator.*

headlong /'hɛdlɒŋ/ adv. **1.** headfirst: *to plunge headlong.* **2.** rashly; without thought. **3.** with great speed; precipitately. –adj. **4.** done or going with the head foremost. **5.** marked by haste; precipitate. **6.** rash; impetuous.

headmaster /'hɛdmastə, hɛd'mastə/ n. the male principal of a school.

headmistress /'hɛdmɪstrəs, hɛd'mɪstrəs/ n. the female principal of a school.

headquarters /'hɛdkwɔtəz, hɛd'kwɔtəz/ pl. n. any centre of operations.

headscarf /'hɛdskaf/ n. (pl. **-scarfs** or **-scarves** /'hɛdskavz/) a square piece of material worn as a covering for the head.

head start n. an initial advantage in a race, competition, etc.

headstone /'hɛdstoʊn/ n. a stone set at the head of a grave.

headstrong /'hɛdstrɒŋ/ adj. bent on having one's own way; wilful.

heads-up n. *Colloq.* a quick issuing of advance notice: *thanks for the heads-up.*

headway /'hɛdweɪ/ n. progress.

headwind /'hɛdwɪnd/ n. a wind that blows directly against the direction of travel.

heady /'hɛdi/ adj. (**-dier, -diest**) **1.** rashly impetuous. **2.** intoxicating.

heal /hil/ v.t. to make whole or sound; restore to health; free from ailment.

health /hɛlθ/ n. **1.** soundness of body; freedom from disease or ailment. **2.** the general condition of the body or mind.

health care n. medical and other services provided for the maintenance of health, prevention of disease, etc. Also, **healthcare**.

healthcare /'hɛlθkɛə/ n. **1.** → **health care**. –adj. **2.** of or relating to such care: *a healthcare organisation.*

health tourism n. travel for the purpose of a medical treatment to a country which offers the service at a cheaper rate or higher standard than that available in the traveller's home country.

healthy /'hɛlθi/ adj. (**-thier, -thiest**) **1.** in a state of good health; free of any sickness or disease. **2.** conducive to good health: *healthy food.* –**healthily**, adv.

heap /hip/ n. **1.** an assemblage of things, lying one on another; a pile. **2.** (sometimes pl.) *Colloq.* a great quantity or number. –v.t. **3.** (oft. fol. by *up, on, together*, etc.) to gather, put, or cast in a heap; pile.

hear /hɪə/ v. (**heard** /hɜd/, **hearing**) –v.t. **1.** to perceive by the ear. **2.** to listen to. **3.** to give a formal, official, or judicial hearing to, as a sovereign, a teacher, an assembly, or a judge does. –v.i. **4.** to have perception of sound by the ear; have the sense of hearing. **5.** to receive information by the ear or otherwise.

hearing /'hɪərɪŋ/ n. **1.** the faculty or sense by which sound is perceived. **2.** *Law* the trial of an action. **3.** earshot.

hearing-impaired /'hɪərɪŋ-ɪmpɛəd/ adj. deficient in the ability to hear, ranging from complete to partial hearing loss.

hearsay /'hɪəseɪ/ n. gossip; rumour.

hearse /hɜs/ n. a funeral vehicle.

heart /hat/ n. **1.** a hollow muscular organ which by rhythmic contraction and dilation keeps the blood in circulation throughout the body. **2.** this organ considered as the seat of life, or vital powers, or of thought, feeling, or emotion. **3.** the seat of emotions and affections (often in contrast to the *head* as the seat of the intellect). **4.** feeling; sensibility. **5.** spirit, courage, or enthusiasm. **6.** the innermost or middle part of anything. **7.** a figure or object with rounded sides meeting in an obtuse point at the bottom and curving inwards to a cusp at the top; a stylised representation of the shape of a heart.

heart attack n. a sudden, severe failure of the heart to function normally; myocardial infarct.

heartburn /'hatbɜn/ n. a burning sensation above the abdomen.

hearten /'hatn/ v.t. to give courage to; cheer.

hearth /haθ/ n. **1.** that part of the floor of a room on which the fire is made. **2.** the fireside; home.

heart-rending /'hat-rɛndɪŋ/ adj. causing acute mental anguish.

heart-throb /'hat-θrɒb/ n. the object of an infatuation.

hearty /'hati/ adj. (**-tier, -tiest**) **1.** warm-hearted; affectionate; cordial; friendly. **2.** enthusiastic or zealous; vigorous. **3.** substantial or satisfying. –**heartily**, adv.

heat /hit/ n. **1.** the quality or condition of being hot. **2.** the sensation of hotness. **3.** hot weather. **4.** warmth or intensity of feeling. **5.** a single course in or division of a race or other contest. **6.** *Zool.* sexual excitement in animals, especially females. –v.t., v.i. **7.** to make or become hot or warm.

heated /'hitəd/ adj. inflamed; vehement; angry.

heath /hiθ/ n. **1.** a tract of open, uncultivated land. **2.** a low, evergreen shrub.

heathen /'hiðən/ n. (pl. **-thens** or **-then**) an irreligious or unenlightened person.

heather /'hɛðə/ n. any of various heaths (def. 2).

heat stroke n. a condition resulting from prolonged exposure to excessive heat, with symptoms such as exhaustion, dizziness, headache, fever, etc., in severe cases progressing to hyperthermia with high fever and, if untreated, potentially coma and death. Also, **heatstroke**.

heatwave /'hitweɪv/ n. a prolonged period of hot weather.

heave /hiv/ v. (**heaved** or, Chiefly Naut., **hove**, **heaving**) −v.t. **1.** to raise or lift with effort or force; hoist. −v.i. **2.** to rise and fall with or as with a swelling motion. **3.** to vomit; retch.

heaven /'hɛvən/ n. **1.** (also upper case) (in many religions and mythologies) a place or state of existence where people (often those who have lived righteously or those chosen by a god or gods) live on after death in happiness. **2.** (chiefly pl.) the sky or firmament. **3.** a place or state of supreme bliss. −**heavenly**, adj.

heavy /'hɛvi/ adj. (**-vier**, **-viest**) **1.** of great weight; hard to lift or carry. **2.** bearing hard upon; burdensome. **3.** connected or concerned with the manufacture of goods of more than the usual weight. **4.** serious; grave. **5.** exceptionally dense in substance. **6.** (of music, literature, etc.) intellectual or deep. −n. (pl. **-vies**) **7.** Colloq. a person who is eminent and influential in the sphere of his or her activities, as an important businessperson, etc.

heavy metal n. **1.** a metal with a density greater than five times that of water, such as lead or mercury; such metals can accumulate to toxic levels in animal tissues. **2.** a style of rock music dominated by electric guitars played at high levels of amplification and with great acoustic distortion. −**heavy-metal**, adj.

heckle /'hɛkəl/ v.t. to badger or torment; harass, especially a public speaker, with questions and gibes.

hectare /'hɛktɛə/ n. a unit of land measurement in the metric system, equal to 10 000 square metres, or about 2½ acres. Symbol: ha

hectic /'hɛktɪk/ adj. characterised by great excitement, passion, activity, confusion, haste.

hedge /hɛdʒ/ n. **1.** a row of bushes or small trees planted close together, especially when forming a fence or boundary. −v. (**hedged**, **hedging**) −v.t. **2.** (oft. fol. by in, off, about, etc.) to enclose with or separate by a hedge. **3.** to protect (a bet, etc.) by taking some offsetting risk. −v.i. **4.** to avoid taking an open or decisive course. **5.** Finance to enter transactions that will protect against loss through a compensatory price movement.

hedgehog /'hɛdʒhɒg/ n. a spiny, nocturnal, insectivorous mammal.

hedonism /'hidənɪzəm, 'hɛ-/ n. the doctrine that pleasure or happiness is the highest good. −**hedonist**, n.

heed /hid/ v.t. to give attention to; regard; notice.

heel[1] /hil/ n. **1.** the back part of the foot, below and behind the ankle. **2.** the part of a stocking, shoe, or the like, covering or supporting the heel. **3.** Colloq. a despicable person; cad. −v.t. **4.** to furnish with heels, as shoes.

heel[2] /hil/ v.i. (of a ship, etc.) to lean.

heeler /'hilə/ n. a cattle or sheep dog which rounds up stock by following at their heels.

hefty /'hɛfti/ adj. (**-tier**, **-tiest**) Colloq. **1.** heavy; weighty. **2.** big and strong; powerful; muscular.

hegemony /hə'gɛməni, hə'dʒɛməni, 'hɛgəməni, 'hɛdʒəməni/, Orig. US /'hɛgəmouni, 'hɛdʒəmouni/ n. (pl. **-monies**) predominant influence exercised by one state over others.

heifer /'hɛfə/ n. a cow that has not produced a calf and is under three years of age.

height /haɪt/ n. **1.** the state of being high. **2.** extent upwards; altitude; stature; distance upwards; elevation. **3.** a high place or level; a hill or mountain. **4.** the highest or culminating point; utmost degree. **5.** high degree, as of a quality.

Heimlich manoeuvre /'haɪmlɪk/ n. a method of helping someone who is choking by applying a sudden squeeze of pressure just below their rib cage, thus forcing air up through the trachea and removing the obstruction.

heinous /'heɪnəs, 'hi-/ adj. hateful.

heir /ɛə/ n. **1.** Law someone who inherits the estate (def. 2b) of a deceased person, normally after it has been reduced by the payment of any debts, liabilities or charges which may pertain to it. **2.** someone to whom something falls or is due. −**heiress**, fem. n.

heirloom /'ɛəlum/ n. any family possession transmitted from generation to generation.

heist /haɪst/ n. a robbery; burglary.

held /hɛld/ v. past tense and past participle of **hold**[1].

helicopter /'hɛlikɒptə, 'hɛlə-/ n. a heavier-than-air craft which is lifted and sustained in the air by horizontal rotating blades.

helicopter parenting n. a style of child rearing in which parents are excessively attentive to and involved in the lives of their children. −**helicopter parent**, n.

helio- a word element meaning 'sun'.

heliotrope /'hiliətroup, 'hiliə-, 'hɛljə-, 'hiljə-/ n. **1.** a European garden plant with small, fragrant purple flowers. **2.** a light tint of purple; reddish lavender. −**heliotropic**, adj.

helipad /'hɛlipæd/ n. an aerodrome or landing place for helicopters.

heliport /'hɛlipɔt/ n. a landing place for helicopters, often the roof of a building.

helium /'hiliəm/ n. an inert gaseous element present in the sun's atmosphere, certain minerals, natural gas, etc., and also occurring as a radioactive decomposition product. Symbol: He

helix /'hiliks, 'hɛl-/ n. (pl. **helices** /'hɛləsiz, 'hil-/ or **helixes**) a spiral. −**helical**, adj.

hell /hɛl/ n. **1.** (also upper case) in some religions, the abode of evil and spirits of the wicked condemned to punishment after death. **2.** any place or state of torment or misery. −interj. **3.** Colloq. an exclamation of annoyance, disgust, etc. −**hellish**, adj.

he'll /hil/ contraction of: **1.** he will. **2.** he shall.

hello /hʌ'lou, hə-/ interj. an exclamation to attract attention, answer a telephone, or express greeting.

helm /hɛlm/ *n.* **1.** the tiller or wheel by which the rudder of a vessel is controlled. **2.** the place or post of control.

helmet /ˈhɛlmət/ *n.* a defensive covering for the head.

help /hɛlp/ *v.t.* **1.** to cooperate effectively with; aid; assist. **2.** to act to improve the likelihood of success of. **3.** to rescue. **4.** to relieve (someone) in need, sickness, pain, or distress. **5.** to refrain from; avoid (with *can* or *cannot*). **6.** to remedy, stop, or prevent. *–n.* **7.** the act of helping; aid or assistance; relief or succour. **8.** a person or thing that helps. *–phr.* **9. help oneself (to)**, to take or appropriate at will.

help desk *n.* a service providing assistance or guidance within a company or organisation, especially in relation to the use of computers and other technical equipment. Also, **helpdesk**.

helpful /ˈhɛlpfəl/ *adj.* **1.** willing or eager to help. **2.** useful. **–helpfully**, *adv.* **–helpfulness**, *n.*

helpless /ˈhɛlpləs/ *adj.* unable to help oneself; weak or dependent.

helter-skelter /ˌhɛltə-ˈskɛltə/ *adv.* in headlong, disorderly haste.

hem /hɛm/ *v.t.* (**hemmed**, **hemming**) **1.** (fol. by *in*, *round*, or *about*) to enclose or confine. **2.** to fold back and sew down the edge of (cloth, a garment, etc.). *–n.* **3.** the edge or border of a garment, etc., especially at the bottom.

hemi- a prefix meaning 'half'.

hemisphere /ˈhɛməsfɪə/ *n.* **1.** half of the terrestrial globe or celestial sphere. **2.** the half of a sphere. **–hemispherical**, *adj.*

hemlock /ˈhɛmlɒk/ *n.* a poisonous herb.

hemp /hɛmp/ *n.* **1.** a tall, Asian herb yielding hashish, etc. **2.** the tough fibre of this plant used for making coarse fabrics, ropes, etc.

hen /hɛn/ *n.* **1.** the female of the domestic fowl. **2.** the female of any bird.

hence /hɛns/ *adv.* as an inference from this fact; for this reason; therefore.

henceforth /hɛnsˈfɔθ/ *adv.* from this time forth; from now on. Also, **henceforwards**.

henchman /ˈhɛntʃmən/ *n.* (*pl.* **-men**) **1.** a trusty attendant or follower. **2.** a ruthless and unscrupulous follower.

Hendra virus /ˈhɛndrə/ *n.* a virus affecting horses and human beings, the natural host being the fruit bat.

henna /ˈhɛnə/ *n.* (the reddish-orange dye from) a small Asian tree.

hepatic /həˈpætɪk/ *adj.* of or relating to the liver.

hepatitis /hɛpəˈtaɪtəs/ *n.* a serious viral disease characterised by inflammation or enlargement of the liver, fever or jaundice, some forms of which are transmitted by infected blood and can therefore be contracted through sexual contact or use of contaminated needles.

hepta- a prefix meaning 'seven'. Also, (*before vowels*), **hept-**.

heptathlon /hɛpˈtæθlən/ *n.* an athletic contest comprising seven different events. **–heptathlete**, *n.*

her /hɜ/ *pron.* **1.** the personal pronoun used, usually after a verb or preposition, to refer to a particular female: *I saw her yesterday*; *give it to her*. **2.** the possessive form of **she**, used before a noun: *that is her book*.

herald /ˈhɛrəld/ *n.* **1.** a messenger; forerunner or harbinger. **2.** someone who proclaims or announces (often used as the name of a newspaper). *–v.t.* **3.** to give tidings of; proclaim. **4.** to usher in. **–heraldic**, *adj.*

heraldry /ˈhɛrəldri/ *n.* (*pl.* **-dries**) **1.** the science of armorial bearings. **2.** a coat of arms; armorial bearings.

herb /hɜb/ *n.* **1.** a flowering plant whose stem above ground does not become woody and persistent. **2.** such a plant when valued for its medicinal properties, flavour, scent, or the like. **–herbal**, **herbaceous**, *adj.*

herbivorous /hɜˈbɪvərəs/ *adj.* feeding on plants. **–herbivore**, *n.*

herd /hɜd/ *n.* a number of animals, especially cattle, kept, feeding, or travelling together; drove; flock.

here /hɪə/ *adv.* **1.** in this place; in this spot or locality (opposed to *there*). **2.** to or towards this place; hither. **3.** at this point; at this juncture.

here- a word element meaning 'this (place)', 'this (time)', etc., used in combination with certain adverbs and prepositions.

hereditary /həˈrɛdətri/ *adj.* **1.** passing, or capable of passing, naturally from parents to offspring. **2.** *Law* descending by inheritance.

heredity /həˈrɛdəti/ *n.* the transmission of genetic characteristics from parents to progeny.

heresy /ˈhɛrəsi/ *n.* **1.** doctrine contrary to the orthodox or accepted doctrine of a church or religious system. **2.** the maintaining of such an opinion or doctrine. **–heretic**, *n.* **–heretical**, *adj.*

heritage /ˈhɛrɪtɪdʒ/ *n.* that which comes or belongs to one by reason of birth; an inherited lot or portion.

hermaphrodite /hɜˈmæfrədaɪt/ *n.* a person or animal with male and female sexual organs and characteristics.

hermetic /hɜˈmɛtɪk/ *adj.* made airtight by fusion or sealing. **–hermetically**, *adv.*

hermit /ˈhɜmət/ *n.* someone who has retired to a solitary place, especially for a life of religious seclusion. **–hermitage**, *n.*

hernia /ˈhɜniə/ *n.* (*pl.* **-nias**) the protrusion of an organ or tissue through an opening in its surrounding tissues, especially in the abdominal region; a rupture.

hero /ˈhɪəroʊ/ *n.* (*pl.* **-roes**) **1.** a person of distinguished courage or performance, especially one who risks injury or death for the sake of others. **2.** the principal male character in a story, play, etc. **–heroic**, *adj.*

heroin /ˈhɛrəwən/ *n.* (*from trademark*) a derivative of morphine, formerly used as a sedative, etc., and constituting a dangerous addictive drug.

heroine /ˈhɛrəwən/ *n.* **1.** a woman of heroic character; a female hero. **2.** the principal female character in a story, play, etc.

heron /ˈhɛrən/ *n.* a wading bird with a long neck, bill, and legs.

herpes /ˈhɜpiz/ *n.* any of certain inflammatory viral infections of the skin or mucous membrane, characterised by clusters of vesicles which tend to spread.

herring /ˈhɛrɪŋ/ n. (pl. **herring** or **herrings**) a food fish of northern seas.

herringbone /ˈhɛrɪŋbəʊn/ n. a pattern consisting of adjoining rows of parallel lines so arranged that any two rows have the form of a V or inverted V.

hers /hɜz/ pron. **1.** the possessive form of **she**, without a noun following: *that book is hers.* **2.** the person(s) or thing(s) belonging to her: *hers is the best work I've seen.*

herself /həˈsɛlf/ pron. **1.** a reflexive form of **she**: *she made herself some dinner.* **2.** a form of **her** or **she** used for emphasis: *she did it herself.* **3.** her normal state of mind: *she didn't feel herself for a few days after the operation.*

hertz /hɜts/ n. the derived SI unit of frequency. *Symbol:* Hz

hesitate /ˈhɛzəteɪt/ v.i. **1.** to hold back in doubt or indecision. **2.** to pause. –**hesitation**, n. –**hesitant**, adj.

hessian /ˈhɛʃən/ n. a strong fabric made from jute, used for sacks, etc.

hetero- a word element meaning 'other' or 'different'. Also, (before vowels), **heter-**.

heterodox /ˈhɛtərədɒks, ˈhetrə-/ adj. not in accordance with established or accepted doctrines or opinions, especially in theology.

heterogeneous /hɛtərouˈdʒiniəs/ adj. composed of parts of different kinds.

heterosexual /hɛtərouˈsɛkʃuəl/ n. **1.** someone who has sexual feelings for people of the opposite sex. –adj. **2.** relating to a heterosexual. –**heterosexuality**, n.

heuristic /hjuˈrɪstɪk/ adj. **1.** serving to find out; furthering investigation. **2.** (of a teaching method) encouraging the student to discover for himself or herself.

hew /hju/ v.t. (**hewed**, **hewed** or **hewn**, **hewing**) to strike forcibly with an axe, sword, or the like; chop; hack.

hex /hɛks/ n. an evil spell or charm.

hexa- a prefix meaning 'six', as in *hexagon*. Also, (before vowels), **hex-**.

hexagon /ˈhɛksəgɒn, -gən/ n. a polygon having six angles and six sides.

hey /heɪ/ interj. an exclamation used to call attention, etc.

heyday /ˈheɪdeɪ/ n. the stage or period of highest vigour or fullest strength.

hi /haɪ/ interj. Colloq. an exclamation, especially of greeting.

hiatus /haɪˈeɪtəs/ n. **1.** a break, with a part missing; an interruption. **2.** a gap or opening.

hibernate /ˈhaɪbəneɪt/ v.i. to spend the winter in close quarters in a dormant condition, as certain animals.

hibiscus /haɪˈbɪskəs/ n. a tree with broad, showy, short-lived flowers.

hiccup /ˈhɪkʌp/ n. **1.** a quick, involuntary inspiration suddenly checked by closure of the glottis, producing a characteristic sound. **2.** a minor problem arising in the course of a planned operation. –v.i. (**-cupped, -cupping**) **3.** to make the sound of a hiccup.

hickory /ˈhɪkəri/ n. (pl. **-ries**) a North American tree bearing sweet, edible nuts.

hide¹ /haɪd/ v. (**hid, hidden** or **hid, hiding**) –v.t. **1.** to conceal from sight; prevent from being seen or discovered. **2.** to conceal from

knowledge; keep secret. –v.i. **3.** to conceal oneself; lie concealed.

hide² /haɪd/ n. **1.** the skin of an animal. **2.** Colloq. impudence.

hideaway /ˈhaɪdəweɪ/ n. **1.** a place of concealment; a refuge. **2.** a retreat, as a holiday home, where one can enjoy uninterrupted relaxation.

hidebound /ˈhaɪdbaʊnd/ adj. narrow and rigid in opinion.

hideous /ˈhɪdiəs/ adj. horrible or frightful to the senses; very ugly.

hiding /ˈhaɪdɪŋ/ n. **1.** a beating. **2.** a defeat.

hierarchy /ˈhaɪəraki/ n. (pl. **-archies**) **1.** any system of persons or things in a graded order, etc. **2.** Science a series of successive terms of different rank.

hiero- a word element meaning 'sacred'. Also, (before a vowel), **hier-**.

hieroglyphic /haɪərəˈglɪfɪk/ adj. Also, **hieroglyphical**. **1.** designating or relating to a writing system, particularly that of the ancient Egyptians, in which many of the symbols are conventionalised pictures of the thing named by the words for which the symbols stand. –n. **2.** (usu. pl.) hieroglyphic writing.

high /haɪ/ adj. **1.** having a great or considerable reach or extent upwards; lofty; tall. **2.** having a specified extent upwards. **3.** situated above the ground or some base; elevated. **4.** of more than average or normal height or depth. **5.** intensified; exceeding the common degree or measure; strong; intense; energetic. **6.** produced by relatively rapid vibrations; shrill. **7.** of great amount, degree, force, etc. **8.** chief; principal; main. **9.** of a period of time, at its fullest point of development. **10.** Colloq. intoxicated or elated with alcohol or drugs. **11.** smelly; bad. –adv. **12.** at or to a high point, place, or level, or a high rank or estimate, a high amount or price, or a high degree. –n. **13.** that which is high; a high level. **14.** Meteorol. a pressure system characterised by relatively high pressure at its centre; an anticyclone.

high-fidelity /haɪ-fəˈdɛlɪti/ adj. (of an amplifier, radio receiver, etc.) reproducing the full audio range of the original sounds with relatively little distortion. Also, **hi-fi**.

high five n. a form of salutation in which one slaps the palm of one's right hand against that of another person, often to express solidarity in victory.

high-five v.t. **1.** to give a high five to (someone). –v.i. **2.** to perform a high five.

high-handed adj. overbearing; arbitrary: *high-handed behaviour.*

highland /ˈhaɪlənd/ n. an elevated region; a plateau.

highlight /ˈhaɪlaɪt/ v.t. **1.** to emphasise or make prominent. **2.** to use a highlighter to emphasise (written or printed text). –n. **3.** a conspicuous or striking part. **4.** (pl.) flecks of colour in hair which gleam in the light.

highlighter /ˈhaɪlaɪtə/ n. a pen which puts a translucent colour over parts of a printed or other page to draw the eye to these parts.

highness /ˈhaɪnəs/ n. **1.** the state of being high; loftiness; dignity. **2.** (upper case) (preceded by Her, His, Your, etc.) a title of honour given to royal or princely personages.

high-pressure *adj.* **1.** having or involving a pressure above the normal. **2.** vigorous; persistent.

high pressure system *n.* See **pressure system**.

high-rise *adj.* → **multistorey**.

high school *n.* → **secondary school**.

high-tech /'haɪ-tɛk/ *adj.* **1.** of or relating to high technology. **2.** ultra-modern, especially using materials or styles associated with high technology.

high technology *n.* highly-sophisticated, innovative technology, especially electronic.

highway /'haɪweɪ/ *n.* a main road, as one between towns.

highwayman /'haɪweɪmən/ *n.* (*pl.* **-men**) (formerly) a robber on the highway, especially one on horseback.

hijab /hə'dʒɑb/ *n.* a scarf-like piece of clothing worn by many Muslim women which covers the hair, neck and shoulders, leaving the face uncovered.

hijack /'haɪdʒæk/ *v.t.* **1.** to seize by force or threat of force (a vehicle, especially a passenger-carrying vehicle, as an aircraft). **2.** to steal (something) in transit, as a lorry and the goods it carries.

hike /haɪk/ *v.i.* **1.** to walk a long distance, especially through country districts, for pleasure. *–n.* **2.** a long walk, especially in the country. **3.** an increase in wages, fares, prices, etc.

hilarious /hə'lɛəriəs/ *adj.* **1.** very funny. **2.** boisterously merry. **–hilarity**, *n.*

hill /hɪl/ *n.* a naturally raised part of the earth's surface, smaller than a mountain. **–hilly**, *adj.*

hillbilly /'hɪlbɪli/ *n.* (*pl.* **-lies**) *Chiefly US* a rustic or yokel living in the backwoods or mountains.

hillock /'hɪlək/ *n.* a small hill.

hilt /hɪlt/ *n.* the handle of a sword or dagger.

him /hɪm/ *pron.* the personal pronoun used, usually after a verb or preposition, to refer to a particular male: *I saw him yesterday*; *give it to him.*

himself /hɪm'sɛlf/ *pron.* **1.** a reflexive form of **he**: *he made himself a cup of tea.* **2.** a form of **him** or **he** used for emphasis: *he did it himself.* **3.** his normal state of mind: *he is now himself again.*

hind[1] /haɪnd/ *adj.* (**hinder**, **hindmost** or **hindermost**) situated behind or at the back; posterior.

hind[2] /haɪnd/ *n.* (*pl.* **hinds** or, especially collectively, **hind**) the female of the deer.

hinder /'hɪndə/ *v.t.* to slow down or make difficult. **–hindrance**, *n.*

hindsight /'haɪndsaɪt/ *n.* perception of the nature and exigencies of a case after the event.

hinge /hɪndʒ/ *n.* **1.** the movable joint or device on which a door, gate, shutter, lid, etc., turns or moves. *–v.i.* (**hinged**, **hinging**) **2.** to depend or turn on, or as if on, a hinge.

hint /hɪnt/ *n.* **1.** an indirect or covert suggestion or implication; an intimation. **2.** a very small or barely perceptible amount. *–v.t.* **3.** to give a hint of. *–v.i.* **4.** (usu. fol. by *at*) to make indirect suggestion or allusion.

hinterland /'hɪntəlænd/ *n.* the land lying behind a coastal district.

hip[1] /hɪp/ *n.* the projecting part of each side of the body formed by the side of the pelvis and the upper part of the femur.

hip[2] /hɪp/ *n.* the ripe fruit of a rose.

hip-hop *n.* **1.** an urban, cultural movement originating in New York's South Bronx, for which rap music, breakdancing and graffiti art are the major expressive forms. **2.** the music associated with hip-hop, usually accompanying rapping. *–adj.* **3.** of or relating to hip-hop. Also, **hip hop.** **–hip-hopper**, *n.*

hippie /'hɪpi/ *n.* a person who rejects conventional social values in favour of principles of universal love, union with nature, etc., sometimes making use of hallucinogenic drugs. Also, **hippy.**

hippopotamus /hɪpə'pɒtəməs/ *n.* (*pl.* **-muses** or **-mi** /-maɪ/) a large herbivorous mammal having a thick hairless body, short legs and large head and muzzle.

hire /haɪə/ *v.t.* **1.** to engage the services of for payment. **2.** to engage the temporary use of for payment. **3.** (oft. fol. by *out*) to grant the temporary use of, or the services of, for a payment.

hire purchase *n.* a system whereby a person pays for a commodity by regular instalments, while having full use of it after the first payment. Also, **hire-purchase.**

hirsute /'hɜsjut/ *adj.* hairy.

his /hɪz/ *pron.* **1.** the possessive form of **he**, used before a noun: *that is his book.* **2.** the possessive form of **he**, without a noun following: *that book is his.* **3.** the person(s) or thing(s) belonging to him: *his are the green ones on the left.*

hiss /hɪs/ *v.i.* **1.** to make or emit a sharp sound like that of the letter *s* prolonged. **2.** to express disapproval or contempt by making this sound. *–n.* **3.** a hissing sound, especially in disapproval.

hissy fit /'hɪsi/ *n. Colloq.* an outburst of bad temper; tantrum.

histamine /'hɪstəmin/ *n.* a substance released by the tissues in allergic reactions.

histology /hɪs'tɒlədʒi/ *n.* the science concerned with the study of the detailed structure of animal and plant tissues.

historic /hɪs'tɒrɪk/ *adj.* important in history: *historic scenes.*

history /'hɪstri, 'hɪstəri/ *n.* (*pl.* **-ries**) **1.** the branch of knowledge dealing with past events. **2.** the record of past events, especially in connection with mankind. **3.** a continuous, systematic written narrative, in order of time, of past events as relating to a particular people, country, period, person, etc. **4.** the aggregate of past events. **–historian**, *n.* **–historical**, *adj.*

histrionics /hɪstri'ɒnɪks/ *pl. n.* artificial or exaggerated behaviour, speech, etc., for effect. **–histrionic**, *adj.*

hit /hɪt/ *v.* (**hit**, **hitting**) *–v.t.* **1.** to come against with an impact or collision. **2.** to succeed in striking with a missile, a weapon, a blow, or the like (intentionally or otherwise). **3.** to have a marked effect on; affect severely. **4.** to reach. *–v.i.* **5.** (oft. fol. by *out*) to strike with a missile, weapon, or the like; deal a blow or blows. *–n.* **6.** an impact or collision, as of one thing against another. **7.** a successful stroke, performance, or production; success. **8.** *Internet* a connection made to a website. **9.** *Colloq.* a shot of heroin or any drug; a fix. *–adj.* **10.** successful; achieving popularity.

hitch /hɪtʃ/ *v.t.* **1.** to make fast, especially temporarily, by means of a hook, rope, strap, etc.; tether. **2.** (usu. fol. by *up*) to raise with jerks. **3.** *Colloq.* to obtain or seek to obtain (a ride) from a passing vehicle. *–n.* **4.** a halt; an obstruction.

hitchhike /'hɪtʃhaɪk/ *v.i.* to travel by obtaining rides in passing vehicles.

hither /'hɪðə/ *adv.* to or towards this place; here.

hitherto /hɪðə'tu/ *adv.* up to this time; until now.

HIV /eɪtʃ aɪ 'vi/ *n.* human immunodeficiency virus; the virus which causes AIDS.

hive /haɪv/ *n.* **1.** a shelter for honey bees; a beehive. **2.** a place swarming with busy occupants.

hives /haɪvz/ *n.* (construed as sing.) any of various eruptive diseases of the skin.

hoard /hɔd/ *n.* **1.** an accumulation of something for preservation or future use. *–v.t.* **2.** to accumulate for preservation or future use, especially in a secluded place.

hoarding /'hɔdɪŋ/ *n.* **1.** a temporary fence enclosing a building during erection. **2.** a large board on which advertisements or notices are displayed; billboard.

hoarfrost /'hɔfrɒst/ *n.* → **frost** (def. 1).

hoarse /hɔs/ *adj.* **1.** having a raucous voice. **2.** husky.

hoary /'hɔri/ *adj.* (**-rier, -riest**) grey or white with age.

hoax /hoʊks/ *n.* a humorous or mischievous deception, especially a practical joke.

hobble /'hɒbəl/ *v.* (**-bled, -bling**) *–v.i.* **1.** to walk lamely; limp. *–v.t.* **2.** to fasten together the legs of (a horse, etc.) so as to prevent free motion.

hobby /'hɒbi/ *n.* (*pl.* **-bies**) a spare-time activity or pastime, etc.

hobgoblin /'hɒbgɒblən/ *n.* anything causing superstitious fear.

hobnob /'hɒbnɒb/ *v.i.* (**-nobbed, -nobbing**) to associate on very friendly terms.

hobo /'hoʊboʊ/ *n.* (*pl.* **-bos** or **-boes**) a tramp or vagrant.

hock¹ /hɒk/ *n.* the joint in the hind leg of the horse, etc., above the fetlock joint.

hock² /hɒk/ *n.* a dry white wine.

hock³ /hɒk/ *v.t. Colloq.* → **pawn¹**.

hockey /'hɒki/ *n.* a ball game in which curved sticks are used to drive the ball.

hod /hɒd/ *n.* a portable trough for carrying mortar, bricks, etc.

hoe /hoʊ/ *n.* **1.** a long-handled implement with a thin, flat blade usually set transversely, used to break up the surface of the ground, destroy weeds, etc. *–v.t.* (**hoed, hoeing**) **2.** to dig, scrape, weed, cultivate, etc., with a hoe.

hog /hɒg/ *n.* **1.** a domesticated pig, especially a castrated boar, bred for slaughter. **2.** *Colloq.* a selfish, gluttonous, or filthy person. *–v.t.* (**hogged, hogging**) **3.** *Colloq.* to appropriate selfishly; take more than one's share of.

hogget /'hɒgət/ *n.* **1.** a young sheep of either sex, older than a lamb, that has not yet been sheared. **2.** the meat of such a sheep.

hogwash /'hɒgwɒʃ/ *n.* meaningless talk; nonsense.

hoick /hɔɪk/ *v.t.* to hoist abruptly.

hoist /hɔɪst/ *v.t.* **1.** to raise or lift, especially by some mechanical appliance. *–n.* **2.** an apparatus for hoisting; a lift.

hold¹ /hoʊld/ *v.* (**held, holding**) *–v.t.* **1.** to have or keep in the hand; keep fast; grasp. **2.** to reserve; retain; set aside. **3.** to bear, sustain, or support with the hand, arms, etc., or by any means. **4.** to keep in a specified state, relation, etc. **5.** to contain or be capable of containing. **6.** to regard or consider. *–v.i.* **7.** to remain or continue in a specified state, relation, etc. **8.** to remain valid; be in force. *–n.* **9.** the act of holding fast by a grasp of the hand or by some other physical means; grasp; grip. **10.** a controlling force, or dominating influence. *–phr.* **11. hold up,** to stop by force in order to rob.

hold² /hoʊld/ *n. Naut.* the interior of a ship below the deck.

holder /'hoʊldə/ *n.* **1.** something to hold a thing with. **2.** someone who has the ownership or use of something. **3.** the payee or endorsee of a bill of exchange or promissory note.

holding /'hoʊldɪŋ/ *n.* **1.** (*oft. pl.*) property owned, especially stocks and shares, and land. *–adj.* **2.** used as an interim measure: *a holding yard.*

holding company *n.* **1.** a company controlling, or able to control, other companies by virtue of share ownership in these companies. **2.** a company which owns stocks or securities of other companies, deriving income from them.

hold-up /'hoʊld-ʌp/ *n.* **1.** a forcible stopping and robbing of a person, bank, etc. **2.** a delay.

hole /hoʊl/ *n.* **1.** an opening through anything; an aperture. **2.** a hollow place in a solid body or mass; a cavity. **3.** *Colloq.* a dirty or unpleasant place: *this town is a hole.* **4.** *Golf* any one of the eighteen stages of a round of golf, including the tee, the fairway and the putting green.

holiday /'hɒlədeɪ/ *n.* **1.** a day fixed by law or custom on which ordinary business is suspended in commemoration of some event or in honour of some person, etc. **2.** (*oft. pl.*) a period of cessation from work, or from recreation; a vacation. *–v.i.* **3.** to take a holiday.

holistic /hoʊ'lɪstɪk/ *adj.* of or relating to a medical approach which treats the whole body rather than just dealing with particular manifestations of a disease or symptoms. Also, **wholistic**.

hollow /'hɒloʊ/ *adj.* **1.** having a hole or cavity within; not solid; empty. **2.** sunken, as the cheeks or eyes. *–v.t.* **3.** to make hollow.

holly /'hɒli/ *n.* (*pl.* **-lies**) a plant with glossy, spiny-edged leaves and red berries.

holocaust /'hɒləkɒst, -kɔst/ *n.* great or wholesale destruction of life, especially by fire.

hologram /'hɒləgræm/ *n.* a negative produced by holography.

holography /hɒ'lɒgrəfi/ *n.* a form of photography in which no lens is used and in which a photographic plate records the interference pattern between two portions of a laser beam.

holster /'hoʊlstə/ *n.* a leather case for a handgun, often attached to a belt.

holy /'houli/ *adj.* **(-lier, -liest) 1.** specially recognised as or declared sacred by religious use or authority; consecrated. **2.** dedicated or devoted to the service of a deity or religion. **–holiness,** *n.*

Holy Grail /houli 'greil/ *n.* **1.** a cup (also taken as a chalice) which according to medieval legend was used by Jesus at the Last Supper. **2.** one's ultimate objective.

homage *n.* **1.** /'homidʒ/ respect or reverence paid or rendered. **2.** /om'aʒ, 'homidʒ/ *Art* a work or a collection of works designed to acknowledge and draw on the work of another artist.

home /houm/ *n.* **1.** a house, or other shelter that is the fixed residence of a person, a family, or a household. **2.** (*oft. upper case*) an institution for the homeless, sick, etc. **3.** the place or region where something is native or most common. **4.** one's native place or own country. *–adv.* **5.** to, towards, or at home.

homegrown terrorism /houm'groun/ *n.* terrorist activities undertaken within a country by people who have lived all or most of their lives in that country. **–homegrown terrorist,** *n.*

home invasion *n.* the holding up of a family in their home.

homeland /'houmlænd/ *n.* **1.** one's native land. **2.** an independent or self-governing territory inhabited by a particular people.

homely /'houmli/ *adj.* **(-lier, -liest)** not good-looking; plain.

homeopathy /houmi'ppəθi/ *n.* a method of treating disease by drugs, given in minute doses, which produce in a healthy person symptoms similar to those of the disease. Also, **homoeopathy. –homeopath** /'houmiəpæθ/, *n.* **–homeopathic** /houmiə'pæθik/, *adj.* **–homeopathically** /houmiə'pæθikli/, *adv.*

home page *n. Internet* the introductory page for a website on the internet, containing information about the site, addresses, menus, etc.

home rule *n.* self-government in internal affairs by the inhabitants of a dependent country.

homesick /'houmsik/ *adj.* ill or depressed from a longing for home.

homespun /'houmspʌn/ *adj.* plain; unpolished; simple.

homestead /'houmstɛd/ *n.* the main residence on a sheep or cattle station or large farm.

home truth *n.* a disagreeable statement of fact that hurts the sensibilities.

home unit *n.* → **unit** (def. 3).

homework /'houmwɜk/ *n.* **1.** the part of a lesson or lessons prepared outside school hours. *–phr.* **2. do one's homework,** *Colloq.* to undertake preparatory work for a meeting, interview, discussion, etc.

homicide /'homəsaid/ *n.* **1.** the killing of one human being by another. **2.** a murderer. **–homicidal,** *adj.*

homily /'homəli/ *n.* (*pl.* **-lies**) a religious discourse addressed to a congregation; a sermon.

hommos /'homəs, 'huməs/ *n.* → **hummus.**

homo- a combining form meaning 'the same'.

homoeo- a word element meaning 'similar' or 'like'. Also, **homeo-, homoio-.**

homoeopathy /houmi'ppəθi/ *n.* → **homeopathy. –homoeopath** /'houmiəpæθ/, *n.*

–homoeopathic /houmiə'pæθik/, *adj.* **–homoeopathically** /houmiə'pæθikli/, *adv.*

homogeneous /houmə'dʒiniəs, homə-/ *adj.* **1.** composed of parts all of the same kind; not heterogeneous. **2.** of the same kind or nature; essentially alike. **–homogeneity,** *n.*

homogenise /hə'modʒənaiz/ *v.t.* to make homogeneous. Also, **homogenize.**

homogenous /hə'modʒənəs/ *adj.* **1.** *Biol.* corresponding in structure because of a common origin. **2.** → **homogeneous.**

homologous /hə'moləgəs/ *adj.* having the same or a similar relation; corresponding, as in relative position, structure, etc.

homonym /'homənim/ *n.* a word like another in sound and perhaps in spelling, but different in meaning, as *meat* and *meet.*

homophobia /houmə'foubiə/ *n.* fear of homosexuals, usually linked with hostility towards them. **–homophobic,** *adj.* **–homophobe,** *n.*

Homo sapiens /,houmou 'sæpiənz/ *n.* the single, surviving species of the genus Homo or modern human beings.

homosexual /,houmə'sɛkʃuəl, ,homə-/ *n.* **1.** someone who has sexual feelings for a person of the same sex. *–adj.* **2.** relating to a homosexual. **–homosexuality,** *n.*

hone /houn/ *n.* **1.** a whetstone of fine, compact texture, especially one for sharpening razors. *–v.t.* **2.** to sharpen on or as on a hone. **3.** to improve by careful attention or practice: *to hone one's skills.*

honest /'onəst/ *adj.* **1.** honourable in principles, intentions, and actions; upright. **2.** open; sincere. **3.** genuine or unadulterated. **–honestly,** *adv.* **–honesty,** *n.*

honey /'hʌni/ *n.* a sweet, viscid fluid produced by bees from the nectar collected from flowers.

honeycomb /'hʌnikoum/ *n.* **1.** a structure of wax containing rows of hexagonal cells, formed by bees for the reception of honey and pollen and of their eggs. *–v.t.* **2.** to pierce with many holes or cavities.

honeydew melon /'hʌnidju/ *n.* a sweet-flavoured, white-fleshed melon with a smooth, pale green rind.

honeyeater /'hʌni,itə/ *n.* a bird with a bill and tongue adapted for extracting the nectar from flowers.

honeymoon /'hʌnimun/ *n.* a holiday spent by a newly married couple before settling down to normal domesticity.

honeysuckle /'hʌnisʌkəl/ *n.* a fragrant, climbing plant.

honk /hoŋk/ *n.* **1.** the cry of the goose. **2.** any similar sound, as a car horn. *–v.i.* **3.** to emit a honk.

honor /'onə/ *n., v.t.* → **honour. –honorable,** *adj.*

honorarium /onə'rɛəriəm/ *n.* (*pl.* **-ariums** or **-aria** /-'rɛəriə/) an honorary reward, as in recognition of professional services on which no price may be set.

honorary /'onərəri, *Orig. US* /'onərɛri/ *adj.* **1.** given for honour only, without the usual duties, privileges, emoluments, etc. **2.** holding a title or position conferred for honour only. **3.** (of a position, job, etc.) unpaid. **4.** (of an obligation) depending on one's honour for fulfilment. —n. **5.** a specialist working in a public hospital.

honorific /ɒnəˈrɪfɪk/ adj. doing or conferring honour.

honour /ˈɒnə/ n. **1.** high public esteem; fame; glory. **2.** credit or reputation for behaviour that is becoming or worthy. **3.** a source of credit or distinction. **4.** (usu. pl.) a mark or observance of public respect: *full military honours.* **5.** an official award conferred on someone as a mark of distinction. **6.** a special privilege or favour. **7.** high-minded character or principles; fine sense of one's obligations. **8.** (pl.) (in universities) scholastic or academic achievement in a degree examination higher than that required for a pass degree. —v.t. **9.** to hold in honour or high respect; revere. **10.** to confer honour or distinction upon. **11.** to accept and pay (a cheque, etc.) when due. **12.** to accept the validity of (a document, etc.). Also, **honor.** —**honourable,** adj.

hood[1] /hʊd/ n. **1.** a soft or flexible covering for the head and neck, either separate or attached to a cloak or the like. **2.** something resembling or suggesting this. **3.** a car bonnet.

hood[2] /hʊd/ n. Colloq. a hoodlum.

-hood a suffix denoting state, condition, character, nature, etc., or a body of persons of a particular character or class.

hoodie /ˈhʊdi/ n. Colloq. a jacket with a hood.

hoodlum /ˈhʌdləm/ n. a petty gangster.

hoodwink /ˈhʊdwɪŋk/ v.t. to deceive.

hoof /hʊf/ n. (pl. **hoofs** /hʊfs/ or **hooves** /hʊvz/) the horny covering protecting the ends of the digits or covering the foot in certain animals, as the ox, horse, etc.

hook /hʊk/ n. **1.** a curved or angular piece of metal or other firm substance catching, pulling, or suspending something. **2.** that which catches; a snare; a trap. **3.** something curved or bent like a hook. **4.** Boxing a curving blow made with the arm bent, and coming in to the opponent from the side. —v.t. **5.** to seize, fasten, or catch hold of and draw in with or as with a hook. —v.i. **6.** to become attached or fastened by or as by a hook; join on.

hookah /ˈhʊkə/ n. a pipe with a long, flexible tube by which the smoke of tobacco, marijuana, etc., is drawn through a vessel of water and thus cooled. Also, **hooka.**

hooked /hʊkt/ adj. **1.** bent like a hook; hook-shaped. **2.** made with a hook. **3.** caught, as a fish. **4.** Colloq. (usu. fol. by on) addicted; obsessed.

hooligan /ˈhuləgən/ n. a hoodlum; young street rough.

hoop /hup/ n. **1.** a circular band or ring of metal, wood, or other stiff material. **2.** something resembling a hoop.

hooray /həˈreɪ, hʊˈreɪ/ interj. an exclamation of joy, applause, or the like.

hoot /hut/ v.i. **1.** to cry out or shout, especially in disapproval or derision. **2.** (of an owl) to utter its cry. **3.** to blow a horn or factory hooter; honk. —n. **4.** the cry of an owl. **5.** any similar sound.

hooves /hʊvz/ n. a plural of **hoof.**

hop[1] /hɒp/ v. (**hopped, hopping**) —v.i. **1.** to spring or leap on one foot. **2.** Colloq. (fol. by in, on or off) to board or alight from a car,

train, etc. —v.t. **3.** Colloq. to jump off (something elevated), or over (a fence, ditch, etc.). —n. **4.** a leap on one foot. **5.** Colloq. a dance, or dancing party.

hop[2] /hɒp/ n. a twining plant whose dried ripe cones are used in brewing, etc.

hope /hoʊp/ n. **1.** expectation of something desired; desire accompanied by expectation. **2.** confidence in a future event; ground for expecting something. —v. (**hoped, hoping**) —v.t. **3.** to look forward to with desire and, to a certain extent, confidence. **4.** to trust in the truth of a matter (with a clause). —v.i. **5.** to have an expectation of something desired. —**hopeless,** adj.

hopeful /ˈhoʊpfəl/ adj. **1.** feeling hope. **2.** expressing hope. **3.** promising advantage or success. —n. **4.** a promising young person. —**hopefulness,** n.

hopefully /ˈhoʊpfəli/ adv. **1.** in a hopeful fashion. **2.** it is hoped.

hopsack /ˈhɒpsæk/ n. a coarse, jute sacking material.

hopscotch /ˈhɒpskɒtʃ/ n. a children's game in which the player hops from one compartment to another of a diagram traced on the ground, without touching a line.

horde /hɔd/ n. a great company or multitude.

horizon /həˈraɪzən/ n. the line or circle which forms the apparent boundary between earth and sky.

horizontal /hɒrəˈzɒntl/ adj. **1.** at right-angles to the vertical; in a horizontal position. **2.** near, on, or parallel to the horizon.

hormone /ˈhɔmoʊn/ n. **1.** any of various substances which are formed in endocrine glands and which activate specifically receptive organs when transported to them by the body fluids. **2.** a synthetic substance having the same effect.

hormone replacement therapy n. the administration of oestrogen and progesterone to women to reduce the risk of osteoporosis and reduce menopausal symptoms. Abbrev.: HRT

horn /hɔn/ n. **1.** a hard, projected, often curved and pointed, hollow and permanent growth (usually one of a pair) on the head of certain mammals. **2.** any horn-like projection or extremity. **3.** Music a wind instrument. **4.** an instrument for sounding a warning signal, as on a car.

hornblende /ˈhɔnblɛnd/ n. a common black or dark-coloured mineral.

hornet /ˈhɔnət/ n. a large, strong, social wasp.

horology /həˈrɒlədʒi/ n. the art or science of making timepieces or of measuring time.

horoscope /ˈhɒrəskoʊp/ n. a forecast of a person's future derived from a study of the relative positions of the sun, moon, planets, etc., at the time of the person's birth.

horrendous /hɒˈrɛndəs, hə-/ adj. dreadful; horrible.

horrible /ˈhɒrəbəl/ adj. **1.** causing or tending to cause horror; dreadful. **2.** extremely unpleasant; deplorable.

horrid /ˈhɒrəd/ adj. **1.** such as to cause horror; dreadful; abominable. **2.** extremely unpleasant or disagreeable.

horrific /hɒˈrɪfɪk, hə-/ adj. causing horror.

horrify /'hɒrɪfaɪ/ v.t. (**-fied, -fying**) to strike with horror; shock intensely.

horror /'hɒrə/ n. **1.** a shuddering fear or abhorrence. **2.** Colloq. something considered atrocious or bad. **3.** a painful or intense aversion or repugnance.

hors d'oeuvre /ɔ 'dɜv/ n. a small piece of food served before a meal; appetiser; canapé.

horse /hɔs/ n. **1.** a large, solid-hoofed quadruped, often used for carrying a rider. **2.** a leather-covered vaulting block, used for gymnastics.

horse float n. a van or trailer for conveying horses by road, rail, etc.

horse flu n. → **equine influenza.**

horseplay /'hɔspleɪ/ n. rough or boisterous play.

horsepower /'hɔspaʊə/ n. a unit for measuring power in the imperial system, defined as 550 foot-pounds per second (equal to 745.7 watts).

horseradish /'hɔsrædɪʃ/ n. a cultivated plant with a pungent root, which is ground and used as a condiment.

horseshoe /'hɔsʃu/ n. **1.** a U-shaped iron plate nailed to a horse's hoof to protect it. **2.** a symbol of good luck.

hortatory /hɔ'teɪtəri, 'hɔtətri/ adj. encouraging; inciting, exhorting.

horticulture /'hɔtəkʌltʃə/ n. the science or art of growing fruit, vegetables, flowers or ornamental plants.

hose /həʊz/ n. **1.** a flexible tube for conveying water, etc., to a desired point. **2.** → **hosiery.** –v.t. **3.** to water, wash, or drench by means of a hose.

hosiery /'həʊʒəri, 'həʊzəri/ n. socks or stockings of any kind. Also, **hose.**

hospice /'hɒspəs/ n. **1.** a hospital for terminally ill patients. **2.** (formerly) a house of shelter or rest for pilgrims, strangers, etc., especially one kept by a religious order.

hospital /'hɒspɪtl/ n. an institution in which sick or injured persons are given medical or surgical treatment.

hospitalise /'hɒspətəlaɪz/ v.t. to place in a hospital. Also, **hospitalize.**

hospitality /hɒspə'tæləti/ n. the reception and entertainment of guests or strangers with liberality and kindness. –**hospitable,** adj.

host¹ /həʊst/ n. **1.** someone who entertains guests in his or her own home or elsewhere. **2.** the landlord of an inn. **3.** an animal or plant from which a parasite obtains nutrition. **4.** a computer containing data which may be accessed by users at other computer terminals linked to it.

host² /həʊst/ n. a multitude or great number of persons or things.

hostage /'hɒstɪdʒ/ n. **1.** a person given or held as a security for the performance of certain actions as the payment of ransom, etc. **2.** a security or pledge.

hostel /'hɒstəl, hɒs'tɛl/ n. a supervised place of low-cost accommodation, usually supplying board and lodging, as for one for students, travellers, etc.

hostess /'həʊstəs/ n. a female host; a woman who entertains guests.

hostile /'hɒstaɪl/ adj. opposed in feeling, action, or character; unfriendly; antagonistic. –**hostility,** n.

hot /hɒt/ adj. (**hotter, hottest**) **1.** having or communicating heat; having a high temperature. **2.** having a sensation of great bodily heat; attended with or producing such a sensation. **3.** new; recent; fresh. **4.** following very closely; close. **5.** Colloq. (of a car) tuned or modified for high speeds. **6.** Colloq. fashionable or popular: this summer's hottest hits. **7.** Colloq. recently stolen or otherwise illegally obtained; wanted by the police. **8.** Colloq. sexually attractive; sexually stimulating.

hotbed /'hɒtbɛd/ n. a place favouring rapid growth, especially of something bad.

hotchpotch /'hɒtʃpɒtʃ/ n. a heterogeneous mixture; a jumble.

hot-desking /'hɒt-dɛskɪŋ/ n. the sharing of a desk between a number of employees, especially those whose job takes them out of the office on a regular basis. –**hot-desk,** v.

hot dog n. **1.** a hot frankfurt served in a split roll. **2.** a short surfboard designed to turn quickly back and forth across the wave. Also, **hot-dog, hotdog.**

hot-dog /'hɒt-dɒg/ v.i. (**-dogged, -dogging**) to perform rapid and difficult manoeuvres with quick changes of direction, while riding a surfboard, skateboard, ski, etc. Also, **hotdog.** –**hot-dogger,** n.

hotel /həʊ'tɛl/ n. a building in which accommodation and food, and usually alcoholic drinks are available; public house.

hothouse /'hɒthaʊs/ n. an artificially heated greenhouse for the cultivation of tender plants.

hotline /'hɒtlaɪn/ n. **1.** a direct telephone connection open to immediate communication in an emergency. **2.** a telephone line which gives direct access to people who wish to ring up to ask advice, give an opinion, etc.

hotplate /'hɒtpleɪt/ n. **1.** a portable appliance for cooking or keeping food warm. **2.** a solid, electrically heated metal plate, usually on top of an electric stove, upon which food, etc., may be heated or cooked.

hot rod n. Colloq. a car (usually an old one) whose engine has been altered for increased speed.

hoummus /'huməs, 'hɒməs/ n. → **hummus.** Also, **hoummos.**

hound /haʊnd/ n. **1.** a dog of any of various breeds used in the chase and commonly hunting by scent. **2.** any dog. –v.t. **3.** to hunt or track with hounds, or as a hound does; pursue. **4.** to harass unceasingly.

hour /'aʊə/ n. **1.** a space of time equal to one 24th part of a mean solar day or civil day; 60 minutes. **2.** a particular or appointed time. **3.** distance normally covered in an hour's travelling.

hourly /'aʊəli/ adj. of, relating to, occurring, or done each successive hour.

house n. /haʊs/ (pl. **houses** /'haʊzəz/) **1.** a building for people to live in, usually one which is self-contained and designed for a single family; a household. **3.** the audience of a theatre, etc. **4. a.** the building in which a legislative or deliberative body meets. **b.** the body itself. **5.** a firm or commercial

establishment. 6. a subdivision of a school, comprising children of all ages and classes. –*v.t.* /haʊz/ (**housed, housing**) **7.** to put or receive into a house; provide with a house.

household /ˈhaʊshoʊld/ *n.* **1.** the people of a house collectively; a family, including servants, etc.; a domestic establishment. –*adj.* **2.** of or relating to a household; domestic. **3.** very common.

house journal *n.* an internal journal of a company, presenting its news to its employees.

housekeeper /ˈhaʊskipə/ *n.* **1.** a paid employee who is hired to run a house, direct the domestic work, catering, etc. **2.** an employee of a hotel responsible for the cleaning staff.

house-sit /ˈhaʊs-sɪt/ *v.* (**-sat, -sitting**) –*v.i.* **1.** to occupy a house, apartment, etc., temporarily and without the payment of rent, for the purpose of providing security or daily maintenance during the absence of the regular occupant. –*v.t.* **2.** to occupy (a house, apartment, etc.) under such an arrangement. –**house-sitter**, *n.* –**house-sitting**, *n.*

house-train /ˈhaʊs-treɪn/ *v.t.* to train (an animal) so that it may be kept inside a house without inconvenience to other occupants; especially to train it to control its natural excretory functions.

house union *n.* a union to which all employees, regardless of profession or trade, may belong by virtue of working for the one employer.

house-warming /ˈhaʊs-wɔmɪŋ/ *n.* a party to celebrate beginning one's occupancy of a new house.

housewife /ˈhaʊswaɪf/ *n.* (*pl.* **-wives**) the woman in charge of a household, especially a wife who does no other job.

housework /ˈhaʊswɜk/ *n.* the work of cleaning, cooking, etc.

housing /ˈhaʊzɪŋ/ *n.* **1.** houses collectively. **2.** the provision of houses for the community. **3.** *Machinery* a frame, plate or the like, that supports a part of a machine, etc.

hove /hoʊv/ *v.* a past tense and past participle of **heave**.

hovel /ˈhɒvəl/ *n.* a small, mean dwelling house; a wretched hut.

hover /ˈhɒvə/ *v.i.* **1.** to hang fluttering or suspended in the air. **2.** to keep lingering about; wait near at hand.

hovercraft /ˈhɒvəkrɑft/ *n.* a vehicle able to travel in close proximity to the ground or water, on a cushion of air.

how /haʊ/ *adv.* **1.** in what way or manner; by what means. **2.** to what extent, degree, etc. **3.** in what state or condition. –*conj.* **4.** concerning the condition or state in which. **5.** concerning the extent or degree to which. **6.** concerning the means or way in which.

however /haʊˈɛvə/ *conj.* **1.** nevertheless; yet; in spite of that. –*adv.* **2.** to whatever extent or degree; no matter how (far, much, etc.). **3.** in whatever condition, state, or manner. **4.** (*used interrogatively*) Also, **how ever**. how in any circumstances.

howl /haʊl/ *v.i.* **1.** to utter a loud, prolonged, mournful cry, as that of a dog or wolf. –*n.* **2.** the cry of a dog, wolf, etc. **3.** a cry or wail, as of pain or rage.

HTML /eɪtʃ ti ɛm ˈɛl/ *n.* hypertext markup language; a computer markup language, similar to SGML, used primarily to create documents for the World Wide Web.

HTTP *n.* hypertext transfer protocol; the protocol used for transferring files on the World Wide Web Also, **http**.

hub /hʌb/ *n.* **1.** the central part of a wheel, as that part into which the spokes are inserted. **2.** a central position around which activity revolves.

huddle /ˈhʌdl/ *v.t.* **1.** to heap or crowd together confusedly. –*v.i.* **2.** to gather or crowd together in a confused mass. –*n.* **3.** a confused heap, mass, or crowd; a jumble.

hue[1] /hju/ *n.* **1.** that property of colour by which the various regions of the spectrum are distinguished, as red, blue, etc. **2.** variety of a colour; a tint.

hue[2] /hju/ *n.* outcry.

huff /hʌf/ *n.* **1.** a sudden swell of anger; a fit of resentment. –*v.t.* **2.** to puff or blow.

hug /hʌg/ *v.t.* (**hugged, hugging**) **1.** to clasp tightly in the arms, especially with affection; embrace. –*n.* **2.** a tight clasp with the arms; a warm embrace.

huge /hjudʒ/ *adj.* extraordinarily large.

hugely /ˈhjudʒli/ *adv.* extremely; immoderately: *he laughed hugely.*

hulk /hʌlk/ *n.* **1.** the body of an old or dismantled ship. **2.** a bulky or unwieldy person or mass of anything.

hull[1] /hʌl/ *n.* **1.** the husk, shell, or outer covering of a seed or fruit. **2.** the calyx of certain fruits, as the strawberry and raspberry. –*v.t.* **3.** to remove the hull of.

hull[2] /hʌl/ *n.* the frame or body of a ship.

hullabaloo /hʌləbəˈlu/ *n.* a clamorous noise or disturbance; an uproar.

hum /hʌm/ *v.i.* (**hummed, humming**) **1.** to make a low, continuous, droning sound. **2.** to be in a state of busy activity.

human /ˈhjumən/ *adj.* **1.** of, relating to, or characteristic of people. –*n.* **2.** a human being.

human being *n.* a member of the human race.

humane /hjuˈmeɪn/ *adj.* characterised by tenderness and compassion for the suffering or distressed.

human immunodeficiency virus *n.* → **HIV**.

humanitarian /hjumænəˈtɛəriən/ *adj.* **1.** having regard to the interests of all humankind; broadly philanthropic. –*n.* **2.** a philanthropist.

humanity /hjuˈmænəti/ *n.* **1.** the human race; humankind. **2.** the quality of being humane; kindness; benevolence.

humankind /hjumənˈkaɪnd/ *n.* the human race.

human resources *pl. n.* the human component of an organisation, etc., seen as one of the elements requiring skilled management to achieve a productive output. *Abbrev.:* HR

human swine influenza *n.* → **pandemic influenza A (H1N1)**. Also, **human swine flu, swine flu**.

humble /ˈhʌmbəl/ *adj.* **1.** low in station, grade of importance, etc.; lowly. **2.** modest; meek; without pride. –*v.t.* **3.** to lower in condition, importance, or dignity; abase.

humbug /ˈhʌmbʌg/ *n.* a quality of falseness or deception.

humdrum /'hʌmdrʌm/ adj. lacking variety; dull.

humerus /'hjumərəs/ n. (pl. **-meri** /-mərai/) (in humans) the single long bone in the arm which extends from the shoulder to the elbow.

humid /'hjuməd/ adj. moist or damp, with liquid or vapour.

humidicrib /hju'mɪdɪkrɪb/ n. Med. an enclosed crib with controlled temperature and humidity.

humidity /hju'mɪdəti/ n. 1. humid condition; dampness. 2. Meteorol. the condition of the atmosphere with regard to its water-vapour content.

humiliate /hju'mɪliert/ v.t. to lower the pride or self-respect of; cause a painful loss of dignity to; mortify. **–humiliation**, n. **–humiliating**, adj. **–humiliatingly**, adv.

humility /hju'mɪləti/ n. the quality of being humble; modest sense of one's own significance.

hummingbird /'hʌmɪŋbɜd/ n. a small bird whose narrow wings vibrate very rapidly, producing a humming sound.

hummock /'hʌmək/ n. a hillock.

hummus /'homəs, 'homəs/ n. a Middle Eastern dish made from ground chickpeas and sesame paste, flavoured with lemon juice and garlic. Also, **hommus**, **hommos**.

humorous /'hjumərəs/ adj. 1. characterised by humour; amusing; funny. 2. having or showing the faculty of humour; droll; facetious.

humour /'hjumə/ n. 1. the quality of being funny. 2. the faculty of perceiving what is amusing or comical. 3. speech or writing showing this faculty. 4. mental disposition or tendency; frame of mind. 5. Physiol. Obs. one of the four chief bodily fluids, blood, choler or yellow bile, phlegm, and melancholy or black bile. –v.t. 6. to comply with the wishes of; indulge. Also, **humor**.

hump /hʌmp/ n. 1. a rounded protuberance, especially on the back. 2. a low, rounded rise of ground; hummock.

humpy /'hʌmpi/ n. a temporary bush shelter used by Aboriginal people; gunyah.

humungous /hju'mʌŋgəs/ adj. Colloq. of huge size or extent.

humus /'hjuməs/ n. the dark organic material in soils, produced by the decomposition of vegetable or animal matter.

humvee /'hʌm'vi/ n. Mil. an off-road vehicle designed for military use.

hunch /hʌntʃ/ v.t. 1. to thrust out or up in a hump. –v.i. 2. (usu. fol. by up) to walk, sit, or stand in a bent position. –n. 3. a hump. 4. Colloq. a premonition or suspicion.

hundred /'hʌndrəd/ n. (pl. **-dreds**, as after a numeral, **-dred**) 1. a cardinal number, ten times ten. –adj. 2. amounting to one hundred in number. **–hundredth**, adj., n.

hundredweight /'hʌndrədwert/ n. (pl. **-weights**, as after a numeral, **-weight**) a unit of weight in the imperial system, equal to 112 lb. (approx. 50.8 kg) and, in the US, to 100 lb. (approx. 45.36 kg). Symbol: cwt

hung /hʌŋ/ v. a past tense and past participle of **hang**.

hunger /'hʌŋgə/ n. 1. the painful sensation or state of exhaustion caused by need of food. 2. strong or eager desire.

hungry /'hʌŋgri/ adj. (**-grier, -griest**) 1. wanting something to eat. 2. wanting something very much. **–hungrily**, adv.

hunk /hʌŋk/ n. a large piece or lump; a chunk.

hunt /hʌnt/ v.t. 1. to chase (game or other wild animals) for the purpose of catching or killing. 2. to search for; seek; endeavour to obtain or find. –v.i. 3. to engage in the chase. 4. (oft. fol. by for or after) to make a search or quest. –n. 5. the act of hunting game or other wild animals; the chase. 6. pursuit; a search.

huntsman /'hʌntsmən/ n. → **tarantula**.

Huon pine /'hjuon/ n. a large coniferous timber tree found in Tasmania.

hurdle /'hɜdl/ n. 1. a barrier in a racetrack, to be leapt by the contestants. 2. a difficult problem to be overcome; obstacle. –v.t. 3. to leap over (a hurdle, etc.) as in a race. 4. to master (a difficulty, problem, etc.).

hurl /hɜl/ v.t. to drive or throw with great force.

hurricane /'hʌrəkən, -kein/ n. a violent tropical cyclonic storm.

hurry /'hʌri/ v. (**-ried, -rying**) –v.i. 1. to move, proceed, or act with haste, often undue haste. –v.t. 2. to drive or move (someone or something) with speed, often with confused haste. –n. 3. need or desire for haste.

hurt /hɜt/ v. (**hurt, hurting**) –v.t. 1. to cause injury or pain to. 2. to affect adversely; harm. –v.i. 3. to cause pain (bodily or mental). –n. 4. a blow that inflicts a wound; bodily injury. 5. injury; damage or harm.

hurtle /'hɜtl/ v.i. to rush violently and noisily.

husband /'hʌzbənd/ n. a man joined in marriage to another person.

husbandry /'hʌzbəndri/ n. the business of a farmer; agriculture; farming.

hush /hʌʃ/ v.t. 1. to make silent; silence. 2. to suppress mention of; keep concealed.

husk /hʌsk/ n. the dry external covering of certain fruits or seeds, especially of an ear of maize.

husky[1] /'hʌski/ adj. (**-kier, -kiest**) 1. Colloq. burly; big and strong. 2. having a semi-whispered vocal tone; somewhat hoarse.

husky[2] /'hʌski/ n. (pl. **-kies**) (also upper case) a strong dog used in a team to pull sledges over snow.

hussy /'hʌsi, 'hʌzi/ n. (pl. **-sies**) 1. an ill-behaved girl. 2. a lewd woman.

hustings /'hʌstɪŋz/ pl. n. the platform from which a political candidate speaks during an election campaign.

hustle /'hʌsəl/ v.i. 1. to proceed or work rapidly or energetically. –v.t. 2. to force roughly or hurriedly. –n. 3. energetic activity.

hut /hʌt/ n. a simple, small house as a beach hut, bushwalker's hut, etc.

hutch /hʌtʃ/ n. a coop for confining small animals.

hyacinth /'haɪəsənθ/ n. a bulbous plant with spikes of fragrant, bell-shaped flowers.

hybrid /'haɪbrəd/ n. 1. the offspring of two animals or plants of different breeds, varieties, species, or genera. 2. anything derived from heterogeneous sources, or composed of elements of different or incongruous kind.

hybrid car *n.* a car which has both an electric and a petrol engine, the latter being required at higher speeds.

hydatid /haɪˈdætəd/ *n.* a cyst with watery contents, produced in humans and animals by a tapeworm in the larval state.

hydrangea /haɪˈdreɪndʒə/ *n.* a shrub with large showy flower clusters.

hydrant /ˈhaɪdrənt/ *n.* an upright pipe with a spout, nozzle, or other outlet, usually in the street, for drawing water from a main or service pipe.

hydraulic /haɪˈdrɒlɪk/ *adj.* operated by or employing water or other liquid.

hydraulic fracturing *n.* (in oil and gas mining) a process by which fractures are made in rock by chemically treated water mixed with sand to natural or man-made openings in order to gain access to oil or gas supplies; fracking.

hydraulics /haɪˈdrɒlɪks/ *n.* the science that deals with the laws governing water or other liquids in motion and their applications in engineering.

hydro-¹ a word element meaning 'water', as in *hydrogen*. Also, **hydr-**.

hydro-² *Chem.* a word element often indicating combination of hydrogen with a negative element or radical. Also, **hydr-**.

hydrocarbon /haɪdrouˈkabən/ *n.* any of a class of compounds containing only hydrogen and carbon.

hydrochlorofluorocarbon /haɪdrouˌklɒrouˌfluːrouˈkabən/ *n.* a chemical containing hydrogen, chlorine, fluorine, and carbon; used instead of the earlier chlorofluorocarbon as a coolant in refrigerators and a propellant in spray cans because it does not damage the ozone layer. *Abbrev.*: HCFC

hydro-electric /ˌhaɪdrou-əˈlɛktrɪk/ *adj.* relating to the generation and distribution of electric energy derived from the energy of falling water.

hydrofluorocarbon /haɪdrouˌfluːrouˈkabən/ *n.* a chemical containing hydrogen, fluorine, and carbon; used as a coolant in refrigerators and a propellant in spray cans because it does not deplete the ozone layer. *Abbrev.*: HFC

hydrofoil /ˈhaɪdrəfɔɪl/ *n.* a boat which, at speed, lifts above the surface of the water on two or more ski-like members.

hydrogen /ˈhaɪdrədʒən/ *n.* a colourless, odourless, flammable gas, which combines chemically with oxygen to form water; the lightest of the known elements. *Symbol*: H

hydroplane /ˈhaɪdrəpleɪn/ *n.* **1.** a plane surface designed to control or facilitate the movement of an aeroplane or boat on or in the water. **2.** a motorboat, with hydrofoils or a shaped bottom, designed to plane along the surface of the water at high speeds.

hydroponics /haɪdrəˈpɒnɪks/ *n.* the cultivation of plants by placing the roots in liquid nutrient solutions rather than in soil. **–hydroponic**, *adj.* **–hydroponically**, *adv.*

hyena /haɪˈinə/ *n.* any of various doglike nocturnal carnivores, feeding chiefly on carrion. Also, **hyaena**.

hyeto- a word element meaning 'rain'.

hygiene /ˈhaɪdʒin/ *n.* **1.** the science which deals with the preservation of health. **2.** the practices, such as keeping oneself clean, which maintain good health.

hygienic /haɪˈdʒinɪk/ *adj.* clean and sanitary.

hygro- a word element meaning 'wet', 'moist'. Also, *(before vowels)*, **hygr-**.

hygrometer /haɪˈgrɒmətə/ *n.* an instrument for determining the humidity of the atmosphere.

hymen /ˈhaɪmən/ *n.* a fold of mucous membrane partially closing the external orifice of the vagina.

hymn /hɪm/ *n.* a song or ode in praise or honour of God, a deity, a nation, etc.

hymnal /ˈhɪmnəl/ *n.* Also, **hymnbook**. **1.** a book of hymns. *–adj.* **2.** of or relating to hymns.

hype /haɪp/ *n. Colloq.* an atmosphere of deliberately stimulated excitement and enthusiasm.

hyper- a prefix meaning 'over', and usually implying excess or exaggeration.

hyperactive /haɪpərˈæktɪv/ *adj.* overactive. **–hyperactivity**, *n.*

hyperbola /haɪˈpɜbələ/ *n.* (*pl.* **-las**) a curve consisting of two distinct and similar branches, formed by the intersection of a plane with a right circular cone when the plane makes a greater angle with the base than does the generator of the cone.

hyperbole /haɪˈpɜbəli/ *n.* obvious exaggeration, for effect; an extravagant statement not intended to be taken literally.

hyperbolic /haɪpəˈbɒlɪk/ *adj.* **1.** having the nature of hyperbole; exaggerated. **2.** of or relating to the hyperbola.

hyperlink /ˈhaɪpəlɪŋk/ *n. Computers* an element of a hypertext document which is connected to another document, or to another place in the same document.

hypertension /haɪpəˈtɛnʃən/ *n.* elevation of the blood pressure, the chief sign of disease of the arteries. **–hypertensive**, *adj.*

hypertext /ˈhaɪpətɛkst/ *n. Computers* text created in HTML which has highlighted links to other documents or other areas in the same document.

hyperthermia /haɪpəˈθɜmiə/ *n.* the acute condition of having an abnormally high body temperature.

hyperventilation /ˌhaɪpəvɛntəˈleɪʃən/ *n.* the excessive exposure of the lungs to oxygen resulting in a rapid loss of carbon dioxide from the blood. **–hyperventilate**, *v.*

hyphen /ˈhaɪfən/ *n.* a short stroke (-) used to connect the parts of a compound word or the parts of a word divided for any purpose. **–hyphenate**, *v.*

hypno- a word element meaning 'sleep' or 'hypnosis'.

hypnosis /hɪpˈnousəs/ *n.* (*pl.* **-noses** /-nousiz/) **1.** *Psychol.* a trance-like mental state induced in a cooperative subject by suggestion. **2.** → **hypnotism**.

hypnotic /hɪpˈnɒtɪk/ *adj.* **1.** relating to hypnosis or hypnotism. *–n.* **2.** an agent or drug that produces sleep; a sedative.

hypnotise /ˈhɪpnətaɪz/ *v.t.* to put in the hypnotic state. Also, **hypnotize**.

hypnotism /ˈhɪpnətɪzəm/ *n.* **1.** the science dealing with the induction of hypnosis. **2.** the induction of hypnosis. **–hypnotist**, *n.*

hypo- a prefix meaning 'under', either in place or in degree ('less', 'less than').

hypochondria /haɪpə'kɒndriə/ n. *Psychol.* a condition characterised by depressed spirits and fancies of ill health, referable to the physical condition of the body or one of its parts. –**hypochondriacal** /haɪpəkɒn'draɪəkəl/, *adj.* –**hypochondriac** n., *adj.*

hypocrisy /hɪ'pɒkrəsi/ n. **1.** the act of pretending to have a character or beliefs, principles, etc., that one does not possess. **2.** pretence of virtue or piety; false goodness.

hypocrite /'hɪpəkrɪt/ n. someone given to hypocrisy; someone who feigns virtue or piety; a pretender. –**hypocritical**, *adj.*

hypodermic /haɪpə'dɜmɪk/ *adj.* **1.** characterised by the introduction of medical remedies under the skin. **2.** lying under the skin, as tissue. –n. **3.** a hypodermic needle.

hypotenuse /haɪ'pɒtənjuz/ n. the side of a right-angled triangle opposite the right angle.

hypothalamus /haɪpə'θæləməs/ n. (*pl.* **-thalami**) the part of the middle brain concerned with emotional expression and bodily responses.

hypothermia /haɪpə'θɜmiə/ n. the acute condition of having an abnormally low body temperature.

hypothesis /haɪ'pɒθəsəs/ n. (*pl.* **-theses** /-θəsiz/) **1.** a proposition (or set of propositions) proposed as an explanation for the occurrence of some specified group of phenomena. **2.** a proposition assumed as a premise in an argument.

hypothetical /haɪpə'θetɪkəl/ *adj.* assumed by hypothesis; supposed.

hysterectomy /hɪstə'rektəmi/ n. (*pl.* **-mies**) the surgical excision of the uterus.

hysteria /hɪs'tɪəriə/ n. an uncontrollable emotional state. –**hysterical**, *adj.*

hysterics /hɪs'terɪks/ *pl. n.* wild laughter.

hystero- a word element meaning 'uterus'. Also, **hyster-**.

I, i

I, i /aɪ/ *n*. the ninth letter of the English alphabet.

-i- an ending for the first element in many compounds, as in *Frenchify*, etc.

I /aɪ/ *pron*. the personal pronoun used by a speaker to refer to himself or herself: *I heard that*.

-ia a suffix of nouns, especially having restricted application in various fields, as in medicine, geography, botany, etc.

-ial variant of **-al¹**, as in *judicial, imperial*.

iamb /ˈaɪæmb, ˈaɪæm/ *n*. a metrical foot of two syllables, a short followed by a long. **–iambic**, *adj*.

-ian variant of **-an**, as in *amphibian*.

-iasis a word element forming names of diseases.

-iatry a combining form meaning 'medical care', as in *psychiatry*.

ibidem /ˈɪbədem, ɪˈbaɪdəm/ *adv*. in the same book, chapter, page, etc.

ibis /ˈaɪbəs/ *n*. (*pl*. **ibis** *or* **ibises**) a wading bird with a long, thin, down-curved bill.

-ible variant of **-able**, as in *credible*.

-ic a suffix forming adjectives from nouns or stems not used as words themselves, meaning 'relating or belonging to'.

-ical a compound suffix forming adjectives from nouns (*rhetorical*), providing synonyms to words ending in *-ic* (*poetical*), and providing an adjective with additional meanings to those in the *-ic* form (*economical*).

ice /aɪs/ *n*. **1.** the solid form of water, produced by freezing; frozen water. **2.** reserve; formality. **3.** *Colloq*. a crystallised, very pure form of methamphetamine hydrochloride. *–v.t*. (**iced, icing**) **4.** to cover with ice. **5.** to cool with ice, as a drink. **6.** to cover (cakes, etc.) with icing. **–icy**, *adj*.

-ice a suffix used in many nouns to indicate state or quality, as in *service, justice*.

iceberg /ˈaɪsbɜg/ *n*. **1.** a large floating mass of ice, detached from a glacier and carried out to sea. **2.** *Colloq*. a regular winter swimmer.

ice cap *n*. a mass of ice which typically feeds a number of glaciers at its edge. Also, **icecap**.

ice cream /ˈaɪs-krim/ *n*. a frozen food made of cream, rich milk, or evaporated milk, sweetened and variously flavoured. Also, **ice-cream**.

ice skate *n*. (a shoe fitted with) a thin metal runner for moving along on ice. **–ice-skate**, *v*.

ichthyo- a word element meaning 'fish'.

ichthyology /ɪkθiˈɒlədʒi/ *n*. the branch of zoology that deals with fishes. **–ichthyologist**, *n*.

-ician a compound suffix especially applied to an expert in a field, as in *geometrician*.

icicle /ˈaɪsɪkəl/ *n*. a pendent tapering mass of ice formed by the freezing of dripping water. **–icicled**, *adj*.

icing /ˈaɪsɪŋ/ *n*. a preparation for covering cakes, etc., usually made from icing sugar with fruit juice, egg white, colouring, etc.

icon /ˈaɪkɒn/ *n*. **1.** a representation in painting, enamel, etc., of some sacred personage, itself venerated as sacred. **2.** a sign or representation which stands for its object by virtue of a resemblance or analogy to it. **3.** *Computers* a picture on a video display unit screen representing an instruction or menu option. **–iconic**, *adj*.

icono- a word element meaning 'likeness' or 'image'.

iconoclast /aɪˈkɒnəklæst/ *n*. **1.** a breaker or destroyer of images, especially those set up for religious veneration. **2.** someone who attacks cherished beliefs as based on error or superstition.

-ics a suffix of nouns, as in *ethics, physics, politics, tactics*.

id /ɪd/ *n*. (in psychoanalysis) the part of the psyche residing in the unconscious which is the source of instinctive energy.

-id¹ a suffix of nouns and adjectives indicating members of a zoological family.

-id² variant of **-ide**.

-id³ a word ending common in adjectives, especially of states which appeal to the senses, as in *torrid, acid*.

ID /aɪ ˈdi/ *Colloq*. *–n*. **1.** a document providing personal details, such as name, address, date of birth, etc. **2.** an identification of a person: *a positive ID*. *–v.t*. (**ID'd, ID'ing**) **3.** to identify (a person).

I'd /aɪd/ contraction of *I would*, or *I had*.

-idae a suffix of the taxonomic names of families in zoology.

-ide a noun suffix in names of chemical compounds. Also, **-id²**.

idea /aɪˈdɪə/ *n*. any conception existing in the mind as the result of mental apprehension or activity.

ideal /aɪˈdɪəl/ *n*. **1.** a conception of something in its highest perfection. **2.** that which exists only in idea. *–adj*. **3.** conceived as constituting a standard of perfection or excellence. **4.** not real or practical.

idealise /aɪˈdɪəlaɪz/ *v.t*. to make ideal; represent in an ideal form or character. Also, **idealize**.

idealism /aɪˈdɪəlɪzəm/ *n*. the cherishing or pursuit of ideals, as for attainment. **–idealist**, *n*. **–idealistic**, *adj*.

ideate /aɪˈdieɪt/ *v.t*. to form in idea, thought, or imagination.

idem /ˈɪdem, ˈaɪdem/ *pron*. the same as previously given or mentioned.

identical /aɪˈdentɪkəl/ *adj*. **1.** agreeing exactly. **2.** same, or being the same one.

identify /aɪˈdentɪfaɪ/ *v.t*. (**-fied, -fying**) **1.** to recognise or establish as being a particular person or thing. **2.** (fol. by *with*) to associate in feeling, interest, action, etc. **3.** to serve as a means of identification for. **–identification**, *n*.

identity /aɪˈdentəti/ *n*. (*pl*. **-ties**) **1.** the state or fact of remaining the same one, as under varying aspects or conditions. **2.** the condition of being oneself or itself, and not another.

identity theft *n*. the appropriation of someone else's identification mechanisms, such as PINs, social security numbers, banking details, etc., to commit fraud or theft.

ideo- a word element meaning 'idea'.

ideology /aɪdiˈɒlədʒi/ *n*. (*pl*. **-gies**) the body of doctrine, myth, and symbols of a social movement, institution, class, or large group. **–ideological**, *adj*. **–ideologist**, *n*.

id est /ɪd ˈɛst/ that is.

idio- a word element meaning 'peculiar' or 'proper to one', as in *idiosyncrasy*.

idiom /ˈɪdiəm/ *n.* **1.** a form of expression peculiar to a language, especially one having a significance other than its literal one. **2.** a distinct style or character, as in music, art, etc. –**idiomatic**, *adj.*

idiosyncrasy /ˌɪdiouˈsɪŋkrəsi/ *n.* (*pl.* **-sies**) any tendency, characteristic, mode of expression, or the like, peculiar to an individual. –**idiosyncratic**, *adj.*

idiot /ˈɪdiət/ *n.* a very foolish or senseless person. –**idiotic**, *adj.* –**idiocy**, *n.*

-idium a diminutive suffix used in scientific terms.

idle /ˈaɪdl/ *adj.* (**idler, idlest**) **1.** unemployed, or doing nothing. **2.** habitually doing nothing or avoiding work. –*v.i.* (**idled, idling**) **3.** to pass time in idleness. **4.** *Machinery* to operate, usually at minimum speed, while the transmission is disengaged.

idol /ˈaɪdl/ *n.* **1.** an image or other material object representing a deity to which religious worship is addressed. **2.** any person or thing blindly adored or revered. –**idolatry**, *n.* –**idolise, idolize**, *v.*

idyll /ˈɪdəl, ˈaɪdəl/ *n.* **1.** a poem or prose composition consisting of a 'little picture', usually describing pastoral scenes. **2.** an episode or scene of simple or poetic charm. –**idyllic**, *adj.*

-ie a suffix used colloquially: **1.** (*with nouns*) as an endearment, or affectionately, especially with and among children: *doggie*. **2.** (*with nouns*) as a familiar abbreviation: *budgie; goalie*. **3.** (*with adjectives*) to form a noun: *greenie*. **4.** (*with adjectives*) as a familiar abbreviation: *indie*.

-ier variant of **-eer**, as in *brigadier*.

-ies a word element representing the plural formation of nouns and third person singular of verbs for words ending in *-y, -ie*, and sometimes *-ey*. See **-s**[2], **-s**[3], **-es**.

if /ɪf/ *conj.* **1.** in case that; granting or supposing that; on condition that. **2.** whether.

-ify variant of **-fy**, used when the preceding stem or word element ends in a consonant, as in *intensify*.

igloo /ˈɪgluː/ *n.* (*pl.* **-loos**) a dome-shaped Inuit hut, built of blocks of hard snow.

igneous rock /ˈɪgniəs/ *n.* rock formed from magma.

ignite /ɪgˈnaɪt/ *v.t.* **1.** to set on fire; kindle. –*v.i.* **2.** to begin to burn.

ignition /ɪgˈnɪʃən/ *n.* **1.** the act of igniting. **2.** the state of being ignited. **3.** (in an internal-combustion engine) the process which ignites the fuel in the cylinder.

ignoble /ɪgˈnoubəl/ *adj.* of low character, aims, etc.; mean; base.

ignominy /ˈɪgnəməni/ *n.* disgrace; dishonour. –**ignominious**, *adj.*

ignoramus /ɪgnəˈreɪməs, ɪgnəˈraːməs/ *n.* (*pl.* **-muses**) an ignorant person.

ignorant /ˈɪgnərənt/ *adj.* destitute of knowledge. –**ignorance**, *n.*

ignore /ɪgˈnɔː/ *v.t.* to refrain from noticing or recognising.

iguana /ɪˈgwaːnə/ *n.* a large tropical American lizard.

il-[1] variant of **in-**[1], (by assimilation) before *l.*

il-[2] variant of **in-**[2], (by assimilation) before *l.*

-ile a suffix of adjectives expressing capability, susceptibility, liability, aptitude, etc., as in *agile, docile, ductile, fragile, prehensile, tensile, volatile*. Also, **-il.**

-ility a compound suffix making abstract nouns from adjectives by replacing the adjective suffixes as in *civility, ability*, etc.

ilk /ɪlk/ *n.* family, class, or kind.

ill /ɪl/ *adj.* (**worse, worst**) **1.** unwell, sick, or indisposed. **2.** evil, wicked, or bad. –*n.* **3.** evil. **4.** harm or injury. **5.** a disease or ailment. –*adv.* **6.** unsatisfactorily or poorly. **7.** with displeasure or offence. **8.** faultily or improperly. –**illness**, *n.*

I'll /aɪl/ contraction of *I will* or *I shall.*

illegal /ɪˈliːgəl/ *adj.* **1.** not legal. –*n.* **2.** *Colloq.* an illegal immigrant. –**illegality**, *n.*

illegal immigrant *n.* an immigrant to a country who is deemed to be illegal because they have arrived without prior authority from the government of that country, as in the form of a visa, or because they have stayed beyond the time allowed by their visa.

illegible /ɪˈlɛdʒəbəl/ *adj.* not legible; impossible or hard to read or decipher.

illegitimate /ɪləˈdʒɪtəmət/ *adj.* **1.** not legitimate. **2.** born out of wedlock.

ill-fated /ˈɪl-feɪtəd/ *adj.* **1.** destined to an unhappy fate. **2.** bringing bad fortune.

ill-gotten /ˈɪl-gɒtn/ *adj.* acquired by evil means, as *ill-gotten gains.*

illicit /ɪˈlɪsət/ *adj.* not permitted or authorised; unlicensed; unlawful.

illiterate /ɪˈlɪtərət, ɪˈlɪtrət/ *adj.* **1.** unable to read and write. –*n.* **2.** an illiterate person.

ill-mannered /ˈɪl-mænəd/ *adj.* having bad manners; impolite; rude.

illuminate /ɪˈljuːməneɪt/ *v.t.* **1.** to supply with light; light up. **2.** to enlighten, as with knowledge. **3.** to decorate (a letter, a page, a manuscript, etc.) with colour, gold, or the like.

illusion /ɪˈluːʒən/ *n.* something that deceives by producing a false impression. –**illusory**, *n.*

illustrate /ˈɪləstreɪt/ *v.t.* **1.** to make clear or intelligible, as by examples. **2.** to furnish (a book, etc.) with drawings or pictorial representations intended for elucidation or adornment. –**illustration**, *n.*

illustrious /ɪˈlʌstriəs/ *adj.* **1.** highly distinguished; renowned; famous. **2.** glorious, as deeds, etc.

im-[1] variant of **in-**[1] used before *b, m*, and *p.*

im-[2] variant of **in-**[2] used before *b, m*, and *p*, as in *immoral*. Also, **em-**.

I'm /aɪm/ contraction of *I am.*

image /ˈɪmɪdʒ/ *n.* **1.** a likeness or similitude of a person, animal, or thing. **2.** an optical counterpart or appearance of an object. **3.** a mental picture or representation; an idea or conception. **4.** the impression a public figure, especially a politician, strives to create for the public. **5.** Also, **spitting image**. a counterpart or copy. **6.** *Rhetoric* a figure of speech, especially a metaphor or a simile. –**imagery**, *n.*

imaginary /ɪˈmædʒənəri, -ənri/, *Orig. US* /-əneri/ *adj.* existing only in the imagination or fancy; not real.

imagination /ɪˌmædʒəˈneɪʃən/ n. the action of imagining, or of forming mental images or concepts of what is not actually present to the senses. **–imaginative**, adj.

imagine /ɪˈmædʒən/ v.t. **1.** to form a mental image of (something not actually present to the senses). **2.** to think, believe, or fancy. **3.** to assume or suppose.

imago /ɪˈmeɪgoʊ/ n. (pl. **imagos** or **imagines** /ɪˈmeɪdʒəniz/) **1.** Entomology an adult insect. **2.** Psychoanalysis an idealised concept of a loved one, formed in childhood and retained uncorrected in adult life.

imam /ɪˈmam/ n. a Muslim religious leader or chief.

imbalance /ɪmˈbæləns/ n. lack of balance.

imbecile /ˈɪmbəsil, -saɪl/ n. **1.** a silly person; fool. **2.** Psychiatry Obsolesc. a person of defective mentality.

imbibe /ɪmˈbaɪb/ v. (**imbibed, imbibing**) –v.t. **1.** to drink in, or drink. –v.i. **2.** to drink; absorb liquid or moisture.

imbroglio /ɪmˈbroʊlioʊ/ n. (pl. **-lios**) an intricate and perplexing state of affairs.

imbue /ɪmˈbju/ v.t. (**-bued, -buing**) to impregnate or inspire, as with feelings, opinions, etc.

imitate /ˈɪməteɪt/ v.t. **1.** to follow or endeavour to follow in action or manner. **2.** to mimic or counterfeit. **3.** to make a copy of; reproduce closely. **–imitation**, n.

immaculate /ɪˈmækjulət, -kjə-/ adj. free from spot or stain; spotlessly clean, as linen.

immanent /ˈɪmənənt/ adj. remaining within; indwelling; inherent.

immaterial /ˌɪməˈtɪəriəl/ adj. **1.** of no essential consequence; unimportant. **2.** not material; spiritual.

immediate /ɪˈmidiət/ adj. **1.** occurring or accomplished without delay; instant. **2.** having no object or space intervening; nearest or next. **–immediacy**, n.

immemorial /ˌɪməˈmɔriəl/ adj. extending back beyond memory, record, or knowledge.

immense /ɪˈmɛns/ adj. **1.** vast; huge; very great. **2.** immeasurable; boundless.

immerse /ɪˈmɜs/ v.t. **1.** to plunge into or place under a liquid; dip; sink. **–immersion**, n.

immigrate /ˈɪməgreɪt/ v.i. to come into a country of which one is not a native for the purpose of permanent residence. **–immigration**, n. **–immigrant**, n., adj.

imminent /ˈɪmənənt/ adj. likely to occur at any moment.

immolate /ˈɪməleɪt/ v.t. to sacrifice.

immoral /ɪˈmɒrəl/ adj. not moral; not conforming to the moral law; not conforming to accepted patterns of conduct. **–immorality**, n.

immortal /ɪˈmɔtl/ adj. **1.** not mortal; not liable or subject to death; undying. **2.** remembered or celebrated through all time. **–immortality**, n. **–immortalise, immortalize**, v.

immune /əˈmjun, ɪ-/ adj. **1.** protected from a disease or the like, as by inoculation. **2.** exempt. **–immunise, immunize**, v. **–immunisation**, n. **–immunity**, n.

immune system n. a complex network of interacting systems within the body which protect it from disease, and which can destroy infected, malignant, or broken-down cells.

immunodeficiency /ˌɪmjənoʊdəˈfɪʃənsi/ n. Med. an impairment in the autoimmune system caused especially by a lack of white blood cells and resulting in reduced immunity to infection. **–immunodeficient**, adj.

immunology /ˌɪmjuˈnɒlədʒi/ n. that branch of medical science which deals with immunity from disease and the production of such immunity. **–immunological**, adj. **–immunologist**, n.

immure /ɪˈmjuə/ v.t. **1.** to enclose within walls. **2.** to imprison.

immutable /ɪˈmjutəbəl/ adj. unchangeable; unalterable; changeless. **–immutability, immutableness**, n. **–immutably**, adv.

imp /ɪmp/ n. **1.** a little devil or demon; an evil spirit. **2.** a mischievous child.

impact n. /ˈɪmpækt/ **1.** the striking of one body against another. **2.** influence or effect exerted by a new idea, concept, ideology, etc. –v.t. /ɪmˈpækt/ **3.** to drive or press closely or firmly into something; pack in. –phr. **4. impact on**, to have an effect on: this law impacts on all of us.

impair /ɪmˈpeə/ v.t. to make worse; diminish in value, excellence, etc.

impala /ɪmˈpalə/ n. (pl. **impalas** or, especially collectively, **impala**) an African antelope.

impale /ɪmˈpeɪl/ v.t. to fix upon a sharpened stake or the like.

impart /ɪmˈpat/ v.t. to give or bestow.

impartial /ɪmˈpaʃəl/ adj. unbiased.

impasse /ˈɪmpas/ n. a position from which there is no escape.

impassive /ɪmˈpæsɪv/ adj. without emotion; apathetic; unmoved.

impatient /ɪmˈpeɪʃənt/ adj. not patient; not bearing pain, opposition, etc., with composure. **–impatience**, n.

impeach /ɪmˈpitʃ/ v.t. **1.** to challenge the credibility of. **2.** to accuse of a grave criminal offence.

impeccable /ɪmˈpɛkəbəl/ adj. faultless or irreproachable.

impecunious /ˌɪmpəˈkjuniəs/ adj. poor; penniless.

impede /ɪmˈpid/ v.t. to obstruct; hinder.

impediment /ɪmˈpɛdəmənt/ n. **1.** some physical defect, especially a speech disorder. **2.** obstruction or hindrance; obstacle.

impel /ɪmˈpɛl/ v.t. (**-pelled, -pelling**) to drive or urge forward.

impend /ɪmˈpɛnd/ v.i. to be imminent.

imperative /ɪmˈpɛrətɪv/ adj. **1.** not to be avoided or evaded. **2.** of the nature of or expressing a command; commanding.

imperfect /ɪmˈpɜfəkt/ adj. **1.** characterised by or subject to defects. **2.** Gram. designating a tense which denotes action going on but not completed, especially in the past. Compare **pluperfect, perfect** (def. 3).

imperial /ɪmˈpɪəriəl/ adj. **1.** of or relating to an empire. **2.** of a commanding quality, manner, or aspect. **3.** (of weights and measures) conforming to the standards legally established in Britain.

imperial system n. a system of non-metric eights and measures set up in Britain and used in Australia before the metric system was introduced in 1970.

imperious /ɪmˈpɪəriəs/ *adj.* domineering, dictatorial, or overbearing.

impersonal /ɪmˈpɜːsənəl/ *adj.* **1.** not personal; without personal reference or connection. **2.** *Gram.* (of a verb) having only third person singular forms, rarely if ever accompanied by an expressed subject.

impersonate /ɪmˈpɜːsəneɪt/ *v.t.* to assume the character of; pretend to be.

impertinent /ɪmˈpɜːtənənt/ *adj.* intrusive or presumptuous.

impervious /ɪmˈpɜːviəs/ *adj.* **1.** not penetrable. **2.** not disposed to be influenced or affected. Also, **imperviable**.

impetigo /ɪmpəˈtaɪgoʊ/ *n.* a contagious skin disease, especially of children.

impetuous /ɪmˈpɛtʃuəs/ *adj.* acting with or characterised by a sudden or rash energy.

impetus /ˈɪmpətəs/ *n.* (*pl.* **-tuses**) moving force; impulse; stimulus.

impinge /ɪmˈpɪndʒ/ *v.i.* (**impinged, impinging**) **1.** to collide. **–phr.** **2.** **impinge on** (or **upon**), to encroach or infringe on.

implacable /ɪmˈplækəbəl/ *adj.* not able to be appeased or pacified.

implant /ɪmˈplænt, -ˈplɑːnt/ *v.t.* to instil or inculcate.

implement *n.* /ˈɪmpləmənt/ **1.** an instrument, tool, or utensil. *–v.t.* /ˈɪmpləmɛnt/ **2.** to put (a plan, proposal, etc.) into effect.

implicate /ˈɪmpləkeɪt/ *v.t.* **1.** to involve as being concerned in a matter, affair, condition, etc. **2.** to imply. **–implication**, *n.*

implicit /ɪmˈplɪsɪt/ *adj.* **1.** (of belief, confidence, obedience, etc.) unquestioning, unreserved, or absolute. **2.** implied, rather than expressly stated.

implore /ɪmˈplɔː/ *v.t.* to call upon in urgent or piteous supplication, as for aid or mercy; beseech.

imply /ɪmˈplaɪ/ *v.t.* (**-plied, -plying**) **1.** to involve as a necessary circumstance. **2.** to indicate or suggest.

import *v.t.* /ɪmˈpɔt, ˈɪmpɒt/ **1.** to bring in from another country, as merchandise or commodities, for sale, use, processing, or re-export. **2.** to convey as a meaning or implication. *–n.* /ˈɪmpɔt/ **3.** that which is imported from abroad. **4.** meaning; implication; purport. **5.** consequence or importance.

important /ɪmˈpɔtənt/ *adj.* **1.** of much significance or consequence. **2.** (fol. by *to*) mattering much. **3.** of considerable influence or authority, as a person, position, etc. **–importance**, *n.*

importune /ɪmˈpɔtʃun, ɪmpɔˈtjun/ *v.t.* to beg urgently or persistently. **–importunate**, *adj.*

impose /ɪmˈpoʊz/ *v.t.* **1.** to lay on or set as something to be borne, endured, fulfilled, etc. **2.** to subject to some penalty, etc. *–v.i.* **3.** to push or force oneself on others. **–imposition**, *n.*

imposing /ɪmˈpoʊzɪŋ/ *adj.* making an impression on the mind, as by great size, stately appearance, etc.

impossible /ɪmˈpɒsəbəl/ *adj.* **1.** not possible; that cannot be, exist, or happen. **2.** that cannot be done or effected. **3.** difficult to deal with: *he's impossible when he hasn't had enough sleep.* **–impossibly**, *adv.* **–impossibility**, *n.*

impost /ˈɪmpoʊst/ *n.* a tax.

impostor /ɪmˈpɒstə/ *n.* someone who practises deception under an assumed character or name. **–imposture**, *n.*

impotent /ˈɪmpətənt/ *adj.* **1.** not potent; lacking power or ability. **2.** (of a male) unable to perform sexual intercourse. **–impotence**, *n.*

impound /ɪmˈpaʊnd/ *v.t.* **1.** to shut up in a pound, as a stray animal. **2.** to seize, take, or appropriate summarily.

impoverish /ɪmˈpɒvərɪʃ, -vrɪʃ/ *v.t.* to reduce to poverty.

imprecate /ˈɪmprəkeɪt/ *v.t.* to call down or invoke (especially evil or curses), as upon a person. **–imprecation**, *n.*

impregnable /ɪmˈprɛgnəbəl/ *adj.* strong enough to resist attack.

impregnate /ˈɪmprɛgneɪt/ *v.t.* **1.** to make pregnant. **2.** to charge with something infused or permeating throughout; saturate.

impresario /ɪmprəˈsɑːrioʊ/ *n.* (*pl.* **-rios**) the organiser or manager of an opera, ballet, or theatre company or orchestra.

impress /ɪmˈprɛs/ *v.t.* **1.** to affect deeply or strongly in mind or feelings, especially favourably; influence in opinion. **2.** to urge, as something to be remembered or done. **3.** to produce (a mark, figure, etc.) by pressure; stamp; imprint.

impression /ɪmˈprɛʃən/ *n.* **1.** a strong effect produced on the intellect, feelings, or conscience. **2.** a notion, remembrance, or belief. **3.** a mark, indentation, figure, etc., produced by pressure. **4.** an imitation, especially one given for entertainment, of the idiosyncrasies of some well-known person or type. **–impressionable**, *adj.*

impressive /ɪmˈprɛsɪv/ *adj.* having the ability to impress; causing admiration or wonder. **–impressively**, *adv.*

imprint *n.* /ˈɪmprɪnt/ **1.** a mark made by pressure; a figure impressed or printed on something. *–v.t.* /ɪmˈprɪnt/ **2.** to impress (a quality, character, or distinguishing mark). **3.** to fix firmly on the mind, memory, etc.

imprison /ɪmˈprɪzən/ *v.t.* to put into or confine in a prison; detain in custody.

impro /ˈɪmproʊ/ *n.* **1.** improvisation, especially in theatre or film, as in creating unscripted dialogue, or in music, as in composing or performing on the spur of the moment. **2.** an instance of such improvisations: *to perform an impro.* Also, **improv**.

impromptu /ɪmˈprɒmptju/ *adj.* made or done without previous preparation.

improper /ɪmˈprɒpə/ *adj.* not done in a proper way, especially morally or legally. **–improperly**, *adv.* **–impropriety**, *n.*

improve /ɪmˈpruːv/ *v.t.* **1.** to bring into a more desirable or excellent condition. *–v.i.* **2.** to increase in value, excellence, etc.; become better. **–improvement**, *n.*

improvise /ˈɪmprəvaɪz/ *v.t.* to prepare or provide offhand or hastily. **–improvisation**, *n.*

impudent /ˈɪmpjudənt, -pjə-/ *adj.* characterised by a shameless boldness.

impugn /ɪmˈpjun/ *v.t.* to call in question; challenge as false.

impulse /ˈɪmpʌls/ *n.* **1.** sudden, involuntary inclination prompting to action, or a particular instance of it. **2.** an impelling action or force. **–impulsive,** *adj.*

impunity /ɪm'pjunɪti/ *n.* exemption from punishment or ill consequences.

impure /ɪm'pjuə/ *adj.* **1.** not pure; mixed with extraneous matter, especially of an inferior or contaminating kind. **2.** modified by admixture, as colour. **3.** mixed or combined with something else: *an impure style of architecture.* **4.** not morally pure; unchaste. **–impurity, impureness,** *n.* **–impurely,** *adv.*

impute /ɪm'pjut/ *v.t.* **1.** to attribute or ascribe. **2.** *Law* to charge. **–imputation,** *n.*

in /ɪn/ *prep.* **1.** a particle expressing inclusion within space, limits, a whole, material or immaterial surroundings, etc. **–adv. 2.** in or into some place, position, state, relation, etc. **–adj. 3.** in one's house or office. **4.** *Colloq.* in favour; on friendly terms: *he's in with the managing director.* **5.** in fashion. **6.** in season.

in-¹ a prefix representing *in,* as in *income, inland,* but used also as a verb-formative with transitive, intensive, or sometimes little apparent force. Compare **en-.** Also, **il-, im-, ir-.**

in-² a prefix corresponding to *un-,* having a negative or privative force, freely used as an English formative, especially of adjectives and their derivatives and of nouns, as in *inattention, indefensible, inexpensive, inorganic.* Also, **il-, im-, ir-.**

inability /ɪnə'bɪlɪti/ *n.* lack of ability; lack of power, capacity, or means.

inaccurate /ɪn'ækjərət/ *adj.* not accurate. **–inaccurately,** *adv.*

inadvertent /ɪnəd'vɜtnt/ *adj.* **1.** not attentive; heedless. **2.** characterised by lack of attention, as actions, etc. **3.** unintentional.

inane /ɪn'eɪn/ *adj.* lacking sense or ideas; silly. **–inanity,** *n.*

inanimate /ɪn'ænəmət/ *adj.* **1.** not animate; lifeless. **2.** spiritless; sluggish; dull.

inappropriate /ɪnə'prouprɪət/ *adj.* not appropriate.

inarticulate /ɪnɑ'tɪkjələt/ *adj.* **1.** not articulate; unclear.: *inarticulate speech.* **2.** unable to produce articulate speech: *inarticulate with rage.* **3.** *Anat., Zool.* not jointed; having no articulation or joint. **–inarticulately,** *adv.* **–inarticulateness,** *n.*

inasmuch as /ɪnəz'mʌtʃ/ *conj.* in view of the fact that; seeing that; since.

inaugurate /ɪn'ɔgjəreɪt/ *v.t.* **1.** to make a formal beginning of; initiate; commence; begin. **2.** to induct into office with formal ceremonies; install. **–inaugural,** *adj.* **–inauguration,** *n.*

inborn /'ɪnbɔn/ *adj.* implanted by nature; innate.

inbox /'ɪnbɒks/ *n. Computers* a folder for receiving incoming emails.

inbreed /ɪn'brid/ *v.t.* (**-bred, -breeding**) to breed (animals) repeatedly within the same strain. **–inbred,** *adj.*

incalculable /ɪn'kælkjuləbəl, -kjə-/ *adj.* that cannot be calculated; beyond calculation.

in camera *phr.* **–camera²**.

incandescence /ɪnkæn'dɛsəns/ *n.* the state of a body caused by approximately white heat, when it may be used as a source of artificial light. **–incandesce,** *v.* **–incandescent,** *adj.*

incantation /ɪnkæn'teɪʃən/ *n.* the chanting or uttering of words supposed to have magical power.

incapable /ɪn'keɪpəbəl/ *adj.* **1.** not able to do anything well: *the shop assistant was completely incapable.* **–phr. 2. incapable of,** not able to do something: *incapable of understanding.*

incapacitate /ɪnkə'pæsɪteɪt/ *v.t.* to make incapable or unfit.

incarcerate /ɪn'kasəreɪt/ *v.t.* to imprison; confine.

incarnate *adj.* /ɪn'kanət, -neɪt/ **1.** embodied in flesh; invested with a bodily, especially a human, form. **2.** personified or typified, as a quality or idea. **–v.t.** /ɪn'kaneɪt/ **3.** to be the embodiment or type of. **–incarnation,** *n.*

incendiary /ɪn'sɛndʒəri/ *adj.* used or adapted for setting property on fire.

incense¹ /'ɪnsɛns/ *n.* an aromatic gum or other substance producing a sweet smell when burnt, used especially in religious ceremonies.

incense² /ɪn'sɛns/ *v.t.* to inflame with wrath; make angry; enrage.

incentive /ɪn'sɛntɪv/ *n.* **1.** that which encourages action, greater effort, etc. **2.** an inducement such as extra money, better conditions, etc., offered to employees to encourage better work.

inception /ɪn'sɛpʃən/ *n.* beginning; start.

incessant /ɪn'sɛsənt/ *adj.* continuing without interruption.

incest /'ɪnsɛst/ *n.* sexual intercourse between persons closely related by blood. **–incestuous,** *adj.*

inch /ɪntʃ/ *n.* **1.** a unit of length in the imperial system, equal to 25.4 mm. **–v.t., v.i. 2.** to move by inches or small degrees.

inchoate /'ɪnkoʊeɪt/ *adj.* just begun.

incidence /'ɪnsədəns/ *n.* **1.** the range of occurrence or influence of a thing, or the extent of its effects. **2.** the falling of a ray of light, etc., on a surface.

incident /'ɪnsədənt/ *n.* **1.** an occurrence or event. **–adj. 2.** naturally appertaining. **3.** falling or striking on something.

incidental /ɪnsə'dɛntl/ *adj.* **1.** happening or likely to happen in fortuitous or subordinate conjunction with something else. **2.** incurred casually and in addition to the regular or main amount.

incinerate /ɪn'sɪnəreɪt/ *v.t.* to reduce to ashes. **–incinerator,** *n.*

incipient /ɪn'sɪpiənt/ *adj.* beginning.

incise /ɪn'saɪz/ *v.t.* to cut into. **–incision,** *n.*

incisive /ɪn'saɪsɪv/ *adj.* penetrating, trenchant, or biting.

incisor /ɪn'saɪzə/ *n.* a tooth in the anterior part of the jaw adapted for cutting.

incite /ɪn'saɪt/ *v.t.* to urge on; stimulate or prompt to action.

incline *v.i.* /ɪn'klaɪn/ **1.** to have a mental tendency; be disposed. **2.** to deviate from the vertical or horizontal; slant. **3.** to tend, in a physical sense; approximate. **–v.t.** /ɪn'klaɪn/ **4.** (fol. by *to*) to dispose (a person) in mind, habit, etc. **5.** to bow (the head, etc.). **6.** to cause to lean or bend in a particular direction. **–n.** /'ɪnklaɪn, ɪn'klaɪn/ **7.** an inclined surface; a slope. **–inclination,** *n.*

include /ɪnˈklud/ v.t. **1.** to contain, embrace, or comprise, as a whole does parts or any part or element. **2.** to place in an aggregate, class, category, or the like. **–inclusive**, adj.

incognito /ɪnkogˈnitoʊ/ adv. with the real identity concealed.

incoherent /ɪnkoʊˈhɪərənt/ adj. **1.** not arranged or connected properly: an incoherent sentence. **2.** (of a person) showing unordered thought or language: incoherent with rage. **–incoherence**, n. **–incoherently**, adv.

income /ˈɪnkʌm, ˈɪŋ-/ n. the returns that come in periodically, especially annually, from one's work, property, business, etc.; revenue; receipts.

income group n. a group of people having similar incomes.

income tax n. an annual government tax on personal incomes, usually graduated and with certain deductions and exemptions.

incommodious /ɪnkəˈmoʊdiəs/ adj. **1.** not affording sufficient room. **2.** inconvenient.

incommunicado /ˌɪnkəmjunəˈkadoʊ/ adj. (especially of a prisoner) deprived of communication with others.

incompatible /ɪnkəmˈpætəbəl/ adj. **1.** not able to exist together in harmony. **2.** (of a computer device) not able to work in conjunction with another specified device. **–incompatibility**, n.

incompetent /ɪnˈkɒmpətənt/ adj. not competent; lacking in skill or ability. **–incompetence**, n. **–incompetently**, adv.

incomplete /ɪnkəmˈplit/ adj. not complete; lacking some part.

incongruous /ɪnˈkɒŋɡruəs/ adj. **1.** out of keeping or place; inappropriate; unbecoming; absurd. **2.** not harmonious in character; lacking harmony of parts. **–incongruity**, n.

inconsequential /ˌɪnkɒnsəˈkwɛnʃəl/ adj. **1.** of no consequence; trivial. **2.** illogical.

inconsiderate /ɪnkənˈsɪdərət/ adj. without proper regard for the rights or feelings of others.

incontinence /ɪnˈkɒntənəns/ n. the inability to exercise voluntary control over natural functions, especially urination and defecation. Also, **incontinency**.

incontinent /ɪnˈkɒntənənt/ adj. **1.** Pathol. lacking control over the normally voluntary excretory functions of the body. **2.** lacking in restraint.

incontrovertible /ˌɪnkɒntrəˈvɜtəbəl/ adj. not able to be argued against.

inconvenient /ɪnkənˈviniənt/ adj. not convenient; awkward, inopportune, disadvantageous, or troublesome. **–inconvenience**, n.

incorporate /ɪnˈkɔpəreɪt/ v.t. **1.** to create or form into a legal corporation. **2.** to form into a society or organisation. **3.** to put or introduce into a body or mass as an integral part or parts.

incorrigible /ɪnˈkɒrədʒəbəl/ adj. **1.** bad beyond correction or reform. **2.** firmly fixed; not easily changed.

increase v.t. /ɪnˈkris/ **1.** to make greater in any respect; augment; add to. **–v.i.** /ɪnˈkris/ **2.** to become greater or more numerous. **–n.** /ˈɪnkris/ **3.** growth or augmentation in numbers. **4.** that by which something is increased.

incredible /ɪnˈkrɛdəbəl/ adj. **1.** seeming too extraordinary to be possible. **2.** not credible; that cannot be believed.

incredulous /ɪnˈkrɛdʒələs/ adj. **1.** not credulous; indisposed to believe; sceptical. **2.** indicating disbelief.

increment /ˈɪnkrəmənt, ˈɪŋ-/ n. **1.** something added or gained; an addition or increase. **2.** an increase in salary resulting from progression within a graduated scale of salaries, designed to reward an employee for increases in skill or experience. **–v.t. 3.** Computers to increase the numerical contents of (a variable).

incriminate /ɪnˈkrɪməneɪt/ v.t. **1.** to imply or provide evidence of the fault of (someone). **2.** to involve in an accusation.

incubate /ˈɪnkjubeɪt, ˈɪŋ-/ v.t. **1.** to sit upon (eggs) for the purpose of hatching. **2.** to maintain (bacterial cultures, etc.) at the most favourable temperature for development. **3.** to keep at even temperature, as prematurely born infants. **–incubator**, n.

inculcate /ˈɪnkʌlkeɪt/ v.t. (usu. fol. by upon or in) to impress by repeated statement or admonition; teach persistently and earnestly; instil.

incumbent /ɪnˈkʌmbənt/ adj. resting on one; obligatory.

incur /ɪnˈkɜ/ v.t. (**-curred**, **-curring**) to run or fall into (some consequence, usually undesirable or injurious).

incursion /ɪnˈkɜʒən/ n. an invasion.

indebted /ɪnˈdɛtəd/ adj. **1.** owing money. **2.** being under an obligation for benefits, favours, assistance. etc., received.

indecent /ɪnˈdisənt/ adj. offending against recognised standards of propriety or good taste; vulgar.

indeed /ɪnˈdid/ adv. in fact; in reality; in truth; truly (used for emphasis, to confirm and amplify a previous statement, to intensify, to indicate a concession or admission, or, interrogatively, to obtain confirmation).

indefatigable /ɪndəˈfætɪɡəbəl/ adj. incapable of being tired out.

indefeasible /ɪndəˈfizəbəl/ adj. not to be annulled or made void.

indefensible /ɪndəˈfɛnsəbəl/ adj. that cannot be justified; inexcusable.

indelible /ɪnˈdɛləbəl/ adj. incapable of being deleted or obliterated.

indelicate /ɪnˈdɛləkət/ adj. offensive to a sense of propriety, or modesty; unrefined.

indemnity /ɪnˈdɛmnəti/ n. (pl. **-ties**) **1.** protection or security against damage or loss. **2.** compensation for damage or loss sustained. **3.** legal protection, as by insurance, from liabilities or penalties incurred by one's actions. **–indemnify**, v.

indent v.t. /ɪnˈdɛnt/ **1.** to form deep recesses in. **2.** to set in or back from the margin, as the first line of a paragraph. **3.** to sever (a document drawn up in duplicate) along an irregular line as a means of identification. **4.** to order, as commodities. **–v.i.** /ɪnˈdɛnt/ **5.** to form a contract. **–n.** /ˈɪndɛnt/ **6.** a tooth-like notch or deep recess; an indentation. **7.** an order for goods. **–indentation**, n.

indenture /ɪnˈdɛntʃə/ n. **1.** an indented document. **2.** a contract by which a person, as an apprentice, is bound to service.

independent /ɪndəˈpɛndənt/ adj. **1.** not influenced by others. **2.** not subject to another's authority or jurisdiction; autonomous; free.

3. not dependent; not depending or contingent on something or someone else for existence, operation, etc. **4.** (of a school) non-government. −*n.* **5.** *Politics* a politician who is not formally affiliated with a political party. −**independence**, *n.*

indeterminate /ɪndəˈtɜːmənət/ *adj.* not determinate; not fixed in extent; indefinite; uncertain.

index /ˈɪndɛks/ *n.* (*pl.* **-dexes** *or* **-dices** /-dəsiːz/) **1.** a detailed alphabetical key to names, places, and topics in a book with reference to their page number, etc., in the book. **2.** something used or serving to point out; a sign, token, or indication. **3.** a number or formula expressing some property, ratio, etc., of a thing indicated. −*v.t.* **4.** to provide with an index, as a book. **5.** to adjust (wages, taxes, etc.) regularly in accordance with changes in commodity and other prices.

indexation /ɪndɛkˈseɪʃən/ *n.* the adjustment of one variable in the light of changes in another variable, especially the adjustment of wages to compensate for rises in the cost of living.

index finger *n.* → **forefinger**.

indicate /ˈɪndəkeɪt, -dɪkeɪt/ *v.t.* **1.** to be a sign of; imply. **2.** to point out or point to; direct attention to. −**indication**, *n.*

indicative /ɪnˈdɪkətɪv/ *adj.* **1.** (fol. by *of*) that indicates; pointing out; suggestive. **2.** *Gram.* mood used in ordinary statements, questions, etc.

indicator /ˈɪndəkeɪtə/ *n.* **1.** something that indicates. **2.** a pointing or directing instrument, as a pointer on an instrument or a flashing light on a car. **3.** a statistic or set of statistics which suggest the state of some aspect of society: *a market indicator.*

indices /ˈɪndəsiːz/ *n.* a plural of **index**.

indict /ɪnˈdaɪt/ *v.t.* to charge with an offence or crime. −**indictment**, *n.*

indie /ˈɪndi/ *adj.* **1.** (of films, CDs, etc.) produced by a company independent of the mainstream companies or studios. **2.** of or relating to a style of popular film or music considered individual and less commercially motivated than mainstream productions.

indifferent /ɪnˈdɪfrənt/ *adj.* **1.** without interest or concern; not caring; apathetic. **2.** neutral in character or quality; neither good nor bad. **3.** not very good. **4.** immaterial or unimportant.

indigenous /ɪnˈdɪdʒənəs/ *adj.* **1.** (sometimes fol. by *to*) originating in and characterising a particular region or country; native. **2.** (*upper case*) of or relating to Aboriginal and Torres Strait Islander people: *Indigenous issues.*

indigent /ˈɪndədʒənt/ *adj.* poor.

indigestion /ɪndəˈdʒɛstʃən, ɪndaɪ-/ *n.* incapability of, or difficulty in, digesting food. −**indigestive**, *adj.*

indignation /ɪndɪɡˈneɪʃən/ *n.* strong displeasure at something deemed unworthy, unjust, or base. −**indignant**, *adj.*

indignity /ɪnˈdɪɡnəti/ *n.* (*pl.* **-ties**) injury to dignity.

indigo /ˈɪndɪɡoʊ/ *n.* (*pl.* **-gos**) a deep violet blue.

indirect /ɪndəˈrɛkt, ɪndaɪˈrɛkt/ *adj.* **1.** not direct in space; not following a straight line: *an indirect route.* **2.** coming or resulting otherwise than directly or immediately: *an indirect effect.*

3. not direct in action; not straightforward: *indirect methods.*

indiscreet /ɪndəsˈkrit/ *adj.* not discreet, not wise or carefully judged: *indiscreet praise.*

indiscretion /ɪndəsˈkrɛʃən/ *n.* **1.** lack of discretion; imprudence. **2.** an indiscreet act or step.

indiscriminate /ɪndəsˈkrɪmənət/ *adj.* not discriminating; making no distinction.

indispensable /ɪndəsˈpɛnsəbəl/ *adj.* absolutely necessary.

indisposed /ɪndəsˈpoʊzd/ *adj.* **1.** sick or ill, especially slightly. **2.** disinclined or unwilling. −**indisposition**, *n.*

individual /ɪndəˈvɪdʒuəl/ *adj.* **1.** single; particular; separate. **2.** relating or peculiar to a single person or thing. **3.** distinguished by peculiar and marked characteristics. −*n.* **4.** a single human being or thing, as distinguished from a group. −**individuality**, *n.* −**individualise, individualize**, *v.* −**individualist**, *n.*

indo- a combining form of **indigo**. Also, **ind-**.

indoctrinate /ɪnˈdɒktrəneɪt/ *v.t.* **1.** to instruct (someone) in some particular teaching or doctrine. **2.** to so instruct (someone) in a manner which leads to their total and uncritical acceptance of the teaching.

indolent /ˈɪndələnt/ *adj.* having or showing a disposition to avoid exertion. −**indolence**, *n.*

indomitable /ɪnˈdɒmətəbəl/ *adj.* that cannot be subdued or overcome, as persons, pride, courage, etc.

indoors /ˈɪndɔːz/ *adj.* inside a house or building. −**indoor**, *adj.*

indubitable /ɪnˈdjubətəbəl/ *adj.* that cannot be doubted; certain. −**indubitably**, *adv.*

induce /ɪnˈdjus/ *v.t.* (**-duced, -ducing**) **1.** to lead or move by persuasion or influence, as to some action, state of mind, etc. **2.** to bring about, produce, or cause. **3.** to initiate (labour) artificially in pregnancy.

inducement /ɪnˈdjusmənt/ *n.* **1.** the act of inducing (defs 1 and 2). **2.** something that induces or persuades; an incentive.

induct /ɪnˈdʌkt/ *v.t.* to lead or bring in; introduce, especially formally, as into an office or position, etc. −**inductee**, *n.*

induction /ɪnˈdʌkʃən/ *n.* **1.** the act of inducting. **2.** a bringing forward or adducing, as of facts, evidence, etc. **3.** the act of inducing. **4.** the artificial initiation of labour in pregnancy.

indulge /ɪnˈdʌldʒ/ *v.* (**-dulged, -dulging**) −*v.t.* **1.** to yield to, satisfy, or gratify (desires, feelings, etc.). **2.** to yield to the wishes or whims of. **3.** *Commerce* to grant an extension of time, for payment or performance, to (a person, etc.) or on (a bill, etc.) −*v.i.* **4.** (oft. fol. by *in*) to indulge oneself; yield to an inclination. −**indulgence**, *n.* −**indulgent**, *adj.*

industrial /ɪnˈdʌstriəl/ *adj.* **1.** of or relating to, of the nature of, or resulting from industry or productive labour. **2.** having highly developed industries. **3.** relating to the workers in industries.

industrial action *n.* organised disruptive action, as a strike or go-slow, taken by a group of workers.

industrial arts *pl. n.* the skills and techniques required in industry, as technical drawing, metal-work, etc.

industrial design *n.* the designing of objects for manufacture.

industrialise /ɪnˈdʌstrɪəlaɪz/ *v.t.* to introduce industry into (an area) on a large scale. Also, **industrialize**. **–industrialisation**, *n.*

industrialist /ɪnˈdʌstrɪələst/ *n.* someone who conducts or owns an industrial enterprise.

industrial park *n.* an area of land planned for light industry and business.

industrial relations *pl. n.* **1.** the management or study of the relations between employers and employees. **2.** the relationship itself usually in a given industry, locality, etc.

industrial union *n.* **1.** a union having the right to enrol as members all of the people employed in a particular industry. **2.** a trade union, or organisation of employers, registered under the appropriate industrial legislation to give it access to industrial tribunals, etc.

industrious /ɪnˈdʌstrɪəs/ *adj.* hardworking; diligent.

industry /ˈɪndəstri/ *n.* (*pl.* **-tries**) **1.** a particular branch of trade or manufacture. **2.** any large-scale business activity. **3.** manufacture or trade as a whole. **4.** assiduous activity at any work or task.

industry standard *n.* a standard which everyone involved in a particular industry agrees to adopt.

-ine¹ an adjective suffix meaning 'of or relating to', 'of the nature of', 'made of', 'like'.

-ine² **1.** a noun suffix denoting some action, procedure, art, place, etc., as in *discipline*, *doctrine*, *medicine*, *latrine*. **2.** a suffix occurring in many nouns of later formation and various meanings, as in *famine*, *routine*.

inebriate /ɪnˈibrɪeɪt/ *v.t.* to make drunk; intoxicate. **–inebriated**, *adj.* **–inebriety**, *n.*

inebriated /ɪˈnibrɪeɪtəd/ *adj.* drunk; intoxicated. **–inebriety**, *n.*

ineffable /ɪnˈɛfəbəl/ *adj.* that cannot be uttered or expressed; inexpressible.

inefficient /ɪnəˈfɪʃənt/ *adj.* not efficient; unable to effect or accomplish in a capable economical way. **–inefficiently**, *adv.*

inept /ɪnˈɛpt/ *adj.* **1.** not apt, fitted, or suitable; unsuitable. **2.** absurd or foolish, as a proceeding, remark, etc. **3.** (of a person) ineffectual; useless.

inert /ɪnˈɜt/ *adj.* having no inherent power of action, motion, or resistance.

inertia /ɪnˈɜʃə/ *n.* **1.** inert condition; inactivity; sluggishness. **2.** *Physics* that tendency of matter to retain its state of rest or of uniform motion in a straight line.

inestimable /ɪnˈɛstəməbəl/ *adj.* that cannot be estimated, or too great to be estimated. **–inestimably**, *adv.*

inevitable /ɪnˈɛvɪtəbəl/ *adj.* that cannot be avoided, evaded, or escaped; certain or necessary.

inexact /ɪnəgˈzækt, ɪnɛg-/ *adj.* not exact; not strictly accurate.

inexorable /ɪnˈɛksərəbəl, ɪnˈɛgz-/ *adj.* unyielding or unalterable.

inexpensive /ɪnəkˈspɛnsɪv/ *adj.* cheap or not expensive: *an inexpensive trip.* **–inexpensively**, *adv.*

inexperienced /ɪnəkˈspɪərɪənst/ *adj.* **1.** not experienced; lacking the knowledge or skill gained through experience. **2.** not knowing much about people, life, etc.

in extremis /ɪn ɛkˈstrimɛs/ *adv.* **1.** in extremity. **2.** near death.

infallible /ɪnˈfæləbəl/ *adj.* not fallible; exempt from liability to error, as persons, their judgement, pronouncements, etc.

infamous /ˈɪnfəməs/ *adj.* of ill fame; having an extremely bad reputation. **–infamy**, *n.*

infant /ˈɪnfənt/ *n.* **1.** a baby. **2.** a child during the earliest period of its life. **3.** *Law* a person who is not of full age, especially someone who has not attained the age of eighteen years. **4.** anything in the first period of existence or the first stage of progress. **–infancy**, *n.*

infantile /ˈɪnfəntaɪl/ *adj.* characteristic of or befitting an infant; babyish; childish.

infantry /ˈɪnfəntri/ *n.* soldiers or military units that fight on foot.

infatuate /ɪnˈfætʃueɪt/ *v.t.* **1.** to affect with folly; make fatuous. **2.** to inspire or possess with a foolish or unreasoning passion, as of love. **–infatuation**, *n.* **–infatuated**, *adj.*

infect /ɪnˈfɛkt/ *v.t.* **1.** to impregnate (a person, organ, wound, etc.) with disease-producing germs. **2.** to taint, contaminate, or affect morally. **–infection**, *n.*

infectious /ɪnˈfɛkʃəs/ *adj.* tending to spread from one to another.

infer /ɪnˈfɜ/ *v.t.* (**-ferred, -ferring**) to derive by reasoning; conclude or judge from premises or evidence. **–inference**, *n.*

inferior /ɪnˈfɪəriə/ *adj.* **1.** (fol. by *to*) lower in station, rank, or degree. **2.** of comparatively low grade; poor in quality. **3.** lower in place or position. **–n. 4.** someone inferior to another or others, as in rank or merit. **–inferiority**, *n.*

inferno /ɪnˈfɜnou/ *n.* (*pl.* **-nos**) hell. **–infernal**, *adj.*

infertile /ɪnˈfɜtaɪl/ *adj.* not fertile. **–infertility**, *n.*

infest /ɪnˈfɛst/ *v.t.* to haunt or overrun in a troublesome manner. **–infestation**, *n.*

infidel /ˈɪnfədɛl/ *n.* **1.** an unbeliever. **2.** someone who does not accept a particular religious faith, especially: **a.** (among Christians) someone who does not accept the Christian faith (formerly applied especially to a Muslim). **b.** (among Muslims) someone who does not accept the Muslim faith.

infidelity /ɪnfəˈdɛləti/ *n.* (*pl.* **-ties**) **1.** unfaithfulness. **2.** a breach of trust.

infiltrate /ˈɪnfɪltreɪt/ *v.t.* **1.** to cause to pass in by, or as by, filtering. **2.** to join (an organisation) for the unstated purpose of influencing it; subvert.

infinite /ˈɪnfənət/ *adj.* **1.** immeasurably great. **2.** unbounded or unlimited; perfect. **–infinity**, *n.*

infinitesimal /ˌɪnfɪnɪˈtɛzməl, -ˈtɛsəməl/ *adj.* indefinitely or exceedingly small.

infinitive /ɪnˈfɪnətɪv/ *n. Gram.* the simple form of the verb (*come, take, eat*) used after certain other verbs (I didn't *eat*), or this simple form preceded by *to* (the **marked infinitive**) (I wanted *to come*).

infirm /ɪnˈfɜm/ *adj.* **1.** feeble in body or health. **2.** not steadfast, unfaltering, or resolute, as persons, the mind, etc. **–infirmity**, *n.*

infirmary /ɪnˈfɜməri/ *n.* (*pl.* **-ries**) a place for the care of the infirm, sick, or injured.

inflame /ɪnˈfleɪm/ *v.t.* **1.** to set on fire. **2.** to kindle or excite (passions, anger, etc.). **3.** to excite inflammation in. –**inflammatory**, *adj.*

inflammable /ɪnˈflæməbəl/ *adj.* capable of being set on fire; combustible.

inflammation /ɪnfləˈmeɪʃən/ *n.* a reaction of the body to injurious agents, commonly characterised by heat, redness, swelling, pain, etc., and disturbed function.

inflate /ɪnˈfleɪt/ *v.t.* **1.** to distend; swell or puff out. **2.** to distend with gas. **3.** to puff up with pride, satisfaction, etc. **4.** to expand (currency, prices, etc.) unduly; raise above the previous or proper amount or value. –*v.i.* **5.** to cause inflation. **6.** to become inflated.

inflation /ɪnˈfleɪʃən/ *n.* **1.** undue expansion or increase of the currency of a country, especially by the issuing of paper money not redeemable in specie. **2.** a substantial rise of prices caused by an undue expansion in paper money or bank credit, or because demand exceeds supply. **3.** the act of inflating. **4.** the state of being inflated. –**inflationary**, *adj.*

inflationary spiral *n.* the situation in which increasing prices lead to increasing wages which lead to increasing prices, and so on.

inflection /ɪnˈflekʃən/ *n.* **1.** modulation of the voice; change in pitch or tone of voice. **2.** *Gram.* a change in the form of a word, generally by affixation, by means of which a change of meaning or relationship to some other word or group of words is indicated. **3.** a bend or angle. Also, **inflexion**. –**inflect**, *v.*

inflict /ɪnˈflɪkt/ *v.t.* **1.** to impose as something that must be borne or suffered. **2.** to impose (anything unwelcome). –**infliction**, *n.*

inflorescence /ɪnfləˈrɛsəns/ *n.* **1.** a flowering or blossoming. **2.** the arrangement of flowers on the axis.

influence /ˈɪnfluəns/ *n.* **1.** invisible or insensible action exerted by one thing or person on another. **2.** power of producing effects by invisible or insensible means. **3.** a thing or person that exerts action by invisible or insensible means. –*v.t.* (**-enced**, **-encing**) **4.** to exercise influence on; modify, affect, or sway. –**influential**, *adj.*

influencer /ˈɪnfluənsə/ *n.* a person with a high public profile who is used to market or promote a product, especially on their social media.

influenza /ɪnfluˈɛnzə/ *n.* an acute, contagious, viral disease marked usually by nasal catarrh and bronchial inflammation. Also, **flu**.

influx /ˈɪnflʌks/ *n.* the act of flowing in; an inflow.

infomercial /ɪnfoʊˈmɜʒəl/ *n.* TV an advertisement of some length, in which the content is overtly instructive.

inform /ɪnˈfɔm/ *v.t.* **1.** to impart knowledge of a fact or circumstance to. **2.** to animate or inspire. –*v.i.* **3.** to give information, especially to furnish incriminating evidence to a prosecuting officer. –**informant**, *n.*

informal /ɪnˈfɔməl/ *adj.* **1.** not according to prescribed or customary forms; irregular. **2.** without formality; unceremonious. **3.** (of a vote) invalid because not correctly marked on the ballot paper, etc. –**informality**, *n.*

information /ɪnfəˈmeɪʃən/ *n.* knowledge communicated or received concerning some fact or circumstance; news. –**informative**, *adj.*

information portal *n.* a website which provides information about an organisation, such as contacts, organisational structure, etc. Also, **enterprise information portal**.

information report *n.* a written or spoken text type or form which presents facts about an entire class of people, animals or objects.

information science *n.* the study of the collection, organisation, and communication of data, usually with computers.

information technology *n.* → **IT**.

infotainment /ɪnfoʊˈteɪnmənt/ *n.* a genre of entertainment comprising television programs, computer games, etc., which presents information of educational value in an entertaining format.

infra /ˈɪnfrə/ *adv.* (in a text) below. Compare **supra**.

infra- a prefix meaning 'below' or 'beneath'.

infraction /ɪnˈfrækʃən/ *n.* breach; violation; infringement.

infra-red /ɪnfrəˈrɛd/ *n.* the part of the invisible spectrum contiguous to the red end of the visible spectrum, comprising radiation of greater wavelength than that of red light.

infrastructure /ˈɪnfrəstrʌktʃə/ *n.* **1.** the basic framework or underlying foundation (as of an organisation or a system). **2.** the buildings or permanent installations associated with an organisation, operation, etc.

infringe /ɪnˈfrɪndʒ/ *v.* (**-fringed**, **-fringing**) –*v.t.* **1.** to violate or transgress. –*v.i.* **2.** (fol. by *on* or *upon*) to encroach or trespass: *Don't infringe on her privacy.* –**infringement**, *n.*

infuriate /ɪnˈfjuriˌeɪt/ *v.t.* to make furious; enrage.

infuse /ɪnˈfjuz/ *v.t.* **1.** (fol. by *into*) to introduce as by pouring; cause to penetrate; instil. **2.** to steep or soak in a liquid to extract soluble properties or ingredients. –**infusion**, *n.*

-ing [1] a suffix of nouns formed from verbs, expressing the action of the verb or its result, product, material, etc., as in *the art of building*, *a new building*. It is also used to form nouns from words other than verbs, as in *offing*.

-ing [2] a suffix forming the present participle of verbs, such participles often being used as adjectives (participial adjectives), as in *warring factions*. Compare **-ing** [1].

ingenious /ɪnˈdʒiniəs/ *adj.* **1.** (of things, actions, etc.) showing cleverness of invention or construction: *an ingenious gadget.* **2.** having inventive faculty; skilful in contriving or constructing. –**ingenuity**, *n.*

ingenuous /ɪnˈdʒɛnjuəs/ *adj.* innocent.

ingest /ɪnˈdʒɛst/ *v.t. Physiol.* to put or take (food, etc.) into the body. –**ingestion**, *n.* –**ingestive**, *adj.*

ingot /ˈɪŋgət/ *n.* the casting obtained when melted metal is poured into a mould.

ingrain /ɪnˈgreɪn/ *v.t.* to fix deeply and firmly, as in the nature or mind. Also, **engrain**.

ingrate /ˈɪngreɪt/ *n.* **1.** an ungrateful person. –*adj.* **2.** ungrateful.

ingratiate /ɪnˈgreɪʃieɪt/ *v.t.* to establish (oneself) in the favour or good graces of others.

ingratitude /ɪn'grætətjud, -tʃud/ n. the state of being ungrateful; unthankfulness.

ingredient /ɪn'gridiənt/ n. something that enters as an element into a mixture.

ingress /'ɪŋgrɛs/ n. **1.** the act of going in or entering. **2.** the right of going in.

inhabit /ɪn'hæbət/ v.t. to live or dwell in (a place), as persons or animals. **–inhabitant**, n.

inhale /ɪn'heɪl/ v.t. to breathe in. **–inhalation**, n.

inherent /ɪn'hɛrənt, ɪn'hɪərənt/ adj. existing in something as a permanent and inseparable element, quality, or attribute. **–inhere**, v. **–inherence**, n.

inherit /ɪn'hɛrət/ v.t. **1.** to take or receive (property, a right, a title, etc.) as the heir of the former owner. **2.** to possess as a hereditary characteristic. **–v.i. 3.** to have succession as heir. **–inheritance**, n.

inhesion /ɪn'hiʒən/ n. inherence.

inhibit /ɪn'hɪbət/ v.t. to restrain, hinder, arrest, or check (an action, impulse, etc.). **–inhibition** /ɪnə'bɪʃən/, n.

inhibited /ɪn'hɪbətəd/ adj. unable or unwilling to behave or express emotions naturally.

inhuman /ɪn'hjumən/ adj. lacking natural human feeling or sympathy for others; brutal. **–inhumanity**, n.

inhumane /ɪnhju'meɪn/ adj. not humane; lacking humanity or kindness. **–inhumanely**, adv.

inhume /ɪn'hjum/ v.t. to bury; inter.

inimical /ɪ'nɪmɪkəl/ adj. **1.** adverse in tendency or effect. **2.** unfriendly or hostile. **–inimicality**, n.

inimitable /ɪ'nɪmɪtəbəl/ adj. incapable of being imitated; surpassing imitation.

iniquity /ɪ'nɪkwəti/ n. (pl. **-ties**) gross injustice; wickedness. **–iniquitous**, adj.

initial /ɪ'nɪʃəl/ adj. **1.** of or relating to the beginning; incipient. **–n. 2.** an initial letter, as of a word. **–v.t.** (**-ialled, -ialling**) **3.** to mark or sign with an initial or initials, especially as an indication of responsibility for or approval of the contents.

initialism /ɪ'nɪʃəlɪzm/ n. an abbreviation formed from the initial letters of a sequence of words, as *ACTU* (from *Australian Council of Trade Unions*) or *LPG* (from *liquefied petroleum gas*).

initiate /ɪ'nɪʃieɪt/ v.t. **1.** to begin, set going, or originate. **2.** to introduce into the knowledge of some art or subject. **3.** to admit with formal rites into secret knowledge, a society, etc. **–initiation**, n.

initiative /ə'nɪʃiətɪv/ n. **1.** an introductory act or step; leading action. **2.** readiness and ability in initiating action; enterprise.

inject /ɪn'dʒɛkt/ v.t. **1.** to force (a fluid) into a passage, cavity, or tissue. **2.** to introduce (something new or different) into a thing. **–injection**, n.

injunction /ɪn'dʒʌŋkʃən/ n. *Law* a judicial process or order requiring the person or persons to whom it is directed to do or (more commonly) not to do a particular thing.

injure /'ɪndʒə/ v.t. **1.** to do or cause harm of any kind to; damage; hurt; impair. **2.** to do wrong or injustice to. **–injurious**, adj. **–injury**, n.

injustice /ɪn'dʒʌstəs/ n. **1.** the quality or fact of being unjust. **2.** unjust action or treatment; violation of another's rights.

ink /ɪŋk/ n. a fluid or viscous substance used for writing or printing.

inkling /'ɪŋklɪŋ/ n. a hint, intimation, or slight suggestion.

inland /'ɪnlænd/ adj. **1.** relating to or situated in the interior part of a country or region. **–adv. 2.** in or towards the interior of a country. **–n. 3.** the interior part of a country, away from the border.

in-law /'ɪn-lɔ/ n. a relative by marriage.

inlay /ɪn'leɪ/ v.t. (**-laid, -laying**) to decorate (an object) with veneers of fine materials set in its surface.

inlet /'ɪnlət/ n. an indentation of a shore line, usually long and narrow, or a narrow passage between islands.

inline skate n. → **rollerblade**.

inmate /'ɪnmeɪt/ n. one of those confined in a hospital, prison, etc.

inn /ɪn/ n. a small hotel that provides lodging, food, etc., for travellers and others.

innards /'ɪnədz/ pl. n. the inward parts of the body; entrails; viscera.

innate /ɪn'eɪt/ adj. **1.** inborn; existing as or if existing in one from birth. **2.** inherent.

inner /'ɪnə/ adj. **1.** situated farther within; interior. **2.** mental or spiritual.

innings /'ɪnɪŋz/ pl. n. (construed as sing.) **1.** *Cricket* **a.** the turn of any one member of the batting team to bat. **b.** one of the major divisions of a match. **2.** any opportunity for some activity; a turn.

innocent /'ɪnəsənt/ adj. **1.** free from any moral wrong; not tainted with sin; pure. **2.** free from legal or specific wrong; guiltless. **3.** free from any quality that can cause physical or moral injury; harmless. **–n. 4.** an innocent person. **–innocence**, n.

innocuous /ɪn'ɒkjuəs/ adj. harmless.

innovate /'ɪnəveɪt/ v.t. to bring in (something new) for the first time. **–innovation**, n. **–innovator**, n.

innovative /'ɪnəvətɪv/ adj. new and original. Also, **innovatory**. **–innovativeness**, n. **–innovatively**, adv.

innuendo /ɪnju'ɛndoʊ/ n. (pl. **-dos** or **-does**) an indirect intimation about a person or thing, especially of a derogatory nature.

innumerable /ɪ'njumərəbəl, ɪ'njumrəbəl/ adj. **1.** very numerous. **2.** incapable of being numbered or definitely counted.

inoculate /ɪ'nɒkjəleɪt/ v.t. to implant (a disease) in a person or animal by the introduction of germs or virus, as through a puncture, in order to produce a mild form of the disease and thus secure immunity. **–inoculation**, n.

inopportune /ɪn'ɒpətjun/ adj. not opportune; inappropriate; untimely.

inordinate /ɪn'ɔdənət/ adj. not within proper limits; excessive.

inorganic /'ɪnɔgænɪk/ adj. **1.** not having the organisation which characterises living bodies. **2.** *Chem.* denoting or relating to compounds not containing carbon, excepting cyanides and carbonates. Compare **organic** (def. 1).

inpatient /'ɪnpeɪʃənt/ n. a patient who is accommodated in a hospital for the duration of their treatment. Also, **in-patient**.

input /'ɪmpʊt/ n. **1.** that which is put in. **2.** information which is fed into a computer before computation. –v.t. (**-put**, **-putting**) **3.** to key (data) into a computer.

input tax credit n. a tax credit for all GST paid on inputs involved in the production and sale of taxable goods and services.

inquest /'ɪnkwɛst/ n. **1.** a legal or judicial inquiry, especially before a jury. **2.** such an inquiry made by a coroner (**coroner's inquest**).

inquire /ɪn'kwaɪə, ən-/ v.i. to seek information by questioning; ask. Also, **enquire**. –**inquiry**, n.

inquisition /ɪnkwə'zɪʃən/ n. **1.** the act of inquiring; inquiry; research. **2.** an investigation, or process of inquiry. –**inquisitor**, n. –**inquisitorial**, adj.

inquisitive /ɪn'kwɪzətɪv/ adj. **1.** inquiring; desirous of or eager for knowledge. **2.** unduly curious; prying.

inroad /'ɪnroʊd/ n. (usu. pl.) forcible or serious encroachment.

insane /ɪn'seɪn/ adj. **1.** not sane; not of sound mind; mentally deranged. **2.** set apart for the care and confinement of mentally deranged persons. **3.** utterly senseless. **4.** Colloq. fantastic; wonderful. –**insanity**, n. –**insanely**, adv.

insatiable /ɪn'seɪʃəbəl/ adj. not satiable; incapable of being satisfied.

inscribe /ɪn'skraɪb/ v.t. **1.** to write or engrave (words, characters, etc.). **2.** to mark (a surface) with words, characters, etc., especially in a durable or conspicuous way. **3.** to address or dedicate (a book, photograph, etc.) informally, especially by a handwritten note. **4.** to enrol, as on an official list. –**inscription**, n.

inscrutable /ɪn'skrutəbəl/ adj. not easily understood; mysterious.

insect /'ɪnsɛkt/ n. Zool. a small, air-breathing arthropod with a body clearly divided into three parts, and with three pairs of legs, and usually two pairs of wings.

insecticide /ɪn'sɛktəsaɪd/ n. a substance or preparation used for killing insects.

insectivorous /ɪnsɛk'tɪvərəs/ adj. adapted to feeding on insects.

insecure /ɪnsə'kjuə/ adj. **1.** exposed to danger; unsafe. **2.** not firm or safe. **3.** not free from fear, doubt, etc. –**insecurity**, n.

inseminate /ɪn'sɛməneɪt/ v.t. to introduce semen into (a female) to cause fertilisation; impregnate. –**insemination**, n.

insensible /ɪn'sɛnsəbəl/ adj. incapable of feeling or perceiving; deprived of sensation; unconscious, as a person after a violent blow.

insensitive /ɪn'sɛnsətɪv/ adj. **1.** not sensitive. **2.** lacking in feeling or sympathy. –**insensitively**, adv. –**insensitivity**, n.

insert v.t. /ɪn'sɜt/ **1.** to put or set in. **2.** to introduce into the body of something. –n. /'ɪnsɜt/ **3.** something inserted, or to be inserted. –**insertion**, n.

inset n. /'ɪnsɛt/ **1.** something inserted; an insert. –v.t. /ɪn'sɛt/ (**-set**, **-setting**) **2.** to set in; insert.

inside prep. /ɪn'saɪd/ **1.** on the inner side of; within. **2.** before the elapse of. –adv. /ɪn'saɪd/ **3.** in or into the inner part. **4.** indoors. **5.** by nature; fundamentally. –n. /'ɪnsaɪd/ **6.** the inner

part; interior. –adj. /'ɪnsaɪd/ **7.** situated or being on or in the inside; interior.

insider /ɪn'saɪdə/ n. **1.** someone who is inside some place, society, etc. **2.** someone who is within a limited circle of persons who understand the actual facts of a case.

insider attack /ɪnsaɪdə ə'tæk/ n. an attack from a person within your own troops, police force, etc., usually an enemy who has infiltrated.

insider trading n. the statutory offence of dealing in a company's securities by someone who through some connection has special information which would materially affect the price of the securities if it were generally known.

insidious /ɪn'sɪdiəs/ adj. stealthily treacherous or deceitful.

insight /'ɪnsaɪt/ n. **1.** an understanding gained or given of something. **2.** penetrating mental vision or discernment; faculty of seeing into inner character or underlying truth.

insignia /ɪn'sɪgniə/ n. (pl. **-nia** or **-nias**) a badge or distinguishing mark of office or honour.

insinuate /ɪn'sɪnjueɪt/ v.t. **1.** to suggest or hint slyly. **2.** instil or infuse subtly or artfully into the mind. **3.** to bring or introduce into a position or relation by indirect or artful methods. –**insinuation**, n.

insipid /ɪn'sɪpəd/ adj. without distinctive, interesting, or attractive qualities.

insist /ɪn'sɪst/ v.i. **1.** to be emphatic, firm, or pertinacious on some matter of desire, demand, intention, etc. **2.** (fol. by on) to lay emphasis in assertion. **3.** (fol. by on) to assert or maintain positively. –**insistent**, adj.

in situ /ɪn 'sɪtʃu/ adv. in the original, actual or appropriate place.

insolent /'ɪnsələnt/ adj. boldly rude or disrespectful; contemptuously impertinent; insulting. –**insolence**, n.

insoluble /ɪn'sɒljubəl/ adj. **1.** incapable of being dissolved: insoluble salts. **2.** that cannot be solved: an insoluble problem. –**insolubility**, **insolubleness**, n. –**insolubly**, adv.

insolvent /ɪn'sɒlvənt/ adj. not solvent; unable to satisfy creditors or discharge liabilities, either because liabilities exceed assets or because of inability to pay debts as they mature.

insomnia /ɪn'sɒmniə/ n. inability to sleep, especially when chronic. –**insomniac**, n.

inspect /ɪn'spɛkt/ v.t. **1.** to look carefully at or over. **2.** to examine officially. –**inspection**, n. –**inspector**, n.

inspire /ɪn'spaɪə/ v.t. **1.** to infuse an animating, quickening, or exalting influence into. **2.** to produce or arouse (a feeling, thought, etc.). **3.** to give rise to, occasion, or cause. **4.** to take (air, gases, etc.) into the lungs in breathing; inhale. –**inspiring**, adj. –**inspiration**, n. –**inspirational**, adj.

inspirit /ɪn'spɪrət/ v.t. to infuse (new) spirit or life into.

install /ɪn'stɔl/ v.t. **1.** to place in position for service or use, as a system of electric lighting, etc. **2.** to establish in any office, position, or place. **3.** Computers: to load (a software application) onto a digital device. –**installation**, n.

instalment /ɪnˈstɔlmənt/ *n.* **1.** any of several parts into which a debt is divided for payment. **2.** a single portion of something furnished or issued by parts at successive times.

instance /ˈɪnstəns/ *n.* **1.** a case of anything. **2.** an example put forth in proof or illustration. –*v.t.* (**-stanced, -stancing**) **3.** to cite as an instance or example.

instant /ˈɪnstənt/ *n.* **1.** an infinitesimal or very short space of time; a moment. **2.** a particular moment. –*adj.* **3.** succeeding without any interval of time; immediate. **4.** (of a food) processed for immediate and simple preparation, as by adding water. –**instancy,** *n.*

instantaneous /ɪnstənˈteɪniəs/ *adj.* occurring, done, or completed in an instant.

instant messaging *n.* text-based, real-time communication between individuals by means of a network of computers or the internet.

instead /ɪnˈstɛd/ *adv.* **1.** (fol. by *of*) in the stead or place; in lieu. **2.** in one's (its, their, etc.) stead.

instep /ˈɪnstɛp/ *n.* the arched upper surface of the human foot between the toes and the ankle.

instigate /ˈɪnstəgeɪt/ *v.t.* to spur on, set on, or incite to some action or course. –**instigation,** *n.*

instil /ɪnˈstɪl/ *v.t.* (**-stilled, -stilling**) to infuse slowly or by degrees into the mind or feelings; insinuate; inject.

instinct /ˈɪnstɪŋkt/ *n.* **1.** innate impulse or natural inclination, or a particular natural inclination or tendency. **2.** a natural aptitude or gift for something. **3.** natural intuitive power. –**instinctive,** *adj.*

institute /ˈɪnstətʃut/ *v.t.* **1.** to set up or establish. **2.** to set in operation. **3.** to establish in an office or position. –*n.* **4.** a society or organisation for carrying on a particular work, as of literary, scientific, or educational character.

institution /ɪnstəˈtʃuʃən/ *n.* **1.** an organisation or establishment for the promotion of a particular object, usually one for some public, educational, charitable, or similar purpose. **2.** any established law, custom, etc. **3.** the act of instituting or setting up; establishment.

institutional /ɪnstəˈtʃuʃənəl/ *adj.* **1.** of, relating to, or established by institution. **2.** of the nature of an institution. **3.** characterised by uniformity and dullness.

institutionalise /ɪnstəˈtʃuʃənəlaɪz/ *v.t.* to make (a person) dependent on an institution, as a prison, mental hospital, etc., to the point where he or she cannot live successfully outside it. Also, **institutionalize.**

instruct /ɪnˈstrʌkt/ *v.t.* **1.** to direct or command; furnish with orders or directions. **2.** to furnish with knowledge, especially by a systematic method; teach; train; educate. **3.** to furnish with information; inform or apprise. –**instructive,** *adj.* –**instructor,** *n.*

instruction /ɪnˈstrʌkʃən/ *n.* **1.** the act or practice of instructing or teaching; education. **2.** (*usu. pl.*) an order or direction. **3.** *Computers* a number or symbol which causes a computer to perform some specified action.

instrument /ˈɪnstrəmənt/ *n.* **1.** a tool or implement. **2.** a contrivance for producing musical sounds. **3.** a thing with or by which something is effected; a means; an agency. **4.** a legal document. **5.** a device for measuring the present value of a quantity under observation. –**instrumental,** *adj.*

insubordinate /ɪnsəˈbɔdənət/ *adj.* disobedient; rebellious. –**insubordination,** *n.*

insubstantial /ɪnsəbˈstænʃəl/ *adj.* not substantial; slight.

insufferable /ɪnˈsʌfərəbəl, -frəbəl/ *adj.* not to be endured; intolerable; unbearable.

insufficient /ɪnsəˈfɪʃənt/ *adj.* not enough; not as much or as many as wanted or needed. –**insufficiency,** *n.* –**insufficiently,** *adv.*

insular /ˈɪnsjulə, ˈɪnfulə/ *adj.* **1.** of or relating to an island or islands. **2.** detached; standing alone. **3.** narrow or illiberal. –**insularity,** *n.*

insulate /ˈɪnʃuleɪt/ *v.t.* **1.** to cover or surround (an electric wire, etc.) with non-conducting material. **2.** to place in an isolated situation or condition; segregate. **3.** to install an insulating material in the roof of (a house), to retain warmth in winter and keep out heat in summer. –**insulation,** *n.* –**insulator,** *n.*

insulin /ˈɪnʃələn, -sjələn/ *n.* a hormone which regulates the metabolism of sugar; produced in the pancreas, a deficiency of insulin produces diabetes.

insult *v.t.* /ɪnˈsʌlt/ **1.** to treat insolently or with contemptuous rudeness; affront. –*n.* /ˈɪnsʌlt/ **2.** an insolent or contemptuously rude action or speech; affront.

insuperable /ɪnˈsupərəbəl, -prəbəl, -ˈsju-/ *adj.* incapable of being passed over, overcome, or surmounted.

insurance /ɪnˈʃɔrəns, -ˈʃʊə-/ *n.* the act, system, or business of insuring property, life, the person, etc., against loss or harm arising in specified contingencies, as fire, accident, death, disablement, or the like, in consideration of a payment proportionate to the risk involved.

insure /ɪnˈʃɔ, -ˈʃʊə/ *v.t.* **1.** to guarantee against risk of loss or harm. **2.** to secure indemnity to or on, in case of loss, damage, or death. **3.** to issue or procure an insurance policy on.

insured /ɪnˈʃɔd, ɪnˈʃʊəd/ *n.* a person covered by an insurance policy.

insurer /ɪnˈʃɔrə, -ˈʃʊə-/ *n.* **1.** a person, institution, etc., that contracts to indemnify against losses, etc., such as an insurance company. **2.** a person who seeks some sort of protection by taking out insurance.

insurgent /ɪnˈsɜdʒənt/ *n.* **1.** someone who rises in forcible opposition to lawful authority. –*adj.* **2.** rising in revolt; rebellious.

insurrection /ɪnsəˈrɛkʃən/ *n.* the act of rising in arms or open resistance against civil or established authority.

intact /ɪnˈtækt/ *adj.* remaining uninjured, unaltered, sound, or whole; unimpaired.

intake /ˈɪnteɪk/ *n.* **1.** the act of taking in. **2.** that which is taken in.

intangible /ɪnˈtændʒəbəl/ *adj.* not tangible.

integer /ˈɪntədʒə/ *n.* Also, **positive integer.** a whole number. **2.** a complete entity.

integral /ˈɪntəgrəl, ɪnˈtɛgrəl/ *adj.* of or relating to a whole; belonging as a part of the whole; constituent or component.

integrate /ˈɪntəgreɪt/ *v.t.* **1.** to bring together (parts) into a whole. **2.** to amalgamate (an ethnic, religious, or other minority group) with the rest of the community. –**integration**, n. –**integrative**, adj.

integrated circuit n. an array of interconnected circuit elements integrated with or deposited on a single semiconductor base.

integrative medicine n. a range of treatments and procedures which combines Western medicine with alternative medicine.

integrity /ɪnˈtɛgrəti/ n. **1.** soundness of moral principle and character; uprightness; honesty. **2.** sound, unimpaired, or perfect condition.

integument /ɪnˈtɛgjumənt/ n. **1.** a skin, shell, rind, or the like. **2.** a covering.

intellect /ˈɪntəlɛkt/ n. the power or faculty of the mind by which one knows, understands, or reasons.

intellectual /ɪntəˈlɛktfuəl/ adj. **1.** of, appealing to or engaging the intellect. **2.** possessing or showing intellect or mental capacity, especially to a high degree. –n. **3.** an intellectual being or person.

intelligence /ɪnˈtɛlədʒəns/ n. **1.** aptitude in grasping truths, facts, meaning, etc. **2.** good mental capacity. **3.** knowledge of an event, circumstance, etc., received or imparted; news; information. **4.** the gathering or distribution of information, especially secret or military information which might prove detrimental to an enemy. **5.** → **artificial intelligence**. –**intelligent**, adj.

intelligentsia /ɪnˌtɛləˈdʒɛntsiə/ pl. n. a class or group of persons having or claiming special enlightenment in views or principles; the intellectuals.

intelligible /ɪnˈtɛlədʒəbəl/ adj. capable of being understood; comprehensible.

intemperate /ɪnˈtɛmpərət, -prət/ adj. **1.** given to or characterised by immoderate indulgence in intoxicating drink. **2.** not temperate; unrestrained or unbridled. –**intemperance**, n.

intend /ɪnˈtɛnd/ v.t. to have in mind as something to be done or brought about.

intense /ɪnˈtɛns/ adj. **1.** of an extreme kind; very great, strong, keen, severe, etc. **2.** having or showing great strength or vehemence of feeling, as a person, the face, language, etc. –**intensify**, v.

intensifier /ɪnˈtɛnsəfaɪə/ n. Gram. a linguistic element or word which increases the semantic effect of a word or phrase but has itself minimal semantic content, as very.

intensity /ɪnˈtɛnsəti/ n. **1.** the quality or condition of being intense. **2.** the degree or extent to which something is intense.

intensive /ɪnˈtɛnsɪv/ adj. **1.** of, relating to, or characterised by intensity. **2.** Econ. of or denoting methods designed to increase effectiveness, as, in agriculture.

intensive care n. medical therapy for the critically ill, usually given under hospital supervision and for a short period of time.

intent¹ /ɪnˈtɛnt/ n. that which is intended; purpose; aim; design; intention.

intent² /ɪnˈtɛnt/ adj. firmly or steadfastly fixed or directed (upon something).

intention /ɪnˈtɛnʃən/ n. the act of determining mentally upon some action or result; a purpose or design. –**intentional**, adj.

inter /ɪnˈtɜ/ v.t. (**-terred**, **-terring**) to deposit (a dead body, etc.) in a grave or tomb; bury, especially with ceremonies.

inter- a prefix meaning 'between', 'among', 'mutually', 'reciprocally', 'together', as in interlope, intermarry.

interact /ɪntərˈækt/ v.i. to act on each other. –**interaction**, n.

interactive /ɪntərˈæktɪv/ adj. **1.** of or relating to things or persons which act on each other. **2.** of or relating to an electronic device, such as a computer, television, etc., which allows for a reciprocal transfer of data, the user providing a stimulus to a responsive central source.

inter alia /ɪntər ˈeɪliə/ adv. among other things.

intercede /ɪntəˈsid/ v.i. to interpose on behalf of one in difficulty or trouble, as by pleading or petition. –**intercession**, n.

intercept /ɪntəˈsɛpt, ˈɪntəsɛpt/ v.t. **1.** to take or seize on the way from one place to another; cut off from the intended destination. **2.** to stop or check (passage, etc.).

interchange /ɪntəˈtʃeɪndʒ/ v. (**-changed**, **-changing**) –v.t. **1.** to put each of (two things) in the place of the other. –v.i. **2.** to change places, as two persons or things, or as one with another. –n. /ˈɪntətʃeɪndʒ/ **3.** the act of interchanging; reciprocal exchange. **4.** any major road junction, especially where motorways converge. **5.** a point, in a public transport system, at which passengers can change from one vehicle to another.

intercom /ˈɪntəkɒm/ n. an intercommunication system.

intercommunication system n. an internal or closed audio system, as within an office complex, school, ship, etc.

intercourse /ˈɪntəkɔs/ n. **1.** dealings or communication between individuals. **2.** interchange of thoughts, feelings, etc. **3.** → **sexual intercourse**.

interdict n. /ˈɪntədɪkt, -daɪt/ **1.** Civil Law any prohibitive act or decree of a court or an administrative officer. –v.t. /ɪntəˈdɪkt, -ˈdaɪt/ **2.** to forbid; prohibit. –**interdictory**, adj. –**interdiction**, n.

interest /ˈɪntrəst, -tərəst/ n. **1.** the feeling of one whose attention or curiosity is particularly engaged by something. **2.** the power of exciting such feeling; interesting quality. **3.** a share in the ownership of property, in a commercial or financial undertaking, or the like. **4.** any right of ownership in property, commercial undertakings, etc. **5.** something in which one has an interest, as of ownership, advantage, attention, etc. **6.** benefit or advantage. **7.** Commerce **a.** payment, or a sum paid, for the use of money borrowed (the principal), or for the forbearance of a debt. **b.** the rate per cent per unit of time represented by such payments. –v.t. **8.** to engage or excite the attention or curiosity of.

interface /ˈɪntəfeɪs/ n. **1.** a surface regarded as the common boundary to two bodies or spaces. **2.** Computers the point at which an interconnection is made between a computer and a peripheral device or other piece of equipment, or between a computer and the person using it: trouble lies at the user interface. **3.** a common boundary or interconnection between two groups of people, organisations, etc. **4.** the point or area at which any two systems or disciplines interact. –v. (**-faced, -facing**) –v.t. **5.** to bring (a computer, piece of equipment, etc.) into an interface: *to interface the computer with the printer.* –v.i. **6.** (of computer systems, equipment, etc.) to interact.

interfere /ɪntəˈfɪə/ v.i. **1.** to interpose or intervene in the affairs of others. **2.** to come into opposition, as one thing with another, especially with the effect of hampering action or procedure: *these interruptions interfere with the work.*

interference /ɪntəˈfɪərəns/ n. **1.** the act or fact of interfering. **2.** *Radio* the jumbling of radio signals by receiving signals other than the desired ones.

intergalactic /ɪntəgəˈlæktɪk/ adj. existing or happening between galaxies.

interim /ˈɪntərəm/ n. **1.** an intervening time; the meantime. –adj. **2.** belonging to or connected with an intervening period of time.

interior /ɪnˈtɪəriə/ adj. **1.** being within; inside of anything; internal; farther towards a centre. **2.** relating to the inland. **3.** inner, private, or secret. –n. **4.** the internal part; the inside. **5.** the inland parts of a region, country, etc.

interject /ɪntəˈdʒɛkt/ v.t. to interpolate; interpose.

interjection /ɪntəˈdʒɛkʃən/ n. **1.** the utterance of ejaculations expressive of emotion; an ejaculation or exclamation. **2.** something, as a remark, interjected. **3.** *Gram.* **a.** (in many languages) a form class, or 'part of speech', comprising words which constitute utterances or clauses in themselves, without grammatical connection. **b.** such a word, as English *ouch!*, *never!*

interlace /ɪntəˈleɪs/ v.t. (**-laced, -lacing**) **1.** to dispose (threads, strips, parts, branches, etc.) so as to intercross one another, passing alternately over and under. **2.** to mingle; blend.

interlock v.i. /ɪntəˈlɒk/ **1.** to engage with each other. **2.** to fit into each other, as parts of machinery, so that all action is simultaneous. –v.t. /ɪntəˈlɒk/ **3.** to lock one with another. **4.** to fit the parts of (something) together so that all must move together, or in the same way. –n. /ˈɪntəlɒk/ **5.** *Textiles* a smooth knitted fabric, especially one made of cotton yarn. –**interlocker,** n.

interlocutor /ɪntəˈlɒkjətə/ n. someone who takes part in a conversation or dialogue. –**interlocutory,** adj. –**interlocution,** n.

interlope /ˈɪntəloup/ v.i. to intrude into the affairs of others.

interlude /ˈɪntəlud/ n. **1.** an intervening episode, period, space, etc. **2.** a period of inactivity; lull.

intermarry /ɪntəˈmæri/ v.i. (**-ried, -rying**) **1.** to become connected by marriage, as two families, tribes, peoples, etc. **2.** to marry within the limits of the family or of near relationship.

intermediate¹ /ɪntəˈmidiət, -dʒət/ adj. being, situated, or acting between two points, stages, things, persons, etc. –**intermediary,** n.

intermediate² /ɪntəˈmidieɪt/ v.i. to act as an intermediary; intervene; mediate. –**intermediation,** n. –**intermediator,** n.

interminable /ɪnˈtɜmənəbəl/ adj. that cannot be terminated; unending.

intermission /ɪntəˈmɪʃən/ n. an interval, especially in the cinema.

intermit /ɪntəˈmɪt/ v.t. (**-mitted, -mitting**) to discontinue temporarily; suspend.

intermittent /ɪntəˈmɪtnt/ adj. alternately ceasing and beginning again.

intern¹ /ɪnˈtɜn/ v.t. to oblige to reside within prescribed limits under prohibition to leave them.

intern² /ˈɪntɜn/ n. **1.** a resident member of the medical staff of a hospital, usually a recent graduate still in partial training. **2.** a person who is receiving practical experience in the workplace as a first step in a career.

internal /ɪnˈtɜnəl/ adj. **1.** situated or existing in the interior of something; interior. **2.** of or relating to the inside or inner part. **3.** existing or occurring within a country; domestic.

internal-combustion engine n. an engine of one or more working cylinders in which the process of combustion takes place within the cylinder.

international /ɪntəˈnæʃənəl/ adj. **1.** between or among nations. **2.** of or relating to different nations or their citizens.

international law n. the body of rules, established by either custom or treaty, generally recognised as binding nations in their conduct towards one another.

International Phonetic Alphabet n. an alphabet designed to provide a consistent and universally understood system of letters and other symbols for writing the speech sounds of all languages. *Abbrev.*: IPA

International System of Units n. an internationally recognised system of metric units, now adopted as the basis of Australia's metric system, in which the seven base units are the metre, kilogram, second, ampere, kelvin, mole and candela. *Abbrev.*: SI See **metric system.** Also, **Système International d'Unités.**

international waters pl. n. those broad sweeps of ocean which are outside any national jurisdiction.

internecine /ɪntəˈnisaɪn/ adj. mutually destructive.

internet /ˈɪntənɛt/ n. **the,** the communications system created by the interconnecting networks of computers around the world. Also, **the Internet, the Net.**

internet cafe n. an establishment which provides connection to the internet for a fee, sometimes also selling coffee and light refreshments. Also, **cyber cafe.**

internet meme /ɪntənɛt ˈmim/ n. a concept, especially one that is quirky or amusing, that spreads swiftly through the internet. Also, **meme.**

internet relay chat n. an online discussion forum available through the internet, in which multiple users can communicate in real-time by means of typing text. *Abbrev.*: IRC Compare **newsgroup.**

internet service provider n. a company that provides access to the internet, usually for a fee. *Abbrev.*: ISP

internet stalking n. → **cyberstalking.** –**internet stalker,** n.

interpellation /ɪnˌtɜpəˈleɪʃən, ɪntəpəˈleɪʃən/ n. a procedure in some legislative bodies of asking a government official to explain an act or policy. –**interpellate,** v.

interplay /'ɪntəpleɪ/ n. reciprocal play, action, or influence.

interpolate /ɪn'tɜːpəleɪt/ v.t. **1.** to alter (a text, etc.) by the insertion of new matter, especially deceptively or without authorisation. **2.** to introduce (something additional or extraneous) between other things or parts. **3.** Maths to insert or find intermediate terms in (a sequence). –**interpolation,** n.

interpose /ɪntə'pəʊz/ v. (-posed, -posing) –v.t. **1.** to place between; cause to intervene. **2.** to put in (a remark, etc.) in the midst of a conversation, discourse, or the like. –v.i. **3.** to come between other things; assume an intervening position or relation. **4.** to put in or make a remark by way of interruption.

interpret /ɪn'tɜːprət/ v.t. **1.** to set forth the meaning of; explain or elucidate. **2.** to explain, construe, or understand in a particular way. **3.** to translate. –**interpretation,** n. –**interpreter,** n.

interregnum /ɪntə'regnəm/ n. (pl. **-nums** or **-na**) **1.** an interval of time between the close of a sovereign's reign and the accession of his or her normal or legitimate successor. **2.** any pause or interruption in continuity.

interrogate /ɪn'terəgeɪt/ v.t. to ask a question or a series of questions of (a person), especially closely or formally. –**interrogation,** n.

interrogative /ɪntə'rɒgətɪv/ adj. **1.** relating to or conveying a question. –n. **2.** Gram. an interrogative word, element, or construction, as 'who?' and 'what?'

interrogatory /ɪntə'rɒgətri/ adj. **1.** interrogative; questioning. –n. (pl. **-tories**) **2.** Law a formal or written question.

interrupt v.i. /ɪntə'rʌpt/ **1.** to cause a break in some otherwise continuous speech, action or process. –v.t. /ɪntə'rʌpt/ **2.** to make a break in (an otherwise continuous extent, course, process, condition, etc.). **3.** to stop (a person) in the midst of doing or saying something, especially as by an interjected remark. –n. /'ɪntərʌpt/ Computers **4.** a command causing the computer to transfer from one program to another. **5.** such a suspension of program. –**interruption,** n. –**interruptive,** adj.

intersect /ɪntə'sekt/ v.t. to cut or divide by passing through or lying across.

intersection /ɪntə'sekʃən, 'ɪntəsekʃən/ n. **1.** the act, fact, or place of intersecting. **2.** a place where two or more roads meet or cross.

intersperse /ɪntə'spɜːs/ v.t. **1.** to scatter here and there among other things. **2.** to diversify with something scattered or introduced here and there. –**interspersion,** n.

interstate adj. /'ɪntəsteɪt/ **1.** between or jointly involving states. –adv. /ɪntə'steɪt/ **2.** to or in another state. **3.** from another state. Compare **intrastate**.

interstice /ɪn'tɜːstəs/ n. a small or narrow space between things or parts; small chink, crevice, or opening.

interval /'ɪntəvəl/ n. **1.** an intervening period of time. **2.** a period of cessation; a pause. **3.** a space intervening between things, points, limits, qualities, etc. **4.** Music the difference in pitch between two notes.

intervene /ɪntə'viːn/ v.i. **1.** to come between in action; intercede. **2.** to fall or happen between other events or periods. **3.** Law to interpose and become a party to a suit pending between other parties. –**intervention,** n.

interview /'ɪntəvjuː/ n. **1.** a meeting of persons face to face, especially for formal conference in business, etc., or for radio and television entertainment, etc. –v.t. **2.** to have an interview with. –**interviewer,** n.

intestate /ɪn'testeɪt, -tət/ adj. (of a person) dying without having made a valid will. –**intestacy,** n.

intestine /ɪn'testɪn, -taɪn/ n. (oft. pl.) the lower part of the alimentary canal; the **large intestine** is the broader and shorter part leading to the anus and the **small intestine** is the narrower and longer part leading away from the stomach. –**intestinal,** adj.

intimate[1] /'ɪntəmət/ adj. **1.** associated in close personal relations. **2.** private; closely personal. **3.** maintaining sexual relations. **4.** (of acquaintance, knowledge, etc.) arising from close personal connection or familiar experience. **5.** detailed; deep. –n. **6.** an intimate friend or associate. –**intimacy,** n.

intimate[2] /'ɪntəmeɪt/ v.t. **1.** to make known indirectly; hint. **2.** to make known, especially formally; announce. –**intimation,** n.

intimidate /ɪn'tɪmədeɪt/ v.t. **1.** to make timid, or inspire with fear; overawe. **2.** to force into or deter from some action by inducing fear. –**intimidation,** n. –**intimidator,** n.

into /'ɪntu/, before consonants /'ɪntə/ prep. **1.** in to; in and to (expressing motion or direction towards the inner part of a place or thing). **2.** Maths being the divisor of.

intolerable /ɪn'tɒlərəbəl/ adj. not tolerable, unable to be endured.

intolerance /ɪn'tɒlərəns/ n. **1.** lack of toleration; indisposition to tolerate contrary opinions or beliefs. **2.** incapacity or indisposition to bear or endure: intolerance of heat. **3.** an abnormal sensitivity or allergy to a food, drug, etc.: a lactose intolerance.

intolerant /ɪn'tɒlərənt/ adj. not tolerant. –**intolerantly,** adv.

intonation /ɪntə'neɪʃən/ n. the pattern or melody of pitch changes revealed in connected speech.

intone /ɪn'təʊn/ v. (-toned, -toning) –v.t. **1.** to utter with a particular tone. –v.i. **2.** to speak or recite in a singing voice, especially in monotone.

intoxicate /ɪn'tɒksəkeɪt/ v.t. **1.** to affect temporarily with loss of control over the physical and mental powers, by means of alcoholic liquor, a drug, or other substance. **2.** to excite mentally beyond self-control or reason. –**intoxication,** n. –**intoxicant,** n.

intra- a prefix meaning 'within'.

intractable /ɪn'træktəbəl/ adj. not docile; stubborn.

intranet /'ɪntrænet/ n. Computers a website or group of websites belonging to an organisation, usually a corporation, and accessible only to organisation members, employees, etc., or people authorised by them.

intransigent /ɪn'trænsədʒənt/ adj. uncompromising, especially in politics.

intransitive verb *n.* **1.** a verb that is never accompanied by a direct object, as *come, sit, lie,* etc. **2.** a verb occurring without a direct object, as *drinks* in the sentence *he drinks only when thirsty.* Compare **transitive verb**.

intrastate /'ɪntrəsteɪt/ *adj.* within a state.

intravenous /ɪntrə'vinəs/ *adj.* within a vein or the veins.

intrepid /ɪn'trɛpəd/ *adj.* fearless.

intricate /'ɪntrəkət/ *adj.* entangled or involved. –**intricacy,** *n.*

intrigue *v.* /ɪn'trig/ (**-trigued, -triguing**) –*v.t.* **1.** to excite the curiosity or interest of by puzzling, novel, or otherwise arresting qualities. –*v.i.* **2.** to use underhand machinations; plot craftily. –*n.* /ɪn'trig, 'ɪntrig/ **3.** the use of underhand machinations to accomplish designs. **4.** a clandestine or illicit love affair.

intrinsic /ɪn'trɪnzɪk, -sɪk/ *adj.* belonging to a thing by its very nature.

intro- a prefix meaning 'inwardly', 'within'.

introduce /ɪntrə'djus/ *v.t.* (**-duced, -ducing**) **1.** to bring into notice, knowledge, use, vogue, etc. **2.** to bring forward with preliminary or preparatory matter. **3.** (fol. by *to*) to bring (a person) to the knowledge or experience of something. **4.** to bring (a person) into the acquaintance of another. **5.** to cause or allow to be established in a new country or geographical region, an animal, a fish, plant, etc., which is native to a different country of origin: *to introduce carp into Australian rivers.* –**introductory,** *adj.*

introduction /ɪntrə'dʌkʃən/ *n.* **1.** the act of introducing. **2.** something introduced. **3.** a preliminary part, as of a book.

introspection /ɪntrə'spɛkʃən/ *n.* observation or examination of one's own mental states or processes. –**introspective,** *adj.*

introvert *n.* /'ɪntrəvɜt/ **1.** *Psychol.* a person concerned chiefly with his or her own self and thoughts. –*v.t.* /ɪntrə'vɜt/ **2.** to turn inwards. –**introversion,** *n.*

intrude /ɪn'trud/ *v.t.* **1.** to thrust or bring in without reason, permission, or welcome. –*v.i.* **2.** to thrust oneself in; come uninvited. –**intrusion,** *n.* –**intrusive,** *adj.*

intuition /ɪntʃu'ɪʃən/ *n.* direct perception of truths, facts, etc., independently of any reasoning process. –**intuitive,** *adj.*

inundate /'ɪnʌndeɪt/ *v.t.* to overspread with or as with a flood. –**inundation,** *n.*

inure /ən'juə, ɪn–/ *phr.* **inure to,** to toughen or harden (someone) to by exercise; accustom to; habituate to: *to inure a person to danger.* Also, **enure.**

invade /ɪn'veɪd/ *v.t.* **1.** to enter as an enemy; go into with hostile intent. **2.** to intrude upon.

invalid¹ /'ɪnvəlɪd, -lɪd/ *n.* **1.** an infirm or sickly person. –*adj.* **2.** deficient in health; weak; sick. **3.** of or for invalids. –*v.t.* **4.** to affect with disease; make an invalid. –*v.i.* **5.** to become an invalid.

invalid² /ɪn'væləd/ *adj.* not valid. –**invalidity,** *n.* –**invalidate,** *v.*

invaluable /ɪn'væljəbəl/ *adj.* that cannot be valued or appraised; of inestimable value.

invasion /ɪn'veɪʒən/ *n.* **1.** the act of invading or entering as an enemy. **2.** infringement by intrusion. –**invasive,** *adj.*

invective /ɪn'vɛktɪv/ *n.* vehement denunciation; an utterance of violent censure or reproach.

inveigh /ɪn'veɪ/ *v.i.* to attack vehemently in words; rail.

inveigle /ɪn'veɪgəl/ *v.t.* (fol. by *into,* sometimes *from, away,* etc.) to draw by beguiling or artful inducements.

invent /ɪn'vɛnt/ *v.t.* to originate as a product of one's own contrivance. –**inventive,** *adj.* –**inventor,** *n.*

invention /ɪn'vɛnʃən/ *n.* **1.** the act of inventing. **2.** *Patent Law* the conception of an idea and the means or apparatus by which the result is obtained. **3.** anything invented or devised. **4.** the act of producing or creating by exercise of the imagination.

inventory /'ɪnvəntri, ɪn'vɛntəri/, *Orig. US* /'ɪnvəntɔri/ *n.* **1.** a detailed descriptive list of articles, with number, quantity, and value of each. **2.** the value of a stock of goods.

inverse /ɪn'vɜs, 'ɪnvɜs/ *adj.* **1.** reversed in position, direction, or tendency. –*n.* **2.** an inverted state or condition. **3.** that which is inverse; the direct opposite.

invert /ɪn'vɜt/ *v.t.* **1.** to turn upside down, inside out, or inwards. **2.** to reverse in position, direction, or order. **3.** to turn or change to the opposite or contrary, as in nature, bearing, or effect. –**inversion,** *n.*

invertebrate /ɪn'vɜtəbrət, -breɪt/ *adj.* **1.** *Zool.* not vertebrate; without a backbone. –*n.* **2.** an invertebrate animal.

invest /ɪn'vɛst/ *v.t.* **1.** to put (money) to use, by purchase or expenditure, in something offering profitable returns, especially interest or income. **2.** to endue or endow. **3.** to install in an office or position; furnish with power, authority, rank, etc. –**investor,** *n.*

investigate /ɪn'vɛstəgeɪt/ *v.t.* to search or inquire into; search or examine into the particulars of; examine in detail. –**investigative,** *adj.*

investigation /ɪnvɛstə'geɪʃən/ *n.* **1.** the act or process of investigating. **2.** a detailed, often official examination of an event, etc., in order to get all the facts. –*phr.* **3. under investigation,** being investigated.

investiture /ɪn'vɛstɪtʃə/ *n.* the formal bestowal of an office or rank, usually involving the giving of insignia.

investment /ɪn'vɛstmənt/ *n.* **1.** the investing of money or capital in order to secure profitable returns, especially interest or income. **2.** a thing invested in. **3.** that which is invested.

inveterate /ɪn'vɛtərət/ *adj.* **1.** confirmed in a habit, practice, feeling, or the like. **2.** firmly established by long continuance.

invidious /ɪn'vɪdiəs/ *adj.* such as to bring odium.

invigorate /ɪn'vɪgəreɪt/ *v.t.* to give vigour to; fill with life and energy.

invincible /ɪn'vɪnsəbəl/ *adj.* that cannot be conquered or vanquished.

inviolable /ɪn'vaɪələbəl/ *adj.* that must not be violated; that is to be kept free from violence or violation of any kind.

inviolate /ɪn'vaɪələt, -leɪt/ *adj.* free from violation, injury, desecration, or outrage.

invisible /ɪn'vɪzəbəl/ *adj.* not visible.

invite /ɪn'vaɪt/ *v.t.* **1.** to ask in a kindly, courteous, or complimentary way, to come or go to some place, gathering, entertainment, etc., or to do something. **2.** to act so as to bring on or render probable. –**invitation**, *n.*

in-vitro fertilisation /ɪn-ˈviːtrəʊ/ *n.* the fertilisation of an ovum by a sperm in a test tube, the resulting embryo to be implanted in a uterus. *Abbrev.*: IVF

invoice /ˈɪnvɔɪs/ *n.* **1.** a written list of merchandise, with prices, delivered or sent to a buyer. **2.** an itemised bill containing the prices which comprise the total charge. –*v.t.* (**-voiced**, **-voicing**) **3.** to present an invoice to (a customer, etc.).

invoke /ɪnˈvəʊk/ *v.t.* **1.** to call for with earnest desire; make supplication or prayer for. **2.** to call on (a divine being, etc.), as in prayer. –**invocation**, *n.*

involuntary /ɪnˈvɒləntri/, *Orig. US* /ɪnˈvɒləntɛri/ *adj.* acting, done or made without one's own volition or choice.

involve /ɪnˈvɒlv/ *v.t.* **1.** to include as a necessary circumstance, condition, or consequence; imply; entail. **2.** to include, contain, or comprehend within itself or its scope. **3.** to bring into an intricate or complicated form or condition. **4.** to implicate, as in guilt or crime, or in any matter or affair. **5.** (*usu. in the passive*) to concern or interest, especially excessively.

inward /ˈɪnwəd/ *adj.* **1.** proceeding or directed towards the inside or interior. **2.** situated within; interior, internal. **3.** relating to the inside or inner part. –*adv.* **4.** → **inwards**.

inwards /ˈɪnwədz/ *adv.* towards the inside or interior, as of a place, a space, or a body. Also, **inward**.

in-your-face /ɪn-jə-ˈfeɪs/ *adj. Colloq.* confronting or provocative. Also, **in your face**.

iodine /ˈaɪədiːn, ˈaɪədaɪn/ *n.* a nonmetallic element used in medicine as an antiseptic. *Symbol*: I

iodo- a word element meaning 'iodine'.

ion /ˈaɪən/ *n. Chem.* an electrically charged atom, radical, or molecule, formed by the loss or gain of one or more electrons. **Positive ions**, created by electron loss, are called *cations* and are attracted to the cathode in electrolysis. **Negative ions**, created by electron gain, are called *anions* and are attracted to the anode.

-ion a suffix of nouns denoting action or process, state or condition, or sometimes things or persons. Compare **-cion**, **-xion**. Also, **-tion**, **-ation**.

iota /aɪˈəʊtə/ *n.* a very small quantity.

IOU /aɪ əʊ ˈjuː/ *n.* a written acknowledgement of a debt, containing the expression 'IOU' (I owe you).

-ious a variant of **-ous**.

IP address *n. Internet* a unique numerical identifier for a computer connected to the internet. Also, **IP number**.

ipso facto /ˈɪpsəʊ ˈfæktəʊ/ *adv.* by the fact itself; by that very fact.

ir-¹ variant of **in-¹**, before *r*, as in *irradiate*.

ir-² variant of **in-²**, before *r*, as in *irrevocable*.

irascible /ɪˈræsəbəl/ *adj.* easily provoked to anger.

irate /aɪˈreɪt/ *adj.* angry; enraged.

ire /ˈaɪə/ *n.* anger; wrath.

iridescent /ɪrəˈdɛsənt/ *adj.* displaying colours like those of the rainbow. –**iridescence**, *n.*

iridology /ɪrəˈdɒlədʒi/ *n.* the diagnosis of the iris to detect pathological changes in the body. –**iridologist**, *n.*

iris /ˈaɪrəs/ *n.* **1.** the coloured part of the eye around the pupil. **2.** a large brightly coloured flower.

irk /ɜːk/ *v.t.* to weary, annoy, or trouble.

iron /ˈaɪən/ *n.* **1.** *Chem.* a ductile, malleable, silver-white metallic element, scarcely known in a pure condition, but abundantly used in its crude or impure forms for making tools, implements, machinery, etc. *Symbol*: Fe **2.** an iron or steel implement used heated for smoothing or pressing cloth, etc. **3.** a metal-headed golf club. **4.** (*pl.*) an iron shackle or fetter. –*adj.* **5.** made of iron. **6.** resembling iron in colour, firmness, etc. –*v.t.* **7.** to smooth or press with a heated iron, as clothes, etc. **8.** to shackle or fetter with irons.

ironbark /ˈaɪənbɑːk/ *n.* any of a group of eucalypts with a characteristic dark deeply fissured bark.

ironic /aɪˈrɒnɪk/ *adj.* relating to, of the nature of, or characterised by irony. Also, **ironical**.

iron lung *n.* a chamber in which alternate pulsations of high and low pressure can be used to force normal lung movements, used especially in some cases of poliomyelitis.

ironman /ˈaɪənmæn/ *n.* **1.** a contestant in a sporting event in which male competitors swim, cycle and run in succession. –*adj.* **2.** of or relating to such an event. Also, **iron man**.

ironwoman /ˈaɪənwʊmən/ *n.* (*pl.* **ironwomen**) **1.** a contestant in a sporting event in which female competitors swim, cycle and run in succession. –*adj.* **2.** of or relating to such an event. Also, **iron woman**.

irony /ˈaɪrəni/ *n.* (*pl.* **-nies**) **1.** a figure of speech or literary device in which the literal meaning is the opposite of that intended. **2.** an outcome of events contrary to what was, or might have been, expected. **3.** an ironic quality.

irradiate /ɪˈreɪdieɪt/ *v.t.* **1.** to shed rays of light upon; illuminate. **2.** to enlighten intellectually or spiritually. **3.** to radiate (light, etc.). **4.** to heat with radiant energy. **5.** to cure or treat by exposure to radiation, as of ultraviolet light. **6.** to expose to radiation. –*v.i.* **7.** to emit rays; shine. **8.** to become radiant. –**irradiation**, *n.* –**irradiant**, *adj.*

irrational /ɪˈræʃənəl/ *adj.* **1.** without the faculty of, or not endowed with, reason. **2.** without, or deprived of, sound judgement. **3.** not rational. **4.** *Maths* not expressible as a ratio of two integers.

irregular /ɪˈrɛɡjələ/ *adj.* **1.** not having an even pace or rhythm: *the patient's pulse was irregular.* **2.** not following an even line. **3.** not usual or normal. –**irregularity**, *n.* –**irregularly**, *adv.*

irrelevant /ɪˈrɛləvənt/ *adj.* **1.** not connected with the current topic or issue: *an irrelevant remark.* **2.** not important because not connected with a situation, person, etc.: *age is irrelevant.* –**irrelevantly**, *adv.* –**irrelevance**, *n.*

irrespective /ɪrəˈspɛktɪv/ *adj.* (fol. by *of*) without regard to something else, especially something specified; independent.

irresponsible /ɪrəˈspɒnsəbəl/ *adj.* not reliable, or not able to be trusted; not responsible. **–irresponsibly,** *adv.*

irrevocable /əˈrevəkəbəl, ɪrəˈvoʊkəbəl/ *adj.* not to be revoked or recalled; that cannot be repealed or annulled.

irrigate /ˈɪrəgeɪt/ *v.t.* 1. to supply (land) with water and thereby promote vegetation. 2. *Med.* to supply (a wound, etc.) with a constant flow of some liquid. **–irrigation,** *n.*

irritable /ˈɪrətəbəl/ *adj.* easily irritated; readily excited to impatience or anger. **–irritability,** *n.*

irritable bowel syndrome *n.* a common intestinal disorder of unknown cause, the symptoms of which may include diarrhoea, constipation, cramping, abdominal pain and bloating. *Abbrev.*: IBS

irritate /ˈɪrəteɪt/ *v.t.* 1. to excite to impatience or anger. 2. *Physiol.*, *Biol.* to excite (a living system) to some characteristic action or function. 3. to bring (a bodily part, etc.) to an abnormally excited or sensitive condition. **–irritation,** *n.* **–irritant,** *n.*, *adj.*

irrupt /ɪˈrʌpt/ *v.i.* to burst or intrude suddenly. **–irruption,** *n.*

Irukandji jellyfish /ɪrəˈkændʒi/ *n.* a small jellyfish, the sting of which is potentially fatal.

is /ɪz/, *weak forms* /z, s/ *v.* 3rd person singular present indicative of **be.**

is- variant of **iso-,** before some vowels.

-isation a noun suffix, combination of **-ise** and **-ation.** Also, **-ization.**

-ise¹ a suffix forming intransitive and transitive verbs. Also, **-ize.**

-ise² a noun suffix indicating quality, condition, or function, as in *merchandise.*

-ish¹ 1. a suffix used to form adjectives from nouns, with the sense of: **a.** 'belonging to' (a people, country, etc.), as in *British, Danish, English, Spanish.* **b.** 'after the manner of', 'having the characteristics of', 'like', as in *babyish, girlish, mulish.* **c.** 'addicted to', 'inclined or tending to', as in *bookish, freakish.* 2. a suffix used to form adjectives from other adjectives, with the sense of 'somewhat', 'rather', as in *oldish, reddish, sweetish.*

-ish² a suffix forming verbs of French origin, as *finish.*

island /ˈaɪlənd/ *n.* 1. a tract of land completely surrounded by water, and not large enough to be called a continent. 2. something resembling an island. 3. a platform in the middle of a street, at a crossing, for the safety of pedestrians.

isle /aɪl/ *n.* a small island.

-ism a suffix of nouns denoting action or practice, state or condition, principles, doctrines, a usage or characteristic, etc., as in *Australianism, baptism, barbarism, criticism, plagiarism, realism.* Compare **-ist, -ise¹.**

isn't /ˈɪzənt/ *v.* contraction of *is not.*

iso- a prefix meaning 'equal'.

isobar /ˈaɪsəbɑ/ *n. Meteorol.* a line drawn on a weather map, etc., connecting all points having the same barometric pressure at a specified time or over a certain period. **–isobaric,** *adj.*

isolate /ˈaɪsəleɪt/ *v.t.* to set or place apart; detach or separate so as to be alone. **–isolation,** *n.*

isomeric /aɪsoʊˈmerɪk/ *adj. Chem.* (of compounds) composed of the same kinds and numbers of atoms which differ from each other in the arrangement of the atoms and, therefore, in one or more properties. **–isomerism,** *n.* **–isomer,** *n.*

isometric /aɪsəˈmetrɪk/ *adj.* 1. relating to or having equality of measure. *–n.* 2. (*pl.*) a system of physical exercises in which muscles are pitted against each other or against a fixed object.

isosceles /aɪˈsɒsəliz/ *adj.* (of a triangle) having two sides equal.

isotope /ˈaɪsətoʊp/ *n.* any of two or more forms of a chemical element, having the same number of protons but different numbers of neutrons in the nucleus. **–isotopic,** *adj.* **–isotopy,** *n.*

issue /ˈɪʃu, ˈɪʃju, ˈɪsju/ *n.* 1. the act of sending, or promulgation; delivery; emission. 2. that which is issued. 3. a point in question or dispute, as between contending parties in an action at law. 4. a point or matter the decision of which is of special or public importance. 5. a distribution of food (rations), clothing, equipment, or ammunition to military personnel. 6. offspring or progeny. 7. a complaint; objection: *do you have an issue with this decision?* 8. *Chiefly Law* the yield or profit from land or other property. *–v.* (**issued, issuing**) *–v.t.* 9. to put out; deliver for use, sale, etc.; put into circulation. 10. to send out; discharge; emit. *–v.i.* 11. to go, pass, or flow out; come forth; emerge. 12. to come or proceed from any source. 13. to arise as a result or consequence; result. 14. *Chiefly Law* to proceed as offspring, or be born or descended. 15. *Chiefly Law* to come as a yield or profit, as from land. *–phr.* 16. **have issues,** to have unresolved personal difficulties and conflicts.

-ist a suffix of nouns, often accompanying verbs ending in *-ise* or nouns ending in *-ism,* denoting someone who does, practises, or is concerned with something, or holds certain principles, doctrines, etc.

isthmus /ˈɪsməs, ˈɪsθməs/ *n.* (*pl.* **-muses**) a narrow strip of land, bordered on both sides by water, connecting two larger bodies of land.

-istic a suffix of adjectives (and in the plural of nouns from adjectives) formed from nouns ending in *-ist,* and having reference to such nouns, or to associated nouns ending in *-ism.*

it /ɪt/ *pron.* a personal pronoun corresponding to *he* and *she,* used: 1. to refer to a thing, or to a person or animal whose sex is not known: *The desk is ready – you can pick it up today; The dog is hungry because it hasn't eaten all day.* 2. to refer to some matter expressed or understood: *How is she handling it?* 3. as the grammatical subject of a clause of which the logical subject is a phrase or clause: *It was agreed that she would go; It's amazing how often he rings her.* 4. in impersonal constructions: *It is raining; It is 5 o'clock.*

IT /aɪ ˈti/ *n.* information technology; the use of computers to produce, store and retrieve information.

Italian parsley /ɪtæljən ˈpɑsli/ *n.* **→ flat-leaf parsley.**

italic /ɪˈtælɪk, aɪ-/ *adj.* 1. designating or relating to a style of printing types in which the letters usually slope to the right (thus, *italic*), patterned upon a compact manuscript hand,

and used for emphasis, etc. –*n.* **2.** (*oft. pl.*) italic type. –**italicise, italicize,** *v.*

itch /ɪtʃ/ *v.i.* **1.** to have or feel a peculiar irritation of the skin which causes a desire to scratch the part affected. **2.** to have a restless desire to do or get something. –*n.* **3.** the sensation of itching. –**itchy,** *adj.*

-ite¹ a suffix of nouns denoting especially **1.** persons associated with a place, tribe, leader, doctrine, system, etc. **2.** minerals and fossils. **3.** chemical compounds, especially salts of acids whose names end in *-ous.* **4.** a member or component of a part of the body.

-ite² a suffix forming adjectives and nouns from adjectives, and some verbs, as in *composite, opposite, requisite, erudite,* etc.

item /'aɪtəm/ *n.* **1.** a separate article or particular. **2.** a separate piece of information or news, as in a newspaper.

itemise /'aɪtəmaɪz/ *v.t.* to state by items; give the particulars of. Also, **itemize.**

iterate /'ɪtəreɪt/ *v.t.* to utter again or repeatedly. –**iteration,** *n.*

itinerant /aɪ'tɪnərənt/ *adj.* **1.** travelling from place to place. **2.** moving on a circuit, as a preacher, judge, or pedlar. –**itinerancy,** *n.* –**itinerate,** *v.*

itinerary /aɪ'tɪnəri, aɪ'tɪnərəri/, *Orig. US* /aɪ-'tɪnəreri/ *n.* (*pl.* **-ries**) **1.** a plan of travel. **2.** an account of a journey.

-ition a noun suffix, **-ite²** plus **-ion.**

-itious an adjective suffix occurring in adjectives associated with nouns in *-ition.*

-itis a noun suffix used in pathological terms denoting inflammation of some part or organ, as in *bronchitis.*

-itive a suffix of adjectives and nouns of adjectival origin, as in *definitive, fugitive.*

it'll /'ɪtl/ contraction of *it will* or *it shall.*

its /ɪts/ *adj., pron.* possessive form of **it.**

it's /ɪts/ contraction of *it is.*

itself /ɪt'sɛlf/ *pron.* **1.** the reflexive form of **it**: *a thermostatically controlled electric fire switches itself off.* **2.** an emphatic form of **it** used: **a.** as object: *the earth gathers its fruits to itself.* **b.** in apposition to a subject or object. **3.** in its normal or usual state.

-ity a suffix forming abstract nouns of condition, characteristics, etc., as in *civility.*

-ium a suffix representing Latin neuter suffix, used especially to form names of metallic elements.

-ive a suffix of adjectives (and nouns of adjectival origin) expressing tendency, disposition, function, connection, etc., as in *active, corrective, destructive.* Compare **-ative.**

I've /aɪv/ contraction of *I have.*

IVF /aɪ vi 'ɛf/ *n.* in-vitro fertilisation; the fertilisation of an ovum by a sperm in a test tube, the resulting embryo to be implanted in a uterus.

ivory /'aɪvəri, 'aɪvri/ *n.* (*pl.* **-ries**) **1.** the hard white substance composing the main part of the tusks of the elephant, walrus, etc. **2.** (*pl.*) *Colloq.* **a.** the keys of a piano, accordion, etc. **b.** dice. **3.** creamy white.

ivy /'aɪvi/ *n.* (*pl.* **ivies**) a climbing plant with smooth, shiny, evergreen leaves.

J, j

J, j /dʒeɪ/ n. the 10th letter of the English alphabet.

jab /dʒæb/ v. (**jabbed, jabbing**) –v.i. **1.** to thrust smartly or sharply, as with the end or point of something. –v.t. **2.** to poke (something) smartly or sharply. –n. **3.** a poke with the end or point of something.

jabber /ˈdʒæbə/ v.i. to utter rapidly, indistinctly, imperfectly, or nonsensically; chatter.

jabiru /dʒæbəˈruː/ n. Australia's only stork, white with glossy green-black head, neck, tail, and a black band across upper and lower wing surfaces, found along the north and east coast.

jacaranda /dʒækəˈrændə/ n. a tall tropical tree with lavender-blue flowers.

jack /dʒæk/ n. **1.** a man or fellow. **2.** a contrivance for raising heavy weights short distances. **3.** any of the four knaves in playing cards. **4.** a knucklebone or plastic imitation used in a children's game. **5.** Colloq. venereal disease. –v.t. **6.** to lift or raise with or as with a jack. –phr. **7. jack up,** Colloq. to refuse; be obstinate; resist.

jackal /ˈdʒækəl/ n. any of several kinds of wild dog.

jackaroo /dʒækəˈruː/ n. **1.** a young man gaining practical experience on a sheep or cattle station. –v.i. **2.** to work as a trainee on such a station. Also, **jackeroo.**

jackass /ˈdʒækæs/ n. **1.** a male donkey. **2.** a very stupid or foolish person.

jacket /ˈdʒækət/ n. **1.** a short coat. **2.** Also, **dust jacket.** a detachable paper cover, usually illustrated in colour, for protecting the binding of a book; dustcover. **3.** the outer casing or covering of a boiler, pipe, tank, etc.

jackhammer /ˈdʒækhæmə/ n. a handheld drill operated by compressed air, used for drilling rocks.

jack-in-the-box /ˈdʒæk-ɪn-ðə-bɒks/ n. a toy consisting of a figure, enclosed in a box, which springs out when the lid is unfastened.

jackknife /ˈdʒæknaɪf/ n. (pl. **-knives**) **1.** a large knife with a blade that folds into the handle. –v.i. (**-knifed, -knifing**) **2.** to bend or fold up, like a jackknife. **3.** (of a semitrailer or a car pulling a caravan, etc.) to go out of control in such a way that the trailer swings round towards the driver's cab.

jackpot /ˈdʒækpɒt/ n. the chief prize to be won in a lottery, a game or contest.

jacuzzi /dʒəˈkuːzi/ n. (from trademark) a type of spa pool, usually not attached to a larger pool.

jade /dʒeɪd/ n. a mineral, sometimes green, highly esteemed as an ornamental stone.

jaded /ˈdʒeɪdəd/ adj. **1.** worn out. **2.** dispirited; losing enthusiasm. **3.** sated: a jaded appetite.

jaffle /ˈdʒæfəl/ n. (from trademark) a sealed toasted sandwich with a savoury or sweet filling.

jagged /ˈdʒægəd/ adj. having notches, teeth, or ragged edges.

jaguar /ˈdʒægjuə/ n. a large, ferocious, spotted wild cat.

jail /dʒeɪl/ n. a prison. Also, **gaol.**

jalopy /dʒəˈlɒpi/ n. (pl. **-pies**) Colloq. an old, decrepit, or unpretentious car.

jam¹ /dʒæm/ v. (**jammed, jamming**) –v.t. **1.** to press or squeeze tightly between bodies or surfaces, so that motion or extrication is made difficult or impossible. **2.** to fill or block up by crowding. **3.** to cause to become wedged, caught, or displaced, so that it cannot work, as a machine, part, etc. **4.** Radio to interfere with (signals, etc.) by sending out others of approximately the same frequency. **5.** (fol. by on) to apply (brakes) forcibly. –v.i. **6.** to become wedged or fixed; stick fast. **7.** to press or push violently, as into a confined space or against one another. **8.** (of a machine, etc.) to become unworkable as through the wedging or displacement of a part. –n. **9.** the act of jamming. **10.** the state of being jammed. **11.** a mass of vehicles, people, or objects jammed together. **12.** Colloq. a difficult or awkward situation; a fix.

jam² /dʒæm/ n. a preserve of boiled and crushed fruit.

jam³ /dʒæm/ n. a meeting of musicians for the spontaneous and improvisatory performance of music. Also, **jam session.**

jamb /dʒæm/ n. a vertical piece forming the side of a doorway, window, or the like.

jangle /ˈdʒæŋgəl/ v.i. **1.** to sound harshly or discordantly. –n. **2.** a harsh or discordant sound.

janitor /ˈdʒænətə/ n. a caretaker.

jape /dʒeɪp/ n. a joke; jest; gibe.

japonica /dʒəˈpɒnɪkə/ n. any of several garden shrubs with white, pink or red flowers.

jar¹ /dʒɑ/ n. a broad-mouthed earthen or glass vessel.

jar² /dʒɑ/ v.i. (**jarred, jarring**) **1.** to produce a harsh, grating sound; sound discordantly. **2.** to have a harshly unpleasant effect upon the nerves, feelings, etc. **3.** to be at variance; conflict; clash.

jargon /ˈdʒɑgən/ n. the language peculiar to a trade, profession, or other group.

jarrah /ˈdʒærə/ n. a large tree of western Australia.

jasmine /ˈdʒæzmən/ n. any of several shrubs or climbing plants with fragrant flowers.

jasper /ˈdʒæspə/ n. a coloured variety of quartz.

jaundice /ˈdʒɔndəs/ n. **1.** a disease characterised by yellowness of the skin, etc. –v.t. (**-diced, -dicing**) **2.** to distort or prejudice, as with pessimism, jealousy, resentment, etc.

jaunt /dʒɒnt/ v.i. **1.** to make a short journey, especially for pleasure. –n. **2.** such a journey.

jaunty /ˈdʒɒnti/ adj. (**-tier, -tiest**) easy and sprightly in manner or bearing.

javelin /ˈdʒævələn/ n. a spear to be thrown by hand.

jaw /dʒɔ/ n. one of the two bones or structures (upper and lower) which form the framework of the mouth.

jay /dʒeɪ/ n. a type of bird.

jaywalk /ˈdʒeɪwɔk/ v.i. to cross a street otherwise than by a pedestrian crossing.

jazz /dʒæz/ n. **1.** a type of popular music marked by frequent improvisation and syncopated rhythms. –v.t. **2.** Colloq. (oft. fol. by up) to put vigour or liveliness into.

jealous /ˈdʒɛləs/ adj. **1.** inclined to or troubled by suspicions or fears of rivalry, as in love or aims. **2.** solicitous or vigilant in maintaining or guarding something. –**jealousy**, *n*.

jeans /dʒinz/ *pl. n.* casual trousers, especially those made of denim.

jeep /dʒip/ *n.* a small military motor vehicle.

jeer /dʒɪə/ *v.i.* to speak or shout derisively; gibe or scoff rudely.

jelly /'dʒɛli/ *n.* (*pl.* **-lies**) **1.** a food preparation of a soft, elastic consistency. –*v.t., v.i.* (**-lied, -lying**) **2.** to bring or come to the consistency of jelly.

jellyfish /'dʒɛlifɪʃ/ *n.* (*pl.* **-fish** *or* **-fishes**) any of various free-swimming marine coelenterates of a soft, gelatinous structure, especially one with an umbrella-like body and long, trailing tentacles.

jemmy /'dʒɛmi/ *n.* (*pl.* **-mies**) a short crowbar.

jeopardy /'dʒɛpədi/ *n.* hazard or risk of loss or harm. –**jeopardise, jeopardize**, *v*.

jerk /dʒɜk/ *n.* **1.** a quick, sharp thrust, pull, throw, or the like. **2.** *Colloq.* a stupid or naive person. –*v.t.* **3.** to move or throw with a quick, suddenly arrested motion.

jerky /'dʒɜki/ *adj.* (**-kier, -kiest**) characterised by jerks or sudden starts; spasmodic. –**jerkily**, *adv.* –**jerkiness**, *n*.

jersey /'dʒɜzi/ *n.* **1.** a close-fitting, usually woollen, outer garment for the upper part of the body; jumper. **2.** a machine-knitted fabric.

jest /dʒɛst/ *n.* **1.** a witticism, joke, or pleasantry. **2.** sport or fun. –*v.i.* **3.** to speak in a playful, humorous, or facetious way; joke.

jet¹ /dʒɛt/ *n.* **1.** a stream of fluid from a nozzle, orifice, etc. **2.** a jet plane. –*v.i.* (**jetted, jetting**) **3.** to spout. **4.** to fly in a jet plane.

jet² /dʒɛt/ *n.* a compact black coal, susceptible of a high polish, used for making beads, jewellery, buttons, etc.

jet lag *n.* bodily discomfort and tiredness caused by the disturbance of normal patterns of eating and sleeping after a long flight across different time zones.

jet plane *n.* an aeroplane operated by jet propulsion.

jet propulsion *n.* a method of producing a propelling force upon an air or water craft through the reaction of a high-velocity jet, usually of heated gases, discharged towards the rear. –**jet-propelled**, *adj*.

jetsam /'dʒɛtsəm/ *n.* goods thrown overboard to lighten a vessel in distress, which sink or are washed ashore. Compare **flotsam**.

jet set *n.* a rich and fashionable social set whose means enable them to travel from resort to resort by jet plane in the pursuit of pleasure.

jettison /'dʒɛtəsən, -zən/ *v.t.* to throw (cargo, etc.) overboard, especially to lighten a vessel or aircraft in distress.

jetty /'dʒɛti/ *n.* (*pl.* **-ties**) a small wharf.

jewel /'dʒuəl/ *n.* a cut and polished precious or semiprecious stone; a gem. –**jeweller**, *n*.

jewellery /'dʒuəlri/ *n.* jewels for personal adornment.

jewfish /'dʒufɪʃ/ *n.* (*pl.* **-fish** *or* **-fishes**) (in Australia) any of several species of large food fishes.

jib /dʒɪb/ *v.i.* (**jibbed, jibbing**) to hold back or baulk at doing something.

jiffy /'dʒɪfi/ *n.* (*pl.* **-fies**) *Colloq.* a very short time. Also, **jiff**.

jig¹ /dʒɪg/ *n.* a device for holding the work in a machine tool.

jig² /dʒɪg/ *n.* **1.** a rapid, lively dance. –*v.t.* (**jigged, jigging**) **2.** to move with a jerky or bobbing motion.

jigger¹ /'dʒɪgə/ *n.* a measure for alcohol used in cocktails.

jigger² /'dʒɪgə/ *v.t.* to break or destroy.

jiggle /'dʒɪgəl/ *v.i.* to move up and down or to and fro with short, quick jerks.

jigsaw puzzle /'dʒɪgsɔ/ *n.* small, irregularly shaped pieces of wood or cardboard, which, when correctly fitted together, form a picture.

jihad /dʒɪhæd, 'dʒɪhad/ *n.* *Islam* spiritual efforts made in the cause of God; at the communal level, a struggle or holy war in support of Islam against unbelievers. Also, **jehad**.

jillaroo /dʒɪlə'ru/ *n.* a female jackaroo. Also, **jilleroo**.

jilt /dʒɪlt/ *v.t.* to cast off (a lover or sweetheart) after encouragement or engagement.

jingle /'dʒɪŋgəl/ *v.i.* **1.** to make clinking or tinkling sounds, as coins, keys, etc., when struck together repeatedly. –*n.* **2.** a clinking or tinkling sound. **3.** a simple, repetitive rhyme set to music, used especially for advertising.

jingoism /'dʒɪŋgoʊɪzəm/ *n.* fervent and excessive patriotism.

jinx /dʒɪŋks/ *Colloq.* –*n.* **1.** a person, thing, or influence supposedly bringing bad luck. –*v.t.* **2.** to bring bad luck to someone; hex.

jitters /'dʒɪtəz/ *phr.* **the jitters**, *Colloq.* nervousness; nerves.

jive /dʒaɪv/ *n.* **1.** jargon used by jazz musicians. **2.** a dance performed to beat music.

job¹ /dʒɒb/ *n.* **1.** an individual piece of work done in the routine of one's occupation or trade. **2.** a post of employment. –*v.i.* (**jobbed, jobbing**) **3.** to work at jobs, or odd pieces of work. –*adj.* **4.** of or for a particular job or transaction. **5.** bought or sold together; lumped together.

job² /dʒɒb/ *v.t.* (**jobbed, jobbing**) *Colloq.* to jab; hit; punch.

job share *n.* an arrangement whereby one job is shared between two or more employees.

jockey /'dʒɒki/ *n.* someone who professionally rides horses in races.

jockstrap /'dʒɒkstræp/ *n.* *Colloq.* a support for the genitals worn by male athletes, dancers, etc.

jocose /dʒə'koʊs/ *adj.* given to or characterised by joking; jesting; humorous.

jocular /'dʒɒkjələ/ *adj.* given to, characterised by, intended for, or suited to joking or jesting.

jocund /'dʒɒkənd/ *adj.* cheerful; merry.

jodhpurs /'dʒɒdpəz/ *pl. n.* riding breeches reaching to the ankle, and fitting closely from the knee down.

joey /'dʒoʊi/ *n.* (*pl.* **-eys**) any young animal, especially a kangaroo.

jog /dʒɒg/ *v.* (**jogged, jogging**) –*v.t.* **1.** to move or shake with a push or jerk. **2.** to stir up by hint or reminder. –*v.i.* **3.** to move with a jolt or jerk. **4.** to run at a slow, regular pace.

jogger /'dʒɒgə/ *n.* **1.** a person who jogs for sport or exercise. **2.** Also, **jogging shoe**. a type of shoe suitable for jogging; runner.

joggle /'dʒɒgəl/ v.t. to shake slightly; move to and fro as by repeated jerks.

John Dory n. a thin, deep-bodied, highly esteemed food fish.

join /dʒɔɪn/ v.t. **1.** (sometimes fol. by *up*) to bring or put together, in contact or connection. **2.** to become a member of. **3.** to come into the company of. –v.i. **4.** to join into or be in contact or connection, or form a junction. **5.** (oft. fol. by *in*) to take part with others. –n. **6.** a place or line of joining; a seam.

joiner /'dʒɔɪnə/ n. a worker in wood who constructs the fittings of a house, furniture, etc. –**joinery,** n.

joint /dʒɔɪnt/ n. **1.** the place or part in which two things, or parts of one thing, are joined or united. **2.** one of the portions into which a carcass is divided by a butcher, especially one ready for cooking. **3.** Colloq. one's house, unit, office, etc. **4.** Colloq. a marijuana cigarette. –adj. **5.** shared by or common to two or more. **6.** sharing or acting in common. –v.t. **7.** to unite by a joint or joints. **8.** to form or provide with a joint or joints. **9.** to divide at a joint, or separate into pieces. –**jointly,** adv.

joist /dʒɔɪst/ n. any of the parallel lengths of timber, steel, etc., used for supporting floors, ceilings, etc.

jojoba /hə'houbə, hou'houbə/ n. an evergreen shrub having edible seeds containing a liquid wax with many uses.

joke /dʒouk/ n. **1.** something said or done to excite laughter or amusement. **2.** an amusing or ridiculous circumstance. –v.i. **3.** to speak or act in a playful or merry way. **4.** to say something in mere sport, rather than in earnest.

joker /'dʒoukə/ n. an extra playing card in a pack, used in some games.

jolly /'dʒɒli/ adj. (**-lier, -liest**) **1.** in good spirits; cheerful. –adv. **2.** Colloq. extremely; very.

jolt /dʒoult/ v.t. **1.** to jar or shake as by a sudden rough thrust. –n. **2.** a jolting shock or movement.

jostle /'dʒɒsəl/ v. (**-tled, -tling**) –v.t. **1.** to strike or push roughly or rudely against; elbow roughly; hustle. –v.i. **2.** (fol. by *with* or *against*) to collide with or strike or push against, as in passing or in a crowd.

jot /dʒɒt/ n. **1.** the least part of something; a little bit. –v.t. (**jotted, jotting**) **2.** (usu. fol. by *down*) to write or mark down briefly.

joule /dʒul/ n. a measure of work or energy in the metric system. Symbol: J

journal /'dʒɜnəl/ n. **1.** a daily record, as of occurrences, experiences, or observations; diary. **2.** a newspaper, especially a daily one. **3.** any periodical or magazine, especially one published by a learned society. **4.** Bookkeeping a book in which transactions are entered.

journalism /'dʒɜnəlɪzəm/ n. the occupation of writing for, editing, and producing newspapers and other periodicals, and television and radio shows. –**journalist,** n.

journey /'dʒɜni/ n. (pl. **-neys**) **1.** a course of travel from one place to another, especially by land. –v.i. (**-neyed, -neying**) **2.** to make a journey; travel.

joust /dʒaust/ n. a combat in which two armoured knights or men-at-arms on horseback opposed each other with lances.

jovial /'dʒouviəl/ adj. endowed with or characterised by a hearty, joyous humour or a spirit of good fellowship.

jowl[1] /dʒaul/ n. **1.** a jaw, especially the under-jaw. **2.** the cheek.

jowl[2] /dʒaul/ n. a fold of flesh hanging from the jaw, as of a fat person.

joy /dʒɔɪ/ n. an emotion of keen or lively pleasure; great gladness; delight.

joyful /'dʒɔɪfəl/ adj. feeling great happiness. Also, **joyous.** –**joyfully,** adv.

joyous /'dʒɔɪəs/ adj. joyful. –**joyously,** adv. –**joyousness,** n.

joystick /'dʒɔɪstɪk/ n. **1.** the control stick of an aeroplane. **2.** a stick used to control the movement of the cursor on a computer screen.

JPEG /'dʒeɪ pɛg/ n. Computers **1.** joint photographic experts group; a standard format used to store images in digital form, used especially for photographic images. **2.** a file stored in this format.

jube /dʒub/ n. a chewy lolly. Also, **jujube.**

jubilant /'dʒubələnt/ adj. expressing or exciting joy; manifesting exultation or gladness. –**jubilation,** n. –**jubilantly,** adv.

jubilate /'dʒubəleɪt/ v.i. to manifest or feel great joy; rejoice; exult. –**jubilation,** n. –**jubilant,** adj.

jubilee /dʒubə'li/ n. the celebration of any of certain anniversaries.

judder /'dʒʌdə/ v.i. to vibrate; shake.

judge /dʒʌdʒ/ n. **1.** a public officer authorised to hear and determine causes in a court of law. **2.** a person appointed to decide in any competition or contest. –v. (**judged, judging**) –v.t. **3.** to try (a person or a case) as a judge does; pass sentence on or in. **4.** to form a judgement or opinion of or upon. –v.i. **5.** to act as a judge; pass judgement. **6.** to make a mental judgement.

judgement /'dʒʌdʒmənt/ n. **1.** the act of judging. **2.** Law the judicial decision of a cause in court. **3.** ability to judge justly or wisely. **4.** the forming of an opinion, estimate, notion, or conclusion, as from circumstances presented to the mind. Also, **judgment.**

judgemental /dʒʌdʒ'mɛntl/ adj. inclined to pass judgement, especially in a dogmatic fashion. Also, **judgmental.**

judicature /'dʒudəkətʃə/ n. **1.** the administration of justice, as by judges or courts. **2.** a body of judges.

judicial /dʒu'dɪʃəl/ adj. **1.** relating to judgement in courts of justice or to the administration of justice. **2.** relating to courts of law or to judges.

judiciary /dʒu'dɪʃəri/ n. (pl. **-aries**) the system of courts of justice in a country.

judicious /dʒu'dɪʃəs/ adj. **1.** using or showing judgement as to action or practical expediency. **2.** having, exercising, or showing good judgement; wise, sensible, or well-advised.

judo /'dʒudou/ n. a style of self-defence derived from jujitsu, employing less violent methods and emphasising the sporting element.

jug /dʒʌg/ n. a vessel in various forms for holding liquids, commonly having a handle.

juggernaut /'dʒʌgənɔt/ n. **1.** anything requiring blind devotion or extreme sacrifice. **2.** any large, relentless, destructive force.

juggle /'dʒʌgəl/ v.t. **1.** to keep (several objects) in continuous motion in the air at the same time by tossing and catching. **2.** to manipulate or alter by artifice or trickery.

jugular /'dʒʌgjulə/ adj. **1.** Anat. of or relating to the throat or neck. –n. **2.** one of the large veins in the neck.

juice /dʒus/ n. **1.** the liquid part of plant or animal substance. **2.** any extracted liquid, especially from a fruit. –**juicy**, adj.

jujitsu /dʒu'dʒɪtsu/ n. a Japanese method of defending oneself without weapons. Also, **jiujitsu**.

jukebox /'dʒukbɒks/ n. a coin-operated machine which plays a select musical item or items.

jumble /'dʒʌmbəl/ v.t. **1.** to mix in a confused mass; put or throw together without order. –n. **2.** a confused mixture.

jumbuck /'dʒʌmbʌk/ n. Colloq. a sheep.

jump /dʒʌmp/ v.i. **1.** to spring clear of the ground or other support by a sudden muscular effort; leap. **2.** to move suddenly or abruptly, as from surprise or shock; start. **3.** to pass abruptly, ignoring intervening stages. –v.t. **4.** to leap or spring over. **5.** to skip or pass over; bypass. –n. **6.** the act of jumping; a leap. **7.** a space or obstacle or apparatus cleared in a leap. **8.** a sudden rise in amount, price, etc. **9.** an abrupt transition from one point or thing to another, with omission of what intervenes.

jumper /'dʒʌmpə/ n. an outer garment, usually of wool, for the upper part of the body; pullover; sweater; jersey.

jumper leads pl. n. a pair of heavy leads used in starting a motor vehicle with a flat battery, by connecting this battery to a charged one.

jumpsuit /'dʒʌmpsut/ n. a close-fitting outer garment covering all of the body and the legs.

jumpy /'dʒʌmpi/ adj. (**-pier**, **-piest**) characterised by or inclined to sudden, involuntary starts, especially from nervousness, fear, excitement, etc.

junction /'dʒʌŋkʃən/ n. **1.** the act of joining; combination. **2.** a place of joining or meeting.

juncture /'dʒʌŋktʃə/ n. **1.** a point of time, especially one made critical or important by a concurrence of circumstances. **2.** the line or point at which two bodies are joined.

jungle /'dʒʌŋgəl/ n. a tropical rainforest with thick, impenetrable undergrowth.

junior /'dʒunjə/ adj. **1.** younger. **2.** of lower rank or standing. –n. **3.** a person who is younger than another. **4.** any minor or child, especially a male. **5.** someone employed as the subordinate of another. **6.** Law any barrister who is not a Senior Counsel or Queen's Counsel.

juniper /'dʒunəpə/ n. any of several coniferous evergreen shrubs or trees.

junk¹ /dʒʌŋk/ n. **1.** any old or discarded material. **2.** anything regarded as worthless.

junk² /dʒʌŋk/ n. a kind of seagoing ship used in Chinese and other waters.

junk bond n. a high-yield security, especially one issued to finance a takeover, and often involving high risk.

junket /'dʒʌŋkət/ n. **1.** a sweet custard-like food. **2.** a feast or merrymaking; a picnic; a pleasure excursion.

junkie /'dʒʌŋki/ n. Colloq. a drug addict. Also, **junky**.

junk mail n. unsolicited mail, usually advertisements or prospectuses.

junta /'dʒʌntə/ n. a small ruling group in a country, either elected or self-chosen, especially one which has come to power after a revolution.

jurisdiction /dʒurəs'dɪkʃən/ n. **1.** the right, power, or authority to administer justice by hearing and determining controversies. **2.** power; authority; control.

jurisprudence /dʒurəs'prudns/ n. **1.** the science or philosophy of law. **2.** a body or system of laws. –**jurisprudent**, n., adj. –**jurisprudential**, adj.

jurist /'dʒurəst, 'dʒuə-/ n. one versed in the law.

juror /'dʒuərə, 'dʒuə-/ n. a member of any jury.

jury /'dʒuəri, 'dʒuri/ n. (pl. **juries**) **1.** a body of persons chosen at random from the community, who are engaged for a trial and sworn to deliver a verdict on questions of fact presented to them. **2.** a body of persons chosen to adjudge prizes, etc., as in a competition.

just /dʒʌst/ adj. **1.** actuated by truth, justice, and lack of bias. **2.** based on right; rightful; lawful. **3.** true; correct. **4.** given or awarded rightly, or deserved, as a sentence, punishment, reward, etc. **5.** in accordance with standards, or requirements. –adv. **6.** within a brief preceding time, or but a moment before. **7.** exactly or precisely: *just what I need*. **8.** by a narrow margin; barely. **9.** only or merely. **10.** actually; truly; positively: *the view is just spectacular*.

justice /'dʒʌstəs/ n. **1.** the quality of being just. **2.** that which is just. **3.** the requital of desert as by punishment or reward. **4.** the maintenance or administration of law, as by judicial or other proceedings. **5.** a judicial officer; a judge or magistrate.

justice of the peace n. **1.** (in Australia) a person authorised to administer oaths, take declarations, and attest instruments. **2.** (in Britain) a lay magistrate with authority to exercise a limited civil and summary criminal jurisdiction. Abbrev.: JP

justify /'dʒʌstəfaɪ/ v.t. (**-fied**, **-fying**) **1.** to show (an act, claim, etc.) to be just, right, or warranted. **2.** to declare guiltless; absolve; acquit. **3.** Typesetting to adjust exactly; make (lines) of the proper length by spacing. –**justification**, n.

jut /dʒʌt/ v.i. (**jutted**, **jutting**) (oft. fol. by *out*) to extend beyond the main body or line; project; protrude.

jute /dʒut/ n. a strong fibre used for making fabrics, cordage, etc.

juvenile /'dʒuvənaɪl/ adj. **1.** relating to, suitable for, characteristic of, or intended for young persons. **2.** young. **3.** inappropriately suggestive of the behaviour or sentiments of a young person. –n. **4.** a young person; a youth.

juvie /'dʒuvi/ Colloq. –adj. **1.** juvenile: *juvie justice*. –n. **2.** juvenile detention: *in juvie*. Also, **juvey**, **juvy**.

juxta- a word element meaning 'near', 'close to', 'beside'.

juxtapose /dʒʌkstə'pouz, 'dʒʌkstəpouz/ v.t. to place in close proximity or side by side. –**juxtaposition**, n.

K, k

K, k /keɪ/ n. the 11th letter of the English alphabet.

K /keɪ/ n. **1.** Also, **k.** *Computers* kilobytes. **2.** a thousand (dollars, etc.).

kaftan /ˈkæftæn/ n. → **caftan**.

kale /keɪl/ n. a kind of cabbage with leaves not forming a head.

kaleidoscope /kəˈlaɪdəskoʊp/ n. an optical instrument in which pieces of coloured glass, etc., in a rotating tube are shown by reflection in continually changing symmetrical forms. –**kaleidoscopic**, *adj.*

Kanaka /kəˈnækə/ n. (*sometimes derog.*) a Pacific islander, especially one brought forcibly to Australia during the 19th century as a labourer.

kangaroo /kæŋgəˈruː/ n. any of several herbivorous marsupials of the Australian region, with powerful hind legs developed for leaping, and very short forelimbs.

kangaroo paw n. a western Australian plant with flowers looking like the paw of a kangaroo, the floral emblem of WA.

kaput /kæˈpʊt, kə-/ adj. *Colloq.* **1.** smashed; ruined. **2.** broken; not working.

karabiner /kærəˈbiːnə/ n. → **carabiner**.

karaoke /kæriˈoʊki/ n. **1.** the entertainment of singing to a karaoke machine: *that restaurant offers karaoke.* –*adj.* **2.** (of bars, restaurants, etc.) equipped with a karaoke machine.

karaoke machine n. a music system which plays simultaneously a video clip of a song with subtitled lyrics and the backing tape of the song, and which is equipped with microphones for the use of a singer.

karate /kəˈrɑːti/ n. a method of defensive fighting in which hands, elbows, feet, and knees are the only weapons used.

karma /ˈkɑːmə/ n. **1.** fate; destiny. **2.** *Colloq.* the quality, mood, or atmosphere of a person or place. –**karmic**, *adj.*

karri /ˈkæri/ n. (*pl.* **-ris**) a tree valued for its hard, durable timber.

kata- variant of **cata-**. Also, **kat-**, **kath-**.

kauri /ˈkaʊri/ n. (*pl.* **-ris**) a tall coniferous tree of NZ, yielding a valuable timber and a resin.

kava /ˈkɑːvə/ n. an intoxicating beverage made from the roots of a Polynesian shrub.

kayak /ˈkaɪæk/ n. an Inuit hunting canoe. –**kayaker**, *n.*

kazoo /kəˈzuː/ n. a short plastic or metal tube with a membrane-covered side hole, into which a person sings or hums. Also, **gazoo**.

kebab /kəˈbæb/ n. **1.** → **shish kebab**. **2.** → **doner kebab**.

keel /kiːl/ n. **1.** a longitudinal timber, or combination of timbers, iron plates, or the like supporting the whole frame of a ship. –*phr.* **2. keel over**, *Colloq.* to collapse suddenly.

keen¹ /kiːn/ adj. **1.** sharp. **2.** characterised by strength and distinctness of perception, as the ear or hearing, the eye, sight, etc. **3.** having or

showing great mental penetration or acumen. **4.** intense, as feeling, desire, etc. **5.** (fol. by *on*) having a fondness or devotion (for).

keen² /kiːn/ v.i. to wail in lamentation for the dead.

keep /kiːp/ v. (**kept**, **keeping**) –v.t. **1.** to maintain in one's action or conduct. **2.** to cause to continue in some place, position, state, course, or action specified. **3.** to have habitually in stock or for sale. **4.** to withhold from use; reserve. **5.** to maintain or carry on, as an establishment, business, etc.; manage. **6.** to maintain or support (a person, etc.). **7.** to save, hold, or retain in possession. –v.i. **8.** to continue in an action, course, position, state, etc. **9.** to continue unimpaired or without spoiling. **10.** (fol. by *away*, *back*, *off*, *out*, etc.) to remain; stay. –n. **11.** subsistence; board and lodging. **12.** the innermost and strongest structure or central tower of a medieval castle. –*phr.* **13. for keeps**, *Colloq.* permanently.

keeping /ˈkiːpɪŋ/ n. just conformity in things or elements associated together.

keepsake /ˈkiːpseɪk/ n. anything kept as a token of remembrance, friendship, etc.

keg /kɛg/ n. a barrel, especially of beer.

kelp /kɛlp/ n. any of the large brown seaweeds.

kelpie /ˈkɛlpi/ n. one of a breed of Australian sheepdogs.

kelvin /ˈkɛlvən/ n. a unit of temperature, equal to one degree Celsius.

Kelvin scale n. a scale of temperature (**Kelvin temperature**), in which zero is equivalent to $-273.16°C$.

ken /kɛn/ n. knowledge.

kennel /ˈkɛnəl/ n. **1.** a house for a dog or dogs. **2.** (*usu. pl., construed as sing.*) an establishment where dogs are bred or boarded.

kept /kɛpt/ v. past tense and past participle of **keep**.

kerb /kɜːb/ n. a line of joined stones, concrete, or the like at the edge of a street, wall, etc.

kerchief /ˈkɜːtʃif, ˈkɜːtʃəf/ n. **1.** a cloth worn or carried on the person. **2.** a cloth worn as a head covering.

kerfuffle /kəˈfʌfəl, -ˈfʊfəl/ n. *Colloq.* argument; commotion; rumpus. Also, **kafoofle**, **kafuffle**, **kerfoofle**.

kernel /ˈkɜːnəl/ n. **1.** the softer, usually edible, part contained in the shell of a nut or the stone of a fruit. **2.** the central part of anything; the nucleus; the core.

kero /ˈkɛroʊ/ n. *Colloq.* → **kerosene**.

kerosene /ˈkɛrəˌsin/ n. a mixture of liquid hydrocarbons, obtained in the distillation of petroleum, used for lamps, engines, heaters. Also, **kerosine**.

kestrel /ˈkɛstrəl/ n. any of several small falcons.

ketchup /ˈkɛtʃəp/ n. any of several sauces or condiments for meat, fish, etc.

kettle /ˈkɛtl/ n. a portable container in which to boil water.

kettledrum /ˈkɛtlˌdrʌm/ n. a hollow metal drum which can be tuned.

key¹ /kiː/ n. (*pl.* **keys**) **1.** an instrument for fastening or opening a lock by moving its bolt. **2.** a means of attaining, understanding, solving, etc. **3.** a systematic explanation of abbreviations, symbols, etc. **4.** something that secures or controls entrance to a place. **5.** a pin, bolt, wedge, or other piece inserted in a hole or space to lock or hold parts of a mechanism or structure together. **6.** one of a set of levers or parts pressed in operating a keyboard, typewriter, musical instrument, etc. **7.** *Music* the keynote or tonic of a scale. *–adj.* **8.** chief; indispensable. **9.** identifying. *–v.t.* (**keyed, keying**) **10.** (oft. fol. by *up*) to bring to a particular degree of intensity of feeling. **11.** to adjust (one's speech, actions, etc.) to external factors, as the level of understanding of one's hearers. **12.** to fasten, secure, or adjust with a key, wedge, or the like, as parts of a mechanism. **13.** to provide with a key or keys. **14.** to give (an advertisement) a letter or number to enable replies to it to be identified. **15.** (oft. fol. by *in*) to enter (data) into a computer by means of a keyboard.

key² /ki/ *n.* **1.** (in the Caribbean area) a reef or low island; cay. **2.** a long low peninsula artificially created, on which houses are built.

keyboard /'kibɔd/ *n.* the row or set of keys on a piano, typewriter, computer, etc. **–keyboarder,** *n.*

keyhole surgery *n.* surgery performed using very small incisions and fibre optics to provide vision.

keynote /'kinoʊt/ *n.* **1.** *Music* the note on which a system of notes is founded; the tonic. **2.** the main interest or determining principle of a conference, political campaign, advertising campaign, etc.

keypad /'kipæd/ *n.* a panel containing a set of keys for entering data or commands into an electronic machine, system, etc.

keystone /'kistoʊn/ *n.* something on which associated things depend.

keystroke /'kistroʊk/ *n.* an instance of pressing down a key on a typewriter or computer keyboard.

khaki /'ka'ki, 'kaki/ *n.* (*pl.* **-kis**) **1. a.** dull yellowish brown. **b.** a dull green with a yellowish or brownish tinge. **2.** stout twilled cotton uniform cloth of this colour, worn especially by soldiers.

kibbutz /kɪ'bʊts/ *n.* (*pl.* **kibbutzim** /kɪ'bʊtsɪm, kɪbʊt'sim/) (in Israel) a communal agricultural settlement.

kick /kɪk/ *v.t.* **1.** to strike with the foot. **2.** to drive, force, make, etc., by or as by kicks. **3.** to strike in recoiling. **4.** *Football* to score (a goal) by a kick. *–v.i.* **5.** to strike out with the foot. **6.** *Colloq.* to resist, object, or complain. **7.** to recoil, as a firearm when fired. *–n.* **8.** the act of kicking; a blow or thrust with the foot. **9.** power or disposition to kick. **10.** the right of or a turn at kicking. **11.** a recoil, as of a gun. **12.** *Colloq.* any thrill or excitement that gives pleasure. **13.** *Colloq.* vigour or energy. *–phr.* **14. kick out,** *Colloq.* to dismiss; get rid of.

kickback /'kɪkbæk/ *n. Colloq.* **1.** a response, usually vigorous. **2.** any sum paid for favours received or hoped for.

kickboxing /'kɪkbɒksɪŋ/ *n.* a form of boxing popular in Asian countries, in which the

opponent can be kicked with the bare feet. **–kickboxer,** *n.* **–kickbox,** *v.*

kid¹ /kɪd/ *n.* **1.** a young goat. **2.** leather made from the skin of a young goat. **3.** *Colloq.* a child or young person.

kid² /kɪd/ *v.t.* (**kidded, kidding**) *Colloq.* to tease; banter; jest with.

kidnap /'kɪdnæp/ *v.t.* (**-napped, -napping**) to carry off (a person) against their will by unlawful force or by fraud, often with a demand for ransom. **–kidnapper,** *n.*

kidney /'kɪdni/ *n.* (*pl.* **-neys**) either of a pair of bean-shaped glandular organs which excrete urine.

kidney bean *n.* a kind of bean with a somewhat kidney-shaped seed.

kikuyu /kaɪ'kuju/ *n.* a perennial grass widely used as a lawn grass.

kill /kɪl/ *v.t.* **1.** to deprive (any living creature or thing) of life. **2.** to destroy. **3.** to defeat or veto (a legislative bill, etc.). *–v.i.* **4.** to inflict or cause death. *–n.* **5.** the act of killing (game, etc.). **6.** an animal or animals killed.

killing /'kɪlɪŋ/ *n. Colloq.* a stroke of extraordinary success, as in a successful speculation in stocks.

kiln /kɪln/ *n.* a furnace or oven for burning, baking, or drying something, especially one for baking bricks.

kilo /'kiloʊ/ *n.* → **kilogram.**

kilo- a prefix denoting 10^3 of a given unit, as in *kilogram.* *Symbol:* k

kilobit /'kɪləbɪt/ *n. Computers* a unit of measurement of computer storage equal to 2^{10} (1024) bits. *Abbrev.:* Kb

kilobyte /'kɪləbaɪt/ *n.* a unit of measurement of computer storage, equal to 2^{10} (1024) bytes. *Symbol:* KB, kbyte

kilogram /'kɪləgræm/ *n.* a unit of weight in the metric system, equal to 1000 grams. *Symbol:* kg Also, **kilo.**

kilohertz /'kɪləhɜts/ *n.* a unit of frequency equal to 1000 hertz; commonly used to express radiofrequency. *Symbol:* kHz

kilojoule /'kɪlədʒul/ *n.* a measure of work or energy in the metric system, equal to 1000 joules or the amount of food needed to produce it. *Symbol:* kJ

kilometre /'kɪləmitə, kə'lɒmətə/ *n.* a unit of length in the metric system, equal to 1000 metres. *Symbol:* km

kilopascal /'kɪləpæskəl/ *n.* a unit of pressure equal to 1000 pascals; used to express the amount of pressure in tyres, pumps, etc. *Symbol:* kPa

kilowatt /'kɪləwɒt/ *n.* a unit of power equal to 1000 watts. *Symbol:* kW

kilowatt hour *n.* a unit of energy equivalent to that transferred or expended in one hour by one kilowatt of power, 3.6×10^6 joules. *Symbol:* kW.h

kilt /kɪlt/ *n.* any short, pleated skirt, especially one worn by men in the Scottish Highlands.

kilter /'kɪltə/ *n.* good condition; order.

kimono /'kɪmənoʊ, kə'moʊnoʊ/ *n.* (*pl.* **-nos**) a wide-sleeved robe characteristic of Japanese costume.

kin /kɪn/ *n.* relatives collectively.

-kin a diminutive suffix, attached to nouns to signify a little object of the kind mentioned.

kind[1] /kaɪnd/ *adj.* of a good or benevolent nature or disposition, as a person. **–kindness, kindliness,** *n.* **–kindly,** *adj., adv.*

kind[2] /kaɪnd/ *n.* **1.** a class or group of individuals of the same nature or character. **2.** nature or character as determining likeness or difference between things. *–phr.* **3. in kind,** in something of the same kind in the same way. **4. kind of,** (*used adverbially*) *Colloq.* after a fashion; to some extent.

kindergarten /ˈkɪndəɡatn/ *n.* **1.** a school for young children, usually under the age of five. **2.** *Chiefly NSW* the first year in primary school.

kindle /ˈkɪndəl/ *v.t.* **1.** to set (a fire, flame, etc.) burning or blazing. **2.** to excite; animate, rouse, or inflame.

kindling /ˈkɪndlɪŋ/ *n.* material for starting a fire.

kindred /ˈkɪndrəd/ *n.* **1.** a body of persons related to one another, or a family, tribe, or people. *–adj.* **2.** associated by origin, nature, qualities, etc.

kinetic /kəˈnɛtɪk, kaɪ-/ *adj.* **1.** relating to motion. **2.** caused by motion.

kinetics /kəˈnɛtɪks, kaɪ-/ *n.* the branch of mechanics which treats of the action of forces in producing or changing the motion of masses.

king /kɪŋ/ *n.* **1.** a male sovereign or monarch. **2.** a chess piece.

kingdom /ˈkɪŋdəm/ *n.* **1.** a state or government having a king or queen as its head. **2.** a realm or province of nature. **3.** *Biol.* a classification of the highest rank, grouping together forms of life which share certain fundamental characteristics.

kingfisher /ˈkɪŋfɪʃə/ *n.* any of numerous fish or insect-eating birds.

king parrot *n.* a large endemic parrot of eastern Australia, the male having a scarlet head, neck and underparts, the female having a light green head and neck.

kingpin /ˈkɪŋpɪn/ *n. Colloq.* the principal person or element in a company or system, etc.

king prawn *n.* a large, edible prawn of eastern Australian waters.

King's Counsel *n.* (in some legal systems) a member of the senior of the two grades of barrister. *Abbrev.:* KC Also, (*when the reigning monarch is a woman*), **Queen's Counsel.**

kink /kɪŋk/ *n.* **1.** a twist or curl, as in a thread, rope, or hair, caused by its doubling or bending upon itself. **2.** a deviation, especially sexual. **–kinky,** *adj.*

kinship /ˈkɪnʃɪp/ *n.* **1.** the state or fact of being of kin; family relationship. **2.** relationship by nature, qualities, etc.

kinship name *n.* → **skin name.**

kiosk /ˈkiɒsk/ *n.* **1.** a small, light structure for the sale of newspapers, cigarettes, etc. **2.** → **canteen** (def. 2).

kip /kɪp/ *n. Colloq.* a sleep.

kipper /ˈkɪpə/ *n.* a smoked fish, especially a herring.

kismet /ˈkɪzmət, ˈkɪs-/ *n.* fate; destiny.

kiss /kɪs/ *v.t.* **1.** to touch or press with the lips, while compressing and then separating them, in token of greeting, affection, etc. *–n.* **2.** the act of kissing.

kiss of life *n.* **1.** mouth-to-mouth resuscitation. **2.** any action, event, etc., which offers new hopes of success to an enterprise previously considered destined to fail.

kit /kɪt/ *n.* **1.** a set or collection of tools, supplies, etc., for a specific purpose. **2.** a set or collection of parts to be assembled.

kitchen /ˈkɪtʃən/ *n.* a room or place equipped for or appropriated to cooking.

kite /kaɪt/ *n.* **1.** a light frame covered with some thin material, to be flown in the wind at the end of a long string. **2.** any of various medium-sized hawks.

kiteboard /ˈkaɪtbɔd/ *n.* **1.** a small surfboard used in kitesurfing. *–v.i.* **2.** to engage in the sport of kitesurfing. **–kiteboarder,** *n.*

kitesurfing /ˈkaɪtsɜfɪŋ/ *n.* the sport of riding a kiteboard whilst being pulled by a motorboat and supported by a large controllable kite. Also, **kiteboarding.**

kith /kɪθ/ *phr.* **kith and kin,** friends and relatives.

kitsch /kɪtʃ/ *n.* pretentious or worthless art, literature, etc.

kitten /ˈkɪtn/ *n.* a young cat.

kitty /ˈkɪti/ *n.* (*pl.* **-ties**) a jointly held fund or collection, usually of small amounts of money.

kiwi /ˈkiwi/ *n.* any of several flightless birds of NZ.

kiwifruit /ˈkiwifrut/ *n.* an oval-shaped, hairy fruit about 7 cm long with a somewhat gooseberry-like flavour; Chinese gooseberry. Also, **Kiwi fruit.**

klaxon /ˈklæksən/ *n.* (*from trademark*) a type of warning hooter with a strident tone, originally used in motor vehicles.

kleptomania /klɛptəˈmeɪniə/ *n. Psychol.* an irresistible desire to steal, without regard to personal needs. **–kleptomaniac,** *n.*

knack /næk/ *n.* a faculty or power of doing something with ease as from special skill; aptitude.

knacker /ˈnækə/ *n.* someone who buys old or useless horses for slaughter. **–knackery,** *n.*

knapsack /ˈnæpsæk/ *n.* a backpack, originally one of leather or canvas. Also, **rucksack.**

knave /neɪv/ *n.* **1.** an unprincipled or dishonest fellow. **2.** *Cards* a playing card bearing the formalised picture of a prince; jack. **–knavery,** *n.* **–knavish,** *adj.*

knead /nid/ *v.t.* to work (dough, etc.) into a uniform mixture by pressing, folding and stretching.

knee /ni/ *n.* **1.** the joint or region in humans between the thigh and the lower part of the leg. *–v.t.* (**kneed, kneeing**) **2.** to strike or touch with the knee.

kneecap /ˈnikæp/ *n.* the flat, movable bone at the front of the knee.

kneejerk /ˈnidʒɜk/ *phr.* **kneejerk reaction,** an instinctive response to an event, situation, etc.

kneel /nil/ *v.i.* (**knelt** or **kneeled, kneeling**) to fall or rest on the knees or a knee.

knell /nɛl/ *n.* the sound made by a bell rung slowly for a death or a funeral.

knew /nju/ *v.* past tense of **know**.

knickerbockers /ˈnɪkəbɒkəz/ *pl. n.* loosely fitting short breeches gathered in at the knee.

knickers /ˈnɪkəz/ *pl. n.* **1.** women's underpants. **2.** → **knickerbockers**.

knick-knack /ˈnɪk-næk/ *n.* **1.** a pleasing trinket. **2.** a bit of bric-a-brac. Also, **nick-nack**.

knife /naɪf/ *n.* (*pl.* **knives**) **1.** a cutting instrument consisting essentially of a thin blade (usually of steel and with a sharp edge) attached to a handle. –*v.t.* (**knifed**, **knifing**) **2.** to apply a knife to; cut, stab, etc., with a knife.

knight /naɪt/ *n.* **1.** *Hist.* a man, usually of noble birth, bound to chivalrous conduct. **2.** a man upon whom a certain dignity, and with it the honorific *Sir*, is conferred by a sovereign for life, because of personal merit or for services rendered to the country. **3.** a chess piece. –*v.t.* **4.** to dub or create (a person) a knight.

knit /nɪt/ *v.* (**knitted** *or* **knit**, **knitting**) –*v.t.* **1.** to make (a garment, fabric, etc.) by interlacing loops of yarn either by hand with knitting needles or by machine. **2.** to join closely and firmly together, as members or parts. –*v.i.* **3.** to perform the action of knitting, especially by hand: *can you knit?* **4.** to become closely and firmly joined together; grow together, as broken bones do. **5.** to contract, as the brow does. –*n.* **6.** fabric produced by interlooping of a yarn or yarns. –*phr.* **7. knit together**, to form a closely bound unit.

knives /naɪvz/ *n.* plural of **knife**.

knob /nɒb/ *n.* **1.** a projecting part, usually rounded, forming the handle of a door, drawer, or the like. **2.** a rounded lump or protuberance. **–knobby, knobbly,** *adj.*

knock /nɒk/ *v.i.* **1.** to strike a sounding blow with the fist, knuckles, or anything hard, especially on a door, as in seeking admittance, giving a signal, etc. **2.** (of an internal-combustion engine) to make a metallic noise as a result of faulty combustion. **3.** (usu. fol. by *against* or *into*) to collide. –*v.t.* **4.** to give a sounding or forcible blow to. **5.** to drive, force or render by a blow or blows. **6.** to strike (a thing) against something else. **7.** *Colloq.* to criticise; find fault with. –*n.* **8.** the act or sound of knocking. –*phr.* **9. knock back**, *Colloq.* **a.** to refuse. **b.** to consume, especially rapidly. **10. knock off**, *Colloq.* to stop an activity, especially work. **11. knock off**, *Colloq.* to stop an activity, especially work. **12. knock out**, to render senseless.

knockback /ˈnɒkbæk/ *n. Colloq.* a refusal; rejection. Also, **knock-back**.

knockout /ˈnɒkaʊt/ *n.* **1.** the act of knocking out. **2.** *Colloq.* a person or thing that excites admiration. **3.** *Colloq.* an extremely good-looking person.

knoll /nɒl/ *n.* a small, rounded hill or eminence; a hillock.

knot /nɒt/ *n.* **1.** an interlacement of a cord, rope, or the like, drawn tight into a lump or knob, as for fastening two cords, etc., together or to something else. **2.** the hard, cross-grained mass of wood at the place where a branch joins the trunk of a tree. **3.** a unit of speed, used in marine and aerial navigation, and in meteorology. –*v.* (**knotted**, **knotting**) –*v.t.* **4.** to tie in

a knot or knots; form a knot or knots in. –*v.i.* **5.** to become tied or tangled in a knot or knots.

know /noʊ/ *v.* (**knew, known, knowing**) –*v.t.* **1.** to perceive or understand as fact or truth, or apprehend with clearness and certainty. **2.** to have fixed in the mind or memory. **3.** to be cognisant or aware of; to be acquainted with (a thing, place, person, etc.), as by sight, experience, or report. **4.** (fol. by *how* before an infinitive) to understand from experience or attainment. –*v.i.* **5.** to have knowledge, or clear and certain perception, as of fact or truth. **6.** to be cognisant or aware, as of some fact, circumstances, or occurrence; have information, as about something.

know-all /ˈnoʊ-ɔl/ *n. Colloq.* someone who claims to know everything, or everything about a particular subject. Also, **know-it-all**.

knowledge /ˈnɒlɪdʒ/ *n.* **1.** familiarity with facts, truths, or principles, as gained from study, examination, research, experience or report. **2.** the body of truths or facts built up by humankind in the course of time. **3.** the fact or state of knowing. **4.** something that is known, or may be known. **5.** the sum of what is known. **6.** *Law or Archaic* sexual intercourse: *carnal knowledge.* **–knowledgeable,** *adj.*

knuckle /ˈnʌkəl/ *n.* **1.** a joint of a finger. –*v.i.* **2.** (fol. by *down*) to apply oneself vigorously or earnestly, as to a task. **3.** (oft. fol. by *down* or *under*) to yield or submit.

knurl /nɜl/ *n.* **1.** a small ridge or the like, especially one of a series. –*v.t.* **2.** to make knurls or ridges on.

koala /koʊˈɑlə/ *n.* a tailless, grey, furry, arboreal marsupial. Also, **koala bear**.

kofta /ˈkɒftə/ *n.* an Indian dish of seasoned minced meat, shaped into small balls and cooked.

kohl /koʊl/ *n.* a powder, used to darken the eyelids, emphasise eyebrows, etc.

komodo dragon /kəˈmoʊdoʊ/ *n.* a giant monitor of the island of Komodo in Indonesia; up to 3.5 m long.

kook /kuk/ *n. Colloq.* a strange or eccentric person. **–kooky,** *adj.*

kookaburra /ˈkʊkəbʌrə/ *n.* either of two Australian kingfishers renowned for their call resembling human laughter.

kosher /ˈkɒʃə, ˈkoʊʃə/ *adj.* fit, lawful, or ritually permitted, according to the Jewish law.

kowtow /kaʊˈtaʊ/ *v.i.* to act in an obsequious manner; show servile deference.

Kris Kringle /krɪs ˈkrɪŋgəl/ *n.* (*sometimes lower case*) → **Secret Santa**. Also, **Kriss Kringle**.

kudos /ˈkjudɒs/ *n.* glory; renown.

kumara /ˈkumərə/ *n.* a sweet potato with a yellow to dark orange flesh. Also, **kumera**.

kumquat /ˈkʌmkwɒt/ *n.* → **cumquat**.

kung-fu /kʊŋ-ˈfu, kʌŋ-ˈfu/ *n.* an ancient Chinese martial art with fluid hand and leg movements used for self-defence and resembling karate.

kurrajong /ˈkʌrədʒɒŋ/ *n.* a tree of eastern Australia, valued as fodder. Also, **currajong**.

kylie /ˈkaɪli/ *n.* a boomerang having one side flat and the other curved. Also, **kiley**.

L, l

L, l /ɛl/ *n.* the 12th letter of the English alphabet.

label /'leɪbəl/ *n.* **1.** a slip of paper or other material for affixing to something to indicate its nature, ownership, destination, etc. **2.** *Colloq.* a trade name, as of a record company, fashion house, etc. –*v.t.* (**-belled, -belling**) **3.** to affix a label to; mark with a label.

labor /'leɪbə/ *n.* → **labour.**

laboratory /lə'bɒrətri/, *Orig. US* /'læbrətɔri/ *n.* (*pl.* **-ries**) a building or part of a building fitted with apparatus for conducting scientific investigations, experiments, tests, etc., or for manufacturing chemicals, medicines, etc.

laborious /lə'bɔriəs/ *adj.* requiring much labour, exertion, or perseverance.

labour /'leɪbə/ *n.* **1.** bodily toil for the sake of gain or economic production. **2.** Also, **labour force**. the workers engaged in this. **3.** work, especially of a hard or fatiguing kind. **4.** the time during which the uterine contractions of childbirth occur. –*v.i.* **5.** to perform labour; exert one's powers of body or mind; work; toil. Also, **labor**.

labour-intensive /'leɪbər-ɪn,tɛnsɪv/ *adj.* of or relating to an industry which, while not needing a very large capital investment in plant, etc., requires a comparatively small labour force (opposed to *capital-intensive*). Also, **labor-intensive**.

labrador /'læbrədɒ/ *n.* one of a breed of dogs with black or golden coats.

labyrinth /'læbərɪnθ, 'læbrənθ/ *n.* an intricate combination of passages in which it is difficult to find one's way or to reach the exit.

lace /leɪs/ *n.* **1.** a netlike ornamental fabric made of threads by hand or machine. **2.** a cord or string for holding or drawing together, as when passed through holes in opposite edges. –*v.t.* (**laced, lacing**) **3.** to fasten, draw together, or compress by means of a lace. **4.** to intermix, as coffee with spirits. –**lacy,** *adj.*

lacerate /'læsəreɪt/ *v.t.* **1.** to tear roughly; mangle. **2.** to hurt. –**laceration,** *n.*

lack /læk/ *n.* **1.** deficiency or absence of something requisite, desirable, or customary. –*v.t.* **2.** to be deficient in, destitute of, or without.

lackadaisical /lækə'deɪzɪkəl/ *adj.* sentimentally or affectedly languishing; weakly sentimental; listless.

lacklustre /'læklʌstə, læk'lʌstə/ *adj.* lacking lustre or brightness; dull.

laconic /lə'kɒnɪk/ *adj.* using few words.

lacquer /'lækə/ *n.* a resinous varnish.

lactate /læk'teɪt/ *v.i.* to produce milk.

lactic acid *n. Chem.* an acid found in sour milk and in muscle tissue after exercise.

lactobacillus /,læktoʊbə'sɪləs/ *n.* (*pl.* **-cilli** /-'sɪlaɪ/) any bacterium which produces large amounts of lactic acid in the fermentation of carbohydrates, especially in milk.

lactose /'læktoʊz, -oʊs/ *n.* a crystalline disaccharide, $C_{12}H_{22}O_{11}$, present in milk, used as a food and in medicine.

lad /læd/ *n.* **1.** a boy or youth. **2.** *Colloq.* a young man typically wearing brand-name clothing and presenting an image of an aggressive troublemaker.

ladder /'lædə/ *n.* **1.** a structure of wood, metal, or rope, commonly consisting of two side-pieces between which a series of bars or rungs are set at suitable distances, forming a means of ascent or descent. **2.** a line or a place in a stocking, etc., where a series of stitches have slipped out or come undone.

lade /leɪd/ *v.t.* (**laded, laden** *or* **laded, lading**) to put (something) on or in as a burden, load, or cargo; load.

laden /'leɪdn/ *adj.* **1.** loaded; burdened. **2.** filled: *a tree laden with fruit.*

ladette /læ'dɛt/ *n. Colloq.* a young female partner of a lad (def. 2), with similar dress style and behaviour.

ladle /'leɪdl/ *n.* **1.** a long-handled utensil with a dish-shaped or cup-shaped bowl for dipping or conveying liquids. –*v.t.* **2.** to dip or convey with or as with a ladle.

lady /'leɪdi/ *n.* (*pl.* **-dies**) **1.** a woman of good family or social position, or of good breeding, refinement, etc. (correlative of *gentleman*). **2.** a polite term for any woman. **3.** a prefix to a title of honour or respect.

ladybird /'leɪdibɜd/ *n.* a beetle of graceful form and delicate colouration. Also, **lady beetle, ladybug.**

lady-in-waiting /,leɪdi-ɪn-'weɪtɪŋ/ *n.* (*pl.* **ladies-in-waiting**) a woman who is in attendance upon a queen or princess.

lag /læg/ *v.i.* (**lagged, lagging**) (oft. fol. by *behind*) to move slowly; fall behind; hang back.

lager /'lagə/ *n.* a German type of beer.

laggard /'lægəd/ *adj.* **1.** lagging; backward; slow. –*n.* **2.** someone who lags; lingerer.

lagoon /lə'gun/ *n.* any small, pond-like body of water.

laid /leɪd/ *v.* past tense and past participle of **lay**[1].

laid-back *adj.* relaxed; at ease. Also, **laidback.**

lain /leɪn/ *v.* past participle of **lie**[2].

lair[1] /lɛə/ *n.* the den or resting place of a wild beast.

lair[2] /lɛə/ *n. Colloq.* a flashily dressed young man of brash and vulgar behaviour.

laird /lɛəd/ *n.* in Scotland, a landed proprietor.

lairy /'lɛəri/ *adj. Colloq.* **1.** exhibitionistic; flashy. **2.** vulgar.

laissez faire /,leɪseɪ 'fɛə/ *n.* **1.** the theory or system of government that holds that economic systems best govern themselves and that governments should therefore intervene as little as possible in economic affairs. **2.** the doctrine of non-interference, especially in the conduct of others. Also, **laisser faire.**

laity /'leɪəti/ *n.* laypeople, as distinguished from members of the clergy.

lake[1] /leɪk/ *n.* a body of water (fresh or salt) of considerable size, surrounded by land.

lake[2] /leɪk/ *n.* a red pigment.

laksa /'lʌksə/ *n.* a spicy Malay dish consisting of fine rice noodles, vegetables, and often seafood, meat or tofu, served in a soup.

lama /'lamə/ *n.* a Buddhist priest or monk.

lamb /læm/ n. a young sheep.

lame /leɪm/ adj. crippled or physically disabled, as a person or animal, especially in the foot or leg so as to limp or walk with difficulty.

lamé /ˈlɑːmeɪ/ n. an ornamental fabric in which metallic threads are woven with silk, wool, artificial fibres, or cotton.

lament /ləˈmɛnt/ v.t. 1. to feel or express sorrow or regret for; mourn for or over. –n. 2. an expression of grief or sorrow. –**lamentable**, adj.

lamina /ˈlæmənə/ n. (pl. -nae /-niː/ or -nas) a thin plate, scale, or layer.

laminate /ˈlæmineɪt/ v.t. 1. to separate or split into thin layers. 2. to construct by placing layer upon layer.

lamington /ˈlæmɪŋtən/ n. a cake confection made by covering a cube of sponge cake in chocolate icing and shredded coconut.

lamp /læmp/ n. any of various devices for using an illuminant, as gas or electricity, or for heating, as by burning alcohol.

lampoon /læmˈpuːn/ n. a malicious or virulent satire upon a person, institution, government, etc., in either prose or verse.

lamprey /ˈlæmpri/ n. (pl. -reys or -rey) an eel-like fish.

lance /lɑːns, læns/ n. 1. a long, shafted weapon with a metal head, used by mounted soldiers in charging. –v.t. (**lanced, lancing**) 2. to pierce with or as with a lance.

land /lænd/ n. 1. the solid substance of the earth's surface. 2. a particular area of the surface of the land, especially with regard to its ownership, quality, appearance, etc. 3. a country or nation. 4. agricultural areas as opposed to urban. 5. Econ. natural resources as a factor of production. –v.t. 6. to bring to or put on land or shore. 7. (fol. by with) to give (someone) a task which they may be unwilling to perform. 8. Colloq. to attain: to land a good job. –v.i. 9. (of an aircraft) to return to the ground after flight. 10. to alight upon the ground after jumping. etc.

landcare /ˈlændkeə/ n. the sustainable management of the environment and natural resources in agriculture. Also, **land care**.

land claim n. 1. a claim for ownership of land. 2. a claim by an Indigenous community for ownership of land under native title.

landfill /ˈlændfɪl/ n. 1. material as garbage, building refuse, etc., deposited under layers of earth to raise the level of the site. 2. the area raised in this fashion.

landing /ˈlændɪŋ/ n. 1. the act of arriving on land as by a plane, etc. 2. the floor at the head or foot of a flight of stairs.

landlady /ˈlændleɪdi/ n. (pl. -ladies) 1. a woman who owns and leases land, buildings, etc. 2. a woman who owns or runs an inn, lodging house, or boarding house.

landline /ˈlændlaɪn/ n. a telecommunications line running under or over the ground. Also, **land-line**.

landlord /ˈlændlɔːd/ n. 1. someone who owns and leases land, buildings, etc., to another. 2. the proprietor of a hotel.

landlubber /ˈlændlʌbə/ n. Naut. someone who lives on land.

landmark /ˈlændmɑːk/ n. 1. a conspicuous object on land that serves as a guide, as to vessels at sea. 2. a prominent or distinguishing feature, part, event, etc.

landmass /ˈlændmæs/ n. a body of land, usually extensive, as a large island or continent, surrounded by water. Also, **land mass**.

land rights pl. n. the rights of the original inhabitants of a country to possess their traditional land.

landscape /ˈlændskeɪp/ n. a view or prospect of rural scenery, more or less extensive, such as is comprehended within the scope or range of vision from a single point of view.

landslide /ˈlændslaɪd/ n. 1. the sliding down of a mass of soil, detritus, or rock on a steep slope. 2. any overwhelming victory.

land tax n. a tax on land the unimproved value of which exceeds a certain sum.

lane /leɪn/ n. 1. a narrow way or passage between fences, walls, or houses. 2. any narrow or well-defined passage, track, channel, or course.

language /ˈlæŋgwɪdʒ, ˈlæŋwɪdʒ/ n. 1. communication in the distinctively human manner, using a system of arbitrary symbols with conventionally assigned meanings, as by voice, writing, or sign language. 2. any set or system of such symbols as used in a more or less uniform fashion by a number of people, who are thus enabled to communicate intelligibly with one another.

languid /ˈlæŋgwəd/ adj. 1. lacking in spirit or interest; indifferent. 2. lacking in vigour or activity; slack; dull. –**languor**, n.

languish /ˈlæŋgwɪʃ/ v.i. 1. to become or be weak or feeble; droop or fade. 2. to lose activity and vigour. 3. to pine with desire or longing for.

lank /læŋk/ adj. 1. meagrely slim; lean; gaunt. 2. (of hair) straight and limp; not resilient or wiry. –**lankly**, adv.

lanky /ˈlæŋki/ adj. (-kier, -kiest) ungracefully tall and thin; rangy. –**lankily**, adv. –**lankiness**, n.

lanolin /ˈlænəlɪn/ n. a fatty substance, extracted from wool, used in ointments. Also, **lanoline**.

lantana /lænˈtɑːnə/ n. a tropical plant which has become a troublesome weed in some areas.

lantern /ˈlæntən/ n. a transparent or translucent case for enclosing a light and protecting it from the wind, rain, etc.

lap¹ /læp/ n. (the part of the clothing that lies on) the front portion of the body from the waist to the knees when one sits.

lap² /læp/ v.t. (**lapped, lapping**) 1. to fold over or about something; wrap or wind round something. 2. to get a lap or more ahead of (a competitor) in racing. –n. 3. a single round or circuit of the course in racing.

lap³ /læp/ v.t. (**lapped, lapping**) 1. (oft. fol. by up) to take up (liquid) with the tongue; lick up. 2. (fol. by up) to receive and accept avidly.

lapel /ləˈpɛl/ n. part of a garment folded back on the breast, especially a continuation of a coat collar.

lapidary /ˈlæpədəri/ n. (pl. -ries) 1. the shaping and polishing of stones, especially precious stones. 2. someone who cuts, polishes, and engraves stones, especially precious stones.

lapis lazuli /læpəs 'læzjəli, -laı/ n. a deep blue stone.

lapse /læps/ n. **1.** a slip or slight error. **2.** a gliding or passing away, as of time. **3.** a falling, or sinking to a lower grade, condition, or degree. –v.i. (**lapsed, lapsing**) **4.** to pass slowly, silently, or by degrees. **5.** to cease to be in force or use.

laptop /'læptɒp/ n. **1.** a portable computer, small enough to be operated while held on one's knees. –adj. **2.** of or relating to a laptop.

larceny /'lasəni/ n. Law the wrongful taking and carrying away of the personal goods of another.

lard /lad/ n. rendered pig fat.

larder /'ladə/ n. a room or place where food is kept; pantry.

large /ladʒ/ adj. being of more than common size, amount, or number.

largesse /la'dʒɛs/ n. generous bestowal of gifts. Also, **largess**.

lark[1] /lak/ n. a singing bird.

lark[2] /lak/ n. a merry or hilarious adventure; prank.

larrikin /'lærəkən/ n. Colloq. **1.** a hoodlum. **2.** an uncultivated, rowdy, but good-hearted person.

larva /'lavə/ n. (pl. **larvae** /'lavi/ or **larvas**) Entomology the young of any insect which undergoes metamorphosis.

laryngitis /lærən'dʒaıtəs/ n. an inflammation of the larynx often causing temporary loss of the voice.

larynx /'lærɪŋks/ n. (pl. **larynges** /lə'rɪndʒiz/ or **larynxes**) Anat., Zool. the cavity at the upper end of the trachea or windpipe containing the vocal cords.

lasagne /lə'sanjə, lə'zanjə/ n. **1.** a form of pasta cut into flat sheets. **2.** a dish made with this, especially with minced meat, tomato, and cheese. Also, **lasagna**.

lascivious /lə'sɪvıəs/ adj. inclined to lust; wanton or lewd.

laser /'leızə/ n. a device for producing a coherent, monochromatic, high-intensity beam of radiation of a frequency within, or near to, the range of visible light.

laser disc n. a grooveless disc on which digitally-encoded data, as music, text, or pictures, is stored as tiny pits in the surface, and is read or played by a laser beam which scans the surface of the disc. Also, **laser disk**.

lash[1] /læʃ/ n. **1.** the flexible part of a whip. **2.** a swift stroke or blow, with a whip, etc., as a punishment. **3.** an eyelash. –v.t. **4.** to strike or beat, now usually with a whip or something slender and flexible. –v.i. **5.** (oft. fol. by out) to strike vigorously at, as with a weapon, whip, or the like.

lash[2] /læʃ/ v.t. to bind or fasten with a rope, cord, or the like.

lass /læs/ n. a girl or young woman.

lassi /'lasi/ n. a sweet or savoury Indian drink made from yoghurt or buttermilk, mixed with water.

lassitude /'læsətjud/ n. weariness.

lasso /læ'su/ n. (pl. **-sos** or **-soes**) a long rope with a running noose at one end, used for catching horses, cattle, etc.

last[1] /last/ adj. **1.** occurring or coming latest, or after all others, as in time, order, or place. **2.** latest; next before the present; most recent. **3.** being the only remaining. **4.** conclusive. –adv. **5.** after all others. **6.** on the most recent occasion. –n. **7.** that which is last.

last[2] /last/ v.i. to go on, or continue in progress, existence or life; endure.

last[3] /last/ n. a model of the human foot, used in shoemaking.

last post n. a signal on a bugle used to give notice to retire for the night, or at military funerals.

latch /lætʃ/ n. a device for holding a door, gate, or the like closed, consisting basically of a bar falling or sliding into a catch, groove, hole, etc.

late /leıt/ adj. **1.** occurring, coming, or being after the usual or proper time. **2.** far advanced in time. **3.** recently deceased. –adv. **4.** after the usual or proper time, or after delay. **5.** until after the usual time or hour; until a late hour at night.

lately /'leıtli/ adv. recently.

latent /'leıtnt/ adj. hidden; concealed; present, but not visible or apparent. –**latency**, n.

lateral /'lætərəl, 'lætrəl/ adj. of or relating to the side; situated at, proceeding from, or directed to a side.

latex /'leıtɛks/ n. a milky liquid in certain plants, as those yielding rubber.

lath /laθ/ n. (pl. **laths** /laðz, laθs/) a thin, narrow strip of wood.

lathe /leıð/ n. a machine for use in working metal, wood, etc.

lather /'læðə/ n. foam or froth made from soap moistened with water, as by a brush for shaving.

latitude /'lætətjud/ n. **1.** Geog. the angular distance north or south from the equator of a point on the earth's surface, measured on the meridian of the point. **2.** freedom from narrow restrictions; permitted freedom of action, opinion, etc.

latrine /lə'trin/ n. a toilet.

latte /'lateı/ n. → cafe latte.

latter /'lætə/ adj. **1.** being the second mentioned of two (opposed to former). **2.** more advanced in time; later. **3.** nearer, or comparatively near, to the end or close. –phr. **4. the latter**, the item or person (out of two) last mentioned.

lattice /'lætəs/ n. a structure of crossed wooden or metal strips with open spaces between, used as a screen, fence, etc.

laud /lɔd/ v.t. to praise; extol.

laugh /laf/ v.i. **1.** to express mirth, amusement, derision, etc., by an explosive, inarticulate sound of the voice, facial expressions, etc. –n. **2.** the act or sound of laughing, or laughter. **3.** the cry of an animal, as the hyena, or the call of a bird, as a kookaburra, that resembles human laughter. **4.** (often ironic) a cause for laughter. –phr. **5. have the (last) laugh**, to prove ultimately successful; win after an earlier defeat. –**laughter**, n.

launch[1] /lɔntʃ/ n. a heavy open or half-decked boat.

launch[2] /lɔntʃ/ v.t. **1.** to set (a boat) afloat; lower into the water. **2.** to set going.

launder /'lɔndə/ v.t. **1.** to wash and iron (clothes, etc.). **2.** to transfer (funds of suspect or illegal origin) usually to a foreign country, and then later to recover them from sources which give them the appearance of being legitimate.

laundromat /ˈlɔndrəmæt/ *n. Orig. US* a public laundry with coin-operated washing machines, dryers, etc. Also, **laundrette**.

laundry /ˈlɔndri/ *n.* (*pl.* **-dries**) **1.** articles of clothing, etc., to be washed. **2.** the room in a house set aside for the washing of clothes. **3.** the act of laundering.

laurel /ˈlɒrəl/ *n.* **1.** a small evergreen tree. **2.** (*usu. pl.*) honour won, as by achievement.

laurel wreath *n.* a wreath made from the foliage of the laurel or bay tree, seen as an emblem of distinction.

lava /ˈlavə/ *n.* the molten or fluid rock (magma), which issues from a volcanic vent.

lavatory /ˈlævətri/ *n.* (*pl.* **-ries**) (a room with) a toilet.

lavender /ˈlævəndə/ *n.* a plant with fragrant, pale purple flowers.

lavish /ˈlævɪʃ/ *adj.* **1.** (oft. fol. by *in*, *with* or *of*) using or bestowing in great abundance or without stint: *lavish in one's praise*. *–v.t.* **2.** to expend or bestow in great abundance or without stint.

law /lɔ/ *n.* **1.** the principles and regulations emanating from a government and applicable to a people. **2.** the profession which deals with law and legal procedure. **3.** (in philosophical and scientific use) a statement of a relation or sequence of phenomena invariable under the same conditions. **–lawful**, *adj.*

lawn[1] /lɔn/ *n.* a stretch of grass-covered land, especially one closely mowed.

lawn[2] /lɔn/ *n.* a thin or sheer linen or cotton fabric, either plain or printed.

lawn bowls *n.* a game in which the players roll biased or weighted balls along a green in an effort to bring them as near as possible to a stationary ball called the jack.

lawyer /ˈlɔɪjə, ˈlɔɪə/ *n.* someone whose profession it is to conduct suits in court or to give legal advice and aid.

lax /læks/ *adj.* **1.** lacking in strictness or severity; careless or negligent. **2.** loose or slack; not tense, rigid, or firm.

laxative /ˈlæksətɪv/ *adj. Med.* mildly purgative.

lay[1] /leɪ/ *v.* (**laid**, **laying**) *–v.t.* **1.** to put or place in a position of rest or recumbency. **2.** to bring forth and deposit. **3.** (fol. by *by*) to put away for future use. **4.** to set. **5.** to present, bring forward, or prefer, as a claim, charge, etc. **6.** to place on or over a surface, as paint; cover or spread with something else. *–v.i.* **7.** to lay eggs. **8.** to apply oneself vigorously. *–n.* **9.** the way or position in which a thing is laid or lies. *–phr.* **10. lay off**, **a.** to put aside. **b.** to dismiss, especially temporarily, as an employee. **c.** *Colloq.* to desist. **11. lay on**, to provide or supply.

lay[2] /leɪ/ *v.* past tense of **lie**[2].

lay[3] /leɪ/ *adj.* belonging to, relating to, or performed by the people or laity, as distinguished from the clergy.

lay-by /ˈleɪbaɪ/ *n.* the reservation of an article by payment of a cash deposit. Also, **layby**.

layer /ˈleɪə/ *n.* a thickness of some material laid on or spread over a surface; a stratum.

layman /ˈleɪmən/ *n.* (*pl.* **-men**) a male layperson.

layout /ˈleɪaʊt/ *n.* an arrangement or plan.

layperson /ˈleɪpɜːsən/ *n.* **1.** one of the laity; someone who is not a member of the clergy. **2.** someone who is not a member of a particular profession. Also, **lay person**.

laze /leɪz/ *v.i.* to be lazy; idle or lounge lazily.

lazy /ˈleɪzi/ *adj.* (**-zier**, **-ziest**) **1.** disinclined to exertion or work; idle. **2.** not spent in work or effort: *a lazy afternoon*.

LDL /ɛl di ˈɛl/ *n.* low-density lipoprotein; a substance which forms the greater part of the cholesterol in the blood and which, in large amounts, can cause a build-up of cholesterol on the artery walls. See **bad cholesterol**. Compare **HDL**.

leach /liːtʃ/ *v.t.* to cause (water, etc.) to percolate through something.

lead[1] /liːd/ *v.* (**led**, **leading**) *–v.t.* **1.** to take or conduct on the way; go before or with to show the way. **2.** to guide in direction, course, action, opinion, etc.; to influence or induce. **3.** to conduct or bring (water, wire, etc.) in a particular course. **4.** to be at the head of, command, or direct (an army, organisation, etc.). **5.** to go through or pass (life, etc.). *–v.i.* **6.** to act as a guide; show the way. **7.** to afford passage to a place, etc., as a road, stairway, or the like. **8.** to go first; be in advance. *–n.* **9.** the first or foremost place; position in advance of others. **10.** the extent of advance. **11.** a thong or line for holding a dog or other animal in check. **12.** a guiding indication; clue. **13.** *Elect.* a single conductor, often flexible and insulated, used in connections between pieces of electrical apparatus. *–adj.* **14.** solo or dominating as in a musical structure.

lead[2] /lɛd/ *n.* **1.** *Chem.* a heavy, comparatively soft, malleable bluish-grey metal. *Symbol*: Pb **2.** a plummet or mass of lead suspended by a line, as for taking soundings.

leaded petrol *n.* petrol that contains small amounts of the metal lead and therefore is environmentally damaging.

leaden /ˈlɛdn/ *adj.* **1.** consisting or made of lead. **2.** inertly heavy, or hard to lift or move, as weight, the limbs, etc.

leader /ˈliːdə/ *n.* **1.** someone who or that which leads. **2.** a principal or important editorial article, as in a newspaper.

leaf /liːf/ *n.* (*pl.* **leaves**) **1.** one of the expanded, usually green, organs borne by the stem of a plant. **2.** any of the sheets of paper, usually printed on both sides, that make up the pages of a book. **3.** a thin sheet of metal, etc. **4.** a sliding, hinged, or detachable flat part, as of a door, tabletop, etc. *–phr.* **5. leaf through**, to turn the pages of quickly.

leaflet /ˈliːflət/ *n.* a small flat or folded sheet of printed matter, as for distribution.

league[1] /liːɡ/ *n.* **1.** a covenant or compact made between persons, parties, states, etc., for the maintenance or promotion of common interests or for mutual assistance or service. **2.** the aggregation of persons, parties, states, etc., associated in such a covenant; a confederacy.

league[2] /liːɡ/ *n.* a former unit of distance.

leak /liːk/ *n.* **1.** an unintended hole, crack, or the like by which fluid, gas, etc., enters or escapes. **2.** an accidental or apparently accidental disclosure of information, etc. *–v.i.* **3.** to let fluid, gas, etc., enter or escape, as through an unintended hole, crack, permeable material, or the like. **4.** to pass in or out in this manner, as water, etc. **5.** (fol. by *out*) to transpire or become known undesignedly. *–v.t.* **6.** to disclose (information, especially of a confidential nature), especially to the media. **–leakage,** *n.*

lean¹ /lin/ *v.i.* (**leaned** *or* **leant** /lɛnt/, **leaning**) **1.** to incline or bend from a vertical position or in a particular direction. **2.** to rest against or on something for support. **3.** to depend or rely.

lean² /lin/ *adj.* **1.** (of persons or animals) scant of flesh; thin; not plump or fat. **2.** (of meat) containing little or no fat.

leap /lip/ *v.* (**leapt** /lɛpt/ *or* **leaped, leaping**) *–v.i.* **1.** to spring through the air from one point or position to another. **2.** to pass, come, rise, etc., as if with a bound. *–v.t.* **3.** to jump over. *–n.* **4.** a spring, jump, or bound; a light springing movement.

leap year *n.* a year containing 366 days, or one day (29 February) more than the ordinary year.

learn /lɜn/ *v.t.* (**learned** /lɜnd/ *or* **learnt, learning**) to acquire knowledge of or skill in by study, instruction, or experience.

learned /ˈlɜnəd/ *adj.* having much knowledge gained by study; scholarly.

lease /lis/ *n.* **1.** an instrument conveying property to another for a definite period, or at will, usually in consideration of rent or other periodical compensation. *–v.t.* **2.** to grant the temporary possession or use of (lands, etc.) to another, usually for compensation at a fixed rate; let. **3.** to take or to hold by a lease, as a flat, house, etc.

leasehold /ˈlishould/ *n.* **1.** a land interest acquired under a lease. *–adj.* **2.** of or relating to land owned by the crown and which is leased out, usually for a specified time period. Compare **freehold.**

leash /liʃ/ *n.* a lead for a dog.

least /list/ *adj.* **1.** little beyond all others in size, amount, degree, etc.; smallest; slightest. *–n.* **2.** that which is least; the least amount, quantity, degree, etc.

leather /ˈlɛðə/ *n.* the skin of animals prepared for use by tanning or a similar process.

leatherjacket /ˈlɛðədʒækət/ *n.* (pl. **-jackets** *or* **-jacket**) any of numerous species of fish, having a roughened skin which can be removed in one piece like a jacket, and a prominent, erectable dorsal spine.

leave¹ /liv/ *v.* (**left, leaving**) *–v.t.* **1.** to go away from, depart from, or quit, as a place, a person, or a thing. **2.** to let stay or be as specified. **3.** to stop attending or participating in (an institution, job, group, etc.). **4.** (fol. by *out*) to omit or exclude. **5.** to give in charge; give for use after one's death or departure. **6.** to have as a remainder after subtraction. *–v.i.* **7.** to go away, depart, or set out.

leave² /liv/ *n.* **1.** permission to do something. **2.** permission to be absent, as from duty. **3.** a farewell.

leaven /ˈlɛvən/ *n.* a mass of fermenting dough reserved for producing fermentation in a new batch of dough.

lecher /ˈlɛtʃə/ *n.* a man whose behaviour exhibits lustfulness and lewdness, especially one who preys on others. **–lechery,** *n.* **–lecherous,** *adj.*

lectern /ˈlɛktən/ *n.* a reading desk in a church, especially that from which the lessons are read.

lecture /ˈlɛktʃə/ *n.* **1.** a discourse read or delivered before an audience, especially for instruction or to set forth some subject. *–v.i.* **2.** to give a lecture. *–v.t.* **3.** to deliver a lecture to or before.

led /lɛd/ *v.* past tense and past participle of **lead¹.**

ledge /lɛdʒ/ *n.* any relatively narrow, horizontal projecting part, or any part affording a horizontal shelf-like surface.

ledger /ˈlɛdʒə/ *n. Bookkeeping* an account book with columns for credits and debits.

lee¹ /li/ *n.* the side or part that is sheltered or turned away from the wind.

lee² /li/ *n.* (*usu. pl.*) that which settles from a liquid, especially from wine.

leech /litʃ/ *n.* a bloodsucking or carnivorous, usually aquatic, worm.

leek /lik/ *n.* a plant allied to the onion, but having a cylindrical bulb.

leer /lɪə/ *n.* a side glance, especially of sly or insulting suggestion or significance.

leeway /ˈliweɪ/ *n. Colloq.* extra space, time, money, etc.

left¹ /lɛft/ *adj.* **1.** belonging or relating to the side of a person or thing which is turned towards the west when facing north (opposed to *right*). *–n.* **2.** a body of persons, political party, etc., holding socialist, progressive or radical views.

left² /lɛft/ *v.* past tense and past participle of **leave¹.**

left-handed /ˈlɛft-hændəd/ *adj.* having the left hand more serviceable than the right; preferring to use the left hand.

leftover /ˈlɛftoʊvə/ *n.* something left over or remaining.

left wing *n.* members of a socialist, progressive, or radical political party or section of a party, generally those favouring extensive political reform.

leg /lɛg/ *n.* **1.** one of the members or limbs which support and move the human or animal body. **2.** something resembling or suggesting a leg in use, position, or appearance. **3.** one of the distinct portions of any course.

legacy /ˈlɛgəsi/ *n.* (pl. **-cies**) **1.** *Law* a gift of property, especially personal property, as money, by will; a bequest. **2.** a consequence: *a legacy of the war in Syria. –adj.* **3.** handed down from one person or group to another: *a legacy project.*

legal /ˈligəl/ *adj.* **1.** appointed, established, or authorised by law; deriving authority from law. **2.** of or relating to law. **3.** connected with the law or its administration. **–legally,** *adv.* **–legality,** *n.*

legalise /ˈligəlaɪz/ *v.t.* to make legal; authorise; sanction. Also, **legalize. –legalisation,** *n.*

legal tender *n.* currency which may be lawfully tendered or offered in payment of money debts and which may not be refused by creditors.

legate /ˈlɛgət/ *n.* an ecclesiastic delegated by the pope as his representative.

legatee /lɛgə'ti/ n. one to whom a legacy is bequeathed.

legation /lə'geɪʃən/ n. (formerly) a diplomatic mission of lesser rank than an embassy.

legend /'lɛdʒənd/ n. **1.** a non-historical or unverifiable story handed down by tradition from earlier times and popularly accepted as historical. **2.** an inscription. **3.** *Colloq.* a person who is well-regarded, especially for excellence in a particular field or activity: *mate, you're a legend!* **–legendary,** *adj.*

leggings /'lɛgɪŋz/ pl. n. a close-fitting covering for the leg, made of stretch material, similar to tights but stopping at the ankle.

legible /'lɛdʒəbəl/ *adj.* able to be read or deciphered, especially with ease, as writing or printing. **–legibility,** *n.*

legion /'lidʒən/ n. **1.** an infantry brigade in the army of ancient Rome. **2.** one of certain military bodies of modern times, as the Foreign Legion. **3.** any great host or multitude, whether of persons or of things.

legislation /lɛdʒəs'leɪʃən/ n. **1.** the act of making or enacting laws. **2.** a law or a body of laws enacted. **–legislate,** *v.* **–legislative,** *adj.*

Legislative Assembly *n.* the lower chamber of certain bicameral parliaments.

Legislative Council *n.* the upper chamber of certain bicameral parliaments.

legislature /'lɛdʒəsleɪtʃə, -lətʃə/ n. the arm of government whose function is to make, amend and repeal laws, as a parliament.

legitimate /lə'dʒɪtəmət/ *adj.* **1.** according to law; lawful. **2.** born in wedlock, or of parents legally married. **3.** genuine; not spurious. **–legitimacy,** *n.*

legume /'lɛgjum/ n. **1.** a pod-bearing plant. **2.** the pod. **–leguminous,** *adj.*

leisure /'lɛʒə/ n. **1.** the condition of having one's time free from the demands of work or duty; ease. **2.** free or unoccupied time.

leisurely /'lɛʒəli/ *adj.* unhurried.

lemming /'lɛmɪŋ/ n. a small rodent noted for its mass migrations in periods of population increase.

lemon /'lɛmən/ n. **1.** a yellowish acid fruit. **2.** clear, light yellow. **3.** *Colloq.* something distasteful, disappointing, or unpleasant.

lemonade /lɛmə'neɪd/ n. a lemon-flavoured carbonated soft drink.

lend /lɛnd/ v.t. (**lent, lending**) **1.** to give the temporary use of (money, etc.) for a consideration. **2.** to grant the use of (something) with the understanding that it (or its equivalent in kind) shall be returned. **3.** to furnish or impart. **4.** to adapt (oneself or itself) to something.

length /lɛŋθ/ n. **1.** the linear magnitude of anything as measured from end to end. **2.** extent from beginning to end of a series, enumeration, account, book, etc. **3.** a piece or portion of a certain or a known length.

lenient /'liniənt/ *adj.* mild, clement, or merciful, as in treatment, spirit, or tendency; gentle.

lens /lɛnz/ n. (*pl.* **lenses**) a piece of transparent substance, usually glass, having two (or two main) opposite surfaces, either both curved or one curved and one plane, used for changing the convergence of light rays, as in magnifying, or in correcting errors of vision.

lentil /'lɛntəl/ n. a plant with flattened seeds which are used for food.

leonine /'liənaɪn/ *adj.* lion-like.

leopard /'lɛpəd/ n. a large, ferocious, spotted carnivore of the cat family.

leotard /'liətad/ n. a close-fitting one-piece garment worn by acrobats, dancers, etc.

leper /'lɛpə/ n. a person affected with leprosy.

leprechaun /'lɛprəkɔn/ n. (in Irish folklore) a little sprite, or goblin.

leprosy /'lɛprəsi/ n. a mildly infectious disease marked by ulcerations, loss of fingers and toes, etc.

lesbian /'lɛzbiən/ n. **1.** a female homosexual. **–adj.** **2.** relating to female homosexuality. **–lesbianism,** *n.*

lesion /'liʒən/ n. an injury; a hurt; a wound.

less /lɛs/ adv. **1.** to a smaller extent, amount, or degree. **–adj.** **2.** smaller in size, amount, degree, etc.; not so large, great, or much. **–prep.** **3.** minus; without.

-less a suffix of adjectives meaning 'without'.

lessee /lɛ'si/ n. one to whom a lease is granted.

lessen /'lɛsən/ v.i. to become less.

lesser /'lɛsə/ *adj.* **1.** less; smaller, as in size, amount, importance, etc. **2.** being the smaller or less important of two.

lesson /'lɛsən/ n. **1.** something to be learned or studied. **2.** a length of time during which a pupil or class studies one subject.

lessor /lɛ'sɔ, 'lɛsɔ/ n. someone who grants a lease.

lest /lɛst/ conj. **1.** for fear that; that…not; so that…not. **2.** (after words expressing fear, danger, etc.) that.

let[1] /lɛt/ v. (**let, letting**) **–v.t.** **1.** to allow or permit. **2.** (occasionally fol. by *out*) to grant the occupancy or use of (land, buildings, rooms, space, etc., or movable property) for rent or hire. **3.** to cause or make. **4.** (as an auxiliary used to propose or order): *let me see.* **–v.i.** **5.** to be rented or leased.

let[2] /lɛt/ n. *Tennis, etc.* an interference with the course of the ball (of some kind specified in the rules) on account of which the stroke or point must be played over again.

-let a diminutive suffix, used often for little objects, as in *booklet, applet.*

lethal /'liθəl/ *adj.* of, relating to, or such as to cause death; deadly.

lethargic /lə'θadʒɪk/ *adj.* having no energy; having a feeling of sleepy laziness. **–lethargy,** *n.*

letter /'lɛtə/ n. **1.** a communication in writing or printing addressed to a person or a number of persons. **2.** one of the marks or signs conventionally used in writing and printing to represent speech sounds; an alphabetical character.

letterbox /'lɛtəbɒks/ n. **1.** a receptacle with a slot for posting mail. **2.** a box or other shaped receptacle for incoming mail at the front gate of a house or on the inside of the front door. **–v.t.** **3.** to distribute pamphlets, etc., throughout (an area) by placing them in letterboxes.

lettuce /'lɛtəs/ n. a leafy plant, much used in salads.

leukaemia /lu'kimiə/ n. a disease, often fatal, characterised by excessive production of white blood cells. Also, **leukemia.**

leukocyte /'lukəsait/ *n.* one of the white or colourless corpuscles of the blood, concerned in the destruction of disease-producing micro-organisms, etc.; white blood cell. Also, **leucocyte**.

levee /'lɛvi/ *n.* a raised riverside.

level /'lɛvəl/ *adj.* **1.** having no part higher than another; having an even surface. **2.** being in a plane parallel to the plane of the horizon; horizontal. **3.** even, equable, or uniform. –*n.* **4.** a device used for determining, or adjusting something to, a horizontal surface. **5.** a position or plane, high or low. –*v.* (**-elled, -elling**) –*v.t.* **6.** to make level. **7.** to bring (something) to the level of the ground. **8.** to bring (two or more things) to an equality of status, condition, etc. **9.** to aim or point at a mark, as a weapon, criticism, etc. –*v.i.* **10.** (oft. fol. by *out*) to arrive at a common level; stabilise.

lever /'livə/ *n.* a bar or rigid piece acted upon at different points by two forces, as a voluntarily applied force (the *power*) and a resisting force (the *weight*), which generally tend to rotate it in opposite directions about a fixed axis or support (the *fulcrum*).

leverage *n.* /'livərɪdʒ, 'lɛvərɪdʒ/ **1.** the action of a lever. **2.** power of action; means of influence. –*v.t.* /'lɛvərɪdʒ/ (**-raged, -raging**) **3.** *Finance* to borrow funds to finance (a company or a specific venture) in the expectation that profits will be greater than the interest on the loan.

levitate /'lɛvəteɪt/ *v.i.* to rise or float in the air, especially through some allegedly supernatural power that overcomes gravity.

levity /'lɛvəti/ *n.* lightness of mind, character, or behaviour; lack of proper seriousness or earnestness.

levy /'lɛvi/ *n.* (*pl.* **-vies**) **1.** a raising or collecting, as of money or troops, by authority or force. –*v.t.* (**-vied, -vying**) **2.** to impose (a tax).

lewd /lud, ljud/ *adj.* inclined to, characterised by, or inciting to lust or lechery.

lexicon /'lɛksəkən/ *n.* **1.** a wordbook or dictionary, especially of Greek, Latin, or Hebrew. **2.** the total stock of words in a given language. –**lexical**, *adj.*

liability /laɪə'bɪləti/ *n.* (*pl.* **-ties**) **1.** *Law* legal responsibility. **2.** an obligation, especially for payment (opposed to *asset*). **3.** something disadvantageous.

liable /'laɪəbəl/ *adj.* **1.** subject, exposed, or open to something possible or likely, especially something undesirable. **2.** under legal obligation; responsible or answerable.

liaison /li'eɪzɒn, -zɒn/ *n.* a connection or communication between people or groups. –**liaise**, *v.*

liana /li'anə/ *n.* a climbing plant or vine.

liar /'laɪə/ *n.* someone who tells lies.

libel /'laɪbəl/ *n.* *Law* defamation by written or printed words, pictures, or in any form other than by spoken words or gestures.

liberal /'lɪbrəl, 'lɪbərəl/ *adj.* **1.** favourable to progress or reform, as in religious or political affairs. **2.** favourable to or in accord with the policy of leaving the individual as unrestricted as possible in the opportunities for self-expression or self-fulfilment. **3.** giving freely or in ample measure. **4.** not strict or rigorous.

–*n.* **5.** a person of liberal principles or views, especially in religion or politics.

liberate /'lɪbəreɪt/ *v.t.* **1.** to set free; release. **2.** to disengage; set free from combination, as a gas. –**liberation**, *n.* –**liberator**, *n.*

libertine /'lɪbətin/ *n.* someone who is free from restraint or control, especially in moral or sexual matters; a dissolute or licentious person.

liberty /'lɪbəti/ *n.* (*pl.* **-ties**) **1.** freedom from control, interference, obligation, restriction, etc. **2.** freedom from captivity, confinement, or physical restraint. **3.** unwarranted or impertinent freedom in action or speech, or a form or instance of it.

libidinous /lə'bɪdənəs/ *adj.* full of lust.

libido /lə'bidou/ *n.* the innate actuating or impelling force in living beings; the vital impulse or urge.

library /'laɪbri, -brəri/, *Orig. US* /-rɛri/ *n.* (*pl.* **-ries**) a place set apart to contain books and other literary material for reading, study, or reference, as a room, set of rooms, or building where books may be read or borrowed. –**librarian**, *n.*

lice /laɪs/ *n.* plural of **louse**.

licence /'laɪsəns/ *n.* **1.** formal permission or leave to do or not to do something. **2.** a certificate of such permission; an official permit. **3.** excessive or undue freedom or liberty.

license /'laɪsəns/ *v.t.* to grant authoritative permission or licence to; authorise. –**licensor**, **licenser**, *n.* –**licensee**, *n.*

licentious /laɪ'sɛnʃəs/ *adj.* sensually unbridled; libertine; lewd.

lichen /'laɪkən/ *n.* a type of plant growing in crust-like patches on rocks, trees, etc.

lick /lɪk/ *v.t.* **1.** (oft. fol. by *off*, *from*, etc.) to pass the tongue over the surface of. **2.** *Colloq.* to overcome; defeat; outdo; surpass. –*n.* **3.** a stroke of the tongue over something. **4.** a place to which wild animals resort to lick salt occurring naturally there.

licorice /'lɪkənʃ, 'lɪkrɪʃ, -rəs/ *n.* the sweet-tasting dried root of a certain plant, or an extract made from it, used in medicine, confectionery, etc. Also, **liquorice**.

lid /lɪd/ *n.* a movable piece, whether separate or hinged, for closing the opening of a vessel, box, etc.; a movable cover.

lie¹ /laɪ/ *n.* **1.** a false statement made with intent to deceive; an intentional untruth; a falsehood. –*v.i.* (**lied, lying**) **2.** to speak falsely or utter untruth knowingly.

lie² /laɪ/ *v.i.* (**lay, lain, lying**) **1.** to be in a recumbent or prostrate position, as on a bed or the ground; recline. **2.** (fol. by *down*) to assume such a position. **3.** to rest in a horizontal position; be stretched out or extended. **4.** to be placed or situated.

liege /lidʒ, liʒ/ *n.* a lord entitled to allegiance and service.

lien /'liən/ *n.* (in law) the right to hold property or to have it sold or applied to pay a claim.

lieu /lu, lju/ *n.* **1.** place; stead. –*phr.* **2. in lieu of**, instead of.

lieutenant /lɛf'tɛnənt, lu'tɛnənt/, *Navy* /lə'tɛnənt/ *n.* **1.** an officer in the army or navy. **2.** someone who holds an office, civil or military, in subordination to a superior, for whom he or she acts.

life /laɪf/ n. (pl. **lives**) **1.** the condition which distinguishes animals and plants from inorganic objects and dead organisms. **2.** the animate existence, or the term of animate existence, of an individual. **3.** the term of existence, activity, or effectiveness of something inanimate, as a machine or a lease. **4.** a living being. **5.** course or mode of existence. **6.** animation, liveliness. **7. a.** a prison sentence covering the rest of the convicted person's natural life. **b.** the maximum possible term of imprisonment that can be awarded by the laws of a state.

life coach n. a person who offers training in dealing with life situations in a way that maximises the client's potential. –**life coaching**, n.

lifeguard /ˈlaɪfgad/ n. someone employed at a place where people swim to rescue and give first aid to those in distress.

life insurance n. insurance providing payment of a specified sum of money to a named beneficiary upon the death of the insured, or to the insured or to a named beneficiary should the insured reach a specified age. Also, **life assurance**.

life jacket n. an inflatable or buoyant sleeveless jacket for keeping a person afloat in water. Also, **life vest**.

lifeline /ˈlaɪflaɪn/ n. **1.** a line or rope for saving life, as one attached to a lifeboat. **2.** any vital line of communication.

lifesaver /ˈlaɪfseɪvə/ n. one of a group of volunteers who patrol surfing beaches, etc., making sure that swimmers remain in designated safe areas, and who are trained in rescue and resuscitation methods. –**lifesaving**, n.

lifesaving /ˈlaɪfseɪvɪŋ/ n. the techniques and practices, especially rescue and resuscitation methods, developed to deal with emergency situations in or near the water, as in swimming pools, lakes, beaches, etc. –**lifesaver**, n.

lifestreaming /ˈlaɪfstrimɪŋ/ n. the online recording of one's daily life, either by a webcam, or by collecting together personal blogs, microblogs, etc.

lifestyle /ˈlaɪfstaɪl/ n. a mode of life chosen by a person or group.

lifestyle drug n. a prescription medicine that is used not to cure illness but to enhance the wellbeing of the healthy by improving looks, sexual performance, etc.

lifetime /ˈlaɪftaɪm/ n. **1.** the time that one's life continues; one's term of life. –adj. **2.** lasting a lifetime.

lift /lɪft/ v.t. **1.** to move or bring (something) upwards from the ground or other support to some higher position; hoist. **2.** to raise in rank, condition, estimation, etc.; elevate or exalt. **3.** Colloq. to steal or plagiarise. –v.i. **4.** to go up; give to upward pressure. **5.** to move upwards or rise; rise and disperse, as clouds, fog, etc. –n. **6.** the act of lifting, raising, or rising. **7.** a moving platform or cage for conveying goods, people, etc., from one level to another, as in a building. **8.** a ride in a vehicle, especially one given free of charge to a traveller on foot. **9.** exaltation or uplift, as in feeling.

lift-off n. Also, **blast-off**. **1.** the start of a rocket's flight from its launching pad. –adj. **2.** removable by lifting: a lift-off lid.

ligament /ˈlɪgəmənt/ n. Anat. a band of tissue, usually white and fibrous, serving to connect bones, hold organs in place, etc.

ligature /ˈlɪgətʃə/ n. a tie or bond.

light[1] /laɪt/ n. **1.** that which makes things visible, or affords illumination. **2.** an illuminating agent or source, as the sun, a lamp, or a beacon. **3.** the illumination from the sun, or daylight. **4.** the aspect in which a thing appears or is regarded. **5.** a traffic light. –adj. **6.** having light or illumination, rather than dark. **7.** pale in colour. –v. (**lit** or **lighted**, **lighting**) –v.t. **8.** to set burning (a candle, lamp, pipe for smoking, etc.); kindle (a fire); ignite (fuel, a match, etc.). –v.i. **9.** to take fire or become kindled. **10.** (oft. fol. by up) to brighten with animation or joy, as the face, eyes, etc.

light[2] /laɪt/ adj. **1.** of little weight; not heavy. **2.** gentle; delicate; exerting only slight pressure. **3.** easy to endure, deal with, or perform. **4.** free from any burden of sorrow or care. **5.** characterised by lack of proper seriousness; frivolous. **6.** having less of a normal standard ingredient: light beer.

light[3] /laɪt/ v.i. (**lighted** or **lit**, **lighting**) **1.** to get down or descend, as from a horse or a vehicle. **2.** (fol. by on or upon) to come by chance, happen, or hit.

lighthouse /ˈlaɪthaʊs/ n. a tower or other structure displaying a light or lights for the guidance of vessels at sea.

lightning /ˈlaɪtnɪŋ/ n. a flashing of light, or a sudden illumination of the sky, caused by the discharge of atmospheric electricity.

lightning strike n. **1.** a hit from a bolt of lightning. **2.** a stoppage of work by employees with little or no warning to employers.

light-pen n. a light sensitive device, made to look like a pen, which by moving the position of a point of light on a display screen, can interact with a computer.

light-year n. the distance traversed by light in one year ($9.460\,55 \times 10^{15}$ metres), used as a unit in measuring stellar distances. Symbol: l.y.

ligneous /ˈlɪgniəs/ adj. of the nature of or resembling wood; woody.

like[1] /laɪk/ prep. **1.** similarly to; in a manner characteristic of. **2.** bearing resemblance to. **3.** for example; as; such as. **4.** indicating a probability of. **5.** desirous of; disposed to (after feel). –n. **6.** (preceded by the) something of a similar nature.

like[2] v.t. **1.** to find agreeable. **2.** (in social media) to indicate support, enthusiasm, etc., for (a post, image, etc.), as by activating a button, tapping on an image, etc. –n. **3.** (in social media) an instance of liking (def. 2): to get hundreds of likes for a photo.

-like a suffix of adjectives, use of **like**[1], as in childlike, lifelike, businesslike, sometimes hyphenated.

likely /ˈlaɪkli/ adj. (**-lier, -liest**) **1.** expected to happen. **2.** able to be reasonably accepted as true but not definitely true. –adv. **3.** probably: you are very likely right. –**likelihood**, n.

liken /ˈlaɪkən/ v.t. to compare.

likewise /'laɪkwaɪz/ *adv.* in like manner.

lilac /'laɪlək/ *n.* a shrub with large clusters of fragrant purple or white flowers.

lilt /lɪlt/ *n.* rhythmic swing or cadence.

lily /'lɪli/ *n.* (*pl.* **-lies**) a scaly-bulbed herb with showy funnel-shaped or bell-shaped flowers.

lima bean /laɪmə/ *n.* a kind of bean with a broad, flat, edible seed.

limb /lɪm/ *n.* **1.** a part or member of an animal body distinct from the head and trunk, as a leg, arm, or wing. **2.** a large or main branch of a tree.

limber /'lɪmbə/ *adj.* **1.** bending readily; flexible; pliant. **2.** characterised by ease in bending the body; supple; lithe. *–v.i.* **3.** (fol. by *up*) to make oneself limber.

limbo /'lɪmbou/ *n.* **1.** (*oft. upper case*) a supposed region on the border of hell or heaven. *–phr.* **2. in limbo**, in a situation where nothing is decided or resolved.

lime¹ /laɪm/ *n.* the oxide of calcium, used in making mortar and cement.

lime² /laɪm/ *n.* a small, greenish yellow, acid fruit allied to the lemon.

limelight /'laɪmlaɪt/ *n.* **1.** (formerly) a strong light, made by heating a cylinder of lime. **2.** the glare of public interest or notoriety.

limerick /'lɪmərɪk/ *n.* a type of humorous verse of five lines.

limestone /'laɪmstoʊn/ *n.* a rock consisting wholly or chiefly of calcium carbonate.

limit /'lɪmət/ *n.* **1.** the final or furthest bound or point as to extent, amount, continuance, procedure, etc. *–v.t.* **2.** (fol. by *to*) to restrict by or as by fixing limits. *–***limitation**, *n.*

limited company *n.* a company which can issue subscription and which may be listed on the stock exchange; there is a minimum number of shareholders but no maximum; on liquidation the liability of the shareholders for the company's debts is limited to any amounts unpaid on their shares. Also, **limited-liability company**.

limited liability *n.* the liability, either by law or contract, only to a limited amount for debts of a trading company or limited partnership.

limousine /'lɪmə'zin, 'lɪməzin/ *n.* any large, luxurious car.

limp¹ /lɪmp/ *v.i.* **1.** to walk with a laboured, jerky movement, as when lame. *–n.* **2.** a lame movement or gait.

limp² /lɪmp/ *adj.* lacking stiffness or firmness.

limpet /'lɪmpət/ *n. Zool.* a marine gastropod mollusc found adhering to rocks.

limpid /'lɪmpəd/ *adj.* clear.

linchpin /'lɪntʃpɪn/ *n.* **1.** a pin inserted through the end of an axle to keep the wheel on. **2.** the key point of a plan, argument, etc. **3.** a key person or event, as in a play, etc. Also, **lynchpin**.

line¹ /laɪn/ *n.* **1.** a mark or stroke long in proportion to its breadth, made with a pen, pencil, tool, etc., on a surface. **2.** something resembling a traced line, as a band of colour, a seam, a furrow, etc. **3.** a row of written or printed letters, words, etc. **4.** a verse of poetry. **5.** a course of action, procedure, thought, etc. **6.** a continuous series of persons or animals in chronological succession, especially in family descent. **7.** a department of activity; a kind of occupation or business. **8.** any transport company or system. **9.** a strip of railway track, a railway, or a railway system. **10.** *Maths* a continuous extent of length, straight or curved, without breadth or thickness; the trace of a moving point. **11.** a supply of commercial goods of the same general class. **12.** the line of arrangement of an army or of the ships of a fleet as drawn up ready for battle. **13.** a thread, string, or the like. **14.** a telephonic channel. *–v.* (**lined, lining**) *–v.i.* **15.** (oft. fol. by *up*) to take a position in a line; range or queue. *–v.t.* **16.** (oft. fol. by *up*) to bring into a line, or into line with others. **17.** to mark with a line or lines.

line² /laɪn/ *v.t.* to provide with a layer of material applied to the inner side.

lineage /'lɪniɪdʒ/ *n.* lineal descent from an ancestor; ancestry or extraction.

lineal /'lɪniəl/ *adj.* being in the direct line, as a descendant, ancestor, etc., or descent, etc.

linear /'lɪniə/ *adj.* **1.** extended in a line. **2.** involving measurement in one dimension only; relating to length. **3.** of or relating to a line or lines. **4.** *Maths* of the first degree, as an equation.

linedance /'laɪndæns/ *n.* a dance, performed to country music, which consists of a repeated sequence of steps performed by a group of dancers facing the same direction in a line. *–***linedancing**, *n.* *–***linedancer**, *n.*

linen /'lɪnən/ *n.* **1.** fabric woven from flax yarns. **2.** clothes or other articles made of linen cloth or some substitute, as cotton.

line of credit *n. Finance* a borrowing facility, usually extended on an indefinite basis so that the borrower can draw on the funds when the need arises, or arranged pending a project for which the money is needed.

liner /'laɪnə/ *n.* one of a commercial line of ships or aeroplanes.

linesman /'laɪnzmən/ *n.* (*pl.* **-men**) **1.** *Sport* a man on the sidelines who assists the referee or umpire in determining whether the ball is still in play. **2.** the member of a surf-lifesaving team who handles the surf-line. Also, **lineman**. *–***lineswoman**, *n.* *–***linesperson**, *n.*

ling /lɪŋ/ *n.* (*pl.* **ling** *or* **lings**) a common fish, reddish-brown in colour with a small feeler on the chin, found around the southern coast of Aust.

-ling a suffix found in some nouns, often pejorative, denoting one concerned with (*hireling, underling*); also diminutive (*princeling, duckling*).

linger /'lɪŋgə/ *v.i.* **1.** to remain or stay on in a place longer than is usual or expected, as if from reluctance to leave it. **2.** to dwell in contemplation, thought, or enjoyment.

lingerie /'lɒnʒəreɪ/ *n.* women's underwear.

lingo /'lɪŋgoʊ/ *n.* (*pl.* **-goes**) *Colloq.* **1.** language. **2.** language or terminology peculiar to a particular field, group, etc.; jargon.

linguine /lɪŋ'gwini/ *n.* (in Italian cookery) a style of pasta in long thin strips.

linguist /'lɪŋgwəst/ *n.* **1.** a person who is skilled in foreign languages. **2.** a person who specialises in linguistics.

linguistics /lɪŋ'gwɪstɪks/ *n.* the science of language. *–***linguistic**, *adj.*

liniment /'lɪnəmənt/ *n.* a liquid preparation, usually oily, for rubbing on or applying to the skin, as for sprains, bruises, etc.

link /lɪŋk/ *n.* 1. one of the rings or separate pieces of which a chain is composed. 2. anything serving to connect one part or thing with another; a bond or tie. 3. one of the 100 wire rods forming the divisions of a surveyor's chain of 66 ft (20.12 m). *–v.t.* 4. to join by or as by a link or links.

linkbait /'lɪŋkbeɪt/ *Internet –v.t.* 1. to create points of interest in (a website) so that other sites will link to it and increase traffic on the site, as by running competitions, etc. *–n.* 2. such an attractive feature of a site. **–link-baiting,** *n.*

links /lɪŋks/ *pl. n.* a golf course.

linoleum /lai'nouliəm/ *n.* a floor covering formed by coating hessian or canvas with linseed oil, powdered cork, and rosin, and adding pigments of the desired colour. Also, **lino.**

linseed /'lɪnsid/ *n.* the seed of flax.

lint /lɪnt/ *n.* a soft material for dressing wounds, etc.

lintel /'lɪntl/ *n.* a horizontal supporting member above an opening such as a window or a door. Also, **lintol.**

lion /'laɪən/ *n.* 1. a large, greyish-tan cat native to Africa and southern Asia, the male of which usually has a mane. *–phr.* 2. **the lion's share,** the largest portion of anything. **–lion-ess,** *fem. n.*

lip /lɪp/ *n.* 1. either of the two fleshy parts or folds forming the margins of the mouth and performing an important function in speech. 2. a lip-like part or structure. 3. any edge or rim.

lipid /'lɪpɪd, 'laɪ-/ *n.* any of a group of organic compounds which make up the fats and other esters which have analogous solubility properties. They have a greasy feel and are insoluble in water, but soluble in alcohols, ethers, and other fat solvents.

liposuction /'laɪpousʌkʃən/ *n.* the removal of fat tissue from the body by means of suction.

lip-read /'lɪp-rid/ *v.t., v.i.* (**-read** /-rɛd/, **-reading**) to understand spoken words by watching the movement of a speaker's lips.

lip-service /'lɪp-sɜvəs/ *n.* insincere profession of devotion or goodwill.

lipstick /'lɪpstɪk/ *n.* a stick or elongated piece of cosmetic preparation for colouring the lips.

lip-sync /'lɪp-sɪŋk/ *v.i.* (**-synched** /-sɪŋkt/ *or* **-synced** /-sɪŋkt/, **-synching** /-sɪŋkɪŋ/ *or* **-syncing** /-sɪŋkɪŋ/) to match lip movements with recorded speech or singing; mime. Also, **lip-synch.**

liquefy /'lɪkwəfaɪ/ *v.t.* (**-fied, -fying**) to make or become liquid. Also, **liquify.**

liqueur /lə'kjuə, lə'kɜ/ *n.* any of a class of alcoholic liquors, usually strong, sweet, and highly flavoured.

liquid /'lɪkwəd/ *adj.* 1. such as to flow like water; fluid. 2. in cash or readily convertible into cash. *–n.* 3. a liquid substance. *–phr.* 4. **go liquid,** to realise assets for cash. **–liquidity,** *n.*

liquidate /'lɪkwədeɪt/ *v.t.* 1. to settle or pay (a debt, etc.). 2. to reduce (accounts) to order; determine the amount of (indebtedness or damages). 3. to convert into cash. 4. to get rid of, especially by killing or other violent means. *–v.i.* 5. to liquidate debts or accounts; go into liquidation. **–liquidation,** *n.*

liquidator /'lɪkwədeɪtə/ *n.* a person appointed to carry out the winding up of a company.

liquor /'lɪkə/ *n.* spirits (as brandy or whisky) as distinguished from fermented beverages (as wine or beer).

liquorice /'lɪkərɪʃ, 'lɪkrɪʃ, -rəs/ *n.* → **licorice.**

lisp /lɪsp/ *n.* 1. a speech defect consisting in pronouncing *s* and *z* like or nearly like the *th* sounds of *thin* and *this*, respectively. *–v.i.* 2. to speak with a lisp.

lissom /'lɪsəm/ *adj.* lithe; limber.

list[1] /lɪst/ *n.* 1. a record consisting of a series of names, words, or the like. *–v.t.* 2. to set down together in a list. 3. to register a security on a stock exchange so that it may be traded there.

list[2] /lɪst/ *v.i.* (of a ship) to careen; incline to one side.

listen /'lɪsən/ *v.i.* 1. to give attention with the ear; attend closely for the purpose of hearing; give ear. *–phr.* 2. **listen up,** *Chiefly US* to pay attention.

listicle /'lɪstɪkəl/ *n.* a type of article in online journalism and blogging which is presented in the form of a list.

listless /'lɪstləs/ *adj.* feeling no inclination towards or interest in anything.

listserv /'lɪstsɜv/ *n. Computers* a mailing list server which automatically sends emails addressed to a mailing list to all addresses on the list, operating in a similar way to a newsgroup but with the messages being accessible only to those included on the mailing list.

lit /lɪt/ *v.* past tense and past participle of **light**[1] and **light**[3].

litany /'lɪtəni/ *n.* (*pl.* **-nies**) 1. a form of prayer consisting of a series of invocations with responses from a congregation. 2. a prolonged recitation; monotonous account.

-lite a word element used in names of minerals, or fossils. Compare **-lith.**

literal /'lɪtrəl, 'lɪtərəl/ *adj.* 1. following the letter, or exact words, of the original, as a translation. 2. in accordance with, involving, or being the natural or strict meaning of the words or word; not figurative or metaphorical. **–literally,** *adv.*

literary /'lɪtərəri, 'lɪtrəri, *Orig. US* /'lɪtəreri/ *adj.* relating to or of the nature of books and writings, especially those classed as literature.

literate /'lɪtərət/ *adj.* 1. able to read and write. 2. having an education; educated. **–literacy,** *n.*

literature /'lɪtrətʃə, 'lɪtərətʃə/ *n.* 1. writings in which expression and form, in connection with ideas of permanent and universal interest, are characteristic or essential features, as poetry, romance, history, biography, essays, etc. 2. *Colloq.* printed matter of any kind, as circulars or advertising matter.

lith- a combining form meaning 'stone'. Also, **litho-.**

-lith a noun termination meaning 'stone'.

lithe /laɪð/ *adj.* pliant; supple.

lithium /'lɪθiəm/ *n.* a soft silver-white metallic element (the lightest of all metals) occurring combined in certain minerals. *Symbol:* Li

lithography /lɪ'θɒɡrəfi/ *n.* the art or process of printing a picture, writing, or the like, from a flat surface of aluminium, zinc or stone, with some greasy or oily substance. **–lithograph,** *n.*

litigant /'lɪtəgənt/ *n.* **1.** one engaged in a lawsuit. *–adj.* **2.** litigating; engaged in a lawsuit.

litigate /'lɪtəgeɪt/ *v.t.* **1.** to contest at law. **2.** to dispute (a point, etc.). *–v.i.* **3.** to carry on a lawsuit. **–litigable,** *adj.* **–litigator,** *n.* **–litigation,** *n.*

litmus /'lɪtməs/ *n.* a colouring substance which is turned red by acid solutions and blue by alkaline solutions.

litmus test *n.* **1.** a test of acidity or alkalinity using litmus paper. **2.** a decisive test of a person's loyalty, character, determination, etc.

litre /'litə/ *n.* a measure of liquid in the metric system. *Symbol:* L

-litre a word element meaning 'litres'.

litter /'lɪtə/ *n.* **1.** things scattered about; scattered rubbish. **2.** a condition of disorder or untidiness. **3.** a number of young brought forth at one birth. **4.** a vehicle carried by people or animals, consisting of a bed or couch, often covered and curtained, suspended between shafts. *–v.t.* **5.** to strew (a place) with scattered objects. **6.** to scatter (objects) in disorder.

litterbug /'lɪtəbʌg/ *n.* someone who drops rubbish, especially in public places.

little /'lɪtl/ *adj.* (**less** or **lesser** or **littler**; **least** or **littlest**) **1.** small in size; not big or large. **2.** small in extent or duration; short; brief. **3.** small in number. **4.** small in amount or degree; not much. *–adv.* (**less**, **least**) **5.** not at all: *he little knows what awaits him.* **6.** rarely; infrequently. *–n.* **7.** that which is little; a small amount, quantity, or degree.

liturgy /'lɪtədʒi/ *n.* (*pl.* **-gies**) a form of public worship; a ritual. **–liturgical,** *adj.*

live¹ /lɪv/ *v.* (**lived** /lɪvd/, **living**) *–v.i.* **1.** to have life, as an animal or plant; be alive. **2.** to continue in existence, operation, memory, etc.; last. **3.** (fol. by *on* or *upon*) to feed or subsist. **4.** to dwell or reside. **5.** to pass life (as specified). *–v.t.* **6.** to pass (life).

live² /laɪv/ *adj.* **1.** being in life; living; alive. **2.** characterised by or indicating the presence of living creatures. **3.** burning or glowing, as a coal. **4.** loaded or unexploded, as a cartridge or shell. **5.** *Elect.* electrically charged. **6.** (of a radio or television program) broadcast or televised at the moment it is being performed.

live feed *n.* a transmission by a media outlet of an event, sporting match, etc., as it is happening.

livelihood /'laɪvlihʊd/ *n.* means of maintaining life; maintenance.

lively /'laɪvli/ *adj.* (**-lier**, **-liest**) **1.** full or suggestive of life or vital energy; active, vigorous, or brisk. **2.** animated, spirited, vivacious, or sprightly. **3.** eventful, stirring, or exciting.

liven /'laɪvən/ *v.t.* (oft. fol. by *up*) to put life into; rouse; cheer.

live pause *n.* a facility on a DVR which can interrupt a program during its telecast and start recording it, making it possible to return to watch it from the point at which it was stopped.

liver /'lɪvə/ *n.* (in humans) a large, reddish brown glandular organ secreting bile and performing various metabolic functions.

liver spot *n.* a brownish patch on the skin, usually of an elderly person.

livery /'lɪvəri/ *n.* (*pl.* **-ries**) **1.** a kind of uniform worn by menservants. **2.** a distinctive dress worn by an official, a member of a company or guild, etc.

livery stable *n.* a stable where horses and vehicles are cared for or let out for hire.

lives /laɪvz/ *n.* plural of **life.**

livestock /'laɪvstɒk/ *n.* the horses, cattle, sheep, and other useful animals kept or bred on a farm or ranch.

live stream *Telecommunications* *–v.t.* **1.** to deliver (media content) directly to the end user by a streaming process as the action is occurring. See **streaming.** *–n.* **2.** such a content delivery. **–live streaming,** *n.*

liveware /'laɪvwɛə/ *n.* the personnel involved with the use of a computer, as programmers, key punch operators, etc. See **software, hardware.**

livid /'lɪvəd/ *adj.* **1.** having a discoloured bluish appearance due to a bruise, etc. **2.** angry; enraged.

living /'lɪvɪŋ/ *adj.* **1.** that lives; alive, or not dead. *–n.* **2.** the act or condition of someone who or that which lives. **3.** means of maintaining life; livelihood.

living fossil *n.* a plant or animal species which has continued to survive in its native habitat since prehistoric times, such as the Wollemi pine, or is almost identical to species only known from the fossil record, such as the platypus.

living room *n.* a room in a house, flat, etc., used both for entertaining and for relaxing, recreation, etc.; lounge room.

lizard /'lɪzəd/ *n.* any of various long-bodied reptiles with tails.

'll a shortening of *will* or *shall.*

llama /'lɑmə/ *n.* a woolly-haired South American ruminant.

lo /loʊ/ *interj. Archaic* look! see! behold!

load /loʊd/ *n.* **1.** that which is laid on or placed in anything for conveyance. **2.** anything borne or sustained. **3.** something that weighs down or oppresses like a burden. **4.** the amount of work required of a person, machine, organisation, etc. **5.** the weight supported by a structure or part. *–v.t.* **6.** to put a load on or in. **7.** to supply abundantly or excessively with something. **8.** to give bias to, especially by fraudulent means. **9.** *Insurance* to increase (a net premium, etc.). See **loading** (def. 2). **10.** to charge (a firearm, camera, etc.)

loading /'loʊdɪŋ/ *n.* **1.** an extra rate paid to employees in recognition of a particular aspect of their employment, as shift work. **2.** *Insurance* an addition to the normal premium on the policy of a person whose life expectancy is considered to be less than the mortality tables would indicate.

loaf¹ /loʊf/ *n.* (*pl.* **loaves** /loʊvz/) **1.** a portion of bread or cake baked in a mass of definite form. **2.** a shaped or moulded mass of food, as of sugar, chopped meat, etc.

loaf² /loʊf/ *v.i.* to lounge or saunter lazily and idly.

loaf³ /loʊf/ *n. Colloq.* the head.

loafer /'loʊfə/ *n.* (*from trademark*) a casual shoe.

loam /loum/ *n.* a loose soil composed of clay and sand.

loan /loun/ *n.* **1.** something lent or provided on condition of being returned, especially a sum of money lent at interest. —*v.t.* **2.** to make a loan of; lend. **3.** to lend (money) at interest.

loath /louθ/ *adj.* reluctant, averse, or unwilling.

loathe /louð/ *v.t.* to feel hatred, disgust, or intense aversion for. —**loathing**, *n.* —**loathsome**, *adj.*

loaves /louvz/ *n.* plural of **loaf**[1].

lob /lob/ *v.t.* (**lobbed, lobbing**) **1.** *Tennis* to strike (a ball) high into the air. **2.** to throw (something) up so that it lands after a high curve.

lobby /'lobi/ *n.* (*pl.* **-bies**) **1.** a corridor, vestibule, or entrance hall. **2.** a group of persons who attempt to influence legislators or other public officials on behalf of some particular cause or interest. —*v.i.* (**-bied, -bying**) **3.** to frequent the lobby of a legislative chamber to influence the members.

lobe /loub/ *n.* a roundish projection.

lobotomy /lə'botəmi/ *n.* (*pl.* **-mies**) the cutting into or across a lobe of the brain.

lobster /'lobstə/ *n.* a large, edible, marine crustacean.

local /'loukəl/ *adj.* **1.** relating to or characterised by place, or position in space. **2.** relating to, characteristic of, or restricted to a particular place or particular places. **3.** relating to or affecting a particular part or particular parts.

local anaesthesia *n.* **1.** drug-induced loss of sensation in a part of the body. **2.** the administration of a drug to produce this effect. Also, **local anesthesia**.

local anaesthetic *n.* **1.** a drug, usually injected, which anaesthetises only part of the body. **2.** the procedure for this. Also, **local anesthetic**.

local area network *n.* a computer networking system which links computers within a limited geographical area to a central computer by means of land lines. *Abbrev.*: LAN Compare **wide area network**.

locale /lou'kal/ *n.* a place or locality, especially with reference to events or circumstances connected with it

local government *n.* the administration of the affairs of a regional district, in Australia usually an area smaller than that of a state such as a shire, municipality, town, etc., by officers elected by the residents and ratepayers of that district.

locality /lou'kæləti/ *n.* (*pl.* **-ties**) a place, spot, or district, with or without reference to things or persons in it.

locate /lou'keit/ *v.t.* to discover the place or location of.

location /lou'keiʃən/ *n.* **1.** a place of settlement or residence. **2.** *Film, TV* a place outside the studio where scenes may be shot. **3.** *Computers* a specific register in the high-speed memory of a computer. —*phr.* **4. on location**, *Film, TV* at a site away from the studio, where filming for a particular scene is taking place.

locavore /'loukəvɔ/ *n.* a person who eats only food that is locally produced.

loch /lok/ *n. Scot* a lake.

lock[1] /lok/ *n.* **1.** a device for securing a door, gate, lid, drawer, or the like, in position when closed. **2.** an enclosed portion of a canal, river, etc., with gates at each end, for raising or lowering vessels from one level to another. **3.** the number of degrees the steering mechanism of a vehicle is able to turn the front wheels from one extreme to the other. —*v.t.* **4.** to fasten or secure (a door, building, etc.) by the operation of a lock. **5.** (fol. by *up, in*, etc.) to shut in a place fastened by a lock or locks, as for security or restraining. **6.** (usu. fol. by *out*) to exclude by or as by a lock. **7.** to join or unite firmly by interlinking or intertwining. —*v.i.* **8.** to become locked. —*phr.* **9. lock down**, to secure (a location) against a perceived threat by cutting off the access and halting movement of people in and around it.

lock[2] /lok/ *n.* a tress or portion of hair.

lockdown /'lokdaun/ *n.* a state of security alert in which access is cut off and movement of people in and around a location is brought to a halt.

locker /'lokə/ *n.* a chest, drawer, compartment, closet, or the like, that may be locked.

locket /'lokət/ *n.* a small case for a miniature portrait, a lock of hair, or other keepsake, usually worn on a chain hung round the neck.

lockjaw /'lokdʒɔ/ *n.* tetanus in which the jaws become firmly locked together.

locomotion /loukə'mouʃən/ *n.* the act or power of moving from place to place.

locomotive /loukə'moutiv/ *n.* a self-propelled vehicle running on a railway track, designed to pull railway carriages or trucks.

locum /'loukəm/ *n.* a temporary substitute for a doctor, lawyer, etc. Also, **locum tenens** /loukəm 'tenənz/.

locus /'loukəs, 'loukəs/ *n.* (*pl.* **loci** /'loki, 'louki, 'loukai/) a place; a locality.

locust /'loukəst/ *n.* **1.** a type of grasshopper which swarms in immense numbers and strips vegetation. **2.** *Colloq.* → **cicada**.

lode /loud/ *n.* a veinlike deposit, usually metal bearing.

lodge /lodʒ/ *n.* **1.** a cabin or hut. **2.** a house or cottage, as in a park or on an estate, occupied by a gatekeeper, caretaker, gardener, or the like. **3.** the meeting place of a branch of a secret society. —*v.* (**lodged, lodging**) —*v.i.* **4.** to have a habitation or quarters, especially temporarily. **5.** to be fixed or implanted. —*v.t.* **6.** to furnish with a habitation or quarters, especially temporarily. **7.** to lay (information, a complaint, etc.) before a court or the like. —**lodgement, lodgment**, *n.*

loft /loft/ *n.* the space between the underside of a roof and the ceiling of a room beneath it.

lofty /'lofti/ *adj.* (**-tier, -tiest**) **1.** extending high in the air; of imposing height. **2.** elevated in style or sentiment, as writings, etc. **3.** haughty; proud.

log /log/ *n.* **1.** an unhewn portion or length of wood. **2.** Also, **logbook**. the official record of significant data concerning a ship's journey, a plane's flight, a machine's operation, etc. —*v.* (**logged, logging**) —*v.t.* **3.** to cut (trees) into logs. **4.** to cut down trees or timber on (land). **5.** to enter in a log. —*v.i.* **6.** to cut down trees and get out logs from the forest for timber.

–phr. **7. log in** (or **on**), to begin a session on a computer, usually gaining access with a username and password. **8. log off** (or **out**), to end a session on a computer.

loganberry /'lougənbəri, -bri/ *n.* (*pl.* **-ries**) a large, dark red, acid berry.

logarithm /'logərɪðəm/ *n.* the exponent of that power to which a fixed number (called the *base*) must be raised in order to produce a given number (called the *antilogarithm*). –**logarithmic**, *adj.*

logic /'lodʒɪk/ *n.* **1.** the system or principles of reasoning applicable to any branch of knowledge or study. **2.** reasons or sound sense, as in utterances or actions. –**logical**, *adj.*

login /'logɪn/ *n. Computers* the act of beginning a computer session, usually by gaining access via a username and password. Also, **log-in**, **logon**, **log-on**.

logistics /lə'dʒɪstɪks/ *n.* (*oft. construed as pl.*) the branch of military science concerned with the mathematics of transportation and supply, and the movement of bodies of troops.

logo /'lougou/ *n.* a trademark or symbol designed to identify a company, organisation, etc.

logo- a word element denoting speech.

logon /'logɒn/ *n. Computers* → **login**. Also, **log-on**.

logout /'logaʊt/ *n. Computers* the act of discontinuing a computer session. Also, **log-out**, **logoff**, **log-off**.

-logy **1.** a combining form naming sciences or bodies of knowledge. **2.** a termination of many nouns referring to writing.

loin /lɔɪn/ *n.* (*usu. pl.*) the part or parts of the body of humans or of quadruped animals on either side of the vertebral column, between the false ribs and hipbone.

loiter /'lɔɪtə/ *v.i.* to linger idly or aimlessly in or about a place.

loll /lɒl/ *v.i.* to recline or lean in a relaxed or indolent manner; lounge.

lollipop /'lolipɒp/ *n.* a kind of boiled sweet or toffee, often a piece on the end of a stick.

lollop /'lɒləp/ *v.i.* to move with bounding, ungainly leaps.

lolly /'loli/ *n.* (*pl.* **-lies**) any sweet, especially a boiled one.

lone /loun/ *adj.* solitary.

lonely /'lounli/ *adj.* (**-lier, -liest**) **1.** destitute of sympathetic or friendly companionship or relationships. **2.** lone; solitary. **3.** away from populated areas: *a lonely stretch of beach.*

lonesome /'lounsəm/ *adj.* depressed by solitude or by a sense of being alone.

long¹ /lɒŋ/ *adj.* (**longer** /'lɒŋgə/, **longest** /'lɒŋgəst/) **1.** having considerable or great extent from end to end; not short. **2.** having considerable or great extent in duration. **3.** having a specified extension in space, duration, etc. **4.** tall. **5.** *Commerce* **a.** owning some commodity or stock. **b.** depending for profit on a rise in prices. *–n.* **6.** something that is long. *–adv.* **7.** for or through a great extent of space or, especially, time. *–phr.* **8. so long**, *Colloq.* goodbye.

long² /lɒŋ/ *v.i.* to have a prolonged or unceasing desire, as for something not immediately (if ever) attainable.

longboard /'lɒŋbɔd/ *n.* **1.** a surfboard, generally over 2.75 metres in length, offering more buoyancy than a shorter board so it can be ridden in smaller surf. **2.** a skateboard which is longer and wider than the average, giving it greater stability.

long COVID *n.* a condition whereby a person who has recovered from COVID-19 continues to experience symptoms such as fatigue, breathlessness, coughing, etc., and sometimes organ damage.

longevity /lɒn'dʒɛvəti/ *n.* long life; great duration of life.

longhand /'lɒŋhænd/ *n.* writing of the ordinary kind, in which the words are written out in full (distinguished from *shorthand*).

longitude /'lɒŋgətjud, 'lɒndʒɪtjud/ *n. Geog.* angular distance east or west on the earth's surface, measured along the equator.

longitudinal /lɒŋgə'tjudənəl/ *adj.* of or relating to longitude or length.

long-life *adj.* **1.** → **UHT**. **2.** of or relating to any product which has been treated to extend its utility beyond the normal length of time.

long service leave *n.* an extended period of leave from employment, earned through long service. *Abbrev.*: LSL

long shot *n.* an attempt which has little hope of success, but which if successful may offer great rewards.

longwinded /'lɒŋwɪndəd/ *adj.* tediously wordy in speech or writing.

loofah /'lufa/ *n.* a bath sponge.

look /lʊk/ *v.i.* **1.** to fix the eyes upon something or in some direction in order to see. **2.** to glance or gaze, in a manner specified. **3.** to use the sight in seeking, searching, examining, watching, etc. **4.** to tend, as in bearing or significance. **5.** to appear or seem. **6.** to direct the mental regard or attention. **7.** to have an outlook or afford a view. **8.** to face or front. *–v.t.* **9.** (fol. by *up, out,* etc.) to try to find; seek. **10.** (fol. by *over*) to view, inspect or examine. **11.** to have the aspect or appearance appropriate to. *–n.* **12.** the act of looking. **13.** a visual search or examination. **14.** way of looking or appearing to the eye or mind; aspect. **15.** (*pl.*) general aspect; appearance. *–phr.* **16. look after**, to take care of. **17. look forward to**, to anticipate with pleasure. **18. look out**, to be on guard.

lookout /'lʊkaʊt/ *n.* **1.** a watch kept, as for something that may come or happen. **2.** a person or group stationed or employed to keep such a watch. **3.** a place on a high vantage point, especially a mountain, from which one can admire the view.

loom¹ /lum/ *n.* a machine or apparatus for weaving yarn or thread into a fabric.

loom² /lum/ *v.i.* to appear indistinctly, or come into view in indistinct and enlarged form.

loop /lup/ *n.* **1.** a folding or doubling of a portion of a cord, lace, ribbon, etc., upon itself, so as to leave an opening between the parts. **2.** anything shaped more or less like a loop. *–v.t.* **3.** to form into a loop or loops.

loophole /'luphoul/ *n.* an outlet, or means of escape or evasion.

loose /lus/ *adj.* **1.** free from bonds, fetters, or restraint. **2.** free or released from fastening or attachment. **3.** not bound together, as papers or flowers. **4.** not put in a package or other container. **5.** lax, as the bowels. **6.** not fitting closely, as garments. **7.** not close or compact in structure or arrangement. **8.** not strict, exact, or precise. *–v.t.* **9.** to let loose, or free from bonds or restraint. **10.** to unfasten, undo, or untie. **11.** to make less tight; slacken or relax. **12.** to render less firmly fixed, or loosen.

loose end *n.* **1.** something left unsettled or incomplete. *–phr.* **2. at a loose end**, without a specific task.

loosen /'lusən/ *v.t.* to make loose or looser.

loot /lut/ *n.* **1.** spoils or plunder taken by pillaging, as in war. **2.** *Colloq.* money. *–v.t.* **3.** to plunder or pillage (a city, house, etc.), as in war.

lop /lɒp/ *v.t.* (**lopped, lopping**) to cut off (protruding parts) of a tree, etc.

lope /loup/ *v.i.* to move or run with a long, easy stride.

lopsided /'lɒpsaɪdəd/ *adj.* heavier, larger, or more developed on one side than on the other; asymmetrical.

loquacious /lə'kweɪʃəs/ *adj.* talkative. **–loquacity,** *n.*

loquat /'loukwɒt, -kwæt, -kət/ *n.* a small, evergreen tree bearing a yellow plum-like fruit.

lord /lɔd/ *n.* **1.** someone who has dominion over others; a master, chief, or ruler. **2.** a titled nobleman, or peer. *–phr.* **3. lord it over someone**, to behave in a high-handed and dictatorial fashion towards someone.

lore /lɔ/ *n.* the body of knowledge, especially of a traditional, anecdotal, or popular nature, on a particular subject.

lorikeet /'lɒrəkit, lɒrə'kit/ *n.* any of various small, brightly coloured, arboreal parrots.

lorry /'lɒri/ *n.* → **truck¹** (def. 2).

lose /luz/ *v.* (**lost, losing**) *–v.t.* **1.** to come to be without, by some chance, and not know the whereabouts of. **2.** to suffer the loss or deprivation of. **3.** to become separated from and ignorant of (the way, etc.). **4.** to leave far behind in a pursuit, race, etc. **5.** to fail to win (a prize, stake, etc.). **6.** to absorb or engross (oneself) in something. *–v.i.* **7.** to suffer loss.

loser /'luzə/ *n.* **1.** someone who has lost a competition or race. **2.** *Colloq.* someone who is repeatedly unsuccessful, especially in social relationships.

loss /lɒs/ *n.* **1.** detriment or disadvantage from failure to keep, have, or get. **2.** that which is lost. **3.** amount or number lost. **4.** a being deprived of or coming to be without something that one has had. **5.** a losing by defeat, or failure to win. **6.** *Commerce* failure to recover the costs of a transaction or the like, in the form of benefits derived. **7.** *Insurance* **a.** occurrence of a risk covered by a contract of insurance so as to result in insurer liability. **b.** that which causes such a loss. **c.** an example of such a loss.

lost /lɒst/ *v.* past tense of **lose**.

lot /lɒt/ *n.* **1.** one of a set of objects drawn from a receptacle, etc., to decide a question or choice by chance. **2.** the decision or choice so made. **3.** one's fate, fortune, or destiny. **4.** a distinct portion or parcel of anything, as land, merchandise, etc. **5.** *Colloq.* a great many or a

great deal. *–phr.* **6. the lot**, the entire amount or quantity.

lotion /'louʃən/ *n.* a liquid containing oils or medicines, to be applied externally to the skin for soothing, healing or cleansing.

lottery /'lɒtəri, 'lɒtri/ *n.* (*pl.* **-ries**) any scheme for the distribution of prizes by chance.

lotus /'loutəs/ *n.* **1.** a plant referred to in Greek legend as yielding a fruit which induced a state of dreamy and contented forgetfulness in those who ate it. **2.** any of various waterlilies.

loud /laud/ *adj.* **1.** striking strongly upon the organs of hearing, as sound, noise, the voice, etc.; strongly audible. **2.** excessively striking to the eye, or offensively showy; as colours, dress or the wearer, etc.; garish.

loudspeaker /laud'spikə, 'laudspikə/ *n.* any of various devices by which speech, music, etc., can be made audible throughout a room, hall, or the like.

lounge /laundʒ/ *v.i.* (**lounged, lounging**) **1.** to pass time idly and indolently. **2.** to recline indolently; loll. *–n.* **3.** a living room. **4.** a large room in a hotel, airport, etc., used by guests or passengers for relaxation purposes or while waiting for a flight, etc. **5.** a sofa or couch.

lounge room *n.* the living room of a private residence.

lour /'lauə/ *v.i.* **1.** to be dark and threatening, as the sky or the weather. **2.** to frown, scowl, or look sullen.

louse /laus/ *n.* (*pl.* **lice** /laɪs/ *for def. 1,* **louses** *for def. 2*) **1.** a small, wingless, bloodsucking insect. **2.** *Colloq.* a despicable person. *–v.t.* **3.** *Colloq.* (fol. by *up*) to spoil.

lousy /'lauzi/ *adj.* (**-sier, -siest**) **1.** infested with lice. **2.** *Colloq.* mean, contemptible or unpleasant. **3.** *Colloq.* inferior; no good.

lout /laut/ *n.* *Colloq.* a rough, uncouth and sometimes violent young man.

louvre /'luvə/ *n.* an arrangement of slats closing a window or other opening.

lovable /'lʌvəbəl/ *adj.* of such a nature as to attract love. Also, **loveable**.

love /lʌv/ *n.* **1.** a strong or passionate affection for another person. **2.** a feeling of warm personal attachment or deep affection. **3.** strong predilection or liking for anything. **4.** *Tennis, etc.* nothing; no score. *–v.t.* (**loved, loving**) **5.** to have love or affection for. *–phr.* **6. in love (with)**, feeling deep affection or passion (for). **7. make love**, to have sexual intercourse.

lovely /'lʌvli/ *adj.* (**-lier, -liest**) charmingly or exquisitely beautiful.

lover /'lʌvə/ *n.* **1.** someone who loves another. **2.** a sexual partner.

loving /'lʌvɪŋ/ *adj.* feeling or showing love and affection. **–lovingly,** *adv.*

low¹ /lou/ *adj.* **1.** situated or occurring not far above the ground, floor, or base. **2.** lying or being below the general level. **3.** designating or relating to regions near the sea level or sea as opposed to highland or inland regions. **4.** rising but slightly from a surface. **5.** lacking in strength or vigour; feeble; weak. **6.** small in amount, degree, force, etc. **7.** assigning or attributing no great amount, value, or excellence. **8.** depressed or dejected. **9.** far down in the scale of rank or estimation; humble.

10. lacking in dignity or elevation, as of thought or expression. **11.** *Biol.* having a relatively simple structure; not complex in organisation. **12.** produced by relatively slow vibrations, as sounds. **13.** not loud. –*adv.* **14.** in or to a low position, point, degree, etc. –*n.* **15.** that which is low; a low level. **16.** *Meteorol.* a pressure system characterised by relatively low pressure at the centre. **17.** a point of least value, amount, etc.

low² /loʊ/ *v.i.* to utter the sound characteristic of cattle.

lowboy /ˈloʊbɔɪ/ *n.* a piece of furniture for holding clothes, similar to a wardrobe, but not so tall.

low-doc loan /ˈloʊ-dɒk/ *n. Colloq.* a loan from a lending institution, such as a bank, for which minimal documentation of the borrower's ability to service the loan is required. Compare **no-doc loan**. Also, **lo-doc loan**.

lowdown /ˈloʊdaʊn/ *n. Colloq.* the actual unadorned facts or truth on some subject.

lower /ˈloʊə/ *adj.* **1.** comparative of **low¹**. –*v.t.* **2.** to reduce in amount, price, degree, force, etc. **3.** to cause to descend, or let down.

lower case *n.* the small letters of the alphabet. *Abbrev.:* l.c.

lower house *n.* in a bicameral parliament, the lower legislative body, usually more numerous and more directly representative of the electorate than the upper house. Also, **lower chamber**.

low-key /ˈloʊ-ki/ *adj.* underplayed; restrained.

lowland /ˈloʊlənd/ *n.* land low with respect to neighbouring country.

lowly /ˈloʊli/ *adj.* (**-lier**, **-liest**) humble in station, condition, or nature.

low pressure system *n.* See **pressure system**.

low profile *n.* a lack of notice or recognition as a result of a deliberate avoidance of publicity or prominence.

loyal /ˈlɔɪəl/ *adj.* **1.** faithful to one's allegiance. **2.** faithful to one's oath, engagements or obligations.

lozenge /ˈlɒzəndʒ/ *n.* a small flavoured confection, often medicated.

LSD /ɛl ɛs ˈdi/ *n.* a hallucinogenic drug, lysergic acid diethylamide.

lubricate /ˈlubrəkeɪt/ *v.t.* to apply some oily, greasy, or other substance to, in order to diminish friction. –**lubricant**, *n.* –**lubrication**, *n.* –**lubricity**, *n.*

lucerne /ˈlusən/ *n.* a forage plant with bluish purple flowers; alfalfa.

lucid /ˈlusəd/ *adj.* **1.** shining or bright. **2.** clear.

luck /lʌk/ *n.* **1.** that which happens to a person, either good or bad, as if by chance, in the course of events. **2.** good fortune; advantage or success considered as the result of chance.

lucky /ˈlʌki/ *adj.* (**-kier**, **-kiest**) **1.** being in a good situation that others might like to be in. **2.** (of a person) usually having good luck. **3.** (a situation, etc.) happening by good luck or having good results. **4.** supposed to bring good luck. –**luckily**, *adv.*

lucrative /ˈlukrətɪv/ *adj.* profitable; remunerative.

lucre /ˈlukə/ *n.* gain or money as the object of sordid desire.

ludicrous /ˈludəkrəs/ *adj.* such as to cause laughter or derision; ridiculous; amusingly absurd.

lug /lʌg/ *v.t.* (**lugged, lugging**) to pull along or carry with effort.

luge /luʒ/ *n.* a type of toboggan ridden while lying on one's back.

luggage /ˈlʌgɪdʒ/ *n.* trunks, suitcases, etc., used in travelling; baggage.

lugubrious /ləˈgubriəs/ *adj.* mournful; doleful; dismal.

lukewarm /ˈlukwɔm/ *adj.* **1.** moderately warm; tepid. **2.** having or showing little ardour or zeal; indifferent.

lull /lʌl/ *v.t.* **1.** to put to sleep or rest by soothing means. **2.** to soothe or quiet. –*n.* **3.** a temporary quiet or stillness.

lullaby /ˈlʌləbaɪ/ *n.* a song intended to put a baby to sleep.

lumbar /ˈlʌmbə/ *adj.* of or relating to the loin or loins.

lumber¹ /ˈlʌmbə/ *n.* **1.** timber sawn or split into planks, boards, etc. –*v.i.* **2.** to cut timber and prepare it for market. –*v.t.* **3.** *Colloq.* to foist off on or leave with, as with something or someone unwelcome or unpleasant.

lumber² /ˈlʌmbə/ *v.i.* to move clumsily or heavily, especially from great or ponderous bulk.

lumberjack /ˈlʌmbədʒæk/ *n. Chiefly US and Canada* someone who works at lumbering.

luminary /ˈluminəri, -mənri/ *Orig.* /ˈlumənri/ *n.* (*pl.* **-ries**) **1.** a celestial body, as the sun or moon. **2.** a person who enlightens humankind or makes some subject clear.

luminescence /lumə'nesəns/ *n.* an emission of light not due directly to incandescence. –**luminescent**, *adj.*

luminous /ˈlumənəs/ *adj.* **1.** radiating or reflecting light; shining. **2.** lighted up or illuminated; well lighted. **3.** clear; readily intelligible. –**luminosity**, *n.*

lump¹ /lʌmp/ *n.* **1.** a piece or mass of solid matter without regular shape. –*v.t.* **2.** to unite into one aggregation, collection, or mass.

lump² /lʌmp/ *v.t. Colloq.* to endure or put up with (a disagreeable necessity).

lunacy /ˈlunəsi/ *n.* insanity. –**lunatic**, *n.*, *adj.*

lunar /ˈlunə/ *adj.* of or relating to the moon.

lunch /lʌntʃ/ *n.* **1.** a meal taken in the middle of the day. –*v.i.* **2.** to eat lunch.

luncheon /ˈlʌntʃən/ *n.* lunch.

lung /lʌŋ/ *n.* either of the two saclike respiratory organs in the thorax of humans and the higher vertebrates.

lunge /lʌndʒ/ *n.* **1.** a thrust, as in fencing. –*v.i.* (**lunged, lunging**) **2.** to make a lunge.

lungfish /ˈlʌŋfɪʃ/ *n.* (*pl.* **-fish** *or* **-fishes**) any of several elongated tropical freshwater fishes that breathes by means of modified lung-like structures as well as gills.

luni- a word element meaning 'moon'.

lupine /ˈlupaɪn/ *adj.* relating to or resembling the wolf.

lurch¹ /lɜtʃ/ *n.* **1.** a sudden leaning or roll to one side, as of a ship or a staggering person. –*v.i.* **2.** to make a lurch; move with lurches; stagger.

lurch² /lɜtʃ/ *phr.* **leave in the lurch**, to leave someone in a helpless situation.

lure /luə, 'ljuə/ n. **1.** anything that attracts, entices, or allures. −v.t. **2.** to decoy; entice; allure.

lurid /'lurəd/ adj. **1.** glaringly vivid or sensational. **2.** wan, pallid, or ghastly in hue.

lurk /lɜk/ v.i. **1.** to remain in or about a place secretly or furtively. −n. **2.** Colloq. a convenient, often unethical, method of performing a task, earning a living, etc.

luscious /'lʌʃəs/ adj. **1.** highly pleasing to the taste or smell. **2.** very luxurious; extremely attractive.

lush¹ /lʌʃ/ adj. **1.** tender and juicy, as plants or vegetation; succulent; luxuriant. **2.** Colloq. characterised by luxury and comfort.

lush² /lʌʃ/ n. Colloq. someone who drinks too much alcohol.

lust /lʌst/ n. **1.** passionate or overwhelming desire. **2.** sexual desire or appetite. −v.i. **3.** (oft. fol. by for or after) to have strong or inordinate desire, especially sexual desire.

lustre /'lʌstə/ n. the state or quality of shining by reflecting light; glitter, glisten, sheen, or gloss. −**lustrous**, adj.

lusty /'lʌsti/ adj. (-tier, -tiest) full of or characterised by healthy vigour.

lute /lut/ n. a stringed musical instrument. −**lutenist**, n.

luxuriant /lʌg'ʒuriənt/ adj. abundant or exuberant in growth, as vegetation.

luxuriate /lʌg'ʒuriet/ v.i. **1.** to indulge in luxury; revel. **2.** to take great delight.

luxury /'lʌkʃəri/ n. (pl. **-ries**) anything conducive to sumptuous living, usually a delicacy, elegance, or refinement of living rather than a necessity. −**luxurious**, adj.

-ly **1.** the normal adverbial suffix, added to almost any descriptive adjective, as in gladly, gradually. **2.** the adverbial suffix applied to units of time, meaning 'per', as in hourly. **3.** adjective suffix meaning 'like', as in saintly, manly.

lychee /'laɪ,tʃi, laɪ'tʃi/ n. a fruit with a thin brittle shell, enclosing a sweet jelly-like pulp and a single seed.

lycra /'laɪkrə/ n. (from trademark) a synthetic knitted fabric with great elasticity.

lye /laɪ/ n. any solution resulting from leaching, percolation, or the like.

lymph /lɪmf/ n. a clear, yellowish, slightly alkaline fluid derived from the tissues of the body and conveyed to the bloodstream by the lymphatic vessels. −**lymphatic**, adj.

lymphoma /lɪm'foumə/ n. (pl. **-mas** or **-mata**) any of various forms of cancer involving the lymph glands.

lynch /lɪntʃ/ v.t. to put (a person) to death without authority or process of law. −**lynching**, n.

lynx /lɪŋks/ n. (pl. **lynxes** or, especially collectively, **lynx**) any of various wildcats having long limbs and short tails.

lyre /'laɪə/ n. a musical instrument of ancient Greece.

lyrebird /'laɪəbɜd/ n. either of two ground-dwelling birds of south-eastern Australia, the males of which have long, lyre-shaped tails.

lyric /'lɪrɪk/ adj. Also, **lyrical**. **1.** (of poetry) having the form and musical quality of a song. **2.** relating to, rendered by, or employing singing. −n. **3.** a lyric poem. **4.** (oft. pl.) the words of a song.

lyricist /'lɪrəsəst/ n. someone who writes the words for songs.

-lyse a word element making verbs of processes represented by nouns in -lysis.

-lysis a word element, especially in scientific terminology, meaning 'breaking down', 'decomposition'.

-lyte a word element denoting something subjected to a certain process (indicated by a noun ending in -lysis).

-lytic a termination of adjectives corresponding to nouns in -lysis.

M, m

M, m /ɛm/ n. the 13th letter of the English alphabet.

ma'am /mæm, mam/, *if unstressed* /məm/ n. madam.

macabre /məˈkab, məˈkabə, -brə/ adj. gruesome; horrible; grim; ghastly.

macadamia /mækəˈdeɪmiə/ n. an ornamental tree which bears edible, hard-shelled nuts.

macadamise /məˈkædəmaɪz/ v.t. to construct (a road) by laying and rolling successive layers of broken stone. Also, **macadamize**.

macaron /mækəˈrɒn, mækəˈrɒ̃/ n. a small cake consisting of two smooth, rounded, soft-centred almond meringues, sandwiched together with a soft filling.

macaroni /mækəˈroʊni/ n. a kind of pasta.

macaroon /mækəˈruːn/ n. a sweet cake or biscuit, usually with coconut.

macaw /məˈkɔː/ n. a large, brightly coloured parrot with a harsh voice.

mace[1] /meɪs/ n. **1.** *Hist.* a club-like weapon of war. **2.** a staff borne as a symbol of office.

mace[2] /meɪs/ n. a spice resembling nutmeg in flavour.

macerate /ˈmæsəreɪt/ v.t. to soften by steeping in a liquid.

mach /mæk/ n. the ratio of the speed of an object to the speed of sound in the medium, usually air.

machete /məˈʃɛti/ n. a large, heavy knife.

machinate /ˈmæʃəneɪt, ˈmækəneɪt/ v.t. to contrive or devise, especially artfully or with evil purpose.

machination /mæʃəˈneɪʃən, mækəˈneɪʃən/ n. (*usu. pl.*) a secret plan or scheme, especially aimed at gaining power or doing something bad: *political machinations.*

machine /məˈʃiːn/ n. **1.** an apparatus consisting of interrelated parts with separate functions, which is used in the performance of some kind of work. **2.** *Mechanics* a device which transmits and modifies force or motion. –v.t. **3.** to make, prepare, or finish with a machine.

machine gun n. a small arm able to fire rapidly and continuously.

machinery /məˈʃiːnəri/ n. **1.** machines or mechanical apparatus. **2.** the parts of a machine, collectively.

machismo /məˈtʃɪzmoʊ, məˈkɪzmoʊ/ n. masculine display emphasising strength.

macho /ˈmætʃoʊ, ˈmækoʊ/ n. **1.** a man who displays machismo. –adj. **2.** showily virile.

-machy a combining form meaning 'combat'.

mackerel /ˈmækərəl/ n. a common iridescent greenish fish with irregular darker markings on the back.

mackintosh /ˈmækəntɒʃ/ n. a raincoat.

McLeod tool /məˈklaʊd/ n. a firefighting implement consisting of a tool with a hardened blade on one side and a rake on the other at the end of a long handle; used for lopping and clearing foliage to create a firebreak; rake-hoe.

macramé /məˈkrɑːmi/ n. a kind of lace or ornamental work made by knotting thread or cord in patterns. Also, **macrame**.

macro[1] /ˈmækroʊ/ adj. broad or overarching (opposed to *micro*): *at the macro level.*

macro[2] /ˈmækroʊ/ n. a single computer command which sets in train a number of other commands to perform a specific task.

macro- a prefix meaning 'long', 'large', 'great', 'excessive'. Also, (*before vowels*), **macr-**.

macrobiotic /mækroʊbaɪˈɒtɪk/ adj. of or relating to a largely vegetarian dietary system intended to prolong life.

macroclimate /ˈmækroʊˌklaɪmət/ n. the climate affecting a large geographical region. Compare **microclimate**.

macro-economics /ˌmækroʊ-ɛkəˈnɒmɪks, -ikə-/ n. (*construed as sing.*) study of the economic system as a whole. Compare **micro-economics**.

macrofauna /ˈmækroʊfɔːnə/ n. small animal organisms found in the soil or at the bottom of bodies of water, measuring at least 1 mm in length and measured in centimetres rather than in microscopic units. Compare **microfauna**.

macroscopic /mækrəˈskɒpɪk/ adj. **1.** visible to the naked eye (opposed to *microscopic*). **2.** comprehensive; concerned with large units or issues.

macular degeneration /ˈmækjələ/ n. a degenerative disease of the eye, which causes a progressive loss of central vision.

mad /mæd/ adj. (**madder, maddest**) disordered in intellect; insane.

madam /ˈmædəm/ n. **1.** (*pl.* **mesdames** /meɪˈdæm, meɪˈdam/ *or* **madams**) a polite term of address to a woman. **2.** (*pl.* **madams**) the woman in charge of a brothel.

mad cow disease n. a fatal virus disease of cattle which attacks the nervous system, and which can cross-infect humans; bovine spongiform encephalopathy.

made /meɪd/ v. **1.** past tense and past participle of **make**. –adj. **2.** assured of success or fortune.

madeira /məˈdɪərə/ n. (*sometimes upper case*) a rich, strong, white wine resembling sherry.

madrigal /ˈmædrɪɡəl/ n. a song with parts for several voices, performed without instrumental accompaniment.

maelstrom /ˈmeɪlstrəm/ n. a restless confusion of affairs, influence, etc.

maestro /ˈmaɪstroʊ/ n. (*pl.* **-tros** *or* **-tri** /-tri/) an eminent musical composer, teacher, or conductor.

magazine /mæɡəˈziːn/ n. **1.** a periodical publication, usually bound and with a paper cover. **2.** a room or place for keeping gunpowder and other explosives. **3.** a metal receptacle for a number of cartridges which is inserted into certain types of automatic weapons. **4.** *Photography* a light-proof enclosure containing film.

magenta /məˈdʒɛntə/ n., adj. reddish purple.

maggot /ˈmæɡət/ n. the legless larva of a fly.

magic /ˈmædʒɪk/ n. **1.** the art of producing effects claimed to be beyond the natural human power. **2.** any extraordinary or irresistible influence. **3.** conjuring. –adj. **4.** of, relating to, or due to magic. –**magician**, n.

magic bullet *n. Colloq.* **1.** any drug or treatment which acts effectively against a disease and has no harmful or unpleasant side effects. **2.** any remedy which is remarkably effective. *The policy was described as a magic bullet in the fight against crime.*

magisterial /mædʒəsˈtɪərɪəl/ *adj.* **1.** of or befitting a magistrate or a magistrate's office. **2.** of the rank of a magistrate.

magistrate /ˈmædʒəstreɪt, -trət/ *n.* a paid judicial officer presiding over a court of the lowest tier, and sometimes also performing other legal duties, for example, acting as coroner. Also, **stipendiary magistrate. –magistracy,** *n.*

magma /ˈmæɡmə/ *n. Geol.* molten material at great heat and pressure, occurring beneath the crust of the earth.

magnanimous /mæɡˈnænəməs/ *adj.* generous in forgiving an insult or injury. **–magnanimity,** *n.*

magnate /ˈmæɡneɪt, ˈmæɡnət/ *n.* a person of eminence or distinction in any field.

magnesium /mæɡˈniːziəm/ *n.* a light, ductile, silver-white metallic element which burns with a dazzling white light, used in lightweight alloys. *Symbol*: Mg

magnet /ˈmæɡnət/ *n.* **1.** a body (as a piece of iron or steel) which possesses the property of attracting certain substances. **2.** a thing or person that attracts, as by some inherent power or charm. **–magnetic,** *adj.* **–magnetism,** *n.* **–magnetise, magnetize,** *v.*

magnetic north *n.* the direction in which the needle of a compass points, differing in most places from true north.

magnetic resonance imaging *n.* a non-invasive imaging technique that produces an image of internal body organs by measurement of the radio frequency emitted by hydrogen nuclei in all tissues after they have been disturbed by an extremely strong magnetic field. *Abbrev.*: MRI

magnetic tape *n.* tape which is used to record sound for a tape-recorder, pictures for a video, or data for a computer.

magneto /mæɡˈniːtoʊ/ *n.* (*pl.* **-tos**) a small electric generator, the poles of which are permanent magnets.

magneto- a combining form of **magnet** or **magnetic**.

magni- a word element meaning 'large', 'great'.

magnification /mæɡnəfəˈkeɪʃən/ *n.* **1.** a magnified copy or reproduction. **2.** (of an optical instrument) the ratio of the linear dimensions of the final image to that of the object.

magnificent /mæɡˈnɪfəsənt/ *adj.* extraordinarily fine.

magnify /ˈmæɡnəfaɪ/ *v.* (**-fied, -fying**) **–v.t. 1.** to increase the apparent size of, as a lens does. **2.** to make greater in size; enlarge. **–v.i. 3.** to increase or be able to increase the apparent size of an object, as a lens does.

magnitude /ˈmæɡnətjuːd/ *n.* **1.** size; extent. **2.** great amount, importance, etc.

magnolia /mæɡˈnoʊliə/ *n.* any of several shrubs and trees, usually with fragrant flowers.

magnum /ˈmæɡnəm/ *n.* (*pl.* **-nums**) a bottle for wine or spirits, holding about 2 normal bottles, or 1.5 litres.

magpie /ˈmæɡpaɪ/ *n.* any of several common black and white birds.

magpie lark *n.* a common Australian black-and-white bird which builds its mud nest high in a tree; peewee.

maharajah /mɑːhəˈrɑːdʒə/ *n.* the title of certain great ruling princes in India. Also, **maharaja**.

maharani /mɑːhəˈrɑːni/ *n.* **1.** the wife of a maharajah. **2.** a female sovereign in her own right. Also, **maharanee**.

mahjong /ˈmɑːˌdʒɒŋ, -ˌdʒɒŋ/ *n.* a game of Chinese origin, usually for four persons, with 136 (or sometimes 144) domino-like pieces or tiles.

mahogany /məˈhɒɡəni/ *n.* (*pl.* **-nies**) **1.** any of certain tropical American trees yielding a hard, reddish brown wood highly esteemed for making fine furniture, etc. **2.** a reddish brown colour.

maid /meɪd/ *n.* **1.** a girl; unmarried woman. **2.** a woman employed for various light domestic duties in houses, hotels, etc.; housemaid.

maiden /ˈmeɪdn/ *n.* **1.** a maid; girl; young unmarried woman; virgin. **–adj. 2.** made, tried, appearing, etc., for the first time.

maiden name *n.* a woman's surname before marriage.

maiden over *n.* (in cricket) an over in which no runs are made.

mail¹ /meɪl/ *n.* **1.** letters, packages, etc., arriving or sent by post. **2.** the system of transmission of letters, etc., by post. **–adj. 3.** of or relating to mail. **–v.t. 4.** to send by mail; place in a post office or post-box for transmission.

mail² /meɪl/ *n.* flexible armour of interlinked rings.

mail merge *n. Computers* a software function for linking a document to a spreadsheet of names and addresses to output a document to multiple recipients.

mail order *n.* an order for goods, etc., received and transmitted by post.

maim /meɪm/ *v.t.* **1.** to deprive of the use of some bodily member; mutilate; cripple. **2.** to impair; make essentially defective.

main /meɪn/ *adj.* **1.** chief; principal; leading. **–n. 2.** a principal pipe or duct in a system used to distribute water, gas, etc. **3.** the chief or principal part or point. **–phr. 4. with might and main,** utmost strength, vigour, force, or effort.

mainframe computer *n.* a powerful computer with a large storage capacity.

mainland /ˈmeɪnlænd, -lənd/ *n.* the principal land mass as distinguished from nearby islands and peninsulas.

mainline /ˈmeɪnlaɪn/ *v.i. Colloq.* to inject a narcotic drug directly into the vein.

mainstream /ˈmeɪnstriːm/ *n.* the dominant trend; chief tendency.

maintain /meɪnˈteɪn, mən-/ *v.t.* **1.** to keep in existence or continuance; preserve; retain. **2.** to affirm; assert.

maintenance /ˈmeɪntənəns/ *n.* **1.** the act of maintaining. **2.** *Law* the money paid for the support of the other spouse or infant children, usually after divorce.

maize /meɪz/ *n.* → **corn**¹ (def. 1).

majesty /ˈmædʒəsti/ *n.* (*pl.* **-ties**) **1.** regal or stately dignity; imposing character; grandeur. **2.** (*usu. upper case*) (preceded by *his, her,* *your*, etc.) a title used when speaking of or to a sovereign. **–majestic**, *adj.*

major /'meɪdʒə/ *adj.* **1.** greater, as in size, amount, extent, importance, rank, etc. **2.** of full legal age. **–n. 3.** an officer in the army. **4.** a field of study chosen by a student to represent their principal interest.

majority /mə'dʒɒrəti/ *n.* (*pl.* **-ties**) **1.** the greater part or number. **2.** the state or time of being of full legal age. **3.** in an election or other vote, the difference in the number of votes received by the winner and the person or group coming second.

majorly /'meɪdʒəli/ *adv. Colloq.* completely: *to be majorly uncool.*

Major Mitchell /'mɪtʃəl/ *n.* a white cockatoo with a scarlet crest, found in dry regions of Australia.

make /meɪk/ *v.* (**made, making**) *–v.t.* **1.** to produce by any action or causative agency. **2.** to cause to be or become; render. **3.** to put into proper condition for use. **4.** to cause, induce, or compel (to do something). **5.** to do; effect. **6.** to become by development; prove to be. **7.** to estimate; reckon. **8.** to arrive at or reach. **9.** to arrive in time for. **10.** *Colloq.* to seduce or have sexual intercourse with. *–v.i.* **11.** to cause oneself, or something understood, to be as specified. **12.** to show oneself in action or behaviour. **13.** to direct or pursue the course; go. *–n.* **14.** style or manner of being made; form; build. *–phr.* **15. make a face,** to grimace. **16. make believe,** to pretend. **17. make do,** to operate or carry on using minimal or improvised resources. **18. make love,** *Colloq.* to have sexual intercourse. **19. make out, a.** to discern; decipher. **b.** to present as; impute to. **20. make tracks,** *Colloq.* to depart. **21. make up, a.** to put together; construct; compile. **b.** to compensate for; make good. **c.** to bring to a definite conclusion, as one's mind. **d.** also, **make it up,** to become reconciled after a quarrel. **e.** to apply cosmetics to, as the face.

makeover /'meɪkoʊvə/ *n.* **1.** cosmetic treatment of the face leading to a very different appearance. **2.** any radical alteration in the structure or appearance of something: *a kitchen makeover; give your old couch a makeover.*

makeshift /'meɪkʃɪft/ *n.* a temporary expedient; substitute.

make-up /'meɪk-ʌp/ *n.* **1.** cosmetics, as those used by a woman to enhance her features. **2.** → **foundation** (def. 5). **3.** the manner of being made up or put together; composition. **4.** physical or mental constitution.

makings /'meɪkɪŋz/ *pl. n.* material of which something may be made.

mal- a prefix meaning 'bad', 'wrongful', 'ill'.

maladjustment /mælə'dʒʌstmənt/ *n.* **1.** a faulty adjustment. **2.** *Psychol.* a failure to function successfully with regard to personal relationships and environment, often a symptom of mental disturbance.

malady /'mælədi/ *n.* (*pl.* **-dies**) any bodily disorder or disease, especially one that is chronic or deep-seated.

malapropism /'mæləprɒp,ɪzəm/ *n.* a word ridiculously misused.

malaria /mə'lɛəriə/ *n.* any of a group of diseases characterised by attacks of chills, fever, and sweating.

malcontent /'mælkəntɛnt/ *adj.* **1.** dissatisfied, especially with the existing administration; inclined to rebellion. *–n.* **2.** a malcontent person.

male /meɪl/ *adj.* **1.** belonging to the sex capable of fertilising female ova. **2.** relating to or characteristic of this sex; masculine. **3.** *Machinery* designating some part, etc., which fits into a corresponding part. *–n.* **4.** a male person or animal.

male chauvinist *n.* a man who discriminates against women.

malevolent /mə'lɛvələnt/ *adj.* wishing evil to another or others; showing ill will.

malformation /mælfɔ'meɪʃən, -fə-/ *n.* faulty or anomalous formation or structure, especially in a living body. **–malformed**, *adj.*

malfunction /mæl'fʌŋkʃən/ *v.i.* **1.** to fail to function properly. *–n.* **2.** failure to function properly.

malibu /'mælɪbu/ *n.* a long surfboard, offering more stability than a short board. Also, **malibu board.**

malice /'mæləs/ *n.* **1.** desire to inflict injury or suffering on another. **2.** *Law* evil intent on the part of someone who commits a wrongful act injurious to others. **–malicious** /mə'lɪʃəs/, *adj.*

malign /mə'laɪn/ *v.t.* **1.** to speak ill of; slander. *–adj.* **2.** having or showing an evil disposition; malevolent.

malignant /mə'lɪgnənt/ *adj.* **1.** very dangerous; harmful in influence or effect. **2.** *Pathol.* deadly; tending to produce death, as a disease, tumour, etc.

malinger /mə'lɪŋgə/ *v.i.* to feign sickness or injury, especially in order to avoid work, etc.

mall /mɔl, mæl/ *n.* **1.** a street or part of a street lined with shops and closed off to traffic. **2.** Also, **shopping mall.** a shopping complex.

malleable /'mæliəbəl/ *adj.* **1.** capable of being extended or shaped by hammering or by pressure with rollers. **2.** adaptable or tractable.

mallee /'mæli/ *n.* **1.** any of various eucalypts having a number of almost unbranched stems arising from a large underground woody tuber. *–phr.* **2. the mallee,** *Colloq.* any remote, isolated or unsettled area.

mallet /'mælət/ *n.* a hammer-like tool.

malnutrition /mælnju'trɪʃən/ *n.* lack of proper nutrition resulting from deficiencies in the diet or the process of assimilation.

malpractice /mæl'præktəs/ *n.* improper professional action.

malt /mɔlt, mɒlt/ *n.* germinated grain (usually barley), used in brewing and distilling.

maltreat /mæl'trit/ *v.t.* to treat badly; handle roughly or cruelly; abuse.

malware /'mælwɛə/ *n. Computers* software created with a destructive intent, such as a virus, trojan horse, worm, etc.

mama /mə'ma/ *n.* mother; mummy.

mamilla /mæ'mɪlə/ *n.* (*pl.* **-millae** /-'mɪli/) the nipple of the breast.

mammal /'mæməl/ *n.* a member of the class of vertebrates whose young feed upon milk from the mother's breast.

mammary /'mæməri/ *adj.* of or relating to the breast.

mammogram /'mæməgræm/ *n.* an X-ray taken of the breasts.

mammoth /'mæməθ/ *n.* **1.** a large, extinct species of elephant. *–adj.* **2.** huge; gigantic.

man /mæn/ *n.* (*pl.* **men**) **1.** an adult male human being. **2.** the human race; humankind. **3.** a male servant; a valet. **4.** one of the pieces used in playing certain games, as chess or draughts. *–v.t.* (**manned, manning**) **5.** to furnish with personnel, as for service or defence. **6.** to take one's place for service, as at a gun, post, etc.

manacle /'mænəkəl/ *n.* (*usu. pl.*) **1.** a shackle for the hand; handcuff. **2.** a restraint. *–v.t.* **3.** to handcuff; fetter.

manage /'mænɪdʒ/ *v.* (**-aged, -aging**) *–v.t.* **1.** to bring about; succeed in accomplishing. **2.** to take charge or care of. **3.** to contrive to get along. *–v.i.* **4.** to conduct affairs.

management /'mænɪdʒmənt/ *n.* **1.** the act or manner of managing. **2.** the person or persons managing an institution, business, etc.

management information system *n.* *Computers* a software package which is designed to provide information for decision-making, usually intended for senior management.

manager /'mænədʒə/ *n.* **1.** a person charged with the management or direction of an institution, a business or the like. **2.** a person in charge of the business affairs of an entertainer, etc. *–managerial*, *adj.*

manchester /'mæntʃəstə, 'mæntʃɛstə/ *n.* household linen.

-mancy a word element meaning 'divination'.

mandarin /'mændərən, mændə'rɪn/ *n.* **1.** (formerly) a public official in the Chinese Empire. **2.** Also, **mandarine**. a small, roundish citrus fruit.

mandate /'mændeɪt/ *n.* **1.** (formerly) a commission given by the League of Nations to administer a territory. **2.** *Politics* the instruction as to policy given or supposed to be given by electors to a legislative body or to one or more of its members.

mandatory /'mændətri, -təri/, *Orig. US* /'mændeɪtəri/ *adj.* obligatory.

mandatory detention *n.* incarceration of an offender or deemed offender which is obligatory rather than resting with the judgement of a court or other official body.

mandatory sentencing *n.* *Law* sentencing which is set down in legislation rather than resting with the judgement of the court.

mandible /'mændəbəl/ *n.* the bone of the lower jaw.

mandolin /'mændə'lɪn/ *n.* a musical instrument with a pear-shaped wooden body and metal strings.

mane /meɪn/ *n.* the long hair growing on the back of or about the neck of some animals.

manga /'mæŋgə/ *n.* the Japanese form of comic book, which has a wide variety of subject areas, catering for both children and adults.

manga movie /'mæŋgə muvi/ *n.* a Japanese animated movie, made in the style of the Japanese comic books; anime.

manganese /'mæŋgə'niz/ *n.* a hard, brittle, greyish-white metallic element used in alloys. *Symbol:* Mn

mange /meɪndʒ/ *n.* any of various skin diseases characterised by loss of hair and scabby eruptions. *–mangy*, *adj.*

manger /'meɪndʒə/ *n.* a box or trough, as in a stable, from which horses or cattle eat.

mangle[1] /'mæŋgəl/ *v.t.* to cut, slash, or crush so as to disfigure.

mangle[2] /'mæŋgəl/ *n.* a machine for pressing water out of cloth by means of rollers.

mango /'mæŋgoʊ/ *n.* (*pl.* **-goes** *or* **-gos**) the ovoid fruit of a tropical tree.

mangrove /'mæŋgroʊv, 'mæn-/ *n.* a tree found in subtropical and tropical countries on salt or brackish mudflats.

manhandle /'mænhændl/ *v.t.* to handle roughly.

manhole /'mænhoʊl/ *n.* a hole, usually with a cover, through which a person may enter a sewer, drain, steam boiler, etc.

man-hour /'mæn-aʊə/ *n.* an hour of work by one person, used as an industrial time unit.

mania /'meɪniə/ *n.* **1.** great excitement or enthusiasm; craze. **2.** *Psychol.* a form of mental illness characterised by great excitement and hyperactivity.

-mania a combining form of **mania**.

maniac /'meɪniæk/ *n.* a person exhibiting wild or violent behaviour, especially one viewed as suffering mental illness.

manic /'mænɪk/ *adj.* **1.** relating to mania. **2.** experiencing manic depression. See **bipolar disorder**. **3.** *Colloq.* frenziedly overactive; agitated.

manic depression *n.* → **bipolar disorder**. *–manic depressive, n.* *–manic-depressive, adj.*

manicure /'mænəkjuə, -kjʊə/ *n.* professional care of the hands and fingernails.

manifest /'mænəfəst, -fɛst/ *adj.* **1.** readily perceived by the eye or the understanding. *–v.t.* **2.** to make manifest. *–n.* **3.** a list of goods or cargo carried, as by a ship, truck, etc. *–manifestation, n.*

manifesto /mænə'fɛstoʊ/ *n.* (*pl.* **-tos** *or* **-toes**) a public declaration, making known intentions, objects, motives, etc.

manifold /'mænəfoʊld/ *adj.* **1.** of many kinds; numerous and varied. **2.** having many different parts, elements, features, forms, etc. **3.** a pipe or chamber with a number of inlets or outlets. *–v.t.* **4.** to make copies of, as with carbon paper.

manipulate /mə'nɪpjəleɪt/ *v.t.* **1.** to handle, manage, or use, especially with skill. **2.** to handle or move (part of the body) as for therapeutic purposes. **3.** to adapt or change (accounts, figures, etc.) to suit one's purpose or advantage.

mankind /mæn'kaɪnd/ *n.* **1.** → **humankind**. **2.** men, as distinguished from women; the male sex.

mannequin /'mænəkən, -kwən/ *n.* **1.** a model of the human figure for displaying or fitting clothes. **2.** → **model** (def. 4).

manner /'mænə/ *n.* **1.** way of doing, being done, or happening. **2.** (*pl.*) ways of behaving, especially with reference to polite standards. **3.** kind; sort. *–phr.* **4. to the manner born**, accustomed or destined by birth (to a high position, etc.).

mannerism /'mænərizəm/ n. a habitual peculiarity of manner.

manoeuvre /mə'nuvə/ n. **1.** a planned and regulated movement of troops, war vessels, etc. **2.** an adroit move; skilful measure. –v. (**-vred, -vring**) **3.** to manipulate with skill or adroitness. –v.i. **4.** to perform a manoeuvre or manoeuvres. **5.** to scheme; intrigue.

manor /'mænə/ n. the main house or mansion on an estate.

manse /mæns/ n. the house and land occupied by a minister or parson.

mansion /'mænʃən/ n. an imposing residence.

manslaughter /'mænslɔtə/ n. Law the killing of a human being unlawfully but without the intention to kill.

mantelpiece /'mæntlpis/ n. the structure around a fireplace.

mantelshelf /'mæntlʃɛlf/ n. (pl. **-shelves**) the projecting part of a mantelpiece.

mantis /'mæntəs/ n. any of various insects which hold the forelegs doubled up as if in prayer. Also, **praying mantis**.

mantle /'mæntl/ n. **1.** Also, **mantua**. a loose, sleeveless cloak. **2.** something that covers, envelops, or conceals. **3.** Geol. a layer of the earth between crust and core, consisting of solid rock.

mantra /'mæntrə/ n. a word, phrase or verse, as a sacred formula in Hinduism and Mahayana Buddhism intoned, often repetitively, to focus the mind. Also, **mantram**, **-mantric**, adj.

manual /'mænjuəl/ adj. **1.** of or relating to the hand or hands. **2.** using or involving human energy, power, etc. –n. **3.** a book, giving information or instructions.

manufacture /mænjə'fæktʃə, 'mænjəfæktʃə/ n. **1.** the making of goods or wares by manufacturing. –v.t. **2.** to make or produce by hand or machinery, especially on a large scale. **3.** to invent fictitiously; concoct; devise.

manuka /mə'nukə, 'manəkə/ n. a small New Zealand tree, valued as a honey plant.

manure /mə'njuə/ n. excrement, especially of animals, used as fertiliser.

manuscript /'mænjəskrɪpt/ n. **1.** a book, document, letter, musical score, etc., written by hand. **2.** an author's copy of a work, written by hand or typewriter, which is used as the basis for typesetting. **3.** writing, as distinguished from print.

many /'mɛni/ adj. **1.** constituting or forming a large number. **2.** relatively numerous (after as, so, too, or how). **3.** (fol. by a or an) being one of a large number. –pron. **4.** a great or considerable number (often followed by a noun with of expressed or understood).

map /mæp/ n. a representation, on a flat surface, of a part or the whole of the earth's surface, the heavens, or a heavenly body.

maple /'meɪpəl/ n. a tree of the north temperate zone from the sap of which **maple syrup** is made.

mar /ma/ v.t. (**marred, marring**) to damage; impair; ruin.

maraca /mə'rækə/ n. a gourd filled with pebbles, seeds, etc., and used as a percussion instrument.

marathon /'mærəθon, -θən/ n. a long-distance race.

maraud /mə'rɔd/ v.i. to rove in quest of plunder. –**marauding**, adj.

marble /'mabəl/ n. **1.** limestone in a more or less crystalline state and capable of taking a polish, occurring in a wide range of colours and markings, and much used in sculpture and architecture. **2.** something resembling marble in hardness, coldness, smoothness, etc. **3.** Games **a.** a little ball of stone, baked clay, glass, etc., used in a children's game. **b.** (pl. construed as sing.) the game itself. –adj. **4.** consisting of marble. **5.** like marble, as being hard, cold, unfeeling, etc. **6.** of variegated or mottled colour. –v.t. **7.** to colour or stain like variegated marble.

march /matʃ/ v.i. **1.** to walk with regular and measured tread, as soldiers; advance in step in an organised body. **2.** to proceed; advance. –v.t. **3.** to cause to march. –n. **4.** the act or course of marching. **5.** a piece of music with a rhythm suited to accompany marching.

marching orders pl. n. orders to leave; dismissal.

mare /mɛə/ n. a female horse.

margarine /madʒə'rin, mag-, 'madʒərən/ n. a butter-like product made from refined vegetable or animal oils.

margin /'madʒən/ n. **1.** a border or edge. **2.** Finance a security, as a percentage in money, deposited with a broker as a provision against loss on transactions on behalf of the investor. **3.** Commerce the difference between the cost and the selling price. **4.** Econ. the point at which the return from economic activity barely covers the cost of production, and below which production is unprofitable. **5.** Banking the excess value of the relative security over the loan for which it is collateral. **6.** that part of a wage, additional to the basic wage, which is offered to recompense an employee for their particular skills. –**marginal**, adj.

marigold /'mærigoʊld/ n. any of various chiefly golden-flowered plants.

marijuana /mærə'wanə/ n. the dried leaves and flowers of Indian hemp, used in cigarettes as a narcotic and intoxicant. Also, **marihuana**.

marina /mə'rinə/ n. a facility offering docking and other services for small craft.

marinade n. /mærə'neɪd/ **1.** a liquid, especially wine or vinegar with oil and seasonings, in which meat, fish, vegetables, etc., may be steeped before cooking. –v.t. /'mærəneɪd/ **2.** → **marinate**.

marinate /'mærəneɪt/ v.t. to let stand in a liquid before cooking or serving in order to impart flavour.

marine /mə'rin/ adj. **1.** of or relating to the sea. **2.** relating to navigation or shipping.

mariner /'mærənə/ n. someone who directs or assists in the navigation of a ship; sailor.

marionette /mæriə'nɛt/ n. a puppet moved by strings attached to its jointed limbs.

marital /'mærətəl/ adj. of or relating to marriage.

maritime /'mærətaɪm/ adj. of or relating to the sea.

maritime climate n. a type of climate characterised by little temperature change, high cloud cover and precipitation, and associated with coastal areas.

mark /mak/ *n.* **1.** a visible trace or impression upon anything. **2.** a sign, token, or indication. **3.** a symbol used in rating conduct, proficiency, attainment, etc., as of pupils in a school. **4.** a recognised or required standard. **5.** something aimed at, as a target. *-v.t.* **6.** to be a distinguishing feature of. **7.** to put a mark or marks on. **8.** to castrate (a lamb, calf, etc.). **9.** to indicate or designate by or as by marks. **10.** to notice or observe. *-v.i.* **11.** to take notice; give attention; consider. *-phr.* **12. mark down**, to reduce the price of. **13. mark up**, to increase the price of.

market /'makət/ *n.* **1.** a meeting of people for selling and buying. **2.** a place where such meetings are held, especially for the sale of food, etc. **3.** a body of persons carrying on extensive transactions in a specified commodity. **4. a.** trade or traffic, particularly as regards a particular commodity. **b.** demand for a particular commodity. **5.** current price or value. *-v.i.* **6.** to deal (buy or sell) in a market. **7.** to dispose of in a market; sell.

marketable /'makətəbəl/ *adj.* readily saleable.

market garden *n.* a garden or smallholding where vegetables and fruit are grown for sale.

marketing /'makətɪŋ/ *n.* **1.** the total process whereby goods are put onto the market. **2.** the act of buying or selling in a market.

market research *n.* the gathering of information by a firm about the preferences, purchasing power, etc., of consumers, especially as a preliminary to putting a product on the market.

markup language /'makʌp/ *n.* a computer language in which various elements of a document, database, etc., are marked with tags, providing a flexible means of arranging and retrieving data. See **HTML**, **SGML**, **XML**.

marlin /'malən/ *n.* any of various species of large, powerful, game fishes.

marmalade /'maməleɪd/ *n.* a jelly-like preserve with fruit (usually citrus) suspended in small pieces.

marmot /'mamət/ *n.* a bushy-tailed, thickset rodent.

maroon[1] /mə'ruːn, mə'run/ *n.* **1.** dark brownish red. *-adj.* **2.** of a dark brownish red colour.

maroon[2] /mə'run/ *v.t.* to put ashore and leave on a desolate island or coast.

marquee /ma'ki/ *n.* a large tent or tentlike shelter, sometimes with open sides.

marriage /'mærɪdʒ/ *n.* **1.** the legal union of two people; wedlock. **2.** the legal or religious ceremony that sanctions or formalises such a union. **3.** any intimate union.

marriage celebrant /'sɛləbrənt/ *n.* someone who performs a marriage, especially in a civil service.

married /'mærid/ *adj.* united in wedlock; wedded.

marron[1] /'mærən/ *n.* a chestnut.

marron[2] /'mærən/ *n.* (*pl.* **marron** *or* **marrons**) a large freshwater crayfish of western Australia.

marrow /'mæroʊ/ *n.* **1.** a soft, fatty vascular tissue in the interior cavities of bones. **2.** a green-skinned elongated fruit widely used as a cooked vegetable.

marry /'mæri/ *v.* (**-ried, -rying**) *-v.t.* **1.** to take in marriage. **2.** to unite in wedlock. *-v.i.* **3.** to enter into the bond of marriage; wed.

Marsala /mə'salə, ma-/ *n.* (*sometimes lower case*) a sweet, dark, fortified wine.

marsh /maʃ/ *n.* a tract of low, wet land.

marshal /'maʃəl/ *n.* **1.** the title of various officials having certain police duties. *-v.t.* (**-shalled, -shalling**) **2.** to arrange in due or proper order; set out in an orderly manner.

marshmallow /'maʃmæloʊ, -mɛl-/ *n.* confection with an elastic, spongy texture.

marsupial /ma'supiəl, -'sjup-/ *n.* any member of the order which includes all of the viviparous but non-placental mammals such as kangaroos, wombats, possums, etc. Most marsupials carry their young in a pouch.

mart /mat/ *n.* market.

martial /'maʃəl/ *adj.* relating to or appropriate for war.

martial art *n.* any of the several methods of unarmed self-defence originating in China, Korea and Japan, as judo, kung-fu, etc.

martial law *n.* the law imposed upon an area by military forces when civil authority has broken down.

martinet /matə'nɛt/ *n.* a rigid disciplinarian, especially a military one.

martini /ma'tini/ *n.* (*from trademark*) a type of cocktail, made from gin and vermouth.

martyr /'matə/ *n.* someone who is put to death or endures great suffering on behalf of any belief, principle, or cause, especially religious.

marvel /'mavəl/ *n.* **1.** something that arouses wonder or admiration. *-v.t.* (**-velled, -velling**) **2.** to wonder at (usually followed by a clause as object).

marvellous /'mavələs/ *adj.* **1.** such as to excite wonder; surprising; extraordinary. **2.** excellent; superb. **3.** improbable or incredible.

marzipan /'mazəpæn/ *n.* a confection made of almond paste.

mascara /mæs'karə/ *n.* a substance used as a cosmetic to colour the eyelashes.

mascot /'mæskɒt/ *n.* a person, animal, or thing supposed to bring good luck.

masculine /'mæskjələn/ *adj.* relating to or characteristic of a man or men.

mash /mæʃ/ *n.* **1.** a soft, pulpy mass. **2.** mashed potatoes. *-v.t.* **3.** to reduce to a soft, pulpy mass, as by heating or pressure.

mashup /'mæʃʌp/ *n.* **1.** a song created by blending two or more songs, usually by overlaying the vocal track of one song onto the music track of another. **2.** *Computers* an application that combines data and functionality, drawing on two or more separate sources for the data and the software. **3.** *Lit.* a blending of a classic text with an element of contemporary fiction genres, as by recontextualising *Jane Eyre* with a zombie theme. Also, **mash-up**. *-***mashupper**, *n.*

mask /mask/ *n.* **1.** a covering for the face, especially one worn for disguise or protection. **2.** anything that disguises or conceals; a disguise; a pretence. *-v.t.* **3.** to disguise or conceal.

masking tape *n.* an adhesive tape used for defining edges and protecting surfaces not to be painted.

masochism /ˈmæsəkɪzəm/ n. a condition in which one compulsively seeks, and sometimes derives pleasure from, suffering, as humiliation, pain, etc. —**masochistic**, adj. —**masochist**, n.

mason /ˈmeɪsən/ n. someone who builds or works with stone.

masonite /ˈmeɪsənaɪt/ n. (from trademark) a kind of wood-fibre material, pressed in sheets and used for partitions, insulation, etc.

masonry /ˈmeɪsənri/ n. (pl. **-ries**) **1.** the art or occupation of a mason. **2.** work constructed by a mason.

masquerade /mæskəˈreɪd, mas-/ n. **1.** a party at which everyone wears a mask. **2.** disguise, or false outward show. —v.i. **3.** to disguise oneself.

mass[1] /mæs/ n. **1.** a body of coherent matter, usually of indefinite shape and often of considerable size. **2.** an aggregation of incoherent particles, parts, or objects regarded as forming one body. —adj. **3.** relating to or involving a large number of people. **4.** large-scale or wide-reaching. —v.i. **5.** to come together in or form a mass or masses. —v.t. **6.** to gather into or dispose in a mass or masses; assemble. —phr. **7. the masses**, the great body of the common people.

mass[2] /mæs/ n. the celebration of the Eucharist.

massacre /ˈmæsəkə/ n. **1.** the unnecessary, indiscriminate slaughter of human beings. —v.t. (**-cred**, **-cring**) **2.** to kill indiscriminately or in a massacre.

massage /ˈmæsaʒ, ˈmæsadʒ/ n. **1.** the act or art of treating the body by rubbing, kneading, etc. —v.t. (**-saged**, **-saging**) **2.** to treat by massage.

masseur /mæˈsɜ/ n. a man who practises massage.

masseuse /mæˈsɜz, məˈsus/ n. a woman who practises massage.

massive /ˈmæsɪv/ adj. consisting of or forming a large mass; bulky and heavy.

mass media n. → **media** (def. 2).

mass-produce /mæs-prəˈdjus/ v.t. (**-duced**, **-ducing**) to manufacture in large quantities by standardised mechanical processes.

mast /mast/ n. a tall spar which supports the yards, sails, etc., of a ship.

mast- variant of **masto-** before vowels.

mastectomy /mæsˈtɛktəmi/ n. (pl. **-mies**) the operation of removing the breast.

master /ˈmastə/ n. **1.** someone who has the power of controlling, using, or disposing of something. **2.** the male head of a household. **3.** a tradesperson qualified to carry on their trade independently and to teach apprentices. **4.** Law an officer of the Supreme Court of Judicature whose main function is to decide preliminary issues in High Court cases. **5.** the head teacher in a particular subject department in a secondary school. **6.** someone who has been awarded a further degree, usually subsequent to a bachelor's degree, at a university (used only in titles or in certain other expressions relating to such a degree). **7.** Music an original recording from which copies, remixes, etc., are made. —adj. **8.** being master. **9.** chief or principal. —v.t. **10.** to conquer or subdue; reduce to subjection. **11.** to rule or direct

as master. **12.** to make oneself master of. —**mastery**, n.

master key n. a key that will open a number of locks whose proper keys are not interchangeable. Also, **pass key**.

master of ceremonies n. a person who directs the entertainment at a party, dinner, etc.

masterpiece /ˈmastəpis/ n. **1.** one's most excellent production, as in an art. **2.** any production of masterly skill. **3.** a consummate example of skill or excellence of any kind.

masterstroke /ˈmastəstroʊk/ n. a masterly action or achievement.

masticate /ˈmæstɪkeɪt/ v.t. to chew.

masto- a word element meaning the breast. Also, **mast-**.

masturbation /mæstəˈbeɪʃən/ n. sexual stimulation not involving intercourse. —**masturbate**, v.

mat /mæt/ n. **1.** a piece of fabric made of plaited or woven rushes, straw, hemp, or other fibre, used to cover a floor, to wipe the shoes on, etc. **2.** a small piece of material, often ornamental, set under a dish of food, a lamp, vase, etc. —v. (**matted**, **matting**) —v.t. **3.** to form into a mat, as by interweaving. —v.i. **4.** to become entangled; form tangled masses.

matador /ˈmætədɔ/ n. the bullfighter who kills the bull in a bullfight.

match[1] /mætʃ/ n. a short, slender piece of wood or other material tipped with a chemical substance which produces fire when rubbed on a rough or chemically prepared surface.

match[2] /mætʃ/ n. **1.** a person or thing that equals or resembles another in some respect. **2.** a contest or game. **3.** a matrimonial compact or alliance. —v.t. **4.** to equal, or be equal to. **5.** to adapt; make to correspond. **6.** to fit together, as two things. —v.i. **7.** to be equal or suitable. **8.** to correspond.

match point n. the final point needed to win a contest.

mate /meɪt/ n. **1.** one joined with another in any pair. **2.** one of a pair of mated animals. **3. a.** a friend. **b.** a form of address: how are you going mate? —v.i. (**mated**, **mating**) **4.** to join as a mate or as mates. **5.** (of animals) to copulate.

material /məˈtɪəriəl/ n. **1.** the substance or substances of which a thing is made or composed. **2.** information, ideas, or the like on which a report, thesis, etc., is based. **3.** a textile fabric. —adj. **4.** formed or consisting of matter; physical; corporeal. **5.** relating to the physical rather than the spiritual or intellectual aspect of things. **6.** (fol. by to) pertinent or essential.

materialise /məˈtɪəriəlaɪz/ v.t. **1.** to assume material or bodily form. **2.** to come into perceptible existence; appear. Also, **materialize**.

materialist /məˈtɪəriəlɪst/ n. someone absorbed in material interests. —**materialistic**, adj.

maternal /məˈtɜnəl/ adj. **1.** of or relating to, befitting, having the qualities of, or being a mother. **2.** related through a mother.

maternity /məˈtɜnəti/ n. the state of being a mother; motherhood.

mathematics /mæθəˈmætɪks/ n. the science that deals with the measurement, properties, and relations of quantities, including arithmetic, geometry, algebra, etc. –**mathematician**, n. –**mathematical**, adj.

maths /mæθs/ n. → **mathematics**.

matilda /mə'tɪldə/ n. Colloq. a swag.

matinee /'mætəneɪ/ n. an entertainment, as a dramatic or musical performance, film, etc., held in the daytime.

matri- a word element meaning 'mother'.

matriarch /'meɪtrɪak/ n. a woman holding a position of leadership in a family or tribal society.

matriarchy /'meɪtrɪaki, 'mæt-/ n. (pl. **-chies**) a form of social organisation in which the mother is head of the family, and in which descent is reckoned in the female line, the children belonging to the mother's clan.

matrices /'meɪtrəsiz/ n. a plural form of **matrix**.

matriculate /mə'trɪkjələɪt/ v.i. to pass matriculation.

matriculation /mətrɪkjə'leɪʃən/ n. a secondary-school examination in which a required level must be reached before qualification for admission to a tertiary education institution.

matrimony /'mætrəməni/, Orig. US /-mouni/ n. the rite, ceremony, or sacrament of marriage. –**matrimonial**, adj.

matrix /'meɪtrɪks/ n. (pl. **matrices** /'meɪtrəsiz/ or **matrixes**) 1. that which gives origin or form to a thing, or which serves to enclose it. 2. a network of communities, organisations, or people, forming an interconnected whole: the social matrix. 3. Maths, Computers a rectangular array of numbers.

matron /'meɪtrən/ n. 1. a married woman. 2. a woman in charge of the sick bay, as in a school or workplace, on board a ship, etc.

matt /mæt/ adj. lustreless and dull in surface.

matter /'mætə/ n. 1. the substance or substances of which physical objects consist or are composed. 2. importance or significance. 3. (preceded by the) the trouble or difficulty. 4. Law statement or allegation. –v.i. 5. to be of importance; signify.

matter-of-fact /mætər-əv-'fækt/ adj. adhering to actual facts; not imaginative; prosaic; commonplace. –**matter-of-factly**, adv.

mattock /'mætək/ n. an instrument for loosening soil.

mattress /'mætrəs/ n. a case filled with soft material, often reinforced with springs, used as or on a bed.

mature /mə'tjuə/ adj. 1. complete in natural growth or development. 2. Commerce having reached the limit of its time; having become payable or due, as a note, insurance policy, etc. –v. (**-tured, -turing**) –v.t. 3. to make mature; ripen. –v.i. 4. to become mature.

maturity /mə'tjurəti/ n. 1. the state of being mature; ripeness. 2. the time when a note or bill of exchange becomes due.

maudlin /'mɔdlən/ adj. tearfully or weakly emotional or sentimental.

maul /mɔl/ v.t. to handle roughly; to injure by rough treatment.

mausoleum /mɔsə'liəm, mɔz-/ n. (pl. **-leums** or **-lea** /-'liə/) 1. a stately and magnificent tomb. 2. a large, old, gloomy building.

mauve /mouv/ n. 1. pale bluish purple. –adj. 2. of the colour of mauve.

maw /mɔ/ n. the mouth, throat, or gullet, especially of an animal.

mawkish /'mɔkɪʃ/ adj. sickly or slightly nauseating.

maxim /'mæksəm/ n. an expression of a general truth, especially relating to conduct.

maxima /'mæksəmə/ n. a plural form of **maximum**.

maximise /'mæksəmaɪz/ v.t. to increase to the greatest possible amount or degree. Also, **maximize**.

maximum /'mæksəməm/ n. (pl. **-mums** or **-ma** /-mə/) the greatest quantity or amount possible, allowable, etc.

may /meɪ/ v. (**might**) used as an auxiliary to express 1. possibility, opportunity, or permission. 2. wish or prayer. 3. contingency, especially in clauses expressing condition, concession, purpose, result, etc.

maybe /'meɪbi, meɪ'bi/ adv. perhaps.

mayday /'meɪdeɪ/ n. an international radio telephonic signal for help, used by ships or aircraft.

mayhem /'meɪhem/ n. 1. Law the crime of violently inflicting a bodily injury. 2. confusion and chaos. Also, **maihem**.

mayonnaise /meɪə'neɪz/ n. a thick dressing used for salads or vegetables.

mayor /mɛə/ n. the principal officer of a municipality; the chief magistrate of a city or borough. –**mayoress**, fem. n.

maze /meɪz/ n. a confusing network of intercommunicating paths or passages; a labyrinth.

me /mi/ personal pron. objective case of the pronoun I.

ME /ɛm 'i/ n. → **chronic fatigue syndrome**.

mea culpa /meɪə 'kulpə/ interj. 1. an expression acknowledging that the speaker is at fault, has made a mistake, etc. –n. 2. an admission of fault.

mead /mid/ n. an alcoholic liquor made by fermenting honey and water.

meadow /'mɛdou/ n. Chiefly Brit. a piece of grassland.

meagre /'migə/ adj. deficient in quantity or quality.

meal¹ /mil/ n. one of the regular repasts of the day, as breakfast, lunch, or dinner.

meal² /mil/ n. the edible part of a grain ground to a (coarse) powder.

mealy-mouthed /'mili-mauðd/ adj. avoiding the use of plain terms, as from timidity, excessive delicacy, or hypocrisy.

mean¹ /min/ v. (**meant, meaning**) –v.t. 1. to have in the mind as in intention or purpose. 2. to intend for a particular purpose, destination, etc. 3. (of words, things, etc.) to have as the signification; signify. –v.i. 4. to be minded or disposed; have intentions.

mean² /min/ adj. 1. inferior in grade, quality or character. 2. penurious, stingy, or miserly. 3. Colloq. powerful, effective.

mean³ /min/ n. 1. something intermediate; that which is midway between two extremes. 2. Maths a quantity having a value intermediate between the values of other quantities; an average. –adj. 3. occupying a middle position.

meander /mi'ændə/ v.i. to proceed by a winding course.

meaning /ˈmiːnɪŋ/ n. what is referred to or indicated by something. –**meaningful**, adj. –**meaningless**, adj.

means /miːnz/ pl. n. **1.** (oft. construed as sing.) an agency, instrumentality, method, etc., used to attain an end. **2.** disposable resources, especially pecuniary resources.

means test n. an evaluation of the income and resources of a person, in order to determine eligibility for part or all of a pension, grant, allowance, etc.

meantime /ˈmiːntaɪm/ n. **1.** the intervening time. –adv. **2.** meanwhile.

meanwhile /ˈmiːnwaɪl, miːnˈwaɪl/ adv. in the intervening time; at the same time.

measles /ˈmiːzəlz/ n. an acute infectious disease occurring mostly in children.

measly /ˈmiːzli/ adj. (**-lier, -liest**) Colloq. wretchedly poor or unsatisfactory.

measure /ˈmɛʒə/ n. **1.** size, dimensions, quantity, etc. **2.** a unit or standard of measurement. **3.** a system of measurement. **4.** any standard of comparison, estimation, or judgement. **5.** an action or procedure intended as a means to an end. –v. (**-ured, -uring**) –v.t. **6.** to ascertain the extent, dimensions, quantity, capacity, etc., of, especially by comparison with a standard. **7.** (oft. fol. by off or out) to mark or lay off or out, or deal out, with reference to measure. –v.i. **8.** to take measurements. **9.** to be of a specified measure. –phr. **10. for good measure**, as an extra and probably unnecessary act, precaution, etc.

measurement /ˈmɛʒəmənt/ n. **1.** the act of measuring. **2.** the extent, size, etc., decided by measuring. **3.** a system of measuring.

meat /miːt/ n. **1.** the flesh of animals as used for food. **2.** the edible part of anything, as a fruit, nut, etc. **3.** the main substance of something, as an argument.

mechanic /məˈkænɪk/ n. a skilled worker with tools or machines.

mechanical /məˈkænɪkəl/ adj. **1.** of or relating to machinery. **2.** relating to, or controlled or effected by, physical forces.

mechanics /məˈkænɪks/ n. **1.** the branch of knowledge concerned (both theoretically and practically) with machinery or mechanical appliances. **2.** the science dealing with the action of forces on bodies and with motion.

mechanise /ˈmɛkənaɪz/ v.t. to introduce machinery into (an industry, etc.). Also, **mechanize**.

mechanism /ˈmɛkənɪzəm/ n. **1.** the machinery, or the agencies or means, by which a particular effect is produced or a purpose is accomplished. **2.** the way in which a thing works or operates.

mechatronics /mɛkəˈtrɒnɪks/ n. (from trademark) a branch of engineering technology which integrates mechanical engineering with electronics, especially in the design and manufacture of products and processes controlled by intelligent computers, such as robots performing certain tasks, air conditioners, cruise control in motor vehicles, etc.

medal /ˈmɛdl/ n. a flat piece of inscribed metal, given as a reward for bravery, merit, etc.

medallion /məˈdæljən/ n. a large medal.

meddle /ˈmɛdl/ v.i. to concern oneself with or in something without warrant or necessity; interfere.

medevac /ˈmɛdivæk/ n. **1.** evacuation of a seriously ill or wounded person, usually by aircraft. –v.t. (**-vaced** /-vækt/, **-vacing** /-vækɪŋ/) **2.** to evacuate (such a seriously ill or wounded person). Also, **medivac**.

media /ˈmiːdiə/ n. **1.** a plural of **medium**. **2.** Also, **mass media**. the means of communication, as radio, television, newspapers, magazines, etc., reaching large numbers of people.

medial /ˈmiːdiəl/ adj. situated in or relating to the middle; median; intermediate.

median /ˈmiːdiən/ adj. **1.** situated in or relating to the middle; medial. –n. **2.** the middle number in a given sequence of numbers.

median strip n. a dividing area, often raised or landscaped, between opposing traffic lanes on a highway.

mediate /ˈmiːdieɪt/ v.i. to act between parties to effect an agreement, compromise, or reconciliation. –**mediator**, n.

medical /ˈmɛdɪkəl/ adj. **1.** of or relating to the science or practice of medicine. –n. **2.** a medical examination.

medical certificate n. a certificate made out by a doctor testifying to the state of a person's health.

medical imaging n. Med. the creation of images of internal organs or parts of the body, as by X-ray, ultrasound or CAT scan, to assist diagnosis and the performance of medical procedures.

medicament /məˈdɪkəmənt/ n. a curative or healing substance.

medicate /ˈmɛdəkeɪt/ v.t. to treat with medicine or medicaments. –**medication**, n.

medicine /ˈmɛdəsən, ˈmɛdsən/ n. **1.** any substance or substances used in treating disease. **2.** the art or science of restoring or preserving health. **3.** the medical profession. –**medicinal**, adj.

medieval /mɛdiˈiːvəl/ adj. of or relating to, characteristic of, or in the style of the Middle Ages. Also, **mediaeval**.

medifraud /ˈmɛdifrɒd/ n. the obtaining of money from a health insurance service on the basis of fraudulent claims.

mediocre /midiˈoʊkə, ˈmidioʊkə/ adj. of middling quality; indifferent; ordinary.

meditate /ˈmɛdəteɪt/ v.i. to engage in thought or contemplation; reflect.

medium /ˈmiːdiəm/ n. (pl. **-dia** /-diə/ or **-diums**) **1.** a middle state or condition; a mean. **2.** an intervening substance, as air, etc., through which a force acts or an effect is produced. **3.** the element in which an organism has its natural habitat. **4.** an agency means, or instrument. –adj. **5.** intermediate in degree, or quality, etc.

medivac /ˈmɛdivæk/ n., v.t. → **medevac**.

medley /ˈmɛdli/ n. a mixture, especially of heterogeneous elements.

meek /miːk/ adj. humbly patient or submissive.

meerkat /ˈmɪəkæt/ n. any of several small, burrowing, southern African carnivores, with dark bands across the back, related to the mongoose.

meet /mit/ v. (**met, meeting**) −v.t. **1.** to come into contact, junction, or connection with. **2.** to go to the place of arrival of, as to welcome. **3.** to come into personal acquaintance with. **4.** to cope or deal effectively with. −v.i. **5.** to come together, face to face, or into company. **6.** to come into contact or form a junction, as lines, planes, areas, etc. **7.** to come together in opposition or conflict. −n. **8.** a meeting, especially for a sporting event.

meet and greet n. **1.** an official occasion to welcome visitors. **2.** an event at which a politician, celebrity, etc., spends time meeting and chatting with members of the public. −v.t. **3.** to welcome (someone) officially. −v.i. **4.** (of a politician, celebrity, etc.) to spend time meeting and chatting with members of the public, usually at a planned and structured event. −**meet-and-greet**, adj.

meeting /'mitɪŋ/ n. an assembly or gathering held.

mega- /'mɛgə-/ **1.** a prefix denoting 10^6 of a given unit, as in megawatt. Symbol: M **2.** a prefix meaning 'great', 'huge'.

megabit /'mɛgəbɪt/ n. a unit of measurement of computer memory size equal to one million bits. Symbol: Mb

megabyte /'mɛgəbaɪt/ n. a unit of measurement of computer memory size, equal to 2^{20} (approximately 10^6) bytes. Symbol: MB Also, **meg**.

megafauna /'mɛgəfɔnə/ n. members of the larger animal species, generally taken to be over 500 kg, especially those that are extinct, as the mammoth, and various Australian marsupials.

megahertz /'mɛgəhɜts/ n. a unit of radiofrequency equal to 1×10^6 hertz. Symbol: MHz

megalitre /'mɛgəlitə/ n. a unit of capacity in the metric system, equal to 1×10^6 litres. Symbol: ML Also, US, **megaliter**.

megalo- a word element denoting largeness or exaggeration.

megalomania /mɛgəlou'meɪniə/ n. a form of mental illness marked by delusions of greatness, wealth, etc.

megaphone /'mɛgəfoun/ n. a device for magnifying sound.

megapixel /mɛgə'pɪksəl/ n. Photography one million pixels, usually in reference to the resolution of a digital camera.

megaton /'mɛgətʌn/ n. **1.** one million tons. **2.** an explosive force equal to that of one million tons of TNT.

megawatt /'mɛgəwɒt/ n. Elect. a unit of power, equal to one million watts. Symbol: MW

meh /mɛ/ Colloq. −interj. **1.** an expression of resigned acceptance, indifference, etc. −adj. **2.** boring; mediocre.

meiosis /maɪ'ousəs/ n. the development process of gametes, consisting of two cell divisions, in the course of which the chromosomes are duplicated only once. −**meiotic**, adj.

melaleuca /mɛlə'lukə/ n. a type of tree or shrub mainly found in Australia, usually on river banks or in swamps.

melancholia /mɛlən'koʊliə/ n. a mental disorder characterised by a profound lack of energy, especially in the morning, and loss of pleasure in one's usual interests and pursuits. Also, **melancholic depression**.

melancholy /'mɛlənkɒli/ n. **1.** a gloomy state of mind, especially when habitual or prolonged; depression. −adj. **2.** affected with, characterised by, or showing melancholy.

melanin /'mɛlənən/ n. any of various dark pigments in the body of humans and certain animals.

melano- a word element meaning 'black'.

melanoma /mɛlə'noumə/ n. a malignant tumour derived from pigment-containing cells especially in skin.

melatonin /mɛlə'tounən/ n. a hormone secreted during the night, which causes lightening of the skin in some animals and the tendency to sleep.

Melba toast /'mɛlbə/ n. very thinly sliced bread, baked in the oven until crisp.

meld /mɛld/ v.t. **1.** to cause to merge or blend. −v.i. **2.** to blend or combine.

melee /'mɛ'leɪ, -'li/ n. **1.** a confused general hand-to-hand fight. **2.** any noisy or confused situation.

mellifluous /mə'lɪfluəs/ adj. sweetly or smoothly flowing.

mellow /'mɛlou/ adj. **1.** soft and full-flavoured from ripeness, as fruit. **2.** soft and rich, as sound, tones, colour, light, etc. **3.** genial; jovial. −v.t., v.i. **4.** to make or become mellow.

melodic /mə'lɒdɪk/ adj. **1.** melodious. **2.** relating to melody as distinguished from harmony and rhythm.

melodrama /'mɛlədramə/ n. a play in which the drama is exaggerated.

melody /'mɛlədi/ n. (pl. **-dies**) musical sounds in agreeable succession or arrangement. −**melodious**, adj.

melon /'mɛlən/ n. any of several large, juicy fruits.

melt /mɛlt/ v. (**melted, melted** or **molten, melting**) −v.i. **1.** to become liquefied by heat. **2.** (oft. fol. by into) to pass, change, or blend gradually. −v.t. **3.** to reduce to a liquid state by heat. **4.** to soften in feeling, as a person, the heart, etc.

member /'mɛmbə/ n. a constituent part of any structural or composite whole.

membrane /'mɛmbreɪn/ n. any thin connecting layer.

meme /mim/ n. → **internet meme**.

memento /mə'mɛntou/ n. (pl. **-tos** or **-toes**) something that serves as a reminder of what is past or gone.

memo /'mɛmou, 'mi-/ n. (pl. **memos**) → **memorandum**.

memoirs /'mɛmwaz/ pl. n. records of one's own life and experiences.

memorabilia /mɛmərə'bɪliə/ pl. n. **1.** matters or events worthy to be remembered. **2.** things saved or collected as souvenirs.

memorable /'mɛmrəbəl, -ərəbəl/ adj. **1.** worthy of being remembered; notable. **2.** easy to remember.

memorandum /mɛmə'rændəm/ n. (pl. **-dums** or **-da** /-də/) **1.** a note made of something to be remembered. **2.** a document which includes the main terms of a shipment of unsold goods and authorises their return within a specified time.

memorial /mə'mɔriəl/ n. something designed to preserve the memory of a person, event, etc.

memorise /'mɛmərʌɪz/ v.t. to commit to memory, or learn by heart. Also, **memorize**.

memory /'mɛmri, 'mɛməri/ n. (pl. **-ries**) **1.** the mental capacity or faculty of retaining or reviving impressions, or of recalling or recognising previous experiences. **2.** a mental impression retained; a recollection. **3.** the state or fact of being remembered. **4.** *Computers* the part of a digital computer in which data and instructions are held until they are required.

memory bank n. a storage device for computer data.

memory stick n. → **USB drive**.

men /mɛn/ n. plural of **man**.

menace /'mɛnəs/ n. **1.** a threat. **2.** *Colloq.* → **nuisance**. –v.t. (**-aced, -acing**) **3.** to serve as a probable cause of evil, etc., to.

menagerie /mə'nædʒəri/ n. a collection of wild or strange animals, especially for exhibition.

mend /mɛnd/ v.t. **1.** to make whole or sound by repairing. **2.** to set right; make better; improve.

mendacious /mɛn'deɪʃəs/ adj. **1.** false or untrue. **2.** lying or untruthful.

menial /'miniəl/ adj. **1.** relating or proper to domestic servants. **2.** of lowly status.

meninges /mə'nɪndʒiz/ pl. n. (sing. **meninx** /'mɪnɪŋks/) the three membranes that surround the brain and spinal cord.

meningitis /mɛnən'dʒʌɪtəs/ n. *Pathol.* inflammation of the meninges.

meningococcal disease /mənɪndʒə'kɒkəl/ n. a form of meningitis caused by meningococcal bacteria, marked by its rapid onset from flu-like symptoms and sometimes fatal outcome.

meningococcus /mənɪndʒə'kɒkəs/ n. a bacterium which can cause meningitis or sepsis. –**meningococcal**, adj.

meno- a word element meaning 'month'.

menopause /'mɛnəpɔz/ n. the period of the cessation of menstruation.

men's business n. **1.** Also, **man's business**. (in Aboriginal societies), matters, especially cultural traditions, which are the exclusive preserve of men, especially ceremonies which are only open to men. **2.** subjects which men may prefer to discuss with other men rather than with women, especially medical matters relating to men, bodily functions, etc. **3.** *Colloq.* (humorous) activities seen to be especially favoured or understood by men. Also, **secret men's business**.

menses /'mɛnsiz/ pl. n. the (approximately) monthly discharge of blood and mucus from the uterus.

menstrual cycle /'mɛnstruəl/ n. (in most primates) the approximately monthly cycle of ovulation and menstruation.

menstruate /'mɛnstrueɪt/ v.i. to discharge the menses. –**menstruation**, n. –**menstrual**, adj.

mensuration /mɛnsʃə'reɪʃən/ n. the act, art, or process of measuring.

-ment a suffix of nouns, often concrete, denoting an action or state resulting (judgement, refreshment), a product (fragment), or means (ornament).

mental /'mɛntl/ adj. **1.** of or relating to the mind. **2.** designated for or relating to the care of those with disordered minds. **3.** *Colloq.* foolish or mad.

mentality /mɛn'tæləti/ n. (pl. **-ties**) **1.** mental capacity or endowment. **2.** outlook; frame of mind: *the mentality of a murderer*.

mention /'mɛnʃən/ v.t. **1.** to refer to briefly or incidentally. –n. **2.** a referring or reference.

mentor /'mɛntɔ/ n. **1.** a wise and trusted counsellor. **2.** (especially in an organisation) a person who is considered to have sufficient experience or expertise to be able to assist others less experienced. –v.t. **3.** to act as a mentor towards: *in our school, the older students mentor the younger ones*. –**mentoring**, n.

menu /'mɛnju, 'mɪnju/ n. **1.** a list of the dishes served at a meal. **2.** *Computers* a range of optional procedures presented to an operator by a computer.

meow /mi'aʊ/ n. **1.** the sound a cat makes. –v.i. **2.** to make such a sound. Also, **miaow, miaou**.

mercantile /'mɜkəntʌɪl/ adj. of or relating to merchants or to trade; commercial.

mercenary /'mɜsənri, -sənəri/, *Orig. US* /'mɜsənɛri/ adj. **1.** working or acting merely for gain. –n. (pl. **-ries**) **2.** a professional soldier serving in a foreign army.

merchandise n. /'mɜtʃəndʌɪs/ **1.** the stock of a store. –v.i. /'mɜtʃəndʌɪz/ **2.** to trade. –v.t. /'mɜtʃəndʌɪz/ **3.** to trade in; buy and sell.

merchandising /'mɜtʃəndʌɪzɪŋ/ n. the promotion and planning of the sales of a product.

merchant /'mɜtʃənt/ n. **1.** someone who buys and sells commodities for profit; a wholesaler. –adj. **2.** relating to trade or commerce.

merchant bank n. a private banking firm engaged chiefly in accepting and endorsing bills of exchange, underwriting new issues of securities and advising on corporate strategy. Compare **retail bank**.

merchant navy n. the vessels of a nation engaged in commerce.

mercurial /mɜ'kjʊriəl/ adj. flighty; fickle; changeable.

mercury /'mɜkjəri/ n. *Chem.* a heavy, silver-white metallic element, remarkable for its fluidity at ordinary temperatures; quicksilver. *Symbol:* Hg

mercy /'mɜsi/ n. (pl. **-cies**) **1.** compassionate or kindly forbearance shown towards an offender, an enemy, or other person in one's power. –phr. **2. at the mercy of**, defenceless or unprotected against. –**merciful**, adj.

mere /mɪə/ adj. (**merest**) being nothing more or better than what is specified.

merely /'mɪəli/ adv. only as specified, and nothing more; simply.

merge /mɜdʒ/ v. (**merged, merging**) –v.t. **1.** to unite or combine. –v.i. **2.** (oft. fol. by in or into) to become swallowed up or absorbed.

merger /'mɜdʒə/ n. a statutory combination of two or more companies by the transfer of the properties to one surviving company.

meridian /mə'rɪdiən/ n. *Geog.* a line of longitude.

meringue /mə'ræŋ/ n. a mixture of sugar and beaten egg whites, baked.

merino /mə'rinoʊ/ n. (pl. **-nos**) one of a variety of sheep valued for its fine wool.

merit /'mɛrət/ n. **1.** claim to commendation; excellence; worth. **2.** (pl.) the substantial right and wrong of a matter unobscured by techni-calities. –*v.t.* **3.** to be worthy of; deserve.

meritorious /ˌmerɪˈtɔːrɪəs/ *adj.* deserving of reward or commendation.

merlot /ˈmɜːloʊ/ *n.* (*sometimes upper case*) **1.** a dark blue grape variety used in winemaking. **2.** the red wine made from this grape variety.

mermaid /ˈmɜːmeɪd/ *n.* an imaginary creature with the torso of a woman and the tail of a fish.

merry /ˈmerɪ/ *adj.* (**-rier, -riest**) full of cheer or gaiety.

merry-go-round /ˈmerɪ-ɡoʊ-ˌraʊnd/ *n.* a ma-chine on which children ride for amusement; roundabout; carousel.

mesh /meʃ/ *n.* **1.** a network or net. **2.** light woven or welded interlocking links or wires, as used for reinforcement, for sieves, etc. –*v.t.* **3.** to catch or entangle in or as in a mesh. **4.** *Machinery* to engage, as gear teeth. –*v.i.* **5.** to become meshed.

mesmerise /ˈmezmeraɪz/ *v.t.* to hypnotise. Also, **mesmerize**. **–mesmeric,** *adj.*

mesne /miːn/ *adj. Law* intermediate or inter-vening.

meso- a word element meaning 'middle'. Also, **mes-**.

mesothelioma /ˌmiːzəʊθiːlɪˈoʊmə, ˌmezə-/ *n.* (*pl.* **-omas** *or* **-omata**) a tumour, usually malig-nant, of the covering of the lung or lining of the chest and abdominal cavities, associated with exposure to airborne asbestos fibres.

mess /mes/ *n.* **1.** a dirty or untidy condition. **2.** excrement, especially of an animal. **3.** a place used by service personnel, etc., for eat-ing, recreation, etc. –*v.t.* **4.** (oft. fol. by *up*) to make dirty or untidy. –*v.i.* **5.** to eat in com-pany, especially as a member of a mess. –*phr.* **6. mess around** (or **about**), to waste time.

message /ˈmesɪdʒ/ *n.* **1.** a communication, as of information, advice, direction, or the like, transmitted through a messenger or other ag-ency. –*v.t.* (**-aged, -aging**) **2.** to communicate with (someone) by text messaging.

message board *n.* **1.** a board, located in a public place, to which messages can be af-fixed. **2.** a location on a website for posting messages available to be read by all visitors to the site.

messaging /ˈmesədʒɪŋ/ *n.* communication by text messages.

messenger /ˈmesəndʒə/ *n.* someone who bears a message or goes on an errand, especially as a matter of duty or business.

met /met/ *v.* past tense and past participle of **meet**.

meta- **1.** a prefix meaning 'among', 'together with', 'after'. **2.** a prefix meaning 'operating at a higher level', as in *metalanguage, metadata.*

metabolism /məˈtæbəlɪzəm/ *n.* the sum of the processes in an organism by which food is built up into living protoplasm and protoplasm is broken down into simpler compounds, with the exchange of energy.

metadata /ˈmetədeɪtə, ˈmetədatə/ *n.* information about data, especially in relation to its structure and organisation.

metal /ˈmetl/ *n.* **1.** any of a class of opaque, ductile, conductive, elementary substances, as silver, copper, etc. **2.** an alloy or mixture composed wholly or partly of such substances.

3. Also, **road metal**. broken stone used for ballast on railway tracks or for surfacing roads; blue metal. **–metallic,** *adj.*

metalanguage /ˈmetələŋɡwɪdʒ/ *n.* a language or code used to discuss a given object language or some aspect of it.

metallurgy /ˈmetələdʒi, məˈtælədʒi/ *n.* **1.** the science of metals and their structures and properties. **2.** the art or science of separating metals from their ores, compounding alloys or working metals. **–metallurgist,** *n.*

metalwork /ˈmetlwɜːk/ *n.* **1.** the art or craft of working with metal. **2.** objects produced by metalwork.

metamorphosis /ˌmetəˈmɔːfəsəs/ *n.* (*pl.* **-phoses** /-fəsiz/) **1.** any complete change in appearance, character, circumstances, etc. **2.** a form resulting from any such change. **–meta-morphic,** *adj.* **–metamorphose,** *v.*

metaphor /ˈmetəfə, -fɔː/ *n.* a figure of speech in which a term is applied to something to which it is not literally applicable, in order to suggest a resemblance. **–metaphorical,** *adj.*

metaphysical /ˌmetəˈfɪzɪkəl/ *adj. Philos.* con-cerned with abstract thought or subjects.

metaphysics /ˌmetəˈfɪzɪks/ *n.* philosophy, especially in its more abstruse branches.

metastasise /məˈtæstəsaɪz/ *v.i.* (especially of cells of malignant tumours, or microorganisms) to spread to other regions by dissemination usually through the blood circulation or lym-phatic systems. Also, **metastasize**.

mete /miːt/ *v.i.* (usu. fol. by *out*) to distribute or apportion by measure; allot.

meteor /ˈmiːtiə, -tiɔː/ *n.* a transient fiery streak in the sky produced by a comet, etc., passing through the earth's atmosphere. **–meteoric,** *adj.*

meteorite /ˈmiːtiəraɪt/ *n.* a mass of stone or metal that has reached the earth from outer space.

meteoroid /ˈmiːtiərɔɪd/ *n.* any of the small bodies, often remnants of comets, travelling through space, which, when encountering the earth's atmosphere, are heated to luminosity, thus becoming meteors.

meteorology /ˌmiːtiəˈrɒlədʒi/ *n.* the science dealing with the atmosphere and its phenom-ena, especially as relating to weather. **–meteor-ologist,** *n.*

meteor shower *n.* a celestial event in which a group of meteoroids enter the earth's atmos-phere at high speed, burning and incandescing from the friction, and appearing as streaks of light radiating from a particular area of the sky.

meter /ˈmiːtə/ *n.* an instrument that measures.

-meter[1] a word element used in names of measuring instruments.

-meter[2] a word element denoting a certain poetic measure or rhythmic pattern.

methadone /ˈmeθədoʊn/ *n.* a powerful anal-gesic drug used for the treatment of drug withdrawal symptoms.

methamphetamine /ˌmeθæmˈfetəmiːn/ *n.* a synthetic drug which acts as a powerful central nervous system stimulant.

methane /ˈmiːθeɪn/ *n.* a colourless, odourless, flammable gas.

methinks /miˈθɪŋks/ v. (impersonal) (**methought**) Archaic and Poetic it seems to me.

metho /ˈmeθoʊ/ n. Colloq. **1.** methylated spirits. **2.** one addicted to drinking methylated spirits.

method /ˈmeθəd/ n. a way of doing something, especially in accordance with a definite plan.

method acting n. an acting technique by which actors try to immerse themselves in the emotional world of the character they are portraying so that the responses required by the part have a feeling of authenticity because they draw on a deeper emotional base. **–method actor,** n.

methodical /məˈθɒdɪkəl/ adj. performed, disposed, or acting in a systematic way. Also, **methodic.**

methodology /meθəˈdɒlədʒi/ n. (pl. **-gies**) a systematic approach to scientific inquiry based on logical principle, employed in various sciences.

methyl alcohol /ˈmeθəl/ n. a colourless, flammable, poisonous liquid used as a fuel, solvent, etc.

methylated spirits /ˈmeθəleɪtəd/ n. a denatured alcohol, used for burning, cleaning, etc.

meticulous /məˈtɪkjələs/ adj. solicitous about minute details; minutely careful.

metre¹ /ˈmitə/ n. a unit of length in the metric system. Symbol: m

metre² /ˈmitə/ n. arrangement of words in rhythmic lines or verses.

-metre a word element meaning metres; or of relating to a metre, as in kilometre.

metric /ˈmetrɪk/ adj. relating to the metre or to the system of measures and weights originally based upon it.

metrication /metrəˈkeɪʃən/ n. the process of conversion from British or imperial units to the metric system. **–metricate,** v.

metric system n. the international standard system of weights and measures based on the number 10. The modern metric system, known as the International System of Units (SI), comprises seven base units: the metre (m), kilogram (kg), second (s), ampere (A), kelvin (K), mole (mol), and candela (cd).

metric ton n. → **tonne.**

metronome /ˈmetrənoʊm/ n. a mechanical contrivance for marking time, as for music.

metropolitan /metrəˈpɒlətən/ adj. of, relating to, or characteristic of a city, or of the people who live in it. **–metropolis,** n.

metrosexual /metroʊˈsekʃuəl/ n. a heterosexual male who devotes such attention to his appearance and presentation as would conventionally be considered feminine, such as the use of cosmetics, hair colouring, etc. **–metrosexuality,** n.

-metry a word element denoting the process of measuring.

mettle /ˈmetl/ n. **1.** the characteristic disposition or temper. **2.** spirit; courage.

mew /mju/ n. **1.** the sound a cat makes. –v.i. **2.** to make this sound.

mews /mjuz/ pl. n. (usu. construed as sing.) a set of stables or garages.

mezzanine /ˈmezənin, mezəˈnin/ n. a low storey between two other storeys.

mica /ˈmaɪkə/ n. any member of a group of minerals that separate readily (by cleavage) into thin, tough, often transparent laminae.

mice /maɪs/ n. plural of **mouse.**

micra /ˈmaɪkrə/ n. a plural of **micron.**

MICR encoding /ˈmaɪkə/ n. a machine-reading system by which characters encoded on documents, as cheques, are read by a magnetically sensitive device.

micro /ˈmaɪkroʊ/ adj. individual or particular (opposed to macro): at the micro level.

micro- /ˈmaɪkroʊ-/ **1.** a prefix meaning: **a.** 'very small'. **b.** 'enlarging' or 'amplifying'. **2.** a prefix denoting 10⁻⁶ of a given unit. Symbol: μ

microbe /ˈmaɪkroʊb/ n. a microorganism, usually one of vegetable nature; a germ.

microbead /ˈmaɪkroʊbid/ n. a microscopic sphere of plastic, a quantity of which is used in cosmetics, toothpaste, etc.; can cause pollution of waterways and oceans, creating a hazard to marine life.

microblog /ˈmaɪkroʊblɒg/ n. **1.** an internet posting which is extremely short, usually up to 140 characters, designed to give a brief but immediate text update. –v.i. (**-blogged**, **-blogging**) **2.** to issue such an internet posting. **–microblogging,** n. **–microblogger,** n.

microclimate /ˈmaɪkroʊˌklaɪmət/ n. the climate affecting a localised region, often created by terrain or conditions which are not prevalent throughout the wider area. Compare **macroclimate. –microclimatic** /ˌmaɪkroʊklaɪˈmætɪk/, adj. **–microclimatically** /ˌmaɪkroʊklaɪˈmætɪkli/, adv.

microcomputer /ˈmaɪkroʊkəmˌpjutə/ n. a computer which has its central processor functions contained on a single printed circuit board constituting a standalone module, usually small in size and cost.

microcopy /ˈmaɪkroʊˌkɒpi/ n. (pl. **-pies**) a greatly reduced photographic copy of a book, page, etc.

microcosm /ˈmaɪkrəkɒzəm/ n. anything regarded as a world in miniature.

microdot /ˈmaɪkroʊˌdɒt/ n. a photograph reduced to the size of a printed or typed dot.

micro-economics /ˌmaɪkroʊ-ekəˈnɒmɪks/ n. (construed as sing.) study of the economic system in terms of its different sectors. Compare **macro-economics.**

microfauna /ˈmaɪkroʊfɔnə/ n. very small animals, usually too small to be seen with the naked eye. Compare **macrofauna.**

microfibre /ˈmaɪkroʊfaɪbə/ n. an extremely fine synthetic textile which is wrinkle resistant and easy to care for.

microfiche /ˈmaɪkroʊfiʃ/ n. a microfilmed transparency about the size and shape of a filing card which may have on it many pages of print.

microfilm /ˈmaɪkroʊfɪlm/ n. **1.** a narrow film, especially of motion-picture stock, on which microcopies are made. **2.** a film reproduction of a large or bulky publication, as a file of newspapers, in miniature form.

microlight aircraft n. an ultralight aircraft with weight shift controls for stabilisation. Also, **microlight.**

micromanage /ˈmaɪkroʊmænɪdʒ/ v.t. (**-managed**, **-managing**) to manage closely by frequently inspecting and controlling the work of (employees), usually to the detriment of efficiency and output. –**micromanager**, *n.* –**micromanagement**, *n.*

micron /'maɪkrɒn/ *n.* (*pl.* -**cra** /-krə/ *or* -**crons**) *Obs.* the millionth part of a metre. *Symbol*: μ

microorganism /maɪkroʊ'ɔːgənɪzəm/ *n.* a microscopic (animal or vegetable) organism.

microphone /'maɪkrəfoʊn/ *n.* an instrument which is capable of transforming the air-pressure waves of sound into changes in electric currents or voltages.

microprocessor /maɪkroʊ'proʊsesə/ *n.* **1.** a small standalone computer, often dedicated to specific functions. **2.** a chip (def. 5) containing a CPU.

microscope /'maɪkrəskoʊp/ *n.* an optical instrument for inspecting objects too small to be seen, or to be seen distinctly and in detail, by the naked eye.

microscopic /maɪkrə'skɒpɪk/ *adj.* **1.** so small as to be invisible or indistinct without the use of the microscope. **2.** of or relating to the microscope or its use.

microwave /'maɪkrəweɪv, 'maɪkroʊ-/ *n.* **1.** an electromagnetic wave of extremely high frequency, approximately comprising the wavelength range from 50 cm to 1 mm. **2.** Also, **microwave oven.** an oven which cooks with unusual rapidity, by passing microwaves through food and generating heat inside it. –*v.t.* **3.** to cook (food) by using a microwave oven.

mid[1] /mɪd/ *adj.* central; at or near the middle point.

mid[2] /mɪd/ *prep.* → **amid.** Also, **'mid.**

mid- a combining form of **middle.**

midair /mɪd'ɛə/ *n.* any elevated position above the ground.

midday /'mɪdeɪ/ *n.* the middle of the day; noon.

middle /'mɪdl/ *adj.* **1.** equally distant from extremes or limits. **2.** medium. –*n.* **3.** the point, part, etc., equidistant from extremes or limits. –*v.t.* (**-died, -dling**) **4.** to place in the middle.

middle-aged /'mɪdl-eɪdʒd/ *adj.* **1.** intermediate in age between youth and old age. **2.** characteristic of or suitable for middle-aged people.

middle class *n.* a social class comprising especially business and professional people and public servants of middle income.

middleman /'mɪdlmæn/ *n.* (*pl.* -**men**) a trader who makes a profit by buying from producers and selling to retailers or consumers. Also, **middle man.**

middling /'mɪdlɪŋ/ *adj.* medium in size, quality, grade, rank, etc.

middy /'mɪdi/ *n.* (*pl.* -**dies**) a medium-sized beer glass.

midge /mɪdʒ/ *n.* any of various small flying insects.

midget /'mɪdʒət/ *n.* something very small of its kind.

midnight /'mɪdnaɪt/ *n.* **1.** the middle of the night; 12 o'clock at night. **2.** resembling midnight, as in darkness. –*phr.* **3. burn the midnight oil,** to study or work far into the night.

midnight sun *n.* the sun visible at midnight in midsummer in arctic and antarctic regions.

midriff /'mɪdrɪf/ *n.* **1.** the middle part of the body, between the chest and the waist. –*adj.*

2. of a dress, blouse, etc., which exposes this part of the body.

midshipman /'mɪdʃɪpmən/ *n.* (*pl.* -**men**) a probationary rank held by naval cadets before qualifying as officers.

midst /mɪdst/ *n.* the middle point, part, or stage.

midstream /'mɪdstriːm/ *n.* **1.** the middle of a stream. –*phr.* **2. in midstream,** *Colloq.* in the middle; at a critical point.

midway *adv.* /mɪd'weɪ/ **1.** to the middle of the way or distance; halfway. –*adj.* /'mɪdweɪ/ **2.** in the middle.

midwife /'mɪdwaɪf/ *n.* (*pl.* -**wives** /-waɪvz/) a nurse who assists women in childbirth. –**midwifery** /mɪd'wɪfəri/ *n.*

mien /miːn/ *n.* air, bearing, or aspect, as showing character, feeling, etc.

miffed /mɪft/ *adj. Colloq.* annoyed; displeased.

might[1] /maɪt/ *v.* past tense of **may.**

might[2] /maɪt/ *n.* effective power or force of any kind. –**mighty,** *adj.*

migraine /'maɪgreɪn, 'miːgreɪn/ *n.* a severe headache often confined to one side of the head and usually associated with nausea.

migrant /'maɪgrənt/ *n.* **1.** someone who migrates. **2.** an immigrant, especially a recent immigrant. –*adj.* **3.** of or relating to migration or migrants.

migrate /maɪ'greɪt/ *v.i.* **1.** to pass periodically from one region to another, as certain birds, fishes, and animals. **2.** (of a person) to move to another country to live. –*v.t.* **3.** *Computers* to transfer (data) from one system to another. –**migration,** *n.*

mike /maɪk/ *n. Colloq.* → **microphone.**

mild /maɪld/ *adj.* **1.** amiably gentle or temperate in feeling or behaviour towards others. **2.** gentle or moderate in force or effect. **3.** moderate in intensity, degree, or character.

mildew /'mɪldjuː/ *n.* **1.** a plant disease usually characterised by a whitish coating. **2.** a fine coating of fungus appearing on materials exposed to moisture.

mile /maɪl/ *n.* **1.** a unit of measurement of length in the imperial system, equal to about 1.6 kilometres. **2.** (*oft. pl.*) a large distance or quantity.

mileage /'maɪlɪdʒ/ *n.* **1.** the total length or distance expressed in miles. **2.** the number of miles travelled by a motor vehicle on a specified quantity of fuel.

milestone /'maɪlstoʊn/ *n.* **1.** a stone set up to mark the distance to or from a town, as along a highway. **2.** a significant point in one's life or career.

milieu /miːˈljɜː/ *n.* medium or environment.

militant /'mɪlətənt/ *adj.* engaged in warfare; warring.

military /'mɪlətri, -təri/, *Orig. US* /-tɛri/ *adj.* **1.** of or relating to the army, armed forces, affairs of war, or a state of war. –*n.* **2.** soldiers generally; the armed forces.

militate /'mɪləteɪt/ *v.i.* to operate (*against* or *in favour of*); have effect or influence.

militia /məˈlɪʃə/ *n.* **1.** a body of people enrolled for military service, called out periodically for drill and exercise but not for actual service only in emergencies. **2.** a body of citizen soldiers as distinguished from professional soldiers. **3.** a member of a militia.

milk /mɪlk/ n. **1.** an opaque white liquid secreted by the mammary glands of female mammals, serving for the nourishment of their young, and, in the case of the cow and some other animals, used for food or as a source of dairy products. −v.t. **2.** to press or draw milk by hand or machine from the udder of (a cow or other animal). **3.** to extract (something) as if by milking; draw. −v.i. **4.** to milk a cow or other animal.

milk bar n. a shop where milk drinks, ice cream, sandwiches, etc., are sold.

milk of magnesia n. a liquid suspension of magnesium hydroxide used medicinally as an antacid or laxative.

milkshake /'mɪlkʃeɪk/ n. a frothy drink made of milk, flavouring, and sometimes ice cream, shaken together. Also, **milk shake**.

milk tooth n. one of the temporary teeth of a mammal which are replaced by the permanent teeth. Also, **baby tooth**.

mill /mɪl/ n. **1.** a building or establishment fitted with machinery, in which any of various mechanical operations or forms of manufacture is carried on. **2.** a machine which does its work by rotary motion. −v.t. **3.** to grind, work, treat, or shape in or with a mill. −v.i. **4.** (oft. fol. by *about*) to move confusedly in a circle. −phr. **5. run of the mill**, conventional; commonplace.

millennial /mə'lenɪəl/ adj. **1.** of or relating to a millennium or the millennium. −n. **2.** a person who was born in the two decades before the 21st century, a member of generation Y.

millennium /mə'lenɪəm/ n. (pl. **-nia** /-nɪə/ or **-niums**) **1.** a period of a thousand years. **2.** a thousandth anniversary.

millet /'mɪlət/ n. a cereal grass.

milli- /'mɪli-/ a prefix denoting 10^{-3} of a given unit. *Symbol:* m

millibar /'mɪliba/ n. in the metric system, a unit of measurement of air pressure, especially in the atmosphere.

milligram /'mɪligræm/ n. in the metric system, a unit of weight equal to 0.001 gram. *Symbol:* mg

millilitre /'mɪlilitə/ n. in the metric system, a unit of measurement of liquid equal to 0.001 litre. *Symbol:* mL, ml

millimetre /'mɪlimitə/ n. in the metric system, a unit of length equal to 0.001 metre. *Symbol:* mm

milliner /'mɪlənə/ n. someone who makes or sells hats for women. −**millinery**, n.

million /'mɪljən/ n. (pl. **-lions**, *as after a numeral*, **-lion**) **1.** a cardinal number, one thousand times one thousand, or 10^6. **2.** a very great number. −adj. **3.** amounting to one million in number. −**millionth**, adj., n.

millionaire /mɪljə'nɛə/ n. a person worth a million or millions, as of pounds, dollars, euros, etc.

millipede /'mɪlipid/ n. any of several kinds of arthropods with segmented bodies and many legs. Also, **millepede**.

millstone /'mɪlstoʊn/ n. **1.** either of a pair of circular stones used for grinding. **2.** a heavy burden.

mime /maɪm/ n. **1.** the art or technique of expressing emotion, character, action, etc., by mute gestures and bodily movements. **2.** a play or performance in mime. **3.** one skilled in mime.

mimic /'mɪmɪk/ v.t. (**-icked**, **-icking**) **1.** to imitate or copy. −n. **2.** someone clever at imitating or mimicking the characteristic voice or gesture of others. −**mimicry** /'mɪmɪkri/, n.

minaret /mɪnə'rɛt, 'mɪnərɛt/ n. a tall, thin tower attached to a mosque.

mince /mɪns/ v. (**minced**, **mincing**) −v.t. **1.** to cut or chop into very small pieces. **2.** to perform or utter with affected elegance. −v.i. **3.** to act, behave, or speak with affected elegance. −n. **4.** minced meat.

mincemeat /'mɪnsmit/ n. **1.** a mixture composed of minced apples, suet, candied peel, etc., with raisins, currants, etc., for filling a pie (**mince pie**). **2.** minced meat. **3.** anything cut up very small.

mind /maɪnd/ n. **1.** that which thinks, feels, and wills, exercises perception, judgement, reflection, etc., as in a human or other conscious being. **2.** intellectual power or ability. **3.** purpose, intention, or will. −v.t. **4.** to apply oneself or attend to. **5.** to be careful, cautious, or wary concerning. **6.** to perceive or notice. **7.** to be careful or wary. **8.** to regard a thing as concerning oneself or as mattering. −phr. **9. make up one's mind**, to come to a decision. **10. out of one's mind**, demented; delirious. **11. to one's mind**, in one's opinion or judgement.

minded /'maɪndəd/ adj. inclined or disposed.

mindful /'maɪndfəl/ adj. (usu. fol. by *of*) attentive; careful.

mind game n. **1.** a contest in which psychological pressure is critical in deciding the outcome. −phr. **2. play mind games**, to exert psychological pressure.

mind map n. a visual representation of the way in which concepts are related around a central key word or idea, used as a tool for the initial exploration of that idea, as a preliminary to developing a strategy, arriving at a decision, etc.

mine¹ /maɪn/ pron. possessive form of **I**, used without a noun following.

mine² /maɪn/ n. **1.** an excavation made in the ground for the purpose of getting out ores, precious stones, coal, etc. **2.** an abounding source or store of anything. **3.** an explosive device. −v. (**mined**, **mining**) −v.i. **4.** to dig a mine. −v.t. **5.** to dig in (ground, etc.) in order to obtain ores, coal, etc. **6.** to extract (ores, coal, etc.) from a mine. **7.** to dig or lay military mines under. −**miner**, n.

mineral /'mɪnərəl, 'mɪnrəl/ n. **1.** a substance obtained by mining; ore. **2.** any of a class of inorganic substances occurring in nature, having a definite chemical composition and crystal structure.

mineralogy /mɪnə'rælədʒi, -'rɒl-/ n. the science of minerals. −**mineralogical**, adj. −**mineralogist**, n.

mineral water n. **1.** water containing dissolved mineral salts or gases. **2.** carbonated water.

minestrone /mɪnə'stroʊni/ n. a soup containing vegetables, herbs, pasta, etc., in chicken or meat stock.

mingle /'mɪŋɡəl/ v. (**-gled**, **-gling**) −v.i. **1.** to become mixed, blended, or united. **2.** to associate or mix in company. –v.t. **3.** to mix or combine; put together in a mixture; blend.

mini /'mɪni/ n. something small in size or dimension, as a skirt or motor vehicle.

mini- a word element meaning 'small' or 'miniature'.

miniature /'mɪnətʃə/ n. **1.** a representation or image of anything on a very small scale. –adj. **2.** on a very small scale; reduced.

mini-budget /'mɪni-bʌdʒət/ n. a budget which seeks to implement government fiscal policies decided upon after the normal budget session.

minibus /'mɪnibʌs/ n. a motor vehicle for carrying between five and ten passengers.

minigolf /'mɪnigɒlf/ n. a form of golf played on a very small course with fancifully contrived obstacles and hazards.

minim /'mɪnəm/ n. Music a note equal in length to one half of a semibreve.

minimise /'mɪnəmaɪz/ v.t. to reduce to the smallest possible amount or degree. Also, **minimize**.

minimum /'mɪnəməm/ n. (pl. **-mums** or **-ma** /-mə/) **1.** the least quantity or amount possible, allowable, etc. **2.** the lowest amount, value, or degree attained or recorded. –**minimal**, adj.

minion /'mɪnjən/ n. a subordinate or employee, usually seen as favoured or servile.

minister /'mɪnəstə/ n. **1.** a person authorised to conduct religious worship; a member of the clergy; a pastor. **2.** a member of the government in charge of a portfolio. –v.i. **3.** to give service, care, or aid. –**ministerial**, adj. –**ministry**, n.

mink /mɪŋk/ n. (pl. **minks** or, especially collectively, **mink**) **1.** a semi-aquatic weasel-like animal. **2.** its valuable fur.

minnow /'mɪnoʊ/ n. (pl. **-nows** or **-now** for defs 1 and 2, **-nows** for def. 3) **1.** a small European cyprinid fish. **2.** any of various other small silvery fishes. **3.** an unimportant, insignificant person or thing.

minor /'maɪnə/ adj. **1.** lesser, as in size, extent, or importance, or being the lesser of two. **2.** under legal age. –n. **3.** a person under legal age.

minority /maɪ'nɒrəti, mə-/ n. (pl. **-ties**) **1.** the smaller part or number. **2.** the state or period of being a minor. **3.** a group of people whose ethnic background, religion, political views, etc., differ from those of the majority of people in the country or community in which they live. –adj. **4.** of or relating to a minority.

minstrel /'mɪnstrəl/ n. one of a class of medieval musicians who sang or recited to the accompaniment of instruments.

mint¹ /mɪnt/ n. **1.** any of several aromatic herbs. **2.** a mint-flavoured sweet.

mint² /mɪnt/ n. **1.** a place where money is coined by public authority. –v.t. **2.** to coin (money). –phr. **3. in mint condition**, in new or perfect condition, as when first issued. –**mintage**, n.

minuet /mɪnju'ɛt/ n. a slow stately dance of French origin.

minus /'maɪnəs/ prep. **1.** less by the subtraction of; decreased by. –adj. **2.** negative; less than zero. –n. **3.** a deficiency or loss.

minuscule /'mɪnəskjul/ adj. very small; tiny.

minute¹ /'mɪnət/ n. **1.** the sixtieth part of an hour; sixty seconds. **2.** a point of time; an instant or moment. **3.** (pl.) the official record of the proceedings at a meeting. **4.** Geom., etc. the sixtieth part of a degree, or sixty seconds.

minute² /maɪ'njut/ adj. **1.** extremely small. **2.** attentive to or concerned with even very small details or particulars.

minutia /maɪ'njuʃə, -tiə/ n. (pl. **-tiae** /-ʃii, -tii/) (usu. pl.) a small or trivial detail.

minx /mɪŋks/ n. a pert, impudent, or flirtatious young woman.

miracle /'mɪrəkəl/ n. a wonderful thing; a marvel. –**miraculous**, adj.

mirage /mə'raʒ/ n. an optical illusion by which reflected images of distant objects are seen, often inverted.

mire /maɪə/ n. **1.** a piece of wet, swampy ground. –v.t. (**mired**, **miring**) **2.** to cause to stick fast in mire.

mirror /'mɪrə/ n. **1.** a reflecting surface, usually glass with a metallic backing; a looking glass. –v.t. **2.** to reflect in or as in a mirror, or as a mirror does.

mirth /mɜθ/ n. rejoicing; joyous gaiety.

mis- a prefix meaning 'ill', 'mistaken', 'wrong', or simply negating.

misadventure /mɪsəd'vɛntʃə/ n. an accident.

misandry /mɪs'ændri/ n. **1.** the hatred of men. **2.** entrenched prejudice against men. Compare **misogyny**. –**misandrist**, n., adj.

misanthropy /mə'zænθrəpi/ n. hatred, dislike, or distrust of humankind.

misappropriate /mɪsə'proʊprieɪt/ v.t. to apply wrongfully or dishonestly to one's own use. –**misappropriation**, n.

misbehave /mɪsbə'heɪv/ v.i. to behave badly. –**misbehaviour**, n.

miscarriage /mɪs'kærɪdʒ, ˌmɪs'kærɪdʒ/ n. **1.** failure to attain the right or desired result. **2.** premature expulsion of a fetus from the uterus, especially before it is viable. **3.** a transmission of goods not in accordance with the contract of shipment. –**miscarry**, v.

miscellaneous /mɪsə'leɪniəs/ adj. consisting of members or elements of different kinds.

miscellany /mə'sɛləni/ n. (pl. **-nies**) a miscellaneous collection.

mischief /'mɪstʃəf/ n. **1.** conduct such as to tease or cause playfully petty annoyance. **2.** an injury due to some cause. –**mischievous**, adj.

miscommunicate /mɪskə'mjunəkeɪt/ v.t. **1.** to fail in communicating (a message, idea, etc.) so that there is no understanding or a wrong understanding on the part of the person receiving the message. –v.i. **2.** to fail in communicating in this way. –**miscommunication**, n.

misconception /mɪskən'sɛpʃən/ n. erroneous conception; a mistaken notion.

misdemeanour /mɪsdə'minə/ n. Law a less serious crime. Compare **felony**. Also, **misdemeanor**.

misdiagnose /mɪsdaɪəg'noʊz/ v.t. to diagnose incorrectly. –**misdiagnosis** /mɪsdaɪəg'noʊsəs/, n.

miser /'maɪzə/ n. a niggardly, avaricious person.

miserable /'mɪzrəbəl, -zərəbəl/ adj. 1. wretchedly unhappy, uneasy, or uncomfortable. 2. attended with or causing misery.

misère /mə'zɛə/ n. Cards a hand which contains no winning card.

misery /'mɪzəri/ n. 1. great distress of mind; extreme unhappiness. 2. wretchedness of condition or circumstances.

misfire /mɪs'faɪə/ v.i. 1. to fail to fire or explode. 2. to fail to have a desired effect; be unsuccessful.

misfit /'mɪsfɪt/ n. someone who feels ill at ease or out of place in a given environment.

misfortune /mɪs'fɔtʃən/ n. bad luck, or difficulty caused by bad luck.

misgiving /mɪs'gɪvɪŋ/ n. a feeling of doubt, distrust, or apprehension.

mishap /'mɪshæp/ n. an unfortunate accident.

mishmash /'mɪʃmæʃ/ n. a hotchpotch; jumble.

mislay /mɪs'leɪ/ v.t. (-laid, -laying) to put in a place afterwards forgotten.

mislead /mɪs'lid/ v.t. (-led, -leading) 1. to lead or guide wrongly; lead astray. 2. to lead into error of conduct, thought, or judgement.

misnomer /mɪs'noumə/ n. a misapplied name or designation.

miso- a word element referring to hate.

misogyny /mə'sɒdʒəni/ n. 1. hatred of women. 2. entrenched prejudice against women. Compare **misandry**. **–misogynist**, n.

misprint /'mɪsprɪnt/ n. a mistake in printing.

miss¹ /mɪs/ v.t. 1. to fail to hit, light upon, meet, catch, receive, obtain, attain, accomplish, see, hear, etc. 2. to perceive the absence or loss of, often with regret. –v.i. 3. to fail to hit, light upon, receive, or attain something. 4. to fail of effect or success; be unsuccessful. 5. Colloq. (of an internal combustion engine) to fail to fire in one or more cylinders. –n. 6. a failure to hit, meet, obtain, or accomplish something. –phr. 7. **miss out**, to fail to receive, especially something desired.

miss² /mɪs/ n. (pl. **misses**) (upper case) the conventional title of respect for an unmarried woman, prefixed to the name.

misshapen /mɪs'ʃeɪpən/ adj. badly shaped; deformed.

missile /'mɪsaɪl/ n. an object or weapon that can be thrown, hurled, or shot.

missing /'mɪsɪŋ/ adj. lacking; absent; not found.

mission /'mɪʃən/ n. 1. a body of persons sent to a foreign country to conduct negotiations, establish relations, or the like. 2. the business with which an agent, envoy, etc., is charged. 3. a missionary post or station. 4. a self-imposed or assigned duty. 5. the goals of an organisation.

missionary /'mɪʃənri/, Orig. US /'mɪʃəneri/. n. a person sent to spread their religious faith, usually among the people of another country or region in which that faith is not widely practised.

missive /'mɪsɪv/ n. 1. a written message; a letter. –adj. 2. sent, especially from an official source.

mist /mɪst/ n. a cloudlike aggregation of minute globules of water suspended in the atmosphere at or near the earth's surface.

mistake /mə'steɪk/ n. 1. an error in action, opinion or judgement. –v.t. (**-took**, **-taken**, **-taking**) 2. to conceive of or understand wrongly.

mister /'mɪstə/ n. (upper case) the conventional title of respect for a man, prefixed to the name, usually written **Mr**.

mistletoe /'mɪsəltou/ n. any of various plants much used in Christmas decorations.

mistreat /mɪs'trit/ v.t. to treat cruelly or in an incorrect way. **–mistreatment**, n.

mistress /'mɪstrəs/ n. 1. a woman who has authority or control. 2. a female head teacher in a particular subject department in a secondary school. 3. a woman who has a continuing sexual relationship with a man outside marriage.

mistrust /mɪs'trʌst/ n. 1. lack of trust or confidence; distrust. –v.t. 2. to regard with mistrust; distrust.

misunderstanding /ˌmɪsʌndə'stændɪŋ, mɪs,ʌn-/ n. disagreement or dissension.

misuse n. /mɪs'jus/ 1. wrong or improper use; misapplication. –v.t. /mɪs'juz/ 2. to ill-use; maltreat.

mite /maɪt/ n. any of various small arachnids, many being parasitic on plants and animals.

mitigate /'mɪtəgeɪt/ v.t. 1. to moderate the severity of (anything distressing). –v.i. 2. to become milder; moderate in severity. **–mitigation**, n.

mitosis /maɪ'tousəs, mə-/ n. an asexual method of cell division in which the chromosomes in the cell nucleus double and then separate to form two identical cells. **–mitotic**, adj.

mitre /'maɪtə/ n. 1. the ceremonial headdress of a bishop. 2. a right-angled joint, as of a picture frame.

mitten /'mɪtn/ n. a kind of hand-covering enclosing the four fingers together and the thumb separately.

mix /mɪks/ v.t. 1. to put together in one mass or assemblage with more or less thorough diffusion of the constituent elements among one another. –v.i. 2. to become mixed. 3. to associate, as in company. –n. 4. a mixing, or a mixed condition; a mixture.

mixed /mɪkst/ adj. 1. composed of different constituents or elements. 2. comprising persons of different ethnic, religious or cultural origins.

mixer /'mɪksə/ n. 1. a kitchen utensil or electrical appliance used for beating. 2. a person with reference to their sociability.

mixture /'mɪkstʃə/ n. any combination of differing elements, kinds, qualities, etc.

mix-up /'mɪks-ʌp/ n. a confused state of things; a muddle; a tangle.

mnemonic /nə'mɒnɪk/ adj. 1. assisting, or intended to assist, the memory. –n. 2. a verse or the like intended to assist the memory.

moa /'mouə/ n. any of various extinct, flightless birds of NZ.

moan /moun/ n. 1. a prolonged, low, inarticulate sound uttered from or as if from physical or mental suffering. –v.i. 2. to utter moans, as of pain or grief.

moat /mout/ n. a deep, wide trench surrounding a fortified place, as a town or a castle, usually filled with water.

mob /mɒb/ n. **1.** a large number, especially of people. **2.** a disorderly, riotous or hostile group of people. **3.** a group of animals: *a mob of sheep.* –v.t. (**mobbed, mobbing**) **4.** to surround and attack with riotous violence.

mobile /ˈmoʊbaɪl/ adj. **1.** movable; moving readily. **2.** of or relating to a mobile phone: *mobile technology.* –n. **3.** a construction or sculpture of delicately balanced movable parts. **4.** a mobile phone. –**mobility,** n.

mobile home n. **1.** a registrable vehicle as a motorhome, van, etc., which is used as a dwelling. **2.** freestanding living quarters which can be moved from one site to another.

mobile phone n. a portable cellular telephone.

mobilise /ˈmoʊbəlaɪz/ v.t. to put (armed forces) into readiness for active service. Also, **mobilize**.

moccasin /ˈmɒkəsən/ n. a slip-on shoe made entirely of soft leather.

mocha /ˈmɒkə/ n. **1.** a choice variety of coffee. **2.** a flavouring obtained from coffee infusion or combined chocolate and coffee infusion.

mock /mɒk/ v.t. **1.** to assail or treat with ridicule or derision. **2.** to mimic, imitate, or counterfeit. –v.i. **3.** (oft. fol. by *at*) to use ridicule or derision; scoff; jeer. –adj. **4.** imitation.

mockery /ˈmɒkəri/ n. **1.** ridicule or derision. **2.** a mere travesty, or mocking pretence.

mockingbird /ˈmɒkɪŋbɜd/ n. any of various scrub birds noted for their ability as mimics.

mockumentary /mɒkjəˈmɛntri/ n. a parody of the documentary genre, which chooses a fictitious subject and treats it with all the mannerisms of the documentary.

mock-up /ˈmɒk-ʌp/ n. a model, built to scale, of a machine, apparatus, or weapon, used in testing, teaching, etc.

modal verb /ˈmoʊdəl/ n. an auxiliary verb that expresses such things as the degree of probability attached by the speaker to the statement (*I might come, the sun will rise*) or the degree of obligation (*he should speak up, the court must decide*).

mod cons pl. n. *Colloq.* modern conveniences.

mode[1] /moʊd/ n. **1.** manner of acting or doing; a method; a way. **2.** the manner of existence or action of anything; a form. **3.** *Statistics* (in a statistical population) the category, value, or interval of the variable having the greatest frequency.

mode[2] /moʊd/ n. a prevailing style or fashion.

model /ˈmɒdl/ n. **1.** a standard or example for imitation or comparison. **2.** a representation, generally in miniature, to show the construction or serve as a copy of something. **3.** a person who poses for a painter, etc. **4.** someone employed in the fashion industry to put on articles of apparel to display them to customers; mannequin. **5.** a typical or specific form or style. –adj. **6.** worthy to serve as a model; exemplary. –v. (**-elled, -elling**) –v.t. **7.** to form or plan according to a model. **8.** to display, especially by wearing. –v.i. **9.** to serve or be employed as a model.

modem /ˈmoʊdɛm, ˈmoʊdəm/ n. an electronic device that facilitates the linking of one computer to another via the telephone system.

moderate /ˈmɒdrət, -ərət/ *for defs 1–3,* /ˈmɒdəreɪt/ *for defs 4 and 5* adj. **1.** not extreme, excessive, or intense. **2.** fair, average or

medium: *a moderate income.* –n. **3.** someone who is moderate in opinion or action, especially in politics or religion. –v.t. **4.** to reduce the excessiveness of; make less violent, severe, intense, or rigorous. –v.i. **5.** to become less violent, severe, intense, or rigorous.

moderation /mɒdəˈreɪʃən/ n. **1.** the quality of being moderate. **2.** the act of moderating.

moderator /ˈmɒdəreɪtə/ n. **1.** someone or something that moderates. **2.** *Internet* a person who oversees all the messages in a forum, deleting any unregistered messages and assisting members. –**moderatorship,** n.

modern /ˈmɒdn/ adj. **1.** of or relating to present and recent time; not ancient or remote. –n. **2.** one whose views and tastes are modern.

modest /ˈmɒdəst/ adj. **1.** having or showing a moderate or humble estimate of one's merits, importance, etc. **2.** moderate. **3.** having or showing regard for the decencies of behaviour, speech, dress, etc. –**modesty,** n.

modicum /ˈmɒdəkəm/ n. a moderate or small quantity.

modify /ˈmɒdəfaɪ/ v. (**-fied, -fying**) –v.t. **1.** to change somewhat the form or qualities of; alter somewhat. **2.** to reduce in degree; moderate; qualify. –v.i. **3.** to change; to become changed. –**modification,** n.

modular /ˈmɒdʒələ/ adj. **1.** of or relating to a module. **2.** composed of standardised units or sections for easy construction or flexible arrangement.

modulate /ˈmɒdʒəleɪt/ v.t. to regulate by or adjust to a certain measure or proportion; soften; tone down. –**modulation,** n.

module /ˈmɒdʒul/ n. **1.** a selected unit of measure used as a basis for planning and standardisation of building materials. **2.** a structural component. **3.** a detachable section of a space vehicle.

mogul /ˈmoʊgəl/ n. an important person.

mohair /ˈmoʊhɛə/ n. a fabric made from the hair of the Angora goat.

mohawk /ˈmoʊhɒk/ adj. of or relating to a hairstyle in which the head is shaved leaving a strip of hair along the centre of the scalp from the forehead to the back of the neck.

moiety /ˈmɔɪəti/ n. (pl. **-ties**) **1.** a half. **2.** *Anthrop.* **a.** one of two units into which a society is divided on the basis of unilineal descent. **b.** one of the two units into which a society is divided on the basis that people in alternate generations are grouped together. **c.** (in Aboriginal culture) a similar division of the Dreaming for those societies with moieties. Compare **section** (def. 5), **subsection** (def. 2).

moist /mɔɪst/ adj. moderately or slightly wet; damp; humid.

moisture /ˈmɔɪstʃə/ n. water or other liquid rendering anything moist.

molar /ˈmoʊlə/ n. a tooth adapted for grinding.

molasses /məˈlæsəz/ n. the thick brown bitter uncrystallised syrup drained from raw sugar.

mole[1] /moʊl/ n. **1.** a small congenital spot or blemish on the human skin.

mole[2] /moʊl/ n. any of various small insectivorous mammals living chiefly underground.

mole[3] /moʊl/ n. the SI base unit of measurement of amount of substance. *Symbol*: mol

molecule /'mɒləkjul/ *n. Physics, Chem.* the smallest physical unit of an element or compound. **–molecular**, *adj.*

molest /mə'lɛst/ *v.t.* **1.** to assault sexually. **2.** to interfere with annoyingly, injuriously, or with hostile intent.

mollify /'mɒləfaɪ/ *v.t.* (**-fied, -fying**) to soften in feeling or temper.

mollusc /'mɒləsk/ *n.* any of a phylum of (usually shelled) invertebrates including the snails, bivalves, squids, octopuses, etc.

mollycoddle /'mɒlikɒdl/ *v.t.* to coddle; pamper.

Molotov cocktail /'mɒlətɒv/ *n.* a homemade bomb, usually a bottle filled with petrol, with a wick which is ignited before the bottle is thrown.

molten /'moʊltn/ *adj.* liquefied by heat; in a state of fusion.

moment /'moʊmənt/ *n.* **1.** an indefinitely short space of time; an instant. **2.** importance or consequence.

momentarily /'moʊməntrəli/, *Chiefly US* /moʊmən'tɛrəli/ *adv.* **1.** for a moment: *to hesitate momentarily.* **2.** *Chiefly US* in a moment; very shortly: *the plane will be in the air momentarily.*

momentary /'moʊməntri/, *Orig. US* /-tɛri/ *adj.* lasting but a moment; very brief.

momentous /moʊ'mɛntəs, mə-/ *adj.* of great importance or consequence.

momentum /mə'mɛntəm/ *n.* (*pl.* **ta** /-tə/) **1.** the quantity of motion of a moving body, equal to the product of its mass and velocity. **2.** impetus, as of a moving body.

mon- variant of **mono-**, before vowels.

monarch /'mɒnək, -ak/ *n.* a hereditary sovereign with more or less limited powers, as a king, queen, emperor, etc.

monarchy /'mɒnəki/ *n.* (*pl.* **-chies**) a government or state in which the supreme power is actually or nominally lodged in a monarch.

monastery /'mɒnəstri, -təri/ *n.* (*pl.* **-ries**) a place occupied by a community of monks living in seclusion from the world under religious vows. **–monastic**, *adj.*

monetarism /'mʌnətərɪzəm/ *n.* an economic theory which holds that a nation's economy is governed by changes in the money supply. **–monetarist**, *adj., n.*

monetary /'mʌnətri, -təri/, *Orig. US* /-tɛri/ *adj.* of or relating to money, or pecuniary matters.

money /'mʌni/ *n.* (*pl.* **-neys** *or* **-nies**) **1.** coin or notes generally accepted in payment of debts and current transactions. **2.** a particular form or denomination of currency. **3.** wealth viewed in terms of money.

moneyed /'mʌnid/ *adj.* having money; wealthy.

money laundering *n.* the illegal practice of transferring funds of illegal origin, usually as cash, into legal enterprises in such a way that they appear to be legitimate. **–money-launderer**, *n.*

money market *n.* a market in which large amounts of money are borrowed and lent for short periods of time (usually less than a month).

money order *n.* an order for the payment of money, as one issued by one post office and payable at another, and requiring proof of ownership before being cashed. Compare **postal note**.

monger /'mʌŋgə/ *n.* (*usu. in compounds*) **1.** a dealer in some commodity: *fishmonger.* **2.** someone who busies himself or herself with something in a sordid or petty way.

mongrel /'mʌŋgrəl/ *n.* **1.** any animal or plant resulting from the crossing of different breeds or varieties. *–adj.* **2.** inferior.

monilia /mə'nɪliə/ *n.* a yeast-like fungus which can cause infection.

monition /mə'nɪʃən/ *n.* **1.** admonition; warning; caution. **2.** an official or legal notice.

monitor /'mɒnətə/ *n.* **1.** a device used to check, observe, or record the operation of a machine or system. **2.** any of several large lizards. **3.** *Computers* the component of a desktop computer which houses the screen; visual display unit. *–v.t.* **4.** to check, observe, or record the operation of (a machine, etc.), without interfering with the operation.

monk /mʌŋk/ *n.* a man who has withdrawn from the world from religious motives and lives under vows of poverty, chastity, and obedience.

monkey /'mʌŋki/ *n.* (*pl.* **-keys**) **1.** a long-tailed member of the mammalian order Primates, living in trees. **2.** any of various mechanical devices. *–v.i.* (**-keyed, -keying**) **3.** *Colloq.* to play or trifle idly.

monkey wrench *n.* a spanner or wrench with an adjustable jaw, for turning nuts of different sizes, etc.

mono- a word element: meaning 'alone', 'single', 'one'.

monochromatic /mɒnəkroʊ'mætɪk/ *adj.* of, producing, or relating to one colour or one wavelength.

monocle /'mɒnəkəl/ *n.* an glass lens for one eye.

monogamy /mə'nɒgəmi/ *n.* the practice of having only one spouse at a time. **–monogamous**, *adj.*

monogram /'mɒnəgræm/ *n.* a character consisting of two or more letters combined or interlaced.

monograph /'mɒnəgræf, -graf/ *n.* a treatise on a particular subject.

monolith /'mɒnəliθ/ *n.* **1.** a single block or piece of stone of considerable size. **2.** something resembling a large block of stone, especially in having a massive, uniform, or unyielding quality or character. **–monolithic**, *adj.*

monologue /'mɒnəlɒg/ *n.* a prolonged talk or discourse by a single speaker.

monophonic /mɒnə'fɒnɪk/ *adj.* of or denoting a system of sound reproduction through only one loudspeaker. Compare **stereophonic**.

monoplane /'mɒnəpleɪn/ *n.* an aeroplane with only one pair of wings.

monopolise /mə'nɒpəlaɪz/ *v.t.* **1.** to acquire, have, or exercise a monopoly of (a market, commodity, etc.). **2.** to keep entirely to oneself. Also, **monopolize**.

monopoly /mə'nɒpəli/ *n.* (*pl.* **-lies**) exclusive control of a commodity or service in a particular market, or a control that makes possible the manipulation of prices.

monorail /'mɒnəreɪl/ *n.* a railway with coaches running on a single (usually overhead) rail.

monosaccharide /mɒnoʊˈsækəraɪd, -rəd/ *n.* a simple sugar, such as glucose.

monosodium glutamate /mɒnəˌsoʊdiəm ˈglutəmeɪt/ *n.* a sodium salt used in cookery to enhance the natural flavour of a dish. Also, **MSG.**

monosyllabic /mɒnəsəˈlæbɪk/ *adj.* **1.** having only one syllable, as a word. **2.** having a vocabulary composed exclusively of monosyllables.

monotheism /ˈmɒnoʊθiˌɪzəm, mɒnoʊˈθiɪzəm/ *n.* the doctrine or belief that there is only one God.

monotone /ˈmɒnoʊtoʊn/ *n.* a single tone without harmony or variation in pitch.

monotony /məˈnɒtəni/ *n.* **1.** lack of variety, or wearisome uniformity, as in occupation, scenery, etc. **2.** sameness of tone or pitch, as in utterance. **–monotonous,** *adj.*

monotreme /ˈmɒnətrim/ *n.* a mammal which both lays eggs and suckles its young, as the platypus and echidna.

monounsaturated /ˌmɒnoʊˈʌnˈsætʃəreɪtəd/ *adj.* of or relating to a fat or oil having only one double bond per molecule, as oleic acid in olive oil. Also, **mono-unsaturated.**

monsoon /mɒnˈsun/ *n.* the rainy season.

monsoon forest *n.* a semi-deciduous tropical forest occurring in areas which experience a monsoon climate, marked by dry periods followed by torrential rain.

monster /ˈmɒnstə/ *n.* **1.** a legendary animal compounded of brute and human shape. *–adj.* **2.** huge; enormous; monstrous.

monstrosity /mɒnˈstrɒsəti/ *n.* (*pl.* **-ties**) something monstrous.

monstrous /ˈmɒnstrəs/ *adj.* **1.** huge; extremely great. **2.** revolting; outrageous; shocking. **3.** deviating greatly from the natural or normal form or type.

montage /mɒnˈtɑʒ, ˈmɒntɑʒ/ *n.* the combination in one picture, etc., of composition elements from several sources.

montane /ˈmɒnteɪn/ *adj.* **1.** mountainous: *a montane region.* **2.** *Biol.* (of a species) found in a mountainous habitat.

month /mʌnθ/ *n.* **1.** approximately one twelfth of a tropical or solar year. **2.** a period of four weeks or of thirty days. **3.** the period (**lunar month**) of a complete revolution of the moon. **–monthly,** *adj., n.*

monument /ˈmɒnjəmənt/ *n.* something erected in memory of a person, event, etc.

monumental /mɒnjəˈmɛntl/ *adj.* **1.** resembling a monument; massive or imposing. **2.** of great importance or significance.

-mony a noun suffix indicating result or condition, as in *parsimony;* but sometimes having the same function as **-ment.**

mooch /mutʃ/ *v.i.* **1.** to hang or loiter about. *–v.t.* **2.** to get without paying or at another's expense; cadge.

mood[1] /mud/ *n.* frame of mind, or state of feeling, as at a particular time.

mood[2] /mud/ *n. Gram.* a set of categories of verb inflection which show the syntactic relation of the verb to other verbs in the sentence, or the speaker's attitude towards the action expressed by the verb.

moody /ˈmudi/ *adj.* (**-dier, -diest**) **1.** given to gloomy or sullen moods; ill-humoured. **2.** exhibiting sharply varied moods; temperamental.

moon /mun/ *n.* **1.** the body which revolves around the earth monthly. **2.** a month. **3.** any planetary satellite. *–v.i.* **4.** *Colloq.* to wander about or gaze idly, dreamily, or listlessly.

moon boot *n.* an orthopaedic shoe, designed to hold the foot rigid to protect an injured or broken ankle.

moonlight /ˈmunlaɪt/ *n.* **1.** the light of the moon. *–adj.* **2.** relating to moonlight. **3.** illuminated by moonlight. *–v.i.* **4.** to work at a second job, often at night, in addition to one's regular employment.

moonshine /ˈmunʃaɪn/ *n.* **1.** the light of the moon. **2.** empty or foolish talk, ideas, etc.; nonsense. **3.** *Colloq.* smuggled or illicitly distilled liquor.

moonstone /ˈmunstoʊn/ *n.* a white translucent variety of feldspar with a bluish pearly lustre, used as a gem.

moonwalk /ˈmunwɔk/ *n.* **1.** a walk on the surface of the moon by an astronaut. **2.** a dance move in which the dancer moves backwards by gliding their feet smoothly along the floor. *–v.i.* **3.** to walk on the surface of the moon. **4.** to perform a moonwalk (def. 2). Also, **moon walk.**

moor[1] /mɔ/ *n.* a tract of open, wasteland; a heath.

moor[2] /mɔ/ *v.t.* to secure (a ship, etc.) in a particular place. **–moorage,** *n.*

moorings /ˈmɔrɪŋz/ *pl. n.* the place where a vessel is or may be moored.

moose /mus/ *n.* (*pl.* **moose**) a large animal of the deer family.

moot /mut/ *adj.* subject to argument or discussion; debatable; doubtful.

moot point *n.* a matter which is uncertain and open to debate.

mop /mɒp/ *n.* **1.** a bundle of coarse yarn, a piece of cloth, or the like, fastened at the end of a stick or handle, used for washing floors, dishes, etc. **2.** a thick mass, as of hair. *–v.t.* (**mopped, mopping**) **3.** to rub, wipe, clean, or remove with a mop. *–phr.* **4. mop up,** to clean up.

mope /moʊp/ *v.i.* to be sunk in listless apathy or dull dejection.

moral /ˈmɒrəl/ *adj.* **1.** relating to or concerned with right conduct or the distinction between right and wrong. **2.** conforming to the rules of right conduct (opposed to *immoral*). *–n.* **3.** the moral teaching or practical lesson contained in a fable, tale, experience, etc. **4.** (*pl.*) principles or habits with respect to right or wrong conduct; ethics.

morale /məˈral/ *n.* mental condition with respect to cheerfulness, confidence, zeal, etc.

moralise /ˈmɒrəlaɪz/ *v.i.* to make moral reflections. Also, **moralize.**

morality /məˈrælɪti/ *n.* conformity to the rules of right conduct.

morass /məˈræs/ *n.* a tract of low, soft, wet ground.

moratorium /mɒrəˈtɔriəm/ *n.* (*pl.* **-toria** /-ˈtɔriə/ or **-toriums**) a general suspension of some type of legal obligation. **–moratory,** *adj.*

moray /'mɒreɪ/ n. (pl. **morays** or **moray**) a type of eel found among rocks and weeds in northern Australia and in the Mediterranean where it is valued as a food.

morbid /'mɔbəd/ adj. **1.** showing a strong interest in gruesome things. **2.** affected by, proceeding from, or characteristic of, disease.

mordant /'mɔdnt/ adj. caustic or sarcastic, as wit, a speaker, etc.

more /mɔ/ adj. **1.** in greater quantity, amount, measure, degree, or number (as the comparative of *much* and *many*). **2.** additional or further. –n. **3.** an additional quantity, amount, or number. **4.** a greater quantity, amount, or degree. –adv. **5.** in or to a greater extent or degree. –phr. **6. more or less**, to a certain extent; approximately.

more-ish /'mɔr-ɪʃ/ adj. of or relating to something of which one would like more.

moreover /mɔr'ouvə/ adv. beyond what has been said; further; besides.

mores /'mɔreɪz/ pl. n. customs or conventions accepted without question and embodying the fundamental moral views of a group.

Moreton Bay bug /'mɔtn/ n. an edible marine crustacean found in northern Australian waters.

morgue /mɔg/ n. a place in which the bodies of persons found dead are exposed for identification.

moribund /'mɔrəbʌnd/ adj. dying.

mornay /'mɔneɪ/ adj. covered with a thick white sauce which has grated cheese added to it.

morning /'mɔnɪŋ/ n. the first part or period of the day.

morocco /mə'rɒkoʊ/ n. a fine leather made from goatskins.

moron /'mɔrɒn/ n. a person of rather low intelligence.

morose /mə'roʊs/ adj. gloomily or sullenly ill-humoured as a person, mood, etc.

-morph a word element meaning 'form', 'shape' or 'structure'.

morpheme /'mɔfim/ n. any of the minimum meaningful elements in a language.

-morphic a word element used as adjective termination corresponding to **-morph**.

morphine /'mɔfin/ n. a drug used to dull pain, induce sleep, etc. Also, **morphia** /'mɔfiə/.

morpho- initial word element corresponding to **-morph**.

morphology /mɔ'fɒlədʒi/ n. the study of form, structure, and the like.

-morphous a word element used as adjective termination corresponding to **-morph**, as in *amorphous*.

morrow /'mɒroʊ/ n. the day next after this or after some other particular day or night.

Morse code /mɔs/ n. a system of dots, dashes, and spaces used to represent the letters of the alphabet, numerals, etc.

morsel /'mɔsəl/ n. a small piece, quantity, or amount of anything; a scrap; a bit.

mortal /'mɔtl/ adj. **1.** liable or subject to death. **2.** of or relating to human beings as subject to death; human. **3.** causing death; fatal. –n. **4.** a being subject to death.

mortality /mɔ'tælɪti/ n. **1.** the condition of being mortal. **2.** relative frequency of death, or death rate, as in a district or community.

mortality table n. an actuarial table compiled by an insurance company from statistics on the life spans of an arbitrarily selected population group or of former policyholders.

mortar[1] /'mɔtə/ n. **1.** a bowl in which drugs, etc., are reduced to powder or paste with a pestle. **2.** a type of cannon.

mortar[2] /'mɔtə/ n. a material which binds bricks, stones, etc., into a compact mass.

mortarboard /'mɔtəbɔd/ n. a kind of cap with a stiff, square top, worn by university graduates, etc.

mortgage /'mɔgɪdʒ/ Law –n. **1.** a security by way of conveyance or assignment of property securing the payment of a debt or the performance of an obligation where the property is redeemable upon payment or performance. –v.t. (-gaged, -gaging) **2.** to put (property, especially houses or land) under a mortgage.

mortice /'mɔtəs/ n. a rectangular cavity in a piece of wood, etc., for receiving a corresponding projection (tenon) on another piece, so as to form a joint. Also, **mortize**.

mortify /'mɔtəfaɪ/ v.t. (-fied, -fying) to humiliate. –**mortification**, n.

mortuary /'mɔtʃəri/ n. (pl. -ries) a place where dead bodies are temporarily kept.

mosaic /moʊ'zeɪk, mə'zeɪk/ n. a picture or decoration made of small pieces of stone, glass, etc., of different colours, inlaid to form a design.

mosh /mɒʃ/ v.i. to move as one of a crush of spectators jostling each other to the music of a live band or act. –**moshing**, n.

mosh pit n. the area in front of the stage on which a band is performing where the audience moshes.

mosque /mɒsk/ n. a Muslim place of worship.

mosquito /məs'kitoʊ/ n. (pl. -toes or -tos) any of various insects the females of which suck the blood of animals.

moss /mɒs/ n. any of various small leafy-stemmed plants growing in tufts in moist places.

most /moʊst/ adj. **1.** in the greatest quantity, amount, measure, degree, or number. –n. **2.** the greatest quantity, amount, or degree. **3.** (construed as pl.) the majority of persons. –adv. **4.** in or to the greatest extent or degree.

-most a suffixal use of **most** found in a series of superlatives, as in *utmost*, *foremost*.

mostly /'moʊstli/ adv. for the most part; in the main.

mote /moʊt/ n. a particle or speck, especially of dust.

motel /moʊ'tɛl/ n. a roadside hotel with self-contained units.

moth /mɒθ/ n. (pl. **moths**) any of a large group of insects similar to the butterflies.

mothball /'mɒθbɔl/ n. a small ball of naphthalene or (sometimes) camphor, stored with clothes, etc., to repel moths.

mother /'mʌðə/ n. **1.** a female parent. **2.** the head or superior of a female religious community. –adj. **3.** relating to or characteristic of a mother. –v.t. **4.** to be the mother of; give origin or rise to. **5.** to care for or protect as a mother does. –**motherly**, adj. –**motherhood**, n.

motherboard /ˈmʌðəbɔd/ n. a printed circuit board plugged into the back of a computer into which other boards (**daughter boards**) can be slotted so that the computer can operate an optional range of peripheral devices. Also, **mother board**.

mother-in-law n. (pl. **mothers-in-law**) the mother of one's spouse.

mother-of-pearl /mʌðər-əv-ˈpɜl/ n. a hard, iridescent substance which forms the inner layer of certain shells, as that of the pearl oyster.

mothership /ˈmʌðəʃɪp/ n. 1. a large ship which services the group of smaller ships with which it sails. 2. a spacecraft which is the main vehicle providing resources and services to a fleet of smaller craft. Also, **mother ship**.

mother tongue n. the language first learned by a person; native language.

motif /mouˈtif, ˈmoutəf/ n. a recurring subject or theme in art, literature, or music.

motion /ˈmouʃən/ n. 1. the process of moving, or changing place or position. 2. a bodily movement or gesture. 3. a proposal formally made to a deliberative assembly. 4. → **faeces**. –v.t. 5. to direct by a significant motion or gesture, as with the hand. –v.i. 6. to make a significant motion; gesture.

motivate /ˈmoutəveɪt/ v.t. to provide with a strong reason for doing something. –**motivated**, adj. –**motivation**, n.

motive /ˈmoutɪv/ n. 1. something that prompts a person to act in a certain way. –adj. 2. causing, or tending to cause, motion.

motley /ˈmɒtli/ adj. exhibiting great diversity of elements.

motocross /ˈmoutəkrɒs/ n. a short distance motorcycle race on rough terrain.

motor /ˈmoutə/ n. 1. a comparatively small and powerful engine, especially an internal-combustion engine. 2. any self-powered vehicle. –adj. 3. causing or imparting motion.

motorcade /ˈmoutəkeɪd/ n. a procession or parade of cars.

motorcycle /ˈmoutəsaɪkəl/ n. a motor vehicle resembling a bicycle.

motorhome /ˈmoutəhoum/ n. a small truck-like vehicle with living accommodation in the style of a caravan behind the driver's cabin. Also, **mobile home**.

motorist /ˈmoutərəst/ n. someone who drives a car.

motor vehicle n. a road vehicle driven by a motor.

motorway /ˈmoutəweɪ/ n. a freeway.

mottled /ˈmɒtld/ adj. spotted or blotched in colouring.

motto /ˈmɒtou/ n. (pl. **-tos** or **-toes**) a maxim adopted as expressing one's guiding principle.

mould¹ /mould/ n. 1. a hollow form or matrix for giving a particular shape to something in a molten or plastic state. 2. something formed in or on a mould. –v.t. 3. to work into a required shape or form; shape.

mould² /mould/ n. a growth of minute fungi forming on vegetable or animal matter.

moulder /ˈmouldə/ v.i. to turn to dust by natural decay.

moult /moult/ v.i. to cast or shed the feathers, skin, or the like, to be succeeded by a new growth. Also, **molt**.

mound /maund/ n. 1. an elevation of earth; a hillock or knoll. 2. a heap or raised mass.

mount¹ /maunt/ v.t. 1. to go up or ascend: to mount the stairs. 2. to get up on (a platform, horse, etc.). 3. to raise or put into position for use, as a gun. 4. to go or put on (guard), as a sentry. 5. (of a male animal) to climb up on (a female) for copulation. 6. to fix on or in a support, backing, setting, etc.: to mount a photograph. 7. to provide (a play, etc.) with scenery, costumes, etc., for production. –v.i. 8. to rise or go to a higher position, level, degree, etc.: tension mounted. –n. 9. a horse, bicycle, etc., used for riding. 10. a support, backing, setting, etc., on or in which something is mounted or fixed.

mount² /maunt/ n. a mountain or hill.

mountain /ˈmauntən/ n. a natural elevation of the earth's surface, higher than a hill.

mountaineer /mauntəˈnɪə/ n. a climber of mountains. –**mountaineering**, n.

mountainous /ˈmauntənəs/ adj. 1. abounding in mountains. 2. of the nature of a mountain.

mountebank /ˈmauntəbæŋk/ n. a charlatan or quack.

mourn /mɔn/ v.i. 1. to feel or express sorrow or grief. –v.t. 2. to grieve or lament over (the dead).

mournful /ˈmɔnfəl/ adj. 1. full of, expressing, or showing sorrow or grief. 2. gloomy, sombre or dreary.

mourning /ˈmɔnɪŋ/ n. the conventional manifestation of sorrow for a person's death, especially by the wearing of black, the hanging of flags at half-mast, etc.

mouse /maus/ n. (pl. **mice** for defs 1 and 2, **mice** or **mouses** for def. 3) 1. any of various small rodents. 2. a quiet, shy person. 3. Computers a handheld device for positioning the cursor on a monitor.

mousepad /ˈmauspæd/ n. Computers a usually foam-backed pad over which a computer mouse is moved, providing more traction than a smooth surface.

moussaka /muˈsakə/ n. a Balkan and Middle Eastern dish based on minced lamb, tomatoes, and eggplant, layered, topped with a thick white sauce and baked.

mousse /mus/ n. 1. any of various preparations of whipped cream, beaten eggs, gelatine, etc., flavoured (sweet or savoury) and usually chilled. 2. any of various cosmetic preparations of similar consistency.

moustache /məˈstaʃ/ n. the hair growing on the upper lip.

mousy /ˈmausi/ adj. (**mousier**, **mousiest**) 1. drab and colourless. 2. quiet as a mouse. Also, **mousey**.

mouth n. /mauθ/ (pl. **mouths** /mauðz/) 1. the opening through which an animal takes in food. 2. a person or other animal as requiring food. 3. utterance or expression. 4. a part of a river or the like where its waters are discharged into some other body of water. –v.t. /mauð/ 5. to utter with unnecessarily noticeable use of the mouth or lips. 6. to form (words) with the lips, uttering no sound.

mouthful /ˈmauθful/ n. (pl. **-fuls**) as much as a mouth can hold.

mouth organ n. → **harmonica**.

mouthpiece /'maʊθpis/ n. **1.** a piece placed at or forming the mouth, as of a receptacle, tube, or the like. **2.** a piece or part, as of an instrument, to which the mouth is applied or which is held in the mouth. **3.** a person, a newspaper, or the like that voices or communicates the sentiments, decisions, etc., of another or others; a spokesperson.

mouth-to-mouth /maʊθ-tə-'maʊθ/ adj. **1.** denoting a method of resuscitation in which air is breathed into the victim's lungs through the mouth. –n. **2.** the method itself.

move /muv/ v.i. **1.** to change place or position. **2.** Commerce to be disposed of by sale, as goods in stock. **3.** (of the bowels) to operate. **4.** to make a formal request, application, or proposal. –v.t. **5.** to change the place or position of. **6.** to prompt, actuate, or impel to some action. **7.** to affect with tender or compassionate emotion; touch. **8.** to propose formally for consideration by a deliberative assembly. –n. **9.** the act of moving; a movement. **10.** a change of abode or residence. –**movable**, **moveable**, adj., n.

movement /'muvmənt/ n. **1.** the act or process or result of moving. **2.** (chiefly pl.) an action or activity, as of a person or a body of persons. **3.** the price change in the market of some commodity or security. **4.** the works of a mechanism, as a watch. **5.** Music a principal division or section of a sonata, symphony, or the like.

movie /'muvi/ n. → **film** (def. 3b).

mow /moʊ/ v.t. (**mowed**, **mown** or **mowed**, **mowing**) **1.** to cut down (grass, grain, etc.) with a scythe or a machine. **2.** to cut down, destroy, or kill indiscriminately.

mozzarella /mɒtsə'relə/ n. a soft, white, ripened cheese, with a plastic curd, giving it a smooth, close texture.

MP3 /ɛm pi 'θri/ n. a digital audio file in which the audio signal is compressed to a size smaller than the original WAV format while still maintaining audio quality. Also, **mp3**.

MP3 player n. a device for downloading, storing, and playing MP3s.

MRI n. magnetic resonance imaging; a technique which produces an image of internal body organs by means of a magnetic scanner.

MSG /ɛm ɛs 'dʒi/ n. → **monosodium glutamate**.

much /mʌtʃ/ adj. **1.** in great quantity, amount, measure, or degree. –n. **2.** a great quantity or amount; a great deal. –adv. **3.** to a great extent or degree; greatly; far. –phr. **4. make much of**, to treat (a person) with great, flattering, or fond consideration.

muck /mʌk/ n. **1.** farmyard dung, decaying vegetable matter, etc., in a moist state; manure. **2.** filth; dirt. –v.t. **3.** (oft. fol. by out) to remove muck from. **4.** Colloq. to spoil; make a mess of. –phr. Colloq. **5. muck about** (or **around**), to idle; potter; fool about. **6. muck up**, to misbehave.

muck-up /'mʌk-ʌp/ n. Colloq. fiasco; muddle.

mucous /'mjukəs/ adj. **1.** relating to, consisting of, or resembling mucus. **2.** containing or secreting mucus.

mucus /'mjukəs/ n. a viscid secretion of the mucous membranes.

mud /mʌd/ n. **1.** wet, soft earth or earthy matter. –phr. Colloq. **2. one's name is mud**, one is in disgrace. **3. throw** (or **sling**) **mud at**, speak ill of; abuse. –**muddy**, adj.

muddle /'mʌdl/ v.t. (**-dled, -dling**) **1.** to mix up or jumble together in a confused or bungling way. –n. **2.** a muddled condition; a confused mental state. –phr. **3. muddle through**, to come to a satisfactory conclusion without planned direction.

mudflat /'mʌdflæt/ n. (oft. pl.) an area of muddy ground covered by water at high tide. Also, **mud flat**.

mudguard /'mʌdgad/ n. a guard or shield shaped to fit over the wheels of a vehicle to prevent splashing of water, mud, etc.

muesli /'mjuzli, 'muzli/ n. a breakfast cereal of oats, wheatgerm, chopped fruit and nuts, etc.

muff /mʌf/ n. **1.** a case covered with fur or other material, in which the hands are placed for warmth. **2.** Colloq. a failure. –v.t., v.i. **3.** to bungle (something).

muffin /'mʌfən/ n. **1.** a type of small, cup-shaped cake, usually sweet, and often containing fruit, nuts, chocolate, etc. **2.** → **English muffin**.

muffin top n. Colloq. the fold of fat around the midriff which, on an overweight woman, spills out over the top of tight-fitting pants or skirts.

muffle /'mʌfəl/ v.t. **1.** to wrap or envelop in a cloak, shawl, scarf, etc. **2.** to wrap with something to deaden or prevent sound. **3.** to deaden (sound) by wrappings or other means.

muffler /'mʌflə/ n. **1.** a heavy neck scarf used for warmth. **2.** any device that reduces noise, especially that on the exhaust of an internal combustion engine.

mufti¹ /'mofti, 'mʌfti/ n. a Muslim legal adviser in religious law.

mufti² /'mʌfti/ n. ordinary clothes, as opposed to a uniform.

mug /mʌg/ n. **1.** a drinking cup, usually cylindrical and commonly with a handle. **2.** Colloq. the face. **3.** Colloq. a fool; someone who is easily duped. –v.t. (**mugged, mugging**) **4.** Colloq. to assault and rob.

muggy /'mʌgi/ adj. (**-gier, -giest**) (of the atmosphere, weather, etc.) damp and close; humid and oppressive.

mulberry /'mʌlbəri, -bri/ n. (pl. **-ries**) **1.** a type of berry. **2.** a dull, dark, reddish purple colour.

mulch /mʌltʃ/ n. straw, leaves, loose earth, etc., spread on the ground.

mule¹ /mjul/ n. **1.** the sterile offspring of a male donkey and a mare, used especially as a beast of burden. **2.** Colloq. a stupid or stubborn person. **3.** Colloq. a courier of illegal drugs.

mule² /mjul/ n. a kind of slipper which leaves the heel exposed.

mulga /'mʌlgə/ n. **1.** any of several species of acacia found in drier parts of Australia. **2.** the bush; back country. **3.** a traditional Aboriginal shield.

mull¹ /mʌl/ v.t. to study or ruminate (over).

mull² /mʌl/ v.t. to heat, sweeten, and spice for drinking, as ale, wine, etc.

mullah /'mʌlə, 'molə/ *n. Islam* someone who is learned in, teaches, or expounds the sacred law. Also, **mulla**.

mullet /'mʌlət/ *n.* (*pl.* **-let** *or* **-lets**) **1.** a type of freshwater fish. **2.** *Colloq.* a type of hairstyle, long at the back and cut short on the top and sides.

multi- a word element meaning 'many'.

multicoloured /'mʌltɪkʌləd/ *adj.* of many colours. Also, **multicolored**.

multicultural /mʌltɪ'kʌltʃərəl/ *adj.* of or relating to a society which embraces a number of different cultures.

multifarious /mʌltə'fɛəriəs/ *adj.* **1.** having many different parts, elements, forms, etc. **2.** of many kinds, or numerous and varied.

multigrade /'mʌltɪgreɪd/ *adj.* denoting a motor oil with a stable viscosity level over a wide range of temperatures.

multilateral /mʌltɪ'lætərəl, -'lætrəl/ *adj.* **1.** having many sides; many-sided. **2.** involving many parties; multipartite.

multilingual /mʌltɪ'lɪŋgwəl/ *adj.* able to speak three or more languages.

multimeter /'mʌltɪmitə/ *n.* a meter for measuring voltages, currents and resistances.

multinational /mʌltɪ'næʃənəl/ *adj.* **1.** of, relating to, or spreading across many nations. –*n.* **2.** a large, usually powerful, company with members from several nations.

multipartite /mʌltɪ'pataɪt/ *adj.* **1.** divided into many parts; having many divisions. **2.** → **multilateral** (def. 2).

multiple /'mʌltəpəl/ *adj.* **1.** consisting of, having, or involving many individuals, parts, elements, relations, etc.; manifold. –*n.* **2.** *Maths* a number which contains another number some number of times without a remainder.

multiple-choice /'mʌltəpəl-tʃɔɪs/ *adj.* offering a number of choices.

multiple personality disorder *n.* a rare psychotic disorder in which the patient develops several distinct, independent personalities which emerge at different times.

multiple sclerosis /sklə'rousəs/ *n.* a disease of the nervous system caused by loss of part of the myelin sheath around certain nerve fibres. *Abbrev.*: MS

multiplicity /mʌltə'plɪsəti/ *n.* a multitude or great number.

multiplier /'mʌltəplaɪə/ *n.* an indicator of the relative sizes of a given initial increase in investment and the total ultimate increase in income.

multiply /'mʌltəplaɪ/ *v.* (**-plied, -plying**) –*v.t.* **1.** to make many or manifold; increase the number, quantity, etc., of. **2.** *Maths* to take by addition a given number of times. **3.** to produce (animals or plants) by propagation. –*v.i.* **4.** to grow in number, quantity, etc.; increase. –**multiplication,** *n.*

multiracial /mʌltɪ'reɪʃəl/ *adj.* of or relating to more than one race (**race²**). –**multiracialism,** *n.*

multistorey /mʌltɪ'stɔri/ *adj.* (of a building) having a considerable number of storeys.

multitude /'mʌltətjud/ *n.* **1.** a great number; host. **2.** a great number of persons gathered together; a crowd or throng. –**multitudinous,** *adj.*

mum¹ /mʌm/ *n. Colloq.* mother.

mum² /mʌm/ *adj.* silent; not saying a word.

mumble /'mʌmbəl/ *v.i.* **1.** to speak indistinctly or unintelligibly. –*v.t.* **2.** to utter indistinctly. –*n.* **3.** a low, indistinct utterance or sound.

mumbo jumbo /mʌmbou 'dʒʌmbou/ *n.* meaningless incantation or ritual.

mummy¹ /'mʌmi/ *n.* (*pl.* **-mies**) the dead body of a human being or animal preserved by embalming.

mummy² /'mʌmi/ *n.* (*pl.* **-mies**) *Colloq.* (*with children*) mother.

mumps /mʌmps/ *pl. n.* (*construed as sing.*) an infectious viral disease causing swelling of the glands.

munch /mʌntʃ/ *v.t., v.i.* to chew steadily or vigorously, and often audibly.

munchies /'mʌntʃiz/ *pl. n.* **1.** *Colloq.* anything to eat, especially snacks between meals. –*phr.* **2. have the munchies,** to experience a craving for food.

mundane /'mʌndeɪn, mʌn'deɪn/ *adj.* ordinary; boring.

mung bean /mʌŋ/ *n.* a bushy annual herb, a chief source of bean sprouts.

municipal /mju'nɪsəpəl, mjunə'sɪpəl/ *adj.* of or relating to a municipality, its government, facilities, etc.

municipal council *n.* a local administrative body which serves a municipality, predominantly in a rural town or city suburban area. Compare **city council**, **shire council**.

municipality /mjunəsə'pæləti/ *n.* (*pl.* **-ties**) **1.** an area of land delineated for the purposes of local government; borough. **2.** the governing body of such a district or community.

munificent /mju'nɪfəsənt/ *adj.* extremely liberal in giving or bestowing; very generous.

munitions /mju'nɪʃənz/ *pl. n.* materials used in war, especially weapons and ammunition.

mural /'mjurəl/ *adj.* **1.** of or relating to a wall; resembling a wall. –*n.* **2.** a painting on a wall.

murder /'mɜdə/ –*n.* **1.** *Law* the unlawful killing of another human being deliberately. **2.** *Colloq.* an uncommonly laborious or difficult task. –*v.t.* **3.** *Law* to kill by an act constituting murder. –**murderous,** *adj.*

murky /'mɜki/ *adj.* (**-kier, -kiest**) cloudy and dirty, as water.

murmur /'mɜmə/ *n.* **1.** any low, continuous sound. **2.** a mumbled or private expression of discontent. –*v.i.* **3.** to make a low or indistinct continuous sound. **4.** to speak in a low tone or indistinctly. **5.** to complain in a low tone, or in private.

muscat /'mʌskət/ *n.* (*also upper case*) **1.** a grape variety. **2.** a type of sweet wine made from this grape. Also, **muscatel**.

muscle /'mʌsəl/ *n.* **1.** a discrete bundle or sheet of contractile fibres having the function of producing movement in the animal body. **2.** muscular strength; brawn. **3.** political or financial strength, especially when exercised in a ruthless fashion. –*phr.* (**-cled, -cling**) **4. muscle in** (**on**), to force one's way in(to).

musclebound /'mʌsəlbaʊnd/ *adj.* having muscles enlarged and inelastic, as from excessive exercise.

muscular /'mʌskjələ/ adj. **1.** of or relating to muscle or the muscles. **2.** having well-developed muscles.

muscular dystrophy /'dɪstrəfi/ n. a disease causing muscular deterioration and wastage.

muse¹ /mjuz/ v.i. to reflect or meditate in silence.

muse² /mjuz/ n. artistic inspiration, especially when identified as a person or object.

museum /mju'ziəm/ n. a building or place for the keeping, exhibition, and study of objects of scientific, artistic, and historical interest.

mush /mʌʃ/ n. **1.** any thick, soft mass. **2.** Colloq. weak or maudlin sentiment or sentimental language.

mushroom /'mʌʃrum/ n. **1.** any of various fleshy edible fungi. **2.** anything of similar shape or correspondingly rapid growth. –adj. **3.** of, relating to, or made of mushrooms. **4.** resembling or suggesting a mushroom in shape. **5.** to spread or grow quickly, as mushrooms.

music /'mjuzik/ n. **1.** an art of organising sound in significant forms to express ideas and emotions through the elements of rhythm, melody, harmony, and colour. **2.** the tones or sounds employed. **3.** musical work or compositions for singing or playing. **4.** the written or printed score of a musical composition. **5.** such scores collectively. –phr. **6. face the music**, to face the consequences, usually unpleasant, of one's actions.

musical /'mjuzikəl/ adj. **1.** of, relating to, or producing music. **2.** pleasing to one's ears, like music. **3.** fond of or skilled in music.

musician /mju'zɪʃən/ n. one skilled in playing a musical instrument.

musk /mʌsk/ n. **1.** a substance secreted by certain animals, having a strong smell, and used in perfumery. **2.** a synthetic imitation of this substance.

musket /'mʌskət/ n. the predecessor of the modern rifle. –**musketeer**, n.

muslin /'mʌzlən/ n. a fine cotton fabric.

mussel /'mʌsəl/ n. an edible bivalve mollusc.

must /mʌst, mʌs/, weak forms /məst, məs/ v. (aux.) **1.** to be obliged or compelled to. **2.** may reasonably be supposed to. –n. **3.** Colloq. anything necessary or vital.

mustard /'mʌstəd/ n. **1.** a pungent powder or paste much used as a food seasoning or condiment. –adj. **2.** brownish-yellow in colour.

mustard gas n. a chemical-warfare agent.

muster /'mʌstə/ v.t. **1.** (oft. fol. by up) to gather, summon, or round up. –v.i. **2.** to come together, collect, or gather. –n. **3.** the act of mustering. –phr. **4. pass muster**, to measure up to specified standards.

musty /'mʌsti/ adj. (-tier, -tiest) having a smell or flavour suggestive of mould.

mutant /'mjutnt/ n. a new type of organism produced as the result of mutation.

mutate /mju'teɪt/ v.i. to change; undergo mutation.

mutation /mju'teɪʃən/ n. **1.** the act or process of changing. **2.** a change or alteration, as in form, qualities, or nature.

mute /mjut/ adj. **1.** silent; refraining from speech or utterance. **2.** incapable of speech. –n. **3.** one unable to utter words. **4.** Also,

mute button. a button on a television or sound amplifier remote control unit which can be used to switch the sound off and on again. **5.** a mechanical device for muffling the tone of a musical instrument. –v.t. (**muted, muting**) **6.** to deaden or muffle the sound of (a musical instrument, etc.).

mutilate /'mjutəleɪt/ v.t. **1.** to deprive (a person or animal, the body, etc.) of a limb or other important part or parts. **2.** to injure, damage or disfigure severely. –**mutilation**, n.

mutiny /'mjutəni/ n. (pl. **-nies**) **1.** revolt or rebellion against constituted authority, especially by soldiers or sailors against their officers. –v.i. (**-nied, -nying**) **2.** to commit mutiny. –**mutinous**, adj.

mutt /mʌt/ n. Colloq. **1.** a dog, especially a mongrel. **2.** a simpleton; a stupid person.

mutter /'mʌtə/ v.i. **1.** to utter words indistinctly or in a low tone; murmur; grumble. **2.** to make a low, rumbling sound. –v.t. **3.** to utter indistinctly or in a low tone.

mutton /'mʌtn/ n. the flesh of sheep, used as food.

mutton-bird /'mʌtn-bɜd/ n. any of various species of petrel.

mutton-chops /'mʌtn-tʃɒps, mʌtn-'tʃɒps/ pl. n. side-whiskers narrow at the top, and broad and trimmed short at the bottom.

mutual /'mjutʃuəl/ adj. **1.** possessed, experienced, performed, etc., by each of two or more with respect to the other or others; reciprocal. **2.** relating to mutual insurance.

mutual insurance n. insurance in which those insured become members of a company who reciprocally engage, by payment of certain amounts into a common fund, to indemnify one another against loss.

muzak /'mjuzæk/ n. (from trademark) recorded background music.

muzzle /'mʌzəl/ n. **1.** the mouth, or end for discharge, of the barrel of a gun, pistol, etc. **2.** the projecting part of the head of an animal, including jaws, mouth, and nose. **3.** a device placed over an animal's mouth to prevent the animal from biting, eating, etc. –v.t. **4.** to put a muzzle on. **5.** to restrain (by physical, legal, or procedural means) from speech or the expression of opinion; gag.

my /maɪ/, weak forms /mi, mə/ pron. **1.** the possessive form corresponding to I and me, used before a noun. –interj. **2.** an exclamation of surprise.

my- a word element meaning 'muscle'. Also, **myo-**.

myc- a word element meaning 'fungus'. Also, **myco-**.

-mycetes a word element meaning 'fungus'.

myelin /'maɪələn/ n. a soft, white, fatty substance surrounding certain nerve fibres.

myna /'maɪnə/ n. **1.** a noisy scavenging bird with yellow legs and beak, native to Asia and introduced into Australia in the 1860s. **2.** any of various Asian birds known for their ability to talk. Also, **mynah, mina**.

myocardial infarct /,maɪoʊkadiəl 'ɪnfakt/ n. → **heart attack**. Also, **myocardial infarction**.

myocardiograph /maɪoʊ'kadɪəgræf, -graf/ n. an apparatus which records the movements of the heart muscle.

myopia /maɪˈoʊpiə/ n. near-sightedness. –**myopic**, adj.

myriad /ˈmɪriəd/ n. **1.** an indefinitely great number: *a myriad of stars.* –adj. **2.** of an indefinitely great number; innumerable: *the myriad stars.*

myrrh /mɜ/ n. an aromatic resinous exudation from certain plants used for incense, perfume, etc.

myrtle /ˈmɜtl/ n. a type of shrub with fragrant white flowers.

myself /maɪˈsɛlf, məˈsɛlf/ pron. **1.** a reflexive form of **I**. **2.** an emphatic form of **me** or **I**, used: **a.** as object. **b.** in apposition to a subject or object. –n. **3.** one's proper or normal self.

mystery /ˈmɪstri, -təri/ n. (pl. **-ries**) **1.** anything that is kept secret or remains unexplained or unknown. **2.** obscure or puzzling character. **3.** any truth unknowable except by divine revelation. –**mysterious**, adj.

mystic /ˈmɪstɪk/ adj. **1.** → **mystical**. –n. **2.** someone who practises or believes in mysticism.

mystical /ˈmɪstɪkəl/ adj. **1.** of or relating to mystics or mysticism. **2.** of occult character, power, or significance. **3.** spiritually significant or symbolic. Also, **mystic**. –**mystically**, adv. –**mysticalness**, n.

mysticism /ˈmɪstəsɪzəm/ n. **1.** belief in the possibility of attaining an immediate spiritual intuition of truths thought to transcend ordinary understanding, or of a direct, intimate union of the soul with a deity or universal soul through contemplation and love. **2.** contemplative practices aimed at achieving such intuition or union.

mystify /ˈmɪstəfaɪ/ v.t. (**-fied, -fying**) **1.** to involve (a subject, etc.) in mystery or obscurity. **2.** to confuse (someone). –**mystification**, n.

mystique /mɪsˈtik/ n. an air of mystery or mystical power surrounding a particular person, object, pursuit, belief, etc.

myth /mɪθ/ n. **1.** a traditional story which attempts to explain natural phenomena. **2.** any invented story. –**mythical**, adj.

mytho- a word element meaning 'myth.'

mythology /məˈθɒlədʒi/ n. myths collectively.

myx- a word element meaning 'slimy'.

N, n

N, n /ɛn/ *n.* the 14th letter of the English alphabet.

naan /nan/ *n.* a slightly leavened Indian bread, usually round. Also, **nan**.

nab /næb/ *v.t.* (**nabbed**, **nabbing**) *Colloq.* to catch or seize, especially suddenly.

nachos /'natʃoʊz/ *pl. n.* a snack consisting of corn chips topped with tomato sauce and melted cheese.

nacre /'neɪkə/ *n.* → mother-of-pearl.

nadir /'neɪdɪə/ *n.* the lowest point.

nag¹ /næg/ *v.* (**nagged**, **nagging**) –*v.t.* **1.** to torment by persistent fault-finding, complaints, or importunities. –*v.i.* **2.** (oft. fol. by *at*) to keep up an irritating or wearisome fault-finding, complaining, or the like. **3.** to cause continual pain, discomfort, or depression, as a headache, feeling of guilt, etc.

nag² /næg/ *n. Colloq.* a horse.

nail /neɪl/ *n.* **1.** a slender piece of metal, usually with one end pointed and the other enlarged, for driving into or through wood, etc., as to hold separate pieces together. **2.** a thin, horny plate, consisting of modified epidermis, growing on the upper side of the end of a finger or toe. –*v.t.* **3.** to fasten with a nail or nails. **4.** *Colloq.* to secure by prompt action; catch or seize.

naive /naɪ'iv, na-/ *adj.* unsophisticated; ingenuous. Also, **naïve**. –**naivety**, *n.*

naked /'neɪkəd/ *adj.* **1.** without clothing or covering; nude. **2.** (of the eye, sight, etc.) unassisted by a microscope, telescope, or other instrument.

naltrexone /næl'trɛksoʊn/ *n.* a drug which acts as a blocking agent to the body's opiate receptors, used to treat drug addiction, especially to heroin.

name /neɪm/ *n.* **1.** a word or a combination of words by which a person, place, or thing, a body or class, or any object of thought, is designated or known. **2.** an appellation, title, or epithet, applied descriptively, in honour, abuse, etc. **3.** a reputation of a particular kind given by common report. –*v.t.* **4.** to give a name to. **5.** to call by a specified name.

namely /'neɪmli/ *adv.* that is to say.

namesake /'neɪmseɪk/ *n.* **1.** someone having the same name as another. **2.** someone named after another.

naming ceremony *n.* (*pl.* -**nies**) **1.** a ceremony at which someone or something is officially named. **2.** an occasion, usually conducted by a civil celebrant, at which a child is named, guardians (or godparents) appointed, etc.

nan /nan/ *n.* → **naan**.

nanna /'nænə/ *n. Colloq.* a grandmother. Also, **nana**, **nan**.

nanny /'næni/ *n.* (*pl.* -**nies**) **1.** a nurse for children. **2.** a grandmother.

nanny goat *n.* a female goat.

nano- **1.** a prefix denoting 10^{-9} of a given unit. *Symbol:* n **2.** a prefix indicating very small size, as in *nanoplankton*.

nanometre /'nænoʊmitə/ *n.* one billionth (10^{-9}) of a metre.

nanoparticle /'nænoʊpatɪkəl/ *n.* a microscopic particle whose size is measured in nanometres.

nanoscience /'nænoʊˌsaɪəns/ *n.* the science concerned with objects of the smallest dimensions.

nanotechnology /'nænoʊˌtɛknɒlədʒi/ *n.* technology generated from nanoscience.

nap¹ /næp/ *v.i.* (**napped**, **napping**) **1.** to have a short sleep; doze. –*n.* **2.** a short sleep; a doze.

nap² /næp/ *n.* the short fuzzy ends of fibres on the surface of cloth.

napalm /'neɪpam, 'næpam/ *n.* an aluminium soap, in the form of a granular powder; mixed with petrol it forms a sticky gel used in flame throwers and fire bombs.

nape /neɪp/ *n.* the back of the neck.

napery /'neɪpəri/ *n.* table linen.

naphthalene /'næfθəlin/ *n.* a white crystalline hydrocarbon used in dyes and as a moth-repellent, etc.

napkin /'næpkən/ *n.* **1.** → **serviette**. **2.** a square or oblong piece of linen, cotton cloth or paper, as for a towel, or a baby's nappy.

nappy /'næpi/ *n.* (*pl.* -**pies**) a piece of cotton towelling, or some disposable material, fastened round a baby to absorb and contain its excrement.

narcissism /'nasəsɪzəm/ *n.* extreme admiration for oneself or one's own attributes; egoism; self-love. –**narcissist**, *n.* –**narcissistic**, *adj.*

narcosis /na'koʊsəs/ *n.* **1.** a state of sleep or drowsiness. **2.** a temporary state of stupor or unconsciousness, especially produced by a drug.

narcotic /na'kɒtɪk/ *n.* any of a class of substances that blunt the senses, relieve pain, induce sleep, etc.

nark /nak/ *n. Colloq.* **1.** an informer. **2.** a scolding, complaining person.

narrate /nə'reɪt/ *v.t.* to give an account of or tell the story of (events, experiences, etc.). –**narrator**, *n.* –**narration**, *n.*

narrative /'nærətɪv/ *n.* a story of events, experiences, or the like, whether true or fictitious.

narrow /'næroʊ/ *adj.* **1.** of little breadth or width; not broad or wide. **2.** limited in extent or space, or affording little room. **3.** lacking breadth of view or sympathy, as persons, the mind, ideas, etc. –*v.i.* **4.** to become narrower. –*v.t.* **5.** to make narrower. –*n.* **6.** a narrow part, place or thing. **7.** (*pl.*) a narrow part of a strait, river, ocean current, etc.

narrowcast /'næroʊkast/ *v.t.* (-**cast** or -**casted**, -**casting**) **1.** to transmit (data) to a limited number of recipients as in cable television where only subscribers' receivers can take the signal. –*n.* **2.** an instance of narrowcasting. –**narrowcasting**, *n.* –**narrowcaster**, *n.*

nasal /'neɪzəl/ *adj.* of or relating to the nose.

nascent /'neɪsənt, 'næsənt/ *adj.* beginning to exist or develop.

nasturtium /nə'stɜʃəm/ *n.* a garden plant with showy flowers.

nasty /'nasti/ *adj.* (**-tier, -tiest**) vicious, spiteful, or ugly.

natal /'neɪtl/ *adj.* of or relating to birth.

natant /'neɪtənt/ *adj.* swimming; floating.

nation /'neɪʃən/ *n.* a body of people associated with a particular territory who are sufficiently conscious of their unity to seek or to possess a government peculiarly their own. **–national**, *adj.*

nationalise /'næʃnəlaɪz/ *v.t.* to bring under the control or ownership of a government as industries, land, etc. Also, **nationalize**.

nationalism /'næʃnəlɪzəm/ *n.* devotion to the interests of one's own nation. **–nationalistic**, *adj.*

nationality /næʃə'næləti, næʃ'næl-/ *n.* (*pl.* **-ties**) the quality of membership in a particular nation (original or acquired).

national service *n.* (in many countries) compulsory service in the armed forces for a particular period.

native /'neɪtɪv/ *adj.* **1.** being the place or environment in which one was born or a thing came into being: *one's native land; a native habitat.* **2.** (oft. fol. by *to*) belonging to a person or thing by birth or nature; inborn; inherent; natural. **3.** (oft. fol. by *to*) of indigenous origin, growth, or production. **4.** belonging or relating to one by reason of one's birthplace or nationality. **5.** born in a particular place or country. **6.** originating naturally in a particular country or region, as animals or plants. *–n.* **7.** one of those descended from the original inhabitants of a place or country, especially as distinguished from strangers, foreigners, colonisers, etc. **8.** someone born in a particular place or country. **9.** an animal or plant indigenous to a particular region.

native title *n.* (in Australia) the right to land or water enjoyed by Indigenous people who have maintained their connection to the land or water and whose possession under their traditional law or customs is recognised by Australian law.

nativity /nə'tɪvəti/ *n.* (*pl.* **-ties**) birth.

natural /'nætʃərəl, 'nætʃrəl/ *adj.* **1.** existing in or formed by nature; not artificial. **2.** of or relating to nature or the created universe. **3.** free from affectation or constraint. **4.** in accordance with the nature of things. **5.** being such by nature; born such. **6.** *Music* neither sharp nor flat; without sharps or flats. *–n.* **7.** *Colloq.* a thing or a person that is by nature satisfactory or successful. **8.** *Music* **a.** a white key on the pianoforte, etc. **b.** the sign ♮, placed before a note cancelling the effect of a previous sharp or flat. **–naturally**, *adv.*

naturalise /'nætʃrəlaɪz/ *v.t.* **1.** to invest (an alien) with the rights and privileges of a subject or citizen; confer the rights and privileges of citizenship upon. **2.** to introduce (animals or plants) into a region and cause to flourish as if native. Also, **naturalize**.

naturalist /'nætʃrələst/ *n.* someone who is versed in or devoted to natural history, especially a zoologist or botanist.

natural language processing *n.* the analysis, interpretation and generation of human languages by computer. *Abbrev.:* NLP

natural resource *n.* a resource (def. 1) which occurs naturally, such as sunlight, wind, soil, water, etc.

nature /'neɪtʃə/ *n.* **1.** the particular combination of qualities belonging to a person or thing by birth or constitution; native or inherent character. **2.** character, kind, or sort. **3.** the material world, especially as surrounding humankind and existing independently of their activities. **4.** the sum total of the forces at work throughout the universe. **5.** reality, as distinguished from any effect of art. **6.** a primitive, wild condition; an uncultivated state.

naturopathy /nætʃə'rɒpəθi/ *n.* a system of treating disease in ways considered natural, especially by use of herbs, natural foods, etc. **–naturopath** /'nætʃərə,pæθ/, *n.* **–naturopathic** /,nætʃərə'pæθɪk/, *adj.*

naught /nɔt/ *n.* destruction, ruin, or complete failure.

naughty /'nɔti/ *adj.* (**-tier, -tiest**) **1.** disobedient; mischievous (especially in speaking to or about children). **2.** improper; obscene.

nausea /'nɔsiə, -ziə/ *n.* sickness at the stomach; a sensation of impending vomiting. **–nauseous**, *adj.* **–nauseate**, *v.*

nautical /'nɔtɪkəl/ *adj.* of or relating to sailors, ships, or navigation.

nave /neɪv/ *n.* the main body, or middle part, lengthwise, of a church.

navel /'neɪvəl/ *n.* a pit or depression in the middle of the surface of the belly.

navigate /'nævəgeɪt/ *v.t.* **1.** to traverse (the sea, a river, etc.) in a vessel, or (the air) in an aircraft. **2.** *Internet* to find one's way around (a website). *–v.i.* **3.** to travel by using a ship or boat, as over the water; sail. **–navigator**, *n.* **–navigation**, *n.* **–navigable**, *adj.*

navigation bar *n. Computers* the bar running along the top, side or bottom of a web page which encloses buttons which take the user to various places on the site.

navy /'neɪvi/ *n.* (*pl.* **-vies**) **1.** the whole body of warships and auxiliaries belonging to a country or ruler. **2.** Also, **navy blue**. a dark blue, as of a naval uniform. **–naval**, *adj.*

nay /neɪ/ *adv.* **1.** no (used in dissent, denial, or refusal). **2.** also; and not only so but: *many good, nay, noble qualities.*

neap /nip/ *adj.* designating those tides, midway between spring tides, which attain the least height.

near /nɪə/ *adv.* **1.** close. **2.** nigh; at, within, or to a short distance. **3.** close at hand in time. **4.** close in relation; closely with respect to connection, similarity, etc. *–adj.* **5.** being close by; not distant. **6.** closely related or connected. *–prep.* **7.** at, within, or to a short distance, or no great distance, from. **8.** close upon (a condition, etc.). **9.** close to (doing something). *–v.t.* **10.** to come or draw near (to); approach.

nearby /nɪə'baɪ/ *adj., adv.* close at hand; not far off.

nearly /'nɪəli/ *adv.* **1.** all but; almost. **2.** with close approximation.

neat /nit/ *adj.* **1.** in a pleasingly orderly condition. **2.** habitually orderly in appearance, etc. **3.** clever, dexterous, or apt. **4.** unadulterated or undiluted, as liquors.

neb /nɛb/ n. **1.** a bill or beak, as of a bird. **2.** the nose, especially of an animal.

nebula /'nɛbjələ/ n. (pl. **-lae** /-li/ or **-las**) Astron. a diffuse, cloudlike patch of gases, particles, etc.

nebulise /'nɛbjəlaɪz/ v.t. **1.** to reduce to fine spray; atomise. **2.** to administer medication to (someone) by means of a nebuliser. Also, **nebulize**.

nebuliser /'nɛbjəlaɪzə/ n. Med. a device which reduces a liquid medication to a fine mist which is then inhaled into the lungs. Also, **nebulizer**.

nebulous /'nɛbjələs/ adj. hazy, vague, indistinct, or confused.

necessary /'nɛsəseri, 'nɛsəsri/ adj. **1.** that cannot be dispensed with. **2.** happening or existing by necessity. –**necessarily**, adv.

necessitate /nə'sɛsəteɪt/ v.t. to make necessary.

necessity /nə'sɛsəti/ n. (pl. **-ties**) **1.** something necessary or indispensable. **2.** an imperative requirement or need for something. **3.** a state of being in difficulty or need; poverty.

neck /nɛk/ n. **1.** that part of an animal's body which is between the head and the trunk and connects these parts. **2.** the slender part of a bottle or any similar object. **3.** any narrow, connecting, or projecting part suggesting the neck of an animal. –v.i. **4.** Colloq. to play amorously.

neckerchief /'nɛkətʃif/ n. a cloth worn round the neck by women or men.

necklace /'nɛkləs/ n. an ornament of precious stones, beads, or the like, worn especially by women round the neck.

necromancy /'nɛkrəˌmænsi/ n. magic.

nectar /'nɛktə/ n. **1.** Bot. the saccharine secretion of a plant. **2.** any delicious drink.

nectarine /'nɛktərən, nɛktə'rin/ n. a form of the common peach, having a skin without down.

nee /neɪ/ adj. born (placed after the name of a married woman to introduce her maiden name). Also, **née** /neɪ/.

need /nid/ n. **1.** a case or instance in which some necessity or want exists; a requirement. **2.** urgent want, as of something requisite. **3.** a condition marked by the lack of something requisite. **4.** destitution; extreme poverty. –v.t. **5.** to have need of; require. –v.i. **6.** to be necessary. **7.** (usu. in negatives and questions) to be under a necessity (followed by infinitive, in certain cases without to; in the 3rd person singular the form is *need*, not *needs*).

needle /'nidl/ n. **1.** a small, slender, pointed instrument, now usually of polished steel, with an eye or hole for thread, used in sewing. **2.** a slender, rodlike implement for use in knitting, or one hooked at the end for use in crocheting, etc. **3.** any of various objects resembling or suggesting a needle. **4.** Bot. a needle-shaped leaf, as of a conifer. –v.t. **5.** to sew or pierce with or as with a needle. **6.** to tease or heckle.

needlework /'nidlwɜk/ n. the process or the product of working with a needle as in sewing or embroidery.

needy /'nidi/ adj. (**-dier, -diest**) in, or characterised by, need or want; very poor.

ne'er-do-well /'nɛə-du-wɛl/ n. a worthless person.

nefarious /nə'fɛəriəs/ adj. wicked.

negate /nə'geɪt/ v.t. to deny; nullify.

negative /'nɛgətɪv/ adj. **1.** expressing or containing refusal or denial. **2.** characterised by the absence of distinguishing or marked qualities or features; lacking positive attributes. **3.** not positive. **4.** Photography denoting an image in which the gradations of light and shade are represented in reverse. **5.** Elect. denoting or relating to the kind of electricity developed on resin, amber, etc., when rubbed with flannel, or that present at the pole from which electrons leave an electric generator or battery, having an excess of electrons. **6.** Chem. tending to gain electrons and become negatively charged. –n. **7.** something negative. –**negativity**, n.

negative gearing n. a financial situation where an investor borrows against an investment, and the loan interest payments exceed the income from the investment, resulting in a negative cash flow and thus taxation benefits.

neglect /nə'glɛkt/ v.t. **1.** to pay no attention to; disregard. **2.** to be remiss in care for or treatment of. –n. **3.** the act or fact of neglecting; disregard. **4.** the fact or state of being neglected; negligence.

negligee /'nɛgləʒeɪ/ n. a woman's dressing-gown, especially a very flimsy one, of nylon, or the like.

negligent /'nɛglədʒənt/ adj. guilty of or characterised by neglect. –**negligence**, n.

negligible /'nɛglədʒəbəl/ adj. so small that it may be neglected or disregarded; very little.

negotiate /nə'goʊʃieɪt/ v.t. **1.** to arrange for or bring about by discussion and settlement of terms. **2.** to clear or pass (an obstacle, etc.). **3.** to transfer (a bill of exchange, etc.) by assignment, endorsement, or delivery. **4.** to dispose of by sale or transfer. –**negotiable**, adj. –**negotiation**, n.

neigh /neɪ/ n. the sound a horse makes; a whinny.

neighbour /'neɪbə/ n. **1.** someone who lives near another. –v.i. **2.** to live or be situated nearby. Also, **neighbor**.

neighbourhood /'neɪbəhʊd/ n. **1.** the region near or about some place or thing. **2.** a district or locality, often with reference to its character or inhabitants. Also, **neighborhood**.

neither /'naɪðə, 'niðə/ adj., pron., conj. not either.

nematode /'nɛmətoʊd/ n. an elongated, smooth worm.

nemesis /'nɛməsəs/ n. (pl. **-meses** /-məsiz/) an agent of retribution or punishment.

neo- a word element meaning 'new', 'recent'.

neologism /ni'ɒlədʒɪzəm/ n. **1.** a new word or phrase. **2.** a new doctrine.

neon /'niɒn/ n. a chemically inert gaseous element occurring in small amounts in the earth's atmosphere, and chiefly used in orange-red tubular electrical discharge lamps. *Symbol*: Ne

neonate /'niouneɪt/ n. a newborn child.

neophyte /'nioufaɪt/ n. **1.** a converted heathen, heretic, etc. **2.** a beginner.

nephew /'nɛfju, 'nɛvju/ n. **1.** a son of one's brother or sister. **2.** a son of one's husband's or wife's brother or sister.

nephritis /nə'fraɪtəs/ n. inflammation of the kidneys.

nephro- a word element referring to the kidneys. Also, **nephr-**.

nepotism /'nɛpətɪzəm/ n. patronage bestowed in consideration of family relationship and not of merit.

nerd /nɜd/ n. Colloq. a person who has an awkward personality and dresses in a conservative way.

nerve /nɜv/ n. **1.** one or more bundles of fibres, forming part of a system which conveys impulses of sensation, motion, etc., between the brain or spinal cord and other parts of the body. **2.** firmness or courage in trying circumstances. **3.** (pl.) nervousness. **4.** Colloq. impertinent assurance.

nervous /'nɜvəs/ adj. **1.** of or relating to the nerves. **2.** characterised by or attended with acute uneasiness or apprehension.

nervous system n. the system of nerves and nerve centres in an animal, comprising two major parts, the central nervous system and the peripheral nervous system. See **central nervous system, peripheral nervous system, somatic nervous system, autonomic nervous system, sympathetic nervous system, parasympathetic nervous system**.

nervy /'nɜvi/ adj. (**-vier, -viest**) **1.** nervous. **2.** excitable; irritable.

-ness a suffix used to form, from adjectives and participles, nouns denoting quality or state (also often, by extension, something exemplifying a quality or state), as in darkness, goodness, kindness.

nest /nɛst/ n. **1.** a structure formed or a place used by a bird for incubation and the rearing of its young. **2.** an assemblage of things lying or set close together, as a series of tables, trays, etc., that fit within each other. –v.i. **3.** to build or have a nest.

nest egg n. money saved as the basis of a fund or for emergencies.

nestle /'nɛsəl/ v.t. to lie close and snug, like a bird in a nest; snuggle or cuddle.

net¹ /nɛt/ n. **1.** a lacelike fabric with a uniform mesh of cotton, silk, etc. **2.** a piece or bag of net for catching fish, butterflies, etc.

net² /nɛt/ adj. **1.** exclusive of deductions, as for charges, expenses, loss, discount, etc. **2.** sold at net prices. **3.** ultimate; conclusive. –n. **4.** net income, profits, or the like. –v.t. (**netted, netting**) **5.** to gain or produce as clear profit. Also, **nett**.

Net /nɛt/ phr. **the → internet**. Also, **the net**.

netball /'nɛtbɔl/ n. a game played by two teams of seven players, in which the players try to gain points by throwing the ball through a hoop attached to a pole at the opposing team's end of a rectangular court. **–netballer, n.**

Net Generation n. the generation born in the 1990s for whom computer use was a central part of life. Also, **net generation**.

nether /'nɛðə/ adj. **1.** lying, or conceived as lying, beneath the earth's surface; infernal. **2.** lower or under.

netizen /'nɛtɪzən/ n. Internet Colloq. a habitual user of the internet.

nettle /'nɛtl/ n. a plant with stinging hairs.

network /'nɛtwɜk/ n. **1.** a system of interconnected people, companies, television stations, etc. **2.** Computers a system of connecting computer systems or peripheral devices, each one remote from the others.

neural /'njurəl/ adj. of or relating to a nerve or the nervous system.

neuro- a word element meaning 'tendon', 'nerve'. Also, **neur-**.

neurodiverse /njuroʊdə'vɜs, -daɪ-/ adj. of or relating to a person with a condition, such as autism, which is considered to be not neurotypical. Also, **neurodivergent**. **–neurodiversity, n.**

neurology /nju'rɒlədʒi/ n. the branch of anatomy or physiology that deals with the nerves or the nervous system. **–neurological, adj. –neurologist, n.**

neuron /'njurɒn/ n. any of the cells which make up the nervous tissue; nerve cell. Also, **neurone**.

neuroplasticity /,njuroʊplæs'tɪsəti/ n. the ability of the brain to change, both in physical structure and in functional organisation, in response to experience, such that functions believed previously to be supported only by particular areas of the brain become supported instead by other areas. **–neuroplastic /njuroʊ'plæstɪk/, adj.**

neuroscience /'njuroʊ,saɪəns/ n. the study of the nervous system. **–neuroscientist, n.**

neurosis /nju'roʊsəs/ n. (pl. **-roses** /-'roʊsiz/) a relatively mild mental illness in which feelings of anxiety, obsessional thoughts, compulsive acts, and physical complaints without objective evidence of disease, in various patterns, dominate the personality. **–neurotic, adj., n.**

neurotoxin /'njuroʊtɒksən/ n. a chemical, often highly toxic, which inhibits the function of the nervous system. **–neurotoxic, adj. –neurotoxicity, n.**

neurotransmitter /njuroʊtrænz'mɪtə/ n. a chemical stored in a nerve cell that transmits information across a synapse.

neurotypical /njuroʊ'tɪpəkəl/ adj. conforming to typical norms of neurological functioning.

neuter /'njutə/ adj. **1.** Gram. of a gender which is neither masculine or feminine. **2.** sexless, or of indeterminate sex.

neutral /'njutrəl/ adj. **1.** (of a person or state) refraining from taking part in a controversy or war between others. **2.** of no particular kind, colour, characteristics, etc.; indefinite. **3.** Chem. exhibiting neither acid nor alkaline qualities. **4.** Elect. neither positive nor negative; not electrified; not magnetised. –n. **5.** Machinery the position or state of disengaged gears or other interconnecting parts. **–neutralise, neutralize, v. –neutrality, n.**

neutron /'njutrɒn/ n. an elementary particle which is a constituent of all atomic nuclei except normal hydrogen. It has zero electric charge and approximately the same mass as the proton.

never /'nɛvə/ adv. not ever; at no time.

nevertheless /nɛvəðə'lɛs/ adv. nonetheless; notwithstanding; however.

new /nju/ adj. **1.** of recent origin or production, or having only lately come or been brought into being. **2.** of a kind now existing or appearing for the first time; novel. **3.** (fol. by to) unfamiliar or strange. **4.** coming or occurring afresh; further; additional. **5.** fresh or unused. **6.** other than the former or the old. *–adv.* **7.** recently or lately. **8.** freshly; anew or afresh.

New Age *n.* a social revolution which replaces traditional attitudes with a new approach based on a loose mysticism, especially in health and medicine and attitudes to the environment.

newbie /'njubi/ *n. Colloq.* **1.** a newcomer to the internet. **2.** a newcomer to any activity.

news /njuz/ *pl. n.* **1.** (*construed as sing.*) a report of any recent event, situation, etc. **2.** the report of events published in a newspaper, journal, radio, television, or any other medium. **3.** information not previously known.

newsagency /'njuzeɪdʒənsi/ *n.* (*pl.* **-cies**) a shop which sells newspapers, magazines, stationery, etc. **–newsagent,** *n.*

newsflash /'njuzflæʃ/ *n.* an announcement of very recent news on radio or television, usually interrupting a scheduled program.

newsgroup /'njuzgrup/ *n. Internet* an online discussion forum for a particular topic, in which users can write and post messages, and read messages posted by others.

newspaper /'njuzpeɪpə/ *n.* a publication issued at regular intervals, usually daily or weekly, and commonly containing news, comment, features, and advertisements; produced in print and digital form.

newsprint /'njuzprɪnt/ *n.* paper used or made to print newspapers on.

newsreel /'njuzril/ *n.* a short film presenting current news events.

newt /njut/ *n.* any of various small, semi-aquatic salamanders.

newton /'njutn/ *n.* the derived SI unit of force. *Symbol:* N

new wave *n.* **1.** a movement or trend to break with traditional concepts in art, literature, politics, etc. **2.** a form of rock music of the 1970s in the style of punk rock, but characterised by greater imaginativeness and performance skills.

next /nɛkst/ *adj.* **1.** immediately following. **2.** nearest. *–adv.* **3.** in the nearest place, time, importance, etc. **4.** on the first subsequent occasion.

next of kin *n.* a person's nearest relative or relatives.

nexus /'nɛksəs/ *n.* (*pl.* **nexus**) a tie or link; a means of connection.

nib /nɪb/ *n.* the point of a pen, especially a small, tapering metallic device having a split tip for drawing up ink and for writing.

nibble /'nɪbəl/ *v.i.* **1.** to bite off small bits. **2.** to evince interest (*at*) without actually accepting. *–v.t.* **3.** to bite off small bits of (a thing). *–n.* **4.** a small morsel or bit. **5. a.** the slight pull on a fishing line which indicates that a fish is attempting to take the bait. **b.** *Colloq.* a slight expression of interest in a proposal.

nice /naɪs/ *adj.* (**nicer, nicest**) **1.** pleasing; agreeable; delightful. **2.** characterised by or requiring great accuracy, precision, skill, or delicacy. **3.** minute, fine, or subtle, as a distinction. **–nicety,** *n.*

niche /niʃ, nɪtʃ/ *n.* **1.** an ornamental recess in a wall, etc. **2.** a place or position suitable or appropriate for a person or thing.

niche market *n.* a section of a market (def. 4), usually small, which can be highly profitable if the product supplied is specially designed to meet targeted needs.

nick[1] /nɪk/ *n.* **1.** a notch, groove, or the like, cut into or existing in a thing. *–v.t.* **2.** to make a nick or nicks in; notch.

nick[2] /nɪk/ *v.t. Colloq.* **1.** to steal. **2.** to capture or arrest.

nickel /'nɪkəl/ *n. Chem.* a hard, silvery-white, ductile and malleable metallic element. *Symbol:* Ni

nickname /'nɪkneɪm/ *n.* a name added to or substituted for the proper name of a person, place, etc., as in ridicule or familiarity.

nicotine /'nɪkə'tin, 'nɪkətɪn/ *n.* a poisonous substance, present in tobacco.

niece /nis/ *n.* **1.** a daughter of one's brother or sister. **2.** a daughter of one's husband's or wife's brother or sister.

nifty /'nɪfti/ *adj.* (**-tier, -tiest**) *Colloq.* smart; stylish; fine.

niggard /'nɪgəd/ *n. Rare* a parsimonious or stingy person. **–niggardly,** *adj.*

niggle /'nɪgəl/ *v.i.* **1.** to make constant petty criticisms. *–v.t.* **2.** to irritate; annoy.

nigh /naɪ/ *adv.* **1.** near in space, time, or relation. *–adj.* (**nigher, nighest** *or* **next**) **2.** being near; not distant; near in relationship. **3.** short or direct.

night /naɪt/ *n.* the interval of darkness between sunset and sunrise.

nightcap /'naɪtkæp/ *n.* an alcoholic or other drink, especially a hot one, taken before going to bed.

nightclub /'naɪtklʌb/ *n.* **1.** a place of entertainment, open during the evening, offering food, drink, cabaret, dancing, etc. **2.** a dance venue which opens from evening till early morning.

nightingale /'naɪtɪŋgeɪl/ *n.* a small migratory bird of the thrush family, noted for the melodious song of the male.

nightly /'naɪtli/ *adj.* **1.** coming, occurring, appearing, or active at night. **2.** coming or occurring each night. *–adv.* **3.** at or by night. **4.** on every night.

nightmare /'naɪtmɛə/ *n.* **1.** a condition during sleep, or a dream, marked by a feeling of suffocation or distress, with acute fear, anxiety, or other painful emotion. **2.** a condition, thought, or experience suggestive of a nightmare in sleep.

nihilism /'naɪəlɪzəm, 'ni-/ *n.* total disbelief in religion or moral principles and obligations, or in established laws and institutions.

nil /nɪl/ *n.* nothing.

nimble /'nɪmbəl/ *adj.* quick and light in movement; moving with ease; agile; active; rapid.

nimbus /'nɪmbəs/ *n.* (*pl.* **-bi** /-baɪ/ *or* **-buses**) a disc or otherwise shaped figure representing a radiance about the head of a divine or sacred personage, etc.; a halo.

nincompoop /'nɪŋkəmpup/ *n.* a fool.

nine /naɪn/ *n.* **1.** a cardinal number, eight plus one. *–adj.* **2.** amounting to nine in number. **–ninth,** *adj.*, *n.*

nineteen /nam'tin, 'namtin/ *n.* **1.** a cardinal number, ten plus nine. *–adj.* **2.** amounting to nineteen in number. *–***nineteenth**, *adj.*, *n.*

ninety /'namti/ *n.* **1.** a cardinal number, ten times nine. *–adj.* **2.** amounting to ninety in number. *–***ninetieth**, *adj.*, *n.*

ninny /'nini/ *n.* (*pl.* *-***nies**) a fool.

nip¹ /nip/ *v.* (**nipped, nipping**) *–v.t.* **1.** to compress sharply between two surfaces or points; pinch or bite. **2.** to check in growth or development. **3.** to affect sharply and painfully or injuriously, as cold does. *–v.i.* **4.** *Colloq.* (fol. by *away*, *off*, *up*, etc.) to move or go suddenly or quickly, or slip.

nip² /nip/ *n.* **1.** a small drink; a sip. **2.** a small measure of spirits.

nipple /'nipəl/ *n.* **1.** a protuberance of the udder or breast where, in the female, the milk ducts discharge; a teat. **2.** something resembling it.

nippy /'nipi/ *adj.* (**-pier, -piest**) biting, as the cold.

niqab /'nikæb/ *n.* a veil worn by some Muslim women, covering the face but leaving the area around the eyes uncovered.

nirvana /ns'vanə, nə-, nıə-/ *n.* **1.** *Buddhism* the ultimate state achieved usually after a series of reincarnations, when all passions and self-delusions have been shed. **2.** *Hinduism* salvation achieved by absorption into Brahman. **3.** any place or state thought of as characterised by complete freedom from pain, worry and the external world.

nit /nit/ *n.* the egg of a parasitic insect attached to a hair, or fibre of clothing; particularly the egg of a louse.

nitrogen /'naitrədʒən/ *n.* a colourless, odourless, gaseous element which forms about four-fifths of the volume of the atmosphere. *Symbol:* N *–***nitrogenous**, *adj.*

nitroglycerine /naitrou'glisərin/ *n.* a colourless, highly explosive oil.

nitty-gritty /'niti-,griti/ *n.* *Colloq.* the hard core of a matter.

nitwit /'nitwit/ *n.* *Colloq.* a slow-witted or foolish person.

nix /niks/ *n.* *Colloq.* nothing.

no¹ /nou/ *interj.* **1.** a word used to express dissent, denial, or refusal, as in response (opposed to *yes*). *–adv.* **2.** not in any degree; not at all (used with a comparative). *–n.* (*pl.* **noes**) **3.** a denial or refusal. **4.** a negative vote or voter (opposed to *aye*).

no² /nou/ *adj.* **1.** not any. **2.** not at all; very far from being.

nobble /'nɒbəl/ *v.t.* *Colloq.* to disable (a horse), as by drugging it.

noble /'noubəl/ *adj.* **1.** distinguished by birth, rank, or title. **2.** belonging to or making up a class (the nobility) possessing a social or political importance passed down from parents to children, in a country or state. **3.** of an exalted moral character or excellence. **4.** of an admirably high quality; notably superior. **5.** *Chem.* inert; chemically inactive. *–n.* **6.** a person of noble birth or rank. *–***nobility**, *n.*

nobleman /'noubəlmən/ *n.* (*pl.* *-***men**) a man of noble birth or rank; a noble. *–***noblewoman**, *n.*

nobody /'noubɒdi, -bədi/ *pron.* **1.** no person. *–n.* (*pl.* *-***bodies**) **2.** a person of no importance, especially socially.

nocturnal /nɒk'tɜnəl/ *adj.* **1.** of or relating to the night. **2.** active by night.

nod /nɒd/ *v.* (**nodded, nodding**) *–v.i.* **1.** to make a slight, quick inclination of the head, as in assent, greeting, command, etc. *–v.t.* **2.** to incline (the head) in a short, quick movement, as of assent, greeting, etc. *–n.* **3.** a short, quick inclination of the head, as in assent, greeting, command, or drowsiness. *–phr.* **4. nod off**, *Colloq.* to go to sleep.

node /noud/ *n.* **1.** a knot, protuberance, or knob. **2.** a centring point of component parts. **3.** *Geom.* a point on a curve or surface, at which there can be more than one tangent line or plane. *–***nodal**, *adj.*

no-doc loan /'nou-dɒk/ *n.* *Colloq.* a loan from a lending institution, such as a bank, for which no evidence is required of the borrower's ability to service the loan, relying simply on the borrower's warranty. Compare **low-doc loan**.

nodule /'nɒdʒul/ *n.* a small rounded mass or lump. *–***nodular**, *adj.*

no-fault *adj.* of or relating to legislation, insurance, etc., which does not depend on the assignation of guilt or blame to any of the parties involved.

no-fly zone *n.* an area over which all or specified aircraft are forbidden to fly.

noggin /'nɒgən/ *n.* **1.** a small measure of spirits. **2.** *Colloq.* the head.

noise /nɔiz/ *n.* **1.** sound, especially of a loud, harsh, or confused kind. **2.** loud shouting, outcry, or clamour. *–***noisy**, *adj.*

noisome /'nɔisəm/ *adj.* offensive.

nomad /'noumæd/ *n.* **1.** one of a people or tribe without fixed abode. **2.** any wanderer. *–***nomadic**, *adj.*

nomenclature /nə'mɛnklətʃə, 'noumənkleitʃə/ *n.* a set or system of names or terms.

nominal /'nɒmənəl/ *adj.* **1.** being such in name only; so-called. **2.** (of a price, consideration, etc.) named as a mere matter of form, being trifling in comparison with the actual value. **3.** *Gram.* used as or like a noun. *–***nominally**, *adv.*

nominate /'nɒməneit/ *v.t.* to propose as a proper person for appointment or election to an office. *–***nomination**, *n.*

nominee /nɒmə'ni/ *n.* a person nominated as to fill an office or stand for election.

-nomy a final word element meaning 'distribution', 'arrangement', 'management', or having reference to laws or government, as in *astronomy, economy, taxonomy*.

non- a prefix indicating: **1.** exclusion from a specified class or group. **2.** objective negation or opposition. **3.** spuriousness or failure to fulfil a claim. **4.** the absence of activity or achievement in the area named.

non-action verb *n.* *Gram.* → **stative verb**.

nonagenarian /nɒnədʒə'nɛəriən, nou-/ *adj.* of the age of 90 years, or between 90 and 100 years old.

nonagon /'nɒnəgɒn, -gən/ *n.* a polygon having nine angles and nine sides.

nonce /nɒns/ *n.* the one or particular occasion or purpose.

nonchalant /'nɒnʃələnt/ *adj.* coolly unconcerned, indifferent, or unexcited; casual. *–***nonchalance**, *n.*

noncommittal /ˈnɒnkəmɪtl/ *adj.* not committing oneself, or not involving committal, to a particular view, course, or the like.

nondescript /ˈnɒndəskrɪpt/ *adj.* of no recognised, definite, or particular type or kind.

none /nʌn/ *pron.* **1.** no one; not one. **2.** not any, as of something indicated. **3.** no part; nothing. **4.** (*construed as pl.*) no, or not any, persons or things. *—adv.* **5.** to no extent; in no way; not at all.

nonentity /nɒnˈɛntəti/ *n.* (*pl.* **-ties**) a person or thing of no importance.

nonetheless /nʌnðəˈlɛs/ *adv.* however.

nonfiction /nɒnˈfɪkʃən/ *n.* a class of writing comprising works dealing with facts and events, rather than imaginative narration: *I like reading biographies and other nonfiction.*

nonflammable /nɒnˈflæməbəl/ *adj.* not easily set alight; slow-burning; not flammable.

nong /nɒŋ/ *n. Colloq.* a fool; an idiot.

nonplus /nɒnˈplʌs/ *v.t.* (**-plussed, -plussing**) **1.** to puzzle completely. *—n.* **2.** a state of utter perplexity.

nonproductive /ˌnɒnprədʌktɪv/ *adj.* not producing goods directly, as employees in charge of personnel, inspectors, etc.

non-renewable resource *n.* a natural resource which, once it is depleted, cannot be replaced or restored, such as fossil fuels. Compare **renewable resource**.

nonsense /ˈnɒnsəns/ *n.* that which makes no sense or is lacking in sense. —**nonsensical**, *adj.*

non sequitur /nɒn ˈsɛkwɪtə/ *n.* an inference or a conclusion which does not follow from the premises.

noodle /ˈnudl/ *n.* a type of pasta, cut into long, narrow, flat strips and served in soups or, with a sauce, as a main dish.

nook /nʊk/ *n.* **1.** a corner, as in a room. **2.** any secluded or obscure corner.

noon /nun/ *n.* midday.

no-one *pron.* nobody.

noose /nus/ *n.* a loop with a running knot, as in a snare, lasso, hangman's halter, etc., which tightens as the rope is pulled.

nor /nɔ/ *conj.* a negative conjunction used: **1.** as the correlative to a preceding *neither: he could neither read nor write.* **2.** to continue the force of a negative, such as *not, no, never,* etc., occurring in a preceding clause. **3.** after an affirmative clause, or as a continuative, in the sense of *and…not: they are happy, nor need we mourn.*

nor' /nɔ/ *n., adj., adv. Chiefly Naut.* north.

norm /nɔm/ *n.* **1.** a standard, model, or pattern. **2.** a mean or average.

normal /ˈnɔməl/ *adj.* **1.** conforming to the standard or the common type; regular, usual, natural, or not abnormal. **2.** serving to fix a standard. *—n.* **3.** the standard or type. **4.** the normal form or state; the average or mean. —**normality**, *n.*

norovirus /ˈnɒrəʊvaɪrəs/ *n.* a virus which causes severe, highly infectious gastroenteritis.

north /nɔθ/ *n.* **1.** a cardinal point of the compass lying in the plane of the meridian and to the right of a person facing the setting sun or west. *—adj.* **2.** lying or proceeding towards the north. **3.** coming from the north, as a wind.

—adv. **4.** towards or in the north. **5.** (of the wind) from the north. Also, *esp. Naut.*, **nor'**. —**northerly**, *adj., n.* —**northern**, *adj.*

nose /noʊz/ *n.* **1.** the part of the face or head which contains the nostrils, affording passage for air in respiration, etc. **2.** this part as the organ of smell. **3.** something regarded as resembling the nose of a person or animal. *—v.t.* **4.** to perceive by or as by the nose or the sense of smell. **5.** to touch or rub with the nose; nuzzle. *—v.i.* **6.** to smell or sniff. **7.** (fol. by *after, for,* etc.) to seek as if by smelling or scent; pry (followed by *about, into,* etc.).

nosedive /ˈnoʊzdaɪv/ *n.* a plunge of an aeroplane with the fore part of the craft vertically downwards.

nosegay /ˈnoʊzɡeɪ/ *n.* a bunch of flowers, or herbs; a bouquet; a posy.

nosh /nɒʃ/ *v.i. Colloq.* to eat; have a snack or a meal.

nostalgia /nɒsˈtældʒə/ *n.* a longing and desire for home, family and friends, or the past. —**nostalgic**, *adj.*

nostril /ˈnɒstrəl/ *n.* one of the external openings of the nose.

nostrum /ˈnɒstrəm/ *n.* **1.** a patent medicine. **2.** a quack medicine.

nosy /ˈnoʊzi/ *adj.* (**-sier, -siest**) *Colloq.* prying; inquisitive. Also, **nosey**.

not /nɒt/ *adv.* a word expressing negation, denial, refusal, or prohibition.

nota bene /noʊtə ˈbɛni, ˈbeɪneɪ/ note well.

notable /ˈnoʊtəbəl/ *adj.* **1.** worthy of note or notice; noteworthy. **2.** prominent, important, or distinguished, as persons.

notary public /noʊtəri ˈpʌblɪk/ *n.* (*pl.* **notaries public**) an official, usually a solicitor, authorised to certify contracts, acknowledge deeds, take affidavits, protest bills of exchange.

notation /noʊˈteɪʃən/ *n.* a system of graphic symbols for a specialised use, other than ordinary writing.

notch /nɒtʃ/ *n.* **1.** a more or less angular cut, indentation, or hollow in a narrow object or surface or an edge. *—v.t.* **2.** to cut or make a notch or notches in. **3.** (fol. by *up*) to score, as in a game.

note /noʊt/ *n.* **1.** a brief record of something set down to assist the memory, or for reference or development. **2.** a short informal letter. **3.** a certificate, as of a government or a bank, passing current as money; a banknote. **4.** importance or consequence. **5.** notice, observation, or heed. **6.** *Music* a sign or character used to represent a sound, the position and form of which indicates the pitch and duration of the sound. **7.** way of speaking or thinking. *—v.t.* **8.** to mark down, as in writing; make a memorandum of. **9.** to observe carefully; give attention or heed to.

notebook /ˈnoʊtbʊk/ *n.* **1.** a book of or for notes. **2.** Also, **notebook computer**. *Computers* a small, lightweight, portable computer.

noteworthy /ˈnoʊtwɜði/ *adj.* worthy of note or notice; notable.

nothing /ˈnʌθɪŋ/ *pron.* **1.** no thing; not anything; naught. *—n.* **2.** a cipher or nought. *—adv.* **3.** in no respect or degree; not at all.

notice /ˈnoʊtəs/ *n.* **1.** information or intelligence. **2.** an intimation or warning. **3.** a note, placard, or the like conveying information or warning. **4.** a notification of the termination, at a specified time, of an agreement, as for renting or employment, given by one of the parties to the agreement. **5.** observation, perception, attention, or heed. –*v.t.* (**-ticed, -ticing**) **6.** to pay attention to or take notice of. **7.** to perceive.

noticeboard /ˈnootəsbod/ *n.* a board, located centrally in a school, office, etc., designed for the display of notices and other information of general interest.

notify /ˈnootəfaɪ/ *v.t.* (**-fied, -fying**) to give notice to, or inform, of something. –**notification,** *n.*

notion /ˈnooʃən/ *n.* a more or less general, vague or imperfect conception or idea of something. –**notional,** *adj.*

not negotiable /nəˈgooʃəbəl/ *adj.* of or relating to a cheque which is crossed, indicating that the person to whom it is given has no better title to it than the person had from whom it was received; popularly and inaccurately held to mean that the cheque can be paid only into the account, the name of which appears on the cheque.

notorious /nəˈtɔːriəs/ *adj.* widely but unfavourably known. –**notoriety,** *n.*

notwithstanding /ˌnɒtwɪθˈstændɪŋ/ *prep.* **1.** in spite of. –*adv.* **2.** nevertheless. –*conj.* **3.** although.

nougat /ˈnuga/ *n.* a hard, paste-like sweet.

nought /nɒt/ *n.* a cipher (0); zero.

noun /naʊn/ *n.* the part of speech comprising words denoting persons, places, things, and such other words as show similar grammatical behaviour, as English *friend, city, desk, whiteness, virtue.*

nourish /ˈnʌrɪʃ/ *v.t.* **1.** to sustain with food or nutriment; supply with what is necessary for maintaining life. **2.** to foster or promote. –**nourishment,** *n.*

nous /naʊs/ *n. Colloq.* common sense.

nouvelle cuisine /nuˈvɛl/ *n.* a style of cooking emphasising small, simple meals, delicately flavoured and garnished.

novel[1] /ˈnɒvəl/ *n.* a fictitious prose narrative of considerable length. –**novelist,** *n.*

novel[2] /ˈnɒvəl/ *adj.* of a new kind, or different from anything seen or known before.

novelty /ˈnɒvəlti/ *n.* (*pl.* **-ties**) **1.** novel character, newness, or strangeness. **2.** a novel thing, experience, or proceeding.

novice /ˈnɒvəs/ *n.* someone who is new to the circumstances, work, etc., in which he or she is placed.

novitiate /noʊˈvɪʃiət, -ieɪt/ *n.* **1.** the state or period of being a novice of a religious order or congregation. **2.** the quarters occupied by religious novices during probation. Also, **noviciate.**

now /naʊ/ *adv.* **1.** at the present time or moment. **2.** (*more emphatically*) immediately or at once. **3.** at the time or moment only just past. **4.** in these present times; nowadays. –*conj.* **5.** now that; since, or seeing that.

nowadays /ˈnaʊədeɪz/ *adv.* at the present day; in these times.

nowhere /ˈnoʊwɛə/ *adv.* in, at, or to no place; not anywhere.

noxious /ˈnɒkʃəs/ *adj.* **1.** harmful or injurious to health or physical wellbeing. **2.** (of an animal, insect, plant, etc.) declared harmful by statute law for compulsory eradication.

nozzle /ˈnɒzəl/ *n.* a projecting spout, terminal discharging pipe, or the like, as of a hose or rocket.

nth /ɛnθ/ *adj.* denoting the last in a series of infinitely decreasing or increasing values, amounts, etc.

nuance /ˈnjuɒns, njuˈɑːns/ *n.* a shade of colour, expression, meaning, feeling, etc.

nub /nʌb/ *n.* **1.** a knob or protuberance. **2.** the point or gist of anything.

nubile /ˈnjubaɪl/ *adj.* (of a girl or young woman) marriageable, especially as to age or physical development.

nuclear /ˈnjukliə/ *adj.* **1.** of, relating to, or forming a nucleus. **2.** relating to, involving, or powered by atomic energy.

nuclear accelerator *n. Physics* a device which accelerates charged particles to velocities which enable them to overcome the coulomb repulsion from the nucleus, thus initiating a nuclear reaction.

nuclear disarmament *n.* the dismantling of nuclear weapons, especially those of major military powers, often coupled with attempts to prevent an increase in the number of nuclear-armed countries.

nuclear fission *n.* the breakdown of an atomic nucleus of an element of relatively high atomic number into two or more nuclei of lower atomic number, with conversion of part of its mass into energy.

nuclear power *n.* → **atomic power.**

nuclear waste *n.* the radioactive by-products of nuclear fission.

nuclear weapon *n.* any weapon in which the explosive power is derived from nuclear fission, nuclear fusion, or a combination of both.

nuclei /ˈnjukliaɪ/ *n.* plural of **nucleus.**

nucleonics /njuklɪˈɒnɪks/ *n.* the techniques of applying nuclear science to industry and to biology, physics, chemistry, and other sciences.

nucleus /ˈnjuklɪəs/ *n.* (*pl.* **-clei** /-klɪaɪ/ or **-cleuses**) **1.** a central part or thing about which other parts or things are grouped. **2.** *Biol.* a differentiated mass (usually rounded) of protoplasm, surrounded by a delicate membrane, present in the interior of nearly all living cells and forming an essential element in their growth metabolism and reproduction. **3.** *Physics* the central core of an atom, composed of protons and neutrons. It has a net positive charge equal to the number of protons.

nude /nud, njud/ *adj.* **1.** naked or unclothed, as a person, the body, etc. **2.** without the usual coverings, furnishings, etc.; bare. –**nudity,** *n.*

nudge /nʌdʒ/ *v.t.* (**nudged, nudging**) **1.** to push slightly or jog, especially with the elbow, as in calling attention or giving a hint or with sly meaning. –*n.* **2.** a slight push or jog.

nudism /ˈnudɪzəm, ˈnju-/ *n.* the practice of going nude as a means of healthful living. –**nudist,** *n.*

nugget /ˈnʌgət/ *n.* a lump of something, especially gold as found in the ground.

nuggety /'nʌgəti/ *adj.* **1.** of or resembling a nugget. **2.** *Colloq.* (of a person) short and sturdy. Also, **nuggetty**.

nuisance /'njusəns/ *n.* **1.** a highly obnoxious or annoying thing or person. **2.** something offensive or annoying to individuals or to the community, to the prejudice of their legal rights.

null /nʌl/ *adj.* **1.** of no effect, consequence, or significance. **2.** being none, lacking, or non-existent. **–nullify,** *v.*

nulla-nulla /ˈnʌlə-nʌlə/ *n.* an Aboriginal club or heavy weapon. Also, **nulla**.

numb /nʌm/ *adj.* deprived of or deficient in the power of sensation and movement.

numbat /'nʌmbæt/ *n.* a small, slender, reddish-brown, diurnal marsupial.

number /'nʌmbə/ *n.* **1.** the sum, total, count, or aggregate of a collection of units or any generalisation of this concept. **2.** the particular numeral assigned to anything in order to fix its place in a series. **3.** a word or symbol, or a combination of words or symbols, used in counting or to denote a total. **4.** a quantity (large or small) of individuals. **5.** (*pl.*) numerical strength or superiority, as in a political party, organisation, etc. **6.** an article of merchandise. *–v.t.* **7.** to ascertain the number of. **8.** to mark with or distinguish by a number or numbers. **9.** to amount to in number. *–v.i.* **10.** to be numbered or included.

numeral /'njumərəl/ *n.* a figure or letter, or a group of figures or letters, denoting a number.

numerate /'njuməreɪt/ *v.t.* to number; count; enumerate.

numerator /'njuməreɪtə/ *n. Maths* that term (usually written above the line) of a fraction which shows how many parts of a unit are taken.

numerical /nju'mɛrɪkəl/ *adj.* **1.** of or relating to number; of the nature of number. **2.** denoting number or a number.

numerous /'njumərəs/ *adj.* very many.

numismatics /njumæz'mætɪks/ *n.* the study and commonly also the collection of coins and medals.

nun /nʌn/ *n.* a woman who has joined a religious order and leads a life of religious observance and service.

nunnery /'nʌnəri/ *n.* (*pl.* **-ries**) a religious house for nuns; a convent.

nuptial /'nʌpʃəl/ *adj.* of or relating to marriage or the marriage ceremony.

nurdle /'nɜdl/ *n.* a pellet of plastic resin used as a base for the manufacture of plastic products; spilt in production processes or during transportation, nurdles constitute a significant marine polluter, being poisonous to marine life.

nurse /nɜs/ *n.* **1.** a person who has the care of the sick or infirm. *–v.t.* **2.** to tend in sickness or infirmity. **3.** to seek to cure (a cold, etc.) by taking care of oneself. **4.** to look after carefully so as to promote growth, development, etc.; foster; cherish (a feeling, etc.). **5.** to hold in the lap while travelling: *he nursed the box for the whole trip.* **6.** to hold in the arms: *he nursed the baby until she fell asleep.* **7.** to breastfeed (an infant). *–v.i.* **8.** to act as nurse; tend the sick or infirm. **9.** to breastfeed an infant.

nurse practitioner *n.* a nurse who is legally qualified to take on some of the responsibilities of a doctor, particularly with regard to prescribing medicines.

nursery /'nɜsri/ *n.* (*pl.* **-ries**) **1.** a room or place set apart for young children. **2.** a place where young trees or other plants are raised for transplanting or for sale.

nurture /'nɜtʃə/ *v.t.* to feed, nourish, or support during the stages of growth, as children or young; rear.

nut /nʌt/ *n.* **1.** a dry fruit consisting of an edible kernel or meat enclosed in a woody or leathery shell. **2.** any of various devices or parts supposed in some way to resemble a nut. **3.** *Colloq.* an enthusiast. **4.** *Colloq.* a foolish or eccentric person. **5.** *Colloq.* an insane person. **6.** a perforated block (usually of metal) with an internal thread or female screw, used to screw on the end of a bolt, etc.

nutmeg /'nʌtmɛg/ *n.* an aromatic spice.

nutrient /'njutriənt/ *adj.* **1.** nourishing; affording nutriment. *–n.* **2.** a nutrient substance.

nutriment /'njutrəmənt/ *n.* that which nourishes; nourishment; food.

nutrition /nju'trɪʃən/ *n.* **1.** the act or process of nourishing or of being nourished. **2.** the process by which the food material taken into an organism is converted into living tissue, etc.

nutritious /nju'trɪʃəs/ *adj.* nourishing, especially in a high degree.

nutritive /'njutrətɪv/ *adj.* serving to nourish; affording nutriment.

nuzzle /'nʌzəl/ *v.i.* **1.** to burrow or root with the nose, as an animal does. **2.** to snuggle or cuddle up with someone or something.

nylon /'naɪlɒn/ *n.* a synthetic material used for yarn, bristles, etc.

nymph /nɪmf/ *n.* **1.** one of a numerous class of inferior divinities of mythology, conceived as beautiful maidens inhabiting the sea, rivers, woods, trees, mountains, meadows, etc. **2.** a beautiful or graceful young woman. **3.** a young, wingless insect.

nymphomania /nɪmfə'meɪniə/ *n.* uncontrollable sexual desire in women. **–nymphomaniac,** *adj., n.*

O, o

O, o /ou/ n. **1.** the 15th letter of the English alphabet. **2.** the Arabic cipher; zero; nought (0).

o' /ə/ prep. an abbreviated form of **of**.

o-¹ Chem. a shortened form of **ortho-**.

o-² variant of **ob-**, before m.

-o an ending for the first element of many compounds, often used as a connective, as in Franco-Italian, speedometer, etc.

-o a suffix used: **1.** in colloquial abbreviations, as arvo for afternoon, combo for combination. **2.** in colloquial responses showing compliance or agreement, as goodo, righto.

oaf /ouf/ n. a lout.

oak /ouk/ n. a large tree which bears acorns.

oar /ɔ/ n. **1.** a long shaft of wood with a blade at one end, used for propelling a boat. –phr. **2. put one's oar in**, to interfere; meddle.

oasis /ou'eisəs/ n. (pl. **oases** /-siz/-) a fertile place in a desert region.

oatcake /'outkeik/ n. a cake, usually thin and brittle, made of oatmeal.

oath /ouθ/ n. (pl. **oaths** /ouðz/) **1.** a solemn appeal to God, or to some revered person or thing, in attestation of the truth of a statement or the binding character of a promise. **2.** a statement or promise strengthened by such an appeal. **3.** any profane expression; a curse.

oats /outz/ pl. n. **1.** a cereal grass cultivated for its edible seed. **2.** the seeds. –phr. **3. sow one's wild oats**, to indulge in the excesses or follies of youth.

ob- a prefix meaning 'towards', 'to', 'on', 'over', 'against', now used also with the sense of 'reversely' or 'inversely'. Also, **o-**, **oc-**, **of-**, **op-**.

obdurate /'ɒbdʒərət/ adj. hardened against persuasions or tender feelings.

obedient /ə'bidiənt/ adj. obeying, or willing to obey. –**obedience**, n.

obeisance /ou'beisəns/ n. deference or homage.

obelisk /'ɒbələsk/ n. a tapering, four-sided shaft of stone.

obese /ou'bis/ adj. excessively fat. –**obesity**, n.

obesity /ou'bisəti/ n. a medical condition in which excess body fat affects the health of the individual, often leading to heart disease and diabetes.

obey /ou'bei/ v.t. **1.** to comply with or fulfil the commands or instructions in action. **2.** (of things) to respond conformably in action to. –v.i. **3.** to be obedient.

obituary /ə'bitʃəri/ n. (pl. **-ries**) a notice of the death of a person, often with a brief biographical sketch, as in a newspaper.

object n. /'ɒbdʒɛkt/ **1.** a visible or tangible thing. **2.** the end towards which effort is directed. **3.** Gram. the noun or its substitute which represents the goal of an action or the ending point of a relation. –v.i. /əb'dʒɛkt/ **4.** to express or feel disapproval; be averse.

objection /əb'dʒɛkʃən/ n. something adduced or said in disagreement or disapproval.

objectionable /əb'dʒɛkʃənəbəl/ adj. that may be objected to; unpleasant; offensive.

objective /əb'dʒɛktɪv/ n. **1.** an end towards which efforts are directed; something aimed at. –adj. **2.** free from personal feelings or prejudice; unbiased. **3.** of or relating to an object or objects. –**objectivity**, n.

obligation /ɒblə'geiʃən/ n. **1.** a binding requirement as to action; duty. **2.** Law an agreement enforceable by law. **3.** a benefit, favour, or service, for which gratitude is due. **4.** the state or fact of being indebted for a benefit, favour, or service. –**obligate**, v.

obligatory /ɒ'blɪgətəri, -tri/ adj. required as a matter of obligation.

oblige /ə'blaidʒ/ v. (**obliged**, **obliging**) –v.t. **1.** to require or constrain, as by law, command, conscience, or necessity. **2.** to place under a debt of gratitude for some benefit, favour, or service. **3.** (fol. by with) to favour or accommodate. –v.i. **4.** to do something as a favour.

obliging /ə'blaidʒɪŋ/ adj. disposed to do favours or services, as a person.

oblique /ə'blik/ adj. **1.** neither perpendicular nor parallel to a given line or surface. **2.** not straight or direct.

obliterate /ə'blɪtəreit/ v.t. to remove all traces of; do away with; destroy.

oblivion /ə'blɪviən/ n. the state of being forgotten.

oblivious /ə'blɪviəs/ adj. (fol. by of or to) unmindful; unconscious.

oblong /'ɒblɒŋ/ adj. **1.** in the form of a rectangle; of greater length than breadth. –n. **2.** an oblong figure.

obnoxious /əb'nɒkʃəs, ɒb-/ adj. objectionable; offensive; odious.

oboe /'oubou/ n. a woodwind instrument.

obscene /əb'sin, ɒb-/ adj. offensive to modesty or decency. –**obscenity**, n.

obscure /əb'skjuə, -'skjuə/ adj. **1.** (of meaning) not clear or plain; uncertain. **2.** inconspicuous or unnoticeable; indistinct. –v.t. **3.** to make obscure, dark, dim, indistinct, etc. –**obscurity**, n. –**obscuration**, n.

obsequious /əb'sikwiəs, ɒb-/ adj. excessively deferential or compliant.

observant /əb'zɜvənt/ adj. quick to notice or perceive; alert.

observatory /əb'zɜvətri/ n. (pl. **-ries**) a place in or from which observations, especially astrological or meteorological, are made.

observe /əb'zɜv/ v.t. **1.** to see, perceive, or notice. **2.** to regard with attention, so as to see or learn something. **3.** to remark; comment. **4.** to show regard for by some appropriate procedure, ceremonies, etc. –**observation**, n.

obsession /əb'sɛʃən/ n. a persistent feeling, idea, or the like, which a person cannot escape. –**obsess**, v. –**obsessive**, adj.

obsessive-compulsive disorder n. a disorder of the mind in which the sufferer has intrusive irrational thoughts and engages in repetitive rituals to find temporary relief.

obsolescent /ɒbsə'lɛsənt/ adj. becoming obsolete. –**obsolescence**, n.

obsolete /'ɒbsəlit/ adj. fallen into disuse, or no longer in use.

obstacle /'ɒbstəkəl/ n. something that stands in the way or obstructs progress.

obstetrics /ɒbˈstetrɪks, əb-/ n. the branch of medicine dealing with childbirth. **–obstetrician**, n. **–obstetric**, adj.

obstinate /ˈɒbstənət/ adj. firmly and often perversely adhering to one's purpose, opinion, etc. **–obstinacy**, n.

obstreperous /əbˈstrepərəs, ɒb-/ adj. resisting control in a noisy manner; unruly.

obstruct /əbˈstrʌkt/ v.t. 1. to block or close up. 2. to interrupt, make difficult, or oppose the passage, progress, course, etc., of. **–obstruction**, n.

obtain /əbˈteɪn/ v.t. 1. to come into possession of; get or acquire. –v.i. 2. to be prevalent, customary, or in vogue.

obtrusive /əbˈtrusɪv, -zɪv/ adj. undesirably obvious.

obtuse /əbˈtjus, ɒb-/ adj. 1. blunt in form; not sharp or acute. 2. not sensitive or observant. 3. Geom., etc. (of an angle) greater than 90° but less than 180°.

obviate /ˈɒbvieɪt/ v.t. to meet and dispose of or prevent (difficulties, etc.).

obvious /ˈɒbviəs/ adj. clearly perceptible or evident.

oc- variant of **ob-** before c.

occasion /əˈkeɪʒən/ n. 1. a particular time, especially as marked by certain circumstances or occurrences. 2. the ground, reason, immediate or incidental cause of some action or result. –v.t. 3. to give occasion or cause for; bring about. –phr. 4. **on occasion**, now and then; occasionally.

occasional /əˈkeɪʒənəl/ adj. 1. occurring or appearing on one occasion or another or now and then. 2. intended for use whenever needed. **–occasionally**, adv.

occlude /əˈklud/ v.t. to close, shut, or stop up (a passage, etc.). **–occlusion**, n.

occult /ˈɒkʌlt, əˈkʌlt/ adj. 1. beyond the bounds of ordinary knowledge. –n. 2. the supernatural.

occupant /ˈɒkjəpənt/ n. a tenant of a house, estate, office, etc. **–occupancy**, n.

occupation /ɒkjəˈpeɪʃən/ n. 1. one's habitual employment; business, trade, or calling. 2. the period during which a country is under the control of foreign military forces.

occupational therapy n. a method of therapy which uses self-care, work and play activities to increase development and independent function, and to prevent disability. **–occupational therapist**, n.

occupy /ˈɒkjəpaɪ/ v.t. (**-pied, -pying**) 1. to take up (space, time, etc.). 2. to engage or employ (the mind, attention, etc., or the person). 3. to take possession of (a place), as by invasion. 4. to hold (a position, office, etc.).

occur /əˈkɜ/ v.i. (**-curred, -curring**) 1. to come to pass, take place, or happen. 2. (usu. fol. by to) to suggest itself in thought. **–occurrence**, n.

ocean /ˈəʊʃən/ n. the vast body of salt water which covers almost three fourths of the earth's surface.

oceanic crust n. Geol. that portion of the earth's lithosphere which forms the floor of much of the oceans. Compare **continental crust**.

ochre /ˈəʊkə/ n. 1. any of a class of natural earths used as pigments. 2. the colour of ochre, ranging from pale yellow to an orange or reddish yellow.

ocker /ˈɒkə/ Colloq. –n. 1. the archetypal uncultivated Australian. –adj. 2. distinctively Australian: an ocker sense of humour. Also, **occa, okker**.

ockie strap /ˈɒki/ n. Colloq. → **octopus strap**.

o'clock /əˈklɒk/ adv. of or by the clock (used in specifying or inquiring the hour of the day).

OCR /əʊ si ˈa, ˈəʊkə/ n. a system of machine reading by a light-sensitive electrical cell of standard character sets encoded on documents such as gas bills, etc.

octa- a word element meaning 'eight'. Also, **oct-, octo-**.

octagon /ˈɒktəgɒn, -gən/ n. a polygon having eight angles and eight sides.

octave /ˈɒktɪv/ n. a series or group of eight.

octet /ɒkˈtet/ n. any group of eight. Also, **octette**.

octopus /ˈɒktəpəs, -pʊs/ n. (pl. **-puses** or **-pi** /-paɪ/) a sea animal with eight arms.

octopus strap n. a stretchable rope with hooks on either end used for securing luggage to roof racks, etc.

ocular /ˈɒkjələ/ adj. of or relating to the eye: ocular movements.

oculist /ˈɒkjələst/ n. an ophthalmologist.

OD /əʊ ˈdi/ Colloq. –n. 1. an overdose, especially of an injected addictive drug. –v.i. (**OD'd, OD-ing**) 2. to give oneself an overdose.

odd /ɒd/ adj. 1. differing in character from what is ordinary or usual. 2. (of a number) leaving a remainder of one when divided by two (opposed to even). 3. additional to a whole mentioned in round numbers; more or less. 4. (of a pair) not matching. 5. occasional or casual. 6. not forming part of any particular group, set, or class. **–oddity**, n.

oddball /ˈɒdbɒl/ n. Colloq. someone who is unusual or peculiar; an eccentric.

oddly /ˈɒdli/ adv. 1. in an odd manner: to be behaving oddly. 2. strangely; unexpectedly: oddly likeable.

oddment /ˈɒdmənt/ n. a left-over article, bit, remnant, or the like.

odds /ɒdz/ pl. n. 1. the amount by which the bet of one party to a wager exceeds that of the other. 2. balance of probability in favour of something occurring or being the case. –phr. 3. **at odds**, in disagreement; at variance. 4. **make no odds**, not to matter; be of no importance. 5. **odds and ends**, odd bits; scraps; remnants; fragments.

ode /əʊd/ n. a lyric poem.

odium /ˈəʊdiəm/ n. hatred or repulsion. **–odious**, adj.

odometer /ɒˈdɒmətə, əʊ-/ n. an instrument for measuring distance passed over, as by a motor vehicle.

odonto- a word element meaning 'tooth'. Also, **odont-**.

odour /ˈəʊdə/ n. 1. that property of a substance which affects the sense of smell. 2. an agreeable scent; fragrance. 3. a bad smell. Also, **odor**. **–odorous**, adj.

o'er /ɔ/ prep., adv. Poetic over.

oesophagus /əˈsɒfəgəs/ n. (pl. **-phagi** /-fəgaɪ/) a tube connecting the mouth or pharynx with the stomach. Also, **esophagus**.

oestrogen /ˈiːstrədʒən, ˈes-/ n. any one of a group of female sex hormones. Also, **estrogen**.

of /ɒv, weak form /əv/ prep. a particle indicating: **1.** distance or direction from, separation, deprivation, riddance, etc.: within a metre of; to cure of. **2.** derivation, origin, or source. **3.** concerning: and what of Marie-Louise? **4.** cause, occasion, or reason. **5.** material, substance, or contents. **6.** a relation of identity. **7.** reference or respect. **8.** the attributing of a quality to.

of- variant of **ob-**, before f.

off /ɒf/ adv. **1.** away from a position occupied, or from contact, connection, or attachment. **2.** as a deduction. **3.** away; distant (in future time). **4.** out of operation or effective existence; disconnected. **5.** away from employment or service. **6.** to fulfilment, or into execution or effect. **7.** on one's way or journey, as from a place. –prep. **8.** away from; so as no longer to be or rest on. **9.** from by subtraction or deduction. **10.** away or disengaged from (duty, work, etc.). **11.** Colloq. refraining from (some food, activity, etc.). –adj. **12.** no longer in effect or operation. **13.** below the normal or expected standard; inferior. **14.** in bad taste; deviating from normal or accepted behaviour. **15.** (of food) tainted. –phr. Also, **on and off**. **16. off and on**, intermittently.

offal /ˈɒfəl/ n. **1.** the inedible parts of a meat carcass after slaughter, excluding the skin. **2.** the internal organs of animals used for food, as brains, heart, kidney, liver, etc.

offbeat /ˈɒfbiːt/ adj. unusual; unconventional.

off-chance n. a remote chance or possibility.

off-colour adj. Colloq. unwell. Also, **off-color**.

offcut /ˈɒfkʌt/ n. that which is cut off, as from paper which has been reduced to a particular size.

offence /əˈfens/ n. **1.** a transgression; a wrong; a sin. **2.** a crime which is not indictable, but is punishable summarily (**summary offence**). **3.** a feeling of resentful displeasure. **4.** the act of attacking; attack or assault. –**offensive**, adj.

offend /əˈfend/ v.t. **1.** to cause resentful displeasure in. **2.** to affect (the sense, taste, etc.) disagreeably. –v.i. **3.** to err in conduct; commit a sin, crime, or fault.

offer /ˈɒfə/ v.t. **1.** to present for acceptance or rejection; proffer. **2.** to propose or volunteer (to do something). **3.** to tender or bid, as a price. –v.i. **4.** to present itself; occur. –n. **5.** a proposal to give or accept something as a price or equivalent for something else; a bid. **6.** the condition of being offered. **7.** something offered.

offering /ˈɒfərɪŋ/ n. something offered.

offhand adv. /ˈɒfˈhænd/ **1.** without previous thought or preparation; extempore. –adj. /ˈɒfhænd/ **2.** informal or casual.

office /ˈɒfəs/ n. **1.** a room or place for the transaction of business, the discharge of professional duties, or the like. **2.** a place where tickets, etc., are sold, information given, etc. **3.** official employment or position.

officer /ˈɒfəsə/ n. someone who holds a position of rank or authority.

official /əˈfɪʃəl/ n. **1.** someone who holds an office or is charged with some form of official duty. –adj. **2.** of or relating to an office or position of duty, trust, or authority.

officialese /əfɪʃəˈliːz/ n. a style of language found in official documents and characterised by pretentiousness, pedantry, obscurity, and the use of jargon.

officiate /əˈfɪʃieɪt/ v.i. to perform the duties of any office or position.

officious /əˈfɪʃəs/ adj. forward in tendering or obtruding one's services upon others.

offing /ˈɒfɪŋ/ phr. **in the offing**, not very distant.

offline /ˈɒflaɪn/ adj. not connected to a computer network. Also, **off-line**.

off-peak adj. of or relating to a period of time of less activity than at the peak time: off-peak train services.

off-putting /ɒf-ˈpʊtɪŋ/ adj. Colloq. disconcerting; discouraging.

off-season adj. denoting a time of year other than the usual or most popular for a specific activity.

offset v.t. /ˈɒfset, ɒfˈset/ (**-set, -setting**) **1.** to balance by something else as an equivalent. –n. /ˈɒfset/ **2.** something that offsets or counterbalances; a compensating equivalent.

offshoot /ˈɒfʃuːt/ n. a shoot from a main stem.

offshore adv. /ɒfˈʃɔː/ **1.** off or away from the shore. **2.** at a distance from the shore. **3.** in or to another country; abroad: to study offshore; to move operations offshore. –adj. /ˈɒfʃɔː, ɒfˈʃɔː/ **4.** moving or tending away from the shore: an offshore wind. **5.** based in an overseas location: offshore processing of asylum seekers. **6.** (of a business) based in a foreign location where the taxation system is not as burdensome as it is in the country where the business is owned.

offside /ɒfˈsaɪd, ˈɒfsaɪd/ adj. Sport in an illegal position.

offsider /ɒfˈsaɪdə/ n. a partner; assistant.

offspring /ˈɒfsprɪŋ/ n. children or young of a particular parent.

off-the-record /ˈɒf-ðə-rekəd/ adj. unofficial.

off-white n. a white colour with a slight touch of grey in it.

often /ˈɒfən, ˈɒftən/ adv. **1.** many times; frequently. **2.** in many cases.

ogle /ˈoʊgəl/ v.t. (**ogled, ogling**) to eye with amorous or impertinently familiar glances.

ogre /ˈoʊgə/ n. a monster, commonly represented as a hideous giant.

oh /oʊ/ interj. an expression denoting surprise, pain, etc., or for attracting attention.

ohm /oʊm/ n. the derived SI unit of resistance. Symbol: Ω, O

-oid a suffix used to form adjectives meaning 'like' or 'resembling', and nouns meaning 'something resembling' what is indicated by the preceding part of the word (and often implying an incomplete or imperfect resemblance).

oil /ɔɪl/ n. **1.** any of a large class of viscous substances, liquid at ordinary temperatures, and insoluble in water. **2.** Painting an oil colour. –v.t. **3.** to smear, lubricate, or supply with oil.

–*adj.* **4.** concerned with the production or use of oil. **5.** using oil, especially as a fuel. –*phr.* **6. the good (or dinkum) oil**, *Colloq.* correct (and usually profitable) information.

oil colour *n.* a colour or paint made by grinding a pigment in oil. Also, **oil color**, **oil paint**.

oilskin /ˈɔɪlskɪn/ *n.* a cotton fabric made waterproof by treatment with oil.

ointment /ˈɔɪntmənt/ *n.* medicated cream for application to the skin.

okay /oʊˈkeɪ/ *Colloq.* –*adj.* **1.** all right. –*adv.* **2.** well; acceptably. –*v.t.* **3.** to endorse; approve; accept. –*n.* **4.** an approval or acceptance. –*interj.* **5.** an exclamation of approval, agreement, delight, etc. Also, **ok**, **OK**.

okra /ˈɒkrə, ˈoʊk-/ *n.* the edible pods of a certain plant, used in soups, etc.

-ol[1] *Chem.* a noun suffix representing 'alcohol'.

-ol[2] variant of **-ole**.

old /oʊld/ *adj.* (**older** *or* **elder**, **oldest** *or* **eldest**) **1.** far advanced in years or life. **2.** having reached a specified age. **3.** long known or in use; familiar. **4.** belonging to a past time. **5.** formerly in use. **6.** deteriorated through age or long use. –*n.* **7.** (used in combination) a person or animal of a specified age or age-group. –*phr.* **8. old hat**, *Colloq.* old-fashioned; out-of-date.

old boy *n.* a former pupil of a specific school.

olden /ˈoʊldən/ *adj.* of old; ancient.

olde-worlde /ˌoʊldi-ˈwɜːldi/ *adj.* excessively quaint or old-fashioned.

old-fashioned /ˈoʊld-fæʃənd/ *adj.* out of fashion.

old girl *n.* a former pupil of a specific school.

old guard *n.* the ultra-conservative members of any group, country, etc.

old hand *n.* one experienced in some activity.

old hat *adj.* old-fashioned; out-of-date; outmoded.

old maid *n.* an elderly or confirmed spinster.

old man *n. Colloq.* **1.** a father, usually one's own. **2.** a husband, usually one's own.

old school *n.* **the**, advocates or supporters of long-established, especially conservative, policies and practices.

old school tie *n.* (*usually derog.*) the network of influences and associations formed among former students of independent schools.

old-timer /ˈoʊld-taɪmə/ *n.* an old person.

old wives' tale *n.* an erroneous idea, superstitious belief, etc., such as is traditionally ascribed to old women.

-ole a noun suffix meaning 'oil'.

oleander /ˌoʊliˈændə, ˌɒli-/ *n.* a poisonous evergreen shrub with rose-coloured or white flowers.

oleo- a word element meaning 'oil'.

olfactory /ɒlˈfæktəri/ *adj.* of or relating to the sense of smell.

oligarchy /ˈɒləgaki/ *n.* (*pl.* **-chies**) a form of government in which the power is vested in a few, or in a dominant class or clique.

oligopoly /ˌɒləˈgɒpəli/ *n. Econ.* a market situation in which a product is supplied by a relatively small number of firms whose actions and policies are constrained by the expected reactions of each other.

olive /ˈɒləv, -lɪv/ *n.* **1.** an evergreen tree cultivated chiefly for its fruit. **2.** the fruit, edible and valuable as a source of oil. **3.** a shade of green or yellowish green. –*adj.* **4.** of the colour olive. **5.** (of the complexion or skin) brownish; darker than fair.

olive branch *n.* a branch of the olive tree (an emblem of peace).

ollie /ˈɒli/ *n.* (in skateboarding, snowboarding, etc.) a manoeuvre in which the rider drives the board into the air from a flat surface without using the hands to hold the board.

Olympic /əˈlɪmpɪk/ *adj.* relating to the Olympic Games.

-oma (*pl.* **-omas** *or* **-omata**) a suffix of nouns denoting a diseased condition of growth (tumour).

ombudsman /ˈɒmbədzmən/ *n.* (*pl.* **-men**) an official appointed to investigate complaints by citizens against the government or its agencies.

omega /əˈmiːgə, ˈɒməgə, əˈmeɪgə/ *n.* **1.** the last letter of the Greek alphabet. **2.** the last of any series; the end.

omelette /ˈɒmlət/ *n.* a dish consisting of eggs beaten and fried. Also, **omelet**.

omen /ˈoʊmən/ *n.* a prophetic sign.

ominous /ˈɒmənəs/ *adj.* portending evil; inauspicious; threatening.

omit /oʊˈmɪt, ə-/ *v.t.* (**omitted**, **omitting**) **1.** to leave out. **2.** to forbear or fail to do, make, use, send, etc. –**omission**, *n.*

omni- a word element meaning 'all'.

omnibus /ˈɒmnɪbəs, -bʌs/ *n.* (*pl.* **-buses**) **1.** → **bus**. **2.** a volume of reprinted works by a single author or related in interest or nature.

omnipotent /ɒmˈnɪpətənt/ *adj.* almighty, or infinite in power.

omnipresent /ˌɒmnəˈprɛzənt/ *adj.* present everywhere at the same time.

omniscient /ɒmˈnɪsiənt, ɒmˈnɪʃənt/ *adj.* knowing all things.

omnivorous /ɒmˈnɪvərəs/ *adj.* **1.** eating both animal and plant foods. **2.** eating all kinds of foods indiscriminately. –**omnivore**, *n.*

on /ɒn/ *prep.* a particle expressing: **1.** position above and in contact with a supporting surface: *on the table.* **2.** contact with any surface: *on the wall.* **3.** support, suspension, dependence, reliance, or means of conveyance: *on foot.* **4.** time or occasion. **5.** with reference to something else: *on the left.* **6.** membership or association. –*adv.* **7.** on oneself or itself: *to put clothes on.* **8.** fast to a thing, as for support: *to hold on.* **9.** forwards, onwards or along, as in any course or process: *to go on.* **10.** with continuous procedure: *to work on.* **11.** into or in active operation or performance: *to turn a machine on.* –*adj.* **12.** operating or in use. **13.** occurring; taking place. –*phr.* **14. be on about**, to be talking about. **15. not on**, *Colloq.* not a possibility; not allowable.

once /wʌns/ *adv.* **1.** at one time in the past; formerly. **2.** a single time. –*conj.* **3.** if or when at any time; if ever. **4.** whenever. –*phr.* **5. all at once**, suddenly. **6. at once**, immediately. **7. once and for all**, finally and decisively. **8. once upon a time**, long ago.

once-over *n. Colloq.* a quick or superficial examination.

oncology /oŋˈkɒlədʒi/ n. the branch of medical science that deals with tumours. —**oncologist**, n.

oncoming /ˈɒnkʌmɪŋ/ adj. approaching.

one /wʌn/ adj. **1.** being a single unit or individual. **2.** some (day, etc., in the future). **3.** single through union, agreement, or harmony. **4.** a certain (often used in naming a person otherwise unknown or undescribed). **5.** a particular (day, night, time, etc. in the past). –n. **6.** the first and lowest whole number. **7.** a unit; a single person or thing. –pron. **8.** a person or thing of number or kind indicated or understood. **9.** (in certain pronominal combinations) a person, unless definitely specified otherwise. **10.** a person indefinitely; anyone. **11.** (to avoid repetition) a person or thing of the kind just mentioned. –phr. **12. one and all**, everybody.

one-off adj. **1.** individual, unique. –n. **2.** an individual or unique item or person.

onerous /ˈoʊnərəs/ adj. burdensome, oppressive, or troublesome.

oneself /wʌnˈsɛlf/ pron. **1.** a person's self (often used for emphasis or reflexively). **2.** one's proper or normal self.

one-time adj. having been (as specified) at one time; former.

one-upmanship /wʌn-ˈʌpmənʃɪp/ n. the art or practice of achieving or demonstrating superiority over others.

onion /ˈʌnjən/ n. **1.** a widely cultivated plant with an edible bulb. **2.** the bulb.

on-lending n. the act of lending out, at a slightly higher rate of interest, money which has just been borrowed.

online /ˈɒnlaɪn/ adj. **1.** of or relating to a computer-controlled device which is directly linked to a computer (opposed to standalone). **2.** having direct access to a computer. **3.** (of information, etc.) able to be accessed directly by connection to a computer database, the internet, etc. –adv. **4.** on the internet: to publish online.

onlooker /ˈɒnlʊkə/ n. a spectator.

only /ˈoʊnli/ adv. **1.** without others or anything further; alone; solely. **2.** as recently as. –adj. **3.** being the single one or the relatively few of the kind. –conj. **4.** but (introducing a single restriction). **5.** except that; but or except for. –phr. **6. only too**, very; extremely.

onomatopoeia /ˌɒnəmætəˈpiə/ n. the use of a word or words which sound like the thing or sound they are describing, such as crunch, splash or buzz. —**onomatopoeic**, adj.

onsell /ɒnˈsɛl/ v.t. (**-sold, -selling**) to sell (assets, securities, etc.) shortly after purchase. —**onselling**, n.

onset /ˈɒnsɛt/ n. **1.** an assault or attack. **2.** a beginning or onset.

onshore adj. /ˈɒnʃɔ, ɒnˈʃɔ/ **1.** towards or located on the shore. –adv. /ɒnˈʃɔ/ **2.** towards the shore.

onside /ɒnˈsaɪd/ adj. in agreement, acting favourably.

onslaught /ˈɒnslɔt/ n. an onset, assault, or attack, especially a vigorous or furious one.

onto /ˈɒntu/ prep. **1.** to a place or position on; upon; on. **2.** aware of (especially something improper or secret).

ontology /ɒnˈtɒlədʒi/ n. **1.** the branch of metaphysics that investigates the nature of being. **2.** Computers the structural framework for a database. —**ontological**, adj.

onus /ˈoʊnəs/ n. a burden; a responsibility.

onward /ˈɒnwəd/ adj. **1.** directed or moving onwards or forwards. –adv. **2.** → **onwards**.

onwards /ˈɒnwədz/ adv. towards a point ahead or in front. Also, **onward**.

oo- a word element meaning 'egg'.

oodles /ˈudlz/ pl. n. Colloq. a large quantity.

oomph /ʊmf/ n. Colloq. vitality; energy.

oops /ʊps, ups/ interj. an exclamation of surprise or shock.

ooze[1] /uz/ v. (**oozed, oozing**) –v.i. **1.** (of moisture, etc.) to percolate or exude, as through pores or small openings. –v.t. **2.** to exude or radiate abundantly.

ooze[2] /uz/ n. soft mud, or slime.

op- variant of **ob-**, before p.

opal /ˈoʊpəl/ n. a mineral, some varieties of which are valued as gems.

opaque /oʊˈpeɪk/ adj. **1.** impenetrable to light. **2.** hard to understand; not clear or lucid; obscure. —**opacity**, n.

open /ˈoʊpən/ adj. **1.** not shut, as a door, gate, etc. **2.** not closed, covered, or shut up, as a house, box, drawer, etc. **3.** not enclosed as by barriers, as a space. **4.** able to be entered, used, shared, competed for, etc., by all. **5.** (of shops, etc.) ready to do business; ready to admit members of the public. **6.** undecided, as a question. **7.** liable or subject. **8.** unobstructed, as a passage, country, stretch of water, view, etc. **9.** exposed to general view or knowledge; frank or flagrant: an open face; open rebellion. **10.** expanded, extended, or spread out. **11.** generous, liberal, or bounteous. **12.** not yet balanced or adjusted, as an account. **13.** (of a cheque) uncrossed. –v.t. **14.** to make, or cause to be, open. **15.** to give access to; make accessible or available, as for use. **16.** to render accessible to knowledge, enlightenment, sympathy, etc. **17.** (sometimes fol. by up) to set in action, begin, start, or commence. –v.i. **18.** to become open. **19.** to afford access (into, to, etc.). **20.** to become receptive to knowledge, sympathy, etc., as the mind. **21.** to disclose or reveal one's knowledge, thoughts, feelings, etc. **22.** to become less compact, less close together, or the like. **23.** to begin, start, or commence; start operations. –n. **24.** an open competition: the Australian open. –phr. **25. the open, a.** an open or clear space. **b.** the open air. **c.** a situation in which hitherto restricted knowledge is extended to all parties: to bring a subject out into the open.

open-and-shut adj. obvious; easily decided.

open day n. a day on which certain institutions, as schools, are open to members of the public and special activities, exhibitions, etc., are arranged for their entertainment.

open door n. admission to all upon equal terms.

open-ended adj. organised or arranged so as to allow for various contingencies; without fixed limits.

opener /ˈoʊpnə, ˈoʊpənə/ n. **1.** someone or something that opens, especially a tin-opener or a bottle opener. **2.** Cricket either of the two people batting who open their side's innings by batting first. –*phr.* **3. for openers,** to begin with.

opening /'oupnɪŋ, 'oupənɪŋ/ *n.* **1.** the act of someone who or that which opens (in any sense). **2.** an open space in solid matter; a gap, hole, or aperture. **3.** the first part or initial stage of anything. **4.** a vacancy. **5.** an opportunity. **6.** a formal or official beginning.

open letter *n.* a letter made public by radio, newspaper, or such, but written as though to a specific person.

open-mouthed /oupən-'mauðd/ *adj.* **1.** having the mouth open. **2.** gaping with surprise or astonishment. **3.** greedy, ravenous, or rapacious.

open order *n.* a voucher, etc., exchangeable for goods up to a specified value from a particular shop.

open-plan *adj.* (of the interior space of a dwelling, office, etc.) not having walls between areas designed for different uses.

open slather *n. Colloq.* a situation in which there are no restraints.

opera¹ /'ɒprə, 'ɒpərə/ *n.* an extended dramatic composition in which music is an essential and predominant factor.

opera² /'ɒpərə/ *n.* plural form of **opus**.

operable /'ɒpərəbəl, 'ɒprə-/ *adj.* **1.** capable of being put into practice. **2.** admitting of a surgical operation.

operate /'ɒpəreɪt/ *v.i.* **1.** to work or run, as a machine does. **2.** to act effectively. **3.** to perform some process of work or treatment. **4.** *Surg.* to perform surgery on a patient. **5.** to carry on transactions in securities, or some commodity, especially speculatively or on a large scale. –*v.t.* **6.** to manage or use (a machine, etc.) at work. –**operation,** *n.*

operating system *n. Computers* the essential program which enables all other programs to be run on a computer, and which establishes an interface between a user and the hardware of the computer.

operational /ɒpə'reɪʃənəl/ *adj.* **1.** of or relating to an operation or operations. **2.** ready for use; in working order.

operations research *n.* the analysis, usually involving mathematical treatment, of a process, problem, or operation to determine its purpose and effectiveness and to gain maximum efficacy. Also, **operational research.**

operative /'ɒpərətɪv, 'ɒprə-/ *adj.* **1.** operating, or exerting force or influence. **2.** engaged in, concerned with, or relating to work or productive activity.

operator /'ɒpəreɪtə/ *n.* **1.** a worker; someone employed or skilled in operating a machine, apparatus, or the like. **2.** someone who deals in shares, currency, etc., especially speculatively or on a large scale. **3.** *Colloq.* someone who successfully manipulates people or situations. **4.** *Maths, Computers, etc.* a symbol, character, word, etc., used to represent a particular action or logical relation, as the word 'and', or the plus symbol (+).

ophthalmic /ɒf'θælmɪk/ *adj.* of or relating to the eye.

ophthalmo- a word element meaning 'eye'.

ophthalmology /ɒfθæl'mɒlədʒi/ *n.* the science dealing with the anatomy, functions, and diseases of the eye. –**ophthalmologist,** *n.*

-opia a word element of nouns denoting a condition of sight or of the visual organs.

opiate /'oupiət, -eɪt/ *n.* **1.** a medicine that contains opium and hence has the quality of inducing sleep. **2.** anything that causes dullness or inaction, or that soothes the feelings.

opinion /ə'pɪnjən/ *n.* a personal view, attitude, or estimation.

opinionated /ə'pɪnjəneɪtəd/ *adj.* obstinate or conceited with regard to one's opinions.

opinion poll *n.* → **gallup poll.**

opium /'oupiəm/ *n.* a narcotic, used in medicine to induce sleep, relieve pain, etc.

opossum /ə'pɒsəm/ *n.* → **possum.**

opponent /ə'pounənt/ *n.* someone who is on the opposite side in a contest, controversy or the like; an adversary.

opportune /'ɒpətjun/ *adj.* **1.** appropriate or favourable. **2.** occurring or coming at an appropriate time; timely.

opportunism /ɒpə'tjunɪzəm, 'ɒpətjunɪzəm/ *n.* the policy or practice of adapting actions, etc., to expediency or circumstances. –**opportunist,** *n.*

opportunistic /ɒpətju'nɪstɪk/ *adj.* **1.** displaying opportunism. **2.** *Med.* (of an illness) developing as a result of a weakness in the immune system. –**opportunistically,** *adv.*

opportunity /ɒpə'tjunəti/ *n.* (*pl.* **-ties**) an appropriate or favourable time or occasion.

opportunity shop *n.* a shop run by a church, charity, etc., for the sale of second hand goods, especially clothes. Also, **op shop.**

oppose /ə'pouz/ *v.t.* **1.** to act or contend in opposition to. **2.** to stand in the way of; hinder. **3.** to set as an obstacle or hindrance. –*v.i.* **4.** to be or act in opposition.

opposite /'ɒpəsət/ *adj.* **1.** placed or lying over against something else or each other, or in a corresponding position from an intervening line, space, or thing. **2.** in a complementary role or position. –*n.* **3.** someone who or that which is opposite or contrary. –*adv.* **4.** on opposite sides.

opposition /ɒpə'zɪʃən/ *n.* **1.** the action of opposing, resisting, or combating. **2.** an opposing group or body.

oppress /ə'prɛs/ *v.t.* **1.** to lie heavily upon, as care, sorrow, etc. **2.** to burden with cruel or unjust impositions or restraints. –**oppression,** *n.* –**oppressive,** *adj.*

opprobrium /ə'proubnəm/ *n.* the disgrace incurred by shameful conduct. –**opprobrious,** *adj.*

op shop /'ɒp ʃɒp/ *n.* a shop that sells second-hand goods, run by a charity. Also, **opportunity shop.**

-opsis a word element indicating apparent likeness.

opt /ɒpt/ *phr.* **1. opt for,** to decide in favour of; choose. **2. opt out,** to decide not to participate.

optical /'ɒptɪkəl/ *adj.* **1.** relating to sight; visual. **2.** acting by means of sight or light, as instruments.

optical scanner *n.* a photoelectric cell that scans printed data and converts it into the electric impulses fed into a computer or data-processing machine.

optician /ɒpˈtɪʃən/ n. a maker or seller of optical glasses and instruments.

optimise /ˈɒptɪmaɪz/ v.t. to make the best of; make the most effective use of. Also, **optimize**. –**optimisation**, n.

optimism /ˈɒptɪmɪzəm/ n. disposition to hope for the best. –**optimistic**, adj.

optimist /ˈɒptɪmɪst/ n. someone who is usually hopeful or who has the habit of expecting that things will turn out well. –**optimistic**, adj. –**optimistically**, adv.

optimum /ˈɒptəməm/ n. (pl. **-ma** /-mə/ or **-mums**) **1.** the best or most favourable point, degree, amount, etc., for the purpose. –adj. **2.** best or most favourable.

option /ˈɒpʃən/ n. **1.** power or liberty of choosing; right of freedom of choice. **2.** something which may be or is chosen; choice. **3.** the right, conferred by an agreement, to buy (or to decline to buy) a property, etc., within a certain time. –**optional**, adj.

optional preferential voting n. a form of preferential voting in which voters may vote for one candidate only, or may choose to indicate preferences for others. Compare **full preferential voting**, **partial preferential voting**.

optometry /ɒpˈtɒmətri/ n. the practice or art of testing the eyes in order to supply suitable glasses. –**optometrist**, n.

opulent /ˈɒpjələnt/ adj. wealthy, rich, or affluent, as persons or places. –**opulence**, n.

opus /ˈoʊpəs/ n. (pl. **opera** /ˈɒpərə/) a work or composition. Abbrev.: op.

or /ɔ/ conj. a particle used: **1.** to connect words, phrases, or clauses representing alternatives: *to be or not to be*. **2.** to connect alternative terms. **3.** often in correlation: *either…or; or…or; whether…or*.

-or[1] **1.** a suffix of nouns denoting a state or condition, a quality or property, etc. **2.** an alternative of **-our**, as in *color, odor*, etc.

-or[2] a suffix of nouns denoting someone who or something that does something, or has some particular function or office. In some cases it is used as an alternative or a substitute for **-er**[1], especially in legal terms (often correlative with forms in **-ee**), as in *lessor, lessee*.

oracle /ˈɒrəkəl/ n. any person or thing serving as an agency of divine communication.

oral /ˈɔrəl/ adj. **1.** uttered by the mouth; spoken. **2.** employing speech, as teachers or methods of teaching. **3.** of or relating to the mouth.

orange /ˈɒrɪndʒ/ n. **1.** a common citrus fruit. **2.** a colour between yellow and red in the spectrum; reddish yellow. –adj. **3.** of or relating to the orange. **4.** reddish yellow.

orange pekoe /ˈpikoʊ/ n. a black tea composed of only the smallest top leaves.

orange stick n. a small stick used in manicure.

orangutan /əˈræŋətæn/ n. a large, long-armed anthropoid ape. Also, **orang-outang**, **orang-utan**.

oration /ɒˈreɪʃən/ n. a formal speech, especially one delivered on a special occasion.

orator /ˈɒrətə/ n. a public speaker, especially one of great eloquence.

oratory /ˈɒrətri/ n. the art of an orator.

orb /ɔb/ n. a sphere or globe.

orbit /ˈɔbət/ n. **1.** the elliptical or curved path described by a planet, satellite, etc., about a body, as the earth or sun. –v.t. **2.** to move or travel in an orbital path around.

orchard /ˈɔtʃəd/ n. a place where fruit trees are grown.

orchestra /ˈɔkəstrə/ n. a group of performers on various musical instruments. –**orchestral**, adj.

orchestrate /ˈɔkəstreɪt/ v.t. **1.** to compose or arrange (music) for performance by an orchestra. **2.** to put together cohesively. –**orchestration**, n.

orchid /ˈɔkəd/ n. a tropical plant noted for its beautiful flowers.

ordain /ɔˈdeɪn/ v.t. to appoint authoritatively; decree; enact.

ordeal /ɔˈdil, ˈɔdil/ n. any severe test or trial.

order /ˈɔdə/ n. **1.** an authoritative direction, injunction, command, or mandate. **2.** the disposition of things following one after another. **3.** a condition in which everything is in its proper place. **4.** proper or satisfactory condition. **5.** any class, kind, or sort. **6.** a direction or commission to make, provide or furnish something. **7.** a quantity of goods purchased. **8.** a written direction to pay money or deliver goods. **9.** *Biol.* the usual major subdivision of a class or subclass. –v.t. **10.** to give an order, direction, or command to. **11.** to give an order for. **12.** to regulate, conduct, or manage. –phr. **13. in order that**, to the end that. **14. in order to**, as a means to. **15. in short order**, speedily; promptly. **16. on order**, ordered but not yet received.

orderly /ˈɔdəli/ adj. **1.** arranged or disposed in order, in regular sequence, or in a tidy manner. **2.** characterised by or observant of order, rule, or discipline. –n. (pl. **-lies**) **3.** a person employed, as in a hospital, for general duties.

ordinal number /ˈɔdənəl/ n. any of the numbers *first, second, third*, etc., which indicate the order in which things occur.

ordinance /ˈɔdənəns/ n. **1.** an authoritative rule or command. **2.** a public injunction or regulation.

ordinary /ˈɔdənəri, ˈɔdənri/, *Orig. US* /-nɛri/ adj. **1.** such as is commonly met with; of the usual kind. **2.** somewhat inferior. –phr. **3. out of the ordinary**, unusual or special: *his new car is nothing out of the ordinary*.

ordnance /ˈɔdnəns/ n. military weapons of all kinds with their equipment, supplies, etc.

ordure /ˈɔdʒʊə/ n. filth; dung; excrement.

ore /ɔ/ n. a metal-bearing mineral or rock.

oregano /ɒrəˈɡanoʊ/ n. a plant of the mint family, used in cookery.

organ /ˈɔɡən/ n. **1.** a keyboard instrument consisting of one or more sets of pipes sounded by means of compressed air. **2.** (in an animal or a plant) a part or member, as the heart, having some specific function.

organdie /ˈɔɡəndi/ n. (pl. **-dies**) a fine, thin stiff cotton fabric.

organic /ɔˈɡænɪk/ adj. **1.** *Chem.* denoting or relating to a class of compounds consisting of all compounds of carbon except for its oxides, sulphides, and metal carbonates. Compare **inorganic** (def. 2). **2.** characteristic of, relating to, or derived from living organisms. **3.** of or relating to farming which does not use chemical fertilisers or pesticides. **4.** of or relating to an organ or the organs of an animal or plant. **5.** characterised by the systematic arrangement of parts.

organisation /ˌɔgənaɪˈzeɪʃən/ *n.* **1.** the act or process of organising. **2.** the state or manner of being organised. **3.** any organised whole. **4.** the administrative personnel or apparatus of a business. Also, **organization.** –**organisational,** *adj.*

organise /ˈɔgənaɪz/ *v.t.* **1.** to systematise. **2.** to give organic structure or character to. **3.** to build a trade union among. –*v.i.* **4.** to combine in an organised company, party, or the like. Also, **organize.**

organism /ˈɔgənɪzəm/ *n.* any form of animal or plant life.

organo- a word element meaning 'organ' or 'organic'.

organza /ɔˈgænzə/ *n.* a fabric made from a mixture of silk or nylon with cotton.

orgasm /ˈɔgæzəm/ *n. Physiol.* a complex series of responses of the genital organs and skin at the culmination of a sexual act.

orgy /ˈɔdʒi/ *n.* (*pl.* **-gies**) **1.** a gathering where people engage in unbridled sexual activity. **2.** wild, drunken, or licentious festivities or revelry.

orient /ˈɔriənt, ˈɒ-/ *v.t.* **1.** → **orientate.** –*phr.* **2. the Orient,** the East, comprising the countries to the east (and south-east) of the Mediterranean.

oriental /ɔriˈɛntl, ɒri-/ *adj.* (*sometimes upper case*) of, relating to, or characteristic of the Orient or East.

orientate /ˈɔriəntæt, ˈɔri-/ *v.t.* to adjust with relation to, or bring into due relation to, surroundings, circumstances, facts, etc. –**orientation,** *n.*

orienteering /ɔriənˈtɪərɪŋ/ *n.* a sport in which competitors race over a course consisting of a number of sites which must be located with the aid of maps, compasses, etc.

orifice /ˈɒrəfəs/ *n.* a mouth-like opening or hole.

origami /ɔrəˈgami/ *n.* the art of folding paper into shapes of flowers, birds, etc.

origin /ˈɒrədʒən/ *n.* **1.** that from which anything arises or is derived; the source. **2.** rise or derivation from a particular source. **3.** birth; parentage; extraction.

original /əˈrɪdʒənəl/ *adj.* **1.** belonging or relating to the origin or beginning of something, or to a thing at its beginning. **2.** new; fresh; novel. **3.** arising or proceeding from a thing itself, or independently of anything else. **4.** being that from which a copy, a translation, or the like is made. –*n.* **5.** a primary form or type from which varieties are derived. –**originality,** *n.*

originate /əˈrɪdʒəneɪt/ *v.i.* **1.** to take its origin or rise; arise; spring. –*v.t.* **2.** to give origin or rise to; initiate; invent.

orlon /ˈɔlɒn/ *n.* (*from trademark*) a synthetic acrylic fabric.

ornament *n.* /ˈɔnəmənt/ **1.** an accessory, article, or detail used to beautify the appearance or general effect. –*v.t.* /ˈɔnəmɛnt/ **2.** to furnish with ornaments. **3.** to be an ornament to. –**ornamental,** *adj.* –**ornamentation,** *n.*

ornate /ɔˈneɪt/ *adj.* elaborately adorned.

ornitho- a word element meaning 'bird'. Also, **ornith-.**

ornithology /ɔnəˈθɒlədʒi/ *n.* the branch of zoology that deals with birds. –**ornithologist,** *n.*

oro- a word element meaning 'mountain'.

orphan /ˈɔfən/ *n.* **1.** a child bereaved by death of both parents, or, less commonly, of one parent. –*v.t.* **2.** to bereave of parents or a parent.

orphanage /ˈɔfənɪdʒ/ *n.* an institution for orphans.

ortho- a word element meaning 'straight', 'upright', 'right', 'correct'.

orthodontics /ɔθəˈdɒntɪks/ *n.* the branch of dentistry that is concerned with the correction of irregularities of the teeth or jaw. –**orthodontist,** *n.*

orthodox /ˈɔθədɒks/ *adj.* of, relating to, or conforming to the approved or accepted form of any doctrine, philosophy, ideology, etc. –**orthodoxy,** *n.*

orthopaedics /ɔθəˈpidɪks/ *n.* the correction or cure of deformities and diseases of the skeletal system. Also, **orthopedics.**

orthoptics /ɔˈθɒptɪks/ *n.* the study and treatment of abnormality of eye muscle function.

orthosis /ɔˈθəʊsəs/ *n.* (*pl.* **-thoses** /-ˈθəʊsiz/) a device applied to the body to modify position or motion, as a supporting collar.

orthotic /ɔˈθɒtɪk/ *adj.* **1.** of or relating to an orthosis. –*n.* **2.** an orthotic device, especially one for the foot.

-ory[1] a suffix of adjectives meaning 'having the function or effect of'.

-ory[2] a suffix of nouns denoting especially a place or an instrument or thing for some purpose.

oscillate /ˈɒsəleɪt/ *v.i.* **1.** to swing or move to and fro, as a pendulum does; vibrate. **2.** to have, produce, or generate oscillations.

oscillation /ɒsəˈleɪʃən/ *n.* **1.** the act or fact of oscillating. **2.** a single swing, or movement in one direction, of an oscillating body, etc.

-ose[1] an adjective suffix meaning 'full of', 'abounding in', 'given to', 'like'.

-ose[2] a noun termination used to form chemical terms, especially names of sugars and other carbohydrates.

-osis (*pl.* **-oses**) a noun suffix denoting action, process, state, condition, etc.

-osity a noun suffix equivalent to **-ose**[1] (or **-ous**) plus **-ity**.

osmium /ˈɒzmiəm/ *n.* a hard, heavy, metallic element used for electric-light filaments, etc. *Symbol:* Os

osmosis /ɒzˈməʊsəs/ *n.* the diffusion of fluids through membranes or porous partitions.

ostensible /ɒsˈtɛnsəbəl/ *adj.* professed; pretended.

ostentation /ɒstɛnˈteɪʃən/ *n.* pretentious show. –**ostentatious,** *adj.*

osteo- a word element meaning 'bone'. Also, (*before vowels*), **oste-.**

osteoarthritis /ˌɒstioʊɑˈθraɪtəs/ *n.* a degenerative type of chronic arthritis. *Abbrev.:* OA

osteopathy /ɒstiˈɒpəθi/ *n.* the curing of disease by manipulation of parts of the body. –**osteopath** /ˈɒstiəˌpæθ/, *n.*

osteoporosis /ˌɒstioʊpəˈroʊsəs/ n. a condition in which bones become thin and brittle, common especially in women past the menopause.

ostracise /ˈɒstrəsaɪz/ v.t. to exclude by general consent from society, privileges, etc. Also, **ostracize**.

ostrich /ˈɒstrɪtʃ/ n. a large flightless bird.

other /ˈʌðə/ adj. **1.** additional or further. **2.** different in nature or kind. **3.** being the remaining one or ones. –pron. **4.** the other one. **5.** another person or thing. –phr. **6. every other**, every alternate. **7. the other day** (**night**, etc.), in recent days (nights, etc.).

otherwise /ˈʌðəwaɪz/ adv. **1.** under other circumstances. **2.** in another manner; differently. **3.** in other respects.

-otic an adjectival form for nouns ending in **-osis**, as *hypnotic* from *hypnosis*, *neurotic* from *neurosis*.

oto- a word element meaning 'ear'.

otter /ˈɒtə/ n. any of various furred, carnivorous, aquatic mammals with webbed feet.

ottoman /ˈɒtəmən/ n. (pl. **-mans**) a cushioned footstool.

ouch /aʊtʃ/ interj. an exclamation expressing sudden pain.

ought /ɔt/ v. (aux.) **1.** was (were) or am (is, are) bound in duty or moral obligation. **2.** was (am, etc.) bound or required on any ground, as of justice, probability, expediency, etc. (usually followed by an infinitive with *to*): *he ought to be punished*.

ouija /ˈwidʒə, -dʒi/ n. (from trademark) a board or table covering marked with words, letters of the alphabet, etc., used during seances.

ounce /aʊns/ n. a unit of weight in the imperial system, equal to about 29 grams.

our /ˈaʊə/ pron., adj. the possessive form corresponding to **we** and **us**, used before a noun. Compare **ours**.

-our a suffix of nouns denoting state or condition, a quality or property, etc. Also, **-or**.

ours /ˈaʊəz/ pron. a form of **our** used without a noun following.

ourselves /aʊəˈsɛlvz/ pl. pron. **1.** a reflexive form of **we**: *we hurt ourselves*. **2.** an emphatic form of **us** or **we** used: **a.** as object: *we used it for ourselves*. **b.** in opposition to a subject or object.

-ous an adjective suffix meaning 'full of', 'characterised by', 'like', etc.

oust /aʊst/ v.t. to expel from a place or position occupied.

out /aʊt/ adv. **1.** forth from, away from, or not in a place, position, state, etc. **2.** into the open. **3.** to exhaustion, extinction, or conclusion; to the end. –adj. **4.** no longer or not burning or furnishing light; extinguished. **5.** not in vogue or fashion. **6.** into or in public notice or knowledge. **7.** on strike. **8.** so as to project or extend. **9.** from a source, ground or cause, material, etc. (with *of*). **10.** in or into a state of dispute. **11.** so as to deprive or be deprived (with *of*). **12.** having used the last (with *of*). **13.** with completeness or effectiveness. **14.** so as to make illegible or indecipherable. **15.** incorrect or inaccurate. **16.** lacking; without. **17.** unconscious; senseless. **18.** not in office or employment; unemployed. **19.** finished; ended. **20.** external; exterior; outer. **21.** (of a homosexual) known publicly to be such. –prep. **22.** out or forth from. **23.** outside; on the exterior of; beyond. –n. **24.** a means of escaping. –v.t. **25.** to expose someone, especially a public figure, as homosexual. –phr. **26. out of it**, Colloq. incapacitated as a result of taking drugs or alcohol.

out- prefixal use of **out** adverb, preposition or adjective, occurring in various senses in compounds, as in *outcast*, *outcome*, *outside*, and serving also to form many transitive verbs denoting a going beyond, surpassing, or out-doing in the particular action indicated.

out-and-out adj. thoroughgoing; thorough; complete; unqualified.

outback /ˈaʊtbæk/ n. (sometimes upper case) remote, sparsely inhabited back country.

outbreak /ˈaʊtbreɪk/ n. **1.** a breaking out; an outburst. **2.** a public disturbance; a riot; an insurrection.

outbuilding /ˈaʊtbɪldɪŋ/ n. a detached building subordinate to a main building.

outburst /ˈaʊtbɜst/ n. a sudden and violent outpouring.

outcast /ˈaʊtkast/ n. a person who is cast out, as from home or society.

outcome /ˈaʊtkʌm/ n. that which results from something; the consequence or issue.

outcrop /ˈaʊtkrɒp/ n. an emerging part.

outcry /ˈaʊtkraɪ/ n. **1.** loud clamour. **2.** widespread protest or indignation.

outdated /ˈaʊtdeɪtəd/ adj. old-fashioned.

outdoors /aʊtˈdɔz/ adv. **1.** out of doors; in the open air. –n. **2. the outdoors**, the world outside buildings; the open air.

outer /ˈaʊtə/ adj. **1.** farther out; external; of or relating to the outside. –n. **2.** that part of a sportsground which is without shelter. –phr. **3. on the outer**, Colloq. excluded from the group; mildly ostracised.

outfit /ˈaʊtfɪt/ n. **1.** a set of articles for any purpose. –v.t. (**-fitted**, **-fitting**) **2.** to furnish with an outfit; fit out; equip.

outflow /ˈaʊtfloʊ/ n. **1.** that which flows out. **2.** any outward movement.

outgoing /ˈaʊtgoʊɪŋ/ adj. **1.** going out; departing. **2.** interested in and responsive to others. –n. **3.** (usu. pl.) an amount of money expended; outlay; expenses.

outgrowth /ˈaʊtgroʊθ/ n. **1.** a natural development, product, or result. **2.** an offshoot.

outing /ˈaʊtɪŋ/ n. an excursion.

outlandish /aʊtˈlændɪʃ/ adj. freakish.

outlaw /ˈaʊtlɔ/ n. **1.** a habitual criminal. –v.t. **2.** to deprive of the benefits and protection of the law. **3.** to prohibit.

outlay n. /ˈaʊtleɪ/ **1.** an amount expended. –v.t. /aʊtˈleɪ/ (**-laid**, **-laying**) **2.** to expend, as money.

outlet /ˈaʊtlɛt, -lət/ n. **1.** an opening or passage by which anything is let out; a vent or exit. **2.** Commerce **a.** a market for goods. **b.** (of a wholesaler or manufacturer) a shop, merchant, or agency selling one's goods.

outline /ˈaʊtlaɪn/ n. **1.** the line, real or apparent, by which a figure or object is defined or bounded; the contour. **2.** a general sketch, account or report, indicating only the main features. –v.t. **3.** to draw the outline of, or draw in

outline, as a figure or object. **4.** to give an outline of (a subject, etc.).

outlook /'aʊtlʊk/ n. the view or prospect from a place.

out-of-the-way adj. **1.** remote; secluded. **2.** unusual.

outpatient /'aʊtpeɪʃənt/ n. a patient receiving treatment at a hospital but not being an inmate. Also, **out-patient**.

outpost /'aʊtpoʊst/ n. any remote settlement.

output /'aʊtpʊt/ n. **1.** the quantity or amount produced, as in a given time. **2.** Computers information obtained from a computer on the completion of a calculation. –v.t. (**-put, -putting**) **3.** to supply from a computer database, file, etc.: we can output the data; I'll output copies for the meeting.

outrage /'aʊtreɪdʒ/ n. **1.** any gross violation of law or decency. –v.t. (**-raged, -raging**) **2.** to affect with a sense of offended right or decency; shock. –**outrageous**, adj. –**outraged**, adj.

outright /'aʊtraɪt/ adj. **1.** complete or total. –adv. **2.** completely; entirely.

outset /'aʊtset/ n. the beginning or start.

outside n. /'aʊtsaɪd/ **1.** the outer side, surface, or part; the exterior. **2.** the space without or beyond an enclosure, boundary, etc. –adj. /'aʊtsaɪd/ **3.** being, acting, done, or originating beyond an enclosure, boundary, etc. **4.** situated on or relating to the outside; exterior; external. **5.** not belonging to or connected with an institution, society, etc. **6.** extremely unlikely or remote. –adv. /aʊt'saɪd/ **7.** on or to the outside, exterior, or space without. –prep. /aʊt'saɪd/ **8.** on or towards the outside of. –phr. **9. at the outside**, at the utmost limit.

outsider /aʊt'saɪdə/ n. someone not belonging to a particular group, set, party, etc.

outskirts /'aʊtskɜːts/ pl. n. outer or bordering parts or districts, as of a city.

outsource /'aʊtsɔːs/ v.t. to contract (work) outside the company rather than employ more in-house staff. –**outsourcing**, n.

outspoken /'aʊtspoʊkən/ adj. free or unreserved in speech.

outstanding /aʊt'stændɪŋ/ adj. prominent; conspicuous; striking.

outstation /'aʊtsteɪʃən/ n. any remote post.

outstrip /aʊt'strɪp/ v.t. (**-stripped, -stripping**) to outdo; surpass; excel.

out-tray n. a tray or other receptacle for outgoing letters, files, job assignments, etc., which have received attention.

outward /'aʊtwəd/ adj. **1.** proceeding or directed towards the outside or exterior. **2.** of or relating to the outside, outer surface, or exterior. –adv. **3.** → **outwards**.

outwardly /'aʊtwədli/ adv. as regards appearance or outward manifestation.

outwards /'aʊtwədz/ adv. towards the outside; out. Also, **outward**.

outwit /aʊt'wɪt/ v.t. (**-witted, -witting**) to get the better of by superior ingenuity or cleverness.

ouzo /'uːzoʊ/ n. an aniseed-flavoured liqueur of Greece.

ova /'oʊvə/ n. plural of **ovum**.

oval /'oʊvəl/ adj. **1.** egg-shaped. –n. **2.** any of various oval things. **3.** a flat area (sometimes elliptical) on which sporting activities can take place.

ovary /'oʊvəri/ n. (pl. **-ries**) Anat., Zool. the female reproductive gland. –**ovarian**, adj.

ovate /'oʊveɪt/ adj. egg-shaped.

ovation /oʊ'veɪʃən/ n. enthusiastic applause.

oven /'ʌvən/ n. a chamber or receptacle for baking or heating.

over /'oʊvə/ prep. **1.** above in place or position; higher up than. **2.** above and to the other side of. **3.** on or upon; so as to rest on or cover. **4.** here and there on or in. **5.** in excess of, or more than. **6.** in preference to. **7.** throughout the duration of. **8.** in reference to, concerning, or about. **9.** by the agency of. –adv. **10.** over the top or upper surface, or edge of something. **11.** so as to cover the surface, or affect the whole surface. **12.** through a region, area, etc. **13.** across any intervening space. **14.** from beginning to end, or all through. **15.** from one person, party, etc., to another. **16.** so as to bring the upper end or side down or under. **17.** in repetition. **18.** in excess or addition. –adj. **19.** higher in authority, station, etc. **20.** serving or intended, as an outer covering. **21.** in excess or addition; surplus; extra. **22.** at an end; done; past. –n. **23.** an amount in excess or addition; an extra. **24.** Cricket the number of balls delivered between successive changes of bowlers. –phr. **25. all over**, **a.** thoroughly; entirely. **b.** done with; finished. **26. all over with**, done with; finished. **27. be over something**, Colloq. to be no longer obsessed by something. **28. be so over something**, Colloq. to be fed up with something. **29. over against**, **a.** opposite to; in front of. **b.** as contrasted with or distinguished from. **30. over and above**, in addition to; besides.

over- prefixal use of **over** preposition, adverb or adjective, occurring in various senses in compounds, especially employed, with the sense of 'over the limit', 'to excess', 'too much', 'too', to form verbs, adjectives, adverbs, and nouns. A hyphen, commonly absent from old or well-established formations, is often used in new coinages, or in any words whose compound parts it may be desirable to set off distinctly.

overall adj. /'oʊvərɔːl/ **1.** covering or including everything. –adv. /oʊvər'ɔːl/ **2.** covering or including everything.

overalls /'oʊvərɔːlz/ pl. n. loose trousers, usually with an attached top or shoulder straps.

overarm /'oʊvərɑːm/ adj. **1.** performed with the arm being raised above the shoulder, as bowling or swimming. –adv. **2.** in an overarm manner.

overawe /oʊvər'ɔː/ v.t. to restrain or subdue by inspiring awe.

overbalance /oʊvə'bæləns/ v. (**-anced, -ancing**) –v.t. **1.** to cause to lose balance or to fall or turn over. –v.i. **2.** to lose (one's balance).

overbearing /oʊvə'bɛərɪŋ/ adj. domineering; dictatorial; haughtily or rudely arrogant.

overboard /'oʊvəbɔːd/ adv. over the side of a ship or boat, especially into or in the water.

overcapitalise /oʊvə'kæpətəlaɪz/ v.t. **1.** to fix the nominal capital (total amount of securities) of (a company) in excess of the limits set by law or by sound financial policy. **2.** to over-estimate the capital value of (a business property or enterprise). **3.** to provide an excessive amount of capital for (a business enterprise). Also, **overcapitalize**.

overcast /ˈoʊvəkɑst/ *adj.* **1.** overspread with clouds, as the sky; cloudy. **2.** dark; gloomy. –*v.* (**-cast, -casting**) –*v.t.* **3.** to overcloud, darken, or make gloomy. –*v.i.* **4.** to become cloudy or dark.

overcharge *v.* (**-charged, -charging**) –*v.t.* /oʊvəˈtʃɑdʒ/ **1.** to charge (a person) too high a price. –*v.i.* /oʊvəˈtʃɑdʒ/ **2.** to make an excessive charge. –*n.* /ˈoʊvətʃɑdʒ/ **3.** a charge in excess of a just price.

overcoat /ˈoʊvəkoʊt/ *n.* **1.** a coat worn over the ordinary clothing, as in cold weather. **2.** an additional coat of paint applied for protection.

overcome /oʊvəˈkʌm/ *v.* (**-came, -come, -coming**) –*v.t.* **1.** to get the better of in a struggle or conflict; conquer; defeat. –*v.i.* **2.** to gain the victory; conquer.

overdo /oʊvəˈdu/ *v.t.* (**-did, -done, -doing**) **1.** to carry to excess or beyond the proper limit. **2.** to cook too much; overcook.

overdose *n.* /ˈoʊvədoʊs/ **1.** an excessive dose. –*v.i.* /oʊvəˈdoʊs/ **2.** to take an overdose of a drug.

overdraft /ˈoʊvədrɑft/ *n.* **1.** a draft in excess of one's credit balance. **2.** the amount of the excess. **3.** the act of overdrawing an account, as at a bank.

overdraw /oʊvəˈdrɔ/ *v.t.* (**-drew, -drawn, -drawing**) to draw upon (an account, allowance, etc.) in excess of the balance standing to one's credit or at one's disposal.

overdue /oʊvəˈdju/ *adj.* past due, as a belated train or a bill not paid by the assigned date.

overflow /oʊvəˈfloʊ/ *v.* (**-flowed, -flown, -flowing**) –*v.i.* **1.** to flow or run over, as rivers, water, etc. **2.** (fol. by *with*) to be filled or supplied in overflowing measure. –*v.t.* **3.** to flow over; flood; inundate. –*n.* **4.** that which flows or runs over. **5.** an excess. **6.** an outlet for excess liquid.

overgrow /oʊvəˈɡroʊ/ *v.* (**-grew, -grown, -growing**) –*v.t.* **1.** to grow over; cover with a growth of something. –*v.i.* **2.** to grow to excess; grow too large.

overhand /ˈoʊvəhænd/ *adj.* **1.** done or delivered overhand. –*adv.* **2.** with the hand over the object.

overhang *v.* (**-hung, -hanging**) –*v.t.* /oʊvəˈhæŋ/ **1.** to hang or be suspended over. **2.** to extend, project, or jut over. –*v.i.* /oʊvəˈhæŋ/ **3.** to hang over; project or jut out over something below. –*n.* /ˈoʊvəhæŋ/ **4.** an overhanging; a projection.

overhaul *v.t.* /oʊvəˈhɔl/ **1.** to investigate or examine thoroughly, as for repair. –*n.* /ˈoʊvəhɔl/ **2.** a thorough examination.

overhead *adv.* /oʊvəˈhɛd/ **1.** over one's head. –*adj.* /ˈoʊvəhɛd/ **2.** situated, operating, or passing overhead, aloft, or above. –*n.* /ˈoʊvəhɛd/ **3.** (*pl.*) the general cost of running a business. **4.** (*pl.*) the general cost which cannot be assigned to particular products or orders.

overhear /oʊvəˈhɪə/ *v.t.* (**-heard, -hearing**) to hear (speech, etc., or a speaker) without the speaker's intention or knowledge.

overkill /ˈoʊvəkɪl/ *n.* the use of more resources or energy than is necessary to achieve one's aim.

overlap *v.* (**-lapped, -lapping**) –*v.t.* /oʊvəˈlæp/ **1.** to cover and extend beyond (something else). **2.** to coincide in part with; correspond partly with. –*v.i.* /oʊvəˈlæp/ **3.** to lap over. –*n.* /ˈoʊvəlæp/ **4.** the extent or amount of overlapping. **5.** an overlapping part.

overleaf /oʊvəˈlif/ *adv.* on the other side of the page or sheet.

overlook /oʊvəˈlʊk/ *v.t.* **1.** to fail to notice, perceive, or consider. **2.** to afford a view down over. **3.** to look after, oversee, or supervise.

overnight *adv.* /oʊvəˈnaɪt/ **1.** during the night. **2.** suddenly; very quickly. –*adj.* /ˈoʊvənaɪt/ **3.** done, occurring, or continuing during the night. **4.** staying for one night. **5.** designed to be used one night or very few nights. **6.** occurring suddenly or rapidly.

overpass /ˈoʊvəpas/ *n.* a bridge over a road or railway.

overpower /oʊvəˈpaʊə/ *v.t.* to overwhelm.

overproof /ˈoʊvəpruf/ *adj.* containing a greater proportion of alcohol than proof spirit does.

overreach /oʊvəˈriʧ/ *v.t.* **1.** to reach or extend over or beyond. **2.** to defeat (oneself) by overdoing matters, often by excessive eagerness or cunning. –*v.i.* **3.** to reach too far.

overriding /ˈoʊvəraɪdɪŋ/ *adj.* prevailing over all other considerations.

overrule /oʊvəˈrul/ *v.t.* to rule against or disallow.

overrun *v.* (**-ran, -run, -running**) –*v.t.* /oʊvəˈrʌn/ **1.** to spread over rapidly and occupy. **2.** to exceed. –*v.i.* /oʊvəˈrʌn/ **3.** to run over; overflow. –*n.* /ˈoʊvərʌn/ **4.** an amount over-running or carried over; excess.

overseas *adv.* /oʊvəˈsiz/ **1.** over, across, or beyond the sea; abroad. –*adj.* /ˈoʊvəsiz/ **2.** situated beyond the sea.

oversee /oʊvəˈsi/ *v.t.* (**-saw, -seen, -seeing**) to direct (work or workers); supervise; manage.

overshadow /oʊvəˈʃædoʊ/ *v.t.* to tower over so as to cast a shadow over.

overshoot /oʊvəˈʃut/ *v.* (**-shot, -shooting**) –*v.t.* **1.** to shoot or go beyond (a point, limit, etc.). –*v.i.* **2.** to shoot over or too far.

oversight /ˈoʊvəsaɪt/ *n.* **1.** failure to notice or take into account. **2.** an omission or mistake. **3.** supervision; watchful care.

oversubscribed /ˈoʊvəsəbskraɪbd/ *adj.* (of share issues) having applications to buy exceeding the number of shares available.

overt /oʊˈvɜt, ˈoʊvɜt/ *adj.* open to view or knowledge; not concealed or secret.

overtake /oʊvəˈteɪk/ *v.* (**-took, -taken, -taking**) –*v.t.* **1.** to come up with or pass. **2.** to come upon suddenly or unexpectedly. –*v.i.* **3.** to pass another vehicle.

overthrow *v.t.* /oʊvəˈθroʊ/ (**-threw, -thrown, -throwing**) **1.** to depose as from a position of power; overcome, defeat, or vanquish. **2.** to throw over; upset; overturn. –*n.* /ˈoʊvəθroʊ/ **3.** the act of overthrowing. **4.** the resulting state.

overtime /ˈoʊvətaɪm/ *n.* **1.** time during which one works before or after regularly scheduled working hours; extra time. **2.** pay for such time.

overtone /'oʊvətoʊn/ *n.* (*usu. pl.*) additional meaning or implication.

overture /'oʊvətʃʊə/ *n.* **1.** an introductory part. **2.** an opening of negotiations, or a formal proposal or offer.

overturn /oʊvə'tɜn/ *v.t.* **1.** to overthrow. **2.** to turn over on its side, face, or back; upset. –*v.i.* **3.** to turn on its side, face, or back; upset; capsize.

overview /'oʊvəvju/ *n.* a general survey which avoids getting down to details.

overwhelm /oʊvə'wɛlm/ *v.t.* **1.** to overcome completely in mind or feeling. **2.** to vanquish; defeat, especially by force of numbers.

overwrought /'oʊvərɔt/ *adj.* worked up or excited excessively.

ovine /'oʊvaɪn/ *adj.* relating to, of the nature of, or like sheep.

oviparous /oʊ'vɪpərəs/ *adj.* producing eggs which hatch outside the mother's body.

ovoid /'oʊvɔɪd/ *adj.* egg-shaped; having the solid form of an egg.

ovulate /'ɒvjəleɪt/ *v.i.* to shed eggs from an ovary or ovarian follicle.

ovum /'oʊvəm/ *n.* (*pl.* **ova** /'oʊvə/) the female reproductive cell.

owe /oʊ/ *v.* (**owed**, **owing**) –*v.t.* **1.** to be indebted for. **2.** to be in debt to. –*v.i.* **3.** to be in debt.

owing /'oʊɪŋ/ *adj.* **1.** owed or due. –*phr.* **2. owing to**, **a.** on account of; because of. **b.** attributable to.

owl /aʊl/ *n.* any of numerous nocturnal birds of prey.

own /oʊn/ *adj.* **1.** belonging or relating to oneself or itself. –*v.t.* **2.** to have or hold in one's possession. **3.** to acknowledge or admit. –*v.i.* **4.** (oft. fol. by *up*) to confess. –*phr.* **5. come into one's own**, **a.** to receive an inheritance. **b.** to be in a situation where particular skills or attributes are evident. **6. get one's own back**,

to have revenge. **7. on one's own**, *Colloq.* on one's own account, responsibility, resources, etc.

ox /ɒks/ *n.* (*pl.* **oxen**) any member of the bovine family.

oxidant /'ɒksədənt/ *n.* the oxidising agent which supplies oxygen, or accepts electrons, in an oxidation reaction.

oxidate /'ɒksədeɪt/ *v.t.* to oxidise. –**oxidative**, *adj.*

oxidation /ɒksə'deɪʃən/ *n.* **1.** the act or process of oxidising. –*adj.* **2.** of or relating to oxidation: *an oxidation potential.*

oxide /'ɒksaɪd/ *n.* a compound, usually containing two elements only, one of which is oxygen.

oxidise /'ɒksədaɪz/ *v.t.* **1.** to convert (an element) into its oxide; to combine with oxygen. **2.** to cover with a coating of oxide, or rust. –*v.i.* **3.** to become oxidised. Also, **oxidize**.

oxygen /'ɒksədʒən/ *n.* a colourless, odourless gaseous element, constituting about one fifth of the volume of the atmosphere and present in a combined state throughout nature. *Symbol*: O

oxymoron /ɒksi'mɔːrɒn/ *n. Rhetoric* a figure of speech by which a locution produces an effect by a seeming self-contradiction, as in *cruel kindness* or *to make haste slowly*. –**oxymoronic** /ɒksimə'rɒnɪk/, *adj.*

oyez /oʊ'jɛs, oʊ'jɛz/ *interj.* hear! attend!

oyster /'ɔɪstə/ *n.* any of various edible marine bivalve molluscs.

Oz /ɒz/ *adj. Colloq.* Australian.

ozone /'oʊzoʊn/ *n. Chem.* a form of oxygen, O_3, having three atoms to the molecule.

ozone depletion *n.* a decline in the amount of ozone in the earth's stratosphere.

ozone layer *n.* a layer of ozone in one of the outer parts of the atmosphere, which partly blocks the harmful rays of the sun. Also, **ozonosphere**.

P, p

P, p /piː/ *n.* the 16th letter of the English alphabet.

pace /peɪs/ *n.* **1.** rate of stepping, or of movement in general. **2.** rate or style of doing anything. **3.** the distance covered in a single step. **4.** manner of stepping; gait. –*v.* (**paced, pacing**) –*v.t.* **5.** to set the pace for, as in racing. **6.** to traverse with paces or steps. –*v.i.* **7.** to walk, especially in a state of nervous excitement. –*phr.* **8. off the pace**, *Colloq.* behind the leader in a race or contest by the specified number of points, length of time, etc.: *two shots off the pace; 25 seconds off the pace.*

pacemaker /ˈpeɪsmeɪkə/ *n. Med.* an instrument implanted beneath the skin to control the rate of the heartbeat.

pachyderm /ˈpækɪdɜm/ *n.* any of the thick-skinned non-ruminant ungulates, as the elephant, hippopotamus, and rhinoceros.

pacific /pəˈsɪfɪk/ *adj.* **1.** peaceable; not warlike. **2.** peaceful; at peace.

pacifism /ˈpæsəfɪzəm/ *n.* opposition to war or violence of any kind. –**pacifist**, *n.*

pacify /ˈpæsəfaɪ/ *v.t.* (**-fied, -fying**) to bring into a state of peace; quiet; calm.

pack[1] /pæk/ *n.* **1.** a quantity of anything wrapped or tied up; a parcel. **2.** a load or burden, as one carried by a person or animal. **3.** a company of certain animals of the same kind. **4.** a group of things, usually abstract. **5.** a complete set, as of playing cards. –*v.t.* **6.** to make into a pack or bundle. **7.** to make into a group or compact mass, as animals, ice, etc. **8.** to press or crowd together within; cram. **9.** (sometimes fol. by *off, away*, etc.) to send off summarily. –*v.i.* **10.** to pack goods, etc., in compact form. **11.** to crowd together, as persons, etc.

pack[2] /pæk/ *v.t.* to collect, arrange, or manipulate (a deliberative body) so as to serve one's own purposes.

package /ˈpækɪdʒ/ *n.* **1.** a bundle or parcel. **2.** a unit, group of parts, or the like, considered as a single entity. –*v.t.* (**-aged, -aging**) **3.** to put into wrappings or a container. **4.** to combine as a single entity. **5.** to present (a person), usually a figure in public life, in a particular way, especially to the media.

packaging /ˈpækɪdʒɪŋ/ *n.* **1.** the box, wrapper, plastic sleeve, etc., in which an item is presented for sale. **2.** the manner in which a public figure or issue is presented, especially to the media.

packet /ˈpækət/ *n.* **1.** a small pack or package. **2.** Also, **data packet**. *Computers* one of several units of data, each including a destination address, into which a message may be divided before being sent over a network link, the components being reassembled at the receiving end to form the original message.

pack ice *n.* an area in polar seas of large blocks of ice driven together over a long period by winds, currents, etc.

pact /pækt/ *n.* an agreement; a compact.

pad[1] /pæd/ *n.* **1.** a cushion-like mass of some soft material, for comfort, protection, or stuffing. **2.** Also, **writing pad**. a number of sheets of paper glued together at one edge. **3.** one of the cushion-like protuberances on the underside of the feet of dogs, foxes, and some other animals. –*v.t.* (**padded, padding**) **4.** to furnish, protect, fill out, or stuff with a pad or padding. **5.** to expand (writing or speech) with unnecessary words or matter.

pad[2] /pæd/ *n.* **1.** a dull sound, as of footsteps on the ground. **2.** a path worn by animals. –*v.i.* (**padded, padding**) **3.** to travel on foot.

paddle[1] /ˈpædl/ *n.* **1.** a short oar held in the hands (not resting in the rowlock) and used especially for propelling canoes. –*v.i.* **2.** to propel a canoe or the like by using a paddle. **3.** to row lightly or gently with oars. –*v.t.* **4.** to propel with a paddle.

paddle[2] /ˈpædl/ *v.i.* to dabble or play in or as in shallow water.

paddleboarding /ˈpædlbɔdɪŋ/ *n.* the activity or sport of riding a stand-up paddleboard. Also, **paddleboard surfing**.

paddock /ˈpædək, ˈpædɪk/ *n.* an enclosed field or piece of land.

paddy /ˈpædi/ *n.* (*pl.* **-dies**) a wet, often flooded field on which rice is grown.

paddywhack /ˈpædiwæk/ *n. Colloq.* **1.** Also, **paddy**. a rage. **2.** a spanking.

pademelon /ˈpædimɛlən/ *n.* any of several species of small wallabies, found in areas of thick scrub or dense, moist undergrowth of eastern Australia and Tasmania. Also, **paddymelon**.

padlock /ˈpædlɒk/ *n.* a portable or detachable lock.

padre /ˈpadreɪ/ *n.* a military or naval chaplain.

paed- a word element meaning 'child'. Also, **paedi-, paedo-**; *US*, **ped-**.

paediatrics /pidiˈætrɪks/ *n.* the study and treatment of the diseases of children. Also, **pediatrics**. –**paediatrician**, *n.* –**paediatric**, *adj.*

paedophile /ˈpɛdəfaɪl, ˈpɪd-/ *n.* an adult who engages in sexual activities with children. Also, **pedophile**. –**paedophilia**, *n.*

pagan /ˈpeɪgən/ *n.* **1.** an irreligious or heathenish person. –*adj.* **2.** heathen; irreligious.

page[1] /peɪdʒ/ *n.* **1.** one side of a leaf of a book, manuscript, letter, or the like. **2.** *Computing* a fixed-length block of data displayed on a computer screen.

page[2] /peɪdʒ/ *n.* **1.** a boy servant or attendant. –*v.t.* (**paged, paging**) **2.** to seek (a person) by calling out their name.

pageant /ˈpædʒənt/ *n.* an elaborate public spectacle. –**pageantry**, *n.*

pagoda /pəˈgoʊdə/ *n.* (in India, Burma, China, etc.) a temple or sacred building, usually more or less pyramidal.

paid /peɪd/ *v.* past tense and past participle of **pay**.

pail /peɪl/ *n.* a bucket.

pain /peɪn/ *n.* **1.** bodily or mental distress. **2.** a distressing sensation in a particular part of the body. **3.** (*pl.*) laborious or careful efforts. –*v.t.* **4.** to inflict pain on; hurt; distress.

painkiller /ˈpeɪnkɪlə/ *n.* a drug which relieves pain. –**painkilling**, *adj.*

painstaking /'peɪnzteɪkɪŋ/ *adj.* assiduously careful.

paint /peɪnt/ *n.* **1.** a substance composed of solid colouring matter mixed with a liquid vehicle or medium, and applied as a coating. *–v.t.* **2.** to execute (a picture, design, etc.) in colours or pigment. **3.** to coat, cover, or decorate (something) with colour or pigment. **4.** to apply like paint, as a liquid medicine, etc. **–painting**, *n.*

painter¹ /'peɪntə/ *n.* someone who paints.

painter² /'peɪntə/ *n.* a rope, usually at the bow, for fastening a boat to a ship, stake, etc.

pair /peə/ *n.* (*pl.* **pairs** *or* **pair**) **1.** two things of a kind, matched for use together. *–v.t.* **2.** to arrange in pairs. **3.** to join in a pair; mate. *–v.i.* **4.** (oft. fol. by *off*) to separate into pairs.

paisley /'peɪzli/ *n.* **1.** a soft fabric made from wool and woven with a colourful and minutely detailed pattern. **2.** any pattern similar to that woven on paisley.

pal /pæl/ *n. Colloq.* a comrade; a chum.

palace /'pæləs/ *n.* the official residence of a sovereign, a bishop, etc. **–palatial**, *adj.*

palaeo- a prefix meaning 'old', 'ancient'. Also, **palae-**, **paleo-**.

palaeontology /ˌpæliɒn'tɒlədʒi, ˌpeɪ-/ *n.* the science of the forms of life existing in former geological periods, as represented by fossil animals and plants. Also, **paleontology**. **–palaeontologist**, *n.*

palatable /'pælətəbəl/ *adj.* agreeable to the taste.

palate /'pælət/ *n.* **1.** the roof of the mouth. **2.** the sense of taste. **–palatal**, *adj.*

palatine /'pælətaɪn/ *adj.* possessing or characterised by royal privileges.

palaver /pə'lavə/ *n.* **1.** a discussion or conference, especially a long and tedious one. **2.** any talk or activity regarded as unnecessary or too lengthy.

pale¹ /peɪl/ *adj.* **1.** of a whitish appearance; without intensity of colour. *–v.t., v.i.* **2.** to make or become pale.

pale² /peɪl/ *n.* **1.** a stake or picket, as of a fence. **2.** a barrier.

palette /'pælət/ *n.* a thin, usually oval or oblong, board or tablet with a thumb hole at one end, used by painters to lay and mix colours on.

palindrome /'pæləndroʊm/ *n.* a word or phrase which reads exactly the same forwards and backwards, as *madam, I'm Adam*. **–palindromic** /pælən'drɒmɪk/, *adj.*

paling /'peɪlɪŋ/ *n.* a long pointed piece of wood, especially as part of a fence.

palisade /pælə'seɪd/ *n.* a fence of pales or stakes set firmly in the ground, as for enclosure or defence.

pall¹ /pɔl/ *n.* **1.** a cloth, often of velvet, for spreading over a coffin, or tomb. **2.** something that covers, shrouds, or overspreads, especially with darkness or gloom.

pall² /pɔl/ *v.i.* (fol. by *on* or *upon*) to have a wearying effect.

pallbearer /'pɔlbeərə/ *n.* one of those who carry or attend the coffin at a funeral.

pallet /'pælət/ *n.* a movable platform on which goods are placed for storage or transportation.

palliate /'pælieɪt/ *v.t.* **1.** to cause (an offence, etc.) to appear less grave or heinous; extenuate; excuse. **2.** to mitigate or alleviate. **–palliative**, *adj.*

palliative care /'pæliətɪv/ *n. Med.* the total care of patients whose disease is not responsive to curative treatment, including attention to the needs of their family, etc.

pallid /'pæləd/ *adj.* pale. **–pallor**, *n.*

palm¹ /pam/ *n.* **1.** that part of the inner surface of the hand which extends from the wrist to the bases of the fingers. *–v.t.* **2.** to conceal in the palm, as in cheating at cards.

palm² /pam/ *n.* **1.** a tropical tall, unbranched tree surmounted by a crown of large fan-shaped leaves. **2.** a palm leaf as an emblem of victory.

palmistry /'paməstri/ *n.* the art or practice of telling fortunes and interpreting character by the lines and configurations of the palm of the hand. **–palmist**, *n.*

palmtop /'pamtɒp/ *n.* a small handheld personal computer.

palomino /pælə'minoʊ/ *n.* (*pl.* **-nos**) a tan or cream-coloured horse with a white mane and tail. Also, **palamino**.

palpable /'pælpəbəl/ *adj.* **1.** readily or plainly seen, heard, perceived, etc.; obvious. **2.** able to be touched or felt.

palpate /'pælpeɪt/ *v.t.* to examine by the sense of touch.

palpitate /'pælpəteɪt/ *v.i.* to pulsate with unnatural rapidity, as the heart. **–palpitation**, *n.*

palsy /'pɔlzi/ *n.* paralysis.

paltry /'pɔltri/ *adj.* (**-trier**, **-triest**) trifling; petty: *a paltry sum.*

pamper /'pæmpə/ *v.t.* to indulge.

pamphlet /'pæmflət/ *n.* a short publication; a booklet.

pan¹ /pæn/ *n.* **1.** a dish commonly of metal, usually broad and shallow. **2.** a depression in the ground, natural or artificial, containing salt water, mineral salts, etc. *–v.t.* (**panned**, **panning**) **3.** to wash (auriferous gravel, sand, etc.) in a pan, to separate the gold or other heavy valuable metal. **4.** *Colloq.* to criticise or reprimand severely.

pan² /pæn/ *v.i.* (**panned**, **panning**) *Film, TV, etc.* (of a camera) to move continuously while shooting.

panacea /pænə'siə/ *n.* **1.** a remedy for all diseases; cure-all. **2.** a solution to all problems: *technology is not the panacea some thought it would be.* **–panacean**, *adj.*

panache /pə'næʃ, -'naʃ/ *n.* a grand or flamboyant manner.

pancake /'pænkeɪk/ *n.* a thin flat cake from batter.

pancreas /'pæŋkriəs/ *n.* a gland situated near the stomach. **–pancreatic**, *adj.*

panda /'pændə/ *n.* a large, black-and-white, bear-like animal which is found mainly in China.

pandemic /pæn'demɪk/ *adj.* (of a disease) prevalent throughout an entire country or continent, or the whole world.

pandemic influenza A (H1N1) /pænˌdemɪk ˌɪnfluˌenzə 'eɪ (eɪtʃ wʌn 'ɛn wʌn)/ *n.* an influenza virus affecting pigs, which can be transmitted from pigs to humans and then transmitted by human-to-human contact, especially the H1N1 subtype of the influenza A virus; symptoms include fever, a sore throat and coughing. Also, **pandemic (H1N1)**, **human swine influenza**.

pandemonium /pændə'mouniəm/ *n.* a place of riotous uproar or lawless confusion.

pander /'pændə/ *v.i.* (fol. by *to*) to indulge.

pane /peɪn/ *n.* **1.** one of the divisions of a window, etc., consisting of a single plate of glass in a frame. **2.** *Philately* a section of a sheet of postage stamps.

panegyric /pænɪ'dʒɪrɪk/ *n.* an oration, discourse, or writing in praise of a person or thing.

panel /'pænəl/ *n.* **1.** a distinct portion or division. **2.** a broad strip of the same or another material set vertically, as for ornament, in or on a woman's dress, etc. **3.** a surface or section of a machine on which controls, dials, etc., are mounted. **4.** the body of persons composing a jury. –*v.t.* (**-elled**, **-elling**) **5.** to arrange in, or furnish with, panels.

pang /pæŋ/ *n.* a sharp pain.

panic /'pænɪk/ *n.* **1.** a sudden demoralising terror, with or without clear cause, often as affecting a group of persons or animals. –*v.* (**-icked**, **-icking**) –*v.t.* **2.** to affect with panic. –*v.i.* **3.** to be stricken with panic.

panoply /'pænəpli/ *n.* (*pl.* **-lies**) a complete covering or array of something.

panorama /pænə'ramə/ *n.* an unobstructed view or prospect over a wide area. –**panoramic**, *adj.*

pansy /'pænzi/ *n.* **1.** a type of garden plant with white, yellow, or purple velvety flowers. **2.** *Colloq.* **a.** an effeminate man. **b.** a male homosexual.

pant /pænt/ *v.i.* **1.** to breathe hard and quickly, as after exertion. –*n.* **2.** the act of panting. **3.** a short, quick, laboured effort of breathing; a gasp.

pantechnicon /pæn'tɛknɪkən/ *n.* a large or medium-sized truck or van with an enclosed back section, especially one used for transporting furniture.

panther /'pænθə/ *n.* (*pl.* **-thers** *or, especially collectively,* **-ther**) the leopard, especially in its black form.

pantihose /'pæntihouz/ *n.* (*construed as pl.*) women's tights, usually made out of fine-mesh material, as for stockings. Also, **pantyhose**.

pantomime /'pæntəmaɪm/ *n.* a form of theatrical entertainment common during the Christmas season.

pantry /'pæntri/ *n.* (*pl.* **-ries**) a room or cupboard in which provisions, especially food, and other household items are kept.

pants /pænts/ *pl. n.* **1.** trousers. **2.** underpants, especially women's.

pap[1] /pæp/ *n.* soft food for infants or invalids.

pap[2] /pæp/ *n.* a teat or nipple.

papa /pə'pa, 'pʌpə/ *n.* → **father**.

papacy /'peɪpəsi/ *n.* **1.** the office, dignity, or jurisdiction of the pope. **2.** the system of ecclesiastical government in which the pope is recognised as the supreme head.

papal /'peɪpəl/ *adj.* of or relating to the pope, the papacy, or the Roman Catholic Church.

paparazzo /papə'ratsi, pæpə-/ *n.* (*pl.* **-razzi**) a press photographer who persistently pursues celebrities in order to photograph them.

papaya /pə'paɪə/ *n.* a melon-like tropical fruit, with pinkish flesh.

paper /'peɪpə/ *n.* **1.** a substance made from rags, straw, wood, or other fibrous material, usually in thin sheets, for writing or printing on, wrapping things in, etc. **2.** negotiable notes, bills, etc., collectively. **3.** a set of questions for an examination, or an individual set of written answers to them. **4.** an essay, article, etc. on a particular topic. **5.** a newspaper or journal. **6.** (*pl.*) documents establishing identity, status, etc. –*v.t.* **7.** to decorate (a wall, room, etc.) with wallpaper.

paperback /'peɪpəbæk/ *n.* a book bound in a flexible paper cover.

papier-mâché /peɪpə-'mæʃeɪ, pæpieɪ-'mæʃeɪ/ *n.* a substance made of pulped paper and glue which becomes hard and strong when dry. Also, **papier-mache**.

papillomavirus /pæpə'loumavaɪrəs/ *n.* any of various small species-specific viruses causing warts.

pappadum /'pæpədʌm/ *n.* a thin, crisp Indian wafer bread, made from spiced potato or rice flour. Also, **pappadam**, **poppadum**.

pappardelle /papə'dɛlə/ *n.* a kind of pasta in flat, very wide strips.

paprika /'pæprɪkə, pə'prikə/ *n.* the dried fruit of a cultivated form of capsicum, ground as a condiment.

papyrus /pə'paɪrəs/ *n.* (*pl.* **-pyri** /-'paɪraɪ/) **1.** a tall aquatic plant of the Nile valley, Egypt, and elsewhere. **2.** a material for writing on, prepared from the pith of this plant.

par /pa/ *n.* **1.** an equality in value or standing. **2.** an average or normal amount, degree, quality, condition, or the like. **3.** *Commerce* **a.** the legally established value of the monetary unit of one country in terms of that of another using the same metal as a standard of value (**mint par of exchange**). **b.** the state of the shares of any business, undertaking, loan, etc., when they may be purchased at the original price (called **issue par**) or at their face value (called **nominal par**). Shares or bonds sold or acquired at a premium are said to be **above par**, and at a discount **below par**. **4.** *Golf* the number of strokes allowed to a hole or course as representing a target standard.

para-[1] a prefix meaning 'beside', 'near', 'beyond', 'aside', 'amiss', and sometimes implying alteration or modification.

para-[2] a prefix of a few words meaning 'guard against', as in *parachute*.

parable /'pærəbəl/ *n.* a short allegorical story, designed to convey some truth or moral lesson.

parabola /pə'ræbələ/ *n. Geom.* a plane curve formed by the intersection of a right circular cone with a plane parallel to a generator of the cone.

paracetamol /pærə'sitəmɒl/ *n.* an analgesic, fever-reducing drug.

parachute /'pærəʃut/ *n.* an apparatus used in descending safely through the air, especially from an aircraft, being umbrella-like in form and rendered effective by the resistance of the air. –**parachutist**, *n.*

parade /pə'reɪd/ *n.* **1.** show, display, or ostentation. **2.** the orderly assembly of troops, etc., for inspection or display. **3.** a public procession. −*v.t.* **4.** to make parade of; display ostentatiously. −*v.i.* **5.** to march or proceed with display. **6.** to promenade in a public place to show oneself.

paradigm /ˈpærədaɪm/ *n. Gram.* the set of all forms containing a particular element, especially the set of all inflected forms of a single root, stem, or theme.

paradise /ˈpærədaɪs/ *n.* **1.** heaven, as the final abode of the righteous. **2.** a place of extreme beauty or delight.

paradox /ˈpærədɒks/ *n.* a statement or proposition seemingly self-contradictory or absurd, and yet expressing a truth. −**paradoxical**, *adj.*

paraffin /ˈpærəfən/ *n. Chem.* any hydrocarbon of the methane series having general formula C_NH_{2N+2}.

paragon /ˈpærəgən, ˈpærəgɒn/ *n.* a model or pattern of excellence, or of a particular excellence.

paragraph /ˈpærəgræf, -grɑf/ *n.* a distinct portion of written or printed matter dealing with a particular point, and usually beginning (commonly with indention) on a new line.

parakeet /ˈpærəkit/ *n.* a small, slender parrot, usually with a long, pointed tail.

paralegal /pærəˈligəl/ *adj.* **1.** of, relating to, or designating a person who is employed by a barrister or a solicitor to conduct administrative and research duties in relation to a case. −*n.* **2.** a person who acts in this capacity.

parallax /ˈpærəlæks/ *n.* the apparent displacement of an observed object due to a change or difference in position of the observer.

parallel /ˈpærəlel/ *adj.* **1.** having the same direction, course, or tendency; corresponding; similar; analogous. **2.** *Geom.* (of straight lines) lying in the same plane but never meeting no matter how far extended. **3.** *Computers, etc.* denoting or relating to a system in which several activities are carried on concurrently. Compare **serial** (def. 4). −*n.* **4.** anything parallel in direction, course, or tendency. **5.** *Geog.* a line of latitude. **6.** *Elect.* a connection of two or more circuits in which all ends having the same instantaneous polarity are electrically connected together and all ends having the opposite polarity are similarly connected. −*v.t.* (**-lleled, -lleling**) **7.** to form a parallel to; be equivalent to; equal.

parallelogram /pærəˈlelɒgræm/ *n.* a quadrilateral the opposite sides of which are parallel, as a square, rectangle or rhombus.

parallel port *n. Computers* a port that enables several bits of data to be sent or received concurrently. Compare **serial port**.

parallel universe *n.* a postulated universe in another space-time continuum parallel to our own.

parallel verb *n.* a verb which expands the range of actions, processes, states, etc., but which is grammatically identical to the preceding verb.

paralysis /pəˈræləsəs/ *n.* (*pl.* **-lyses** /-ləsiz/) **1. a.** loss of power of a voluntary muscular contraction. **b.** a disease characterised by this; palsy. **2.** a more or less complete crippling, as of powers or activities. −**paralyse**, *v.* −**paralytic**, *n., adj.*

paramedical /pærəˈmedɪkəl/ *adj.* related to the medical profession in a supplementary capacity.

parameter /pəˈræmətə/ *n.* any constituent variable quality.

paramount /ˈpærəmaʊnt/ *adj.* chief in importance; supreme; pre-eminent.

paramour /ˈpærəmɔ/ *n.* an illicit lover.

paranoia /pærəˈnɔɪə/ *n.* a psychotic disorder characterised by systematised delusions. −**paranoid**, *adj.* −**paranoiac**, *adj.*

parapet /ˈpærəpət/ *n.* any protective wall or barrier at the edge of a roof, bridge, etc.

paraphernalia /pærəfəˈneɪliə/ *pl. n.* **1.** personal belongings. **2.** (*sometimes construed as sing.*) any collection of miscellaneous articles.

paraphrase /ˈpærəfreɪz/ *n.* **1.** a restatement of the sense of a text or passage, as for clearness. −*v.t., v.i.* **2.** to restate; render in, or make, a paraphrase. −**paraphrastic**, *adj.*

paraplegia /pærəˈplidʒə/ *n.* paralysis of the lower part of the body. −**paraplegic**, *adj., n.*

parasite /ˈpærəsaɪt/ *n.* an animal or plant which lives on or in an organism of another species (the host), from the body of which it obtains nutriment. −**parasitic** /pærəˈsɪtɪk/, *adj.*

parasol /ˈpærəsɒl/ *n.* a woman's small or light sun umbrella; a sunshade.

parasympathetic nervous system *n. Physiol., Anat.* that part of the autonomic nervous system which consists of nerves arising from the cranial and lumbar regions, and which functions in opposition to the sympathetic nervous system, thus inhibiting heartbeat, contracting the pupil of the eye, etc.

parataxis /pærəˈtæksəs/ *n.* the placing together of sentences, clauses, or phrases without a conjunctive word.

paratrooper /ˈpærətrupə/ *n.* a soldier who reaches a battle by landing from an aeroplane by parachute.

parboil /ˈpabɔɪl/ *v.t.* to boil partially, or for a short time.

parcel /ˈpasəl/ *n.* **1.** a quantity of something wrapped or packaged together; a package or bundle. **2.** a quantity of something, as of a commodity for sale. **3.** a part or portion of anything. −*v.t.* (**-celled, -celling**) **4.** (usu. fol. by *out*) to divide into or distribute in parcels or portions.

parch /patʃ/ *v.t.* to make dry, especially to excess.

parchment /ˈpatʃmənt/ *n.* the skin of sheep, goats, etc., prepared for use as a writing material, etc.

pardon /ˈpadn/ *n.* **1.** courteous indulgence or allowance, as in excusing fault or seeming rudeness. **2.** *Law* a remission of penalty. −*v.t.* **3.** to remit the penalty of (an offence). **4.** to release (a person) from liability for an offence. **5.** to make courteous allowance for, or excuse (an action or circumstance, or a person).

pare /peə/ *v.t.* to cut off the outer coating, layer, or part of.

parent /ˈpeərənt/ *n.* **1.** a father or a mother. **2.** an author or source. −**parental**, *adj.* −**parentage**, *n.* −**parenthood**, *n.*

parenthesis /pəˈrenθəsəs/ *n.* (*pl.* **-theses** /-θəsiz/) **1. a.** a set of the upright brackets ( ), used to mark off an interjected explanatory or qualifying remark, indicate groupings in mathematics, etc. **b.** either of these brackets ( ) individually; round bracket. **2. a.** *Gram.* a qualifying or explanatory word, phrase, etc., which interrupts the syntactic construction without otherwise affecting it and shown in writing by commas, parentheses, or dashes. **b.** a phrase, sentence, comment, etc., which is inserted into a conversation or written passage, and which is not directly related to the main subject **3.** an interval; interlude. *–phr.* **4. in parenthesis**, as an aside **–parenthetic, parenthetical,** *adj.*

parfait /pɑ'feɪ/ *n.* a dessert, served in a tall glass, made from layers of ice cream, fruit, jelly, syrup, nuts, etc.

pariah /pə'raɪə/ *n.* an outcast.

parietal /pə'raɪətl/ *adj. Anat.* referring to the side of the skull, or to any wall or wall-like structure.

parish /'pærɪʃ/ *n.* an ecclesiastical district having its own church and minister. **–parishioner,** *n.*

parity /'pærəti/ *n.* **1.** equality, as in amount, status, or character. **2.** equivalence; correspondence; similarity or analogy. **3.** *Computers* a method of checking information in a computer, by counting the number of digits present in a binary number.

parity pricing *n.* the policy of basing the local price of a commodity on an agreed international price where such exists.

park /pɑk/ *n.* **1.** an area of land within a town, set aside for public use, often landscaped with trees and gardens, and with recreational and other facilities. *–v.t.* **2.** to put or leave (a car, etc.) for a time in a particular place, as at the side of the road.

parka /'pɑkə/ *n.* a strong waterproof jacket with a hood.

Parkinson's disease /'pɑkənsənz/ *n.* a form of paralysis characterised by tremor, muscular rigidity, and weakness of movement. Also, **Parkinsonism.**

parlance /'pɑləns/ *n.* way of speaking, or language; idiom; vocabulary.

parley /'pɑli/ *n.* a discussion.

parliament /'pɑləmənt/ *n.* (*usu. upper case*) an assembly of elected representatives, often comprising an upper and lower house, which forms the legislature of a nation or constituent state. **–parliamentary,** *n.* **parliamentarian,** *n.*

parlour /'pɑlə/ *n.* a room for the reception and entertainment of visitors. Also, **parlor.**

parmesan /'pɑməzən/ *n.* a hard, dry, strongtasting cheese.

parochial /pə'roʊkiəl/ *adj.* **1.** of or relating to a parish or parishes. **2.** confined to or interested only in some particular narrow district or field.

parody /'pærədi/ *n.* (*pl.* **-dies**) **1.** a humorous or satirical imitation of a serious piece of literature or writing. **2.** a poor imitation; a travesty. *–v.t.* (**-died, -dying**) **3.** to imitate (a composition, author, etc.) in such a way as to ridicule.

parole /pə'roʊl/ *n.* the liberation of a person from prison, conditional upon good behaviour, prior to the end of the maximum sentence imposed upon that person.

-parous a word element forming an adjective termination meaning 'bringing forth','bearing', 'producing', as in *oviparous, viviparous.*

paroxysm /'pærəksɪzəm/ *n.* any sudden, violent outburst; a fit of violent action or emotion.

parquetry /'pɑkətri/ *n.* mosaic work of wood used for floors, wainscoting, etc.

parrot /'pærət/ *n.* any of numerous hook-billed, fleshy-tongued, often gaily coloured birds.

parry /'pæri/ *v.t.* (**-ried, -rying**) to ward off (a thrust, stroke, weapon, etc.), as in fencing.

parse /pɑz/ *v.t.* to describe (a word or series of words) grammatically, telling the part of speech, inflectional form, syntactic relations, etc.

parsimony /'pɑsəməni/, *Orig. US* /-moʊni/ *n.* extreme or excessive economy or frugality. **–parsimonious,** *adj.*

parsley /'pɑsli/ *n.* a garden herb used to garnish or season food.

parsnip /'pɑsnɪp/ *n.* **1.** a plant with a large, whitish, edible root. **2.** the root.

parson /'pɑsən/ *n.* a member of the clergy.

part /pɑt/ *n.* **1.** a portion or division of a whole, separate in reality, or in thought only; a piece, fragment, fraction, or section. **2.** (*usu. pl.*) a region, quarter, or district. **3.** one of the sides to a contest, question, agreement, etc. **4.** a character sustained in a play or in real life; a role. **5.** a parting in the hair. *–v.t.* **6.** to divide (a thing) into parts; break; cleave; divide. **7.** to comb (the hair) away from a dividing line. **8.** to put or keep asunder (two or more parts, persons, etc., or one part, person, etc., from another); draw or hold apart; separate. *–v.i.* **9.** to go apart from each other or one another, as persons. *–adj.* **10.** in part; partial.

partake /pɑ'teɪk/ *v.i.* (**-took, -taken, -taking**) (sometimes fol. by *in*) to take or have a part or share in common with others; participate.

partial /'pɑʃəl/ *adj.* **1.** relating to or affecting a part. **2.** being such in part only; not total or general; incomplete. **3.** biased or prejudiced in favour of a person, group, side, etc., as in a controversy. **–partiality,** *n.*

partial preferential voting *n.* a form of preferential voting in which voters must indicate their order of preference for a minimum number of candidates. Compare **full preferential voting, optional preferential voting.**

participate /pɑ'tɪsəpeɪt/ *v.i.* (sometimes fol. by *in*) to take or have a part or share, as with others; share. **–participant,** *n.*, *adj.* **–participation,** *n.*

participle /'pɑtəsɪpəl/ *n.* an adjective form derived from verbs. **–participial,** *adj.*

particle /'pɑtɪkəl/ *n.* **1.** a minute portion, piece, or amount; a very small bit. **2.** a small word of functional or relational use, such as an article, preposition, or conjunction, whether of a separate form class or not.

particular /pə'tɪkjələ/ *adj.* **1.** relating to some one person, thing, group, class, occasion, etc., rather than to others or all; special, not general. **2.** attentive to or exacting about details or small points.

particulate /pə'tɪkjələt/ *adj.* existing as, composed of, or relating to particles.

partisan /'pɑtəzən, pɑtə'zæn/ *n.* an adherent or supporter of a person, party, or cause.

partition /pɑ'tɪʃən/ *n.* **1.** division into or distribution in portions or shares. **2.** separation, as of two or more things. **3.** something that separates. *–v.t.* **4.** to divide into parts or portions.

partner /'patnə/ n. **1.** a sharer or partaker; an associate. **2.** *Law* one associated with another or others as a principal or a contributor of capital in a business or a joint venture. **3.** See **silent partner**. **4.** one of two people in a romantic or sexual relationship. –v.t. **5.** to associate as a partner or partners. **6.** to be, or act as, the partner of. –**partnership,** n.

partridge /'patrɪdʒ/ n. (pl. **-tridges** or, especially collectively, **-tridge**) a game bird.

part-time adj. **1.** of, relating to, or occupying less than all normal working hours (opposed to full-time). **2.** not being one's chief occupation. –adv. **3.** during less than all normal working hours. –**part-timer,** n.

parturition /patʃə'rɪʃən/ n. the act of bringing forth young; childbirth.

party /'pati/ n. (pl. **-ties**) **1.** a group gathered together for some purpose, as for amusement or entertainment. **2.** (oft. upper case) a number or body of persons ranged on one side, or united in purpose or opinion, in opposition to others, as in politics, etc. **3.** someone who participates in some action or affair. **4.** a person in general. –phr. **5. be (a) party to,** to help, take part in, or be involved in. –**partying,** n.

party machine n. the organisation behind a political party which influences the choice of candidates, runs elections, and manages fundraising.

parvenu /'pavənu, -nju/ n. **1.** someone who has risen above their class or to a position above their qualifications. –adj. **2.** being, resembling, or characteristic of a parvenu.

pascal /'pæskəl/ n. the derived SI unit of pressure. Symbol: Pa

pashmina /pæʃ'minə/ n. **1.** a fine woollen fabric made from the underbelly fur of Himalayan goats, sometimes blended with silk. **2.** a shawl made from this fabric.

paspalum /pæs'pæləm/ n. a grass widespread in Australia.

pass /pas/ v.t. **1.** to go by or move past (something). **2.** to go by without acting upon or noticing; leave unmentioned. **3.** to go or get through. **4.** to undergo successfully (an examination, etc.). **5.** to exist through; live during; spend. **6.** to convey, transfer, or transmit; deliver. **7.** to discharge or void, as excrement. **8.** to sanction or approve. **9.** to express or pronounce, as an opinion or judgement. –v.i. **10.** to go or move onwards; proceed; make one's, or its, way. **11.** to elapse, as time. **12.** to die. **13.** to go on or take place; happen; occur. **14.** to be interchanged, as between two persons. **15.** to go or get through something, such as a barrier, test, examination, etc. **16.** to go unheeded, uncensured, or unchallenged. –n. **17.** a narrow route across a relatively low notch or depression in a mountain barrier. **18.** a permission or licence to pass, go, come, or enter. **19.** the passing of an examination, etc., especially without honours. **20.** the transference of a ball, etc., from one player to another, as in football.

passage /'pæsɪdʒ/ n. **1.** an indefinite portion of a writing, speech, or the like, usually one of no great length; a paragraph, verse, etc. **2.** the act of passing. **3.** liberty, leave, or right to pass. **4.** that by which a person or thing passes; a means of passing; a way, route, avenue, channel, etc. **5.** a voyage across the sea from one port to another.

passata /pə'satə/ n. a fine tomato sauce in the Italian style, made from sieved tomatoes. Compare **sugo**.

passbook /'pasbʊk/ n. a bankbook.

passé /pa'seɪ/ adj. antiquated, or out-of-date.

passenger /'pæsəndʒə/ n. someone who travels by some form of conveyance.

passerine /'pæsəraɪn/ adj. belonging to the order of perching birds.

passion /'pæʃən/ n. **1.** any kind of feeling or emotion, as hope, fear, joy, grief, anger, love, desire, etc., especially when of compelling force. **2.** a strong or extravagant fondness, enthusiasm, or desire for anything. **3.** the object of such a fondness or desire. –**passionate,** adj.

passionfruit /'pæʃənfrut/ n. (the edible fruit of) a type of climbing vine.

passive /'pæsɪv, -səv/ adj. **1.** not acting, or not attended with or manifested in open or positive action. **2.** suffering action, acted upon, or being the object of action (opposed to active). **3.** produced by or due to external agency. **4.** suffering, receiving, or submitting without resistance. **5.** *Gram.* denoting a verb form or voice, in which the subject is represented as being acted on, as was hit in the sentence He was hit. **6.** (of a communications satellite) only able to reflect signals, and not retransmit them.

passive aggressive adj. **1.** deliberately uncooperative; employing methods that frustrate the objectives of others without confronting them with outright refusal. –n. **2.** a person who behaves in such a manner.

passive smoking n. the inhaling by a non-smoker of the smoke produced by cigarette, cigar and pipe smokers, seen as detrimental to health. –**passive smoker,** n.

passport /'paspot/ n. an official document granting permission to the person specified to visit foreign countries, and authenticating the holder's identity, citizenship and right to protection while abroad.

password /'paswɜd/ n. **1.** a secret word or expression used to gain access to a restricted area or to distinguish a friend from an enemy. **2.** *Computers* a private code, usually a word or expression, used to gain access to a computer system.

past /past/ adj. **1.** gone by in time. **2.** belonging to, or having existed or occurred in time previous to this. –n. **3.** the time gone by. **4.** the events of that time. –adv. **5.** so as to pass by or beyond. **6.** ago. –prep. **7.** beyond in time, position or amount.

pasta /'pæstə, 'pas-/ n. any of the several preparations made from a dough or paste of wheat flour, salt, water, and sometimes egg, such as spaghetti, macaroni, etc.

paste /peɪst/ n. **1.** a mixture of flour and water, often with starch, etc., used for causing paper, etc., to adhere. **2.** any material or preparation in a soft or plastic mass. **3.** a brilliant, heavy glass, used for making artificial gems. –v.t. **4.** to fasten or stick with paste or the like.

pastel /'pæstl/ *n*. **1.** a soft, subdued shade. **2.** a crayon. **3.** the art of drawing with such crayons.

pasteurise /'pæstʃəraɪz/ *v.t.* to swiftly heat (milk, etc.) to a high temperature and then swiftly cool to a low temperature, in order to destroy certain microorganisms and prevent or arrest fermentation. Also, **pasteurize**.

pastie /'pæsti, 'pasti/ *n*. a type of pie in which a circular piece of pastry is folded around a filling of vegetables, meat, etc. and baked. Also, **pasty, Cornish pastie**.

pastille /pæs'til, 'pæstl/ *n*. a lozenge.

pastime /'pastaɪm/ *n*. that which serves to make time pass agreeably.

pastor /'pastə/ *n*. a minister or member of the clergy with reference to his or her congregation.

pastoral /'pastərəl, -trəl/ *adj*. **1.** of or relating to the raising of stock, especially sheep or cattle, on rural properties. **2.** used for pasture, as land. **3.** relating to the country or life in the country. **4.** relating to a minister or pastor, or to their duties, etc. **5.** (especially in a school) of or relating to guidance provided to students regarding personal wellbeing and moral and ethical concerns. –*n*. **6.** a poem, play, or the like, dealing with the life of shepherds, commonly in a conventional or artificial manner, or with simple rural life generally.

pastoralism /'pastərəlɪzəm/ *n*. the process of developing land for pasture for the grazing of domesticated or partially domesticated animals, especially for meat or wool production. –**pastoralist**, *n*.

pastrami /pəs'trami/ *n*. a highly seasoned shoulder cut of smoked beef, usually sold sliced.

pastry /'peɪstri/ *n*. (*pl*. **-tries**) **1.** a mixture of flour, water, butter, etc., cooked as a crust for pies and tarts. **2.** an article of food made with pastry, such as pie or tart.

pasture /'pastʃə/ *n*. ground covered with grass, etc., used or suitable for the grazing of cattle, etc.; grassland.

pasty¹ /'peɪsti/ *adj*. (**-tier, -tiest**) of or like paste in consistency, colour, etc.

pasty² /'pæsti, 'pasti/ *n*. (*pl*. **-ties**) → **pastie**.

PA system *n*. → **public-address system**.

pat¹ /pæt/ *v.t.* (**patted, patting**) **1.** to strike lightly with something flat. –*n*. **2.** a light stroke or blow with something flat. **3.** a small mass of something, as butter, shaped by patting or other manipulation.

pat² /pæt/ *adj*. **1.** exactly to the point or purpose. **2.** apt; opportune; ready. –*adv*. **3.** exactly or perfectly.

patch /pætʃ/ *n*. **1.** a piece of material used to mend a hole or break, or strengthen a weak place. **2.** a small piece or scrap of anything. **3.** *Colloq*. an area of responsibility: *stay out of my patch!* **4.** *Computers* a correction (usually temporary) made by the user to a computer program supplied by a software publisher, allowing the program to be customised for special uses; hotfix. **5.** Also, **skin patch**. *Med*. an adhesive dressing which slowly dispenses medicine or other needed chemicals which are absorbed through the skin of the body. –*v.t.* **6.** to mend or strengthen with or as with a patch or patches. **7.** (usu. fol. by *up*) to repair or restore, especially in a hasty or makeshift way. **8.** *Telecommunications* to connect (a telephone or radio caller) to another caller or location: *patch me through to head office*.

patchwork /'pætʃwɜk/ *n*. work made of pieces of cloth or leather of various colours or shapes sewn together.

pate /peɪt/ *n*. the head.

pâté /'pæteɪ, 'pa-/ *n*. a paste or spread made of finely minced liver, meat, fish, etc.

patella /pə'telə/ *n*. (*pl*. **-las** or **-lae** /-li/) *Anat*. the kneecap.

patent /'peɪtnt/ *n*. **1.** a government grant to an inventor, for a stated period of time, conferring a monopoly of the exclusive right to make, use, and vend an invention or discovery. –*adj*. **2.** of a kind specially protected by a patent. **3.** open to view or knowledge; manifest; evident; plain. –*v.t.* **4.** to take out a patent on; obtain the exclusive rights to (an invention) by a patent.

patent leather *n*. leather lacquered to produce a hard, glossy, smooth finish.

paternal /pə'tɜnəl/ *adj*. **1.** fatherly. **2.** related on the father's side.

paternity /pə'tɜnəti/ *n*. the state of being a father; fatherhood.

path /paθ/ *n*. **1.** a way beaten or trodden by the feet of humans or animals. **2.** a course of action, conduct, or procedure.

pathetic /pə'θetɪk/ *adj*. exciting pity or sympathetic sadness.

pathogen /'pæθədʒən/ *n*. a disease-producing organism. –**pathogenic**, *adj*.

pathology /pə'θɒlədʒi/ *n*. **1.** the science that deals with the origin, nature, and course of diseases. **2.** Also, **clinical pathology**. the study of diseased body organs, tissues, or cells, using laboratory tests. –**pathologist**, *n*. –**pathological**, *adj*.

pathos /'peɪθɒs/ *n*. the quality or power, as in speech, music, etc., of evoking a feeling of pity or sympathetic sadness.

patient /'peɪʃənt/ *n*. **1.** someone who is under medical or surgical treatment. –*adj*. **2.** quietly persevering or diligent. **3.** quietly enduring strain, annoyance, etc. –**patience**, *n*.

patina /'pætənə, pə'tinə/ *n*. **1.** a film or encrustation, usually green, caused by oxidisation on the surface of old bronze, and esteemed as ornamental. **2.** a similar film or colouring on some other substance. **3.** a surface calcification of implements, usually indicating great age.

patio /'pætioʊ, 'peɪioʊ/ *n*. (*pl*. **-tios**) an area, usually paved, adjoining a house, used for outdoor living.

patri- a word element meaning 'father'.

patriarch /'peɪtriak, 'pæt-/ *n*. **1.** the male head of a family or tribal line. **2.** a person regarded as the father or founder of an order, class, etc.

patriarchy /'peɪtriaki, 'pæt-/ *n*. (*pl*. **-archies**) a form of social organisation in which the father is head of the family, and in which descent is reckoned in the male line, the children belonging to the father's clan.

patrician /pə'trɪʃən/ *n*. **1.** a member of the original senatorial aristocracy in ancient Rome. **2.** any noble or aristocrat.

patricide /'pætrəsaɪd/ *n*. **1.** someone who kills their father. **2.** the act of killing one's father. –**patricidal**, *adj*.

patriot /ˈpeɪtrɪət, ˈpæt-/ n. a person who loves their country, zealously supporting and defending it and its interests. **–patriotism**, n.

patriotic /peɪtrɪˈɒtɪk, pætr-/ adj. 1. having a strong feeling of love and loyalty towards one's own country. 2. relating to patriotic feelings. **–patriotically**, adv.

patrol /pəˈtroʊl/ v.i. (**-trolled, -trolling**) 1. to go the rounds in a camp or garrison, as a guard. –n. 2. a person or a body of persons charged with patrolling. 3. the act of patrolling.

patron /ˈpeɪtrən/ n. 1. someone who supports with their patronage a shop, hotel, or the like. 2. a protector or supporter, as of a person, cause, institution, art, or enterprise. **–patronage**, n.

patronise /ˈpætrənaɪz/ v.t. 1. to favour (a shop, restaurant, etc.) with one's patronage; to trade with. 2. to treat in a condescending way. Also, **patronize**.

patter¹ /ˈpætə/ v.i. 1. to strike or move with a succession of slight tapping sounds. 2. the act of pattering.

patter² /ˈpætə/ n. the glib and rapid speech used by a salesperson, etc., to attract attention or amuse.

pattern /ˈpætn/ n. 1. a decorative design, as for china, wallpaper, textile fabrics, etc. 2. style or type in general. 3. anything fashioned or designed to serve as a model or guide for something to be made. –v.t. 4. to make after a pattern.

patty /ˈpæti/ n. (pl. **-ties**) 1. a little pie. 2. a savoury mixture formed into a flattened ball, usually fried.

paucity /ˈpɔsəti/ n. smallness of quantity.

paunch /pɒntʃ/ n. the belly.

pauper /ˈpɔpə/ n. a very poor person.

pause /pɔz/ n. 1. a temporary stop or rest, especially in speech or action. –v.i. 2. to make a pause; stop; wait; hesitate.

pave /peɪv/ v.t. 1. to cover or lay (a road, walk, etc.) with stones, bricks, tiles, wood, concrete, etc., so as to make a firm, level surface. 2. to prepare (the way) for.

pavement /ˈpeɪvmənt/ n. a walk or footway, especially a paved one, at the side of a street or road.

pavilion /pəˈvɪljən/ n. a light, more or less open structure for purposes of shelter, pleasure, etc., as in a park.

pavlova /pævˈloʊvə/ n. a dessert made of a large soft-centred meringue.

paw /pɔ/ n. 1. the foot of an animal with nails or claws. –v.t. 2. to strike or scrape with the paws or feet. 3. a pivoted bar adapted to engage with the teeth of a ratchet or the like.

pawn¹ /pɔn/ v.t. to deposit as security, as for money borrowed.

pawn² /pɔn/ n. Chess one of the 16 pieces of lowest value, usually moving one square straight ahead, but capturing diagonally.

pawnbroker /ˈpɔnbroʊkə/ n. someone who lends money at interest on pledged personal property. **–pawnbroking**, n.

pawpaw /ˈpɔpɔ/ n. a large melon-like tropical fruit with orange flesh.

pay /peɪ/ v. (**paid, paying**) –v.t. 1. to discharge (a debt, obligation, etc.), as by giving or doing something. 2. to give compensation for. 3. to

yield a recompense or return to; be profitable to. 4. to give or render (attention, regard, court, compliments, etc.) as if due or fitting. 5. to make (a call, visit, etc.). –v.i. 6. to give money, etc., due. 7. to yield a return or profit; be advantageous or worthwhile. 8. to suffer, or be punished, as for something; make amends. –n. 9. payment, as of wages, salary, or stipend. 10. paid employ. –phr. 11. **pay out, a.** to disburse; hand out (money). **b.** Colloq. to reprimand or criticise (someone). 12. **pay out** (or **away**), Naut., etc. to let out (a rope, etc.) as by slackening. 13. **put paid to**, put an end to; prevent. **–payable**, adj. **–payment**, n.

pay-and-display adj. 1. of or relating to a ticket vending machine in a parking area, where the driver must purchase a ticket and display it on the dashboard of the vehicle. 2. of, relating to, or using this system of payment for parking.

pay-as-you-go tax n. a form of withholding tax in which tax is deducted from income before it is paid to the recipient. Also, **PAYG tax**.

pay-per-view n. 1. a system by which one can view films, programs, etc., on television as one pays for them. –adj. 2. of or relating to this system: pay-per-view movies.

payroll /ˈpeɪroʊl/ n. 1. a roll or list of persons to be paid, with the amounts due. 2. the aggregate of these amounts. 3. the total number of people employed by a firm.

pay TV n. a television service to viewers who pay a subscription either as a monthly charge or as a fee for a particular program. Also, **pay television**.

paywall /ˈpeɪwɔl/ n. Internet a system for blocking access to content on a website, requiring payment from the user for the content to be released. Also, **pay wall**.

PC¹ /pi ˈsi/ n. a personal computer.

PC² /pi ˈsi/ adj. politically correct.

PCB /pi si ˈbi/ n. polychlorinated biphenyl; one of a group of highly toxic chemicals, used in making plastics and electrical insulators.

PDF /pi di ˈɛf/ Computers –n. 1. a format in which documents may be saved and sent to others for viewing. 2. a document in this format. –adj. 3. of or relating to this format or a file stored in this format. –v.t. (**PDFed, PDFing**) 4. to save (an electronic document) in this format. Also, **pdf**; (in filenames), **.pdf**.

pea /pi/ n. a small, round, highly nutritious seed, widely used as a vegetable.

peace /pis/ n. 1. freedom from war, hostilities, strife or dissension. 2. a state of being tranquil or serene. **–peaceable**, adj.

peaceful /ˈpisfəl/ adj. 1. quiet and without worry or trouble. 2. without violence. **–peacefully**, adv.

peach /pitʃ/ n. a juicy, drupaceous fruit.

peacock /ˈpikɒk/ n. the male of the peafowl distinguished for its long, colourful tail.

peafowl /ˈpifaʊl/ n. a peacock or peahen.

peahen /ˈpihɛn/ n. the female peafowl.

peak /pik/ n. 1. the pointed top of a mountain. 2. the highest point. 3. the maximum point or degree of anything. 4. a projecting front piece, or visor, of a cap.

peak body *n.* an organisation which represents a group of enterprises engaged in similar activities: *the peak body of the advertising industry.*

peal /pil/ *n.* **1.** a loud, prolonged sound of bells. **2.** any other loud, prolonged sound as of cannon, thunder, applause, laughter, etc. –*v.i.* **3.** to sound forth in a peal; resound.

peanut /'pinʌt/ *n.* the fruit (pod) or the edible seed of a leguminous plant native to Brazil, the pod of which is forced underground in growing, where it ripens. Also, **groundnut**.

pear /peə/ *n.* an edible fruit, typically rounded but elongated and growing smaller towards the stem.

pearl /pɜl/ *n.* **1.** a hard, smooth, often highly lustrous concretion, white or variously coloured, secreted within the shell of various molluscs, and often valuable as a gem. **2.** something precious or choice.

pear-shaped /'peə-ʃeɪpt/ *adj.* **1.** having an oval shape tapering towards one end, as a pear. –*phr.* **2. go pear-shaped**, *Colloq.* (of a plan, enterprise, etc.) to fail after a promising beginning.

peasant /'pezənt/ *n.* one of a class of persons, of inferior social rank, living in the country and engaged usually in agricultural labour. –**peasantry**, *n.*

peat /pit/ *n.* a highly organic soil (more than fifty per cent combustible) of partially decomposed vegetable matter, in marshy or damp regions.

pebble /'pebəl/ *n.* a small, rounded stone, especially one worn by the action of water.

pecan /'pikæn, pɪ'kæn/ *n.* (the oval, smooth-skinned nut of) a type of hickory tree.

peccadillo /pekə'dɪloʊ/ *n.* (pl. **-loes** or **-los**) a petty sin or offence; a trifling fault.

peck¹ /pek/ *n.* a dry measure in the imperial system, equal to 8 quarts or $9.092 \, 18 \times 10^{-3} \, \text{m}^3$.

peck² /pek/ *v.t.* **1.** to strike or indent with the beak, as a bird does, or with some pointed instrument, especially with quick, repeated movements. **2.** to kiss in a hasty dabbing manner. –*v.i.* **3.** to make strokes with the beak or a pointed instrument. –*n.* **4.** a pecking stroke. **5.** a hasty kiss.

peckish /'pekɪʃ/ *adj. Colloq.* mildly hungry.

pectin /'pektən/ *n.* an organic acid which occurs in pipe fruits. –**pectic**, *adj.*

pectoral /'pektərəl/ *adj.* of or relating to the breast or chest; thoracic.

peculiar /pə'kjulia, -ljə/ *adj.* **1.** strange, odd, or queer. **2.** (fol. by *to*) belonging characteristically. –**peculiarly**, *adv.* –**peculiarity**, *n.*

pecuniary /pə'kjuniəri, -nəri/, *Orig. US* /pə'kjuniɛri/ *adj.* **1.** consisting of or given or exacted in money. **2.** of or relating to money.

-ped a word element meaning 'foot', serving to form adjectives and nouns, as *biped*, *quadruped*. Compare **-pod**.

pedagogue /'pedəgɒg/ *n.* a teacher. –**pedagogy**, *n.*

pedal /'pedl/ *n.* **1.** a lever worked by the foot. –*v.* (**-alled, -alling**) –*v.t.* **2.** to work or use the pedals of, as in playing an organ or propelling a bicycle. –*v.i.* **3.** to operate the pedals.

pedant /'pednt/ *n.* someone who makes an excessive or tedious show of learning or exacting precision. –**pedantic**, *adj.*

peddle /'pedl/ *v.t.* to carry about for sale, often from door to door.

peddler /'pedlə/ *n.* **1.** someone who trades in drugs or others illicit or socially undesirable goods. **2.** → **pedlar**.

-pede a word element meaning 'foot', as in *centipede*.

pederasty /'pedəræsti/ *n.* sexual relations between a male adult and a boy. Also, **paederasty**. –**pederast**, *n.*

pedestal /'pedəstl/ *n.* **1.** a supporting structure or piece, especially for something on display; base. –*phr.* **2. put** (or **place**) (or **set**) **someone on a pedestal**, to hold someone in high esteem; idealise someone.

pedestrian /pə'destriən/ *n.* **1.** someone who goes or travels on foot. –*adj.* **2.** prosaic; dull.

pedicel /'pedəsɛl/ *n. Bot.* a small stalk.

pedicure /'pedəkjuə, -kjʊə/ *n.* professional care or treatment of the feet.

pedigree /'pedəgri/ *n.* an ancestral line, or line of descent, especially as recorded.

pediment /'pedəmənt/ *n. Archit.* a low triangular gable.

pedlar /'pedlə/ *n.* (formerly) someone who travelled from place to place selling things.

pedometer /pə'dɒmətə/ *n.* an instrument for recording the number of steps taken in walking.

pedosphere /'pedousfiə/ *n.* the earth's envelope where soil is naturally formed and soil-forming processes are active.

peduncle /pə'dʌŋkəl/ *n.* a flower stalk or something similar.

peek /pik/ *v.i.* **1.** to peep; peer. –*n.* **2.** a peeking look.

peel /pil/ *v.t.* to strip off the skin, rind, bark, etc.

peep¹ /pip/ *v.i.* **1.** to look through or as through a small aperture. **2.** to peer, as from a hiding place. –*n.* **3.** a peeping look or glance.

peep² /pip/ *n.* **1.** a peeping cry or sound. –*v.i.* **2.** to utter a shrill little cry; cheep; squeak.

peer¹ /pɪə/ *n.* **1.** a person of the same civil rank or standing; an equal before the law. **2.** someone who ranks with another in respect to endowments or other qualifications; an equal in any respect. **3.** a member of the nobility. –**peerless**, *adj.*

peer² /pɪə/ *v.i.* to look narrowly, as in the effort to discern clearly.

peer-to-peer *adj. Computers* of or relating to a computer network that relies on the power of the computers in the network, rather than on the computer power provided by a server alone to a network of clients. Also, **p2p**.

peevish /'pivɪʃ/ *adj.* cross, querulous, or fretful.

peewee /'piwi/ *n.* → **magpie lark**.

peg /peg/ *n.* **1.** a pin of wood or other material driven or fitted into something, as to fasten parts together, to hang things on, or to mark some point, etc. –*v.t.* (**pegged, pegging**) **2.** to drive or insert a peg into. **3.** to fasten with or as with pegs. **4.** (oft. fol. by *out*) to mark with pegs. **5.** *Colloq.* to identify as a particular type, having certain abilities, etc.: *I pegged him as a cricketer.* –*phr.* **6. have someone pegged**, *Colloq.* to have summed up the character or nature of someone.

peignoir /'peɪnwɑ/ n. **1.** a dressing-gown. **2.** a negligee.

pejorative /pə'jɒrətɪv/ adj. deprecatory.

Peking duck /pi'kɪŋ/ n. in Chinese cooking, a dish consisting of small pancakes wrapped around pieces of crisp roast duck skin and spring onions, cucumber and hoisin sauce, the flesh of the duck being traditionally served separately.

peleton /'pɛlətɒn/ n. → **peloton**.

pelican /'pɛləkən/ n. a bird with a large fish-catching bill.

pelican crossing n. a pedestrian crossing at which the lights can be activated by the pedestrian, and which usually incorporates a flashing orange signal after the red signal to indicate that caution is required.

pellet /'pɛlət/ n. a round or spherical body, especially one of small size.

pellicle /'pɛlɪkəl/ n. a thin skin; a film.

pellucid /pə'lusəd/ adj. **1.** allowing the passage of light; translucent. **2.** clear in meaning.

pelmet /'pɛlmət/ n. a short ornamental drapery or board, placed across the top of a window in order to hide the curtain rail.

peloton /'pɛlətɒn/ n. the main group of cyclists in a race. Also, **peleton**.

pelt[1] /pɛlt/ v.t. **1.** to assail with repeated blows or with missiles. –v.i. **2.** (of rain) to fall very heavily. –n. **3.** the act of pelting. –phr. **4. full pelt**, the utmost energy or speed.

pelt[2] /pɛlt/ n. the skin of an animal.

pelvis /'pɛlvəs/ n. the basin-like cavity in the lower part of the trunk of many vertebrates. –**pelvic**, adj.

pen[1] /pɛn/ n. **1.** any instrument for writing with ink. **2.** Ornith. a large feather of the wing or tail; a quill feather; a quill. –v.t. (**penned, penning**) **3.** to write with a pen; set down in writing.

pen[2] /pɛn/ n. an enclosure for domestic animals or livestock.

penal /'pinəl/ adj. of or relating to punishment, as for offences or crimes.

penalty /'pɛnəlti/ n. (pl. **-ties**) **1.** a punishment imposed or incurred for a violation of law or rule. **2.** consequence or disadvantage attached to any action, condition, etc. –**penalise, penalize**, v.

penalty corner n. Hockey a corner (def. 8) given as a penalty for an infringement by a player on the defending team.

penalty rate n. a rate of pay determined by an award, higher than the usual rate, in compensation for working outside the normal spread of hours.

penalty shootout n. Hockey, etc., Soccer a method of deciding a match after a tied game, in which each team is given equal opportunity to score penalty goals, the team scoring the greatest number being declared the winner.

penalty shot n. Hockey, Soccer, etc. a shot at goal awarded to one side as a penalty for an infringement by a player on the other side.

penance /'pɛnəns/ n. punishment undergone in token of penitence for sin.

pence /pɛns/ n. plural of **penny**, used especially when value is indicated.

penchant /'pɛntʃənt, pɒ̃'ʃɒ̃/ n. a strong inclination; a taste or liking for something.

pencil /'pɛnsəl/ n. **1.** a thin tube of wood, etc., with a core of graphite, chalk, the like, for drawing or writing. –v.t. (**-cilled, -cilling**) **2.** to use a pencil on. **3.** to execute, draw, colour, or write with or as with a pencil.

pendant /'pɛndənt/ n. a hanging ornament, as of a necklace or earring.

pendent /'pɛndənt/ adj. **1.** hanging or suspended. **2.** overhanging; jutting or leaning over.

pending /'pɛndɪŋ/ prep. **1.** until. **2.** during. –adj. **3.** remaining undecided.

pendulous /'pɛndʒələs/ adj. **1.** hanging. **2.** swinging freely. **3.** vacillating.

pendulum /'pɛndʒələm/ n. a body so suspended from a fixed point as to move to and fro by the action of gravity and acquired kinetic energy.

penetrate /'pɛnətreɪt/ v.t. **1.** to pierce into or through. **2.** to enter the interior of. **3.** to reach (a wide number of buyers, customers, etc): to penetrate a market. –**penetrable**, adj. –**penetrative**, adj.

penguin /'pɛŋgwən, 'pɛŋgwən/ n. a flightless aquatic bird of the Southern Hemisphere, with webbed feet, and wings reduced to flippers.

penicillin /pɛnə'sɪlən/ n. a powerful antibacterial substance.

peninsula /pə'nɪnʃələ, pə'nɪnsjələ/ n. a piece of land almost surrounded by water.

penis /'pinəs/ n. the male organ of copulation and urination.

penitent /'pɛnətənt/ adj. repentant; contrite; sorry for sin or fault and disposed to atonement and amendment. –**penitence**, n. –**penitential**, adj.

penitentiary /pɛnə'tɛnʃəri/ n. (pl. **-ries**) **1.** US a prison. –adj. **2.** of or relating to penance; penitential.

pen-name n. a name assumed to write under; an author's pseudonym.

pennant /'pɛnənt/ n. **1.** Also, **pendant, pennon**. a long triangular flag, borne on naval or other vessels or used in signalling, etc. **2.** any flag serving as an emblem, as of success in an athletic contest.

penny /'pɛni/ n. (pl. **pennies** or, especially collectively, **pence**) a former unit of currency. Abbrev.: d. –**penniless**, adj.

pension[1] /'pɛnʃən/ n. a fixed periodical payment made in consideration of past services, injury or loss sustained, merit, poverty, etc. –**pensioner**, n.

pension[2] /pɒ̃'sjɒ̃, 'pɛnsiɒn/ n. (in France and some other countries) **1.** a boarding house or small hotel. **2.** room and board. Compare **pensione**.

pensione /pɛnsi'oʊneɪ/ n. (in Italy) **1.** a boarding house or small hotel. **2.** room and board. Compare **pension**[2].

pensive /'pɛnsɪv/ adj. deeply or sadly thoughtful.

pent- a word element meaning 'five'. Also, (before consonants), **penta-**.

pentagon /'pɛntəgɒn, -gən/ n. a polygon having five angles and five sides.

pentathlon /pɛnˈtæθlən/ n. an athletic contest comprising five different events. –**pentathlete**, n.

penthouse /ˈpɛnthaʊs/ n. (pl. **-houses** /-haʊzəz/) a separate flat on the top floor or floors of a tall building.

pent-up adj. confined; restrained: *pent-up emotions.*

penultimate /pəˈnʌltəmət/ adj. next to the last.

penumbra /pəˈnʌmbrə/ n. (pl. **-bras** or **-brae** /-bri/) the partial or imperfect shadow outside the complete shadow (umbra) of an opaque body.

penury /ˈpɛnjəri/ n. 1. extreme poverty; destitution. 2. dearth or insufficiency. –**penurious**, adj.

peony /ˈpiəni/ n. (pl. **-nies**) a garden plant with large showy flowers.

people /ˈpipəl/ n. 1. (construed as sing., with pl. **peoples**) the whole body of persons constituting a community, tribe, race, or nation: *this is a united people.* 2. the common people; populace. –v.t. 3. to furnish with people; populate.

people smuggling n. the illegal business of transporting people to a country which they are not authorised to enter as immigrants. –**people smuggler**, n.

pep /pɛp/ n. Colloq. vigour.

pepita /pəˈpitə/ n. a pumpkin seed which has been shelled, roasted and salted; eaten as a snack.

pepper /ˈpɛpə/ n. 1. a pungent condiment obtained from the dried berries of various plants used either whole or ground. 2. any species of capsicum, as its fruit (red or green, hot or sweet) as the capsicum or common pepper of the garden. –v.t. 3. to season with or as with pepper. 4. to sprinkle as with pepper; dot.

peppercorn /ˈpɛpəkɔn/ n. the berry of the pepper plant, often dried and used as a condiment.

peppermint /ˈpɛpəmənt/ n. 1. a herb cultivated for its aromatic pungent oil. 2. a lozenge or confection flavoured with peppermint.

pepperoni /pɛpəˈroʊni/ n. a type of salami, much used on pizzas. Also, **peperoni**.

pepper spray n. an aerosol spray derived from capsicum, which irritates the face, especially the eyes; used by police to subdue offenders. Also, **capsicum spray**.

peptic /ˈpɛptɪk/ adj. relating to or concerned in digestion; digestive.

per /pɜ/, weak form /pə/ prep. through; by; for each.

per- a prefix meaning 'through', 'thoroughly', 'utterly', 'very', as in *pervert, pervade, perfect.*

perambulate /pəˈræmbjəleɪt/ v.i. to walk or travel about.

perambulator /pəˈræmbjəleɪtə/ n. → **pram**.

per annum /pɜr ˈænəm, pər ˈænəm/ adv. by the year; yearly.

per capita /pə ˈkæpətə/ adv. by the individual person.

perceive /pəˈsiv/ v.t. 1. to gain knowledge of through one of the senses; discover by seeing, hearing, etc. 2. to apprehend with the mind; understand. –**perception**, n. –**perceptive**, adj.

per cent adv. 1. by the hundred; for or in every hundred (used in expressing proportions, rates of interest, etc.). –n. 2. a stock which bears a specified rate of interest. Symbol: % Also, **percent**.

percentage /pəˈsɛntɪdʒ/ n. 1. a rate or proportion per hundred. 2. a proportion in general.

percentile /pəˈsɛntaɪl/ n. one of the values of a variable which divides the distribution of the variable into 100 groups having equal frequencies.

perceptible /pəˈsɛptəbəl/ adj. capable of being perceived; cognisable; appreciable.

perch¹ /pɜtʃ/ n. 1. a pole or rod usually fixed horizontally to serve as a roost for birds. 2. a rod, or linear measurement in the imperial system of 5½ yards or 16½ feet, equal to 5.0292 m. –v.i. 3. to alight or rest upon a perch, as a bird. 4. to settle or rest in some elevated position, as if on a perch.

perch² /pɜtʃ/ n. (pl. **perch** or **perches**) any of a number of species of Australian food and sport fishes, mainly freshwater but some marine.

percipient /pəˈsɪpiənt/ adj. 1. perceiving. 2. having perception. –n. 3. someone who or that which perceives.

percolate /ˈpɜkəleɪt/ v.i. 1. to pass through a porous substance; filter; ooze. 2. to become known gradually.

percolator /ˈpɜkəleɪtə/ n. a kind of coffeepot in which boiling water is forced up a hollow stem, filters through ground coffee, and returns to the pot below.

percussion /pəˈkʌʃən/ n. 1. the striking of one body against another with some violence; impact. 2. Music the instruments in an orchestra which are played by striking.

perdition /pɜˈdɪʃən/ n. a condition of final spiritual ruin or damnation.

peremptory /pəˈrɛmptri, -təri/ adj. 1. imperative. 2. imperious or dictatorial. 3. Law that precludes or does not admit of debate, question, etc.

perennial /pəˈrɛniəl/ adj. 1. lasting for an indefinitely long time; enduring. 2. Bot. having a life cycle lasting more than two years. –n. 3. a perennial plant.

perentie /pəˈrɛnti/ n. the largest Aust. lizard, dark in colour with large pale yellow spots; found in arid areas of northern and central Aust. Also, **perenti**.

perfect adj. /ˈpɜfəkt/ 1. in a state proper to a thing when completed; having all essential elements, characteristics, etc.; lacking in no respect; complete. 2. in a state of complete excellence; without blemish or defect. 3. Gram. designating a tense denoting an action or state brought to a close prior to some temporal point of reference. Compare **pluperfect**, **imperfect** (def. 2). –v.t. /pɜˈfɛkt/ 4. to bring to completion, complete, or finish. 5. to make perfect or faultless, bring to perfection. –**perfection**, n.

perfidy /ˈpɜfədi/ n. (pl. **-dies**) a deliberate breach of faith or trust; faithlessness; treachery. –**perfidious**, adj.

perforate /ˈpɜfəreɪt/ v.t. to make a hole or holes through by boring, punching or other process. –**perforation**, n.

perforce /pəˈfɔs/ adv. of necessity.

perform /pə'fɔm/ v.t. **1.** to carry out; execute; do. **2.** to act (a play, a part, etc.), as on the stage. **3.** to render (music), as by playing or singing. –v.i. **4.** to fulfil a command, promise, or undertaking. **5.** to execute or do something. **6.** to act in a play. **7.** to perform music. **8.** to go through any performance. **9.** to display anger.

performance /pə'fɔmɒns/ n. **1.** a musical, dramatic or other entertainment. **2.** the act of performing. **3.** the way in which something reacts under certain conditions or fulfils the purpose for which it was intended.

performance-enhancing drug n. a drug taken by an athlete or other competitive sportsperson to improve performance. Also, **performance enhancing drug.**

perfume /'pɜfjum/ n. a substance, extract, or preparation for diffusing or imparting a fragrant or agreeable smell.

perfunctory /pə'fʌŋktəri/ adj. performed merely as an uninteresting or routine duty; mechanical; indifferent, careless.

pergola /pə'həps, 'pɜgələ/ n. a shelter formed of trellises supported on posts, over which vines or other plants are grown.

perhaps /pə'hæps, præps/ adv. maybe; possibly.

peri- a prefix meaning 'around', 'about', 'beyond'.

peril /'perəl/ n. exposure to injury, loss, or destruction; risk; jeopardy; danger. –**perilous**, adj.

perimeter /pə'rɪmətə/ n. the circumference, border, or outer boundary of a two-dimensional figure.

period /'pɪəriəd/ n. **1.** an indefinite portion of time, or of history, life, etc., characterised by certain features or conditions. **2.** any specified division or portion of time. **3.** an episode of menstruation. **4.** → **full stop.** –adj. **5.** relating to, denoting, characteristic of, imitating, or representing a past period or the fashions current during a specific period of history.

periodic /pɪəri'ɒdɪk/ adj. **1.** occurring or appearing at regular intervals. **2.** intermittent.

periodical /pɪəri'ɒdɪkəl/ n. a magazine, journal, etc., issued at regularly recurring intervals.

peripheral /pə'rɪfərəl/ adj. **1.** relating to, situated in, or constituting the periphery. **2.** of minor importance; not essential; superficial. –n. **3.** → **peripheral device.** –**peripherally**, adv.

peripheral nervous system n. Physiol., Anat. a system of nerves and ganglia leading from the spinal cord and brain (the central nervous system) to the organs of the body, conveying sensory information from within and outside the body to the central nervous system and motor instructions from it in response. See **autonomic nervous system**, **somatic nervous system.**

periphery /pə'rɪfəri/ n. (pl. **-ries**) **1.** the external boundary of any surface or area. **2.** the external surface, or outside, of a body.

periphrastic /peri'fræstɪk/ adj. circumlocutory; roundabout.

periscope /'perəskoup/ n. an optical instrument by which a view at the surface of water, etc., may be seen from below or behind. –**periscopic**, adj.

perish /'perɪʃ/ v.i. **1.** to suffer death, or lose life, through violence, privation, etc. **2.** to pass away; decay and disappear. **3.** to rot.

perishable /'perɪʃəbəl/ adj. **1.** liable to perish; subject to decay or destruction. –n. **2.** (usu. pl.) a perishable thing, as food.

perjure /'pɜdʒə/ v.t. to render (oneself) guilty of swearing falsely, or of wilfully making a false statement under oath or solemn affirmation. –**perjury**, n.

perk¹ /pɜk/ v.i. (fol. by up) to become lively or vigorous, as after depression or sickness.

perk² /pɜk/ n. Colloq. any fringe benefit, bonus, or other income, in cash or in kind, that an employee receives in addition to his or her normal salary.

perky /'pɜki/ adj. (**-kier**, **-kiest**) jaunty; brisk; pert.

permaculture /'pɜməkʌltʃə/ n. a system, usually applied to farming, housing, infrastructure, etc., the elements of which are economically viable and environmentally sound, thus making the whole system sustainable in the long term.

permafrost /'pɜməfrɒst/ n. ground that is always frozen

permanent /'pɜmənənt/ adj. lasting or intended to last indefinitely; remaining unchanged; not temporary; enduring; abiding. –**permanence**, n.

permanent residence n. a visa status which gives holders the right to stay permanently in their chosen country. Abbrev.: PR Also, **permanent residency.** –**permanent resident**, n.

permeable /'pɜmiəbəl/ adj. capable of being permeated. –**permeability**, n.

permeate /'pɜmieɪt/ v.t. **1.** to penetrate through the pores, interstices, etc., of. **2.** to be diffused through; pervade; saturate.

permission /pə'mɪʃən/ n. the act of permitting; formal or express allowance or consent.

permissive /pə'mɪsɪv/ adj. **1.** tolerant. **2.** sexually and morally tolerant.

permit v.t. /pə'mɪt/ (**-mitted**, **-mitting**) **1.** to allow (a person, etc.) to do something. **2.** to let (something) be done or occur. –n. /'pɜmɪt/ **3.** a written order granting leave to do something. **4.** an authoritative or official certificate of permission; a licence.

permutation /pɜmjə'teɪʃən/ n. Maths **1.** the act of changing the order of elements arranged in a particular order (as, abc into acb, bac, etc.), or of arranging a number of elements in groups made up of equal numbers of the elements in different orders (as, a and b in ab and ba). **2.** any of the resulting arrangements or groups.

pernicious /pə'nɪʃəs/ adj. **1.** ruinous; highly hurtful. **2.** deadly; fatal.

peroxide /pə'rɒksaɪd/ n. Chem. that oxide of an element or radical which contains an unusually large amount of oxygen.

perpendicular /pɜpən'dɪkjələ/ adj. **1.** vertical; upright. **2.** Geom. meeting a given line or surface at right angles.

perpetrate /'pɜpətreɪt/ v.t. to perform, execute, or commit (a crime, deception, etc.). –**perpetration**, n. –**perpetrator**, n.

perpetual /pə'petʃuəl/ adj. continuing or enduring forever or indefinitely. –**perpetuate**, v. –**perpetuity**, n.

perplex /pə'plɛks/ v.t. to cause to be puzzled over what is not understood or certain; bewilder; confuse mentally.

perquisite /'pɜːkwəzət/ n. an incidental emolument, fee, or profit over and above fixed income, salary, or wages.

per se /pɜː 'seɪ/ adv. by or in itself; intrinsically.

persecute /'pɜːsɪkjuːt/ v.t. 1. to harass persistently. 2. to oppress with injury or punishment for adherence to principles or religious faith. –**persecution**, n.

persevere /pɜːsə'vɪə/ v.i. to persist in anything undertaken; maintain a purpose in spite of difficulty or obstacles. –**perseverance**, n.

persimmon /'pɜːsəmən, pə'sɪmən/ n. (a tree bearing) an astringent plumlike fruit.

persist /pə'sɪst/ v.i. 1. to continue steadily or firmly in some state, purpose, course of action, or the like, especially in spite of opposition. 2. (of something not wanted or liked) to go on and on: *her toothache persisted for hours.*

persistent /pə'sɪstənt/ adj. 1. continuing in spite of difficulties or opposition. 2. (of something unwanted or disliked) going on and on. –**persistence**, n. –**persistently**, adv.

person /'pɜːsən/ n. 1. a human being, whether man, woman, or child. 2. the living body of a human being, often including the clothes worn. 3. *Gram.* (in some languages) a category of verb inflection and of pronoun classification, distinguishing between the speaker (**first person**), the one addressed (**second person**), and anyone or anything else (**third person**). –*phr.* 4. **in person**, in one's own bodily presence.

-person a noun suffix used to avoid the specification or implication of sex, as in *chairman*, *salesman*; hence *chairperson*, *salesperson*.

personable /'pɜːsənəbəl/ adj. of pleasing personal appearance and manner; comely; presentable.

personage /'pɜːsənɪdʒ/ n. 1. a person of distinction or importance. 2. any person.

personal /'pɜːsənəl/ adj. 1. of or relating to a particular person; individual; private. 2. a. relating to the physical presence or involvement of a person: *a personal appearance at the concert*; *a personal interest in the shop*. b. relating to what serves the advantage of a particular person: *personal gain*. 3. relating to, directed to, or aimed at, a particular person: *a personal attack*. 4. relating to the person, body, or bodily aspect: *personal hygiene*.

personal best n. 1. *Sport* (in timed or measured events) an athlete's best performance. 2. one's greatest achievement in any field of activity. *Abbrev.*: PB

personal computer n. a microcomputer designed for individual use, for such applications as word processing, accounting, etc. Also, **PC**.

personal digital assistant n. a handheld computer which stores a diary, organiser, address book, calendar, etc., and which can be linked to other digital services and equipment. *Abbrev.*: PDA

personal identification number n. → PIN.

personality /pɜːsə'næləti/ n. (pl. **-ties**) 1. a distinctive or notable personal character. 2. a well-known or prominent person; celebrity.

personal organiser n. 1. a folder or wallet containing a diary, address book, etc. 2. a small electronic device used to record appointments, store telephone numbers, etc. 3. a computer program comprising features such as a diary, address book, etc. Also, **personal organizer**.

personify /pə'sɒnəfaɪ/ v.t. (**-fied, -fying**) 1. to attribute personal nature or character to (an inanimate object or an abstraction), as in speech or writing. 2. to be an embodiment of; typify. –**personification**, n.

personnel /pɜːsə'nɛl/ n. the body of persons employed in any work, undertaking, or service.

perspective /pə'spɛktɪv/ n. 1. the art of depicting on a flat surface, various objects, architecture, landscape, etc., in such a way as to express dimensions and spatial relations. 2. a mental view or prospect.

perspex /'pɜːspɛks/ n. (*from trademark*) a plastic substitute for glass.

perspicacious /pɜːspə'keɪʃəs/ adj. having keen mental perception; discerning.

perspire /pə'spaɪə/ v.i. to excrete watery fluid through the pores; sweat. –**perspiration**, n.

persuade /pə'sweɪd/ v.t. 1. to prevail on (a person, etc.), by advice, urging, reasons, inducements, etc., to do something. 2. to induce to believe; convince. –**persuasion**, n. –**persuasive**, adj.

pert /pɜːt/ adj. bold; saucy.

pertain /pə'teɪn/ v.i. to have reference or relation; relate.

pertinacious /pɜːtə'neɪʃəs/ adj. extremely persistent.

pertinent /'pɜːtənənt/ adj. relating or relating to the matter in hand; relevant.

perturb /pə'tɜːb/ v.t. to disturb or disquiet greatly in mind; agitate.

peruse /pə'ruːz/ v.t. 1. to read through, as with thoroughness or care: *to peruse a document*. 2. to read in a leisurely fashion. –**perusal**, n.

perv /pɜːv/ *Colloq.* –n. 1. a sexual pervert; a person with unusual sexual desires. 2. a person who habitually watches others voyeuristically: *you are such a perv.* –v.i. 3. (fol. by *on*) to look at lustfully.

pervade /pə'veɪd/ v.t. 1. to extend its presence, activities, influence, etc., throughout. 2. to go, pass, or spread through. –**pervasive**, adj.

perverse /pə'vɜːs/ adj. wilfully determined or disposed to go counter to what is expected or desired; contrary.

perversion /pə'vɜːʒən/ n. 1. the act of perverting. 2. a perverted form of something. 3. *Psychol.* unnatural or abnormal condition of the sexual instincts (**sexual perversion**).

pervert v.t. /pə'vɜːt/ 1. to turn away from the right course. 2. to lead astray morally. 3. to distort. –n. /'pɜːvɜːt/ 4. someone who has sexual habits which are generally unacceptable.

pervious /'pɜːviəs/ adj. 1. admitting of passage or entrance; permeable. 2. accessible to reason, feeling, etc.

pessary /'pɛsəri/ n. (pl. **-ries**) *Med.* 1. an instrument worn in the vagina to remedy uterine displacement. 2. a vaginal suppository.

pessimism /'pɛzəmɪzəm, 'pɛs-/ n. disposition to take the gloomiest possible view.

pessimist /'pɛzəməst, 'pesəməst/ n. someone who usually expects that things will turn out badly. **–pessimistic**, adj. **–pessimistically**, adv.

pest /pɛst/ n. a noxious, destructive, or troublesome thing or person; nuisance.

pester /'pɛstə/ v.t. to harass with petty annoyances; torment.

pesticide /'pɛstəsaɪd/ n. a chemical substance for destroying pests, such as mosquitoes, flies, etc.

pestilence /'pɛstələns/ n. a deadly epidemic disease. **–pestilential**, adj.

pestilent /'pɛstələnt/ adj. 1. infectious, as a disease; pestilential. 2. destructive to life; deadly; poisonous.

pestle /'pɛsəl/ n. an instrument for breaking up and grinding substances in a mortar.

pesto /'pɛstoʊ/ n. a thick green sauce made of basil, pine nuts, garlic, parmesan cheese and oil, used in Italian cooking.

pet /pɛt/ n. 1. any domesticated or tamed animal that is cared for affectionately. –adj. 2. treated as a pet, as an animal. 3. favourite. –v.t. (**petted, petting**) 4. to treat as a pet; fondle; indulge.

petal /'pɛtl/ n. one of the floral leaves, usually brightly coloured, of a flower or blossom.

PET bottle /pi i 'ti, pɛt/ n. a soft-drink bottle made of plastic which can be recycled for other uses.

peter /'pitə/ v.i. (fol. by out) to diminish gradually and then disappear or cease.

petite /pə'tit/ adj. (of women) small.

petition /pə'tɪʃən/ n. 1. a formally drawn-up request addressed to a person or a body of persons in authority or power, soliciting some favour, right, mercy, or other benefit. –v.t. 2. to address a formal petition to (a sovereign, a legislative body, etc.).

petrel /'pɛtrəl/ n. a seabird.

petrify /'pɛtrəfaɪ/ v.t. (**-fied, -fying**) 1. to convert into stone or a stony substance. 2. to stupefy or paralyse with astonishment, horror, fear, or other strong emotion.

petrodiesel /'pɛtroʊdizəl/ n. diesel obtained from petroleum. Compare **biodiesel**.

petrol /'pɛtrəl/ n. a mixture of volatile liquid hydrocarbons, used as a solvent and extensively as a fuel in internal-combustion engines.

petroleum /pə'troʊliəm/ n. an oily, usually dark-coloured liquid (a form of bitumen or mixture of various hydrocarbons). Also, **rock-oil**.

petrol sniffing n. the deliberate inhalation of petrol fumes in order to induce intoxication. **–petrol sniffer**, n.

petrol station n. → **service station**

petticoat /'pɛtikoʊt/ n. a skirt, especially an underskirt, worn by women and girls; a slip.

petty /'pɛti/ adj. (**-tier, -tiest**) 1. of small importance; trifling; trivial. 2. having or showing narrow ideas, interests, etc.

petty cash n. a small cash fund set aside to meet incidental expenses, as for office supplies.

petulant /'pɛtʃələnt/ adj. moved to or showing sudden, impatient irritation, especially over some trifling annoyance.

petunia /pə'tjunjə/ n. a plant with funnel-shaped flowers of various colours.

pew /pju/ n. (in a church) one of an assemblage of fixed bench-like seats (with backs), accessible by aisles, for the use of the congregation.

pewter /'pjutə/ n. any of various alloys in which tin is the chief constituent, originally one of tin and lead.

pH /pi 'eɪtʃ/ n. a measure of acidity or alkalinity, as of soil, water, etc., on a scale, running from 1 (extreme acidity) to 14 (extreme alkalinity).

-phagous a word element forming an adjective termination meaning 'eating', 'feeding on'.

phallus /'fæləs/ n. 1. an image of the erect male reproductive organ. 2. Anat. the penis, clitoris, or the sexually undifferentiated embryonic organ out of which each develops. **–phallic**, adj.

phantom /'fæntəm/ n. 1. an image appearing in a dream or formed in the mind. 2. an apparition or spectre.

pharmaceutical /fɑmə'sjutɪkəl/ adj. relating to pharmacy. Also, **pharmaceutic**.

pharmaceutics /fɑmə'sjutɪks/ n. → **pharmacy** (def. 1).

pharmacology /fɑmə'kɒlədʒi/ n. the science of drugs, their preparation, uses, and effects.

pharmacy /'fɑməsi/ n. (pl. **-cies**) 1. the art or practice of preparing and dispensing drugs and medicines. 2. a dispensary; chemist's shop. **–pharmacist**, n.

pharyngitis /færən'dʒaɪtəs/ n. inflammation of the mucous membrane of the pharynx.

pharynx /'færɪŋks/ n. (pl. **pharynxes** or **pharynges** /fə'rɪndʒiz/) the tube or cavity, with its surrounding membrane and muscles, which connects the mouth with the oesophagus.

phase /feɪz/ n. 1. a stage of change or development. –phr. (**phased, phasing**) 2. **phase in**, to introduce gradually and synchronise into a system, or the like. 3. **phase out**, to withdraw gradually from a system.

pheasant /'fɛzənt/ n. a large, long-tailed, gallinaceous bird.

phenomenon /fə'nɒmənən/ n. (pl. **-mena** /-mənə/) 1. a fact, occurrence, or circumstance observed or observable. 2. something that impresses the observer as extraordinary; a remarkable thing or person. **–phenomenal**, adj.

phial /'faɪəl/ n. a small bottle.

phil- a word element meaning 'loving', as in philanthropy. Also, **philo-**.

-phil → **-phile**.

philander /fə'lændə/ v.i. (of a man) to make love, especially without serious intentions.

philanthropy /fə'lænθrəpi/ n. love of humankind, especially as manifested in deeds of practical beneficence. **–philanthropist**, n. **–philanthropic**, adj.

philately /fə'lætəli/ n. the collecting and study of postage stamps, etc. **–philatelic**, adj. **–philatelist**, n.

-phile a word element meaning 'loving', 'friendly', or 'lover', 'friend'. Also, **-phil**.

-philia a word element forming a noun termination meaning 'fondness', 'craving' or 'affinity for'.

philistine /ˈfɪləstaɪn/ *n.* (*sometimes upper case*) someone looked down on as lacking in and indifferent to culture, aesthetic refinement, etc.

philology /fəˈlɒlədʒi/ *n.* linguistics.

philosophical /fɪləˈsɒfɪkəl/ *adj.* **1.** of or relating to philosophy. **2.** rationally or sensibly calm in trying circumstances.

philosophy /fəˈlɒsəfi/ *n.* (*pl.* **-phies**) **1.** the study or science of the truths or principles underlying all knowledge and being (or reality). **2.** a system of principles for guidance in practical affairs. **3.** philosophical spirit or attitude; wise composure throughout the vicissitudes of life. **–philosopher,** *n.*

-philous a word element forming an adjective termination meaning 'loving'.

philtre /ˈfɪltə/ *n.* a love potion.

phishing /ˈfɪʃɪŋ/ *n.* a form of internet fraud in which an email purporting to be from a legitimate sender, such as a bank, government institution, etc., encourages the recipient to provide personal information, passwords, etc., ostensibly to confirm or update information which the legitimate organisation already has. **–phisher,** *n.*

phlegm /flɛm/ *n. Physiol.* the thick mucus secreted in the respiratory passages and discharged by coughing, etc.

phlegmatic /flɛgˈmætɪk/ *adj.* **1.** not easily excited to action or feeling; sluggish or apathetic. **2.** cool or self-possessed.

-phobe a word element used as a noun termination meaning 'someone who fears or dreads'.

phobia /ˈfoʊbiə/ *n.* any extreme or irrational fear or dread.

-phobia a word element used as a noun termination meaning 'fear' or 'dread', often excessive, or with implication of aversion or hatred.

phoenix /ˈfiːnɪks/ *n.* a mythical bird.

phone /foʊn/ *n., v.t., v.i.* → **telephone.**

phonetic /fəˈnɛtɪk/ *adj.* of or relating to speech sounds and their production.

phonetics /fəˈnɛtɪks/ *n.* the science of speech sounds and their production. **–phonetician,** *n.*

phoney /ˈfoʊni/ *adj.* (**-nier, -niest**) *Colloq.* not genuine; spurious; counterfeit, or bogus; fraudulent. Also, **phony.**

phosphorescence /fɒsfəˈrɛsəns/ *n.* the property of being luminous at temperatures below incandescence. **–phosphorescent,** *adj.*

phosphorus /ˈfɒsfərəs/ *n. Chem.* a solid non-metallic element used in matches and in fertilisers. *Symbol:* P **–phosphoric,** *adj.*

photo /ˈfoʊtoʊ/ *n.* (*pl.* **-tos**) → **photograph.**

photo- **1.** a word element meaning 'light' as in *photosynthesis, photoelectron.* **2.** a word element meaning 'photograph' or 'photographic' as in *photocopy.*

photobomb /ˈfoʊtoʊbɒm/ *v.t.* **1.** to upstage (the intended subject of a photograph) by appearing in it, usually in some theatrical or distracting way. **2.** to ruin (a photograph) by such behaviour as a prank. **–n.** **3.** a picture with such an unwanted inclusion. **–photo-bombing,** *n.*

photochemical /foʊtoʊˈkɛmɪkəl/ *adj.* of, relating to, or produced by the action of light triggering a chemical process: *photochemical smog.*

photocopy /ˈfoʊtoʊkɒpi/ *n.* (*pl.* **-copies**) **1.** a photographic reproduction of written or printed material. **–v.t.** (**-copied, -copying**) **2.** to make a photocopy of. **–photocopier,** *n.*

photoelectric cell /ˌfoʊtoʊəˈlɛktrɪk/ *n.* a device used for the detection of light.

photogenic /foʊtoʊˈdʒɛnɪk, -ˈdʒiːnɪk/ *adj. Photography* (of a person) suitable for being photographed for artistic purposes, etc.

photograph /ˈfoʊtəgræf, -graf/ *n.* **1.** a picture produced by photography. **–v.t.** **2.** to take a photograph of.

photography /fəˈtɒgrəfi/ *n.* the process or art of producing images of objects on sensitised surfaces by the chemical action of light or of other forms of radiant energy. **–photographer,** *n.* **–photographic,** *adj.*

photon /ˈfoʊtɒn/ *n.* a quantum of light energy, proportional to the frequency of the radiation.

photo shoot *n.* a session during which a professional photographer takes shots of fashion models, a location, etc., as for a magazine, advertisement, website, etc. Also, **photoshoot.**

photoshop /ˈfoʊtoʊʃɒp/ *v.t.* (**-shopped, -shopping**) (*from trademark*) to alter a (digital image) on a computer.

photostat /ˈfoʊtəstæt/ (*from trademark*) **–n.** **1.** a special camera for making facsimile copies of maps, drawings, pages of books or manuscripts, etc., which photographs directly as a positive on sensitised paper. **2.** a copy so made. **–v.t.** (**-statted, -statting**) **3.** to make such a copy or copies of.

photosynthesis /foʊtoʊˈsɪnθəsəs/ *n.* the synthesis of complex organic materials by plants from carbon dioxide, water, and inorganic salts using sunlight as the source of energy and with the aid of a catalyst such as chlorophyll. **–photosynthetic,** *adj.*

phrase /freɪz/ *n.* **1.** *Gram.* a sequence of two or more words arranged in a grammatical construction and acting as a unit in the sentence. **2.** a characteristic, current, or proverbial expression. **3.** a group or sequence making up a recognisable entity. **–v.t.** **4.** to express or word in a particular way. **–phrasal,** *adj.*

phraseology /freɪziˈɒlədʒi/ *n.* manner or style of verbal expression; characteristic language. **–phraseological,** *adj.*

phrenology /frəˈnɒlədʒi/ *n.* the theory that one's mental powers are indicated by the shape of the skull.

-phyll a word element used as a noun termination meaning 'leaf'. Also, **-phyl.**

phyllo- a word element meaning 'leaf'. Also, (*before vowels*), **phyll-.**

-phyllous a word element used as an adjective termination meaning 'having leaves', 'leaved', or implying some connection with a leaf, as in *diphyllous.*

phylo- a word element meaning 'tribe'.

phylum /ˈfaɪləm/ *n.* (*pl.* **phyla** /ˈfaɪlə/) *Biol.* a primary division of the animal or vegetable kingdom.

physical /ˈfɪzɪkəl, ˈfɪzɪkəl/ *adj.* **1.** relating to the body; bodily. **2.** of or relating to material nature; material. **3.** of or relating to the physics.

physician /fəˈzɪʃən/ *n.* one legally qualified to practise medicine.

physics /ˈfɪzɪks/ *n.* the science dealing with natural laws and processes, and the states and properties of matter and energy, other than those restricted to living matter and to chemical changes. **–physicist,** *n.*

physiognomy /fɪzi'ɒnəmi/ *n.* (*pl.* **-mies**) the face or countenance, especially as considered as an index to the character.

physiology /fɪzi'ɒlədʒi/ *n.* the science dealing with the functioning of living organisms or their parts. **–physiologist,** *n.* **–physiological,** *adj.*

physiotherapy /ˌfɪzioʊ'θerəpi/ *n.* the treatment of disease or bodily weaknesses or defects by physical remedies, such as massage, gymnastics, etc. Also, **physio.** **–physiotherapist,** *n.*

physique /fə'zik/ *n.* human bodily structure or type.

pi /paɪ/ *n.* (*pl.* **pis**) *Maths* the ratio (3.141 592) of the circumference of a circle to its diameter.

piano /pi'ænoʊ/ *n.* (*pl.* **-nos**) a musical instrument in which hammers, operated from a keyboard, strike upon metal strings. **–pianist,** *n.* **–pianistic,** *adj.*

piano accordion *n.* an accordion having a piano-like keyboard for the right hand.

pianoforte /piænoʊ'fɔːteɪ, pianoʊ-/ *n.* → **piano.**

picador /'pɪkədɔː/ *n.* a bullfighter on horseback who opens the bullfight by enraging the bull by pricking it with sharp lances.

picaresque /pɪkə'resk/ *adj.* of or relating to rogues.

piccolo /'pɪkəloʊ/ *n.* (*pl.* **-los**) a small flute, sounding an octave higher than the ordinary flute.

pick¹ /pɪk/ *v.t.* **1.** to choose or select carefully. **2.** to choose (one's way or steps), as over rough ground or through a crowd. **3.** to steal the contents of (a person's pocket, purse, etc.). **4.** to open (a lock) with a pointed instrument, a wire, or the like, as for robbery. **5.** to pierce, indent, dig into, or break up (something) with a pointed instrument. **6.** to pluck or gather. **7.** *Music* to pluck (the strings of an instrument). *–v.i.* **8.** to strike with or use a pointed instrument or the like on something. **9.** to eat with dainty bites. *–n.* **10.** the choicest or most desirable part, example, or examples. **11.** → **plectrum.** *–phr.* **12. pick on,** *Colloq.* **a.** to annoy; tease; bully. **b.** to single out (a person), often indiscriminately, for something unpleasant, as punishment or criticism. **13. pick out, a.** to distinguish (a thing) from surrounding or accompanying things. **b.** to make out (sense or meaning). **c.** to extract by picking. **14. pick someone's brains,** to find out as much as one can, from someone else's knowledge of a subject. **15. pick to pieces,** to criticise, especially in petty detail. **16. pick up, a.** to take up. **b.** to learn by occasional opportunity or without special teaching. **c.** to get casually. **d.** to take (a person or thing) into a car, ship, etc., or along with one. **e.** to bring into the range of reception, observation, etc. **f.** to accelerate, especially in speed. **g.** *Colloq.* to improve. **h.** *Colloq.* to arrest. **–picker,** *n.*

pick² /pɪk/ *n.* a hand tool for loosening and breaking up soil, etc.

pickaxe /'pɪkæks/ *n.* a pick.

picket /'pɪkət/ *n.* **1.** a pointed post, stake, pale, or peg. **2.** a person or a body of persons stationed by a trade union or the like in front of a place of work and attempting to dissuade or prevent workers from entering the building during a strike. *–v.i.* **3.** to stand or march by a place of employment as a picket.

pickle /'pɪkəl/ *n.* **1.** (*oft. pl.*) vegetables, as cucumbers, onions, cauliflowers, etc., preserved in vinegar, brine, etc., and eaten as a relish. **2.** a liquid or marinade prepared with salt or vinegar for the preservation of fish, meat, vegetables, etc., or for the hardening of wood, leather, etc. **3.** *Colloq.* a predicament. *–v.t.* **4.** to preserve or steep in pickle.

pickpocket /'pɪkpɒkət/ *n.* someone who steals from the pockets, handbags, etc., of people in public places.

picnic /'pɪknɪk/ *n.* **1.** an outing or excursion, typically one in which those taking part carry food with them and share a meal in the open air. **2.** *Colloq.* an enjoyable experience or time. **3.** *Colloq.* an easy undertaking. *–v.i.* (**-nicked, -nicking**) **4.** to hold, or take part in, a picnic. **–picnicker,** *n.*

pictogram /'pɪktəgræm/ *n.* a written symbol representing something by a stylised drawing of it or something associated with it and not by its name or the sound of its name. Also, **pictograph.**

pictorial /pɪk'tɔːriəl/ *adj.* relating to, expressed in, or of the nature of, a picture or pictures.

picture /'pɪktʃə/ *n.* **1.** a representation, upon a surface, usually flat, as a painting, drawing or photograph, etc. **2.** any visible image, however produced. *–v.t.* **3.** to form a mental image of. *–phr.* **4. the pictures,** a cinema.

picturesque /pɪktʃə'resk/ *adj.* visually charming or quaint.

piddle /'pɪdl/ *v.i. Colloq.* to urinate.

pide /'pideɪ/ *n.* **1.** a Turkish flatbread. **2.** a dish consisting of this bread wrapped around various fillings, as meat, spinach, cheese, etc., and baked; Turkish pizza.

pidgin /'pɪdʒən/ *n.* a language used for communication between groups having different first languages, and which typically has features deriving from those languages. Also, **pigeon.**

pie /paɪ/ *n.* a baked dish consisting of a sweet (fruit, etc.) or savoury filling (meat, fish, etc.), enclosed in or covered by pastry.

piebald /'paɪbɔld/ *adj.* having patches of black and white or of other colours.

piece /pis/ *n.* **1.** a limited portion or quantity, of something. **2.** one of the parts, fragments, or shreds into which something may be divided or broken. **3.** an individual article of a set or collection. **4.** any of the counters, discs, blocks, or the like, of wood, ivory, or other material, used in any of a number of board games, as draughts, backgammon, or chess. **5.** an amount of work forming a single job. **6.** a musical composition, usually a short one. **7.** *Mil.* a firearm. *–v.t.* (**pieced, piecing**) **8.** (*usu. fol. by together*) to mend (something broken); reassemble. **9.** to fit together, as pieces or parts.

piecemeal /'pismil/ *adv.* piece by piece; gradually.

pier /pɪə/ *n.* **1.** a structure built out into the water to serve as a landing place for ships. **2.** one of the supports of a span of a bridge or of two adjacent spans.

pierce /pɪəs/ *v.t.* (**pierced**, **piercing**) **1.** to penetrate or run into or through (something), as a sharp-pointed instrument does; puncture. **2.** to penetrate with the eye or mind; see into or through. **3.** to sound sharply through (the air, stillness, etc.) as a cry. –**piercer**, *n.* –**piercingly**, *adv.*

piety /'paɪəti/ *n.* reverence for God, or regard for religious obligations.

piffle /'pɪfəl/ *n. Colloq.* nonsense.

pig /pɪg/ *n.* **1.** an omnivorous non-ruminant mammal; a sow, hog, or boar; a swine. Compare **hog**. **2.** *Colloq.* a greedy, dirty person. **3.** *Colloq.* (*derog.*) a police officer. **4.** *Metallurgy* an oblong mass of metal that has been run while still molten into a mould of sand or the like.

pigeon /'pɪdʒən/ *n.* a bird with a compact body and short legs, often bred for racing, etc.

pigeonhole /'pɪdʒənhoʊl/ *n.* **1.** one of a series of small compartments in a desk, cabinet, or the like, used for papers, etc. –*v.t.* **2.** to put away for reference at some indefinite future time. **3.** to assign a definite place in some orderly system.

piggyback /'pɪgibæk/ *adv.* sitting on the back or shoulders of another.

pig-headed /'pɪg-hɛdəd/ *adj.* stupidly obstinate.

piglet /'pɪglət/ *n.* a little pig.

pigment /'pɪgmənt/ *n.* **1.** a colouring matter or substance. **2.** *Biol.* any substance whose presence in the tissues or cells of animals or plants colours them. –**pigmentation**, *n.*

pigtail /'pɪgteɪl/ *n.* a braid of hair hanging down the back of the head.

pike¹ /paɪk/ *n.* (*pl.* **pike** *or* **pikes**) any of various elongated fishes.

pike² /paɪk/ *n.* a sharp point; a spike.

pike³ /paɪk/ *n.* a jackknife dive.

pikelet /'paɪklət/ *n.* a small thick, sweet pancake.

piker /'paɪkə/ *n.* someone who, from lack of courage or from diffidence, does anything in a contemptibly small or cheap way.

Pilates /pə'lɑtiz/ *n.* a fitness regimen that introduces comprehensive stretching and strengthening movements into an exercise routine. Also, **Pilates method**.

pilchard /'pɪltʃəd/ *n.* a small abundant fish.

pilchers /'pɪltʃəz/ *pl. n.* flannel or plastic pants or a plastic wrapper worn by an infant over a nappy.

pile¹ /paɪl/ *n.* **1.** an assemblage of things laid or lying one upon another in a more or less orderly fashion. –*v.t.* **2.** (oft. fol. by *up* or *on*) to lay or dispose in a pile. **3.** (fol. by *up*) to accumulate. –*v.i.* **4.** (fol. by *up*) to accumulate, as money, debts, evidence, etc.

pile² /paɪl/ *n.* a heavy timber, stake or pole, sometimes pointed at the lower end, driven vertically into the ground or the bed of a river, etc., to support a superstructure or form part of a wall.

pile³ /paɪl/ *n.* **1.** hair, especially soft, fine hair or down. **2.** a raised surface on cloth.

pile⁴ /paɪl/ *n.* (*usu. pl.*) → **haemorrhoid**.

pilfer /'pɪlfə/ *v.t.* **1.** to steal (a small amount or object). –*v.i.* **2.** to practise petty theft. –**pilferer**, *n.* –**pilferage**, *n.*

pilgrim /'pɪlgrəm/ *n.* someone who journeys, especially a long distance, to some sacred place as an act of devotion. –**pilgrimage**, *n.*

pill /pɪl/ *n.* a small globular or rounded mass of medicinal substance, to be swallowed whole; tablet.

pillage /'pɪlɪdʒ/ *v.t.* (**-laged**, **-laging**) **1.** to strip of money or goods by open violence, as in war; plunder. –*n.* **2.** the act of plundering, especially in war.

pillar /'pɪlə/ *n.* an upright supporting part.

pillion /'pɪljən/ *n.* an extra seat behind the driver's seat on a bicycle, etc.

pillory /'pɪləri/ *n.* (*pl.* **-ries**) **1.** a wooden framework erected on a post, with holes for securing the head and hands, used to expose an offender to public derision. –*v.t.* (**-ried**, **-rying**) **2.** to expose to public ridicule or abuse.

pillow /'pɪloʊ/ *n.* a bag or case filled with feathers, down, or other soft material, commonly used as a support for the head during sleep or rest.

pilot /'paɪlət/ *n.* **1.** a person duly qualified to steer ships into or out of a harbour or through certain difficult waters. **2.** someone who controls an aeroplane, balloon, or other aircraft. **3.** a guide or leader. **4.** a sample episode for a television series. –*v.t.* **5.** to steer. **6.** to guide or conduct, as through unknown places, intricate affairs, etc.

pimp /pɪmp/ *n.* someone who solicits for a prostitute or brothel; a procurer.

pimple /'pɪmpəl/ *n.* a small, usually inflammatory swelling or elevation of the skin.

pin /pɪn/ *n.* **1.** a small, slender, sometimes tapered or pointed piece of wood, metal, etc., used to fasten, or hold things together, etc. **2.** a short, slender piece of wire with a point at one end and a head at the other, for fastening things together, as cloth or paper. –*v.t.* (**pinned**, **pinning**) **3.** to fasten or attach with a pin or pins, or as if with a pin. **4.** Also, **pin down**. to hold (a person, etc.) fast in a spot or position.

PIN /pɪn/ *n.* personal identification number; a sequence of numbers and/or letters used as part of an identification procedure in electronic banking, etc. Also, **PIN number**.

pinafore /'pɪnəfɔ/ *n.* an apron. Also, **pinny**.

piñata /pɪn'jɑtə/ *n.* a pottery jar or hollow papier-mâché figure of an animal or other object, filled with sweets or small gifts, which is held aloft by a rope and struck with a stick by a blindfolded child or other person, usually as part of birthday or other festivities.

pinball /'pɪnbɔl/ *n.* a game played on a sloping board, in which a ball, driven by a spring, hits objects which electrically record the score.

pince-nez /'pæns-neɪ, 'pɪns-neɪ/ *n.* a pair of spectacles kept in place by a spring which pinches the nose.

pincers /'pɪnsəz/ *n.* (*pl. or sing.*) **1.** a gripping tool consisting of two pivoted limbs forming a pair of jaws and a pair of handles. **2.** *Zool.* a grasping organ or pair of organs resembling this.

pinch /pɪntʃ/ *v.t.* **1.** to compress between the finger and thumb, the jaws of an instrument, or any two opposed surfaces. **2.** to cramp within narrow bounds or quarters. **3.** to stint the supply or amount of (a thing). **4.** *Colloq.* to steal. **5.** *Colloq.* to arrest. *–v.i.* **6.** to exert a sharp or painful compressing force. **7.** to cause sharp discomfort or distress. **8.** the act of pinching; nip; squeeze. **9.** a very small quantity of anything. **10.** sharp or painful stress, as of hunger, need, or any trying circumstances.

pincushion /'pɪnkʊʃən/ *n.* a small cushion in which pins are stuck, in readiness for use.

pine¹ /paɪn/ *n.* an evergreen coniferous trees with long needle-shaped leaves.

pine² /paɪn/ *v.i.* (fol. by *for*) to suffer with longing, or long painfully.

pineapple /'paɪnæpəl/ *n.* an edible juicy tropical fruit being a large collective fruit developed from a spike or head of flowers, and surmounted by a crown of leaves.

pine nut *n.* the edible nut found in the pine cone of any of several pine trees.

ping-pong /'pɪŋ-pɒŋ/ *n.* (*from trademark*) → **table tennis**.

pinion¹ /'pɪnjən/ *n. Machinery* a small cogwheel engaging with a larger cogwheel or with a rack.

pinion² /'pɪnjən/ *n.* **1.** the end section of a bird's wing. *–v.t.* **2.** to cut off the pinion of (a wing) or bind (the wings), in order to prevent a bird from flying. **3.** to bind (a person's arms or hands) so as to deprive them of their use.

pink¹ /pɪŋk/ *n.* **1.** a light tint of crimson; pale reddish purple. **2.** the highest form or degree: *in the pink of condition*. *–adj.* **3.** of the colour pink. *–phr.* **4. in the pink**, *Colloq.* in good health and spirits.

pink² /pɪŋk/ *v.t.* **1.** to pierce with a rapier or the like; stab. **2.** to finish at the edge with a scalloped, notched, or other ornamental pattern.

pinnacle /'pɪnəkəl/ *n.* **1.** a lofty peak. **2.** the highest or culminating point.

PIN number /pɪn/ *n.* → **PIN**.

pinot /'pinoʊ/ *n.* (*sometimes upper case*) **1.** any of various purple or white Burgundian grape varieties. **2.** any wine made from these grape varieties.

pinot grigio /pinoʊ 'gridʒoʊ/ *n.* (*sometimes upper case*) an Italian style of white wine made from the pinot grape.

pinot noir /pinoʊ 'nwa/ *n.* (*sometimes upper case*) a red wine made from pinot grapes.

pint /paɪnt/ *n.* a measure of liquid in the imperial system, equal to almost 600 millilitres.

pin-up *n. Colloq.* **1.** a picture, usually pinned to the wall, of an attractive member of the opposite sex. **2.** the person depicted.

pioneer /paɪə'nɪə/ *n.* **1.** one of those who first enter or settle a region, thus opening it for occupation and development by others. **2.** one of those who are first or earliest in any field of inquiry, enterprise, or progress. *–v.i.* **3.** to act as a pioneer. *–v.t.* **4.** to open or prepare (a way, etc.), as a pioneer does. **5.** to open a way for. **6.** to be a pioneer in.

pious /'paɪəs/ *adj.* **1.** having or displaying religious fervour or conscientiousness in religious observance. **2.** respectful or dutiful. **3.** sanctimonious.

pip¹ /pɪp/ *n.* **1.** one of the spots on dice, playing cards, or dominoes. **2.** *Mil. Colloq.* a badge of rank worn on the shoulders of certain commissioned officers.

pip² /pɪp/ *n.* a small seed, especially of a fleshy fruit, as an apple or orange.

pip³ /pɪp/ *n.* **1.** a brief high-pitched sound made by a radio receiver, echo-sounder, or the like. **2.** the signal on the screen of a radar set or the like.

pipe¹ /paɪp/ *n.* **1.** a hollow cylinder of metal, wood, or other material, for the conveyance of water, gas, steam, etc., or for some other purpose; a tube. **2.** a tube of wood, clay, hard rubber, or other material, with a small bowl at one end, used for smoking tobacco, opium, crack cocaine, ice, etc. **3.** *Music* **a.** a musical wind instrument. **b.** one of the wooden or metal tubes from which the sounds of an organ are produced. *–v.i.* **4.** to play on a pipe. *–v.t.* **5.** to convey by means of pipes. **6.** to utter in a shrill tone. **7.** to trim or finish (a garment, etc.) with piping. *–phr.* **8. put that in your pipe and smoke it!**, *Colloq.* an exclamation indicating that an unpleasant ultimatum has been given.

pipe² /paɪp/ *n.* a large cask, of varying capacity, for wine, etc.

pipe bomb *n.* an improvised bomb made from a hollow tube packed with explosive and projectiles such as shotgun pellets or nails.

pipedream /'paɪpdrim/ *n.* a futile hope, far-fetched fancy, or fantastic story.

pipeline /'paɪplaɪn/ *n.* **1.** pipe(s) used for the transmission of petroleum, etc. *–phr.* **2. in the pipeline**, on the way; in preparation.

pipette /pɪ'pet/ *n.* a slender graduated tube for measuring and transferring liquids from one vessel to another. Also, **pipet**.

pipi /'pɪpi/ *n.* an edible, smooth-shelled burrowing, bivalve mollusc.

piping /'paɪpɪŋ/ *n.* **1.** the act of someone who or that which pipes. **2.** a cordlike ornamentation made of icing, used on cakes, pastry, etc. **3.** a tubular band of material, sometimes containing a cord, for trimming garments, etc., as along edges and seams.

pipsqueak /'pɪpskwik/ *n. Colloq.* a small or insignificant person or thing.

piquant /'pikənt, pi'kɒnt/ *adj.* **1.** agreeably pungent or sharp in taste or flavour; biting; tart. **2.** agreeably stimulating, interesting, or attractive. *–***piquancy**, *n.*

pique /pik/ *v.t.* (**piqued, piquing**) **1.** to affect with sharp irritation and resentment, especially by some wound to pride. **2.** to excite (interest, curiosity, etc.). *–n.* **3.** anger, resentment, or ill feeling, as resulting from a slight or injury, especially to pride or vanity; offence taken.

piranha /pə'ranə/ *n.* a small fish noted for its voracious habits.

pirate /'paɪrət/ *n.* **1.** someone who robs or commits illegal violence at sea or on the shores of the sea. **2.** any plunderer. **3.** someone who appropriates and reproduces without authorisation, as for his or her own profit, the literary, artistic, or other work or any invention of another. **4.** Also, **pirate radio**. a radio station broadcasting on an unauthorised wavelength, and often operating outside territorial waters or in a foreign country so as to avoid payment of copyright fees or other legal restrictions. *–v.t.* **5.** to appropriate and reproduce (a literary work, video, CD, computer program, etc.) without authorisation or legal right. **–piracy**, *n.*

pirouette /pɪruˈɛt/ *n.* a whirling about on one foot or on the points of the toes, as in dancing.

piscatorial /pɪskəˈtɔːriəl/ *adj.* of or relating to fishing.

pisci- a word element meaning 'fish'.

piss /pɪs/ *Colloq.* (*taboo*) *–v.i.* **1.** to urinate. *–n.* **2.** urine. **3.** an act of passing water; urination. *–phr.* **4. piss off**, (*oft. used imperatively in dismissal*) (*sometimes offensive*) to go away: *I'm sick of your complaining – just piss off!; the party was boring so we pissed off.* **5. piss someone off**, **a.** to send someone away. **b.** to annoy someone intensely.

pistachio /pəˈstɑːʃioʊ, pəˈstæʃioʊ/ *n.* (*pl.* **-chios**) a hard-shelled nut with an edible greenish kernel.

pistil /ˈpɪstl/ *n. Bot.* the seed-bearing organ of a flower.

pistol /ˈpɪstl/ *n.* a short firearm intended to be held and fired with one hand.

piston /ˈpɪstən/ *n.* a movable disc or cylinder fitting closely within a tube or hollow cylinder, and capable of being driven alternately forwards and backwards in the tube by pressure, as in an internal-combustion engine.

pit¹ /pɪt/ *n.* **1.** a hole or cavity in the ground. **2.** *Mining* an excavation made in digging for some mineral deposit. **3.** a natural hollow or depression in the body. **4.** an enclosure for combats, as of dogs or cocks. **5.** any of the stalls beside the motor-racing track in which competing cars undergo running repairs, are refuelled, etc., during a race. *–v.t.* (**pitted, pitting**) **6.** to mark with pits or depressions. **7.** to set in active opposition, as one against another.

pit² /pɪt/ *n.* the stone of a fruit.

pita /ˈpiːtə/ *n.* a small, flat, round, slightly leavened bread forming a pocket, which, when opened, can be filled with food. Also, **pita bread, pitta**.

pitch¹ /pɪtʃ/ *v.t.* **1.** to set up or erect (a tent, camp, etc.). **2.** *Music* to set at a particular pitch, or determine the key or keynote of (a tune, etc.). **3.** to throw, fling or toss. *–v.i.* **4.** to plunge or fall forward or headlong. **5.** to plunge with alternate fall and rise of bow and stern, as a ship, aeroplane, etc. (opposed to *roll*). *–n.* **6.** relative point, position, or degree. **7.** height (now chiefly in certain specific uses). **8.** *Acoustics, Music* the apparent predominant frequency of a sound from an acoustic source, musical instrument, etc. **9.** the act or manner of pitching. **10.** inclination or slope, as of ground or a roof. **11.** *Sport* the whole area of play, usually of grass, of cricket, football, hockey, etc. **12.** a sales talk. *–phr. Colloq.* **13. cruel** (or **queer**) **someone's pitch**, to spoil someone's opportunity or plan. **14. pitch in**, to contribute or join in.

pitch² /pɪtʃ/ *n.* any of various dark-coloured tenacious or viscous substances used for covering the seams of vessels after caulking, for making pavements, etc.

pitchblende /ˈpɪtʃblɛnd/ *n.* a mineral; the principal ore of uranium and radium.

pitcher /ˈpɪtʃə/ *n.* a container, usually with a handle and spout or lip, for holding and pouring liquids.

pitchfork /ˈpɪtʃfɔːk/ *n.* a fork for lifting and pitching hay, etc.

piteous /ˈpɪtiəs/ *adj.* such as to excite or deserve pity.

pitfall /ˈpɪtfɔːl/ *n.* any trap or danger for the unwary.

pith /pɪθ/ *n.* **1.** the soft, spongy lining of the rind of oranges and other citrus fruits. **2.** *Bot.* the central cylinder of soft tissue in the stems of certain plants. **3.** the important or essential part; essence.

pithy /ˈpɪθi/ *adj.* (**pithier, pithiest**) full of vigour, substance, or meaning; terse.

pitiable /ˈpɪtiəbəl/ *adj.* **1.** deserving to be pitied; such as justly to excite pity; lamentable; deplorable. **2.** such as to excite a contemptuous pity; miserable; contemptible.

pitiful /ˈpɪtəfəl/ *adj.* **1.** such as to excite or deserve pity. **2.** such as to excite contempt by smallness, poor quality, etc.

pitta /ˈpɪtə/ *n.* → **pita**. Also, **pitta bread**.

pittance /ˈpɪtns/ *n.* **1.** a small allowance or sum for living expenses. **2.** a scanty income or remuneration.

pituitary gland /pəˈtʃuːətri/ *n.* a small, oval, endocrine gland attached to the base of the brain.

pity /ˈpɪti/ *n.* **1.** sympathetic or kindly sorrow excited by the suffering or misfortune of another, often leading one to give relief or to show mercy. *–v.t.* (**pitied, pitying**) **2.** to feel pity or compassion for. **–pitiless**, *adj.*

pivot /ˈpɪvət/ *n.* **1.** a pin or short shaft on the end of which something rests and turns, or upon and about which something rotates or oscillates. **2.** that on which something turns, hinges, or depends. *–v.i.* **3.** to turn on or as on a pivot.

pixel /ˈpɪksəl/ *n. Computers* the smallest element of a graphic image which can be produced in a visual display unit.

pixie /ˈpɪksi/ *n.* **1.** a fairy or sprite. *–phr.* **2. away (or off) with the pixies**, *Colloq.* no longer in tune with reality. Also, **pixy**.

pixilation /pɪksəˈleɪʃən/ *n.* an animation technique in which the animator photographs real objects and people frame by frame to achieve unusual effects of motion.

pizza /ˈpiːtsə, ˈpɪtsə/ *n.* an Italian dish made from yeast dough formed into a flat, round shape, covered with any of a variety of foods and baked in an oven; usually cut into wedge-shaped pieces for serving.

placard /ˈplækɑːd/ *n.* a written or printed notice to be posted in a public place or carried, as in a demonstration.

placate /pləˈkeɪt/ *v.t.* to appease; pacify. **–placatory**, *adj.*

place /pleɪs/ *n.* **1.** a particular portion of space, of definite or indefinite extent. **2.** any part or spot. **3.** a space or seat for a person, as in a theatre, train, etc. **4.** position, situation, or circumstances. **5.** a short street, a court, etc. **6.** a job, post, or office. **7.** a function or duty. **8.** a region. **9.** an area, especially one regarded as an entity. **10.** stead or lieu. **11.** *Arithmetic* **a.** the position of a figure in a series, as in decimal notation. **12.** *Sport* **a.** a position among the leading competitors, usually the first three, at the finish of a race. **b.** the position of the second or third (opposed to *win*). *–v.t.* (**placed**, **placing**) **13.** to put in a particular place; set. **14.** to fix (confidence, esteem, etc.) in a person or thing. **15.** to appoint (a person) to a post or office. **16.** to put or set in a particular place, position, situation, or relation. **17.** to identify by connecting with the proper place, circumstances, etc.

placebo /plə'sibou/ *n.* (*pl.* **-bos** *or* **-boes**) *Med.* a medicine which performs no physiological function but may benefit the patient psychologically.

placenta /plə'sentə/ *n.* (*pl.* **-tas** *or* **-tae** /-ti/) *Zool.*, *Anat.* the organ providing for the nourishment of the fetus and the elimination of its waste products.

placid /'plæsəd/ *adj.* pleasantly calm.

placket /'plækət/ *n.* an opening at the top of a skirt, or in a dress, blouse, or shirt.

plagiarism /'pleɪdʒərəzəm/ *n.* the appropriation or imitation of another's ideas and manner of expressing them, as in art, literature, etc., to be passed off as one's own. **–plagiarist**, *n.* **–plagiaristic**, *adj.* **–plagiarise**, **plagiarize**, *v.*

plagioclase /'pleɪdʒiou,kleɪz, -,kleɪs/ *n.* an important constituent of many igneous rocks.

plague /pleɪg/ *n.* **1.** an epidemic disease of high mortality; a pestilence. **2.** any cause of trouble or vexation. *–v.t.* (**plagued**, **plaguing**) **3.** to trouble or torment in any manner.

plaid /plæd/ *n.* any fabric woven of different coloured yarns in a cross-barred pattern.

plain /pleɪn/ *adj.* **1.** clear or distinct to the eye or ear. **2.** clear to the mind; evident, manifest, or obvious. **3.** conveying the meaning clearly or simply; easily understood. **4.** without special pretensions, superiority, elegance, etc.; ordinary. **5.** not beautiful; unattractive. **6.** without pattern, device, or colouring. **7.** flat or level. *–adv.* **8.** simply; absolutely. **9.** clearly or intelligibly. *–n.* **10.** an area of land not significantly higher than adjacent areas and with relatively minor differences in elevation within the area.

plaint /pleɪnt/ *n.* *Law* a statement of grievance made to a court for the purpose of asking redress.

plaintiff /'pleɪntəf, -tɪf/ *n.* *Law* someone who brings an action in a civil case.

plaintive /'pleɪntɪv/ *adj.* expressing sorrow or melancholy discontent; mournful.

plait /plæt/ *n.* **1.** a braid, as of hair or straw. *–v.t.* **2.** to braid (hair, etc.).

plan /plæn/ *n.* **1.** a scheme of action or procedure. **2.** a design or scheme of arrangement. **3.** a representation of a thing drawn on a plane, as a map or diagram. *–v.t.* (**planned**, **planning**) **4.** to arrange a plan or scheme for (any work, enterprise, or proceeding). **5.** to form a plan, project, or purpose of. *–phr.* **6.** off (the) plan, from the architect's plan of a proposed building before it is built: *to buy a unit off plan.*

plane¹ /pleɪn/ *n.* **1.** a flat or level surface. **2.** *Maths* a surface such that the straight line joining any two distinct points in it lies entirely within it. **3.** an aeroplane. *–adj.* **4.** flat or level, as a surface.

plane² /pleɪn/ *n.* **1.** a tool with an adjustable blade for paring, smoothing, or finishing the surface of wood, etc. *–v.t.* **2.** to smooth or dress with or as with a plane.

planet /'plænət/ *n.* *Astron.* a celestial body revolving around the sun and visible by its reflected light, large enough to exert sufficient gravity on itself to achieve a rounded shape, and to clear its orbit of all asteroids, comets, and other space debris. **–planetary**, *adj.*

plangent /'plændʒənt/ *adj.* **1.** beating or dashing, as waves. **2.** resounding loudly.

plank /plæŋk/ *n.* a long, flat piece of timber thicker than a board.

plankton /'plæŋktən/ *n.* the mass of very small animal and plant organisms that float or drift in the water, especially at or near the surface.

plant /plænt, plant/ *n.* **1.** any member of the vegetable group of living organisms. **2.** a herb or other small vegetable growth, in contrast to a tree or a shrub. **3.** the equipment, including the fixtures, machinery, tools, etc., and often the buildings, necessary to carry on any industrial business. **4.** *Colloq.* **a.** something or someone intended to trap, decoy, or lure, as criminals. **b.** a spy. *–v.t.* **5.** to put or set in the ground for growth, as seeds, young trees, etc. **6.** to implant (ideas, sentiments, etc.); introduce and establish (principles, doctrines, etc.) **7.** to insert or set firmly in or on the ground or some other body or surface. **8.** to put or place. **9.** *Colloq.* to hide or conceal, as stolen goods. **10.** to place (evidence) so that it will be discovered and incriminate an innocent person.

plantar /'plæntə/ *adj.* of or relating to the sole of the foot.

plantation /plæn'teɪʃən, plan'teɪʃən/ *n.* a farm or estate, especially in a tropical or semitropical country, on which cotton, tobacco, coffee, sugar, or the like is cultivated, usually by resident labourers.

plaque /plak, plæk/ *n.* **1.** a plate or tablet of metal, porcelain, etc., as on a wall or set in a piece of furniture, for ornamentation or, if inscribed, commemoration. **2.** a film on teeth harbouring bacteria.

plasma /'plæzmə/ *n.* **1.** *Anat.*, *Physiol.* the liquid part of blood or lymph, as distinguished from the corpuscles. **2.** *Physics* a highly ionised gas which, because it contains an approximately equal number of electrons and positive ions, is electrically neutral and highly conducting; used in a plasma display panel. **3.** *Astrophysics* **a.** a system of charged particles large enough to behave collectively, as in the sun. **b.** the ionised region of the earth's upper atmosphere.

plasma display *n.* a system for illuminating tiny coloured fluorescent lights in a plasma display panel, each set of three having one red, one green and one blue, to produce a pixel and from many pixels to form an image; used for television screens, computer screens, etc.

plasma display panel *n.* a panel with numerous cells filled with plasma (def. 2) which is activated by passing an electronic current through it to produce light photons which are then amplified by the phosphorus material on the inside wall of the cell. See **plasma display**.

plasma screen *n.* a screen for a television set, computer, etc., which uses plasma display.

plasma TV *n.* a television which has a plasma screen. Also, **plasma television**, **plasma**.

plaster /'plastə/ *n.* **1.** a pasty composition, as of lime, sand, water, and often hair, used for covering walls, ceilings, etc., where it hardens in drying. **2.** an adhesive bandage. *–v.t.* **3.** to cover (walls, etc.) with plaster. **4.** to overspread with anything, especially thickly or to excess.

plasterboard /'plastəbod/ *n.* plaster in paper-covered sheets, used for walls.

plastic /'plæstɪk/ *adj.* **1.** capable of being moulded or of receiving form. **2.** produced by moulding. **3.** pliable; impressionable. *–n.* **4.** any of a group of synthetic or natural organic materials which may be shaped when soft and then hardened. **5.** *Colloq.* credit or debit cards as a means of making a payment: *have you brought your plastic?*

plastic explosive *n.* an explosive substance in the form of a malleable, dough-like material.

plasticine /'plæstəsin/ *n.* (*from trademark*) a plastic modelling compound, in various colours.

plastic money *n.* credit cards collectively. Also, **plastic**.

plastic surgery *n.* the reconstruction or repair by surgery of part of the body for restorative or cosmetic purposes.

plate /pleɪt/ *n.* **1.** a shallow, usually circular dish, now usually of earthenware or porcelain, from which food is eaten. **2.** a plate of sandwiches, cakes, etc., prepared and brought to a social occasion. **3.** domestic dishes, utensils, etc., of gold or silver. **4.** a thin, flat sheet or piece of metal or other material, especially of uniform thickness. **5.** a sheet of metal for printing from. **6.** plated metallic ware. **7.** *Dentistry* a piece of metal, vulcanite, or plastic substance, with artificial teeth attached. *–v.t.* **8.** to coat (metal) with a thin film of gold, silver, nickel, etc., by mechanical or chemical means. *–phr.* **9. plate up**, to arrange food on an individual plate or plates for serving.

plateau /'plætoʊ/ *n.* (*pl.* **-eaus** or **-eaux** /-oʊz/) **1.** a tabular surface of high elevation, often of considerable extent. **2.** any period of minimal growth or decline.

plateau indexation *n.* a form of indexation in which wages below a certain value are increased on a proportional basis, and wages above that value by a fixed amount.

platelet /'pleɪtlət/ *n.* one of many small, cell-like fragments formed from special white blood cells, which help blood to clot in wounds.

platform /'plætfɔm/ *n.* **1.** a raised flooring or structure. **2.** a plan or set of principles. **3. a.** *Computers* an operating system. **b.** a telecommunications system: *an SMS platform.*

platinum /'plætənəm/ *n. Chem.* a heavy, greyish white, highly malleable and ductile metallic element. *Symbol:* Pt

platitude /'plætɪtjud/ *n.* a flat, dull, or trite remark.

platonic /plə'tonɪk/ *adj.* purely spiritual; free from sensual desire.

platoon /plə'tun/ *n.* a group of soldiers forming a unit.

platter /'plætə/ *n.* a large, shallow dish.

platypus /'plætəpʊs/ *n.* (*pl.* **-puses** or **-pi** /paɪ/ or, *especially collectively*, **-pus**) an amphibious, egg-laying monotreme with webbed feet and a muzzle like the bill of a duck.

plaudit /'plɔdət/ *n.* (*usu. pl.*) a demonstration or round of applause, as for some approved or admired performance.

plausible /'plɔzəbəl/ *adj.* having an appearance of truth or reason.

play /pleɪ/ *n.* **1.** a dramatic composition or piece; a drama. **2.** exercise or action by way of amusement or recreation. **3.** fun, jest, or trifling, as opposed to earnest. **4.** a set manoeuvre in the playing of a game: *a set play.* **5.** action, activity, or operation. **6.** freedom of movement, as within a space, as of a part of a mechanism. *–v.t.* **7.** to act or sustain (a part) in a dramatic performance or in real life. **8.** to engage in (a game, pastime, etc.). **9.** to contend against in a game. **10.** to perform on (a musical instrument): *to play the piano.* **11.** to perform (music) on an instrument or instruments: *to play a song from a record.* **12.** to cause (a record, cassette, etc.) to produce the sound recorded on it. **13.** to cause (a song, etc.) to be produced by a record or cassette player, etc. **14.** to do, perform, bring about, or execute. *–v.i.* **15.** to exercise or employ oneself in diversion, amusement, or recreation. **16.** (fol. by *with*) to amuse oneself or toy. **17.** to take part or engage in a game. **18.** to perform on a musical instrument. **19.** (fol. by *on* or *upon*) to work on (the feelings, weaknesses, etc., of another) for one's own purposes. *–phr.* **20. play around**, **a.** to behave in a lighthearted or irresponsible manner. **b.** (oft. fol. by *with*) to experiment with something in order to solve a problem, familiarise oneself, or produce a different result. **21. play it safe**, to act cautiously. *–***player**, *n.*

playground /'pleɪgraʊnd/ *n.* **1.** an outside area with equipment like swings, slides, etc., for children to play on. **2.** an outside area at a school, where students can play at recess and lunch.

playhouse /'pleɪhaʊs/ *n.* **1.** a theatre. **2.** a one-room imitation house built for children to play in.

playing card *n.* one of the conventional set of 52 cards, in 4 suits (diamonds, hearts, spades, and clubs), used in playing various games of chance and skill.

plaything /'pleɪθɪŋ/ *n.* a thing to play with; a toy.

playwright /'pleɪraɪt/ *n.* a writer of plays.

plaza /'plazə/ *n.* a public square.

plea /pli/ *n.* **1.** an excuse; a pretext. **2.** *Law* an allegation made by, or on behalf of, a party to a legal suit, in support of his or her claim or defence. **3.** an appeal or entreaty.

plea bargaining *n.* the negotiation for an agreement between the prosecution and the defence in a law suit that the accused will face only specified charges or reduced penalties if a plea of guilty is entered.

plead /plid/ *v.* (**pleaded** or **plead** /plɛd/ or, *Chiefly US*, **pled**, **pleading**) *–v.i.* **1.** to make earnest appeal or entreaty. **2.** *Law* **a.** to make any allegation or plea in an action at law. **b.** to address a court as an advocate. –*v.t.* **3.** to allege or urge in defence, justification, or excuse. **4.** *Law* **a.** to maintain (a cause, etc.) by argument before a court. **b.** to allege or set forth (something) formally in an action at law. **c.** to allege or cite in legal defence.

pleasant /'plɛzənt/ *adj.* **1.** pleasing, agreeable, or affording enjoyment; pleasurable. **2.** (of persons, manners, disposition, etc.) agreeable socially.

pleasantry /'plɛzəntri/ *n.* (*pl.* **-ries**) **1.** good-humoured raillery; pleasant humour in conversation. **2.** a conventional, polite remark: *to exchange pleasantries.*

please /pliz/ –*v.t.* **1.** to act to the pleasure or satisfaction of. **2.** to be the pleasure or will of; seem good to. –*v.i.* **3.** to be agreeable; give pleasure or satisfaction. **4.** to find something agreeable; like, wish or choose: *go where you please.* –*interj.* **5.** (as a polite addition to requests, etc.) if you are willing: *please come here.*

pleasurable /'plɛʒərəbəl/ *adj.* such as to give pleasure; agreeable; pleasant.

pleasure /'plɛʒə/ *n.* **1.** the state or feeling of being pleased. **2.** enjoyment or satisfaction derived from what is to one's liking; gratification; delight.

pleat /plit/ *n.* **1.** a fold made by doubling cloth upon itself. –*v.t.* **2.** to fold or arrange in pleats.

plebeian /plə'biən/ *adj.* **1.** belonging or relating to the common people. –*n.* **2.** a plebeian person.

plebiscite /'plɛbəsaɪt, -sət/ *n.* a direct vote of all the qualified electors in regard to some important issue.

plectrum /'plɛktrəm/ *n.* (*pl.* **-trums** *or* **-tra** /-trə/) a piece of metal, plastic, etc., for plucking strings of a guitar, etc.

pledge /plɛdʒ/ *n.* **1.** a solemn promise of something, or to do or refrain from doing something. **2.** anything given or regarded as a security of something. **3.** a toast. –*v.t.* (**pledged, pledging**) **4.** to bind by or as by a pledge. **5.** to promise solemnly, or engage to give, maintain, etc. **6.** to give or deposit as a pledge; pawn.

plenary /'plinəri/ *adj.* **1.** full; complete; entire; absolute; unqualified. **2.** attended by all qualified members, as a council. **3.** (of a conference session) scheduled without parallel sessions, and so likely to be attended by most of those registered as participants, usually to hear a prominent invited speaker.

plenipotentiary /ˌplɛnəpə'tɛnʃəri/ *n.* (*pl.* **-ries**) **1.** a person, especially a diplomatic agent, invested with full power or authority to transact business. –*adj.* **2.** invested with full power or authority.

plenitude /'plɛnətjud/ *n.* abundance.

plenteous /'plɛntiəs/ *adj.* plentiful.

plentiful /'plɛntəfəl/ *adj.* existing in great plenty; abundant.

plenty /'plɛnti/ *n.* **1.** a full or abundant supply. **2.** abundance.

plethora /'plɛθərə/ *n.* overfullness.

pleur- a word element meaning 'side', sometimes 'rib'. Also, (*before consonants*), **pleuro-**.

pleurisy /'plʊrəsi/ *n.* an inflammation of the membrane surrounding the lungs.

pliable /'plaɪəbəl/ *adj.* **1.** easily bent; flexible; supple. **2.** easily influenced; yielding; adaptable.

pliant /'plaɪənt/ *adj.* pliable.

pliers /'plaɪəz/ *pl. n.* small pincers with long jaws, for bending wire, etc.

plight[1] /plaɪt/ *n.* condition, state, or situation (usually bad).

plight[2] /plaɪt/ *v.t.* to give in pledge.

plinth /plɪnθ/ *n. Archit.* the lower square part of the base of a column.

plod /plɒd/ *v.i.* (**plodded, plodding**) **1.** to walk heavily; trudge; move laboriously. **2.** to work with dull perseverance; drudge.

plonk[1] /plɒŋk/ *v.t.* (oft. fol. by *down*) to place or drop heavily or suddenly.

plonk[2] /plɒŋk/ *n. Colloq.* cheap wine.

plop /plɒp/ *v.i.* (**plopped, plopping**) to make a sound like that of a flat object striking water without a splash.

plot[1] /plɒt/ *n.* **1.** a secret plan or scheme to accomplish some purpose, especially a hostile, unlawful, or evil purpose. **2.** the plan, scheme, or main story of a play, novel, poem, or the like. –*v.t.* (**plotted, plotting**) **3.** to plan secretly (something hostile or evil). **4.** to determine and mark (points), as on graph paper, by means of measurements or coordinates. –*phr.* **5. lose the plot**, *Colloq.* (of a person) to cease to understand fully what is going on in a certain situation, job, etc., and thus fail to act effectively.

plot[2] /plɒt/ *n.* a small piece or area of ground.

plough /plaʊ/ *n.* **1.** an agricultural implement for cutting and turning over the soil. –*v.t.* **2.** to furrow, remove, etc., or make (a furrow, groove, etc.) with or as with a plough. –*v.i.* **3.** to till the soil with a plough; work with a plough.

ploy /plɔɪ/ *n.* a manoeuvre or stratagem.

pluck /plʌk/ *v.t.* **1.** to pull off or out from the place of growth, as fruit, flowers, feathers, etc. **2.** to pull with sudden force or with a jerk. **3.** to sound (the strings of a musical instrument) by pulling at them with the fingers or a plectrum. –*n.* **4.** the act of plucking; a pull, tug, or jerk. **5.** the heart, liver, and lungs, especially of an animal used for food. **6.** courage or resolution in the face of difficulties.

plucky /'plʌki/ *adj.* (**-kier, -kiest**) having or showing pluck or courage; brave. –**pluckily**, *adv.* –**pluckiness**, *n.*

plug /plʌg/ *n.* **1.** a piece of rubber or plastic for stopping the flow of water from a basin, bath or sink. **2.** a device, usually with three prongs, which by insertion in a socket establishes contact between an electrical appliance and a power supply. **3.** any object or piece of material, as cork, plastic, etc., used to stop up a hole, to fill a gap, etc. –*v.t.* (**plugged, plugging**) **4.** to stop or fill with or as with a plug. **5.** *Colloq.* to mention (a publication, product or the like) favourably and often, repetitively as in a lecture, radio show, etc. **6.** (fol. by *in*) to connect (an electrical device) with an outlet.

plum /plʌm/ *n.* **1.** a purplish-coloured stone fruit. **2.** a good or choice thing, as one of the best parts of anything, a fine situation or appointment, etc.

plumage /'plumɪdʒ/ n. feathers collectively.

plumb /plʌm/ n. **1.** a small mass of lead or heavy material, used for various purposes. –adj. **2.** true according to a plumbline; perpendicular. –adv. **3.** in a perpendicular or vertical direction. **4.** exactly, precisely, or directly. –v.t. **5.** to make vertical. **6.** to sound (the ocean, etc.) with, or as with, a plumbline. –phr. **7. out of plumb, a.** not perpendicular. **b.** not functioning properly.

plumbing /'plʌmɪŋ/ n. the system of pipes and other apparatus for conveying water, liquid wastes, etc., as in a building. –**plumber**, n.

plumbline /'plʌmlaɪn/ n. a string to one end of which is attached a metal bob, used to determine perpendicularity, find the depth of water, etc.

plume /plum/ n. **1.** a feather. **2.** a flow of matter, especially a waste material or other pollutant, spreading from a source. –v.t. (**plumed, pluming**) **3.** to furnish, cover, or adorn with plumes or feathers. **4.** (fol. by on or upon) to display or feel satisfaction with or pride in (oneself); pride (oneself) complacently.

plummet /'plʌmət/ n. **1.** a plumbline. –v.i. **2.** to plunge.

plump[1] /plʌmp/ adj. well filled out or rounded in form; somewhat fleshy or fat.

plump[2] /plʌmp/ v.i. **1.** to fall heavily or suddenly and directly. **2.** (oft. fol. by for) to vote exclusively for or choose one out of a number.

plunder /'plʌndə/ v.t. **1.** to rob of goods or valuables by open force, as in war, hostile raids, etc. –n. **2.** the act of plundering; pillage. **3.** that which is taken in plundering; loot.

plunge /plʌndʒ/ v. (**plunged, plunging**) –v.t. **1.** to cast or thrust forcibly or suddenly into a liquid, etc. –v.i. **2.** to cast oneself, or fall as if cast, into water, a deep place, etc. **3.** to rush or dash with headlong haste. **4.** to throw oneself impetuously or abruptly into some condition, situation, matter, etc. **5.** to descend abruptly or precipitously, as a cliff, a road, etc. –n. **6.** the act of plunging.

plunk /plʌŋk/ v.t. **1.** to pluck (a stringed instrument or its strings); twang. **2.** to throw, push, put, etc., heavily or suddenly.

pluperfect /plu'pɜfəkt/ adj. Gram. perfect with respect to a temporal point of reference in the past. Compare **perfect, imperfect**.

plural /'plurəl/ adj. consisting of, containing, or relating to more than one.

plurality /plu'ræləti/ n. more than half of the whole; the majority.

plus /plʌs/ prep. **1.** with the addition of; with. –adj. **2.** involving or denoting addition. **3.** positive. –n. (pl. **-ses** or **-sses**) **4.** a plus quantity. **5.** an advantage, asset, or gain.

plush /plʌʃ/ n. **1.** a fabric of silk, cotton, wool, etc., having a longer pile than that of velvet, often used to make soft toys. –adj. **2.** (of a room, furnishings, or the like) luxurious and costly.

plutocracy /plu'tɒkrəsi/ n. (pl. **-cies**) the rule or power of wealth or of the wealthy.

plutonium /plu'tooniəm/ n. Chem. a radioactive element. Symbol: Pu

pluvial /'pluviəl/ adj. **1.** of or relating to rain; rainy. **2.** Geol. due to rain.

ply[1] /plaɪ/ v. (**plied, plying**) –v.t. **1.** to use; employ busily, or work with or at. **2.** to carry on, practise, or pursue. **3.** to supply with something pressingly offered. **4.** to address persistently or importunately, as with questions, solicitations, etc.; importune. **5.** to traverse (a river, etc.), especially on regular trips. –v.i. **6.** to travel or run regularly over a fixed course or between certain places, as a vessel or vehicle.

ply[2] /plaɪ/ n. (pl. **plies**) **1.** a fold; a thickness. **2.** a strand of yarn.

plywood /'plaɪwʊd/ n. a material consisting of an odd number of thin sheets or strips of wood glued together with the grains (usually) at right angles.

pneumatic /nju'mætɪk/ adj. **1.** of or relating to air, or gases in general. **2.** operated by air, or by pressure or exhaustion of air. **3.** containing air; filled with compressed air, as a tyre.

pneumonia /nju'mooniə/ n. inflammation of the lungs.

poach[1] /pootʃ/ v.i. **1.** to take game or fish illegally. **2.** to encroach on another's rights; take something belonging to another.

poach[2] /pootʃ/ v.t. to simmer in liquid in a shallow pan.

pock /pɒk/ n. a pustule on the body in an eruptive disease, as smallpox.

pocket /'pɒkət/ n. **1.** a small bag inserted in a garment, for carrying a purse or other small articles. **2.** money, means, or financial resources. **3.** a small isolated area. –adj. **4.** small enough to go in the pocket; diminutive: a pocket edition of a novel. –v.t. **5.** to put into one's pocket. **6.** to take possession of as one's own, often dishonestly.

pocket-dial v.i. (**-dialled** or, esp. US, **-dialed**, **-dialling** or, esp. US, **-dialing**) to make an unintended call from a mobile phone by accidentally activating the phone's speed dial while the phone is in one's pocket. –**pocket-dialling**, n.

pocket money n. **1.** a small weekly allowance of money. **2.** money for minor personal expenses.

pod[1] /pɒd/ n. a more or less elongated, two-valved seed vessel, as that of the pea.

pod[2] /pɒd/ n. a small herd or school, especially of seals or whales.

-pod a word element meaning 'footed', as in cephalopod.

podcast /'pɒdkast/ (from trademark) –v.t. (**-cast** or **-casted**, **-casting**) **1.** to deliver (a radio program) over the internet as a file to be stored and played as required on a computer or MP3 player. –n. **2.** such a program. –**podcasting**, n., adj.

poddy /'pɒdi/ n. (pl. **-dies**) a handfed calf.

podiatry /pə'daɪətri/ n. the investigation and treatment of foot disorders. –**podiatrist**, n. –**podiatric**, adj.

podium /'poodiəm/ n. (pl. **-dia** /-diə/) a small platform for the conductor of an orchestra, for a public speaker, for the recipients of awards, medals, etc.

pod slurping n. the downloading of large quantities of data to an MP3 player or memory stick from a computer, especially when done illegally after gaining unauthorised access to a computer.

poem /'pouəm/ *n.* a composition in verse, especially one characterised by artistic construction and imaginative or elevated thought.

poet /'pouət/ *n.* **1.** someone who composes poetry. **2.** someone having the gift of poetic thought, imagination, and creation, together with eloquence of expression.

poetic /pou'ɛtɪk/ *adj.* **1.** possessing the qualities or the charm of poetry. **2.** of or relating to poets or poetry. –**poetically**, *adv.*

poetry /'pouətri/ *n.* the art of rhythmical composition, written or spoken, for exciting pleasure by beautiful, imaginative, or elevated thoughts.

pogrom /'pɒgrəm/ *n.* an organised massacre, especially of Jews.

poignant /'pɔɪnjənt, 'pɔɪnənt/ *adj.* keenly distressing to the mental or physical feelings. –**poignancy**, *n.*

poinciana /pɔɪnsi'anə, -'ænə/ *n.* a tree or shrub with showy orange or scarlet flowers.

poinsettia /pɔɪn'sɛtiə/ *n.* a perennial with variously lobed leaves and brilliant usually scarlet bracts.

point /pɔɪnt/ *n.* **1.** a sharp or tapering end, as of a dagger. **2.** a mark made as with a sharp end of something. **3.** a mark of punctuation. **4.** a decimal point, etc. **5.** something that has position but not extension, as the intersection of two lines. **6.** any definite position, as in a scale, course, etc. **7.** each of the 32 positions indicating direction marked at the circumference of the card of a compass. **8.** a degree or stage. **9.** a particular instant of time. **10.** the important or essential thing. **11.** a particular aim, end, or purpose. **12.** a dance shoe with a stiffened toe worn by a ballerina to enable her to dance on the tip of her toes. **13.** a single unit, as in counting, scoring a game, etc. **14.** *Commerce* a unit of price quotation in share transactions on the stock exchange. –*v.t.* **15.** to direct (the finger, a weapon, the attention, etc.) at, to, or upon something. **16.** (fol. by *out*) to direct attention to. –*v.i.* **17.** to indicate position or direction, or direct attention, with or as with the finger. **18.** to aim. **19.** to have a tendency, as towards something. **20.** to face in a particular direction, as a building. –**pointy**, *adj.*

point-blank *adj.* **1.** aimed or fired straight at the mark at close range; direct. **2.** straightforward, plain, or explicit.

pointy /'pɔɪnti/ *adj.* (**-tier**, **-tiest**) **1.** being pointed at the end: *pointy shoes; a pointy nose.* –*phr.* **2. at the pointy end**, at the moment of engagement or crisis.

poise /pɔɪz/ *n.* **1.** a state of balance or equilibrium, as from equality or equal distribution of weight. **2.** composure; self-possession. –*v.* (**poised**, **poising**) –*v.t.* **3.** to balance evenly; adjust, hold, or carry in equilibrium. **4.** to hold supported or raised, as in position for casting, using, etc. –*v.i.* **5.** to be balanced; rest in equilibrium. **6.** to hang supported or suspended.

poison /'pɔɪzən/ *n.* **1.** any substance (liquid, solid, or gaseous) which by reason of an inherent deleterious property tends to destroy life

or impair health. –*v.t.* **2.** to administer poison to (a person or animal). –**poisonous**, *adj.*

poke /pouk/ *v.t.* **1.** to thrust against or into (something) with the finger or arm, a stick, etc.; prod. **2.** to thrust obtrusively. –*v.i.* **3.** to make a thrusting or pushing movement with the finger, a stick, etc. **4.** (oft. fol. by *about* or *around*) to pry; search curiously. –*n.* **5.** a thrust or push. –*phr.* **6. better than a poke in the eye with a blunt stick** (or **a dead mullet**), an interjection, said grudgingly of some small benefit received, or humorously of a great one.

poker[1] /'poukə/ *n.* a metal rod for poking or stirring a fire.

poker[2] /'poukə/ *n.* a card game, usually involving gambling.

poker machine *n.* a coin-operated gambling machine.

pokie /'pouki/ *n.* *Colloq.* a poker machine.

poky /'pouki/ *adj.* (**-kier**, **-kiest**) (of a place) small and cramped. Also, **pokey**.

polar /'poulə/ *adj.* of or relating to a pole, as of the earth, a magnet, an electric cell, etc.

polar bear *n.* a large white bear of the arctic regions.

polarisation /poulərar'zeɪʃən/ *n.* **1.** *Optics* a state, or the production of a state, in which rays of light, or similar radiation, exhibit different properties in different directions. **2.** the state of being polarised: *the polarisation of the electorate.* Also, **polarization**.

polarise /'poulərarz/ *v.t.* **1.** to cause polarisation in. **2.** to cause (a community, organisation, etc.) to divide on an issue. **3.** to bring about sharp division in: *to polarise the tax debate.* Also, **polarize**. –**polarisable**, *adj.* –**polariser**, *n.*

polarity /pə'lærəti/ *n.* (*pl.* **-ties**) **1.** in physics, the possession of a positive or negative pole, or both poles, by magnets, batteries, etc. **2.** the possession of two directly opposite ideas, principles or qualities.

polaroid /'poulərɔɪd/ *n.* (*from trademark*) a material which allows only light polarised in a particular direction to pass.

pole[1] /poul/ *n.* **1.** a long, rounded, usually slender piece of wood, metal, etc. –*v.t.* (**poled**, **poling**) **2.** to push, strike, propel, etc., with a pole.

pole[2] /poul/ *n.* **1.** each of the extremities of the axis of the earth or of any more or less spherical body. **2.** each of the two points in which the extended axis of the earth cuts the celestial sphere, about which the stars seem to revolve (**celestial pole**). **3.** *Physics* each of the two regions or parts of a magnet, electric battery, etc., at which certain opposite forces are manifested or appear to be concentrated. **4.** one of two completely opposed or contrasted principles, tendencies, etc.

poleaxe /'poulæks/ *n.* an axe, usually with a hammer opposite the cutting edge, used in felling or stunning animals.

polecat /'poulkæt/ *n.* a mammal of the weasel family.

polemic /pə'lɛmɪk/ *n.* **1.** a controversial argument; argumentation against some opinion, doctrine, etc. –*adj.* Also, **polemical**. **2.** of or relating to dispute or controversy; controversial.

police /pə'liːs/ *n.* (*construed as pl.*) **1. the police**, an organised civil force for maintaining order, preventing and detecting crime, and enforcing the laws. **2.** the members of such a force. *–v.t.* (**-liced, -licing**) **3.** to regulate, control, or keep in order by police or as a police force does.

policy[1] /'pɒləsi/ *n.* (*pl.* **-cies**) **1.** a definite course of action adopted as expedient or from other considerations. **2.** prudence, practical wisdom, or expediency.

policy[2] /'pɒləsi/ *n.* (*pl.* **-cies**) a document embodying a contract of insurance.

polio /'pouliou/ *n.* → **poliomyelitis**.

poliomyelitis /ˌpouliˌouməˈlaɪtəs/ *n.* an acute viral disease resulting in paralysis.

-polis a word element meaning 'city'.

polish /'pɒlɪʃ/ *v.t.* **1.** to make smooth and glossy, especially by friction. **2.** to render finished, refined or elegant. **3.** *Colloq.* (fol. by *off*) to finish, or dispose of quickly. *–n.* **4.** a substance used to give smoothness or gloss. **5.** the act of polishing. **6.** smoothness and gloss of surface. **7.** superior or elegant finish imparted; refinement; elegance.

polite /pə'laɪt/ *adj.* showing good manners towards others, as in behaviour, speech, etc.; courteous; civil.

politic /'pɒlətɪk/ *adj.* **1.** sagacious; prudent; judicious. **2.** shrewd; artful; expedient.

political /pə'lɪtɪkəl/ *adj.* **1.** relating to politics. **2.** relating to or connected with a political party, or its principles, aims, activities, etc. **3.** of or relating to, the state or its government. *–***politically**, *adv.*

politically correct *adj.* conforming to current beliefs about correctness in language and behaviour with regard to policies on sexism, racism, ageism, etc. *–***political correctness**, *n.*

politics /'pɒlətɪks/ *n.* (*construed as sing. or pl.*) **1.** the science or art of political government. **2.** the practice or profession of conducting political affairs. **3.** political affairs. **4.** the use of underhand or unscrupulous methods in obtaining power or advancement within an organisation. *–***politician**, *n.* *–***politicise**, **politicize**, *n.*

polity /'pɒləti/ *n.* (*pl.* **-ties**) **1.** a particular form or system of government (civil, ecclesiastical, or other). **2.** government or administrative regulation.

polka /'pɒlkə/ *n.* a lively dance.

poll /poul/ *n.* **1.** the registering of votes, as at an election. **2.** the number of votes cast. **3.** an analysis of public opinion on a subject, usually by selective sampling. **4.** the head, especially the part of it on which the hair grows. *–v.t.* **5.** to receive at the polls, as votes. **6.** to take or register the votes of, as persons. **7.** to cut off or cut short the hair, etc., of (a person, etc.); crop; clip; shear. **8.** to cut off or cut short the horns of (cattle).

pollard /'pɒləd/ *n.* **1.** a tree cut back nearly to the trunk, so as to produce a dense mass of branches. **2.** an animal, as a stag, ox, or sheep, without horns.

pollen /'pɒlən/ *n.* the fertilising element of flowering plants, consisting of fine, powdery, yellowish grains or spores.

pollinate /'pɒləneɪt/ *v.t.* to convey pollen for fertilisation to.

pollute /pə'luːt/ *v.t.* to make foul or unclean. *–***pollutant**, *n.*

pollution /pə'luːʃən/ *n.* **1.** the act of polluting. **2.** the results of this polluting, as city smog, etc.

polo /'poulou/ *n.* a game resembling hockey, played on horseback.

poltergeist /'pɒltəɡaɪst/ *n.* a ghost or spirit which manifests its presence by noises, knockings, etc.

poltroon /pɒl'truːn/ *n.* a wretched coward.

poly- a word element or prefix, meaning 'much', 'many'. Compare **mono-**.

polyandry /pɒli'ændri/ *n.* the practice or the condition of having more than one husband at one time.

polycarbonate /pɒli'kɑːbəneɪt/ *n.* a strong, transparent thermoplastic resin, used to make shatterproof glass, lightweight spectacle lenses, etc.

polyester /'pɒliɛstə/ *n.* a synthetic polymer used in fabrics, etc.

polygamy /pə'lɪɡəmi/ *n.* the practice or condition of having more than one spouse at one time. *–***polygamous**, *adj.*

polyglot /'pɒliɡlɒt/ *adj.* knowing many or several languages, as a person.

polygon /'pɒliɡɒn, -ɡən/ *n.* a closed, plane figure having three or more sides and angles.

polygyny /pə'lɪdʒəni/ *n.* the practice or the condition of having more than one wife at one time.

polyhedron /pɒli'hidrən/ *n.* (*pl.* **-drons** or **-dra** /-drə/) a solid figure having many faces.

polymer /'pɒləmə/ *n.* a compound of high molecular weight derived either by the combination of many smaller molecules or by the condensation of many smaller molecules eliminating water, alcohol, etc. *–***polymerise**, **polymerize**, *v.*

polyp /'pɒləp/ *n.* **1.** *Zool.* an animal form with a more or less fixed base and free end with mouth and tentacles. **2.** a projecting growth from a mucous surface.

polysaccharide /pɒli'sækəraɪd/ *n.* a carbohydrate, as starch, cellulose, etc., containing more than three monosaccharide units per molecule, which can be broken down by acids or enzymes to monosaccharides.

polysemy /pə'lɪsəmi/ *n.* the acquisition and retention of many meanings by one word, as in the case of the word *tank* which referred to a receptacle for liquids and then additionally to a military vehicle.

polystyrene /pɒli'staɪrin/ *n.* a clear plastic, easily coloured and moulded and used as an insulating material.

polytheism /'pɒliθiˌɪzəm/ *n.* the doctrine of, or belief in, many gods or more gods than one.

polythene /'pɒləθin/ *n.* a plastic used for containers, electrical insulation, packaging, etc.

polyunsaturated /ˌpɒliʌn'sætʃəreɪtəd/ *adj.* *Chem.* **1.** of or relating to a fat or oil which has two or more double bonds per molecule. **2.** of or relating to foods based on polyunsaturated fat, oils, and believed not to increase cholesterol levels in the blood.

polyurethane /ˌpɒliˈjʊərəθeɪn/ n. a substance used in making foam products for insulation, decoration, etc.

Pom /pɒm/ n. Colloq. (sometimes derog.) (also lower case) a person who is resident in or has migrated from the British Isles, especially England. Also, **Pommy**.

pomander /pəˈmændə/ n. a mixture of aromatic substances, often in the form of a ball.

pomegranate /ˈpɒməɡrænət/ n. a several-chambered, many-seeded fruit.

pommel /ˈpʌməl, ˈpɒməl/ n. **1.** a terminating knob, as on the top of a tower, hilt of a sword, etc. **2.** the protuberant part at the front and top of a saddle. Also, **pummel**.

Pommy /ˈpɒmi/ n. (pl. **-mies**) Colloq. (sometimes derog.) (also lower case) → **Pom**. Also, **Pommie**.

pomp /pɒmp/ n. stately or splendid display.

pompom /ˈpɒmpɒm/ n. an ornamental tuft or ball of feathers, wool, or the like.

pompous /ˈpɒmpəs/ adj. **1.** characterised by ostentatious parade of dignity or importance. **2.** (of language, style, etc.) ostentatiously lofty.

ponce /pɒns/ Colloq. –n. **1.** → **pimp**. –v.i. (**ponced**, **poncing**) **2.** (fol. by about) to flounce; behave in a foolishly effeminate fashion. –**poncy**, adj.

poncho /ˈpɒntʃoʊ/ n. (pl. **-chos**) a blanket-like cloak.

pond /pɒnd/ n. a body of water smaller than a lake, often one artificially formed.

ponder /ˈpɒndə/ v.i. **1.** to consider deeply; meditate. –v.t. **2.** to weigh carefully in the mind, or consider carefully.

ponderable /ˈpɒndərəbəl/ adj. capable of being weighed; having appreciable weight.

ponderous /ˈpɒndərəs, -drəs/ adj. **1.** of great weight; heavy; massive. **2.** without graceful lightness or ease; dull.

pontiff /ˈpɒntɪf/ n. **1.** a high or chief priest. **2.** Eccles. **a.** a bishop. **b.** the bishop of Rome (the pope). –**pontifical**, adj.

pontificate /pɒnˈtɪfəkeɪt/ v.i. to speak in a pompous manner. –**pontification**, n.

pontoon¹ /pɒnˈtun/ n. a boat, or some other floating structure, used as one of the supports for a temporary bridge over a river.

pontoon² /pɒnˈtun/ n. a card game; twenty-one; blackjack.

pony /ˈpoʊni/ n. (pl. **-nies**) a small horse.

ponytail /ˈpoʊniteɪl/ n. a bunch of hair tied at the back of the head.

poo /pu/ n. Colloq. (euphemistic) → **faeces**.

poodle /ˈpudl/ n. one of a breed of intelligent pet dogs with thick curly hair.

poofter /ˈpʊftə/ n. Colloq. (sometimes derog.) a male homosexual.

pool¹ /pul/ n. **1.** a small body of standing water; pond. **2.** a swimming pool.

pool² /pul/ n. **1.** an association of competitors who control to control the production, market, and price of a commodity for mutual benefit, although they appear to be rivals. **2.** a combination of interests, funds, etc., for common advantage. **3.** a facility or service that is shared by a number of people. **4.** Also, **pocket**

billiards. any of various games played on a billiard table in which the object is to drive all the balls into the pockets with the cue ball. –v.t. **5.** to put (interests, money, etc.) into a pool, or common stock or fund, as for a financial venture, according to agreement.

poop¹ /pup/ n. an enclosed space in the back part of a ship.

poop² /pup/ v.t. Colloq. to tire or exhaust.

poop³ /pup/ n. Colloq. excrement.

poor /pɔ/ adj. **1.** having little or nothing in the way of wealth, goods, or means of subsistence. **2.** of an inferior, inadequate, or unsatisfactory kind; not good. **3.** humble. **4.** unfortunate.

pop¹ /pɒp/ v. (**popped**, **popping**) –v.i. **1.** to make a short, quick, explosive sound or report. **2.** to burst open with such a sound. **3.** (fol. by in, into, out, etc.) to come or go quickly, suddenly or unexpectedly. **4.** (of the ears) to adjust to a sudden change in air pressure. –v.t. **5.** to cause to make a sudden, explosive sound. **6.** Colloq. to take (a pill or recreational drug) orally. **7.** to force air into the Eustachian tubes so as to adjust the pressure on the eardrums of (the ears). –n. **8.** a short, quick, explosive sound. –phr. **9. a pop**, Colloq. each.

pop² /pɒp/ adj. **1.** denoting or relating to a type of commercial modern music with wide popular appeal, especially among the young, and usually being tuneful, repetitive and having an insistent rhythmic beat. **2.** denoting or relating to a singer or player of such music.

pop³ /pɒp/ n. Colloq. father, or grandfather.

popcorn /ˈpɒpkɔn/ n. any of several varieties of maize whose kernels burst open and puff out when subjected to dry heat.

pope /poʊp/ n. (oft. upper case) the bishop of Rome as head of the Roman Catholic Church.

poplar /ˈpɒplə/ n. a tall, spire-shaped tree.

poplin /ˈpɒplən/ n. a strong, finely ribbed cotton material.

pop music n. a type of commercial music having great but ephemeral popularity, especially among the young, and often characterised by an insistent rhythmic beat.

poppadum /ˈpɒpʌdʌm/ n. → **pappadum**. Also, **poppadom**.

poppet /ˈpɒpət/ n. a term of endearment for a girl or child.

poppy /ˈpɒpi/ n. (pl. **-pies**) a plant with showy flowers of various colours.

pop quiz n. a test, usually in a classroom situation, of which the participants have not been given prior warning.

populace /ˈpɒpjələs/ n. the inhabitants of an area; population.

popular /ˈpɒpjələ/ adj. **1.** regarded with favour or approval by associates, acquaintances, the general public, etc. **2.** of, relating to, or representing the people, or the common people. –**popularity**, n.

populate /ˈpɒpjəleɪt/ v.t. **1.** to inhabit. **2.** to furnish with inhabitants, as by colonisation; people. **3.** Computers to enter data into (a field of a database, etc.).

population /pɒpjəˈleɪʃən/ n. **1.** the total number of persons inhabiting a country, town, or any district or area. **2.** the body of inhabitants of a place. **3.** the act or process of populating.

populous /ˈpɒpjələs/ *adj.* full of people or inhabitants, as a region; well populated.

pop-up *adj.* **1.** equipped with a pop-up mechanism: *a pop-up card.* **2.** (of a shop, restaurant, bar, etc.) operating for a brief period only, often for a specific short-term marketing or advertising purpose; guerilla.

porcelain /ˈpɔːsəlɪn, ˈpɔːslən/ *n.* a vitreous, more or less translucent, ceramic material; china.

porch /pɔːtʃ/ *n.* an exterior appendage to a building, forming a covered approach or vestibule to a doorway.

porcine /ˈpɔːsaɪn/ *adj.* **1.** of or resembling swine. **2.** swinish, hoggish, or piggish.

porcupine /ˈpɔːkjəpaɪn/ *n.* any of various rodents covered with stout spines or quills.

pore[1] /pɔː/ *v.t.* (usu. fol. by *over*, *on*, or *upon*) to meditate or ponder intently.

pore[2] /pɔː/ *n.* a minute opening or orifice, as in the skin or a leaf, a rock, etc.

pork /pɔːk/ *n.* the flesh of pigs.

pork-barrelling *n.* the practice of supplying an inappropriate share of government money to a person, company, institution, etc., in return for political support.

pornography /pɔːˈnɒɡrəfi/ *n.* obscene literature, art, or photography, designed to excite sexual desire. **–pornographer**, *n.* **–pornographic**, *adj.*

porous /ˈpɔːrəs/ *adj.* **1.** having pores. **2.** permeable by water, air, etc. **3.** allowing easy passage in and out: *porous borders.*

porphyry /ˈpɔːfəri/ *n.* (*pl.* **-ries**) an igneous rock.

porpoise /ˈpɔːpəs/ *n.* (*pl.* **-poises** *or, especially collectively,* **-poise**) **1.** any of various cetaceans, usually blackish above and paler underneath, with a blunt, rounded snout. **2.** → **dolphin**.

porridge /ˈpɒrɪdʒ/ *n.* an oatmeal breakfast dish.

port[1] /pɔːt/ *n.* **1.** a town or place where ships load or unload. **2.** a place along the coast where ships may take refuge from storms.

port[2] /pɔːt/ *n.* the left-hand side of a ship or aircraft facing forward (opposed to *starboard*).

port[3] /pɔːt/ *n.* any of a class of very sweet, fortified wines, mostly dark red.

port[4] /pɔːt/ *n.* **1.** *Naut.* a porthole. **2.** a steel door in the side of a ship for loading and discharging cargo and baggage. **3.** *Computers* an interface to which a peripheral device is connected.

port[5] /pɔːt/ *v.t.* **1.** *Mil.* to carry (a rifle, etc.) with both hands, in a slanting direction across the front of the body with the barrel or like part near the left shoulder. **2.** to carry (something).

port[6] /pɔːt/ *n.* a portmanteau; suitcase.

portable /ˈpɔːtəbəl/ *adj.* **1.** capable of being transported or conveyed. **2.** (of benefits, superannuation, etc.) capable of being transferred with a change in job, especially from one department of the public service to another.

portal /ˈpɔːtl/ *n.* **1.** a door, gate, or entrance. **2.** → **web portal**.

portend /pɔːˈtɛnd/ *v.t.* to indicate beforehand, as an omen does.

portent /ˈpɔːtɛnt/ *n.* an indication of something about to happen, especially something momentous. **–portentous**, *adj.*

porter /ˈpɔːtə/ *n.* a person employed to carry bags and other loads, as at a railway station, hotel, etc.

portfolio /pɔːtˈfoʊlioʊ/ *n.* (*pl.* **-lios**) **1.** a portable case for loose papers, prints, etc. **2.** *Govt* **a.** the office or post of a minister of state or member of a cabinet. **b.** the public service department or departments for which a minister is responsible. **3.** an itemised account or list of financial assets, as securities, shares, discount paper, etc., of an investment organisation, bank or other investor. **4.** a collection of an artist's drawings, photographs, etc., which may be shown to prospective employers, etc., as examples of their work.

porthole /ˈpɔːthoʊl/ *n.* a usually circular aperture in the side of a ship, for admitting light and air.

portion /ˈpɔːʃən/ *n.* **1.** a part of any whole, whether actually separated from it or not. **2.** the part of a whole allotted to or belonging to a person or group; a share. **–v.t. 3.** (oft. fol. by *out*) to divide into or distribute in portions or shares; parcel.

portly /ˈpɔːtli/ *adj.* (**-lier**, **-liest**) stout.

portmanteau /pɔːtˈmæntoʊ/ *n.* (*pl.* **-teaus** *or* **-teaux**) a case for clothing.

portrait /ˈpɔːtrət, ˈpɔːtreɪt/ *n.* a painting, drawing or photograph of a person.

portray /pɔːˈtreɪ/ *v.t.* **1.** to represent by a drawing, painting, carving, or the like. **2.** to represent dramatically, as on the stage. **–portrayal**, *n.*

pose /poʊz/ *v.i.* **1.** to affect a particular character as with a view to the impression made on others. **2.** to assume or hold a position or attitude for some artistic purpose. **–v.t. 3.** to present: *the fire poses a threat to nearby residents.* **–n. 4.** attitude or posture of body. **5.** a studied attitude or mere affectation, as of some character, quality, sentiment, or course.

posh /pɒʃ/ *adj. Colloq.* **1.** elegant; luxurious; smart; first-class. **2.** having or affecting the speech, dress, and manners thought to be typical of an upper class.

position /pəˈzɪʃən/ *n.* **1.** condition with reference to place; location. **2.** proper or appropriate place. **3.** a post of employment. **4.** mental attitude; way of viewing a matter; stand. **5.** condition (of affairs, etc.). **–v.t. 6.** to put in a particular or appropriate position; place.

positive /ˈpɒzətɪv/ *adj.* **1.** explicitly laid down or expressed. **2.** admitting of no question. **3.** confident in opinion or assertion, as a person; fully assured. **4.** absolute. **5.** characterised by optimism or hopefulness. **6.** *Elect.* having a deficiency of electrons. **7.** *Chem.* having fewer electrons than the neutral form or molecule, with a resultant positive charge. **8.** *Maths* denoting a quantity greater than zero.

positive discrimination *n.* discrimination which works actively to favour a previously disadvantaged group in society.

posse /ˈpɒsi/ *n.* (formerly, in the US) the body of citizens that a sheriff is empowered to call to assist in preserving the peace, making arrests, and serving writs.

possess /pə'zɛs/ v.t. **1.** to have as property; to have belonging to one. **2.** to have as a faculty, quality, or the like. **3.** (of a spirit, especially an evil one) to occupy and control, or dominate from within, as a person. **–possessory**, adj.

possession /pə'zɛʃən/ n. **1.** the act or fact of possessing. **2.** ownership. **3.** a thing possessed. **4.** control over oneself, one's mind, etc.

possessive /pə'zɛsɪv/ adj. exerting or seeking to exert excessive influence on the affections, behaviour, etc., of others.

possible /'pɒsəbəl/ adj. **1.** capable of existing, happening, being done, being used, etc. **2.** that might happen, work, or be the case, but without certainty: a possible cure for cancer. **–possibility**, n.

possum /'pɒsəm/ n. a herbivorous, largely arboreal, marsupial.

post¹ /poust/ n. **1.** a strong piece of timber, metal, or the like, set upright as a support, a point of attachment, a mark, a place for displaying notices, etc. –v.t. **2.** to affix (a notice, etc.) to a post, wall, or the like.

post² /poust/ n. a position of duty, employment, or trust to which one is assigned or appointed.

post³ /poust/ n. **1.** a single collection or delivery of letters, packages, etc. **2.** the letters, packages, etc., themselves; mail. –v.t. **3.** to place (a letter, etc.) in a post-box, post office, etc., for transmission. **4.** Bookkeeping **a.** to transfer (an entry or item), as from the journal to the ledger. **b.** to enter (an item) in due place and form. **5.** to supply with up-to-date information; inform. **6.** Internet to send (a message) electronically to a mailing list or newsgroup. **–postage**, n.

post⁴ /poust/ n. an examination held after the main examination.

post- a prefix meaning 'behind', 'after'.

postal note n. an order for the payment of a small amount of money, bought from and generally cashed at a post office. Compare **money order**. Also, **postal order**.

postbox /'poustbɒks/ n. a letterbox (def. 1), especially one on a public thoroughfare.

postcode /'poustkoud/ n. a group of numbers or letters added as part of the address and intended to facilitate the delivery of mail.

postcolonial /poustkə'louniəl/ adj. following a period of colonialism: postcolonial nationalism.

postcolonialism /poustkə'louniəlɪzəm/ n. **1.** an attitude of mind typical of those who have experienced colonial rule. **2.** a philosophical, literary, or artistic theory that frames subjects in the context of the cultural aftermath of colonial rule. **–postcolonialist**, adj.

postdate /poust'deɪt/ v.t. **1.** to date (a document, cheque, invoice, etc.) with a date later than the current date. **2.** to follow in time.

poster /'poustə/ n. a large placard or bill, often incorporating photographs or illustrations, and posted for advertisement or publicity or for decorative purposes.

poster child n. (pl. **poster children**) **1.** a child who is regarded as a focus of some community sentiment or aspiration, especially one with appealing looks who is used for advertising for donations. **2.** any person, organisation, or entity, regarded as representative of a cause, development, etc.

posterior /pɒs'tɪəriə/ adj. **1.** situated behind, or hinder (opposed to anterior). –n. **2.** the hinder parts of the body; the buttocks.

posterity /pɒ'stɛrəti/ n. succeeding generations collectively.

postgraduate /poust'grædʒuət/ n. someone studying at a university for a higher degree.

posthaste /poust'heɪst/ adv. with all possible speed or promptness.

posthumous /'pɒstʃəməs/ adj. **1.** (of books, music, medals, etc.) published or awarded after a person's death. **2.** arising, existing, or continuing after one's death.

posting /'poustɪŋ/ n. the transfer of service personnel away to another unit or command.

postmark /'poustmak/ n. an official mark stamped on letters or other mail, to cancel the postage stamp, indicate the place and date of sending.

post-mortem adj. /'poust-mɒtəm/ **1.** subsequent to death, as an examination of the body. –n. /poust-'mɒtəm/ **2.** a post-mortem examination.

post-obit /poust-'oubət, -'ɒbət/ adj. effective after a particular person's death.

post office n. **1.** the authority responsible for a country's postal and telecommunications services. **2.** a local office of this authority for receiving, distributing, and transmitting mail, selling postage stamps, providing telecommunications services, etc. **–post-office**, adj.

postpone /poust'poun, pous'poun/ v.t. to put off to a later time; defer.

postscript /'poustskrɪpt/ n. a paragraph, sentence, etc., added to a letter which has already been concluded and signed by the writer. Abbrev.: PS

postulate /'pɒstʃəleɪt/ v.t. **1.** to ask, demand, or claim. **2.** to claim or assume the existence or truth of, especially as a basis for reasoning.

posture /'pɒstʃə/ n. **1.** the relative disposition of the various parts of anything. **2.** the position of the body and limbs as a whole. –v.t. **3.** to place in a particular posture or attitude; dispose in postures.

posy /'pouzi/ n. (pl. **-sies**) a bouquet.

pot /pɒt/ n. **1.** an earthen, metallic, or other container, usually round and deep, used for domestic or other purposes. **2.** a type of basket for trapping fish or crustaceans. **3.** a medium-sized beer glass. **4.** Colloq. marijuana. –v.t. (**potted**, **potting**) **5.** to put into a pot. **6.** to preserve or cook (food) in a pot. **7.** to plant in a pot of soil. **8.** Colloq. to capture, secure, or win. –phr. **9. pot out**, to replant (a potted plant) into a garden bed. **10. pot up**, to replant (a potted plant) into a bigger pot.

potable /'poutəbəl/ adj. fit or suitable for drinking.

potash /'pɒtæʃ/ n. **1.** potassium carbonate, especially the crude impure form obtained from wood ashes. **2.** potassium.

potassium /pə'tæsiəm/ n. a silvery-white metallic element whose compounds are used as fertiliser and in special hard glasses. Symbol: K **–potassic**, adj.

potato /pə'teɪtou/ n. (pl. **-toes**) the edible tuber of a cultivated plant.

potch /pɒtʃ/ n. an opal which may have colour, but lacks the fine play of colour which distinguishes gem-quality opal.

potent /ˈpoʊtnt/ adj. **1.** powerful; mighty. **2.** having sexual power. **–potency,** n.

potentate /ˈpoʊtnteɪt/ n. someone who possesses great power.

potential /pəˈtɛnʃəl/ adj. **1.** possible as opposed to actual. **2.** capable of being or becoming; latent. **–n. 3.** a possibility or potentiality.

potentiate /pəˈtɛnʃieɪt/ v.t. to increase the effect or potency of, especially by working in conjunction with: *a drug potentiated by alcohol.* **–potentiation,** n. **–potentiator,** n.

pothole /ˈpɒthoʊl/ n. **1.** a deep hole; a pit. **2.** a hole in the surface of a road.

potion /ˈpoʊʃən/ n. a drink or draught, especially one of a medicinal, poisonous, or magical kind.

pot luck n. Colloq. **1.** whatever food happens to be at hand without special preparation or buying. **2.** an unpredictable situation. **–phr. 3. take pot luck,** to accept whatever is on offer. Also, **potluck, pot-luck.**

potoroo /pɒtəˈru/ n. a small, long-nosed, Australian animal with a pointed head like a bandicoot, found in low thick scrub and grassland.

potpourri /pɒtˈpʊəri, poʊpəˈri/ n. (pl. **-ris**) a mixture of dried petals, spices, etc., kept in a jar for the fragrance.

potter[1] /ˈpɒtə/ n. someone who makes earthen pots or other vessels. **–pottery,** n.

potter[2] /ˈpɒtə/ v.i. to busy or occupy oneself in an ineffective manner.

potty[1] /ˈpɒti/ adj. Colloq. foolish; crazy.

potty[2] /ˈpɒti/ n. Colloq. a chamber-pot.

pouch /paʊtʃ/ n. **1.** a bag, sack, or similar receptacle, especially one for small articles. **2.** something shaped like or resembling a bag or pocket. **3.** Zool. a bag-like or pocket-like part, as the sac beneath the bill of pelicans, or the receptacle for the young of marsupials.

pouf /puf, pʊf/ n. a stuffed cushion of thick material forming a low seat.

poultice /ˈpoʊltəs/ n. a soft, moist mass of some substance, as bread, meal, linseed, etc., applied as a medicament to the body.

poultry /ˈpoʊltri/ n. domestic fowls collectively, as chickens, turkeys, etc.

pounce /paʊns/ v.i. (**pounced, pouncing**) **1.** to swoop down suddenly and lay hold, as a bird does on its prey. **–n. 2.** a sudden swoop, as on prey.

pound[1] /paʊnd/ v.t. **1.** to strike repeatedly and with great force, as with an instrument, the fist, heavy missiles, etc. **–v.i. 2.** to strike heavy blows repeatedly. **3.** to beat or throb violently, as the heart. **–n. 4.** the act of pounding.

pound[2] /paʊnd/ n. (pl. **pounds** or, especially collectively, **pound**) **1.** a unit of weight in the imperial system, equal to just under half a kilogram. *Symbol:* lb **2.** a unit of money used in Australia until 1966 and still used in Britain and some other countries. *Symbol:* £

pound[3] /paʊnd/ n. **1.** an enclosure maintained by public authorities for confining stray or homeless animals. **2.** a place of confinement or imprisonment.

pour /pɔ/ v.t. **1.** to send (a fluid, or anything in loose particles) flowing or falling, as from a container or into, over, or on something. **–v.i.**

2. to issue, move, or proceed in great quantity or number. **3.** to rain heavily. **–n. 4.** the act or process of pouring molten metal, concrete, etc., into a mould.

pout /paʊt/ v.i. to thrust out or protrude the lips, especially in displeasure or sullenness.

poverty /ˈpɒvəti/ n. **1.** the condition of being poor with respect to money, goods, or means of subsistence. **2.** a shortage of something needed or wanted: *a poverty of ideas.*

poverty line n. officially, the level of income below which one cannot afford to obtain the necessities of life.

powder /ˈpaʊdə/ n. **1.** any solid substance in the state of fine, loose particles, as produced by crushing, grinding, or disintegration; dust. **–v.t. 2.** to reduce to powder; pulverise. **3.** to sprinkle or cover with, or as with, powder.

power /ˈpaʊə/ n. **1.** ability to do or act; capability of doing or effecting something. **2.** great or marked ability to do or act; strength; might; force. **3.** the possession of control or command over others; dominion; authority; ascendancy or influence. **4.** legal ability, capacity, or authority. **5.** a state or nation having international authority or influence. **6.** mechanical energy as distinguished from hand labour. **7.** Maths the product obtained by multiplying a quantity by itself one or more times.

power board n. a single moulded plastic unit comprising a number of power points. Also, **powerboard.**

powerful /ˈpaʊəfəl/ adj. **1.** having great force or influence. **2.** having great physical strength. **–powerfully,** adv.

powerful owl n. a large endemic owl of southeastern Australia.

powerless /ˈpaʊələs/ adj. **1.** not having any or enough power. **2.** not having the ability to do things.

power nap n. a short sleep taken during the day in order to restore one's energy.

power of attorney n. a written document given by one person or party to another authorising the latter to act for the former.

power play n. tactics designed to intimidate an opposition. **–power player,** n.

powwow /ˈpaʊwaʊ/ n. Colloq. any conference or meeting.

pox /pɒks/ n. **1.** a disease characterised by multiple skin pustules, as smallpox. **2.** Colloq. any venereal disease.

practicable /ˈpræktɪkəbəl/ adj. capable of being put into practice, done, or effected, especially with the available means or with reason or prudence; feasible.

practical /ˈpræktɪkəl/ adj. **1.** relating or relating to practice or action. **2.** relating to or connected with the ordinary activities, business, or work of the world. **3.** adapted for actual use. **4.** mindful of the results, usefulness, advantages or disadvantages, etc., of action or procedure. **5.** matter-of-fact; prosaic. **6.** being such in practice or effect; virtual. **–practically,** adv. **–practicality,** n.

practice /ˈpræktəs/ n. **1.** habitual or customary performance. **2.** repeated performance or systematic exercise for the purpose of acquiring skill or proficiency. **3.** the action or process of performing or doing something (opposed to *theory* or *speculation*). **4.** the exercise of a profession or occupation, especially law or medicine.

practise /'præktəs/ v. (**-tised, -tising**) −v.t. **1.** to carry out, perform, or do habitually or usually. **2.** to exercise or pursue as a profession, art, or occupation. **3.** to perform or do repeatedly in order to acquire skill or proficiency. −v.i. **4.** to pursue a profession, especially law or medicine. **5.** to exercise oneself by performance tending to give proficiency.

practising /'præktəsɪŋ/ adj. **1.** actively pursuing a particular profession in which one is qualified to work. **2.** actively observing or following a particular religion, philosophy, way of life, etc.

practitioner /præk'tɪʃənə/ n. one engaged in the practice of a profession or the like.

pragmatic /præg'mætɪk/ adj. **1.** concerned with practical consequences or values. **2.** relating to the affairs of a state or community. Also, **pragmatical**. **−pragmatist**, n.

pragmatics /præg'mætɪks/ n. Ling. the study of the forms of communication that exist outside what is conveyed in words.

prairie /'preəri/ n. an extensive or slightly undulating treeless tract of land.

praise /preɪz/ n. **1.** the act of expressing approval or admiration. −v.t. (**praised, praising**) **2.** to express approval or admiration of. **−praiseworthy**, adj.

praline /'pralɪn/ n. a confection of nuts and caramelised sugar.

pram /præm/ n. a small, four-wheeled vehicle used for carrying a baby.

prance /præns, prans/ v.i. (**pranced, prancing**) **1.** to spring, or move by springing, from the hind legs, as a horse. **2.** to move or go in an elated manner; swagger.

prang /præŋ/ v.t. **1.** Colloq. to crash (a car or the like). −n. **2.** a crash in a motor vehicle or the like.

prank /præŋk/ n. a trick or practical joke.

prate /preɪt/ v.i. to talk too much; talk foolishly or pointlessly; chatter; babble.

prattle /'prætl/ v.i. to talk or chatter in a simple-minded or foolish way; babble.

prawn /prɒn/ n. a shrimp-like crustacean, often used as food.

pray /preɪ/ v.t. **1.** to make earnest or devout petition to (a person, God, etc.). −v.i. **2.** to make entreaty or supplication, as to a person or for a thing.

prayer /preə/ n. **1.** a devout petition to, or any form of spiritual communion with, God or an object of worship. **2.** a petition or entreaty.

praying mantis n. → **mantis**.

pre- a prefix applied freely to mean 'prior to', 'in advance of' (*prewar*), also 'early', 'beforehand' (*prepay*), 'before', 'in front of' (*preoral, prefrontal*), and in many figurative meanings, often attached to stems not used alone (*prevent, preclude, preference, precedent*).

preach /pritʃ/ v.t. **1.** to proclaim or make known by sermon (the gospel, good tidings, etc.). −v.i. **2.** to deliver a sermon. **−preacher**, n.

preamble /pri'æmbəl/ n. an introductory statement; a preface.

precarious /prə'keəriəs/ adj. **1.** uncertain; unstable; insecure. **2.** dangerous; perilous.

precaution /prə'kɔʃən/ n. **1.** a measure taken beforehand to ward off possible evil or secure good results. **2.** caution employed beforehand; prudent foresight.

precede /pri'sid/ v.t. to go before, as in place, order, rank, importance, or time.

precedence /'presədəns, pri'sidəns/ n. **1.** the act or fact of preceding. **2.** priority in order, rank, importance, etc.

precedent /'prisədənt, 'pre-/ n. a preceding instance or case which may serve as an example for or a justification in subsequent cases.

precentor /prə'sentə/ n. someone who leads a church choir or congregation in singing.

precept /'prisept/ n. a commandment or direction given as a rule of action or conduct.

precession /pri'seʃən/ n. the act or fact of preceding; precedence.

precinct /'prisɪŋkt/ n. a place or space of definite or understood limits.

precious /'preʃəs/ adj. **1.** of great price or value; valuable; costly. **2.** dear or beloved.

precipice /'presəpəs/ n. a steep cliff.

precipitant /prə'sɪpətənt/ adj. **1.** hasty; rash. **2.** unduly sudden or abrupt.

precipitate v.t. /prə'sɪpəteɪt/ **1.** to hasten the occurrence of; bring about in haste or suddenly. **2.** Chem. to separate (a substance) in solid form from a solution, as by means of a reagent. **3.** to cast down headlong; fling or hurl down. −adj. /prə'sɪpətət/ **4.** proceeding rapidly or with great haste. **5.** exceedingly sudden or abrupt: *a precipitate exit*. −n. /prə'sɪpətət/ **6.** Chem. a substance precipitated from a solution. **−precipitately**, adv.

precipitation /prəsɪpə'teɪʃən/ n. **1.** the act of precipitating. **2.** Meteorol. falling products of condensation in the atmosphere, as rain, snow, hail.

precipitous /prə'sɪpətəs/ adj. extremely or impassably steep.

precis /'preɪsi/ n. (pl. **-cis** /-siz/ or **-cises** /-siz/) an abstract or summary.

precise /prə'saɪs/ adj. **1.** definite or exact; definitely or strictly stated, defined, or fixed. **2.** carefully distinct, as the voice. **3.** exact in measuring, recording, etc., as an instrument. **4.** excessively or rigidly particular; puritanical. **−precision**, n.

preclude /pri'klud/ v.t. to shut out or exclude.

precocious /prə'koʊʃəs/ adj. **1.** forward in development, especially mental development, as a child. **2.** (of a child) cheeky; forward; impertinent.

preconceive /prikən'siv/ v.t. to conceive beforehand; form an idea of in advance. **−preconception**, n.

precursor /.pri'kɜsə/ n. someone who or that which precedes; a predecessor.

precycle /'prisaɪkəl/ v.i. to anticipate the causes of waste and take action to prevent it. **−precycling**, n. **−precycler**, n.

predatory /'predətəri, -tri/ adj. **1.** of, relating to, or characterised by plundering, pillaging, or robbery. **2.** Zool. habitually preying upon other animals. **−predator**, n.

predecessor /'pridəsesə/ n. someone who precedes another in an office, position, etc.

predestine /pri'destɪn/ v.t. to determine beforehand; predetermine.

predetermine /pridə'tɜmən/ v.t. to determine or decide beforehand.

predicament /prə'dɪkəmənt/ n. an unpleasant, trying, or dangerous situation.

predicate v.t. /'prɛdɪkeɪt/ **1.** to proclaim; declare; affirm or assert. –n. /'prɛdɪkət/ **2.** Gram. (in many languages) the active verb in a sentence or clause together with all the words it governs and those which modify it, as *is here* in *Jack is here*. –**predicative**, adj.

predict /prə'dɪkt/ v.t. **1.** to foretell; prophesy. –v.i. **2.** to foretell the future. –**prediction**, n.

predilection /pridə'lɛkʃən/ n. a predisposition of the mind in favour of something.

predispose /pridəs'pouz/ v.t. **1.** to give a previous inclination or tendency to. **2.** to render subject, susceptible, or liable.

predominate /prə'domɪneɪt/ v.i. **1.** to be the stronger or leading element. **2.** (oft. fol. by *over*) to have or exert controlling power. –**predominant**, adj.

pre-eminent /pri-'ɛmənənt/ adj. superior to or surpassing others; distinguished beyond others.

pre-empt /pri-'ɛmpt/ v.t. **1.** to occupy (land) in order to establish a prior right to buy. **2.** to acquire or appropriate beforehand. –**pre-emptive**, adj.

preen /prin/ v.t. **1.** to trim or dress with the beak, as a bird does its feathers. **2.** to prepare, dress, or array (oneself) carefully in making one's toilet.

preface /'prɛfəs/ n. **1.** a preliminary statement by the author or editor of a book. **2.** something preliminary or introductory. –v.t. (**-aced, -acing**) **3.** to provide with or introduce by a preface. **4.** to serve as a preface to this. **5.** to introduce by something preliminary: *he prefaced his remarks to the farmers with a reference to the recent welcome rain.*

prefect /'prifɛkt/ n. a person appointed to any of various positions of command, authority, or superintendence. –**prefecture**, n.

prefer /prə'fɜ/ v.t. (**-ferred, -ferring**) **1.** to set or hold before or above other persons or things in estimation; like better; choose rather. **2.** to put forward or present (a statement, suit, charge, etc.) for consideration or sanction. **3.** to put forward or advance, as in rank or office. **4.** to favour: *to prefer kicking with your right foot.* –**preferable**, adj. –**preferably**, adv.

preference /'prɛfərəns, 'prɛfrəns/ n. **1.** the act of preferring one thing above another. **2.** the state of being preferred. **3.** that which is preferred. **4.** a prior right or claim, as to payment of dividends, or to assets upon dissolution. **5.** a vote, usually specified in rank, given to a candidate in a preferential voting system. –v.t. (**-enced, -encing**) **6.** to direct one's voting preferences to: *the Greens will preference Labor in the election.* –**preferential**, adj.

preference share n. Stock Exchange a share which ranks before ordinary shares in the entitlement to dividends, usually at a fixed rate of interest. Also, US, **preferred stock.**

preferential voting /prɛfə'rɛnʃəl/ n. a system of voting which enables the voter to indicate his or her order of preference for candidates in the ballot. Compare **first-past-the-post.**

prefix n. /'prifɪks/ **1.** Gram. an affix which is put before a word, stem, or word element to

add to or qualify its meaning (as *un-* in *unkind*). –v.t. /pri'fɪks, 'prifɪks/ **2.** to fix or put before or in front. **3.** Gram. to add as a prefix. –**prefixal**, adj.

pregnant /'prɛgnənt/ adj. **1.** being with child or young, as a woman or female mammal; having a fetus in the womb. **2.** full of meaning; highly significant. –**pregnancy**, n.

prehensile /pri'hɛnsaɪl/ adj. adapted for seizing, grasping, or laying hold of anything.

prehistory /pri'hɪstəri/ n. the history of humanity in the period before recorded events. –**prehistoric**, adj.

prejudice /'prɛdʒədəs/ n. **1.** any preconceived opinion or feeling, favourable or unfavourable. **2.** disadvantage resulting from some judgement or action of another. **3.** resulting injury or detriment. –v.t. (**-diced, -dicing**) **4.** to affect with a prejudice, favourable or unfavourable. **5.** to affect disadvantageously or detrimentally. –**prejudicial**, adj.

prejudiced /'prɛdʒədəst/ adj. **1.** having preconceived opinions which affect the ability to make a fair judgement about a particular matter. **2.** having an unreasonable dislike or hatred of a particular racial, religious or other group.

prelate /'prɛlət/ n. an ecclesiastic of a high order, as an archbishop, bishop, etc.

preliminary /prə'lɪmənəri/ adj. **1.** introductory; preparatory. –n. (pl. **-naries**) **2.** something preliminary.

prelude /'prɛljud/ n. **1.** a preliminary to an action, event, condition, or work of broader scope and higher importance. **2.** Music a piece which precedes a more important movement. –v.t. **3.** to serve as a prelude or introduction to.

premarital /pri'mærətl/ adj. before marriage.

premature /'prɛmətʃə, prɛmə'tjuə/ adj. coming into existence or occurring too soon.

premeditate /pri'mɛdəteɪt/ v.t. to plan beforehand.

premenstrual /pri'mɛnstruəl/ adj. **1.** of or relating to the time in the menstrual cycle immediately preceding menstruation. **2.** suffering from the symptoms of premenstrual syndrome.

premenstrual syndrome n. a syndrome affecting some women just before menstruation, with a variety of symptoms such as tension, irritability, pelvic discomfort and headache. Abbrev.: PMS

premenstrual tension n. the symptoms of tension, irritableness, etc., associated with premenstrual syndrome. Abbrev.: PMT

premier /'prɛmiə/ n. **1.** the leader of a state government. –adj. **2.** first in rank; chief; leading. **3.** earliest.

premiere /prɛmi'ɛə/ n. a first public performance of a play, etc.

premise /'prɛməs/ n. **1.** (pl.) **a.** the property forming the subject of a conveyance. **b.** a house or building with the grounds, etc., belonging to it. **2.** Also, **premiss.** Logic a proposition (or one of several) from which a conclusion is drawn. –v.t. **3.** to set forth beforehand, as by way of introduction or explanation.

premium /'primiəm/ n. **1.** a bonus, prize, or the like. **2.** the amount paid or agreed to be paid, in one sum or periodically, as the consideration for a contract of insurance. **3.** a sum above the nominal or par value of a thing. **4.** Stock

Exchange the amount that a buyer is prepared to pay for the right to subscribe for a new or rights issue of stocks or shares in a company. *–adj.* **5.** of highest quality; best. *–phr.* **6. at a premium, a.** in high esteem; in demand. **b.** at a high price.

premonition /prɛmə'nɪʃən, pri-/ *n.* **1.** a forewarning. **2.** → **presentiment**.

prenatal /ˌpri'neɪtl/ *adj.* before birth; during pregnancy: *a prenatal clinic*. Also, **antenatal**. **–prenatally**, *adv*.

prenuptial agreement /pri'nʌptʃəl/ *n.* a legal contract made by two people before their wedding, detailing various financial or domestic arrangements, in particular outlining a settlement in the event of a divorce.

preoccupy /pri'ɒkjəpaɪ/ *v.t.* (**-pied, -pying**) to absorb or engross to the exclusion of other things.

prepaid /'pripeɪd/ *adj.* paid before incurring a cost, as for a service, such as mobile phone use.

preparation /prɛpə'reɪʃən/ *n.* **1.** a proceeding, measure, or provision by which one prepares for something. **2.** homework, or, especially in a boarding school, individual work supervised by a teacher. **3.** the act of preparing. **4.** something prepared, manufactured, or compounded.

prepare /prə'pɛə/ *v.t.* **1.** to make ready, or put in due condition, for something. **2.** to get ready for eating, as a meal, by due assembling, dressing, or cooking. **3.** to manufacture, compound, or compose. **–preparatory**, *adj*.

preponderant /prə'pɒndərənt, pri-, -drənt/ *adj.* superior in weight, force, influence, number, etc.; preponderating; predominant.

preponderate /prə'pɒndəreɪt, pri-/ *v.i.* to be superior in power, force, influence, number, amount, etc.; predominate.

preposition /prɛpə'zɪʃən/ *n.* (in some languages) one of the major form-classes, or parts of speech, comprising words placed before nouns to indicate their relation to other words or their function in the sentence. *By, to, in, from* are prepositions in English.

prepossessing /pripə'zɛsɪŋ/ *adj.* impressing favourably beforehand or at the outset.

preposterous /prə'pɒstərəs/ *adj.* directly contrary to nature, reason, or common sense; absurd, senseless, or utterly foolish.

prepuce /'pripjus/ *n.* the fold of skin which covers the head of the penis or clitoris; foreskin. **–preputial**, *adj*.

prerogative /prə'rɒgətɪv/ *n.* an exclusive right or privilege.

presage *n.* /'prɛsɪdʒ/ **1.** an omen. *–v.t.* /'prɛsɪdʒ, prə'seɪdʒ/ (**-saged, -saging**) **2.** to forecast; predict.

presbyter /'prɛzbətə, 'prɛspətə/ *n. Christian Church* **1.** (in the early Christian church) an office-bearer exercising teaching, priestly, and administrative functions. **2.** (in hierarchical churches) a priest. **3.** (in certain Protestant churches, such as the Presbyterian Church) a lay officer with governing, teaching, or administrative duties. **–presbyteral** /prɛz'bɪtərəl/, *adj.* **–presbyterate** /prɛz'bɪtərət/, *n*.

preschool /'priskul/ *n.* a school for children too young to start going to an ordinary school, usually under the age of five.

prescience /'prɛsɪəns/ *n.* knowledge of things before they exist or happen.

prescribe /prə'skraɪb/ *v.t.* **1.** to lay down, in writing or otherwise, as a rule or a course to be followed; appoint, ordain, or enjoin. **2.** *Med.* to designate or order for use, as a remedy or treatment.

prescription /prə'skrɪpʃən/ *n.* **1.** *Med.* a direction (usually written) by the doctor to the pharmacist for the preparation and use of a medicine or remedy. **2.** *Law* the process of acquiring a right by uninterrupted assertion of the right over a long period of time.

prescriptive /prə'skrɪptɪv/ *adj.* **1.** that prescribes; giving directions or injunctions. **2.** depending on or arising from effective prescription, as a right or title.

presence /'prɛzəns/ *n.* **1.** the state or fact of being present, as with others or in a place. **2.** personal appearance or bearing, especially of a dignified or imposing kind. **3.** a divine or spiritual being.

present¹ /'prɛzənt/ *adj.* **1.** being, existing, or occurring at this time or now. **2.** being here or there, rather than elsewhere. *–n.* **3.** the present time.

present² *v.t.* /prə'zɛnt/ **1.** to furnish or endow with a gift or the like, especially by formal act. **2.** afford or furnish (an opportunity, possibility, etc.). **3.** to hand or send in, as a bill or a cheque for payment. **4.** to introduce (a person) to another. **5.** to show or exhibit. **6.** to level or aim (a weapon, especially a firearm). *–n.* /'prɛzənt/ **7.** a thing presented as a gift; a gift.

presentable /prə'zɛntəbəl/ *adj.* of sufficiently good appearance, or fit to be seen.

presentation /prɛzən'teɪʃən/ *n.* **1.** the act of presenting. **2.** an address or report on a particular topic, especially one supported by images, digital data, exhibits, etc. **3.** the presenting of a bill, note, or the like.

presentiment /prə'zɛntəmənt/ *n.* a feeling or impression of something about to happen, especially something evil; a foreboding.

presently /'prɛzəntli/ *adv.* **1.** in a little while or soon. **2.** at this time, currently.

preservative /prə'zɜvətɪv/ *n.* a chemical substance used to preserve foods, etc., from decomposition or fermentation.

preserve /prə'zɜv/ *v.t.* **1.** to keep safe from harm or injury; save. **2.** to keep up; maintain. **3.** to prepare (food or any perishable substance) so as to resist decomposition or fermentation. **4.** to keep (accrued superannuation benefits) in a superannuation or rollover fund until retirement age has been reached. *–n.* **5.** something that preserves. **6.** that which is preserved. **7.** a spread made by boiling fruit, etc., with sugar.

preset *v.t.* /ˌpri'sɛt/ (**-set, -setting**) **1.** to set in advance: *to preset an oven to roast a joint four hours later. –adj.* /'prisɛt/ **2.** determined in advance to follow a certain course or the like: *a preset missile*.

preside /prə'zaɪd/ *v.i.* to occupy the place of authority or control.

president /'prɛzədənt/ *n.* **1.** (*oft. upper case*) the highest official in a republic. **2.** an officer appointed or elected to preside over an organised body of persons, as a council, society, etc. **–presidency**, n. **–presidential**, adj.

press¹ /prɛs/ v.t. **1.** to act upon with weight or force. **2.** to compress or squeeze, as to alter in shape or size. **3.** to make flat by subjecting to weight. **4.** to iron (clothes, etc.). **5.** to urge (a person, etc.). –v.i. **6.** to exert weight, force, or pressure. **7.** to compel haste. **8.** to crowd or throng. –n. **9.** printed publications collectively, especially newspapers and periodicals. **10.** *Printing* machine used for printing. **11.** an establishment for printing books, etc. **12.** any of various instruments or machines for exerting pressure. **13.** a crowd, throng, or multitude. **14.** pressure or urgency, as of affairs or business. **15.** an upright case, or piece of furniture, for holding clothes, books, etc.

press² /prɛs/ v.t. to force into service, especially naval or military service; to impress.

pressure /'prɛʃə/ n. **1.** the exertion of force upon a body by another body in contact with it; compression. **2.** *Physics* the force per unit area exerted at a given point. **3.** the act of pressing. **4.** harassment; oppression. **5.** a constraining or compelling force or influence. **6.** urgency, as of affairs or business.

pressure system n. *Meteorol.* an atmospheric circulation system which may be a low pressure system such as a cyclone or depression, or a high pressure system such as an anticyclone.

pressurise /'prɛʃəraɪz/ v.t. to maintain normal air pressure in (the cockpit or cabin of) an aeroplane designed to fly at high altitudes. Also, **pressurize**.

prestige /prɛs'tiʒ/ n. reputation or influence arising from success, achievement, rank, or other circumstances. **–prestigious**, adj.

presume /prə'zjum/ v.t. **1.** to take for granted, assume, or suppose. –v.i. **2.** to act or proceed with unwarrantable or impertinent boldness. **–presumption**, n.

presumptuous /prə'zʌmptʃuəs/ adj. unwarrantedly or impertinently bold; forward.

pretence /prə'tɛns/ n. **1.** pretending or feigning; make-believe. **2.** a false show of something. **3.** a piece of make-believe. **4.** the act of pretending or alleging, now especially falsely. **5.** an alleged or pretended reason or excuse, or a pretext. **6.** insincere or false profession. **7.** the putting forth of a claim. **8.** the claim itself. **9.** (fol. by *to*) pretension.

pretend /prə'tɛnd/ v.t. **1.** to put forward a false appearance of; feign. **2.** to allege or profess, especially insincerely or falsely. –v.i. **3.** to make believe. **4.** (fol. by *to*) to lay claim.

pretension /prə'tɛnʃən/ n. the assumption of or a claim to dignity or importance. **–pretentious**, adj. **–pretentiousness**, n.

pretentious /prə'tɛnʃəs/ adj. **1.** characterised by assumption of dignity or importance. **2.** making an exaggerated outward show; ostentatious.

preter- a prefix meaning 'beyond', 'more than'.

preterite /'prɛtərət, 'prɛtrət/ adj. *Gram.* designating a tense usually denoting an action or state which was completed in the past.

preterm /'pritɜm/ adj. **1.** (of a baby) born or occurring following a pregnancy has reached its full term. **2.** (of an election) held before the parliament or other body for which members

are elected has reached its full term. Also, **pre-term**.

pretext /'pritɛkst/ n. that which is put forward to conceal a true purpose or object; an ostensible reason.

pretty /'prɪti/ adj. (**-tier, -tiest**) **1.** fair or attractive to the eye in a feminine or childish way. **2.** (of things, places, etc.) pleasing to the eye, especially without grandeur. –adv. **3.** moderately. **4.** quite; very. –v.t. (**-tied, -tying**) **5.** to make pretty.

pretzel /'prɛtsəl/ n. **1.** a crisp, dry biscuit. **2.** a soft bun, sweet or savoury, in a tie shape.

prevail /prə'veɪl/ v.i. **1.** to be widespread or current; to exist everywhere or generally. **2.** to be or prove superior in strength, power, or influence. **3.** (fol. by *on, upon,* or *with*) to use persuasion or inducement successfully.

prevalent /'prɛvələnt/ adj. widespread. **–prevalence**, n.

prevaricate /prə'værəkeɪt/ v.i. to act or speak evasively; equivocate; quibble.

prevent /prə'vɛnt/ v.t. to keep from doing or occurring; hinder. **–prevention**, n.

preventive /prə'vɛntɪv/ adj. **1.** *Med.* warding off disease. **2.** serving to prevent or hinder. Also, **preventative**.

preview /'privju/ n. a previous view; a view in advance, as of a film.

previous /'priviəs/ adj. coming or occurring before something else; prior.

prey /preɪ/ n. **1.** an animal hunted or seized for food, especially by a carnivorous animal. **2.** a person or thing that falls a victim to an enemy, a disease, or any adverse agency. –v.i. **3.** to seek for and seize prey, as an animal does. –phr. **4. easy prey**, someone who will easily fall victim to a deception or imposition.

price /praɪs/ n. **1.** the sum or amount of money or its equivalent for which anything is bought, sold, or offered for sale. **2.** that which must be given, done, or undergone in order to obtain a thing. –v.t. (**priced, pricing**) **3.** to fix the price of.

price-fixing /'praɪs-fɪksɪŋ/ n. the setting of a price, usually a high price, for a commodity or service by agreement between business competitors so as to increase their profits. **–price-fixer**, n.

price index n. an indicator used to show the general level of prices.

priceless /'praɪsləs/ adj. valuable.

prick /prɪk/ n. **1.** a puncture made by a needle, thorn, or the like. **2.** the act of pricking. **3.** *Colloq.* (taboo) **a.** the penis. **b.** an unpleasant or despicable person. –v.t. **4.** to pierce with a sharp point; puncture. **5.** to cause to stand erect or point upwards. –v.i. **6.** to perform the action of piercing or puncturing something. **7.** (fol. by *up*) to rise erect or point upwards, as the ears of an animal.

prickle /'prɪkəl/ n. **1.** a sharp point. **2.** a small, pointed process growing from the bark of a plant; a thorn. –v.t. **3.** to prick. **4.** to cause a pricking sensation in.

pride /praɪd/ n. **1.** high or inordinate opinion of one's own dignity, importance, merit, or superiority. **2.** the state or feeling of being proud. **3.** self respect. **4.** the best or most admired part of anything. **5.** a company of lions. –v.t.

6. (usu. fol. by *on* or *upon*) to indulge or plume (oneself) in a feeling of pride.

priest /priːst/ *n.* one whose office it is to perform religious rites, and especially to make sacrificial offerings.

prig /prɪg/ *n.* someone who is precise to an extreme in attention to principle or duty, especially in a self-righteous way.

prim /prɪm/ *adj.* (**primmer, primmest**) affectedly precise or proper.

primacy /ˈpraɪməsi/ *n.* **1.** the state of being first in order, rank, importance, etc. **2.** *Eccles.* the office, rank, or dignity of a primate.

prima-facie evidence /praɪməˈfeɪʃi, praɪməˈfeɪʃi/ *n.* (in law) evidence sufficient to establish a fact, or to raise a presumption of fact, unless rebutted.

primal /ˈpraɪməl/ *adj.* first; original; primeval.

primary /ˈpraɪməri, ˈpraɪmri/ *adj.* **1.** first or highest in rank or importance; chief; principal. **2.** constituting, or belonging to, the first stage in any process. **3.** original, not derived or subordinate; fundamental; basic. **–primarily,** *adv.*

primary colour *n.* any of three colours (usually said to be red, yellow and blue) regarded as basic, and which can produce all other colours by mixing. Also, **primary color.**

primary forest *n. Ecol.* forest that has not been logged or cleared in the past (opposed to *secondary forest*).

primary industry *n.* any industry such as dairy farming, forestry, mining, etc., which is involved in the growing, producing, extracting, etc., of natural resources.

primary school *n.* a school for full-time elementary instruction of children from the age of five or six to about twelve years, varying between Australian states.

primate *n.* **1.** /ˈpraɪmət/ *Eccles.* an archbishop. **2.** /ˈpraɪmeɪt/ any mammal of the order Primates, that includes humans, apes, monkeys, etc.

prime /praɪm/ *adj.* **1.** first in importance, excellence, or value. **2.** first or highest in rank, dignity, or authority; chief; principal; main. **3.** original; fundamental. **4.** typical: *a prime example.* –*n.* **5.** the most flourishing stage or state. **6.** the choicest or best part of anything. –*v.t.* **7.** to prepare or make ready for a particular purpose or operation. **8.** to supply (a firearm) with powder for communicating fire to a charge. **9.** to pour water into (a pump) so as to swell the sucker and so act as a seal, making it work effectively. **10.** to cover (a surface) with a preparatory coat or colour, as in painting. **11.** to supply or equip with information, words, etc., for use.

prime minister *n.* (*oft. upper case*) the first or principal minister of certain governments; the chief of the cabinet or ministry. **–prime ministry,** *n.*

primer /ˈpraɪmə, ˈprɪmə/ *n.* **1.** an elementary book for teaching children to read. **2.** any, often small, book of elementary principles.

primeval /praɪˈmiːvəl/ *adj.* of or relating to the first age or ages, especially of the world. Also, **primaeval.**

primitive /ˈprɪmətɪv/ *adj.* **1.** early in the history of the world or of humankind. **2.** characteristic

of early ages or of an early state of human development. **3.** unaffected or little affected by civilising influences. **4.** being in its or the earliest period; early.

primogeniture /praɪmoʊˈdʒɛnətʃə/ *n. Law* the principle of inheritance or succession by the firstborn, specifically the eldest son.

primordial /praɪˈmɔːdiəl/ *adj.* relating to or existing at or from the very beginning.

primrose /ˈprɪmroʊz/ *n.* a garden plant usually with yellow flowers.

prince /prɪns/ *n.* **1.** a non-reigning male member of a royal family. **2.** a sovereign or monarch; a king. **3.** the ruler of a small state, lower in rank than a king.

princess /ˈprɪnsɛs/ *n.* **1.** a non-reigning female member of a royal family. **2.** a female sovereign. **3.** the consort of a prince.

principal /ˈprɪnsəpəl/ *adj.* **1.** first or highest in rank, importance, value, etc.; chief; foremost. –*n.* **2.** a chief or head. **3.** something of principal or chief importance. **4.** *Law* a person authorising another (an agent) to represent him or her. **5.** a person primarily liable for an obligation (opposed to an *endorser*). **6.** the main body of an estate, etc., as distinguished from income. **7.** *Commerce* a capital sum, as distinguished from interest or profit.

principality /prɪnsəˈpæləti/ *n.* (*pl.* **-ties**) a state ruled by a prince.

principle /ˈprɪnsəpəl/ *n.* **1.** an accepted or professed rule of action or conduct. **2.** a fundamental, primary, or general truth, on which other truths depend. **3.** guiding sense of the requirements and obligations of right conduct. **4.** a rule or law exemplified in natural phenomena, in the construction or operation of a machine, the working of a system, or the like.

print /prɪnt/ *v.t.* **1.** to produce (a text, a picture, etc.) by applying inked types, blocks, or the like, with direct pressure to paper or other material. **2.** to write in letters like those commonly used in print. **3.** to produce or fix (an impression, mark, etc.) as by pressure. **4.** *Photography* to produce a positive picture from (a negative) by the transmission of light. **5.** *Computers* (oft. fol. by *out*) to produce (a result, data, etc.) in a legible form on paper. –*n.* **6.** the state of being printed. **7.** printed lettering, especially with reference to character, style, or size. **8.** printed matter. **9.** a design, usually in colour, pressed on woven cotton with engraved rollers. **10.** the cloth so treated. **11.** *Photography* a picture made from a negative.

printer /ˈprɪntə/ *n.* **1.** a person or firm engaged in the printing industry. **2.** *Computers* a machine that prints on paper information sent by means of electrical or mechanical signals.

printout /ˈprɪntaʊt/ *n.* results, data, or the like printed automatically by a computer in legible form.

prior[1] /ˈpraɪə/ *adj.* **1.** preceding in time, or in order; earlier or former; anterior or antecedent. –*adv.* **2.** (fol. by *to*) previously.

prior[2] /ˈpraɪə/ *n.* the superior of certain monastic orders and houses.

priority /praɪˈɒrəti/ *n.* (*pl.* **-ties**) **1.** the state of being earlier in time, or of preceding something else. **2.** precedence in order, rank, etc.

3. *Computers* the position in rank of an interrupt system in gaining the attention of the computer when there is more than one interrupt system.

prise /praɪz/ *v.t.* to raise, move, or force with or as with a lever. Also, **prize**.

prism /ˈprɪzəm/ *n.* **1.** *Optics* a transparent prismatic body (especially one with triangular bases) used for decomposing light into its spectrum or for reflecting light beams. **2.** *Geom.* a solid whose bases or ends are any congruent and parallel polygons, and whose sides are parallelograms. –**prismatic**, *adj.*

prison /ˈprɪzən/ *n.* a public building for the confinement or safe custody of criminals and others committed by law.

prisoner /ˈprɪzənə, ˈprɪznə/ *n.* **1.** someone who is confined in prison or kept in custody, especially as the result of legal action. **2.** someone who is caught or captured: *to be kept as a prisoner by the kidnappers.*

prison officer *n.* an official having charge of prisoners in a jail; warder.

prissy /ˈprɪsi/ *adj.* (**-sier, -siest**) *Colloq.* precise; prim; affectedly nice.

pristine /ˈprɪstin/ *adj.* **1.** so clean as to appear new: *the house was in pristine condition.* **2.** of or relating to the earliest period or state; original; primitive. **3.** having its original purity.

private /ˈpraɪvət/ *adj.* **1.** belonging to some particular person or persons; belonging to oneself; being one's own. **2.** confined to or intended only for the person or persons immediately concerned; confidential. **3.** not holding public office employment, as a person. **4.** (of a company) having the right to transfer its shares restricted, the number of its members limited to 50, and prohibited from using public subscription for its shares or debentures. **5.** removed from or out of public view of knowledge; secret. **6.** without the presence of others; alone; secluded. **7.** (of a member of parliament) not holding a government post. –*n.* **8.** a soldier of the lowest military rank. –**privacy**, *n.*

private enterprise *n.* **1.** business or commercial activities independent of state ownership or control. **2.** the principle of free enterprise.

private sector *n.* that sector of an economy which is owned and operated by individuals and privately-owned companies (opposed to the *public sector*).

privation /praɪˈveɪʃən/ *n.* lack of the usual comforts or necessaries of life, or an instance of this. –**privative**, *adj.*

privatise /ˈpraɪvətaɪz/ *v.t.* to change the status of (land, industries, etc.) from that of state to private ownership. Also, **privatize**. –**privatisation**, *n.*

privet /ˈprɪvət/ *n.* a shrub with evergreen leaves and small, heavily perfumed, white flowers, now considered noxious.

privilege /ˈprɪvəlɪdʒ/ *n.* **1.** a right or immunity enjoyed by a person or persons beyond the common advantages of others. **2.** a prerogative, advantage, or opportunity enjoyed by anyone in a favoured position (as distinct from a right). –*v.t.* (**-leged, -leging**) **3.** to grant a privilege to.

privy /ˈprɪvi/ *adj.* **1.** (usu. fol. by *to*) participating in the knowledge of something private or secret. –*n.* (*pl.* **privies**) **2.** an outhouse serving as a toilet. **3.** *Law* a person participating directly in a legal transaction, or claiming through or under such a one. –**privity**, *n.*

prize¹ /praɪz/ *n.* **1.** a reward of victory or superiority, as in a contest or competition. **2.** that which is won in a lottery or the like.

prize² /praɪz/ *v.t.* to value or esteem highly.

prize³ /praɪz/ *v.t.* → **prise**.

pro¹ /proʊ/ *adv.* **1.** in favour of a proposition, opinion, etc. (opposed to *con*). –*n.* (*pl.* **pros**) **2.** an argument, consideration, vote, etc., for something (opposed to *con*).

pro² /proʊ/ *n.* (*pl.* **pros**) *Colloq.* a professional.

pro-¹ a prefix indicating favour for some party, system, idea, etc., having *anti-* as its opposite. **2.** a prefix of priority in space or time having especially a meaning of advancing or projecting forwards or outwards, having also extended figurative meanings, including substitution, and attached widely to stems not used as words, as *provision*, *prologue*, *proceed*, *produce*, *protract*.

proactive /proʊˈæktɪv/ *adj.* taking the initiative, rather than waiting until things happen and then reacting. –**proactively**, *adv.*

probability /prɒbəˈbɪləti/ *n.* (*pl.* **-ties**) **1.** the quality or fact of being probable. **2.** a likelihood or chance of something. **3.** a probable event, circumstance, etc. **4.** *Statistics* the relative frequency of the occurrence of an event as measured by the ratio of the number of cases or alternatives favourable to the event to the total number of cases or events. –**probabilistic**, *adj.*

probable /ˈprɒbəbl/ *adj.* **1.** likely to occur or prove true. **2.** affording ground for belief. –**probably**, *adv.*

probate /ˈproʊbeɪt/ *n. Law* the official proving of a will as authentic or valid.

probation /prəˈbeɪʃən/ *n.* **1.** the act of testing. **2.** *Law* a method of dealing with offenders, especially young persons guilty of minor crimes or first offences, by allowing them to go at large conditionally under supervision.

probation order *n. Law* a form of bond by which an offender is not imprisoned but must report on a regular basis to a probation officer.

probe /proʊb/ *v.t.* **1.** to search into or examine thoroughly; question closely. **2.** to examine or explore as with a probe. –*n.* **3.** the act of probing. **4.** a slender surgical instrument for exploring the depth or direction of a wound, sinus, or the like.

probiotic /proʊbaɪˈɒtɪk/ *adj.* **1.** of or relating to a food containing live bacteria which have health-promoting properties. –*n.* **2.** such a food.

probity /ˈproʊbəti/ *n.* integrity; uprightness; honesty.

problem /ˈprɒbləm/ *n.* **1.** any question or matter involving doubt, uncertainty, or difficulty. **2.** a question proposed for solution or discussion. –**problematic**, *adj.*

pro bono /proʊ ˈboʊnoʊ/ *adj.* **1.** (especially of legal work) performed without charge. –*adv.* **2.** without charging a fee.

proboscis /prə'bɒskəs, prə'bousəs/ n. (pl. **-boscises** /-'bɒskəsəz, -'bɒsəsəz/ or **-boscides** /-'bɒskədiz, -'bɒsədiz/) 1. an elephant's trunk. 2. any long flexible snout.

procedural /prə'sidʒərəl/ adj. 1. of or relating to procedure. 2. of or relating to a text type or form which shows how something can be done, as a recipe.

procedure /prə'sidʒə/ n. 1. the act or manner of proceeding in any action or process; conduct. 2. a surgical operation or other medical technique performed on part of the body for a diagnostic or therapeutic purpose.

proceed v.i. /prə'sid/ 1. to go on with or carry on any action or process. 2. (fol. by *against*) to take legal proceedings. 3. to be carried on, as an action, process, etc. 4. to go or come forth; issue. –n. /'prousid/ 5. (*usu. pl.*) the sum derived from a sale or other transaction.

proceeding /prə'sidɪŋ/ n. 1. action, course of action, or conduct. 2. (*pl.*) records of the doings of a society. 3. *Law* a. the instituting or carrying on of an action at law. b. a legal step or measure.

process /'prouses/ n. 1. a systematic series of actions directed to some end. 2. the whole course of the proceedings in an action at law. 3. a prominence or protuberance. 4. the action of going forward or on. 5. the condition of being carried on. 6. course or lapse, as of time. –v.t. 7. to treat or prepare by some particular process, as in manufacturing. 8. *Computers* to manipulate data in order to abstract the required information. 9. to apply a process to: *to process an application.*

procession /prə'sɛʃən/ n. the proceeding or moving along in orderly succession, in a formal or ceremonious manner, of a line or body of persons, animals, vehicles, etc.

proclaim /prə'kleɪm/ v.t. to announce or declare, publicly and officially. –**proclamation**, n.

proclivity /prə'klɪvəti/ n. natural or habitual inclination or tendency.

procrastinate /prou'kræstəneɪt/ v.i. to defer action; delay. –**procrastination**, n. –**procrastinator**, n.

procreate /'proukrieɪt/ v.t. 1. to beget or generate (offspring). 2. to produce; bring into being.

proctor /'prɒktə/ n. (in certain universities) an official charged with various duties, especially with the maintenance of discipline.

procure /prə'kjuə/ v.t. 1. to obtain or get by care, effort, or the use of special means. 2. to effect; cause; bring about, especially by unscrupulous or indirect means.

prod /prɒd/ v.t. (**prodded**, **prodding**) 1. to poke or jab with something pointed. –n. 2. the act of prodding; a poke or jab. 3. any of various pointed instruments, as a goad.

prodigal /'prɒdɪgəl/ adj. 1. wastefully or recklessly extravagant. –n. 2. a spendthrift.

prodigious /prə'dɪdʒəs/ adj. 1. extraordinary in size, amount, extent, degree, force, etc. 2. wonderful or marvellous.

prodigy /'prɒdədʒi/ n. (pl. **-gies**) a person, especially a child, endowed with extraordinary gifts or powers.

produce v.t. /prə'djus/ (**-duced**, **-ducing**) 1. to bring into existence. 2. to make; create.

3. *Econ.* to create (something having an exchangeable value). 4. to yield. 5. to bring forward. 6. to bring (a play, film, etc.) before the public. 7. to extend or prolong (a line, etc.). –n. /'prɒdjus/ 8. that which is produced; yield; product. 9. agricultural or natural products collectively. –**production**, n. –**productive**, adj.

producer /prə'djusə/ n. someone who supervises the production of a film, play, television or radio show, etc., with particular responsibility for administrative and financial aspects.

product /'prɒdʌkt/ n. 1. a thing produced by any action or operation, or by labour; an effect or result. 2. something produced; a thing produced by nature or by a natural process. 3. *Maths* the result obtained by multiplying two or more quantities together.

productivity /prɒdʌk'tɪvəti/ n. efficiency of production, as measured by a comparison of product output with input cost.

profane /prə'feɪn/ adj. characterised by irreverence or contempt for God or sacred things; irreligious, especially speaking or spoken in manifest or implied contempt for sacred things. –**profanity**, n.

profess /prə'fɛs/ v.t. 1. to lay claim to (a feeling, etc.), often insincerely; pretend to. 2. to declare openly; announce or affirm; avow or acknowledge.

profession /prə'fɛʃən/ n. a vocation requiring knowledge of some department of learning or science.

professional /prə'fɛʃnəl, -ʃənəl/ adj. 1. following an occupation as a means of livelihood or for gain. 2. relating or appropriate to a profession. 3. following as a business an occupation ordinarily engaged in as a pastime. –n. 4. someone belonging to one of the learned or skilled professions. 5. someone who makes a business of an occupation, etc., especially of an art or sport, in which amateurs engage for amusement or recreation.

professor /prə'fɛsə/ n. a teacher of the highest rank, usually holding a chair in a particular branch of learning, in a university or college.

proffer /'prɒfə/ v.t. to put before a person for acceptance; offer.

proficient /prə'fɪʃənt/ adj. well advanced or expert in any art, science, or subject; skilled. –**proficiency**, n.

profile /'proufaɪl/ n. 1. the outline or contour of the human face, especially as seen from the side. 2. the outline of something seen against a background. 3. a vivid and concise sketch of the biography and personality of an individual. 4. an analysis of the traits and characteristics of a person from the facts available, as of a criminal to assist in their capture. –v.t. (**-filed**, **-filing**) 5. to compile a profile of.

profit /'prɒfət/ n. 1. (*oft. pl.*) pecuniary gain resulting from the employment of capital in any transaction: **a. gross profit**, gross receipts less the immediate costs of production. **b. net profit**, the amount remaining after deducting all costs from gross receipts. **c.** the ratio of such pecuniary gain to the amount of capital invested. 2. *Econ.* the surplus left to the producer or employer after deducting wages, rent, cost of raw materials, etc. 3. advantage;

benefit; gain. *–v.i.* **4.** to gain advantage or benefit. **5.** to make profit.

profitable /'prɒfətəbəl/ *adj.* **1.** yielding profits; remunerative. **2.** beneficial or useful. **–profitability**, *n.*

profiteer /prɒfə'tɪə/ *n.* someone who seeks or exacts exorbitant profits, as by taking advantage of public necessity.

profiterole /prə'fɪtəroʊl/ *n.* a small ball of pastry cooked, then filled with cream, jam, cheese, or the like.

profligate /'prɒfləgət/ *adj.* utterly and shamelessly immoral.

pro forma /proʊ 'fɔmə/ *adv.* according to form; as a matter of form. **–pro-forma**, *adj.*

profound /prə'faʊnd/ *adj.* **1.** penetrating or entering deeply into subjects of thought or knowledge. **2.** deep. **–profundity**, *n.*

profuse /prə'fjus/ *adj.* **1.** extravagant. **2.** abundant; in great amount. **–profusion**, *n.*

progeny /'prɒdʒəni/ *n.* offspring; issue; descendants. **–progenitor**, *n.*

progesterone /prə'dʒɛstəroʊn/ *n.* a hormone which prepares the uterus for the fertilised ovum and helps to maintain pregnancy.

prognosis /prɒg'noʊsəs/ *n.* (*pl.* **-noses** /-'noʊsiz/) **1.** a forecasting of the probable course and termination of a disease. **2.** a particular forecast made. **–prognostic**, *adj.*

prognosticate /prɒg'nɒstəkeɪt/ *v.t.* to prophesy.

program /'proʊgræm/ *n.* **1.** a plan or policy to be followed. **2.** a list of items, pieces, performers, etc., in a musical, theatrical, or other entertainment. **3.** an entertainment with reference to its pieces or numbers. **4.** a prospectus or syllabus. **5.** *Computers* a set of instructions written in a computer language, which need to be compiled into a code in order to run. *–v.* (**-grammed, -gramming**) *–v.t.* **6.** to insert instructions into a (device) in order to make it perform a certain task: *to program the video.* *–v.i.* **7.** to plan a program. **8.** to write a computer program. Also, **programme**. **–programmer**, *n.*

programming language *n.* → **computer language**.

progress *n.* /'proʊgrɛs/ **1.** advancement in general. **2.** growth or development; continuous improvement. **3.** course of action, of events, of time, etc. *–v.i.* /prə'grɛs/ **4.** to advance.

progression /prə'grɛʃən/ *n.* **1.** forward or onward movement. **2.** a passing successively from one member of a series to the next; succession; sequence.

progressive /prə'grɛsɪv/ *adj.* **1.** favouring or advocating progress, improvement, or reform, especially in political matters. **2.** progressing or advancing. **3.** denoting or relating to a form of taxation in which the rate increases with certain increases in the taxable income.

prohibit /prə'hɪbət/ *v.t.* to forbid (an action, a thing) by authority. **–prohibition**, *n.*

prohibitive /prə'hɪbətɪv/ *adj.* **1.** that prohibits or forbids something. **2.** serving to prevent the use, purchase, etc., of something. Also, **prohibitory**.

project *n.* /'proʊdʒɛkt, 'prɒ-/ **1.** something that is contemplated, devised, or planned; a plan; a scheme; an undertaking. *–v.t.* /prə'dʒɛkt/ **2.** to propose, contemplate, or plan. **3.** to throw,

cast, or impel forwards or onwards. **4.** to communicate; convey; make known (an idea, impression, etc.). **5.** to cause (a figure or image) to appear as on a background. **6.** to cause to jut out or protrude. *–v.i.* /prə'dʒɛkt/ **7.** to extend or protrude beyond something else. **–projection**, *n.*

projectile /prə'dʒɛktaɪl/ *n.* an object set in motion by an exterior force which then continues to move by virtue of its own inertia.

projector /prə'dʒɛktə/ *n.* an apparatus for throwing an image on a screen, as of a slide; a film projector, etc.

prokaryote /proʊ'kærioʊt/ *n.* any organism which has cells without a distinct nucleus but containing single-strand DNA, such as bacteria; moneran. Compare **eukaryote**. **–prokaryotic** /proʊkæri'ɒtɪk/, *adj.*

prolapse /'proʊlæps/ *n.* a falling down of an organ or part, as the uterus, from its normal position.

prolate /'proʊleɪt/ *adj.* elongated along the polar diameter.

proletariat /proʊlə'tɛəriət/ *n.* **1.** the unpropertied class; that class which is dependent for support on the sale of its labour. **2.** the working class, or wage-earners in general.

proliferate /prə'lɪfəreɪt/ *v.i.* to grow or produce by multiplication of parts. **–proliferation**, *n.*

prolific /prə'lɪfɪk/ *adj.* **1.** producing offspring, young, fruit, etc., especially abundantly; fruitful. **2.** abundantly productive of or fruitful in something specified.

prolix /'proʊlɪks/ *adj.* tediously long.

prologue /'proʊlɒg/ *n.* an introductory speech, often in verse, calling attention to the theme of a play.

prolong /prə'lɒŋ/ *v.t.* to make longer.

promenade /prɒmə'nad, prɒmə'neɪd, 'prɒmənad, 'prɒməneɪd/ *n.* **1.** a walk, especially in a public place, as for pleasure or display. *–v.i.* **2.** to take a promenade.

prominent /'prɒmənənt/ *adj.* **1.** standing out so as to be easily seen; conspicuous; very noticeable. **2.** important; leading; well-known. **–prominence**, *n.*

promiscuous /prə'mɪskjuəs/ *adj.* **1.** having many sexual partners.. **2.** indiscriminate. **–promiscuity**, *n.*

promise /'prɒməs/ *n.* **1.** an express assurance on which expectation is to be based. **2.** indication of future excellence or achievement. *–v.t.* **3.** to engage or undertake by promise (with an infinitive or clause). **4.** to make a promise of. *–v.i.* **5.** (oft. fol. by *well* or *fair*) to afford ground for expectation.

promissory note /'prɒməsəri/ *n.* a written promise to pay a specified sum of money to a person designated or to his or her order, or to the bearer, at a time fixed or on demand.

promontory /'prɒməntri/ *n.* (*pl.* **-ries**) a high point of land or rock projecting into the sea or other water beyond the line of coast; a headland.

promote /prə'moʊt/ *v.t.* **1.** to advance in rank, dignity, position, etc. **2.** to further the growth, development, progress, etc., of; encourage. **–promotion**, *n.*

prompt /prɒmpt/ *adj.* **1.** done, performed, delivered, etc., at once or without delay. **2.** ready in action; quick to act as occasion demands. −*v.t.* **3.** to move or incite to action. **4.** to assist (a person speaking) by suggesting something to be said. −*v.i.* **5.** *Theatre* to supply offstage cues and effects. −*n.* **6.** *Commerce* a limit of time given for payment for merchandise purchased, the limit being stated on a note of reminder called a **prompt note**. **7.** something that prompts. **8.** *Computers* a message from a computer, appearing as words or symbols on the screen, which indicates to the user that the computer is ready for further instructions.

promulgate /'prɒmᵊlgeɪt/ *v.t.* **1.** to make known by open declaration. **2.** to set forth or teach publicly (a creed, doctrine, etc.).

prone /proʊn/ *adj.* **1.** having a natural inclination or tendency to something; disposed; liable. **2.** having the front or ventral part downwards; lying face downwards. **3.** lying flat; prostrate.

prong /prɒŋ/ *n.* one of the pointed divisions or tines of a fork.

pronoun /'proʊnaʊn/ *n.* a word used as a substitute for a noun. −**pronominal**, *adj.*

pronounce /prᵊ'naʊns/ *v.* (**-nounced**, **-nouncing**) −*v.t.* **1.** to enunciate or articulate (words, etc.). **2.** to utter or sound in a particular manner in speaking. **3.** to declare (a person or thing) to be as specified. **4.** to utter or deliver formally or solemnly. −*v.i.* **5.** (usu. fol. by *on*) to give an opinion or decision. −**pronunciation**, *n.*

pronounced /prᵊ'naʊnst/ *adj.* **1.** strongly marked. **2.** clearly indicated.

proof /pruf/ *n.* **1.** evidence sufficient to establish a thing as true, or to produce belief in its truth. **2.** the establishment of the truth of anything; demonstration. **3.** an arithmetical operation serving to check the correctness of a calculation. **4.** the arbitrary standard strength, as of alcoholic liquors. **5.** *Photography* a trial print from a negative. **6.** *Printing* a trial impression of composed type, taken to correct errors and mark alterations. −*adj.* **7.** impenetrable, impervious, or invulnerable. **8.** of tested or proved strength or quality.

-proof a suffix meaning 'insulated from', 'impervious to', 'not affected by', etc., as in *waterproof*.

proofread /'prufrid/ *v.t.* (**-read** /'prufrɛd/, **-reading**) to read (printers' proofs, etc.) in order to detect and mark errors.

prop¹ /prɒp/ *v.t.* (**propped, propping**) **1.** (oft. fol. by *up*) to support, or prevent from falling, with or as with a prop. **2.** to support or sustain. −*n.* **3.** a stick, rod, pole, beam, or other rigid support. **4.** a person or thing serving as a support or stay.

prop² /prɒp/ *n. Theatre* an item of furniture, ornament, or decoration in a stage setting; any object handled or used by an actor in performance. Also, **property**.

propaganda /prɒpᵊ'gændᵊ/ *n.* dissemination of ideas, information or rumour for the purpose of injuring or helping an institution, a cause or a person.

propagate /'prɒpᵊgeɪt/ *v.t.* **1.** to cause (plants, animals, etc.) to multiply by any process of natural reproducing from the parent stock. **2.** to transmit (traits, etc.) in reproduction, or through offspring. **3.** to spread (a report, doctrine, practice, etc.) from person to person; disseminate. **4.** to cause to extend to a greater distance, or transmit through space or a medium.

propane /'proʊpeɪn/ *n.* a gaseous hydrocarbon found in petroleum.

propel /prᵊ'pɛl/ *v.t.* (**-pelled, -pelling**) to drive, or cause to move, forwards.

propellant /prᵊ'pɛlᵊnt/ *n.* **1.** a propelling agent. **2.** *Aeronautics* one or more substances used in rocket motors for the chemical generation of gas at the controlled rates required to provide thrust. Also, **propellent**.

propellent /prᵊ'pɛlᵊnt/ *adj.* **1.** propelling; driving forward. −*n.* **2.** → **propellant**.

propeller /prᵊ'pɛlᵊ/ *n.* a device having a revolving hub with radiating blades, for propelling a ship, aircraft, etc. Also, **propellor**.

propensity /prᵊ'pɛnsᵊti/ *n.* a natural or habitual inclination or tendency.

proper /'prɒpᵊ/ *adj.* **1.** adapted or appropriate to the purpose or circumstances; fit; suitable. **2.** conforming to established standards of behaviour or manners; correct or decorous. **3.** belonging or relating exclusively or distinctly to a person or thing. **4.** strict; accurate.

proper noun *n.* a noun that is not usually preceded by an article or other limiting modifier and, when written, is spelt with an initial capital; in meaning applicable only to a single person or thing, or to several persons or things which constitute a unique class only by virtue of having the same name. Compare **common noun**. Also, **proper name**.

property /'prɒpᵊti/ *n.* (*pl.* **-ties**) **1.** that which one owns; the possession or possessions of a particular owner. **2.** a piece of land owned. **3.** Also, **country property**. a farm, station, orchard, etc. **4.** an essential or distinctive attribute or quality of a thing. **5.** → **prop²**.

property trust *n. Law* a unit trust which invests in property (mainly real estate).

prophecy /'prɒfᵊsi/ *n.* (*pl.* **-cies**) a prediction.

prophesy /'prɒfᵊsaɪ/ *v.* (**-sied, -sying**) −*v.t.* **1.** to foretell or predict. −*v.i.* **2.** to make predictions. −**prophetic**, *adj.*

prophet /'prɒfᵊt/ *n.* **1.** someone who speaks for God or a deity, or by divine inspiration. **2.** someone who foretells or predicts what is to come.

prophylactic /prɒfᵊ'læktɪk/ *adj.* **1.** defending or protecting from disease, as a drug. −*n.* **2.** a contraceptive, especially a condom. −**prophylaxis**, *n.*

propinquity /prᵊ'pɪŋkwᵊti/ *n.* **1.** nearness in place; proximity. **2.** nearness of relation; kinship.

propitiate /prᵊ'pɪʃieɪt/ *v.t.* to make favourably inclined; appease.

propitious /prᵊ'pɪʃᵊs/ *adj.* presenting favourable conditions; favourable.

proponent /prᵊ'poʊnᵊnt/ *n.* **1.** someone who puts forward a proposition or proposal. **2.** someone who supports a cause or doctrine.

proportion /prᵊ'pɔʃᵊn/ *n.* **1.** comparative relation between things or magnitudes as to size, quantity, number, etc.; ratio. **2.** proper relation between things or parts. **3.** (*pl.*) dimensions. **4.** a portion or part, especially in its relation to the whole. **5.** symmetry; harmony; balanced relationship. **–proportional,** *adj.* **–proportionate,** *adj.*

proportional representation *n.* a system of electing representatives to a legislative assembly in which there are a number of members representing any one electorate. The number of successful candidates from each party is directly proportional to the percentage of the total vote won by the party.

propose /prə'pouz/ *v.t.* **1.** to put forward (a matter, subject, case, etc.) for consideration, acceptance, or action. **2.** to present (a person) for some position, office, membership, etc. **3.** to propound (a question, riddle, etc.). **–proposal,** *n.* **–proposition,** *n.*

propound /prə'paund/ *v.t.* to put forward for consideration, acceptance, or adoption.

proprietary /prə'praiətri/ *adj.* **1.** belonging to a proprietor or proprietors. **2.** manufactured and sold only by the owner of the patent, formula, brand name, or trademark associated with the product.

proprietary limited company *n.* a company with a limit of 50 shareholders, which cannot issue shares for public conscription and which is not listed on the stock exchange; shareholders enjoy limited liability, on liquidation. Also, **proprietary company.**

proprietor /prə'praiətə/ *n.* **1.** the owner of a business establishment, a hotel, newspaper, etc. **2.** someone who has the exclusive right or title to something; an owner, as of property. **–proprietorship,** *n.*

propriety /prə'praiəti/ *n.* **1.** conformity to established standards of behaviour or manners. **2.** appropriateness to the purpose or circumstances; suitability.

propulsion /prə'pʌlʃən/ *n.* the act of propelling or driving forward or onward.

pro rata /prou 'ratə/ *adv.* **1.** in proportion; according to a certain rate. *–adj.* **2.** proportionate.

prorogue /prə'roug/ *v.t.* to discontinue meetings of (parliament or similar legislative body) until the next session.

prosaic /prou'zeiik, prə-/ *adj.* commonplace or dull; matter-of-fact.

proscenium /prə'siniəm/ *n. (pl.* **-nia** /-niə/) (in the modern theatre) the decorative arch or opening between the stage and the auditorium.

prosciutto /prə'ʃutou/ *n.* a dry-cured, spiced ham, often sold very thinly sliced.

proscribe /prou'skraib/ *v.t.* **1.** to denounce or condemn (a thing) as dangerous; to prohibit. **2.** to banish, exile or outlaw.

prose /prouz/ *n.* the ordinary form of spoken or written language, without metrical structure (as distinguished from poetry or verse).

prosecute /'prɒsəkjut/ *v.t. Law* **1.** to institute legal proceedings against (a person, etc.). **2.** to seek to enforce or obtain by legal process. **3.** to conduct criminal proceedings in court against. **–prosecution,** *n.* **–prosecutor,** *n.*

proselyte /'prɒsəlait/ *n.* someone who has come over or changed from one opinion, religious belief, sect, or the like to another; a convert.

prosody /'prɒsədi, 'prɒz-/ *n.* the science or study of the writing of poetry.

prospect /'prɒspɛkt/ *n.* **1.** (*usu. pl.*) an apparent probability of advancement, success, profit,

etc. **2.** the outlook for the future. **3.** something in view as a source of profit. **4.** a view or scene presented to the eye, especially of scenery. *–v.t.* **5.** to search or explore (a region), as for gold. *–v.i.* **6.** to search or explore a region for gold or the like. **–prospector,** *n.*

prospective /prə'spɛktiv/ *adj.* **1.** of or in the future. **2.** potential; likely; expected.

prospectus /prə'spɛktəs/ *n.* **1.** a circular or advertisement inviting applications from the public to subscribe for securities of a corporation or proposed corporation. **2.** a pamphlet issued by a school or other institution giving details about itself.

prosperous /'prɒspərəs, -prəs/ *adj.* **1.** having or characterised by continued good fortune; flourishing; successful. **2.** well-to-do or well-off. **–prosper,** *v.* **–prosperity,** *n.*

prostate gland /'prɒsteit/ *n.* the composite gland which surrounds the urethra of males at the base of the bladder.

prosthesis /prɒs'θisəs, prəs-/ *n. (pl.* **-theses** /-'θisiz/) **1.** the addition of an artificial part to supply a defect of the body. **2.** such a part, as an artificial limb. **–prosthetics,** *n.*

prostitute /'prɒstətjut/ *n.* a person, especially a woman, who engages in sexual intercourse for money as a livelihood.

prostrate *v.t.* /prɒs'treit/ **1.** to throw down level with the ground. *–adj.* /'prɒstreit/ **2.** submissive. **3.** *Bot.* (of a plant or stem) lying flat on the ground.

protagonist /prə'tægənəst/ *n.* the leading character in a play, novel, etc.

protea /'proutiə/ *n.* any of various southern African shrubs or trees with large showy flowers.

protean /prə'tiən, 'proutiən/ *adj.* readily assuming different forms or characters.

protect /prə'tɛkt/ *v.t.* **1.** to defend or guard from attack, invasion, annoyance, insult, etc.; cover or shield from injury or danger. **2.** *Econ.* to guard (a country's industry) from foreign competition by imposing import duties. **–protective,** *adj.* **–protection,** *n.* **–protector,** *n.*

protection money *n.* money extorted by criminals from victims, ostensibly to buy protection for them from other criminals.

protection racket *n.* a criminal scheme based on the extortion of protection money.

protectorate /prə'tɛktərət, -trət/ *n.* **1.** the relation of a strong state towards a weaker state or territory which it protects and partly controls. **2.** a state or territory so protected.

protégé /'proutəʒei/ *n.* someone who is under the protection or friendly patronage of another.

protein /'proutin/ *n. Biochem.* any of the polymers formed from amino acids, which are found in all cells and which include enzymes, plasma and proteins.

protest *n.* /'proutɛst/ **1.** an expression or declaration of objection or disapproval. **2.** a demonstration or meeting of people to express objection to or disapproval of something. *–v.i.* /prə'tɛst, 'prou-/ **3.** to give formal expression to objection or disapproval; remonstrate. *–v.t.* /prə'tɛst, 'prou-/ **4.** to declare solemnly or formally; affirm; assert.

protestation /prɒtəs'teiʃən, prou-/ *n.* a solemn declaration or affirmation.

protist /'prootast/ n. Biol. one of a variety of eukaryotic organisms, including some algae, protozoans, and moulds. Also, **protistan**.

protistan /proo'tustan/ n. **1.** → **protist**. –adj. **2.** of or relating to a protist.

proto- a word element meaning 'first', 'earliest form of', as prototype.

protocol /'prootakol/ n. **1.** the customs and regulations dealing with the ceremonies and etiquette of the diplomatic corps and others at a court or capital. **2.** Computers a set of rules governing the format in which messages are sent from one computer to another, as in a network.

proton /'prooton/ n. a positively-charged elementary particle present in every atomic nucleus.

protoplasm /'prootaplæzam/ n. the living matter of all vegetable and animal cells and tissues.

prototype /'prootataip/ n. the original or model after which anything is formed. –**prototypical**, adj.

protozoan /proota'zooan/ adj. an animal consisting of one cell.

protract /pra'trækt/ v.t. **1.** to prolong. **2.** Surveying, etc. to plot; to draw by means of a scale and protractor.

protractor /pra'trækta/ n. a flat semicircular instrument, graduated around the circular edge, used to measure or mark off angles.

protrude /pra'trud/ v.i. to project; jut out. –**protrusion**, n.

protuberant /pra'tjubarant, -brant/ adj. bulging. –**protuberance**, n.

proud /praud/ adj. **1.** (oft. fol. by of, an infinitive, or a clause) feeling pleasure or satisfaction over something conceived as highly honourable or creditable to oneself. **2.** having or showing self-respect or self-esteem. **3.** (of things) stately, majestic, or magnificent. **4.** projecting beyond the surrounding elements or objects.

prove /pruv/ v.t. (**proved**, **proved** or **proven** /'pruvan, 'proovan/, **proving**) **1.** to establish the truth or genuineness of, as by evidence or argument. **2.** to put to the test; try or test. **3.** to determine the characteristics of by scientific analysis. **4.** Cookery to cause (dough) to rise in a warm place before baking.

provedore /prova'do/ n. someone who provides supplies as for a ship, tuckshop, etc. Also, **provedor**, **providore**, **providor**.

provenance /'provanans/ n. the place of origin, as of a work of art, etc.

provender /'provanda/ n. dry food for livestock, as hay; fodder.

proverb /'provab/ n. a short popular saying, long current, embodying some familiar truth or useful thought in expressive language. –**proverbial**, adj.

provide /pra'vaid/ –v.t. **1.** to furnish or supply. –v.i. **2.** (oft. fol. by for) to supply means of support, etc.

provided /pra'vaidad/ conj. on the condition or supposition (that).

providence /'provadans/ n. **1.** the foreseeing care and guardianship of God over his creatures. **2.** provident or prudent management of resources; economy.

provident /'provadant/ adj. having or showing foresight; careful in providing for the future.

provider /pra'vaida/ n. **1.** a person who supplies a means of support; breadwinner. **2.** a company which provides access to a service: mobile phone provider. **3.** → **internet service provider**.

providing /pra'vaidiŋ/ conj. → **provided**.

providore /'provada/ n. → **provedore**.

province /'provans/ n. **1.** an administrative division or unit of a country. **2.** the sphere or field of action of a person, etc.; one's office, function, or business. –phr. **3. the provinces**, the parts of a country outside the capital or the largest cities. –**provincial**, adj.

provision /pra'vɪʒən/ n. **1.** a clause in a legal instrument, a law, etc., providing for a particular matter; stipulation; proviso. **2.** arrangement or preparation beforehand, as for the doing of something, the meeting of needs, the supplying of means, etc. **3.** (pl.) supplies of food.

provisional /pra'vɪʒənəl/ adj. temporary; conditional.

proviso /pra'vaizoo/ n. (pl. **-sos** or **-soes**) a stipulation or condition.

provoke /pra'vook/ v.t. **1.** to anger, enrage, exasperate, or vex. **2.** to stir up, arouse, or call forth. **3.** to give rise to, induce, or bring about. –**provocation**, n. –**provocative**, adj.

provost /'provast/ n. a person appointed to superintend or preside. –**provostship**, n.

prow /prau/ n. the forepart of a ship or boat above the waterline; the bow.

prowess /'praues, prau'es/ n. **1.** valour; bravery. **2.** outstanding ability.

prowl /praul/ v.i. to rove or go about stealthily in search of prey, plunder, etc.

proximate /'proksamat/ adj. next; nearest.

proximity /prok'simati/ n. nearness.

proximo /'proksamoo/ adv. in or of the next or coming month. Abbrev.: prox. Compare ultimo.

proxy /'proksi/ n. (pl. **-xies**) the agency of a person acting as a deputy for another.

proxy server n. Internet a server which acts as a buffer between the user and the internet, performing a range of functions such as storing frequently used data in a cache to speed access, imposing restrictions on access to some users, or hiding IP addresses to ensure anonymity. Also, **proxy**.

prude /prud/ n. a person who affects extreme modesty or propriety. –**prudery**, n.

prudence /'prudns/ n. **1.** cautious practical wisdom; good judgement; discretion. **2.** provident care in management; economy or frugality. –**prudential**, adj. –**prudent**, adj.

prune¹ /prun/ n. a purplish black dried fruit.

prune² /prun/ v.t. to cut or lop superfluous or undesired twigs, branches, or roots from; to trim.

prurient /'pruriant/ adj. inclined to or characterised by lascivious thought.

pry /prai/ v.i. (**pried**, **prying**) **1.** to look closely or curiously, peer, or peep. **2.** to search or inquire curiously or inquisitively into something.

psalm /sam/ n. a sacred or solemn song, or hymn.

psephology /səˈfɒlədʒi/ n. the study of elections by analysing their results, trends, etc.

pseudo- a word element meaning 'false', 'pretended'.

pseudonym /ˈsjudənɪm/ n. an assumed name adopted by an author to conceal his or her identity; pen-name.

pseudoscience /ˈsjudoʊsaɪəns/ n. an apparently scientific approach to the process or presentation of a theory, invention, product, etc., which on close analysis is shown to have no scientific validity. –**pseudoscientist**, n. –**pseudoscientific**, adj. –**pseudoscientifically**, adv.

psych /saɪk/ phr. Colloq. **1. psych up**, to use psychological means to put (a person, team, etc.) into a frame of mind which maximises performance, as in a race, competition, etc. **2. psych out**, to gain advantage over (an opponent) by undermining their confidence using psychological means.

psyche /ˈsaɪki/ n. the human soul, spirit, or mind.

psychedelic /saɪkəˈdɛlɪk/ adj. **1.** denoting or relating to a mental state of enlarged consciousness, involving a sense of aesthetic joy and increased perception transcending verbal concepts. **2.** Colloq. having bright colours and imaginative patterns, as materials.

psychiatry /səˈkaɪətri, saɪ-/ n. the practice or the science of treating mental diseases. –**psychiatric**, adj. –**psychiatrist**, n.

psychic /ˈsaɪkɪk/ adj. Also, **psychical. 1.** of or relating to the human soul or mind; mental (opposed to physical). **2.** Psychol. relating to super- or extra-sensory mental functioning, such as clairvoyance, telepathy. –n. **3.** a person specially susceptible to psychic influences.

psycho- a word element representing 'psyche' (as in psychology and psychoanalysis). Also, **psych-**.

psychoanalysis /ˌsaɪkoʊəˈnæləsəs/ n. a technical procedure for investigating unconscious mental processes, and for treating neuroses. –**psychoanalyse**, v.

psychological /saɪkəˈlɒdʒɪkəl/ adj. **1.** of or relating to psychology. **2.** relating to the mind or to mental phenomena.

psychology /saɪˈkɒlədʒi/ n. **1.** the science of mind, or of mental states and processes; the science of human nature. **2.** the science of human and animal behaviour. –**psychologist**, n.

psychopathic /saɪkəˈpæθɪk/ adj. denoting a personality outwardly normal but characterised by a diminished sense of social responsibility, inability to establish deep human relationships, and sometimes, abnormal or dangerous acts. –**psychopath**, n.

psychopathy /saɪˈkɒpəθi/ n. **1.** mental disease or disorder. **2.** a psychopathic personality.

psychosis /saɪˈkoʊsəs/ n. (pl. **-choses** /-ˈkoʊsiz/) any major, severe form of mental illness. –**psychotic**, adj.

psychosomatic /ˌsaɪkoʊsəˈmætɪk/ adj. denoting a physical disorder which is caused by or notably influenced by the emotional state of the patient.

ptomaine /təˈmeɪn/ n. any of a class of basic nitrogenous substances, some of them very poisonous, produced during putrefaction of animal or plant proteins. Also, **ptomain**.

pub /pʌb/ n. Colloq. a hotel, especially one that is primarily a provider of alcoholic drinks rather than accommodation.

puberty /ˈpjubəti/ n. sexual maturity; the earliest age at which a person is capable of procreating offspring.

pubic /ˈpjubɪk/ adj. relating to the lower part of the abdomen, or groin.

public /ˈpʌblɪk/ adj. **1.** relating to or used by the people of a community or the people as a whole. –n. **2. the public**, the people of a community. –phr. **3. go public**, to make known things which were previously secret or private. **4. in public**, in front of other people. **5. the general public**, all the people. –**publicly**, adv.

public-address system n. an electronic system consisting of microphone, amplifier, and a loudspeaker, which serves to amplify sound. Also, **PA, PA system**.

publican /ˈpʌblɪkən/ n. the owner or manager of a pub or hotel.

publication /pʌbləˈkeɪʃən/ n. **1.** the publishing of a book, ebook, periodical, blog, images, sheet music, sound recordings, or the like. **2.** that which is published, as a book or the like.

public company n. a company with the capacity to invite the public to subscribe for shares or debentures, the share capital of which must not be less than a statutory minimum.

publicise /ˈpʌbləsaɪz/ v.t. to announce publicly; bring to the attention of people in general. Also, **publicize**.

publicity /pʌbˈlɪsəti/ n. **1.** the measures, process, or business of securing public notice. **2.** advertisement matter, as leaflets, films, etc., intended to attract public notice. –**publicist**, n.

public relations n. (functioning as sing. or pl.) the practice of promoting goodwill among the public for a company, government body, individual or the like; the practice of working to present a favourable image.

public sector n. that sector of an economy which is owned and operated by government and government authorities (opposed to the private sector).

public service n. the structure of government departments and personnel responsible for the administration of policy and legislation. Also, Chiefly Brit., **civil service**. –**public servant**, n.

publish /ˈpʌblɪʃ/ v.t. **1.** to issue, or cause to be issued, in print or digital formats, for sale or distribution to the public, as a book, ebook, blog, periodical, images, sheet music, sound recordings, or the like. **2.** to make publicly or generally known.

puce /pjus/ n. dark or purplish brown.

pucker /ˈpʌkə/ v.t., v.i. to draw or gather into wrinkles or irregular folds.

pudding /ˈpʊdɪŋ/ n. **1.** a sweet or savoury dish made in many forms and of various ingredients. **2.** a course in a meal following the main or meat course.

puddle /ˈpʌdl/ n. **1.** a small pool of water, especially dirty water, as in a road after rain. **2.** a small pool of any liquid.

puerile /'pjʊəraɪl, 'pjurɑɪl/ *adj.* **1.** of or relating to a child or boy. **2.** childishly foolish, irrational, or trivial.

puff /pʌf/ *n.* **1.** a short, quick blast, as of wind or breath. **2.** an inflated or distended part of a thing; a swelling; a protuberance. **3.** inflated or exaggerated praise, especially as uttered or written from interested motives. –*v.i.* **4.** to blow with short, quick blasts, as the wind. **5.** to emit puffs or whiffs of vapour or smoke. **6.** (usu. fol. by *up*) to become inflated or distended. –*v.t.* **7.** to send forth (air, vapour, etc.) in short quick blasts. **8.** to inflate or distend, especially with air. –*phr.* **9. out of puff**, *Colloq.* out of breath.

puffin /'pʌfən/ *n.* a seabird with a brightly coloured bill.

puff pastry *n.* a rich, flaky pastry used for pies, tarts, etc.; rough puff pastry; flaky pastry. Also, *US,* **puff paste.**

puffy /'pʌfi/ *adj.* (**-fier, -fiest**) inflated or distended.

pug /pʌg/ *n.* a breed of dog.

pugilist /'pjudʒələst/ *n.* a boxer.

pugnacious /pʌg'neɪʃəs/ *adj.* given to fighting; quarrelsome; aggressive.

pull /pʊl/ *v.t.* **1.** to draw or haul towards oneself or itself, in a particular direction, or into a particular position. **2.** to draw, rend, or tear (apart, to pieces, etc.). **3.** to draw or pluck away from a place of growth, attachment, etc. **4.** to cause to form, as a grimace. **5.** to strain, as a ligament. –*v.i.* **6.** (oft. fol. by *at*) to exert a drawing, tugging, or hauling force. –*n.* **7.** the act of pulling or drawing. **8.** force used in pulling; pulling power. **9.** *Colloq.* influence, as with persons able to grant favours. –*phr.* **10. pull in**, (of a vehicle, driver, etc.) to move to the side of the road in order to stop. **11. pull out. a.** to leave; depart. **b.** (of a vehicle, driver, etc.) to move out of a lane or stream of traffic, as in preparing to overtake. **c.** *Colloq.* to withdraw, as from an agreement or enterprise. **12. pull through**, *Colloq.* to recover, as from an illness, period of adversity, or the like. **13. pull up. a.** to stop. **b.** to correct or rebuke.

pull-down menu *n. Computers* a computer menu which is instantly accessible and which leaves the screen exactly as it was once an option has been chosen. Also, **drop-down menu.**

pullet /'pʊlət/ *n.* a young hen.

pulley /'pʊli/ *n.* (*pl.* **-leys**) a wheel with a grooved rim for carrying a line, turning in a frame or block and serving to change the direction of or transmit power, as in pulling at one end of the line to raise a weight at the other end.

pullover /'pʊloʊvə/ *n.* → **jumper.**

pulmonary /'pʌlmənri, 'pʊl-/ *adj.* of or relating to the lungs.

pulp /pʌlp/ *n.* **1.** the succulent part of a fruit. **2.** any soft, moist, slightly cohering mass, as that into which linen, wood, etc., are converted in the making of paper.

pulpit /'pʊlpət/ *n.* a platform or raised structure in a church, from which the priest or minister, etc., delivers a sermon, etc.

pulsate /pʌl'seɪt/ *v.i.* **1.** to expand and contract rhythmically, as the heart; beat; throb. **2.** to vibrate; quiver.

pulse¹ /pʌls/ *n.* **1.** the regular throbbing of the arteries caused by the successive contractions of the heart, especially as felt in an artery at the wrist. **2.** a single stroke, vibration, or undulation. **3.** a throb of life, emotion, etc. –*v.i.* **4.** to beat or throb; pulsate.

pulse² /pʌls/ *n.* the edible seeds of certain leguminous plants, as peas, beans, etc.

pulverise /'pʌlvəraɪz/ *v.t.* to reduce to dust or powder, as by pounding, grinding, etc. Also, **pulverize.**

puma /'pjumə/ *n.* a large tawny wild cat.

pumice /'pʌməs/ *n.* a porous or spongy form of volcanic glass, used, especially when powdered, as an abrasive, etc. Also, **pumice stone.** –**pumiceous**, *adj.*

pummel /'pʌməl/ *v.t.* (**-melled** or, *Chiefly US,* **-meled, -melling** or, *Chiefly US,* **-meling**) to beat or thrash with rapid blows, as with the fists.

pump¹ /pʌmp/ *n.* **1.** an apparatus or machine for raising, driving, exhausting, or compressing fluids, as by means of a piston, plunger, or rotating vanes. –*v.t.* **2.** to raise, drive, etc., with a pump. **3.** (sometimes fol. by *out*) to free from water, etc., by means of a pump. **4.** to seek to elicit information from, as by artful questioning. –*v.i.* **5.** to work a pump; raise or move water, etc., with a pump. **6.** to operate as a pump does.

pump² /pʌmp/ *n.* a type of shoe.

pumpkin /'pʌmpkən/ *n.* a large, usually orange, vegetable.

pun /pʌn/ *n.* a play on words.

punch¹ /pʌntʃ/ *n.* **1.** a thrusting blow, especially with the fist. –*v.t.* **2.** to give a sharp thrust or blow to, especially with the fist.

punch² /pʌntʃ/ *n.* a tool or apparatus for piercing, or perforating tickets, leather, etc., or stamping materials, impressing a design, forcing nails beneath a surface, driving bolts out of holes, etc.

punch³ /pʌntʃ/ *n.* a beverage consisting of wine or spirits mixed with water, fruit juice, etc.

punchline /'pʌntʃlaɪn/ *n.* the culminating sentence, line, phrase, or the like of a joke, especially that on which the whole joke depends.

punctilious /pʌŋk'tɪliəs/ *adj.* strict in the observance of forms in conduct or actions.

punctual /'pʌŋktʃuəl/ *adj.* strictly observant of an appointed or regular time; not late. –**punctuality,** *n.*

punctuation /pʌŋktʃu'eɪʃən/ *n.* the practice, art, or system of inserting marks or points in writing or printing in order to make the meaning clear. –**punctuate,** *v.*

puncture /'pʌŋktʃə/ *v.t.* to prick, pierce, or perforate.

pundit /'pʌndət/ *n.* someone who sets up as an expert.

pungent /'pʌndʒənt/ *adj.* sharply affecting the organs of taste, as if by a penetrating power; biting; acrid.

punish /'pʌnɪʃ/ *v.t.* **1.** to subject to a penalty, or to pain, loss, confinement, death, etc., for some offence, transgression, or fault. **2.** to handle severely or roughly, as in a fight. **–punishment**, *n*. **–punitive**, *adj*.

punk /pʌŋk/ *n*. **1.** *Chiefly US Colloq*. something or someone worthless, degraded, or bad. **2.** a follower of punk rock and an associated style of dress and behaviour.

punk rock *n*. a type of rock music usually associated with aggression and rebelliousness.

punnet /'pʌnət/ *n*. a small, shallow container, as for strawberries.

punt¹ /pʌnt/ *n*. **1.** a shallow, flat-bottomed, square-ended boat. **2.** a ferry for carrying vehicles across rivers, etc.

punt² /pʌnt/ *v.i.* to gamble; wager.

puny /'pjuni/ *adj*. (**-nier**, **-niest**) of less than normal size or strength; weakly.

pup /pʌp/ *n*. **1.** a young dog, under one year; a puppy. **2.** a young seal.

pupa /'pjupə/ *n*. (*pl*. **-pae** /-pi/ *or* **-pas**) an insect in the non-feeding, usually immobile, transformation stage between the larva and the imago. **–pupal**, *adj*.

pupil¹ /'pjupəl/ *n*. someone who is under an instructor or teacher; a student.

pupil² /'pjupəl/ *n*. the expanding and contracting opening in the iris of the eye, through which light passes to the retina.

puppet /'pʌpət/ *n*. **1.** a doll. **2.** *Theatre* an artificial figure of a person, animal or object, usually in miniature and capable of articulated movement, controlled by a puppeteer. **–puppeteer**, *n*. **–puppetry**, *n*.

puppy /'pʌpi/ *n*. (*pl*. **-pies**) **1.** a young dog. **2.** the young of certain other animals, as the shark. **3.** a presuming, conceited, or empty-headed young man.

purchase /'pɜtʃəs/ *v.t.* **1.** to acquire by the payment of money or its equivalent; buy. **–n*. **2.** something which is purchased or bought.

purdah /'pɜdə/ *n*. (in some Muslim and Hindu communities) the custom of women remaining secluded, especially from men who are not their relatives, remaining in a particular part of their home and wearing clothing that completely covers them when they are in public.

pure /'pjuə, pjuə/ *adj*. **1.** free from extraneous matter, or from mixture with anything of a different, inferior, or contaminating kind. **2.** abstract or theoretical (opposed to *applied*). **3.** unqualified; absolute; utter; sheer. **4.** being that and nothing else; mere. **5.** clean, spotless, or unsullied. **6.** untainted with evil; innocent. **–purify**, *v*. **–purity**, *n*.

puree /'pjureɪ/ *n*. a cooked and sieved vegetable or fruit.

purgative /'pɜgətɪv/ *adj*. purging; cleansing; specifically, causing evacuation of the bowels.

purgatory /'pɜgətri/ *n*. any condition, situation, or place of temporary suffering, expiation, or the like.

purge /pɜdʒ/ *v.t.* (**purged**, **purging**) **1.** to cleanse; rid of whatever is impure or undesirable; purify. **–n*. **2.** the elimination from political activity, as by killing, of political opponents and others.

purism /'pjurɪzəm/ *n*. scrupulous or excessive observance of or insistence on purity in language, style, etc. **–purist**, *n*.

puritan /'pjurətən/ *n*. someone who aspires to great purity or strictness of life in moral and religious matters. **–puritanical**, *adj*.

purl /pɜl/ *n*. a stitch used in hand knitting to make a rib effect.

purloin /pɜ'lɔɪn/ *v.t.* to steal.

purple /'pɜpəl/ *n*. **1.** any colour having components of both red and blue, especially a dark shade of such a colour. **–adj*. **2.** of the colour of purple. **–v.t.* **3.** to make purple.

purport *v.t.* /pɜ'pɔt, 'pɜpɔt/ **1.** to profess or claim. **2.** to convey to the mind as the meaning or thing intended; express; imply. **–n*. /'pɜpɔt, -pət/ **3.** tenor, import, or meaning. **4.** purpose or object.

purpose /'pɜpəs/ *n*. **1.** the object for which anything exists or is done, made, used, etc. **2.** an intended or desired result; end or aim. **3.** intention or determination. **–phr*. **4. on purpose**, by design; intentionally. **–purposive**, *adj*.

purr /pɜ/ *v.i.* to utter a low, continuous murmuring sound expressive of satisfaction, as a cat does.

purse /pɜs/ *n*. **1.** a small bag, pouch, or case for carrying money on the person. **2.** a sum of money offered as a prize.

purser /'pɜsə/ *n*. an officer, especially on board a ship, charged with keeping accounts, etc.

pursuance /pə'sjuəns/ *n*. the following or carrying out of some plan, course, injunction, or the like.

pursuant /pə'sjuənt/ *adv*. (fol. by *to*) according. Also, **pursuantly**.

pursue /pə'sju/ *v.t.* (**-sued**, **-suing**) **1.** to follow with the view of overtaking, capturing, killing, etc.; chase. **2.** to strive to gain; seek to attain or accomplish (an end, object, purpose, etc.). **3.** to carry on (a course of action, train of thoughts, etc.). **4.** to continue to discuss (a subject, topic, etc.). **–pursuit**, *n*.

purvey /pə'veɪ/ *v.t.* to provide, furnish, or supply (especially food or provisions). **–purveyance**, *n*. **–purveyor**, *n*.

purview /'pɜvju/ *n*. range of operation, activity, concern, etc.

pus /pʌs/ *n*. a yellow-white substance produced by suppuration and found in abscesses, sores, etc. **–pussy**, *adj*.

push /puʃ/ *v.t.* **1.** to exert force upon or against (a thing) in order to move it away. **2.** to press or urge (a person, etc.) to some action or course. **3.** to peddle (narcotics). **–v.i*. **4.** to exert a thrusting force upon something. **5.** to use steady force in moving a thing away; shove. **–n*. **6.** the act of pushing; a shove or thrust. **7.** a determined pushing forward or advance. **8.** the pressure of circumstances. **9.** *Colloq*. persevering energy; enterprise.

pushover /'puʃoʊvə/ *n. Colloq*. anything done easily.

pusillanimous /pjusə'lænəməs/ *adj*. faint-hearted; cowardly.

puss /pus/ *n*. a cat.

pussy /'pusi/ *n*. (*pl*. **-sies**) a cat.

pussyfoot /'pusifut/ *v.i.* **1.** to go with a soft, stealthy tread like that of a cat. **2.** to act cautiously or timidly, as if afraid to commit oneself on a point at issue. **–pussyfooter**, *n*. **–pussyfooting**, *n*.

pustule /ˈpʌstjul/ n. a small elevation of the skin containing pus. –**pustular**, adj.

put /pʊt/ v.t. (**put, putting**) 1. to move or place (anything) so as to get it into or out of some place or position. 2. to bring into some relation, state, etc. 3. to set at a particular place, point, amount, etc., in a scale of estimation. 4. to express or state. 5. to set, give, or make. 6. to throw or cast, especially with a forward motion of the hand when raised close to the shoulder. –phr. 7. **put across**, to communicate; cause to be understood; explain effectively. 8. **put down**, a. to write down. b. to repress or suppress. c. (usu. fol. by to) to ascribe or attribute. d. to pay as a lump sum. e. to destroy an animal, for reasons of disease, etc. f. to nominate. 9. **put in**, a. Naut. to enter a port or harbour. b. (oft. fol. by for) to apply. c. to devote, as time, work, etc. 10. **put off**, a. to postpone. b. to disgust or cause to dislike. 11. **put on**, a. to assume sincerely or falsely. b. to dress in (clothing). c. to produce; stage. d. to cause to speak on the telephone. 12. **put out**, a. to extinguish (fire, etc.). b. to confuse or embarrass. c. Naut. to go out to sea. 13. **put up**, a. to erect. b. to provide (money, etc.). c. to give lodging to. d. (fol. by to) to persuade to do.

putative /ˈpjutətɪv/ adj. commonly regarded as such; reputed; supposed.

put option n. Stock Exchange the right to sell a parcel of shares at an agreed price within a specified period.

putrefy /ˈpjutrəfaɪ/ v.i. (**-fied, -fying**) to become putrid; rot. –**putrefaction**, n.

putrid /ˈpjutrɪd/ adj. 1. in a state of foul decay or decomposition. 2. offensively or disgustingly objectionable or bad.

putt /pʌt/ v.t. Golf to strike (the ball) gently and carefully so as to make it roll along the putting green into the hole.

putty /ˈpʌti/ n. 1. a kind of cement, of dough-like consistency, used for securing panes of glass, stopping up holes in woodwork, etc. 2. any person or thing easily moulded, influenced, etc.

puzzle /ˈpʌzəl/ n. 1. a toy or other contrivance designed to amuse by presenting difficulties to be solved by ingenuity or patient effort. 2. something puzzling; a puzzling matter or person. –v.t. 3. to cause to be at a loss;

bewilder; confuse. 4. (fol. by out) to solve (a problem) or resolve (a difficulty) by careful study and reflection.

pygmy /ˈpɪgmi/ n. (pl. **-mies**) Colloq. (chiefly derog.) a small or dwarfish person. Also, **pigmy**.

pyjamas /pəˈdʒaməz/ n. (construed as pl.) nightclothes consisting of loose trousers and jacket.

pylon /ˈpaɪlɒn/ n. 1. a steel tower or mast carrying high-tension, telephonic or other cables and lines. 2. a relatively tall structure at either side of a gate, bridge, or avenue, marking an entrance or approach.

pyramid /ˈpɪrəmɪd/ n. 1. Archit. a massive structure built of stone, with square (or polygonal) base, and sloping sides meeting at an apex, such as those built by the ancient Egyptians. 2. anything of such form. 3. Geom. a solid having a triangular, square, or polygonal base, and triangular sides which meet in a point. 4. Econ. a multi-company structure in which one company controls two or more companies, each of which may itself control a number of companies, and so on.

pyre /ˈpaɪə/ n. 1. a pile or heap of wood or other combustible material. 2. such a pile for burning a dead body.

pyrex /ˈpaɪrɛks/ n. (from trademark) a heat-resistant glassware for baking, frying, etc.

pyrites /paɪˈraɪtiz/ n. any of various sulphides, as of iron, tin, etc.

pyro- a word element meaning 'of, relating to, or concerned with fire'. Also, (before vowels), **pyr-**.

pyrogenic /paɪrouˈdʒɛnɪk/ adj. 1. producing heat or fever. 2. produced by fire, as igneous rocks.

pyromania /paɪrəˈmeɪniə/ n. a mania for setting things on fire. –**pyromaniac**, n.

pyrotechnics /paɪrouˈtɛknɪks/ n. 1. the art of making fireworks. 2. the making and use of fireworks for display, military purposes, etc. 3. a brilliant or sensational display, as of rhetoric, etc. Also (for defs 1 and 2), **pyrotechny** /ˈpaɪroutɛkni/.

python /ˈpaɪθən/ n. any of various non-venomous snakes, generally large and with vestiges of hind limbs, which kill by constriction.

Q, q

Q, q /kjuː/ *n.* the 17th letter of the English alphabet.

QR code /kjuː 'ɑː koʊd/ *n.* quick response code; a data matrix bar code which, when scanned by a mobile phone, connects to a website for the downloading of information, as for example, a QR code at a transport terminal which connects the user to a timetable.

qua /kweɪ, kwɑː/ *adv.* as; as being; in the character or capacity of.

quack¹ /kwæk/ *v.i.* to utter the cry of a duck, or a sound resembling it.

quack² /kwæk/ *n.* someone who pretends professionally or publicly to skill, knowledge, or qualifications which he or she does not possess; a charlatan. **–quackery,** *n.*

quad¹ /kwɒd/ *n. Colloq.* → **quadrangle** (def. 2).

quad² /kwɒd/ *n. Colloq.* → **quadruplet.**

quad bike *n.* a four-wheeled motorcycle designed to travel over rough terrain.

quadrangle /ˈkwɒdræŋgəl/ *n.* **1.** a plane figure having four angles and four sides, as a square. **2.** a quadrangular space or court wholly or nearly surrounded by a building or buildings, as in a school, college, etc. **–quadrangular,** *adj.*

quadrant /ˈkwɒdrənt/ *n.* the quarter of a circle; an arc of 90°.

quadraphonic /kwɒdrə'fɒnɪk/ *adj.* of or relating to four-channel sound reproduction. Compare **stereophonic.** Also, **quadrasonic.**

quadrasonic /kwɒdrə'sɒnɪk/ *adj.* → **quadraphonic.**

quadrate /ˈkwɒdrət/ *adj.* **1.** square; rectangular. *–n.* **2.** a square, or something square or rectangular.

quadratic /kwɒd'rætɪk/ *adj.* **1.** square. **2.** *Algebra* involving the square and no higher power of the unknown quantity.

quadri- a word element meaning 'four'. Also, (*before vowels*), **quadr-.**

quadriceps /ˈkwɒdrəsɛps/ *n.* the great muscle of the front of the thigh, which extends the leg and is considered as having four points of connection. Also, **quads.**

quadrilateral /kwɒdrə'lætrəl, -'lætərəl/ *adj.* **1.** having four sides. *–n.* **2.** a plane figure having four sides and four angles.

quadrille /kwə'drɪl/ *n.* a square dance for four couples.

quadriplegia /kwɒdrə'plidʒə/ *n.* a condition in which the arms and legs are paralysed. **–quadriplegic,** *n.*, *adj.*

quadruped /ˈkwɒdrəpɛd/ *adj.* **1.** four-footed. *–n.* **2.** an animal, especially a mammal, having four feet. **–quadrupedal,** *adj.*

quadruple /kwɒ'drupəl, 'kwɒdrəpəl/ *adj.* **1.** fourfold; consisting of four parts. *–v.t.* **2.** to make four times as great. *–v.i.* **3.** to become four times as great.

quadruplet /kwɒ'druplət/ *n.* **1.** any group or combination of four. **2.** one of four children born at one birth.

quaff /kwɒf/ *v.t.* to drink (a beverage, etc.), copiously and heartily.

quagmire /ˈkwɒgmaɪə, 'kwæg-/ *n.* a piece of miry or boggy ground.

quail¹ /kweɪl/ *n.* (*pl.* **quails** *or, especially collectively,* **quail**) a small ground-dwelling bird.

quail² /kweɪl/ *v.i.* to lose heart or courage in difficulty or danger; shrink with fear.

quaint /kweɪnt/ *adj.* strange or odd in an interesting, pleasing, or amusing way.

quake /kweɪk/ *v.i.* **1.** (of persons) to shake from cold, weakness, fear, anger, or the like. *–n.* **2.** an earthquake.

qualify /ˈkwɒləfaɪ/ *v.* (**-fied, -fying**) *–v.t.* **1.** to invest with proper or necessary qualities, skills, etc.; make competent. **2.** to attribute some quality or qualities to; characterise, call, or name. **3.** to modify in some way. *–v.i.* **4.** to make or show oneself competent for something. **–qualification,** *n.*

qualitative /ˈkwɒlə,teɪtɪv, 'kwɒlətətɪv/ *adj.* relating to or concerned with quality or qualities.

quality /ˈkwɒləti/ *n.* (*pl.* **-ties**) **1.** a characteristic, property, or attribute. **2.** high grade; superior excellence. *–adj.* **3.** of fine quality: *a quality wine.*

qualm /kwɑm/ *n.* an uneasy feeling or a pang of conscience as to conduct.

quandary /ˈkwɒndəri/ *n.* (*pl.* **-ries**) a state of embarrassing perplexity or uncertainty, especially as to what to do; a dilemma.

quandong /ˈkwɒndɒŋ/ *n.* an Australian tree with fruit which can be eaten raw or made into jams and jellies.

quantify /ˈkwɒntəfaɪ/ *v.t.* (**-fied, -fying**) to determine the quantity of; measure.

quantitative /ˈkwɒntə,teɪtɪv, 'kwɒntətətɪv/ *adj.* of or relating to the describing or measuring of quantity.

quantity /ˈkwɒntəti/ *n.* (*pl.* **-ties**) **1.** a particular, indefinite, or considerable amount of anything. **2.** amount or measure.

quantum /ˈkwɒntəm/ *n.* (*pl.* **-ta**) a particular quantity or amount.

quantum mechanics *n. Physics* the branch of mechanics which deals with the dynamics of atomic and subatomic systems which do not obey Newtonian laws. **–quantum mechanical,** *adj.*

quantum number *n.* one of a set of integers or half-integers which defines the energy state of a system, or its components, in quantum mechanics.

quantum physics *n.* the branch of physics that uses quantum theory.

quantum theory *n.* a theory concerning the behaviour of physical systems which states that a system has certain properties, such as energy and momentum in discrete amounts (quanta).

quarantine /ˈkwɒrəntin/ *n.* **1.** a strict isolation designed to prevent the spread of disease. *–v.t.* **2.** to put in or subject to quarantine.

quarrel /ˈkwɒrəl/ *n.* **1.** an angry dispute or altercation. *–v.t.* (**-relled, -relling**) **2.** to disagree angrily, squabble, or fall out. **–quarrelsome,** *adj.*

quarry¹ /ˈkwɒri/ *n.* (*pl.* **-ries**) **1.** an excavation or pit, usually open to the air, from which building stone, slate, or the like is obtained by cutting, blasting, etc. –*v.t.* (**-ried, -rying**) **2.** to obtain (stone, etc.) from, or as from, a quarry.

quarry² /'kwɒri/ *n.* (*pl.* **-ries**) an animal or bird hunted or pursued.

quart /kwɔt/ *n.* a liquid measure of capacity in the imperial system, equal to a quarter of a gallon, or approximately 1.137 litres.

quarter /'kwɔtə/ *n.* **1.** one of the four equal or equivalent parts into which anything is or may be divided. **2.** *Astron.* a fourth of the moon's period or monthly revolution. **3.** a region, district, or place. **4.** (*usu. pl.*) a place of stay; lodgings; residence. **5.** a part or member of a community, government, etc., which is not specified. –*v.t.* **6.** to divide into four equal or equivalent parts. **7.** to provide with lodgings in a particular place.

quarterback /'kwɔtəbæk/ *n.* **1.** *American Football* a back (**back**¹ def. 4) who lines up immediately behind the centre and directs the offensive play of the team. –*v.i.* **2.** to play in this position.

quarterdeck /'kwɔtədek/ *n.* the upper deck between the mainmast and the stern.

quarterly /'kwɔtəli/ *adj.* **1.** occurring, done, etc., at the end of every quarter of a year. –*n.* (*pl.* **-lies**) **2.** a periodical issued every three months.

quartermaster /'kwɔtəmastə/ *n.* *Mil.* a regimental officer in charge of quarters, rations, clothing, equipment, and transport.

quartet /kwɔ'tɛt/ *n.* a group of four singers or players.

quartile /'kwɔtail/ *n.* *Statistics* (in a frequency distribution) one of the values of a variable which divides the distribution of the variable into four groups having equal frequencies.

quarto /'kwɔtoʊ/ *n.* (*pl.* **-tos**) **1.** a volume printed from sheets folded twice to form four leaves or eight pages. *Abbrev.*: 4to, 4° **2.** a paper size.

quartz /kwɒts/ *n.* one of the commonest minerals, having many varieties which differ in colour, lustre, etc.

quartz-crystal *adj.* (of a watch, clock, etc.) regulated by a specially prepared quartz crystal, which gives great accuracy. Also, **quartz**.

quartzite /'kwɒtsait/ *n.* a granular rock consisting essentially of quartz in interlocking grains. –**quartzitic** /kwɒt'sitik/, *adj.*

quasar /'kweisa/ *n.* *Astron.* one of many extremely luminous extragalactic objects lying close to the edge of the known universe, comprising a highly active galactic nucleus common when the universe was young.

quash¹ /kwɒʃ/ *v.t.* to put down or suppress completely; subdue.

quash² /kwɒʃ/ *v.t.* to make void, annul, or set aside (a law, indictment, decision, etc.).

quasi /'kweizi/ *adj.* **1.** resembling; as it were. –*adv.* **2.** seemingly, but not actually.

quasi- /'kweizi-/ a prefix meaning 'resembling', 'seeming'.

quaternary /kwə'tɜnəri/ *adj.* **1.** consisting of four. **2.** arranged in fours.

quaver /'kweivə/ *v.i.* **1.** to shake tremulously, quiver, or tremble (now said usually of the voice). –*n.* **2.** a quavering or tremulous shake, especially in the voice. **3.** *Music* a note equal in length to half a crotchet.

quay /ki/ *n.* an artificial landing place for vessels unloading or loading cargo, etc.

queasy /'kwizi/ *adj.* (**-sier, -siest**) inclined to nausea.

queen /kwin/ *n.* **1.** the wife or consort of a king. **2.** a female sovereign or monarch. **3.** a fertile female of ants, bees, wasps, or termites. **4.** a chess piece. **5.** *Colloq.* a male homosexual. –*adj.* **6.** (of a bed, mattress, etc.) slightly smaller than king-size.

Queen's Counsel *n.* (in some legal systems) a senior barrister who has received a commission to act as adviser to the crown, as a form of recognition of his or her eminence. *Abbrev.*: QC Also, (*when the reigning monarch is a man*), **King's Counsel**.

queer /'kwiə/ *adj.* **1.** strange from a conventional point of view; singular or odd. **2.** out of the normal state of feeling physically. **3.** *Colloq.* mentally unbalanced or deranged. **4.** *Colloq.* (*sometimes derog.*) homosexual. –*n.* **5.** *Colloq.* (*sometimes derog.*) a male homosexual.

quell /kwɛl/ *v.t.* **1.** to suppress (disorder, mutiny, etc.); put an end to; extinguish. **2.** to quiet or allay (feelings, etc.).

quench /kwɛntʃ/ *v.t.* **1.** to slake, as thirst; allay; satisfy. **2.** to suppress; stifle; subdue; overcome.

querulous /'kwɛrələs/ *adj.* full of complaints; complaining.

query /'kwiəri/ *n.* (*pl.* **-ries**) **1.** a question; an inquiry. **2.** a doubt; uncertainty. –*v.t.* (**-ried, -rying**) **3.** to ask or inquire about. **4.** to question (a statement, etc.) as doubtful or obscure. **5.** to ask questions of.

quest /kwɛst/ *n.* a search or pursuit made in order to find or obtain something.

question /'kwɛstʃən/ *n.* **1.** a sentence in an interrogative form, addressed to someone in order to elicit information. **2.** a matter for investigation. **3.** (fol. by *of*) a matter or point of uncertainty or difficulty; a case. –*v.t.* **4.** to ask a question or questions of; interrogate. **5.** to ask or enquire. **6.** to make a question of; doubt. **7.** to challenge; dispute.

questionable /'kwɛstʃənəbəl/ *adj.* doubtful.

question mark *n.* a mark indicating a question, as (?).

questionnaire /kwɛstʃən'ɛə, kɛs-/ *n.* a list of questions, usually printed on a form, as for statistical purposes, or to obtain opinions on some subject.

queue /kju/ *n.* **1.** a file or line of people, vehicles, etc., waiting in turn. –*v.i.* (**queued, queuing** *or* **queueing**) **2.** to form in a line while waiting.

quibble /'kwibəl/ *n.* **1.** trivial, petty, or carping criticism. –*v.i.* **2.** to make petty criticisms.

quiche /kiʃ/ *n.* a savoury custard tart.

quick /kwik/ *adj.* **1.** done, proceeding, or occurring with promptness or rapidity. **2.** hasty; impatient. **3.** lively or keen, as feelings. **4.** of ready intelligence. **5.** *Finance* readily convertible into cash; liquid, as assets. –*n.* **6.** living persons. **7.** the sensitive flesh under the nails of the human hand: *nails bitten down to the quick.* –*adv.* **8.** in a quick manner.

quicksand /'kwɪksænd/ n. an area of soft or loose wet sand of considerable depth, apt to engulf persons, animals, etc.

quicksilver /'kwɪksɪlvə/ n. mercury.

quid /kwɪd/ n. (pl. **quid** or **quids**) Colloq. **1.** (formerly) a pound in money. **2.** money, especially a large amount.

quid pro quo /kwɪd prɒʊ 'kwɒʊ/ n. one thing in return for another.

quiescent /kwi'ɛsənt/ adj. being at rest, quiet, or still; inactive or motionless. **–quiescence,** n.

quiet /'kwaɪət/ n. **1.** freedom from disturbance or tumult; tranquillity; rest; repose. **2.** making no disturbance or trouble. **3.** free from disturbing emotions, etc.; mentally peaceful. **4.** refraining or free from activity, especially busy or vigorous activity. **5.** motionless or still; moving gently. **6.** making no noise or sound, especially no disturbing sound. **7.** restrained in speech, manner, etc.; saying little. **8.** Commerce commercially inactive. –v.t. **9.** to make quiet. –v.i. **10.** to become quiet.

quill /kwɪl/ n. **1.** one of the large feathers of the wing or tail of a bird. **2.** a feather, as of a goose, formed into a pen for writing. **3.** one of the hollow spines on a porcupine or hedgehog.

quilt /kwɪlt/ n. **1.** a cover for a bed. –v.t. **2.** to stitch together (two pieces of cloth with a soft interlining), usually in an ornamental pattern. **3.** to pad or line with some material.

quince /kwɪns/ n. a hard, yellowish, acid fruit.

quinine /'kwɪnin, kwə'nin/ n. a bitter substance, used to treat malaria.

quinoa /'kinwa, kwə'nɒʊə/ n. a plant of the goosefoot family, cultivated for its seeds which are ground and eaten as a cereal.

quinque- a word element meaning 'five'.

quintessence /kwɪn'tɛsəns/ n. **1.** the pure and concentrated essence of a substance. **2.** the most perfect embodiment of something.

quintessential /kwɪntə'sɛnʃəl/ adj. of, relating to, or embodying a quintessence. **–quintessentially,** adv.

quintet /kwɪn'tɛt/ n. a set of five singers or players.

quintuple /'kwɪntəpəl, kwɪn'tjupəl/ adj. **1.** fivefold; consisting of five parts. –v.t. **2.** to make five times as great. –v.i. **3.** to become five times as great.

quintuplet /kwɪn'tʌplət/ n. **1.** any group or combination of five. **2.** one of five children born at one birth.

quip /kwɪp/ n. **1.** a clever or witty saying. –v.i. (**quipped, quipping**) **2.** to utter quips. –adv.

quire /'kwaɪə/ n. **1.** a set of 24 uniform sheets of paper. **2.** Bookbinding a section of pages in proper sequence after the printed sheet or sheets have been folded.

quirk /kwɜk/ n. **1.** a trick or peculiarity. **2.** a sudden twist, turn, or curve.

quisling /'kwɪzlɪŋ/ n. someone who betrays their own country.

quit /kwɪt/ v. (**quit** or **quitted, quitting**) –v.t. **1.** to stop, cease, or discontinue. **2.** to depart from; leave. **3.** to give up; let go; relinquish. –v.i. **4.** to cease from doing something; stop. **5.** to depart or leave. **6.** to give up one's job or position; resign. –adj. **7.** (usu. fol. by of) released from obligation, penalty, etc.; free, clear, or rid.

quite /kwaɪt/ adv. **1.** completely, wholly, or entirely. **2.** actually, really, or truly. **3.** Colloq. to a considerable extent or degree.

quiver¹ /'kwɪvə/ v.i., v.t. to shake with a slight but rapid motion; vibrate tremulously; tremble.

quiver² /'kwɪvə/ n. a case for holding arrows.

quixotic /kwɪk'sɒtɪk/ adj. extravagantly chivalrous or romantic. **–quixotically,** adv.

quiz /kwɪz/ v.t. (**quizzed, quizzing**) **1.** to question closely. **2.** to examine or test (a student or class) informally by questions. –n. (pl. **quizzes**) **3.** a general knowledge test.

quizzical /'kwɪzɪkəl/ adj. Rare odd, queer, or comical: a quizzical hat.

quoin /kɔɪn/ n. an external solid angle of a wall or the like.

quoit /kɔɪt/ n. **1.** Also, **deck quoit**. a flattish ring thrown in play to encircle a peg stuck in the ground. **2.** (pl., construed as sing.) the game so played.

quokka /'kwɒkə/ n. a small wallaby with small, rounded ears, found in considerable numbers on Rottnest Island, off WA.

quoll /kwɒl/ n. a marsupial with a long tail and spots, about the size of a cat.

quorum /'kwɔrəm/ n. the number of members of a body required to be present to transact business legally.

quota /'kwɒʊtə/ n. **1.** a proportional part or share of a fixed total amount or quantity. **2.** the number of persons of a particular group allowed to immigrate to a country, join an institution, etc.

quotation /kwɒʊ'teɪʃən/ n. **1.** that which is quoted; a passage quoted from a book, speech, etc. **2.** an estimate of costs given in advance of work being done.

quotation mark n. one of the marks used to indicate the beginning and end of a quotation, usually consisting of an inverted comma (') at the beginning and an apostrophe (') at the end, or double marks of this kind. Also, **speech mark**.

quote /kwɒʊt/ v.t. **1.** to repeat (a passage, etc.) from a book, speech, etc. **2.** to bring forward, adduce, or cite. **3.** Commerce **a.** to state (a price). **b.** to state the current price of. –n. **4.** a quotation.

quotient /'kwɒʊʃənt/ n. (in mathematics) the result of division.

R, r

R, r /a/ n. the 18th letter of the English alphabet.

rabbi /'ræbaɪ/ n. (pl. **-bis**) the spiritual leader of a Jewish community.

rabbit /'ræbət/ n. **1.** a small, long-eared, burrowing mammal. –v.i. (**-bited, -biting**) **2.** to hunt rabbits.

rabble /'ræbəl/ n. **1.** a disorderly crowd; a mob. **2. the rabble**, (*derog.*) the lowest class of people.

rabid /'ræbəd/ adj. **1.** irrationally extreme in opinion or practice. **2.** furious or raging; violently intense. **3.** affected with or relating to rabies; mad.

rabies /'reɪbiz/ n. a fatal, infectious disease of the brain, transmitted by the bite of an afflicted animal, generally a dog.

raccoon /rə'kun/ n. any of several small nocturnal carnivores with a bushy ringed tail.

race[1] /reɪs/ n. **1.** a contest of speed, as in running, riding, driving, sailing, etc. **2.** (*pl.*) a series of races, especially horseraces or greyhound races run at a set time over a regular course. **3.** any contest or competition. **4.** a narrow passageway. –v. (**raced, racing**) –v.i. **5.** to engage in a contest of speed; run a race. **6.** to engage in or practise horseracing. **7.** to run, move, or go swiftly. –v.t. **8.** to run a race with; try to beat in a contest of speed. **9.** to cause to run in a race or races.

race[2] /reɪs/ n. **1.** a group of persons connected by common descent. **2.** *Ethnology* a subdivision of a stock, characterised by a more or less unique combination of physical traits which are transmitted in descent.

racial /'reɪʃəl/ adj. **1.** relating to or characteristic of race or extraction, or a race or races. **2.** relating to the relations between people of different races.

racism /'reɪsɪzəm/ n. **1.** the belief that human races have distinctive characteristics which determine their respective cultures, usually involving the idea that one's own race is superior. **2.** behaviour or language based on this kind of belief in relation to a person or persons of a particular race, colour, descent, or ethnic origin. **3.** such behaviour or language used against people of a different nationality. –**racist**, n., adj.

rack[1] /ræk/ n. **1.** a framework of bars, wires, or pegs on which articles are arranged or deposited. **2.** an apparatus or instrument formerly in use for torturing persons by stretching the body. **3.** violent strain. –v.t. **4.** to strain in mental effort.

rack[2] /ræk/ n. wreck; destruction.

rack[3] /ræk/ v.i. *Colloq.* (fol. by *off*) to leave; go.

racket[1] /'rækət/ n. **1.** a loud noise. **2.** *Colloq.* an organised illegal activity.

racket[2] /'rækət/ n. → **racquet**.

raconteur /rækən'tɜ/ n. a person skilled in relating stories and anecdotes.

racquet /'rækət/ n. a light bat having a network of cord or nylon, stretched in a more or less elliptical frame, used in tennis, etc. Also, **racket**.

racy /'reɪsi/ adj. (**-cier, -ciest**) **1.** vigorous; lively; spirited. **2.** suggestive; risqué.

radar /'reɪda/ n. a device to determine the presence and location of an object by measuring the time for the echo of a radio wave to return from it, and the direction from which it returns.

radial /'reɪdiəl/ adj. of, like, or relating to a radius or a ray.

radial-ply tyre n. a pneumatic tyre with flexible walls.

radian /'reɪdiən/ n. the supplementary SI unit of measurement of plane angle. *Symbol:* rad

radiant /'reɪdiənt/ adj. emitting rays of light; shining; bright.

radiate /'reɪdieɪt/ v.i. **1.** to spread or move like rays or radii from a centre. **2.** to emit rays, as of light or heat. –v.t. **3.** (of persons) to exhibit abundantly (good humour, benevolence, etc.).

radiation /reɪdi'eɪʃən/ n. *Physics* the emission and propagation of particles or waves such as by a radioactive substance.

radiator /'reɪdieɪtə/ n. a device which radiates heat.

radical /'rædɪkəl/ adj. **1.** going to the root or origin; fundamental. **2.** thoroughgoing or extreme. **3.** favouring extreme political, religious, social or other reforms. **4.** *Maths* relating to or forming a root. –n. **5.** someone who holds or follows extreme political principles, especially left-wing political principles; an extremist. –**radically**, adv.

radii /'reɪdiaɪ/ n. plural of **radius**.

radio /'reɪdioʊ/ n. (pl. **-dios**) **1.** wireless telegraphy or telephony. **2.** an apparatus for receiving radio broadcasts; a wireless. –v.t. (**-dioed, -dioing**) **3.** to transmit (a message) by radio. **4.** to send a message to (a person) by radio.

radio- a word element meaning: **1.** radio. **2.** radial. **3.** radium, radioactive, or radiant energy.

radioactivity /reɪdioʊæk'tɪvəti/ n. the property of spontaneous disintegration possessed by certain elements due to changes in their atomic nuclei. –**radioactive**, adj.

radiofrequency /reɪdioʊ'frikwənsi/ n. (pl. **-cies**) any frequency of electromagnetic radiation within the radio band often used for broadcasting.

radiography /reɪdi'ɒgrəfi/ n. the production of images by the action of X-rays on a photographic plate, especially as used in medicine. –**radiographer**, n.

radiology /reɪdi'ɒlədʒi/ n. the science dealing with X-rays or rays from radioactive substances, especially for medical uses. –**radiologist**, n.

radio station n. an organisation engaged in broadcasting radio programs on a fixed frequency.

radio telescope n. a large parabolic reflector used to gather radio signals emitted by celestial bodies or spacecraft and focus them for reception by a receiver.

radiotherapy /reɪdioʊ'θɛrəpi/ n. *Med.* treatment of disease by means of X-rays or of radioactive substances. –**radiotherapist**, n.

radish /'rædɪʃ/ n. the crisp, pungent, edible root of a plant.

radium /ˈreɪdɪəm/ n. a naturally occurring radioactive metallic element. *Symbol:* Ra

radius /ˈreɪdɪəs/ n. (pl. **-dii** /-dɪaɪ/ or **-diuses**) **1.** a straight line extending from the centre of a circle or sphere to the circumference or surface. **2.** *Anat.* that one of the two bones of the forearm which is on the thumb side.

raffia /ˈræfɪə/ n. a fibre used for making matting, baskets, hats, and the like.

raffle /ˈræfəl/ n. **1.** a lottery in which the prizes are usually goods rather than money. −v.i. **2.** (sometimes fol. by *off*) to dispose of by a raffle.

raft[1] /raft/ n. a more or less rigid floating platform made of buoyant materials, assembled for the conveyance of people, goods, etc.

raft[2] /raft/ n. a collection or set of items: *a whole raft of issues.*

rafter /ˈraftə/ n. one of the sloping timbers or members sustaining the outer covering of a roof.

rag[1] /ræg/ n. **1.** a comparatively worthless fragment of cloth, especially one resulting from tearing or wear. **2.** a shred, scrap, or fragmentary bit of anything. **3.** *Colloq.* a newspaper or magazine, especially one considered as being of little value.

rag[2] /ræg/ v.t. (**ragged, ragging**) *Colloq.* to tease; torment.

ragamuffin /ˈrægəmʌfən/ n. a ragged child.

rage /reɪdʒ/ n. **1.** angry fury; violent anger. **2.** the object of widespread enthusiasm. −v.i. (**raged, raging**) **3.** to show or feel violent anger.

ragged /ˈrægəd/ adj. **1.** clothed in tattered garments. **2.** torn or worn to rags; tattered. **3.** full of rough or sharp projections; jagged.

raglan /ˈræglən/ adj. (of a garment or sleeve) having no shoulder seam, the sleeve continuing up to the collar.

raid /reɪd/ n. **1.** a sudden onset or attack, as upon something to be seized or suppressed. −v.t. **2.** to make a raid on. **−raider,** n.

rail[1] /reɪl/ n. **1.** a bar of wood or metal fixed more or less horizontally for any of various purposes. **2.** one of a pair of steel bars that provide a guide and running surface for the wheels of vehicles. **3.** the railway, as a means of transportation.

rail[2] /reɪl/ v.i. (oft. fol. by *at* or *against*) to utter bitter complaint or vehement denunciation.

raillery /ˈreɪləri/ n. good-humoured ridicule; banter.

railroad /ˈreɪlroʊd/ −n. **1.** *US* a railway. −v.t. *Colloq.* **2.** to send or push forward with great or undue speed: *to railroad a bill through parliament.* **3.** to coerce, especially by unfair means: *he was railroaded out of office.*

railway /ˈreɪlweɪ/ n. **1.** a permanent road or way, laid or provided with rails on which vehicles run for the transporting of passengers, goods, and mail. **2.** the company owning or operating it.

raiment /ˈreɪmənt/ n. *Archaic or Poetic* clothing; apparel; attire.

rain /reɪn/ n. **1.** water in drops falling from the sky to the earth. **2.** (pl.) the seasonal rainfalls in tropical regions. −v.i. **3.** (of rain) to fall. **4.** to fall like rain. −v.t. **5.** to offer, bestow, or give abundantly. −phr. **6. rain cats and dogs,** to rain heavily.

rainbow /ˈreɪnboʊ/ n. **1.** a bow or arc of prismatic colours appearing in the sky opposite the sun, due to the refraction and reflection of the sun's rays in drops of rain. **2.** the spectrum. −adj. **3.** multicoloured.

rainbow serpent n. (*sometimes upper case*) (in Aboriginal mythology) a spirit of creation which appeared as a great snake in the Dreaming, fashioned the earth, and then returned to a spot east of the Kimberley at a place where the rainbow meets the earth. Also, **rainbow snake, rainbow spirit.**

rainfall /ˈreɪnfɔl/ n. **1.** a fall or shower of rain. **2.** the amount of water falling as rain, snow, etc., within a given time and area.

rainforest /ˈreɪnfɒrəst/ n. dense forest found in tropical and temperate areas.

raise /reɪz/ v.t. (**raised, raising**) **1.** to move to a higher position; lift up; elevate. **2.** to cause to rise or stand up. **3.** to build; erect. **4.** to cause to be or appear. **5.** to cultivate, produce, breed (crops, plants, animals, etc.). **6.** to bring up; rear (children, etc.). **7.** to give rise to; bring up or about. **8.** to give vigour to; animate (the mind, spirits, hopes). **9.** to gather together; collect. **10.** to increase in degree, intensity, pitch, or force. **11.** to increase in amount, as rent, prices, wages, etc. **12.** to increase the price of (a commodity, stock, etc.). −n. **13.** a rise (in wages). **14.** a raising, lifting, etc.

raisin /ˈreɪzən/ n. a dried grape.

rake[1] /reɪk/ n. **1.** a long-handled tool with teeth, used for various purposes. −v.t. **2.** to gather together, draw, or remove with or as with a rake. **3.** (oft. fol. by *up*) to collect, especially with difficulty. −v.i. **4.** to use a rake. **5.** to search as with a rake. **6.** (fol. by *against, over,* etc.) to scrape or sweep.

rake[2] /reɪk/ n. *Archaic* a profligate or dissolute man.

rake-hoe n. → **McLeod tool.**

rally /ˈræli/ v. (**-lied, -lying**) −v.t. **1.** to bring together or into order again. **2.** to draw or call (persons) together for common action. −v.i. **3.** to come together for common action. **4.** to come to the assistance of a person, party, or cause. **5.** to acquire fresh strength or vigour. −n. (pl. **-lies**) **6.** a recovery from dispersion or disorder, as of troops. **7.** a renewal or recovery of strength, activity, etc. **8.** a drawing or coming together of persons, as for common action. **9.** *Finance* a sharp rise in price and active trading, after a declining market. **10.** *Tennis, etc.* the return of the ball by both sides a number of times consecutively.

ram /ræm/ n. **1.** an uncastrated male sheep. **2.** any of various devices for battering, crushing, driving, or forcing something. −v.t. (**rammed, ramming**) **3.** to drive or force by heavy blows. **4.** to push firmly.

RAM /ræm/ n. random-access memory; a computer memory which is so structured that each item can be accessed equally quickly.

ramble /ˈræmbəl/ v.i. **1.** to wander about in a leisurely manner. −n. **2.** a walk without a definite route, taken for pleasure.

ramification /ræməfəˈkeɪʃən/ n. **1.** a division or subdivision springing or derived from a main stem or source. **2.** one of a number of results, especially one which complicates an issue.

ramp /ræmp/ n. **1.** a sloping surface connecting two different levels. −v.i. **2.** to act violently; rage; storm.

rampage n. /'ræmpeɪdʒ/ **1.** violent or furious behaviour. −v.i. /ræm'peɪdʒ/ (**-paged, -paging**) **2.** to rush, move, or act furiously or violently.

rampant /'ræmpənt/ adj. in full sway; unchecked.

ram raid n. a robbery involving gaining access to a property, such as a shop, service station, etc., by driving a vehicle into the front window.

ramraid /'ræmreɪd/ v.t. to gain access to (a property, as a shop, service station, etc.) as part of a ram raid.

ramrod /'ræmrɒd/ n. any person or thing considered as exemplifying or exercising stiffness or unyielding rigidity.

ramshackle /'ræmʃækəl/ adj. loosely made or held together; rickety; shaky.

ran /ræn/ v. past tense of **run**.

ranch /ræntʃ, rantʃ/ n. a farm for cattle, horses, or the like, generally having extensive grazing land.

rancid /'rænsəd/ adj. having a rank, unpleasant, stale smell or taste.

rancour /'ræŋkə/ n. bitter, rankling resentment or ill will; hatred; malice. Also, **rancor**. −**rancorous**, adj.

random /'rændəm/ adj. **1.** not according to a pattern or method. **2.** Colloq. **a.** (of a person) eccentric; odd. **b.** (of an occurrence) strangely coincidental. **c.** (of a film, plot, etc.) strange, unpredictable, or confusing. −n. **3.** Colloq. an unknown person or outsider. −phr. **4. at random**, in a haphazard way; without definite aim, purpose, or method. −**randomness**, n.

random-access memory n. → **RAM**.

random breath test n. a breath test to detect the presence of alcohol in the driver's system, applied to randomly selected motorists. Abbrev.: RBT

random drug test n. a test to detect the presence of drugs in someone's system, usually by saliva, blood or urine sampling, applied to randomly selected motorists, athletes, workers, etc. −**random drug testing**, n.

randy /'rændi/ adj. (**-dier, -diest**) Colloq. sexually aroused.

rang /ræŋ/ v. past tense of **ring²**.

ranga /'ræŋə/ n. Colloq. (mildly derog.) a red-headed person.

range /reɪndʒ/ n. **1.** the extent or scope of the operation or efficacy of something. **2.** an area in which shooting at targets is practised. **3.** Statistics the difference between the smallest and largest varieties in a statistical distribution. **4.** a row or line, as of persons or things. **5.** the region over which something is distributed, is found, or occurs. **6.** a chain of mountains. **7.** a form of large stove for cooking. −v. (**ranged, ranging**) −v.t. **8.** to dispose systematically; set in order; arrange. **9.** to make straight, level, or even, as lines of type. **10.** to pass over or through (an area or region) in all directions, as in exploring or searching. −v.i. **11.** to vary within certain limits. **12.** to

have range of operation. **13.** to extend, run or go in a certain direction. **14.** to move about or through a region in all directions, as persons, animals, etc.

ranger /'reɪndʒə/ n. a person employed to patrol a public reserve, wildlife park, etc.

rank¹ /ræŋk/ n. **1.** position or standing in the social scale or in any graded body, especially a high position. **2.** a row, line, or series of things or persons. −v.t. **3.** to assign to a particular position, station, class, etc. −v.i. **4.** to take up or occupy a place in a particular rank, class, etc.

rank² /ræŋk/ adj. **1.** growing with excessive luxuriance. **2.** having an offensively strong smell or taste. **3.** utter; unmistakable. **4.** grossly coarse or indecent.

rankle /'ræŋkəl/ v.i. to produce or continue to produce within the mind keen irritation or bitter resentment.

ransack /'rænsæk/ v.t. to search thoroughly or vigorously through.

ransom /'rænsəm/ n. **1.** the redemption of a prisoner, slave, kidnapped person, captured goods, etc., for a price. **2.** the sum or price paid or demanded. −v.t. **3.** to redeem from captivity, bondage, detention, etc., by paying a price demanded.

rant /rænt/ v.i. to talk in a wild or vehement way.

rap¹ /ræp/ v. (**rapped, rapping**) −v.t. **1.** to strike, especially with a quick, smart, or light blow. **2.** (usu. fol. by out) to utter sharply or vigorously. **3.** Colloq. to accelerate (a motor vehicle). −v.i. **4.** to knock smartly or lightly. −n. **5.** a quick, smart, or light blow.

rap² /ræp/ Colloq. −n. **1.** a sustained rhythmic spiel or verbal improvisation, often rhyming, performed as an accompaniment to dance music. −v.i. (**rapped, rapping**) **2.** to perform a rap. −**rapper**, n.

rapacious /rə'peɪʃəs/ adj. greedy in a violent and unpleasant way. −**rapacity**, n.

rap dancing n. a form of street dancing involving jerky movements of the limbs.

rape /reɪp/ n. **1.** the crime of having sexual intercourse with a person against their will. −v.t. (**raped, raping**) **2.** to commit the crime or act of rape on.

rapid /'ræpəd/ adj. **1.** moving or acting with great speed; swift. −n. **2.** (usu. pl.) a part of a river where the current runs very swiftly. −**rapidity**, n.

rapier /'reɪpiə/ n. a slender sword used only for thrusting.

rap music n. Orig. US the music of pop songs in a funk style in which the lyrics are rhythmically spoken rather than sung and have a strong rhyme pattern. Also, **rap**.

rapport /ræ'pɔ/ n. relation; connection, especially harmonious or sympathetic relation.

rapt /ræpt/ adj. **1.** deeply engrossed or absorbed. **2.** transported with emotion; enraptured.

rapture /'ræptʃə/ n. ecstatic joy or delight; joyful ecstasy.

rare¹ /reə/ adj. **1.** few in number. **2.** of low density or pressure. **3.** remarkable or unusual, especially in excellence or greatness.

rare² /reə/ adj. (of meat) not thoroughly cooked; underdone.

rarefied /'rɛərəfaɪd/ adj. **1.** belonging to or reserved for a small group; esoteric. **2.** (of air) having only a small amount of oxygen present. **3.** (of language) arcane; lofty. Also, **rarified**.

rarefy /'rɛərəfaɪ/ v.t. (**-fied, -fying**) to make or become rare, more rare, or less dense. **–rarefaction**, n.

raring /'rɛərɪŋ/ adj. ready; eager.

rarity /'rɛərəti/ n. (pl. **-ties**) something rare, unusual, or uncommon.

rascal /raskəl/, Esp. Victoria and Qld /'ræskəl/ n. a base, dishonest person.

rash¹ /ræʃ/ adj. acting too hastily or without due consideration.

rash² /ræʃ/ n. **1.** an eruption or efflorescence on the skin. **2.** a proliferation.

rasher /'ræʃə/ n. a thin slice of bacon.

rash shirt n. → **surf shirt** (def. 1). Also, Colloq., **rashie**.

rasp /rasp, ræsp/ v.t. **1.** to scrape or abrade with a rough instrument. **2.** to utter with a grating sound. –v.i. **3.** to scrape or grate. **4.** to make a grating sound. –n. **5.** a coarse form of file, having separate point-like teeth. **–raspy**, adj.

raspberry¹ /'razbəri, -bri/ n. (pl. **-ries**) a small red, black, or pale yellow berry.

raspberry² /'razbəri, -bri/ n. (pl. **-ries**) Colloq. a sound expressing derision or contempt, made with the tongue and lips.

rat /ræt/ n. **1.** any of certain long-tailed rodents. **2.** Colloq. someone who abandons friends or associates, especially in time of trouble. –v.i. (**ratted, ratting**) Colloq. **3.** to desert one's party or associates, especially in time of trouble. **4.** to inform (on). –phr. **5. rat through**, to sort through in a careless or hasty manner. **6. smell a rat**, Colloq. to be suspicious.

ratatouille /rætə'tui/ n. a type of vegetable casserole or stew.

ratchet /'rætʃət/ n. a mechanism having a toothed bar and wheel which engages with a pivoted bar.

rate /reɪt/ n. **1.** a certain quantity or amount of one thing considered in relation to a unit of another thing and used as a standard or measure. **2.** a fixed charge per unit of quantity. **3.** degree of speed, of travelling, working, etc. **4.** (usu. pl.) a tax on property, imposed by a local authority and used for the maintenance and supply of services. –v.t. **5.** to estimate the value or worth of; appraise. **6.** to fix at a certain rate, as of charge or payment. –v.i. **7.** to have value, standing, etc. **–rateable, ratable**, adj.

rather /'raðə/ adv. **1.** more so than not; to a certain extent; somewhat. **2.** in preference; as a preferred or accepted alternative.

ratify /'rætəfaɪ/ v.t. (**-fied, -fying**) to confirm by expressing consent, approval, or formal sanction.

rating /'reɪtɪŋ/ n. **1.** classification according to grade or rank. **2.** a person's or firm's credit standing.

ratio /'reɪʃioʊ/ n. (pl. **-tios**) proportional relation; rate; quotient of two numbers.

ration /'ræʃən/ n. **1.** a fixed allowance of provisions or food. –v.t. **2.** to put on, or restrict to, rations.

rational /'ræʃnəl, 'ræʃənəl/ adj. **1.** agreeable to reason; reasonable; sensible. **2.** endowed with the faculty of reason. **3.** proceeding or derived from reason, or based on reasoning. **4.** Maths expressible as the quotient of two integers. **–rationality**, n.

rationale /ræʃə'nal/ n. a reasoned exposition of principles.

rationalise /'ræʃnəlaɪz/ v.t. **1.** Psychol. to invent a rational, acceptable explanation for (behaviour). **2.** to reorganise (resources, the components of a business, etc.) to promote efficiency, economy, etc. –v.i. **3.** to employ reason; think in a rational or rationalistic manner. **4.** to reorganise and integrate (an industry), especially when this results in job losses. **5.** to justify one's behaviour by plausible explanations. Also, **rationalize**.

rat-race n. **1.** the struggle for success, especially in career, fiercely competitive and often unscrupulous. **2.** the frantic pace of city life.

rat run n. Colloq. a circuitous route through suburban streets, usually taken by a driver wishing to avoid major thoroughfares. **–rat-running**, n.

ratshit /'rætʃɪt/ adj. Colloq. (taboo) no good. Also, **RS**.

rattan /rə'tæn/ n. the tough stems of certain palms, used for wickerwork, canes, etc.

rattle /'rætl/ v.i. **1.** to give out a rapid succession of short sharp sounds. –v.t. **2.** to cause to rattle. **3.** to utter or perform in a rapid or lively manner: to rattle off a speech. **4.** Colloq. to disconcert or confuse (a person). –n. **5.** a rapid succession of short, sharp sounds, as from the collision of hard bodies. **6.** an instrument contrived to make a rattling sound, as a child's toy.

rattlesnake /'rætlsneɪk/ n. any of various venomous American snakes with a rattling mechanism at the end of the tail.

raucous /'rɔkəs/ adj. hoarse; harsh-sounding, as a voice.

raunchy /'rɔntʃi/ adj. (**-chier, -chiest**) coarse; earthy; lusty. **–raunchiness**, n.

ravage /'rævɪdʒ/ n. **1.** havoc; ruinous damage. –v.t. (**-aged, -aging**) **2.** to work havoc upon; damage or mar by ravages.

rave /reɪv/ v.i. **1.** to talk wildly, as in delirium. –n. **2.** extravagantly enthusiastic praise. –adj. **3.** praising with extravagant enthusiasm.

ravel /'rævəl/ v. (**-elled, -elling**) –v.t. **1.** to tangle or entangle. –v.i. **2.** to become separated thread by thread or fibre by fibre; fray. **3.** to become tangled.

raven /'reɪvən/ n. **1.** a large, glossy black bird with a loud harsh call. –adj. **2.** lustrous black.

ravenous /'rævənəs/ adj. extremely hungry.

ravine /rə'vin/ n. a long, deep, narrow valley, especially one worn by water.

ravioli /rævi'ooli/ n. small pieces of filled pasta.

ravish /'rævɪʃ/ v.t. **1.** to fill with strong emotion, especially joy. **2.** to seize and carry off by force.

ravishing /'rævəʃɪŋ/ adj. entrancing; enchanting.

raw /rɔ/ adj. **1.** not having undergone processes of preparing, dressing, finishing, refining, or manufacture. **2.** denoting figures, etc., before adjustments have been made. **3.** painfully open, as a sore, wound, etc. **4.** *Colloq.* harsh or unfair.

ray¹ /reɪ/ *n.* **1.** a narrow beam of light. **2.** *Maths* one of a system of straight lines emanating from a point.

ray² /reɪ/ *n.* a flat fish living on the sea bottom.

rayon /'reɪɒn/ *n.* a synthetic textile.

raze /reɪz/ *v.t.* to tear down, demolish, or level to the ground.

razor /'reɪzə/ *n.* **1.** a sharp-edged instrument used especially for shaving hair from the skin. –*v.t.* **2.** to apply a razor to.

razorback /'reɪzəbæk/ *n.* a sharp ridge.

razor wire *n.* coiled stainless-steel wire having pieces of protruding metal with razor-sharp points attached at intervals along the wire.

re /ri, reɪ/ *prep.* in the case of; with reference to.

're *v.* a contracted form of **are**.

re- a prefix indicating repetition. **2.** a prefix indicating withdrawal or backward motion.

reach /riːtʃ/ *v.t.* **1.** to get to, or get as far as in, moving, going, travelling, etc. **2.** to stretch or extend so as to touch or meet. **3.** to establish communication with. –*v.i.* **4.** to make a stretch, as with the hand or arm. **5.** to extend in operation or effect. **6.** to stretch in space; extend in direction, length, distance, etc. –*n.* **7.** the act of reaching. **8.** the extent or distance of reaching. **9.** a continuous stretch or extent of something. –**reachable**, *adj.*

react /ri'ækt/ *v.i.* **1.** to act in return on an agent or influence; act reciprocally upon each other, as two things. **2.** to act in opposition, as against some force. –**reactor**, *n.* –**reactive**, *adj.*

reaction /ri'ækʃən/ *n.* **1.** the act or an instance of reacting. **2.** *Commerce* a drop in the market after an advance in prices.

reactionary /ri'ækʃənri/, *Orig. US* /ri'ækʃənɛri/ *n.* (*pl.* **-ries**) **1.** a person opposed to progress or reform. –*adj.* **2.** opposing progressive policies; conservative.

read¹ /riːd/ *v.* (**read** /rɛd/, **reading** /'riːdɪŋ/) –*v.t.* **1.** to observe, and apprehend the meaning of (something written, printed, etc.). **2.** to render in speech (something written, printed, etc.). **3.** to understand or take (something read or observed) in a particular way. **4.** to introduce (something not expressed or directly indicated) into what is read or considered. **5.** to register or indicate, as a thermometer or other instrument. **6.** (of a computer) to take (information) from a peripheral device into the central computer. –*v.i.* **7.** to read or peruse writing, printing, etc., or papers, books, etc. **8.** to utter aloud, or render in speech, written or printed words that one is perusing. **9.** to obtain knowledge or learn of something by reading. **10.** to be capable of being read or interpreted (as stated). **11.** (of a computer) to take in information. –*n.* **12.** the act or process of reading.

read² /rɛd/ *adj.* having knowledge gained by reading.

readout /'riːdaʊt/ *n.* → **digital display**.

read-write /riːd-'raɪt/ *adj.* of or relating to a computer, etc., which reads and then restores memory data.

ready /'rɛdi/ *adj.* (**-dier, -diest**) **1.** completely prepared or in due condition for immediate action or use. **2.** willing. **3.** prompt or quick in

perceiving, comprehending, speaking, writing, etc. **4.** present or convenient. –*v.t.* (**-died, -dying**) **5.** to make ready; prepare. –*n.* **6.** *Colloq.* ready money. **7.** the condition or position of being ready. –**readily**, *adv.*

reagent /ri'eɪdʒənt/ *n.* a substance which, on account of the reactions it causes, is used in chemical analysis.

real /riːl/ *adj.* **1.** true. **2.** genuine; not counterfeit, artificial, or imitation. **3.** *Law* denoting or relating to immoveable property of a freehold type, as lands and tenements excluding leaseholds (opposed to *personal*). –*adv. & adj. Colloq.* an intensifier with the sense of 'very': *real cute.*

real estate *n.* property in the form of land, buildings, etc.: *a valuable piece of real estate.*

real estate agent *n.* a person who acts as an intermediary between the buyer and the vendor of real estate; real estate broker.

realise /'riːəlaɪz/ *v.t.* **1.** to grasp or understand clearly. **2.** to make real, or give reality to (a hope, fear, plan, etc.). **3.** to convert into cash or money. **4.** to obtain as a profit or income for oneself by trade, labour, or investment. –*v.i.* **5.** to convert property or goods into cash or money. **6.** to realise a profit. Also, **realize**.

realism /'riːəlɪzəm/ *n.* **1.** the taking of a practical rather than a moral view in human problems, etc. **2.** the tendency to view or represent things as they really are. –**realistic**, *adj.*

reality /ri'æləti/ *n.* (*pl.* **-ties**) **1.** the state or fact of being real. **2.** resemblance to what is real. **3.** that which is real. –*phr.* **4. in reality**, in fact; actually.

reality check *n. Colloq.* **1.** an appraisal of the facts of a situation, often providing a contrast with expectations. **2.** any event which triggers such an appraisal of one's expectations, beliefs, etc.

reality TV *n.* a television program format which uses actual footage of events as they occur, often in a contrived situation and with some competitive element providing the motivation for people to interact. Also, **reality television**.

real-life *adj.* that actually occurs or has occurred; not fictional.

really /'riːli/ *adv.* **1.** in reality; actually. **2.** genuinely or truly. **3.** indeed.

realm /rɛlm/ *n.* the region, sphere, or domain within which anything rules or prevails.

real-time *adj.* **1.** of or relating to an analytical or computing device which processes information and outputs results at the same rate at which the original information is presented. **2.** of or relating to computer simulations which reproduce the speed of the event being simulated. –*n.* **3.** a method using real-time processing. Also, **realtime**.

realtor /'riːəltə, -tɔ/ *n. Chiefly US* → **real estate agent**.

realty /'riːəlti/ *n.* → **real estate**.

ream /riːm/ *n.* a standard quantity among paper dealers meaning 20 quires or 500 sheets (formerly 480 sheets).

reap /riːp/ *v.t.* to gather or take (a crop, harvest, etc.).

rear¹ /rɪə/ *n.* **1.** the back of anything, as opposed to the front. **2.** the space or position behind anything. *–adj.* **3.** situated at or relating to the rear.

rear² /rɪə/ *v.t.* **1.** to care for and support up to maturity. **2.** to raise to an upright position. *–v.i.* **3.** to rise on the hind legs, as a horse or other animal.

reason /'riːzən/ *n.* **1.** a ground or cause, as for a belief, action, fact, event, etc. **2.** the mental powers concerned with drawing conclusions or inferences. **3.** sound judgement or good sense. *–v.i.* **4.** to think or argue in a logical manner. *–v.t.* **5.** (oft. fol. by *out*) to think out (a problem, etc.) logically. **6.** (fol. by *that*) to conclude or infer. **7.** to bring, persuade, etc., by reasoning.

reasonable /'riːzənəbəl/ *adj.* **1.** endowed with reason. **2.** agreeable to reason or sound judgement. **3.** moderate, or moderate in price.

reassure /riə'ʃɔ/ *v.t.* to restore (a person, etc.) to assurance or confidence.

rebate /'riːbeɪt/ *n.* **1.** a return of part of an original amount paid for some service or merchandise. *–v.t.* **2.** to allow as a discount. **–rebatable, rebateable,** *adj.*

rebel *n.* /'rɛbəl/ **1.** someone who refuses allegiance to, resists, or rises in arms against, the established government or ruler. *–adj.* /'rɛbəl/ **2.** of or relating to rebels. *–v.i.* /rə'bɛl/ **(-belled, -belling) 3.** to rise in arms or active resistance against one's government or ruler.

rebellion /rə'bɛljən/ *n.* the act of rebelling.

rebellious /rə'bɛljəs/ *adj.* **1.** fighting against a government or other organised authority. **2.** not wanting to obey any kind of authority. **–rebelliousness,** *n.*

rebound *v.i.* /rə'baʊnd/ **1.** to bound or spring back from force of impact. *–n.* /'riːbaʊnd, rə-'baʊnd/ **2.** the act of rebounding; recoil.

rebuff /rə'bʌf/ *n.* **1.** a peremptory refusal of a request, offer, etc.; a snub. **2.** a check to action or progress. *–v.t.* **3.** to give a rebuff to.

rebuke /rə'bjuːk/ *v.t.* **1.** to reprove or reprimand. *–n.* **2.** a reproof; a reprimand.

rebut /rə'bʌt/ *v.t.* **(-butted, -butting)** to refute by evidence or argument. **–rebuttal,** *n.*

recalcitrant /rə'kælsətrənt/ *adj.* **1.** resisting authority or control. *–n.* **2.** a recalcitrant person. **–recalcitrance, recalcitrancy,** *n.*

recall /rə'kɔl/ *v.t.* **1.** to recollect or remember. **2.** to call back; summon to return. *–n.* /'riːkɔl/ **3.** the act of recalling. **4.** memory; recollection.

recant /rə'kænt/ *v.t., v.i.* to withdraw or disavow (a statement, etc.), especially formally; retract.

recap /'riːkæp/ *v.t., v.i.* **(-capped, -capping)** to recapitulate.

recapitulate /riːkə'pɪtʃəleɪt/ *v.t.* **1.** to review by way of an orderly summary, as at the end of a speech or discourse. *–v.i.* **2.** to sum up statements or matters.

recede /rə'siːd/ *v.i.* **1.** to go or move back, to or towards a more distant point. **2.** to slope backwards.

receipt /rə'siːt/ *n.* **1.** a written acknowledgement of having received money, goods, etc., specified. **2.** (*pl.*) the amount or quantity received. **3.** the state of being received. *–v.t.* **4.** to give a receipt for (money, goods, etc.). *–v.i.* **5.** to give a receipt, as for money or goods.

receive /rə'siːv/ *v.t.* **1.** to take into one's hand or one's possession. **2.** to take into the mind;

apprehend mentally. **3.** to meet with; experience. **4.** to greet or welcome (guests, etc.) upon arriving. **5.** to accept as authoritative, valid, true, or approved. *–v.i.* **6.** to receive something. **7.** *Radio, TV* to convert incoming electromagnetic waves into the original signal. **–receival,** *n.*

receiver /rə'siːvə/ *n.* **1.** a device or apparatus which receives electrical signals, and renders them perceptible to the senses. **2.** *Commerce* a person appointed to receive money due. **3.** someone who knowingly receives stolen goods.

recent /'riːsənt/ *adj.* lately happening, done, made, etc.

receptacle /rə'sɛptəkəl/ *n.* that which serves to receive or hold something.

reception /rə'sɛpʃən/ *n.* **1.** the act of receiving. **2.** a manner of being received. **3.** a function or occasion when people are formally received. **4.** a place, office, desk, or the like where callers are received, as in an office or hotel.

receptionist /rə'sɛpʃənəst/ *n.* a person employed to receive and direct callers, as in an office or hotel.

receptive /rə'sɛptɪv/ *adj.* able or quick to receive ideas, etc.

recess *n.* /rə'sɛs, 'riːsɛs/ **1.** a part or space that is set back or recedes. **2.** withdrawal or cessation for a time from the usual occupation, work, or activity. *–v.t.* /rə'sɛs/ **3.** to place or set in a recess. **4.** to make a recess or recesses in. *–v.i.* /rə'sɛs/ **5.** to take a recess.

recession /rə'sɛʃən/ *n.* **1.** a receding part of a wall, etc. **2.** a period of adverse economic circumstances, usually less severe than a depression.

recessive /rə'sɛsɪv/ *adj.* tending to recede; receding.

recipe /'rɛsəpi/ *n.* any formula, especially one for preparing a dish in cookery.

recipient /rə'sɪpiənt/ *n.* someone who or that which receives; a receiver.

reciprocal /rə'sɪprəkəl/ *adj.* relating to two people or groups who feel the same way about each other or who agree to act in a way that gives each other help. **–reciprocally,** *adv.*

reciprocate /rə'sɪprəkeɪt/ *v.t.* **1.** to give, feel, etc., in return. **2.** to give and receive reciprocally; interchange. *–v.i.* **3.** to make return, as for something given. **–reciprocity,** *n.*

recite /rə'saɪt/ *v.t.* **1.** to repeat the words of, as from memory, especially in a formal manner. *–v.i.* **2.** to recite or repeat something from memory. **–recital, recitation,** *n.*

reckless /'rɛkləs/ *adj.* utterly careless of the consequences of action.

reckon /'rɛkən/ *v.t.* **1.** to count, compute, or calculate as to number or amount. **2.** to esteem or consider (as stated). **3.** *Colloq.* to think or suppose. *–v.i.* **4.** to count; make a computation or calculation. **5.** to settle accounts, as with a person. **6.** to count, depend, or rely (*on*), as in expectation. **7.** to think; suppose.

reclaim /rə'kleɪm/ *v.t.* **1.** to claim or demand the return or restoration of (something or someone): *to reclaim baggage; to reclaim someone's affection.* **2.** to bring (wild, waste, or marshy land) into a condition for cultivation or other use. **–reclamation**, *n.*

recline /rə'klaın, ri-/ *v.i.* **1.** to lean or lie back; rest in a recumbent position. *–v.t.* **2.** to cause to lean back on something.

recluse /rə'klus/ *n.* a person who lives in seclusion or apart from society, often for religious meditation. **–reclusiveness**, *n.*

recognise /'rɛkəgnaız/ *v.t.* **1.** to identify from knowledge of appearance or character. **2.** to perceive as existing or true; realise. **3.** to acknowledge or treat as valid. Also, **recognize**. **–recognition**, *n.*

recoil *v.i.* /rə'kɔıl/ **1.** to draw back, as in alarm, horror, or disgust. **2.** to spring or fly back, as from force of impact, as a firearm. *–n.* /rə'kɔıl, 'rikɔıl/ **3.** the act of recoiling.

recollect /rɛkə'lɛkt/ *v.t.* to recall to mind, or recover knowledge of by an act or effort of memory; remember.

recommend /rɛkə'mɛnd/ *v.t.* to present as worthy of confidence, acceptance, use, etc. **–recommendation**, *n.*

recompense /'rɛkəmpɛns/ *v.* (**-pensed, -pensing**) *–v.t.* **1.** to make compensation to (a person, etc.); repay. *–v.i.* **2.** to repay or reward a person for service, aid, etc. *–n.* **3.** compensation made, as for loss, injury, or wrong.

reconcile /'rɛkənsaıl/ *v.t.* to bring into agreement or harmony; make compatible or consistent. **–reconciliation**, *n.*

recondition /rikən'dıʃən/ *v.t.* to restore to a good or satisfactory condition; repair; overhaul.

reconnoitre /rɛkə'nɔıtə/ *v.t.* (**-tred, -tring**) to examine or survey (a region, etc.) for engineering, geological, military, or other purposes. **–reconnaissance**, *n.*

reconstitute /ri'kɒnstətjut/ *v.t.* to constitute again; reconstruct; recompose: *reconstituted milk; a reconstituted committee.* **–reconstitution** /rikɒnstə'tjuʃən/, *n.*

record *v.t.* /rə'kɔd/ **1.** to set down or register in some permanent form. *–v.i.* /rə'kɔd/ **2.** to record something. *–n.* /'rɛkɔd/ **3.** an account in writing or the like preserving the memory or knowledge of facts or events. **4.** information or knowledge preserved in writing or the like. **5.** *Computers* a self-contained group of data. **6.** a disc, especially one made from a vinyl polymer, on which sound has been recorded in a spiral groove, to be played using a stylus on a record-player. **7.** the highest or farthest recorded degree attained. *–adj.* /'rɛkɔd/ **8.** making or affording a record. *–phr.* **9. off the record**, unofficially; without intending to be quoted.

recorder /rə'kɔdə/ *n.* **1.** a recording or registering apparatus or device. **2.** a soft-toned flute played in vertical position.

recount *v.t.* /rə'kaʊnt/ **1.** to relate or narrate. *–n.* /'rikaʊnt/ **2.** a written or spoken text type or form which typically records events in the order in which they happened.

recoup *v.t.* /rə'kup, ri-/ **1.** to obtain an equivalent for; compensate for. **2.** to regain or recover. **3.** to reimburse or indemnify. *–v.i.* /rə'kup, ri-/ **4.** to obtain an equivalent, as for something lost. *–n.* /'rikup/ **5.** the act of recouping.

recourse /rə'kɔs/ *n.* **1.** resort or application to a person or thing for help or protection. **2.** *Commerce* the right to resort to a person for pecuniary compensation. An endorsement **without recourse** is one by which a payee or holder of a negotiable instrument merely transfers the instrument without assuming any liability upon it.

recover /rə'kʌvə/ *v.t.* **1.** to get again, or regain (something lost or taken away). **2.** to make up for or make good (loss, damage, etc., to oneself). **3.** to regain the strength, composure, balance, etc., of (oneself). *–v.i.* **4.** to regain a former (and better) state or condition. **–recovery**, *n.*

recreation /rɛkri'eıʃən/ *n.* **1.** refreshment by means of some pastime, agreeable exercise, or the like. **2.** a pastime, diversion, exercise, or other resource affording relaxation and enjoyment. **–recreational**, *adj.*

recriminate /rə'krıməneıt/ *v.t.* to accuse in return.

recruit /rə'krut/ *n.* **1.** a newly secured member of any body or class. *–v.t., v.i.* **2.** to enlist (people) for service in the armed forces.

rectangle /'rɛktæŋgəl/ *n.* a parallelogram with all its angles right angles, especially one in which adjacent sides are equal. **–rectangular**, *adj.*

recti- a word element meaning 'straight', 'right'. Also, (*before vowels*), **rect-**.

rectify /'rɛktəfaı/ *v.t.* (**-fied, -fying**) **1.** to make, put, or set right; remedy; correct. **2.** *Elect.* to change (an alternating current) into a direct current.

rectitude /'rɛktətjud/ *n.* rightness of principle or practice.

rector /'rɛktə/ *n. Church of England* a minister who has the charge of a parish.

rectum /'rɛktəm/ *n.* (*pl.* **-ta** /-tə/) the comparatively straight terminal section of the intestine, ending in the anus.

recumbent /rə'kʌmbənt/ *adj.* lying down; reclining; leaning.

recuperate /rə'kupəreıt/ *v.i.* **1.** to recover from sickness or exhaustion. **2.** to recover from pecuniary loss.

recur /ri'kɜ, rə-/ *v.i.* (**-curred, -curring**) to occur again, as an event, experience, etc.

recursive /rə'kɜsıv/ *adj.* permitting or relating to an operation that may be repeated indefinitely.

recycle /ri'saıkəl/ *v.t.* **1.** to treat (waste, empty bottles, tins, etc.) so that new products can be manufactured from them. **2.** to prepare (something) for a second use, often with some adaptation or reconstruction. **–recyclable**, *adj.*

red /rɛd/ *adj.* (**redder, reddest**) **1.** of a spectral hue beyond orange in the spectrum. **2.** (*oft. upper case*) ultraradical politically, especially communist. *–n.* **3.** any of the hues adjacent to orange in the spectrum, such as scarlet, vermilion, cherry. **4.** red wine, as opposed to white wine. *–phr.* **5. the red**, **a.** red ink as used in bookkeeping and accounting practice for recording deficits. **b.** loss or deficit.

-red a noun suffix denoting condition, as in *hatred, kindred*.

red-back *n.* a small, highly venomous, Australian spider.

red-bellied black snake *n.* a venomous snake of eastern Australian forests and scrubs, glossy black above and pale pink to red below, growing to two metres or more in length.

red blood cell *n.* → erythrocyte.

red-blooded /'rɛd-blʌdəd/ *adj.* vigorous; virile.

red card *n. Sport* a red card shown by a referee to a player who has committed a serious infringement of the rules as an indication that the player is to leave the field for the remainder of the game. Compare **yellow card**.

red carpet *n.* highly favoured or deferential treatment.

red dwarf *n. Astron.* a type of small, relatively cool, very faint star.

redeem /rə'dim/ *v.t.* **1.** to buy or pay off; clear by payment. **2.** to recover (something pledged or mortgaged) by payment or other satisfaction. **3.** to convert (paper money) into specie. **4.** to make up for; make amends for. **5.** to obtain the release or restoration of, as from captivity, by paying a ransom. –**redemption**, *n.*

red-handed /rɛd-'hændəd/ *adj., adv.* in the very act of a crime or other deed.

red herring *n.* something to divert attention; a false clue.

red-letter day *n.* a memorable or especially happy occasion.

red light *n.* **1.** a red lamp, used as a signal to mean 'stop'. **2.** a warning signal. **3.** the symbol of a brothel.

red-light camera *n.* a camera positioned at an intersection with traffic lights to photograph the numberplate of any motor vehicle that goes through a red light.

redolent /'rɛdələnt/ *adj.* **1.** having a pleasant smell; fragrant. **2.** (fol. by *of*) odorous or smelling. **3.** (fol. by *of*) suggestive; reminiscent.

redoubtable /rə'daʊtəbəl/ *adj.* that is to be feared; formidable.

redound /rə'daʊnd/ *v.i.* to come back or recoil, as upon a person.

red-pencil *v.t.* (**-cilled** or, *Chiefly US*, **-ciled**, **-cilling** or, *Chiefly US*, **-ciling**) to correct or edit (manuscript or typescript) with or as with a red pencil.

redress /rə'drɛs/ *n.* **1.** the setting right of what is wrong. **2.** compensation for wrong or injury. –*v.t.* **3.** to set right; remedy or repair (wrongs, injuries, etc.). **4.** to adjust evenly again, as a balance.

red tape *n.* **1.** excessive attention to formality and routine. **2.** official procedures.

reduce /rə'djus/ *v.* (**-duced**, **-ducing**) –*v.t.* **1.** to bring down to a smaller extent, size, amount, number, etc. **2.** to lower in degree, intensity, etc. **3.** to lower in price. **4.** to bring to a certain state, condition, arrangement, etc. **5.** to bring under control or authority; subdue. **6.** to thin (paints, etc.) with oil or turpentine. –*v.i.* **7.** to become reduced.

reduction /rə'dʌkʃən/ *n.* **1.** the act of reducing. **2.** the amount by which something is reduced or diminished. **3.** a copy on a smaller scale.

redundant /rə'dʌndənt/ *adj.* **1.** being in excess. **2.** denoting or relating to an employee who is

or becomes superfluous to the needs of the employer.

reed /rid/ *n.* **1.** the straight stalk of any of various tall grasses. **2.** anything made from such a stalk or from something similar.

reef /rif/ *n.* a narrow ridge of rocks or sand, often of coral debris, at or near the surface of water.

reefer /'rifə/ *n. Colloq.* a marijuana cigarette.

reef knot *n.* a kind of flat knot.

reek /rik/ *n.* **1.** a strong, unpleasant smell. –*v.i.* **2.** to smell strongly and unpleasantly.

reel¹ /ril/ *n.* **1.** a cylinder, frame, or other device, turning on an axis, on which to wind something. –*v.t.* **2.** to draw with a reel, or by winding. **3.** (fol. by *off*) to say, write, or produce in an easy, continuous way.

reel² /ril/ *v.i.* **1.** to sway or rock under a blow, shock, etc. **2.** to sway about in standing or walking, as from dizziness, intoxication, etc.; stagger.

reel³ /ril/ *n.* a lively dance popular in Scotland.

reel-to-reel *n.* **1.** a tape recorder which uses reels of tape rather than cassettes or cartridges. –*adj.* **2.** of or relating to such a system of recording.

re-enact /ri-ən'æct/ *v.t.* to act out again (a past event, especially one of historical importance). –**re-enactment**, *n.*

refectory /rə'fɛktri/ *n.* (*pl.* **-ries**) a dining hall in an institution.

refer /rə'fɜ/ *v.* (**-ferred, -ferring**) –*v.t.* **1.** to direct for information or anything required. **2.** (of a medical practitioner) to direct (a patient) to another doctor, usually a specialist, for further consultation or treatment. **3.** to hand over or submit for information, consideration, decision, etc. **4.** to direct anyone for information, especially about one's character, abilities, etc. –*v.i.* **5.** to have relation; relate; apply. **6.** to direct a remark or mention. –**referral**, *n.*

referee /rɛfə'ri/ *n.* **1.** one to whom something is referred, especially for decision or settlement; arbitrator; umpire. –*v.t.* **2.** to preside over as referee; act as referee in.

reference /'rɛfrəns/ *n.* **1.** the act or fact of referring. **2.** a directing of attention; allusion. **3.** direction or a direction to some source of information. **4.** use or recourse for purposes of information. **5.** a written or verbal testimonial given as to the character, abilities, etc., of a person, especially a job applicant. **6.** a person who supplies such a testimony; referee. **7.** relation, regard, or respect. –*phr.* **8. terms of reference**, the scope allowed to an investigating body.

referendum /rɛfə'rɛndəm/ *n.* (*pl.* **-da** /-də/ or **-dums**) the principle or procedure of referring or submitting measures proposed or passed by a legislative body to the vote of the electorate for approval or rejection.

refine /rə'faɪn/ *v.t.* **1.** to bring to a fine or a pure state; free from impurities. **2.** to make elegant or cultured. –*v.i.* **3.** to become pure. **4.** to become more fine, elegant, or polished.

reflect /rə'flɛkt/ *v.t.* **1.** to cast back (light, heat, sound, etc.) after incidence. **2.** to give back or show an image of; mirror. **3.** to reproduce; show. –*v.i.* **4.** to be turned or cast back, as light. **5.** to cast back light, heat, etc. **6.** to be reflected or mirrored. **7.** to serve or tend to bring reproach or discredit. **8.** to think, ponder, or meditate. –**reflective**, *adj.*

reflex /'rifleks/ *adj.* **1.** occurring in reaction; responsive. **2.** bent or turned back. –*n.* **3.** *Physiol.* a reflex action or movement.

reflexive /rə'fleksɪv/ *adj. Gram.* **1.** (of a verb) having identical subject and object, as *shave* in *he shaved himself*. **2.** (of a pronoun) indicating identity of object with subject, as *himself* in the example above.

reform /rə'fɔm/ *n.* **1.** the improvement or amendment of what is wrong, corrupt, etc. –*v.t.* **2.** to improve by alteration, substitution, abolition, etc. **3.** to cause (a person) to abandon wrong or evil ways of life or conduct. –*v.i.* **4.** to abandon evil conduct or error.

reformatory /rə'fɔmətri/, *Orig. US* /rə'fɔmətəri/ *n.* (*pl.* **-ries**) a penal institution for the reformation of young offenders. Also, **reform school**.

refraction /rə'frækʃən/ *n. Physics* the change of direction of a ray of light, heat, or the like, in passing obliquely from one medium into another.

refractory /rə'fræktəri/ *adj.* stubborn; unmanageable.

refrain¹ /rə'freɪn/ *v.i.* (oft. fol. by *from*) to forbear; keep oneself back.

refrain² /rə'freɪn/ *n.* a phrase or verse recurring at intervals in a song or poem, especially at the end of each stanza; chorus.

refresh /rə'freʃ/ *v.t.* **1.** (oft. *reflexive*) to reinvigorate by rest, food, etc. **2.** to stimulate (the memory). **3.** *Computers* to update the image on (a computer screen). –*v.i.* **4.** to become fresh or vigorous again; revive.

refreshment /rə'freʃmənt/ *n.* that which refreshes, especially food or drink.

refrigerate /rə'frɪdʒəreɪt/ *v.t.* to make or keep cold or cool.

refrigerator /rə'frɪdʒəreɪtə/ *n.* a cabinet or room in which food, drink, etc., is kept cool.

refuge /'refjudʒ/ *n.* shelter or protection from danger, trouble, etc.

refugee /refju'dʒi/ *n.* someone who flees for refuge or safety, especially to a foreign country.

refund *v.t.* /rə'fʌnd/ **1.** to give back or restore (especially money); repay. **2.** to make repayment to; reimburse. –*n.* /'rifʌnd/ **3.** a repayment. –**refundable**, *adj.*

refurbish /ri'fɜbɪʃ/ *v.t.* to renovate.

refusal /rə'fjuzəl/ *n.* **1.** the act of refusing. **2.** priority in refusing or taking something; option.

refuse¹ /rə'fjuz/ *v.t.* **1.** to decline to accept (something offered). **2.** to deny (a request, demand, etc.). **3.** to express a determination not (to do something). –*v.i.* **4.** to decline acceptance, consent, or compliance.

refuse² /'refjus/ *n.* that which is discarded as worthless or useless; rubbish.

refute /rə'fjut/ *v.t.* to prove to be false.

regal /'rigəl/ *adj.* **1.** of or relating to a king; royal. **2.** (of a woman) tall, dignified, and elegant.

regale /rə'geɪl/ *v.t.* to entertain agreeably; delight.

regard /rə'gad/ *v.t.* **1.** to look upon or think of with a particular feeling. **2.** to have or show

respect or concern for. **3.** to take into account; consider. **4.** to look at; observe. **5.** to relate to; concern. –*v.i.* **6.** to pay attention. –*n.* **7.** reference; relation. **8.** a point or particular. **9.** thought; attention; concern. **10.** look; gaze. **11.** respect; deference. **12.** kindly feeling; liking. **13.** (*pl.*) sentiments of esteem or affection.

regatta /rə'gætə/ *n.* a boat race.

regenerate *v.t.* /rə'dʒɛnəreɪt/ **1.** to re-create, reconstitute, or make over, especially in a better form or condition. –*v.i.* /rə'dʒɛnəreɪt/ **2.** to come into existence or be formed again. **3.** to reform; become regenerate. –*adj.* /rə-'dʒɛnərət/ **4.** reconstituted in a better form. **5.** reformed. –**regeneration**, *n.*

regent /'ridʒənt/ *n.* someone who exercises the ruling power in a kingdom during the minority, absence, or disability of the sovereign. –**regency**, *n.*

reggae /'regeɪ/ *n.* a type of modern music, originating in the West Indies, with a strong bass part and guitar chords played on the unaccented beat.

regift /ri'gɪft/ *v.t.* to present (something which one has received as a gift) to another person as a gift from oneself. –**regifting**, *n.* –**regifter**, *n.*

regime /reɪ'ʒim/ *n.* a mode or system of rule or government.

regimen /'redʒəmən/ *n.* **1.** a prevailing system. **2.** a regulated course of diet, exercise, etc.

regiment *n.* /'redʒəmənt/ **1.** *Mil.* a unit of ground forces. –*v.t.* /'redʒəmənt/ **2.** to form into an organised body or group; organise or systematise. –**regimentation**, *n.* –**regimental**, *adj.*

region /'ridʒən/ *n.* **1.** any more or less extensive, continuous part of a surface or space. **2.** a district without respect to boundaries or extent.

register /'redʒəstə/ *n.* **1.** a record of acts, occurrences, etc. **2.** *Commerce* a ship's official document of identification which must be produced when a ship is entering or leaving a port. **3.** a mechanical device by which data is automatically recorded, as a cash register. **4.** *Computers* a device capable of holding digital information until it is required. –*v.t.* **5.** to enter or have entered formally in a register. **6.** to indicate or show, as on a scale. **7.** to show (surprise, joy, anger, etc.). –*v.i.* **8.** to enter one's name, or cause it to be entered, in an electoral or other register; enrol. **9.** *Colloq.* to make an impression. –**registrant**, *n.* –**registration**, *n.* –**registrable**, *adj.*

registered /'redʒəstəd/ *adj. Commerce* officially listing the owner's name with the issuing company and suitably inscribing the certificate, as with bonds to evidence title.

registered nurse *n.* a nurse who holds a degree in nursing from a university, or who qualified under the former system of intensive hospital training. *Abbrev.:* RN Compare **enrolled nurse**.

registrar /'redʒəstra/ *n.* **1.** someone who keeps a record; an official recorder. **2.** an employee of a limited company who is responsible for registering the issues of securities.

registry /'redʒəstri/ *n.* (*pl.* **-ries**) a place where a register is kept; an office of registration.

regnant /'regnənt/ *adj.* reigning; ruling.

regress /ri'grɛs/ v.i. to move in a backward direction; go back. **–regression**, n. **–regressive**, adj.

regret /rə'grɛt/ v.t. (**-gretted, -gretting**) 1. to feel sorry about (anything disappointing, unpleasant, etc.). 2. to think of with a sense of loss. –n. 3. a sense of loss, disappointment, dissatisfaction, etc. 4. the feeling of being sorry for some fault, act, omission, etc., of one's own.

regrowth /ri'groʊθ/ n. 1. a growing again: *this forest is undergoing regrowth.* 2. new hair growth, especially that which contrasts in colour with previously dyed hair.

regular /'rɛgjələ/ adj. 1. usual; normal; customary. 2. conforming in form or arrangement; symmetrical. 3. adhering to rule or procedure. 4. recurring at fixed times. 5. orderly; well-ordered. 6. *Colloq.* complete; thorough: *a regular troublemaker.* –n. 7. *Colloq.* a regular customer.

regulate /'rɛgjəleɪt/ v.t. 1. to control or direct by rule, principle, method, etc. 2. to adjust to some standard or requirement; as amount, degree, etc. **–regulation**, n.

regurgitate /rə'gɜdʒəteɪt/ v.t. 1. to cause to surge or rush back. 2. to bring back (food), digested or partially digested, into the mouth. 3. to repeat (information) without thought or independent analysis.

rehabilitate /rihə'bɪləteɪt/ v.t. 1. to restore to a good condition, or alter to an improved state.

rehash v.t. /ri'hæʃ/ 1. to work up (old material) in a new form. –n. /'rihæʃ/ 2. something rehashed.

rehearse /rə'hɜs/ v.t. 1. to perform in private by way of practice. –v.i. 2. to rehearse a play, part, etc. **–rehearsal**, n.

rehydrate /ri'haɪdreɪt/ v.t. 1. to replenish the fluid in (dehydrated plants). 2. to replenish the bodily fluids of. 3. to reconstitute (dried food, etc.) by adding or soaking in water. –v.i. 4. to replenish one's bodily fluids, as by drinking.

reign /reɪn/ n. 1. the period or term of ruling, as of a sovereign. –v.i. 2. to possess or exercise sovereign power or authority.

reimburse /rim'bɜs/ v.t. to make repayment to for expense or loss incurred.

rein /reɪn/ n. 1. a long, narrow strap for guiding a horse. 2. any means of curbing, controlling, or directing; a check; restraint. –v.t. 3. to curb; restrain; control.

reincarnation /ˌrinka'neɪʃən/ n. rebirth of the soul in a new body.

reindeer /'reɪndɪə/ n. (pl. **-deer** or **-deers**) a large deer.

reinforce /rim'fɔs/ v.t. 1. to strengthen; make more forcible or effective. 2. to augment; increase.

reinstate /rin'steɪt/ v.t. to put back or establish again, as in a former position or state.

reinvent /rin'vɛnt/ v.t. 1. to produce (a device, solution, etc.), believing it to be original, when it has in fact been invented before. –phr. 2. **reinvent oneself**, to create a new character, appearance, role, etc., for oneself: *when she turned thirty she reinvented herself as an intellectual.* 3. **reinvent the wheel**, to attempt to work out again a method, solution, procedure, etc., which is already known and widely adopted.

reiterate /ri'ɪtəreɪt/ v.t. to repeat; say or do again or repeatedly.

reject v.t. /rə'dʒɛkt/ 1. to refuse to have, take, recognise, etc. 2. to refuse to accept (someone) as a friend, member of a group, etc. 3. to cast out or off. –n. /'ridʒɛkt/ 4. something rejected, as an imperfect article. 5. *Colloq.* (derog.) a person despised by a particular group.

rejoice /rə'dʒɔɪs/ v.i. to be glad; take delight (in).

rejoinder /rə'dʒɔɪndə/ n. 1. an answer to a reply; response. 2. *Law* the defendant's answer to the plaintiff's replication.

rejuvenate /rə'dʒuvəneɪt/ v.t. to make young again.

-rel a noun suffix having a diminutive or pejorative force.

relapse /rə'læps/ v.i. 1. to fall or slip back into a former state, practice, etc. –n. 2. the act of relapsing.

relate /rə'leɪt/ v.t. 1. to tell. 2. to bring into or establish association, connection, or relation. –v.i. 3. to have reference (to). 4. to have some relation (to).

related /rə'leɪtəd/ adj. 1. of a similar kind or having some connection. 2. part of the same family.

relation /rə'leɪʃən/ n. 1. an existing connection; a particular way of being related. 2. connection between persons by blood or marriage. 3. a relative. 4. reference; regard; respect.

relationship /rə'leɪʃənʃɪp/ n. 1. a particular connection. 2. a connection between people by blood or marriage. 3. an emotional connection between people, sometimes involving sexual relations.

relative /'rɛlətɪv/ n. 1. someone who is connected with another or others by blood or marriage. 2. something having, or standing in, some relation to something else, as opposed to *absolute*. –adj. 3. considered in relation to something else; comparative. 4. having relation or connection. 5. correspondent; proportionate.

relative atomic mass n. the average mass of the atoms of an element in its naturally occurring state, relative to the mass of an atom of the carbon-12 isotope taken as exactly 12. Compare **atomic mass**. Also, **atomic weight**.

relativity /rɛlə'tɪvəti/ n. 1. the state or fact of being relative. 2. (pl.) the relative differences in wages between groups of workers.

relax /rə'læks/ v.t. 1. to make lax, or less tense, rigid, or firm. 2. to diminish the force of. –v.i. 3. to become less tense, rigid, or firm. 4. to become less strict or severe; grow milder. 5. to slacken in effort, application, etc.; take relaxation.

relay n. /'rileɪ/ 1. a set of persons relieving others or taking turns; a shift. 2. Also, **relay race**. a race between two or more teams, each member running, swimming, etc., one of the lengths of the distance. 3. an automatic device for operating the controls of a larger piece of equipment. –v.t. /rə'leɪ, 'rileɪ/ 4. to carry forward by or as by relays.

release /rə'lis/ v.t. 1. to free from confinement, bondage, obligation, pain, etc. 2. to allow to become known, be issued or exhibited. –n. 3. liberation from anything that restrains or fastens. 4. some device for effecting such liberation. **5.** the releasing of something for public exhibition or sale. **6.** the article so released.

relegate /'rɛləgeɪt/ v.t. to send or consign to some obscure position, place, or condition.

relent /rə'lɛnt/ v.i. to soften in feeling, temper, or determination.

relevant /'rɛləvənt/ adj. bearing upon or connected with the matter in hand; to the purpose; pertinent. **–relevance**, n.

reliable /rə'laɪəbəl/ adj. that may be relied on; trustworthy.

reliant /rə'laɪənt/ adj. confident; trustful. **–reliance**, n.

relic /'rɛlɪk/ n. **1.** a surviving memorial of something past. **2.** a surviving trace of something.

relief /rə'lif/ n. **1.** deliverance, alleviation, or ease through the removal of pain, distress, oppression, etc. **2.** something affording a pleasing change, as from monotony. **3.** the person or persons relieving another or others. **4.** prominence, distinctness, or vividness due to contrast.

relieve /rə'liv/ **1.** to ease or alleviate (pain, distress, anxiety, need, etc.). **2.** to free from anxiety, fear, pain, etc. **3.** to make less tedious, unpleasant, or monotonous. **4.** to bring into relief or prominence. **5.** to release (one on duty) by coming as or providing a substitute. **6.** to take the place of (an absent worker). –phr. **7. relieve oneself**, to empty the bowels or bladder.

religion /rə'lɪdʒən/ n. recognition on the part of human beings of a controlling superhuman power entitled to obedience, reverence, and worship.

religious /rə'lɪdʒəs/ adj. **1.** of, relating to, or concerned with religion. **2.** scrupulously faithful; conscientious.

relinquish /rə'lɪŋkwɪʃ/ v.t. to renounce or surrender (a possession, right, etc.).

relish /'rɛlɪʃ/ n. **1.** pleasurable appreciation of anything; liking. **2.** something appetising or savoury added to a meal, as chutney. **3.** a taste or flavour. –v.t. **4.** to take pleasure in; like; enjoy.

relive /ˌri'lɪv/ v.t. to repeat former experiences, in fact or memory.

reluctant /rə'lʌktənt/ adj. unwilling; disinclined.

rely /rə'laɪ/ v.i. (**-lied, -lying**) (fol. by on or upon) to depend confidently; put trust in.

remain /rə'meɪn/ v.i. **1.** to continue in the same state; continue to be (as specified). **2.** to stay in a place. **3.** to be left after the removal, departure, loss, etc., of another or others. –n. (pl.) **4.** that which remains or is left; a remnant. **5.** what remains of a person after death; dead body.

remainder /rə'meɪndə/ n. **1.** that which remains or is left. **2.** a copy of a book remaining in the publisher's stock when the sale has practically ceased, frequently sold at a reduced price. –v.t. **3.** to dispose of or sell as a publisher's remainder.

remains /rə'meɪnz/ pl. n. **1.** that which remains or is left. **2.** what remains of a person after death; dead body.

remand /rə'mænd, -'mand/ v.t. **1.** to send back, remit, or consign again. **2.** the state of being remanded.

remark /rə'mak/ v.t. **1.** to say casually, as in making a comment. **2.** to note; perceive. –v.i. **3.** (fol. by on or upon) to make a remark or observation. –n. **4.** a casual or brief expression of thought or opinion.

remarkable /rə'makəbəl/ adj. worthy of remark or notice.

remediate /rə'midieɪt/ v.t. to correct (a fault or impairment).

remediation /rəmidi'eɪʃən/ n. **1.** the act or process of remedying. **2.** the restoration of an environment to its pristine state, as by the removal of pollutants, etc.

remedy /'rɛmədi/ n. (pl. **-dies**) **1.** something that corrects or removes an evil of any kind. –v.t. (**-died, -dying**) **2.** to cure or heal. **3.** to put right, or restore to the natural or proper condition. **–remedial**, adj.

remember /rə'mɛmbə/ v.t. **1.** to recall to the mind by an act or effort of memory. **2.** to retain in the memory; bear in mind. **3.** to mention to another as sending kindly greetings. –v.i. **4.** to possess or exercise the faculty of memory. **–remembrance**, n.

remind /rə'maɪnd/ v.t. to cause to remember.

reminiscence /rɛmə'nɪsəns/ n. the act or process of remembering one's past. **–reminiscent**, adj. **–reminisce**, v.

remiss /rə'mɪs/ adj. characterised by negligence or carelessness.

remit /rə'mɪt/ v. (**-mitted, -mitting**) –v.t. **1.** to transmit or send (money, etc.) to a person or place. **2.** to refrain from exacting, as a payment or service. **3.** to slacken; abate. **4.** to give back. **5.** to put back into a previous position or condition. –v.i. **6.** to transmit money, etc., as in payment. **7.** to slacken; abate. **–remission**, n.

remittance /rə'mɪtns/ n. **1.** the remitting of money, etc., to a recipient at a distance. **2.** money or its equivalent sent from one place to another.

remix /'rimɪks/ n. **1.** a recorded version of a piece of music containing a mix of the original recording tracks which is different from that used for the earlier published version. –v.t. **2.** to mix again.

remnant /'rɛmnənt/ n. a part, quantity, or number (usually small) remaining.

remonstrance /rə'mɒnstrəns/ n. a protest. **–remonstrate**, v.

remorse /rə'mɔs/ n. deep and painful regret for wrongdoing; compunction.

remote /rə'moʊt/ **1.** far apart; far distant in space. **2.** out-of-the-way; retired; secluded. **3.** distant in time. **4.** far off; removed. **5.** slight or faint. **6.** abstracted; cold and aloof. –n. **7.** → **remote control** (def. 2).

remote control n. **1.** the control of a system by means of electrical, radio, or other signals from a point at a distance from the system. **2.** a usually handheld device for the control of domestic appliances such as televisions, VCRs, air conditioners, etc.

remove /rə'muv/ v.t. **1.** to move from a place or position; take away; take off. **2.** to take, withdraw, or separate (from). –v.i. **3.** to move from one place to another, especially to another locality or residence. —*n.* **4.** the act of removing. **5.** a step or degree, as in a graded scale. —**removal**, *n.*

removed /rə'muvd/ *adj.* remote; separate; not connected with; distinct from.

remunerate /rə'mjunərəɪt/ *v.t.* to pay, recompense, or reward for work, trouble, etc. —**remuneration**, *n.* —**remunerative**, *adj.*

renaissance /rə'neɪsəns, rə'næsəns/ *n.* a new birth or revival, especially one in the world of art or learning.

renal /'rinəl/ *adj.* of or relating to the kidneys.

rend /rɛnd/ *v.t.* (**rent**, **rending**) to tear apart, split, or divide.

render /'rɛndə/ *v.t.* **1.** to make, or cause, to be or become. **2.** to do; perform. **3.** to present for consideration, approval, payment, action, etc., as an account. **4.** to pay as due (a tax, tribute, etc.). **5.** to give in return or requital. —**rendition**, *n.*

rendezvous /'rɒndeɪvu, rɒndeɪ'vu/ *n.* an appointment to meet at a fixed place and time.

renegade /'rɛnəgeɪd/ *n.* someone who deserts a party or cause for another.

renege /rə'nɛg, -'nɪg/ *v.i. Colloq.* to go back on one's word.

renew /rə'nju/ *v.t.* **1.** to begin or take up again, as acquaintance, conversation, etc. **2.** to make effective for an additional period. **3.** to restore or replenish. —*v.i.* **4.** to begin again; recommence. **5.** to renew a lease, note, etc. —**renewal**, *n.*

renewable resource *n.* a natural resource which is not finite but can be renewed, such as the sun, wind, or biomass. Compare **non-renewable resource**.

renounce /rə'naʊns/ *v.t.* **1.** to give up or put aside voluntarily. **2.** to repudiate; disown.

renovate /'rɛnəveɪt/ *v.t.* **1.** to make new or as if new again; restore to good condition; repair. **2.** to reinvigorate; refresh; revive. —**renovation**, *n.* —**renovator**, *n.*

renown /rə'naʊn/ *n.* widespread and high repute; fame. —**renowned**, *adj.*

rent[1] /rɛnt/ *n.* **1.** a return or payment made periodically by a tenant to an owner or landlord for the use of land or building. **2.** profit or return derived from any differential advantage in production. —*v.t.* **3.** to grant the possession and enjoyment of (property) in return for payments to be made at agreed times. **4.** to take and hold (property) in return for payments to be made at agreed times. —*v.i.* **5.** to be leased or let for rent.

rent[2] /rɛnt/ *n.* **1.** an opening made by rending or tearing; slit; fissure. —*v.* **2.** past tense and past participle of **rend**.

rental /'rɛntl/ *n.* **1.** an amount received or paid as rent. **2.** an income arising from rents received. —*adj.* **3.** relating to rent. **4.** available for rent.

renunciation /rənʌnsi'eɪʃən/ *n.* the formal abandoning of a right, title, etc.

rep /rɛp/ *n. Colloq.* **1.** a travelling salesperson. **2.** *Sport* a player, athlete, etc., who is selected to represent their region or division in sport. **3.** a union representative.

repair[1] /rə'pɛə/ *v.t.* **1.** to restore to a good or sound condition after decay or damage; mend.

—*n.* **2.** the act, process, or work of repairing. **3.** the good condition resulting from repairing.

repair[2] /rə'pɛə/ *v.i.* to take oneself or go, as to a place.

reparable /'rɛpərəbəl, 'rɛprəbəl/ *adj.* capable of being repaired or remedied.

reparation /rɛpə'reɪʃən/ *n.* the making of amends for wrong or injury done.

repartee /rɛpa'ti/ *n.* speech or talk characterised by quickness and wittiness of reply.

repast /rə'past/ *n.* a taking of food; a meal.

repatriate /ri'pætrieɪt/ *v.t.* to bring or send back (a person) to his or her own country. —**repatriation**, *n.*

repay /ri'peɪ/ *v.t.* (**-paid**, **-paying**) **1.** to pay back or refund (money, etc.). **2.** to make return for.

repeal /rə'pil/ *v.t.* **1.** to revoke or withdraw formally or officially. —*n.* **2.** the act of repealing; revocation.

repeat /rə'pit/ *v.t.* **1.** to say or utter again. **2.** to say or utter in reproducing the words, etc., of another. **3.** to do, make, perform, etc., again. —*v.i.* **4.** to do or say something again. **5.** something repeated. **6.** an order for goods identical to a previous order. **7.** a duplicate or reproduction of something.

repeated /rə'pitəd/ *adj.* done or said again and again. —**repeatedly**, *adv.*

repel /rə'pɛl/ *v.t.* (**-pelled**, **-pelling**) **1.** to drive or force back (an assailant, invader, etc.). **2.** to keep off or out; fail to mix with. **3.** to excite feelings of distaste or aversion in. —**repellent**, *adj.*, *n.*

repent /rə'pɛnt/ *v.i.* **1.** to feel self-reproach, compunction, or contrition for past conduct. —*v.t.* **2.** to feel sorry for; regret. —**repentance**, *n.* —**repentant**, *adj.*

repercussion /ripə'kʌʃən/ *n.* an after-effect, often an indirect result, of some event or action.

repertoire /'rɛpətwa/ *n.* the list of dramas, operas, parts, pieces, etc., which a company, actor, singer or the like, is prepared to perform.

repertory /'rɛpətri/ *n.* (*pl.* **-ries**) a theatrical company.

repetition /rɛpə'tɪʃən/ *n.* **1.** the act of repeating. **2.** a repeated action, performance, production, or presentation. —**repetitious**, **repetitive**, *adj.*

repetition strain injury *n.* → **RSI**. Also, **repetitive strain injury**, **repetitive stress injury**.

replace /rə'pleɪs/ *v.t.* **1.** to fill or take the place of; substitute for (a person or thing). **2.** to provide a substitute or equivalent in the place of. **3.** to restore to a former or the proper place. —**replacement**, *n.*

replay *n.* /'ripleɪ/ **1.** (in sport) a match, contest, etc. which is played again because of some difficulty or disagreement. **2.** (in television coverage of sport) the playing again of some highlight of a game, often immediately after it has happened. —*v.t.* /ri'pleɪ, 'ripleɪ/ **3.** to repeat (a sporting event, match, etc. or a sequence from it) on radio or television.

replenish /rə'plɛnɪʃ/ *v.t.* to bring back to a state of fullness or completeness.

replete /rə'plit/ *adj.* stuffed or gorged with food and drink.

replica /'rɛplɪkə/ *n.* any copy or reproduction.

replication /ˌrɛpləˈkeɪʃən/ n. **1.** a reply to an answer. **2.** a reproduction, copy, or duplication. **–replicate**, v.

reply /rəˈplaɪ/ v. (**-plied, -plying**) **–v.i. 1.** to make answer in words or writing; answer; respond. **2.** to respond by some action, performance, etc. **–v.t. 3.** to return as an answer. **–n.** (pl. **-plies**) **4.** an answer or response.

report /rəˈpɔt/ n. **1.** an account brought back or presented. **2.** a statement generally circulated; rumour. **3.** repute; reputation. **4.** a loud noise, as from an explosion. **–v.t. 5.** to relate as what has been learned by observation or investigation. **6.** to give or render a formal account or statement of. **7.** to lay a charge against (a person), as to a superior. **8.** to relate or tell. **–v.i. 9.** to make a report. **10.** to present oneself duly, as at a place.

reporter /rəˈpɔtə/ n. **1.** someone employed to gather and report news for a newspaper, news agency, or broadcasting organisation. **2.** someone who prepares official reports, as of legal or legislative proceedings.

repose /rəˈpoʊz/ n. **1.** the state of reposing or resting; rest; sleep. **2.** dignified calmness, as of manner or demeanour. **–v.i. 3.** to lie at rest; take rest. **–v.t. 4.** (oft. used reflexively) to lay to rest; rest; refresh by rest.

repository /rəˈpɒzətri/ n. (pl. **-ries**) a receptacle or place where things are deposited, stored, or offered for sale.

repossess /ˌripəˈzɛs/ v.t. **1.** to possess again; regain possession of. **2.** to put again in possession of something.

reprehensible /ˌrɛprəˈhɛnsəbəl/ adj. (of behaviour) deserving harsh criticism: reprehensible conduct.

represent /ˌrɛprəˈzɛnt/ v.t. **1.** to serve to express, designate, stand for, or denote, as a word, symbol, or the like; symbolise. **2.** to speak and act for by delegated authority. **3.** to present in words; set forth; describe; state. **4.** to serve as an example or specimen of; exemplify. **5.** to be the equivalent of; correspond to.

representative /ˌrɛprəˈzɛntətɪv/ adj. **1.** serving to represent; representing. **2.** representing a constituency or community or the people generally in legislation or government. **3.** characterised by, founded on, or relating to representation of the people in government. **–n. 4.** someone who or that which represents another or others. **5.** an agent or deputy.

repress /rəˈprɛs/ v.t. to keep under control, check, or suppress.

reprieve /rəˈpriv/ v.t. **1.** to relieve temporarily from any evil. **–n. 2.** respite from impending punishment, especially from execution of a sentence of death.

reprimand /ˈrɛprəmand, -mænd/ n. **1.** a severe reproof, especially a formal one by a person in authority. **–v.t. 2.** to reprove severely, especially in a formal way.

reprisal /rəˈpraɪzəl/ n. retaliation, or an act of retaliation.

reproach /rəˈproʊtʃ/ v.t. **1.** to find fault with (a person, etc.); blame; censure. **–n. 2.** an expression of upbraiding, censure or reproof. **3.** a cause or occasion of disgrace or discredit.

reprobate /ˈrɛprəbeɪt/ n. **1.** an abandoned, unprincipled, or reprehensible person. **–adj. 2.** morally depraved; unprincipled; bad.

reproduce /ˌriprəˈdjus/ v. (**-duced, -ducing**) **–v.t. 1.** to make a copy, representation, duplicate, or close imitation of. **2.** to produce another or more individuals of (some animal or plant kind). **3.** to produce, form, make, or bring about again or anew in any manner. **–v.i. 4.** to reproduce its kind, as an animal or plant; propagate. **5.** to turn out (well, etc.) when copied. **–reproductive**, adj. **–reproducible**, adj. **–reproducer**, n. **–reproduction**, n.

reproof /rəˈpruf/ n. an expression of censure or rebuke.

reprove /rəˈpruv/ v.t. **1.** to address words of disapproval to (a person, etc.); rebuke; blame. **–v.i. 2.** to speak in reproof; administer a reproof. **–reproval**, n.

reptile /ˈrɛptaɪl/ n. any of various creeping or crawling animals, as the lizards, snakes, etc.

republic /rəˈpʌblɪk/ n. a nation in which the head of the state is a president, usually either elected or nominated and so deemed a representative of the people, not a hereditary monarch. **–republican**, n., adj.

repudiate /rəˈpjudieɪt/ v.t. **1.** to reject as having no authority or binding force. **2.** to refuse to acknowledge and pay, as a debt (said specifically of a state, municipality, etc.).

repugnant /rəˈpʌgnənt/ adj. distasteful or objectionable. **–repugnance**, n.

repulse /rəˈpʌls/ v.t. **1.** to drive back, or repel, as an assailant, etc. **2.** to reject or refuse, especially rudely (an offer, etc.). **3.** to disgust: the thought of it repulsed him. **–repulsion**, n. **–repulsive**, adj.

reputable /ˈrɛpjətəbəl/ adj. held in good repute; honourable.

reputation /ˌrɛpjəˈteɪʃən/ n. the estimation in which a person or thing is held.

repute /rəˈpjut/ n. estimation in the view of others; reputation.

reputed /rəˈpjutəd/ adj. accounted or supposed to be such.

request /rəˈkwɛst/ n. **1.** the act of asking for something. **–v.t. 2.** to ask for, especially politely or formally. **3.** to make request to, ask, or beg (a person, etc.) to do something.

requiem /ˈrɛkwiəm, ˈreɪkwiəm/ n. any musical service, hymn, or dirge for the repose of the dead.

require /rəˈkwaɪə/ v.t. **1.** to have need of; need. **2.** to ask for authoritatively or imperatively; demand. **3.** to place under an obligation or necessity.

requisite /ˈrɛkwəzət/ adj. **1.** needed or demanded by the nature of things or by conditions; indispensable. **–n. 2.** a necessary thing; something requisite.

requisition /ˌrɛkwəˈzɪʃən/ n. **1.** an authoritative or official demand. **2.** the state of being required for use or called into service. **–v.t. 3.** to require or take for use; press into service.

requite /rəˈkwaɪt/ v.t. to give or do in return. **–requital**, n.

reroute /riˈrut/, Chiefly US and Computers /riˈraʊt/ v.t. (**rerouted, rerouting** or **rerouting**) **1.** to direct (a road, river, etc.) into a different course. **2.** Finance to send (funds) to a different location. **3.** *Computers* to alter the connections for (computer hardware): *to reroute a computer on a network.* **4.** *Internet* to redirect (traffic) by adjusting a browser, IP address, etc. Also, **re-route.**

rescind /rɪˈsɪnd/ *v.t.* to invalidate (an act, measure, etc.) by a later action or a higher authority. –**rescission**, *n.*

rescue /ˈrɛskju/ *v.t.* (**-cued, -cuing**) **1.** to free or deliver from confinement, violence, danger, or evil. –*n.* **2.** the act of rescuing.

research /rəˈsɜːtʃ, ˈrisɜːtʃ/ *n.* **1.** diligent and systematic inquiry or investigation into a subject in order to discover facts or principles. –*v.i.* **2.** to make researches; investigate carefully. –*v.t.* **3.** to investigate carefully. –*adj.* **4.** of or relating to research.

resemble /rəˈzɛmbəl/ *v.t.* to be like or similar to. –**resemblance**, *n.*

resent /rəˈzɛnt/ *v.t.* to feel or show a sense of injury or insult. –**resentful**, *adj.* –**resentfulness**, *n.* –**resentment**, *n.*

reservation /rɛzəˈveɪʃən/ *n.* **1.** the making of some exception or qualification. **2.** tract of public land set apart for a special purpose. **3.** the allotting or the securing of accommodation at a hotel, on a train or boat, etc.

reserve /rəˈzɜːv/ *v.t.* **1.** to keep back or save for future use, disposal, treatment, etc. **2.** to secure or book in advance, as accommodation, theatre seats, etc. **3.** *Law* to delay handing down (a judgement or decision), especially to give time for better consideration of the issues involved. –*n.* **4.** an amount of capital retained by a company to meet contingencies. **5.** something reserved, as for some purpose or contingency; a store or stock. **6.** a tract of public land set apart for a special purpose, as a nature reserve. **7.** reticence or silence. **8.** → **reserve price**. –*adj.* **9.** kept in reserve; forming a reserve.

reserve bank *n.* the national banking organisation of a country, which administers the monetary policy of a government, receives revenue, pays government expenditure and issues money, both paper and coin, as legal tender.

reserved /rəˈzɜːvd/ *adj.* **1.** kept in reserve. **2.** characterised by reserve, as the disposition, manner, etc.

reserve price *n.* the lowest price at which a person is willing that their property shall be sold at auction. Also, **reserve.**

reservoir /ˈrɛzəvwɑ, ˈrɛzəvɔ/ *n.* a natural or artificial place where water is collected and stored for use.

reshuffle /ˌriˈʃʌfəl/ *v.t.* to make a new allocation of jobs, especially within a government or cabinet.

reside /rəˈzaɪd/ *v.i.* **1.** to dwell permanently or for a considerable time. **2.** (fol. by *in*) to rest or be vested, as powers, rights, etc. –**resident**, *adj.*, *n.*

residence /ˈrɛzədəns/ *n.* **1.** the place, especially the house, in which one resides. **2.** a large house. **3.** the time during which one resides in a place. –*phr.* **4. in residence**, living or staying in a place of official or other duty. –**residential**, *adj.*

residency /ˈrɛzədənsi/ *n.* (*pl.* **-cies**) **1.** → **residence**. **2.** the dwelling place of officials or

diplomats representing the heads of state of foreign countries.

residue /ˈrɛzədʒu/ *n.* that which remains after a part is taken, disposed of, or gone; remainder; rest. –**residual**, *adj.*

resign /rəˈzaɪn/ *v.i.* **1.** (oft. fol. by *from*) to give up an office or position. **2.** to submit; yield. –*v.t.* **3.** to give up (an office, position, etc.) formally. **4.** to submit (oneself, one's mind, etc.) without resistance. –**resignation**, *n.*

resilient /rəˈzɪliənt, -ˈzɪljənt/ *adj.* **1.** returning to the original form or position after being bent, compressed, or stretched. **2.** readily recovering, as from sickness, depression, or the like; buoyant; cheerful. –**resilience**, *n.*

resin /ˈrɛzən/ *n.* any of a class of organic substances used in medicine and in the making of varnishes and plastics.

resist /rəˈzɪst/ *v.t.* **1.** to withstand, strive against, or oppose. –*v.i.* **2.** to act in opposition; offer resistance.

resistance /rəˈzɪstəns/ *n.* **1.** the opposition offered by one thing, force, etc., to another. **2.** *Elect.* the property of a device which opposes the flow of an electric current.

resolute /ˈrɛzəlut/ *adj.* firmly resolved or determined; set in purpose or opinion.

resolution /rɛzəˈluʃən/ *n.* **1.** a resolve or determination. **2.** the mental state or quality of being resolved or resolute; firmness of purpose. **3.** the act or process of resolving or separating into constituent or elementary parts.

resolve /rəˈzɒlv/ *v.t.* **1.** to fix or settle on by deliberate choice and will; determine (to do something). **2.** to separate into constituent or elementary parts. **3.** (oft. *reflexive*) to convert or transform by any process. **4.** to settle, determine, or state formally in a vote or resolution, as of a deliberative assembly. **5.** to deal with (a question, a matter of uncertainty, etc.) conclusively; explain; solve (a problem). **6.** to clear away or dispel (doubts, etc.), as by explanation. –*v.i.* **7.** (oft. fol. by *on* or *upon*) to come to a determination; make up one's mind; determine. **8.** to break up or disintegrate. –*n.* **9.** a resolution or determination made. **10.** determination; firmness of purpose.

resonance /ˈrɛzənəns/ *n.* **1.** the state or quality of being resonant. **2.** the prolongation of sound by reflection; reverberation.

resonant /ˈrɛzənənt/ *adj.* **1.** resounding or re-echoing, as sounds, places, etc. **2.** deep and full of resonance.

resonate /ˈrɛzəneɪt/ *v.i.* to resound.

resort /rəˈzɔt/ *v.i.* **1.** to have recourse for use, service, or help. –*n.* **2.** a place frequented, especially by the public generally. **3.** a resorting to some person or thing for aid, service, etc.; recourse. **4.** a person or thing resorted to for aid, service, etc.

resound /rəˈzaʊnd/ *v.i.* **1.** to re-echo or ring with sound. **2.** to be echoed, or ring, as sounds. –*v.t.* **3.** to re-echo (a sound). **4.** to proclaim loudly (praises, etc.).

resource /rəˈzɔs, ˈrisɔs, ˈrisɔs, ˈrizɔs/ *n.* **1.** a source of supply, support, or aid. **2.** a source of information. **3.** (oft. *pl.*) money, or any property which can be converted into money;

assets. **4.** capability in dealing with a situation or in meeting difficulties.

resourceful /rə'zɔːsfəl, rə'sɔsfəl/ *adj.* full of resource; ingenious; skilful in overcoming difficulties. **–resourcefully**, *adv.* **–resourcefulness**, *n.*

respect /rə'spɛkt/ *n.* **1.** a particular, detail, or point (in phrases preceded by *in*). **2.** (preceded by *in* or *with*) relation or reference. **3.** esteem or deferential regard felt or shown. **4.** (*pl.*) deferential, respectful, or friendly compliments. *–v.t.* **5.** to hold in esteem or honour. **6.** to treat with consideration; refrain from interfering with.

respectable /rə'spɛktəbəl/ *adj.* **1.** worthy of respect or esteem. **2.** having socially accepted standards of moral behaviour. **3.** of presentable appearance; decently clothed.

respective /rə'spɛktɪv/ *adj.* relating individually or severally to each of a number of persons, things, etc.; particular.

respectively /rə'spɛktɪvli/ *adv.* with respect to each of a number in the stated or corresponding order.

respiration /rɛspə'reɪʃən/ *n.* the inhalation and exhalation of air; breathing. **–respiratory** /rə'spɪrətri, 'rɛsprətri/, *adj.*

respirator /'rɛspəreɪtə/ *n.* **1.** a device worn over the mouth, or nose and mouth, to prevent the breathing in of poisonous or harmful substances, etc. **2.** an apparatus to induce artificial respiration.

respite /'rɛspət, 'rɛspaɪt, rə'spaɪt/ *n.* **1.** a delay or cessation for a time, especially of anything distressing or trying; an interval of relief. *–v.t.* **2.** to relieve temporarily.

resplendent /rə'splɛndənt/ *adj.* shining brilliantly; gleaming; splendid.

respond /rə'spɒnd/ *v.i.* to answer; give a reply.

respondent /rə'spɒndənt/ *n. Law* a defendant, especially in appellate and divorce cases.

response /rə'spɒns/ *n.* answer or reply, whether in words, in some action, etc.

responsibility /rəspɒnsə'bɪləti/ *n.* (*pl.* **-ties**) **1.** the state or fact of being responsible. **2.** something for which one is responsible. **3.** ability to meet debts or payments.

responsible /rə'spɒnsəbəl/ *adj.* **1.** (oft. fol. by *to* or *for*) answerable or accountable, as for something within one's power, control, or management. **2.** able to discharge obligations or pay debts. **3.** reliable in business or other dealings; showing reliability.

responsive /rə'spɒnsɪv/ *adj.* responding readily to influences, appeals, efforts, etc.

rest¹ /rɛst/ *n.* **1.** refreshing ease or inactivity after exertion or labour. **2.** relief or freedom, especially from anything that wearies, troubles, or disturbs. **3.** cessation or absence of motion. **4.** a pause or interval. **5.** a support, or supporting device. *–v.i.* **6.** to refresh oneself, as by sleeping, lying down, or relaxing. **7.** to be quiet or still. **8.** to cease from motion, come to rest, or stop. **9.** to remain without further action or notice. **10.** (fol. by *in, on, against*, etc.) to lie, sit, lean, or be set. **11.** (fol. by *on* or *upon*) to be based or founded. **12.** (fol. by *in* or *with*) to be a responsibility, as something to be done. *–v.t.* **13.** to give rest to; refresh with rest. **14.** to base, or let depend, as on some

ground of reliance. **15.** to bring to rest; halt; stop.

rest² /rɛst/ *n.* that which is left or remains; the remainder.

restaurant /'rɛstərɒnt/ *n.* an establishment where meals are served to customers.

restitution /rɛstə'tjuʃən/ *n.* the restoration of property or rights previously taken away or surrendered.

restive /'rɛstɪv/ *adj.* impatient of control, restraint, or delay.

restless /'rɛstləs/ *adj.* **1.** characterised by or showing inability to remain at rest: *a restless mood.* **2.** unquiet or uneasy, as a person, the mind, heart, etc. **3.** never at rest, motionless, or still; never ceasing. **4.** without rest; without restful sleep: *a restless night.* **5.** characterised by unceasing activity; averse to quiet or inaction, as persons. **–restlessly**, *adv.* **–restlessness**, *n.*

restore /rə'stɔ/ *v.t.* **1.** to bring back to a former, original, or normal condition. **2.** to put back to a former place, or to a former position, rank, etc. **3.** to give back. **–restoration**, *n.*

restrain /rə'streɪn/ *v.t.* to hold back from action; keep in check or under control.

restraint /rə'streɪnt/ *n.* **1.** a means of restraining. **2.** the state or fact of being restrained.

restrict /rə'strɪkt/ *v.t.* to confine or keep within limits, as of space, action, choice, quantity, etc. **–restriction**, *n.* **–restrictive**, *adj.*

restrictive practice *n.* a practice on the part of the members of an association such as a trade union, tending to limit the freedom of choice of their coworkers or employers.

restructure /ri'strʌktʃə/ *v.t.* **1.** to change the organisation or structure of. **2.** (in business, manufacturing, etc.) to change the pattern of employment, distribution, etc., especially when this results in job losses. **3.** to reformulate, as when redrafting a document, policy, award, etc. *–n.* **4.** the act or process of restructuring. **–restructuring**, *n.*

result /rə'zʌlt/ *n.* **1.** that which results; the outcome, consequence, or effect. *–v.i.* **2.** to spring, arise, or proceed as a consequence. **3.** to terminate or end in a specified manner or thing.

resume /rə'zjum/ *v.t.* **1.** to take up or go on with again after interruption. *–v.i.* **2.** to go on or continue after interruption.

résumé /'rɛzjəmeɪ/ *n.* **1.** a short written summary of one's education and previous employment; CV. **2.** a summing up; a summary. Also, **resumé**.

resurrect /rɛzə'rɛkt/ *v.t.* **1.** to raise from the dead; bring to life again. *–v.i.* **2.** to rise from the dead.

resuscitate /rə'sʌsəteɪt/ *v.t.* to revive, especially from apparent death or from unconsciousness. **–resuscitation**, *n.*

retail /'riteɪl/ *n.* **1.** the sale of commodities to household or ultimate consumers, usually in small quantities (opposed to *wholesale*). *–adj.* **2.** relating to, connected with, or engaged in sale at retail. *–adv.* **3.** at a retail price or in a retail quantity. *–v.t.* **4.** to sell directly to the consumer. *–v.i.* **5.** to be sold at retail.

retail bank *n.* a bank which deals with transactions made by individual customers rather than businesses or other banks. Compare **merchant bank**. –**retail banking**, n.

retain /rə'teɪn/ v.t. **1.** to continue to use, practise, etc. **2.** to continue to hold or have. **3.** to keep in mind; remember. –**retention**, n.

retainer /rə'teɪnə/ n. **1.** a fee paid to secure services, as of a barrister. **2.** a reduced rent paid during absence as an indication of future requirement.

retaliate /rə'tælieɪt/ v.i. to return like for like, especially evil for evil.

retard /rə'tad/ v.t. **1.** to delay the progress of; hinder or impede. **2.** to delay or limit (a person's intellectual or emotional development).

retch /rɛtʃ/ v.i. **1.** to make the sound and spasmodic movement of being about to vomit. **2.** the act or an instance of retching.

retentive /rə'tɛntɪv/ adj. **1.** tending or serving to retain something. **2.** having power or capacity to retain.

reticent /'rɛtəsənt/ adj. disposed to be silent; not inclined to speak freely.

reticulate adj. /rə'tɪkjələt/ **1.** netted; covered with a network. **2.** like a network or net. –v.t. /rə'tɪkjəleɪt/ **3.** to form into a network. –v.i. /rə'tɪkjəleɪt/ **4.** to form a network. –**reticulately**, adv. –**reticulation**, n.

retina /'rɛtənə/ n. (pl. **-nas** or **-nae** /-ni/) the innermost coat of the posterior part of the eyeball, serving to receive the image.

retinue /'rɛtənju/ n. a body of people in attendance upon an important personage.

retire /rə'taɪə/ v.i. **1.** to withdraw, or go away or apart, to a place of abode, shelter, or seclusion. **2.** to go to bed. **3.** to withdraw from office, business, or active life. –**retirement**, n.

retort /rə'tɔt/ v.t. **1.** to reply in retaliation. –n. **2.** a severe, incisive, or witty reply.

retrace /rə'treɪs/ v.t. to trace back; go back over.

retract[1] /rə'trækt/ v.t. to draw back or in. –**retractable**, adj.

retract[2] /rə'trækt/ v.t. to withdraw or revoke (a decree, promise, etc.).

retread v.t. /ˌri'trɛd/ (**-treaded, -treading**) **1.** to recondition (a worn motor-vehicle tyre) by moulding a fresh tread on to it. –n. /'ritrɛd/ **2.** a retreaded tyre.

retreat /rə'trit/ n. **1.** the act of withdrawing, as into safety or privacy. **2.** a place of refuge, seclusion, or privacy. –v.i. **3.** to withdraw, retire, or draw back, especially for shelter or seclusion.

retrench /rə'trɛntʃ/ v.t. **1.** to sack or dismiss, as part of an effort to economise. –v.i. **2.** to economise; reduce expenses.

retribution /rɛtrə'bjuʃən/ n. requital according to merits or deserts, especially for evil.

retrieve /rə'triv/ v.t. **1.** to recover or regain. **2.** to bring back to a former and better state; restore.

retriever /rə'trivə/ n. any of several breeds of dog for retrieving game.

retro /'rɛtroʊ/ adj. of or relating to fashion or popular music of previous times which has become fashionable again.

retro- a prefix meaning 'backwards'.

retroactive /rɛtroʊ'æktɪv/ adj. operative with respect to past occurrences, as a statute; retrospective.

retrofit /'rɛtroʊfɪt/ v.t. **1.** to fit out anew as part of repairs or maintenance. **2.** to fit out at a later time as part of a secondary stage of development.

retrograde /'rɛtrəgreɪd/ adj. **1.** moving backwards. **2.** returning to an earlier and inferior state.

retrogress /rɛtrə'grɛs/ v.i. to go backwards into a worse or earlier condition. –**retrogression**, n. –**retrogressive**, adj.

retrospect /'rɛtrəspɛkt/ n. contemplation of the past. –**retrospection**, n.

retrospective /rɛtrə'spɛktɪv/ adj. **1.** looking or directed backwards. **2.** retroactive, as a statute.

retrospectivity /ˌrɛtroʊspɛk'tɪvəti/ n. **1.** the quality of being retrospective. **2.** (in union or other agreements) the dating of the effectiveness of the agreement to a time prior to the date of the discussion concerning the agreement.

retrovirus /'rɛtroʊvaɪrəs/ n. any of a family of viruses including HIV and a number of viruses suspected of causing cancer.

return /rə'tɜn/ v.i. **1.** to go or come back, as to a former place, position, state, etc. **2.** to make reply; retort. –v.t. **3.** to put, bring, take, give, or send back. **4.** to yield (a profit, revenue, etc.), as in return for labour, expenditure, or investment. **5.** to elect, as to a legislative body. **6.** to turn back or in the reverse direction. –n. **7.** the act or fact of returning. **8.** response or reply. **9.** (oft. pl.) a yield or profit. **10.** the report or statement of financial condition. **11.** Econ. yield per unit as compared to the cost per unit involved in a specific industrial process. –adj. **12.** sent, given, or done in return. **13.** done or occurring again. –phr. **14. by return**, by the next post.

returning officer n. an official responsible for the organisation of an election, the accuracy of the count, the reading of the results, etc.

reunion /ri'junjən/ n. a gathering of relatives, friends, or associates after separation.

rev /rɛv/ n. **1.** a revolution (in an engine or the like). –v.t. (**revved, revving**) **2.** to change, especially to increase the speed of (in a specified way).

revamp /ri'væmp/ v.t. to renovate.

reveal /rə'vil/ v.t. **1.** to make known; disclose; divulge. **2.** to lay open to view; display; exhibit. –**revelation** /rɛvə'leɪʃən/, n. –**revelatory** /rɛvə'leɪtəri/, adj.

reveille /rə'væli/ n. a signal to waken soldiers or sailors for the day's duties.

revel /'rɛvəl/ v.i. (**-elled, -elling**) **1.** (fol. by in) to take great pleasure or delight. –n. **2.** (oft. pl.) an occasion of merrymaking or noisy festivity with dancing, etc. –**revelry**, n.

revenge /rə'vɛndʒ/ n. **1.** retaliation for injuries or wrongs; vengeance. –v.t. (**-venged, -venging**) **2.** to take vengeance on behalf of (a person) or for (a wrong).

revenue /'rɛvənju/ n. **1.** the income of a government from taxation, excise duties, customs, or other sources, appropriated to the payment of the public expenses. **2.** the return or yield from any kind of property; income. **3.** an amount of money regularly coming in.

reverberate /rə'vɜbəreɪt/ *v.i.* to re-echo or resound.

revere /rə'vɪə/ *v.t.* to regard with respect tinged with awe; venerate. **–reverence**, *n.* **–reverent**, *adj.*

reverend /'revrənd, 'revərənd/ *adj.* **1.** (*oft. upper case*) an epithet of respect for a member of the clergy. **–n. 2.** *Colloq.* a member of the clergy.

reverie /'revəri/ *n.* a state of dreamy meditation or fanciful musing.

reverse /rə'vɜs/ *adj.* **1.** opposite or contrary in position, direction, order, or character. **2.** producing a rearward motion. **–n. 3.** the opposite or contrary of something. **4.** the back or rear of anything. **5.** an adverse change of fortune. **6.** *Motor Vehicles* reverse gear. **–v.t. 7.** to turn inside out or upside down. **8.** to turn in the opposite direction; send on the opposite course. **9.** to revoke or annul (a decree, judgement, etc.). **10.** to drive (a motor vehicle) backwards. **–v.i. 11.** to turn or move in the opposite or contrary direction.

reverse-cycle *adj.* of or relating to an air conditioner able to cool an area in summer and heat it in winter.

reverse-engineer *v.t.* to analyse the construction of (a product), especially as a preliminary to designing a similar product.

reversible /rə'vɜsəbəl/ *adj.* **1.** capable of being reversed or of reversing. **2.** capable of re-establishing the original condition after a change by the reversal of that change. **3.** (of a fabric, garment, etc.) woven or printed so that either side may be exposed. **–n. 4.** a garment, especially a coat, that may be worn with either side exposed. **–reversibility** /rəvɜsə'bɪləti, ri-/, **reversibleness**, *n.* **–reversibly**, *adv.*

revert /rə'vɜt/ *v.i.* **1.** to return to a former habit, practice, belief, condition, etc. **2.** *Law* to go back or return to the former owner or his or her heirs. **–reversion**, *n.*

review /rə'vju/ *n.* **1.** a critical article or report on some literary work, film, play, opera, etc. **2.** a periodical publication containing articles on current events or affairs, books, art, etc. **3.** contemplation or consideration of past events, circumstances, or facts. **4.** a general survey of something, especially in words. **–v.t. 5.** to view, look at, or look over again. **6.** to look back upon; view retrospectively. **7.** to present a survey of in speech or writing. **8.** to discuss (a book, etc.) in a critical review.

revile /rə'vaɪl/ *v.t.* to address, or speak of, abusively.

revise /rə'vaɪz/ *v.t.* **1.** to amend or alter. **2.** to go over (a subject, book, etc.) again or study in order to fix it in the memory, as before an examination. **–revision**, *n.*

revitalise /ri'vaɪtəlaɪz/ *v.t.* to introduce new vigour and strength into. Also, **revitalize**. **–revitalisation**, *n.*

revive /rə'vaɪv/ *v.t.* **1.** to bring back into notice, use, or currency. **2.** to restore to life or consciousness. **–revival**, *n.*

revocable /'revəkəbəl/ *adj.* able to be revoked.

revoke /rə'voʊk/ *v.t.* to take back or withdraw; annul, cancel, or reverse. **–revocation**, *n.*

revolt /rə'voʊlt/ *v.i.* **1.** to break away from or rise against constituted authority; rebel. **2.** to turn away in mental rebellion, utter disgust, or abhorrence. **–v.t. 3.** to affect with disgust or abhorrence. **–n. 4.** an insurrection or rebellion. **5.** the state of those revolting.

revolution /revə'luʃən/ *n.* **1.** a complete overthrow of an established government or political system. **2.** procedure or course as if in a circuit. **3.** a single turn of this kind.

revolutionary /revə'luʃənəri, -ʃənri/ *adj.* **1.** subversive to established procedure, principles, etc. **–n.** (*pl.* **-ries**) **2.** someone who advocates or takes part in a revolution.

revolutionise /revə'luʃənaɪz/ *v.t.* to bring about a revolution in; effect a radical change in. Also, **revolutionize**.

revolve /rə'vɒlv/ *v.i.* **1.** to turn round or rotate, as on an axis. **2.** to move in a circular or curving course, or orbit.

revolver /rə'vɒlvə/ *n.* a pistol which can be fired repeatedly without reloading.

revue /rə'vju/ *n.* a collection of skits, dances, and songs.

revulsion /rə'vʌlʃən/ *n.* **1.** a sudden and violent change of feeling or reaction in sentiment. **2.** a violent dislike or aversion for something.

reward /rə'wɔd/ *n.* something given or received in return for service, merit, hardship, etc.

rewarding /rə'wɔdɪŋ/ *adj.* giving satisfaction that the effort made was worthwhile.

-rhagia a word element meaning 'bursting forth'.

rhapsody /'ræpsədi/ *n.* (*pl.* **-dies**) an exalted or exaggerated expression of feeling or enthusiasm.

rheo- a word element meaning 'something flowing', 'a stream', 'current'.

rhesus monkey /'risəs/ *n.* a monkey much used in medical research, common in India.

rhetoric /'retərɪk/ *n.* **1.** (in prose or verse) the use of exaggeration or display, in an unfavourable sense. **2.** (originally) the art of oratory. **–rhetorical**, *adj.*

rhetorical question /rə'tɒrɪkəl/ *n.* a question designed to produce an effect and not to draw an answer.

rheumatism /'rumətɪzəm/ *n.* any of various ailments of the joints or muscles, as certain chronic disabilities of the joints (**chronic rheumatism**) and certain painful conditions of the muscles (**muscular rheumatism**). **–rheumatic**, *adj.*

rhinestone /'raɪnstoʊn/ *n.* an artificial gem made of paste.

rhino /'raɪnoʊ/ *n.* (*pl.* **-nos**) → **rhinoceros**.

rhino- a word element meaning 'nose'. Also, **rhin-**.

rhinoceros /raɪ'nɒsərəs, raɪ'nɒsrəs/ *n.* (*pl.* **-ceroses** *or, especially collectively,* **-ceros**) any of various large mammals with one or two upright horns on the snout.

rhinoplasty /'raɪnoʊ,plæsti/ *n.* plastic surgery of the nose.

rhizo- a word element meaning 'root'.

rhizome /'raɪzoʊm/ *n.* a root-like subterranean stem.

rhodium /'roʊdiəm/ *n.* a silvery-white metallic element of the platinum family. *Symbol*: Rh

rhodo- a word element meaning 'rose'. Also, **rhod-**.

rhododendron /roudə'dɛndrən/ *n.* any of several evergreen and deciduous shrubs and trees much cultivated for ornament.

-rhoea a word element meaning 'flow', 'discharge'.

rhombus /'rɒmbəs/ *n.* (*pl.* **-buses** *or* **-bi** /-baɪ/) an oblique-angled parallelogram with all sides equal.

rhubarb /'rubab/ *n.* **1.** a garden plant with edible leafstalks. **2.** the word supposedly spoken by actors to simulate noisy conversation in the background.

rhyme /raɪm/ *n.* **1.** agreement in the terminal sounds of lines of verse, or of words. **2.** a word agreeing with another in terminal sound. **3.** verse or poetry having correspondence in the terminal sounds of the line. *–v.i.* (**rhymed, rhyming**) **4.** to form a rhyme, as one word or line with another. *–phr.* **5. rhyme or reason,** logic; explanation; meaning.

rhythm /'rɪðəm/ *n.* **1.** movement or procedure with uniform recurrence of a beat, accent, or the like. **2.** procedure marked by the regular recurrence of particular elements, phases, etc. *–***rhythmic, rhythmical,** *adj.*

rhythm and blues *n.* a style of music which first became popular in the early 1960s, using both vocal and instrumental elements based on the guitar, and derived ultimately from the African-American blues style but with a quicker tempo and more complex rhythms. *Abbrev.:* R & B

rib¹ /rɪb/ *n.* **1.** one of a series of long, slender, curved bones, occurring in pairs, more or less enclosing the thoracic cavity. **2.** some thing or part resembling a rib in form, position, or use, as a supporting or strengthening part. *–v.t.* (**ribbed, ribbing**) **3.** to furnish or strengthen with ribs.

rib² /rɪb/ *v.t.* (**ribbed, ribbing**) *Colloq.* to tease; ridicule; make fun of. *–***ribbing,** *n.*

ribald /'rɪbəld, 'raɪ-, 'raɪbɔld/ *adj.* coarsely mocking or abusive; wantonly irreverent. *–***ribaldry,** *n.*

ribbon /'rɪbən/ *n.* **1.** a woven strip or band of fine material, used for ornament, tying, etc. **2.** anything resembling or suggesting a ribbon or woven band. **3.** a band of material charged with ink, or supplying ink, for the impression in a typewriter. **4.** *Sport* an award for success in a competition.

riboflavin /raɪbou'fleɪvən/ *n.* vitamin B₂, one of the vitamins in the vitamin B complex.

rice /raɪs/ *n.* the starchy seeds or grain of a species of grass, an important food.

rice paper *n.* a thin, edible paper made from the straw of rice.

rich /rɪtʃ/ *adj.* **1.** abundantly supplied with resources, means, or funds. **2.** abounding in natural resources. **3.** (fol. by *in* or *with*) abounding. **4.** of great value or worth; valuable. **5.** (of wine, gravy, etc.) strong and full flavoured. **6.** (of colour) deep, strong, or vivid. **7.** (of sound, the voice, etc.) full and mellow in tone. **8.** *Colloq.* ridiculous, absurd, or preposterous. *–n.* **9.** (usu. preceded by *the*) rich people collectively.

riches /'rɪtʃəz/ *pl. n.* wealth.

Richter scale /'rɪktə skeɪl/ *n.* a scale used to measure the energy of disturbances in the earth, such as earthquakes.

rickets /'rɪkəts/ *n.* a childhood disease, caused by malnutrition and often resulting in deformities.

rickety /'rɪkəti/ *adj.* liable to fall or collapse; shaky.

rickshaw /'rɪkʃɔ/ *n.* a small two-wheeled hooded vehicle drawn by one or more people.

ricochet /'rɪkəʃeɪ/ *n.* the motion of an object or projectile which rebounds one or more times from the surface or surfaces it strikes.

ricotta /rə'kɒtə/ *n.* a soft cottage cheese with a fresh bland flavour.

rid /rɪd/ *v.t.* (**rid** *or* **ridded, ridding**) **1.** (fol. by *of*) to clear, disencumber, or free of something objectionable. *–phr.* **2. get rid of,** to get free, or relieved of.

riddance /'rɪdns/ *n.* a relieving or deliverance from something.

ridden /'rɪdn/ *v.* past participle of **ride**.

riddle¹ /'rɪdl/ *n.* **1.** a question or statement so framed as to exercise one's ingenuity in answering it or discovering its meaning. **2.** a puzzling question, problem, or matter.

riddle² /'rɪdl/ *v.t.* to pierce with many holes.

ride /raɪd/ *v.* (**rode, ridden, riding**) *–v.i.* **1.** to sit on and manage a horse or other animal in motion. **2.** to be carried on something as if on horseback. **3.** to be borne along on or in a vehicle or any kind of conveyance. **4.** to turn or rest on something. **5.** to work or move (*up*) from the proper position, as a skirt, or the like. **6.** to have a specified character for riding purposes. *–v.t.* **7.** to sit on and manage (a horse or other animal, or a bicycle or the like) so as to be carried along. **8.** to ride over, along or through (a road, boundary, region, etc.). *–n.* **9.** a journey or excursion on a horse, etc., or on or in a vehicle. *–phr.* **10. ride out,** to sustain or endure successfully.

rider /'raɪdə/ *n.* **1.** someone who rides. **2.** an addition or amendment to a document, etc. *–***riderless,** *adj.*

ridge /rɪdʒ/ *n.* **1.** a long, narrow elevation of land, or a chain of hills or mountains. **2.** any raised narrow strip, as on cloth, etc. **3.** the horizontal line in which the tops of the rafters of a roof meet. *–v.t.* (**ridged, ridging**) **4.** to provide with or form into a ridge or ridges.

ridicule /'rɪdəkjul/ *n.* **1.** words or actions intended to excite contemptuous laughter at a person or thing; derision. *–v.t.* **2.** to deride; make fun of.

ridiculous /rə'dɪkjələs/ *adj.* absurd, preposterous, or laughable.

riesling /'rizlɪŋ, 'rislɪŋ/ *n.* (*oft. upper case*) a dry white wine.

rife /raɪf/ *adj.* of common or frequent occurrence; prevalent.

riffle /'rɪfəl/ *v.t.* to make (pages, etc.) flutter and shift, as when looking quickly through them.

riffraff /'rɪfræf/ *n.* worthless or low persons.

rifle¹ /'raɪfəl/ *n.* a shoulder firearm.

rifle² /'raɪfəl/ *v.t.* to ransack and rob (a place, receptacle, etc.).

rift /rɪft/ *n.* a fissure; a cleft; a chink.

rig /rɪg/ *v.t.* (**rigged, rigging**) **1.** (usu. fol. by *out* or *up*) to furnish or provide with equipment, etc.; fit. **2.** (oft. fol. by *up*) to prepare or put together, especially as a makeshift. **3.** to manipulate fraudulently. –*n.* **4.** an apparatus for some purpose; equipment; outfit. **5.** Also, **rig-out**. *Colloq.* costume or dress, especially when odd or conspicuous.

rigging /ˈrɪgɪŋ/ *n.* the ropes, chains, etc., employed to support and work the masts, yards, sails, etc., on a ship.

right /raɪt/ *adj.* **1.** in accordance with what is just or good. **2.** in conformity with fact, reason, or some standard or principle; correct. **3.** in good health or spirits, as persons. **4.** in a satisfactory state; in good order. **5.** most convenient, desirable, or favourable. **6.** belonging or relating to the side of a person or thing which is turned towards the east when the face is towards the north (opposed to *left*). **7.** belonging or relating to the political right. **8.** *Geom.* having the axis perpendicular to the base. **9.** *Colloq.* unquestionable; unmistakable; true. –*n.* **10.** a just claim or title, whether legal, prescriptive, or moral. **11.** that which is due to anyone by just claim. **12.** *Finance* **a.** the privilege, usually pre-emptive, which accrues to the owners of the stock of a company to subscribe for additional stock or shares at an advantageous price. **b.** (*oft. pl.*) a privilege of subscribing for a stock or bond. **13.** that which is ethically good and proper and in conformity with the moral law. **14.** that which accords with fact, reason, or propriety. **15.** the right side or what is on the right side. **16.** a body of persons, political party, etc., holding conservative views. –*adv.* **17.** quite or completely. **18.** immediately. **19.** exactly, precisely, or just. **20.** correctly or accurately. **21.** properly or fittingly. **22.** advantageously, favourably, or well. **23.** towards the right hand; to the right. **24.** very (used in certain titles). –*v.t.* **25.** to bring or restore to an upright or the proper position. **26.** to set in order or put right. **27.** to redress (wrong, etc.). –*v.i.* **28.** to resume an upright or the proper position.

right angle *n.* an angle of 90°.

right-click *v.i.* to activate a computer function by pressing on the right-hand button on the mouse.

righteous /ˈraɪtʃəs/ *adj.* **1.** characterised by uprightness or morality. **2.** in accordance with right; upright or virtuous.

right-handed /raɪt-ˈhændəd/ *adj.* preferring to use the right hand. –**right-handedly**, *adv.* –**right-handedness**, *n.*

right of way *n.* **1.** the legal or customary right of a person, motor vehicle or vessel to proceed ahead of another. **2.** a right of passage, as over another's land.

right wing *n.* the members of a conservative or reactionary political party or group. –**right-wing**, *adj.* –**right-winger**, *n.*

rigid /ˈrɪdʒəd/ *adj.* stiff or unyielding; not pliant or flexible; hard.

rigmarole /ˈrɪgmərool/ *n.* a long and complicated process.

rigor mortis /rɪgə ˈmɔtəs/ *n.* the stiffening of the body after death.

rigour /ˈrɪgə/ *n.* **1.** strictness, severity, or harshness, as in dealing with persons. **2.** severity of life; hardship. Also, **rigor**. –**rigorous**, *adj.*

rile /raɪl/ *v.t.* (**riled**, **riling**) to irritate or vex.

rim /rɪm/ *n.* **1.** the outer edge, border, or margin, especially of a circular object. –*v.t.* (**rimmed**, **rimming**) **2.** to furnish with a rim, border, or margin. –**rimless**, *adj.*

rime /raɪm/ *n.* a rough, white icy covering deposited on trees, etc.

rind /raɪnd/ *n.* a thick and firm coat or covering, as of fruits, cheeses, etc.

ring¹ /rɪŋ/ *n.* **1.** a circular band of metal or other material, especially one for wearing on the finger. **2.** anything having the form of a circular band. **3.** a circular course. **4.** an enclosed circular or other area, as one in which some sport or exhibition takes place. **5.** a group of persons cooperating for selfish or illegal purposes. –*v.* (**ringed**, **ringing**) –*v.t.* **6.** to surround with a ring; encircle. **7.** to form into a ring. –*v.i.* **8.** to form a ring or rings. **9.** to move in a ring or a constantly curving course.

ring² /rɪŋ/ *v.* (**rang**, **rung**, **ringing**) –*v.i.* **1.** to give forth a clear, resonant sound when set in sudden vibration by a blow or otherwise, as a bell, glass, etc. **2.** to seem (true, false, etc.) in the effect produced on the mind. **3.** to cause a bell or bells to sound, especially as a summons. **4.** to be filled with sound; re-echo with sound, as a place. –*v.t.* **5.** to cause to ring. **6.** to proclaim, usher in or out, summon, signal, etc., by or as by the sound of a bell. **7.** to telephone. –*n.* **8.** a resonant sound or note. **9.** a telephone call. **10.** a characteristic or inherent quality. –*phr.* **11. ring a bell**, to arouse a memory; sound familiar. **12. ring off**, to end a telephone conversation. **13. ring the changes**, to vary the manner of performing an action, especially one that is often repeated; execute a number of manoeuvres or variations. **14. ring up**, **a.** to telephone. **b.** to record (the cost of an item) on a cash register.

ringbark /ˈrɪŋbak/ *v.t.* to cut away the bark in a ring around a tree trunk or branch, in order to kill the tree or the affected part.

ringer¹ /ˈrɪŋə/ *n.* a station hand, especially a stockman or drover.

ringer² /ˈrɪŋə/ *n. Colloq.* **1.** an athlete, horse, etc., entered in a competition under false representations as to identity or ability. **2.** a person or thing that closely resembles another.

ringer³ /ˈrɪŋə/ *n.* the fastest shearer of a group.

ring-in *n. Colloq.* **1.** someone who or that which does not belong in a group or set. **2.** a person substituted for another at the last minute. **3.** a thing substituted for another at the last minute, as a horse fraudulently substituted for another in a race.

ringlet /ˈrɪŋlət/ *n.* a curled lock of hair.

ringmaster /ˈrɪŋmastə/ *n.* one in charge of the performances in the ring of a circus.

ringside /ˈrɪŋsaɪd/ *n.* any place providing a close view.

ringtone /ˈrɪŋtoʊn/ *n. Telecommunications* **1.** a tone returned by receiving equipment that tells a caller that the called telephone is ringing. **2.** the sound produced by a mobile phone to indicate that a call is being received, originally a ringing sound, but now any of various recorded sounds, fragments of music, etc. Also, **ring tone**, **ringing tone**.

ringworm /ˈrɪŋwɜm/ *n.* → **tinea**.

rink /rɪŋk/ *n.* **1.** a sheet of ice for skating. **2.** a smooth floor for rollerskating.

rinse /rɪns/ *v.t.* (**rinsed, rinsing**) **1.** to put through clean water, as a final stage in cleansing. *–n.* **2.** an act or instance of rinsing. **3.** any liquid preparation used for impermanently tinting the hair.

riot /ˈraɪət/ *n.* **1.** any disturbance of the peace by an assembly of persons. **2.** an unbridled outbreak, as of emotions, passions, etc. **3.** a brilliant display. **4.** *Colloq.* someone who or that which causes great amusement, enthusiasm, etc. *–v.i.* **5.** to take part in a riot or disorderly public outbreak. *–phr.* **6. run riot**, to act without control or restraint. **–riotous,** *adj.*

rip[1] /rɪp/ *v.* (**ripped, ripping**) *–v.t.* **1.** to cut or tear apart or off in a rough or vigorous manner. *–v.i.* **2.** *Colloq.* to move along with violence and great speed. *–n.* **3.** a rent made by ripping; a tear.

rip[2] /rɪp/ *n.* a fast current, especially one at a beach, which can take swimmers out to sea.

ripcord /ˈrɪpkɔd/ *n.* a cord or ring which opens a parachute during a descent.

ripe /raɪp/ *adj.* complete in natural growth or development.

ripen /ˈraɪpən/ *v.i.* **1.** to become ripe. *–v.t.* **2.** to make ripe.

rip-off *n.* an excessive charge or exorbitant price; swindle. **–rip off,** *v.*

riposte /rəˈpɒst/ *n.* a quick, sharp return in speech or action. Also, **ripost.**

ripper /ˈrɪpə/ *n. Colloq.* something or someone exciting extreme admiration.

ripping /ˈrɪpɪŋ/ *adj. Colloq.* excellent, splendid, or fine.

ripple /ˈrɪpəl/ *v.i.* to form small waves or undulations on the surface, as water.

rise /raɪz/ *v.* (**rose, risen, rising**) *–v.i.* **1.** to get up from a lying, sitting, or kneeling posture; assume a standing position. **2.** to get up from bed. **3.** to become active in opposition or resistance; revolt or rebel. **4.** to spring up or grow. **5.** to move from a lower to a higher position; move upwards; ascend. **6.** to come above the horizon, as a heavenly body. **7.** to extend directly upwards. **8.** to attain higher rank, importance, etc. **9.** to prove oneself equal to a demand, emergency, etc. **10.** to become animated or cheerful, as the spirits. **11.** to swell or puff up, as dough from the action of yeast. **12.** to increase in amount, as prices, etc. **13.** to increase in price or value, as commodities. **14.** to increase in degree, intensity, or force, as colour, fever, etc. **15.** to become louder or of higher pitch, as the voice. **16.** to adjourn, or close a session, as a deliberative body or court. *–v.t.* **17.** to cause to rise. *–n.* **18.** the act of rising; upward movement or ascent. **19.** appearance above the horizon, as of the sun or moon. **20.** elevation or advance in rank, position, fortune, etc. **21.** an increase in amount, as of wages, salary, etc. **22.** an increase in degree or intensity, as of temperature. **23.** origin, source, or beginning. **24.** extension upwards. **25.** upward slope, as of ground or a road. *–phr.* **27. get** (or **take**) **a rise out of**, to provoke to anger, annoyance, etc., by banter, mockery, deception, etc.

risk /rɪsk/ *n.* **1.** a hazard or dangerous chance. **2.** *Insurance* **a.** the hazard or chance of loss. **b.** the amount which the insurance company may lose. **c.** the type of loss, as life, fire, theft, etc., against which insurance policies are drawn. *–v.t.* **3.** to expose to the chance of injury or loss, or hazard. **4.** to venture upon; take or run the risk of.

risotto /rəˈzɒtoʊ, rəˈsɒtoʊ/ *n.* (*pl.* **-tos**) an Italian dish of rice fried in butter with onion, flavoured with parmesan, and other flavourings.

risqué /ˈrɪskeɪ, rɪsˈkeɪ/ *adj.* daringly close to indelicacy or impropriety.

rissole /ˈrɪsoʊl/ *n.* a small fried ball, roll, or cake of minced meat or fish.

rite /raɪt/ *n.* a formal or ceremonial act or procedure prescribed or customary in religious or other solemn use.

ritual /ˈrɪtʃuəl/ *n.* **1.** an established or prescribed procedure, code, etc., for a religious or other rite. **2.** any solemn or customary action, code of behaviour, etc., regulating social conduct.

rival /ˈraɪvəl/ *n.* **1.** someone who is in pursuit of the same object as another, or strives to equal or outdo another; a competitor. *–adj.* **2.** being a rival. *–v.t.* (**-valled, -valling**) **3.** to strive to equal or outdo.

river /ˈrɪvə/ *n.* **1.** a defined watercourse of considerable size and length, whether flowing or dry according to the seasons, and whether a single channel or a number of diverging or converging channels. **2.** any abundant stream or copious flow.

rivet /ˈrɪvət/ *n.* **1.** a metal pin or bolt. *–v.t.* **2.** to fasten or fix firmly.

rivulet /ˈrɪvjələt/ *n.* a small stream.

roach[1] /roʊtʃ/ *n.* → **cockroach.**

roach[2] /roʊtʃ/ *n. Colloq.* the butt of a cigarette or joint (def. 4).

road /roʊd/ *n.* **1.** a way, usually open to the public for the passage of vehicles, persons, and animals. **2.** a way or course.

roadhog /ˈroʊdhɒg/ *n.* a motorist who drives without consideration for other road users.

roadhouse /ˈroʊdhaʊs/ *n.* an inn, hotel, restaurant, etc., on a main road.

roadie /ˈroʊdi/ *n. Colloq.* a road manager for a band.

roadkill /ˈroʊdkɪl/ *n.* the remains of any animal or animals struck and killed by a motor vehicle and lying on or beside a road.

road rage *n.* uncontrolled violent behaviour by a motorist, usually directed towards another motorist, resulting from the tensions and frustrations of driving.

roadrunner /ˈroʊdrʌnə/ *n.* a terrestrial cuckoo of the south western US.

road toll *n.* the tally of traffic accident deaths.

road train *n.* a group of articulated motor vehicles, used for transportation, especially of cattle.

roadway /ˈroʊdweɪ/ *n.* a way used as a road; a road.

roam /roʊm/ *v.i.* to walk, go, or travel about without fixed purpose or direction.

roan /roʊn/ *adj.* (chiefly of horses) brown sprinkled with grey or white.

roar /rɔ/ *v.i.* **1.** to utter a loud, deep sound, especially of excitement, distress, or anger. **2.** to laugh loudly or boisterously. **3.** to make a loud noise or din, as thunder, cannon, waves, wind, etc. –*v.t.* **4.** to utter or express in a roar. –*n.* **5.** the sound of roaring.

roast /rəʊst/ *v.t.* **1.** to bake (meat or other food) by dry heat, as in an oven. **2.** to brown by exposure to heat, as coffee. **3.** *Colloq.* to criticise, rebuke or ridicule severely. –*n.* **4.** a piece of roasted meat; roasted meat.

rob /rɒb/ *v.t.* (**robbed, robbing**) to deprive of something by unlawful force or threat of violence; steal from. **–robber,** *n.* **–robbery,** *n.*

robe¹ /rəʊb/ *n.* any long, loose garment.

robe² /rəʊb/ *n.* → **wardrobe**.

robin /'rɒbən/ *n.* **1.** any of various birds of Australasia and PNG, the male of some species having a red breast, similar to, but much brighter than, the unrelated European robin. **2.** any of several small birds of Europe and North America having a red or reddish breast.

robot /'rəʊbɒt/ *n.* **1.** a mechanical self-controlling apparatus designed to carry out a specific task, which would normally be performed by a human. **2.** *Computers* → **web crawler**.

robust /'rəʊbʌst, rə'bʌst/ *adj.* **1.** strong and healthy, hardy, or vigorous. **2.** suited to or requiring bodily strength or endurance. **3.** able to withstand critical analysis: *a robust report; a robust argument*.

rock¹ /rɒk/ *n.* **1.** *Geol.* mineral matter of various composition, assembled in masses or considerable quantities in nature. **2.** a large piece of stone. **3.** a stone of any size. **4.** something resembling or suggesting a rock. **5.** a firm foundation or support. –*phr.* **6. on the rocks**, **a.** *Colloq.* into or in a state of disaster or ruin. **b.** (of drinks) with ice-cubes.

rock² /rɒk/ *v.i.* **1.** to move or sway to and fro or from side to side. **2.** to cause to rock. –*n.* **3.** → **rock music**. **4.** → **rock'n'roll**.

rock-and-roll /rɒk-ən-'rəʊl/ *n.* → **rock'n'roll**.

rock art *n.* **1.** the art of creating pictures on rock surfaces by painting, drawing, or carving out sections of rock, traditionally practised by Australian Aboriginal peoples. **2.** a picture created on a rock surface.

rock bottom *n.* the lowest level, especially of fortune.

rock climbing *n.* the sport of climbing on steep rock faces, both sheer and uneven, using specialised ropes and equipment. Also, **rockclimbing. –rock climber,** *n.*

rocker /'rɒkə/ *n.* **1.** one of the curved pieces on which a cradle or a rocking chair rocks. **2.** any of various devices that operate with a rocking motion. –*phr.* **3. off one's rocker,** *Colloq.* crazy; mad; demented.

rockery /'rɒkəri/ *n.* (*pl.* **-ries**) a garden, or part of a garden, featuring rocks and plants which favour a rocky soil and are suited to dry, sunny conditions.

rocket¹ /'rɒkət/ *n.* **1.** *Aeronautics* a structure propelled by an emission of heated gas from the rear. –*v.i.* (**-eted, -eting**) **2.** to move like a rocket.

rocket² /'rɒkət/ *n.* a plant with bitter-tasting green leaves, commonly used in salads.

rocking chair *n.* a chair mounted on rockers, or on springs, so as to permit a rocking back and forth.

rocking horse *n.* a toy horse, mounted on rockers.

rockmelon /'rɒkmɛlən/ *n.* a type of melon with orange-coloured flesh; cantaloupe.

rock music *n.* any contemporary music which has developed from 1950s rock'n'roll.

rock'n'roll /rɒk-ən-'rəʊl/ *n.* a form of pop music of the 1950s which has a twelve bar blues form, and a heavily accented rhythm. Also, **rock, rock-and-roll, rock-'n'-roll.**

rock pool *n.* a swimming pool beside the sea which may be either artificially constructed or naturally occurring but which is made entirely or almost entirely of rocks in the locality, and which is filled and freshened by the recurring tides. Also, **rockpool.**

rock salt *n.* a common salt (sodium chloride), occurring in extensive, irregular beds in rock-like masses.

rocky road *n.* a confection made from chocolate, marshmallow and nuts.

rococo /rə'kəʊkəʊ/ *adj.* tastelessly or clumsily florid.

rod /rɒd/ *n.* **1.** a stick, wand, staff, shaft, or the like, of wood, metal, or other material. **2.** a pole used in angling or fishing. **3.** a stick used as an instrument of punishment. **4.** a wand or staff carried as a symbol of office, authority, power, etc.

rode /rəʊd/ *v.* past tense of **ride**.

rodent /'rəʊdnt/ *n.* one of the order of gnawing or nibbling mammals, that includes the mice, squirrels, beavers, etc.

rodeo /rəʊ'deɪoʊ, 'rəʊdioʊ/ *n.* (*pl.* **-deos**) a public exhibition, sometimes competitive, showing the skills of riding horses or steers bareback, roping calves and other similar activities deriving from work on a cattle station.

roe /rəʊ/ *n.* the mass of eggs, or spawn, of the female fish.

roesti /'rɒsti/ *n.* → **rosti**.

roger /'rɒdʒə/ *interj.* an expression of agreement, comprehension, etc.

rogue /rəʊg/ *n.* **1.** a dishonest person. **2.** a playfully mischievous person; rascal; scamp. **3.** an animal, especially an elephant, which is dangerously unpredictable, and tends to live apart from its group. –*adj.* **4.** having deviated from acceptable practice; not operating under normal controls: *a rogue cop; a rogue program*.

roister /'rɒɪstə/ *v.i.* to act in a swaggering, boisterous, or uproarious manner.

role /rəʊl/ *n.* **1.** the part or character which an actor presents in a play. **2.** proper or customary function.

roll /rəʊl/ *v.i.* **1.** to move along a surface by turning over and over, as a ball or a wheel. **2.** (oft. fol. by *along*) to move or be moved on wheels, as a vehicle or its occupants. **3.** to extend in undulations, as land. **4.** to continue with or have a deep, prolonged sound, as thunder, etc. **5.** to turn over, or over and over, as a person or animal lying down. **6.** to sway or rock from side to side, as a ship (opposed to *pitch*). **7.** to form into a roll, or curl up from itself. **8.** (fol. by *out*, etc.) to spread out from being rolled up; unroll. **9.** to spread out as under a roller. –*v.t.* **10.** to cause to roll. **11.** to cause to turn round in different directions, as the eyes. **12.** to make by forming a roll. **13.** to wrap or envelop, as in some covering. **14.** to operate upon so as to spread out, level, compact, or the like, as with a roller, rolling pin, etc. *−n.* **15.** a list, register, or catalogue. **16.** anything rolled up in cylindrical form. **17.** Also, **bread roll**. a small cake of bread. **18.** a deep, prolonged sound, as of thunder, etc. **19.** the continuous sound of a drum rapidly beaten. **20.** a single throw of dice. **21.** *Colloq.* a wad of paper currency.

rolled gold *n.* metal covered with a thin coating of gold.

roller /'roʊlə/ *n.* **1.** a cylinder, wheel, or the like, upon which something is rolled along. **2.** a cylinder of plastic, wire, etc., around which hair is rolled to set it. **3.** a cylindrical body for rolling over something to be spread out, levelled, crushed, compacted, impressed, linked, etc. **4.** any of various other revolving cylindrical bodies.

rollerblade /'roʊləbleɪd/ *(from trademark)* *−n.* **1.** one of a pair of rollerskates designed in imitation of an ice-skating shoe with a single row of rollers instead of a skate; inline skate. *−v.i.* **2.** to move on rollerblades. Also, **blade**.

roller-coaster /'roʊlə-koʊstə/ *n.* **1.** an amusement park ride, on a steep twisting track. *−adj.* **2.** experiencing severe fluctuations in direction or momentum, and apparently proceeding without control: *a roller-coaster economy.*

rollerskate /'roʊləskeɪt/ *n.* **1.** a form of skate running on small wheels or rollers. *−v.i.* **2.** to move on rollerskates. **−rollerskater**, *n.* **−rollerskating**, *n.*

rollicking /'rɒlɪkɪŋ/ *adj.* swaggering and jolly.

rolling strike *n.* industrial action by employees against their employer in which groups of employees go on strike consecutively.

rollout /'roʊlaʊt/ *n.* the launch of a new product, service, etc.: *the rollout of the new software was well publicised.* Also, **roll-out**.

rollover /'roʊloʊvə/ *adj.* **1.** of or relating to the investment of a superannuation payout with a government-approved institution that allows the deferral of lump sum tax. **2.** *Computers* of or relating to text or an image which appears when the cursor is rolled over a particular area on a computer screen. *−n.* **3.** *Computers* a rollover image or block of text. Also, **roll-over**.

roly-poly /,roʊli-'poʊli/ *adj.* **1.** plump. *−n.* *(pl.* **-lies)** **2.** a type of pudding.

ROM /rɒm/ *n.* *Computers* read-only memory; a computer storage device which holds data that can be read, but not altered, by program instructions.

Roman blind /roʊmən 'blaɪnd/ *n.* a window blind which pulls in soft folds to provide a horizontal pleated effect.

romance /rə'mæns, 'roʊmæns/ *n.* **1.** a tale depicting heroic or marvellous achievements. **2.** a made-up story; fanciful or extravagant invention or exaggeration. **3.** romantic character or quality. **4.** a romantic affair or experience; a love affair. *−v.i.* **(-manced, -mancing)** **5.** to think or talk romantically.

Roman numerals *pl. n.* the numerals in the ancient Roman system of notation, still used for

certain limited purposes. The common basic symbols are $I (= 1)$, $V (= 5)$, $X (= 10)$, $L (= 50)$, $C (= 100)$, $D (= 500)$, and $M (= 1000)$.

romantic /rə'mæntɪk/ *adj.* **1.** of, relating to, or of the nature of romance. **2.** proper to romance rather than to real or practical life. **3.** displaying or expressing love, emotion, strong affection, etc. **4.** imaginary, fictitious, or fabulous. *−n.* **5.** a romantic person.

romanticise /rə'mæntɪsaɪz/ *v.t.* **1.** to invest with a romantic character. *−v.i.* **2.** to have romantic ideas. Also, **romanticize**.

romp /rɒmp/ *v.i.* **1.** to play or frolic in a lively or boisterous manner. *−phr.* **2.** **romp home** (or **in**), to win easily.

rompers /'rɒmpəz/ *pl. n.* a one-piece loose outer garment for a baby.

roo /ru/ *n.* *Colloq.* a kangaroo.

roof /ruf/ *n. (pl.* **roofs** /rufs, ruvz/) **1.** the external upper covering of a house or other building. **2.** something which in form or position resembles the roof of a house.

rook[1] /rʊk/ *n.* **1.** a large black European bird like a crow. *−v.t.* **2.** to cheat; fleece; swindle.

rook[2] /rʊk/ *n.* a chess piece; castle.

rookery /'rʊkəri/ *n. (pl.* **-ries)** **1.** a colony of rooks. **2.** any instance of cheating, sharp practice, exorbitant prices, etc.

rookie /'rʊki/ *n.* *Colloq.* a raw recruit.

room /rum/ *n.* **1.** a portion of space within a building or other structure, separated by walls or partitions from other parts. **2.** space, or extent of space, occupied by or available for something. **3.** opportunity or scope for or to do something. *−v.i.* **4.** to occupy a room or rooms; to share a room; lodge.

roomy /'rumi/ *adj.* **(-mier, -miest)** affording ample room; spacious; large.

roost /rust/ *n.* **1.** a perch upon which domestic fowls rest at night. *−v.i.* **2.** to settle or stay, especially for the night.

rooster /'rustə/ *n.* a domestic cock.

root[1] /rut/ *n.* **1.** a part of the body of a plant which grows downwards into the soil, fixing the plant and absorbing nutriment and moisture. **2.** the embedded portion of a hair, tooth, nail, etc. **3.** the fundamental or essential part. **4.** the base or point of origin of something. **5.** *(pl.)* a person's real home and environment. **6.** *Maths* a quantity which, when multiplied by itself a certain number of times, produces a given quantity. *−v.i.* **7.** to send out roots and begin to grow. **8.** to become fixed or established. *−v.t.* **9.** to fix by, or as if by, roots. **10.** (fol. by *up, out,* etc.) to pull, tear, or dig up by the roots. **11.** *Colloq.* to break; ruin. **12.** *Colloq.* to have sexual intercourse with.

root[2] /rut/ *v.i.* **1.** (fol. by *around*) to poke, pry, or search, as if to find something. *−v.t.* **2.** (fol. by *up,* etc.) to unearth; bring to light.

rope /roʊp/ *n.* **1.** a strong, thick line or cord. **2.** death by hanging as a punishment. **3.** *(pl.)* methods; procedure; operations of a business, etc. *−v.t.* **(roped, roping)** **4.** to tie, bind, or fasten with a rope. **5.** *Colloq.* (fol. by *in*) to draw, entice, or inveigle into something.

ropeable /'roʊpəbəl/ *adj.* *Colloq.* extremely angry or bad-tempered. Also, **ropable**.

rort /rɔt/ *n.* *Colloq.* **1.** an incident or series of incidents involving reprehensible or suspect behaviour, especially by officials or politicians. **2.** a wild party. *–v.t.* **3.** to take wrongful advantage of; abuse: *to rort the system.*

rosary /'rouzəri/ *n.* (*pl.* **-ries**) **1.** a string of beads used for counting prayers in reciting them. **2.** the series of prayers recited.

rose[1] /rouz/ *n.* **1.** any of various showy-flowered shrubs. **2.** the flower of any such shrubs. **3.** an ornament shaped like or suggesting a rose. **4.** the traditional reddish colour of the rose. **5.** a perforated cap or plate at the end of a water pipe or the spout of a watering-can, etc., to break a flow of water into a spray.

rose[2] /rouz/ *v.* past tense of **rise**.

rosé /rou'zeɪ/ *n.* a light wine of a translucent pale red colour.

rosella /rou'zɛlə/ *n.* any of a number of brilliantly coloured parrots.

rosemary /'rouzməri/ *n.* an evergreen shrub used as a herb in cookery.

rosette /rou'zɛt/ *n.* any arrangement, part, object, or formation more or less resembling a rose.

rosin /'rɒzən/ *n.* a hard, brittle resin used in making varnish, for rubbing on violin bows, etc.

roster /'rɒstə/ *n.* a list of persons or groups with their turns or periods of duty. –**rostered**, *adj.*

rosti /'rɒsti/ *n.* in Swiss cooking, grated potato mixed with other ingredients, as cheese, bacon, egg, tomato, vegetables, and then fried on both sides. Also, **rösti**, **roesti** /'rɜsti/.

rostrum /'rɒstrəm/ *n.* (*pl.* **-trums** *or* **-tra** /-trə/) any platform, stage, or the like, for public speaking.

rosy /'rouzi/ *adj.* (**-sier**, **-siest**) **1.** pink or pinkish red. **2.** (of persons, the cheeks, lips, etc.) having a fresh, healthy redness. **3.** bright or promising. **4.** cheerful or optimistic.

rot /rɒt/ *v.* (**rotted**, **rotting**) *–v.i.* **1.** to undergo decomposition; decay. *–v.t.* **2.** to cause to rot. *–n.* **3.** rotting or rotten matter. **4.** any of various diseases characterised by decomposition. **5.** *Colloq.* nonsense.

rotary /'routəri/ *adj.* **1.** turning round as on an axis, as an object. **2.** having a part or parts that rotate, as a machine.

rotate /rou'teɪt/ *v.t.* **1.** to cause to turn round like a wheel on its axis. *–v.i.* **2.** to turn round as on an axis. **3.** to proceed in a fixed routine of succession. –**rotation**, *n.*

rote /rout/ *phr.* **by rote**, in a mechanical way without thought of the meaning.

rotisserie /rou'tɪsəri/ *n.* a mechanical spit on which meat, poultry, and game can be cooked.

rotten /'rɒtn/ *adj.* **1.** in a state of decomposition or decay; putrid. **2.** *Colloq.* wretchedly bad, unsatisfactory, or unpleasant. **3.** contemptible. **4.** *Colloq.* extremely drunk.

rotund /rou'tʌnd/ *adj.* rounded; plump.

rotunda /rə'tʌndə/ *n.* a round building, especially one with a dome.

rouge /ruʒ/ *n.* **1.** any of various red cosmetics for colouring the cheeks or lips. *–v.t.* (**rouged**, **rouging**) **2.** to colour with rouge.

rough /rʌf/ *adj.* **1.** uneven from projections, irregularities, or breaks of surface; not smooth. **2.** shaggy. **3.** acting with or characterised by violence. **4.** bad-mannered or rude. **5.** *Colloq.* severe, hard, or unpleasant. **6.** without refinements, luxuries, or ordinary comforts or

conveniences. **7.** requiring exertion or strength rather than intelligence or skill, as work. **8.** unpolished, as language, verse, style, etc. **9.** made or done without any attempt at exactness, completeness, or thoroughness. *–n.* **10.** that which is rough. **11.** the rough, hard, or unpleasant side or part of anything. *–adv.* **12.** in a rough manner; roughly. *–v.t.* **13.** (oft. fol. by *up*) to treat roughly or harshly. **14.** (fol. by *in* or *out*) to cut, shape, or sketch roughly. –**roughness**, *n.*

roughage /'rʌfɪdʒ/ *n.* the coarser parts of food, of little nutritive value, but aiding digestion.

roughhouse /'rʌfhaus/ *Colloq.* *–n.* **1.** noisy, disorderly behaviour or play. *–v.i.* **2.** to engage or take part in a roughhouse. *–adj.* **3.** resembling a roughhouse; boisterous; violent: *roughhouse tactics.*

roughly /'rʌfli/ *adv.* **1.** in a crude, harsh or violent manner. **2.** approximately; about.

rouleau /'rulou/ *n.* (*pl.* **-leaux** *or* **-leaus** /-louz/) a number of coins put up in cylindrical form in a paper wrapping.

roulette /ru'lɛt/ *n.* **1.** a gambling game played at a table. **2.** a small wheel, especially one with sharp teeth, mounted in a handle, for making lines of marks, dots, or perforations.

round /raund/ *adj.* **1.** circular, as a disc. **2.** ring-shaped, as a hoop. **3.** curved like part of a circle, as an outline. **4.** spherical or globular, as a ball. **5.** free from angularity; curved, as parts of the body. **6.** full, complete, or entire. **7.** roughly correct. **8.** considerable in amount. *–n.* **9.** something round. **10.** any complete course, series, or succession. **11.** (*sometimes pl.*) a circuit of any place, series of places, etc., covered in a customary or predetermined way. **12.** a distribution of drink, etc., to all the members of a company. **13.** a standard cut of beef from the lower part of the butt. **14. a.** (of bread) a slice. **b.** a sandwich. *–adv.* **15.** in a circle, ring, or the like, or so as to surround something. **16.** on all sides, or about, whether circularly or otherwise. **17.** in a circular or rounded course. **18.** throughout, or from beginning to end of, a recurring period of time. **19.** by a circuitous or roundabout course. **20.** with change to another or opposite direction, course, opinion, etc. *–prep.* **21.** so as to encircle, surround, or envelop. **22.** around; about. **23.** in the vicinity of. **24.** so as to make a turn or partial circuit about or to the other side of. *–v.t.* **25.** to free from angularity or flatness. **26.** to encircle or surround. *–v.i.* **27.** to become free from angularity; become plump. **28.** to develop to completeness or perfection. *–phr.* **29. a round of applause**, a single outburst of cheering, clapping, etc. **30. round on** (or **upon**), to attack, usually verbally, with sudden and often unexpected vigour. **31. round the bend** (or **twist**), *Colloq.* insane. **32. round up**, to collect (cattle, people, etc.) in a particular place or for a particular purpose.

roundabout /'raundəbaut/ *n.* **1.** → **merry-go-round**. **2.** a road junction at which the flow of traffic is facilitated by moving in one direction only round a circular arrangement. *–adj.* **3.** circuitous or indirect.

rounders /'raundəz/ *pl. n.* (*construed as sing.*) a game played with bat and ball.

roundly /ˈraʊndli/ *adv.* vigorously or briskly.

round table *n.* a number of persons assembled for conference or discussion of some subject, and considered as meeting on equal terms.

rouse¹ /raʊz/ *v.t.* to bring or come out of a state of sleep, unconsciousness, inactivity, fancied security, apathy, depression, etc.

rouse² /raʊs/ *v.i.* (fol. by *on*, *at*) scold, upbraid.

rouseabout /ˈraʊsəbaʊt/ *n.* a general hand on a station, in a hotel, etc. Also, **roustabout**.

rout¹ /raʊt/ *n.* 1. a defeat attended with disorderly flight. 2. a clamour or fuss. –*v.t.* 3. to defeat utterly.

rout² /raʊt/ *v.t.* to turn over or dig up with the snout, as swine.

route /rut/, *Chiefly US and Computers* /raʊt/ *n.* 1. a way or road taken or planned for passage or travel. 2. *Computers* any path, such as that between hosts in a computer network. –*v.t.* (**routed, routeing** *or* **routing**) 3. to send or forward by a particular route.

router /ˈraʊtə/ *n. Computers* a device used in connecting networks which configures the best route between hosts; gateway.

routine /ruˈtin/ *n.* 1. a customary or regular course of procedure. 2. *Computers* a set of orders which cause a digital computer to perform some simple function. –*adj.* 3. of the nature of, proceeding by, or adhering to routine. –**routinely**, *adv.*

rove /roʊv/ *v.i.* to wander about without definite destination.

row¹ /roʊ/ *n.* a number of persons or things arranged in a straight line.

row² /roʊ/ *v.i.* 1. to use oars or the like for propelling a boat. –*v.t.* 2. to propel (a boat, etc.) by or as by the use of oars. –*n.* 3. an act of rowing.

row³ /raʊ/ *n.* 1. a noisy dispute or quarrel; commotion. 2. *Colloq.* noise or clamour.

rowdy /ˈraʊdi/ *adj.* (**-dier, -diest**) rough and disorderly.

rowlock /ˈrɒlək/ *n.* a device on which an oar rests and swings.

royal /ˈrɔɪəl/ *adj.* 1. of or relating to a sovereign, king, queen, or the like, or sovereignty. 2. established or chartered by, or existing under the patronage of, a sovereign.

royalist /ˈrɔɪəlɪst/ *n.* a supporter or adherent of a king or a royal government.

royalty /ˈrɔɪəlti/ *n.* (*pl.* **-ties**) 1. royal persons collectively. 2. royal status, dignity, or power; sovereignty. 3. a compensation or portion of proceeds paid to the owner of a right, as a patent, for the use of it. 4. an agreed portion of the proceeds from his or her work, paid to an author, composer, etc.

-rrhagia variant of **-rhagia**. Also, **-rrhage**, **-rrhagy**.

RSI /ar ɛs ˈaɪ/ *n.* repetition strain injury; an injury resulting in inflammation of the tendon sheath of a muscle, caused by the excessive repetition of a movement over a period of time.

rub /rʌb/ *v.* (**rubbed, rubbing**) –*v.t.* 1. to subject (an object) to pressure and friction, especially in order to clean, smooth, polish, etc. 2. to move, spread, or apply (something) with pressure and friction over something else. 3. (fol. by *together*, etc.) to move (things) with pressure and friction over each other. 4. (fol.

by *off*, *out*, etc.) to remove or erase by rubbing. 5. to chafe or abrade. –*v.i.* 6. to exert pressure and friction on something. 7. to admit of being rubbed (*off*, etc.). –*n.* 8. the act of rubbing. 9. a difficulty; source of doubt or difficulty. –*phr.* 10. **rub it in**, to remind someone repeatedly of their mistakes, failures or shortcomings. 11. **rub off on**, to be transferred to, especially as a result of repeated close contact.

rubber¹ /ˈrʌbə/ *n.* 1. an elastic material, derived from the latex of certain plants. 2. a synthetic material resembling rubber. 3. a piece of rubber for erasing pencil marks, etc.

rubber² /ˈrʌbə/ *n. Bridge, Whist, etc.* a set of games.

rubberneck /ˈrʌbənɛk/ *n. Colloq.* an extremely or excessively curious person. Also, **rubbernecker**.

rubber plant *n.* an ornamental house plant.

rubber stamp *n.* 1. a device of rubber for printing dates, etc., by hand. 2. *Colloq.* someone who gives approval without consideration, or without demur.

rubbish /ˈrʌbɪʃ/ *n.* 1. waste or refuse material; debris; litter. 2. worthless stuff; trash. 3. nonsense. –*v.t.* 4. *Colloq.* to speak of scornfully; criticise; denigrate.

rubble /ˈrʌbəl/ *n.* rough fragments of broken stone.

rubella /ruˈbɛlə/ *n.* a contagious disease, usually mild, accompanied by fever, often some sore throat, and a rash resembling that of scarlet fever, causing birth defects in the first three months of pregnancy; German measles.

rubric /ˈrubrɪk/ *n.* a title, heading, direction, or the like, in a manuscript, book, etc.

ruby /ˈrubi/ 1. a red gemstone. 2. deep red; carmine. –*adj.* 3. ruby-coloured. 4. made from or containing a ruby.

ruck /rʌk/ *n.* 1. *Aust. Rules* a group of three players who do not have fixed positions. 2. *Rugby Football* a group of players struggling for the ball in no set pattern of play.

rucksack /ˈrʌksæk/ *n.* → **knapsack**.

ruction /ˈrʌkʃən/ *n. Colloq.* a disturbance, quarrel or row.

rudder /ˈrʌdə/ *n.* a board or plate of wood or metal hinged vertically at the stern of a boat or ship as a means of steering. –**rudderless**, *adj.*

ruddy /ˈrʌdi/ *adj.* (**-dier, -diest**) 1. reddish. –*adv.* 2. *Colloq.* extremely.

rude /rud/ *adj.* 1. discourteous or impolite. 2. without culture, learning, or refinement.

rudimentary /rudəˈmɛntəri, -tri/ *adj.* 1. relating to rudiments or first principles; elementary. 2. undeveloped.

rudiments /ˈrudəmənts/ *pl. n.* the elements or first principles of a subject.

rue¹ /ru/ *v.t.* (**rued, ruing**) to feel sorrow over; repent of; regret bitterly.

rue² /ru/ *n.* a yellow-flowered herb.

ruff /rʌf/ *n.* 1. a collar of lace, etc., gathered into deep, full, regular folds. 2. a collar of long or specially marked hairs or feathers, on the neck of an animal or bird.

ruffian /ˈrʌfiən/ *n.* a violent, lawless man; a rough brute.

ruffle /ˈrʌfəl/ *v.t.* 1. to destroy the smoothness or evenness of. 2. to annoy, disturb, or irritate. 3. to draw up (cloth, lace, etc.) into a ruffle by gathering along one edge. –v.i. **4.** to be or become ruffled. –n. **5.** a break in the smoothness or evenness of some surface. **6.** a strip of cloth, lace, etc., drawn up by gathering along one edge, and used as a trimming on dress, etc.

rug /rʌg/ n. **1.** a small, often thick, carpet. **2.** a thick, warm blanket. –v.t. (**rugged**, **rugging**) **3.** (usu. fol. by *up*) to dress (oneself) in thick clothing, etc.

Rugby football /'rʌgbi/ n. either of two forms of football, **Rugby League** and **Rugby Union**, played by teams of 13 and 15 players respectively.

rugged /'rʌgəd/ adj. **1.** roughly broken, rocky, hilly, or otherwise difficult of passage. **2.** severe, hard, or trying.

ruin /'ruən/ n. **1.** (pl.) the remains of a fallen building, town, etc., or of anything in a state of destruction or decay. **2.** a ruined building, town, etc. **3.** fallen and wrecked or decayed state; ruinous condition. **4.** the downfall, decay, or destruction of anything. **5.** the complete loss of means, position, or the like. –v.t. **6.** to reduce to ruin. –**ruinous**, adj.

rule /rul/ n. **1.** a principle or regulation governing conduct, action, procedure, arrangement, etc. **2.** that which customarily or normally occurs or holds good. **3.** control, government, or dominion. –v. (**ruled**, **ruling**) –v.t. **4.** to control or direct; exercise dominating power or influence over. **5.** to declare judicially; decree. **6.** to mark with lines, especially parallel straight lines, with the aid of a ruler or the like. –v.i. **7.** to exercise dominating power or influence. **8.** to prevail or be current. –phr. **9. rule out,** to exclude; refuse to admit.

ruler /'rulə/ n. **1.** someone who or that which rules or governs. **2.** a strip of wood, metal, or other material with a graduated straight edge, used in drawing lines, measuring, etc.

rum /rʌm/ n. an alcoholic spirit.

rumba /'rʌmbə/ n. a dance, originally from Cuba. Also, **rhumba**.

rumble /'rʌmbəl/ v.i. **1.** to make a deep, heavy, continuous, resonant sound, as thunder, etc. **2.** to fight. –n. **3.** Colloq. a fight, especially between teenage gangs.

rumbustious /rʌm'bʌstʃəs/ adj. boisterous; noisy.

ruminant /'rumənənt/ n. any of the cloven-hoofed, cud-chewing quadrupeds, as cattle, sheep, goats, etc.

ruminate /'ruməneɪt/ v.i. to meditate or muse; ponder.

rummage /'rʌmɪdʒ/ v. (**-maged, -maging**) –v.t. **1.** to search thoroughly or actively through (a place, receptacle, etc.). **2.** (fol. by *out* or *up*) to find by searching. –v.i. **3.** to search actively, as in a place or receptacle. –n. **4.** miscellaneous articles; odds and ends. **5.** a rummaging search.

rummy /'rʌmi/ n. a card game.

rumour /'rumə/ n. **1.** a story or statement in general circulation without confirmation or certainty as to facts. –v.t. **2.** to circulate, report, or assert by a rumour. Also, **rumor**.

rump /rʌmp/ n. the hinder part of the body of an animal.

rumple /'rʌmpəl/ v.t. **1.** to draw or crush into wrinkles; crumple. –v.i. **2.** to become wrinkled or crumpled.

rumpus /'rʌmpəs/ n. Colloq. disturbing noise; uproar.

run /rʌn/ v. (**ran, run, running**) –v.i. **1.** to move quickly on foot, so as to go more rapidly than in walking. **2.** to move easily or swiftly. **3.** to make a short, quick, or casual journey, as for a visit, etc. **4.** to stand as a candidate for election. **5.** to traverse a route, as a public conveyance. **6.** to melt and flow, as solder, varnish, etc. **7.** to flow, stream, or be wet with a liquid. **8.** to recur or be inherent. **9.** to come undone, as stitches or a fabric; ladder. **10.** to be in operation or continue operating. **11.** to exist or occur within a specified range of variation. **12.** to pass into a certain state or condition; become. –v.t. **13.** to cause (an animal, etc.) to move quickly on foot. **14.** to cause (a vehicle, etc.) to move. **15.** to traverse (a distance or course) in running. **16.** to perform by or as by running. **17.** to run or get past or through: *to run the lights.* **18.** to keep (livestock), as on pasture. **19.** to cause to move, especially quickly or cursorily. **20.** to convey or transport, as in a vessel or vehicle. **21.** to keep operating or in service, as a machine. **22.** to expose oneself to or be exposed to (a risk, etc.). **23.** to bring, lead, or force into some state, action, etc. **24.** to conduct, administer, or manage, as a business, an experiment, or the like. –n. **25.** an act, instance, or spell of running. **26.** a running pace. **27.** an act or instance of escaping, running away, etc. **28.** a quick, short trip. **29.** the amount of something produced in any uninterrupted period of operation. **30.** a line or place in knitted or sewn work where a series of stitches have slipped or come undone; a ladder. **31.** freedom to range over, go through, or use. **32.** any rapid or easy course or progress. **33.** a continuous course of some condition of affairs, etc. **34.** a continuous series of something. **35.** any continued or extensive demand, call, or the like. **36.** a series of sudden and urgent demands for payment, as on a bank. **37.** the ordinary or average kind. **38.** an enclosure within which domestic animals may range about. **39.** the area and habitual route covered by a vendor who delivers goods to houses, etc. **40.** a large area of grazing land; a rural property. **41.** a score unit in cricket. –phr. **42. in the long run,** ultimately. **43. run down, a.** to slow up before stopping, as a clock or other mechanism. **b.** to knock down and injure, as a vehicle or driver; run over. **c.** to denigrate; make adverse criticism of. **d.** to reduce, as stocks. **e.** to find, especially after extensive searching. **44. run in, a.** to operate (new machinery, especially a motor vehicle) carefully for an initial period, so that the machine becomes ready for full operation without damage. **b.** Colloq. → arrest. **45. run off, a.** to depart or retreat quickly. **b.** to produce by a printing or similar process. **c.** to write or otherwise create quickly. **46. run over, a.** to knock down and injure, as a vehicle or driver. **b.** to exceed (a time-limit or the like). **c.** to review, rehearse, or recapitulate. **47. run up, a.** to amass or incur, as a bill. **b.** to make, especially quickly, as something sewn. **48. the runs**, *Colloq.* diarrhoea.

run-down *adj.* /ˈrʌn-ˈdaʊn/ **1.** in a poor or deteriorated state of health; depressed, sick, or tired. **2.** fallen into disrepair. –*n.* /ˈrʌn-daʊn/ **3.** a cursory review or summary of points of information: *a brief run-down of past events.*

rung[1] /rʌŋ/ *v.* past tense and past participle of **ring**[2].

rung[2] /rʌŋ/ *n.* one of the rounded pieces forming the steps of a ladder.

runnel /ˈrʌnəl/ *n.* a small channel, as for water.

runner /ˈrʌnə/ *n.* **1.** one acting as collector, agent, or the like for a bank, broker, etc. **2.** one whose business it is to solicit patronage or trade. **3.** something in or on which something else runs or moves, as the strips of wood that guide a drawer, etc. **4.** a long, narrow strip, as of material. **5.** a plant which spreads by sending out long stems which grow roots and form new plants, or these stems themselves. **6.** → **jogger** (def. 2).

runner-up /ˈrʌnər-ˈʌp/ *n.* (*pl.* **runners-up**) the competitor, player, or team finishing in second place.

running /ˈrʌnɪŋ/ *adj.* **1.** that runs; moving or passing rapidly or smoothly. **2.** creeping or climbing, as plants. **3.** slipping or sliding easily, as a knot or a noose. **4.** operating, as a machine. **5.** cursive, as handwriting. **6.** going or carried on continuously; sustained. **7.** following in succession (placed after the noun). **8.** discharging matter, especially fluid, as a sore. –*phr.* **9. in the running**, having a chance of success.

running account *n.* an account kept with a shop, business, etc., so that goods can be supplied as needed, the total debt being paid at agreed intervals.

running stitch *n.* a small, even stitch used for seams, gathering, quilting, etc.

runny /ˈrʌni/ *adj.* **1.** (of matter) fluid or tending to flow. **2.** tending to flow with or discharge liquid.

run-off /ˈrʌn-ɒf/ *n.* **1.** a deciding final contest held after a principal one. **2.** something which runs off, as rain which flows off from the land in streams.

run-of-the-mill /ˈrʌn-əv-ðə-mɪl/ *adj.* ordinary; mediocre; commonplace.

runout campaign /ˈrʌnaʊt/ *n.* a vigorous program to sell previous model cars before the release of the latest model.

runt /rʌnt/ *n.* the smallest in a litter.

runway /ˈrʌnweɪ/ *n.* **1.** a paved or cleared strip on which aeroplanes land and take off; airstrip. **2.** → **catwalk** (def. 2).

rupture /ˈrʌptʃə/ *n.* **1.** the state of being broken or burst. –*v.t.* **2.** to break or burst (a blood vessel, etc.). **3.** to cause a breach of (relations, etc.).

rural /ˈrʊrəl/ *adj.* of, relating to, or characteristic of the country (as distinguished from towns or cities).

ruse /ruz/ *n.* a trick, stratagem, or artifice.

rush[1] /rʌʃ/ *v.i.* **1.** to move or go with speed, rash haste, or violence. –*v.t.* **2.** to send or drive with speed or violence. **3.** to perform, complete, or organise (some process or activity) with special haste. **4.** to attack with a rush. –*n.* **5.** the act of rushing; a rapid, impetuous, or headlong onward movement. **6.** a sudden coming or access. **7.** a hurried state, as from pressure of affairs. **8.** a period of intense activity. **9.** (fol. by *on*) a great demand for a commodity, etc. –*adj.* **10.** requiring or performed with haste. **11.** characterised by rush or press of work, traffic, etc.

rush[2] /rʌʃ/ *n.* **1.** any of several grass-like herbs with pithy or hollow stems, found in wet or marshy places. **2.** a stem of such a plant, used for making chair bottoms, mats, baskets, etc.

rusk /rʌsk/ *n.* a crisp cake, given especially to babies when teething, and invalids.

russet /ˈrʌsət/ *n.*, *adj.* reddish brown; light brown; yellowish brown.

rust /rʌst/ *n.* **1.** the red or orange coating which forms on the surface of iron when exposed to air and moisture. **2.** rust colour; reddish brown or orange. –*v.i.* **3.** to grow rusty, as iron does; corrode. **4.** to deteriorate or become impaired, as through inaction or disuse. –*v.t.* **5.** to impair as if with rust.

rustic /ˈrʌstɪk/ *adj.* **1.** rural. **2.** made of roughly dressed limbs or roots of trees, as garden seats, etc. –*n.* **3.** an unsophisticated country person.

rustle /ˈrʌsəl/ *v.* (**-tled, -tling**) –*v.t.* **1.** to make a succession of slight, soft sounds, as of parts rubbing gently one on another, as leaves, silks, papers, etc. **2.** to move or stir so as to cause a rustling sound. **3.** to steal (cattle, etc.). **4.** *Colloq.* (oft. fol. by *up*) to move, bring, get, etc., by energetic action. –*n.* **5.** the sound made by anything that rustles.

rut[1] /rʌt/ *n.* **1.** any furrow, groove, etc. **2.** a fixed or established way of life; a dull routine.

rut[2] /rʌt/ *n.* the periodically recurring sexual excitement of the deer, goat, sheep, etc.

ruthless /ˈruθləs/ *adj.* without pity or compassion; pitiless; merciless.

-ry a suffix of abstract nouns of condition, practice and collectives.

rye /raɪ/ *n.* **1.** a widely cultivated cereal grass. **2.** its seeds or grain. **3.** an American whisky distilled from rye.

S, s

S, s /ɛs/ n. the 19th letter of the English alphabet.

's¹ an ending which marks the possessive singular of nouns, as in *man's*.

's² an ending which marks the possessive plural of nouns, as in *men's*.

's³ colloquial reduction of: **1.** is: *he's here*. **2.** has. **3.** does. **4.** us.

-s¹ a suffix serving to form adverbs, as *always*, *evenings*, *needs*, *unawares*. Compare **-ways**.

-s² an ending which marks the third person singular indicative active of verbs, as in *hits*.

-s³ 1. an ending which marks the regular plural of nouns, as in *dogs*. **2.** a quasi-plural ending occurring in nouns for which there is no proper singular, as *trousers*, *shorts*, *scissors*.

Sabbath /'sæbəθ/ n. **1.** the seventh day of the week (Saturday) as the day of rest and religious observance among the Jews and certain Christian sects. **2.** the first day of the week (Sunday), similarly observed by most Christians in commemoration of the resurrection of Christ.

sabbatical /sə'bætɪkəl/ n. a year, term, or other period of freedom from duties, granted to a university teacher or someone in one of certain other professional areas, often after seven years of service, as for study or travel. Also, **sabbatical leave**.

sable /'seɪbəl/ n. **1.** a small mammal of the weasel family valued for its dark brown fur. *-adj.* **2.** made of the fur or hair of the sable. **3.** *Poetic* black; very dark.

sabotage /'sæbətaʒ/ n. **1.** malicious injury to work, tools, machinery, etc. **2.** any malicious attack on or undermining of a cause. *-v.t.* (**-taged**, **-taging**) **3.** to injure or attack by sabotage. **-saboteur**, n.

sabre /'seɪbə/ n. **1.** a heavy one-edged sword. **2.** a light sword for fencing and duelling.

sac /sæk/ n. a bag-like structure in an animal or plant, as one containing fluid.

saccharide /'sækəraɪd/ n. any sugar or other carbohydrate, especially a simple sugar.

saccharin /'sækərən, -krən/ n. a very sweet crystalline compound. Also, **saccharine**.

saccharine /'sækərən, -krən/ adj. **1.** of a sugary sweetness. *-n.* **2.** → **saccharin**.

sachet /'sæʃeɪ/ n. a small sealed bag used for packaging a variety of goods.

sack¹ /sæk/ n. **1.** a large bag of stout woven material. **2.** a woman's loose-fitting, unbelted dress. *-v.t.* **3.** *Colloq.* to dismiss or discharge, as from employment. *-phr.* **4. the sack**, *Colloq.* dismissal or discharge, as from employment.

sack² /sæk/ v.t. **1.** to pillage or loot after capture; plunder. *-n.* **2.** the plundering of a captured place; pillage.

sacrament /'sækrəmənt/ n. something regarded as possessing a sacred character or a mysterious significance.

sacred /'seɪkrəd/ adj. **1.** relating to or connected with religion (opposed to *profane* and

secular). **2.** properly immune from violence, interference, etc., as a person or their office.

sacred site n. **1.** (in Australia) a site that is sacred to Aboriginal people or is otherwise of significance according to Aboriginal tradition. **2.** a site or institution that has particular religious, cultural or historical significance.

sacrifice /'sækrəfaɪs/ n. **1.** the offering of life (animal, plant, or human) or some material possession, etc., to a deity, as in propitiation or homage. **2.** the surrender or destruction of something prized or desirable for the sake of something considered as having a higher or more pressing claim. **3.** the thing so surrendered or devoted. **4.** a loss incurred in selling something below its value. *-v.t.* (**-ficed**, **-ficing**) **5.** to make a sacrifice or offering of. **6.** to dispose of (goods, etc.) regardless of profit. **-sacrificial**, adj.

sacrilege /'sækrəlɪdʒ/ n. the violation of anything sacred or held sacred. **-sacrilegious**, adj.

sacro- a word element meaning 'holy'.

sacrosanct /'sækrəsæŋkt/ adj. especially or superlatively sacred or inviolable.

sad /sæd/ adj. (**sadder**, **saddest**) **1.** sorrowful or mournful. **2.** causing sorrow. **-sadly**, adv. **-sadness**, n.

saddle /'sædl/ n. **1.** a seat for a rider on the back of a horse or other animal. **2.** a similar seat on a bicycle, machine, etc. **3.** something resembling a saddle in shape or position. *-v.t.* **4.** to put a saddle upon (a horse, etc.). **5.** to load or charge, as with a burden.

sadism /'sædɪzəm, 'seɪ-/ n. **1.** sexual gratification gained through causing physical pain and humiliation. **2.** any enjoyment in inflicting mental or physical pain. **-sadistic**, adj. **-sadist**, n.

sadomasochism /ˌseɪdoʊ'mæsəkɪzəm, ˌsædoʊ-/ n. a disturbed condition of the mind marked by the presence of sadistic and masochistic tendencies. **-sadomasochistic**, adj. **-sadomasochist**, n.

safari /sə'fari/ n. (pl. **-ris**) a journey; an expedition, especially for hunting.

safe /seɪf/ adj. **1.** secure from liability to harm, injury, danger, or risk. **2.** involving no risk of mishap, error, etc. *-n.* **3.** any receptacle or structure for the storage or preservation of articles. *-phr.* **4. play safe**, to act cautiously.

safe-conduct /seɪf-'kɒndʌkt/ n. a conducting in safety.

safe-deposit adj. providing safekeeping for valuables.

safeguard /'seɪfgad/ n. **1.** something serving as a protection or defence, or ensuring safety. *-v.t.* **2.** to guard; protect; secure.

safe sex n. any sexual practices in which precautions are taken to prevent the transmission of sexually transmitted diseases.

safety /'seɪfti/ n. **1.** the state of being safe; freedom from injury or danger. **2.** the quality of insuring against hurt, injury, danger, or risk.

safety belt n. → **seatbelt**.

safety pin n. a pin bent back on itself to form a spring, with a guard to cover the point.

safflower /'sæflaʊə/ n. a thistlelike herb cultivated for its oil which is used in cookery, cosmetics, etc.

saffron /'sæfrɒn, 'sæfrən/ n. a crocus having handsome purple flowers with orange stigmas used to colour food and as a spice.

sag /sæg/ v.i. (**sagged, sagging**) 1. to sink or bend downwards by weight or pressure, especially in the middle. 2. to decline, as in price. −n. 3. the degree of sagging. 4. a place where anything sags; a depression. 5. moderate decline in prices.

saga /'sagə/ n. any narrative or legend of heroic exploits.

sagacious /sə'geɪʃəs/ adj. having acute mental discernment and keen practical sense; shrewd. −**sagacity**, n.

sage[1] /seɪdʒ/ n. 1. a profoundly wise person. −adj. 2. named or mentioned before. (**sager, sagest**) 2. wise, judicious, or prudent.

sage[2] /seɪdʒ/ n. a perennial plant used for seasoning in cookery.

sago /'seɪgoʊ/ n. starchy food used in making puddings, and other dishes.

said /sɛd/ v. 1. past tense and past participle of say. −adj. 2. named or mentioned before.

sail /seɪl/ n. 1. an expanse of canvas or similar material spread to the wind to make a vessel move through the water. 2. some similar piece or apparatus. 3. a voyage or excursion, especially in a sailing vessel. −v.i. 4. to travel in a vessel conveyed by the action of wind, steam, etc. 5. to move along in a manner suggestive of a sailing vessel. −v.t. 6. to sail upon, over, or through. 7. to navigate (a ship, etc.). −**sailor**, n.

sailboard /'seɪlbɔd/ n. 1. a lightweight, polyurethane surfboard, equipped with a mast and sail, on which the rider stands to manoeuvre the sail. −v.i. 2. to ride on a sailboard.

saint /seɪnt/ n. a person of great holiness. Abbrev.: S, (plural SS), St

sake[1] /seɪk/ n. 1. cause, account, or interest. 2. purpose or end.

sake[2] /'saki/ n. a Japanese alcoholic drink made from fermented rice. Also, **saki**.

sal /sæl/ n. Chiefly Pharmaceutical salt.

salacious /sə'leɪʃəs/ adj. lustful or lecherous.

salad /'sæləd/ n. a dish of uncooked vegetables, typically served with a savoury dressing.

salad days pl. n. days of youthful inexperience.

salamander /'sæləmændə/ n. 1. any of various tailed amphibians, most of which have an aquatic larval stage but are terrestrial as adults. 2. a mythical lizard or other reptile, or a being supposedly able to live in fire.

salami /sə'lami/ n. a kind of sausage, originally Italian, often flavoured with garlic.

salary /'sæləri/ n. (pl. **-ries**) a fixed periodical payment, usually monthly, paid to a person for regular work or services. −**salaried**, adj.

sale /seɪl/ n. 1. the act of selling. 2. the quantity sold. 3. a special disposal of goods, as at reduced prices. 4. transfer of property for money or credit. −phr. 5. **for sale** or **on sale**, offered to be sold; offered to purchasers.

salesperson /'seɪlzpɜsən/ n. (pl. **-people** or **-persons**) someone employed to sell goods, as in a shop, etc.

sales tax n. a tax imposed on the seller of goods in respect of goods sold, but generally passed on to the ultimate consumer in the retail price.

salient /'seɪliənt/ adj. prominent or conspicuous.

saline /'seɪlaɪn, -lin/ adj. 1. containing or tasting like common table salt. −n. 2. a saline health drink or medicine.

salinity /sə'lɪnəti/ n. 1. the degree of salt present in a substance. 2. a level of salt rising from the substratum to the surface of the earth which turns surface freshwater into brackish water and reduces the value of the soil for agriculture.

saliva /sə'laɪvə/ n. a fluid consisting of the secretions produced by glands which discharge into the mouth. −**salivate**, v.

sallow /'sæloʊ/ adj. of a yellowish, sickly hue or complexion.

sally /'sæli/ n. (pl. **-lies**) 1. a sudden rush of troops from a besieged place upon an enemy. −phr. 2. **sally forth**, to set out briskly or energetically.

salmon /'sæmən/ n. (pl. **-mon** or **-mons**) 1. a marine and freshwater food fish with pink flesh. 2. Also, **salmon pink**. light yellowish-pink.

salon /'sælɒn/ n. 1. a drawing room or reception room in a large house. 2. a fashionable business establishment or shop.

saloon /sə'lun/ n. a room or place for general use for a specific purpose.

salsa /'sælsə/ n. 1. a type of lively popular dance music originating in Latin America and blending Cuban rhythms with elements of jazz, rock, and soul music. 2. a hot Mexican sauce usually based on tomatoes and chilli.

salt /sɒlt, sɔlt/ n. 1. a crystalline compound, sodium chloride, NaCl, occurring as a mineral, a constituent of sea water, etc., and used for seasoning food, as a preservative, etc. 2. Chem. a compound which upon dissociation yields cations (positively charged) of a metal, and anions (negatively charged) of an acid radical. 3. (pl.) any of various salts used as purgatives. 4. wit; pungency. −v.t. 5. to season with salt. 6. to cure, preserve, or treat with salt. −adj. 7. containing salt; having the taste of salt. 8. overflowed with or growing in salt water.

saltbush /'sɒltbʊʃ/ n. any of various drought-resistant plants used as grazing plants in arid areas.

saltcellar /'sɒltsɛlə/ n. a shaker or vessel for salt.

salt pan n. a small basin flooded by salt deposits.

saltpetre /sɒlt'pitə/ n. a white salt used in making gunpowder, etc.

salubrious /sə'lubriəs/ adj. 1. (especially of air, climate, etc.) favourable to health. 2. (of a place) attractive and prosperous.

salutary /'sæljətri/, Orig. US /'sæljətɛri/ adj. promoting or conducive to some beneficial purpose.

salutation /sæljə'teɪʃən/ n. something uttered, written, or done by way of saluting.

salute /sə'lut/ v.t. 1. to address with expressions of goodwill, respect, etc.; greet. 2. Mil., Navy to pay respect to or honour by some formal act, as by raising the right hand to the side of the headgear, presenting arms, firing cannon, dipping colours, etc. *–n.* **3.** an act of saluting. **4. → Australian salute.**

salvage /ˈsælvɪdʒ/ **1.** the saving of anything from fire, danger, etc., or the property so saved. *–v.t.* (**-vaged, -vaging**) **2.** to save from shipwreck, fire, etc.

salvation /sælˈveɪʃən/ *n.* **1.** the state of being saved or delivered. **2.** a source, cause, or means of deliverance.

salve /sav, sælv/ *n.* **1.** a healing ointment. *–v.t.* **2.** to soothe as if with salve.

salver /ˈsælvə/ *n.* a tray.

salvo /ˈsælvoʊ/ *n.* (*pl.* **-vos** *or* **-voes**) a discharge of artillery or other firearms, often intended as a salute.

salwar kameez /salwa kəˈmiz/ *n.* a South Asian set of matching garments comprising baggy pants, a long tunic, and scarf. Also, **shalwar kameez.**

samba /ˈsæmbə/ *n.* a ballroom dance of Brazilian (ultimately African) origin.

same /seɪm/ *adj.* **1.** identical with what is about to be or has just been mentioned. **2.** being one or identical, though having different names, aspects, etc. **3.** agreeing in kind, amount, etc.; corresponding. **4.** unchanged in character, condition, etc. *–pron.* **5.** the same person or thing. *–phr.* **6. the same,** with the same manner (used adverbially).

sample /ˈsæmpəl, ˈsampəl/ *n.* **1.** a small part of anything or one of a number, intended to show the quality, style, etc., of the whole; a specimen. **2.** *Music* a digitally encoded recording of sound which may be reproduced, often at a different pitch or speed, as part of a new recording. *–adj.* **3.** serving as a specimen. *–v.t.* **4.** to take a sample or samples of; test or judge by a sample. **5.** *Music* to digitally record (a sound) or take a small section of (an existing digital recording) for incorporation into a new recording, often varying the pitch, speed, etc., in the process.

sampler /ˈsæmplə/ *n.* **1.** someone who samples something. **2.** a piece of cloth embroidered with various devices, serving to show a beginner's skill in needlework. **3.** *Music* a device that digitally encodes external sounds and reproduces them at different pitches, accessed by electronic keyboards or other such controlling devices.

samurai /ˈsæmərai, ˈsæmjərai/ *n.* (*pl.* **-rai**) (in feudal Japan) a member of a military class.

sanatorium /sænəˈtɔriəm/ *n.* (*pl.* **-toriums** *or* **-toria** /-ˈtɔriə/) an establishment for the treatment of invalids, convalescents, etc.

sanctimonious /sæŋktəˈmoʊniəs/ *adj.* making a show of holiness; affecting sanctity.

sanction /ˈsæŋkʃən/ *n.* **1.** countenance or support given to an action, etc. **2.** something serving to support an action, etc. *–v.t.* **3.** to authorise, countenance, or approve. **4.** to ratify or confirm.

sanctity /ˈsæŋktəti/ *n.* **1.** holiness, saintliness, or godliness. **2.** sacred or hallowed character.

sanctuary /ˈsæŋktʃəri, ˈsæŋktʃuəri/, *Orig. US* /ˈsæŋktʃuɛri/ *n.* (*pl.* **-ries**) **1.** a sacred or holy place. **2.** a place of protection from something. **3.** the protection given by such a place.

sand /sænd/ *n.* **1.** the more or less fine debris of rocks, consisting of small, loose grains, often

of quartz. **2.** a dull reddish yellow colour. *–v.t.* **3.** to smooth or polish with sand or sandpaper.

sandal /ˈsændl/ *n.* any of various kinds of low shoes or slippers.

sandalwood /ˈsændlwʊd/ *n.* the fragrant central wood of any of certain Asiatic and Australian trees.

sandbar /ˈsændba/ *n.* a bar of sand formed in a river or sea by the action of tides or currents.

sandpaper /ˈsændpeɪpə/ *n.* **1.** strong paper coated with a layer of sand or the like, used for smoothing or polishing. *–v.t.* **2.** to smooth or polish with or as with sandpaper.

sandshoe /ˈsænʃu, ˈsændʃu/ *n.* a rubber-soled canvas shoe, worn especially for sports, etc., and as casual wear.

sandsoap /ˈsændsoʊp/ *n.* a soap with mildly abrasive power.

sandstone /ˈsændstoʊn/ *n.* a rock formed by the consolidation of sand.

sandwich /ˈsænwɪtʃ, -wɪdʒ/ *n.* **1.** two slices of bread or toast, plain or buttered, with a layer of meat, cheese, salad or the like between. *–v.t.* **2.** to insert or hem in between two other things.

sane /seɪn/ *adj.* **1.** free from mental derangement. **2.** having or showing reason, sound judgement, or good sense. **–sanity,** *n.*

sang /sæŋ/ *v.* past tense of **sing**.

sangfroid /sɒŋˈfrwa/ *n.* coolness of mind; calmness; composure.

sanguine /ˈsæŋgwən/ *adj.* hopeful or confident.

sanitarium /sænəˈtɛəriəm/ *n.* (*pl.* **-tariums** *or* **-taria** /-ˈtɛəriə/) **→ sanatorium.**

sanitary /ˈsænətri/ *adj.* **1.** of or relating to health. **2.** favourable to health; free from dirt, germs, etc.

sanitary napkin *n.* a soft, absorbent, disposable pad worn during menstruation to absorb the discharge from the uterus. Also, **sanitary pad.**

sanitation /sænəˈteɪʃən/ *n.* a drainage system.

sank /sæŋk/ *v.* past tense of **sink**.

sap¹ /sæp/ *n.* **1.** the juice or vital circulating fluid, especially of a woody plant. **2.** *Colloq.* a fool or weak person.

sap² /sæp/ *v.t.* (**sapped, sapping**) to undermine; weaken or destroy insidiously.

sapling /ˈsæplɪŋ/ *n.* a young tree.

sapphire /ˈsæfaɪə/ *n.* **1.** a transparent blue gemstone. **2.** a deep blue. *–adj.* **3.** resembling sapphire; deep blue.

sapro- a word element meaning 'rotten'. Also, (*before vowels*), **sapr-**.

saprophyte /ˈsæprəfaɪt/ *n.* any vegetable organism that lives on dead organic matter, as certain fungi and bacteria. **–saprophytic** /sæprəˈfɪtɪk/, *adj.*

sarc- a word element meaning 'flesh'. Also, (*before consonants*), **sarco-**.

sarcasm /ˈsakæzəm/ *n.* harsh or bitter derision or irony. **–sarcastic,** *adj.*

sarcoma /saˈkoʊmə/ *n.* (*pl.* **-mata** /-mətə/) any of various malignant tumours originating in the connective tissue, attacking especially the bones.

sarcophagus /saˈkɒfəgəs/ *n.* (*pl.* **-phagi** /-fəgaɪ/ *or* **-phaguses**) a stone coffin.

sardine /sɑˈdin/ *n.* (*pl.* **-dines** *or* **-dine**) the young of the common pilchard, often preserved in oil and canned for food.

sardonic /sɑˈdɒnɪk/ *adj.* bitterly ironic; sarcastic; sneering.

sari /ˈsɑri/ *n.* (*pl.* **-ris**) a long piece of cotton or silk, the principal outer garment of Hindu women. Also, **saree**.

sarong /səˈrɒŋ/ *n.* a garment consisting of a piece of cloth enveloping the lower part of the body like a skirt.

SARS /sɑz/ *n.* severe acute respiratory syndrome; an acute form of pneumonia.

SARS-CoV-2 /ˌsɑz-koo vi-'tu/ *n.* the coronavirus which causes COVID-19. Also, **SARS-2**.

sarsaparilla /sɑspəˈrɪlə/ *n.* **1.** a climbing plant having a root used medicinally. **2.** an extract or other preparation made of it.

sartorial /sɑˈtɔriəl/ *adj.* of or relating to clothes or dress, generally men's.

sash[1] /sæʃ/ *n.* a long band or scarf of silk, etc.

sash[2] /sæʃ/ *n.* a movable framework in which panes of glass are set, as in a window or the like.

sashay /sæˈʃeɪ/ *v.i. Colloq.* to strut, move exaggeratedly.

sashimi /sæˈʃimi/ *n.* a Japanese dish of fresh seafood fillets cut into bite-sized, oblong strips, and eaten raw with soy sauce and Japanese horseradish.

sassafras /ˈsæsəfræs/ *n.* any of several Australian trees with fragrant bark.

sassy /ˈsæsi/ *adj.* (**-sier, -siest**) *Colloq.* saucy.

sat /sæt/ *v.* past tense and past participle of **sit**.

satanic /səˈtænɪk/ *adj.* characteristic of or befitting Satan; extremely wicked; diabolical. Also, **satanical**.

satay /ˈsæteɪ/ *n.* **1.** Also, **satay sauce**. a spicy peanut-based sauce used in South-East Asian cookery. **2.** a dish consisting of pieces of marinated meat, chicken or seafood grilled on a skewer and served with satay sauce or a similar hot, spicy sauce.

satchel /ˈsætʃəl/ *n.* a bag with a shoulder strap, used for carrying schoolbooks.

sate /seɪt/ *v.t.* to satisfy (any appetite or desire) to the full.

satellite /ˈsætəlaɪt/ *n.* **1.** a small body which revolves round a planet; a moon. **2.** a human-made device for launching into orbit round the earth, another planet, or the sun, for purposes of communication, research, etc.

satellite TV *n.* a television service in which a signal is transmitted via an artificial satellite to a satellite dish and then to the television set of a householder.

satiate /ˈseɪʃieɪt/ *v.t.* to satisfy to the full.

satin /ˈsætɪn/ *n.* **1.** a very smooth, glossy fabric. *–adj.* **2.** smooth; glossy.

satire /ˈsætaɪə/ *n.* the use of irony, sarcasm, ridicule, etc., in exposing, denouncing, or deriding vice, folly, etc. **–satirical, satiric,** *adj.*

satirise /ˈsætəraɪz/ *v.t.* to make the object of satire. Also, **satirize**.

satisfaction /sætəsˈfækʃən/ *n.* **1.** the state of being satisfied. **2.** the cause of being satisfied. **3.** the opportunity of repairing a supposed

wrong, as by a duel. **4.** payment, as for debt; discharge, as of obligations.

satisfactory /sætəsˈfæktəri/ *adj.* giving satisfaction or fulfilling a particular demand or requirement. **–satisfactorily,** *adv.*

satisfy /ˈsætəsfaɪ/ *v.* (**-fied, -fying**) *–v.t.* **1.** to fulfil the desires, expectations, needs, or demands of. **2.** to fulfil (a desire, expectation, want, etc.). **3.** to discharge fully (a debt, etc.). **4.** to pay (a creditor). *–v.i.* **5.** to give satisfaction. **–satisfied,** *adj.*

saturate /ˈsætʃəreɪt/ *v.t.* to soak, impregnate, or imbue thoroughly or completely.

saturnine /ˈsætənaɪn/ *adj.* gloomy; taciturn.

satyr /ˈseɪtə, ˈsætə/ *n.* in classical mythology, a god, part human, part goat.

sauce /sɔs/ *n.* **1.** any preparation, usually liquid or soft, eaten as a relish or appetising accompaniment to food. **2.** *Colloq.* impertinence; impudence.

saucepan /ˈsɔspən/ *n.* a container for boiling, stewing, etc.

saucer /ˈsɔsə/ *n.* a small, round, shallow dish to hold a cup.

saucy /ˈsɔsi/ *adj.* (**-cier, -ciest**) cheeky; impertinent.

sauerkraut /ˈsaʊəkraʊt/ *n.* cabbage cut fine, salted, and allowed to ferment until sour.

sauna /ˈsɔnə/ *n.* **1.** a type of steam bath. **2.** a room or device for taking such a bath.

saunter /ˈsɔntə/ *v.i.* **1.** to walk with a leisurely gait; stroll. *–n.* **2.** a leisurely walk or ramble; a stroll.

-saur a word element meaning 'lizard'.

sauro- a word element meaning 'lizard'.

sausage /ˈsɒsɪdʒ/ *n.* minced meat packed into a special skin.

sausage roll *n.* a roll of baked pastry filled with sausage meat.

sauté /ˈsouteɪ/ *v.t.* (**sautéed, sautéing**) to cook in a small amount of fat; pan fry.

sauterne /souˈtɜn, sə-/ *n.* (*sometimes upper case*) a rich sweet white table wine.

sauvignon blanc /ˌsouvinjõ ˈblõk/ *n.* (*sometimes upper case*) **1.** a highly regarded grape variety grown for the production of white wine. **2.** a white wine made from this grape.

savage /ˈsævɪdʒ/ *adj.* **1.** uncivilised; wild. **2.** fierce, ferocious, or cruel; untamed. *–n.* **3.** an uncivilised human being. *–v.t.* (**-vaged, -vaging**) **4.** to assail violently. **–savagery,** *n.*

save[1] /seɪv/ *v.t.* **1.** to rescue from danger. **2.** to avoid the spending, consumption, or waste of. **3.** to set apart, reserve, or lay by. **4.** to prevent the occurrence, use, or necessity of. *–v.i.* **5.** (*oft. fol. by up*) to accumulate or put aside money, etc., as the result of economy. *–n.* **6.** the act or instance of saving, especially in sports.

save[2] /seɪv/ *prep.* **1.** except; but. *–conj.* **2.** except; but.

saveloy /ˈsævəlɔɪ/ *n.* → **frankfurt**.

saving /ˈseɪvɪŋ/ *adj.* **1.** that saves; rescuing; preserving. **2.** redeeming. *–n.* **3.** a reduction or lessening of expenditure or outlay. **4.** (*pl.*) sums of money saved by economy and laid away. *–prep.* **5.** except.

savings account *n.* an account with a savings bank or permanent building society on which a rate of interest is paid and money can be withdrawn at short notice.

savings bank *n.* a bank which mainly accepts deposits from individual customers and invests them, and lends money for housing. In Australia the distinction between savings banks and trading banks has now been abolished.

saviour /'seɪvjə/ *n.* someone who saves, rescues, or delivers. Also, **savior**.

savoir faire /ˌsævwa 'fɛə/ *n.* knowledge of what to do in any situation; tact.

savour /'seɪvə/ *n.* **1.** a particular taste or smell. **2.** distinctive quality or property. *–v.t.* **3.** to perceive by taste or smell, especially with relish. **4.** to give oneself to the enjoyment of. Also, **savor**.

savoury /'seɪvəri/ *adj.* **1.** piquant, pungent, or salty to the taste; not sweet. *–n. (pl.* **-vouries) 2.** a non-sweet, usually salty, bite-sized morsel on a small biscuit, etc. Also, **savory**.

savvy /'sævi/ *adj.* (**-vier, -viest**) well-informed or experienced.

saw¹ /sɔ/ *n.* **1.** a tool or device for cutting, typically a thin blade of metal with a series of sharp teeth. *–v.* (**sawed, sawn** *or* **sawed, sawing**) *–v.t.* **2.** to cut or divide with a saw. *–v.i.* **3.** to cut as a saw does.

saw² /sɔ/ *v.* past tense of **see¹**.

sax /sæks/ *n. Colloq.* a saxophone.

saxophone /'sæksəfoʊn/ *n.* a musical wind instrument consisting of a conical metal tube (usually brass) with keys and a mouthpiece. **–saxophonist** /sæk'sɒfənəst/, *n.*

say /seɪ/ *v.* (**said, saying**) *–v.t.* **1.** to utter or pronounce; speak. **2.** to express in words; state; declare. **3.** to assume as a hypothesis or an estimate. *–v.i.* **4.** to speak; declare; express an opinion. *–n.* **5.** *Colloq.* the right or opportunity to say, speak or decide.

saying /'seɪɪŋ/ *n.* something said, especially a proverb.

scab /skæb/ *n.* **1.** the encrustation which forms over a sore during healing. **2.** someone who continues to work during a strike. *–v.i.* (**scabbed, scabbing**) **3.** to become covered with a scab. **4.** to act or work as a scab.

scabbard /'skæbəd/ *n.* a sheath or cover for the blade of a sword, dagger, or the like.

scabies /'skeɪbiz, -biiz/ *n.* any of several infectious skin diseases occurring in sheep and cattle, and in humans, caused by parasitic mites; itch.

scaffold /'skæfəld, -oʊld/ *n.* any raised framework or platform. Also, **scaffolding**.

scald /skɔld/ *v.t.* **1.** to burn or affect painfully with, or as with, hot liquid or steam. **2.** to subject to the action of boiling or hot liquid. *–n.* **3.** a burn caused by hot liquid or steam.

scale¹ /skeɪl/ *n.* **1.** one of the thin, flat, horny or hard plates that form the covering of certain animals, as fishes. **2.** any thin plate-like piece, lamina, or flake such as peels off from a surface. *–v.t.* **3.** to remove the scales or scale from.

scale² /skeɪl/ *n.* (*usu. pl.*) a balance, or any of various other more or less complicated devices for weighing.

scale³ /skeɪl/ *n.* **1.** a succession or progression of steps or degrees. **2.** a graduated line, as on a map, representing proportionate size. **3.** an instrument with graduated spaces, for measuring, etc. **4.** the proportion which the representation of an object bears to the object. **5.** *Music* a succession of notes ascending or descending according to fixed intervals, especially such a series beginning on a particular note. *–v.t.* **6.** to climb by, or as by, a ladder; climb up or over. **7.** (*oft. fol. by down*) to reduce in amount according to a fixed scale or proportion.

scallop /'skɒləp/ *n.* **1.** any of various bivalve molluscs having fluted shell valves. **2.** the large muscle of certain kinds of such molluscs, valued as a food. **3.** one of a series of rounded projections along the edge of pastry, a garment, cloth, etc. **4.** a thin slice of potato dipped in batter and deep-fried. *–v.t.* **5.** to finish (an edge) with scallops.

scallywag /'skæliwæg/ *n.* (*oft. used indulgently of children*) a scamp; rascal. Also, **scalawag, scallawag**.

scalp /skælp/ *n.* **1.** the skin of the upper part of the head. *–v.t.* **2.** to cut or tear the scalp from. **3.** *Colloq.* **a.** to buy and sell so as to make small, quick profits, as stocks. **b.** to buy (tickets) cheaply and sell at other than official rates.

scalpel /'skælpəl/ *n.* a light knife used in surgery.

scam /skæm/ *Colloq.* *–n.* **1.** a ruse or confidence trick. *–v.t.* (**scammed, scamming**) **2.** to practise a confidence trick on (someone). **3.** to get (something) from someone by plausible deceit rather than paying: *he scammed some cakes from the tuckshop.* **–scammer,** *n.*

scamp /skæmp/ *n.* a mischievous child.

scamper /'skæmpə/ *v.i.* to run or go hastily or quickly.

scan /skæn/ *v.* (**scanned, scanning**) *–v.t.* **1.** to glance at or run through hastily. **2.** *Radar* to sweep a region with a beam from a radar transmitter. **3.** *Computers* to examine every item in (a record or file). **4.** *Med.* to examine an area, organ, or system of the body using a moving detector or moving beam of radiation to produce an image of that body part, sometimes after an injection of a radioactive substance which has the ability to enhance the image of a particular tissue. *–v.i.* **5.** (of verse) to conform to the rules of metre. *–n.* **6.** the act of scanning; close examination or scrutiny.

scandal /'skændl/ *n.* **1.** a disgraceful or discreditable action, circumstance, etc. **2.** damage to reputation; disgrace. **3.** malicious gossip.

scandalise /'skændəlaɪz/ *v.t.* to shock or horrify by something considered immoral or improper. Also, **scandalize**.

scanner /'skænə/ *n.* **1.** a machine used to find medical problems in the body, as by X-ray, sound waves, etc. **2.** a machine used to read the price of an item from a bar code. **3.** a machine which reads images and stores them as computer data.

scant /skænt/ *adj.* **1.** barely sufficient in amount or quantity. **2.** barely amounting to as much as indicated.

-scape a suffix indicating a view or expanse of the particular location indicated.

scapegoat /'skeɪpgoʊt/ n. someone who is made to bear the blame for others.

scapula /'skæpjələ/ n. (pl. **-lae** /-li/) Anat. a shoulderblade.

scar¹ /ska/ n. **1.** the mark left by a healed wound, sore, or burn. –v.t. (**scarred, scarring**) **2.** to mark with a scar.

scar² /ska/ n. a precipitous rocky place; a cliff.

scarab /'skærəb/ n. a type of beetle. Also, **scarab beetle**.

scarce /skɛəs/ adj. seldom met with; rare.

scarcely /'skɛəsli/ adv. barely; hardly.

scare /skɛə/ v. (**scared, scaring**) –v.t. **1.** to strike with sudden fear or terror. –v.i. **2.** to become frightened. –n. **3.** a sudden fright or alarm, especially with little or no ground.

scarecrow /'skɛəkroʊ/ n. an object, usually a figure of a man in old clothes, set up to frighten crows, etc., away from crops.

scarf /skaf/ n. (pl. **scarfs** or **scarves** /skavz/) a long, broad strip of silk, wool, lace, etc., worn about the neck, shoulders, or head for ornament or protection.

scarify /'skærəfaɪ, 'skɛər-/ v.t. (**-fied, -fying**) to make scratches or superficial incisions in.

scarlet /'skalət/ n. **1.** bright red colour inclining towards orange. –adj. **2.** of the colour scarlet.

scarlet fever n. a contagious disease, now chiefly of children.

scarp /skap/ n. a steep face on the side of a hill.

scarper /'skapə/ v.i. Colloq. to run away; depart suddenly, especially leaving behind debts or other commitments.

scat /skæt/ v.i. (**scatted, scatting**) Colloq. (usu. in the imperative) to go off hastily.

scathing /'skeɪðɪŋ/ adj. intended to hurt the feelings.

scato- a word element indicating faeces or excrement.

scatter /'skætə/ v.t. **1.** to throw loosely about; distribute at irregular intervals. **2.** to separate and drive off in various directions; disperse. –v.i. **3.** to separate and disperse; go in different directions. –n. **4.** the act of scattering. **5.** that which is scattered.

scattergun /'skætəgʌn/ n. a gun, such as a shotgun, which does not shoot a single missile but many smaller missiles in a scatter. –phr. **2. scattergun approach**, an approach to a problem, argument, etc., which relies on a broad range of not necessarily well-directed counter measures as a tactic, rather than a single well-directed one.

scavenge /'skævəndʒ/ v. (**-enged, -enging**) –v.t. **1.** to search for, and take (anything usable) from discarded material. –v.i. **2.** to search amongst refuse or any discarded material for anything usable, as food, clothing, etc. –**scavenger**, n.

scenario /sə'narioʊ/ n. (pl. **-rios**) an outline of the plot of a dramatic work.

scene /sin/ n. **1.** the place where any action occurs. **2.** any view or picture. **3.** an exhibition or outbreak of excited or violent feeling before others. **4.** a unit of dramatic action within a play. **5.** an episode, situation, or the like, as described in writing. **6.** the setting of a story or the like.

scenery /'sinəri/ n. (pl. **-ries**) **1.** the general appearance of a place. **2.** hangings, draperies,

structures, etc., on the stage in a theatre, intended to represent some place or furnish decorative background.

scenic /'sinɪk/ adj. of or relating to natural scenery; having fine scenery.

scent /sɛnt/ n. **1.** distinctive smell, especially when agreeable. **2.** a track or trail as indicated by such a smell. **3.** → **perfume**. –v.t. **4.** to perceive or recognise by the sense of smell. **5.** to impregnate or sprinkle with perfume.

sceptic /'skɛptɪk/ n. someone who mistrusts and who maintains a doubting pessimistic attitude towards people, plans, ideas, etc. –**sceptical**, adj. –**scepticism**, n.

sceptre /'sɛptə/ n. a rod or wand borne in the hand as an emblem of regal or imperial power.

schedule /'ʃɛdʒul, 'skɛdʒul/ n. **1.** a plan of procedure for a specified project. **2.** a list of items to be dealt with during a specified time. **3.** a timetable. –v.t. **4.** to enter in a schedule. **5.** to plan for a certain date.

schema /'skimə/ n. (pl. **-mata** /-mətə/) a diagram, plan, or scheme. –**schematic**, adj.

scheme /skim/ n. **1.** a plan or design to be followed, as for building operations, etc. **2.** a policy or plan officially adopted by a company, business, etc., as for pensions, loans, etc. **3.** an underhand plot; intrigue. **4.** any system of correlated things, parts, etc., or the manner of its arrangement. –v.t. **5.** to devise as a scheme; plan. –v.i. **6.** to plot.

schism /'skɪzəm, 'fɪzəm, 'sɪzəm/ n. division or disunion, especially into mutually opposed parties.

schizo /'skɪtsoʊ/ n., adj. Colloq. **1.** schizophrenic. **2.** (a person) having an unpredictable character.

schizo- a word element referring to cleavage. Also, (before vowels), **schiz-**.

schizophrenia /skɪtsə'friniə/ n. any of various psychotic disorders characterised by breakdown of integrated personality functioning, withdrawal from reality, emotional dullness and distortion, and disturbances in thought and behaviour. –**schizophrenic**, n., adj.

schlep /ʃlɛp/ Chiefly US Colloq. –v.t. (**schlepped, schlepping**) **1.** to carry; cart or lug. –phr. **2. schlep around**, to traipse or trudge around. Also, **shlep**.

schmaltz /ʃmɔlts, ʃmælts/ n. Colloq. excessive sentimentality, especially in the arts. Also, **schmalz**. –**schmaltzy**, adj.

schmick /ʃmɪk/ adj. Colloq. **1.** highly approved; excellent. **2.** the smallest amount of knowledge: not to have a schmick.

schnapper /'ʃnæpə/ n. → **snapper**.

schnapps /ʃnæps/ n. a type of gin.

scholar /'skɒlə/ n. **1.** a learned or erudite person. **2.** a student; pupil. –**scholarly**, adj.

scholarship /'skɒləʃɪp/ n. **1.** learning; knowledge acquired by study; the academic attainments of a scholar. **2.** the sum of money or other aid granted to a scholar.

scholastic /skə'læstɪk/ adj. of or relating to schools, scholars, or education.

school¹ /skul/ n. **1.** a place or establishment where instruction is given, especially one for children. **2.** a department or faculty in a university or similar educational institution. **3.** a body of scholars, artists, writers, etc., or who are united by a similarity of method, style, principles, etc. −*v.t.* **4.** to educate in or as in a school.

school² /skul/ *n.* a large number of fish, porpoises, whales, or the like, feeding or migrating together.

schoolyard /'skuljad/ *n.* the playground of a school.

schooner /'skunə/ *n.* **1.** a sailing vessel with two or more masts. **2.** a large glass of beer.

sciatica /sai'ætikə/ *n.* any painful disorder extending from the hip down the back of the thigh and surrounding area.

science /'saiəns/ *n.* **1.** systematised knowledge in general. **2.** a particular branch of knowledge.

science fiction *n.* a form of fiction which draws imaginatively on scientific knowledge and speculation.

scientific /saiən'tifik/ *adj.* **1.** of or relating to science or the sciences. **2.** systematic or accurate.

scientific method *n.* a method of research in which you identify a problem, collect the relevant data, formulate a hypothesis on the basis of this data, and, finally, test the hypothesis to prove if it is valid.

scientist /'saiəntəst/ *n.* one versed in or devoted to science.

scintillate /'sintəleit/ *v.i.* **1.** to twinkle, as the stars. **2.** to be witty, brilliant in conversation.

scion /'saiən/ *n.* a descendant.

scissors /'sizəz/ *pl. n.* a cutting instrument consisting of two blades (with handles) so pivoted together that their edges work against each other (often called *a pair of scissors*).

sclero- a word element meaning 'hard'. Also, (*before vowels*), **scler-**.

sclerophyll /'sklerəfil, 'sklɪə-/ *n.* **1.** *Bot.* any of various plants, typically found in low rainfall areas, having tough leaves which help to reduce water loss. −*adj.* **2.** of or relating to such plants.

sclerophyll forest *n.* a forest comprising sclerophyll plants.

scoff¹ /skɒf/ *v.i.* (oft. fol. by *at*) to jeer.

scoff² /skɒf/ *v.t.*, *v.i. Colloq.* to eat greedily and quickly.

scold /skould/ *v.t.* **1.** to find fault with; chide. −*v.i.* **2.** to find fault; reprove. −*n.* **3.** a person, especially a woman, who is habitually abusive.

scoliosis /skɒli'ousəs/ *n.* abnormal lateral curvature of the spine, more common in females than males, and developing at any age but often accelerating in puberty in periods of growth spurts.

scone /skɒn/ *n.* **1.** a small light plain cake, usually eaten split open and spread with butter, etc. **2.** *Colloq.* the head.

scoop /skup/ *n.* **1.** a ladle or ladle-like utensil. **2.** an item of news, etc., published or broadcast in advance of, or to the exclusion of, rival newspapers, broadcasting organisations, etc. −*v.t.* **3.** to take up or out with, or as with a scoop.

scoot /skut/ *v.i. Colloq.* to dart; go swiftly or hastily.

scooter /'skutə/ *n.* **1.** a child's vehicle with two wheels, one in front of the other, and a tread between them, steered by a handlebar

and propelled by pushing against the ground with one foot. **2.** a small, low motorcycle.

scope /skoup/ *n.* **1.** extent or range of view, operation, etc. **2.** space for movement or activity. −*v.t.* **3.** to assess the extent, range or ramifications of (a proposal, idea, etc.).

-scope a word element referring to instruments for viewing.

-scopy a word element for forming abstract action nouns related to *-scope*.

scorch /skɔtʃ/ *v.t.* **1.** to affect in colour, taste, etc., by burning slightly. **2.** to parch or shrivel with heat. −*v.i.* **3.** to be or become scorched.

score /skɔ/ *n.* **1.** the record of points made by the competitors in a game or match. **2.** the aggregate of points made by a side or individual. **3.** a notch or scratch. **4.** (*pl.* **score**) a group or set of twenty. **5.** account, reason, or ground. **6.** *Music* **a.** a written or printed piece of music. **b.** the background music to a film, play, etc. −*v.t.* **7.** to make a score of. **8.** to make notches, cuts, or lines in or on. −*v.i.* **9.** to make a point or points in a game or contest. **10.** to keep score, as of a game.

scorn /skɔn/ *n.* **1.** open or unqualified contempt; disdain. −*v.t.* **2.** to treat or regard with scorn.

scorpion /'skɔpiən/ *n.* any of numerous arachnids having a long narrow abdomen terminating in a venomous sting.

scotch /skɒtʃ/ *v.t.* **1.** to injure so as to make harmless. **2.** to put an end to; stamp out.

scot-free /skɒt-'fri/ *adj.* free from penalty.

scoundrel /'skaundrəl/ *n.* an unprincipled, dishonourable person; a villain.

scour¹ /'skauə/ *v.t.* **1.** to cleanse or polish by hard rubbing. −*n.* **2.** act of scouring.

scour² /'skauə/ *v.t.* to range over, as in search.

scourge /skɜdʒ/ *n.* **1.** a cause of affliction or calamity. −*v.t.* (**scourged**, **scourging**) **2.** to punish or chastise severely; afflict; torment.

scout /skaut/ *n.* **1.** a person sent out to obtain information. −*v.t.* **2.** *Colloq.* (usu. fol. by *out* or *up*) to seek; search for.

scowl /skaul/ *v.i.* **1.** to have a gloomy or threatening look. −*n.* **2.** a scowling expression, look, or aspect.

scrabble /'skræbəl/ *v.i.* **1.** to scratch or scrape, as with the claws or hands. **2.** to struggle to gain possession of something. −*n.* **3.** a scrabbling or scramble.

scraggly /'skrægli/ *adj.* (**-lier**, **-liest**) irregular; ragged; straggling.

scraggy /'skrægi/ *adj.* (**-gier**, **-giest**) **1.** lean or thin. **2.** meagre.

scram /skræm/ *v.i.* (**scrammed**, **scramming**) *Colloq.* to get out quickly; go away.

scramble /'skræmbəl/ *v.i.* **1.** to make one's way hurriedly by use of the hands and feet, as over rough ground. **2.** to struggle with others for possession. **3.** to mix together confusedly. −*n.* **4.** a climb or progression over rough, irregular ground, or the like. **5.** any disorderly struggle or proceeding.

scrap¹ /skræp/ *n.* **1.** a small piece or portion; a fragment. −*adj.* **2.** discarded or left over. −*v.t.* (**scrapped**, **scrapping**) **4.** to discard as useless or worthless.

scrap² /skræp/ *Colloq.* —*n.* **1.** a fight or quarrel. —*v.i.* (**scrapped, scrapping**) **2.** to fight or quarrel.

scrapbook /'skræpbʊk/ *n.* a blank book in which photos, newspaper cuttings, etc., are pasted.

scrape /skreɪp/ *v.* (**scraped, scraping**) —*v.t.* **1.** to free from an outer layer by rubbing a sharp instrument over the surface. **2.** to remove (an outer layer, adhering matter, etc.) in this way. **3.** (fol. by *up* or *together*) to collect by or as by scraping, or laboriously, or with difficulty. **4.** to rub harshly on or across (something). —*v.i.* **5.** to scrape something. **6.** to practise laborious economy or saving. —*n.* **7.** a scraped place. **8.** an embarrassing situation. **9.** a fight; struggle; scrap.

scratch /skrætʃ/ *v.t.* **1.** to dig, scrape, or to tear (*out, off,* etc.) with the claws, the nails, etc. **2.** to rub or scrape lightly with the fingernails, etc., as to relieve itching. **3.** to erase or strike out (writing, a name, etc.). —*v.i.* **4.** to use the nails, claws, etc., for tearing, digging, etc. **5.** to relieve itching by rubbing with the nails, etc. **6.** to make a slight grating noise, as a pen. —*n.* **7.** a mark produced by scratching, such as one on the skin. **8.** an act of scratching. —*phr.* **9. from scratch**, from the beginning. **10. up to scratch**, satisfactory.

scratchie /'skrætʃi/ *n.* a type of instant lottery ticket from which the purchaser scratches off a film which conceals a number of pictures, symbols, etc., a prize being won if a certain set of these is revealed. Also, **scratch card**, **scratch ticket**.

scrawl /skrɔl/ *v.t., v.i.* **1.** to write or draw in a sprawling awkward manner. —*n.* **2.** awkward or careless handwriting.

scrawny /'skrɔni/ *adj.* (**-nier, -niest**) lean; thin; scraggy.

scream /skrim/ *v.i.* **1.** to utter a loud, sharp, piercing cry or sound. —*n.* **2.** a loud, sharp, piercing cry or sound. **3.** *Colloq.* someone or something that is very funny.

screech /skritʃ/ *v.i.* **1.** to utter a harsh, shrill cry. —*n.* **2.** a harsh, shrill cry.

screed /skrid/ *n.* a long speech or piece of writing; harangue.

screen /skrin/ *n.* **1.** a covered frame or the like, movable or fixed, serving as a shelter, partition, etc. **2.** something affording a surface for displaying films, slides, etc. **3.** films collectively. **4.** the component of a television, computer monitor, etc., on which the visible image is displayed. **5.** anything that shelters, protects, or conceals. —*v.t.* **6.** to shelter, protect, or conceal with, or as with, a screen. **7.** to project (pictures, etc.) on a screen. **8.** to check the loyalty, character, ability, etc., of applicants, employees, (etc.).

screen grab *n.* an image taken from a computer screen and saved as a pdf file.

screenplay /'skrinpleɪ/ *n.* the script of a film, including details of camera positions and movement, action, dialogue, lighting, etc.

screen-print *v.t.* → **silk-screen**.

screensaver /'skrinseɪvə/ *n. Computers* a program which is activated when the mouse or keyboard has not been used for a specified length of time, replacing the screen's contents with either a blank screen or an animated graphic; designed to save power and to entertain. Also, **screen saver**.

screw /skru/ *n.* **1.** a metal device to hold things together, having a slotted head and a tapering body with a helical ridge. **2.** *Colloq.* (*taboo*) an act of sexual intercourse. —*v.t.* **3.** to force, press, hold fast, stretch tight, etc., by or as by means of a screw. **4.** to work (a screw, etc.) by turning. **5.** to twist; contort; distort. **6.** to force. **7.** *Colloq.* (*taboo*) to have sexual intercourse with. —*v.i.* **8.** to turn as or like a screw. **9.** (fol. by *on, together, off,* etc.) to be adapted for being connected or taken apart by means of a screw or screws.

screwdriver /'skrudraɪvə/ *n.* a tool fitting into the slotted head of a screw for driving in or withdrawing it by turning.

scribble /'skrɪbəl/ *v.t.* **1.** to write hastily or carelessly. **2.** to make meaningless marks. —*n.* **3.** a hasty or careless piece of writing or drawing.

scribe /skraɪb/ *n.* **1.** a copyist, as someone who formerly made copies of manuscripts, etc. **2.** someone who writes or types something which another dictates: *He injured his arm and so needed a scribe for the exam.*

scrimp /skrɪmp/ *v.t.* to be sparing of or in; stint.

scrip /skrɪp/ *n.* **1.** a writing, especially a receipt or certificate. **2.** *Finance* a certificate representing a provisional purchase of shares or stock where the purchase price is paid in parts according to an agreed schedule of payments.

script /skrɪpt/ *n.* the working text of a play, film, etc.

scripture /'skrɪptʃə/ *n.* any writing or book, of a sacred nature, especially the Bible.

scroll /skroʊl/ *n.* **1.** a roll of parchment or paper, especially one with writing on it. **2.** an ornament, having a spiral or coiled form. —*v.t.* **3.** *Computers* to move (text, images, etc.) up, down, left or right on a computer screen in order to view material which is outside the limits of the screen.

scrooge /skrudʒ/ *n.* a miserly, ill-tempered person.

scrotum /'skroʊtəm/ *n.* (*pl.* **-ta** /-tə/ or **-tums**) the pouch of skin that contains the testicles.

scrounge /skraʊndʒ/ *v.t.* (**scrounged, scrounging**) to obtain by borrowing, foraging, or pilfering.

scrub¹ /skrʌb/ *v.* (**scrubbed, scrubbing**) —*v.t.* **1.** to rub hard with a brush, cloth, etc., or against a rough surface, in washing. **2.** *Colloq.* to cancel; get rid of. —*v.i.* **3.** to cleanse things by hard rubbing. —*n.* **4.** the act of scrubbing.

scrub² /skrʌb/ *n.* **1.** low trees or shrubs, collectively, especially when stunted and of poor quality. **2.** a tract of land covered with such vegetation.

scrub turkey *n.* → **brush turkey**.

scruff /skrʌf/ *n.* the nape or back of the neck.

scruffy /'skrʌfi/ *adj.* (**-fier, -fiest**) *Colloq.* unkempt or dirty; shabby. —**scruffily**, *adv.* —**scruffiness**, *n.*

scrumptious /'skrʌmpʃəs/ *adj. Colloq.* deliciously tasty; superlatively fine or nice; splendid.

scrupulous /'skrupjələs/ *adj.* punctiliously or minutely careful, precise, or exact.

scrutineer /ˈskruːtəˈnɪə/ n. someone who is authorised, especially by a candidate at an election, to inspect the counting of votes by electoral officers.

scrutinise /ˈskruːtənaɪz/ v.t. to examine closely or critically. Also, **scrutinize**. –**scrutiny**, n.

SCSI /ˈskʌzi/ n. small computer system interface; an interface standard for connecting peripheral devices to a computer system.

scuba /ˈskuːbə/ n. a portable breathing device for free-swimming divers.

scud /skʌd/ v.i. (**scudded**, **scudding**) to run or move quickly or hurriedly.

scuff /skʌf/ v.t. **1.** to mar by scraping or hard use, as shoes, furniture, etc. –n. **2.** a type of slipper or sandal without a back.

scuffle /ˈskʌfəl/ v.i. **1.** to struggle or fight in a scrambling, confused manner. –n. **2.** a confused struggle or fight.

scull¹ /skʌl/ n. **1. a.** an oar worked from side to side over the stern of a boat as a means of propulsion. **b.** one of a pair of oars operated, one on each side, by one person. **2.** a boat propelled by a scull or sculls, especially a light racing boat propelled by one rower with a pair of oars. –v.t. **3.** to propel or convey by means of a scull or sculls. –v.i. **4.** to propel a boat with a scull or sculls. **5.** to swim while floating on the front or the back, with the arms close to the body, using only a wrist movement. –**sculler**, n.

scull² /skʌl/ v.t. Colloq. to consume (a drink) at one draught. Also, **skol**.

scullery /ˈskʌləri/ n. (pl. **-ries**) a small room where the rough, dirty work of a kitchen is done.

sculpture /ˈskʌlptʃə/ n. **1.** the fine art of forming figures or designs by carving, moulding, etc. **2.** a piece of such work. –v.t. Also, **sculpt**. **3.** to carve, make, or execute by sculpture. –**sculptor**, n.

scum /skʌm/ n. **1.** a film of foul or extraneous matter on a liquid. **2.** low, worthless persons: scum of the earth.

scunge /skʌndʒ/ n. Colloq. dirt, mess, slime, etc.

scungies /ˈskʌndʒiz/ pl. n. (from trademark) men's or women's briefs worn under board shorts, sports uniforms or similar garments.

scupper /ˈskʌpə/ v.t. to sink (a ship) deliberately.

scurrilous /ˈskʌrələs/ adj. grossly or indecently abusive.

scurry /ˈskʌri/ v.i. (**-ried**, **-rying**) to go or move quickly or in haste.

scurvy /ˈskɜːvi/ n. **1.** a disease caused by a diet lacking in vitamin C. –adj. (**-vier**, **-viest**) **2.** low, mean, or contemptible.

scuttle¹ /ˈskʌtl/ v.i. (oft. fol. by off, away, etc.) to run with quick, hasty steps; hurry.

scuttle² /ˈskʌtl/ v.t. to sink (a vessel) by cutting a hole below the waterline or opening the valves in the hull.

scythe /saɪð/ n. an agricultural implement for mowing grass, etc., by hand.

SDTV /ˌɛs di ti ˈviː/ n. standard definition TV; a type of digital TV which produces picture and sound quality similar to that of analog TV. Compare **HDTV**.

sea /siː/ n. **1.** the salt waters that cover the greater part of the earth's surface. **2.** a division of these waters. **3.** a large lake or landlocked body of water. –phr. Also, **all at sea**. **4.** at **sea, a.** sailing on or in the ocean. **b.** bewildered; confused.

sea anemone n. any of several marine coelenterates.

seabird /ˈsiːbɜːd/ n. a bird frequenting the sea or coast.

sea breeze n. a thermally produced wind blowing during the day from the cool ocean surface on to the adjoining warm land.

sea change n. **1.** a complete or radical transformation. **2.** a move from a city environment to a rural location, especially near the coast, as part of a lifestyle change, usually to escape the stress and other deleterious aspects of city life. –**sea changer**, n.

seafood /ˈsiːfuːd/ n. any saltwater fish or shellfish which is used for food.

seafront /ˈsiːfrʌnt/ n. the side or edge of land and buildings bordering on the sea.

seagoing /ˈsiːɡoʊɪŋ/ adj. designed or fit for going to sea, as a vessel.

seagull /ˈsiːɡʌl/ n. a gull, especially any of the marine species. See **gull**.

seahorse /ˈsiːhɔːs/ n. any of a number of small fishes with a prehensile tail and a beaked head that is turned at right angles to the body.

seal¹ /siːl/ n. **1.** a device affixed to a document as evidence of authenticity or attestation. **2.** anything that effectively closes a thing. **3.** a road surface of hard material, as tar, bitumen, etc. –v.t. **4.** to approve, authorise, or confirm. **5.** to close by any form of fastening that must be broken before access can be had. **6.** to decide irrevocably. **7.** to surface a road with tar, bitumen, etc.

seal² /siːl/ n. (pl. **seals** or, especially collectively, **seal**) any of several furred, amphibious mammals with flippers for limbs.

sea level n. the horizontal plane or level corresponding to the surface of the sea when halfway between mean high and low water, widely used as a base from which to indicate the height of locations on land.

seam /siːm/ n. **1.** the line formed by sewing together pieces of cloth, leather, or the like. **2.** any line between abutting edges; a crack or fissure; a groove. –v.t. **3.** to join with a seam; sew the seams of. **4.** to furrow; mark with wrinkles, scars, etc. –v.i. **5.** to become cracked, fissured, or furrowed.

sea monkey n. a form of shrimp, the eggs of which, when put into water, produce live shrimp after a few hours; sold as a novelty pet.

seamstress /ˈsiːmstrəs/ n. a woman whose occupation is sewing. Also, **sempstress**.

seamy /ˈsiːmi/ adj. (**-mier**, **-miest**) disagreeable; vulgar; sordid.

seance /ˈseɪɒns/ n. a meeting of people seeking to communicate with spirits of the dead with the help of a medium. Also, **séance**.

seaplane /ˈsiːpleɪn/ n. an aeroplane that can land on water.

sear /sɪə/ v.t. to burn or char the surface of.

search /sɜːtʃ/ v.t. **1.** to go or look through carefully in seeking to find something. **2.** to examine (a person) for concealed objects by going through their pockets or the like. **3.** to bring or find (out) by a search. –v.i. **4.** to seek. –n. **5.** the act of searching. **6.** Law examination by a purchaser of records and registers at the Land Titles Office to find encumbrances affecting title to property.

search engine n. Computers software which enables a user to find items on a database on the internet.

search function n. Internet a facility provided on a website allowing a user to enter a term which will then be matched in the text of the whole site or a specified subset.

search warrant n. a court order authorising the searching of a house, etc., as for stolen goods or other evidence of a crime.

seashell /'siʃel/ n. the shell of any marine mollusc.

seashore /'siʃɔ/ n. land along the sea or ocean.

seasickness /'sisikns/ n. nausea caused by the motion of a vessel at sea.

season /'sizən/ n. **1.** a period of the year characterised by particular conditions of weather, temperature, etc. **2.** the period of the year when something is best or available. **3.** any period of time. **4.** a suitable, proper, fitting, or right time. **5.** Agric. fertile period in female stock; time for mating. –v.t. **6.** to heighten or improve the flavour of (food) by adding condiments, spices, herbs, or the like. **7.** to prepare (timber) for use by drying and hardening it. –v.i. **8.** to become seasoned, matured, hardened, or the like.

seasonable /'sizənəbəl/ adj. **1.** suitable to the season. **2.** timely; opportune.

seasonal /'sizənəl/ adj. periodical.

seasoning /'sizəniŋ/ n. something that seasons, especially salt, spices, herbs, or other condiments.

season ticket n. a ticket valid any number of times for a specified period, usually at a reduced rate.

seat /sit/ n. **1.** something for sitting on, as a chair or bench. **2.** the part of a chair or the like on which one sits. **3.** the part of the body on which one sits; the buttocks. **4.** manner of sitting, as on horseback. **5.** an established place or centre, as of government. **6.** site, location, or locality. **7.** a parliamentary constituency. –v.t. **8.** to place on a seat or seats. **9.** to find seats for.

seatbelt /'sitbelt/ n. a belt attached to the frame of a motor vehicle for securing a driver or passenger against sudden turns, stops, collision, etc. Also, **safety belt**.

sea urchin n. a small globe-shaped sea creature with a spiny shell.

seaweed /'siwid/ n. any plant or plants growing in the ocean, especially marine algae.

sebaceous /sə'beiʃəs/ adj. **1.** relating to, of the nature of, or resembling tallow or fat. **2.** secreting a fatty substance.

secant /'sikənt/ n. Maths a straight line which cuts a circle or other curve.

secateurs /'sekətəz, 'sekətɜz, sekə'tɜz/ pl. n. a scissor-like cutting instrument for pruning shrubs, etc.

secede /sə'sid/ v.i. to withdraw formally from an alliance or association, as from a political or religious organisation. –**secession**, n.

seclude /sə'klud/ v.t. to shut off or keep apart; place in or withdraw into solitude. –**seclusion**, n.

second¹ /'sekənd/ adj. **1.** an ordinal number, next after the first in order, place, time, rank, value, quality, etc. **2.** alternate. **3.** additional; further. –n. **4.** someone who or that which comes next to or after the first, in order, quality, rank, etc. **5.** (sometimes pl.) Commerce a product or material that is below the normal or required standard. –v.t. **6.** to support, back up, or assist. –adv. **7.** in the second place, group, etc.

second² /'sekənd/ n. **1.** a sixtieth part of a minute of time. **2.** Geom., etc. the sixtieth part of a minute of a degree. **3.** a moment or instant.

second³ /sə'kɒnd/ v.t. to transfer (someone) temporarily to another post or organisation. –**secondment**, n.

secondary /'sekəndri/, Orig. US /-deri/ adj. **1.** next after the first in order, place, time, importance, etc. **2.** derived or derivative; not primary or original. **3.** of or relating to the processing of primary products. **4.** of minor importance; subordinate; auxiliary.

secondary colour n. a colour produced by mixing two or more primary colours, as orange, green, or violet. Also, **secondary color**.

secondary forest n. Ecol. forest that has regrown after logging or clearing activities (opposed to primary forest).

secondary industry n. an industry involved in the production of manufactured goods.

secondary school n. a school providing post-primary education; a high school.

second cousin n. See **cousin**.

second-hand adj. **1.** previously used or owned: second-hand books. –adv. **2.** after having been owned by another person: we bought our fridge second-hand.

second nature n. habit, tendency, etc., so long practised that it is inalterably fixed in one's character.

second person n. See **person** (def. 3).

seconds /'sekəndz/ pl. n. **1.** the plural of **second**. **2.** (at a meal) **a.** a second helping. **b.** a second course.

second sight n. a supposed faculty of seeing distant objects and future events; clairvoyance.

second wind n. the restoration of more comfortable breathing after one has got over an initial stress.

secret /'sikrət/ adj. **1.** done, made, or conducted without the knowledge of others. –n. **2.** something secret, hidden, or concealed. **3.** the reason or explanation, not immediately or generally apparent. –phr. **4. in secret**, secretly. –**secretive**, adj. –**secrecy**, n.

secret agent n. a spy.

secretariat /sekrə'teəriət/ n. the officials or office entrusted with maintaining records and performing secretarial duties, especially for an international organisation.

secretary /'sekrətri/, Orig. US /-teri/ n. (pl. **-taries**) **1.** a person who conducts correspondence, keeps records, etc., for an individual or an organisation. **2.** → **private secretary**.

secretary-general /sekrətri-'dʒenrəl/ n. (pl. **secretaries-general**) the head of a secretariat.

secrete /sə'krit/ v.t. **1.** Biol. to separate off, prepare, or elaborate from the blood, as in the physiological process of secretion. **2.** to hide or conceal; keep secret. **–secretion,** *n.*

Secret Santa /ˈsænta/ *n.* a ritual by which a group of people exchange gifts at Christmas, each person giving a present to one other randomly selected member of the group, the gifts being limited to a certain price; Kris Kringle.

secret service *n.* official service of a secret nature.

sect /sɛkt/ *n.* a body of persons adhering to a particular religious faith; a religious denomination.

-sect a word element meaning 'cut', as in *intersect.*

section /ˈsɛkʃən/ *n.* **1.** one of a number of parts that fit together to make a whole. **2.** the act of cutting; separation by cutting. **3.** a representation of an object as it would appear if cut by a plane. **4.** → **block** (def. 8b). **5.** (in some Aboriginal tribes) one of four exogamous kinship and totemic groups, sometimes overlapping with a moiety system. Compare **moiety** (def. 2), **subsection** (def. 2).

sector /ˈsɛktə/ *n.* **1.** *Geom.* a plane figure bounded by two radii and the included arc of a circle, ellipse, or the like. **2.** any field or division of a field of activity.

secular /ˈsɛkjələ/ *adj.* of or relating to the world, or to things not religious, sacred, or spiritual; temporal; worldly.

secure /səˈkjuə, sə'kjuə/ *adj.* **1.** free from or not exposed to danger; safe. **2.** not liable to fall, yield, become displaced, etc., as a support or a fastening. **3.** free from care; without anxiety. **4.** sure; certain. **–v.t. 5.** to get hold or possession of; obtain. **6.** to make secure or certain. **7.** to assure a creditor of (payment) by the pledge or mortgaging of property.

secure server *n. Computers* a website in which data is protected by its formatting to prevent information such as a purchaser's credit card number or a respondent's personal information being obtained by someone else.

security /səˈkjuərəti/ *n.* (*pl.* **-ties**) **1.** freedom from danger, risk, etc.; safety. **2.** freedom from worry or doubt; confidence. **3.** something that secures or makes safe; a protection; a defence. **4.** an assurance; guarantee. **5.** *Law* something given or deposited as a guarantee for the fulfilment of a promise or an obligation, the payment of a debt, etc. **6.** (*usu. pl.*) stocks and shares, etc.

sedan /səˈdæn/ *n.* a car with two rows of seating, four or two doors, and a separate boot. Also, **saloon car.**

sedate /səˈdeɪt/ *adj.* **1.** calm, quiet, or composed. **–v.t. 2.** to calm or put to sleep by means of sedatives. **–sedation,** *n.*

sedative /ˈsɛdətɪv/ *adj.* **1.** tending to calm or soothe. **–n. 2.** a sedative agent or remedy.

sedentary /ˈsɛdəntri/, *Orig.* *US* /-teri/ *adj.* **1.** characterised by or requiring a sitting posture. **2.** taking little exercise.

sediment /ˈsɛdəmənt/ *n.* matter which settles to the bottom of a liquid.

sedition /səˈdɪʃən/ *n.* incitement of discontent or rebellion against the government.

seduce /səˈdjus/ *v.t.* (**-duced, -ducing**) **1.** to induce to have sexual intercourse. **2.** to win over; entice. **–seduction,** *n.* **–seductive,** *adj.*

see¹ /si/ *v.* (**saw, seen, seeing**) **–v.t. 1.** to observe, be aware of, or perceive, with the eyes. **2.** to perceive or be aware of with any or all of the senses. **3.** to have experience or knowledge of. **4.** to view, or visit or attend as a spectator. **5.** to discern with the intelligence; perceive mentally; understand. **6.** to ascertain, find out, or learn, as by inquiry. **7.** to visit. **8.** to accompany or escort. **9.** to ensure. **–v.i. 10.** to have or use the power of sight. **11.** to understand; discern. **12.** to inquire or find out. **13.** to give attention or care.

see² /si/ *n.* the seat, centre of authority, office, or jurisdiction of a bishop.

seed /sid/ *n.* (*pl.* **seeds** or **seed**) **1.** the propagative part of a plant, especially as preserved for growing a new crop. **2.** (*usu. pl.*) the germ or beginning of anything. **3.** a player who has been seeded. **–v.t. 4.** to sow (land) with seed. **5.** to modify (the ordinary drawing of lots for position in a tournament, as at tennis) by distributing certain outstanding players so that they will not meet in the early rounds of play. **–v.i. 6.** to produce or shed seed.

seed bank *n.* a store of seeds as a source for their future planting should they become extinct in the natural world.

seedling /ˈsidlɪŋ/ *n.* a young plant developed from the embryo after germination of a seed.

seedy /ˈsidi/ *adj.* (**-dier, -diest**) rather disreputable or shabby.

seek /sik/ *v.t.* (**sought, seeking**) **1.** to go in search or quest of. **2.** to try or attempt (followed by an infinitive). **3.** to ask for; request.

seem /sim/ *v.i.* to appear to be; appear (to be, feel, do, etc.).

seemly /ˈsimli/ *adj.* (**-lier, -liest**) fitting or becoming with respect to propriety or good taste; decent; decorous.

seep /sip/ *v.i.* to pass gradually, as liquid, through a porous substance; ooze.

seer /sɪə/ *n.* someone who foretells future events; a prophet.

seesaw /ˈsiˌsɔ/ *n.* **1.** a plank or beam balanced at the middle so that its ends may rise and fall alternately. **–v.i. 2.** to move in the manner of a seesaw.

seethe /sið/ *v.i.* (**seethed, seething**) to surge or foam, as a boiling liquid.

segment *n.* /ˈsɛgmənt/ **1.** *Geom.* a part cut off from a figure (especially a circular or spherical one) by a line or a plane. **2.** one of the parts into which anything naturally separates or is naturally divided. **–v.t., v.i.** /sɛgˈment/ **3.** to separate or divide into segments.

segregate /ˈsɛgrəgeɪt/ *v.t.* **1.** to separate or set apart from the others or from the main body; isolate. **–v.i. 2.** to separate or go apart.

segue /ˈsɛgweɪ/ *n.* any smooth transition, as from one topic of discussion to another.

seismic /ˈsaɪzmɪk/ *adj.* relating to, of the nature of, or caused by an earthquake. Also, **seismal, seismical. –seismically,** *adv.*

seismo- a word element meaning 'seismic'.

seize /siz/ *v.t.* **1.** to lay hold of suddenly or forcibly; grasp. **2.** to take possession of by legal authority; confiscate. **3.** to take advantage of promptly. **–v.i. 4.** (fol. by *up*) to become jammed or stuck solid, as an engine through excessive heat.

seizure /ˈsiːʒə/ n. **1.** the act of seizing. **2.** a sudden attack, as of disease.

seldom /ˈsɛldəm/ adv. rarely; infrequently; not often.

select /səˈlɛkt/ v.t. **1.** to choose in preference to another or others. –adj. **2.** selected; chosen in preference to others.

selection /səˈlɛkʃən/ n. **1.** the act of selecting or the fact of being selected; choice. **2.** a thing or a number of things selected. **3.** a range of things from which selection may be made.

selective /səˈlɛktɪv/ adj. **1.** making selection. **2.** choosing the best in anything; discriminating. **3.** marked by selection. **4.** Educ. of or relating to a school to which entry is restricted to those applicants who successfully complete a pre-scribed test or series of tests. –**selectivity**, n.

seleno- a word element meaning 'moon', as in selenology.

self /sɛlf/ n. (pl. **selves**) **1.** a person or thing referred to with respect to individuality; one's own person. –pron. (pl. **selves**) **2.** myself, himself, etc.

self- prefixal use of **self**, expressing principally reflexive action or relation.

self-assurance n. self-confidence. –**self-assured**, adj.

self-centred adj. engrossed in one's self; selfish.

self-confidence n. confidence in one's own judgement, ability, power, etc., sometimes to an excessive degree.

self-conscious adj. excessively conscious of oneself as an object of observation to others.

self-contained adj. containing in oneself or itself all that is necessary; independent.

self-control n. control of oneself or one's actions, feelings, etc.

self-defence n. the act of defending one's own person, reputation, etc.

self-esteem n. one's sense of one's own worth.

self-evident adj. evident in itself without proof; axiomatic.

self-government n. political independence of a country, people, region, etc.

selfie /ˈsɛlfi/ n. Colloq. a photograph one has taken of oneself using a digital device, such as the smartphone, usually with the intention of posting it on a social network.

self-important adj. having or showing an exaggerated opinion of one's own importance; conceited or pompous.

self-interest n. regard for one's own interest or advantage, especially with disregard of others.

selfish /ˈsɛlfɪʃ/ adj. devoted to or caring only for oneself, one's welfare, interests, etc.

selfless /ˈsɛlfləs/ adj. unselfish. –**selflessly**, adv. –**selflessness**, n.

self-made adj. having succeeded in life, un-aided by inheritance, class background, or other people.

self-opinionated adj. obstinate in one's own opinion.

self-possessed adj. having or showing con-trol of one's feelings, behaviour, etc.

self-raising flour n. wheat flour with baking powder already added.

self-respect n. proper esteem or regard for the dignity of one's character.

self-righteous adj. thinking that one is right or righteous.

selfsame /ˈsɛlfseɪm/ adj. (the) very same; identical.

self-satisfaction n. satisfaction with oneself, one's achievements, etc.; smugness. –**self-satisfied**, adj.

self-seeking adj. selfish.

self-service adj. (of a service station, restau-rant, shop, etc.) operating on the principle that the customers perform part or all of the service themselves. Also, **self-serve**.

self-starter n. someone who acts on personal initiative and does not require external motiva-tion as an encouragement to work.

self-sufficient adj. able to supply one's own needs.

sell /sɛl/ v. (**sold**, **selling**) –v.t. **1.** to give up or make over for a consideration; dispose of to a purchaser for a price. **2.** to deal in; keep for sale. –v.i. **3.** to sell something; engage in selling. **4.** to be on sale; find purchasers. –n. **5.** Colloq. an act of selling or salesmanship. –phr. **6. sell out**, **a.** to sell all of. **b.** Colloq. to betray. **7. sell up**, to liquidate by selling the assets (of). –**seller**, n.

sellout /ˈsɛlaʊt/ n. Colloq. **1.** a betrayal. **2.** a play, show, etc., for which all seats are sold.

selvage /ˈsɛlvɪdʒ/ n. the edge of woven fabric finished to prevent fraying, often in a narrow tape effect, different from the body of the fab-ric. Also, **selvedge**.

selves /sɛlvz/ n. plural of **self**.

semantic /səˈmæntɪk/ adj. relating to meaning.

semaphore /ˈsɛməfɔː/ n. a system of signalling by hand, in which a flag is held in each hand at arm's length in various positions.

semblance /ˈsɛmbləns/ n. an outward aspect or appearance.

semen /ˈsiːmən/ n. the impregnating fluid pro-duced by male reproductive organs; seed; sperm.

semester /səˈmɛstə/ n. (in educational institu-tions) one of two divisions of the academic year. See **term**.

semi- a prefix modifying the latter element of the word, meaning 'half' in its precise and less precise meanings, as in semitone.

semibreve /ˈsɛmibriːv/ n. Music a note half the length of a breve, and worth four crotchets.

semicolon /ˈsɛmiˌkoʊlən, ˈsɛmikoʊlən/ n. a mark of punctuation (;) used to indicate a more distinct separation between parts of a sentence than that indicated by a comma.

semiconductor /ˌsɛmikənˈdʌktə/ n. **1.** a sub-stance whose electrical conductivity at normal temperatures is intermediate between that of a metal and an insulator. **2.** a device, as a tran-sistor, which is based on the electronic prop-erties of such substances.

semidetached /ˌsɛmidəˈtætʃt/ adj. of or relat-ing to a pair of houses joined by a common wall but detached from other buildings.

seminal /ˈsɛmənəl/ adj. **1.** highly original and influential. **2.** of or relating to semen.

seminar /ˈsɛmənɑː/ n. a meeting organised to discuss a specific topic.

seminary /ˈsɛmənri/, Orig. US /ˈsɛmənɛri/ n. (pl. **-ries**) Roman Catholic Church a college for the education of men for the priesthood or ministry.

semiquaver /'sɛmikweɪvə/ n. a note equivalent to half a quaver.

semitone /'sɛmitoʊn/ n. Music the smallest interval in the chromatic scale of Western music.

semitrailer /sɛmi'treɪlə/ n. an articulated goods vehicle.

semolina /sɛmə'linə/ n. the large, hard parts of wheat grains used for making puddings, etc.

senate /'sɛnət/ n. 1. a legislative assembly of a state or nation. 2. a governing, advisory, or disciplinary body, as in certain universities. –**senator**, n.

send /sɛnd/ v. (**sent, sending**) –v.t. 1. to cause to go; direct or order to go. 2. to cause to be conveyed or transmitted to a destination. 3. (fol. by *forth, out*, etc.) to give forth, as light, smell, or sound. –v.i. 4. to dispatch a message, messenger, etc. –phr. 5. **send up**, *Colloq.* to mock or ridicule; satirise.

senile /'sɛnaɪl, 'sinaɪl/ adj. mentally or physically infirm due to old age.

senior /'sinjə/ adj. 1. older or elder. 2. of higher rank or standing, especially by virtue of longer service. –n. 3. a person who is older than another. –**seniority**, n.

Senior Counsel n. (in some legal systems) a member of the senior of the two ranks of barrister. *Abbrev.*: SC Compare **junior** (def. 6).

sensation /sɛn'seɪʃən/ n. 1. the operation or function of the senses; perception through the senses. 2. a mental condition produced through or as through an organ of sense. 3. a state of excited feeling or interest caused among a number of persons. 4. a cause of such feeling or interest.

sensational /sɛn'seɪʃənəl/ adj. 1. able to produce a sensation. 2. (of a book, film, etc.) sensationalised. 3. *Colloq.* very pleasing, exciting or excellent.

sensationalism /sɛn'seɪʃənəlɪzəm/ n. the exploitation of cheap emotional excitement by popular newspapers, novels, etc. –**sensationalist**, n., adj. –**sensationalise, sensationalize**, v.

sense /sɛns/ n. 1. each of the special faculties connected with bodily organs by which human beings and other animals perceive external objects and their own bodily changes (commonly reckoned as sight, hearing, smell, taste, and touch). 2. a feeling or perception produced through the organs of touch, taste, etc. 3. any more or less vague perception or impression. 4. sound practical intelligence; common sense. 5. what is sensible or reasonable. 6. the meaning, or one of the meanings, of a word, statement, or a passage. –v.t. 7. to perceive by or as by the senses. –phr. 8. **in a sense**, according to one interpretation.

sensibility /sɛnsə'bɪləti/ n. (pl. **-ties**) 1. mental susceptibility or responsiveness. 2. (pl.) emotional capacities.

sensible /'sɛnsəbəl/ adj. 1. having, using, or showing good sense or sound judgement. 2. (usu. fol. by *of*) cognisant; keenly aware.

sensitive /'sɛnsətɪv/ adj. 1. readily affected by external agencies or influences. 2. easily affected, pained, annoyed, etc. 3. (of an issue, topic, etc.) arousing strong feelings or reaction.

sensory /'sɛnsəri/ adj. relating to sensation.

sensual /'sɛnfuəl/ adj. relating to or given to the gratification of the senses or the indulgence of appetite.

sensuous /'sɛnfuəs/ adj. readily affected through the senses.

sent /sɛnt/ v. past tense and past participle of **send**.

sentence /'sɛntəns/ n. 1. a word or a sequence of words arranged in a grammatical construction expressing an independent statement, inquiry, command, or the like, as, *Fire!* or *Summer is here* or *Who's there?* 2. *Law* **a.** a judicial judgement or decree, especially the judicial determination of the punishment to be inflicted on a convicted criminal. **b.** the punishment itself. –v.t. (**-tenced, -tencing**) 3. to pronounce sentence upon.

sententious /sɛn'tɛnʃəs/ adj. moralising.

sentient /'sɛntiənt, 'sɛnʃənt/ adj. having the power of perception by the senses.

sentiment /'sɛntəmənt/ n. 1. mental attitude with regard to something; opinion. 2. refined or tender emotion. 3. the thought or feeling intended to be conveyed by words.

sentimental /sɛntə'mɛntl/ adj. 1. relating to or dependent on sentiment. 2. weakly emotional.

sentimental value n. the value which something often of little or no monetary value has because of its ability to arouse sentiments.

sentinel /'sɛntənəl/ n. one on watch.

sentry /'sɛntri/ n. (pl. **-tries**) a soldier stationed at a place to keep guard; a sentinel.

sepal /'sipəl/ n. any of the individual leaves or parts of the calyx of a flower.

separate v.t. /'sɛpəreɪt/ 1. to keep apart or divide, as by an intervening barrier, space, etc. 2. to part or divide (an assemblage, mass, compound, etc.) into individuals, components, or elements. 3. (fol. by *from* or *out*) to take by such parting or dividing. –v.i. /'sɛpəreɪt/ 4. (oft. fol. by *from*) to part company; withdraw from personal association. 5. become disconnected or disengaged. 6. to become parted from a mass or compound, as crystals. –adj. /'sɛprət/ 7. separated or disconnected. 8. unconnected or distinct.

sepia /'sipiə/ n. 1. a brown pigment. 2. *Photography* a brown-coloured image. –adj. 3. of a brown similar to that from sepia ink.

sepsis /'sɛpsəs/ n. local or generalised bacterial invasion of the body.

sept- a prefix meaning 'seven'. Also, **septem-, septe-, septi-**.

septic /'sɛptɪk/ adj. relating to or of the nature of sepsis; infected.

septicaemia /sɛptə'simiə/ n. the invasion and persistence of disease-causing bacteria in the bloodstream. Also, **septicemia**.

septic tank n. a tank in which solid organic sewage is decomposed and purified by bacteria.

septum /'sɛptəm/ n. (pl. **septa** /'sɛptə/) *Biol.* a dividing wall, membrane, or the like in a plant or animal structure.

sepulchre /'sɛpəlkə/ n. a tomb, grave, or burial place.

sequel /'sikwəl/ n. 1. a literary work, film, etc., complete in itself, but continuing a preceding work. 2. an event or circumstance following something.

sequence /'sikwəns/ n. **1.** the following of one thing after another; succession. **2.** order of succession. **3.** a continuous or connected series.

sequester /sə'kwɛstə, si-/ v.t. to remove or withdraw into solitude or retirement; seclude. **–sequestration,** n.

sequin /'sikwən/ n. a small shining disc or spangle used to ornament a dress, etc.

serenade /sɛrə'neɪd/ n. **1.** a song sung in the open air at night, as by a man under the window of his lover. –v.t. **2.** to entertain with a serenade.

serendipity /sɛrən'dɪpəti/ n. the ability to make desirable but accidental discoveries. **–serendipitous,** adj.

serene /sə'rin/ adj. calm; peaceful; tranquil. **–serenity,** n.

serf /sɜf/ n. a person required to render services to a lord.

serge /sɜdʒ/ n. cotton, rayon, or silk in a twill weave.

sergeant /'sadʒənt/ n. **1.** an officer in the army. **2.** a police officer ranking above a constable.

serial /'stəriəl/ n. **1.** anything published, broadcast, etc., in instalments at regular intervals. –adj. **2.** published in instalments or successive parts. **3.** of, relating to, or arranged in a series. **4.** of or relating to someone who repeats an offence or misdemeanour a number of times: a serial killer.

serial number n. an individual number given to a particular person, article, etc., for identification.

serial port n. Computers a port which enables data to be sent or received one bit at a time. Compare **parallel port**.

series /'stəriz/ n. (pl. **-ries**) **1.** a number of things, events, etc., arranged or occurring in spatial, temporal, or other succession; a sequence. **2.** a set of something: a new series of stamps. **3.** a number of programs on radio or television which are linked in some way, either by subject matter or by being about the same group of people.

serious /'stəriəs/ adj. **1.** of grave or solemn disposition or character; thoughtful. **2.** being in earnest; not trifling. **3.** weighty or important.

sermon /'sɜmən/ n. **1.** a discourse for the purpose of religious instruction or exhortation, especially one based on a text of Scripture and delivered from a pulpit. **2.** a long, tedious speech.

sero- a word element representing **serum**.

serotonin /sɛrə'toʊnən/ n. a hormone found in the brain, intestines, and platelets; deficiencies linked to mood disorders, anxiety, etc.

serpent /'sɜpənt/ n. a snake. **–serpentine,** adj.

serrated /sə'reɪtəd/ adj. having a notched or grooved edge.

serum /'stərəm/ n. (pl. **sera** /'stərə/ or **serums**) the clear, pale yellow liquid which separates from the clot in the coagulation of blood.

servant /'sɜvənt/ n. a person in the service of another.

serve /sɜv/ v.i. **1.** to act as a servant. **2.** to wait at table; hand food to guests. **3.** to render assistance; help. **4.** to go through a term of service. **5.** Tennis, etc. to put the ball in play. –v.t. **6.** to be in the service of; work for. **7.** to render service to; help. **8.** to go through (a term of service, imprisonment, etc.). **9.** to answer the requirements of; suffice. **10.** to wait upon; set food before. **11.** to set (food) on a table. **12.** (of a male animal) to mate with. **13.** Law to make legal delivery of (a process or writ). –n. **14.** the act, manner, or right of serving, as in tennis.

server /'sɜvə/ n. **1.** something used for serving food: cake server. **2.** Tennis, etc. the player who puts the ball in play. **3.** Computers **a.** a program which provides services to another computer via a network. **b.** the computer on which the program operates.

servery /'sɜvəri/ n. an area in which food is set out on plates.

service /'sɜvəs/ n. **1.** an act of helpful activity. **2.** the supplying or supplier of any articles, commodities, activities, etc., required or demanded. **3.** occupation or employment as a servant. **4.** (pl.) Mil. the armed forces. **5.** the act of servicing a piece of machinery, especially a motor vehicle. **6.** public religious worship according to prescribed form and order. **7.** Tennis, etc. the act or manner of putting the ball in play. –adj. **8.** of service; useful. **9.** of, relating to, or used by servants, tradespeople, etc. **10.** of or relating to the armed forces. –v.t. (**-viced, -vicing**) **11.** to make fit for service; restore to condition for service. **12.** (of a male animal) to inseminate (a female animal). **13.** to meet interest and other payments on, as a government debt.

serviceable /'sɜvəsəbəl/ adj. capable of doing good service.

service lift n. a goods lift.

service station n. a commercial premises selling fuel, oil, etc., for motor vehicles, and sometimes offering mechanical repairs. Also, **petrol station**.

serviette /sɜvi'ɛt/ n. a piece of cloth or paper used at table to protect the clothes, etc.; napkin; dinner napkin; table napkin.

servile /'sɜvaɪl/ adj. obsequious.

serving /'sɜvɪŋ/ n. a portion of food or drink; a helping.

servitude /'sɜvətjud/ n. slavery; bondage.

sesame /'sɛsəmi/ n. the small edible seeds of a tropical plant.

sesqui- a word element meaning 'one and a half'.

session /'sɛʃən/ n. a period of time during which a person or group of persons performs an activity.

set /sɛt/ v. (**set, setting**) –v.t. **1.** to put in a particular place, position, condition or relation. **2.** to apply. **3.** to put (a price or value) upon something. **4.** to incite or urge to attack. **5.** to fix, appoint, or ordain. **6.** to prescribe or assign, as a task. **7.** to put in the proper position, order, or condition for use; adjust or arrange. **8.** to adjust the settings of (a device) for operation. **9.** to adjust according to a standard. **10.** to cause to sit; seat. **11.** to put into a fixed, rigid, or settled state, as the countenance, the muscles, or the mind. **12.** to cause (something, as mortar) to become firm or hard. **13.** to change into a curd. **14.** to cause (hair, etc.) to assume a desired shape, style, or form. **15.** Surg. to put (a broken or dislocated bone) back in position. **16.** *Music* to fit, as words to music. *–v.i.* **17.** to pass below the horizon; sink. **18.** to become set. *–n.* **19.** the act or state of setting. **20.** a number of things customarily used together or forming a complete assortment, outfit, or collection. **21.** a number or group of persons associating or classed together. **22.** fixed direction or bent, as of the mind, etc. **23.** a radio or television receiving apparatus. **24.** a construction representing a place in which action takes place in a film, television or theatre production, or the like. *–adj.* **25.** fixed beforehand. **26.** fixed; rigid. **27.** resolved or determined; habitually or stubbornly fixed. **28.** ready; prepared; organised. *–phr.* **29. dead set**, *Colloq.* true; certain. **30. set about**, to begin; start. **31. set off, a.** to explode. **b.** to cause to explode. **c.** to begin; start, as on a journey. **d.** to intensify or improve by contrast. **e.** *Banking* to hold a credit balance on (one account) against a debit balance on another account held by the same person, company, etc. **32. set out, a.** to arrange. **b.** to state or explain methodically. **c.** to start, as on a journey. **33. set to, a.** to apply oneself; begin, as to work. **b.** to start to fight.

seti- a word element meaning 'bristle'.

set square *n.* a flat piece of wood, plastic, or the like, in the shape of a right-angled triangle, used in mechanical drawing.

settee /sɛˈti, səˈti/ *n.* a seat for two or more persons.

setter /ˈsɛtə/ *n.* one of a breed of long-haired hunting dogs.

setting /ˈsɛtɪŋ/ *n.* **1.** the surroundings or environment of anything. **2.** the articles required for setting a single place at a table.

settle[1] /ˈsɛtl/ *v.t.* **1.** to agree upon (a time, price, conditions, etc.). **2.** to pay (a bill, account due, or the like). **3.** to close (an account) by payment. **4.** to take up residence in (a country, place, house, etc.). **5.** to cause to take up residence. **6.** to furnish (a place) with inhabitants or settlers. **7.** to establish in a way of life, a business, etc. **8.** to bring to rest; quiet (the nerves, stomach, etc.). **9.** to cause to sink down gradually. *–v.i.* **10.** (oft. fol. by *on* or *upon*) to decide; arrange. **11.** (oft. fol. by *up*) to make a financial arrangement; pay. **12.** to take up residence in a new country or place. **13.** to come to rest in a particular place. **14.** to sink to the bottom, as sediment.

settle[2] /ˈsɛtl/ *n.* a long seat or bench.

settlement /ˈsɛtlmənt/ *n.* **1.** the act of settling. **2.** a colony, especially in its early stages.

settler /ˈsɛtlə/ *n.* someone who settles in a new country or region, especially someone who takes up portions of the land for agriculture.

set-top box *n.* a device, connected to a conventional television set, which receives and decodes digital television broadcasts.

seven /ˈsɛvən/ *n.* **1.** a cardinal number, six plus one. *–adj.* **2.** amounting to seven in number. **–seventh**, *adj.*, *n.*

seventeen /sɛvənˈtin/ *n.* **1.** a cardinal number, ten plus seven. *–adj.* **2.** amounting to seventeen in number. **–seventeenth**, *adj.*, *n.*

seventy /ˈsɛvənti/ *n.* (*pl.* **-ties**) **1.** a cardinal number, ten times seven. *–adj.* **2.** amounting to seventy in number. **–seventieth**, *adj.*, *n.*

sever /ˈsɛvə/ *v.t.* **1.** to divide into parts, especially forcibly; cut; cleave. **2.** to break off or dissolve (ties, relations, etc.). **–severance**, *n.*

several /ˈsɛvrəl/ *adj.* **1.** being more than two or three, but not many. **2.** respective; individual. **3.** separate; different.

severance pay *n.* money paid by a firm to employees or directors in compensation for loss of employment.

severe /səˈvɪə/ *adj.* **1.** harsh; harshly extreme. **2.** serious; stern. **3.** rigidly restrained in style or taste; simple; plain. **4.** rigidly exact, accurate, or methodical. **–severity**, *n.*

sew /soʊ/ *v.* (**sewed**, **sewn** *or* **sewed**, **sewing**) *–v.t.* **1.** to join or attach by a thread or the like, as with a needle. **2.** to make, repair, etc., (a garment) by such means. *–v.i.* **3.** to work with a needle and thread, or with a sewing machine.

sewage /ˈsuɪdʒ/ *n.* the waste matter that passes through sewers.

sewer /ˈsuə/ *n.* an artificial conduit, usually underground, for carrying off waste water and refuse, as from a town or city.

sewerage /ˈsurɪdʒ, ˈsuərɪdʒ/ *n.* **1.** the removal of waste water and refuse by means of sewers. **2.** the pipes and fittings conveying sewage.

sex /sɛks/ *n.* **1.** the sum of the anatomical and physiological differences with reference to which the male and the female are distinguished. **2.** the character of being either male or female: *persons of both sexes.* **3.** men collectively or women collectively. *–v.t.* **4.** to ascertain the sex of. *–phr.* **5. have sex**, to have sexual intercourse.

sex- a word element meaning 'six'.

sexist /ˈsɛksəst/ *adj.* **1.** of an attitude which stereotypes a person according to gender, or sexual preference, rather than judging on individual merits. *–n.* **2.** a person who displays sexist attitudes. **–sexism**, *n.*

sexual /ˈsɛkʃuəl/ *adj.* **1.** of or relating to sex. **2.** occurring between or involving the two sexes.

sexual harassment *n.* persistent unwelcome sexual advances, obscene remarks, etc., especially when made by superiors in the workplace and when employment status is dependent upon compliance.

sexual intercourse *n.* a sexual act between two people, usually one in which a man's penis enters a woman's vagina. Also, **intercourse**.

sexualise /ˈsɛkʃuəlaɪz/ *v.t.* **1.** to make sexual in nature: *to sexualise a relationship.* **2.** to imbue with sexual character: *to sexualise a marketing campaign.* Also, **sexualize**. **–sexualisation**, *n.* **–sexualised**, *adj.*

sexuality /sɛkʃuˈæləti/ *n.* sexual character; possession of sex.

sexy /ˈsɛksi/ *adj.* (**sexier**, **sexiest**) **1.** sexually interesting or exciting; having sex appeal. **2.** having or involving a predominant or intense concern with sex.

SGML /ɛs dʒi ɛm ˈɛl/ *n.* standard generalised markup language; a computer markup language designed a standard for multiple applications or operating systems.

shabby /ˈʃæbi/ *adj.* (**-bier**, **-biest**) **1.** having the appearance impaired by wear, use, etc. **2.** meanly ungenerous or unfair; contemptible, as persons, actions, etc.

shack /ʃæk/ *n.* **1.** a rough cabin; shanty. *–phr.* **2. shack up with,** *Colloq.* to live with.

shackle /'ʃækəl/ *n.* **1.** a ring or fastening of iron or the like for securing the wrist, ankle, etc.; a fetter. **2.** anything that serves to prevent freedom of procedure, thought, etc. *–v.t.* **3.** to put a shackle or shackles on; confine or restrain.

shade /ʃeɪd/ *n.* **1.** the comparative darkness caused by the interception of rays of light. **2.** comparative obscurity. **3.** a spectre or ghost. **4.** anything used for protection against excessive light, heat, etc. **5.** degree of darkening of a colour. **6.** a slight variation, amount, or degree. *–v.t.* **7.** to produce shade in or on. **8.** to screen. *–v.i.* **9.** to pass or change by slight graduations, as one colour or one thing into another.

shades /ʃeɪdz/ *pl. n. Colloq.* sunglasses.

shadow /'ʃædoʊ/ *n.* **1.** a dark figure or image cast by a body intercepting light. **2.** an instance or area of comparative darkness. **3.** shelter; protection. **4.** a slight suggestion; a trace. *–v.t.* **5.** to follow (a person) about secretly. *–adj.* **6.** *Govt* of or relating to members of the chief opposition party, as *shadow cabinet, shadow ministry.*

shaft /ʃaft/ *n.* **1.** a long pole or rod forming the body of various weapons, as a spear, lance, or arrow. **2.** something directed as in sharp attack. **3.** a ray or beam. **4.** the handle of a long implement. **5.** either of the parallel bars of wood between which the animal drawing a vehicle is placed. **6.** any vertical enclosed space, as in a building.

shag¹ /ʃæg/ *n.* rough, matted hair, wool, or the like.

shag² /ʃæg/ *n.* any of various marine cormorants.

shag³ /ʃæg/ *Colloq.* (**shagged, shagging**) **1.** to have sexual intercourse with. *–n.* **2.** an act of sexual intercourse.

shag pile *n.* carpet pile which is long and thick.

shah /ʃa/ *n.* a king (especially used as a title of the former rulers of Iran).

shake /ʃeɪk/ *v.* (**shook, shaken, shaking**) *–v.i.* **1.** to move or sway with short, quick, irregular vibratory movements. **2.** to tremble with emotion, cold, etc. **3.** to totter; become unsteady. *–v.t.* **4.** to shake (something). **5.** to bring, throw, force, rouse, etc., by or as by shaking. **6.** to agitate or disturb profoundly in feeling. *–n.* **7.** the act of shaking. **8.** tremulous motion. **9.** → **milkshake**. **10.** (*pl.*) *Colloq.* a state of trembling, especially that induced by alcoholism, drugs or nervous disorder.

shale /ʃeɪl/ *n.* a layered, easily split rock formed by the consolidation of clay.

shall /ʃæl/ *v.* (*modal*) **1.** used, generally in the first person, to indicate simple future time. **2.** used, generally in the second and third persons, to indicate promise or determination.

shallot /ʃə'lɒt/ *n.* a plant of the lily family whose small bulbs are used in cookery.

shallow /'ʃæloʊ/ *adj.* **1.** of little depth; not deep. *–n.* **2.** (*usu. pl.*) a shallow part of a body of water.

shalwar kameez /ʃalwa kə'miz/ *n.* → **salwar kameez**.

sham /ʃæm/ *n.* **1.** something that is not what it purports to be; a spurious imitation. *–adj.*

2. pretended; counterfeit. *–v.t.* (**shammed, shamming**) **3.** to assume the appearance of.

shamble /'ʃæmbəl/ *v.i.* to walk or go awkwardly; shuffle.

shambles /'ʃæmblz/ *n.* any place or thing in confusion or disorder.

shame /ʃeɪm/ *n.* **1.** the painful feeling arising from the consciousness of something dishonourable, improper, ridiculous, etc., done by oneself or another. **2.** disgrace; ignominy. *–v.t.* **3.** to cause to feel shame; make ashamed.

shammy /'ʃæmi/ *n.* (*pl.* **-mies**) → **chamois** (defs 2 and 3).

shampoo /ʃæm'pu/ *v.t.* (**-pooed, -pooing**) **1.** to wash, especially with a cleaning preparation. *–n.* **2.** a preparation used for shampooing.

shamrock /'ʃæmrɒk/ *n.* a plant with three-lobed leaflets.

shandy /'ʃændi/ *n.* a mixed drink of beer with ginger beer or lemonade.

shanghai¹ /'ʃæŋhaɪ, ʃæŋ'haɪ/ *v.t.* (**-haied, -haiing**) **1.** *Naut.* to obtain (a person) for the crew of a ship by unscrupulous means. **2.** *Colloq.* to involve (someone) in an activity, usually without their knowledge or consent.

shanghai² /'ʃæŋhaɪ/ *n.* a child's catapult.

shank /ʃæŋk/ *n.* that part of the leg in humans between the knee and the ankle.

shan't /ʃant/ *v. Colloq.* contraction of *shall not.*

shanty /'ʃænti/ *n.* (*pl.* **-ties**) a roughly built hut.

shape /ʃeɪp/ *n.* **1.** the quality of a thing depending on its outline or external surface. **2.** a particular or definite form or nature. **3.** something used to give form, as a mould or a pattern. *–v.t.* **4.** to give definite form, shape, or character to; fashion or form. *–v.i.* **5.** (oft. fol. by *up*) to develop; assume a definite form or character.

shard /ʃad/ *n.* a fragment, especially of broken earthenware.

share /ʃɛə/ *n.* **1.** the portion or part allotted or belonging to, or contributed or owed by, an individual or group. **2.** one of the equal fractional parts into which the capital stock of a limited company is divided, generally classed as either **ordinary shares** or **preference shares**. *–v.t.* (**shared, sharing**) **3.** to use, participate in, enjoy, etc., jointly.

sharebroker /'ʃɛəbroʊkə/ *n.* → **stockbroker**.

sharia /'ʃariə, ʃə'riə/ *n.* **1.** Islamic law. *–adj.* **2.** of or relating to this system. Also, **shariah**.

shark /ʃak/ *n.* any of a group of elongate (mostly marine) fishes, certain species of which are large, ferocious, and dangerous to humans.

sharp /ʃap/ *adj.* **1.** having a thin cutting edge or a fine point; well adapted for cutting or piercing. **2.** terminating in an edge or point; not blunt or rounded. **3.** clearly outlined; distinct. **4.** keen or acute. **5.** shrewd to the point of dishonesty. **6.** stylish or elegant, especially in an ostentatious manner. **7.** *Music* higher in pitch by a semitone, or too high in pitch: *B sharp. –adv.* **8.** keenly or acutely. **9.** abruptly or suddenly. **10.** punctually. *–n.* **11.** *Music* **a.** a note that is one semitone above a given note. **b.** the music sign '♯' which raises a note by a semitone when it is placed before it.

sharper /'ʃapə/ *n.* a shrewd swindler.

shashlik /'ʃæʃlɪk/ *n.* → **shish kebab**. Also, **shashlick, shaslick**.

shatter /ˈʃætə/ v.t. **1.** to break in pieces, as by a blow. –v.i. **2.** to break suddenly into fragments.

shave /ʃeɪv/ v.t. (**shaved**, **shaved** or **shaven**, **shaving**) **1.** to remove hair from (the face, legs, etc.) **2.** to cut or scrape away the surface of with a sharp-edged tool. –n. **3.** a narrow miss or escape.

shaving /ˈʃeɪvɪŋ/ n. (oft. pl.) a very thin piece or slice, especially of wood.

shawl /ʃɔl/ n. a piece of material, worn as a covering for the shoulders, head, etc.

she /ʃi/ **1.** the personal pronoun used to refer to a particular female: she is my cousin. –n. (pl. **shes**) **2.** any woman or any female person or animal (correlative to he). –adj. **3.** female or feminine, especially of animals.

sheaf /ʃif/ n. (pl. **sheaves**) any bundle, cluster, or collection.

shear /ʃɪə/ v.t. (**sheared** or **shore**, **shorn** or **sheared**, **shearing**) **1.** to remove by or as by cutting with a sharp instrument. **2.** to cut the hair, fleece, wool, etc., from. –n. **3.** (pl.) scissors of large size.

sheath /ʃiθ/ n. (pl. **sheaths** /ʃiðz, ʃiθs/) **1.** a case or covering for the blade of a sword, dagger, or the like. **2.** any similar covering.

shed[1] /ʃed/ n. **1.** a slight or rough structure built for shelter, storage, etc. **2.** a large, strongly built structure, often open at the sides or end.

shed[2] /ʃed/ v.t. (**shed**, **shedding**) **1.** to emit and let fall (tears). **2.** to cast off or let fall by natural process (leaves, hair, feathers, skin, shell, etc.).

she'd /ʃid/ contraction of: **1.** she had. **2.** she would.

sheen /ʃin/ n. lustre; brightness; radiance.

sheep /ʃip/ n. (pl. **sheep**) **1.** a ruminant mammal, closely allied to the goat, valuable for its flesh, fleece, etc. **2.** a meek, timid, or stupid person.

sheepdog /ˈʃipdɒg/ n. a dog trained to guard and round up sheep.

sheepish /ˈʃipɪʃ/ adj. awkwardly bashful or embarrassed.

sheepshank /ˈʃipʃæŋk/ n. a kind of knot, hitch, or bend made on a rope to shorten it temporarily.

sheer[1] /ʃɪə/ adj. **1.** transparently thin. **2.** unmixed with anything else. **3.** extending down or up very steeply.

sheer[2] /ʃɪə/ v.i. to deviate from a course, as a ship; swerve.

sheet /ʃit/ n. **1.** a large rectangular piece of linen, cotton, etc., used on a bed, commonly one of a pair spread immediately above and below the sleeper. **2.** a broad, thin mass, layer, or covering. **3.** an oblong or square piece of paper.

sheikh /ʃeɪk, ʃik/ n. (oft. upper case) (in Arab and other Muslim use) **1.** a chief or head; the head person of a village or tribe. **2.** the head of a Muslim religious body. Also, **sheik**.

shelf /ʃelf/ n. (pl. **shelves**) **1.** a thin slab of wood or other material fixed horizontally to a wall, or in a frame, for supporting objects. **2.** a shelf-like surface or projection; a ledge.

shelf life n. the period in which a product may remain on the shelf before being purchased, and still be marketable.

shell /ʃel/ n. **1.** a hard outer covering of an animal, as the hard case of a mollusc. **2.** any of various objects resembling a shell in some respect. **3.** the material constituting any of various kinds of shells. **4.** the exterior surface of an egg. **5.** an enclosing case or cover suggesting a shell. **6.** a cartridge. **7.** a hollow projectile for a cannon, etc., filled with explosive charge which explodes during flight or upon impact. –v.t. **8.** to take out of the shell, pod, etc. **9.** to remove the shell of.

she'll /ʃil/, weak form /ʃəl/ contraction of: **1.** she will. **2.** she shall.

shellfish /ˈʃelfɪʃ/ n. (pl. **-fish** or **-fishes**) an aquatic animal (not a fish in the ordinary sense) having a shell, especially such as oysters, mussels, etc., and (less commonly in Australia) crustaceans such as lobsters, prawns, etc.

shelter /ˈʃeltə/ n. **1.** something which affords protection or refuge; a place of refuge or safety. **2.** protection. –v.t. **3.** to be a shelter for; afford shelter to. –v.i. **4.** to take shelter; find a refuge.

shelve[1] /ʃelv/ v.t. **1.** to put on a shelf or shelves. **2.** to lay or put aside from consideration.

shelve[2] /ʃelv/ v.i. to slope gradually.

shepherd /ˈʃepəd/ n. **1.** a person who minds sheep. **2.** someone who watches over or protects a group of people. –v.t. **3.** to tend or guard as a shepherd.

sherbet /ˈʃɜbət/ n. **1.** a powdered confection. **2.** Also, **sorbet**. a frozen fruit-flavoured mixture.

sheriff /ˈʃerəf/ n. Law an officer of the Supreme Court with duties relating to service and execution of processes, summoning of juries, etc.

sherry /ˈʃeri/ n. (pl. **-ries**) a fortified and blended wine.

shiatsu /ʃiˈætsu/ n. → acupressure.

shied /ʃaɪd/ v. past tense and past participle of **shy**.

shield /ʃild/ n. **1.** anything used or serving to protect, especially a piece of armour carried on the left arm. **2.** Heraldry a shield-shaped escutcheon on which armorial bearings are displayed. –v.t. **3.** to protect with or as with a shield. –v.i. **4.** to act or serve as a shield.

shift /ʃift/ v.i. **1.** to move from one place, position, etc., to another. **2.** to transfer from one place, position, person, etc., to another. –n. **3.** a shifting from one place, position, person, etc., to another; a transfer. **4.** the portion of the day scheduled as a day's work when a factory, etc., operates continuously during the 24 hours, or works both day and night. **5.** an expedient; ingenious device. **6.** a woman's loose-fitting dress. –phr. **7. make shift**, to manage to get along or succeed.

shiftless /ˈʃiftləs/ adj. lacking in resource.

shiftwork /ˈʃiftwɜk/ n. **1.** a system of work which is regularly carried out at hours outside the normal spread of hours in addition to work within the spread, so that work performed by one employee or group of employees during a shift (usually of eight hours) is continued by another employee or group for the following shift, etc. **2.** an arrangement of an employee's working hours under which, over a period of time, the employee works on different shifts. **–shiftworker**, n.

shifty /'ʃɪfti/ adj. (**-tier, -tiest**) furtive.

shilling /'ʃɪlɪŋ/ n. (in Australia until 1966) a coin equal to $\frac{1}{20}$ of a pound.

shimmer /'ʃɪmə/ n. **1.** a subdued, tremulous light or gleam. –v.i. **2.** to shine with a shimmer.

shin /ʃɪn/ n. **1.** the front part of the leg from the knee to the ankle. –v.t., v.i. (**shinned, shinning**) **2.** to climb by holding fast with the hands or arms and legs and drawing oneself up.

shine /ʃaɪn/ v. (**shone** or **shined, shining**) –v.i. **1.** to give forth, or glow with, light; shed or cast light. **2.** to be bright with reflected light; glisten; sparkle. **3.** to excel; be conspicuous. –v.t. **4.** to cause to shine. –n. **5.** radiance; light. **6.** lustre; polish. **7.** sunshine; fair weather. **8.** Colloq. a liking; fancy. **–shiny**, adj.

shiner /'ʃaɪnə/ n. Colloq. a black eye.

shingle[1] /'ʃɪŋgəl/ n. a thin piece of wood, slate, etc., used to cover the roofs and sides of houses.

shingle[2] /'ʃɪŋgəl/ n. small, water-worn stones or pebbles such as on the seashore.

shingles /'ʃɪŋgəlz/ n. (construed as sing. or pl.) a viral disease of the skin.

shining /'ʃaɪnɪŋ/ adj. **1.** giving out or reflecting bright light. **2.** excellent: a shining example.

ship /ʃɪp/ n. **1.** any vessel intended or used for navigating the water, especially one of large size and not propelled by oars, paddles, or the like. –v.t. (**shipped, shipping**) **2.** to send or transport by ship, rail, etc. **3.** to bring (an object) into a ship or boat.

-ship a suffix of nouns denoting condition, character, office, skill, etc., as in kingship, friendship, statesmanship.

shipment /'ʃɪpmənt/ n. **1.** the act of shipping goods, etc. **2.** that which is shipped.

shipshape /'ʃɪpʃeɪp/ adj. in good order.

shiralee /'ʃɪrə'li, 'ʃɪrəˌli/ n. → **swag** (def. 1).

shiraz /ʃə'ræz/ n. (sometimes upper case) **1.** a red grape variety grown in Australia for the making of dry red table wines as well as sweet red wines. **2.** a wine made from such grapes.

shire /'ʃaɪə/ n. an area of land delineated for the purposes of local government.

shire council n. the local administrative body which serves a shire. Compare **city council, municipal council**.

shirk /ʃɜk/ v.t. to evade (work, duty, etc.).

shirt /ʃɜt/ n. a garment for the upper part of the body.

shirty /'ʃɜti/ adj. Colloq. bad-tempered.

shish kebab /'ʃɪʃ kəbæb/ n. a dish consisting of cubes of meat, marinated, and grilled on a skewer, often with onion, tomato, green pepper, etc. Also, **kebab**.

shit /ʃɪt/ Colloq. (taboo) –v. (**shitted** or **shat** or **shit, shitting**) –v.i. **1.** to defecate. –v.t. **2.** (sometimes fol. by off) to anger or disgust. –n. **3.** faeces; dung; excrement. **4.** the act of defecating. –interj. **5.** an exclamation expressing anger, disgust, disappointment, disbelief, etc.

shithouse /'ʃɪthaʊs/ Colloq. (taboo) –n. **1.** a toilet. –adj. **2.** foul; wretchedly bad.

shiver /'ʃɪvə/ v.i. **1.** to shake or tremble with cold, fear, excitement, etc. –phr. **2. the shivers**, a fit or attack of shivering.

shoal[1] /ʃoʊl/ n. a sandbank or sandbar in the bed of a body of water, especially one which shows at low water.

shoal[2] /ʃoʊl/ n. a group of fish crowded fairly close together.

shock[1] /ʃɒk/ n. **1.** a sudden and violent blow, or impact, collision, or encounter. **2.** something that shocks mentally, emotionally, etc. **3.** a sudden collapse of the nervous mechanism caused by violent physical or psychic factors. **4.** the physiological effect produced by the passage of an electric current through the body. –v.t. **5.** to strike with intense surprise, horror, disgust, etc. **6.** to cause a shock in. –adj. **7.** causing intense surprise, horror, etc.

shock[2] /ʃɒk/ n. a thick, bushy mass, as of hair.

shock jock n. a radio or television presenter who deliberately antagonises at least some part of their audience by their manner of presentation, choice of words, or body language.

shoddy /'ʃɒdi/ adj. (**-dier, -diest**) of poor quality or badly made.

shoe /ʃu/ n. (pl. **shoes**) **1.** an external covering, usually of leather, for the foot. **2.** some thing or part resembling a shoe in form, position, or use. –v.t. (**shod, shoeing**) **3.** to provide or fit with a shoe or shoes.

shoehorn /'ʃuhɔn/ n. a shaped piece of horn, metal, or the like, inserted in a shoe at the heel to make it slip on more easily.

shogun /'ʃoʊgən/ n. (in Japan) **1.** originally, a military chief, the title originating in the 8th century. **2.** in later history, a member of a quasi-dynasty, holding real power while the imperial dynasty remained theoretically and ceremonially supreme.

shone /ʃɒn/ v. past tense and past participle of **shine**.

shook /ʃʊk/ v. past tense of **shake**.

shoosh /ʃʊʃ/ interj. Colloq. hush (a command to be quiet or silent).

shoot /ʃut/ v. (**shot** /ʃɒt/, **shooting**) –v.t. **1.** to hit, wound, or kill with a missile discharged from a weapon. **2.** to send forth (arrows, bullets, etc.) from a bow, firearm, or the like. **3.** to send forth like an arrow or bullet. **4.** to pass rapidly along with. **5.** Photography to photograph or film. –v.i. **6.** to send forth missiles, from a bow, firearm, or the like. **7.** (fol. by ahead, away, into, off, etc.) to move, start to move, or pass suddenly or swiftly; dart; be propelled. **8.** (oft. fol. by up) to grow, especially rapidly. –n. **9.** an act of shooting with a bow, firearm, etc. **10.** a young branch, stem, twig, or the like.

shooting star n. a falling star.

shop /ʃɒp/ n. **1.** a building where goods are sold retail. **2.** a place for doing certain work; a workshop. –v.i. (**shopped, shopping**) **3.** to visit shops for purchasing or examining goods. –phr. **4. all over the shop**, Colloq. all over the place; in confusion. **5. talk shop**, to discuss one's trade, profession, or business.

shop floor n. **1.** that part of a factory where the machines, etc., are situated. **2.** workers collectively, especially factory workers.

shopfront /'ʃɒpfrʌnt/ n. **1.** that part of a shop which faces the street, etc. **2.** that part of an organisation which deals directly with the public.

shoplift /'ʃɒplɪft/ v.t. to steal (goods) from a shop while appearing to be a legitimate shopper.

shoplifting /'ʃɒplɪftɪŋ/ n. the crime of stealing goods from a shop while appearing to be a legitimate customer. Also, **shop stealing**.

shopping /'ʃɒpɪŋ/ n. **1.** the act of one someone who shops. **2.** the articles bought.

shopping mall n. → **mall** (def. 2).

shop steward n. a trade-union official representing workers in a factory, workshop, etc.

shore[1] /ʃɔ/ n. land along the edge of a sea, lake, large river, etc.

shore[2] /ʃɔ/ v.t. (usu. fol. by up) to support or prop.

shorn /ʃɔn/ v. past participle of **shear**.

short /ʃɔt/ adj. **1.** having little length; not long. **2.** having little height; not tall; low. **3.** brief; not extensive. **4.** rudely brief; curt; hurting. **5.** below the standard in extent, quantity, duration, etc. **6.** (fol. by on) deficient in. **7.** Commerce not possessing at the time of sale commodities or stocks that one sells. –adv. **8.** on the nearer side of an intended or particular point. **9.** Commerce without possessing at the time the stocks etc., sold. –n. **10.** something that is short. –v.t. **11.** Colloq. to short-circuit. –phr. **12. for short**, by way of abbreviation. **13. in short**, briefly.

shortage /'ʃɔtɪdʒ/ n. deficiency in quantity.

shortbread /'ʃɔtbrɛd/ n. a thick, crisp biscuit, rich in butter.

short-change v.t. (**-changed**, **-changing**) Colloq. **1.** to give less than proper change to. **2.** to cheat.

short circuit n. an abnormal connection of relatively low resistance, whether made accidentally or intentionally, between two points of different potential in an electrical circuit.

shortcoming /'ʃɔtkʌmɪŋ/ n. a failure or defect in conduct, condition, etc.

short cut n. a shorter or quicker way.

shorten /'ʃɔtn/ v.t. to make short or shorter.

shortening /'ʃɔtnɪŋ/ n. butter, lard, or other fat, used to make pastry, etc.

shorthand /'ʃɔthænd/ n. **1.** a method of rapid handwriting using extremely simple strokes in place of letters. –adj. **2.** using shorthand. **3.** written in shorthand.

shorthanded /ʃɔt'hændəd/ adj. not having the necessary number of workers, helpers, etc.

short list n. a list of especially favoured candidates for a position, promotion, etc., who have been selected from a larger group of applicants.

shortly /'ʃɔtli/ adv. in a short time; soon.

shorts /ʃɔts/ pl. n. short trousers, not extending beyond the knee.

short-sighted /'ʃɔt-saɪtəd/ adj. unable to see far; near-sighted; myopic.

short-staffed /ʃɔt-'staf/ adj. not having the usual number of personnel present.

short-tempered /ʃɔt-'tɛmpəd/ adj. having a hasty temper; inclined to become angry on little provocation.

short-term adj. **1.** covering a comparatively short period of time. **2.** having a maturity within a comparatively short time.

short-winded /ʃɔt-'wɪndəd/ adj. short of breath; liable to difficulty in breathing.

shot[1] /ʃɒt/ n. **1.** the act of shooting. **2.** small pellets of lead as used in a sportsman's gun. **3.** a person who shoots. **4.** anything like a shot. **5.** a heavy metal ball which competitors cast as far as possible in shot-putting contests. **6.** an aimed stroke, throw, or the like, as in games, etc. **7.** an attempt or try. **8.** Colloq. an injection of a drug, vaccine, etc. **9.** a small measure of alcoholic liquor. **10.** Photography a photograph.

shot[2] /ʃɒt/ v. **1.** past tense and past participle of **shoot**. –adj. **2.** woven so as to present a play of colours, as silk.

shotgun /'ʃɒtgʌn/ n. a gun for firing small shot to kill small game.

shot-put /'ʃɒt-pʊt/ n. **1.** the athletic exercise of casting a heavy metal ball (the **shot**) as far as possible. **2.** the ball itself.

should /ʃʊd/ v. **1.** past tense of **shall**. **2.** (specially used) **a.** to denote duty, propriety, or expediency. **b.** to make a statement less direct or blunt. **c.** to emphasise the uncertainty in conditional and hypothetical clauses.

shoulder /'ʃoʊldə/ n. **1.** either of two corresponding parts of the human body, situated at the top of the trunk and extending respectively from the right side and left side of the neck to the upper joint of the corresponding arm. **2.** a corresponding part in animals. **3.** a shoulder-like part or projection. **4.** either of two strips of land bordering a road. –v.t. **5.** to push, as with the shoulder, especially roughly. **6.** to take upon or support with the shoulder. **7.** to assume as a burden, or responsibility. –v.i. **8.** to push with the shoulder.

shoulderblade /'ʃoʊldəbleɪd/ n. Anat. either of two flat bones forming the back part of the shoulder.

shout[1] /ʃaʊt/ v.i. **1.** to call or cry out loudly and vigorously. –v.t. **2.** to express by a shout or shouts. –n. **3.** a loud call or cry.

shout[2] /ʃaʊt/ v.t. **1.** to pay for something for (another person); treat. –n. **2.** one's turn to shout.

shove /ʃʌv/ v.t. **1.** to move along by force from behind. **2.** to push roughly or rudely; jostle. –v.i. **3.** to push. –n. **4.** an act of shoving.

shovel /'ʃʌvəl/ n. **1.** an implement similar to a spade in use and appearance. –v.t. (**-elled**, **-elling**) **2.** to take up and cast or remove with a shovel.

show /ʃoʊ/ v. (**showed**, **shown** or **showed**, **showing**) –v.t. **1.** to cause or allow to be seen; exhibit; display; present. **2.** to point out. **3.** to guide; escort. **4.** to indicate; register. **5.** to make evident by appearance, behaviour, etc. –v.i. **6.** to be seen; be or become visible. –n. **7.** a display. **8.** ostentatious display. **9.** an indication; trace. **10.** any undertaking, organisation, etc.; affair. –phr. **11. show off**, to exhibit for approval or admiration, or ostentatiously.

show business n. the entertainment industry, especially that part concerned with variety.

showdown /'ʃoʊdaʊn/ *n.* a confrontation of parties for the final settlement of a contested issue.

shower /'ʃaʊə/ *n.* **1.** a brief fall, as of rain, hail, sleet or snow. **2. a.** an apparatus for spraying water for bathing. **b.** a washing of the body in the water sprayed from such an apparatus. *–v.t.* **3.** to pour (something) down in a shower. *–v.i.* **4.** to rain in a shower. **5.** (of a person) to take a shower (def. 2b).

shower tea *n.* → **bridal shower**.

show-off *n. Colloq.* one given to pretentious display or exhibitionism.

showroom /'ʃoʊrum/ *n.* a room used for the display of goods or merchandise.

showy /'ʃoʊi/ *adj.* (**-wier, -wiest**) **1.** making an imposing display: *showy flowers.* **2.** ostentatious; gaudy.

shrank /ʃræŋk/ *v.* past tense of **shrink**.

shrapnel /'ʃræpnəl/ *n.* **1.** shell (def. 7) fragments. **2.** *Colloq.* small change, especially silver.

shred /ʃrɛd/ *n.* **1.** a piece cut or torn off, especially in a narrow strip. *–v.* (**shredded** or **shred, shredding**) *–v.t.* **2.** to cut or tear into small pieces, especially small strips; reduce to shreds. *–v.i.* **3.** to tear; be reduced to shreds.

shrew /ʃru/ *n.* **1.** any of various small, insectivorous mouse-like mammals. **2.** a woman of violent temper and speech.

shrewd /ʃrud/ *adj.* astute or sharp.

shriek /ʃrik/ *n.* **1.** a loud, sharp, shrill cry. *–v.i.* **2.** to cry out sharply in a high voice.

shrift /ʃrɪft/ *phr.* **short shrift**, little consideration in dealing with someone or something.

shrill /ʃrɪl/ *adj.* **1.** high-pitched and piercing. *–v.t., v.i.* **2.** to cry in a shrill manner. *–***shrilly**, *adv.*

shrimp /ʃrɪmp/ *n.* **1.** any of various small, long-tailed, chiefly marine, crustaceans, esteemed as a table delicacy. **2.** *Colloq.* a diminutive person.

shrine /ʃraɪn/ *n.* any structure or place consecrated or devoted to some saint or deity.

shrink /ʃrɪŋk/ *v.* (**shrank** or **shrunk, shrunk** or **shrunken, shrinking**) *–v.i.* **1.** to draw back, as in retreat or avoidance. **2.** to become reduced in extent or compass. *–v.t.* **3.** to cause to shrink or contract. *–***shrinkage**, *n.*

shrink-wrap *v.t.* (**-wrapped, -wrapping**) to enclose (an object) in a flexible plastic wrapping which shrinks to the shape of the object, sealing it in. *–***shrink-wrapped**, *adj.*

shrivel /'ʃrɪvəl/ *v.i.* (**-elled** or, *Chiefly US*, **-eled, -elling** or, *Chiefly US*, **-eling**) to contract and wrinkle, as from great heat or cold.

shroud /ʃraʊd/ *n.* **1.** a white cloth or sheet in which a corpse is wrapped for burial. **2.** something which covers or conceals. *–v.t.* **3.** to cover; hide from view.

shrub /ʃrʌb/ *n.* a woody perennial plant smaller than a tree, usually having permanent stems branching from or near the ground.

shrug /ʃrʌg/ *v.t., v.i.* (**shrugged, shrugging**) **1.** to raise and lower (the shoulders), expressing indifference, disdain, etc. *–n.* **2.** this movement.

shudder /'ʃʌdə/ *v.i.* **1.** to tremble with a sudden convulsive movement, as from horror, fear, or cold. *–n.* **2.** such a movement.

shuffle /'ʃʌfəl/ *v.i.* **1.** to walk without lifting the feet. **2.** to move this way and that. **3.** to mix (cards in a pack) so as to change their relative position. *–n.* **4.** the act of shuffling.

shun /ʃʌn/ *v.t.* (**shunned, shunning**) to keep away from.

shunt /ʃʌnt/ *v.t.* to move or turn aside or out of the way.

shush /ʃʊʃ/ *interj.* → **shoosh**.

shut /ʃʌt/ *v.* (**shut, shutting**) *–v.t.* **1.** to put (a door, cover, etc.) in position to close or obstruct. **2.** (oft. fol. by *up*) to close the doors of. **3.** to close by folding or bringing the parts together. *–v.i.* **4.** to become shut or closed; close. *–phr.* **5. shut in**, to confine; enclose. **6. shut out**, to bar; exclude. **7. shut up**, *Colloq.* to stop talking; become silent.

shutter /'ʃʌtə/ *n.* a hinged or otherwise movable cover for a window or other opening.

shuttle /'ʃʌtl/ *n.* **1.** the sliding container that carries the lower thread in a sewing machine. *–v.t., v.i.* **2.** to move quickly to and fro like a shuttle.

shuttlecock /'ʃʌtlkɒk/ *n.* a piece of cork, or similar light material, with feathers stuck in one end, intended to be struck to and fro.

shy /ʃaɪ/ *adj.* (**shyer** or **shier, shyest** or **shiest**) **1.** bashful; retiring. **2.** easily frightened away; timid. *–v.i.* (**shied, shying**) **3.** to draw back; recoil.

Siamese twins /saɪə'miz/ *pl. n.* → **conjoined twins**.

sibilant /'sɪbələnt/ *adj.* hissing.

sibling /'sɪblɪŋ/ *n.* a brother or sister.

sic /sɪk/ *adv.* so; thus (often used parenthetically to show that something, especially a mistake, has been copied exactly from the original).

sick /sɪk/ *adj.* **1.** affected with nausea. **2.** affected with any disorder of health; ill, unwell, or ailing. **3.** of or appropriate to sick persons. **4.** macabre: *a sick joke. –n.* **5.** vomit. *–phr.* **6. sick up**, to vomit. *–***sicken**, *v.* *–***sickness**, *n.*

sick bay *n.* a place in a school where students go if they are ill or injured.

sickie /'sɪki/ *n. Colloq.* a day taken off work with pay, because of genuine or feigned illness.

sickle /'sɪkəl/ *n.* an implement for cutting grain, grass, etc., consisting of a curved, hooklike blade mounted in a short handle.

sick leave *n.* leave of absence granted because of illness.

side /saɪd/ *n.* **1.** one of the surfaces or lines bounding a thing. **2.** one of the two surfaces of an object other than the front, back, top, and bottom. **3.** either of the two lateral (right and left) parts of a thing. **4.** the space immediately beside someone or something. **5.** one of two or more parties concerned in a case, contest, etc. *–adj.* **6.** being at or on one side. **7.** coming from one side. **8.** directed towards one side. **9.** subordinate. *–phr.* (**sided, siding**) **10. side with** (or **against**), to place oneself with (or against) a side or party to support or oppose an issue.

-side a combining form used to indicate a locality which is specified.

sideboard /'saɪdbɔd/ *n.* a piece of furniture for holding articles of table service.

sideburn /'saɪdbɜn/ n. (oft. pl.) a short amount of facial hair extending from the hairline to below the ear of a man, usually worn with an unbearded chin. Also, **sidelever**, **sideboard**.

sidecar /'saɪdka/ n. a small car attached on one side to a motorcycle and supported on the other by a wheel of its own; used for a passenger, parcels, etc.

side effect n. any effect produced other than those originally intended, especially an unpleasant or harmful effect.

sideline /'saɪdlaɪn/ n. **1.** a line at the side of something. **2.** an additional or auxiliary line of goods or of business. **3.** Sport **a.** a line or mark defining the limit of play on the side of the field in football, etc. **b.** (pl.) the area immediately beyond any of the sidelines. –v.t. **(-lined, -lining) 4.** Sport to cause (a player) to become a non-participant, an observer from the sidelines: *the accident sidelined him for eight months.* **5.** to put outside the group involved in the main activity of an enterprise, organisation, etc. –phr. **6. on the sidelines, a.** not playing in a contest or game. **b.** not involved in the main action.

sidelong /'saɪdloŋ/ adj. **1.** directed to one side. –adv. **2.** towards the side; obliquely.

sidero- a word element meaning 'iron', 'steel'. Also, (before vowels), **sider-**.

sidestep /'saɪdstɛp/ v. **(-stepped, -stepping)** –v.i. **1.** to step to one side, as in avoidance. –v.t. **2.** to avoid by stepping to one side. –n. **3.** an act or instance of sidestepping.

sidetrack /'saɪdtræk/ v.i., v.t. **1.** to move from the main subject or course. –n. **2.** an act of sidetracking; a diversion; distraction. **3.** a temporary road constructed as a detour.

sideways /'saɪdweɪz/ adv. **1.** with the side foremost. **2.** towards or from one side. –adj. **3.** towards or from one side. Also, **sidewise**.

sidle /'saɪdl/ v.i. to edge along furtively.

SIDS /sɪdz/ n. sudden infant death syndrome; the sudden unexplained death of an apparently healthy baby, usually while asleep; cot death.

siege /sidʒ/ n. the operation of reducing and capturing a fortified place by surrounding it, cutting off supplies, and other offensive operations.

siemens /'simənz/ n. (pl. **-mens**) the SI unit of electrical conductance. Symbol: S

siesta /si'ɛstə/ n. a midday or afternoon rest or nap.

sieve /sɪv/ n. an instrument, with a meshed or perforated bottom, used for separating coarse from fine parts of loose matter, for straining liquids, etc.

sievert /'sivɜt/ n. the SI derived unit of radiation dose. Symbol: Sv

sift /sɪft/ v.t. **1.** to separate the coarse parts of (flour, ashes, etc.) with a sieve. **2.** to scatter by means of a sieve. **3.** to examine closely.

sigh /saɪ/ v.i. **1.** to let out one's breath audibly, as from sorrow, weariness, relief, etc. **2.** to yearn or long. –v.t. **3.** to express with a sigh. –n. **4.** the act or sound of sighing.

sight /saɪt/ n. **1.** the power or faculty of seeing; vision. **2.** the act or fact of seeing. **3.** range of vision. **4.** a view; glimpse. **5.** something seen or to be seen; spectacle. –v.t. **6.** to get sight of.

–phr. **7. set one's sights on,** to adopt as an ambition or goal.

sign /saɪn/ n. **1.** a token; indication. **2.** a symbol used technically instead of the word or words which it represents, as an abbreviation. **3.** a movement that expresses an idea or feeling. **4.** an inscribed board, space, etc., serving for information, advertisement, warning, etc. –v.t. **5.** to affix a signature to. **6.** to communicate by a sign. –v.i. **7.** to write one's signature, as a token of agreement, obligation, receipt, etc. **8.** to make a sign or signal.

signal /'sɪgnəl/ n. **1.** a gesture, act, light, etc., serving to warn, direct, command, or the like. **2.** an act, event, or the like, which precipitates an action. **3.** a token; indication. **4.** Radio, etc. the impulses, waves, sounds, etc., transmitted or received. –adj. **5.** serving as a sign. –v. **(-nalled, -nalling)** –v.t. **6.** to make a signal to. **7.** to make known by a signal. –v.i. **8.** to make communication by a signal or signals.

signatory /'sɪgnətri/ adj. **1.** that has signed, or has joined in signing, a document. –n. (pl. **-ries) 2.** a signer, or one of the signers, of a document, as a treaty.

signature /'sɪgnətʃə/ n. **1.** a person's name written by himself or herself or by a deputy, as in signing a letter or other document. **2.** the act of signing a document.

signet /'sɪgnət/ n. a small official seal.

significance /sɪg'nɪfəkəns/ n. **1.** importance; consequence. **2.** meaning; import. –**significant,** adj.

signify /'sɪgnəfaɪ/ v. **(-fied, -fying)** –v.t. **1.** to make known by signs, speech, or action. **2.** to be a sign of; mean; portend. –v.i. **3.** to be of importance or consequence.

sign language n. a communication system using gestures rather than speech or writing, as that used with the hearing-impaired.

silence /'saɪləns/ n. **1.** absence of any sound or noise; stillness. –v.t. **(-lenced, -lencing) 2.** to put or bring to silence; still. –interj. **3.** be quiet! –**silent,** adj.

silent partner n. a partner having no active or public part in the conduct of a business.

silhouette /sɪlu'ɛt, sɪlə'wɛt/ n. a dark image outlined against a lighter background.

silic- a word element meaning 'flint', 'silica', 'silicon'. Also, **silici-, silico-**.

silica /'sɪlɪkə/ n. silicon dioxide, appearing as quartz, sand, flint, and agate.

silicon /'sɪlɪkən/ n. a nonmetallic element used in steelmaking, etc.; widely used as a semiconductor in solid-state electronics. Symbol: Si

silk /sɪlk/ n. **1.** the fine, soft, lustrous fibre obtained from the cocoon of the silkworm. **2.** thread or cloth made of this fibre. **3.** any fibre or filamentous matter resembling silk. –adj. **4.** made of silk. **5.** of or relating to silk. –phr. **6. take silk,** to become a Queen's Counsel. –**silken,** adj.

silk-screen v.t. to produce by silk-screen printing.

silk-screen printing n. a process of printing from stencils, which may be photographically made or cut by hand, through a fine mesh of silk, metal or other material. –**silk-screen print,** n.

silkworm /ˈsɪlkwɜːm/ n. a caterpillar of certain moth families which spins a fine, soft fibre (silk) to form a cocoon, in which it is enclosed while in the pupal stage.

sill /sɪl/ n. the horizontal piece or member beneath a window, door, or other opening.

silly /ˈsɪli/ adj. (-lier, -liest) 1. lacking good sense; foolish; stupid. 2. absurd or ridiculous. –n. (pl. -lies) 3. Colloq. a silly person.

silo /ˈsaɪloʊ/ n. (pl. -los) a tower-like structure for storing grain.

silt /sɪlt/ n. earthy matter, fine sand, or the like, carried by moving or running water and deposited as a sediment. –siltation, n.

silver /ˈsɪlvə/ n. 1. Chem. a white ductile metallic element, used for making mirrors, coins, ornaments, table utensils, etc. Symbol: Ag 2. coin made of silver or of a metal resembling silver; money. 3. silverware: table articles made of or plated with silver. 4. a lustrous greyish-white or whitish-grey; colour of metallic silver. –adj. 5. consisting or made of silver; plated with silver. 6. of or relating to silver. 7. (of coins) made of a metal or alloy resembling silver. 8. having the colour silver, or tinted with silver. 9. indicating the 25th event of a series, as a wedding anniversary.

silverbeet /ˈsɪlvəbiːt/ n. a form of beet with large leaves and a long fleshy stalk, used as a vegetable; spinach. Also, silver beet.

silver bullet n. a certain and effective remedy, as a drug, defence system, etc., usually seen as an unrealistic ideal.

silverfish /ˈsɪlvəfɪʃ/ n. (pl. -fishes or, especially collectively, -fish) any of certain small, wingless insects damaging to books, wallpaper, etc.

silver plate n. 1. a thin silver coating deposited on the surface of another metal. 2. silver-plated tableware.

silverside /ˈsɪlvəsaɪd/ n. a cut of beef from the outside portion of a full butt, usually boiled or pickled.

SIM card /sɪm/ n. a circuit-bearing card inserted into a mobile phone which contains the subscriber's authorisation to use a certain mobile phone network.

simian /ˈsɪmiən/ adj. of or relating to an ape or monkey.

similar /ˈsɪmələ/ adj. having likeness or resemblance, especially in a general way. –similarity, n.

simile /ˈsɪməli/ n. a figure of speech directly expressing a resemblance, in one or more points, of one thing to another, as a man like an ox.

similitude /səˈmɪlətjuːd/ n. 1. likeness; resemblance. 2. a likening or comparison; a parable or allegory.

simmer /ˈsɪmə/ v.i., v.t. to cook in a liquid just below the boiling point. –n. 2. state or process of simmering. –phr. 3. simmer down, Colloq. to become calm or calmer.

simper /ˈsɪmpə/ v.i. to smile in a silly, self-conscious way.

simple /ˈsɪmpəl/ adj. 1. easy to understand, deal with, use, etc. 2. not elaborate or artificial. 3. not complex or complicated. 4. sincere; innocent. 5. unlearned; ignorant. 6. Chem. a. composed of one substance or element:

a simple substance. b. not mixed. –simplicity, n.

simple interest n. interest which is not compounded, that is, interest calculated only on the original capital invested or the original amount of the loan.

simpleton /ˈsɪmpəltən/ n. a fool.

simplify /ˈsɪmpləfaɪ/ v.t. (-fied, -fying) to make less complex or complicated; make plainer or easier.

simplistic /sɪmˈplɪstɪk/ adj. characterised by extreme simplification, especially if misleading; oversimplified.

simply /ˈsɪmpli/ adv. 1. in a simple manner. 2. plainly; unaffectedly. 3. not deceitfully or craftily. 4. merely; only. 5. absolutely: simply irresistible.

simulation /sɪmjəˈleɪʃən/ n. 1. assumption of a particular appearance or form. 2. Computers a. the technique of establishing a routine for one computer to make it function as nearly as possible like another computer. b. the representation of physical systems, phenomena, etc., by computers. 3. the practice of constructing a model of a machine in order to test behaviour. –simulate, v.

simulator /ˈsɪmjəleɪtə/ n. a training or experimental device that simulates movement, flight, etc.

simulcast /ˈsɪmʌlkast, ˈsaɪ-/ n. simultaneous broadcast of the same program by two separate radio stations or by a radio and a television station.

simultaneous /sɪmlˈteɪniəs/ adj. existing, occurring, or operating at the same time.

sin /sɪn/ n. 1. transgression of divine law. 2. an act regarded as such transgression. –v.i. (sinned, sinning) 3. to do a sinful act.

sin-bin n. Colloq. → penalty box. Also, sin bin, sinbin.

since /sɪns/ adv. 1. (oft. preceded by ever) from then till now. 2. between a particular past time and the present; subsequently. 3. ago; before now. –prep. 4. continuously from or counting from. 5. between a (past time or event) and the present. –conj. 6. in the period following the time when. 7. because; inasmuch as.

sincere /sɪnˈsɪə, sən-/ adj. free from any element of deceit, dissimulation, duplicity or hypocrisy. –sincerity, n.

sine /saɪn/ n. Maths a trigonometric function defined for an acute angle in a right-angled triangle as the ratio of the side opposite the angle to the hypotenuse.

sinecure /ˈsɪnəkjʊə, ˈsaɪnəkjʊə/ n. an office requiring little or no work, especially one yielding profitable returns.

sinew /ˈsɪnjuː/ n. 1. a tendon. 2. strength; vigour.

sing /sɪŋ/ v. (sang or sung, sung, singing) –v.i. 1. to utter words or sounds in succession with musical modulations of the voice. 2. to produce melodious sounds, as certain birds, insects, etc. 3. to make a short ringing, whistling, or whizzing sound. –v.t. 4. to utter with musical modulations of the voice, as a song. 5. to bring, send, put, etc., with or by singing. –n. 6. a singing, ringing, or whistling sound, as of a bullet.

Singapore noodles /'sɪŋəpɔ/ *pl. n.* **1.** thin round noodles in the Asian style. **2.** (*construed as sing.*) a dish based on these noodles in a style originating in Singapore, with a sauce, and including vegetables, prawns and chicken.

singe /sɪndʒ/ *v.i.*, *v.t.* (**singed**, **singeing**) **1.** to burn superficially. *–n.* **2.** a superficial burn.

single /'sɪŋgəl/ *adj.* **1.** one only; separate; individual. **2.** of or relating to one person, family, etc. **3.** alone; solitary. **4.** without a spouse or permanent partner. **5.** consisting of one part, element, or member. **6.** sincere; honest. *–v.t.* **7.** (usu. fol. by *out*) to pick or choose out from others. *–n.* **8.** something single or separate; a single one.

single-handed *adj.* acting or working alone or unaided.

single-minded *adj.* having or showing undivided purpose.

singlet /'sɪŋlət, 'sɪŋglət/ *n.* a short garment, with or without sleeves, usually worn next to the skin.

singsong /'sɪŋsɒŋ/ *n.* **1.** an informal gathering at which the company sing; community singing. *–adj.* **2.** characterised by a regular rising and falling intonation.

singular /'sɪŋgjələ/ *adj.* **1.** being the only one of the kind; unique. **2.** separate; individual. **3.** *Gram.* designating the number category that normally implies one person, thing, or collection.

sinister /'sɪnəstə/ *adj.* threatening or portending evil; ominous.

sink /sɪŋk/ *v.* (**sank** *or, Chiefly US,* **sunk**, **sunk** *or* **sunken**, **sinking**) *–v.i.* **1.** to descend gradually to a lower level, as water, flames, etc. **2.** to become submerged. **3.** to pass or fall into some lower state, as of fortune, estimation, etc. **4.** to decrease in amount, extent, degree, etc., as value, prices, rates, etc. **5.** (fol. by *in*, *into*, etc.) to enter or permeate the mind; become understood. **6.** to fall in; become hollow, as the cheeks. **7.** (usu. fol. by *in* or *into*) to be or become deeply absorbed in a mental state. *–v.t.* **8.** to cause to sink. **9.** to suppress; ignore; omit. **10.** to invest (money), now especially unprofitably. **11.** to make (a hole, shaft, well, etc.) by excavating or boring downwards; hollow out (any cavity). *–n.* **12.** a basin with a water supply and outlet. **13.** a low-lying area where waters collect. **14.** a place of vice or corruption.

sinker /'sɪŋkə/ *n.* a weight of lead, etc., for sinking a fishing line, fishing net, or the like in the water.

sinking fund *n.* a fund into which regular payments are made, either for the purpose of liquidating a debt by degrees, or for meeting future commitments.

sinuous /'sɪnjuəs/ *adj.* having many curves, bends, or turns; winding.

sinus /'saɪnəs/ *n.* (*pl.* **-nuses**) one of the hollow cavities in the skull connecting with the nasal cavities.

-sion a suffix having the same function as **-tion**, as in *compulsion*.

sip /sɪp/ *v.i.*, *v.t.* (**sipped**, **sipping**) **1.** to drink a little at a time. *–n.* **2.** an act of sipping. **3.** a small quantity taken by sipping.

siphon /'saɪfən/ *n.* **1.** a tube through which liquid flows over the wall of a tank or reservoir to a lower elevation by atmospheric pressure. *–v.t.*, *v.i.* **2.** to convey or pass through a siphon. Also, **syphon**.

sir /sɜ/ *n.* a respectful term of address used to a man.

sire /'saɪə/ *n.* **1.** the male parent of an animal. *–v.t.* **2.** to beget.

siren /'saɪrən/ *n.* **1.** *Classical Myth.* one of several sea nymphs, part woman and part bird, who supposedly lured mariners to destruction by their seductive singing. **2.** a device used as a whistle, fog signal, warning sound on an ambulance, fire-engine, etc. *–adj.* **3.** of or like a siren.

sirloin /'sɜlɔɪn/ *n.* the portion of the loin of beef in front of the rump, used whole as a roast or cut into steaks.

sissy /'sɪsi/ *n.* (*pl.* **-sies**) a timid or cowardly person. Also, **cissy**.

sister /'sɪstə/ *n.* **1.** a daughter of the same parents. **2.** a female associate. **3.** a female member of a religious community. *–adj.* **4.** being a sister; related by, or as by, sisterhood.

sister-in-law /'sɪstər-ɪn-lɔ/ *n.* (*pl.* **sisters-in-law**) **1.** one's husband's or wife's sister. **2.** one's sibling's wife. **3.** the wife of one's spouse's sibling.

sit /sɪt/ *v.* (**sat**, **sitting**) *–v.i.* **1.** to rest on the lower part of the body; be seated. **2.** to be situated; dwell. **3.** to remain quiet or inactive. **4.** to fit or be adjusted, as a garment. **5.** to occupy a seat in an official capacity, as a judge or bishop. **6.** to be convened or in session, as an assembly. *–v.t.* **7.** to cause to sit; seat (often with *down*). **8.** to sit upon (a horse, etc.). **9.** to provide seating room for; seat.

sitar /'sɪta, 'sɪta/ *n.* a guitar-like instrument of India, having a long neck and usually three strings. Also, **sittar**.

sitcom /'sɪtkɒm/ *n.* a comedy based on the situations of ordinary life.

sit-down strike *n.* a strike during which workers refuse either to leave their place of employment or to work or to allow others to work until the strike is settled. Also, **sit-down**.

site /saɪt/ *n.* **1.** the area on which anything, as a building, is, has been or is to be situated. *–v.t.* **2.** to locate; place; provide with a site.

site map *n.* **1.** a map of a building site showing the location of different buildings, areas of interest, etc. **2.** *Computers* a map of a website showing the various pages and links between them.

sitting duck *n.* any particularly easy mark to shoot at.

situate /'sɪtʃueɪt/ *v.t.* to give a site to; locate.

situation /sɪtʃu'eɪʃən/ *n.* **1.** manner of being situated; a location or position with reference to environment. **2.** a place or locality. **3.** the state of affairs; combination of circumstances. **4.** a position or post of employment.

SI unit /ɛs 'aɪ/ *n.* a unit of the International System of Units.

six /sɪks/ *n.* **1.** a cardinal number, five plus one. *–adj.* **2.** amounting to six in number. *–sixth*, *adj.*, *n.*

sixteen /sɪks'tin/ *n.* **1.** a cardinal number, ten plus six. *–adj.* **2.** amounting to sixteen in number. *–sixteenth*, *adj.*, *n.*

sixth sense *n.* a power of perception beyond the five senses; intuition.

sixty /'sɪksti/ *n.* (*pl.* **-ties**) **1.** a cardinal number, ten times six. *–adj.* **2.** amounting to sixty in number. **–sixtieth**, *adj.*, *n.*

size[1] /saɪz/ *n.* **1.** the dimensions, proportions, or magnitude of anything. *–v.t.* **2.** to separate or sort according to size. **3.** to make of a certain size. *–phr.* **4. size up**, to form an estimate of.

size[2] /saɪz/ *n.* any of various gelatinous or glutinous preparations used for glazing or coating paper, cloth, etc.

sizzle /'sɪzəl/ *v.i.* **1.** to make a hissing sound, as in frying or burning. *–n.* **2.** a sizzling sound.

skate /skeɪt/ *n.* **1.** a steel blade attached to the bottom of a shoe, enabling a person to glide on ice. **2.** → **rollerskate**. *–v.i.* **3.** to glide over ice, the ground, etc., on skates. **–skater**, *n.*

skateboard /'skeɪtbɔd/ *n.* a short plank on rollerskate wheels, ridden, usually standing up, as a recreation. **–skateboarder**, *n.*

skein /skeɪn/ *n.* a length of thread or yarn wound in a coil.

skeleton /'skɛlətn/ *n.* **1.** the bones of a human or other animal body considered together. **2.** *Colloq.* a very lean person or animal. **3.** a supporting framework, as of a leaf, building, or ship. *–adj.* **4.** of or relating to a skeleton. **–skeletal**, *adj.*

skeleton key *n.* a key which may open various locks. Also, **pass key**.

skerrick /'skɛrɪk/ *n.* a very small quantity; a scrap.

sketch /skɛtʃ/ *n.* **1.** a simply or hastily executed drawing or painting. **2.** a rough design, plan, or draft, as of a literary work. **3.** a brief or hasty outline of facts, occurrences, etc. *–v.t.* **4.** to make a sketch of. *–v.i.* **5.** to make a sketch or sketches.

skew /skju/ *v.i.* **1.** to turn aside or swerve; take an oblique course. *–v.t.* **2.** to give an oblique direction to; shape or form obliquely. **3.** to distort.

skewer /'skjuə/ *n.* **1.** a long pin of wood or metal for putting through meat to hold it together or in place while being cooked. *–v.t.* **2.** to fasten with, or as with, skewers.

ski /ski/ *n.* (*pl.* **skis**) **1.** one of a pair of long, slender pieces of hard wood, metal, or plastic, one fastened to each shoe, used for travelling or gliding over snow, and often (especially as a sport) down slopes. *–v.i.* (**ski'd** *or* **skied**, **skiing**) **2.** to travel on or use skis.

skid /skɪd/ *n.* **1.** a plank, bar, log, or the like, especially one of a pair, on which something heavy may be slid or rolled along. **2.** an act of skidding. *–v.i.* (**skidded**, **skidding**) **3.** to slide along without rotating, as a wheel to which a brake has been applied. **4.** to slide forward under its own momentum, as a car when the wheels have been braked.

skilful /'skɪlfəl/ *adj.* having skill; good at doing something. **–skilfully**, *adv.*

skill /skɪl/ *n.* the ability that comes from knowledge, practice, aptitude, etc., to do something well.

skilled /skɪld/ *adj.* **1.** showing, involving, or requiring skill, as work. **2.** of or relating to workers performing a specific operation

requiring apprenticeship or other special training or experience.

skillet /'skɪlət/ *n.* a small frying pan.

skillshare /'skɪlʃɛə/ *v.i.* **1.** to share one's acquired skills with other people, as between students. *–n.* **2.** the process of such sharing.

skim /skɪm/ *v.* (**skimmed**, **skimming**) *–v.t.* **1.** to take up or remove (floating matter) from a liquid with a spoon, ladle, etc. **2.** to clear (liquid) thus. **3.** to move or glide lightly over or along the surface of (the ground, water, etc.). **4.** *Colloq.* to take the details of (a plastic card) so as to steal money from the account of the owner. *–v.i.* **5.** to pass or glide lightly along over or near a surface. *–n.* **6.** the act of skimming. **7.** that which is skimmed off, such as the cream from skim milk.

skim milk *n.* milk from which the cream has been removed. Also, **skimmed milk**.

skimming /'skɪmɪŋ/ *n.* **1.** (*usu. pl.*) something that is removed by skimming. **2.** *Colloq.* the practice of taking the details of (a plastic card) so as to steal money from the account of the owner.

skimp /skɪmp/ *v.t.* **1.** to be sparing with; scrimp. *–v.i.* **2.** (oft. fol. by *on*) to be extremely thrifty.

skimpy /'skɪmpi/ *adj.* (**-pier, -piest**) hardly enough in quantity, size, etc.: *a skimpy meal*; *a skimpy jumper*. **–skimpily**, *adv.* **–skimpiness**, *n.*

skin /skɪn/ *n.* **1.** the external covering of an animal body, especially when soft and flexible. **2.** any outer coating, or surface layer, as an investing membrane, the rind or peel of fruit, or a film on liquid. *–v.t.* (**skinned**, **skinning**) **3.** to strip or deprive of skin; flay; peel. **4.** to strip off, as or like skin.

skindiving /'skɪndaɪvɪŋ/ *n.* underwater swimming with an aqualung or snorkel, and foot fins.

skinflint /'skɪnflɪnt/ *n.* a mean person.

skink /skɪŋk/ *n.* any of various harmless, generally smooth-scaled lizards.

skin name *n.* a name which identifies an Aboriginal person to a particular section or subsection. See **section** (def. 5), **subsection** (def. 2). Also, **kinship name**.

skinny /'skɪni/ *adj.* (**-nier, -niest**) **1.** lean; emaciated. **2.** of or like skin. **3.** *Colloq.* having less than the usual fat content: *a skinny cappuccino*.

skint /skɪnt/ *adj.* *Colloq.* completely without money; broke.

skip[1] /skɪp/ *v.* (**skipped**, **skipping**) *–v.i.* **1.** to spring, jump, or leap lightly; gambol. **2.** to pass from one point, thing, subject, etc., to another, disregarding or omitting what intervenes. **3.** to use a skipping-rope. *–v.t.* **4.** to jump lightly over. **5.** to miss out, as part of a continuum or one of a series. **6.** *Colloq.* to leave hastily, or flee from, as a place. *–n.* **7.** a skipping movement; a light jump.

skip[2] /skɪp/ *n.* a container designed to be attached to a crane or cable for transporting materials or refuse in building operations.

skipper /'skɪpə/ *n.* a captain or leader, as of a team.

skirmish /'skɜmɪʃ/ *n.* **1.** any brisk encounter. *–v.i.* **2.** to engage in a skirmish.

skirt /skɜt/ *n.* **1.** the lower part of a garment, hanging from the waist. **2.** a separate garment,

skirting board *n.* a line of boarding protecting an interior wall next to the floor. Also, **skirting**.

skit /skɪt/ *n.* a slight parody, satire, or caricature, especially dramatic or literary.

skite /skaɪt/ *Colloq.* –*v.i.* **1.** to boast; brag. –*n.* **2.** a boast; brag. **3.** Also, **skiter.** a boaster; braggart.

skittish /ˈskɪtɪʃ/ *adj.* restlessly or excessively lively.

skittle /ˈskɪtl/ *n.* **1.** (*pl.*) a game played with bottle-shaped pieces of wood and a ball to knock them down. –*v.t.* (**skittled, skittling**) **2.** to knock over or send flying, in the manner of skittles.

skivvy /ˈskɪvi/ *n.* (*pl.* **-vies**) a close-fitting stretch garment with long sleeves.

skulduggery /skʌlˈdʌɡəri/ *n.* dishonourable proceedings; mean dishonesty or trickery. Also, **skullduggery**.

skulk /skʌlk/ *v.i.* to lie or keep in hiding, as for some evil or cowardly reason.

skull /skʌl/ *n.* the bony framework of the head, enclosing the brain and supporting the face.

skunk /skʌŋk/ *n.* **1.** a small, striped, fur-bearing, bushy-tailed, North American mammal which ejects a fetid fluid when attacked. **2.** *Colloq.* a thoroughly contemptible person.

sky /skaɪ/ *n.* (*pl.* **skies**) (*oft. pl.*) the region of the clouds or the upper air.

skyboard /ˈskaɪbɔd/ *n.* **1.** a lightweight board similar to a snowboard, used for skysurfing. –*v.i.* **2.** to skydive on such a skyboard.

skydive /ˈskaɪdaɪv/ *v.i.* (**-dived, -diving**) **1.** to engage in the sport of skydiving. –*n.* **2.** an instance of skydiving. –**skydiver,** *n.*

skydiving /ˈskaɪdaɪvɪŋ/ *n.* the sport of free-falling from an aeroplane for a great distance, controlling one's course by changes in body position, before releasing one's parachute.

skylight /ˈskaɪlaɪt/ *n.* an opening in a roof or ceiling, fitted with glass or other such translucent material, for admitting daylight.

sky marshal *n.* a guard placed on an aeroplane to maintain security. Also, **air marshal**.

skyrocket /ˈskaɪrɒkət/ *n.* **1.** a firework that ascends into the air and explodes at a height. –*v.i.* **2.** to move like a skyrocket.

skyscraper /ˈskaɪskreɪpə/ *n.* a tall building of many storeys, especially one for office or commercial use.

skysurf /ˈskaɪsɜf/ *v.i.* to skydive on a skyboard. Also, **skyboard.** –**skysurfer,** *n.* –**skysurfing,** *adj.*, *n.*

slab /slæb/ *n.* a broad, flat, somewhat thick piece of stone, wood, or other solid material.

slack /slæk/ *adj.* **1.** not tense or taut; loose. **2.** indolent; negligent; remiss. –*n.* **3.** a slack condition, interval, or part. –*v.t.*, *v.i.* **4.** to make or become slack. –*phr.* **5. cut someone some slack,** *Colloq.* to show leniency towards someone.

slacks /slæks/ *pl. n.* long trousers, worn by either men or women as informal wear.

slag /slæɡ/ *n.* matter separated during the reduction of a metal from its ore.

slain /sleɪn/ *v.* past participle of **slay**.

slake /sleɪk/ *v.t.* to allay (thirst, desire, wrath, etc.) by satisfying.

slalom /ˈslɑləm, ˈslæləm/ *n.* a downhill skiing race with a winding course.

slam /slæm/ *v.t.*, *v.i.* (**slammed, slamming**) **1.** to shut with force and noise. **2.** to dash, strike, etc., with violent and noisy impact. –*n.* **3.** a violent and noisy closing, dashing, or impact.

slander /ˈslændə, ˈslɑndə/ *n.* **1.** a malicious, false, and defamatory statement or report. –*v.t.* **2.** to utter slander concerning; defame.

slang /slæŋ/ *n.* language differing from standard or written speech in vocabulary and construction, involving extensive metaphor, ellipsis, humorous usage, etc., less conservative and more informal than standard speech, and sometimes regarded as being in some way inferior.

slant /slænt, slɑnt/ *v.i.* **1.** to slope; be directed or lie obliquely. –*v.t.* **2.** to slope; direct or turn so as to make (something) oblique. **3.** to distort or give partisan emphasis to (a newspaper story, article, etc.). –*n.* **4.** slanting or oblique direction; slope. **5.** a mental leaning or tendency; especially unusual or unfair; bias.

slap /slæp/ *n.* **1.** a smart blow, especially with the open hand or with something flat. –*v.t.* (**slapped, slapping**) **2.** to strike with a slap.

slapdash /ˈslæpdæʃ/ *adv.*, *adj.* carelessly hasty or offhand.

slapstick /ˈslæpstɪk/ *n.* comedy featuring rough play and clowning.

slap-up *adj. Colloq.* first-rate; excellent.

slash /slæʃ/ *v.t.* **1.** to cut with a violent sweep or by striking violently and at random. **2.** to cut, reduce, or alter, especially drastically. –*v.i.* **3.** to make a sweeping, cutting stroke. –*n.* **4.** a sweeping stroke. **5.** a cut or wound made with such a stroke; a gash. **6.** Also, **forward slash.** a short diagonal line (/), used in writing or typing to separate or enclose words or characters; solidus.

slash-and-burn *adj.* of or relating to a method of cultivation of land, especially in developing countries, in which natural vegetation is cut down and burned as a preliminary to sowing crops, resulting in degradation of the soil.

slat /slæt/ *n.* **1.** a long, thin, narrow strip of wood, metal, etc., used as a support for a bed, as one of the horizontal laths of a venetian blind, etc. –*v.t.* (**slatted, slatting**) **2.** to furnish or make with slats.

slate¹ /sleɪt/ *n.* **1.** a fine-grained rock formed by the compression of mudstone, that tends to split along parallel cleavage planes, usually at an angle to the planes of stratification. **2.** a thin piece or plate of this rock or a similar material, used especially for roofing, or for writing on. **3.** a dull, dark bluish grey. –*v.t.* **4.** to write or set down for nomination or appointment: *I've slated you for the job of marketing manager.*

slate² /sleɪt/ *v.t.* to censure or reprimand severely.

slather /ˈslæðə/ *v.t.* **1.** to use in large quantities; to lavish. –*phr.* **2. open slather,** complete freedom; free rein.

slaughter /ˈslɔtə/ n. **1.** the killing or butchering of cattle, sheep, etc., especially for food. **2.** the killing by violence of great numbers of persons. −v.t. **3.** to slaughter (people or animals).

slave /sleɪv/ n. **1.** someone who is the property of and wholly subject to another. −v.i. **2.** to work like a slave; drudge. −**slavery**, n. −**slavish**, adj.

slaver /ˈslævə/ v.i. to let saliva run from the mouth; slobber.

slay /sleɪ/ v.t. (**slew** or **slayed**, **slain** or **slayed**, **slaying**) to kill by violence.

sleazy /ˈslizi/ adj. (**-zier**, **-ziest**) **1.** of dubious moral character, especially in relation to sexual matters. **2.** shabby, shoddy, untidy, or grubby.

sled /sled/ n. a vehicle mounted on runners for travelling over snow, etc.

sledge¹ /sledʒ/ n. any of various vehicles mounted on runners for travelling or conveying loads over snow, ice, rough ground, etc.

sledge² /sledʒ/ v.t. (**sledged**, **sledging**) to abuse and ridicule.

sledgehammer /ˈsledʒhæmə/ n. a large heavy hammer, often held with both hands; sledge.

sleek /slik/ adj. **1.** smooth; glossy, as hair, an animal, etc. **2.** well-fed or well-groomed. **3.** suave; insinuating.

sleep /slip/ v. (**slept**, **sleeping**) −v.i. **1.** to take the repose or rest afforded by the natural suspension, complete or partial, of consciousness. **2.** to be dormant, quiescent, or inactive, as faculties. −v.t. **3.** to have beds or sleeping accommodation for. **4.** (fol. by away or out) to spend or pass (time, etc.) in sleep. −n. **5.** the state of a person, animal, or plant that sleeps. **6.** a period of sleeping. **7.** the mucous congealed in the corners of the eyes, especially after sleep.

sleep apnoea /ˈæpniə/ n. a temporary cessation of breathing during sleep, often caused by obstruction of the air passages, as by enlarged tonsils, etc.

sleeper /ˈslipə/ n. **1.** a timber, concrete, or steel beam forming part of a railway track, serving as a foundation or support for the rails. **2.** a bed, place, or compartment in a carriage on a passenger train. **3.** a small ring, bar, etc., worn in the ear lobe after piercing to prevent the hole from closing. **4.** Colloq. **a.** someone or something that unexpectedly achieves success or fame. **b.** a book, item of manufacture, etc., which has slow but constant sales.

sleeper cell n. a small group of people, committed to a cause, who infiltrate a community waiting for an instruction to carry out sabotage, undertake a specific terrorist activity, etc.

sleeping partner n. → **silent partner**.

sleep mode n. a state of low activity in which an electronic device not being used, especially a computer, consumes less electric power but is not turned off.

sleepover /ˈslipoʊvə/ n. (with children) a night spent at a friend's home.

sleepwalk /ˈslipwɔk/ v.i. to walk or perform other activities while asleep. −**sleepwalking**, n. −**sleepwalker**, n.

sleet /slit/ n. snow or hail and rain falling together.

sleeve /sliv/ n. **1.** the part of a garment that covers the arm, varying in form and length but commonly tubular. **2.** something resembling this.

sleigh /sleɪ/ n. a vehicle on runners, drawn by horses, dogs, etc., and used for transport on snow or ice.

sleight /slaɪt/ n. skill; dexterity.

slender /ˈslendə/ adj. **1.** small in circumference in proportion to height or length. **2.** small in size, amount, extent, etc.

sleuth /sluθ/ n. Colloq. a detective.

slew¹ /slu/ v. past tense of **slay**.

slew² /slu/ v.t. **1.** to turn or twist (something), especially upon its own axis or without moving it from its place. **2.** to cause to swing round. −v.i. **3.** to swerve awkwardly; swing round; twist. **4.** Colloq. to relax vigilance. −n. **5.** such a movement. **6.** the position reached by slewing.

slew³ /slu/ n. Colloq. a large number: a whole slew of DVDs.

slice /slaɪs/ n. **1.** a thin, broad, flat piece cut from something. **2.** any of various implements with a thin, broad blade or part, as for turning food in a frying pan, etc. −v.t. (**sliced**, **slicing**) **3.** to cut into slices; divide into parts. **4.** to cut (off, away, from, etc.) as or like a slice.

slick /slɪk/ adj. **1.** smooth of manners, speech, etc. **2.** ingenious; cleverly devised. −n. **3.** a patch or film of oil or the like, as on the sea.

slide /slaɪd/ v. (**slid**, **slid** or **slidden**, **sliding**) −v.i. **1.** to move along in continuous contact with a smooth or slippery surface. **2.** to slip, as one losing foothold or as a vehicle skidding. **3.** (fol. by in, out, away, etc.) to slip easily, quietly, or unobtrusively. −v.t. **4.** to cause to slide, as over a surface or with a smooth, gliding motion. −n. **5.** the act of sliding. **6.** a single image for projection in a projector; transparency. **7.** Also, **hair slide**. a clip for holding a woman's hair in place. **8.** that which slides, as part of a machine.

slide rule n. a device for rapid arithmetic calculation.

sliding scale n. a variable scale, especially of industrial costs, as wages, raw materials, etc., which may be adapted to demand.

slight /slaɪt/ adj. **1.** small in amount, degree, etc. **2.** frail; flimsy. −v.t. **3.** to treat with indifference; ignore or snub. −n. **4.** an instance of slighting treatment; an affront.

slim /slɪm/ adj. (**slimmer**, **slimmest**) **1.** slender, as in girth, or form; slight in build or structure. −v.i. (**slimmed**, **slimming**) **2.** to make oneself slim, as by dieting, exercise, etc.

slime /slaɪm/ n. **1.** thin, glutinous mud. **2.** a viscous secretion of animal or vegetable origin. **3.** Colloq. servility; quality of being ingratiating. −**slimy**, adj.

sling /slɪŋ/ n. **1.** an instrument for hurling stones, etc., by hand, consisting of a piece for holding the missile, with two strings attached. **2.** a bandage used to suspend an injured part of the body, as an arm or hand, by looping round the neck. **3.** a strap, band, or the like forming a loop by which something is suspended or carried. −v. (**slung**, **slinging**) −v.t. **4.** to throw, cast or hurl; fling, as from the hand. **5.** to suspend. −v.i. **6.** to give money as a bribe.

slingshot /ˈslɪŋʃɒt/ n. a catapult.

slink /slɪŋk/ v.i. (**slunk**, **slinking**) to move stealthily, as to evade notice.

slip¹ /slɪp/ v. (**slipped, slipping**) –v.i. **1.** to pass or go smoothly or easily; glide; slide. **2.** to slide suddenly and involuntarily, as on a smooth surface; to lose one's foothold. **3.** to move, slide, or start from place, position, fastening, the hold, etc. **4.** to go, come, get, etc., easily or quickly. **5.** (oft. fol. by *up*) to make a slip, mistake, or error. –v.t. **6.** to cause to slip, pass, put, draw, etc., with a smooth, easy, or sliding motion. **7.** to untie or undo (a knot). **8.** to escape (one's memory, notice, knowledge, etc.). –*phr.* **9. let slip**, to say or reveal unintentionally. **10. slip away**, to depart quietly so as to not draw attention to oneself. –n. **11.** the act of slipping. **12.** a mistake, often inadvertent, as in speaking or writing. **13.** the eluding of a pursuer, notice, etc. **14.** a woman's sleeveless underdress. **15.** a pillowcase.

slip² /slɪp/ n. **1.** any long, narrow piece or strip, as of wood, paper, land, etc. –*phr.* Also, **a slip of a thing. 2. a slip of a** (**person**), a young person, especially one of slender form.

slipper /ˈslɪpə/ n. a light shoe into which the foot may be easily slipped for indoor wear.

slippery /ˈslɪpəri, ˈslɪpri/ adj. (**-rier, -riest**) **1.** tending to cause slipping or sliding, as ground, surfaces, things, etc. **2.** likely to slip away or escape.

slippery dip n. a construction bearing an inclined smooth slope for children to slide down for amusement; slide. Also, **slippery slide**.

slipshod /ˈslɪpʃɒd/ adj. untidy, or slovenly; careless or negligent.

slip-stitch n. one of a series of stitches used for dress hems, etc., in which only a few threads of material are caught up from the outer material, and the stitches which hold it are invisible from the outside.

slipstream /ˈslɪpstriːm/ n. an air current behind any moving object.

slit /slɪt/ v.t. (**slit, slitting**) **1.** to cut apart or open along a line; make a long cut, fissure, or opening in. –n. **2.** a straight, narrow cut, opening, or aperture.

slither /ˈslɪðə/ v.i. to slide down or along a surface, especially unsteadily or with more or less friction or noise. –**slithery**, adj.

sliver /ˈslɪvə/ n. a slender piece, as of wood, split, broken, or cut off, usually lengthwise or with the grain; splinter.

slob /slɒb/ n. Colloq. a stupid, clumsy, uncouth, or slovenly person.

slobber /ˈslɒbə/ v.i. **1.** to let saliva, etc., run from the mouth; slaver; dribble. **2.** to indulge in mawkish sentimentality. –n. **3.** saliva or liquid dribbling from the mouth; slaver.

slog /slɒg/ Colloq. –v. (**slogged, slogging**) –v.t. **1.** to hit hard, as in boxing, cricket, etc. –v.i. **2.** to deal heavy blows. **3.** to toil. –n. **4.** a strong blow with little finesse. **5.** a spell of hard work or walking.

slogan /ˈsloʊgən/ n. a distinctive cry or phrase of any party, class, body, or person.

slop /slɒp/ v.t., v.i. (**slopped, slopping**) **1.** to spill or splash. –n. **2.** (oft. pl.) the dirty water, liquid refuse, etc., of a household or the like.

slope¹ /sloʊp/ v.i. **1.** to take or have an inclined or slanting direction, especially downwards or

upwards from the horizontal. –v.t. **2.** to direct at a slope or inclination; incline from the horizontal. –n. **3.** inclination or slant, especially downwards or upwards. **4.** an inclined surface.

slope² /sloʊp/ v.i. Colloq. to move or go.

sloppy /ˈslɒpi/ adj. (**-pier, -piest**) **1.** muddy, slushy, or very wet. **2.** Colloq. weak, silly, or maudlin. **3.** Colloq. loose, careless, or slovenly.

sloppy joe /ˈdʒoʊ/ n. a loose, thick sweater.

slosh /slɒʃ/ n. **1.** → **slush.** –v.i. **2.** to splash in slush, mud, or water. –v.t. **3.** (oft. fol. by *in, on, round,* etc.) to pour, stir, spread, etc., a liquid or similar.

sloshed /slɒʃt/ adj. Colloq. drunk.

slot /slɒt/ n. **1.** a narrow, elongated depression or aperture, especially one to receive or admit something. **2.** a position within a system. –v.t. (**slotted, slotting**) **3.** to provide with a slot or slots; make a slot in. **4.** (usu. fol. by *in*) to insert into a slot.

slothful /ˈsloʊθfəl, ˈslɒθfəl/ adj. sluggardly; indolent; lazy.

slouch /slaʊtʃ/ v.i. **1.** to sit, stand, or walk in an awkward, drooping posture. –v.t. **2.** to cause to droop or bend down. –n. **3.** a drooping or bending forward of the head and shoulders.

slouch hat n. an army hat of soft felt.

slough /slʌf, slɒf/ v.t. (fol. by *off*) to cast.

sloven /ˈslʌvən/ n. someone who is habitually untidy or dirty. –**slovenly**, adj.

slow /sloʊ/ adj. **1.** taking or requiring a comparatively long time. **2.** sluggish in nature, disposition, or function. **3.** dull of perception or understanding, as a person, the mind, etc. **4.** slack, as trade. **5.** showing a time earlier than the correct time, as a clock. –adv. **6.** in a slow manner; slowly. –v.t., v.i. **7.** to make or become slow or slower.

slow food n. food which is the end product of a chain of local agriculture and processing, prepared in the context of a traditional cuisine.

slowmo /ˈsloʊmoʊ/ n. Colloq. (in film or television) slow motion. Also, **slow-mo, slo-mo**.

slow motion n. the process or technique used in film or television production in which images are made to move more slowly than their originals, as a result of having been photographed at a greater number of frames per second than normal, or being projected more slowly than normal.

sludge /slʌdʒ/ n. mud, mire.

slug¹ /slʌg/ n. **1.** any of various slimy, elongated terrestrial gastropods related to the terrestrial snails, but having no shell or only a rudimentary one. **2.** a piece of lead or other metal for firing from a gun.

slug² /slʌg/ v.t. (**slugged, slugging**) **1.** to strike heavily. –n. **2.** a heavy blow, especially with the fist.

sluggard /ˈslʌgəd/ n. someone who is habitually lazy.

sluggish /ˈslʌgɪʃ/ adj. inactive, slow, or of little energy or vigour.

sluice /sluːs/ n. **1.** any contrivance for regulating a flow from or into a receptacle. **2.** a channel or a drain. –v.t. (**sluiced, sluicing**) **3.** to flush or cleanse with a rush of water.

slum /slʌm/ *n.* (*oft. pl.*) an overpopulated, squalid part of a city, inhabited by the poorest people.

slumber /ˈslʌmbə/ *v.i.* **1.** to sleep, especially deeply. –*n.* **2.** (*oft. pl.*) sleep, especially deep sleep.

slump /slʌmp/ *v.i.* **1.** to drop heavily and limply. **2.** to fall suddenly and markedly, as prices, the market, etc. –*n.* **3.** a decline in prices or sales.

slur /slɜ/ *v.t.* (**slurred, slurring**) **1.** (oft. fol. by *over*) to pass over lightly, or without due mention or consideration. **2.** to pronounce (a syllable, word, etc.) indistinctly. –*n.* **3.** a disparaging remark; a slight. **4.** a blot or stain, as upon reputation.

slurp /slɜp/ *v.i., v.t.* **1.** to eat or drink noisily. –*n.* **2.** the noise produced by eating in such a manner.

slush /slʌʃ/ *n.* **1.** snow in a partly melted state. **2.** *Colloq.* silly, sentimental, or weakly emotional writing, talk, etc.

slush fund *n.* money collected unofficially, sometimes by secret or deceitful means, by an individual or an organisation for a special purpose.

slushy /ˈslʌʃi/ *adj.* (**-shier, -shiest**) **1.** of or relating to slush. –*n.* Also, **slushie**. **2.** a semifrozen drink consisting of flavoured liquid to which finely crushed ice is added.

slut /slʌt/ *n.* (*derog.*) a woman who has many sexual partners.

sly /slaɪ/ *adj.* (**slyer** or **slier, slyest** or **sliest**) cunning or wily.

smack¹ /smæk/ *n.* **1.** a taste or flavour, especially a slight flavour distinctive or suggestive of something. –*v.i.* **2.** (oft. fol. by *of*) to have a taste, flavour, trace, or suggestion.

smack² /smæk/ *v.t.* **1.** to strike smartly, especially with the open hand or anything flat. **2.** to bring, put, throw, send, etc., with a sharp, resounding blow or a smart stroke. **3.** to come or strike smartly or forcibly, as against something. –*n.* **4.** a smart, resounding blow, especially with something flat. **5.** a resounding or loud kiss. **6.** *Colloq.* heroin. –*adv.* **7.** *Colloq.* directly; straight.

small /smɔl/ *adj.* **1.** of limited size; not big; little. **2.** not great in amount, degree, extent, duration, value, etc. **3.** of minor importance, moment, weight, or consequence. –*adv.* **4.** in a small manner. **5.** into small pieces. –*n.* **6.** that which is small. **7.** the lower central part of the back.

small fry *n.* young or unimportant persons or objects.

smallgoods /ˈsmɔlɡʊdz/ *pl. n.* processed meats, as salami, frankfurts, etc.

smallpox /ˈsmɔlpɒks/ *n.* an acute, highly contagious disease caused by a virus and characterised by a pustular sore which often leaves permanent pits or scars.

smarmy /ˈsmami/ *adj.* flattering; unctuous.

smart /smat/ *v.i.* **1.** to be a source of sharp local and usually superficial pain, as a wound. **2.** to suffer keenly from wounded feelings. –*adj.* **3.** sharp or keen, as pain. **4.** sharply severe, as blows, strokes, etc. **5.** sharply brisk, vigorous, or active. **6.** clever. **7.** dashingly or effectively neat or trim in appearance, as persons, dress,

etc. **8.** socially elegant, or fashionable. **9.** (of a device or set of devices) controlled with computer software so that it performs some functions without the human input usually required. –*n.* **10.** sharp local pain, usually superficial, as from a wound or sting.

smart alec /ˈælɪk/ *n. Colloq.* someone who is ostentatious in the display of knowledge or skill. Also, **smart aleck**.

smart card *n.* a plastic card containing integrated circuits capable of storing digital information, used for performing financial transactions, accessing restricted areas, accessing secure computer records, etc. Also, **smart-card**.

smartphone /ˈsmatfoʊn/ *n.* a mobile phone with access to the internet and the functionality of a personal computer. Also, **smart phone**.

smash /smæʃ/ *v.t.* **1.** to break to pieces with violence and often with a crashing sound. –*v.i.* **2.** to break to pieces from a violent blow or collision. –*n.* **3.** a smashing or shattering, or the sound of it. **4.** a destructive collision.

smashed /smæʃt/ *adj. Colloq.* incapacitated as a result of taking drugs, alcohol, etc.

smashing /ˈsmæʃɪŋ/ *adj. Colloq.* excellent or extremely good; first-rate.

smattering /ˈsmætərɪŋ/ *n.* a slight or superficial knowledge of something.

smear /smɪə/ *v.t.* **1.** to rub or spread with oil, grease, paint, dirt, etc. **2.** to rub something over (a thing) so as to cause a smear. –*n.* **3.** a mark or stain made by, or as by, smearing.

smell /smɛl/ *v.* (**smelt** or **smelled, smelling**) –*v.t.* **1.** to perceive through the nose, by means of the olfactory nerves; inhale the odour of. **2.** to test by the sense of smell. **3.** to perceive, detect, or discover by shrewdness or sagacity. –*v.i.* **4.** to have the sense of smell. **5.** to give out an odour. **6.** to give out an offensive odour. **7.** to seem or be unpleasant or bad. –*n.* **8.** the faculty or sense of smelling. **9.** that quality of a thing which is or may be smelled; odour. **10.** an unpleasant odour. **11.** the act of smelling.

smelt /smɛlt/ *v.t.* **1.** to fuse or melt (ore) in order to separate the metal contained. **2.** to obtain or refine (metal) in this way.

smidgen /ˈsmɪdʒən/ *n.* a very small quantity; a bit. Also, **smidgin, smidgeon**.

smile /smaɪl/ *v.i.* **1.** to assume a facial expression, characterised especially by a widening of the mouth, indicative of pleasure, favour, kindliness, amusement, derision, scorn, etc. –*v.t.* **2.** to assume or give (a smile). **3.** to express by a smile. **4.** (fol. by *on* or *upon*) to look with favour, or support. –*n.* **5.** the act of smiling; a smiling expression of the face.

smirch /smɜtʃ/ *v.t.* **1.** to discolour or soil with some substance, as soot, dust, dirt, etc., or as the substance does. –*n.* **2.** a dirty mark or smear.

smirk /smɜk/ *v.i.* **1.** to smile in a condescending or knowing way. –*n.* **2.** such a smile.

smite /smaɪt/ *v.t.* (**smote, smitten** or **smit, smiting**) **1.** to strike or hit hard, as with the hand, a stick or weapon, etc. **2.** to affect suddenly and strongly with a specified feeling. **3.** to impress favourably; charm.

smith /smɪθ/ *n.* a worker in metal.

smithereens /smɪðə'rinz/ *pl. n. Colloq.* small fragments.

smock /smɒk/ *n.* any loose overgarment.

smog /smɒg/ *n.* a mixture of smoke and fog. **–smoggy,** *adj.*

smoke /smoʊk/ *n.* **1.** the visible exhalation given off by a burning or smouldering substance. **2.** something resembling this, as vapour or mist, flying particles, etc. **3.** an act or spell of smoking tobacco, or the like. **4.** that which is smoked, as a cigar or cigarette. *–v.i.* **5.** to give off or emit smoke. **6.** to draw into the mouth and puff out the smoke of tobacco or the like. *–v.t.* **7.** to draw into the mouth and puff out the smoke of tobacco, etc., from (a cigarette, pipe, etc.). **8.** to expose to smoke.

smoked /smoʊkt/ *adj.* (of food items) treated with smoke to preserve them or to add flavour: *smoked ham; smoked almonds.*

smokescreen /'smoʊkskrin/ *n.* a mass of dense smoke produced to conceal an area, vessel, or aeroplane from the enemy.

smoking ceremony *n.* an Aboriginal cleansing ritual in which green leaves from local plants are burnt creating smoke which is said to cleanse and heal the area; often used to prepare a site for a new purpose, or after a death to remove spirits.

smoking gun *n.* **1.** a gun that has just been fired. **2.** a piece of incontrovertible evidence which points to the perpetrator of a crime, the cause of a disaster, etc.

smooch /smutʃ/ *v.i. Colloq.* to kiss; cuddle.

smoodge /smudʒ/ *v.i.* (**smoodged, smoodging**) *Colloq.* **1.** to kiss; caress. **2.** to flatter; curry favour.

smooth /smuð/ *adj.* **1.** free from projections or irregularities of surface such as would be perceived in touching or stroking. **2.** of uniform consistency. **3.** pleasant, agreeable, or ingratiatingly polite. *–v.t.* **4.** (sometimes fol. by *down*) to make smooth of surface, as by scraping, planing, pressing, stroking, etc. **5.** (oft. fol. by *away* or *out*) to remove (projections, etc.) in making something smooth. **6.** a smooth part or place.

smorgasbord /'smɔgəzbɒd/ *n.* a buffet meal of various dishes.

smother /'smʌðə/ *v.t.* **1.** to stifle or suffocate, especially by smoke or by depriving of the air necessary for life. **2.** to extinguish or deaden (fire, etc.) by covering so as to exclude air. *–v.i.* **3.** to become stifled or suffocated. *–n.* **4.** an overspreading profusion of anything.

smoulder /'smoʊldə/ *v.i.* **1.** to burn or smoke without flame. **2.** to exist or continue in a suppressed state or without outward demonstration. Also, *US,* **smolder.**

SMS /ɛs ɛm 'ɛs/ *n.* (*pl.* **SMSs** or **SMSes** or **SMS's**) **1.** short messaging service; a communications service which enables a user to key in the text of a message on a mobile phone and send it to another mobile phone where it can be read on the screen. **2.** → **text message.** *–v.t.* (**SMS'ed** or **SMSed, SMS'ing** or **SMSing**) **3.** to send (a text message) especially in SMS. **4.** to send (a person) a text message especially in SMS.

SMS code *n.* a code designed to reduce the length of words when sending SMS messages, such as *u* for *you*, *b4* for *before*, etc.

smudge /smʌdʒ/ *n.* **1.** a dirty mark or smear. *–v.t.* (**smudged, smudging**) **2.** to mark with dirty streaks or smears.

smug /smʌg/ *adj.* (**smugger, smuggest**) complacently proper, righteous, clever, etc.

smuggle /'smʌgəl/ *v.t.* to import or export (goods) secretly, without payment of legal duty or in violation of law.

smut /smʌt/ *n.* **1.** a black or dirty mark; a smudge. **2.** indecent talk or writing; obscenity.

snack /snæk/ *n.* **1.** a small portion of food or drink; a light meal. **2.** *Colloq.* anything easily done.

snag[1] /snæg/ *n.* **1.** any sharp or rough projection. **2.** any obstacle or impediment. **3.** a small hole or ladder caused by a snag. *–v.t.* (**snagged, snagging**) **4.** to ladder; catch upon, or damage by, a snag.

snag[2] /snæg/ *n. Colloq.* a sausage.

snag[3] /snæg/ *n. Colloq.* sensitive new-age guy; a man who displays sensitivity in personal relationships. Also, **SNAG.**

snail /sneɪl/ *n.* **1.** a small slow-moving animal with a soft body and a coiled shell, often found in gardens. **2.** a slow or lazy person; a sluggard.

snail mail *n.* (*humorous*) the ordinary post (as opposed to email).

snake /sneɪk/ *n.* **1.** a scaly, limbless, usually slender reptile, occurring in venomous and non-venomous forms. **2.** a treacherous person. **3.** something resembling a snake in form or manner. *–v.i.* **4.** to move, twist, or wind in the manner of a snake.

snap /snæp/ *v.i.* **1.** to move, strike, shut, catch, etc., with a sharp sound, as a lid. **2.** to break suddenly, especially with a sharp, cracking sound. **3.** to make a quick or sudden bite or snatch. **4.** to utter a quick, sharp speech, reproof, retort, etc. *–v.t.* **5.** (usu. fol. by *up* or *off*) to seize with, or as with, a quick bite or snatch. **6.** to bring, strike, shut, open, operate, etc., with a sharp sound or movement. **7.** to break suddenly, especially with a crackling sound. **8.** *Photography* to take a snapshot of. *–n.* **9.** a sharp, crackling or clicking sound, or a movement or action causing such a sound. **10.** a catch or the like operating with such a sound. **11.** a quick or sudden bite or snatch, as at something. **12.** a short spell, as of cold weather. **13.** (**snapped, snapping**) → **snapshot.** *–adj.* **14.** denoting devices closing by pressure on a spring catch, or articles using such devices. **15.** made, done, taken, etc., suddenly or offhand.

snapper /'snæpə/ *n.* a marine food fish widely distributed in Australian and NZ coastal waters. Also, **schnapper.**

snapshot /'snæpʃɒt/ *n.* a photograph taken quickly without any formal arrangement of the subject, mechanical adjustment of the camera, etc.

snare /snɛə/ *n.* anything serving to entrap, entangle, or catch unawares; a trap.

snarl[1] /snal/ *v.i.* **1.** to growl angrily or viciously, as a dog. *–n.* **2.** the act of snarling. **–snarling,** *adj.*

snarl[2] /snal/ *n.* **1.** a tangle, as of thread or hair. *–v.t.* **2.** to bring into a tangled condition, as thread, hair, etc; tangle.

snatch /snætʃ/ v.i. **1.** (usu. fol. by *at*) to make a sudden effort to seize something, as with the hand. –v.t. **2.** (oft. fol. by *up*, *from*, *out of*, *away*, etc.) to seize by a sudden or hasty grasp. –n. **3.** the act of snatching. **4.** a bit, scrap, or fragment of something.

snazzy /'snæzi/ adj. (**-zier**, **-ziest**) *Colloq.* very smart; strikingly fashionable; stylish.

sneak /snik/ v. (**sneaked** *or*, *Colloq.*, **snuck**, **sneaking**) –v.i. **1.** (fol. by *about*, *along*, *in*, *off*, *out*, etc.) to go in a stealthy or furtive manner; slink; skulk. **2.** to act in a furtive, underhand, or mean way. –v.t. **3.** to move, put, pass, etc., in a stealthy or furtive manner. –n. **4.** someone who sneaks; a sneaking, underhand, or contemptible person.

sneaker /'snikə/ n. a shoe with a rubber or other soft sole, worn for sport or as part of casual attire.

sneer /snɪə/ v.i. **1.** to smile or curl the lip in a manner that shows scorn, contempt, etc. –n. **2.** an act of sneering.

sneeze /sniz/ v.i. **1.** to emit air or breath suddenly, forcibly, and audibly through the nose and mouth by involuntary, spasmodic action. –n. **2.** an act or sound of sneezing.

snick /snik/ v.t. to cut, snip, or nick.

snicker /'snikə/ n., v.i. → **snigger**.

snide /snaɪd/ adj. derogatory in a nasty, insinuating manner.

sniff /snif/ v.i. **1.** to draw air through the nose in short, audible inhalation. –v.t. **2.** to draw in or up through the nose by sniffing, as air, smells, liquid, powder, etc.; inhale. –n. **3.** an act of sniffing; a single short, audible inhalation.

sniffle /'snifəl/ v.i. to sniff repeatedly, as from a cold in the head or in repressing tearful emotion. –**sniffling**, n., adj.

snigger /'snigə/ v.i. **1.** to laugh in a half-suppressed, indecorous or disrespectful, manner. –n. **2.** such a laugh.

snip /snip/ v.t. (**snipped**, **snipping**) **1.** to cut with a small, quick stroke, or a succession of such strokes, with scissors or the like. –n. **2.** the act of snipping, as with scissors. **3.** a small cut, notch, slit, etc., made by snipping.

snipe /snaɪp/ n. **1.** any of several small shorebirds having plump bodies, striped heads and long, straight bills, frequenting swamps and wet grasslands in many parts of the world. –v.i. **2.** to shoot at individual soldiers, etc., as opportunity offers from a concealed or long-range position. –phr. **3. snipe at**, to make critical or damaging comments about (someone) without entering into open conflict. –**sniper**, n.

snippet /'snipət/ n. a small piece snipped off; a small bit, scrap, or fragment.

snivel /'snivəl/ v.i. (**-elled** *or*, *Chiefly US*, **-eled**, **-elling** *or*, *Chiefly US*, **-eling**) **1.** to weep or cry with sniffing. **2.** to draw up mucus audibly through the nose.

snob /snob/ n. someone who affects social importance and exclusiveness. –**snobbish**, **snobby**, adj.

snooker /'snukə/ n. a game played on a billiard table with fifteen red balls and six balls of other colours.

snoop /snup/ *Colloq.* –v.i. **1.** to prowl or pry; go about in a sneaking, prying way; pry in a

mean, sly manner. –n. **2.** an act or instance of snooping. **3.** someone who snoops.

snooze /snuz/ *Colloq.* –v.i. **1.** to sleep; slumber; doze; nap. –n. **2.** a rest; nap.

snore /snɔ/ v.i. **1.** to breathe during sleep with hoarse or harsh sounds. –n. **2.** an act of snoring, or the sound made.

snorkel /'snɔkəl/ n. a tube enabling a person swimming underwater to breathe.

snort /snɔt/ v.i. **1.** to force the breath violently through the nostrils with a loud, harsh sound, as a horse, etc. **2.** to express contempt, indignation, etc., by such a sound. –n. **3.** the act or sound of snorting.

snot /snot/ n. *Colloq.* mucus from the nose.

snout /snaʊt/ n. the part of an animal's head projecting forward and containing the nose and jaws; the muzzle.

snow /snoʊ/ n. **1.** the aqueous vapour of the atmosphere precipitated in partially frozen crystalline form and falling to the earth in white flakes. **2.** something resembling snow. –v.i. **3.** (of snow) to fall: *it snowed last night.* **4.** to descend like snow. –v.t. **5.** (fol. by *in*, *over*, *under*, *up*, etc.) to cover, obstruct, isolate, etc., with snow.

snowboard /'snoʊbɔd/ n. **1.** a board for gliding over the snow, which resembles a surfboard in that the rider stands on it, the feet being strapped to it as with skis. –v.i. **2.** to glide over the snow on a snowboard. –**snowboarder**, n. –**snowboarding**, n.

snub /snʌb/ v.t. (**snubbed**, **snubbing**) **1.** to treat with disdain or contempt. **2.** to check or rebuke sharply. –n. **3.** an act of snubbing; a sharp rebuke. –adj. **4.** (of the nose) short, and turned up at the tip.

snuff[1] /snʌf/ n. a preparation of powdered tobacco, usually taken into the nostrils by inhalation.

snuff[2] /snʌf/ v.t. (fol. by *out*) to extinguish.

snuffle /'snʌfəl/ v.i. **1.** to speak through the nose or with a nasal twang. **2.** to sniff; snivel. –n. **3.** an act of snuffling.

snug /snʌg/ adj. (**snugger**, **snuggest**) **1.** comfortable or cosy, as a place, living quarters, etc. **2.** fitting closely, as a garment.

snuggle /'snʌgəl/ v.i. **1.** (oft. fol. by *up*, *in*, etc) to lie or press closely, as for comfort or from affection; nestle; cuddle. –n. **2.** a cuddle; embrace.

so /soʊ/ adv. **1.** in the way or manner indicated, described, or implied. **2.** as stated or reported. **3.** to that extent; in that degree. **4.** for a given reason; hence; therefore. **5.** in the way that follows; in this way. –conj. **6.** *Colloq.* consequently; with the result that. **7.** (oft. fol. by *that*) under the condition that. –pron. **8.** such as has been stated. –phr. **9. and so on**, et cetera. **10. or so**, about thus: *twenty or so.*

soak /soʊk/ v.i. **1.** to lie in and become saturated or permeated with water or some other liquid. **2.** (usu. fol. by *in*, *through*, *out*, etc.) to pass, as a liquid, through pores or interstices. –v.t. **3.** to place and keep in liquid in order to saturate thoroughly; steep. **4.** to permeate thoroughly, as liquid or moisture. **5.** (oft. fol. by *up*) to take in or up by absorption. –n. **6.** the act of soaking. **7.** the liquid in which anything is soaked.

soap /soup/ n. **1.** a substance used for washing and cleansing purposes, usually made by treating a fat with an alkali (as sodium or potassium hydroxide), and consisting chiefly of the sodium or potassium salts of the acids contained in the fat. *-v.t.* **2.** to rub, cover or treat with soap.

soapbox /'soupboks/ n. a box, usually wooden, in which soap has been packed, especially one used as a temporary platform by speakers addressing a street audience.

soap opera n. *Colloq.* a television series, usually dealing with domestic problems, especially in a highly emotional manner. Also, **soapie, soap**.

soar /sɔ/ v.i. to fly at a great height, without visible movements of the pinions, as a bird.

sob /sɒb/ v.i. **(sobbed, sobbing) 1.** to weep with a sound caused by a convulsive catching of the breath. *-n.* **2.** the act of sobbing; a convulsive catching of the breath in weeping.

sober /'soubə/ adj. **1.** not intoxicated or drunk. **2.** quiet or sedate in demeanour, as persons. **3.** free from excess, extravagance, or exaggeration. *-v.i., v.t.* **4.** to make or become sober. **-sobriety,** n.

soccer /'sɒkə/ n. a form of football in which there are eleven players in a team, the ball is spherical, and the use of the hands and arms is prohibited except to the goalkeeper.

sociable /'souʃəbəl/ adj. inclined to associate with or be in the company of others.

social /'souʃəl/ adj. **1.** relating to, devoted to, or characterised by friendly companionship or relations. **2.** of or relating to the life and relation of human beings in a community. *-n.* **3.** a social gathering or party.

social distancing n. (esp. in epidemiology) the practice of maintaining a distance between individuals, as a means of limiting transmission of an infectious disease.

socialise /'souʃəlaɪz/ v.t. **1.** to make social; educate to conform to society. *-v.i.* **2.** to go into society; frequent social functions. Also, **socialize**.

socialism /'souʃəlɪzəm/ n. a theory or system of social organisation which advocates the vesting of the ownership and control of the means of production, capital, land, etc., in the community as a whole. **-socialist,** n., adj.

socialite /'souʃəlaɪt/ n. a member of the social elite, or someone who aspires to be such.

social media n. online social networks used to disseminate information through online social interaction.

social network n. **1.** a supportive group of friends, relatives, acquaintances, etc. **2.** such a group whose point of contact is an online website. **-social networker,** n. **-social networking,** n.

social sciences pl. n. a broad group of subjects, as economics, social science, sociology, etc., relating to human social function.

social security n. the provision by the state for the economic and social welfare of the public by means of old-age pensions, sickness and unemployment benefits.

social service n. organised welfare efforts carried on under professional rules by trained personnel.

social studies pl. n. a broad group of subjects, as economics, social history, sociology, etc., relating to man's function as a social being, especially as taught in schools. Also, **social science**.

social welfare n. a system of services set up by a state or other organisation for the benefit of the community in areas such as health, housing, etc.

social work n. organised work directed towards the bettering of social conditions in the community, as by seeking to improve the condition of the poor, to promote the welfare of children, etc.

society /sə'saɪəti/ n. (pl. **-ties**) **1.** a body of individuals living as members of a community. **2.** human beings collectively regarded as a body divided into classes according to worldly status. **3.** an organisation of persons associated together for religious, benevolent, literary, scientific, political, patriotic, or other purposes. **4.** any community. *-adj.* **5.** of or relating to polite society.

socio- a word element representing 'social', 'sociological'.

sociology /sousi'ɒlədʒi/ n. the systematic study of the origin, development, organisation, and functioning of human society; the science of the fundamental laws of social relations, institutions, etc. **-sociologist,** n. **-sociological,** adj.

sock¹ /sɒk/ n. (pl. **socks** or **sox**) a woven or knitted covering for the foot and lower leg, worn inside a shoe.

sock² /sɒk/ v.t. *Colloq.* to strike or hit hard.

socket /'sɒkət/ n. a hollow part or piece for receiving and holding some part or thing.

soda /'soudə/ n. **1.** sodium (in expressions such as *carbonate of soda*). **2.** soda water. **3.** a drink made with soda water, served with fruit or other syrups, ice cream, etc. **4.** *US* a soft drink.

soda water n. an effervescent beverage consisting of water charged with carbon dioxide.

sodden /'sɒdn/ adj. soaked with liquid or moisture.

sodium /'soudiəm/ n. a soft, silver-white metallic element which oxidises rapidly in moist air, occurring in nature only in the combined state. *Symbol:* Na

sodium bicarbonate /baɪ'kabənət/ n. a white crystalline compound used in cookery, medicine, etc.

sodium chloride n. common salt, NaCl.

sodomy /'sɒdəmi/ n. anal intercourse.

sofa /'soufə/ n. a long upholstered seat; couch.

soft /sɒft/ adj. **1.** yielding readily to touch or pressure; easily penetrated, divided, or altered in shape; not hard or stiff. **2.** smooth and agreeable to the touch; not rough or coarse. **3.** low in sound. **4.** gentle, mild. **5.** not strong or robust; delicate. **6.** *Colloq.* not hard, trying, or severe; involving little effort. **7.** (of water) relatively free from mineral salts that interfere with the action of soap. **8.** (of drugs) nonaddictive, as marijuana and LSD. **-softness,** n.

softball /'sɒftbɔl/ n. a form of baseball played with a larger and softer ball, in which the pitcher delivers the ball underarm.

soft drink *n.* a drink which is not alcoholic or intoxicating, as ginger beer, lemonade, etc.

soft goods *pl. n.* merchandise such as textiles, furnishings, etc.

soft pedal *n.* a pedal, as on a piano, for lessening the volume.

soft sell *n.* a method of selling or advertising which is quietly persuasive and subtle. Compare **hard sell**. –**soft-sell**, *v.*

soft serve *n.* a gelatine confection, similar to but softer than ice cream, usually served in a cone. Also, **soft serve ice cream**. –**soft-serve**, *adj.*

soft target *n.* an enemy target without military protection.

software /ˈsɒftwɛə/ *n.* programs which enable a computer to perform a desired operation or series of operations (opposed to *hardware*).

soggy /ˈsɒgi/ *adj.* (**-gier, -giest**) **1.** soaked; thoroughly wet. **2.** damp and heavy, as undercooked bread.

soil¹ /sɔɪl/ *n.* **1.** that portion of the earth's surface in which plants grow. **2.** a particular kind of earth. **3.** the ground or earth.

soil² /sɔɪl/ *v.t., v.i.* to make or become dirty or foul, especially on the surface.

soiree /ˈswaˈreɪ, ˈswareɪ/ *n.* an evening party or social gathering: *a musical soiree.* Also, **soirée**.

sojourn /ˈsɒudʒɜn, ˈsɒdʒɜn, ˈsʌdʒ-, -ən/ *v.i.* **1.** to dwell for a time in a place; make a temporary stay. –*n.* **2.** a temporary stay.

solace /ˈsɒləs/ *n.* **1.** comfort in sorrow or trouble. **2.** something that gives comfort. –*v.t.* (**-aced, -acing**) **3.** to comfort, console, or cheer (a person, oneself, the heart, etc.).

solar /ˈsɒulə/ *adj.* **1.** of or relating to the sun. **2.** determined by the sun. **3.** proceeding from the sun, as light or heat. **4.** operating by the light or heat of the sun, as a device or mechanism.

solar energy *n.* energy derived from the sun, as for home heating, industrial use, etc.

solar heating *n.* the use of solar energy to provide heating for air or water in a building. –**solar-heated**, *adj.*

solar panel *n.* a panel which is part of a solar heating system.

solar plexus /ˈplɛksəs/ *n. Anat.* a network of nerves situated at the upper part of the abdomen, behind the stomach and in front of the aorta.

solar system *n.* the sun together with all the planets, satellites, asteroids, etc., revolving around it.

sold /sɒuld/ *v.* past tense and past participle of **sell**.

solder /ˈsɒldə/ *n.* **1.** any of various fusible alloys, applied in a melted state to metal surfaces, joints, etc., to unite them. –*v.t.* **2.** to unite with solder or some other substance or device.

soldier /ˈsɒuldʒə/ *n.* **1.** someone who serves in an army for pay; one engaged in military service. –*v.i.* **2.** to act or serve as a soldier.

sole¹ /sɒul/ *adj.* **1.** being the only one or ones; only. **2.** belonging or relating to one individual or group to the exclusion of all others; exclusive.

sole² /sɒul/ *n.* **1.** the bottom or under surface of the foot. **2.** the corresponding under part of a shoe, boot, or the like.

sole³ /sɒul/ *n.* (*pl.* **sole** *or* **soles**) a flat-bodied fish with a hooklike snout.

solecism /ˈsɒləsɪzəm/ *n.* **1.** a use of language regarded as substandard or non-standard. **2.** any error, impropriety, or inconsistency.

solemn /ˈsɒləm/ *adj.* **1.** grave, sober, or mirthless. **2.** serious or earnest. **3.** of a formal or ceremonious character. –**solemnity**, *n.*

solenoid /ˈsɒlənɔɪd/ *n. Elect.* an electrical conductor wound as a helix, a current passing through which establishes a magnetic field.

soli-¹ a word element meaning 'alone', 'solitary'.

soli-² a word element meaning 'sun'.

solicit /səˈlɪsət/ *v.t.* **1.** to seek for by entreaty, earnest or respectful request, formal application, etc. **2.** to entreat or petition (a person, etc.) for something or to do something. –*v.i.* **3.** to make petition or request, as for something desired. **4.** to accost another with immoral intention. **5.** to endeavour to obtain orders or trade, as for a business house. –**solicitation**, *n.*

solicitor /səˈlɪsətə/ *n.* a member of that branch of the legal profession whose services consist of advising clients, representing them before the lower courts, and preparing cases for barristers to try in the higher courts.

solicitor-general *n.* (*pl.* **solicitors-general** *or* **solicitor-generals**) the second legal officer of the government whose principal functions are to appear on behalf of the government in litigation to which the government is a party and to offer such legal advice to the government as is requested by the attorney-general.

solicitous /səˈlɪsətəs/ *adj.* (fol. by *about, for,* etc., or a clause) anxious or concerned over something.

solid /ˈsɒləd/ *adj.* **1.** having three dimensions (length, breadth, and thickness), as a geometrical body or figure. **2.** having the interior completely filled up, free from cavities, or not hollow. **3.** without openings or breaks. **4.** firm, hard, or compact in substance. **5.** dense, thick, or heavy in nature or appearance. **6.** whole or entire. **7.** financially sound or strong. –*n.* **8.** a body or magnitude having three dimensions (length, breadth, and thickness). **9.** a solid substance or body. –**solidity**, *n.* –**solidify**, *v.*

solidarity /sɒləˈdærəti/ *n.* union or fellowship arising from common responsibilities and interests.

solid-state *adj. Electronics* of or relating to electronic devices which are composed of components in the solid state, as transistors, integrated circuits, etc.

solidus /ˈsɒlədəs/ *n.* (*pl.* **-di** /-daɪ/) a short, sloping line (/) representing the old long form of the letter 's' (abbreviation of solidus) generally used as a dividing line, as in dates, fractions, etc.; forward slash; slash.

soliloquy /səˈlɪləkwi/ *n.* (*pl.* **-quies**) the act of talking when alone or as if alone.

solipsism /ˈsɒlɪpsɪzəm/ *n.* the theory that the self is the only object of verifiable knowledge, or that nothing but the self exists.

solitaire /'splətεə/ n. 1. a game played by one person alone. 2. a precious stone set by itself.

solitary /'splətri/ adj. 1. quite alone. 2. done without assistance or accompaniment. 3. secluded, or lonely. 4. spending a lot of time alone or liking to spend time alone.

solitude /'splətjud/ n. the state of being or living alone.

solo /'soulou/ n. 1. any performance, as a dance, by one person. —adj. 2. performed alone; not combined with other parts of equal importance; not concerted. —adv. 3. alone; without a companion or partner.

so long interj. Colloq. goodbye.

solstice /'splstəs/ n. Astron. the shortest (winter) or longest (summer) day of the year.

soluble /'spljəbəl/ adj. 1. capable of being dissolved or liquefied. 2. capable of being solved or explained.

solution /sə'luʃən/ n. 1. a particular instance or method of solving; an explanation or answer. 2. the fact of being dissolved; dissolved state. 3. a homogeneous molecular mixture of two or more substances.

solve /splv/ v.t. 1. to clear up or explain; find the answer to. 2. to work out the answer or solution to (a mathematical problem).

solvent /'splvənt/ adj. 1. able to pay all just debts. 2. having the power of dissolving; causing solution. —n. 3. the component of a solution which dissolves the other component. —**solvency**, n.

somatic /sou'mætɪk/ adj. of the body; bodily; physical.

somatic nervous system n. Physiol., Anat. the part of the peripheral nervous system involved with the voluntary control of body movements through the action of skeletal muscles, and with reception of external stimuli. Compare **autonomic nervous system**.

sombre /'spmbə/ adj. gloomily dark, shadowy, or dimly lit.

sombrero /spm'brεərou/ n. (pl. -ros) a broad-brimmed hat, as worn in Mexico.

some /sʌm/, weak form /səm/ adj. 1. being an undetermined or unspecified one. 2. certain (with plural nouns). 3. of a certain unspecified number, amount, degree, etc. —pron. 4. certain persons, instances, etc., not specified.

-some[1] suffix found in some adjectives showing especially a tendency, as in quarrelsome, burdensome.

-some[2] collective suffix used with numerals, as in twosome, threesome, foursome.

-some[3] a word element meaning 'body', as in chromosome.

somebody /'sʌmbɒdi, 'sʌmbədi/ pron. 1. some person. —n. (pl. -bodies) 2. a person of some note or importance.

somehow /'sʌmhaʊ/ adv. in some way not specified, apparent, or known.

someone /'sʌmwʌn/ pron., n. → **somebody**.

somersault /'sʌməsɔlt, -splt/ n. an acrobatic movement of the body in which it describes a complete revolution, heels over head.

something /'sʌmθɪŋ/ pron. some thing; a certain thing which is not named.

sometimes /'sʌmtaɪmz/ adv. on some occasions; now and then.

somewhat /'sʌmwɒt/ adv. in some measure or degree; to some extent.

somewhere /'sʌmwεə/ adv. in, at or to some place not specified, determined, or known.

somnambulism /spm'næmbjəlɪzəm/ n. sleep-walking.

son /sʌn/ n. 1. a male child or person in relation to his parents. 2. any male descendant. 3. someone related as if by ties of sonship.

sonar /'souna/ n. an echo sounder. Also, SONAR.

sonata /sə'natə/ n. Music an extended instrumental composition.

song /spŋ/ n. 1. a short metrical composition combining words and music. 2. poetical composition; poetry. 3. the musical or tuneful sounds produced by certain birds, insects, etc.

sonic /'spnɪk/ adj. 1. of or relating to sound. 2. denoting a speed approximating that of the propagation of sound.

son-in-law n. (pl. **sons-in-law**) the husband of one's daughter or son.

sonnet /'spnət/ n. Prosody a poem of 14 lines.

sonorous /'spnərəs/ adj. loud, deep, or resonant, as a sound.

-sonous a word element used in adjectives to refer to sounds.

sook /suk/ n. (usually of children) a timid, shy, cowardly person.

soon /sun/ adv. 1. within a short period after this (or that) time, event, etc. 2. promptly or quickly.

soot /sut/ n. a black powder produced during the combustion of coal, wood, oil, etc.

soothe /suð/ v.t. (**soothed, soothing**) 1. to tranquillise or calm. 2. to mitigate, assuage, or allay, as pain, sorrow, doubt, etc.

sop /spp/ n. 1. something given to pacify or quiet, or as a bribe. —v. (**sopped, sopping**) —v.t. 2. to drench. 3. (usu. fol. by up) to take up (water, etc.) by absorption. —v.i. 4. to become or be soaking wet.

sophism /'spfɪzəm/ n. a specious but fallacious argument.

sophisticated /sə'fɪstəkeɪtəd/ adj. 1. (of a person, ideas, tastes, manners, etc.) altered by education, experience, etc., worldly-wise; refined; artificial. 2. of intellectual complexity; reflecting a high degree of skill, intelligence, etc.; subtle. —**sophisticate**, n.

sophistication /səfɪstə'keɪʃən/ n. 1. sophisticated character, ideas, tastes, or ways. 2. advanced refinement or complexity.

-sophy a word element referring to systems of thought, as in philosophy.

soporific /sppə'rɪfɪk/ adj. causing or tending to cause sleep.

soppy /'sppi/ adj. (-pier, -piest) Colloq. excessively sentimental; mawkish; silly.

soprano /sə'pranou/ n. (pl. -nos or -ni /-ni/) the highest singing voice in women and boys.

sorbet /'sɔbeɪ, 'sɔbət/ n. a light frozen dish made with fruit, egg whites, etc., served between the courses of a meal to clear the palate or as a dessert.

sorcery /'sɔsəri/ n. magic, especially black magic. —**sorcerer**, n.

sordid /'sɔdəd/ adj. 1. dirty or filthy; squalid. 2. morally mean or ignoble.

sore /sɔ/ adj. **1.** physically painful or sensitive, as a wound. **2.** suffering bodily pain. **3.** causing very great suffering, misery, hardship, etc. -n. **4.** a sore spot or place on the body, especially an ulceration.

sorghum /'sɔgəm/ n. a cereal grass of many varieties, used as food for humans and animals.

sorrow /'sɒroʊ/ n. **1.** distress caused by loss, affliction, disappointment, etc. **2.** a cause or occasion of grief or regret. -v.i. **3.** to feel sorrow; grieve.

sorry /'sɒri/ adj. (-**rier**, -**riest**) **1.** feeling regret, compunction, sympathy, pity, etc. **2.** of a deplorable, pitiable, or miserable kind.

sort /sɔt/ n. **1.** a particular kind, species, variety, class, group, or description, as distinguished by the character or nature. -v.t. **2.** to arrange according to sort, kind, or class; separate into sorts; classify. **3.** to separate or take (out) from other sorts, or from others. -phr. **4.** of sorts, of a mediocre or poor kind. **5.** out of sorts, not in a normal condition of good health, spirits, or temper. **6.** sort of, to a certain extent; in some way; as it were. **7.** sort out, to find a solution for: to sort out a problem.

sorted /'sɔtəd/ adj. Colloq. effectively dealt with; resolved: there was a problem with the bill but it's sorted now.

SOS /ɛs oʊ 'ɛs/ n. a call for help.

so-so adj. indifferent; neither very good nor very bad.

sotto voce /sɒtoʊ 'voʊtʃeɪ/ adv. in a low tone intended not to be overheard.

sou' /saʊ/ n., adj., adv. Chiefly Naut. south.

soufflé /'suflẽɪ/ n. a light baked dish made fluffy with beaten eggwhites combined with egg yolks, white sauce, and fish, cheese, or other ingredients.

sought /sɔt/ v. past tense and past participle of **seek**.

soul /soʊl/ n. **1.** the spiritual part of a human being as believed to survive death. **2.** the seat of the feelings or sentiments. **3.** the embodiment of some quality. **4.** a human being; person.

soul music n. commercial African American blues music which combines gospel music with a blues style.

sound¹ /saʊnd/ n. **1.** the sensation produced in the organs of hearing when certain vibrations (**soundwaves**) are caused in the surrounding air. **2.** a noise, vocal utterance, musical note, or the like. **3.** mere noise, without meaning. -v.i. **4.** to make or emit a sound. **5.** to be heard, as a sound. **6.** to convey a certain impression when heard or read. -v.t. **7.** to cause (an instrument, etc.) to make or emit a sound. **8.** to give forth (a sound).

sound² /saʊnd/ adj. **1.** free from injury, defect, etc. **2.** financially strong, secure, or reliable. -adv. **3.** in a sound manner.

sound³ /saʊnd/ v.t. **1.** to measure or try the depth of (water, a deep hole, etc.) by letting down a lead or plummet at the end of a line or by some equivalent means. **2.** (oft. fol. by out) to seek to elicit the views or sentiments of (a person) by indirect inquiries, suggestive allusions, etc.

sound⁴ /saʊnd/ n. an inlet, arm, or recessed portion of the sea.

soundtrack /'saʊndtræk/ n. **1.** a strip at the side of a cinema film which carries the sound recording. **2.** such a recording, especially when transferred on to a CD or cassette.

soup /sup/ n. **1.** a liquid food made with various ingredients, by boiling or simmering. -phr. **2.** soup up, Colloq. to modify (an engine, especially of a car) in order to increase its power.

soupçon /'supsɒn/ n. a very small amount.

sour /'saʊə/ adj. **1.** having an acid taste, such as that of vinegar, lemon juice, etc.; tart. **2.** acidified or affected by fermentation; fermented. **3.** distasteful or disagreeable; unpleasant.

source /sɔs/ n. **1.** any thing or place from which something comes, arises, or is obtained; origin. -v.t. **2.** (**sourced**, **sourcing**) **2.** to establish the source of. **3.** to obtain (a product) from a particular producer.

souse /saʊs/ v.t. (**soused**, **sousing**) **1.** to plunge into water or other liquid. -n. **2.** Colloq. a drunkard.

south /saʊθ/ n. **1.** a cardinal point of the compass directly opposite to the north. -adj. **2.** lying or proceeding towards the south. **3.** coming from the south, as a wind. -adv. **4.** towards or in the south. **5.** from the south. Also, esp. Naut., **sou'** /saʊ/. -southerly, adj., n. -southern, adj.

southern lights pl. n. the aurora of the Southern Hemisphere.

souvenir /suvə'nɪə/ n. something given or kept for remembrance; a memento.

souvlaki /suv'laki/ pl. n. a Greek dish of diced lamb and vegetables cooked on skewers.

sovereign /'sɒvrən/ n. **1.** a monarch; a king or queen. **2.** a former British gold coin. -adj. **3.** having supreme rank, power, or authority. -sovereignty, n.

sow¹ /soʊ/ v. (**sowed**, **sown** or **sowed**, **sowing**) -v.t. **1.** to scatter (seed) over land, earth, etc., for growth; plant (seed, and hence a crop). **2.** to scatter seed over (land, earth, etc.) for the purpose of growth. -v.i. **3.** to sow seed, as for the production of a crop.

sow² /saʊ/ n. an adult female pig.

soybean /'sɔɪbin/ n. a leguminous plant with an oil-yielding seed used as food. Also, **soy**, **soya bean**.

soy sauce n. a salty dark brown sauce, made by fermenting soybeans in brine. Also, **soya sauce**.

spa /spa/ n. **1.** a mineral spring, or a locality in which such springs exist. **2.** a spa bath or spa pool.

spa bath n. a bath equipped with submerged water jets which create water turbulence.

space /speɪs/ n. **1.** the unlimited or indefinitely great general receptacle of things, commonly conceived as an expanse extending in all directions. **2.** that part of the universe which lies outside the earth's atmosphere. **3.** extent or area; a particular extent of surface. **4.** the area or position for a person to stand, sit, etc. **5.** extent, or a particular extent, of time. -v.t. (**spaced**, **spacing**) **6.** to set some distance apart.

space age *n.* the period in human history when exploration of and travel in space has been possible.

spacecraft /'speiskraft/ *n.* a vehicle capable of travelling in space.

space shuttle *n.* a re-usable rocket-propelled spacecraft designed to transport equipment and personnel from earth into space and back.

spacious /'speiʃəs/ *adj.* containing much space, as a house, room, court, street, etc.; amply large.

spade¹ /speid/ *n.* **1.** a tool for digging. **2.** some implement, piece, or part resembling this.

spade² /speid/ *n.* a black figure shaped like an inverted heart with a short stem at the cusp opposite the point, used on playing cards.

spadework /'speidwɜk/ *n.* preliminary or initial work, especially of a laborious or tedious nature.

spaghetti /spə'gɛti/ *n.* a kind of pasta.

spam /spæm/ *(from trademark)* –*n.* **1.** a type of cooked tinned meat. **2.** *Colloq.* unsolicited email, especially advertising material. –*v.t.* **(spammed, spamming) 3.** *Colloq.* to send (someone) spam (def. 2). **–spammer**, *n.* **–spamming**, *n.*

span /spæn/ *n.* **1.** the distance between the tip of the thumb and the tip of the little finger when the hand is fully extended. **2.** the distance or space between two supports of a bridge, beam, or similar structure. **3.** the full extent, stretch, or reach of anything. –*v.t.* **(spanned, spanning) 4.** to encircle with the hand or hands, as the waist. **5.** to extend over or across (a space, a river, etc.).

spangle /'spæŋgəl/ *n.* **1.** any small, bright drop, object, spot, or the like. –*v.t.* **2.** to decorate with spangles.

spaniel /'spænjəl/ *n.* a small dog usually with a long, silky coat and drooping ears.

spank¹ /spæŋk/ *v.t.* **1.** to strike (a person, usually a child) with the open hand, a slipper, etc., especially on the buttocks, as in punishment. –*n.* **2.** a blow given in spanking; a smart or resounding slap.

spank² /spæŋk/ *v.i.* to move quickly, vigorously, or smartly.

spanner /'spænə/ *n.* a tool for catching upon or gripping and turning or twisting the head of a bolt, a nut, a pipe, or the like, commonly consisting of a bar of metal with fixed or adjustable jaws.

spa pool *n.* a small pool, sometimes part of a larger pool, in which heated water is agitated and aerated to massage the user's muscles.

spar¹ /spa/ *n. Naut.* a stout pole such as those used for masts, etc.; a mast, yard, boom, gaff, or the like.

spar² /spa/ *v.i.* **(sparred, sparring)** to box with light blows, especially while seeking an opening in an opponent's defence.

spare /speə/ *v.* **(spared, sparing)** –*v.t.* **1.** to refrain from harming or destroying. **2.** to save from strain, discomfort, annoyance, or the like. **3.** to part with or let go, as from a supply, especially without inconvenience or loss. **4.** to use economically or frugally. –*v.i.* **5.** to use economy; be frugal. –*adj.* **(sparer, sparest) 6.** kept in reserve, as for possible use. **7.** being in excess of present need; free for other use. **8.** lean or thin, as a person. –*n.* **9.** a spare thing, part, etc., as an extra tyre for emergency use.

spare part *n.* a part which replaces a faulty, worn, or broken part of a machine, especially a motor vehicle. Also, **spare**.

spark /spak/ *n.* **1.** an ignited or fiery particle such as is thrown off by burning wood, etc., or produced by one hard body striking against another. **2.** *Elect.* the light produced by a sudden discontinuous discharge of electricity. –*v.i.* **3.** to emit or produce sparks.

sparkle /'spakəl/ *v.i.* **1.** to emit little sparks, as burning matter. **2.** to shine with little gleams of light. **3.** to effervesce, as wine. –*n.* **4.** a little spark or fiery particle.

spark plug *n.* a device inserted in the cylinder of an internal-combustion engine, containing two terminals between which passes the electric spark for igniting the explosive gases. Also, **sparking plug**.

sparrow /'spærou/ *n.* a common small bird inhabiting urban areas and farmland, native to Europe, Asia and North Africa, and widely introduced elsewhere.

sparse /spas/ *adj.* thinly scattered or distributed.

spasm /'spæzəm/ *n.* a sudden, involuntary muscular contraction.

spasmodic /spæz'mɒdɪk/ *adj.* **1.** relating to or of the nature of a spasm. **2.** very brief or irregular; intermittent: *spasmodic appearances*. **–spasmodically**, *adv.*

spastic /'spæstɪk/ *n.* a person who has cerebral palsy.

spat¹ /spæt/ *n.* a petty quarrel.

spat² /spæt/ *v.* past tense and past participle of **spit¹**.

spate /speit/ *n.* a sudden, almost overwhelming, outpouring.

spatial /'speiʃəl/ *adj.* of or relating to space.

spatio- a word element meaning 'space'.

spatter /'spætə/ *v.t.* **1.** to scatter or dash in small particles or drops. **2.** to splash with something in small particles.

spatula /'spætʃələ/ *n.* a broad, flexible blade, used for mixing and spreading.

spawn /spɔn/ *v.i.* **1.** to shed the sex cells, especially as applied to animals that shed eggs and sperm directly into water. –*v.t.* **2.** to give birth to; give rise to.

spay /spei/ *v.t.* to remove the ovaries of (a female animal).

SP bookmaker *n.* an unlicensed bookmaker operating off racetracks paying the starting price odds.

speak /spik/ *v.* **(spoke, spoken, speaking)** –*v.i.* **1.** to utter words or articulate sounds with the ordinary (talking) voice. **2.** to deliver an address, discourse, etc. **3.** to make communication by any means. –*v.t.* **4.** to utter orally and articulately. **5.** to use, or be able to use, in oral utterance, as a language.

speaker /'spikə/ *n.* **1.** *(usu. upper case)* the presiding officer of the lower house of a parliament, as in the House of Representatives. **2.** a loudspeaker.

spear /spiə/ *n.* **1.** a weapon for thrusting or throwing, being a long staff with a sharp head, as of iron or steel. –*v.t.* **2.** to pierce with or as with a spear.

spearmint /ˈspɪəmɪnt/ n. an aromatic herb much used for flavouring.

spec builder /spɛk/ n. someone who builds houses, etc., as a speculative enterprise, rather than under contract.

special /ˈspɛʃəl/ adj. **1.** of a distinct or particular character. **2.** being a particular one. **3.** relating or peculiar to a particular person, thing, instance, etc. **4.** extraordinary; exceptional. –phr. **5. on special,** Colloq. available at a bargain price.

specialise /ˈspɛʃəlaɪz/ v.i. **1.** to pursue some special line of study, work, etc. –v.t. **2.** to invest with a special character, function, etc. **3.** to adapt to special conditions. **4.** to restrict payment of (a negotiable instrument) by endorsing over to a specific payee. Also, **specialize.** –**specialisation,** n.

specialist /ˈspɛʃələst/ n. someone who is devoted to one subject, or to one particular branch of a subject or pursuit.

speciality /spɛʃiˈæləti/ n. (pl. **-ties**) **1.** an article of unusual or superior design or quality. **2.** an article with such strong consumer demand that it is at least partially removed from price competition. Also, **specialty.**

specialty /ˈspɛʃəlti/ n. (pl. **-ties**) **1.** a special study, line of work, or the like. **2.** an article particularly dealt in, manufactured, etc. **3.** → **speciality.**

specie /ˈspiʃi/ n. coin; coined money.

species /ˈspisiz, -ʃiz/ n. (pl. **species**) **1.** a group of individuals having some common characteristics or qualities; distinct sort or kind. **2.** Biol. the basic category of biological classification, intended to designate a single kind of animal or plant, any variations existing among the individuals being regarded as not affecting the essential sameness which distinguishes them from all other organisms within the category.

speciesism /ˈspisizɪzəm/ n. human discrimination against other animal species, especially in regard to the exploitation of certain animals for human benefit.

specific /spəˈsɪfɪk/ adj. **1.** specified, precise, or particular. **2.** peculiar or proper to something, as qualities, characteristics, effects, etc. **3.** of a special or particular kind. **4.** Commerce denoting customs or duties levied in fixed amounts per unit (number, volume, weight, etc.). –n. **5.** something specific, as a statement, quality, etc. –**specificity,** n.

specification /spɛsəfəˈkeɪʃən/ n. **1.** the act of specifying. **2.** a statement of particulars.

specify /ˈspɛsəfaɪ/ v.t. (**-fied, -fying**) **1.** to mention or name specifically or definitely; state in detail. **2.** to name or state as a condition.

specimen /ˈspɛsəmən/ n. a part or an individual taken as exemplifying a whole mass or number.

specious /ˈspiʃəs/ adj. apparently good or right but without real merit; superficially pleasing.

speck /spɛk/ n. **1.** a small spot differing in colour or substance from that of the surface or material upon which it appears. –v.t. **2.** to mark with, or as with, a speck or specks.

speckle /ˈspɛkəl/ n. **1.** a small speck, spot, or mark, as on skin. –v.t. **2.** to mark with, or as with, speckles.

spectacle /ˈspɛktəkəl/ n. **1.** anything presented to the sight or view, especially something of a striking kind. **2.** (pl.) a device to aid defective vision or to protect the eyes from light, dust, etc., consisting usually of two glass lenses set in a frame which rests on the nose.

spectacular /spɛkˈtaʃələ/ adj. relating to a display or sight which is unusual in a very exciting and impressive way. –**spectacularly,** adv.

spectator /spɛkˈteɪtə, ˈspɛkteɪtə/ n. someone who looks on; an onlooker.

spectra /ˈspɛktrə/ n. plural of **spectrum.**

spectre /ˈspɛktə/ n. a ghost; phantom.

spectro- a word element representing **spectrum.**

spectrum /ˈspɛktrəm/ n. **1.** Optics the band of colours (red, orange, yellow, green, blue, indigo, violet) observed when white light passes through a prism. **2.** a range of interrelated values, objects, opinions, etc.

speculate /ˈspɛkjəleɪt/ v.i. **1.** (oft. fol. by on, upon, or a clause) to engage in thought or reflection, or meditate. **2.** to indulge in conjectural thought. **3.** Commerce to buy and sell commodities, shares, etc., in the expectation of profit through a change in their market value. –**speculation,** n. –**speculative,** adj. –**speculator,** n.

sped /spɛd/ v. past tense and past participle of **speed.**

speech /spitʃ/ n. **1.** the faculty or power of speaking; oral communication. **2.** that which is spoken. **3.** a form of communication in spoken language, made by a speaker before an audience for a given purpose. **4.** the form of utterance characteristic of a particular people or region; a language or dialect. **5.** manner of speaking, as of a person.

speech pathology n. the assessment, diagnosis, and management of disorders of speech and language in children and adults. Also, **speech therapy.** –**speech pathologist,** n.

speed /spid/ n. **1.** rapidity in moving, going, travelling. **2.** Physics the ratio of the distance covered by a moving body to the time taken. **3.** Colloq. amphetamines. –v. (**sped** or **speeded, speeding**) –v.t. **4.** (usu. fol. by up) to increase the rate of speed of. –v.i. **5.** to move, go, pass, or proceed with speed or rapidity. **6.** to drive a vehicle at a rate exceeding the maximum permitted by law. **7.** (fol. by up) to increase the rate of speed or of progress.

speed camera n. a computerised camera positioned to monitor traffic and photograph the numberplate of any vehicle that exceeds the speed limit.

speed dial n. a feature of a phone in which preentered telephone numbers are accessed and dialled by pressing one button.

speed-dial adj. **1.** of or relating to speed dial. –v.t. (**-dialled** or, esp. US, **-dialed, -dialling** or, esp. US, **-dialing**) **2.** to telephone (someone) using a speed-dial facility.

speedometer /spiˈdɒmətə/ n. a device attached to a motor vehicle or the like to indicate the rate of travel. Also, **speedo.**

speed reading /ˈspid ridɪŋ/ n. reading at a fast speed while maintaining comprehension, using any of various techniques which enable this process, as by assimilating several phrases or sentences at once.

speleology /spiːliˈɒlədʒi/ n. the exploration and study of caves. Also, **spelaeology**.

spell¹ /spɛl/ v. (**spelt** or **spelled, spelling**) –v.t. **1.** to name, write, or otherwise give (as by signals), in order, the letters of (a word, syllable, etc.). **2.** (of letters) to form (a word, syllable, etc.). –v.i. **3.** to name, write, or give the letters of words, etc.

spell² /spɛl/ n. a form of words supposed to possess magic power.

spell³ /spɛl/ n. **1.** a continuous course or period of work or other activity. **2.** Colloq. an interval or space of time, usually indefinite or short. **3.** an interval or period of rest. –v.t. **4.** to give an interval of rest to.

spellchecker /ˈspɛltʃɛkə/ n. a computer program which checks the spelling of words.

spelling /ˈspɛlɪŋ/ n. the manner in which words are spelt.

spencer /ˈspɛnsə/ n. a kind of woman's vest, worn for extra warmth.

spend /spɛnd/ v. (**spent, spending**) –v.t. **1.** to pay out, disburse, or expend; dispose of (money, wealth, resources, etc.). **2.** to pass (time, or some period of time). **3.** to use up: *he has spent all his anger.* –v.i. **4.** to spend money, etc.

spendthrift /ˈspɛndθrɪft/ n. someone who spends their possessions or money extravagantly or wastefully; a prodigal.

sperm /spɜːm/ n. a male reproductive cell; a spermatozoon.

-sperm a terminal combining form of **sperm**, as in *angiosperm*.

spermatozoon /ˌspɜːmətəˈzoʊɒn/ n. (pl. **-zoa** /-ˈzoʊə/) a mature male reproductive cell.

spew /spjuː/ v.i. **1.** to discharge the contents of the stomach through the mouth; vomit. –v.t. **2.** to eject from the stomach through the mouth; vomit.

SPF /ˌɛs piː ˈɛf/ n. the effectiveness of a sunscreen preparation in protecting the skin from ultraviolet radiation, indicated on a scale, usually from 2 to 15. Also, **sun protection factor**.

sphere /sfɪə/ n. **1.** a round body whose surface is at all points equidistant from the centre. **2.** any rounded body approximately of this form; a globular mass, shell, etc. **3.** a field of activity or operation.

-sphere a word element representing **sphere**.

spherical /ˈsfɛrɪkəl/ adj. **1.** having the form of a sphere; globular. **2.** of or relating to a sphere or spheres.

sphincter /ˈsfɪŋktə/ n. Anat. a circular band of voluntary or involuntary muscle which encircles an orifice of the body or one of its hollow organs.

spice /spaɪs/ n. **1.** any of a class of pungent or aromatic substances of vegetable origin, as pepper, cinnamon, cloves, and the like, used as seasoning, preservatives, etc. **2.** piquancy, or interest. –v.t. **3.** to prepare or season with a spice or spices. –**spicy**, adj.

spick-and-span /spɪk-ən-ˈspæn/ adj. **1.** neat and clean. **2.** perfectly new; fresh. Also, **spick and span**.

spider /ˈspaɪdə/ n. **1.** any of the eight-legged wingless, predatory, insect-like arachnids most of which spin webs that serve as nests and as traps for prey. **2.** any of various things resembling or suggesting a spider. **3.** an aerated soft drink to which ice cream is added.

spiel /spil, ʃpil/ n. a salesperson's, conjurer's, or swindler's patter.

spigot /ˈspɪgət/ n. a small peg or plug for stopping the vent of a cask, etc.

spike /spaɪk/ n. **1.** a stiff, sharp-pointed piece or part. –v.t. **2.** to fasten or secure with a spike or spikes. **3.** to pierce with or impale on a spike. **4.** to set or stud with something suggesting spikes. **5.** to make ineffective, or frustrate the action or purpose of. **6.** Colloq. to add alcoholic liquor to a drink.

spill¹ /spɪl/ v. (**spilt** or **spilled, spilling**) –v.t. **1.** to cause or allow (liquid, or any matter in grains or loose pieces) to run or fall from a container, especially accidentally or wastefully. –v.i. **2.** (of a liquid, loose particles, etc.) to run or escape from a container, especially by accident or in careless handling. –n. **3.** a spilling, as of liquid. **4.** a quantity spilt. **5.** a throw or fall from a horse, vehicle, or the like. **6.** Politics the declaring vacant of a number of positions when one of them falls vacant.

spill² /spɪl/ n. a slender piece of wood or twisted paper, for lighting candles, lamps, etc.

spin /spɪn/ v. (**spun, spinning**) –v.t. **1.** to cause to turn round rapidly, as on an axis; twirl; whirl. **2.** to make (yarn) by drawing out, twisting, and winding fibres. **3.** to form (any material) into thread. **4.** to produce, fabricate, or evolve in a manner suggestive of spinning thread, as a story. –v.i. **5.** to turn round rapidly, as on an axis, as the earth, a top, etc. **6.** to produce a thread from the body, as spiders, silkworms, etc. –n. **7.** a spinning motion given to a ball or the like when thrown or struck. **8.** a rapid run, ride, drive, or the like, as for exercise or enjoyment. **9.** Colloq. the particular slant deliberately given to a media story so as to achieve the desired outcome in terms of public awareness and acceptance.

spinach /ˈspɪnɪtʃ/ n. Also, **English spinach**. an annual herb cultivated for its succulent leaves. **2.** a form of beet with large, firm, strongly veined green leaves and a long fleshy stalk, used as a vegetable; silverbeet.

spinal cord /ˈspaɪnəl/ n. the cord of nervous tissue extending through the spinal column.

spin control n. a method of controlling the point of view presented in the media, especially in relation to politics.

spindle /ˈspɪndl/ n. **1.** the rod on a spinning wheel by which the thread is twisted and on which it is wound. **2.** any similar rod or pin.

spindly /ˈspɪndli/ adj. (**-dlier, -dliest**) long or tall and slender.

spin-dry /ˈspɪn draɪ/ v.t. (**-dried, -drying**) to dry (laundry) by spinning it in a tub.

spine /spaɪn/ n. **1.** the vertebral or spinal column; the backbone. **2.** any backbone-like part. **3.** a stiff, pointed process or appendage. **4.** Bookbinding the part of a book's cover that holds the front and back together. –**spinal**, adj.

spinechilling /ˈspaɪntʃɪlɪŋ/ adj. terrifying.

spinifex /'spɪnəfeks/ *n.* spiny-leaved tussock-forming grasses of inland Australia.

spinnaker /'spɪnəkə/ *n.* a large triangular sail with a light boom (**spinnaker boom**).

spinning top *n.* a child's toy, having a point on which it is made to spin.

spinning wheel *n.* a device for spinning wool, flax, etc., into yarn or thread consisting essentially of a single spindle driven by a large wheel operated by hand or foot.

spin-off *n.* **1.** an object, product or enterprise derived as an incidental or secondary development of a larger enterprise. **2.** *Econ.* a new company formed by an already existing company, with shareholders in the existing company entitled to subscribe for shares in the new company.

spinster /'spɪnstə/ *n.* a woman who has never been married.

spiny /'spaɪni/ *adj.* (**-nier, -niest**) **1.** having many spines; thorny, as a plant. **2.** covered with spines, as an animal.

spiny anteater /'spaɪni/ *n.* → **echidna**.

spiral /'spaɪrəl/ *n.* **1.** a plane curve traced by a point which runs continuously round and round a fixed point or centre while constantly receding from or approaching it. **2.** a spiral or helical object, formation, or form. **3.** *Econ.* a reciprocal interaction of price and cost changes forming an overall economic change upwards (**inflationary spiral**) or downwards (**deflationary spiral**). *–adj.* **4.** resembling or arranged in a spiral or spirals. *–v.* (**-ralled, -ralling**) *–v.i.* **5.** to take a spiral form or course. *–v.t.* **6.** to cause to take a spiral form or course.

spiralise /'spaɪrəlaɪz/ *v.t.* to shred (vegetables) into ribbon or noodle-like lengths which form loose curls. Also, **spiralize**. **–spiraliser**, *n.*

spire /spaɪə/ *n.* a tall, tapering structure erected on a tower, roof, etc.

spirit /'spɪrət/ *n.* **1.** the vital principle in human beings, animating the body or mediating between body and soul. **2.** the incorporeal part of a human being. **3.** a supernatural, incorporeal being. **4.** (*pl.*) feelings with respect to exaltation or depression. **5.** fine or brave vigour or liveliness; mettle. **6.** the true or general meaning or intent of a statement, etc. (opposed to *letter*). **7.** (*oft. pl.*) a strong distilled alcoholic liquor. **8.** *Pharmaceutical* a solution in alcohol of an essential or volatile principle. *–adj.* **9.** relating to something which works by burning alcoholic spirits. *–v.t.* **10.** to carry (*away, off,* etc.) mysteriously or secretly. **–spirited,** *adj.*

spiritual /'spɪrətʃuəl, -tʃəl/ *adj.* **1.** of or relating to the spirit or soul as opposed to the physical body. **2.** of or relating to sacred, religious, or supernatural things. *–n.* **3.** a traditional religious song, especially of African Americans.

spiro-¹ a word element referring to respiration.

spiro-² a word element meaning 'coil', 'spiral'.

spirulina /spɪrə'linə/ *n.* a human and animal food supplement made from organisms which contain unusually high amounts of protein.

spit¹ /spɪt/ *v.* (**spat** *or* **spit, spitting**) *–v.i.* **1.** to eject saliva from the mouth. **2.** to sputter. **3.** to fall in scattered drops or flakes, as rain or snow. *–v.t.* **4.** to eject (saliva, etc.) from the

mouth. **5.** to throw out or emit, especially violently. *–n.* **6.** saliva, especially when ejected. **7.** the act of spitting. *–phr.* **8. dead spit,** *Colloq.* the image, likeness, or counterpart of a person, etc.

spit² /spɪt/ *n.* **1.** any of various rods, pins, or the like used for particular purposes. **2.** a narrow point of land projecting into the water. *–v.t.* (**spitted, spitting**) **3.** to thrust a spit into or through, as roasting meat.

spite /spaɪt/ *n.* **1.** a keen, ill-natured desire to humiliate, annoy, or injure another. *–v.t.* **2.** to annoy or thwart, out of spite. *–phr.* **3. in spite of,** in disregard or defiance of; notwithstanding.

spiteful /'spaɪtfəl/ *adj.* wanting to hurt or upset someone else because one feels angry or jealous. **–spitefully,** *adv.* **–spitefulness,** *n.*

spittle /'spɪtl/ *n.* saliva; spit.

spittoon /spɪ'tun/ *n.* a bowl, etc., for spitting into.

splash /splæʃ/ *v.t.* **1.** to wet or soil by dashing masses or particles of water, mud, or the like; spatter. **2.** to dash (water, etc.) about in scattered masses or particles. **3.** *Colloq.* to display or print very noticeably, as in a newspaper. *–v.i.* **4.** to dash a liquid or semiliquid substance about. **5.** to fall, move, or go with a splash or splashes. *–n.* **6.** the act of splashing. **7.** the sound of splashing. **8.** a striking show, or an ostentatious display; sensation or excitement.

splat /splæt/ *n.* a slapping sound as made with something wet.

splatter /'splætə/ *v.i., v.t.* to splash.

splay /spleɪ/ *v.t.* **1.** to spread out, expand, or extend. *–v.i.* **2.** to spread or flare.

spleen /splin/ *n.* **1.** *Anat.* a gland-like organ, in the upper left of the abdomen, which modifies the blood. **2.** ill humour, peevish temper, or spite. **–splenetic,** *adj.*

splendid /'splɛndəd/ *adj.* **1.** gorgeous; magnificent; sumptuous. **2.** strikingly admirable or fine.

splendour /'splɛndə/ *n.* brilliant or gorgeous appearance, colouring, etc. Also, **splendor.**

splice /splaɪs/ *v.t.* (**spliced, splicing**) to join together or unite, especially by the interweaving of strands.

splint /splɪnt/ *n.* **1.** a thin piece of wood or other rigid material used to immobilise a fractured or dislocated bone. *–v.t.* **2.** to support as if with splints.

splinter /'splɪntə/ *n.* **1.** a rough piece of wood, bone, etc., usually comparatively long, thin, and sharp, split or broken off from a main body. *–v.t., v.i.* **2.** to split or break into splinters.

split /splɪt/ *v.* (**split, splitting**) *–v.t.* **1.** to divide into distinct parts or portions. **2.** to separate (a part) by such division. **3.** to make (a vote) less effective by offering more than one candidate with a similar policy. *–v.i.* **4.** to break or part lengthways, or suffer longitudinal division. **5.** to part, divide, or separate in any way. **6.** to become separated off by such a division, as a piece or part from a whole. **7.** *Colloq.* to leave hurriedly. *–n.* **8.** the act of splitting. **9.** a crack, rent, or fissure caused by splitting. **10.** (*usu. pl.*) the feat of separating the legs while sinking to the floor, until they extend at right angles to the body. *–adj.* **11.** that has undergone splitting; parted lengthwise; cleft.

split-level *adj.* denoting or relating to a building or room with a floor at more than one level.

split personality *n.* **1.** (in popular use) → **schizophrenia. 2.** (in popular use) → **multiple personality disorder. 3.** *Colloq.* an unpredictable or extremely changeable personality.

splotch /splɒtʃ/ *n.* a large, irregular spot; blot; stain.

splurge /splɜdʒ/ *v.i.* (**splurged, splurging**) *Colloq.* to be extravagant.

splutter /'splʌtə/ *v.i.* **1.** to talk hastily and confusedly or incoherently, as in excitement or embarrassment. **2.** to fly or fall in particles or drops; spatter, as a liquid.

spoil /spɔɪl/ *v.* (**spoiled** *or* **spoilt, spoiling**) *–v.t.* **1.** to damage or impair (a thing) irreparably. **2.** to impair in character or disposition. *–v.i.* **3.** to become spoiled, bad, or unfit for use. *–n.* **4.** (*oft. pl.*) booty, loot, or plunder taken in war or robbery. **5.** treasures won or accumulated.

spoilsport /'spɔɪlspɔt/ *n.* someone who interferes with the pleasure of others.

spoke[1] /spoʊk/ *v.* past tense of **speak**.

spoke[2] /spoʊk/ *n.* one of the bars, rods, or rungs radiating from the hub of a wheel and supporting the rim.

spoken /'spoʊkən/ *v.* **1.** past participle of **speak.** *–adj.* **2.** (in compounds) speaking, or using speech, as specified.

spokesperson /'spoʊkspɜsən/ *n.* someone who speaks for another or others.

sponge /spʌndʒ/ *n.* **1.** the light, yielding, porous, fibrous skeleton or framework of certain animals, or colonies of this group, from which the living matter has been removed, characterised by readily absorbing water, and becoming soft when wet while retaining toughness. **2.** someone who or that which absorbs something freely, as a sponge does water. **3.** a light, sweet cake. *–v.* (**sponged, sponging**) *–v.t.* **4.** to wipe or rub with a wet sponge, in order to clean or moisten. **5.** (fol. by *off, away*, etc.) to remove with a wet sponge. *–v.i.* **6.** *Colloq.* to live at the expense of others.

sponsor /'spɒnsə/ *n.* **1.** someone who vouches or is responsible for a person or thing. **2.** a person, firm, or other organisation that finances a radio or television program in return for advertisement. *–v.t.* **3.** to act as sponsor for.

spontaneous /spɒn'teɪniəs/ *adj.* **1.** natural and unconstrained. **2.** independent of external agencies.

spoof /spuf/ *n.* *Colloq.* parody; hoax.

spook /spuk/ *n.* *Colloq.* a ghost; a spectre. **–spooky,** *adj.* **–spookily,** *adv.*

spooked /spukt/ *adj.* frightened; on edge; nervous.

spooky /'spuki/ *adj.* (**-kier, -kiest**) *Colloq.* like or suggesting a ghost; eerie: *a spooky noise.* **–spookily,** *adv.* **–spookiness,** *n.*

spool /spul/ *n.* any cylindrical piece or appliance on which something is wound.

spoon /spun/ *n.* **1.** a utensil consisting of a bowl or concave part and a handle, for taking up or stirring liquid or other food, or other

matter. *–v.t.* **2.** to take up or transfer in or as in a spoon. *–v.i.* **3.** to show affection, especially in an openly sentimental manner.

spoonerism /'spunərɪzəm/ *n.* a slip of the tongue whereby initial or other sounds of words are transposed, as in 'our queer old dean' for 'our dear old queen'.

spoor /spɔ/ *n.* a track or trail, especially that of a wild animal pursued as game.

sporadic /spə'rædɪk/ *adj.* appearing or happening at intervals; occasional.

spore /spɔ/ *n.* a germ, germ cell, seed, or the like.

sporo- a word element meaning 'seed'. Also, **spor-**.

sporran /'spɒrən/ *n.* (in Scottish Highland costume) a large pouch, commonly of fur, worn hanging from the belt over the front of the kilt.

sport /spɔt/ *n.* **1.** an activity pursued for exercise or pleasure, usually requiring some degree of physical prowess. **2.** pleasant pastime. **3.** something sported with or tossed about like a plaything. **4.** *Colloq.* a term of address, usually between males. **5.** *Colloq.* someone who is pursuits involving betting or gambling. *–v.i.* **6.** to amuse oneself with some pleasant pastime or recreation. *–v.t.* **7.** to have or wear, especially ostentatiously, proudly, etc.

sporting /'spɔtɪŋ/ *adj.* **1.** exhibiting qualities especially esteemed in those who engage in sports, such as fairness, good humour when losing, etc. **2.** willing to take a chance. **3.** even or fair; involving reasonable odds, as a gamble.

sports /spɔts/ *adj.* **1.** of, relating to, or devoted to a sport or sports. **2.** (of garments, etc.) suitable for outdoor or informal use.

sports car *n.* a high-powered car, usually a two-seater with a low body, built for speed and manoeuvring ability.

sports drink *n.* a drink which contains sugars, salts and water; designed to rehydrate the body during or after periods of intense physical exertion. Also, **sport drink.**

sportsman /'spɔtsmən/ *n.* (*pl.* **-men**) **1.** a man who engages in sport, especially in an open-air sport and with some expertise. **2.** someone who exhibits sporting qualities.

sportsperson /'spɔtspɜsən/ *n.* (*pl.* **-people**) a person who engages in sport, usually with a degree of expertise.

sportswoman /'spɔtswʊmən/ *n.* (*pl.* **-women**) a woman who engages in sport, especially in an open-air sport and with some expertise.

spot /spɒt/ *n.* **1.** a mark made by foreign matter; a stain. **2.** a blemish of the skin, as a pimple. **3.** a relatively small, usually roundish, part of a surface differing from the rest in appearance or character. **4.** a moral blemish; flaw. **5.** a place or locality. **6.** *Colloq.* a small quantity of something. **7.** *Colloq.* a predicament. *–v.* (**spotted, spotting**) *–v.t.* **8.** to stain with spots. **9.** to see or perceive, especially suddenly, by chance, or when it is difficult to do so. *–v.i.* **10.** to make a spot; cause a stain. *–adj.* **11.** *Commerce* made, paid, delivered, etc., at once.

spot check *n.* **1.** an inspection made without warning, as of motor vehicles, etc. **2.** a check made on a random sample, as of manufactured articles.

spotlight /'spɒtlaɪt/ n. Theatre a strong light with a narrow beam thrown upon a particular spot on the stage.

spot-on adj. Colloq. absolutely right or accurate; excellent.

spot price n. (in commodities trading) the price agreed on for immediate delivery of the commodity.

spouse /spaʊs, spaʊz/ n. one's husband or wife.

spout /spaʊt/ v.i. **1.** to discharge or emit (a liquid, etc.) in a stream, with some force. −v.i. **2.** to discharge a liquid, etc., in a jet or continuous stream. **3.** to issue with force, as liquid through a narrow orifice. −n. **4.** a tube by which a liquid is discharged or poured.

sprain /spreɪn/ v.t. to overstrain or wrench (a joint) so as to injure without fracture or dislocation.

sprang /spræŋ/ v. past tense of **spring**.

sprat /spræt/ n. a small, herring-like marine fish.

sprawl /sprɔl/ v.i. **1.** to be stretched out in irregular or ungraceful movements, as the limbs. **2.** to lie or sit with the limbs stretched out in a careless or ungraceful posture. **3.** to spread out in a straggling or irregular manner, as vines, buildings, handwriting, etc. −v.t. **4.** to stretch out (the limbs) as in sprawling.

spray[1] /spreɪ/ n. **1.** water or other liquid broken up into small particles and blown or falling through the air. −v.t. **2.** to scatter in the form of fine particles. **3.** to direct a spray of particles, missiles, etc., upon. −v.i. **4.** to scatter spray; discharge a spray. **5.** to issue as spray.

spray[2] /spreɪ/ n. a single flower or small bouquet of flowers designed to be pinned to one's clothes as an adornment.

spray can n. → **aerosol**.

spread /sprɛd/ v. (**spread, spreading**) −v.t. **1.** to draw or stretch out to the full width. **2.** to distribute in a sheet or layer. **3.** to overlay, cover, or coat with something. **4.** to diffuse or disseminate, as knowledge, news, disease, etc. −v.i. **5.** to become stretched out or extended. **6.** to be capable of being spread or applied in a thin layer, as a soft substance. **7.** to become diffused or disseminated. −n. **8.** expansion; extension; diffusion. **9.** a stretch, expanse, or extent of something. **10.** a cloth covering for a bed, table, or the like, especially a bedspread. **11.** any food preparation for spreading on bread, etc. **12.** Stock Exchange **a.** the difference between the highest and the lowest prices at which business has been done during one day. **b.** the difference between the prices quoted by a stockjobber for buying and selling. **13.** a pair of facing pages of a book, magazine, or the like, or any part of them.

spread-eagle v.t. to stretch out. −**spread-eagled**, adj.

spreadsheet /'sprɛdʃit/ n. a computer program for organising large amounts of numerical data in tabular formats.

spree /spri/ n. a session or period of excessive indulgence: a spending spree.

sprig /sprɪg/ n. a shoot, twig, or small branch.

sprightly /'spraɪtli/ adj. (**-lier, -liest**) animated, vivacious, or lively.

spring /sprɪŋ/ v. (**sprang** or **sprung, sprung, springing**) −v.i. **1.** to rise or move suddenly and lightly as by some inherent power. **2.** to go or come suddenly as if with a leap. **3.** (oft. fol. by up) to come into being; rise or arise. −v.t. **4.** to cause to spring. **5.** to bring out, disclose, produce, make, etc., suddenly. **6.** to equip or fit with springs. **7.** to leap over. **8.** to make a surprise attack on (someone). −n. **9.** a leap, jump, or bound. **10.** elasticity or springiness. **11.** an issue of water from the earth. **12.** a beginning or cause of origin. **13.** the season of the year between winter and summer. **14.** the first and freshest period. **15.** an elastic contrivance which recovers its shape after being compressed, bent, etc. −adj. **16.** of, relating to, characteristic of, or suitable for the season of spring. **17.** resting on or containing springs.

springboard /'sprɪŋbɔd/ n. **1.** a projecting semiflexible board used for diving. **2.** a flexible board used as a take-off in vaulting, tumbling, etc., to increase the height of leaps.

springbok /'sprɪŋbɒk/ n. (pl. **-boks** or, especially collectively, **-bok**) a gazelle of southern Africa which has a habit of springing upwards. Also, **springbuck**.

spring roll n. a Chinese delicacy consisting of a savoury filling wrapped in a thin dough and deep fried.

sprinkle /'sprɪŋkəl/ v.t. **1.** to scatter, as a liquid or a powder, in drops or particles. **2.** to disperse or distribute here and there. **3.** to overspread with drops or particles of water, powder, or the like. −n. **4.** a sprinkling.

sprint /sprɪnt/ v.i. **1.** to race at full speed, especially for a short distance, as in running, rowing, etc. −n. **2.** a short race at full speed.

sprite /spraɪt/ n. **1.** an elf, fairy, or goblin. **2.** an icon which moves around a screen in computer graphics.

spritzig /'sprɪtsɪg/ adj. (of wine) showing a slight degree of gassiness.

sprocket /'sprɒkət/ n. Machinery one of a set of projections on the rim of a wheel which engage the links of a chain.

sprout /spraʊt/ v.i. **1.** to begin to grow. **2.** (of a seed, plant, the earth, etc.) to put forth buds or shoots. −n. **3.** a shoot of a plant. **4.** → **brussels sprout**.

spruce[1] /sprus/ n. an evergreen tree with short angular needle-shaped leaves.

spruce[2] /sprus/ adj. (**sprucer, sprucest**) **1.** smart in dress or appearance. −v.i. (**spruced, sprucing**) **2.** (usu. fol. by up) to make oneself spruce.

sprung /sprʌŋ/ v. past tense and past participle of **spring**.

spry /spraɪ/ adj. (**spryer** or **sprier, spryest** or **spriest**) active; nimble; brisk.

spud /spʌd/ n. Colloq. a potato.

spume /spjum/ n. foam; froth; scum.

spun /spʌn/ v. past tense and past participle of **spin**.

spun glass n. → **fibreglass**.

spunk /spʌŋk/ n. Colloq. **1.** pluck; spirit; mettle. **2.** a good-looking person. −**spunky**, adj.

spunky /'spʌŋki/ adj. (**-kier, -kiest**) Colloq. **1.** plucky; spirited: a spunky attitude. **2.** good-looking; attractive. −**spunkily**, adv. −**spunkiness**, n.

spur /spɜ/ n. **1.** a pointed device attached to a rider's boot heel, for goading a horse onwards, etc. **2.** a stiff, usually sharp, horny point on the leg of various birds and animals. –v.t. (**spurred**, **spurring**) **3.** to prick with, or as with, spurs or a spur, as to urge on. –phr. **4. on the spur of the moment**, suddenly; without premeditation.

spurious /'spjuriəs/ adj. not genuine or true.

spurn /spɜn/ v.t. to reject with disdain.

spurt /spɜt/ v.i. **1.** to gush or issue suddenly in a stream or jet, as a liquid. **2.** to show marked activity or energy for a short period. –n. **3.** a forcible gush of water, etc., as from a confined place. **4.** a sudden outburst, as of feeling.

sputter /'spʌtə/ v.i. **1.** to emit particles of anything in an explosive manner, as a candle does in burning. –v.t. **2.** to emit (anything) in small particles, as if by spitting.

spy /spaɪ/ n. (pl. **spies**) **1.** someone who keeps secret watch on the actions of others. **2.** one employed by a government to obtain secret information or intelligence. –v. (**spied**, **spying**) –v.i. **3.** to make secret observations. –v.t. **4.** to find (out) by observation or scrutiny. **5.** to catch sight of; see.

spyglass /'spaɪglas/ n. a small telescope.

spyware /'spaɪweə/ n. software which, once installed on a computer, secretly collects information as the user goes about their normal computer tasks, as tracking internet viewing for advertising purposes, copying files from the hard disk, or copying logins and passwords.

squabble /'skwɒbəl/ v.i. **1.** to engage in a petty quarrel. –n. **2.** a petty quarrel.

squad /skwɒd/ n. any small group or party of persons engaged in a common enterprise, etc.

squadron /'skwɒdrən/ n. an air force unit.

squalid /'skwɒlɪd/ adj. foul and repulsive.

squall¹ /skwɔl/ n. a sudden strong wind which dies away rapidly.

squall² /skwɔl/ v.i. to cry out loudly; scream violently.

squalor /'skwɒlə/ n. filth and misery.

squander /'skwɒndə/ v.t. (oft. fol. by away) to spend (money, time, etc.) extravagantly or wastefully.

square /skweə/ n. **1.** a four-sided plane figure, or rectangle, with four equal sides and four right angles. **2.** anything having this form or a form approximating to it. **3.** Maths the second power of a number or quantity. **4.** Colloq. someone who is ignorant of or uninterested in the latest fads. –v. (**squared**, **squaring**) –v.t. **5.** to reduce to square, rectangular, or cubic form. **6.** Maths to multiply (a number or quantity) by itself. **7.** (oft. fol. by off) to make straight, level, or even. –v.i. **8.** (oft. fol. by with) to accord or agree. –adj. (**squarer**, **squarest**) **9.** of the form of a right angle; having some part or parts rectangular. **10.** at right angles, or perpendicular. **11.** designating a unit representing an area in the form of a square. **12.** of a specified length on each side of a square. **13.** leaving no balance of debt on either side; having all accounts settled. **14.** just, fair, or honest. **15.** conservative. –adv. **16.** so as to be square; in square or rectangular form. –phr. **17. square up**, to pay or settle a bill, debt, etc.

square bracket n. either of the two parenthetical marks: [ ].

square dance n. a dance by couples arranged in a square or in some set form.

square root n. Maths the quantity of which a given quantity is the square.

squash¹ /skwɒʃ/ v.t. **1.** to press into a flat mass or pulp; crush. –n. **2.** the act or sound of squashing. **3.** the fact of being squashed. **4.** something squashed or crushed. **5.** a game for two players, played in a small walled court with light racquets and a small rubber ball.

squash² /skwɒʃ/ n. a vegetable similar to the pumpkin.

squat /skwɒt/ v.i. (**squatted** or **squat**, **squatting**) **1.** to assume a posture close to the ground with the knees bent and the back more or less straight. **2.** to occupy a building without title or right. –adj. **3.** low and thick or broad. –n. **4.** a squatting position or posture.

squatter /'skwɒtə/ n. **1.** (formerly) someone who settled on crown land to run stock. **2.** someone who occupies a building without right or title.

squawk /skwɔk/ v.i. **1.** to utter a loud, harsh cry, as a duck. –n. **2.** a loud, harsh cry or sound.

squeak /skwik/ n. **1.** a short, sharp, shrill cry. –v.i. **2.** to utter or emit a squeak or squeaky sound.

squeal /skwil/ n. **1.** a more or less prolonged, sharp, shrill cry, as of pain, fear, etc. –v.i. **2.** to utter or emit a squeal or squealing sound.

squeamish /'skwimɪʃ/ adj. easily nauseated or sickened.

squeeze /skwiz/ v.t. **1.** to press forcibly together; compress. **2.** to apply pressure to as in order to extract something. **3.** to thrust forcibly; force by pressure; cram. **4.** (usu. fol. by out or from) to force out, extract, or procure by pressure. –v.i. **5.** to exert a compressing force. **6.** (fol. by through, in, out, etc.) to force a way through some narrow or crowded place. –n. **7.** the act of squeezing. **8.** a restriction, demand, or pressure, as imposed by a government. **9.** a small quantity or amount of anything obtained by squeezing. **10.** Also, **main squeeze**. Colloq. a girlfriend or boyfriend.

squelch /skwɛltʃ/ v.t. **1.** to strike or press with crushing force; crush down; squash. –v.i. **2.** to make a splashing sound.

squid /skwɪd/ n. (pl. **squid** or **squids**) any of various slender cephalopods with ten tentacles.

squint /skwɪnt/ v.i. **1.** to look with the eyes partly closed. **2.** to look or glance obliquely or sideways; look askance. –v.t. **3.** to close (the eyes) partly. –n. **4.** a disorder of the eye. **5.** a looking obliquely or askance. –adj. **6.** looking obliquely.

squire /'skwaɪə/ n. **1.** (formerly) a personal attendant, as of a person of rank. –v.t. **2.** to attend as or in the manner of a squire.

squirm /skwɜm/ v.i. to wriggle or writhe.

squirrel /'skwɪrəl/ n. **1.** any of various arboreal, bushy-tailed rodents. **2.** a person who hoards objects of little value.

squirt /skwɜt/ v.i. **1.** to eject liquid in a jet from a narrow orifice. **2.** to issue in a jet-like stream. –v.t. **3.** to cause (liquid) to issue in a jet from a narrow orifice. **4.** to wet or spatter with a liquid so ejected. *–n.* **5.** a jet, as of water.

stab /stæb/ *v.* (**stabbed, stabbing**) *–v.t.* **1.** to pierce or wound with, or as with, a pointed weapon. **2.** to thrust or plunge (a knife, etc.) into something. *–v.i.* **3.** to thrust with or as with a knife or other pointed weapon. *–n.* **4.** the act of stabbing. **5.** a sudden, usually painful sensation.

stable¹ /ˈsteɪbəl/ *n.* **1.** a building for the lodging and feeding of horses, cattle, etc. **2.** a collection of animals belonging in such a building. **3.** any centre of production or connected group of such centres, as a group of newspapers, car factories, etc. *–v.t.* **4.** to put or lodge in or as in a stable.

stable² /ˈsteɪbəl/ *adj.* not likely to fall or give way, as a structure, support, foundation, etc.; firm; steady. **–stability,** *n.* **–stabilise, stabilize,** *v.*

staccato /stəˈkɑːtoʊ/ *adj. Music* detached, disconnected, or abrupt.

stack /stæk/ *n.* **1.** any more or less orderly pile or heap. **2.** *Colloq.* a great quantity or number. **3.** that part of a library in which the main holdings of a library are kept. *–v.t.* **4.** to pile or arrange in a stack. **5.** to cover or load with something in stacks or piles. **6.** to bring a large number of one's own supporters to (a meeting) in order to outvote those of opposing views. **7.** to crash (a motor vehicle, bicycle, etc.). *–v.i.* **8.** (fol. by *up*) to accumulate; add up.

stackhat /ˈstækhæt/ *n. Colloq.* (*from trademark*) a safety helmet designed to be used when cycling, skateboarding, etc.

stadium /ˈsteɪdiəm/ *n.* (*pl.* **-dia** /-diə/ *or* **-diums**) a sporting facility, often, though not necessarily, enclosed, comprising an arena, tiers or seats for spectators, parking, etc.

staff /stɑːf/ *n.* (*pl.* **staffs** *or* **staves** /steɪvz/ *for defs 1, 2 and 4,* **staffs** *for def. 3*) **1.** a pole or rod to aid in walking. **2.** something which serves to support or sustain. **3.** a body of persons charged with carrying out the work of an establishment or executing some undertaking. **4.** *Music* → **stave** (def. 1). *–v.t.* **5.** to provide with a staff.

stag /stæg/ *n.* **1.** an adult male deer. *–adj.* **2.** *Colloq.* for or of men only.

stage /steɪdʒ/ *n.* **1.** a single step or degree in a process; a particular period in a process of development. **2.** a raised platform or floor. **3.** the theatre, the drama, or the dramatic profession. **4.** the scene of any action. *–v.t.* (**staged, staging**) **5.** to put, represent, or exhibit on or as on a stage. **6.** to arrange; set up, as for a particular event.

stagecoach /ˈsteɪdʒkoʊtʃ/ *n.* a coach that runs regularly over a fixed route.

stagflation /stægˈfleɪʃən/ *n.* a situation in the economy in which stagnant economic growth is accompanied by inflation.

stagger /ˈstægə/ *v.i.* **1.** to walk, move, or stand unsteadily; sway. *–v.t.* **2.** to cause to reel, as with shock. **3.** to arrange in some other order or manner than the regular, uniform, or usual one, especially at such intervals that there is a continuous overlapping. *–n.* **4.** the act of staggering.

stagnant /ˈstægnənt/ *adj.* not running or flowing, as water, air, etc.

stagnate /ˈstægneɪt, stægˈneɪt/ *v.i.* **1.** to become foul from standing, as a pool of water. **2.** to become inactive, sluggish, or dull. **3.** to make no progress; stop developing.

staid /steɪd/ *adj.* of settled or sedate character; not flighty or capricious.

stain /steɪn/ *n.* **1.** a semipermanent discolouration produced by foreign matter; a spot. **2.** a cause of reproach; blemish. **3.** a solution or suspension of colouring matter in water, spirit, or oil. *–v.t.* **4.** to discolour with spots or streaks of foreign matter. *–v.i.* **5.** to become stained; take a stain.

stair /steə/ *n.* a series or flight of steps; a stairway.

staircase /ˈsteəkeɪs/ *n.* a flight of stairs.

stairwell /ˈsteəwel/ *n.* the vertical shaft or opening containing a stairway.

stake¹ /steɪk/ *n.* **1.** a stick or post pointed at one end, for driving into the ground. **2.** a post, especially one to which a person is bound for execution, usually by burning. *–v.t.* **3.** (oft. fol. by *off* or *out*) to mark with stakes. **4.** to protect, separate, or close off by a barrier of stakes. **5.** to support with a stake or stakes, as a plant. **6.** (fol. by *out*) to surround (a building, etc.) for the purposes of a raid, a siege or keeping watch.

stake² /steɪk/ *n.* **1.** that which is wagered in a game, race, or contest. **2.** an interest held in something. *–v.t.* **3.** to put at risk upon the result of a game, the event of a contingency, etc.; wager. *–phr.* **4. at stake,** involved; in a state of being staked or at hazard.

stalactite /ˈstæləktaɪt/ *n.* a calcium deposit shaped like an icicle, hanging from the roof of a cave.

stalagmite /ˈstæləgmaɪt/ *n.* a calcium deposit shaped like an inverted stalactite, formed on the floor of a cave.

stale /steɪl/ *adj.* not fresh; flat, as beverages; dry or hardened, as bread.

stalemate /ˈsteɪlmeɪt/ *n.* any position in which no action can be taken; a deadlock.

stalk¹ /stɔːk/ *n.* the stem or main axis of a plant.

stalk² /stɔːk/ *v.i.* **1.** to pursue or approach game, etc., stealthily. **2.** to walk with slow, stiff, or haughty strides. *–v.t.* **3.** to pursue (game, a person, etc.) stealthily. **4.** to harass (someone) by persistently and obsessively following them, telephoning them, etc. **5.** to harass (someone) through the use of the internet, email, chat rooms, or other digital communications devices. **–stalker,** *n.*

stall /stɔːl/ *n.* **1.** a compartment in a stable or shed, for the accommodation of one animal. **2.** a booth, bench, table, or stand on which merchandise is displayed or exposed for sale. *–v.t.* **3.** to bring to a standstill; check the progress or motion of, especially of a vehicle or an engine by unintentionally overloading it or giving an inadequate fuel supply. **4.** to to put off, avoid or deceive: *stall the visitors until next week. –v.i.* **5.** to come to a standstill; be brought to a stop, especially unintentionally.

stallion /ˈstæljən/ *n.* a male horse not castrated.

stalwart /ˈstɔːlwət/ *adj.* **1.** strong and brave. **2.** firm, dependable, or unyielding. *–n.* **3.** a stalwart person.

stamen /ˈsteɪmən/ *n.* (*pl.* **stamens** *or* **stamina** /ˈstæmənə/) *Bot.* the pollen-bearing organ of a flower, consisting of the filament and the anther.

stamina /ˈstæmənə/ *n.* strength of physical constitution.

stammer /ˈstæmə/ *v.i.* **1.** to speak with spasmodic repetitions of syllables or sounds. *–n.* **2.** a stammering mode of utterance.

stamp /stæmp/ *v.t.* **1.** to strike or beat with a forcible downward thrust of the foot. **2.** to bring (the foot) down forcibly or smartly on the ground, floor, etc. **3.** to impress with a particular mark or device, as to indicate genuineness, approval, ownership, etc. **4.** to impress (a design, figure, words, etc.) on something; imprint deeply or permanently on anything. **5.** to affix an adhesive paper stamp to (a letter, etc.). *–v.i.* **6.** to bring the foot down forcibly or smartly, as in crushing something, expressing rage, etc. *–n.* **7.** the act or an instance of stamping. **8.** a die, engraved block, or the like, for impressing a design, characters, words, or marks. **9.** an official mark indicating genuineness, validity, etc., or payment of a duty or charge. **10.** a small adhesive piece of paper printed with a distinctive design, issued by a government for a fixed sum, for attaching to documents, goods subject to duty, letters, etc., to show that a charge has been paid. **11.** a similar piece of paper issued privately for various purposes.

stamp duty *n.* a tax imposed on certain legal documents, as cheques, receipts, conveyances, etc., on which a stamp is impressed or affixed.

stampede /stæmˈpiːd/ *n.* **1.** a sudden scattering or headlong flight, especially of a body of cattle or horses in fright. *–v.i.* **2.** to scatter or flee in a stampede. *–v.t.* **3.** to cause to stampede.

stance /stæns, stɑːns/ *n.* the position or bearing of the body while standing.

stand /stænd/ *v.* (**stood**, **standing**) *–v.i.* **1.** to take or keep an upright position on the feet (opposed to *sit*, *lie*, etc.). **2.** to have a specified height when in this position. **3.** to cease moving; halt; stop. **4.** to take a position or stand as indicated. **5.** to adopt a certain course or attitude. **6.** (of things) to be in an upright position (opposed to *lie*). **7.** (of an account, score, etc.) to show a specified position of the parties concerned. **8.** to resist change, decay, or destruction. **9.** to become or be a candidate, as for parliament. *–v.t.* **10.** to cause to stand; set upright; set. **11.** to endure or undergo without hurt or damage, or without giving way. **12.** to tolerate: *I will stand no nonsense*. *–n.* **13.** the act of standing. **14.** a coming to a position of rest. **15.** a determined opposition to or support for some cause, circumstance, or the like. **16.** a raised platform or other structure. **17.** a framework on or in which articles are placed for support, exhibition, etc. **18.** a standing growth, as of grass, wheat, etc. *–phr.* **19. stand by**, **a.** to wait in a state of readiness. **b.** to aid, uphold, or sustain. **20. stand down**, **a.** to withdraw, as from a contest. **b.** to dismiss (employees) who are not involved in direct strike action but who are not able to carry out

their normal duties as a result. **21. stand in**, to act as a substitute or representative. **22. stand out**, to be prominent or conspicuous.

standalone /ˈstændəloʊn/ *adj.* **1.** of or relating to a computerised device which does not need to be linked up to a larger computer system. *–n.* **2.** such a device. Also, **stand-alone**.

standard /ˈstændəd/ *n.* **1.** anything taken by general consent as a basis of comparison; an approved model. **2.** a certain commodity in which the basic monetary unit is stated, historically usually either gold or silver. **3.** a grade or level of excellence, achievement, or advancement. **4.** a level of quality which is regarded as normal, adequate, or acceptable. **5.** *Mil.* any of various military or naval flags. **6.** an upright support or supporting part. *–adj.* **7.** serving as a basis of weight, measure, value, comparison, or judgement. **8.** of recognised excellence or established authority. **9.** normal, adequate, acceptable, or average.

standard deviation *n.* *Statistics* the square root of the average of the squares of a set of deviations about an arithmetic mean.

standardise /ˈstændədaɪz/ *v.t.* **1.** to bring to or make of an established standard size, weight, quality, strength, or the like. **2.** to compare with or test by a standard. Also, **standardize**.

stand-by *n.* (*pl.* **-bys**) **1.** something or someone upon which one can rely; a chief support. **2.** something kept in a state of readiness for use, as for an emergency.

stand-in *n.* a substitute.

standing /ˈstændɪŋ/ *n.* **1.** position or status, as to rank, credit, reputation, etc. **2.** good position, financial viability, or credit. **3.** length of existence, continuance, residence, membership, experience, etc. *–adj.* **4.** performed in or from a stationary or an erect position. **5.** continuing in operation, force, use, etc.

standing committee *n.* **1.** a committee that may be appointed without a term, to oversee an aspect of the running of an institution. **2.** *Parliamentary Procedure* a committee, the members of which are appointed at the beginning of each parliamentary session, which has a continuing responsibility for a general sphere of government activity.

standing order *n.* any of the rules ensuring continuity of procedure during the meetings of an assembly, especially the rules governing the conduct of business in parliament.

stand-out *Colloq.* *–n.* **1.** a person in a team, competition, etc., who impresses as having abilities greater than all the others. *–adj.* **2.** outstanding; obvious: *a stand-out choice*. **3.** brilliant, excellent: *a stand-out season*. Also, **standout**.

standpoint /ˈstændpɔɪnt/ *n.* **1.** the point at which one stands to view something. **2.** the mental position from which one views and judges things.

standstill /ˈstændstɪl/ *n.* the condition of standing still; a halt, pause or stop.

stand-up paddleboard *n.* a surfboard designed so that the rider stands up on it and propels and steers it with a paddle. *Abbrev.:* SUP

stank /stæŋk/ *v.* a past tense of **stink**.

stanza /'stænzə/ n. a group of lines of verse, forming a regularly repeated metrical division of a poem.

staphylococcus /stæfələ'kɒkəs/ n. (pl. **-cocci** /-'kɒksaɪ/) any of certain species of bacteria.

staple¹ /'steɪpəl/ n. 1. a bent piece of wire used to bind papers, sections of a book, etc., together. –v.t. 2. to secure or fasten by a staple or staples.

staple² /'steɪpəl/ n. 1. a principal commodity grown or manufactured in a locality. 2. a principal item, thing, feature, element, or part. –adj. 3. principally used.

stapler /'steɪplə/ n. a stapling machine.

star /sta/ n. 1. any of the heavenly bodies appearing as apparently fixed luminous points in the sky at night. 2. (pl.) a horoscope. 3. a conventional figure considered as representing a star of the sky. 4. a prominent actor, singer, or the like. –adj. 5. brilliant, prominent, or distinguished; chief. –v. (**starred**, **starring**) –v.t. 6. to set with, or as with, stars; spangle. 7. to present or feature (an actor, etc.) as a star. 8. to mark with a star or asterisk, as for special notice. –v.i. 9. (of an actor, etc.) to appear as a star.

starboard /'stabəd/ n. Naut. the side of a ship to the right of a person looking towards the bow (opposed to port).

starch /statʃ/ n. 1. a white, tasteless solid, chemically a carbohydrate, occurring in the form of minute grains in the seeds, tubers, and other parts of plants. 2. a commercial preparation of this substance. 3. stiffness or formality, as of manner. –v.t. 4. to stiffen or treat with starch.

star-crossed /'sta-krɒst/ adj. having much bad luck, as if brought about by the influence of the stars.

stare /stɛə/ v.i. (**stared**, **staring**) 1. to gaze fixedly, especially with the eyes wide open. 2. to stand out boldly or obtrusively to view. –n. 3. a staring gaze; a fixed look with the eyes wide open.

starfish /'stafɪʃ/ n. (pl. **-fish** or **-fishes**) a marine animal having the body radially arranged, usually in the form of a star.

stark /stak/ adj. 1. sheer, utter, downright, or arrant. 2. harsh, grim, or desolate to the view, as places, etc. –adv. 3. utterly, absolutely, or quite.

starling /'stalɪŋ/ n. a small bird, introduced and now widespread in eastern Australia.

start /stat/ v.i. 1. to begin to move, go, or act. 2. to begin any procedure or course of action, such as a journey. 3. to begin to exist or happen for the first time. 4. (of a process or performance) to begin. 5. to move with a sudden, involuntary jerk or twitch, as from a shock of surprise, alarm, or pain. –v.t. 6. to set moving, going, or acting. 7. to set in operation; establish. 8. to enter upon or begin. –n. 9. the beginning or outset of anything. 10. the first part of anything. 11. a sudden, involuntary jerking movement of the body. 12. a lead or advance of specified amount, as over competitors or pursuers. 13. a spurt of activity.

starting gun n. a type of gun which does not shoot a projectile, but makes a loud noise when fired; used to start a race. Also, **starter gun**.

starting price n. the betting odds on a horse, greyhound, etc., at the time when a race begins.

startle /'statl/ v.t. 1. to cause to start involuntarily, as under a sudden shock. –v.i. 2. to start involuntarily, as from a surprise or alarm.

starve /stav/ v.i. 1. to die or perish from hunger. 2. (fol. by for) to pine or suffer for lack of something specified. –v.t. 3. to cause to starve. –**starvation**, n.

stash /stæʃ/ v.t. 1. to put away, as for safekeeping or in a prepared place. –n. 2. a hoard.

-stat a word element meaning 'standing', 'stationary'.

state /steɪt/ n. 1. the condition of a person or thing, as with respect to circumstances or attributes. 2. condition with respect to constitution, structure, form, phase, or the like. 3. a particular condition of mind or feeling. 4. a particularly tense, nervous, or excited condition. 5. a body of people occupying a definite territory and organised under one government, especially a sovereign government. –adj. 6. of or relating to the supreme civil government or authority. 7. characterised by, attended with, or involving ceremony. –v.t. 8. to declare definitely or specifically. 9. to set forth formally in speech or writing.

stately /'steɪtli/ adj. (**-lier**, **-liest**) dignified or majestic; imposing in magnificence, elegance, etc.

statement /'steɪtmənt/ n. 1. something stated. 2. Commerce an abstract of an account, as one rendered to show the balance due.

statesman /'steɪtsmən/ n. (pl. **-men**) someone who exhibits ability of the highest kind in directing the affairs of a government or in dealing with important public issues. –**statesmanlike**, adj. –**stateswoman**, n.

static /'stætɪk/ adj. 1. relating to or characterised by a fixed or stationary condition. 2. of or relating to static electricity. 3. Econ. relating to fixed relations, or different combinations of fixed quantities. –n. Also, **atmospherics**. 4. Radio extraneous noises, crackling, etc., caused by electrical currents picked up by the receiver.

static electricity n. 1. electricity at rest, as that produced by friction. 2. electricity in the atmosphere which interferes with the sending and receiving of radio messages, etc.

station /'steɪʃən/ n. 1. the place in which anything stands. 2. the place at which something stops. 3. a place equipped for some particular kind of work, service, or the like. 4. a large rural establishment for raising sheep or cattle. 5. standing, as of persons or things, in a scale of estimation, rank, or dignity. 6. the wavelength on which a radio or television program is broadcast; a frequency or channel. –adj. 7. of or relating to a sheep or cattle station. –v.t. 8. to assign a station to; place or post in a station or position.

stationary /'steɪʃənri, 'steɪʃənəri/, Orig. US /'steɪʃəneri/ adj. standing still; not moving.

stationery /ˈsteɪʃənri, ˈsteɪʃənəri/, *Orig. US* /ˈsteɪʃəneri/ *n.* writing materials, as pens, pencils, paper, etc. **–stationer,** *n.*

station hand *n.* an employee involved in routine work on a rural property or station.

station wagon *n.* a car with an extended interior, allowing extra space behind the rear seat, and a door or tailgate at the back.

statistic /stəˈtɪstɪk/ *n.* a numerical fact.

statistics /stəˈtɪstɪks/ *n.* **1.** (*construed as sing.*) the science which deals with the collection, classification, and use of numerical facts or data, bearing on a subject or matter. **2.** (*construed as pl.*) the numerical facts or data themselves. **–statistician,** *n.* **–statistical,** *adj.*

stative verb /ˈsteɪtɪv/ *n. Gram.* a verb which indicates a state or condition which is not changing, as in *I own a house*, or *I hate vegetables.* Compare **dynamic verb.** Also, **non-action verb.**

stats /stæts/ *pl. n. Colloq.* statistics.

statue /ˈstætʃu/ *n.* a solid image of a person or animal, usually made out of stone, wood or bronze.

stature /ˈstætʃə/ *n.* **1.** the height of an animal body, especially a human. **2.** degree of development or achievement attained.

status /ˈsteɪtəs, ˈstætəs/ *n.* **1.** condition, position, or standing socially, professionally, or otherwise. **2.** the relative standing, position, or condition of anything.

status quo *n.* the existing or previously existing state or condition.

statute /ˈstætʃut/ *n.* **1.** a law made by a legislature. **2.** a permanent rule established by an institution, corporation, etc., for the conduct of its internal affairs. **–statutory,** *adj.*

statutory declaration /ˈstætʃətri/ *n.* a written statement declared before and witnessed by an authorised official.

staunch¹ /stɔntʃ/ *v.t.* to stop the flow of (a liquid, especially blood).

staunch² /stɔntʃ/ *adj.* characterised by firmness or steadfastness.

stave /steɪv/ *n.* Also, **staff. 1.** *Music* a set of horizontal lines on which music is written. *–v.t.* (**staved** *or* **stove, staving**) **2.** (oft. fol. by *in*) to break a hole in; crush inwards. *–phr.* **3. stave off,** to put, ward, or keep off, as by force or evasion.

stay¹ /steɪ/ *v.i.* **1.** to remain in a place, situation, company, etc. **2.** to pause or wait, as for a moment. **3.** to hold back, detain, or restrain. **4.** to remain through or during (a period of time, etc.). **5.** to remain to the end of. *–n.* **6.** a sojourn or temporary residence.

stay² /steɪ/ *n.* **1.** a prop; a brace. **2.** (*pl.*) a corset.

stay³ /steɪ/ *n. Chiefly Naut.* rope used to support a mast.

STD¹ /es ti ˈdi/ *n.* any disease such as syphilis, gonorrhoea, AIDS, herpes, etc., which is transmitted through sexual contact; sexually transmitted disease.

STD² /es ti ˈdi/ *n.* **1.** subscriber trunk dialling; a system for making direct long-distance telephone calls without going through an operator. *–adj.* **2.** of or relating to this system: *an STD call.*

stead /stɛd/ *n.* the place of a person or thing as occupied by a successor or substitute.

steadfast /ˈstɛdfast, -fəst/ *adj.* **1.** firm in purpose, resolution, faith, attachment, etc., as a person. **2.** unwavering, as resolution, faith, adherence, etc.

steady /ˈstɛdi/ *adj.* (**-dier, -diest**) **1.** firmly placed or fixed; stable. **2.** uniform; continuous. **3.** settled, staid, or sober. *–n.* (*pl.* **-dies**) **4.** *Colloq.* a regular boyfriend or girlfriend. *–v.* (**-died, -dying**) *–v.t.* **5.** to make steady, as in position, movement, action, character, etc. *–v.i.* **6.** to become steady. *–adv.* **7.** in a firm or steady manner.

steak /steɪk/ *n.* a slice of meat or fish, usually cut thick and across the grain of the muscle.

steal /stil/ *v.* (**stole, stolen, stealing**) *–v.t.* **1.** to take or take away dishonestly or wrongfully, especially secretly. **2.** (fol. by *away, from, in, into,* etc.) to move, bring, convey, or put secretly or quietly. *–v.i.* **3.** to commit or practise theft. **4.** to move, go, or come secretly, quietly, or unobserved. *–n.* **5.** *Colloq.* something acquired at a cost well below its true value.

stealth /stɛlθ/ *n.* secret, clandestine, or surreptitious procedure. **–stealthy,** *adj.*

steam /stim/ *n.* **1.** water in the form of gas or vapour. **2.** water changed to this form by boiling, and extensively used for the generation of mechanical power, for heating purposes, etc. *–v.i.* **3.** to emit or give off steam or vapour. **4.** to become covered with condensed steam, as a surface. *–v.t.* **5.** to expose to or treat with steam, as in order to heat, cook, soften, renovate, or the like. *–adj.* **6.** heated by or heating with steam. **7.** operated by steam.

steamroller /ˈstimroʊlə/ *n.* a heavy locomotive, originally steam-powered, having a roller or rollers, for crushing or levelling materials in road-making.

steed /stid/ *n.* a horse, especially one for riding.

steel /stil/ *n.* **1.** iron in a modified form, artificially produced, and possessing a hardness, elasticity, strength, etc., which vary with the composition and the heat treatment. *–adj.* **2.** relating to or made of steel. **3.** like steel in colour, hardness, or strength. *–v.t.* **4.** to cause to resemble steel in some way.

steel wool *n.* fine threads or shavings of steel, tangled into a small pad, and used for scouring, polishing, etc.

steep¹ /stip/ *adj.* **1.** having a relatively high gradient, as a hill, an ascent, stairs, etc. **2.** *Colloq.* unduly high, or exorbitant, as a price or amount.

steep² /stip/ *v.t.* **1.** to soak in water or other liquid. *–v.i.* **2.** to lie soaking in a liquid.

steeple /ˈstipəl/ *n.* a lofty tower, especially one with a spire, attached to a church, temple, or the like, and often containing bells.

steeplechase /ˈstipəltʃeɪs/ *n.* a horserace over a course furnished with artificial ditches, hedges, and other obstacles.

steer¹ /stɪə/ *v.t.* **1.** to guide the course of (anything in motion) by a rudder, helm, wheel, etc. *–v.i.* **2.** to direct the course of a vessel, vehicle, aeroplane, or the like by the use of a rudder or other means. **3.** (of a vessel, etc.) to admit of being steered.

steer² /stɪə/ *n.* a castrated male bovine, especially one raised for beef; ox; bullock.

steerage /ˈstɪərɪdʒ/ *n.* (in a passenger ship) the part allotted to the passengers who travel at the cheapest rate.

steering committee *n.* a committee, especially one of a legislative body, entrusted with the preparation of the agenda of a conference, session, etc.

stego- a word element meaning 'cover'.

stegosaurus /stɛgəˈsɔrəs/ *n.* a huge plant-eating dinosaur, with a heavy and bony armour. Also, **stegosaur**.

stein /staɪn/ *n.* an earthenware mug, especially for beer.

stellar /ˈstɛlə/ *adj.* **1.** of or relating to the stars; consisting of stars. **2.** starlike.

stem¹ /stɛm/ *n.* **1.** the ascending part of a plant which ordinarily grows in an opposite direction to the root. **2.** something resembling or suggesting the stem of a plant, flower, etc. *–v.* (**stemmed, stemming**) *–v.t.* **3.** to remove the stem from (a fruit, etc.). *–v.i.* **4.** (usu. fol. by *from*) to originate.

stem² /stɛm/ *v.t.* (**stemmed, stemming**) to stop, hold back or plug.

stem cell *n.* an unspecialised form of cell, capable of dividing and giving rise to various specialised cells.

stench /stɛntʃ/ *n.* an offensive smell; stink.

stencil /ˈstɛnsəl/ *n.* **1.** a thin sheet of paper, cardboard or metal cut through so as to reproduce a design, letters, etc., when colour is rubbed through it. **2.** the letters, designs, etc., produced. *–v.t.* (**-cilled, -cilling**) **3.** to produce (letters, etc.) by means of a stencil.

steno- a word element meaning 'little', 'narrow'.

stenographer /stəˈnɒgrəfə/ *n.* someone who is skilled in taking dictation in shorthand. **–stenography,** *n.*

stenotype /ˈstɛnətaɪp/ *n.* (*from trademark*) a keyboard instrument resembling a typewriter, used in a system of phonetic shorthand.

step /stɛp/ *n.* **1.** a movement made by lifting the foot and setting it down again in a new position, as in walking, running, marching, or dancing. **2.** the space passed over or measured by one movement of the foot in stepping. **3.** pace uniform with that of another or others, or in time with music. **4.** a move or proceeding, as towards some end or in the general course of action. **5.** a degree on a scale. **6.** a support for the foot in ascending or descending. *–v.i.* (**stepped, stepping**) **7.** to move by a step or steps. **8.** to tread (*on* or *upon*), by intention or accident. **9.** to move or set (the foot) in taking a step. **10.** (sometimes fol. by *off* or *out*) to measure (a distance, ground, etc.) by steps. **11.** to make or arrange in the manner of a series of steps. *–phr.* **12. step down, a.** to decrease. **b.** to resign; relinquish a position, etc.

step- a prefix indicating connection between members of a family by the remarriage of a parent, and not by blood.

stepladder /ˈstɛplædə/ *n.* a ladder having flat steps or treads in place of rungs and a hinged support to keep it upright.

steppe /stɛp/ *n.* an extensive grassland plain, especially one without trees.

stepping stone *n.* **1.** a stone in shallow water, a marshy place, or the like, used for stepping on in crossing. **2.** any means of advancing or rising.

-ster a suffix of personal nouns, often derogatory, referring especially to occupation or habit, as in *songster, gamester, trickster*, also having less apparent connotations, as in *youngster, roadster*.

stereo /ˈstɛriou, ˈstɪəriou/ *n.* (*pl.* **stereos**) **1.** stereophonic sound reproduction. **2.** any system, equipment, etc., for reproducing stereophonic sound. *–adj.* **3.** relating to stereophonic sound, stereoscopic photography, etc.

stereo- a word element referring to hardness, solidity, three-dimensionality. Also, (*before some vowels*), **stere-**.

stereophonic /stɛriəˈfɒnɪk, stɪə-/ *adj.* **1.** of or relating to a three-dimensional auditory perspective. **2.** of or relating to the multi-channel reproduction or broadcasting of sound which simulates three-dimensional auditory perspective.

stereotype /ˈstɛriətaɪp, ˈstɪə-/ *n.* **1.** a process for making metal plates for use in printing from moulds. **2.** a plate made by this process. **3.** a standardised idea or concept. *–v.t.* **4.** to make a stereotype of. **5.** to characterise according to conventional ideas or prejudices.

sterile /ˈstɛraɪl/ *adj.* **1.** free from living germs or micro-organisms. **2.** incapable of producing, or not producing, offspring. **–sterility,** *n.* **–sterilise, sterilize,** *v.*

sterling /ˈstɜːlɪŋ/ *adj.* **1.** consisting of or relating to British money. **2.** (of silver) being of standard quality, 92½ per cent pure silver.

stern¹ /stɜːn/ *adj.* firm, strict, or uncompromising.

stern² /stɜːn/ *n.* the hinder part of anything.

sternum /ˈstɜːnəm/ *n.* (*pl.* **-nums** or **-na** /-nə/) *Anat.* the breastbone.

steroid /ˈstɛrɔɪd/ *n.* **1.** any of a large group of chemical substances found in the body, including many hormones. **2.** a hormone used by athletes, etc., to develop their muscles.

stet /stɛt/ *v.i.* let it stand (a direction on a printer's proof, a manuscript, or the like to retain cancelled matter).

stetho- a word element meaning 'chest'. Also, (*before vowels*), **steth-**.

stethoscope /ˈstɛθəskoup/ *n.* an instrument used to convey sounds in the chest or other parts of the body to the ear of the examiner.

stevedore /ˈstivədɔ/ *n.* a firm or individual engaged in the loading or unloading of a vessel.

stew /stju/ *v.t.* **1.** to cook (food) by simmering or slow boiling. *–v.i.* **2.** to undergo cooking by simmering or slow boiling. *–n.* **3.** a preparation of meat, fish or other food cooked by stewing.

steward /ˈstjuəd/ *n.* **1.** someone who manages another's property or financial affairs. **2.** any attendant on a ship or aircraft who waits on passengers. *–v.i.* **3.** to act or serve as steward.

stick¹ /stɪk/ *n.* **1.** a relatively long and slender piece of wood. **2.** an elongated, stick-like piece of some material. *–phr.* **3. the sticks**, remote and little developed areas.

stick² /stɪk/ *v.* (**stuck, sticking**) *–v.t.* **1.** to pierce or puncture with a pointed instrument, as a dagger, spear, or pin; stab. **2.** to thrust (something pointed) in, into, through etc. **3.** to fasten in position by, or as by, something thrust through. **4.** to place in a specified position. **5.** to fasten or attach by causing to adhere. **6.** to endure; tolerate. *–v.i.* **7.** to have the point piercing, or embedded in something. **8.** to remain attached by adhesion. **9.** to remain firm in resolution, opinion, statement, attachment, etc. **10.** (fol. by *at* or *to*) to keep steadily at a task, undertaking, or the like. **11.** to be at a standstill, as from difficulties. *–phr.* **12. stick out, a.** to go beyond a surface or area. **b.** to be obvious. **13. stick up**, *Colloq.* to rob, especially at gunpoint. **14. stick up for**, to speak or act in favour of; defend; support.

sticker /'stɪkə/ *n.* an adhesive label, usually with an advertisement, publicity slogan, or other message printed on it.

stick insect *n.* any of certain insects with long, slender, twig-like bodies.

stickler /'stɪklə/ *n.* (fol. by *for*) a person who insists on something unyieldingly.

stickybeak /'stɪkibik/ *n.* someone who pries.

sticky tape *n.* an adhesive tape, made of cellulose and usually transparent.

stiff /stɪf/ *adj.* **1.** rigid or firm in substance. **2.** not moving or working easily. **3.** rigidly formal. **4.** lacking ease and grace; awkward. **5.** severe, as a penalty. **6.** relatively firm in consistency, as semisolid matter. *–n.* **7.** *Colloq.* a corpse. *–adv.* **8.** in a rigid state.

stifle /'staɪfəl/ *v.* (**stifled, stifling**) *v.t.* **1.** to kill by impeding respiration; smother. **2.** to suppress, crush, or stop. *–v.i.* **3.** to become stifled or suffocated. **4.** to suffer from difficulty in breathing, as in a close atmosphere.

stigma /'stɪgmə/ *n.* (pl. **stigmata** /'stɪgmətə, stɪg'matə/ or **stigmas**) a mark of disgrace; a stain, as on one's reputation. **–stigmatic**, *adj.*

stile /staɪl/ *n.* a series of steps or the like for ascending and descending in getting over a fence, etc., which remains closed to cattle.

stiletto /stə'lɛtoʊ/ *n.* **1.** a dagger having a narrow blade, thick in proportion to its width. **2.** a high heel on a woman's shoe, or the shoe itself.

still[1] /stɪl/ *adj.* **1.** remaining in place or at rest. **2.** free from sound or noise. **3.** tranquil; calm. **4.** not effervescent or sparkling, as wine. *–n.* **5.** a single photographic picture, especially a print of one of the frames of a film. *–adv.* **6.** up to this or that time. **7.** even or yet (with comparatives or the like). **8.** even then; yet; nevertheless. *–conj.* **9.** and yet; but yet; nevertheless. *–v.t.* **10.** to calm, appease, or allay.

still[2] /stɪl/ *n.* a distilling apparatus.

stillbirth /'stɪlbɜθ/ *n.* the birth of a dead child or organism.

still life *n.* (pl. **still lifes**) a picture representing inanimate objects, such as fruit, flowers, etc.

stilt /stɪlt/ *n.* **1.** one of two poles, each with a support for the foot at some distance above the ground. **2.** one of several high posts underneath any structure built above land or over water.

stilted /'stɪltəd/ *adj.* stiffly dignified or formal, as speech, literary style, etc.; pompous.

stimulant /'stɪmjələnt/ *n.* **1.** *Physiol., Med.* something that temporarily quickens some vital process or the functional activity of some organ or part. **2.** any beverage or food that stimulates.

stimulate /'stɪmjəleɪt/ *v.t.* **1.** to rouse to action or effort. **2.** to invigorate by an alcoholic or other stimulant. *–v.i.* **3.** to act as a stimulus or stimulant.

stimulus /'stɪmjələs/ *n.* (pl. **-li** /-li, -laɪ/ or **-luses**) something that incites to action or exertion, or quickens action, feeling, thought, etc.; an incentive.

sting /stɪŋ/ *v.* (**stung, stinging**) *–v.t.* **1.** to affect painfully or irritatingly. *–v.i.* **2.** to use or have a sting, as bees. **3.** to cause a sharp, smarting pain, as some plants, an acrid liquid or gas, etc. **4.** to feel a smarting pain, as from the sting of an insect or from a blow. *–n.* **5.** any sharp or smarting wound, hurt, or pain (physical or mental). **6.** anything, or an element in anything, that wounds, pains, or irritates.

stingray /'stɪŋreɪ/ *n.* any of the rays having a long flexible tail armed near the base with a strong, serrated bony spine with which they can inflict severe and very painful wounds.

stingy /'stɪndʒi/ *adj.* (**-gier, -giest**) reluctant to give or spend; niggardly.

stink /stɪŋk/ *v.i.* (**stank** or **stunk, stunk, stinking**) **1.** to emit a strong offensive smell. *–n.* **2.** a strong offensive smell; stench.

stint /stɪnt/ *v.t.* **1.** to limit, often unduly. *–v.i.* **2.** to be sparing or frugal. *–n.* **3.** a period of time, usually short, allotted to a particular activity.

stipend /'staɪpɛnd/ *n.* fixed or regular pay; periodic payment; salary.

stipendiary magistrate /staɪ'pɛndəri/ *n.* → **magistrate**.

stipple /'stɪpəl/ *v.t.* to paint, engrave, or draw by means of dots or small touches.

stipulate /'stɪpjəleɪt/ *v.i.* **1.** to make an express demand or arrangement (*for*), as a condition of agreement. *–v.t.* **2.** to require as an essential condition in making an agreement.

stir /stɜ/ *v.* (**stirred, stirring**) *–v.t.* **1.** to move or agitate (a liquid, or any matter in separate particles or pieces). **2.** to move, especially in some slight way. **3.** (oft. fol. by *up*) to rouse from inactivity. **4.** to affect strongly; excite. *–v.i.* **5.** to move, especially slightly or lightly. **6.** to touch on controversial topics in a deliberate attempt to incite a heated discussion. *–n.* **7.** the act of stirring or moving, or the sound made. **8.** a state or occasion of general excitement; a commotion.

stir-fry /'stɜ-fraɪ/ *v.t.* (**-fried, -frying**) **1.** to fry lightly in a little hot fat or oil, while stirring continually. *–n.* **2.** a dish prepared by stir-frying.

stirrup /'stɪrəp/ *n.* a loop, ring, or other contrivance of metal, wood, leather, etc., suspended from the saddle of a horse to support the rider's foot.

stitch /stɪtʃ/ *n.* **1.** a loop or portion of thread disposed in place by one movement in sewing, knitting, etc., or the mode of disposing it. **2.** a sudden, sharp pain in the side, brought on by physical exertion. *–v.t.* **3.** to work upon, join, or fasten with stitches.

stoat /stoʊt/ *n.* the ermine in its brown summer phase.

stock /stɒk/ *n.* **1.** an aggregate of goods kept on hand by a merchant, business firm, manufacturer, etc., for the supply of customers. **2.** a quantity of something accumulated, as for future use. **3.** a breed, variety, or other related group of animals or plants. **4.** the handle of a whip, etc. **5.** a long stick used in skiing. **6.** the raw material from which anything is made. **7.** *Finance* **a.** the capital of a company converted from fully paid shares. **b.** the shares of a particular company. –*adj.* **8.** having as one's job the care of a concern's goods: *a stock clerk.* **9.** of the common or ordinary type; in common use. **10.** designating or relating to livestock raising; stock farming. **11.** *Theatre* relating to repertory plays or pieces. **12.** to furnish with stock, as a farm with horses, cattle, etc. **13.** to fasten to or provide with a stock, as a rifle, plough, bell, anchor, etc. –*phr.* **14.** take stock, **a.** to make an inventory of stock on hand. **b.** to make an appraisal of resources, prospects, etc.

stockade /stɒˈkeɪd/ *n.* a defensive barrier consisting of strong posts or timbers fixed upright in the ground.

stockbroker /ˈstɒkbroʊkə/ *n.* a broker who buys and sells stocks and shares for customers for a commission.

stock exchange *n.* (*oft. upper case*) **1.** a company or other association whose members are stockbrokers and whose function is to maintain a market on which its members may deal in securities as agents for clients or as principals on their own account. **2.** a building or place where stocks and shares are bought and sold.

Stockholm syndrome /ˈstɒkhoʊm/ *n.* the tendency of hostages to form a sympathetic bond with their captors.

stocking /ˈstɒkɪŋ/ *n.* a close-fitting covering for the foot and leg.

stock-in-trade /stɒk-ɪn-ˈtreɪd/ *n.* goods, assets, etc., necessary for carrying on a business.

stockman /ˈstɒkmən/ *n.* (*pl.* **-men**) a man employed to tend livestock, especially cattle. –**stockwoman**, *n.*

stock market *n.* a market where stocks and shares are bought and sold; a stock exchange. Also, **stockmarket**.

stockpile /ˈstɒkpaɪl/ *n.* **1.** a large supply of essential materials, held in reserve for use during a period of shortage, etc. –*v.t.* **2.** to accumulate for future use.

stock-still /stɒk-ˈstɪl/ *adj.* motionless.

stocktake /ˈstɒkteɪk/ *n.* **1.** an instance of stocktaking. –*v.i.* (**-taken**, **-taking**) **2.** to conduct a stocktaking. –**stocktaker**, *n.*

stocktaking /ˈstɒkteɪkɪŋ/ *n.* **1.** the examination and listing of goods, assets, etc., in a shop, business, etc. **2.** a reappraisal or reassessment of one's position, progress, prospects, etc.

stockworker /ˈstɒkwɜːkə/ *n.* a person employed to tend livestock, especially cattle.

stocky /ˈstɒki/ *adj.* (**-kier**, **-kiest**) of solid and sturdy form or build; thickset, often short.

stoic /ˈstoʊɪk/ *adj.* noted for calm or silent strength and courage; impassive. Also, **stoical**.

stoke /stoʊk/ *v.t.* **1.** to poke, stir up, and feed a fire). **2.** to tend a fire or furnace. –**stoker**, *n.*

stole[1] /stoʊl/ *v.* past tense of **steal**.

stole[2] /stoʊl/ *n.* a type of long scarf.

stolen /ˈstoʊlən/ *v.* past participle of **steal**.

stolen children *pl. n.* (in Australia) members of the stolen generations of Aboriginal and Torres Strait Islander children.

stolen generations *pl. n.* (in Australia) Aboriginal children who were removed from their families and communities, by government or non-government agencies, in order to enforce integration into white society; the practice continued in some areas until the 1960s. Also, **stolen generation**.

stolid /ˈstɒlɪd/ *adj.* not easily moved or stirred mentally; impassive; unemotional.

stomach /ˈstʌmək/ *n.* **1.** (in humans and other vertebrates) a sac-like enlargement of the alimentary canal, forming an organ of storage, dilution, and digestion. **2.** the part of the body containing the stomach; the belly or abdomen. –*v.t.* **3.** to take into or retain in the stomach. **4.** to endure or tolerate.

stomato- a word element referring to the mouth. Also, (*before vowels*), **stomat-**.

-stome a word element referring to the mouth.

stomp /stɒmp/ *v.i. Colloq.* to stamp.

stone /stoʊn/ *n.* **1.** the hard substance of which rocks consist. **2.** a piece of rock of small or moderate size. **3.** (*pl.* **stone**) a unit of weight in the imperial system, equal to a little more than six kilograms. **4.** something resembling a small stone or pebble. –*adj.* **5.** made of or relating to stone. –*v.t.* **6.** to throw stones at; drive by pelting with stones. **7.** to free from stones, as fruit. –*adv.* **8.** extremely: *stone deaf; stone cold sober.* –**stony**, *adj.*

stoned /stoʊnd/ *adj. Colloq.* completely drunk or under the influence of drugs.

stonefish /ˈstoʊnfɪʃ/ *n.* (*pl.* **-fish** or **-fishes**) a highly venomous fish, camouflaged to resemble weathered coral or rock, having erectile dorsal spines capable of inflicting an extremely painful and sometimes fatal sting.

stood /stʊd/ *v.* past tense and past participle of **stand**.

stooge /stuːdʒ/ *n.* someone who acts on behalf of another, especially in an obsequious, corrupt, or secretive fashion.

stool /stuːl/ *n.* **1.** a seat without arms or a back. **2.** the mass of matter evacuated at each movement of the bowels; faeces.

stoop[1] /stuːp/ *v.i.* **1.** to bend the head and shoulders, or the body generally, forwards and downwards from an erect position. **2.** to condescend; deign. –*v.t.* **3.** to bend (oneself, one's head, etc.) forwards and downwards. –*n.* **4.** the act of stooping; a stooping movement. **5.** a stooping position or carriage of body.

stoop[2] /stuːp/ *n.* a step or set of steps at the entrance to a building.

stop /stɒp/ *v.* (**stopped, stopping**) –*v.t.* **1.** to cease from, leave off, or discontinue. **2.** to cause to cease; put an end to. **3.** to cut off, intercept, or withhold. **4.** to prevent from proceeding, acting, operating, continuing, etc. **5.** (*oft. fol. by up*) to block, obstruct, or close (a passageway, channel, opening, duct, etc.). **6.** *Banking* to notify a banker not to honour (a cheque) on presentation. –*v.i.* **7.** to cease moving, proceeding, speaking, acting, operating, etc.; to pause; desist. **8.** to cease; come to an end. **9.** to stay: *We'll stop at Dungog for the night.* —*n.* **10.** the act of stopping. **11.** a stay or sojourn made at a place, as in the course of a journey. **12.** a place where buses or other vehicles halt. **13.** any piece or device that serves to check or control movement or action in a mechanism. **14.** *Banking* an order to stop a cheque. **15.** → **full stop.** —*phr.* **16. stop by,** to call somewhere briefly on the way to another destination.

stopcock /'stɒpkɒk/ *n.* a valve, with a tapered plug operated by a handle, used to control the flow of a liquid or gas from a receptacle or through a pipe.

stopover /'stɒpoʊvə/ *n.* any brief stop in the course of a journey.

stop payment *n.* an order by the drawer of a cheque to a financial institution not to pay a specified cheque.

stopper /'stɒpə/ *n.* a plug or piece for closing a bottle, tube, or the like.

stop press *n.* news inserted in a newspaper after printing has begun.

stopwatch /'stɒpwɒtʃ/ *n.* a watch in which the timing mechanism can be stopped or started at any instant.

stop-work meeting *n.* a meeting of employees held during working time to consult with unions or management over conditions of work, etc.

storage /'stɔrɪdʒ/ *n.* **1.** the state or fact of being stored. **2.** *Computers* the capacity of a device to hold information. **3.** a place where something is stored.

store /stɔ/ *n.* **1.** a large shop with many departments or branches. **2.** a supply or stock (of something), especially one for future use. **3.** a shop. **4.** measure of esteem or regard. **5.** a computer memory. —*v.t.* **6.** to lay up or put away, as a supply for future use (often with *up* or *away*).

storehouse /'stɔhaʊs/ *n.* a house or building in which things are stored.

storey /'stɔri/ *n.* (*pl.* **-reys** or **-ries**) a complete horizontal section of a building, having one continuous or approximately continuous floor.

stork /stɔk/ *n.* any of various long-legged, long-necked, long-billed wading birds.

storm /stɔm/ *n.* **1.** a disturbance of the normal condition of the atmosphere, manifesting itself by winds of unusual force or direction, often accompanied by rain, snow, hail, thunder and lightning, or flying sand or dust. **2.** a violent assault on a fortified place, strong position, or the like. **3.** a violent outburst or outbreak. —*v.i.* **4.** to rage or complain with violence or fury. **5.** to rush to an assault or attack. —*v.t.* **6.** to subject to or as to a storm.

stormwater /'stɔmwɔtə/ *n.* a sudden, excessive run-off of water following a storm.

story /'stɔri/ *n.* (*pl.* **-ries**) **1.** narrative designed to interest or amuse the hearer or reader; a tale. **2.** the plot, or succession of incidents of a novel, poem, drama, etc. **3.** *Media* a news item. **4.** *Colloq.* a lie; a fib.

stout /staʊt/ *adj.* **1.** bulky or thickset. **2.** bold, hardy, or dauntless. —*n.* **3.** any of various beers brewed by the top-fermentation method but darker and heavier than ales.

stove¹ /stoʊv/ *n.* an apparatus for furnishing heat, as for comfort, cooking, or mechanical purposes.

stove² /stoʊv/ *v.* a past tense and past participle of **stave.**

stow /stoʊ/ *v.t.* to put in a place or receptacle as for storage or reserve; pack.

stowaway /'stoʊəweɪ/ *n.* someone who hides aboard a ship or other conveyance, as to get a free trip.

straddle /'strædl/ *v.i.* **1.** to walk, stand, or sit with the legs wide apart. —*v.t.* **2.** to walk, stand, or sit with one leg on each side of.

strafe /straf, streɪf/ *v.t.* to bombard heavily.

straggle /'strægəl/ *v.i.* **1.** to stray from the road, course, or line of march. **2.** to go, come, or spread in a scattered, irregular fashion.

straight /streɪt/ *adj.* **1.** without a bend, crook, or curve. **2.** (of a line) lying evenly between its points. **3.** evenly formed or set. **4.** honest, honourable, or upright. **5.** *Colloq.* **a.** conforming to orthodox forms of behaviour, as avoidance of illegal drugs, etc. **b.** heterosexual. **6.** right or correct. **7.** undiluted, as an alcoholic beverage; neat. —*adv.* **8.** in a straight line. **9.** honestly, honourably, or virtuously. **10.** in the proper order or condition, as a room. —*n.* **11.** a straight form or position. **12.** *Colloq.* a conservative person.

straightaway /streɪtə'weɪ/ *adv.* immediately. Also, **straight away.**

straightforward /streɪt'fɔwəd/ *adj.* **1.** free from crookedness or deceit; honest. **2.** without difficulty; uncomplicated.

strain¹ /streɪn/ *v.t.* **1.** to exert to the utmost. **2.** to impair, injure, or weaken by stretching or overexertion, as a muscle. **3.** to make excessive demands upon. **4.** to pass (liquid matter) through a filter, sieve, or the like, in order to hold back the denser or solid constituents. —*v.i.* **5.** to stretch one's muscles, nerves, etc., to the utmost. —*n.* **6.** any force or pressure tending to alter shape, cause fracture, etc. **7.** an injury to a muscle, tendon, etc., due to excessive tension or use; a sprain. **8.** severe, trying, or wearing pressure or effect. **9.** (*sing.* or *pl.*, *oft.* collective *pl.*) a passage of music or song as rendered or heard.

strain² /streɪn/ *n.* **1.** any of the different lines of ancestry united in a family or an individual. **2.** a variety, especially of micro-organisms.

strainer /'streɪnə/ *n.* a filter, sieve, or the like for straining liquids.

strait /streɪt/ *n.* **1.** (*oft. pl. with sing. sense*) a narrow passage of water connecting two large bodies of water. **2.** (*oft. pl.*) a position of difficulty, distress, or need.

straitjacket /'streɪtdʒækət/ *n.* a kind of coat for confining the arms of violently insane persons, etc. Also, **straightjacket.**

straitlaced /'streɪtleɪst/ *adj.* excessively strict in conduct or morality; puritanical; prudish.

strand¹ /strænd/ *v.t.* **1.** (*usu. in the passive*) to bring into a helpless position. —*v.i.* **2.** to be driven or run ashore, as a ship, etc. —*n.* **3.** *Poetic* the seashore.

strand² /strænd/ *n.* **1.** each of a number of strings or yarns which are twisted together to form a rope, cord, or the like. **2.** a thread of the texture of anything, as cloth.

strange /streɪndʒ/ *adj.* **1.** unusual, extraordinary, or curious; odd; queer. **2.** situated, belonging, or coming from outside one's own or a particular locality.

stranger /'streɪndʒə/ *n.* **1.** a person with whom one has, or has hitherto had, no personal acquaintance. –*phr.* **2. no stranger to ...**, a person accustomed to (something specified).

strangle /'stræŋɡəl/ *v.t.* to kill by stopping the breath.

strap /stræp/ *n.* **1.** a long, narrow piece or object; strip; band. –*v.t.* (**strapped, strapping**) **2.** to fasten or secure with a strap or straps.

strapping /'stræpɪŋ/ *adj. Colloq.* tall, robust, and strongly built.

strata /'strɑtə/ *n.* **1.** a plural of **stratum**. –*adj.* **2.** of or relating to or sold under a strata title: *a strata unit.*

stratagem /'strætədʒəm/ *n.* a plan, scheme, or trick for deceiving the enemy.

strata title *n.* a system of registration of strata of air space in multistorey buildings, similar to the registration of titles under the Torrens system.

strategic /strə'tidʒɪk/ *adj.* important in strategy.

strategy /'strætədʒi/ *n.* (*pl.* **-gies**) the method of conducting operations, especially by the aid of manoeuvring or stratagem.

strati- a word element representing **stratum**.

stratify /'strætəfaɪ/ *v.t.* (**-fied, -fying**) to form in strata or layers.

strato- a word element meaning 'low and horizontal'.

stratosphere /'strætəsfɪə/ *n.* the region of the atmosphere at an altitude of about 20 to 50 km above the earth. –**stratospheric** /ˌstrætəs'ferɪk/, *adj.*

stratum /'strɑtəm/ *n.* (*pl.* **strata** /'strɑtə/ *or* **stratums**) a layer of material, formed either naturally or artificially, often one of a number of parallel layers placed one upon another.

stratus /'streɪtəs/ *n.* (*pl.* **strati** /'streɪtaɪ/) a continuous horizontal sheet of cloud, resembling fog but not resting on the ground, usually of uniform thickness and comparatively low altitude.

straw /strɔ/ *n.* **1.** a single stalk or stem, especially of certain species of grain, chiefly wheat, rye, oats, and barley. **2.** a mass of such stalks, especially after drying and threshing, used as fodder, as material for hats, etc. **3.** a hollow paper tube, plant stem, etc., used in drinking some beverages, etc. –*adj.* **4.** of, relating to, or made of straw.

strawberry /'strɔbəri, -bri/ *n.* (*pl.* **-ries**) a small, red, fleshy fruit.

straw company *n.* a company set up not to produce anything but simply as a legal device to obtain some benefit, especially tax benefits.

straw poll *n.* an unofficial vote taken to obtain some indication of the general drift of opinion. Also, **straw vote**.

stray /streɪ/ *v.i.* **1.** (fol. by *away, off, from, into, to,* etc.) to wander. **2.** to deviate, as from the set or right course; go astray; get lost. –*n.* **3.** a domestic animal found wandering at large or without an owner. –*adj.* **4.** straying, or having strayed, as a domestic animal. **5.** found or

occurring apart from others, or as an isolated or casual instance.

streak /strik/ *n.* **1.** a long, narrow mark, smear, band of colour, or the like. **2.** a vein or strain of anything. –*v.t.* **3.** to mark with a streak or streaks. –*v.i.* **4.** to become streaked. **5.** to flash or go rapidly, like a streak of lightning.

stream /strim/ *n.* **1.** a body of water flowing in a channel or bed. **2.** any flow of water or other liquid or fluid. **3.** prevailing direction; drift. –*v.i.* **4.** to flow, pass, or issue in a stream, as water, tears, blood, etc. **5.** (fol. by *with*) to send forth or throw off a stream; run or flow. –*v.t.* **6.** to transmit a digitised form of (media content) by streaming. **7.** to send forth or discharge in a stream.

streamer /'strimə/ *n.* **1.** a long, narrow flag or pennant. **2.** a long, narrow strip of paper, usually brightly coloured, thrown in festivities, or used for decorating rooms or the like.

streaming /'strimɪŋ/ *n. Computers* the process of transmitting digital data in a continuous, steady flow, so that it may be processed and displayed as it is being received, rather than being stored and only displayed when the entire file has been received and processed.

streamline /'strimlaɪn/ *v.t.* **1.** to make streamlined. **2.** to simplify, especially to improve efficiency.

streamlined /'strimlaɪnd/ *adj.* **1.** having a shape designed to offer the least possible resistance in passing through the air, etc. **2.** simplified, especially to improve efficiency.

street /strit/ *n.* a public way or road, paved or unpaved, in a town or city, sometimes including a pavement or pavements, with houses, shops, etc., along it.

street race *n.* a motor vehicle race conducted, often illegally, on ordinary streets as opposed to a purpose-built racing track. –**street racer**, *n.* –**street racing**, *n.*

street smart *adj.* used to dealing with the people on the street, especially in business transactions, and therefore keenly aware of and prepared for the sordid and underhand aspects of urban life. Also, **street-smart**.

streetwise /'stritwaɪz/ *adj.* skilled in living in an urban environment.

strength /streŋθ/ *n.* **1.** the quality or state of being strong; bodily or muscular power; vigour, as in robust health. **2.** something that makes strong; a support or stay.

strenuous /'strɛnjuəs/ *adj.* characterised by vigorous exertion.

streptococcus /ˌstrɛptə'kɒkəs/ *n.* (*pl.* **-cocci** /ˌstrɛptə'kɒkaɪ, -'kɒki/) any of certain species of bacteria. –**streptococcal**, *adj.*

stress /strɛs/ *v.t.* **1.** to lay stress or emphasis on; emphasise. –*n.* **2.** importance or significance attached to a thing; emphasis. **3.** emphasis in music, rhythm, etc. **4.** the physical pressure, pull, or other force exerted on one thing by another. **5.** severe nervous tension caused by disturbing physiological or psychological factors.

-stress a feminine equivalent of **-ster**.

stressful /'strɛsfəl/ *adj.* causing anxiety and tension.

stretch /stretʃ/ *v.t.* **1.** to draw out or extend. **2.** to lengthen, widen, distend, or enlarge by tension. **3.** to extend or force beyond the natural or proper limits; strain. –*v.i.* **4.** (usu. fol. by *out*) to recline at full length. **5.** to extend the hand, or reach, as for something. **6.** to extend over a distance, area, period of time, or in a particular direction. **7.** to stretch oneself by extending the limbs, straining the muscles, etc. **8.** to become stretched, or admit of being stretched, to greater length, width, etc., as any elastic material. –*n.* **9.** the act of stretching. **10.** the state of being stretched. **11.** capacity for being stretched. **12.** a continuous length, distance, tract, or expanse. **13.** an extent in time or duration. –*adj.* **14.** made to stretch in order to fit different shapes and sizes, as clothing.

stretcher /'stretʃə/ *n.* **1.** a light, folding bed. **2.** a bed-like device designed for transporting an ill or injured person.

strew /struː/ *v.t.* (**strewed, strewed** *or* **strewn, strewing**) to let fall in separate pieces or particles over a surface; scatter or sprinkle.

stricken /'strɪkən/ *adj.* smitten or afflicted, as with disease, trouble, or sorrow.

strict /strɪkt/ *adj.* **1.** demanding close conformity to requirements or principles. **2.** closely or rigorously enforced or maintained. **3.** exact or precise.

stricture /'strɪktʃə/ *n.* a remark or comment, especially an adverse criticism.

stride /straɪd/ *v.* (**strode, stridden, striding**) –*v.i.* **1.** to walk with long steps. **2.** to take a long step. –*v.t.* **3.** to walk with long steps along, on, through, over, etc. **4.** to pass over or across by one stride. –*n.* **5.** a long step in walking. **6.** (*pl.*) *Colloq.* trousers.

strident /'straɪdnt/ *adj.* making or having a harsh sound; grating; creaking.

strife /straɪf/ *n.* conflict, discord, or variance.

strike /straɪk/ *v.* (**struck, striking**) –*v.t.* **1.** to deal a blow or stroke to. **2.** to deal or inflict (a blow, stroke, etc.). **3.** to drive or thrust forcibly. **4.** to produce (fire, sparks, light, etc.) by percussion, friction, etc. **5.** to cause (a match) to ignite by friction. **6.** to come into forcible contact or collision with. **7.** to fall upon (something), as light or sound. **8.** to enter the mind of; occur to. **9.** to impress strongly. **10.** to come upon or find (ore, oil, etc.) in prospecting, boring, or the like. **11.** to send down or put forth (a root, etc.), as a plant, cutting, etc. **12.** to balance (a ledger, etc.). **13.** (in various technical uses) to make level or smooth. **14.** (fol. by *off, out*, etc.) to efface or cancel with, or as with, the stroke of a pen. **15.** (usu. fol. by *off*) to remove or separate with a cut. **16.** to indicate (the hour of day) by a stroke or strokes, as a clock. **17.** to assume (an attitude or posture). **18.** to reach by agreement, as a compromise. **19.** (usu. fol. by *up*) to enter upon or form (an acquaintance, etc.). –*v.i.* **20.** to deal or aim a blow or stroke. **21.** come into forcible contact. **22.** to make an impression on the mind, senses, etc., as something seen or heard. **23.** (of an orchestra or band) to begin to play. **24.** to take root, as a slip of a plant. **25.** to go, proceed, or advance, especially in a new direction. **26.** (of an employee or employees) to engage in a strike. –*n.*

27. an act of striking. **28.** a concerted stopping of work or withdrawal of workers' services in order to compel an employer to accede to demands.

string /strɪŋ/ *n.* **1.** a line, cord, or thread, used for tying parcels, etc. **2.** a number of objects, as beads or pearls, threaded or arranged on a cord. **3.** any series of things arranged or connected in a line or following closely one after another. **4.** (in musical instruments) a tightly stretched cord or wire which produces a note when caused to vibrate. –*v.* (**strung, stringing**) –*v.t.* **5.** to furnish with or as with a string or strings. **6.** to extend or stretch (a cord, etc.) from one point to another. **7.** to thread on, or as on, a string. **8.** to connect in, or as in, a line; arrange in a series or succession. **9.** to deprive of a string or strings; strip the strings from. –*v.i.* **10.** to form into a string or strings, as glutinous substances do when pulled. –*phr.* **11. string along** (or **on**), *Colloq.* to deceive (someone) in a progressive series of falsehoods; con.

stringent /'strɪndʒənt/ *adj.* **1.** narrowly binding; rigorously exacting; strict; severe. **2.** (of the money market) tight; characterised by a shortage of loan money.

strip¹ /strɪp/ *v.* (**stripped, stripping**) –*v.t.* **1.** to deprive of covering. **2.** to deprive of clothing; make bare or naked. **3.** to take away or remove. **4.** to deprive or divest. –*v.i.* **5.** to strip something; especially, to strip oneself of clothes.

strip² /strɪp/ *n.* a narrow piece, comparatively long and usually of uniform width.

stripe /straɪp/ *n.* **1.** a relatively long, narrow band of a different colour, appearance, weave, material, or nature from the rest of a surface or thing. **2.** a strip, or long, narrow piece of anything. –*v.t.* **3.** to mark or provide with a stripe or stripes.

stripling /'strɪplɪŋ/ *n.* a youth just passing from boyhood to manhood.

strip search *n.* a type of body-search in which the suspect is required to take off their clothes.

striptease /'strɪptiːz/ *n.* an act in which someone strips before an audience.

strive /straɪv/ *v.i.* (**strove** *or* **strived, striven** /'strɪvən/ *or* **strived, striving**) **1.** to make strenuous efforts towards any end. **2.** to struggle vigorously, as in opposition or resistance.

strobe lighting /stroʊb/ *n.* flashing light of great intensity, as at a dance, etc.

strode /stroʊd/ *v.* past tense of **stride**.

stroganoff /'strɒgənɒf/ *n.* a Russian dish of meat cooked in a sauce of sour cream and mushrooms.

stroke¹ /stroʊk/ *n.* **1.** an act of striking; a blow. **2.** something likened to a blow in its effect, as an attack of apoplexy or paralysis. **3.** *Med.* a sudden interruption to the supply of blood to the brain, caused by haemorrhage, thrombosis or embolism. **4.** a single complete movement, especially one continuously repeated in some process. **5.** a movement of a pen, pencil, brush, or the like. **6.** a mark traced by or as if by a pen, pencil, brush, or the like.

stroke² /stroʊk/ *v.t.* **1.** to pass the hand or an instrument over (something) lightly or with little pressure; rub gently, as in soothing or caressing. *—n.* **2.** the act or an instance of stroking; a stroking movement.

stroll /strəʊl/ *v.i.* **1.** to walk leisurely as inclination directs; ramble. *—n.* **2.** a leisurely walk; a ramble; a saunter.

stroller /ˈstrəʊlə/ *n.* a light collapsible chair on wheels, used for carrying small children. Also, **pushchair, pusher.**

strong /strɒŋ/ *adj.* **1.** physically vigorous or robust. **2.** mentally powerful or vigorous. **3.** of great moral power, firmness, or courage. **4.** powerful in influence, authority, resources. **5.** well-supplied or rich in something specified. **6.** of great force, effectiveness, potency, or cogency. **7.** containing alcohol, or much alcohol. **8.** intense, as light or colour. **9.** strenuous or energetic; forceful or vigorous. **10.** of an unpleasant or offensive flavour or smell. **11.** *Commerce* characterised by steady or advancing prices. *—adv.* **12.** in a strong manner. **13.** in number: *the team was fifteen strong.*

stronghold /ˈstrɒŋhəʊld/ *n.* a strong or well-fortified place; a fortress.

strop /strɒp/ *n.* **1.** material used for sharpening razors. *—v.t.* (**stropped, stropping**) **2.** to sharpen on, or as on, a strop.

stroppy /ˈstrɒpi/ *adj.* (**-pier, -piest**) *Colloq.* rebellious and difficult to control.

strove /strəʊv/ *v.* past tense of **strive.**

struck /strʌk/ *v.* past tense and a past participle of **strike.**

structure /ˈstrʌktʃə/ *n.* **1.** arrangement of parts, elements or constituents. **2.** something built or constructed. **3.** anything composed of parts arranged together in some way; an organisation. *—v.t.* **4.** to give form or organisation to. **—structural,** *adj.*

strudel /ˈstruːdəl/ *n.* a very thin sheet of pastry, spread with a sweet filling, rolled up and baked.

struggle /ˈstrʌgəl/ *v.i.* **1.** to contend with an adversary or opposing force. *—n.* **2.** the act or process of struggling.

strum /strʌm/ *v.* (**strummed, strumming**) *—v.t.* **1.** to play on (a stringed musical instrument) unskilfully or carelessly. **2.** to play (chords, etc., especially on a guitar) by sweeping across the strings with the fingers or with a plectrum. *—v.i.* **3.** to play chords on a stringed instrument unskilfully or as a simple accompaniment.

strumpet /ˈstrʌmpət/ *n. Obs.* a prostitute.

strung /strʌŋ/ *v.* past tense and past participle of **string.**

strut¹ /strʌt/ *v.i.* (**strutted, strutting**) to walk with a vain, pompous bearing, as with head erect and chest thrown out, as if expecting to impress observers.

strut² /strʌt/ *n.* a structural part designed to take pressure.

strychnine /ˈstrɪknin, -nən/ *n.* a colourless crystalline poison.

stub /stʌb/ *n.* **1.** a short remaining piece. *—v.t.* (**stubbed, stubbing**) **2.** to strike, as one's toe, against something projecting from a surface. *—phr.* **3. stub out,** to extinguish (a cigarette) by pressing the lighted end against a hard surface.

stubble /ˈstʌbəl/ *n.* any short, rough growth, as of beard.

stubborn /ˈstʌbən/ *adj.* unreasonably obstinate; obstinately perverse.

stubby /ˈstʌbi/ *adj.* (**-bier, -biest**) **1.** short and thick or broad. *—n.* (*pl.* **-bies**) **2.** a small squat beer bottle.

stubby holder *n.* a lightweight casing designed as insulation for a stubby (def. 2) or can. Also, **stubby cooler.**

stuck /stʌk/ *v.* past tense and past participle of **stick².**

stud¹ /stʌd/ *n.* **1.** a boss, knob, nail head, or other protuberance projecting from a surface or part, especially as an ornament. **2.** a kind of small button or fastener. *—v.t.* (**studded, studding**) **3.** to set with or as with studs, bosses, or the like. **4.** to set or scatter (objects) at intervals over a surface.

stud² /stʌd/ *n.* **1.** an establishment in which horses cattle, etc., are kept for breeding. **2.** retained for breeding purposes.

student /ˈstjuːdnt/ *n.* someone who studies.

studio /ˈstjuːdiəʊ/ *n.* (*pl.* **-dios**) **1.** a room or place in which some form of art is pursued. **2.** a room or set of rooms specially equipped for broadcasting radio or television programs or making recordings.

study /ˈstʌdi/ *n.* (*pl.* **-dies**) **1.** application of the mind to the acquisition of knowledge, as by reading, investigation, or reflection. **2.** a thorough examination and analysis of a particular subject. **3.** a room, in a house or other building, set apart for private study, reading, writing, or the like. **4.** something produced as an educational exercise. *—v.* (**-died, -dying**) *—v.i.* **5.** to apply oneself to the acquisition of knowledge, as by reading, investigation, practice, etc. *—v.t.* **6.** to apply oneself to acquiring a knowledge of (a branch of learning, science, or art, or a subject), especially systematically. **7.** to examine or investigate carefully and in detail. **—studious,** *adj.*

stuff /stʌf/ *n.* **1.** the material of which anything is made. **2.** material to be worked upon, or to be used in making something. **3.** matter or material indefinitely. **4.** worthless matter or things. *—v.t.* **5.** to fill (a receptacle), especially by packing the contents closely together. **6.** to fill (a chicken, turkey, piece of meat, etc.) with seasoned breadcrumbs or other savoury matter. **7.** to thrust or cram (something) tightly into a receptacle, cavity, or the like. **8.** (usu. fol. by *up*) to stop up or plug; block or choke. **9.** *Colloq.* to cause to fail; render useless. *—v.i.* **10.** to cram oneself with food.

stuffing /ˈstʌfɪŋ/ *n.* that with which anything is or may be stuffed.

stuffy /ˈstʌfi/ *adj.* (**-fier, -fiest**) **1.** close or ill-ventilated, as a room; oppressive from lack of freshness, as the air, etc. **2.** conceited. **3.** old-fashioned; immune to new ideas.

stumble /ˈstʌmbəl/ *v.i.* **1.** to strike the foot against something in walking, running, etc., so as to stagger or fall; trip. **2.** to walk or go unsteadily. *—n.* **3.** the act of stumbling. *—phr.* **4. stumble on** (or **upon**) (or **across**), to find accidentally or unexpectedly.

stump /stʌmp/ *n.* **1.** something left after a part has been cut off, as of a tree, leg, etc. **2.** a short remnant of a pencil, candle, cigar, etc. **3.** *Cricket* each of the three upright sticks which, with the two bails laid on the top of them, form a wicket. *–v.t.* **4.** to clear of stumps, as land. **5.** to nonplus, embarrass, or render completely at a loss. *–v.i.* **6.** to walk heavily or clumsily, as if with a wooden leg.

stun /stʌn/ *v.t.* (**stunned**, **stunning**) **1.** to deprive of consciousness or strength by or as by a blow, fall, etc. **2.** to strike with astonishment; astound; amaze.

stung /stʌŋ/ *v.* past tense and past participle of **sting**.

stun gun *n.* a weapon which administers a mild electric shock to a person, sufficient to temporarily stun them.

stunt¹ /stʌnt/ *v.t.* to check the growth or development of.

stunt² /stʌnt/ *n.* a performance serving as a display of strength, activity, skill, or the like, as in athletics, etc.; a feat.

stunt double *n.* someone whose job is to perform hazardous or acrobatic feats, especially one who replaces a film actor in scenes requiring such feats.

stuntman /ˈstʌntmæn/ *n.* a male stunt double.

stuntwoman /ˈstʌntwʊmən/ *n.* a female stunt double.

stupefy /ˈstjupəfaɪ/ *v.t.* (**-fied, -fying**) to put into a state of stupor.

stupendous /stjuˈpɛndəs/ *adj.* such as to cause amazement.

stupid /ˈstjupəd/ *adj.* **1.** lacking intelligence. **2.** showing a lack of good sense: *a stupid thing to do*.

stupor /ˈstjupə/ *n.* a state of suspended or deadened sensibility.

sturdy /ˈstɜdi/ *adj.* (**-dier, -diest**) strongly built, stalwart, or robust.

sturgeon /ˈstɜdʒən/ *n.* (pl. **-geon** *or* **-geons**) a large fish of the Nthn Hemisphere, valued for their flesh and as a source of caviar.

stutter /ˈstʌtə/ *v.t.*, *v.i.* **1.** to utter (sounds) in which the rhythm is interrupted by blocks or spasms, repetitions, or prolongation. *–n.* **2.** unrhythmical and distorted speech.

sty¹ /staɪ/ *n.* (pl. **sties**) a pen or enclosure for pigs.

sty² /staɪ/ *n.* (pl. **sties**) → **stye**.

stye /staɪ/ *n.* a small inflammation on the eyelid. Also, **sty**.

style /staɪl/ *n.* **1.** a particular kind, sort, or type, as with reference to form, appearance, or character. **2.** a particular, distinctive, or characteristic mode of action. **3.** a mode of fashion, as in dress, especially good or approved fashion; elegance; smartness. **4.** the features of a literary composition belonging to the form of expression other than the content. **5.** a manner or tone adopted in speaking to others. **6.** the rules of spelling, punctuation, capitalisation, etc., observed by a publishing house, newspaper, etc. **7.** a descriptive or distinguishing appellation, especially a recognised title. *–v.t.* (**styled, styling**) **8.** to call by a particular style or appellation (as specified). **9.** to design in accordance with a given or new style. **–stylistic**, *adj.*

stylise /ˈstaɪlaɪz/ *v.t.* to bring into conformity with a particular style. Also, **stylize**.

stylish /ˈstaɪlɪʃ/ *adj.* smart; elegant.

stylus /ˈstaɪləs/ *n.* **1.** a needle tipped with diamond, sapphire, etc., for reproducing the sound of a gramophone record. **2.** *Computers* a pen-shaped instrument used to write, draw, etc., directly onto a touch-sensitive computer screen, the resultant text or image being digitised by the computer's software. **3.** any of various pointed instruments used in drawing, tracing, stencilling, etc.

suave /swɑv/ *adj.* (of persons or their manner, speech, etc.) smoothly agreeable or polite; agreeably or blandly urbane.

sub /sʌb/ *n.* a submarine.

sub- a prefix meaning 'under', 'not quite', or 'somewhat', also attached to stems not used independently, with various extensions of meaning (*subject, subtract, subvert*).

subcommittee /ˈsʌbkəˌmɪti/ *n.* a secondary committee appointed out of a main committee.

subconscious /sʌbˈkɒnʃəs/ *adj.* **1.** existing or operating beneath or beyond consciousness. *–n.* **2.** the totality of mental processes of which the individual is not aware; unreportable mental activities.

subcontract *Law* *–n.* /sʌbˈkɒntrækt/ **1.** a contract by which one agrees to render services or to provide materials necessary for the performance of another contract. *–v.i., v.t.* /sʌbkən-ˈtrækt/ **2.** to make a subcontract (for). **–subcontractor**, *n.*

subculture /ˈsʌbkʌltʃə/ *n.* *Sociology* a distinct network of behaviour, beliefs and attitudes existing within a larger culture.

subcutaneous /sʌbkjuˈteɪniəs/ *adj.* situated or lying under the skin, as tissue.

subdivide /sʌbdəˈvaɪd, sʌbdəˈvaɪd/ *–v.t.* **1.** to divide (a part, or an already divided whole) into smaller parts; divide anew after a first division. *–v.i.* **2.** to become separated into subdivisions.

subdue /səbˈdju/ *v.t.* **1.** to overpower by superior force; overcome. **2.** to bring into mental subjection. **3.** to reduce the intensity, force, or vividness of.

subeditor /sʌbˈedətə/ *n.* **1.** *Journalism* someone who edits and corrects material written by others. **2.** an assistant or subordinate editor.

subheading /ˈsʌbhɛdɪŋ/ *n.* **1.** a title or heading of a subdivision or subsection in a chapter, treatise, essay, newspaper article, etc. **2.** a subordinate division of a heading or title. Also, **subhead**.

subject *n.* /ˈsʌbdʒɛkt/ **1.** something that forms a matter of thought, discourse, investigation, etc. **2.** a branch of knowledge organised into a system so as to form a suitable course of study. **3.** someone who is under the dominion or rule of a sovereign, state, etc. **4.** *Gram.* the word or words of a sentence which represent the person or object performing the action expressed in the predicate, as, *she* in *she raised her hat*. **5.** someone who or that which undergoes, or may undergo, some action. *–adj.* /ˈsʌbdʒɛkt/ **6.** (oft. fol. by *to*) being under domination, control, or influence. **7.** being under dominion, rule, or authority. **8.** (fol. by *to*) open or exposed. **9.** (fol. by *to*) being dependent or conditional upon something. *–v.t.* /səbˈdʒɛkt/ **10.** (usu. fol. by *to*) to make subject. **–subjection**, *n.*

subjective /səbˈdʒɛktɪv/ *adj.* belonging to the thinking subject rather than to the object of thought (opposed to *objective*).

sub judice /sʌb ˈdʒuːdəsi/ *adv.* before a judge or court of law; under judicial consideration.

subjugate /ˈsʌbdʒəgeɪt/ *v.t.* to bring under complete control or into subjection; subdue; conquer.

sublet /sʌbˈlɛt/ *v.t.* (**-let**, **-letting**) to let to another person, the party letting being himself or herself a lessee.

sublimate /ˈsʌbləmeɪt/ *v.t. Psychol.* to deflect (sexual or other biological energies) into socially constructive or creative channels.

sublime /səˈblaɪm/ *adj.* **1.** supreme or perfect. –*n.* **2.** that which is sublime.

subliminal /səˈblɪmənəl/ *adj. Psychol.* (of stimuli, etc.) being or operating below the threshold of consciousness or perception.

submarine /ˈsʌbmərin, sʌbməˈrin/ *n.* **1.** a type of vessel that can be submerged and navigated under water. –*adj.* **2.** situated, occurring, operating, or living under the surface of the sea or any large body of water.

submerge /səbˈmɜːdʒ/ *v.* (**-merged**, **-merging**) –*v.t.* **1.** to cover with or as with water; immerse. –*v.i.* **2.** to sink or plunge under water.

submissive /səbˈmɪsɪv/ *adj.* **1.** inclined or ready to submit. **2.** marked by or indicating submission.

submit /səbˈmɪt/ *v.* (**-mitted**, **-mitting**) –*v.t.* **1.** to yield in surrender, compliance, or obedience. **2.** to state or urge with deference (usually followed by a clause). **3.** to refer to the decision or judgement of another or others. –*v.i.* **4.** to yield in surrender, compliance, obedience, etc.

suborder /ˈsʌbˌɔːdə/ *n.* a group of related plants or animals ranking above a family and below an order.

subordinate *adj.* /səˈbɔːdənət/ **1.** of lesser importance; secondary. **2.** subject to or under the authority of a superior. –*n.* /səˈbɔːdənət/ **3.** a subordinate person or thing. –*v.t.* /səˈbɔːdəneɪt/ **4.** to place in a lower order or rank. **5.** to make subordinate.

subpoena /səˈpinə/ *Law* –*n.* **1.** the usual writ process for the summoning of witnesses. –*v.t.* (**-naed**, **-naing**) **2.** to serve with a subpoena.

subprime /sʌbˈpraɪm/ *adj. US* of, relating to, or designating a loan, usually a housing loan, which is risky because the borrower is less than ideal or has an ability to repay which has not been accurately assessed.

subroutine /ˈsʌbrutin/ *n. Computers* a section of a program which can be called up as required from various points in the main program, returning the user to the point at which it was called up.

subscribe /səbˈskraɪb/ *v.t.* **1.** to write or inscribe (something) beneath or at the end of a thing; sign (one's name) to a document, etc. –*v.i.* **2.** to obtain a subscription to a magazine, newspaper, etc. **3.** to give or pay money as a contribution, payment, etc. **4.** to assent by, or as by, signing one's name.

subscript /ˈsʌbskrɪpt/ *n.* something written below.

subscription /səbˈskrɪpʃən/ *n.* **1.** a monetary contribution towards some object or a payment for shares, a book, a periodical, etc. **2.** the dues paid by a member of a club, society, etc. **3.** something subscribed.

subsection /ˈsʌbsɛkʃən/ *n.* **1.** a part or division of a section. **2.** one of eight exogamous kinship groups within some Aboriginal tribes having a kinship system with sections; equivalent to half a section. Compare **moiety** (def. 2c), **section** (def. 5).

subsequent /ˈsʌbsəkwənt/ *adj.* occurring or coming later or after.

subservient /səbˈsɜːviənt/ *adj.* (of persons, their conduct, etc.) servile; excessively submissive; obsequious.

subside /səbˈsaɪd/ *v.i.* to sink to a low or lower level.

subsidiary /səbˈsɪdʒəri/ *adj.* **1.** serving to assist or supplement. **2.** subordinate or secondary.

subsidise /ˈsʌbsədaɪz/ *v.t.* to furnish or aid with a subsidy. Also, **subsidize**.

subsidy /ˈsʌbsədi/ *n.* (*pl.* **-dies**) a direct pecuniary aid furnished by a government to a private industrial undertaking, a cultural organisation, or the like.

subsist /səbˈsɪst/ *v.i.* to continue alive; live, as on food, resources, etc., especially when these are limited.

subsistence /səbˈsɪstəns/ *n.* **1.** the state or fact of subsisting. **2.** means of supporting life; a living or livelihood.

substance /ˈsʌbstəns/ *n.* **1.** that of which a thing consists; matter or material. **2.** a species of matter of definite chemical composition. **3.** substantial or solid character or quality. **4.** the meaning or gist, as of speech or writing.

substantial /səbˈstænʃəl/ *adj.* **1.** of a corporeal or material nature; real or actual. **2.** of ample or considerable amount, quantity, size, etc. **3.** of solid character or quality; firm, stout, or strong. **4.** wealthy or influential.

substantiate /səbˈstænʃieɪt/ *v.t.* to establish by proof or competent evidence.

substantive /ˈsʌbstəntɪv, ˈsʌbstəntɪv/ *n.* **1.** *Gram.* a noun, pronoun, or other word or phrase having nominal function in a sentence. –*adj.* **2.** *Gram.* of or relating to substantives. **3.** real or actual. **4.** of considerable amount or quantity. **5.** *Law* relating to the rules of right which courts are called on to apply, as opposed to rules of procedure. –**substantively**, *adv.*

substitute /ˈsʌbstətjut/ *n.* **1.** a person or thing acting or serving in place of another. –*v.t.* **2.** to put (one person or thing) in the place of another. –*v.i.* **3.** to act as substitute.

subsume /səbˈsjum/ *v.t.* **1.** to consider (an idea, term, proposition, etc.) as part of a more comprehensive one. **2.** bring (a case, instance, etc.) under a rule.

subter- a prefix meaning 'position underneath', with figurative applications, as in *subterfuge*.

subterfuge /ˈsʌbtəfjudʒ/ *n.* an artifice or expedient employed to escape the force of an argument, to evade unfavourable consequences, hide something etc.

subterranean /sʌbtəˈreɪniən/ *adj.* existing, situated, or operating below the surface of the earth; underground.

subtitle /'sʌbtaɪtl/ n. **1.** a secondary or subordinate title of a literary work, usually of explanatory character. **2.** *Film* one of a series of captions projected on to the lower part of the screen which translate and summarise the dialogue of foreign language films.

subtle /'sʌtl/ adj. **1.** fine or delicate, often when likely to elude perception or understanding. **2.** requiring mental acuteness, penetration, or discernment. **3.** insidious in operation, as poison, etc. –**subtlety**, n.

subtract /səb'trækt/ v.t. **1.** to withdraw or take away, as a part from a whole. –v.i. **2.** to take away something or a part, as from a whole. –**subtraction**, n.

suburb /'sʌbɜb/ n. a more or less self-contained district of a town or city. –**suburban**, adj.

suburbia /sə'bɜbiə/ n. the suburbs collectively especially as they embody the middle range of community standards and values.

subvert /səb'vɜt/ v.t. to cause the downfall, ruin, or destruction of. –**subversion**, n. –**subversive**, adj.

subway /'sʌbweɪ/ n. an underground passage or tunnel enabling pedestrians to cross beneath a street, railway line, etc.

succeed /sək'sid/ v.i. **1.** to have the desired result. **2.** to accomplish what is attempted or intended. **3.** to achieve success in a particular field. **4.** (oft. fol. by *to*) to follow or replace another by descent, election, appointment, etc. **5.** to come next after something else in an order or series. –v.t. **6.** to come after and take the place of, as in an office or estate. **7.** to come next after in an order or series, or in the course of events; follow. –**succession**, n. –**successive**, adj.

success /sək'sɛs/ n. **1.** the favourable or prosperous end to attempts or endeavours. **2.** the gaining of wealth, position, or the like. **3.** a thing or a person that is successful. –**successful**, adj.

successor /sək'sɛsə/ n. someone who or that which succeeds or follows. –**succession**, n.

succinct /sək'sɪŋkt/ adj. characterised by conciseness or verbal brevity.

succour /'sʌkə/ n. help; relief; aid; assistance. Also, **succor**.

succulent /'sʌkjələnt/ adj. full of juice; juicy.

succumb /sə'kʌm/ v.i. to give way to superior force; yield.

such /sʌtʃ/ adj. **1.** of the kind, character, degree, extent, etc., of that or those indicated or implied. **2.** (*preceding an adjective used attributively*) so, or in such a manner or degree. **3.** an intensifier with the sense of 'to a high degree': *he is such a nice man.* **4.** (*with omission of an indication of comparison*) of such extreme a kind; so great, good, bad, etc.: *she is such a liar.* **5.** being the person or thing, or the persons or things, indicated. **6.** Also, **such and such**. being definite or particular, but not named or specified. –pron. **7.** the person or thing, or the persons or things, indicated. –phr. **8.** as such, **a.** as being what is indicated; in that capacity. **b.** in itself or themselves.

suck /sʌk/ v.t. **1.** to draw into the mouth by action of the lips and tongue which produces a partial vacuum. **2.** to draw (water, moisture, air, etc.) by any process resembling this. **3.** to

apply the lips or mouth to, and draw upon by producing a partial vacuum, especially for extracting fluid contents. **4.** to hold in the mouth and dissolve in the saliva, assisted by the action of the tongue, etc. –v.i. **5.** to draw or be drawn by, or as by, suction. –n. **6.** the act or instance of sucking.

sucker /'sʌkə/ n. *Colloq.* a person easily deceived or imposed upon; dupe.

suckle /'sʌkəl/ v.t. **1.** to nurse at the breast. –v.i. **2.** to suck at the breast.

sucrose /'sukrouz, -ous/ n. the sugar obtained from the sugar cane, the sugar beet, etc.

suction /'sʌkʃən/ n. **1.** the act, process, or condition of sucking. **2.** the tendency to suck a substance into an interior space when the atmospheric pressure is reduced in the space. **3.** the act or process of sucking a gas or liquid by such means.

sudden /'sʌdn/ adj. **1.** happening, coming, made, or done quickly, without warning or unexpectedly. –phr. **2. all of a sudden**, suddenly.

sudden infant death syndrome n. → SIDS.

sudoku /sə'doʊku/ n. a logic puzzle in which the solution depends on correctly inserting digits from 1 to 9 in a grid so that each row and each column and each marked subset within the grid has only one occurrence of each digit.

suds /sʌdz/ pl. n. soapy water; lather.

sue /su/ v. (**sued, suing**) –v.t. **1.** to institute process in law against. –v.i. **2.** to institute legal proceedings, or bring suit.

suede /sweɪd/ n. kid or other leather finished on the flesh side with a soft, napped surface.

suet /'suət/ n. hard animal fat used in cookery, etc.

suffer /'sʌfə/ v.i. **1.** to undergo or feel pain or distress. **2.** to endure patiently or bravely. –v.t. **3.** to undergo, experience, or be subjected to. **4.** to tolerate or allow.

sufferance /'sʌfərəns, 'sʌfrəns/ phr. **on sufferance**, reluctantly tolerated.

suffice /sə'faɪs/ v.i. (**-ficed, -ficing**) **1.** to be enough or adequate. –phr. **2. suffice (it) to say**, let it be enough to say.

sufficient /sə'fɪʃənt/ adj. that suffices. –**sufficiency**, n.

suffix /'sʌfɪks/ n. *Gram.* a word part added to the end of a word, as *-ness* in *kindness*.

suffocate /'sʌfəkeɪt/ v.t. **1.** to kill by preventing the access of air to the blood. –v.i. **2.** to become suffocated; stifle; smother.

suffrage /'sʌfrɪdʒ/ n. the right of voting, especially in political elections.

suffuse /sə'fjuz/ v.t. to overspread with or as with a liquid, colour, etc.

sugar /'ʃʊgə/ n. **1.** a sweet crystalline substance extensively used for food purposes. **2.** a member of the same class of carbohydrates. –v.t. **3.** to cover, sprinkle, mix, or sweeten with sugar.

sugar beet n. a variety of beet cultivated for the sugar it yields.

sugar cane n. a tall grass of tropical and warm regions, constituting the chief source of sugar. Also, **sugarcane**.

suggest /'sə'dʒɛst/ v.t. **1.** to place or bring (an idea, proposition, plan, etc.) before a person's mind for consideration or possible action. **2.** to propose (a person or thing) as suitable or possible.

suggestible /sə'dʒestəbəl/ *adj.* open to influence by suggestion.

suggestion /sə'dʒestʃən/ *n.* **1.** an idea or plan put forward for someone to consider. **2.** something that indicates that something is the case without being definite. **3.** a slight sign of something.

suggestive /sə'dʒestɪv/ *adj.* such as to suggest something improper or indecent.

sugo /'sugoʊ/ *n.* a tomato sauce in the Italian style, made from coarsely chopped tomatoes. Compare **passata**.

suicide /'suəsaɪd/ *n.* **1.** someone who intentionally takes their own life. **2.** the intentional taking of one's own life. –*v.i.* **3.** to commit suicide. –**suicidal**, *adj.*

suicide bomber *n.* a person who carries out a bomb attack in the knowledge that the detonation will kill them. –**suicide bombing**, *n.*

suicide vest *n.* a jacket packed with explosives and armed with a detonator, designed to be worn by a suicide bomber and set off at the required location.

suit /sut/ *n.* **1.** a set of garments, vestments, or armour, intended to be worn together. **2.** the act or process of suing in a court of law; legal prosecution. **3.** a number of things forming a series or set. –*v.t.* **4.** to make appropriate, adapt, or accommodate, as one thing to another. **5.** to be appropriate or becoming to. –*v.i.* **6.** to be appropriate or suitable; accord. **7.** to be satisfactory, agreeable, or acceptable.

suitable /'sutəbəl/ *adj.* such as to suit; appropriate; fitting; becoming.

suitcase /'sutkeɪs/ *n.* a portable rectangular travelling bag, usually with stiffened frame, for carrying clothes, etc.

suite /swit/ *n.* **1.** a company of followers or attendants; a train or retinue. **2.** a number of things forming a series or set.

sulfur /'sʌlfə/ *n.* → **sulphur**.

sulk /sʌlk/ *v.i.* to hold aloof in a sullen, morose, ill-humoured, or offended mood.

sullen /'sʌlən/ *adj.* showing ill humour by a gloomy silence or reserve.

sully /'sʌli/ *v.t.* (**-lied**, **-lying**) to soil, stain, or tarnish.

sulphur /'sʌlfə/ *n. Chem.* a nonmetallic element which exists in several forms. *Symbol:* S Also, **sulfur**. –**sulphuric**, *adj.* –**sulphurous**, *adj.*

sultan /'sʌltən/ *n.* the sovereign of a Muslim country.

sultana /sʌl'tanə, səl-/ *n.* **1.** a wife of a sultan. **2.** a small, green, seedless grape. **3.** a raisin made from such a grape.

sultry /'sʌltri/ *adj.* (**-trier**, **-triest**) oppressively hot and close or moist; sweltering.

sum /sʌm/ *n.* **1.** the aggregate of two or more numbers, magnitudes, quantities, or particulars as determined by mathematical process. **2.** a quantity or amount, especially of money. **3.** a series of numbers or quantities to be added up. **4.** the total amount, or the whole. –*v.t.* (**summed**, **summing**) **5.** (oft. fol. by *up*) to combine into an aggregate or total. **6.** to bring into or contain in a brief and comprehensive statement. –*adj.* **7.** denoting or relating to a sum.

sum- occasional variant of **sub-** (by assimilation) before *m.*

summary /'sʌməri/ *n.* (*pl.* **-ries**) **1.** a brief and comprehensive presentation of facts or statements. –*adj.* **2.** brief and comprehensive; concise. **3.** direct and prompt; unceremoniously fast. **4.** (of legal proceedings, jurisdiction, etc.) conducted without or exempt from the various steps or delays of full proceedings. –**summarise**, **summarize**, *v.*

summer /'sʌmə/ *n.* **1.** the warmest season of the year, between spring and autumn. –*adj.* **2.** of, relating to, or characteristic of summer.

summit /'sʌmɪt/ *n.* **1.** the highest point or part. **2.** a meeting or conference between heads of state or the heads of any other organisation. –*adj.* **3.** (in diplomacy) between heads of state.

summon /'sʌmən/ *v.t.* **1.** to call as with authority. **2.** (oft. fol. by *up*) to call into action; rouse; call forth.

summons /'sʌmənz/ *n.* (*pl.* **-monses**) an authoritative command, message, or signal by which one is summoned.

sump /sʌmp/ *n.* a pit, well, or the like in which water or other liquid is collected.

sumptuous /'sʌmptʃuəs/ *adj.* luxuriously fine; splendid or superb.

sun /sʌn/ *n.* **1.** the star which is the central body of the solar system. **2.** sunshine. **3.** something likened to the sun in brightness, splendour, etc. **4.** to warm, dry, etc., in the sunshine. –*v.i.* (**sunned**, **sunning**) **5.** to expose oneself to the sun's rays. –**sunny**, *adj.*

sunbake /'sʌnbeɪk/ *v.i.* to expose one's body to the sun.

sunblock /'sʌnblɒk/ *n.* → **sunscreen** (def. 2).

sunburn /'sʌnbɜn/ *n.* superficial inflammation of the skin, caused by excessive or too sudden exposure to the sun's rays. –**sunburnt**, *adj.*

suncream /'sʌnkrim/ *n.* → **sunscreen** (def. 2).

sundae /'sʌndeɪ/ *n.* a portion of ice cream with fruit or other syrup poured over it.

sunder /'sʌndə/ *v.t.*, *v.i.* to separate; part; divide.

sundial /'sʌndaɪəl/ *n.* an instrument for indicating the time of day by the position of a shadow cast by the sun.

sundries /'sʌndriz/ *pl. n.* sundry things or items.

sundry /'sʌndri/ *adj.* **1.** various. –*phr.* **2.** all and sundry, everyone collectively and individually.

sunflower /'sʌnflaʊə/ *n.* a tall plant grown for its showy flowers, and for its seeds, valuable as a source of oil.

sung /sʌŋ/ *v.* past tense and past participle of **sing**.

sunglasses /'sʌnglasəz/ *pl. n.* spectacles having tinted, darkened, or polaroid lenses to protect the eyes from the glare of the sun.

sunk /sʌŋk/ *v.* a past tense and past participle of **sink**.

sunrise /'sʌnraɪz/ *n.* the rise or ascent of the sun above the horizon in the morning.

sunrise industry *n.* industry based on innovative local technology, especially electronic.

sunscreen /'sʌnskrin/ *n.* **1.** an awning, etc., which provides a screen against the sun. **2.** Also, **sunblock**, **suncream**, **blockout**. a lotion or cream which, when applied to the skin, protects it against damage from the rays of the sun.

sunset /'sʌnsɛt/ n. the setting or descent of the sun below the horizon in the evening.

sunshine /'sʌnʃaɪn/ n. **1.** the shining of the sun; the direct light of the sun. **2.** cheerfulness, happiness, or prosperity.

sunspot /'sʌnspɒt/ n. **1.** one of the relatively dark patches which appear periodically on the surface of the sun. **2.** a discolouration and roughening of part of the skin, usually as a result of exposure to the sun.

sunstroke /'sʌnstroʊk/ n. a condition caused by excessive exposure to the sun, marked by prostration.

suntan /'sʌntæn/ n. brownness of the skin induced by exposure to the sun.

sup¹ /sʌp/ v.i. (**supped, supping**) to eat the evening meal; take supper.

sup² /sʌp/ v.t. (**supped, supping**) to take (liquid food, or any liquid) into the mouth in small quantities, as from a spoon or a cup.

super /'supə/ n. Colloq. **1.** → **superannuation**. **2.** high-grade petrol. **3.** a superintendent. **4.** a supervisor. –adj. **5.** of a superior quality, grade, size, etc.

super- a prefix meaning 'superior to' or 'over-', applied variously.

superannuate /supər'ænjueɪt/ v.t. to allow to retire from service or office on a pension, on account of age or infirmity.

superannuation /ˌsupərænjuˈeɪʃən/ n. **1.** a pension or allowance to a superannuated person. **2.** a sum paid periodically as contribution to a superannuation fund.

superannuation fund n. a retirement fund to which an employee (and usually also his or her employer) contributes during the period of his or her employment, and which provides benefits during illness and after retirement. Also, **provident fund**.

superannuation guarantee n. the contribution made by an employer into an employee's superannuation fund.

superb /sə'pɜb, su-/ adj. admirably fine or excellent.

superbug /'supəbʌg/ n. a bacterium which has adapted so that it has become resistant to all existing antibiotics.

supercilious /supə'sɪliəs/ adj. haughtily disdainful or contemptuous.

supercomputer /'supəkəmpjutə/ n. the fastest type of computer, particularly suited to carrying out complex mathematical calculations very quickly, and used for specialised applications such as meteorological research. –**supercomputing**, n.

supercontinent /supə'kɒntənənt/ n. any great landmass that existed in the geological past and split into smaller landmasses.

superficial /supə'fɪʃəl/ adj. **1.** being at, on, or near the surface. **2.** concerned with or comprehending only what is on the surface or obvious. **3.** shallow; not profound or thorough. **4.** apparent, rather than real.

superfluous /su'pɜfluəs/ adj. being over and above what is sufficient or required.

superfood /'supəfud/ n. a nutrient-dense food of which only a small amount has to be

consumed in order to gain the health benefits thought to be associated.

supergene /'supədʒin/ n. a group of genes on a chromosome which are viewed collectively because they are inherited together and have related functions.

superimpose /supərɪm'poʊz/ v.t. **1.** to impose, place, or set on or over something else. **2.** (fol. by on or upon) to put or join as an addition.

superintend /supərɪn'tɛnd, suprɪn-/ v.t., v.i. to oversee and direct (work, processes, affairs, etc.). –**superintendent**, n.

superior /sə'pɪəriə, su-/ adj. **1.** higher in station, rank, degree, or grade. **2.** of higher grade or quality. **3.** greater in quantity or amount. **4.** showing a consciousness or feeling of being above others in such respects. –n. **5.** one superior to another or others. –**superiority**, n.

superlative /su'pɜlətɪv/ adj. surpassing all other or others.

supermarket /'supəmakət/ n. a large, usually self-service, retail store or market.

supernatural /supə'nætʃrəl, -'nætʃərəl/ adj. **1.** not explicable in terms of natural laws or phenomena. **2.** of or relating to supernatural beings, as ghosts, spirits, etc. **3.** abnormal; extraordinary; unprecedented. –n. **4.** supernatural forces, effects, and beings collectively.

supernova /supə'noʊvə/ n. (pl. **-vas** or **-vae** /-vi/) Astron. the sudden gravitational collapse of a giant star resulting in an explosion of stellar matter and energy into space and leaving a black hole or neutron star as a remnant.

superordinate /supər'ɔdənət/ adj. **1.** higher in rank, degree, etc. –n. **2.** someone who or something which is superordinate.

superpower /'supəpaʊə/ n. an extremely powerful and influential nation.

superscript /'supəskrɪpt/ adj. **1.** written above, as a mark over a letter or a correction of a word. –n. **2.** a superscript or superior letter, figure, etc.

supersede /supə'sid/ v.t. **1.** to set aside, as void, useless, or obsolete, now usually in favour of something mentioned. **2.** to succeed to the position, function, office, etc., of; supplant.

supersize /'supəsaɪz/ v.t. **1.** to increase in magnitude to an unusual degree: to supersize one's income. –adj. **2.** unusually large: supersize ice creams.

supersonic /supə'sɒnɪk/ adj. (of velocities) above the velocity of sound in the medium.

superstar /'supəsta/ n. a singer, actor, or show business personality who is very famous.

superstition /supə'stɪʃən/ n. **1.** a belief or notion entertained, regardless of reason or knowledge, of the ominous significance of a particular thing, circumstance, occurrence, proceeding, or the like. **2.** any blindly accepted belief or notion. –**superstitious**, adj.

superstructure /'supəstrʌktʃə/ n. all of an edifice above the basement or foundation.

supertax /'supətæks/ n. **1.** a tax in addition to a normal tax, as one upon income above a certain amount. **2.** → **surtax**.

supervise /'supəvaɪz/ v.t. to oversee (a process, work, workers, etc.) during execution or performance. –**supervision**, n. –**supervisor**, n.

supper /'sʌpə/ n. **1.** a light meal taken late at night. **2.** Chiefly Brit. and US the evening meal. **3.** any evening meal often one forming part of a social entertainment.

supplant /səˈplænt, -ˈplɑnt/ v.t. to take the place of (another).

supple /ˈsʌpəl/ adj. bending readily or easily.

supplement n. /ˈsʌpləmənt/ **1.** something added to complete a thing, supply a deficiency, or reinforce or extend a whole. –v.t. /ˈsʌpləmɛnt/ **2.** to complete, add to, or extend by a supplement; form a supplement or addition to. –**supplementary**, adj.

supplicate /ˈsʌplɪkeɪt/ v.i. to pray humbly; make humble and earnest entreaty or petition.

supply /səˈplaɪ/ v. (**-plied, -plying**) –v.t. **1.** to furnish (a person, establishment, place, etc.) with what is lacking or requisite. **2.** to furnish or provide (something wanting or requisite). –v.i. **3.** to fill the place of another, temporarily, or as a substitute. –n. (pl. **-plies**) **4.** the act of supplying, furnishing, providing, satisfying, etc. **5.** a quantity of something provided or on hand, as for use; a stock or store. **6.** Econ. **a.** the quantity of a commodity, etc., that is in the market and available for purchase, or that is available for purchase at a particular price. **b.** the willingness of sellers to offer various quantities of a good or service at specific prices. See **demand** (def. 5).

supply bill n. Parliamentary Procedure a bill to secure the money which the government needs to carry out its business.

supply-side economics n. management of the national economy which seeks to overcome a recession by stimulating the production of goods and the supply of services.

support /səˈpɔt/ v.t. **1.** to sustain or withstand (weight, etc.) without giving way. **2.** to undergo or endure, especially with patience or submission; tolerate. **3.** to give help or strength to. **4.** to sustain (a person, the mind, spirits, courage, etc.) under trial or affliction. **5.** to maintain (a person, family, establishment, institution, etc.) by supplying with things necessary to existence; provide for. **6.** to uphold (a person, cause, policy, etc.). **7.** to like (a particular sports team, etc.) and want them to win competitions: *he supports the local football team.* –n. **8.** the act of supporting. **9.** the state of being supported. **10.** maintenance, as of a person, family, etc., with necessities, means, or funds. **11.** a thing or a person that supports. –**supportive**, adj.

suppose /səˈpoʊz/ v.t. **1.** to assume (something), without reference to its being true or false, for the sake of argument or for the purpose of tracing the consequences. **2.** to assume as true, or believe, in the absence of positive knowledge or of evidence to the contrary. **3.** to think, with reference to mere opinion. **4.** (of facts, circumstances, etc.) to require logically; imply; presuppose. –v.i. **5.** to assume something; presume; think. –**supposition**, n.

supposed /səˈpoʊzd, səˈpoʊzəd/ adj. merely thought to be such.

suppository /səˈpɒzɪtri/ n. (pl. **-ries**) a medicinal substance inserted into the rectum or vagina to be dissolved therein.

suppress /səˈprɛs/ v.t. **1.** to keep in or repress. **2.** to quell; crush; vanquish or subdue.

suppressant /səˈprɛsənt/ n. something, especially a medication, which acts to suppress or reduce the intensity of a specific symptom: *a cough suppressant.*

suppurate /ˈsʌpjəreɪt/ v.i. to produce or discharge pus.

supra /ˈsuprə/ adv. above.

supra- a prefix meaning 'above', equivalent to **super-**, but emphasising situation or position.

supreme /suˈprim, sə-/ adj. **1.** highest in rank or authority. **2.** greatest, utmost, or extreme. –**supremacy**, n.

sur-¹ a prefix corresponding to **super-**.

sur-² occasional variant of **sub-** (by assimilation) before r.

surcharge n. /ˈsɜtʃadʒ/ **1.** an additional sum added to the usual cost, in restaurants, etc. –v.t. /ˈsɜtʃadʒ, sɜˈtʃadʒ/ (**-charged, -charging**) **2.** to subject to an additional or extra charge (for payment). **3.** to show an omission in (an account) of something that operates as a charge against the accounting party.

sure /ʃɔ/ adj. (**surer, surest**) **1.** free from apprehension or doubt as to the reliability, character, action, etc., of something. **2.** confident, as of something expected. **3.** worthy of confidence; reliable. **4.** firm or stable. **5.** unerring; never missing, slipping, etc.: *a sure aim.* **6.** inevitable. –adv. **7.** Colloq. surely, undoubtedly, or certainly.

surely /ˈʃɔli/ adv. **1.** in a sure manner. **2.** (used in emphatic utterances that are not necessarily sustained by fact): *Surely you can see that this rule is unfair?* **3.** inevitably or without fail.

surety /ˈʃɔrəti, ˈʃʊrəti/ n. security against loss or damage; security for the fulfilment of an obligation, the payment of a debt, etc.; a pledge, guarantee, or bond.

surf /sɜf/ n. **1.** the swell of the sea which breaks upon a shore or upon shoals. –v.i. **2.** to engage in surfing. –v.t. **3.** Computers to explore (an information network): *to surf the internet.*

surface /ˈsɜfəs/ n. **1.** the outer face, or outside, of a thing. **2.** extent or area of outer face; superficial area. –adj. **3.** of, on, or relating to the surface. **4.** superficial; external; apparent, rather than real. **5.** of, on, or relating to land and/or sea. –v. (**-faced, -facing**) –v.t. **6.** to finish as to surface; give a particular kind of surface to; make even or smooth. –v.i. **7.** to rise to the surface.

surfboard /ˈsɜfbɔd/ n. a long, narrow board used by surfers in riding waves towards the shore.

surfeit /ˈsɜfət/ n. **1.** excess; an excessive amount. **2.** general disgust caused by excess or satiety.

surfing /ˈsɜfɪŋ/ n. **1.** the sport in which one paddles a surfboard out over the surf, and then attempts to ride on or with a wave towards the shore. **2.** Also, **body-surfing**. the sport of swimming in the surf, and especially of riding waves, allowing oneself to be carried along by the force of the water.

surf lifesaving n. lifesaving which is appropriate for emergency situations occurring on surf beaches.

surf shirt n. **1.** a garment worn with a swimming costume to protect the upper body from sunburn, usually made from a light synthetic fabric and having short or long sleeves; rash shirt. **2.** a loose, short-sleeved, men's casual shirt, usually brightly patterned.

surf ski *n.* a small narrow craft propelled usually by one rider using a double ended paddle.

surge /sɜdʒ/ *n.* **1.** a strong forward or upward movement, rush, or sweep, like that of swelling or rolling waves. *–v.i.* (**surged, surging**) **2.** to rise or roll in waves, or like waves.

surgeon /ˈsɜdʒən/ *n.* **1.** a medical practitioner who has undertaken postgraduate studies to specialise in surgery. **2.** any medical practitioner qualified to practise surgery.

surgery /ˈsɜdʒəri/ *n.* (*pl.* **-ries**) **1.** the art, practice, or work of treating diseases, injuries, or deformities by manual operation or instrumental appliances. **2.** the consulting room of a medical practitioner, dentist, or the like. **–surgical**, *adj.*

surgical appliance /ˈsɜdʒɪkəl/ *n.* any device designed to be worn to support a damaged or deformed part of the body.

surly /ˈsɜli/ *adj.* (**-lier, -liest**) churlishly rude or ill-humoured.

surmise *v.t.* /sɜˈmaɪz/ **1.** to think or infer without certain or strong evidence. *–n.* /sɜˈmaɪz, ˈsɜmaɪz/ **2.** a matter of conjecture.

surmount /sɜˈmaʊnt/ *v.t.* **1.** to get over or across (barriers, obstacles, etc.). **2.** to be on top of or above.

surname /ˈsɜneɪm/ *n.* the name which a person has in common with the other members of his or her family, as distinguished from his or her given name; a family name.

surpass /sɜˈpas/ *v.t.* to go beyond in amount, extent, or degree.

surplus /ˈsɜpləs/ *n.* **1.** that which remains above what is used or needed. **2.** *Accounting* the excess of assets over liabilities accumulated throughout the existence of a business, excepting assets against which stock certificates have been issued.

surprise /səˈpraɪz/ *v.t.* **1.** to strike with a sudden feeling of wonder. **2.** to catch (a person, etc.) in the act of doing something; discover (a thing) suddenly. **3.** to assail, attack, or capture suddenly or without warning. *–n.* **4.** a sudden and unexpected event, action, or the like. **5.** the state or feeling of being surprised as by something unexpected. *–adj.* **6.** sudden and unexpected.

surreal /səˈril/ *adj.* of dreamlike experience, especially in art. **–surrealism**, *n.*

surrender /səˈrɛndə/ *v.t.* **1.** to yield (something) to the possession or power of another. *–v.i.* **2.** to give oneself up, as into the power of another or of an emotion, course of action, etc.; submit or yield. *–n.* **3.** the act of surrendering.

surreptitious /sʌrəpˈtɪʃəs/ *adj.* obtained, done, made, etc., by stealth.

surrogate *n.* /ˈsʌrəgət/ **1.** a substitute. *–v.t.* /ˈsʌrəgeɪt/ **2.** to put into the place of another as a successor, substitute, or deputy; substitute for another. **–surrogacy**, *n.*

surround /səˈraʊnd/ *v.t.* **1.** to enclose on all sides, or encompass. *–n.* **2.** a border which surrounds.

surroundings /səˈraʊndɪŋz/ *pl. n.* all that is around or near someone or something.

surtax /ˈsɜtæks/ *n.* **1.** one of a graded series of additional taxes levied on incomes exceeding a certain amount. **2.** an additional or extra tax on something already taxed.

surveillance /sɜˈveɪləns/ *n.* watch kept over a person, etc.

survey *v.t.* /sɜˈveɪ, ˈsɜveɪ/ **1.** to take a general or comprehensive view of. **2.** to view in detail, especially to inspect or examine formally or officially in order to ascertain condition, value, etc. **3.** to collect sample opinions, facts, figures or the like in order to estimate the total overall situation. *–n.* /ˈsɜveɪ/ (*pl.* **-veys**) **4.** the act of surveying; a comprehensive view. **5.** a formal or official examination. **6.** a partial poll or gathering of sample opinions, facts or figures in order to estimate the total or overall situation.

survive /səˈvaɪv/ *v.i.* **1.** to remain alive or in existence after the death of someone or after the cessation of something or the occurrence of some event; continue to live. *–v.t.* **2.** to outlive. **–survivor**, *n.* **–survival**, *n.*

susceptible /səˈsɛptəbəl/ *adj.* **1.** (fol. by *of* or *to*) capable of receiving, admitting, undergoing, or being affected by, something. **2.** impressionable. **–susceptibility**, *n.*

sushi /ˈsuʃi, ˈsuʃi/ *n.* (in Japanese cuisine) any of various preparations of boiled Japanese rice flavoured with a sweetened rice vinegar and combined with toppings or fillings of raw seafood, vegetables, nori, etc.

suspect *v.t.* /səˈspɛkt/ **1.** to imagine to be guilty, false, counterfeit, undesirable, defective, bad, etc., with insufficient proof or with no proof. **2.** to imagine to be the case or to be likely; surmise. *–v.i.* /səˈspɛkt/ **3.** to imagine something, especially something evil, wrong, or undesirable, to be the case; have suspicion. *–n.* /ˈsʌspɛkt/ **4.** one suspected; a person suspected of a crime, offence, or the like. *–adj.* /ˈsʌspɛkt/ **5.** suspected; open to suspicion.

suspend /səˈspɛnd/ *v.t.* **1.** to hang by attachment to something above. **2.** to defer or postpone. **3.** to cause to cease, or bring to a stop or stay, usually for a time. **4.** to debar, usually for a time, from the exercise of an office or function or the enjoyment of a privilege. *–v.i.* **5.** to come to a stop, usually temporarily; cease from operation for a time. **6.** to stop payment; be unable to meet financial obligations.

suspender /səˈspɛndə/ *n.* a strap with fastenings to support women's stockings.

suspense /səˈspɛns/ *n.* a state of mental uncertainty, as in awaiting a decision or outcome, usually with more or less apprehension or anxiety.

suspension /səˈspɛnʃən/ *n.* **1.** the act of suspending. **2.** the state of being suspended. **3.** stoppage of payment of debts, etc., through financial inability, or insolvency. **4.** something on or by which something else is hung. **5.** the arrangement of springs, etc., in a motor vehicle, which limits the effect of the jolting of the wheels, etc.

suspicion /səˈspɪʃən/ *n.* **1.** the act of suspecting; imagination of the existence of guilt, fault, falsity, defect, or the like, on slight evidence or without evidence. **2.** a vague notion of something. **3.** a slight trace. **–suspicious**, *adj.*

suss /sʌs/ *Colloq.* –*adj.* **1.** suspect; dubious; unreliable: *her story sounded pretty suss to me.* **2.** suspicious: *to be suss about the offer.* –*phr.* **3. suss out**, to investigate directly, especially in a situation involving a particular challenge or presenting probable difficulties.

sustain /sə'steɪn/ *v.t.* **1.** to hold or bear up from below. **2.** to bear (a burden, charge, etc.). **3.** to undergo, experience, or suffer (injury, loss, etc.). **4.** to keep up or keep going, as an action or process. **5.** to supply with food and drink, or the necessities of life, as persons. **6.** to support by aid or countenance, as a person or cause.

sustainable /sə'steɪnəbəl/ *adj.* **1.** able to be sustained. **2.** designed or developed to have the capacity to continue operating perpetually, by avoiding adverse effects on the natural environment and depletion of natural resources. –**sustainability**, *n.* –**sustainably**, *adv.*

sustainable development *n.* economic development designed to meet present needs while also taking into account future costs, including costs to the environment and depletion of natural resources.

sustenance /'sʌstənəns/ *n.* means of sustaining life; nourishment.

suture /'sutʃə/ *n.* **1.** a sewing together, or a joining as by sewing. –*v.t.* **2.** to unite by or as by a suture.

svelte /svɛlt, sfɛlt/ *adj.* slender, especially gracefully slender in figure; lithe.

swab /swɒb/ *n.* **1.** a piece of sponge, cloth, or cottonwool, used for cleaning parts of the body, such as the mouth, or applying a medicine, etc. –*v.t.* (**swabbed**, **swabbing**) **2.** to clean or wipe (a wound, etc.) with a swab.

swaddle /'swɒdl/ *v.t.* to bind (an infant, especially a newborn infant) with long, narrow strips of cloth.

swag /swæg/ *n.* **1.** a bundle or roll containing the belongings of a traveller through the bush, a miner, etc. **2.** *Colloq.* an unspecified but large number or quantity.

swagger /'swægə/ *v.i.* to walk or strut with a defiant or insolent air.

swagman /'swægmən/ *n.* (formerly) a man who travelled the country on foot, living on occasional jobs or gifts.

swallow[1] /'swɒloʊ/ *v.t.* **1.** to take into the stomach through the throat or gullet (oesophagus), as food, drink, or other substances. **2.** to take in so as to envelop. **3.** *Colloq.* to accept without question or suspicion. –*v.i.* **4.** to perform the act of swallowing. –*n.* **5.** the act of swallowing.

swallow[2] /'swɒloʊ/ *n.* a small, migratory, long-winged bird notable for its swift, graceful flight.

swam /swæm/ *v.* past tense of **swim**.

swamp /swɒmp/ *n.* **1.** a piece or tract of wet, spongy land. –*v.t.* **2.** to flood or drench with water or the like.

swan /swɒn/ *n.* a large, stately swimming bird with a long, slender neck.

swank /swæŋk/ *n. Colloq.* dashing smartness, as in bearing, appearance, etc.; style. –**swanky**, *adj.*

swap /swɒp/ *v.* (**swapped**, **swapping**) –*v.t.* **1.** to exchange, barter, or trade, as one thing for another. –*v.i.* **2.** to make an exchange. –*n.* **3.** an exchange. Also, **swop**.

swarm[1] /swɔm/ *n.* **1.** a body of bees settled together, as in a hive. **2.** a great number of things or persons, especially in motion. –*v.i.* **3.** to move about, along, forth, etc., in great numbers, as things or persons. **4.** (fol. by *with*) (of a place) to be thronged or overrun; abound or teem.

swarm[2] /swɔm/ *v.i., v.t.* (usu. fol. by *up*) to climb (a tree, pole, or the like) by clasping it with the hands or arms and legs and drawing oneself up; shin.

swarthy /'swɔði/ *adj.* (**-thier**, **-thiest**) dark-coloured, now especially as the skin, complexion, etc., of a person.

swashbuckler /'swɒʃbʌklə/ *n.* a swaggering swordsman or bully. Also, **swasher**.

swat /swɒt/ *v.t.* (**swatted**, **swatting**) *Colloq.* to hit with a smart or violent blow.

swathe /sweɪð/ *v.t.* (**swathed**, **swathing**) **1.** to wrap, bind, or swaddle with bands of some material. –*n.* **2.** a band of linen or the like in which something is wrapped; a wrapping; a bandage.

sway /sweɪ/ *v.i.* **1.** to move to and fro, as something fixed at one end or resting on a support; swing to and fro. **2.** to fluctuate or vacillate, as in opinion. **3.** to cause to sway. **4.** to cause (the mind, etc., or the person) to incline or turn in a specified way. –*n.* **5.** rule; dominion. **6.** dominating power or influence.

swear /sweə/ *v.* (**swore**, **sworn**, **swearing**) –*v.i.* **1.** to make a solemn declaration with an appeal to God or some superhuman being in confirmation of what is declared. **2.** to engage or promise on oath or in a solemn manner. **3.** to use profane or taboo oaths or language. –*v.t.* **4.** to declare or affirm by swearing by a deity, some sacred object, etc. **5.** to affirm or say with solemn earnestness or great emphasis. **6.** to promise or undertake on oath or in a solemn manner; vow. –*phr.* **7. swear in**, to admit to office or service by administering an oath.

sweat /swɛt/ *v.* (**sweat** *or* **sweated**, **sweating**) –*v.i.* **1.** to excrete watery fluid through the pores of the skin, as from heat, exertion, etc.; perspire, especially freely or profusely. **2.** *Colloq.* to exert oneself strenuously; work hard. –*v.t.* **3.** to exude (moisture, etc.) in drops or small particles. **4.** (oft. fol. by *out* or *off*) to send forth or get rid of with or like perspiration. –*n.* **5.** the process of sweating or perspiring. **6.** the secretions of sweat glands; the product of sweating. –*phr.* **7. sweat it out**, *Colloq.* to hold out; endure until the end.

sweated /'swɛtəd/ *adj.* underpaid and overworked.

sweater /'swɛtə/ *n.* a knitted jumper, usually of wool.

sweatshirt /'swɛtʃɜt/ *n.* a loose pullover.

sweep /swip/ *v.* (**swept**, **sweeping**) –*v.t.* **1.** to move, drive, or bring, by passing a broom, brush, or the like over the surface occupied, or as the broom or other object does. **2.** to pass or draw (something) over a surface, or about, along, etc., with a steady, continuous stroke or movement. **3.** to clear or clean (a floor, room, chimney, path, etc.) of dirt, litter, etc., by means of a broom or the like. –*v.i.* **4.** to sweep a floor, room, etc., as with a broom, or as a broom does. **5.** (fol. by *down*, *over*, etc.) to move steadily and strongly or swiftly. **6.** to walk in long, trailing garments. **7.** to extend in a continuous or curving stretch, as a road, a shore, fields, etc. –*n.* **8.** the act of sweeping, especially a moving, removing, clearing, etc., by or as by the use of a broom. **9.** a swinging or curving movement or stroke, as of the arm or a weapon, oar, etc. **10.** a continuous extent or stretch. **11.** the motion of the spot across the screen of a cathode-ray tube.

sweepstake /'swipsteık/ *n.* a method of gambling, as on the outcome of a horserace, in which each participant contributes a stake, usually by buying a numbered ticket entitling the winner to draw the name of a competitor, the winnings being provided from the stake money. Also, **sweepstakes**.

sweet /swit/ *adj.* **1.** pleasing to the taste, especially having the pleasant taste or flavour characteristic of sugar, honey, etc. **2.** pleasing or agreeable; yielding pleasure or enjoyment; delightful. **3.** pleasant in disposition or manners; amiable; kind or gracious as a person, action, etc. **4.** dear; beloved; precious. –*adv.* **5.** in a sweet manner; sweetly. –*n.* **6.** that which is sweet. **7.** Also, **sweetie**. any of various small confections made wholly or partly from sugar. **8.** (*oft. pl.*) any sweet dish, as a pudding, tart, etc., served at the end of a meal. **9.** a beloved person; darling; sweetheart.

sweetbread /'switbred/ *n.* **1.** the pancreas of an animal, especially a calf or a lamb, used for food. **2.** the thymus gland likewise so used.

sweet corn *n.* the unripe and tender ears of maize, especially when used as a table vegetable and when the kernels have been removed from the cob.

sweetheart /'swithat/ *n.* a beloved person (often used in affectionate address).

sweetmeat /'switmit/ *n.* a sweet delicacy.

sweet potato *n.* a plant cultivated for its edible root.

sweet tooth *n.* *Colloq.* a strong liking for sweets, sweet dishes, etc.

swell /swɛl/ *v.i.* (**swelled**, **swollen** *or* **swelled**, **swelling**) **1.** to grow in bulk, as by absorption of moisture, by inflation, by addition of material in the process of growth, or the like. **2.** to rise in waves, as the sea. **3.** to grow in amount, degree, force, or the like. **4.** to increase in amount, degree, force, etc. **5.** to puff up with pride. –*n.* **6.** increase in bulk. **7.** a part that bulges out, or a protuberant part. **8.** a wave, especially when long and unbroken, or such waves collectively. **9.** a gradually rising elevation of the land. **10.** increase in amount, degree, force, etc. **11.** a person of high social standing. –*adj.* *Colloq.* **12.** (of things) stylish; elegant; grand. **13.** first-rate; excellent.

swelling /'swɛlıŋ/ *n.* a swollen part; a protuberance or prominence.

swelter /'swɛltə/ *v.i.* to suffer or languish with oppressive heat.

swept /swɛpt/ *v.* past tense and past participle of **sweep**.

swerve /swɜv/ *v.i.* to turn aside abruptly in movement or direction.

swift /swıft/ *adj.* **1.** moving with great speed or velocity; fleet; rapid. –*n.* **2.** any of several rapidly flying birds.

swill /swıl/ *n.* **1.** liquid or partly liquid food for animals, especially kitchen refuse given to pigs. **2.** any liquid matter; slops. –*v.t.* **3.** to wash or cleanse by flooding with water.

swim /swım/ *v.* (**swam**, **swum**, **swimming**) –*v.i.* **1.** to move on or in water or other liquid in any way, especially on the surface. **2.** to be immersed or steeped in, or overflowed or flooded with, a liquid. **3.** to be dizzy or giddy; have a whirling sensation; seem to whirl. –*v.t.* **4.** to perform (a particular stroke) in swimming. –*phr.* **5. in the swim**, actively engaged in current affairs, social activities, etc.

swimmers /'swıməz/ *pl. n. Colloq.* → **swimming costume**.

swimming costume *n.* a garment or garments worn for swimming. Also, **bathers**, **swimmers**, **swimsuit**, **togs**, **cossie**, **cozzie**.

swimmingly /'swımıŋli/ *adv.* without difficulty; with great success.

swimsuit /'swımsut/ *n.* → **swimming costume**.

swindle /'swındl/ *v.t.* **1.** to cheat (a person) out of money, etc. –*n.* **2.** a fraudulent transaction or scheme.

swine /swaın/ *n.* (*pl.* **swine**) **1.** the domestic pig. **2.** a contemptible person.

swine flu *n.* → **human swine influenza**.

swing /swıŋ/ *v.* (**swung**, **swinging**) –*v.t.* **1.** to cause to move to and fro, sway, or oscillate, as something suspended from above. **2.** to cause to move in alternate directions, or in either direction, about a fixed point or line of support, as a door on its hinges. **3.** to suspend so as to hang freely, as a hammock or a door. **4.** to sway, influence, or manage as desired. –*v.i.* **5.** to move to and fro, as something suspended from above, as a pendulum. **6.** to move to and fro on a swing, as for amusement. **7.** to move in alternate directions, as a gate on its hinges. **8.** to move in a curve as if about a central point, as around a corner. **9.** to change or shift one's attention, opinion, interest, etc.; fluctuate. **10.** to aim at or hit something with a sweeping movement of the arm. **11.** *Colloq.* to be lively or modern. –*n.* **12.** the act or the manner of swinging; movement in alternate directions, or in a particular direction. **13.** the amount of such movement. **14.** active operation. **15.** a seat suspended from above as in a loop of rope or between ropes or rods, in which one may sit and swing to and fro for amusement. **16.** Also, **swing music**. a smooth, orchestral type of jazz popular in the 1930s, often arranged for big bands.

swipe /swaıp/ *n.* **1.** *Colloq.* a sweeping stroke; a stroke with full swing of the arms, as in cricket or golf. –*v.t.* **2.** *Colloq.* to strike with a sweeping blow. **3.** *Colloq.* to steal. **4.** to move (a card with a magnetic strip) through the slot of an electronic device. –*v.i.* **5.** *Colloq.* to make a sweeping stroke.

swirl /swɜl/ *v.i.* to move about or along with a whirling motion.

swish /swıʃ/ *v.i.* **1.** to move with or make a sibilant sound. –*n.* **2.** a swishing movement or sound. *–adj.* Also, **swishy**. **3.** *Colloq.* smart; stylish; glamorous.

switch /swɪtʃ/ *n.* **1.** a slender, flexible shoot, rod, etc., used especially in whipping, beating, etc. **2.** *Elect.* a device for turning on or off or directing an electric current, or making or breaking a circuit. **3.** *Colloq.* → **switchboard**. *–v.t.* **4.** to whip or beat with a switch or the like; lash. **5.** to move, swing, or whisk (a cane, a fishing line, etc.) like a switch or with a swift, lashing stroke. **6.** to exchange; shift. *–v.i.* **7.** to strike with or as with a switch. **8.** to change direction or course; turn, shift, or change. *–phr.* **9. switch off**, to cause an electric current or appliance to stop. **10. switch on**, to cause (an electric current) to flow or (an electric appliance) to operate.

switchboard /'swɪtʃbɔd/ *n.* an arrangement of switches, plugs, and jacks mounted on a board or frame enabling an operator to make temporary connections between telephone users.

swivel /'swɪvəl/ *n.* a fastening device which allows the thing fastened to turn round freely upon it.

swollen /'swoʊlən/ *v.* past participle of **swell**.

swoon /swun/ *v.i.* to faint; lose consciousness.

swoop /swup/ *v.i.* **1.** to sweep through the air, as a bird or a bat, especially down upon prey. **2.** (oft. fol. by *down* or *on* or *upon*) to come down in a sudden swift attack. *–v.t.* **3.** (oft. fol. by *up*) to take, lift, or remove, with, or as with, a sweeping motion. *–n.* **4.** the act of swooping; a sudden, swift descent. *–phr.* **5. at** (or **in**) **one fell swoop**, in a single action or smoothly coordinated series of actions.

sword /sɔd/ *n.* a weapon with a long, straight or slightly curved blade, sharp-edged on one side or both sides, with one end pointed and the other fixed in a hilt or handle.

swordfish /'sɔdfɪʃ/ *n.* (pl. **-fish** or **-fishes**) a large marine game fish with the upper jaw elongated into a swordlike weapon.

swore /swɔ/ *v.* past tense of **swear**.

sworn /swɔn/ *v.* **1.** past participle of **swear**. *–adj.* **2.** bound by or as by an oath.

swot /swɒt/ *Colloq. –v.i.* (**swotted**, **swotting**) **1.** to study hard. *–n.* **2.** someone who studies hard. Also, **swat**.

swum /swʌm/ *v.* past participle of **swim**.

swung /swʌŋ/ *v.* past tense and past participle of **swing**.

sy- variant of **syn-**.

sycamore /'sɪkəmɔ/ *n.* **1.** (in Europe) a maple grown as a shady ornamental tree and for its wood. **2.** a tree of western Asia, related to the common fig and bearing an edible fruit.

sycophant /'sɪkəfænt, -fənt, 'saɪ-/ *n.* a self-seeking flatterer; a fawning, servile parasite.

syl- variant of **syn-** (by assimilation) before *l*.

syllable /'sɪləbəl/ *n.* **1.** *Phonetics* a segment of speech uttered with a single impulse of air pressure from the lungs. **2.** the least portion or amount of speech or writing. **–syllabic**, *adj.*

syllabus /'sɪləbəs/ *n.* (pl. **-buses** or **-bi** /-baɪ/) an outline or summary of a course of studies, lectures, etc.

sym- variant of **syn-**, before *b*, *p*, and *m*, as in *sympathy*.

symbiosis /sɪmbaɪ'oʊsəs, -bi-/ *n.* *Biol.* the living together of two species of organisms. **–symbiotic** /sɪmbaɪ'ɒtɪk/, *adj.*

symbol /'sɪmbəl/ *n.* something used or regarded as standing for or representing something else; an emblem, token, or sign. **–symbolic**, *adj.*

symbolise /'sɪmbəlaɪz/ *v.t.* **1.** to be a symbol of; stand for, or represent, as a symbol does. **2.** to represent by a symbol or symbols. Also, **symbolize**.

symmetry /'sɪmətri/ *n.* the correspondence, in size, form, and arrangement, of parts on opposite sides of a plane, line, or point. **–symmetrical**, *adj.*

sympathetic /sɪmpə'θɛtɪk/ *adj.* **1.** characterised by, proceeding from, exhibiting, or feeling sympathy; sympathising; compassionate. **2.** (oft. fol. by *to* or *towards*) looking with favour or liking upon.

sympathetic nervous system *n.* *Anat.*, *Physiol.* that portion of the autonomic nervous system which is made up of a system of nerves and ganglia which arise from the thoracic and lumbar regions of the spinal cord, and which supply the walls of the vascular system and the various viscera and glands where they function in opposition to the parasympathetic nervous system, as in accelerating heartbeat, dilating the pupil of the eye, etc.

sympathise /'sɪmpəθaɪz/ *v.i.* **1.** (oft. fol. by *with*) to feel a compassionate sympathy, as for suffering or trouble. **2.** to agree, correspond, or accord. Also, **sympathize**.

sympathy /'sɪmpəθi/ *n.* **1.** the fact or the power of entering into the feelings of another. **2.** community of or agreement in feeling. **3.** agreement, consonance, or accord. **4.** *Physiol.* the relation between parts or organs whereby a condition, affection, or disorder of one part induces some effect in another.

symphony /'sɪmfəni/ *n.* (pl. **-nies**) *Music* an elaborate instrumental composition written for an orchestra.

symposium /sɪm'poʊziəm/ *n.* (pl. **-siums** or **-sia** /-ziə/) a meeting or conference for discussion of some subject.

symptom /'sɪmptəm/ *n.* a sign or indication of something.

symptomatic /sɪmptə'mætɪk/ *adj.* (oft. fol. by *of*) of the nature of or constituting a symptom; indicative.

syn- a prefix having the same function as **co-** (def. 1), as in *synthesis*, *synoptic*. Also, **sy-**, **syl-**, **sym-**, **sys-**.

synagogue /'sɪnəgɒg/ *n.* a Jewish house of worship.

synapse /'saɪnæps/ *n.* *Biol.* the region of contact between the processes of two or more nerve cells, across which an impulse passes.

synchronise /'sɪŋkrənaɪz/ *v.i.* **1.** to occur at the same time, or coincide or agree in time. *–v.t.* **2.** to cause to synchronise. Also, **synchronize**. **–synchronisation**, *n.*

syncopate /'sɪŋkəpeɪt/ *v.t.* to place (accents) on musical beats which are normally unaccented. **–syncopation**, *n.*

syndicate *n.* /'sɪndɪkət, 'sɪndəkət/ **1.** a combination of persons, as business associates, commercial firms, etc., formed for the purpose of carrying out some project, especially one requiring large resources of capital. –v.t. /'sɪndəkeɪt/ **2.** to combine into a syndicate. **3.** *Journalism* to publish simultaneously, or supply for simultaneous publication, in a number of newspapers or other periodicals in different places.

syndrome /'sɪndroʊm/ n. the pattern of symptoms in a disease or the like; a number of characteristic symptoms occurring together.

synergy /'sɪnədʒi/ n. (pl. **-gies**) combined action. –**synergetic**, adj.

synonym /'sɪnənɪm/ n. a word having the same, or nearly the same, meaning as another in the language, as *joyful, elated, glad.*

synopsis /sə'nɒpsəs/ n. (pl. **-opses** /-ɒpsiz/) a brief or condensed statement giving a general view of some subject.

synoptic chart /sə'nɒptɪk/ n. a chart showing distribution of meteorological conditions over a region at a given moment.

syntax /'sɪntæks/ n. *Gram.* the patterns of formation of sentences and phrases from words in a particular language.

synthesis /'sɪnθəsəs/ n. (pl. **-theses** /-θəsiz/) **1.** the combination of parts or elements, as material substances or objects of thought, into a complex whole (opposed to *analysis*). **2.** a complex whole made up of parts or elements combined.

synthesise /'sɪnθəsaɪz/ v.t. **1.** to make up by combining parts or elements. **2.** to combine into a complex whole. **3.** *Chem.* to manufacture (a complex product, especially a product resembling one of natural origin) by combining simple substances. Also, **synthesize**.

synthesiser /'sɪnθəsaɪzə/ n. a machine which creates speech or music by combining the controlled outputs of a number of electronic circuits. Also, **synthesizer**.

synthetic /sɪn'θetɪk/ adj. **1.** of, relating to, or involving synthesis (opposed to *analytic*). **2.** (of materials, etc.) made by chemical process, as opposed to being of natural origin.

synthetic drug n. **1.** a drug which is made in a laboratory rather than extracted from a natural source. **2.** such a drug which mimics

the effects of an illegal drug such as cocaine or marijuana.

syphilis /'sɪfələs/ n. a chronic, infectious venereal disease contracted by contact or congenitally.

syphon /'saɪfən/ n., v.i., v.t. → **siphon**.

syringe /sə'rɪndʒ, 'sɪrɪndʒ/ n. *Med.* a small tube used for injecting fluids into the body, etc.

syrup /'sɪrəp/ n. any of various sweet, more or less viscid liquids.

sys- variant of **syn-**, before *s*.

system /'sɪstəm/ n. **1.** an assemblage or combination of things or parts forming a complex or unitary whole. **2.** a coordinated body of methods, or a complex scheme or plan of procedure. **3.** *Biol.* the entire human or animal body. **4.** a method or scheme of classification. **5.** (*also pl.*) *Computers* (in data-processing) the interrelation of personnel, procedure, hardware, and software, which combine to accomplish a set of specific functions. **6. the system**, society at large or an organisation within it.

system administrator n. a person responsible for maintaining a multi-user computer system.

systematic /sɪstə'mætɪk/ adj. having, showing, or involving a system, method, or plan.

systematise /'sɪstəmətaɪz/ v.t. to arrange in or according to a system; reduce to a system; make systematic. Also, **systematize**.

systemic /sɪs'temɪk, sɪs'timɪk/ adj. relating to or affecting the whole bodily system.

system operator n. a person who assists in the maintenance of a computer system.

systems analysis n. the analysis of an activity or project, usually with the aid of a computer, to determine its aims, methods and effectiveness. –**systems analyst**, n.

systems engineer n. an engineer who is concerned with the design of systems in the light of systems analysis and information theory.

systole /'sɪstəli/ n. *Physiol.* the normal rhythmical contraction of the heart, especially that of the ventricles, which drives the blood into the aorta and the pulmonary artery. Compare **diastole**. –**systolic** /sɪs'tɒlɪk/, adj.

T, t

T, t /ti/ *n.* the 20th letter of the English alphabet.

-t a suffix forming the past tense or past participle of certain verbs; an equivalent of **-ed**. See **-ed¹**, **-ed²**.

tab¹ /tæb/ *n.* **1.** a small flap, strap, loop, or similar appendage, as on a garment, etc. **2.** a stiffened projection from a file, document, or the like, for ready identification; tag. **3.** a graphic representation of this on a computer screen, which, when clicked, opens the document to which it is linked.

tab² /tæb/ *n.* a key on a typewriter or computer keyboard which is depressed to set the point at which the line or section of the line of type begins.

tabby /'tæbi/ *n.* (*pl.* **-bies**) a cat with a striped or brindled coat.

tabernacle /'tæbənækəl/ *n.* **1.** the tent used by the Jews as a portable sanctuary before their final settlement in Palestine. **2.** any place of worship, especially one designed for a large congregation.

table /'teɪbəl/ *n.* **1.** an article of furniture consisting of a flat top resting on legs or on a pillar. **2.** a flat or plane surface; a level area. **3.** an arrangement of words, numbers, or signs, or combinations of them, as the multiplication tables, to exhibit a set of facts or relations in a definite, compact, and comprehensive form. *–v.t.* (**-bled**, **-bling**) **4.** to enter in or form into a table or list. **5.** to place or lay on a table.

tableau /'tæbloʊ/ *n.* (*pl.* **-leaux** /-loʊz, -loʊ/ *or* **-leaus**) a picturesque grouping of persons or objects; a striking scene.

tableland /'teɪbəlænd/ *n.* an elevated and generally level region.

tablespoon /'teɪbəlspun/ *n.* a large spoon.

tablet /'tæblət/ *n.* **1.** a small, flat or flattish, cake or piece of some solid or solidified substance, as a drug, chemical or the like. **2.** *US* a writing pad. **3.** a small, flat slab or surface, especially one bearing or intended to bear an inscription, carving, or the like. **4.** Also, **tablet computer**. *Computers* a small, portable computer which has one side as a touch screen, and an on-screen virtual keyboard.

table tennis *n.* a miniature tennis game usually played indoors on a table, with small bats and a hollow celluloid or plastic ball; ping-pong.

tabloid /'tæblɔɪd/ *n.* **1.** a newspaper, about one half the page size of a broadsheet, emphasising pictures and concise writing, and often characterised by a sensationalised editorial approach. *–adj.* **2.** having mass appeal due to being sensationalist in nature: *the tabloid press; tabloid television.*

taboo /təˈbu, tæ-/ *adj.* **1.** forbidden to general use; placed under a prohibition or ban. *–n.* (*pl.* **-boos**) **2.** a prohibition or interdiction of anything; exclusion from use or practice. *–v.t.* (**-booed**, **-booing**) **3.** to put under a taboo; prohibit or forbid.

tabouli /təˈbuli/ *n.* a salad of cracked wheat, chopped parsley, mint, tomato, oil, lemon juice, etc. Also, **tabouleh**, **tabbouli**.

tabular /'tæbjələ/ *adj.* **1.** relating to or of the nature of a table or tabulated arrangement. **2.** having the form of a table, tablet, or tablature.

tabulate /'tæbjəleɪt/ *v.t.* to put or form into a table, scheme, or synopsis; formulate tabularly.

tacit /'tæsət/ *adj.* **1.** silent; saying nothing. **2.** not openly expressed, but implied.

taciturn /'tæsətɜn/ *adj.* inclined to silence, or reserved in speech.

tack /tæk/ *n.* **1.** a short, sharp-pointed nail or pin. **2.** a long temporary stitch. **3.** *Naut.* **a.** the direction or course of a ship in relation to the position of its sails. **b.** a course obliquely against the wind. **4.** a course of action or conduct, especially one differing from some preceding or other course. **5.** the equipment collectively which pertains to the saddling and harnessing of horses. *–v.t.* **6.** to fasten by a tack or tacks. **7.** (usu. fol. by *on* or *on to*) to append or annex. *–v.i.* **8.** *Naut.* to change the course of a ship by bringing its head into the wind and then causing it to fall off on the other side.

tackle /'tækəl/ *n.* **1.** equipment, apparatus, or gear, especially for fishing. **2.** a mechanism or apparatus, as a rope and block or a combination of ropes and blocks, for hoisting, lowering, and shifting objects or materials. **3.** an act of tackling, as in football. *–v.t.* (**-led**, **-ling**) **4.** to undertake to deal with, master, solve, etc. **5.** *Rugby Football, etc.* to seize and pull down (an opponent having the ball).

tacky /'tæki/ *adj.* (**-kier**, **-kiest**) *Colloq.* **1.** shabby; dowdy. **2.** superficially attractive but lacking quality or craftsmanship. **3.** in bad taste; vulgar. *–***tackiness**, *n.*

taco /'takoʊ, 'tækoʊ/ *n.* a dish of Mexican origin consisting of a flat piece of crisp corn bread folded around a spicy savoury filling.

tact /tækt/ *n.* a keen sense of what to say or do to avoid giving offence.

tactic /'tæktɪk/ *n.* a plan or procedure for achieving a desired end. *–***tactical**, *adj.*

tactile /'tæktaɪl/ *adj.* of or relating to the organs or sense of touch.

tad /tæd/ *n.* a small amount.

tadpole /'tædpoʊl/ *n.* the aquatic larva or immature form of frogs, toads, etc.

tae bo /taɪ 'boʊ/ *n.* an aerobic exercise regime using martial arts sequences at a rapid pace.

taekwondo /taɪkwɒn'doʊ/ *n.* a Korean martial art, similar to karate. Also, **tae kwon do**.

taffeta /'tæfətə/ *n.* a shiny silk or rayon fabric of plain weave.

tag¹ /tæg/ *n.* **1.** a piece or strip of strong paper, leather, or the like, for attaching by one end to something as a mark or label. **2.** any small hanging or loosely attached part or piece; tatter. **3.** *Internet* a caption to a digital photograph viewed online. **4.** the identifying mark or signature of a graffitist; tag-name. *–v.* (**tagged**, **tagging**) *–v.t.* **5.** to append as a tag to something else. **6.** to identify (a digital picture viewed online) by a caption. *–v.i.* **7.** *Colloq.* (usu. fol. by *along*) to follow closely; go along or about as a follower.

tag² /tæg/ n. a game in which one child chases others so as to touch another one who then becomes the pursuer.

tagine /ta'ʒin/ n. (in Moroccan cookery) a slow-cooked stew, usually featuring meat or poultry with vegetables and spices, traditionally cooked in a shallow earthenware dish with a tall, cone-shaped lid; often served with couscous. Also, **tajine**.

tai chi /taɪ 'tʃi/ n. a form of stylised exercises based on Chinese martial arts which emphasises the smooth transition of one movement into another while retaining balance.

tail /teɪl/ n. 1. the hindmost part of an animal especially when forming a distinct flexible appendage to the trunk. 2. something resembling or suggesting this in shape or position. 3. the hinder, bottom, or concluding part of anything; the rear. 4. (pl.) Colloq. the reverse of a coin. 5. Colloq. the buttocks. 6. Colloq. a person who follows another, especially someone who is employed to do so in order to observe or hinder escape. –v.t. 7. to dock the tail of. 8. Colloq. to follow in order to hinder escape or to observe.

tailor /'teɪlə/ n. 1. someone whose business it is to make or mend outer garments, especially for men. 2. Also, **tailer, taylor**. an Australian sport fish.

tailwind /'teɪlwɪnd/ n. a favourable wind blowing from behind an aircraft or vessel, etc., thus increasing its speed.

taint /teɪnt/ n. 1. a trace of infection, contamination, or the like. –v.t. 2. to infect, contaminate, or corrupt. 3. to sully or tarnish.

taipan /'taɪpæn/ n. a long-fanged, highly venomous snake.

take /teɪk/ v. (**took, taken, taking**) –v.t. 1. to get into one's hands, possession, control, etc. 2. to seize, catch, or capture. 3. to select; pick out from a number. 4. to obtain by making payment. 5. (fol. by away, etc.) to carry off or remove. 6. to subtract or deduct. 7. to carry or convey. 8. to have recourse to (a vehicle, etc.) as a means of progression or travel. 9. to conduct or lead. 10. to absorb or become impregnated with (a colour, etc.). 11. to proceed to deal with in some manner. 12. to proceed to occupy. 13. to occupy, use up, or consume (space, material, time, etc.). 14. to attract and hold. 15. to write down (notes, a copy, etc.). 16. to make (a reproduction, picture, or photograph of something). 17. to make or perform (a measurement, observation, etc.). 18. to assume the obligation of (a vow, pledge, etc.); perform or discharge (a part, service, etc.). 19. to assume or adopt as one's own (a part or side in a contest, etc.); assume or appropriate as if by right. 20. to accept and comply with (advice, etc.). 21. Gram. to have by usage, either as part of itself or with it in construction (a particular form, accent, etc., or a case, mode, etc.), as a word or the like. –v.i. 22. to catch or engage, as a mechanical device. 23. to strike root, or begin to grow, as a plant. 24. to adhere, as ink, etc. 25. to have the intended result or affect as a medicine, inoculation, etc. 26. to become (sick or ill). –n. 27. an act or instance of taking. 28. that which is taken. 29. the quantity of fish, etc. taken at one time. 30. Film, etc. a scene or a portion of

a scene photographed at one time without any interruption or break. 31. Colloq. a cheat; swindle. –phr. 32. **take off, a.** to remove, as of clothing; to undress. **b.** to leave the ground, as an aeroplane. **c.** Colloq. to imitate or mimic. 33. **take place, to** happen; occur.

takeover /'teɪkoʊvə/ n. acquisition of control, especially of a business company, by the purchase of the majority of its shares.

takings /'teɪkɪŋz/ pl. n. quantity or amount of money received, as from sales in a shop.

talc /tælk/ n. a soft greenish grey mineral used in making lubricants, talcum powder, electrical insulation, etc. Also, **talcum** /'tælkəm/.

talcum powder n. powdered talc, usually perfumed for toilet use.

tale /teɪl/ n. a narrative purporting to relate the facts about some real or imaginary event.

talent /'tælənt/ n. a special natural ability or aptitude.

talisman /'tæləzmən/ n. (pl. **-mans**) any amulet or charm.

talk /tɔk/ v.i. 1. to speak or converse; perform the act of speaking. 2. to make information known by means of spoken words. –v.t. 3. to express in words: to talk sense. 4. to discuss: to talk politics. –n. 5. the act of talking; speech; conversation, especially of a familiar or informal kind. 6. a lecture or informal speech. 7. report or rumour; gossip.

talkative /'tɔkətɪv/ adj. liking to talk a lot.

tall /tɔl/ adj. 1. of more than average height. 2. having a particular height: a man 1.9 metres tall.

tallow /'tæloʊ/ n. the fatty tissue or suet of animals.

tally /'tæli/ n. (pl. **-lies**) 1. anything on which a score or account is kept. –v.t. (**-lied, -lying**) 2. to count or reckon up.

talon /'tælən/ n. a claw, especially of a bird of prey.

tambourine /tæmbə'rin/ n. a small drum with several pairs of metal discs (jingles) inserted into the frame.

tame /teɪm/ adj. 1. changed from the wild or savage state; domesticated. 2. tractable, docile, or submissive, as a person, the disposition, etc. 3. spiritless or pusillanimous. 4. only mildly risqué; weak or relatively inoffensive: a tame joke. –v.t. 5. to make tame; domesticate; make tractable; subdue. 6. to soften; tone down.

tam-o'-shanter /tæm-ə-'ʃæntə/ n. a cap, of Scottish origin.

tamp /tæmp/ v.t. to force in or down by repeated, somewhat light strokes.

tamper /'tæmpə/ v.i. (fol. by with) to meddle, especially for the purpose of altering, damaging, misusing, etc.

tampon /'tæmpɒn/ n. 1. a plug of cotton or the like inserted into an orifice, wound, etc., as to stop haemorrhage. 2. a similar device used internally to absorb menstrual flow.

tan /tæn/ v.t. (**tanned, tanning**) 1. to convert (a hide) into a leather, especially by soaking or steeping in a bath prepared from bark, as wattle, etc., or synthetically. 2. to make brown by exposure to ultraviolet rays, as of the sun. 3. Colloq. to beat or thrash. –n. 4. a light brown colour. 5. the brown colour imparted to the skin by exposure to the sun or open air; suntan.

tandem /'tændəm/ adv. **1.** one behind another; in single file. −n. **2.** a bicycle for two riders, having twin seats, pedals, etc.

tandoori /tæn'dʊəri/ adj. in Indian cooking, relating to dishes traditionally cooked in a cylindrical clay oven (**tandoor oven**).

tang /tæŋ/ n. **1.** a strong taste or flavour. **2.** a pungent or distinctive smell.

tangent /'tændʒənt/ adj. **1.** touching. −n. **2.** a sudden divergence from one course, thought, etc., to another.

tangerine /tændʒə'rin/ n. a small, loose-skinned variety of mandarin.

tangible /'tændʒəbəl/ adj. **1.** discernible by the touch; material or substantial. **2.** real or actual, rather than imaginary or visionary.

tangle /'tæŋgəl/ v.t. **1.** to bring together into a mass of confusedly interlaced or intertwisted threads, strands, or other like parts; snarl. −v.i. **2.** to be or become tangled. −n. **3.** a tangled condition.

tango /'tæŋgoʊ/ n. (pl. **-gos**) **1.** a dance of Spanish-American origin. −v.i. (**-goed**, **-going**) **2.** to dance the tango.

tank /tæŋk/ n. **1.** a large receptacle or structure for holding water or other liquid or a gas. **2.** Mil. an armoured, self-propelled combat vehicle, armed with cannon, and machine-guns and moving on caterpillar tracks.

tankard /'tæŋkəd/ n. a large drinking cup, now usually with a handle and (sometimes) a hinged cover.

tanker /'tæŋkə/ n. a ship, aircraft, road or rail vehicle designed to carry oil or other liquid in bulk.

tannin /'tænən/ n. a substance used in tanning.

tantalise /'tæntəlaɪz/ v. to torment with, or as with, the sight of something desired but out of reach; tease by arousing expectations that are repeatedly disappointed. Also, **tantalize**.

tantamount /'tæntəmaʊnt/ adj. equivalent, as in value, force, effect, or signification.

tantrum /'tæntrəm/ n. a fit of ill temper or passion.

tap¹ /tæp/ v.t. (**tapped**, **tapping**) **1.** to strike lightly but audibly; strike with slight blows. −n. **2.** a light but audible blow.

tap² /tæp/ n. **1.** any device for controlling the flow of liquid from a pipe or the like by opening or closing an orifice; a cock. **2.** an instrument for cutting the thread of a female screw. **3.** a connection, usually secretly made, to a telephone line, which enables interested parties to overhear or record the conversations on that line. −v.t. (**tapped**, **tapping**) **4.** to draw off (liquid) by drawing out or opening a tap, or by piercing the container; draw liquid from (any vessel or reservoir). **5.** to gain or effect secret access to. **6.** to open outlets from (power lines, roads, pipes, etc.).

tape /teɪp/ n. **1.** a long narrow strip of linen, cotton, or the like, used for tying garments, etc. **2.** a long narrow strip of paper, metal, etc. **3.** the ribbon of white paper on which a ticker prints quotations or news. −v.t. **4.** to furnish with a tape or tapes. **5.** to tape-record.

tape machine n. (formerly) a telegraphic instrument which automatically printed share prices, market reports, etc., on a tape (**ticker tape**).

tape measure n. a long strip or ribbon, as of linen or steel, marked with subdivisions of the foot or metre for measuring.

taper /'teɪpə/ v.i. **1.** to become gradually slenderer towards one end. −v.t. **2.** to make gradually smaller towards one end. **3.** to reduce gradually. −n. **4.** gradual diminution of width or thickness in an elongated object. **5.** gradual decrease of force, capacity, etc. **6.** a long wick coated with wax, tallow, or the like, as for use in lighting candles or gas.

tape recorder n. a device for recording an electrical signal, especially one produced by sound.

tapestry /'tæpəstri/ n. (pl. **-ries**) a fabric consisting of a warp upon which coloured threads are woven by hand to produce a design, often pictorial, and used for wall hangings, furniture coverings, etc.

tapeworm /'teɪpwɜm/ n. a parasitic flat or tapelike worm.

tapioca /tæpi'oʊkə/ n. a granular farinaceous food substance used for making puddings, etc.

taproot /'tæprut/ n. Bot. a main root descending downwards and giving off small lateral roots.

tar¹ /ta/ n. **1.** any of various dark-coloured viscid products obtained by the destructive distillation of certain organic substances, such as coal, wood, etc. −v.t. (**tarred**, **tarring**) **2.** to smear or cover with, or as with, tar.

tar² /ta/ n. Colloq. a sailor.

tarantula /tə'ræntʃələ/ n. a large spider.

tardy /'tadi/ adj. (**-dier**, **-diest**) **1.** moving or acting slowly; slow; sluggish. **2.** late or behindhand.

tare /tɛə/ n. **1.** the weight of the wrapping, receptacle, or conveyance containing goods. **2.** the weight of a vehicle without cargo, passengers, etc.

target /'tagət/ n. **1.** a device, usually marked with concentric circles, to be aimed at in shooting practice or contests. **2.** a goal to be reached. −v.t. (**-eted** or **-etted**, **-eting** or **-etting**) **3.** to have as a target: nuclear submarines can target the US.

tariff /'tærəf/ n. **1.** an official list or table showing the duties or customs imposed by a government on exports or, less commonly, imports. **2.** any duty in such a list or system.

tarmac /'tamæk/ n. **1.** → **tarmacadam**. **2.** a road or airport runway.

tarmacadam /tamə'kædəm/ n. a road-surfacing mixture consisting of small stones or gravel bound together with tar or a mixture of tar and bitumen.

tarnish /'tanɪʃ/ v.t. **1.** to dull or alter the lustre of (especially a metallic surface); discolour. **2.** to diminish or destroy the purity of; stain; sully. −n. **3.** tarnished condition; discolouration; alteration of the lustre.

tarot /'tæroʊ/ n. a pack of cards, usually used in fortune-telling.

tarpaulin /ta'pɔlən/ n. a protective covering of canvas or other material waterproofed with tar, paint, or wax.

tarragon /'tærəgən/ n. a herb with aromatic leaves used for flavouring.

tarry /'tæri/ v.i. (**-ried, -rying**) **1.** to remain or stay, as in a place. **2.** to delay or be tardy in acting, starting, coming, etc.; linger or loiter. **3.** to wait.

tart¹ /tat/ adj. sour or acid.

tart² /tat/ n. a saucer-shaped shell of pastry with a sweet or savoury filling and no top crust.

tart³ /tat/ n. **1.** a female prostitute. –phr. **2. tart up**, to adorn; make attractive, especially with cheap ornaments and cosmetics.

tartan /'tatn/ n. a woollen or worsted cloth woven with stripes of different colours and widths crossing at right angles, worn chiefly by the Scottish Highlanders.

tartar /'tata/ n. **1.** a hard substance deposited on the teeth. **2.** the deposit from wines.

tartare sauce /'tatə, 'tata/ n. a mayonnaise dressing usually with added chopped pickles, onions, olives, capers, and green herbs, etc., often served with fish. Also, **tartar sauce**.

taser /'teizə/ n. (from trademark) a form of stun gun which fires projectiles with a wire attached through which an electric current passes. Also, **taser gun**. –**tasered**, adj.

task /task/ n. **1.** a definite piece of work assigned or falling to a person; a duty. **2.** a matter of considerable labour or difficulty. –v.t. **3.** to subject to severe or excessive labour or exertion.

Tasmanian devil /tæz'meinian/ n. a carnivorous marsupial of Tasmania having a black coat with white markings.

Tasmanian tiger n. → **thylacine**.

tassel /'tæsəl/ n. **1.** a clasp consisting commonly of a bunch of threads, small cords, or strand hanging from a roundish knob or head. **2.** something resembling this.

taste /teist/ v.t. **1.** to try the flavour or quality of (something) by taking some into the mouth. **2.** to eat or drink a little of. **3.** to perceive or distinguish the flavour of. **4.** to have or get experience, especially a slight experience. –v.i. **5.** (usu. fol. by of) to smack or savour. –n. **6.** the act of tasting food, drink, or the like. **7.** the sense by which the flavour or savour of things is perceived when they are brought into contact with special organs of the tongue. **8.** a small quantity tasted; a morsel, bit, or sip. **9.** a relish, liking, or predilection for something. **10.** the sense of what is fitting, harmonious, or beautiful; the perception and enjoyment of what constitutes excellence in the fine arts, literature, etc. **11.** a slight experience or a sample of something.

tastebud /'teistbʌd/ n. any of a number of small, flask-shaped bodies on the tongue, etc., the special organs of taste.

tasteless /'teistləs/ adj. **1.** (of food) not having much taste or flavour. **2.** unsuitable for the situation or likely to give offence.

tasty /'teisti/ adj. (**-tier, -tiest**) pleasing to the taste; savoury; appetising.

tatter /'tætə/ n. **1.** a torn piece hanging loose from the main part, as of a garment, etc. **2.** a separate torn piece.

tatting /'tætiŋ/ n. the process or work of making a kind of knotted lace of cotton or linen thread with a shuttle.

tattle /'tætl/ v.i. to let out secrets.

tattoo¹ /tæ'tu/ n. (pl. **-toos**) an outdoor military pageant or display.

tattoo² /tæ'tu/ n. (pl. **-toos**) an indelible pattern made on the skin.

taught /tɔt/ v. past tense and past participle of **teach**.

taunt /tɔnt/ v.t. to reproach or provoke in a sarcastic or insulting manner.

taupe /tɔp, toup/ n. dark grey.

taut /tɔt/ adj. tightly drawn; tense.

tautology /tɔ'tɒlədʒi/ n. (pl. **-gies**) needless repetition of an idea.

tavern /'tævən/ n. premises where food and alcoholic drink are served.

taw /tɔ/ n. a choice or fancy playing marble.

tawdry /'tɔdri/ adj. (**-rier, -riest**) (of finery, etc.) gaudy; showy and cheap.

tawny /'tɔni/ adj. (**-nier, -niest**) of a dark yellowish or yellowish brown colour.

tawny frogmouth n. a medium-sized Australian night bird, with differently coloured mottled plumage, and a low but penetrating call.

tax /tæks/ n. **1.** a compulsory monetary contribution demanded by a government for its support and levied on incomes, property, goods purchased, etc. –v.t. **2.** to impose tax on. **3.** to lay a burden on; make serious demands. –**taxable**, adj.

taxation /tæk'seiʃən/ n. **1.** the act of taxing. **2.** the revenue raised by taxes.

tax avoidance n. the taking of lawful measures to minimise one's tax liabilities. Compare **tax evasion**.

tax-deductible /'tæks-dədʌktəbəl/ adj. of or relating to any expense, loss, etc., which can be legally claimed as a deduction from taxable income.

tax evasion n. the illegal non-payment or underpayment of taxes, as by making inaccurate declarations of taxable income. Compare **tax avoidance**.

tax file number n. an official unique identification number allocated to each taxpayer. Also, **TFN**.

taxi /'tæksi/ n. (pl. **taxis**) Also, **taxicab**. **1.** a car for public hire. –v.i. (**taxied, taxiing** or **taxying**) **2.** (of an aeroplane) to move over the surface of the ground or water under its own power.

taxidermy /'tæksə,dɜmi/ n. the art of preparing and preserving the skins of animals, and stuffing and mounting them in lifelike form. –**taxidermist**, n.

tax indexation n. the indexing of tax scales in accordance with certain economic variables such as the consumer price index.

taxonomy /tæk'sɒnəmi/ n. classification, especially in relation to its principles or laws.

tax return n. a statement of personal income required annually by tax authorities, used in assessing a person's tax liability.

tax shelter n. an investment, allowance, etc., used by a person or company to reduce or avoid tax liability.

T cell n. a white blood cell derived from or processed by the thymus, responsible for cellular immune reactions.

tea /ti/ *n.* **1.** the dried and prepared leaves of a shrub, widely grown in China, Japan, India, etc., from which a somewhat bitter, aromatic beverage is made by infusion in boiling water. **2.** any of various infusions prepared from the leaves, flowers, etc., of other plants, and used as beverages or medicines. **3.** a light meal taken in the late afternoon. **4.** the main evening meal.

teach /titʃ/ *v.t.* (**taught, teaching**) **1.** to impart knowledge of or skill in; give instruction in. **2.** to impart knowledge or skill to; give instruction to. –**teacher**, *n.*

teak /tik/ *n.* a large tree tree native to India and South-East Asia, with a hard, durable, yellowish brown, resinous wood.

teal /til/ **1.** a small freshwater duck. –*n.* **2.** a deep greenish-blue colour. –*adj.* **3.** of the colour of teal.

tea light *n.* a small candle, often in a metal or plastic casing.

team /tim/ *n.* **1.** a number of persons associated in some joint action, especially one of the sides in a match. **2.** two or more horses, oxen, or other animals harnessed together to draw a vehicle, plough or the like. –*v.t.* **3.** to join together in a team.

team spirit *n.* the camaraderie and loyalty which members of a team display towards each other.

tear[1] /tɪə/ *n.* a drop of fluid appearing in or flowing from the eye, chiefly as the result of emotion, especially grief.

tear[2] /tɛə/ *v.* (**tore, torn, tearing**) –*v.t.* **1.** to pull apart or in pieces by force, especially so as to leave ragged or irregular edges. **2.** to pull or pluck violently or with force. **3.** to rend or divide. –*v.i.* **4.** to become torn. **5.** *Colloq.* to move or go with violence or great haste. –*n.* **6.** the act of tearing. **7.** a rent or fissure.

tease /tiz/ *v.t.* (**teased, teasing**) **1.** to worry or irritate by persistent petty requests, trifling raillery, or other annoyances often in jest. **2.** to pull apart or separate the adhering fibres of. **3.** to flirt with, especially insincerely. –*n.* **4.** the act of teasing. **5.** the state of being teased. **6.** someone who or that which teases or annoys.

teat /tit/ *n.* **1.** the protuberance on the breast or udder in female mammals (except the monotremes), where the milk ducts discharge; a nipple. **2.** something resembling a teat, especially for feeding a baby from a bottle.

techie /ˈtɛki/ *n. Colloq.* someone with a professional or passionate interest in technology, especially computing. Also, **tech**.

technical /ˈtɛknɪkəl/ *adj.* **1.** belonging or relating to an art, science, or the like. **2.** skilled in, or familiar in a practical way with, a particular art, trade, etc., as a person. **3.** relating to or connected with the mechanical or industrial arts and the applied sciences.

technicality /tɛknəˈkæləti/ *n.* (*pl.* **-ties**) a literal, often narrow-minded interpretation of a rule, law, etc.; quibble.

technician /tɛkˈnɪʃən/ *n.* **1.** one skilled in the technique of an art, as music or painting. **2.** a person skilled and knowledgeable in a particular technical area: *a telephone technician.*

technicolour /ˈtɛknɪkʌlə, -nə-/ *n.* a process of making cinema films in colour by superimposing the three primary colours to produce a final coloured print. Also, **technicolor**.

technique /tɛkˈnik/ *n.* method of performance; way of accomplishing.

technocracy /tɛkˈnɒkrəsi/ *n.* (*pl.* **-cies**) government by experts in technical fields, as engineering, economics, etc. –**technocrat**, *n.*

technology /tɛkˈnɒlədʒi/ *n.* **1.** the branch of knowledge that deals with science and engineering, or its practice, as applied to industry; applied science. **2.** equipment of a technologically sophisticated nature, such as computers, internet connections, audiovisual equipment, etc.: *The technology has failed us in this demonstration.* –**technological**, *adj.* –**technologist**, *n.*

technology park *n.* an industrial park devoted to high-technology industries. Also, **high technology park**.

tectonic /tɛkˈtɒnɪk/ *adj.* **1.** of or relating to building or construction. **2.** of or relating to the structure or conditions of the earth's crust, or the forces acting upon it.

tectonic plate *n. Geol.* a section of the earth's crust and uppermost part of the mantle, which moves in relation to the other plates causing earthquakes, volcanoes, mountain-building and the formation of oceanic trenches.

teddy bear /ˈtɛdi/ *n.* a stuffed toy bear.

tedium /ˈtidiəm/ *n.* the state of being wearisome. –**tedious**, *adj.*

tee /ti/ *Golf* –*n.* **1.** the starting place, usually a hard mound of earth, at the beginning of each fairway. **2.** a small plastic or wooden object, on which the ball is placed and from which it is driven at the beginning of a hole. –*v.i.* (**teed, teeing**) **3.** (fol. by *off*) to strike the ball from a tee.

teem[1] /tim/ *v.i.* (fol. by *with*) to abound or swarm; be prolific or fertile.

teem[2] /tim/ *v.i.* **1.** to empty or pour out; discharge. **2.** to rain very hard.

teenager /ˈtineɪdʒə/ *n.* a person in his or her teens. –**teenage**, *adj.*

teens /tinz/ *pl. n.* the period of one's life between the ages of 12 and 20.

teepee /ˈtipi/ *n.* a tent of the indigenous people of North America, usually made of skins. Also, **tepee**.

teeter /ˈtitə/ *v.i.* **1.** to seesaw. **2.** to move unsteadily.

teeth /tiθ/ *n.* plural of **tooth**.

teethe /tið/ *v.i.* (**teethed, teething**) to grow teeth; cut one's teeth.

teetotal /ˈtitoutl, tiˈtoutl/ *adj.* of or relating to, advocating, or pledged to total abstinence from intoxicating drink. –**teetotaller**, *n.* –**teetotally**, *adv.*

telco /ˈtɛlkoʊ/ *n.* a telecommunications company.

tele- **1.** a word element meaning 'distant', especially 'transmission over a distance', as in *telegraph.* **2.** a word element referring to television, as in *telemovie, teletext.* **3.** a word element referring to the use of telecommunications, as in *telecommute, telebanking.*

telecast /ˈtɛləkast, ˈtɛli-/ *v.i., v.t.* (**telecast** or **telecasted, telecasting**) **1.** to broadcast by television. –*n.* **2.** a television broadcast.

telecommunications /ˌtɛləkəmjunəˈkeɪʃənz, ˌteli-/ *pl. n.* the science or technology of telegraphic or telephonic communications by line or radio transmission.

teleconference /ˈtelikɒnfərəns/ *n.* a conference in which the people at locations remote from each other can take part using an audio and video telecommunications system. **–teleconferencing**, *n.*

telefraud /ˈtelifrɒd/ *n.* the swindling of people by scams that involve contact by telephone.

telegram /ˈtɛləgræm/ *n.* a communication sent by telegraph; a telegraphic message.

telegraph /ˈtɛləgræf, -graf/ *n.* a system or device for sending messages by electric signals along wire. **–telegraphic**, *adj.* **–telegraphy** /təˈlɛgrəfi/ *n.*

telemarketing /ˈtelimakətɪŋ/ *n.* the selling of goods or services by contacting potential customers on the telephone. **–telemarketer**, *n.*

telemovie /ˈtelimuvi/ *n.* a film produced especially for television.

teleology /tiliˈɒlədʒi, tɛl-/ *n.* the doctrine that the universe is tending towards a final purpose, and that there is evidence of this in nature which is proof of the existence of the being who established what this purpose should be.

telepathy /təˈlɛpəθi/ *n.* communication of one mind with another by some means other than the normal use of the senses. **–telepathic** /tɛləˈpæθɪk/, *adj.* **–telepathically** /tɛləˈpæθɪkli/, *adv.*

telephone /ˈtɛləfoʊn/ *n.* 1. an apparatus, system, or process for transmission of sound or speech to a distant point, especially by an electrical device. –*v.t.* 2. to contact (a person) by telephone: *I'll telephone him later.* –*v.i.* 3. to send a message by telephone: *she telephoned last night.* **–telephonic** /tɛləˈfɒnɪk/, *adj.* **–telephony** /təˈlɛfəni/, *n.*

teleprinter /ˈtɛliprɪntə, ˈtɛlə-/ *n.* an instrument with a typewriter keyboard which sends and receives messages by changing typed information into electrical signals. Also, **teletype**.

teleprocessing /ˈteliˌproʊsɛsɪŋ/ *n.* the processing of information held at another place, by means of an online computer.

telescope /ˈtɛləskoʊp/ *n.* 1. an optical instrument for making distant objects appear nearer and larger. –*v.* (**-scoped, -scoping**) –*v.t.* 2. to force together, one into another, or force into something else, in the manner of the sliding tubes of a jointed telescope. 3. to condense; shorten. –*v.i.* 4. to slide together, or into something else in the manner of the tubes of a jointed telescope. **–telescopic**, *adj.*

teletype /ˈtɛlitaɪp, ˈtɛlə-/ *n.* (*from trademark*) → **teleprinter**.

televise /ˈtɛləvaɪz/ *v.t.* to broadcast by television.

television /ˈtɛləvɪʒən/ *n.* 1. the broadcasting of a still or moving image via radio waves to receivers which project it electronically on a screen. 2. a television receiver; television set. Also, **TV**.

television station *n.* an organisation engaged in broadcasting, on a fixed channel, television programs of news, entertainment, propaganda, etc.

telex /ˈtɛlɛks/ *n.* an international two-way communications system which uses the public telecommunications network to link teleprinters at remote locations.

tell /tɛl/ *v.* (**told, telling**) –*v.t.* 1. to give an account or narrative of; narrate; relate (a story, tale, etc.). 2. to make known by speech or writing (a fact, news, information, etc.); communicate. 3. to utter (the truth, a lie, etc.). 4. to recognise or distinguish. –*v.i.* 5. to give an account or report. 6. (fol. by *of*) to give evidence or be an indication. 7. (usu. fol. by *on*) to disclose something secret or private; play the informer. 8. to produce a marked or severe effect.

teller /ˈtɛlə/ *n.* someone employed in a bank to receive or pay out money over the counter.

tellurian /tɛlˈjuriən, təˈlu-/ *adj.* of or characteristic of the earth or an inhabitant of the earth.

temerity /təˈmɛrəti/ *n.* reckless boldness.

temper /ˈtɛmpə/ *n.* 1. a particular state of mind or feelings. 2. heat of mind or passion, shown in outbursts of anger, resentment, etc. 3. *Metallurgy* the particular degree of hardness and elasticity imparted to steel, etc., by tempering. –*v.t.* 4. to moderate or mitigate. 5. to bring to a proper, suitable, or desirable state by, or as by, blending. 6. to heat and cool or quench (metal) to bring to the proper degree of hardness, elasticity, etc.

tempera /ˈtɛmpərə/ *n.* paint made from pigment ground in water and mixed with an emulsion of egg yolk or some similar substance.

temperament /ˈtɛmprəmənt/ *n.* the individual peculiarity of physical organisation by which the manner of thinking, feeling, and acting of every person is permanently affected; natural disposition.

temperamental /tɛmprəˈmɛntl/ *adj.* 1. moody, irritable or sensitive. 2. liable to behave erratically; unstable; unreliable.

temperance /ˈtɛmpərəns, ˈtɛmprəns/ *n.* 1. habitual moderation. 2. total abstinence from alcoholic drink.

temperate /ˈtɛmpərət, ˈtɛmprət/ *adj.* 1. moderate or self-restrained. 2. not excessive.

temperate climate *n.* a climate without extremes of temperature or precipitation.

temperate rainforest *n.* a coniferous or broadleaf forest occurring in coastal mountains with high rainfall. Compare **tropical rainforest**.

temperature /ˈtɛmprətʃə/ *n.* 1. a measure of the degree of hotness or coldness of a body or substance. 2. *Physiol.* **a.** the degree of heat of a living body, especially the human body. **b.** the excess of this above the normal (which in the adult human being is about 37°C or about 98.4°F).

tempest /ˈtɛmpəst/ *n.* a violent storm.

tempestuous /tɛmˈpɛstʃuəs/ *adj.* tumultuous; turbulent. **–tempestuously**, *adv.* **–tempestuousness**, *n.*

template /ˈtɛmplət, -leɪt/ *n.* 1. a formula or example. 2. a pattern, mould, or the like, usually consisting of a thin plate of wood, metal, or plastic, used as a guide in mechanical work or for transferring a design onto a work surface, etc.

temple[1] /ˈtɛmpəl/ *n.* a building erected as a place of worship, especially a large or imposing one.

temple[2] /ˈtɛmpəl/ *n.* the flattened region on either side of the human forehead.

tempo /ˈtɛmpoʊ/ *n.* (*pl.* **-pos** *or* **-pi** /-piː/) *Music* relative rapidity or rate of movement.

temporal /ˈtɛmpərəl, ˈtɛmprəl/ *adj.* **1.** of or relating to time. **2.** relating to or concerned with the present life or this world; worldly.

temporary /ˈtɛmpri, -prəri/, *Orig. US* /ˈtɛmpəreri/ *adj.* **1.** lasting for a short time only; not permanent. **2.** lasting or in use for a limited time: *a temporary job.*

temporise /ˈtɛmpəraɪz/ *v.i.* **1.** to act indecisively or evasively to gain time or delay matters. **2.** to comply with the time or occasion; yield temporarily or ostensibly to the current of opinion or circumstances. Also, **temporize.**

tempt /tɛmpt/ *v.t.* **1.** to induce or persuade by enticement or allurement. **2.** to render strongly disposed (to do something). **–temptation,** *n.*

tempura /tɛmˈpʊrə/ *n.* a Japanese food made from seafood or vegetables coated in a light batter and deep-fried in oil.

ten /tɛn/ *n.* **1.** a cardinal number, nine plus one. *–adj.* **2.** amounting to ten in number. **–tenth,** *adj.*, *n.*

tenable /ˈtɛnəbəl/ *adj.* capable of being held, maintained, or defended, as against attack or objection.

tenacious /təˈneɪʃəs/ *adj.* **1.** (oft. fol. by *of*) holding fast; characterised by keeping a firm hold. **2.** highly retentive. **3.** pertinacious, persistent, stubborn, or obstinate. **–tenacity,** *n.*

tenant /ˈtɛnənt/ *n.* someone who holds land, a house, or the like, of another (the landlord) for a period of time, as a lessee or occupant for rent. **–tenancy,** *n.*

tend[1] /tɛnd/ *v.i.* to be disposed or inclined in action, operation, or effect (to do something). **–tendency,** *n.*

tend[2] /tɛnd/ *v.t.* **1.** to attend to by work or services, care, etc. **2.** to look after.

tendentious /tɛnˈdɛnʃəs/ *adj.* having or showing a definite tendency, bias, or purpose.

tender[1] /ˈtɛndə/ *adj.* **1.** soft or delicate in substance; not hard or tough. **2.** weak or delicate in constitution; not strong or hardy; fragile. **3.** warm and affectionate. **4.** gentle. **5.** acutely or painfully sensitive.

tender[2] /ˈtɛndə/ *v.t.* **1.** to present formally for acceptance; make formal offer of. *–n.* **2.** the act of tendering; an offer of something for acceptance. **3.** *Commerce* an offer made in writing by one party to another to execute certain work, supply certain commodities, etc., at a given cost.

tendon /ˈtɛndən/ *n. Anat.* a cord or band of dense, tough, inelastic, white fibrous tissue, serving to connect a muscle with a bone or part; a sinew. **–tendinous,** *adj.*

tendonitis /tɛndənˈaɪtəs/ *n.* inflammation of a tendon. Also, **tendinitis.**

tendril /ˈtɛndrəl/ *n. Bot.* a leafless curly organ of climbing plants.

tenement house /ˈtɛnəmənt/ *n.* a house divided into flats, especially one in the poorer, crowded parts of a large city.

tenet /ˈtɛnət/ *n.* any opinion, principle, doctrine, dogma, or the like, held as true.

tennis /ˈtɛnəs/ *n.* a game in which a ball is hit with racquets backwards and forwards over a net.

tenon /ˈtɛnən/ *n.* a projection shaped on an end of a piece of wood, etc., for insertion in a corresponding cavity (mortice) in another piece.

tenor /ˈtɛnə/ *n.* **1.** the course of thought or meaning which runs through something written or spoken; purport; drift. **2.** *Music* the highest natural male voice.

tenpin bowling /ˈtɛnpɪn/ *n.* a form of bowling played with ten wooden pins at which a ball is bowled to knock them down.

tense[1] /tɛns/ *adj.* **1.** stretched tight, as a cord, fibre, etc.; drawn taut; rigid. **2.** in a state of mental or nervous strain, as a person. *–v.t., v.i.* **3.** to make or become tense.

tense[2] /tɛns/ *n. Gram.* a category of verb inflection found in some languages which specifies the time and length of occurrence of the action or state expressed by the verb.

tensile /ˈtɛnsaɪl/ *adj.* **1.** of or relating to tension. **2.** capable of being stretched or drawn out; ductile. **–tensility,** *n.*

tension /ˈtɛnʃən/ *n.* **1.** the act of stretching or straining. **2.** mental or emotional strain; intense suppressed anxiety, suspense, or excitement.

tent /tɛnt/ *n.* a portable shelter of strong cloth, formerly usually of canvas.

tentacle /ˈtɛntəkəl/ *n. Zool.* any of various slender, flexible processes or appendages in animals, especially invertebrates, which serve as organs of touch, etc.; a feeler.

tentative /ˈtɛntətɪv/ *adj.* **1.** of the nature of, or made or done as, a trial, experiment, or attempt; experimental. **2.** hesitant; cautious; diffident.

tenterhooks /ˈtɛntəhʊks/ *phr.* **on tenterhooks,** in a state of painful suspense or anxiety.

tenuous /ˈtɛnjuəs/ *adj.* flimsy; lacking a firm or sound basis; weak; vague.

tenure /ˈtɛnjə/ *n.* **1.** the holding or possessing of anything. **2.** a period of office or employment that terminates, possibly subject to certain conditions, only on resignation or retirement. **3.** the period or terms of holding something.

tepid /ˈtɛpəd/ *adj.* moderately warm.

teppanyaki /tɛpənˈjaki/ *n.* a Japanese dish in which pieces of meat or fish are roasted on a hot iron plate.

terabyte /ˈtɛrəbaɪt/ *n. Computers* a measure of computer memory equal to 2^{40} (approximately 10^{12}) bytes.

tercentenary /tɜsənˈtinəri, -ˈtɛn-/ *adj.* of or relating to a 300th anniversary.

teriyaki /tɛriˈjaki/ *n.* a Japanese dish consisting of meat, chicken or seafood, marinated in a mixture containing soy sauce, and grilled.

term /tɜm/ *n.* **1.** any word or group of linguistic forms naming something, especially as used in some particular field of knowledge. **2.** the time or period through which something lasts or is fixed to last. **3.** each of certain stated periods of the year into which instruction is regularly organised for students or pupils in universities, colleges, and schools. **4.** (*pl.*) conditions with regard to payment, price, charge, rates, wages, etc. **5.** (*pl.*) footing or standing. *–v.t.* **6.** to apply a particular term or name to; name; call; designate. *–phr.* **7. a contradiction in terms**, a statement which is self-contradictory.

terminal /'tɜmənəl/ *adj.* **1.** situated at or forming the end or extremity of something. **2.** relating to, situated, at or forming the terminus of a railway. **3.** occurring at or causing the end of life. *–n.* **4.** a terminal part or structure; end or extremity. **5.** the end of a railway line, shipping route, air route, etc., at which large scale loading and unloading of passengers, goods, etc., takes place. **6.** *Elect.* the mechanical device by means of which an electrical connection to an apparatus is established. **7.** → **computer terminal**. **8.** *Archit., etc.* a carving or the like at the end of something.

terminally /'tɜmənəli/ *adv.* incurably: *terminally ill.*

terminate /'tɜməneɪt/ *v.t.* **1.** bring to an end; put an end to. **2.** to end (a pregnancy) by causing the fetus to be expelled before it is viable. *–v.i.* **3.** to end, conclude, or cease. **–terminable**, *adj.* **–termination**, *n.*

terminating building society *n.* an association of individuals who make regular payments to a common fund, from which each obtains a housing loan, the order usually being determined by ballot; the society is terminated when the last house is paid for.

terminology /tɜmə'nɒlədʒi/ *n.* (*pl.* **-gies**) the system of terms belonging to a science, art, or subject; nomenclature.

terminus /'tɜmənəs/ *n.* (*pl.* **-ni** /-naɪ/ *or* **-nuses**) the station or town at the end of a railway line, bus route, etc.

termite /'tɜmaɪt/ *n.* a social insect, sometimes very destructive to buildings, etc.; white ant.

tern /tɜn/ *n.* a seabird.

ternary /'tɜnəri/ *adj.* consisting of or involving three; threefold; triple.

terrace /'tɛrəs/ *n.* **1.** one of a series of flat levels formed across a slope, mountain side, etc., usually for the purposes of cultivation. **2.** an open (usually paved) area connected with a house and serving as an outdoor living area. **3. a.** a row of adjoining, identical houses, usually of 19th-century construction, and often with two storeys and iron lace decoration. **b.** one such house.

terracotta /tɛrə'kɒtə/ *n.* a hard, usually unglazed earthenware of fine quality.

terrain /tə'reɪn/ *n.* a tract of land, especially as considered with reference to its natural features, military advantages, etc.

terra nullius /tɛrə 'nʊliəs/ *n.* territory belonging to no state, that is, not inhabited by a community with a social and political organisation.

terrestrial /tə'rɛstriəl/ *adj.* **1.** relating to, consisting of, or representing the earth. **2.** of or relating to the land as distinct from the water.

terrible /'tɛrəbəl/ *adj.* **1.** exciting or fitted to excite terror or great fear; dreadful; awful. **2.** very bad.

terrier /'tɛriə/ *n.* a small dog.

terrific /tə'rɪfɪk/ *adj.* **1.** extraordinarily great, intense, etc. **2.** *Colloq.* very good.

terrify /'tɛrəfaɪ/ *v.t.* (**-fied**, **-fying**) to fill with terror; make greatly afraid.

territory /'tɛrətri, -tɔri/, *Orig. US* /-tɔri/ *n.* (*pl.* **-ries**) **1.** any tract of land; region or district.

2. the lands and waters belonging to or under the jurisdiction of a state, sovereign, etc. **3.** any separate tract of land belonging to a nation. **4.** the field of action, thought, etc.; domain or province of something. **–territorial**, *adj.*

terror /'tɛrə/ *n.* **1.** intense, sharp, overpowering fear. **2.** *Colloq.* a person or thing that is a particular nuisance.

terrorise /'tɛrəraɪz/ *v.t.* to fill or overcome with terror. Also, **terrorize**.

terrorism /'tɛrərɪzəm/ *n.* the use of methods to induce terror, especially the use of violence to achieve political ends. **–terrorist**, *n.*, *adj.* **–terroristic**, *adj.*

terry towelling *n.* cotton fabric with loops on one or both sides.

terse /tɜs/ *adj.* **1.** neatly or effectively concise; brief and pithy, as language. **2.** abrupt or bad-tempered, especially in one's speech.

tertiary /'tɜʃəri/ *adj.* of the third order, rank, formation, etc.; third.

tertiary education *n.* all forms of formal education beyond secondary education.

terylene /'tɛrəlin/ *n.* (*from trademark*) a synthetic polyester fibre.

tessellate /'tɛsəleɪt/ *v.t.* to form of small squares or blocks, as floors, pavements, etc.; form or arrange in a chequered or mosaic pattern.

test /tɛst/ *n.* **1.** that by which the presence, quality, or genuineness of anything is determined; a means of trial. **2.** *Educ.* a form of examination for evaluating the performance and capabilities of a student or class. *–v.t.* **3.** to subject to a test of any kind; try.

testament /'tɛstəmənt/ *n.* **1.** *Law* a formal declaration, usually in writing, of a person's wishes as to the disposition of his or her property after his or her death. **2.** (*upper case*) either of the two main divisions of the Bible. **3.** something which serves as proof or evidence of some quality: *her behaviour was a testament to her maturity.*

testate /'tɛsteɪt, 'tɛstət/ *adj.* *Law* having made and left a valid will. **–testacy**, *n.*

testes /'tɛstiz/ *n.* plural of **testis**.

testicle /'tɛstɪkə/ *n.* the male sex gland, either of two oval glands situated in the scrotum.

testify /'tɛstəfaɪ/ *v.* (**-fied**, **-fying**) *–v.i.* **1.** to bear witness; give or afford evidence. **2.** to make solemn declaration. *–v.t.* **3.** to bear witness to; affirm as fact or truth.

testimonial /tɛstə'moʊniəl/ *n.* **1.** a writing certifying to a person's character, conduct, or qualifications. **2.** something given or done as an expression of esteem, admiration, or gratitude.

testimony /'tɛstəməni/, *Orig. US* /-moʊni/ *n.* (*pl.* **-nies**) **1.** *Law* the statement or declaration of a witness under oath or affirmation, usually in court. **2.** evidence.

testis /'tɛstəs/ *n.* (*pl.* **testes** /'tɛstiz/) → **testicle**.

testosterone /tɛs'tɒstəroʊn/ *n.* a male sex hormone, secreted by the testes, which stimulates development of masculine characteristics.

test tube *n.* a hollow cylinder of thin glass with one end closed, used in chemical tests.

testy /'tɛsti/ *adj.* (**-tier**, **-tiest**) touchy.

tetanus /ˈtɛtnəs, ˈtɛtənəs/ *n.* an infectious, often fatal disease, marked by spasms and muscle rigidity.

tether /ˈtɛðə/ *n.* **1.** a rope, chain, or the like, by which an animal is fastened, as to a stake, so that its range of movement is limited. –*v.t.* **2.** to fasten or confine with or as with a tether. –*phr.* **3. the end of one's tether**, the limit of one's possibilities, patience, or resources.

tetra- a word element meaning 'four'.

tetragon /ˈtɛtrəgən, -gɒn/ *n.* a plane figure having four angles; a quadrangle.

text /tɛkst/ *n.* **1.** the main body of matter in a book or manuscript. **2.** the actual wording of anything written or printed. –*v.t.* **3.** to send (someone) a text message. –**textual**, *adj.* –**texter**, *n.*

texta /ˈtɛkstə/ *n.* (*from trademark*) → **felt pen**.

textaholic /tɛkstəˈhɒlɪk/ *n. Colloq.* someone who sends an excessive number of text messages. –**textaholism**, *n.*

textbook /ˈtɛkstbʊk/ *n.* a book used by students for a particular branch of study.

textile /ˈtɛkstaɪl/ *n.* a woven material.

text message *n.* a message sent by mobile phone using SMS. –**text messaging**, *n.*

texture /ˈtɛkstʃə/ *n.* **1.** the characteristic appearance or essential quality of something, especially as conveyed to the touch. **2.** the structure of the surface of any work of art, or the simulation of the surface structure of the skin, garment, etc., of the object represented in paint, stone, or other medium.

-th¹ a noun suffix referring to condition, quality, or action, added to words (*warmth*) and to stems related to words (*depth*, *length*).

-th² the suffix of ordinal numbers (*fourth*, *sixth*, *tenth*), the form *-th* being added in some cases to altered stems of the cardinal numbers (*fifth*, *twelfth*).

than /ðæn/, *weak form* /ðən/ *conj.* **1.** a particle used after comparative adjectives and adverbs and certain other words, such as *other*, *otherwise*, *else*, etc., to introduce the second member of a comparison. –*prep.* **2.** in comparison with.

thank /θæŋk/ *v.t.* **1.** to give thanks to; express gratitude to. –*n.* **2. thanks**, **a.** feelings of being grateful or words showing one is grateful: *filled with thanks.* **b.** thank you.

thankful /ˈθæŋkfəl/ *adj.* feeling or showing thanks. –**thankfully**, *adv.* –**thankfulness**, *n.*

thank you *interj.* the customary expression of gratitude or acknowledgement.

that /ðæt/, *weak form* /ðət/ *pron.* (*pl.* **those**) **1.** a demonstrative pronoun used to indicate: **a.** a person, thing, idea, etc., as pointed out or present, before mentioned, about to be mentioned, supposed to be understood, or by way of emphasis: *that is my husband.* **b.** of two or more persons, things, etc., already mentioned, to the one more remote in place, time, or thought (often opposed to *this*): *That is the one I want.* **2.** a relative pronoun used as the subject or object of a relative clause: *How old was the car that was stolen?* –*adj.* **3.** a demonstrative adjective used to indicate: **a.** a person, place, thing, idea, etc., as pointed out or present, before mentioned, supposed to be understood, or by way of emphasis: *That man*

is my husband. **b.** of two or more persons, things, etc., already mentioned, the one more remote in place, time, or thought (opposed to *this*): *It was that one, not this one.* –*adv.* **4.** an adverb used with adjectives and adverbs of quality or extent to indicate precise degree or extent: *that much*; *that far.* –*conj.* **5.** a conjunction used to introduce a clause as the subject or object of the principal verb or as the necessary complement to a statement made: *That he will come is certain*; *I know that you will do it.*

thatch /θætʃ/ *n.* **1.** a material, as straw, rushes, leaves, or the like, used to cover roofs, haystacks, etc. –*v.t.* **2.** to cover with or as with thatch.

thaw /θɔ/ *v.i.* to pass from a frozen to a liquid or semiliquid state; melt.

the¹ /ðɪ/ *before a vowel,* /ðə/ *before a consonant – definite article* **1.** used before nouns with a specifying or particularising effect, opposed to *a* or *an*. **2.** used before adjectives substantively and denoting an individual, a class or number of individuals, or an abstract notion.

the² /ðɪ/ *before a vowel,* /ðə/ *before a consonant –adv.* (used to modify an adjective or adverb in the comparative degree) **1.** signifying 'in or by that', 'on that account', 'in or by so much', or 'in some or any degree': *he looks the better for his holiday.* **2.** used correlatively, in one instance with relative force and in the other with demonstrative force, and signifying 'by how much … by so much' or 'in what degree … in that degree': *the more, the merrier.*

theatre /ˈθɪətə, ˈθɪətə/ *n.* **1.** a building or room designed to house dramatic presentations, stage entertainments, or the like. **2.** dramatic performances as a branch of art; the drama. **3.** a room or hall, fitted with tiers of seats rising like steps, as used for lectures, anatomical demonstrations, etc. **4.** a room in a hospital or elsewhere in which surgical operations are performed. **5.** a place of action; field of operations.

theatrical /θiˈætrəkəl/ *adj.* **1.** of or relating to the theatre. **2.** suggestive of the theatre or of acting. Also, **theatric**.

theft /θɛft/ *n.* the act of stealing.

their /ðɛə/ *pron.* the possessive form of **they** used before a noun: *Those are their bags.*

theirs /ðɛəz/ *pron.* **1.** the possessive form of **they**, used without a noun following: *those books are theirs.* **2.** the person(s) or thing(s) belonging to them: *Theirs is the red car parked around the back.*

theism /ˈθiːɪzəm/ *n.* the belief in one god as the creator and ruler of the universe.

them /ðɛm/, *weak form* /ðəm/ *pron.* **1.** the personal pronoun used, usually after a verb or preposition, to refer to a number of people or things: *I'll put them in my bag*; *Get it from them tomorrow.* **2.** a personal pronoun used, usually after a verb or preposition, to refer to a single person when the sex of the person is unknown: *If anyone needs a new form, I am happy to supply them with one.*

theme /θiːm/ *n.* a subject of discourse, discussion, meditation, or composition; a topic.

themself /ðəmˈsɛlf/ *pron.* a reflexive form of **they** used as a singular pronoun when the sex of the person being referred to is unknown: *A child might hurt themself on this equipment.*

themselves /ðəm'sɛlvz/ *pl. pron.* **1.** a reflexive form of **they. 2.** a form of **them** or **they** used for emphasis: *They did it themselves.*

then /ðɛn/ *adv.* **1.** at that time. **2.** next in order of time. **3.** in that case; in those circumstances.

thence /ðɛns/ *adv.* **1.** from that place. **2.** from that time. **3.** from that source; for that reason; therefore.

theocracy /θi'ɒkrəsi/ *n. (pl.* **-cies**) a form of government in which a deity is recognised as the supreme civil ruler.

theodolite /θi'ɒdəlaɪt/ *n. Surveying* an instrument for measuring horizontal or vertical angles.

theology /θi'ɒlədʒi/ *n.* the science or study of divine things or religious truth; divinity. **–theologian,** *n.* **–theological,** *adj.*

theorem /'θɪərəm/ *n.* a rule or law, especially one expressed by an equation or formula.

theoretical /θɪə'rɛtɪkəl/ *adj.* **1.** of, relating to, or consisting in theory; not practical. **2.** existing only in theory; hypothetical.

theorise /'θɪəraɪz/ *v.i.* **1.** to form a theory or theories. **2.** to speculate or conjecture. Also, **theorize.**

theory /'θɪəri/ *n. (pl.* **-ries**) **1.** a coherent group of general propositions used as principles of explanation for a class of phenomena. **2.** that department of a science or art which deals with its principles or methods, as distinguished from the practice of it. **3.** conjecture or opinion.

therapeutic /θɛrə'pjutɪk/ *adj.* relating to the treating or curing of disease.

therapy /'θɛrəpi/ *n.* the treatment of disease, disorder, defect, etc., as by some remedial or curative process. **–therapist,** *n.*

there /ðɛə/ *adv.* **1.** in or at that place. **2.** into or to that place; thither.

there- a word element meaning 'that (place)', 'that (time)', etc., used in combination with certain adverbs and prepositions.

thereby /ðɛə'baɪ, 'ðɛəbaɪ/ *adv.* by that; by means of that.

therefore /'ðɛəfɔ, ðɛə'fɔ/ *adv.* in consequence of that; as a result; consequently.

thereupon /ðɛərə'pɒn, 'ðɛərəpɒn/ *adv.* immediately following that.

thermal /'θɜməl/ *adj.* of or relating to heat or temperature. Also, **thermic.**

thermodynamics /ˌθɜmoʊdaɪ'næmɪks/ *n.* the science concerned with the relations between heat and mechanical energy or work, and the conversion of one into the other.

thermometer /θə'mɒmətə/ *n.* an instrument for measuring temperature.

thermonuclear /ˌθɜmoʊ'njuklɪə/ *adj.* designating, or capable of producing, extremely high temperatures resulting from, caused by, or associated with nuclear fusion.

thermonuclear reaction *n.* a nuclear fusion reaction that takes place between atomic nuclei which form part of a substance which has been heated to a temperature of several million degrees Celsius.

thermos /'θɜmɒs, -məs/ *n. (from trademark)* a vessel which keeps its contents at a constant temperature. Also, **thermos flask.**

thermostat /'θɜməstæt/ *n.* a device which establishes and maintains a desired temperature automatically.

thesaurus /θə'sɔrəs, -'zɔ-/ *n. (pl.* **-ruses** *or* **-ri** /-raɪ/) **1.** a storehouse or repository, as of words or knowledge. **2.** a dictionary of synonyms.

these /ðiz/ *pron., adj.* plural of **this.**

thesis /'θisəs/ *n. (pl.* **theses** /'θisiz/) **1.** a proposition laid down or stated, especially one to be discussed and proved or to be maintained against objections. **2.** a subject for a composition or essay. **3.** a dissertation, as one presented by a candidate for a diploma or degree, especially a postgraduate degree.

thespian /'θɛspiən/ *n.* an actor.

thew /θju/ *n. (usu. pl.)* muscle or sinew.

they /ðeɪ/ *pron.* **1.** the personal pronoun used to refer to a number of people or things, not including the speaker or the person spoken to. It is the plural of **he, she** and **it. 2.** a personal pronoun used to refer to a single person when the sex of the person is unknown: *If anyone wants to go, they should let me know.*

thiamine /'θaɪəmin/ *n.* a vitamin (B₁) required by the nervous system.

thick /θɪk/ *adj.* **1.** having relatively great extent from one surface or side to its opposite; not thin. **2.** measuring as specified between opposite surfaces, or in depth, or in a direction perpendicular to that of the length and breadth. **3.** set close together; compact; dense. **4.** having relatively great consistency; viscous. **5.** (of an accent or dialect) very pronounced.

thicket /'θɪkət/ *n.* a thick or dense growth of shrubs, bushes, or small trees; a thick coppice.

thief /θif/ *n. (pl.* **thieves**) someone who steals.

thieve /θiv/ *v.t.* to take by theft; steal. **–thievery,** *n.*

thigh /θaɪ/ *n.* that part of the leg between the hip and the knee in humans.

thimble /'θɪmbəl/ *n.* a small cap, usually of metal, worn on the finger to push the needle in sewing.

thin /θɪn/ *adj.* (**thinner, thinnest**) **1.** having relatively little extent from one surface or side to its opposite; not thick. **2.** of small cross-section in comparison with the length; slender. **3.** having little flesh; spare; lean. **4.** not dense; sparse; scanty. **5.** having relatively slight consistency, as a liquid; fluid; rare or rarefied, as air, etc. **6.** easily seen through, transparent, or flimsy. **–v.t.** (**thinned, thinning**) **7.** (oft. fol. by *down, out,* etc.) to make thin or thinner.

thing /θɪŋ/ *n.* **1.** a material object without life or consciousness; an inanimate object. **2.** that which is or may become an object of thought, whether material or ideal, animate or inanimate, actual, possible, or imaginary.

think /θɪŋk/ *v.* (**thought, thinking**) **–v.t.** **1.** to form or conceive in the mind; have in the mind as an idea, conception, or the like. **2.** to form or have an idea or conception of (a thing, fact, circumstance, etc.). **3.** to hold as an opinion; believe; suppose. **4.** to consider (something) to be (as specified). **–v.i.** **5.** to use the mind, especially the intellect, actively; cogitate or meditate. **6.** (fol. by *of*) to form or have an idea or mental image. **7.** to reflect upon the matter in question. **8.** to have a belief or opinion as indicated.

think tank *n.* a group, usually of highly qualified specialists, dedicated to the solving of particular problems and the generating of productive ideas.

thinner /'θɪnə/ *n.* a volatile liquid added to paints or varnishes to facilitate application and to aid penetration by lowering the viscosity.

third /θɜd/ *adj.* **1.** an ordinal number, next after the second in order, place, time, rank, value, quality, etc. –*n.* **2.** someone who or that which comes next after the second. **3.** a third part, especially of one.

third party *n.* any person other than the principals to some transaction, proceeding, or agreement.

third-party property damage insurance *n.* a form of insurance which covers the owner or driver of a vehicle for the damage which the vehicle insured might cause to someone else's vehicle or property.

third person *n.* See **person** (def. 3).

thirst /θɜst/ *n.* **1.** an uneasy or painful sensation of dryness in the mouth and throat caused by need of drink. **2.** strong or eager desire; craving. –**thirsty**, *adj.*

thirteen /θɜ'tin/ *n.* **1.** a cardinal number, ten plus three. –*adj.* **2.** amounting to thirteen in number. –**thirteenth**, *adj.*, *n.*

thirty /'θɜti/ *n.* (*pl.* **-ties**) **1.** a cardinal number, ten times three. –*adj.* **2.** amounting to thirty in number. –**thirtieth**, *adj.*, *n.*

this /ðɪs/ *pron.* (*pl.* **these**) **1.** a demonstrative pronoun used to indicate: **a.** a person, thing, idea, etc., as pointed out, present, or near, as before mentioned or supposed to be understood, as about to be mentioned, or by way of emphasis: *This is my husband.* **b.** one of two or more persons, things, etc., already mentioned, referring to the one nearer in place, time, or thought: *This is the one.* –*adj.* (*pl.* **these**) **2.** a demonstrative adjective used to indicate: **a.** a person, place, thing, idea, etc., as pointed out, present, or near, before mentioned, supposed to be understood, or by way of emphasis: *This man is my husband.* **b.** one of two or more persons, things, etc., already mentioned, referring to the one nearer in place, time, or thought: *this one, not that one.* –*adv.* **3.** an adverb used with adjectives and adverbs of quality or extent to indicate precise degree or extent: *this much; this far.*

thistle /'θɪsəl/ *n.* any of various prickly plants.

thither /'ðɪðə/ *adv.* to or towards that place or point.

thong /θɒŋ/ *n.* **1.** a narrow strip of hide or leather, used as a fastening, as the lash of a whip, etc. **2.** a sandal held loosely on the foot by two strips of leather, rubber, etc., passing between the first and second toes and over either side of the foot; flip-flop.

thorax /'θɔræks/ *n.* (*pl.* **thoraces** /'θɔrəsiz, θɒ'reɪsiz/ *or* **thoraxes**) *Anat.* (in humans and the higher vertebrates) the part of the trunk between the neck and the abdomen, containing the cavity (enclosed by the ribs, etc.) in which the heart, lungs, etc., are situated; the chest. –**thoracic**, *adj.*

thorn /θɔn/ *n.* a sharp-pointed excrescence on a plant; a prickle.

thorough /'θʌrə/ *adj.* **1.** carried out through the whole of something; fully executed; complete or perfect. **2.** thoroughgoing in action or procedure; leaving nothing undone.

thoroughbred /'θʌrəbred/ *adj.* **1.** of pure or unmixed breed, stock, etc., as a horse or other animal. –*n.* **2.** a thoroughbred animal.

thoroughfare /'θʌrəfeə/ *n.* a road, street, or the like, open at both ends, especially a main road.

those /ðəʊz/ *pron.*, *adj.* plural of **that**.

though /ðəʊ/ *conj.* **1.** (*introducing a subordinate clause, which is oft. marked by ellipsis*) notwithstanding that; in spite of the fact that. **2.** even if; granting that. **3.** if (usually in *as though*). –*adv.* **4.** for all that; however. Also, *Poetic*, **tho'**.

thought /θɔt/ *v.* **1.** past tense and past participle of **think**. –*n.* **2.** the product of mental activity; that which one thinks. **3.** the capacity or faculty of thinking. **4.** meditation.

thoughtful /'θɔtfəl/ *adj.* **1.** occupied with or given to thought; contemplative. **2.** characterised by or manifesting thought: *a thoughtful essay.* **3.** careful, heedful, or mindful **4.** showing consideration for others; considerate. –**thoughtfully**, *adv.* –**thoughtfulness**, *n.*

thoughtless /'θɔtləs/ *adj.* **1.** not taking thought; unthinking, careless, or heedless. **2.** lacking in consideration for others; inconsiderate. –**thoughtlessly**, *adv.* –**thoughtlessness**, *n.*

thought police *n. Colloq.* (*derog.*) authoritarians who wish to regulate the way people think, especially in relation to political correctness.

thousand /'θaʊzənd/ *n.* (*pl.* **-sands**, *as after a numeral*, **-sand**) **1.** a cardinal number, ten times one hundred. –*adj.* **2.** amounting to one thousand in number. –**thousandth**, *adj.*, *n.*

thrall /θrɔl/ *n.* a slave.

thrash /θræʃ/ *v.t.* **1.** to beat soundly by way of punishment; administer a beating to. –*v.i.* **2.** to beat, toss, or plunge wildly or violently about.

thread /θred/ *n.* **1.** a fine cord, especially that used for sewing. **2.** the helical ridge of a screw. **3.** that which runs through the whole course of something, connecting successive parts, as the sequence of events in a narrative. –*v.t.* **4.** to pass the end of a thread through the eye of (a needle). **5.** to fix (beads, etc.) upon a thread that is passed through; string.

threadbare /'θredbeə/ *adj.* **1.** (of fabric, etc.) worn thin; shabby. **2.** meagre, scanty, or poor.

threading /'θredɪŋ/ *n.* **1.** the passing of a thread through something, as a needle. **2.** a beauty treatment for the removal of unwanted hair so as to improve an untidy hairline, in which hairs are caught and pulled out by a twisted cotton thread which is rolled over them.

threat /θret/ *n.* **1.** a declaration of an intention or determination to inflict punishment, pain or loss on someone. **2.** an indication of probable evil to come. –**threaten**, *v.*

three /θri/ *n.* **1.** a cardinal number, two plus one. –*adj.* **2.** amounting to three in number.

3D /θri'di/ *adj.* **1.** three-dimensional. *–n.* **2.** a three-dimensional form or appearance. Also, **3-D.**

three-dimensional /θri-də'mɛnʃənəl/ *adj.* **1.** having or seeming to have, the dimension of depth as well as height and breadth. **2.** realistic; lifelike.

3D printing *n.* a process by which a three-dimensional solid object can be produced from a digital model. **–3D printer,** *n.*

thresh /θrɛʃ/ *v.t.* to separate the grain or seeds from (a cereal plant, etc.) by some mechanical means, as by the action of a threshing machine.

threshold /'θrɛʃhoʊld/ *n.* **1.** the entrance to a house or building. **2.** any place or point of entering or beginning. **3.** *Psychol., Physiol.* the point at which a stimulus becomes perceptible or is of sufficient intensity to produce an effect.

threw /θru/ *v.* past tense of **throw.**

thrice /θrais/ *adv.* three times.

thrift /θrift/ *n.* economical management; economy; frugality. **–thrifty,** *adj.*

thrill /θril/ *v.t.* **1.** to effect with a sudden wave of keen emotion, so as to produce a tremor or tingling sensation through the body. *–v.i.* **2.** to be stirred by a thrill of emotion or excitement. *–n.* **3.** a tremor or tingling sensation passing through the body as the result of sudden keen emotion or excitement. **4.** thrilling property or quality, as of a story.

thriller /'θrilə/ *n.* a book, play, or film, dealing with crime, mystery, etc., in an exciting or sensational manner.

thrive /θraiv/ *v.i.* (**thrived** *or* **throve, thrived** *or* **thriven** /'θrivən/, **thriving**) to grow or develop vigorously; flourish.

throat /θroʊt/ *n.* **1.** the passage from the mouth to the stomach or to the lungs. **2.** the front of the neck below the chin and above the collarbones.

throb /θrob/ *v.i.* (**throbbed, throbbing**) **1.** to beat with increased force or rapidity, as the heart under the influence of emotion or excitement; palpitate. *–n.* **2.** the act of throbbing. **3.** any pulsation or vibration.

throes /θroʊz/ *pl. n.* **1.** any violent disturbance or struggle: *death throes. –phr.* **2. in the throes of,** engaged in; fully preoccupied with.

thrombosis /θrɒm'boʊsəs/ *n.* coagulation of the blood in the heart, arteries, veins, or capillaries.

throne /θroʊn/ *n.* the chair or seat occupied by a sovereign, bishop, or other exalted personage on ceremonial occasions.

throng /θrɒŋ/ *n.* a multitude of people crowded or assembled together; a crowd.

throttle /'θrɒtl/ *n.* **1.** a lever, pedal, or other device to control the amount of fuel being fed to an engine. *–v.t.* (**-tled, -tling**) **2.** to stop the breath of by compressing the throat; strangle.

through /θru/ *prep.* **1.** in at one end, side, or surface, and out at the other. **2.** by the means or instrumentality of. **3.** by reason of or in consequence of. *–adv.* **4.** in at one end, side, or surface and out at the other. **5.** from the beginning to the end. **6.** to the end. *–adj.* **7.** that extends, goes, or conveys through the whole of a long distance with little or no interruption, obstruction, or hindrance. Also, **thro, thro', thru.**

throughout /θru'aʊt/ *prep.* **1.** in or to every part of; everywhere in. *–adv.* **2.** in every part.

throw /θroʊ/ *v.t.* (**threw, thrown, throwing**) **1.** to project or propel forcibly through the air by a sudden jerk or straightening of the arm; propel or cast in any way. **2.** to put hastily. **3.** to shape on a potter's wheel. **4.** to deliver (a blow or punch). **5.** to cast (dice). **6.** (of a horse, etc.) to cause to fall off. **7.** *Colloq.* to astonish; disconcert; confuse. **8.** to arrange or host (a social event). *–n.* **9.** an act of throwing or casting; a cast or fling.

throwback /'θroʊbæk/ *n.* reversion to an ancestral type or character.

thru /θru/ *prep., adv., adj.* (*often used in advertising*) → **through.**

thrush¹ /θrʌʃ/ *n.* a type of migratory bird, of medium size, not brightly coloured, noted for its song.

thrush² /θrʌʃ/ *n.* a disease characterised by whitish spots and ulcers on the membranes of the mouth, throat, vagina, etc., due to a parasitic fungus; monilia.

thrust /θrʌst/ *v.* (**thrust, thrusting**) *–v.t.* **1.** to push forcibly; shove; put or drive with force. *–v.i.* **2.** to push against something. **3.** to make a thrust, lunge, or stab at something. *–n.* **4.** the act of thrusting; a forcible push or drive; a lunge or stab.

thud /θʌd/ *n.* **1.** a dull sound, as of a heavy blow or fall. *–v.i., v.t.* (**thudded, thudding**) **2.** to beat or strike with a dull sound of heavy impact.

thug /θʌg/ *n.* a brutal, vicious, or murderous ruffian, robber, or gangster.

thumb /θʌm/ *n.* **1.** the short, thick inner digit of the human hand, next to the forefinger. *–v.t.* **2.** to soil or wear with the thumbs in handling, as the pages of a book. **3.** (oft. fol. by *through*) to run through (the pages of a book, etc.) quickly.

thumbnail /'θʌmneil/ *n.* **1.** the nail of the thumb. Also, **thumbnail sketch. a.** a concise or rudimentary drawing. **b.** a brief description of a person or account of an event. **3.** a small computer graphics image which offers a preview of a full-size image.

thump /θʌmp/ *n.* **1.** a blow with something thick and heavy, producing a dull sound; a heavy knock. *–v.t.* **2.** to strike or beat with something thick and heavy, so as to produce a dull sound; pound. **3.** *Colloq.* to punch; thrash severely.

thunder /'θʌndə/ *n.* **1.** the loud noise which accompanies a flash of lightning, due to violent disturbance of the air by a discharge of electricity. *–v.i.* **2.** to speak in a very loud tone.

thus /ðʌs/ *adv.* **1.** in the way just indicated; in this way. **2.** accordingly; consequently.

thwack /θwæk/ *v.t.* to strike or beat vigorously with something flat; whack.

thwart /θwɔt/ *v.t.* **1.** to oppose successfully; prevent from accomplishing a purpose; frustrate (a purpose, etc.); baffle. *–adj.* **2.** adverse; unfavourable.

thylacine /'θailəsin/ *n.* a carnivorous, wolf-like marsupial of Tasmania, now thought to be extinct, with a tan-coloured coat with black stripes across the back. Also, **Tasmanian tiger.**

thyme /taɪm/ n. any of various plants of the mint family with aromatic leaves used for seasoning.

thymus /'θaɪməs/ n. Anat. a ductless gland lying near the base of the neck.

thyroid gland /'θaɪrɔɪd/ n. Anat. a two-lobed gland lying on either side of the trachea. Its internal secretion is important in regulating body growth.

TIA /ti aɪ 'eɪ/ n. Pathol. transient ischaemic attack; a small stroke (**stroke¹** def. 3), usually caused by a temporary disruption in the flow of blood to the brain tissue, the symptoms being minor and temporary but sometimes being an indicator that a more severe stroke will follow.

tiara /ti'ɑrə/ n. a small jewelled ornamental crown worn by women.

tibia /'tɪbɪə/ n. (pl. **tibias** or **tibiae** /'tɪbi:/) Anat. the inner of the two bones of the lower leg, extending from the knee to the ankle; shinbone.

tic /tɪk/ n. a sudden, painless, purposeless muscular contraction in the face or extremities.

tick¹ /tɪk/ n. **1.** a slight, sharp recurring click or beat, as of a clock. **2.** a small mark, as a hooked, sloping dash (formed by two strokes at an acute angle) indicating that something has been done or is correct. –v.i. **3.** to emit or produce a tick, like that of a clock. –v.t. **4.** to mark (an item, etc.) with a tick, as to indicate examination or correctness. –phr. **5. tick off**, Colloq. to rebuke; scold.

tick² /tɪk/ n. a bloodsucking mite-like animal.

ticket /'tɪkət/ n. **1.** a slip, usually of paper or cardboard, serving as evidence of the holder's title to some service, right, or the like. **2.** a label or tag. **3.** a list of candidates nominated or put forward by a political party, faction, etc. **4.** a summons issued for a traffic or parking offence. **5.** a preliminary recording of transactions prior to their entry into more permanent books of account. **6.** Colloq. the right or proper thing: that's the ticket!

tickle /'tɪkəl/ v.t. **1.** to touch or stroke lightly with the fingers, a feather, etc., so as to excite a tingling or itching sensation in; titillate. **2.** to poke in some sensitive part of the body so as to excite spasmodic laughter.

ticklish /'tɪklɪʃ/ adj. **1.** sensitive to tickling. **2.** requiring careful handling or action; risky; difficult. **3.** unstable or easily upset, as a boat; unsteady.

tidal power n. the energy which can be harvested from the tides in the ocean by trapping water at high tide and running it through a turbine system as the tide goes out. Also, **tidal energy**.

tidal wave /'taɪdəl/ n. (in non-technical use) a tsunami.

tiddler /'tɪdlə/ n. a very small fish.

tiddly /'tɪdli/ adj. (**-lier**, **-liest**) Colloq. slightly drunk.

tide /taɪd/ n. **1.** the periodic rise and fall of the waters of the ocean and its inlets, about every 12 hours and 26 minutes, due to the attraction of the moon and sun. **2.** a tendency, trend, current, etc., as of events, ideas, public opinion, etc. –phr. (**tided**, **tiding**) **3. tide someone over**, to help someone to get over a period of difficulty, distress, etc. –**tidal**, adj.

tidings /'taɪdɪŋz/ pl. n. news or information.

tidy /'taɪdi/ adj. (**-dier**, **-diest**) **1.** neat; trim; orderly. **2.** Colloq. considerable. –v.t., v.i. (**-died**, **-dying**) **3.** (oft. fol. by up) to make tidy or neat.

tie /taɪ/ v. (**tied**, **tying**) –v.t. **1.** to bind or fasten with a cord, string, or the like, drawn together and knotted. **2.** to draw together the parts of with a knotted string or the like. **3.** to draw together into a knot, as a cord. **4.** to fasten, join, or connect in any way. **5.** to confine, restrict, or limit. **6.** to bind or oblige, as to do something. –v.i. **7.** to make the same score; be equal in a contest. –n. **8.** that with which anything is tied. **9.** a narrow, decorative band, as of cotton or silk, worn round the neck, commonly under a collar, and tied in front. **10.** anything that fastens, secures, or unites. **11.** something that restricts one's freedom of action. **12.** a state of equality in points, votes, etc., as among competitors.

tier /tɪə/ n. a row, range, or rank.

tiff /tɪf/ n. a slight or petty quarrel.

TIFF /tɪf/ n. Computers **1.** tagged image file format; a data format for bitmapped image files. **2.** a file stored in this format.

tiger /'taɪgə/ n. a large feline, tawny-coloured and striped with black.

tiger snake n. a highly venomous snake of southern Australia.

tight /taɪt/ adj. **1.** firmly or closely fixed in place; not easily moved; secure. **2.** drawn or stretched so as to be tense; taut. **3.** fitting closely, especially too closely. **4.** of such close or compacted texture, or fitted together so closely, as to be impervious to water, air, steam, etc. **5.** strict; firm; rigid. **6.** Colloq. mean with money; stingy; parsimonious. **7.** Colloq. intoxicated; drunk; tipsy. **8.** Commerce (of a commodity) difficult to obtain. **9.** Finance (of credit) not easily obtained. –**tighten**, v. –**tightly**, adv.

-tight a suffix meaning 'impervious to', as in watertight.

tightrope /'taɪtroʊp/ n. a rope or wire stretched tight, on which acrobats perform feats of balancing. Also, **tightwire**.

tights /taɪts/ pl. n. a close-fitting, finely woven garment covering the body from the waist downwards and the legs.

tiki /'tiki/ n. a carved image representing an ancestor, worn as an amulet in some Polynesian cultures.

tilde /'tɪldə/ n. a mark (~) placed over a letter, as over the letter 'n' in Spanish to indicate a palatal nasal sound, as in señor.

tile /taɪl/ n. **1.** a thin slab or shaped piece of baked clay used for covering roofs, lining walls, paving floors, etc. –v.t. (**tiled**, **tiling**) **2.** to cover with or as with tiles.

till¹ /tɪl/ prep. **1.** up to the time of; until. **2.** (with a negative) before. –conj. **3.** to the time that or when; until. **4.** (with a negative) before.

till² /tɪl/ v.t. to work (land); cultivate.

till³ /tɪl/ n. (in a shop, etc.) a container as a box, drawer, or the like, in which cash is kept.

tilt /tɪlt/ v.t. **1.** to cause to lean, incline, slope or slant. –v.i. **2.** to move into or assume a sloping position or direction. **3.** (fol. by at) to strike, thrust, or charge with a lance or the like. –n.

4. an act or instance of tilting. **5.** the state of being tilted; a sloping position.

timber /'tɪmbə/ *n.* wood, especially when suitable for building houses, ships, etc., or for use in carpentry, joinery, etc.

timbre /'tɪmbə, 'tæmbə/ *n.* the characteristic quality of a sound.

time /taɪm/ *n.* **1.** the system of those relations which any event has to any other as past, present, or future; indefinite continuous duration regarded as that in which events succeed one another. **2.** a limited extent of time, as between two successive events. **3.** (*oft. pl.*) the period or era now (or then) present. **4.** a prescribed or allotted period, as of one's life, for payment of a debt, etc. **5.** a particular or definite point in time. **6.** a particular part of a year, day, etc. **7.** the period in which an action is completed, especially a performance in a race. **8.** each occasion of a recurring action or event. **9.** (*pl.*) used as a multiplicative word in phrasal combinations expressing how many instances of a quantity or factor are taken together. **10.** *Music, etc.* tempo; relative rapidity of movement. *–adj.* **11.** of, relating to, or showing the passage of time. **12.** *Commerce* payable a stated period of time after presentment. *–v.t.* **13.** to ascertain or record the time, duration, or rate of. **14.** to appoint or choose the moment or occasion for.

time clause *n.* **1.** *Law* a clause in a contract which limits it or some aspect of it to a certain time period. **2.** *Gram.* a subordinate clause which specifies the time at which the action of the main clause takes place, as in *When you arrive, go straight to bed.*

time line *n.* **1.** a representation of historical events in the form of a line with date divisions and important events marked on it. **2.** a schedule with deadlines indicated. Also, **timeline**.

timely /'taɪmli/ *adj.* (**-lier, -liest**) occurring at a suitable time; seasonable; opportune; well-timed.

timepiece /'taɪmpis/ *n.* a clock or a watch.

time share *n.* a share in a holiday resort property, entitling the owner to occupy the resort unit for a specified time each year. **–timeshare,** *adj.*

time sheet *n.* a sheet, card or digital file recording the hours worked by an employee. Also, **timesheet**.

timeshift /'taɪmʃɪft/ *v.i.* **1.** to record a television program in order to view it at a time of one's own convenience. *–v.t.* **2.** to record (a program) in this way. **–timeshifting,** *n.*

timetable /'taɪmteɪbəl/ *n.* **1.** a schedule showing the times at which railway trains, buses, aeroplanes, etc., arrive and depart. **2.** any plan listing the times at which certain things are due to take place.

time trial *n.* a race in which participants race against the clock, the race being decided on who completes the course in the fastest time.

timid /'tɪməd/ *adj.* subject to fear; easily alarmed; timorous; shy.

timing /'taɪmɪŋ/ *n.* **1.** the controlling of the speed of an action, event, etc. **2.** the mechanism which ensures that the valves in an internal-combustion engine open and close at the correct time.

timorous /'tɪmərəs/ *adj.* **1.** full of fear; fearful. **2.** subject to fear; timid.

timpani /'tɪmpəni/ *pl. n.* (*sing.* **-pano** /-pənoʊ/) a set of kettledrums.

tin /tɪn/ *n.* **1.** a low-melting, metallic element. *Symbol:* Sn **2.** any shallow metal pan, especially one used in baking. **3.** a hermetically sealed container for food, especially one made of tin plate. *–v.t.* (**tinned, tinning**) **4.** to cover or coat with a thin deposit of tin. **5.** to pack or preserve in tins, as foods.

tincture /'tɪŋktʃə/ *n. Pharmaceutical* a solution of a medicinal substance in alcohol.

tinder /'tɪndə/ *n.* any dry substance that readily takes fire from a spark.

tine /taɪn/ *n.* a sharp projecting point or prong, as of a fork or deer's antler. Also, **tyne**.

tinea /'tɪniə/ *n.* any of several contagious skin diseases affecting various parts of the body and caused by fungi.

ting /tɪŋ/ *v.t., v.i.* to cause to make, or to make, a high, clear, ringing sound.

tinge /tɪndʒ/ *v.t.* (**tinged, tingeing** *or* **tinging**) **1.** to impart a trace or slight degree of some colour to; tint. *–n.* **2.** a slight degree of colouration.

tingle /'tɪŋgəl/ *v.i.* **1.** to have a prickling or stinging sensation. *–n.* **2.** a tingling sensation.

tinker /'tɪŋkə/ *n.* **1.** a mender of pots, kettles, pans, etc., usually an itinerant. *–v.i.* **2.** to busy oneself with something, especially a machine or an appliance, usually without useful results.

tinkle /'tɪŋkəl/ *v.i.* **1.** to give forth or make a succession of short, light, ringing sounds. *–n.* **2.** a tinkling sound.

tinnitus /'tɪnətəs, tə'naɪtəs/ *n.* a ringing or similar sensation of sound in the ears, due to disease of the auditory nerve, etc.

tinny¹ /'tɪni/ *adj.* (**-nier, -niest**) characteristic of tin, as sounds; lacking resonance.

tinny² /'tɪni/ *adj.* (**-nier, -niest**) *Colloq.* lucky.

tinsel /'tɪnsəl/ *n.* an inexpensive glittering metallic substance used in pieces, strips, threads, etc., to produce a sparkling effect.

tint /tɪnt/ *n.* **1.** a colour, or a variety of a colour; hue. **2.** a colour diluted with white. *–v.t.* **3.** to apply a tint or tints to; colour slightly or delicately; tinge.

tiny /'taɪni/ *adj.* (**-nier, -niest**) very small; minute; wee.

-tion a suffix used to form abstract nouns. Also, **-ation, -cion, -ion, -sion, -xion**.

tip¹ /tɪp/ *n.* **1.** a slender or pointed extremity, especially of anything long or tapered. **2.** the top, summit, or apex.

tip² /tɪp/ *v.* (**tipped, tipping**) *–v.t.* **1.** to cause to assume a slanting or sloping position; incline; tilt. **2.** (*oft. fol. by over or up*) to overthrow, overturn, or upset. *–v.i.* **3.** (*usu. fol. by over or up*) to tumble or topple. *–n.* Also, **rubbish tip**. **4.** a place where waste material is deposited; dump; rubbish dump.

tip³ /tɪp/ *n.* **1.** a small present of money given to someone, as a waiter, porter, etc., for performing a service; a gratuity. **2.** a useful hint or idea. *–v.t.* (**tipped, tipping**) **3.** to give a small present of money to.

tipple /'tɪpəl/ *v.t.* to drink (wine, spirits, etc.), especially repeatedly.

tipsy /'tɪpsi/ *adj.* (**-sier**, **-siest**) slightly intoxicated.

tiptoe /'tɪptoʊ/ *n.* **1.** the tip or end of a toe. *–v.i.* (**-toed**, **-toeing**) **2.** to move or go on tiptoe, as with caution or stealth.

tirade /taɪ'reɪd, tə'reɪd/ *n.* a prolonged outburst of denunciation.

tire /'taɪə/ *v.t.* **1.** (sometimes fol. by *out*) to reduce or exhaust the strength of, as by exertion; make weary; fatigue. *–v.i.* **2.** to have the strength reduced or exhausted, as by labour or exertion; become fatigued. **3.** (usu. fol. by *of*) to have one's appreciation, interest, patience, etc., exhausted; become or be weary.

tired /'taɪəd/ *adj.* **1.** weakened by effort, work, etc., and needing to sleep. *–phr.* **2. tired of**, bored with. **–tiredness**, *n.*

tiresome /'taɪəsəm/ *adj.* **1.** such as to tire one; wearisome. **2.** annoying or exasperating. **–tiresomely**, *adv.*

'tis /tɪz/ *Archaic* contraction of *it is.*

tissue /'tɪʃu/ *n.* **1.** *Biol.* the substance of which an organism or part is composed. **2.** a woven fabric, especially one of light or gauzy texture, originally woven with gold or silver. **3.** any of several kinds of soft gauze-like papers used for various purposes. **4.** a paper handkerchief.

tit[1] /tɪt/ *n.* a small bird.

tit[2] /tɪt/ *n. Colloq.* a female breast.

titanic /taɪ'tænɪk/ *adj.* of enormous size.

titanium /taɪ'teɪniəm/ *n.* a metallic element. *Symbol:* Ti

titbit /'tɪtbɪt/ *n.* **1.** a delicate bit of food. **2.** a choice or pleasing bit of anything.

tithe /taɪð/ *n.* (*oft. pl.*) the tenth part of the annual produce of agriculture, etc., due or paid as a tax.

titian /'tɪʃən, 'ti-/ *n.* a reddish brown colour.

titillate /'tɪtəleɪt/ *v.t.* **1.** to tickle; excite a tingling or itching sensation in, as by touching or stroking lightly. **2.** to excite agreeably.

titivate /'tɪtəveɪt/ *v.i.* **1.** to make oneself smart or spruce. *–v.t.* **2.** to make smart or spruce.

title /'taɪtl/ *n.* **1.** the distinguishing name of a book, poem, picture, piece of music, or the like. **2.** a descriptive or distinctive appellation, especially one belonging to a person by right of rank, office, attainment, etc. **3.** *Sport* the championship. **4.** established or recognised right to something. **5.** *Law* **a.** legal right to the possession of property, especially real property. **b.** the instrument constituting evidence of such right.

title deed *n. Law* a deed or document containing or constituting evidence of ownership.

titter /'tɪtə/ *v.i.* to laugh in a low, half-restrained way, as from nervousness or in ill-suppressed amusement.

tittle-tattle /'tɪtl-tætl/ *n.* gossip.

titular /'tɪtʃələ/ *adj.* **1.** of, relating to, or of the nature of a title. **2.** existing or being such in title only.

tix /tɪks/ *pl. n. Colloq.* tickets.

tizz /tɪz/ *n. Colloq.* a state of somewhat hysterical confusion and anxiety, often expressed in frantic but ineffectual activity.

tizzy /'tɪzi/ *adj.* (**-zier**, **-ziest**) *Colloq.* gaudy, vulgar.

to /tu/, *weak form* /tə/ *prep.* **1.** expressing motion or direction towards something. **2.** indicating limit of movement or extension. **3.** expressing a point or limit in time. **4.** expressing aim, purpose, or intention. **5.** expressing limit in degree or amount. **6.** indicating addition or amount. **7.** expressing comparison or opposition. **8.** expressing reference or relation. **9.** expressing relative position. **10.** indicating proportion or ratio. **11.** connecting transitive verbs with their indirect or distant objects, and adjectives, nouns, and intransitive or passive verbs with a following noun which limits their action or application. **12.** used as the ordinary sign or accompaniment of the infinitive. *–adv.* **13.** towards a person, thing, or point implied or understood. **14.** to consciousness; to one's senses.

toad /toʊd/ *n.* a terrestrial amphibian similar to a frog.

toadstool /'toʊdstul/ *n.* a usually poisonous fungus, similar to a mushroom.

toast[1] /toʊst/ *n.* bread in slices browned on both surfaces by heat.

toast[2] /toʊst/ *n.* **1.** a person whose health is proposed and drunk. **2.** a call on another or others to drink to some person or thing. **3.** words of congratulation, appreciation, loyalty, etc., spoken before drinking. *–v.t.* **4.** to drink to the health of, or in honour of.

tobacco /tə'bækoʊ/ *n.* a plant whose leaves are prepared for smoking or chewing or as snuff.

toboggan /tə'bɒgən/ *n.* a light sledge with low runners.

today /tə'deɪ/ *n.* **1.** this present day. *–adv.* **2.** on this present day.

toddle /'tɒdl/ *v.i.* to go with short, unsteady steps, as a child or an old person.

toddy /'tɒdi/ *n.* (*pl.* **-dies**) a drink made of spirits and hot water.

to-do /tə'du/ *n.* (*pl.* **to-dos**) bustle; fuss.

toe /toʊ/ *n.* **1.** (in humans) one of the terminal members or digits of the foot. **2.** an analogous part in other animals. **3.** a part resembling a toe in shape or position.

toff /tɒf/ *n. Colloq.* (*usually derog.*) a rich, upper-class, usually well-dressed person.

toffee /'tɒfi/ *n.* a sweet made of sugar or treacle.

tofu /'toʊfu/ *n.* a curd made from white soybeans, usually formed into small blocks; bean curd.

toga /'toʊgə/ *n.* (*pl.* **-gas**) the loose outer garment of the citizens of ancient Rome.

together /tə'gɛðə/ *adv.* **1.** into or in one gathering, company, mass, place, or body. **2.** at the same time; simultaneously. **3.** in cooperation; with united action. *–adj.* **4.** capable and calm.

toggle /'tɒgəl/ *n.* **1.** a transverse pin, bolt, or rod placed through an eye of a rope, link of a chain, or the like, for various purposes. **2.** *Computers* a key or command that has the reverse effect on each successive use.

togs /tɒgz/ *pl. n. Colloq.* **1.** clothes. **2.** → **swimming costume**.

toil /tɔɪl/ *n.* **1.** hard and continuous work; exhausting labour or effort. *–v.i.* **2.** to engage in severe and continuous work; labour arduously.

toilet /'tɔɪlət/ *n.* **1.** a receptacle for the disposal of urine and waste matter from the bowel, especially one connected to a drain in which the waste is flushed away with water. **2.** a room where people go to use a toilet. **3.** the act or process of dressing, including bathing, arranging the hair, etc.

toiletry /ˈtɔɪlətri/ n. (pl. **-ries**) an article or substance used in dressing or hygiene.

token /ˈtoʊkən/ n. **1.** something serving to represent or indicate some fact, event, feeling, etc.; sign. **2.** a characteristic mark or indication; symbol. **3.** a ticket, metal disc, etc., certified as having a particular value, for payment or exchange, as for ferry fares, etc. **4.** a particular act or event, especially as an instance of a class or type.

told /toʊld/ v. **1.** past tense and past participle of **tell.** –phr. **2. all told,** in all.

tolerant /ˈtɒlərənt/ adj. **1.** willing to put up with behaviour or conditions one doesn't like or agree with. **2.** willing to accept other people's beliefs and customs. –**tolerance,** n.

tolerate /ˈtɒləreɪt/ v.t. **1.** to allow; permit. **2.** to bear without repugnance; put up with. **3.** Med. to endure or resist the action of (a drug, poison, etc.). –**tolerable,** adj. –**toleration,** n.

toll[1] /toʊl/ v.t. **1.** to cause (a large bell) to sound with single strokes slowly and regularly repeated, as for summoning a congregation to church, or especially for announcing a death. –v.i. **2.** to sound with single strokes slowly and regularly repeated, as a bell.

toll[2] /toʊl/ n. **1.** Also, **tollage.** a payment exacted by the state, the local authorities, etc., for some right or privilege, as for passage along a road or over a bridge. **2.** cost, especially in terms of death or loss.

tom /tɒm/ n. the male of various animals.

tomahawk /ˈtɒməhɔk/ n. a small, short-handled axe.

tomato /təˈmatoʊ/ n. (pl. **-toes**) a widely cultivated plant bearing a slightly acid, pulpy fruit, commonly red, sometimes yellow, used as a vegetable.

tomb /tum/ n. an excavation in earth or rock for the reception of a corpse.

tomboy /ˈtɒmbɔɪ/ n. an adventurous, athletic girl.

tombstone /ˈtumstoʊn/ n. a stone, usually bearing an inscription, set to mark a tomb or grave.

tome /toʊm/ n. a book, especially a large or scholarly one.

tomfoolery /tɒmˈfuləri/ n. foolish or silly behaviour.

tomorrow /təˈmɒroʊ/ n. **1.** the day after this day. –adv. **2.** on the morrow; on the day after this day.

tom-tom /ˈtɒm-tɒm/ n. a type of drum.

ton /tʌn/ n. a unit of mass in the imperial system equal to about 1016 kg. –**tonnage,** n.

tone /toʊn/ n. **1.** any sound considered with reference to its quality, pitch, strength, source, etc. **2.** quality or character of sound. **3.** a particular quality, way of sounding, modulation, or intonation of the voice. **4.** stress of voice on a syllable of a word. **5.** Music an interval equivalent to two semitones. **6.** a variety of colour; a tint; a shade. **7.** Physiol. the state of tension or firmness proper to the organs or tissues of the body. **8.** style, distinction, or elegance. –v. (**toned, toning**) –v.t. **9.** to sound

with a particular tone. **10.** to give the proper tone to. **11.** to modify the tone or character of. –v.i. **12.** (fol. by *with* or *in with*) to harmonise in tone or colour. –**tonal,** adj.

tongs /tɒŋz/ pl. n. (*sometimes construed as sing.*) any of various implements consisting of two arms fastened together, for seizing, holding, or lifting something.

tongue /tʌŋ/ n. **1.** an organ in humans and most vertebrates occupying the floor of the mouth and often freely movable, being the principal organ of taste, and, in humans, of articulate speech. **2.** the faculty or power of speech. **3.** the language of a particular people, country, or locality. **4.** something resembling or suggesting an animal's tongue in shape, position, or function.

tonic /ˈtɒnɪk/ n. **1.** a medicine that invigorates or strengthens. **2.** anything invigorating physically, mentally, or morally. **3.** Music the first degree of the scale; the keynote. –adj. **4.** relating to, maintaining, increasing, or restoring the tone or healthy condition of the system or organs, as a medicine. **5.** invigorating physically, mentally, or morally. **6.** characterised by distinctions of tone or accent.

tonic water n. effervescent water, often added to spirits.

tonight /təˈnaɪt/ n. **1.** this present or coming night; the night of this present day. –adv. **2.** on this present night; on the night of this present day.

tonne /tɒn/ n. a measure of mass in the metric system, equal to 1000 kilograms. Symbol: t

tonsil /ˈtɒnsəl/ n. Anat. either of two prominent oval masses of lymphoid tissue situated one on each side of the inside of the throat.

tonsillitis /tɒnsəˈlaɪtəs/ n. inflammation of the tonsils.

tonsure /ˈtɒnʃə/ n. the shaving of the head, or of some part of it, as a religious practice or rite.

too /tu/ adv. **1.** in addition; also; furthermore; moreover. **2.** to an excessive extent or degree.

took /tʊk/ v. past tense of **take.**

tool /tul/ n. **1.** an instrument, especially one held in the hand, for performing or facilitating mechanical operations, as a hammer, saw, file, etc. **2.** a person used by another for that person's own ends. **3.** Colloq. a stupid person. –v.t. **4.** to work or shape with a tool.

toolbar /ˈtulbɑ/ n. Computers a rectangular bar, usually at the top of a computer screen, containing buttons marked with icons or words which enable specific computer functions.

toolkit /ˈtulkɪt/ n. **1.** a collection of tools kept together for some particular work such as plumbing, electrical repair, etc. **2.** the toolbox, sheath or any other storage device for holding such tools.

toot /tut/ v.i. **1.** (of a horn) to give forth its characteristic sound. –v.t. **2.** to cause (a horn, etc.) to sound by blowing it.

tooth /tuθ/ n. (pl. **teeth** /tiθ/) **1.** (in most vertebrates) one of the hard bodies or processes usually attached in a row to each jaw, used for chewing, etc. **2.** any projection resembling or suggesting a tooth.

toothpaste /ˈtuθpeɪst/ n. a preparation for cleaning teeth in the form of paste.

tootle /'tutl/ *v.i. Colloq.* to go, walk, or drive.

top¹ /tɒp/ *n.* **1.** the highest point or part of anything. **2.** the highest or leading place, position, rank, etc. **3.** the highest point, pitch, or degree. **4.** a covering or lid, as of a box, car, etc. **5.** a blouse, T-shirt, jumper, jacket or other outer garment, sometimes with sleeves, which covers the torso. *–adj.* **6.** relating to, situated at, or forming the top; highest; uppermost; upper. **7.** highest in degree; greatest. **8.** foremost, chief, or principal. **9.** *Colloq.* the best; excellent. *–v.t.* (**topped, topping**) **10.** to furnish with a top; put a top on. **11.** to be at or constitute the top of. **12.** to reach the top of. **13.** to surpass, excel, or outdo. **14.** to remove the top of; crop; prune.

top² /tɒp/ *n.* → **spinning top**.

topaz /'toupæz/ *n.* a mineral occurring in crystals of various colours, and used as a gem.

topiary /'toupiəri/ *adj.* (of hedges, trees, etc.) clipped or trimmed into shapes.

topic /'tɒpɪk/ *n.* a subject of conversation or discussion.

topical /'tɒpɪkəl/ *adj.* **1.** relating to or dealing with matters of current or local interest. **2.** relating to the subject of a discourse, composition, or the like.

topnotch /'tɒpnɒtʃ/ *adj. Colloq.* excellent.

topo- a word element meaning 'place'.

topography /tə'pɒgrəfi/ *n.* (*pl.* **-phies**) the relief features or surface configuration of an area. *–***topographic**, *adj.*

topple /'tɒpəl/ *v.i.* to fall forwards as having too heavy a top.

topsoil /'tɒpsɔɪl/ *n.* the surface or upper part of the soil.

topsy-turvy /tɒpsi-'tɜvi/ *adj.* turned upside down; inverted; reversed.

top-up *n.* a further supply of something, usually a liquid, to replenish a container: *a top-up for your glass of champagne.*

tor /tɔ/ *n.* a rocky eminence; a hill.

torch /tɔtʃ/ *n.* **1.** a small portable electric lamp powered by dry batteries. **2.** a flame carried in the hand to give light. **3.** any of various lamplike devices which produce a hot flame and are used for soldering, burning off paint, etc.

tore /tɔ/ *v.* past tense of **tear²**.

toreador /'tɒriədɔ/ *n.* a bullfighter.

torment *v.t.* /tɔ'mɛnt/ **1.** to afflict with great bodily or mental suffering. *–n.* /'tɔmɛnt/ **2.** a state of great bodily or mental suffering; agony; misery. **3.** great pain or suffering.

torn /tɔn/ *v.* past participle of **tear²**.

tornado /tɔ'neɪdoʊ/ *n.* (*pl.* **-does** or **-dos**) a violent whirlwind.

torpedo /tɔ'pidoʊ/ *n.* (*pl.* **-does** or **-dos**) **1.** a self-propelled cigar-shaped missile containing explosives. *–v.t.* (**-doed, -doing**) **2.** to damage, or destroy with a torpedo or torpedoes.

torpor /'tɔpə/ *n.* lethargic dullness or indifference; apathy. *–***torpid**, *adj.*

torque /tɔk/ *n. Mechanics* that which produces or tends to produce torsion or rotation.

Torrens title /'tɒrənz/ *n.* a system whereby title to land is authorised by one document issued by a government department.

torrent /'tɒrənt/ *n.* a stream of water flowing with great rapidity and violence. *–***torrential**, *adj.*

torrent file *n.* a file created using software which sets up a network of peer-to-peer file sharers who each supply a small part of the file, greatly increasing the speed of delivery.

torrid /'tɒrəd/ *adj.* **1.** oppressively hot, parching, or burning. **2.** ardent; passionate.

torsion /'tɔʃən/ *n.* **1.** the act of twisting. **2.** the resulting state.

torso /'tɔsoʊ/ *n.* (*pl.* **-sos**) the trunk of the human body.

tort /tɔt/ *n. Law* **1.** any wrong other than a criminal wrong, as negligence, defamation, etc. **2.** (*pl.*) the field of study of torts.

tortilla /tɔ'tijə/ *n.* (in Mexico, etc.) a thin, round, unleavened pancake prepared from corn meal, cooked on a flat plate of iron, earthenware, or the like.

tortoise /'tɔtəs/ *n.* a slow-moving reptile, with a hard shell into which it can retract its head and feet.

tortoiseshell /'tɔtəfɛl/ *n.* a hard, brown, mottled substance obtained from the shell of a type of tortoise, or a synthetic equivalent.

tortuous /'tɔtʃuəs/ *adj.* **1.** full of twists, turns, or bends. **2.** not direct or straightforward.

torture /'tɔtʃə/ *n.* **1.** the act of inflicting excruciating pain, especially from sheer cruelty or in hatred, revenge, or the like. **2.** extreme anguish of body or mind; agony. *–v.t.* (**-tured, -turing**) **3.** to subject to torture. *–***torturous**, *adj.*

toss /tɒs/ *v.t.* **1.** to throw, pitch, or fling, especially to throw lightly or carelessly. *–v.i.* **2.** to pitch, rock, sway, or move irregularly, as a flag or plumes in the breeze. **3.** to move restlessly about. *–n.* **4.** the act of tossing.

tosser /'tɒsə/ *n.* **1.** someone or something that tosses. **2.** *Colloq.* a stupid person.

tot¹ /tɒt/ *n.* a small child.

tot² /tɒt/ *v.t.* (**totted, totting**) *Colloq.* (oft. fol. by *up*) to add.

total /'toutl/ *adj.* **1.** constituting or comprising the whole; entire; whole. **2.** complete in extent or degree; absolute; unqualified; utter. *–n.* **3.** the total amount; sum; aggregate. *–v.t.* (**-talled, -talling**) **4.** to bring to a total; add up. **5.** to reach a total of; amount to. *–***totally**, *adv.*

totalisator /'toutləɪˌzeɪtə/ *n.* a form of betting, as on horseraces, in which those who bet on the winners divide the bets or stakes, less a percentage for the management, taxes, etc. Also, **totalizator**.

totalitarian /toʊˌtælə'tɛəriən/ *adj.* of or relating to a centralised government in which those in control grant neither recognition nor tolerance to parties of differing opinion.

totality /toʊ'tæləti/ *n.* (*pl.* **-ties**) **1.** the state of being total. **2.** that which is total.

tote /toʊt/ *v.t. Colloq.* to carry, as on the back or in the arms, as a burden or load.

totem /'toʊtəm/ *n.* an object or natural phenomenon, often an animal, assumed as the token or emblem of a clan, family, or related group. *–***totemic**, *adj.*

totter /'tɒtə/ *v.i.* **1.** to walk or go with faltering steps, as if from extreme weakness. **2.** to sway or rock on the base or ground, as if about to fall.

toucan /'tukæn/ *n.* a strikingly coloured bird with a huge beak.

touch /tʌtʃ/ *v.t.* **1.** to put the hand, finger, etc., on or into contact with (something) to feel it. **2.** to come into or be in contact with. **3.** to affect with some feeling or emotion. **4.** *Colloq.* to apply to for money. –*v.i.* **5.** to come into or be in contact with something. **6.** (fol. by *on* or *upon*) to speak or write about briefly or casually in the course of a discourse, etc. –*n.* **7.** the act of touching. **8.** that sense by which anything material is perceived by means of the contact with it of some part of the body. **9.** the sensation or effect caused by touching something, regarded as a quality of the thing. **10.** a slight stroke or blow. **11.** a slight attack, as of illness or disease. **12.** manner of execution in artistic work. **13.** a slight amount.

touchpad /'tʌtʃpæd/ *n.* **1.** a control panel used to operate an appliance. **2.** *Computers* a small, pressure-sensitive pad on some computers, used to control the cursor by moving a fingertip across the pad.

touch-type *v.i.* to type without looking at the keys of the typewriter or computer keyboard.

touchy /'tʌtʃi/ *adj.* (**-chier, -chiest**) **1.** easily annoyed or offended. **2.** likely to give rise to strong emotions: *a touchy subject; a touchy situation.*

tough /tʌf/ *adj.* **1.** not easily broken or cut. **2.** (of food) difficult to cut or chew. **3.** capable of great endurance; sturdy; hardy. **4.** difficult to perform, accomplish, or deal with; hard, trying, or troublesome. **5.** vigorous; severe; violent.

toupee /'tupei/ *n.* a wig worn to cover a bald spot.

tour /tʊə, 'tuə, tɔ/ *v.i.* **1.** to travel from place to place. –*n.* **2.** a travelling around from place to place. **3.** a long journey including the visiting of a number of places in sequence. **4.** *Chiefly Mil.* a period of duty at one place.

tourism /'tʊərɪzəm, 'tuə-, 'tɔ-/ *n.* the occupation of providing local services, as entertainment, lodging, food, etc., for tourists.

tourist /'tʊərəst, 'tuə-, 'tɔ-/ *n.* someone who tours, especially for pleasure.

tournament /'tɔnəmənt/ *n.* **1.** a meeting for contests in athletic or other sports. **2.** a trial of skill in some game, in which competitors play a series of contests.

tourniquet /'tɔnəkei, 'tuə-/ *n.* any device for forcibly compressing a blood vessel, as to stop bleeding.

tousle /'taʊzəl/ *v.t.* **1.** to disorder or dishevel. **2.** to handle roughly.

tout /taʊt/ *v.i.* **1.** to solicit business, employment, votes, etc., importunately. **2.** *Racing* to sell betting information, take bets, etc., especially in public places. –*n.* **3.** someone who touts.

tow /toʊ/ *v.t.* **1.** to drag or pull (a boat, car, etc.) by means of a rope or chain. –*n.* **2.** the act of towing.

towards /tə'wɔdz, tɔdz/ *prep.* **1.** in the direction of (with reference to either motion or position). **2.** with respect to; as regards. **3.** as a help or contribution to. Also, **toward**.

$2 shop /tu 'dɒlə/ *n.* a shop which sells a wide range of inexpensive goods. Also, **two-dollar shop**.

towel /'taʊəl, taʊl/ *n.* a cloth or the like for wiping and drying something wet.

towelling /'taʊəlɪŋ, 'taʊlɪŋ/ *n.* any of various absorbent fabrics used for towels, and also for beachwear and the like.

tower /'taʊə/ *n.* **1.** a building or structure high in proportion to its width. **2.** any of various tower-like structures, contrivances, or objects. –*v.i.* **3.** to rise or extend far upwards. **4.** (fol. by *over, above,* etc.) to surpass, as in ability, etc.

town /taʊn/ *n.* **1.** a distinct densely populated area of considerable size, having some degree of self-government, usually smaller than a city. **2.** urban life, opposed to rural. **3.** the main shopping, business, or entertainment centre of a large town, contrasted with the suburbs. **4.** an urban community; the people of a town.

town hall *n.* a hall or building belonging to a town, used for the transaction of the town's business, etc., and often also as a place of public assembly.

townhouse /'taʊnhaʊs/ *n.* a dwelling, sharing a common wall with another, sold under strata title, and each with ground floor access. Also, **town house**.

township /'taʊnʃɪp/ *n.* a small town or settlement.

toxic /'tɒksɪk/ *adj.* **1.** of, relating to, affected with, or caused by a toxin or poison. **2.** poisonous. **3.** detrimental to a good outcome; extremely disadvantageous. –**toxicity** /tɒk'sɪsəti/, *n.* –**toxically**, *adv.*

toxic debt *n.* debt which, although initially acquired as a legitimate business transaction, proves subsequently to be financially worthless.

toxico- a combining form of **toxic**.

toxicology /tɒksə'kɒlədʒi/ *n.* the science of poisons, their effects, antidotes, detection, etc. –**toxicologist**, *n.*

toxin /'tɒksən/ *n.* **1.** a specific poisonous product generated by a disease-producing microorganism. **2.** any of various organic poisons.

toy /tɔɪ/ *n.* **1.** an object for playing with, usually by children; a plaything. –*adj.* **2.** of or like a toy, especially in size. –*v.i.* **3.** to act idly, absent-mindedly, or without seriousness. **4.** (usu. fol. by *with*) to trifle; deal with as unimportant.

trace[1] /treɪs/ *n.* **1.** a mark, token, or evidence of the former presence, existence, or action of something; a vestige. **2.** a mark, indication, or evidence. **3.** a scarcely discernible quantity of something; a very small amount. **4.** a record traced by a self-registering instrument. –*v.t.* (**traced, tracing**) **5.** to follow the footprints, track, or traces of. **6.** to follow the course, development, or history of. **7.** to copy (a drawing, plan, etc.) by following the lines of the original on a superimposed transparent sheet. **8.** to make a plan, diagram, or map of. –**traceable**, *adj.*

trace[2] /treɪs/ *n.* each of the two straps, ropes, or chains by which a carriage, wagon, or the like is drawn by a harness horse or other draught animal.

trace element *n. Biochem.* a chemical element, found in plants and animals in minute quantities, which is a critical factor in physiological processes.

tracery /ˈtreɪsəri/ *n.* any delicate interlacing work of lines, threads, etc.

traceur /treɪˈsɜ/ *n.* a person who undertakes the sport of parkour.

trachea /trəˈkiə/ *n.* (*pl.* **-cheas** *or* **-cheae** /-ˈkiː/) the principal passage for conveying air to and from the lungs; the windpipe.

track /træk/ *n.* **1.** a road, path, or trail. **2.** the structure of rails, sleepers, etc., on which a railway train or the like runs; a railway line. **3.** the mark, or series of marks, left by anything that has passed along. **4.** a rough roadway or path. **5.** a route, usually only roughly defined. **6.** the sports which are performed on a track, collectively; athletics. **7.** an endless jointed metal band around the wheels of some heavy vehicles. **8.** a course of action or conduct; a method of proceeding. **9.** a course laid out for running or racing. **10.** one of the distinct sections of a record, CD, etc., containing a piece, or section of music, etc. –*v.t.* **11.** to hunt by following the tracks of. **12.** (fol. by *down*) to catch or find, after pursuit or searching. **13.** to follow (a track, course, etc.).

track record *n.* an account of a person's successes or failures in a specific field.

tracksuit /ˈtræksut/ *n.* a loose, two-piece overgarment worn by athletes in training, between events, etc.

tract¹ /trækt/ *n.* a stretch or extent, as of land, water, etc.

tract² /trækt/ *n.* a brief treatise or pamphlet suitable for general distribution, especially one dealing with some topic of practical religion.

tractable /ˈtræktəbəl/ *adj.* easily managed, or docile.

traction /ˈtrækʃən/ *n.* **1.** the act of drawing or pulling. **2.** the adhesive friction of a body, as of a wheel on a rail.

tractor /ˈtræktə/ *n.* a motor vehicle, usually having tyres with deep treads, used to draw farm implements.

trade /treɪd/ *n.* **1.** the buying and selling, or exchanging, of commodities, either by wholesale or by retail, within a country or between countries. **2.** market: *the tourist trade.* **3.** commercial occupation (as against professional). **4.** a skilled occupation, especially one requiring manual labour. –*v.t.* **5.** to give in return; exchange; barter. –*v.i.* **6.** to carry on trade. –*phr.* **7. trade in**, to part in part exchange, as in a transaction. –**tradeable**, *adj.*

trade barrier *n.* a restraint placed on the free flow of goods between two or more countries, thus reducing the overall volume of trade.

trade gap *n.* the difference between the value of a country's imports and of its exports, when the former is a larger figure.

trademark /ˈtreɪdmak/ *n.* the name, symbol, figure, letter, word, or mark adopted and used by a manufacturer or merchant in order to designate the goods he or she manufactures or sells, and to distinguish them from those manufactured or sold by others. Any mark entitled to registration under the provisions of a statute is a trademark. Also, **trade mark**.

trade name *n.* **1.** the name or style under which a commercial enterprise does business.

2. a word or phrase used in trade whereby a business or enterprise or a particular class of goods is designated, but which is not technically a trademark, either because it is not susceptible of exclusive appropriation as a trademark or because it is not affixed to goods sold in the market. **3.** Also, **brand name**. the name by which an article or substance is known to the trade.

trade-off /ˈtreɪd-ɒf/ *n.* a concession made in a negotiation in return for one given.

trade price *n.* the price at which goods are sold to members of the same trade, or to retail dealers by wholesalers.

trade union *n.* an organisation of employees for mutual aid and protection, and for dealing collectively with employers. Also, **trades union**. –**trade unionism**, *n.* –**trade unionist**, *n.*

trading bank /ˈtreɪdɪŋ/ *n.* a bank which offers a wide variety of financial services to both individual and corporate customers, including cheque accounts, loans for commercial ventures, etc. In Australia the distinction between trading banks and savings banks has now been abolished.

trading stamp *n.* a stamp with a certain value given as a premium by a seller to a customer, specified quantities of these stamps being exchangeable for various articles when presented to the issuers of the stamps.

tradition /trəˈdɪʃən/ *n.* the handing down of statements, beliefs, legends, customs, etc., from generation to generation, especially by word of mouth or by practice. –**traditional**, *adj.*

traditional custodian *n.* a person who is entitled, by Indigenous tradition, to have certain cultural knowledge.

traditional owner *n.* a person who has, in accordance with Indigenous tradition, social, economic, and spiritual affiliations with, and responsibilities for, the lands claimed or any part of them.

traduce /trəˈdjus/ *v.t.* (**-duced, -ducing**) to speak evil or maliciously and falsely of.

traffic /ˈtræfɪk/ *n.* **1.** the coming and going of persons, vehicles, ships, etc., along a way of passage or travel. **2.** trade; buying and selling; commercial dealings. **3.** dealings or exchanges of anything between parties, people, etc. –*v.i.* (**-ficked, -ficking**) **4.** to carry on dealings of an illicit or improper kind.

tragedy /ˈtrædʒədi/ *n.* (*pl.* **-dies**) **1.** a dramatic composition of serious or sombre character, with an unhappy ending. **2.** a disaster or calamity.

tragic /ˈtrædʒɪk/ *adj.* **1.** characteristic or suggestive of tragedy. **2.** dreadful, calamitous, or fatal. –*n.* **3.** *Colloq.* someone who is excessively devoted to a particular celebrity, sport, hobby, etc.: *a cricket tragic.* –**tragically**, *adv.*

trail /treɪl/ *v.t.* **1.** to draw or drag along behind. –*v.i.* **2.** to be drawn or dragged along the ground or some other surface, as when hanging from something moving. **3.** to hang down loosely from something. –*n.* **4.** a path or track made across a wild region, over rough country, or the like, by the passage of people or animals. **5.** the track, scent, or the like, left by an animal, person, or thing, especially as followed by a hunter, hound, or other pursuer.

trail bike *n.* → **dirt bike**.

trailblazer /'treɪlbleɪzə/ *n.* **1.** a person who blazes a trail. **2.** a leader or innovator in a particular field. –**trailblaze**, *v.* –**trailblazing**, *adj.*, *n.*

trailer /'treɪlə/ *n.* **1.** a vehicle designed to be towed by a motor vehicle, and used in transporting loads. **2.** *Film* an advertisement for a forthcoming film, usually consisting of extracts from it.

train /treɪn/ *n.* **1.** a set of railway carriages or wagons, whether self-propelled or connected to a locomotive. **2.** a line or procession of persons, vehicles, etc., travelling together. **3.** an elongated part of a skirt or dress trailing behind on the ground. **4.** a succession or series of proceedings, events, circumstances, etc. **5.** a succession of connected ideas; a course of reasoning. –*v.t.* **6.** to make proficient by instruction and practice, as in some art, profession, or work. **7.** to make (a person, etc.) fit by proper exercise, diet, etc., as for some athletic feat or contest. **8.** to discipline and instruct (an animal) to perform specified actions. –*v.i.* **9.** to undergo discipline and instruction, drill, etc. **10.** to get oneself into condition by exercise, etc.

trainee /treɪ'ni/ *n.* **1.** a person receiving training. –*adj.* **2.** receiving training.

trainer /'treɪnə/ *n.* **1.** someone who trains others in a particular skill or activity. **2.** someone who prepares racehorses for racing. **3.** someone who trains athletes in a sport. **4.** equipment used in training, especially that which simulates the conditions of a sport. **5.** a shoe which is designed for use in sport.

train wreck *n.* **1.** the wreck of a train. **2.** *Colloq.* a complete disaster.

traipse /treɪps/ *v.i.* to walk (about) aimlessly.

trait /treɪt, treɪ/ *n.* a distinguishing feature or quality; characteristic.

traitor /'treɪtə/ *n.* someone who betrays their country by violating their allegiance; one guilty of treason.

trajectory /trə'dʒɛktəri/ *n.* (*pl.* -**ries**) the curve described by a projectile in its flight.

tram /træm/ *n.* a passenger vehicle moving on tracks laid in urban streets. Also, **tramcar.**

trammel /'træməl/ *n.* (*usu. pl.*) anything that impedes or hinders free action; a restraint.

tramp /træmp/ *v.i.* **1.** to tread or walk with a firm, heavy, resounding step. **2.** to go about as a vagrant or tramp. –*n.* **3.** the act of tramping. **4.** a person who travels about on foot from place to place, especially a vagrant living on occasional jobs or gifts of money or food.

trample /'træmpəl/ *v.t.* to tread heavily, roughly, or carelessly on or over.

trampoline /'træmpəlin, træmpə'lin/ *n.* a frame with tightly stretched material attached to it by springs, on which one jumps for pleasure or sport.

trance /træns, trans/ *n.* **1.** a dazed or bewildered condition. **2.** a fit of complete mental absorption or deep musing. **3.** an unconscious hypnotic condition.

tranche /træntʃ, trantʃ/ *n.* an additional block of stock, as bonds, etc., supplementary to an already existing issue.

trank /træŋk/ *n. Colloq.* any drug which acts as a depressant to the central nervous system, used as a recreational drug. –**tranked**, *adj.*

tranquil /'træŋkwəl/ *adj.* **1.** free from commotion or tumult; peaceful; quiet; calm. **2.** free from or unaffected by disturbing emotions; unruffled. –**tranquillity**, *n.* –**tranquillise**, **tranquillize**, *v.*

trans- **1.** a prefix meaning 'across', 'beyond'. **2.** a prefix meaning 'across' in the sense of changing from one state to another, as in *transgender, transsexual.*

transact /trænz'ækt/ *v.t.* to carry through (affairs, business, negotiations, etc.) to a conclusion or settlement.

transaction /trænz'ækʃən/ *n.* **1.** the act of transacting. **2.** an instance or process of transacting something. **3.** that which is transacted; an affair; a piece of business.

transcend /træn'sɛnd/ *v.t.* to go or be above or beyond; surpass or exceed. –**transcendent**, *adj.*

transcendental /trænsen'dɛntl/ *adj.* transcending ordinary or common experience, thought, or belief.

transcribe /træn'skraɪb/ *v.t.* **1.** to make a copy of in writing. **2.** to reproduce in writing or print as from speech. **3.** to write out in other characters; transliterate. –**transcript**, *n.* –**transcription**, *n.*

trans fat /'trænz/ *n.* fat composed of trans fatty acid.

trans fatty acid *n.* a type of unsaturated fat occurring naturally in meat and dairy products, but also created in the production of margarine; thought to increase the risk of coronary heart disease.

transfer *v.t.* /træns'fɜ/ (-**ferred**, -**ferring**) **1.** to convey or remove from one place, person, etc., to another. **2.** *Law* to make over or convey. –*n.* /'trænsfɜ/ **3.** the means or system of transferring. **4.** the act of transferring. **5.** a drawing, pattern, etc., which may be transferred to a surface, especially by direct contact. **6.** *Law* a conveyance, by sale, gift, or otherwise, of real or personal property, to another. **7.** *Finance* the act of having the ownership of a stock or registered bond transferred upon the books of the issuing company or its agent. **8.** *Finance* a deed completed when stocks and shares change hands, which is registered with the company issuing the shares. –**transferable**, *adj.* –**transference**, *n.* –**transferral**, *n.*

transfigure /træns'fɪgə/ *v.t.* to change in outward form or appearance; transform, change, or alter.

transfix /træns'fɪks/ *v.t.* **1.** to pierce through, as with a pointed weapon, or as the weapon does. **2.** to make motionless with amazement, terror, etc.

transform /træns'fɔm/ *v.t.* **1.** to change in form. **2.** to change in appearance, condition, nature, or character, especially completely or extensively. –**transformation**, *n.*

transformer /træns'fɔmə/ *n. Elect.* an electric device which transforms electric energy from circuit to circuit, usually also changing voltage and current.

transfuse /træns'fju:z/ v.t. **1.** to pour from one container into another. **2.** Med. to transfer (blood) from the veins or arteries of one person or animal into those of another. –**transfusion**, n.

transgender /trænz'dʒɛndə/ adj. of or relating to a person whose gender identity is different from their physiological gender as designated at birth.

transgress /trænz'grɛs/ v.t. to go beyond the limits imposed by (a law, command, etc.). –**transgression**, n.

transient /'trænziənt/ adj. **1.** not lasting or enduring. **2.** remaining for only a short time, as a guest at a hotel. –n. **3.** someone who or that which is transient. –**transience**, n.

transistor /træn'zɪstə/ n. **1.** Electronics a miniature solid-state device for amplifying or switching. **2.** a radio equipped with transistors.

transit /'trænzət/ n. **1.** the act or fact of passing across or through; passage from one place to another. **2.** conveyance from one place to another, as of persons or goods.

transition /træn'zɪʃən/ n. passage from one position, state, stage, etc., to another.

transitive verb /'trænzətɪv/ n. **1.** a verb which can only be used with a direct object. **2.** a verb used with a direct object, as *drink* in the sentence *She drinks water* where *water* is the direct object. Compare **intransitive verb**.

transitory /'trænzətri/ adj. passing away; not lasting, enduring, permanent or eternal.

translate /trænz'leɪt/ v.t. **1.** to turn (something written or spoken) from one language into another. **2.** to express in other terms; interpret; explain. –**translator**, n. –**translation**, n.

transliterate /trænz'lɪtəreɪt/ v.t. to change (letters, words, etc.) into corresponding characters of another alphabet or language.

translucent /trænz'lusənt/ adj. transmitting light imperfectly, as frosted glass.

transmission /trænz'mɪʃən/ n. **1.** the act of transmitting. **2.** that which is transmitted. **3.** Machinery **a.** the transmitting or transferring of motive force. **b.** a device for this purpose, especially the mechanism for transmitting power from the engine to the wheels of a motor vehicle.

transmit /trænz'mɪt/ v.t. (-mitted, -mitting) **1.** to send over or along, as to a recipient or destination; forward, dispatch, or convey. **2.** to communicate, as information, news, etc. **3.** to broadcast (a radio or television program). **4.** to convey or pass along.

transmogrify /trænz'mɒɡrəfaɪ/ v.t. (-fied, -fying) to change as by magic; transform.

transmute /trænz'mjut/ v.t. to change from one nature, substance, or form into another; transform.

transnational /trænz'næʃənəl/ adj. **1.** operating on a nationwide basis. **2.** → **multinational**.

transom /'trænsəm/ n. a lintel.

transparency /træns'pɛərənsi/, -'pær-/ n. (pl. -cies) **1.** Also, **transparence**. the property or quality of being transparent. **2.** a transparent positive photographic image used for projection. **3.** (of a government or other organisation)

the policy or practice of making all operations clearly manifest, and of being accountable to the public for all such operations.

transparent /træns'pɛərənt, -'pær-/ adj. **1.** having the property of transmitting rays of light through its substance so that bodies situated beyond or behind can be distinctly seen. **2.** open, frank, or candid. **3.** easily seen through or understood. **4.** open to public scrutiny, as government or business dealings.

transpire /træns'paɪə/ v.i. **1.** to occur, happen, or take place. **2.** to emit or give off waste matter, etc., through the surface, as of the body, of leaves, etc.

transplant v.t. /træns'plænt, -'plant/ **1.** to remove (a plant) from one place and plant it in another. **2.** Surg. to transfer (an organ or a portion of tissue) from one part of the body to another or from one person or animal to another. –n. /'trænsplænt, -plant/ **3.** a transplanting. **4.** something transplanted.

transport v.t. /træns'pɔt, 'trænspɔt/ **1.** to carry or convey from one place to another. **2.** to carry away by strong emotion. –n. /'trænspɔt/ **3.** the act or method of transporting or conveying; conveyance. **4.** a system of conveying passengers or freight. **5.** a means of transporting or conveying, as a ship, large truck, aeroplane, etc. **6.** strong emotion; ecstatic joy, bliss, etc. –**transportation**, n. –**transportable**, adj.

transpose /træns'pouz/ v.t. **1.** to alter the relative position or order of (a thing in a series, or a series of things). **2.** to cause (two or more things) to change places; interchange. **3.** Music to reproduce in a different key.

transsexual /trænz'sɛkʃuəl/ adj. **1.** of or relating to someone who has changed sex. –n. **2.** someone who has undergone a sex change operation. **3.** someone who feels himself or herself, though physically of one sex, to be of the other sex in psychological disposition. Also, **transexual**.

transversal /trænz'vɜsəl/ n. Geom. a line intersecting two or more lines.

transverse /'trænzvɜs, trænz'vɜs/ adj. lying or being across or in a crosswise direction.

transvestism /trænz'vɛstɪzəm/ n. the desire to wear clothing typical of the opposite sex. –**transvestite**, n., adj.

trap /træp/ n. **1.** a contrivance used for catching game or other animals, as a mechanical device that springs shut suddenly. **2.** any device, stratagem, or the like for catching someone unawares. **3.** any of various mechanical contrivances for preventing the passage of steam, water, etc. **4.** a carriage, especially a light two-wheeled one. –v.t. (trapped, trapping) **5.** to catch in a trap.

trapdoor /'træpdɔ/ n. a door or the like, flush, or nearly so, with the surface of a floor, ceiling, roof, etc.

trapdoor spider n. a burrowing spider.

trapeze /trə'piz/ n. an apparatus for gymnastics, consisting of a short horizontal bar attached to the ends of two suspended ropes.

trapezium /trə'piziəm/ n. (pl. -ziums or -zia /-ziə/) a quadrilateral plane figure in which only one pair of opposite sides is parallel.

trapezoid /'træpəzɔɪd, trə'pizɔɪd/ *n. Geom.*
1. (especially in the UK) a quadrilateral plane
figure of which no two sides are parallel.
2. (especially in the US) a quadrilateral plane
figure of which two sides are parallel.

trappings /'træpɪŋz/ *pl. n.* articles of equipment
or dress, especially of an ornamental character.

trash /træʃ/ *n.* **1.** anything worthless or useless;
rubbish. *–v.t. Colloq.* **2.** to destroy utterly,
especially as an act of vandalism. **3.** to subject
to scathing criticism.

trauma /'trɔmə/ *n.* (*pl.* -**mas** *or* -**mata** /-mətə/)
1. a bodily injury. **2.** *Psychol.* a startling experience which has a lasting effect on mental
life; a severe shock. –**traumatic**, *adj.* –**trau-
matise**, **traumatize**, *v.*

travail /'træveɪl/ *n.* physical or mental toil or
exertion, especially when painful.

travel /'trævəl/ *v.i.* (-**elled**, -**elling**) **1.** to move
or go from one place or point to another. *–n.*
2. the act of travelling; journeying, especially
in distant or foreign places. **3.** (*pl.*) journeys.
4. *Machinery* the complete movement of a
moving part in one direction, or the distance
traversed. –**traveller**, *n.*

travel advisory *n.* a notice, especially one
issued by a government authority, giving advice
on the degree of risk involved in travelling
to certain parts of the world affected by war,
diseases, etc.

traverse /trə'vɜs, 'trævɜs/ *v.t.* **1.** to pass across,
over, or through. **2.** to go to and fro over
or along, as a place. **3.** *Law* to deny formally,
in pleading at law. *–n.* **4.** the act of traversing.
5. something that crosses, obstructs, or
thwarts; obstacle. **6.** a place where one may
traverse or cross; a crossing. *–adj.* **7.** lying,
extending, or passing across; cross; transverse.

travesty /'trævəsti/ *n.* (*pl.* -**ties**) any grotesque
or debased likeness or imitation.

trawl /trɔl/ *n.* Also, **trawl net**. **1.** a strong fishing net dragged along the sea bottom in
trawling. *–v.i.* **2.** to fish with a trawl. **3.** to troll.

tray /treɪ/ *n.* a flat container or receptacle with
slightly raised edges used for carrying things.

treachery /'trɛtʃəri/ *n.* violation of faith; betrayal of trust; treason. –**treacherous**, *adj.*

treacle /'trikəl/ *n.* the dark, viscous, uncrystallised syrup obtained in refining sugar.

tread /trɛd/ *v.t.* (**trod**, **trodden** *or* **trod**,
treading) **1.** to step or walk on, about, in, or
along. **2.** to trample or crush underfoot. **3.** to
domineer harshly over; crush. *–n.* **4.** a treading, stepping, or walking, or the sound of this.
5. manner of treading or walking. **6.** a single
step as in walking. **7.** the horizontal upper
surface of a step. **8.** that part of a wheel, tyre,
or runner which touches the road, rail, etc.

treadle /'trɛdl/ *n.* a lever or the like worked by
the foot, as to impart motion to a machine.

treadmill /'trɛdmɪl/ *n.* **1.** a machine with a
continuous, rotating track for walking or running on. **2.** a monotonous or wearisome round,
as of work or life.

treason /'trizən/ *n.* violation by a subject of his
or her allegiance to his or her sovereign or to
the state; high treason.

treasure /'trɛʒə/ *n.* **1.** wealth or riches stored or
accumulated, especially in the form of precious
metals or money. **2.** any thing or person

greatly valued or highly prized. *–v.t.* **3.** to
regard as precious; prize; cherish.

treasurer /'trɛʒərə/ *n.* **1.** someone who has
charge of the funds of a company, private
society, or the like. **2.** an officer of a state, city,
etc., entrusted with the receipt, care, and disbursement of public money.

treasury /'trɛʒəri/ *n.* (*pl.* -**ries**) **1.** a place
where public revenues, or the funds of a
company, etc., are deposited, kept, and dis-
bursed. **2.** (*upper case*) the department of
government which has control over the collection, management, and disbursement of the
public revenue.

treat /trit/ *v.t.* **1.** to act or behave towards in
some specified way. **2.** to deal with. **3.** to
subject to some agent or action in order to
bring about a particular result. *–v.i.* **4.** to carry
on negotiations with someone, with a view to
a settlement, discuss terms of settlement, or
negotiate. **5.** anything that affords particular pleasure or enjoyment. **6.** one's turn to
pay, as for a joint outing, etc. –**treatment**, *n.*

treatise /'tritəs/ *n.* a book or writing dealing
with some particular subject.

treaty /'triti/ *n.* (*pl.* -**ties**) a formal agreement
between two or more independent states in
reference to peace, alliance, commerce, etc.

treble /'trɛbəl/ *adj.* **1.** threefold; triple. **2.** *Music*
of the highest pitch or range, as a voice part,
voice, singer, or instrument.

tree /tri/ *n.* a perennial plant having a permanent,
woody, self-supporting main stem or trunk,
usually growing to a considerable height, and
usually developing branches at some distance
from the ground.

tree change *n.* a move from a city environment
to a rural location away from the coast, as part
of a lifestyle change, usually to escape stress
and other deleterious aspects of city life. –**tree
changer**, *n.*

tree kangaroo *n.* any of the medium-sized
kangaroos of north-eastern Queensland and
New Guinea, highly adapted to living in trees.

trek /trɛk/ *n.* a journey, especially a difficult one
on foot.

trellis /'trɛləs/ *n.* a frame or structure of lattice-
work; a lattice.

tremble /'trɛmbəl/ *v.i.* **1.** (of persons, the body,
etc.) to shake involuntarily with quick, short
movements, as from fear, excitement, weakness, cold, etc. **2.** to be tremulous, as light,
sound, etc.

tremendous /trə'mɛndəs/ *adj.* **1.** extraordinarily great in size, amount, degree, etc.
2. extraordinary; unusual; remarkable.

tremor /'trɛmə/ *n.* **1.** involuntary shaking of the
body or limbs, as from fear, weakness, etc.;
a fit of trembling. **2.** any tremulous or vibratory movement; a vibration. **3.** a trembling or
quivering effect, as of light, etc. **4.** a tremulous
sound or note.

tremulous /'trɛmjələs/ *adj.* **1.** (of persons, the
body, etc.) characterised by trembling. **2.** (of
things) vibratory or quivering.

trench /trɛntʃ/ *n.* a deep furrow, ditch, or cut.

trenchant /'trɛntʃənt/ *adj.* incisive or keen, as
language or a person; cutting.

trencher /'trɛntʃə/ *n.* → **mortarboard**.

trend /trɛnd/ *n.* **1.** the general course, drift, or tendency. **2.** style; fashion. *–v.i.* **3.** (of a topic on a social network) to appear at an increasingly high level of frequency: *The election is trending on Twitter.* **–trendy**, *adj.*

trepidation /trɛpəˈdeɪʃən/ *n.* tremulous alarm or agitation; perturbation.

trespass /ˈtrɛspəs/ *n.* **1.** *Law* **a.** an unlawful act causing injury to the person, property, or rights of another, committed with force or violence, actual or implied. **b.** a wrongful entry upon the lands of another. **2.** an encroachment or intrusion. *–v.i.* **3.** to commit trespass.

tress /trɛs/ *n.* (*usu. pl.*) any long lock or curl of hair.

-tress a suffix forming some feminine agent-nouns, corresponding to masculine nouns in *-ter, -tor*.

trestle /ˈtrɛsəl/ *n.* a frame used as a support, consisting typically of a horizontal beam or bar fixed at each end to a pair of spreading legs.

trevally /trəˈvæli/ *n.* a sport and food fish.

tri- a word element meaning 'three'.

triad /ˈtraɪæd/ *n.* a group of three.

triage /ˈtriaʒ/ *n.* the sorting of casualties according to the urgency of treatment required.

trial /ˈtraɪəl, traɪl/ *n.* **1.** *Law* **a.** the examination before a judicial tribunal of the facts put in issue in a cause (often including issues of law as well as of fact). **b.** the determination of a person's guilt or innocence by due process of law. **2.** the act of trying or testing, or putting to the test. **3.** a contest or competition. **4.** an attempt or effort to do something. **5.** tentative or experimental action in order to ascertain results; an experiment. **6.** an affliction or trouble. *–v.t.* (**trialled**, **trialling**) **7.** to put (a plan, procedure, etc.) into operation, often on a small scale, to test its feasibility.

triangle /ˈtraɪæŋgəl/ *n.* **1.** a geometrical plane figure formed by three (usually) straight lines which meet two by two in three points, thus forming three angles. **2.** *Music* a triangular percussion instrument. **–triangular**, *adj.*

triathlon /traɪˈæθlɒn/ *n.* an athletic contest comprising three events, usually swimming, cycling, and running. **–triathlete**, *n.*

tribe /traɪb/ *n.* a group of people united by such features as descent, language and land ownership. **–tribal**, *adj.*

tribulation /trɪbjəˈleɪʃən/ *n.* grievous trouble; severe trial or experience.

tribunal /traɪˈbjunəl/ *n.* **1.** a body set up to investigate and resolve disputes. **2.** a court of justice. **3.** a place or seat of judgement.

tributary /ˈtrɪbjətri/ *n.* (*pl.* **-taries**) **1.** a stream contributing its flow to a larger stream or other body of water. *–adj.* **2.** furnishing subsidiary aid; contributory; auxiliary. **3.** paying or required to pay tribute.

tribute /ˈtrɪbjut/ *n.* **1.** a personal offering, testimonial, compliment, or the like given as if due, or in acknowledgement of gratitude, esteem, or regard. **2.** a stated sum or other valuable consideration paid by one sovereign or state in acknowledgement of submission or as the price of peace, security, protection, or the like.

triceps /ˈtraɪsɛps/ *n. Anat.* a muscle having three heads, or points of origin, especially the extending muscle at the back of the upper arm.

triceratops /traɪˈsɛrətɒps/ *n.* a large plant-eating dinosaur with a heavily armoured neck and three horns on the skull.

trick /trɪk/ *n.* **1.** a crafty or fraudulent device, expedient, or proceeding. **2.** the art or knack of doing something. **3.** a clever or dexterous feat, as for exhibition or entertainment. **4.** *Cards* the cards collectively which are played and won in one round. *–v.t.* **5.** to deceive by trickery. **–trickery**, *n.*

trickle /ˈtrɪkəl/ *v.i.* **1.** to flow or fall by drops, or in a small, broken, or gentle stream. **2.** to come, go, pass, or proceed bit by bit, slowly, irregularly, etc. *–n.* **3.** a trickling flow or stream.

tricky /ˈtrɪki/ *adj.* (**-kier**, **-kiest**) **1.** given to or characterised by deceitful or clever tricks; clever; wily. **2.** deceptive, requiring careful handling or action. **–trickily**, *adv.* **–trickiness**, *n.*

tricycle /ˈtraɪsɪkəl/ *n.* a cycle with three wheels.

trident /ˈtraɪdnt/ *n.* a three-pronged instrument or weapon.

tried /traɪd/ *v.* past tense and past participle of **try**.

triennial /traɪˈɛniəl/ *adj.* **1.** lasting three years. **2.** occurring every three years.

trifle /ˈtraɪfəl/ *n.* **1.** an article or thing of small value. **2.** a small, inconsiderable amount; a matter of slight importance. **3.** a dessert of sponge, jelly, cream, etc. *–v.i.* **4.** (usu. fol. by *with*) to deal lightly or without due seriousness or respect. **–trifling**, *adj.*

trigger /ˈtrɪgə/ *n.* **1.** (in firearms) a small projecting piece which when pressed by the finger liberates the mechanism and discharges the weapon. **2.** a stimulus or cause: *the trigger for a general election.* *–v.t.* **3.** to start or precipitate (something), as a chain of events or a scientific reaction.

trigonometry /trɪgəˈnɒmətri/ *n.* the branch of mathematics that deals with the relations between the sides and angles of triangles and the calculations, etc., based on these.

trill /trɪl/ *v.i.* **1.** to resound vibrantly, or with a rapid succession of sounds, as the voice, song, laughter, etc. **2.** to execute a shake or trill with the voice or on a musical instrument. *–n.* **3.** the act or sound of trilling.

trillion /ˈtrɪljən/ *n.* (*pl.* **-lions**, as after a numeral, **-lion**) **1.** a million times a million, or 10^{12}. **2.** (*becoming obsolete*) a million times a million times a million, or 10^{18}.

trilogy /ˈtrɪlədʒi/ *n.* (*pl.* **-gies**) a series or group of three related dramas, operas, novels, etc.

trim /trɪm/ *v.t.* (**trimmed**, **trimming**) **1.** to reduce to a neat or orderly state by clipping, paring, pruning, etc. **2.** to modify (opinions, etc.) according to expediency. **3.** to decorate or deck with ornaments, etc. **4.** to upholster and line the interior of cars, etc. *–n.* **5.** proper condition or order. **6.** dress, array, or equipment. **7.** material used for decoration; decorative trimming. **8.** a trimming by cutting, clipping, or the like. **9. a.** the upholstery, knobs, handles, and other equipment inside a car. **b.** ornamentation on the exterior of a car, especially in chromium or a contrasting colour. *–adj.* (**trimmer**, **trimmest**) **10.** pleasingly neat or smart in appearance. **11.** in good condition or order. **12.** healthily slim.

trimaran /'traɪməræn/ n. a boat with a main middle hull and two outer hulls.

trimming /'trɪmɪŋ/ n. anything used to decorate or enhance.

trinity /'trɪnəti/ n. (pl. **-ties**) a group of three; a triad.

trinket /'trɪŋkət/ n. **1.** any small fancy article, bit of jewellery, or the like, usually of little value. **2.** anything trifling.

trio /'triou/ n. (pl. **trios**) any group of three persons or things.

trip /trɪp/ n. **1.** a journey or voyage. **2.** Colloq. a period under the influence of a hallucinatory drug. **3.** a stumble. –v. (**tripped**, **tripping**) –v.i. **4.** to stumble. **5.** to make a slip or mistake, as in a statement; make a wrong step in conduct. **6.** to step lightly or nimbly; skip; dance. –v.t. **7.** (oft. fol. by up) to cause to stumble. **8.** (oft. fol. by up) to cause to make or catch in a slip or error.

tripartite /traɪ'pɑtaɪt/ adj. divided into or consisting of three parts.

tripe /traɪp/ n. **1.** the first and second divisions of the stomach of a ruminant, especially of the ox kind, prepared for use as food. **2.** Colloq. anything poor or worthless, especially written work; nonsense; rubbish.

triple /'trɪpəl/ adj. threefold; consisting of three parts.

triplet /'trɪplət/ n. **1.** one of three children born at one birth. **2.** any group or combination of three. **3.** a thin bar of opal set between two layers of plastic, or one layer of potch and one of crystal.

triplicate v.t. /'trɪpləkeɪt/ **1.** to make threefold; triple. –adj. /'trɪpləkət/ **2.** threefold; triple; tripartite.

tripod /'traɪpɒd/ n. **1.** a stool, pedestal, or the like with three legs. **2.** a three-legged stand, as for a camera.

triptych /'trɪptɪk/ n. Art a set of three panels or compartments side by side, bearing pictures, carvings, or the like.

trite /traɪt/ adj. made commonplace by constant use or repetition.

triumph /'traɪʌmf, 'traɪəmf/ n. **1.** the act or fact of being victorious, or triumphing; victory; conquest. **2.** a notable achievement; striking success. –v.i. **3.** to achieve success. **–triumphal**, adj.

triumphant /traɪ'ʌmfənt/ adj. having achieved victory or success; victorious.

trivet /'trɪvət/ n. a small metal plate with short legs put under a hot platter or dish at the table.

trivia /'trɪviə/ pl. n. **1.** inessential, unimportant, or inconsequential things; trivialities. **2.** inconsequential and often arcane items of information.

trivia game n. a quiz in which contestants attempt to answer questions on areas of general knowledge such as literature, science, entertainment, sport and popular culture.

trivial /'trɪviəl/ adj. of little importance; trifling; insignificant. **–triviality**, n.

-trix a suffix of feminine agent-nouns, as in executrix.

trochee /'trouki/ n. Prosody a group of two syllables, a long followed by a short, or an accented followed by an unaccented. **–trochaic**, adj.

trod /trɒd/ v. past tense and past participle of **tread**.

trodden /'trɒdn/ v. past participle of **tread**.

troglodyte /'trɒglədaɪt/ n. a cave-dweller.

troll[1] /troʊl/ v.i. **1.** to fish with a moving line, as one trailed behind a boat. **2.** Internet to behave in the manner of a troll (def. 3). –n. **3.** Internet someone who posts messages in an internet discussion forum, chat room, etc., that are designed to be upsetting.

troll[2] /trɒl/ n. an imaginary figure in fairytales, either a dwarf or giant, who lives underground.

trolley /'trɒli/ n. (pl. **-leys**) any of various kinds of low carts or vehicles.

trollop /'trɒləp/ n. **1.** an untidy or slovenly woman. **2.** an immoral woman; prostitute.

trombone /trɒm'boun/ n. a brass wind instrument consisting of a cylindrical metal tube expanding into a bell and bent twice in U shape, usually equipped with a slide. **–trombonist**, n.

troop /trup/ n. **1.** an assemblage of persons or things; a company or band. **2.** (pl.) a body of soldiers, etc. –v.i. **3.** to walk as if on a march.

trope /troup/ n. Rhetoric a figure of speech.

trophy /'troufi/ n. (pl. **-phies**) anything taken in war, hunting, etc., especially when preserved as a memento; a spoil or prize.

tropic /'trɒpɪk/ n. **1.** Geog. either of two corresponding parallels of latitude on the terrestrial globe, one (**tropic of Cancer**) about 23½° north, and the other (**tropic of Capricorn**) about 23½° south of the equator, being the boundaries of the Torrid Zone. –phr. **2. the tropics**, the regions lying between and near these parallels of latitude. **–tropical**, adj.

tropical rainforest n. rainforest occurring in tropical areas. Compare **temperate rainforest**.

trot /trɒt/ v.i. (**trotted**, **trotting**) **1.** (of a horse, etc.) to go at a gait between a walk and a run. **2.** to go at a quick, steady gait; move briskly, bustle, or hurry. –n. **3.** a jogging gait between a walk and a run. –phr. **4. the trots**, **a.** races for trotting or pacing horses; a trotting meeting. **b.** Colloq. diarrhoea.

troth /troʊθ/ n. one's word or promise.

trotter /'trɒtə/ n. **1.** an animal which trots; a horse bred and trained for harness racing. **2.** the foot of an animal, especially of a sheep or pig, used as food.

troubadour /'trubədɔ/ n. a minstrel.

trouble /'trʌbəl/ v.t. (**-bled**, **-bling**) **1.** to disturb in mind; distress; worry. **2.** to put to inconvenience, exertion, pains, or the like. –n. **3.** molestation, harassment, annoyance, or difficulty. **4.** unfortunate position or circumstances; misfortunes. **5.** disturbance; disorder; unrest. **6.** disturbance of mind, distress, or worry. **–troublesome**, adj.

trough /trɒf/ n. **1.** an open, box-like receptacle, usually long and narrow, as for containing water or food for animals, or for any of various other purposes. **2.** Meteorol. an elongated area of relatively low pressure.

trounce /traʊns/ v.t. **1.** to beat or thrash severely. **2.** to defeat thoroughly.

troupe /trup/ n. a troop, company, or band, especially of actors, singers, or the like.

trousers /'traʊzəz/ pl. n. an outer garment covering the lower part of the trunk and each leg separately, extending to the ankles.

trousseau /'trusoʊ/ n. (pl. **-seaux** or **-seaus** /-soʊz/) a bride's outfit of clothes, linen, etc.

trout /traʊt/ n. (pl. **trouts** or **trout**) a game and food fish.

trowel /'traʊəl/ n. **1.** any of various tools consisting of a plate of metal or other material, usually flat, fitted into a short handle, used for spreading, shaping, or smoothing plaster or the like. **2.** a small garden spade.

troy weight /trɔɪ/ n. an imperial system for measuring the mass of precious metals and gems.

truant /'truənt/ n. a pupil who stays away from school without permission. –**truancy**, n.

truce /trus/ n. a suspension of hostilities, as between armies, by agreement, for a specified period; an armistice.

truck[1] /trʌk/ n. **1.** any of various vehicles for carrying goods, etc. **2.** a motor vehicle with cab (def. 2) and tray or compartment for carrying goods; lorry. –v.t. **3.** to transport by a truck or trucks.

truck[2] /trʌk/ n. dealings.

truculent /'trʌkjələnt/ adj. **1.** fierce; cruel. **2.** aggressive; belligerent.

trudge /trʌdʒ/ v.i. to walk laboriously or wearily.

true /tru/ adj. (**truer**, **truest**) **1.** being in accordance with the actual state of things; conforming to fact; not false. **2.** real or genuine. **3.** firm in allegiance; loyal; faithful; trusty. **4.** exact, correct, or accurate. **5.** legitimate or rightful. **6.** exactly or accurately shaped, formed, fitted, or placed, as a surface, instrument, or part of a mechanism. **7.** Navig. (of a bearing) fixed in relation to the earth's axis rather than the magnetic poles. –adv. **8.** in a true manner; truly or truthfully. **9.** exactly or accurately. –**truly**, adv.

true-blue adj. **1.** unchanging; unwavering; staunch; true. **2.** staunchly conservative.

truffle /'trʌfəl/ n. **1.** any of various subterranean edible fungi. **2.** a type of confection.

truffle dog n. a dog trained to sniff out truffles under the ground so that they can be dug out.

truism /'truɪzəm/ n. a self-evident, obvious truth. –**truistic**, **truistical**, adj.

trump /trʌmp/ Cards –n. **1.** any playing card of a suit that for the time outranks the other suits, such a card being able to take any card of another suit. –v.t. **2.** to take with a trump.

trumpet /'trʌmpət/ n. **1.** Music any of a family of musical wind instruments with a penetrating, powerful tone, consisting of a tube, now usually metallic, and commonly once or twice curved round upon itself, having a cup-shaped mouthpiece at one end and a flaring bell at the other. –v.t. **2.** to sound on a trumpet.

truncate /trʌŋ'keɪt, 'trʌŋkeɪt/ v.t. to shorten by cutting off a part; cut short.

truncheon /'trʌnʃən/ n. a short club carried by a police officer.

trundle /'trʌndəl/ v. (**-dled**, **-dling**) –v.t. **1.** to cause (a ball, hoop, etc.) to roll along; roll. –v.i. **2.** Colloq. to walk in a leisurely fashion.

trunk /trʌŋk/ n. **1.** the main stem of a tree, as distinct from the branches and roots. **2.** a box or chest for holding clothes and other articles, as for use on a journey. **3.** the body of a human being or of an animal, excluding the head and limbs. **4.** (pl.) Obs. men's shorts, either

tight-fitting or loose, worn by athletes, swimmers, etc. **5.** the long, flexible, cylindrical nasal appendage of the elephant.

trunk line n. Telecommunications a telephone line or channel between two exchanges in different parts of a country or of the world, which is used to provide connections between subscribers making long-distance calls.

truss /trʌs/ v.t. **1.** to tie, bind, or fasten. **2.** Building Trades, etc. a combination of members, as beams, bars, ties, or the like, so arranged as to form a rigid framework and support. **3.** Med. an apparatus for maintaining a hernia in a reduced state.

trust /trʌst/ n. **1.** reliance on the integrity, justice, etc., of a person, or on some quality or attribute of a thing; confidence. **2.** confident expectation of something; hope. **3.** the state of being relied on, or the state of one to whom something is entrusted. **4.** the obligation or responsibility imposed on one in whom confidence or authority is placed. **5.** Law **a.** a fiduciary relationship in which one person (the trustee) holds the title to property (the **trust estate** or **trust property**) for the benefit of another (the beneficiary). **b.** Also, **trust fund**. a fund of securities, cash or other assets, held and administered under such a relationship. **6.** Commerce **a.** a combination of industrial or commercial companies having a central committee or board of trustees, controlling a majority or the whole of the stock of each of the constituent companies, thus making it possible to manage the concerns so as to economise expenses, defeat competition, etc. **b.** a monopolistic organisation or combination in restraint of trade whether in the form of a trust (def. 6a), contract, association or otherwise. –v.t. **7.** to have trust or confidence in; rely on. **8.** to expect confidently, hope (usually followed by a clause or an infinitive).

trustee /trʌs'ti/ n. Law **1.** a person, usually one of a body of persons, appointed to administer the affairs of a company, institution, etc. **2.** a person who holds the title to property for the benefit of another.

trustworthy /'trʌstwɜːði/ adj. worthy of trust or confidence; reliable.

truth /truθ/ n. **1.** that which is true; the true or actual facts of a case. **2.** a verified or indisputable fact, proposition, principle, or the like.

try /traɪ/ v.t. (**tried**, **trying**) **1.** to attempt to do or accomplish. **2.** to test the quality, value, fitness, accuracy, etc, of. **3.** Law to examine and determine judicially, as a cause; determine judicially the guilt or innocence of (a person). **4.** to put to a severe test; strain the endurance, patience, etc., of; subject to grievous experiences, affliction, or trouble. –n. (pl. **tries**) **5.** an attempt, endeavour, or effort. **6.** Rugby Football a score of four points (in Rugby League) or five points (in Rugby Union) earned by placing the ball on the ground in the opponents' in-goal area.

trying /'traɪŋ/ adj. annoying; distressing.

tryst /trɪst/ n. an appointment, especially between lovers.

tsar /zɑ/ n. **1.** an emperor or king. **2.** (usu. upper case) (formerly) the emperor of Russia. Also, **czar**, **tzar**.

T-shirt /'ti-ʃɜt/ n. a lightweight top, usually short-sleeved and collarless, made from a knitted fabric. Also, **t-shirt, tee-shirt**.

tsunami /su'nami, sə-, tsu-, tsə-/ n. a large, often destructive sea wave or series of waves caused by an underwater earthquake, landslide, or volcanic eruption.

tuan /'tjuən/ n. a small mouse-like marsupial, mostly tree-dwelling, with a hairy-tipped tail.

tub /tʌb/ n. **1.** a vessel or receptacle for bathing in. **2.** any of various vessels resembling or suggesting a tub.

tuba /'tjubə/ n. a brass wind instrument of low pitch.

tubby /'tʌbi/ adj. (**-bier, -biest**) short and fat.

tube /tjub/ n. **1.** a hollow usually cylindrical body of metal, glass, rubber, or other material, used for conveying or containing fluids, and for other purposes. **2.** a small, collapsible, metal or plastic cylinder closed at one end and having the open end provided with a cap, for holding paint, toothpaste, or other semiliquid substance to be squeezed out by pressure. **–tubular**, adj.

tuber /'tjubə/ n. Bot. a fleshy, usually oblong or rounded thickening or outgrowth (as the potato) of a subterranean stem or shoot. **–tuberous**, adj.

tuberculosis /təbɜkju'lousəs/ n. an infectious disease, especially of the lungs.

tuck /tʌk/ v.t. **1.** to thrust into some narrow space or close or concealed place. **2.** to draw up in folds or a folded arrangement. **–n. 3.** a tucked piece or part. **4.** Sewing a fold, or one of a series of folds, made by doubling cloth upon itself, and stitching parallel with the edge of the fold.

tucker¹ /'tʌkə/ n. Colloq. food.

tucker² /'tʌkə/ v.t. Colloq. to weary; tire.

tuckshop /'tʌkʃɒp/ n. → canteen (def. 2).

-tude a suffix forming abstract nouns.

tuft /tʌft/ n. a bunch of small, usually soft and flexible things, as feathers, hairs, etc., fixed at the base with the upper part loose.

tug /tʌg/ v.t. (**tugged, tugging**) to pull at with force or effort.

tugboat /'tʌgbout/ n. a strongly-built vessel with a powerful engine, designed for towing other vessels.

tuition /tju'ɪʃən/ n. teaching or instruction, as of pupils.

tulip /'tjuləp/ n. a plant with large, showy, cup-shaped or bell-shaped flowers of various colours.

tulle /tjul/ n. a thin silk or nylon net, used in millinery, dressmaking, etc.

tumble /'tʌmbəl/ v.i. **1.** to roll or fall over or down as by losing footing, support, or equilibrium. **2.** to fall rapidly, as stock market prices. **–n. 3.** an act of tumbling; a fall; a downfall. **4.** tumbled condition; disorder or confusion.

tumefy /'tjuməfaɪ/ v.t. (**-fied, -fying**) to make swollen.

tumescent /tju'mɛsənt/ adj. swelling.

tummy /'tʌmi/ n. (pl. **-mies**) Colloq. the stomach.

tumour /'tjumə/ n. an abnormal or diseased swelling in any part of the body. Also, **tumor**.

tumult /'tjumʌlt/ n. **1.** the commotion or disturbance of a multitude, usually with noise; an uproar. **2.** agitation of mind; a mental or emotional disturbance. **–tumultuous**, adj.

tuna /'tjunə/ n. a large, fast-swimming, marine food fish.

tundra /'tʌndrə/ n. one of the vast, nearly level, treeless plains of the arctic regions of Europe, Asia, and North America.

tune /tjun/ n. **1.** a succession of musical sounds forming an air or melody, with or without the harmony accompanying it. **2.** the state of being in the proper pitch. **3.** accord; agreement. **–v.t. (tuned, tuning) 4.** (oft. fol. by up) to adjust (a musical instrument) to a correct or given standard of pitch. **5.** to bring into harmony. **6.** (oft. fol. by up) to adjust (an engine, machine or the like) for proper or improved running. **7.** Radio to adjust a receiving apparatus so as to receive (the signals of a sending station).

tuner /'tjunə/ n. the part of a radio receiver which produces an output suitable for feeding into an amplifier.

tungsten /'tʌŋstən/ n. a rare metallic element Symbol: W

tunic /'tjunɪk/ n. **1.** a coat worn as part of a military or other uniform. **2.** a loose, sleeveless dress, especially as worn by girls as part of a school uniform.

tunnel /'tʌnəl/ n. **1.** an underground passage. **–v.t. (-nelled, -nelling) 2.** to make or form a tunnel through or under.

tunny /'tʌni/ n. (pl. **-ny** or **-nies**) a marine food fish.

turban /'tɜbən/ n. a form of headdress consisting of a scarf wound around the head.

turbid /'tɜbəd/ adj. **1.** (of liquids) opaque or muddy with particles of extraneous matter. **2.** disturbed; confused.

turbine /'tɜbaɪn/ n. any of a class of hydraulic motors in which a vaned wheel or runner is made to revolve by the impingement of a free jet of fluid (**impulse turbine or action turbine**) or by the passage of fluid which completely fills the motor (**reaction turbine or pressure turbine**).

turbo- /'tɜbou-/ adj. a prefix indicating: **1.** driven by a turbine. **2.** of or relating to a turbine.

turbocharged /'tɜboutʃadʒd/ adj. **1.** (of an engine) fitted with a turbocharger. **2.** (of a computer game) programmed to operate at high speed. **3.** (of an activity) conducted at an accelerated pace.

turbocharger /'tɜboutʃadʒə/ n. a supercharger which uses an exhaust-driven turbine to boost the air-intake pressure in an internal-combustion engine.

turbulent /'tɜbjələnt/ adj. disturbed; agitated; troubled; stormy. **–turbulence**, n.

turd /tɜd/ n. Colloq. (taboo) **1.** a piece of excrement. **2.** an unpleasant person.

tureen /tə'rin, tju-/ n. a large deep dish with a cover, for holding soup, etc.

turf /tɜf/ n. (pl. **turfs or turves** /tɜvz/) **1.** the covering of grass, etc., with its matted roots, forming the surface of grassland. **2.** a piece cut or torn from the surface of grassland, with the grass, etc., growing on it; a sod. **–v.t. 3.** to cover with turf or sod. –*phr.* **4. turf out**, *Colloq.* to throw out; eject.

turgid /'tɜdʒəd/ *adj.* **1.** pompous or bombastic, as language, style, etc. **2.** swollen; distended.

turkey /'tɜki/ *n.* a large gallinaceous bird.

Turkish bread /tɜkɪʃ/ *n.* → **pide** (def. 1).

Turkish pizza *n.* → **pide** (def. 2).

turmeric /'tɜmərɪk, 'tjumərɪk/ *n.* **1.** the aromatic rhizome of a tropical Asian plant. **2.** a powder prepared from it, used as a condiment (especially in curry powder), a yellow dye, a medicine, etc.

turmoil /'tɜmɔɪl/ *n.* a state of commotion or disturbance; tumult; agitation; disquiet.

turn /tɜn/ *v.t.* **1.** cause to move round on an axis or about a centre; rotate. **2.** to reverse the position or posture of. **3.** to change or alter the course of; to divert; deflect. **4.** to change or alter the nature, character, or appearance of. **5.** (fol. by *into* or *to*) to change or convert. **6.** to put or apply to some use or purpose. **7.** to get beyond or pass (a certain age, time, amount, etc.). **8.** to bring into a rounded or curved form. **9.** to form or express gracefully. **10.** to cause to go; send; drive. **11.** to maintain a steady flow or circulation of (money or articles of commerce). **12.** to curve, bend, or twist. –*v.i.* **13.** to move round on an axis or about a centre; rotate. **14.** to direct the face or gaze towards or away from something, or in a particular direction. **15.** to direct or set one's course towards or away from something or in a particular direction. **16.** to apply one's efforts, interest, etc., to something; devote oneself to something. **17.** to shift the body about as if on an axis. **18.** to assume a curved form; bend. **19.** to be affected with nausea, as the stomach. **20.** to change or alter, as in nature, character, or appearance. **21.** to become sour, fermented, or the like, as milk, etc. **22.** (fol. by *into* or *to*) to be changed, transformed, or converted. –*n.* **23.** a movement of rotation, whether total or partial. **24.** the time for action or proceeding which comes in due rotation or order to each of a number of persons, etc. **25.** a place where a road, river, or the like turns. **26.** a single revolution, as of a wheel. **27.** change or a change in nature, character, condition, circumstances, etc. **28.** a passing or twisting of one thing round another as of a rope round a mast. **29.** a distinctive form or style imparted. **30.** a short walk, ride, or the like which includes a going and a returning, especially by different routes. **31.** natural inclination, bent, tendency, or aptitude. **32.** a spell or bout of action. **33.** an attack of illness or the like. **34.** an act of service or disservice (with *good*, *bad*, *kind*, etc.). **35.** *Colloq.* a nervous shock, as from fright or astonishment. –*phr.* **36. turn down**, **a.** to fold. **b.** to lessen the intensity of; moderate. **c.** to refuse or reject (a person, request, etc.). **37. turn off**, **a.** to stop the flow of (water, gas, etc.) as by closing a valve, etc. **b.** to switch off (a radio, light, etc.). **c.** to branch off; diverge; change direction. **d.** to arouse antipathy or revulsion in. **38. turn on**, **a.** to cause (water, gas, etc.) to flow as by opening a valve, etc. **b.** to switch on (a radio, light, etc.). **c.** Also, **turn upon**. to become suddenly hostile; attack without warning. **d.** *Colloq.* to excite or interest (a person).

39. turn out, **a.** to extinguish or put out (a light, etc.). **b.** to come to be; become ultimately. **40. turn over**, **a.** to move or be moved from one side to another. **b.** to meditate; ponder. **c.** *Commerce* to purchase and then sell (goods or commodities). **d.** *Commerce* to do business or sell goods to the amount of (a specified sum). **e.** *Commerce* to invest or recover (capital) in some transaction or in the course of business.

turnaround /'tɜnəraʊnd/ *n.* **1.** a reversal in circumstances, especially as losing to winning. **2.** the time taken to perform a task. Also, **turnround**.

turnip /'tɜnəp/ *n.* a plant with a thick, fleshy, edible root.

turnover /'tɜnoʊvə/ *n.* **1.** the aggregate of worker replacements in a given period in a given business or industry. **2.** the total amount of business done in a given time. **3.** the rate at which items are sold or stock used up and replaced.

turnstile /'tɜnstaɪl/ *n.* a horizontally revolving gate which allows people to pass one at a time.

turntable /'tɜnteɪbəl/ *n.* the rotating disc on which the record in a gramophone rests.

turpentine /'tɜpəntaɪn/ *n.* an oil used for dissolving paint, etc., originally from the resin of various trees, now usually made from petroleum.

turpitude /'tɜpətjud/ *n.* **1.** shameful depravity. **2.** a depraved or shameful act.

turquoise /'tɜkwɔɪz/ *n.* **1.** a sky blue or greenish blue compact opaque mineral. **2.** a greenish blue or bluish green.

turret /'tʌrət/ *n.* a small tower, usually one forming part of a larger structure.

turtle /'tɜtl/ *n.* any of various reptiles having the body enclosed in a shell from which the head, tail, and four legs protrude.

tusk /tʌsk/ *n.* (in certain animals) a tooth developed to great length, usually as one of a pair, as in the elephant, walrus, wild boar, etc.

tussive /'tʌsɪv/ *adj.* of or relating to a cough.

tussle /'tʌsəl/ *v.i.* **1.** to struggle or fight roughly or vigorously; wrestle; scuffle. –*n.* **2.** a rough struggle as in fighting or wrestling; a scuffle.

tussock /'tʌsək/ *n.* a tuft or clump of growing grass or the like.

tutelage /'tjutəlɪdʒ/ *n.* **1.** the office or function of a guardian; guardianship. **2.** instruction. –**tutelary**, *adj.*

tutor /'tjutə/ *n.* **1.** one employed to instruct another in some branch or branches of learning, especially a private instructor. **2.** a university teacher who supervises the studies of certain undergraduates assigned to him or her. –*v.t.* **3.** to act as a tutor to.

tutorial /tju'tɔriəl/ *n.* a period of instruction given by a university tutor to an individual student or a small group of students.

tutti-frutti /tuti-'fruti/ *n.* an ice cream or confection containing chopped mixed fruits and sometimes nuts.

tutu /'tutu/ *n.* a short, full, ballet skirt.

tuxedo /tʌk'sidoʊ/ *n.* (*pl.* **-dos**) a man's black jacket for formal occasions.

TV /ti 'vi/ *n.* → **television**.

twain /twein/ n. Archaic two: never the twain; cut in twain.

twang /twæŋ/ v.i. **1.** to give out a sharp, ringing sound, as the string of a musical instrument when plucked. —n. **2.** the sharp, ringing sound produced by plucking or suddenly releasing a tense string. **3.** a sharp, nasal tone, as of the human voice.

tweak /twik/ v.t. **1.** to seize and pull with a sharp jerk and twist. **2.** to make minor adjustments to for best effect or maximum performance.

twee /twi/ adj. Colloq. affected; excessively dainty.

tweed /twid/ n. a coarse wool cloth in a variety of weaves and colours.

tweeny /ˈtwini/ n. a child, especially a girl, between the ages of 8 or 9 and 13 or 14. Also, **tween**, **tweener**, **tweenie**.

tweet¹ /twit/ n. **1.** the weak chirp of a young or small bird. —v.i. **2.** to utter a tweet or tweets.

tweet² /twit/ v.i. **1.** to post a message on the social network formerly known as Twitter (now X). —v.t. **2.** to post such a message to (someone). —n. **3.** such a message.

tweezers /ˈtwizəz/ pl. n. small pincers for plucking out hairs, taking up small objects, etc.

twelve /twelv/ n. **1.** a cardinal number, ten plus two. —adj. **2.** amounting to twelve in number. —**twelfth**, adj., n.

twenty /ˈtwenti/ n. (pl. **-ties**) **1.** a cardinal number, ten times two. —adj. **2.** amounting to twenty in number. —**twentieth**, adj., n.

24/7 /twenti-fə ˈsevən/ Colloq. —adv. **1.** continuously; uninterruptedly: This channel broadcasts news 24/7. —adj. **2.** uninterrupted; constant: 24/7 broadcasting of tennis.

twi- a word element meaning 'two', or 'twice'.

twice /twais/ adv. two times.

twiddle /ˈtwidl/ v.t. to turn round and round, especially with the fingers.

twig¹ /twig/ n. **1.** a slender shoot of a tree or other plant. **2.** a small dry, woody piece fallen from a branch.

twig² /twig/ v.i.v. (**twigged**, **twigging**) Colloq. to understand.

twilight /ˈtwailait/ n. the light from the sky when the sun is below the horizon, especially in the evening.

twill /twil/ n. a fabric woven with the weft threads so crossing the warp as to produce an effect of parallel diagonal lines.

twin /twin/ n. **1.** one of two children or animals born at a single birth. —adj. **2.** being two, or one of two, children or animals born at the same birth. **3.** being two persons or things closely related or associated or much alike; forming a pair or couple.

twine /twain/ n. **1.** a strong thread or string composed of two or more strands twisted together. —v. (**twined**, **twining**) —v.t. **2.** to twist together. —v.i. **3.** to wind in a sinuous or meandering course.

twinge /twindʒ/ n. a sudden, sharp pain.

twinkle /ˈtwiŋkəl/ v.i. **1.** to shine with quick, flickering, gleams of light, as stars, distant lights, etc. **2.** to sparkle in the light. **3.** (of the eyes) to be bright with amusement, pleasure, etc. —n. **4.** a twinkling with light. **5.** a twinkling brightness in the eyes.

twirl /twɜl/ v.t. **1.** to cause to rotate rapidly; spin; whirl; swing circularly. —v.i. **2.** to rotate rapidly; whirl.

twist /twist/ v.t. **1.** to combine, as two or more strands or threads, by winding together. **2.** to entwine (one thing) with or in another; wind or twine (something) about a thing. **3.** to alter in shape, as by turning the ends in opposite directions, so that parts previously in the same straight line and plane are situated in a spiral curve. **4.** to change the proper form or meaning; pervert. —v.i. **5.** to be or become intertwined. **6.** to wind or twine about something. **7.** to take a spiral form or course; wind, curve, or bend. **8.** to turn or rotate, as on an axis. —n. **9.** a curve, bend, or turn. **10.** a peculiar bent, bias, or the like, as in the mind or character. **11.** a sudden, unexpected alteration to the course of events, as in a play. **12.** a vigorous dance of the 1960s.

twit¹ /twit/ v.t. (**twitted**, **twitting**) **1.** to taunt, gibe at, or banter by references to anything embarrassing. **2.** to reproach or upbraid.

twit² /twit/ n. Colloq. a fool.

twitch /twitʃ/ v.t. **1.** to give a short, sudden pull or tug at; jerk. —n. **2.** a quick, jerky movement of the body, or of some part of it.

twitter /ˈtwitə/ v.i. to utter a succession of small, tremulous sounds, as a bird.

two /tu/ n. **1.** a cardinal number, one plus one. —adj. **2.** amounting to two in number.

two-dimensional /tu-də'menʃənəl/ adj. having two dimensions, as height and width.

two-up /ˈtu-ʌp/ n. a gambling game in which two coins are spun in the air and bets are laid on whether they will fall heads or tails.

-ty¹ a suffix of numerals denoting multiples of ten, as twenty.

-ty² a suffix of nouns denoting quality, state, etc., as unity, enmity.

tycoon /tar'kun/ n. a businessperson having great wealth and power.

tyke /taik/ n. Colloq. a mischievous child.

tyne /tain/ n. → **tine**.

type /taip/ n. **1.** a kind, class, or group as distinguished by a particular characteristic. **2.** the general form, style, or character distinguishing a particular kind, class or group. **3.** the pattern or model from which something is made. **4.** Printing **a.** a rectangular piece or block, now usually of metal, having on its upper surface a letter or character in relief. **b.** a printed character or printed characters. —v.t. **5.** to produce (a document, etc.) by means of a computer or typewriter. **6.** to be a type or symbol of. —v.i. **7.** to write by means of a computer or typewriter.

typecast /ˈtaipkast/ v.t. (**-cast**, **-casting**) to cast (an actor, etc.) continually in the same kind of role, especially because of some physical characteristic.

typeface /ˈtaipfeis/ n. → **face** (def. 8).

typescript /ˈtaipskript/ n. a typewritten copy of a literary composition, a document, or the like.

typeset /ˈtaipset/ v.t. (**-set**, **-setting**) Printing to set in type.

typewriter /ˈtaipraitə/ n. a machine for writing mechanically in letters and characters, either operated by hand or powered by electricity.

typhoid fever /ˈtaɪfɔɪd/ *n.* an infectious, often fatal, fever. Also, **typhoid**.

typhoon /taɪˈfuːn/ *n.* a tropical cyclone or hurricane.

typhus /ˈtaɪfəs/ *n.* an acute infectious disease marked by great prostration, severe nervous symptoms, and a characteristic eruption of reddish spots on the body, now regarded as due to a specific microorganism transmitted by lice and fleas. Also, **typhus fever**. –**typhous**, *adj.*

typical /ˈtɪpɪkəl/ *adj.* **1.** relating to, of the nature of, or serving as a type or emblem; symbolic. **2.** of the nature of or serving as a type or representative specimen. **3.** conforming to the type.

typify /ˈtɪpəfaɪ/ *v.t.* (**-fied, -fying**) to serve as the typical specimen of; exemplify.

typist /ˈtaɪpəst/ *n.* someone who operates a computer keyboard or typewriter.

typo /ˈtaɪpoʊ/ *n.* (*pl.* **typos**) *Colloq.* a typographical or keying error.

typography /taɪˈpɒɡrəfi/ *n.* **1.** the work or process of printing with types. **2.** the general character of printed matter. –**typographical**, *adj.*

tyrannosaurus /təˌrænəˈsɔrəs/ *n.* a great carnivorous dinosaur which walked erect on its powerful hind limbs. Also, **tyrannosaur**.

tyranny /ˈtɪrəni/ *n.* **1.** arbitrary or unrestrained exercise of power; despotic abuse of authority. **2.** the government or rule of a tyrant or absolute ruler. **3.** undue severity or harshness. –**tyrannical**, *adj.* –**tyrannise, tyrannize**, *v.*

tyrant /ˈtaɪrənt/ *n.* **1.** a king or ruler who exercises power oppressively or unjustly. **2.** any person who exercises power despotically.

tyre /ˈtaɪə/ *n.* a band of metal or (usually inflated) rubber, fitted round the rim of a wheel as a running surface.

tzar /zɑ/ *n.* → **tsar**.

tzatziki /tsætˈsiki, zætˈziki/ *n.* in Greek cooking, a dip made from yoghurt, chopped cucumber and garlic.

U, u

U, u /juː/ *n.* the 21st letter of the English alphabet.

ubiquity /juːˈbɪkwəti/ *n.* the state or capacity of being everywhere at the same time; omnipresence. **–ubiquitous**, *adj.*

udder /ˈʌdə/ *n.* a mammary gland, especially when pendulous and with more than one teat, as in cows.

UFO /juː ef ˈoʊ, ˈjuːfoʊ/ *n.* (*pl.* **UFOs** *or* **UFO's**) unidentified flying object.

ugg boot /ˈʌg/ *n.* a comfortable shoe made from sheepskin with the soft fleece being on the inside of the boot and the leather on the outside. Also, **ug boot**, **ugh boot**.

ugly /ˈʌgli/ *adj.* (**-lier, -liest**) **1.** repulsive; offensive to the sense of beauty. **2.** troubling; threatening disadvantage or danger.

UHT /juː eɪtʃ ˈtiː/ *adj.* ultra heat treated; (of milk products) treated by heating briefly to a high temperature and then packaged in hermetically sealed containers; long-life.

ukulele /juːkəˈleɪli/ *n.* a small, four-stringed, guitar-like musical instrument. Also, **ukelele**.

ulcer /ˈʌlsə/ *n.* a sore open either to the surface of the body or to a natural cavity, and accompanied by the disintegration of tissue and the formation of pus, etc. **–ulcerous**, *adj.* **–ulcerate**, *v.*

-ule a diminutive suffix of nouns.

-ulent an adjective suffix meaning 'full of (some thing or quality), as in *fraudulent*.

ulna /ˈʌlnə/ *n.* (*pl.* **-nae** /-niː/ *or* **-nas**) *Anat.* that one of the two bones of the forearm which is on the side opposite to the thumb.

-ulose variant of **-ulous** in scientific terms.

-ulous a suffix forming adjectives meaning 'tending to'.

ulterior /ʌlˈtɪəriə/ *adj.* intentionally kept concealed.

ultimate /ˈʌltəmət/ *adj.* **1.** forming the final aim or object. **2.** coming at the end, as of a course of action, a process, etc. *–n.* **3.** the final point; final result. **4.** a fundamental fact or principle.

ultimatum /ʌltəˈmeɪtəm/ *n.* (*pl.* **-tums** *or* **-ta** /-tə/) a final proposal or statement of conditions.

ultimo /ˈʌltəmoʊ/ *adv.* in or of the month preceding the present. *Abbrev.:* ult., ulto Compare **proximo**.

ultra- a prefix meaning: **1.** beyond (in space or time). **2.** excessive; excessively.

ultralight /ˈʌltrəlaɪt/ *adj.* **1.** extremely lightweight. **2.** of or relating to an ultralight aircraft. *–n.* **3.** an ultralight aircraft.

ultralight aircraft *n.* a powered aircraft of limited weight, designed to carry not more than two people. Also, **ultralight**, **ultralight plane**.

ultramarine /ʌltrəməˈriːn/ *n.* a deep blue colour.

ultrasound /ˈʌltrəsaʊnd/ *n.* sound vibrations above the audible limit, used in medicine as a means of diagnosis or therapy, as in the imaging of internal organs of the body or deep-heat treatment.

ultraviolet /ʌltrəˈvaɪələt, -ˈvaɪlət/ *adj.* beyond the violet, as the invisible rays of the spectrum lying outside the violet end of the visible spectrum.

ululate /ˈjuːljəleɪt/ *v.i.* to howl, as a dog or wolf. **–ululation**, *n.*

umami /uˈmami/ *n.* a taste category, distinguished from sweet, sour, salt, and bitter, which is described as being the taste of freshness common to savoury food such as meat, cheese, mushrooms, etc.; associated with Japanese cuisine.

umbel /ˈʌmbəl/ *n. Bot.* a flower cluster in which several stalks or pedicels spread from a common cluster. **–umbelliferous**, *adj.*

umber /ˈʌmbə/ *n.* a brown pigment.

umbilical cord /ʌmˈbɪləkəl, ʌmbəˈlaɪkəl/ *n. Anat.* a cord connecting the embryo or fetus with the placenta of the mother, and transmitting nourishment from the mother.

umbrage /ˈʌmbrɪdʒ/ *n.* offence given or taken; resentful displeasure.

umbrella /ʌmˈbrɛlə/ *n.* **1.** a portable shade or screen for protection from sunlight, rain, etc. **2.** any general protection or cover.

umpire /ˈʌmpaɪə/ *n.* **1.** a person selected to see that a game is played in accordance with the rules. **2.** a person to whose decision a controversy between parties is referred; an arbiter or referee.

un-¹ a prefix meaning 'not', freely used as an English formative, giving a negative or opposite force. *Note:* Of the words in *un-¹*, only a selected number are separately entered, since in most formations of this class, the meaning, spelling, and pronunciation may readily be determined by reference to the simple word from which each is formed.

un-² a prefix freely used in English to form verbs expressing a reversal of some action or state, or removal, deprivation, release, etc.

unaccountable /ʌnəˈkaʊntəbəl/ *adj.* not to be accounted for or explained.

unanimous /juˈnænəməs/ *adj.* of one mind; in complete accord; agreed.

unassuming /ʌnəˈsjumɪŋ/ *adj.* unpretending; modest.

unbelievable /ʌnbəˈlivəbəl/ *adj.* **1.** not believable; not able to be accepted as true. **2.** *Colloq.* wonderful; excellent. **–unbelievably**, *adv.*

uncanny /ʌnˈkæni/ *adj.* **1.** such as to arouse superstitious uneasiness; unnaturally strange. **2.** abnormally good.

uncertain /ʌnˈsɜtn/ *adj.* **1.** not sure. **2.** not definitely known or decided upon: *the results are still uncertain.* **3.** not to be depended on: *uncertain weather.* **–uncertainty**, *n.* **–uncertainly**, *adv.*

uncle /ˈʌŋkəl/ *n.* **1.** a brother of one's father or mother. **2.** the husband of one's aunt or uncle.

unconscionable /ʌnˈkɒnʃənəbəl/ *adj.* **1.** unreasonably excessive. **2.** not in accordance with what is just or reasonable. **3.** not guided by conscience; unscrupulous.

unconscious /ʌnˈkɒnʃəs/ *adj.* **1.** not conscious; unaware. **2.** temporarily devoid of consciousness. **3.** occurring below the level of conscious thought. **4.** unintentional. *–phr.* **5. the unconscious**, *Psychol.* an organisation of the mind containing all psychic material not available in the immediate field of awareness.

uncouth /ʌnˈkuːθ/ *adj.* awkward, clumsy, or bad-mannered, as persons, behaviour, actions, etc.

uncrossed /ʌnˈkrɒst/ *adj.* (of a cheque) not crossed; negotiable.

unction /ˈʌŋkʃən/ *n.* the act of anointing, especially for medical purposes or as a religious rite.

unctuous /ˈʌŋkʃuəs/ *adj.* oily; greasy.

under /ˈʌndə/ *prep.* **1.** beneath and covered by. **2.** at a point or position lower than or farther down than. **3.** subject to. **4.** below in degree, amount, price, etc.; less than. **5.** below in rank, dignity, or the like. **6.** authorised, warranted, or attested by. **7.** in accordance with. –*adv.* **8.** under or beneath something. **9.** in a lower place. **10.** in a lower degree, amount, etc. **11.** in a subordinate position or condition. –*phr.* **12. go under, a.** to sink in or as in water. **b.** to fail, especially of a business.

under- a prefixal attributive use of *under*, as to indicate: **1.** a place or situation below or beneath, as in *underbrush*, *undertow*, or lower in grade or dignity, as in *understudy*. **2.** a lesser degree, extent, or amount, as in *undersized*. **3.** an insufficiency, as in *underfeed*.

underachieve /ʌndəˈtʃiːv/ *v.i.* to fail to perform as well as one's innate ability suggests. –**underachiever**, *n.* –**underachievement**, *n.*

underarm /ˈʌndəraːm/ *adj. Cricket, Tennis, etc.* executed with the hand below the shoulder as in bowling, service, etc.

undercapitalise /ʌndəˈkæpətəlaɪz/ *v.t.* to provide insufficient capital for (a business venture). Also, **undercapitalize**.

undercarriage /ˈʌndəkærɪdʒ/ *n.* the portions of an aeroplane beneath the body.

undercurrent /ˈʌndəkʌrənt/ *n.* **1.** a current below the surface. **2.** an underlying or concealed condition or tendency.

undercut /ʌndəˈkʌt/ *v.t.* (-**cut**, -**cutting**) to sell or work at a lower price than.

underdeveloped /ʌndədəˈvɛləpt/ *adj.* less fully developed than average.

underdog /ˈʌndədɒg/ *n.* **1.** a victim of oppression. **2.** the loser or expected loser in a competitive situation, fight, etc.

underfelt /ˈʌndəfɛlt/ *n.* a thick felt laid under a carpet to make it more resilient.

undergo /ʌndəˈgoʊ/ *v.t.* **1.** to be subjected to; experience; pass through. **2.** to endure; sustain; suffer.

undergraduate /ʌndəˈgrædʒuət/ *n.* a student in a university or college who has not completed a first degree.

underground /ˈʌndəgraʊnd/ *adj.* **1.** existing, situated, operating, or taking place beneath the surface of the ground. **2.** hidden or secret; not open. –*n.* **3.** the place or region beneath the surface of the ground; the underworld. **4.** a secret organisation, etc.

underground economy *n.* cash economy, operating as a means of tax evasion.

undergrowth /ˈʌndəgroʊθ/ *n.* shrubs or small trees growing beneath or among large trees.

underhand /ˈʌndəhænd/ *adj.* secret and crafty or dishonourable.

underlie /ʌndəˈlaɪ/ *v.t.* (-**lay**, -**lain**, -**lying**) **1.** to lie under or beneath. **2.** to be at the basis of. –**underlying**, *adj.*

underline /ʌndəˈlaɪn/ *v.t.* to mark with a line or lines underneath, as writing, etc.

undermine /ʌndəˈmaɪn, ˈʌndəmaɪn/ *v.t.* to weaken insidiously; destroy gradually.

underneath /ʌndəˈniːθ/ *prep.* **1.** under; beneath. –*adv.* **2.** beneath; below. –*adj.* **3.** lower.

underpants /ˈʌndəpænts/ *pl. n.* an article of underwear in the form of close-fitting short trousers, with or without legs.

underprivileged /ʌndəˈprɪvəlɪdʒd/ *adj.* denied the enjoyment of the normal privileges or rights of a society because of poverty and low social status.

undersecretary /ʌndəˈsɛkrətri/ *n.* (*pl.* -**ries**) the permanent head in certain government departments.

undersigned /ˈʌndəsaɪnd/ *n.* the person or persons who have signed at the end of a document.

understand /ʌndəˈstænd/ *v.* (-**stood**, -**standing**) –*v.t.* **1.** to perceive the meaning of; grasp the idea of; comprehend. **2.** to be thoroughly familiar with; apprehend clearly the character or nature of. **3.** to regard or take as a fact, or as settled. –*v.i.* **4.** to perceive what is meant.

understanding /ʌndəˈstændɪŋ/ *n.* **1.** the act of someone who understands; comprehension; personal interpretation. **2.** superior intelligence; superior power of recognising the truth. **3.** a mutual comprehension of each other's meaning, thoughts, etc. **4.** a mutual agreement of a private or unannounced kind. –*adj.* **5.** sympathetically discerning; tolerant.

understate /ʌndəˈsteɪt/ *v.t.* to state or represent less strongly than is desirable or necessary; state with too little emphasis. –**understatement**, *n.*

understorey /ˈʌndəstɔːri/ *n.* lower-level growth in forests, especially the plants and seedlings protected by the forest canopy.

understudy /ˈʌndəstʌdi/ *n.* an actor or actress who stands by to replace a performer when the latter is unable to appear.

undertake /ʌndəˈteɪk/ *v.t.* (-**took**, -**taken**, -**taking**) **1.** to take on oneself (some task, performance, etc.); attempt. **2.** to lay oneself under a formal obligation to perform or execute (some task, duty, etc.).

undertaker /ˈʌndəteɪkə/ *n.* one whose business it is to prepare the dead for burial and to take charge of funerals.

undertaking /ˈʌndəteɪkɪŋ/ *n.* a task, enterprise, etc., undertaken.

undertone /ˈʌndətoʊn/ *n.* **1.** a low or subdued tone, as of utterance. **2.** an underlying quality, element, or tendency.

undertow /ˈʌndətoʊ/ *n.* the backward flow or draught of the water, below the surface, from waves breaking on a beach.

underwear /ˈʌndəweə/ *n.* clothes worn under outer clothes, especially those worn next to the skin.

underworld /ˈʌndəwɜːld/ *n.* **1.** the lower, degraded, or criminal part of human society. **2.** the lower or nether world.

underwrite /ˈʌndəraɪt/ *v.t.* (-**wrote**, -**written**, -**writing**) **1.** to agree to meet the expense of; undertake to finance. **2.** to guarantee the sale of (shares or bonds to be offered to the public for subscription). **3.** *Insurance* to write one's name at the end of (a policy of insurance), thereby becoming liable in case of certain losses specified therein.

undo /ʌn'du/ *v.t.* (**-did, -done, -doing**) **1.** to unfasten and open (something closed, locked, barred, etc.). **2.** to untie or loose (strings, etc.). **3.** to reverse the doing of; cause to be as if never done. **4.** to bring to ruin or disaster; destroy.

undress /ʌn'drɛs/ *v.t., v.i.* to remove the clothes (of).

undulate /'ʌndʒəleɪt/ *v.i.* to have a wavy motion. **–undulation,** *n.*

unduly /ʌn'dʒuli/ *adv.* **1.** excessively. **2.** inappropriately; improperly; unjustifiably.

unearned income /ʌn'ɜnd/ *n.* income earned other than through personal efforts, as from investments, inheritance, property, etc.; such income is sometimes taxed at a higher level than earned income.

unearth /ʌn'ɜθ/ *v.t.* to uncover or bring to light by digging, searching, or discovery.

uneasy /ʌn'izi/ *adj.* (**-sier, -siest**) not easy in body or mind; disturbed.

unemployed /ʌnəm'plɔɪd/ *adj.* without work or employment.

unerring /ʌn'ɜrɪŋ/ *adj.* **1.** not erring; without error or mistake. **2.** unfailingly right, exact, or sure.

unexplored /ʌnək'splɔd/ *adj.* **1.** not explored; uncharted. **2.** not analysed; unknown.

unfaithful /ʌn'feɪθfəl/ *adj.* not faithful.

unfeeling /ʌn'filɪŋ/ *adj.* unsympathetic; callous; hard-hearted.

unfit /ʌn'fɪt/ *adj.* **1.** not suitable, deserving or good enough: *unfit to be eaten.* **2.** unqualified or incompetent: *an unfit parent.* **3.** not physically fit or in due condition.

unforeseen /ʌnfɔ'sin, -fə-/ *adj.* not predicted; unexpected.

unfortunate /ʌn'fɔtʃənət/ *adj.* **1.** tending to suffer mishaps or misfortune: *an unfortunate child.* **2.** constituting a misfortune.: *an unfortunate accident.* **3.** likely to have undesirable results: *an unfortunate decision.* **4.** unsuitable: *an unfortunate choice of words.* –*n.* **5.** an unfortunate person. **–unfortunately,** *adv.*

unfriend /ʌn'frɛnd/ *v.t.* to delete (someone) as a friend from a site on a social network. Also, **defriend.**

ungainly /ʌn'geɪnli/ *adj.* not graceful.

unguent /'ʌŋgwənt/ *n.* any soft preparation or salve; an ointment.

unhappy /ʌn'hæpi/ *adj.* **1.** not happy: *an unhappy expression on her face; an unhappy marriage.* **2.** not pleased or satisfied: *unhappy with the standard of one's work.* **–unhappily,** *adv.* **–unhappiness,** *n.*

unhealthy /ʌn'hɛlθi/ *adj.* (**-thier, -thiest**) **1.** not healthy; in a state of poor health. **2.** likely to lead to ill health, or not conducive to good health: *unhealthy food.* **–unhealthily,** *adv.*

uni /'juni/ *n. Colloq.* a university.

uni- a word element meaning 'one', 'single'.

unicameral /juni'kæmərəl/ *adj.* having a single parliamentary chamber. Compare **bicameral.** **–unicameralism,** *n.* **–unicameralist,** *n.*

unicorn /'junəkɔn/ *n.* a mythological animal with a single long horn.

uniform /'junəfɔm/ *adj.* **1.** having always the same form or character; unvarying. **2.** regular; even. **3.** agreeing with one another in form, character, appearance, etc.; alike; of the same form, character, etc., with another or others. –*n.* **4.** a distinctive dress of uniform style, materials, and colour worn by and identifying all the members of a group or organisation. **–uniformity,** *n.*

unify /'junəfaɪ/ *v.t.* (**-fied, -fying**) to form into one; make a unit of; reduce to unity. **–unification,** *n.*

unilateral /juni'lætərəl, -'lætrəl, junə-/ *adj.* **1.** relating to, occurring on, or affecting one side only. **2.** affecting one side, party, or person only. **3.** concerned with or considering only one side of a matter or question; one-sided.

unimpressed /ʌnɪm'prɛst/ *adj.* **1.** not impressed; unmoved: *unimpressed by the sales pitch.* **2.** (*rhetorical*) extremely displeased: *decidedly unimpressed with the opposition.*

uninstall /ʌnɪn'stɔl/ *v.t.* **1.** to remove from any office, position, place, etc. **2.** *Computers* to remove (a software application).

uninterested /ʌn'ɪntrəstəd/ *adj.* **1.** having or showing no feeling of interest; indifferent. **2.** not personally concerned in something.

union /'junjən/ *n.* **1.** the act of uniting two or more things into one. **2.** the state of being so united; conjunction; combination. **3.** something formed by uniting two or more things; a combination. **4.** a number of persons, societies, states, or the like, joined together or associated for some common purpose. **5.** → **trade union.**

unionise /'junjənaɪz/ *v.t.* to organise into a trade union. Also, **unionize.**

unionist /'junjənɪst/ *n.* a trade unionist.

unique /ju'nik/ *adj.* **1.** of which there is only one; sole. **2.** having no like or equal.

unisex /'junisɛks/ *adj.* of a style of dress, etc., which does not adhere to the traditional differentiations between the sexes.

unison /'junəsən/ *n.* **1.** coincidence in pitch of two or more notes, voices, etc. **2.** accord.

unit /'junət/ *n.* **1.** a single thing or person; any group of things or persons regarded as an individual. **2.** any specified amount of a quantity, as of length, volume, force, momentum, time, by comparison with which any other quantity of the same kind is measured or estimated. **3.** Also, **home unit.** one of a number of dwelling apartments in the same building, each owned under separate title, frequently by the occupier. Compare **flat²** (def. 1).

unite /ju'naɪt/ *v.t.* **1.** to join in so as to form one connected whole; join, combine, or incorporate in one; cause to be one. **2.** to associate (persons, etc.) by some bond or tie; join in action, interest, opinion, feeling, etc. –*v.i.* **3.** to join together so as to form one connected whole; become one; combine.

unit price *n.* a price per agreed unit, as per kilogram, per dozen, etc.

unity /'junəti/ *n.* **1.** the state or fact of being one; oneness. **2.** the oneness of a complex or organic whole or of an interconnected series. **3.** freedom from diversity or variety. **4.** oneness of mind, feeling, etc., as among a number of persons; concord, harmony, or agreement.

universal /junə'vɜsəl/ *adj.* **1.** extending over, including, proceeding from, all or the whole (of something specified or implicit); without exception. **2.** applicable to many individuals or single cases; general. **3.** affecting, concerning, or involving all. **4.** of or relating to the universe, all nature, or all existing things. **5.** *Machinery, etc.* adapted or adaptable for all or various uses, angles, sizes, etc. *–n.* **6.** that which may be applied throughout the universe to many things.

universe /'junəvɜs/ *n.* **1.** all of space, and all the matter and energy which it contains; the cosmos. **2.** a world or sphere in which something exists or prevails.

university /junə'vɜsəti/ *n.* (*pl.* **-ties**) an institution of higher learning, conducting teaching and research at the undergraduate and postgraduate level.

unkempt /ʌn'kɛmpt/ *adj.* in an uncared-for, neglected, or untidy state; rough.

unleaded petrol *n.* petrol that does not contain the metal lead and is therefore not as environmentally damaging as petrol with lead.

unless /ʌn'lɛs, ən-/ *conj.* except on condition that; except when; if…not.

unload /ʌn'loud/ *v.t.* to take the load from; remove the burden, cargo, or freight from.

unnerve /ʌn'nɜv/ *v.t.* to deprive of nerve, strength, or physical or mental firmness; break down the self-control of; upset.

unprepossessing /ʌnpripə'zɛsɪŋ/ *adj.* not impressive; ordinary.

unravel /ʌn'rævəl/ *v.t.* (**-elled** or, *Chiefly US*, **-eled**, **-elling** or, *Chiefly US*, **-eling**) to disentangle; disengage the threads or fibres of (a woven or knitted fabric, a rope, etc.).

unreal /ʌn'ril/ *adj.* **1.** not real; not substantial; imaginary; artificial; unpractical or visionary. **2.** *Colloq.* **a.** unbelievably awful. **b.** unbelievably wonderful.

unreasonable /ʌn'rizənəbəl/ *adj.* **1.** not reasonable; not endowed with reason. **2.** not guided by reason or good sense. **3.** not agreeable to or willing to listen to reason. **4.** not based on or in accordance with reason or sound judgement. **5.** exceeding the bounds of reason; immoderate; exorbitant: *unreasonable expense.* –**unreasonably**, *adv.*

unrequited /ʌnrə'kwaɪtəd/ *adj.* (used especially of affection) not returned or reciprocated.

unrest /ʌn'rɛst/ *n.* strong, almost rebellious, dissatisfaction and agitation.

unruly /ʌn'ruli/ *adj.* not submissive or conforming to rule; ungovernable. –**unruliness**, *n.*

unsavoury /ʌn'seɪvəri/ *adj.* socially or morally unpleasant or offensive. Also, **unsavory.**

unscathed /ʌn'skeɪðd/ *adj.* not harmed in any way.

unscrew /ʌn'skru/ *v.t.* **1.** to draw the screw or screws from; unfasten by withdrawing screws. **2.** to loosen, remove or withdraw (a screw, lid, etc.) by turning. **3.** to be capable of being unscrewed: *This part unscrews.* **4.** to become unscrewed: *The cap unscrewed in my bag and toothpaste went everywhere.*

unscrupulous /ʌn'skrupjələs/ *adj.* untroubled by conscience; lacking sound moral principles.

unsecured /ʌnsə'kjuəd/ *adj.* **1.** not made secure or fastened. **2.** not insured against loss, as by a mortgage, bond, pledge, etc.

unsettle /ʌn'sɛtl/ *v.t.* to shake or weaken (beliefs, feelings, etc.); derange (the mind, etc.).

unsightly /ʌn'saɪtli/ *adj.* not pleasing to the sight; forming an unpleasing sight.

unsound /ʌn'saund/ *adj.* not sound; diseased, defective or weak.

unstable /ʌn'steɪbəl/ *adj.* not stable; likely to fall or give way. –**instability**, *n.*

unsteady /ʌn'stɛdi/ *adj.* not stable, firm or steady. –**unsteadily**, *adv.*

untenable /ʌn'tɛnəbəl/ *adj.* incapable of being maintained against arguments, as an opinion, scheme, etc.

unthinkable /ʌn'θɪŋkəbəl/ *adj.* **1.** inconceivable; unimaginable. **2.** not to be considered; utterly out of the question.

untidy /ʌn'taɪdi/ *adj.* (**-dier**, **-diest**) not tidy or neat –**untidily**, *adv.* –**untidiness**, *n.*

untie /ʌn'taɪ/ *v.* (**untied**, **untying**) *–v.t.* **1.** to loosen or unfasten (anything tied); let or set loose by undoing a knot. **2.** to undo the string or cords of. **3.** to free from or as from bonds or restraint. *–v.i.* **4.** to become untied.

until /ʌn'tɪl/ *conj.* **1.** up to the time that or when; till. **2.** (with negatives) before: *not until he's finished.* *–prep.* **3.** onward to, or till (a specified time); up to the time of (some occurrence). **4.** (with negatives) before: *not until evening.*

untimely /ʌn'taɪmli/ *adj.* **1.** occurring at an unsuitable or inopportune time; ill-timed: *her untimely arrival.* **2.** premature: *his untimely demise.*

unto /'ʌntu/ *prep. Archaic* to (in its various uses, except as the accompaniment of the infinitive).

untoward /ʌntə'wɔd/ *adj.* **1.** unfavourable or unfortunate. **2.** unseemly.

unusual /ʌn'juʒuəl/ *adj.* not usual, common or ordinary. –**unusually**, *adv.*

unwieldy /ʌn'wildi/ *adj.* **1.** not readily handled or managed in use or action, as from size, shape, or weight. **2.** ungainly; awkward.

unwitting /ʌn'wɪtɪŋ/ *adj.* unaware; unconscious.

unwritten law *n.* **1.** the body of law which rests for its authority on custom, convention, etc., as distinguished from law originating in written command, judicial decision, statute, or decree. **2.** a custom or social convention.

unzip /ʌn'zɪp/ *v.t.* (**-zipped**, **-zipping**) **1.** to open the zip of (a garment). **2.** *Computers →* **decompress** (def. 2).

up /ʌp/ *adv.* **1.** to, towards, or in a more elevated position. **2.** into the air. **3.** to or in an erect position. **4.** out of bed. **5.** to or at any point that is considered higher, as the north, a capital city, or the like. **6.** to or at a higher point or degree in a scale, as of rank, size, value, pitch, etc. **7.** to or at a point of equal advance, extent, etc. **8.** well advanced or versed, as in a subject. **9.** to a state of maturity. **10.** to a state of completion; to an end. *–prep.* **11.** to, towards, or at a higher place on or in. **12.** to, towards, near, or at a higher station, condition, or rank in. *–adj.* **13.** upwards; going or directed upwards. **14.** travelling towards a terminus or centre. **15.** standing and speaking. **16.** out of bed. **17.** well informed or advanced, as in a subject. **18.** (especially of a computer) operational. **19.** appearing before a court or the like on some charge. **20.** in a leading or advanced position. *–v.t.* (**upped, upping**) *Colloq.* **21.** to make larger; step up. **22.** to go better than (a preceding wager). *–interj.* **23.** a command to rise or stand up.

up- a prefixal, attributive use of *up*, in its various meanings.

upbraid /ʌpˈbreɪd/ *v.t.* to reproach for some fault or offence; reprove severely; chide.

upbringing /ˈʌpbrɪŋɪŋ/ *n.* the bringing up or rearing of a person from childhood.

up-country /ˈʌp-kʌntri/ *adj.* **1.** being or living remote from the coast or border; interior. *–adv.* **2.** towards or in the interior of a country.

update *v.t.* /ʌpˈdeɪt/ **1.** to bring up to date. *–n.* /ˈʌpdeɪt/ **2.** the act of updating. **3.** an updated version; revision.

up-end /ʌp-ˈend/ *v.t.* **1.** to set on end. **2.** to upset.

up-front /ʌp-frʌnt/ *adj.* **1.** Also, **upfront.** placed in a position of leadership or responsibility: *the up-front leader.* **2.** straightforward; open. **3.** (of money) payable in advance: *an up-front fee.*

upgrade /ʌpˈgreɪd/ *v.t.* (**-graded, -grading**) **1.** to improve. **2.** to allocate to (someone) a seat on a plane, etc., in a class higher than the one ticketed. **3.** such a seat reallocation: *to give someone an upgrade.* **4.** *Computers* a new version of a product, usually software, designed to replace a previous version of the product.

upheave /ʌpˈhiv/ *v.t.* **1.** to heave or lift up; raise up or aloft. **2.** to disturb or change violently or radically. **–upheaval,** *n.*

uphold /ʌpˈhoʊld/ *v.t.* (**-held, -holding**) to support or maintain, as by advocacy or agreement.

upholstery /ʌpˈhoʊlstri, -stəri/ *n.* the cushions, furniture coverings and other material used to stuff and cover furniture and cushions.

upkeep /ˈʌpkip/ *n.* (the cost of) the maintenance of an establishment, machine, etc.

uplift /ʌpˈlɪft/ *v.t.* **1.** to lift up; raise; elevate. **2.** to exalt emotionally or spiritually.

upload /ˈʌploʊd/ *Computers –v.t.* **1.** to transfer or copy (data) from a computer to a larger system, as from a personal computer to a network or mainframe computer. *–n.* **2.** the act or process of uploading data. **3.** the data uploaded in such an operation.

up-market /ˈʌp-makət/ *adj.* superior in style or production; pretentious. Compare **down-market.**

upon /əˈpɒn/ *prep.* **1.** up and on; upwards so as to get or be on. **2.** on, in any of various senses.

upper /ˈʌpə/ *adj.* **1.** higher (than something implied) or highest, as in place, or position, or in a scale. **2.** forming the higher of a pair of corresponding things or sets. **3.** (of a surface) facing upwards. *–n.* **4.** anything which is higher than another, as of a pair) or highest. **5.** the part of a shoe or boot above the sole.

upper class *n.* the class of people socially and conventionally regarded as being higher or highest in the social hierarchy and commonly identified by wealth or aristocratic birth.

upright /ˈʌpraɪt/ *adj.* **1.** erect or vertical, as in position or posture. **2.** righteous, honest, or just. *–n.* **3.** something standing erect or vertical, as a piece of timber.

uprising /ˈʌpraɪzɪŋ, ʌpˈraɪzɪŋ/ *n.* an insurrection or revolt.

uproar /ˈʌprɔ/ *n.* violent and noisy disturbance.

uproarious /ʌpˈrɔriəs/ *adj.* **1.** characterised by or in a state of uproar; tumultuous. **2.** extremely funny.

upscale /ˈʌpskeɪl/ *adj. Colloq.* **1.** of high quality; superior: *upscale decor.* **2.** affluent: *an upscale suburb.*

upsell /ˈʌpsel/ *v.t.* (**-sold, -selling**) to effect the sale of (a product) which is more expensive than the one the customer intended to buy. **–upselling,** *n.*

upset *v.t.* /ʌpˈset/ (**-set, -setting**) **1.** to overturn; knock or tip over; capsize. **2.** to disturb (someone) mentally or emotionally; distress. **3.** to put out of order. **4.** to make feel sick in the stomach. **5.** to defeat (a competitor or opponent), especially contrary to expectation. *–n.* /ˈʌpset/ **6.** a physical upsetting or being upset; overthrow. **7.** an emotional disturbance. **8.** a defeat, especially unexpected. *–adj.* /ˈʌpset, ʌpˈset/ **9.** emotionally disturbed; distressed.

upshot /ˈʌpʃɒt/ *n.* the final issue, the conclusion, or the result.

upstage /ʌpˈsteɪdʒ/ *adv.* **1.** on or to the back of the stage. *–v.t.* (**-staged, -staging**) **2.** to steal attention (from another) by some manoeuvre.

upstairs *adv.* /ʌpˈsteəz/ **1.** up the stairs; to or on an upper floor. **2.** *Colloq.* to or in a higher rank or office. *–adj.* /ˈʌpsteəz/ **3.** on or relating to an upper floor.

upstanding /ʌpˈstændɪŋ/ *adj.* straightforward, open, or independent; upright; honourable.

upstart /ˈʌpstat/ *n.* someone who has risen suddenly from a humble position to wealth or power, or to assumed consequence.

upstream /ʌpˈstrim/ *adv.* towards or in the higher part of a stream; against the current.

uptake /ˈʌpteɪk/ *n.* the action of understanding or comprehension; mental grasp.

uptight /ˈʌptaɪt/ *adj. Colloq.* tense, nervous, or irritable.

up-to-date /ˈʌp-tə-deɪt/ *adj.* extending to the present time; including the latest facts.

upturn /ˈʌptɜn/ *n.* an upward turn, or a changing and rising movement, as in prices, business, etc.

upward /ˈʌpwəd/ *adj.* **1.** directed, tending, or moving towards a higher point or level; ascending. *–adv.* **2.** → **upwards**

upwards /ˈʌpwədz/ *adv.* towards a higher place, position, level or degree. Also, **upward.**

upwind /ʌpˈwɪnd/ *adv.* towards or in the direction from which the wind is blowing.

uranium /juˈreɪniəm/ *n.* a white, lustrous, radioactive, metallic element, one isotope of which is the basis of the atomic bomb and nuclear reactors. *Symbol:* U

urano- a word element meaning 'heaven'.

urban /ˈɜbən/ *adj.* of, relating to, or comprising a city or town.

urban consolidation *n.* the encouragement of development within existing urbanised areas, limiting development on non-urbanised land, so as to maximise the use of existing infrastructure.

urbane /ɜ'beɪn/ *adj.* having the refinement and manners considered to be characteristic of city-dwellers; civilised; sophisticated.

urchin /'ɜtʃən/ *n.* a small boy or youngster, especially someone who is mischievous and impudent, or ragged and shabbily dressed.

-ure a suffix of abstract nouns indicating action, result, and instrument, as in *legislature, pressure.*

urea /ju'riə, 'juriə/ *n.* a colourless crystalline substance occurring in the urine of mammals, amphibians, and some fishes and reptiles.

urethra /ju'riθrə/ *n.* (*pl.* **-thrae** /-θri/ *or* **-thras**) *Anat.* the membranous tube which extends from the bladder to the exterior. In the male it conveys semen as well as urine.

urge /ɜdʒ/ *v.t.* (**urged, urging**) **1.** to endeavour to induce or persuade; entreat or exhort earnestly. **2.** to press, push, or hasten (the course, activities, etc.). *–n.* **3.** the fact of urging or being urged. **4.** an involuntary, natural, or instinctive impulse.

urgent /'ɜdʒənt/ *adj.* **1.** pressing; compelling or requiring immediate action or attention; imperative. **2.** insistent or earnest in solicitation. **–urgency,** *n.*

-urgy a word element meaning 'a technology', as in *metallurgy.*

urinal /'juranəl, ju'raɪnəl/ *n.* a fixture, room, or building for discharging urine in.

urinate /'jurəneɪt/ *v.i.* to discharge urine.

urine /'jurən, -aɪn/ *n.* the secretion of the kidneys (in mammals, a fluid). **–urinary,** *adj.*

URL /ju ar 'ɛl/ *n. Internet* the address of a web page on the internet.

urn /ɜn/ *n.* **1.** a kind of vase, of various forms, especially one with a foot or pedestal. **2.** a vessel with a tap, used for heating water, tea, coffee, etc., in quantity.

urogenital /jurou'dʒɛnətl/ *adj.* of or relating to the urinary and genital organs.

ursine /'ɜsaɪn/ *adj.* **1.** of or relating to a bear or bears. **2.** bear-like.

us /ʌs/, *weak forms* /əs, əz/ *pron.* the personal pronoun used, usually after a verb or preposition, by a speaker to refer to himself or herself along with at least one other person: *Could you please take us home?*

usage /'jusɪdʒ, 'juzɪdʒ/ *n.* **1.** customary way of doing; a custom or practice. **2.** customary manner of using a language or any of its forms, especially standard practice in a given language. **3.** usual conduct or behaviour. **4.** the act or fact of using or employing; use. Also, **useage.**

usance /'juzəns/ *n.* **1.** *Commerce* the length of time, exclusive of days of grace, allowed by custom or usage for the payment of foreign bills of exchange. **2.** *Econ.* the income of benefits of every kind derived from the ownership of wealth.

USB /ju ɛs 'bi/ *n. Computers* universal serial bus; a standard for connection sockets.

USB drive /ju ɛs 'bi draɪv/ *n.* a small portable data storage device that plugs into the USB port of a computer; memory stick. Also, **USB, USB stick, flash drive.**

USB stick *n. Computers* a memory stick for USB portals.

use *v.* /juz/ (**used, using**) *–v.t.* **1.** to employ for some purpose; put into service. **2.** to avail oneself of; apply to one's own purposes. **3.** to act or behave towards, or treat (a person) in some manner. **4.** to exploit (a person) for one's own ends. **5.** to operate or put into effect. *–v.i.* **6.** *Colloq.* to take drugs, especially heroin. *–n.* /jus/ **7.** the act of employing or using, or putting into service. **8.** the state of being employed or used. **9.** a way of being employed or used; a purpose for which something is used. **10.** the power, right, or privilege of employing or using something. **11.** help; profit; resulting good. **12.** custom; practice. **13.** way of using or treating; treatment.

use-by date *n.* the date by which the manufacturer of a product recommends that it should be used, usually stamped onto the packaging.

used¹ /juzd/ *adj.* **1.** worn; showing signs of wear. **2.** second-hand.

used² /just/ *phr.* **used to, 1.** accustomed or inured to: *used to hard work.* **2.** (sometimes fol. by infinitive or infinitive implied) an auxiliary expressing habitual past action: *I used to sing; She plays now but she used not to.*

useful /'jusfəl/ *adj.* being of use or service; serving some purpose.

user /'juzə/ *n.* **1.** someone who uses something: *a road user; a computer user.* **2.** *Colloq.* a drug user, especially someone who takes heroin. **3.** *Colloq.* a person who selfishly exploits others.

user-friendly /'juzə-frɛndli/ *adj.* of or relating to equipment, especially computer programs or equipment, designed to provide minimal difficulty for the inexperienced operator.

user group *n.* a group of people linked by their use of a particular product, sometimes forming an association for the sharing of information about that product. Also, **usergroup.**

userid /'juzərar'di/ *n.* a personal identification code entered into a computer when signing on. Also, **username.**

username /'juzəneɪm/ *n.* → **userid.**

user-pays principle *n.* the principle that the cost of a government service should be borne mainly by the people who benefit from it.

usher /'ʌʃə/ *n.* **1.** someone who escorts persons to seats in a church, theatre, etc. **2.** an attendant who keeps order in a law court. *–v.t.* **3.** to conduct or escort, as an attendant does.

usual /'juʒuəl/ *adj.* **1.** habitual or customary: *with his usual good humour.* **2.** such as is commonly met with or observed in experience; ordinary: *the usual January weather.* **3.** in common use; common: *to say the usual things.* *–n.* **4.** that which is usual or habitual. **–usually,** *adv.*

usurp /ju'sɜp, ju'zɜp/ *v.t.* to seize and hold (an office or position, power, etc.) by force or without right.

usury /'juʒəri/ *n.* the lending, or practice of lending money at an exorbitant rate of interest.

ute /jut/ *n.* → **utility** (def. 4).

utensil /ju'tɛnsəl/ *n.* any instrument, vessel, or implement.

uterus /'jutərəs/ *n.* (*pl.* **uteri** /'jutəraɪ/ *or* **uteruses**) that portion of the female reproductive system in which the fertilised ovum

implants itself and develops until birth; womb.
–**uterine**, *adj.*

utilise /'jutǝlaɪz/ *v.t.* to put to use; turn to profitable account. Also, **utilize**.

utilitarian /juˌtɪlǝ'tɛǝrɪǝn/ *adj.* **1.** relating to or consisting in utility; concerning practical or material things. **2.** having regard to utility or usefulness rather than beauty, ornamentality, etc.

utility /ju'tɪlǝti/ *n.* (*pl.* **-ties**) **1.** the state or character of being useful. **2.** something useful; a useful thing. **3.** a public service, as a bus or railway service, gas or electricity supply, or the like. **4.** Also, **utility truck, ute.** a small truck with an enclosed cabin and a rectangular tray which has sides and is sometimes covered by a tarpaulin.

utility program *n. Computers* a computer program designed to carry out a routine process, as sorting data, copying files, etc.

utmost /'ʌtmoʊst/ *adj.* **1.** of the greatest or highest degree, quantity, or the like; greatest. **2.** being at the farthest point or extremity; farthest. –*n.* **3.** the greatest degree or amount.

4. the highest, greatest, or best of one's power. Also, **uttermost**.

utopia /ju'toʊpɪǝ/ *n.* (*sometimes upper case*) a place or state of ideal perfection. –**utopian**, *adj.*

utter[1] /'ʌtǝ/ *v.t.* **1.** to give audible expression to (words, etc.); speak or pronounce. **2.** to express or make known in any manner. **3.** to make publicly known; publish. **4.** to put into circulation, as coins, notes, etc., and especially counterfeit money, forged cheques, etc. –**utterance**, *n.*

utter[2] /'ʌtǝ/ *adj.* complete; total; absolute. –**utterly**, *adv.*

U-turn /'ju-tɜn/ *n.* a sharp turn executed by the driver of a motor vehicle so that the vehicle faces the direction from which it was travelling.

uvula /'juvjǝlǝ/ *n.* (*pl.* **-las** *or* **-lae** /-li/) the small, fleshy, conical body projecting downwards from the middle of the soft palate. –**uvular**, *adj.*

uxorious /ʌk'sɔrɪǝs/ *adj.* excessively or foolishly fond of one's wife.

V, v

V, v /viː/ *n.* the 22nd letter of the English alphabet.

vacant /ˈveɪkənt/ *adj.* 1. having no contents; empty; void. 2. having no occupant. 3. free from work, business, etc., as time. –**vacancy**, *n.*

vacate /vəˈkeɪt, veɪˈkeɪt/ *v.t.* 1. to make vacant; cause to be empty or unoccupied. 2. to give up the occupancy of.

vacation /vəˈkeɪʃən, veɪˈkeɪʃən/ *n.* 1. a part of the year when law courts, universities, etc., are suspended or closed. 2. an extended period of exemption from work, or of recreation.

vaccinate /ˈvæksəneɪt/ *v.t.* to inoculate with the modified virus of a disease, as a preventive measure. –**vaccination**, *n.*

vaccine /ˈvækˈsin, ˈvæksɪn/ *n.* the modified virus of a disease, used for preventive inoculation.

vacillate /ˈvæsəleɪt/ *v.i.* 1. to sway unsteadily; waver; stagger. 2. to fluctuate. –**vacillation**, *n.*

vacuous /ˈvækjuəs/ *adj.* 1. empty; without contents. 2. empty of ideas or intelligence; stupidly vacant. –**vacuity**, *n.*

vacuum /ˈvækjum/ *n.* (*pl.* **vacuums** *or* **vacua** /ˈvækjuə/) 1. a space entirely void of matter. 2. an enclosed space from which air (or other gas) has been removed, as by an air pump. 3. → **vacuum cleaner**.

vacuum cleaner *n.* a machine for cleaning floors, carpets, etc., which functions by sucking up dirt and dust.

vagabond /ˈvægəbɒnd/ *n.* someone who is without a fixed abode and wanders from place to place.

vagary /ˈveɪɡəri/ *n.* (*pl.* **-ries**) 1. an extravagant idea or notion. 2. a wild, capricious, or fantastic action; a freak. 3. uncertainty: *the vagaries of life.*

vagina /vəˈdʒaɪnə/ *n. Anat.* the passage leading from the uterus to the vulva in a female mammal. –**vaginal**, *adj.*

vagrant /ˈveɪɡrənt/ *n.* 1. someone who wanders from place to place and has no settled home or means of support; tramp. –*adj.* 2. wandering or roaming from place to place. –**vagrancy**, *n.*

vague /veɪɡ/ *adj.* 1. not definite in statement or meaning; not explicit or precise. 2. indistinct to the sight or other sense, or perceptible or recognisable only in an indefinite way. 3. (of persons, etc.) indefinite in statement; not clear in thought or understanding.

vain /veɪn/ *adj.* 1. without real value or importance; hollow, idle or worthless. 2. futile; useless; ineffectual. 3. having an excessive pride in one's own appearance, qualities, gifts, achievements, etc.; conceited.

vainglory /veɪnˈɡlɔːri/ *n.* inordinate elation or pride in one's achievements, abilities, etc. –**vainglorious**, *adj.*

valance /ˈvæləns/ *n.* a short curtain.

valedictory /ˌvæləˈdɪktəri/ *adj.* 1. bidding farewell. 2. of or relating to an occasion of leave-taking. –*n.* (*pl.* **-ries**) 3. a valedictory speech. –**valediction**, *n.*

valency /ˈveɪlənsi/ *n.* (*pl.* **-cies**) *Chem.* the combining capacity of an atom.

-valent a word element meaning 'having worth or value', used especially in scientific terminology to refer to valency.

valerian /vəˈlɪəriən, -ˈlɪə-/ *n.* 1. a herb with white or pink flowers. 2. a drug consisting of or made from its root, used to calm nerves.

valet /ˈvæleɪ, ˈvælət/ *n.* 1. a male servant who is his employer's personal attendant, caring for the employer's clothing, etc. 2. someone who performs similar services for patrons of a hotel, etc.

valet parking *n.* a service provided in a hotel, etc., in which patrons drive to the door and leave their cars for an attendant to park.

valetudinarian /ˌvælətjudəˈnɛəriən/ *n.* 1. an invalid. 2. someone who is constantly or excessively concerned about the state of their health.

valiant /ˈvæliənt/ *adj.* brave, courageous, or stout-hearted.

valid /ˈvæləd/ *adj.* 1. sound, just, or well-founded. 2. having force, weight, or cogency; authoritative. 3. legally sound, effective, or binding. –**validity**, *n.* –**validate**, *v.*

valley /ˈvæli/ *n.* an elongated depression, usually with an outlet, between uplands, hills, or mountains, especially one following the course of a stream.

valour /ˈvælə/ *n.* bravery or heroic courage, especially in battle. Also, **valor**.

valuable /ˈvæljuəbəl, ˈvæljubəl/ *adj.* 1. of monetary worth. 2. of considerable use, service, or importance.

valuation /væljuˈeɪʃən/ *n.* an estimating or fixing of the value of a thing.

value /ˈvælju/ *n.* 1. that property of a thing because of which it is esteemed, desirable, or useful, or the degree of this property possessed; worth, merit, or importance. 2. the worth of a thing as measured by the amount of other things for which it can be exchanged, or as estimated in terms of a medium of exchange. 3. force, import, or significance. –*v.t.* (**-ued, -uing**) 4. to estimate the value of; rate at a certain value or price; appraise. 5. to consider with respect to worth, excellence, usefulness, or importance. 6. to regard or esteem highly.

value-add /ˈvæljuˈæd/ *v.i.* to add to the value of a product or service at any stage of production. –**value-added**, *adj.* –**value-adding**, *n.*

valve /vælv/ *n.* 1. any device for closing or modifying the passage through a pipe, outlet, inlet, or the like, in order to control the flow of liquids, gases, etc. 2. *Anat.* a membranous fold or other structure which permits blood to flow in one direction only. 3. *Electronics* an electrical device which can be used for controlling a flow of electricity.

vamp[1] /væmp/ *n.* 1. the front part of the upper of a shoe or boot. 2. anything patched up or pieced together. –*v.t.* 3. (oft. fol. by *up*) to patch up or repair; renovate.

vamp[2] /væmp/ *n.* a woman who uses her charms to seduce and exploit men.

vampire /ˈvæmpaɪə/ *n.* 1. a supernatural being, in the common belief a reanimated corpse of a person improperly buried, supposed to suck blood of sleeping persons at night. **2.** Also, **vampire bat**. a bat which feeds on the blood of animals including humans.

van /væn/ *n.* a covered vehicle, usually large in size, for moving furniture, goods, etc.

vanadium /vəˈneidiəm/ *n.* a rare element used as an ingredient of steel. *Symbol:* V

vandal /ˈvændl/ *n.* someone who wilfully or ignorantly destroys or damages anything. **–vandalism**, *n.* **–vandalise, vandalize,** *v.*

vane /vein/ *n.* a flat piece of metal, etc., especially one which moves with the wind and indicates its direction.

vanguard /ˈvængad/ *n.* the leading position in any field.

vanilla /vəˈnilə/ *n.* a tropical orchid whose podlike fruit yields an extract used in flavourings, perfumery, etc.

vanish /ˈvæniʃ/ *v.i.* to disappear from sight, or become invisible, especially quickly.

vanity /ˈvænəti/ *n.* (*pl.* **vanities**) **1.** the quality of being personally vain. **2.** Also, **vanity unit**. an item of bathroom furniture consisting of a cabinet with a bench top and an inset basin.

vanquish /ˈvæŋkwiʃ/ *v.t.* to conquer or defeat in battle or conflict.

vantage point /ˈvæntidʒ, ˈvan-/ *n.* a position or place affording an advantageous or clear view or perspective.

vapid /ˈvæpəd/ *adj.* having lost life, sharpness, or flavour; insipid; flat.

vaporise /ˈveipəraiz/ *v.t.* to cause to pass into the gaseous state. Also, **vaporize**.

vapour /ˈveipə/ *n.* **1.** a visible exhalation, as fog, mist, condensed steam, smoke, etc. **2.** a substance in the gaseous state; a gas. Also, **vapor**.

variable /ˈvɛəriəbəl/ *adj.* **1.** apt or liable to vary or change; changeable. **2.** inconsistent or fickle, as a person. *–n.* **3.** something variable. **4.** *Maths* a symbol, or the quantity or function which it signifies, which may represent any one of a given set of numbers and other objects. **–variability**, *n.*

variance /ˈvɛəriəns/ *n.* the state or fact of varying; divergence or discrepancy.

variant /ˈvɛəriənt/ *adj.* **1.** being an altered or different form of something. *–n.* **2.** a variant form.

variation /vɛəriˈeiʃən/ *n.* **1.** the act or process of varying; change in condition, character, degree, etc. **2.** amount or rate of change. **3.** a different form of something; a variant.

varicose /ˈværəkous, -kəs/ *adj.* abnormally or unusually enlarged, swollen, or dilated.

variegate /ˈvɛəriəgeit, ˈvɛərə-/ *v.t.* to make varied in appearance; mark with different colours, tints, etc.

variety /vəˈraiəti/ *n.* (*pl.* **-ties**) **1.** the state or character of being various or varied; diversity, or absence of uniformity or monotony. **2.** a number of things of different kinds. **3.** a kind or sort. **4.** a different form, condition, or phase of something.

various /ˈvɛəriəs/ *adj.* **1.** differing one from another, or of different kinds, as two or more things. **2.** several or many.

varnish /ˈvaniʃ/ *n.* **1.** a preparation which, when applied to the surface of wood, metal, etc., dries and leaves a hard, more or less glossy,

usually transparent coating. *–v.t.* **2.** to apply varnish to.

vary /ˈvɛəri/ *v.* (**-ried, -rying**) *–v.t.* **1.** to change or alter, as in form, appearance, character, substance, degree, etc. **2.** to cause to be different, one from another. **3.** to diversify (something); relieve from uniformity or monotony. *–v.i.* **4.** to be different, or show diversity. **5.** to undergo change in form, appearance, character, substance, degree, etc. **6.** to change in succession, follow alternately, or alternate. **7.** (usu. fol. by *from*) to diverge; deviate.

vas /væs/ *n.* (*pl.* **vasa** /ˈveisə/) *Anat., Zool., Bot.* a vessel or duct.

vascular /ˈvæskjələ/ *adj.* relating to, composed of, or provided with vessels or ducts which convey fluids, as blood, lymph, or sap.

vas deferens /væs ˈdefərenz/ *n.* (*pl.* **vasa deferentia** /ˌveisə defəˈrenʃiə/) *Anat.* the duct of the testicle which transports sperm to the penis.

vase /vaz/ *n.* a hollow vessel used as a container for flowers.

vasectomy /vəˈsektəmi/ *n.* (*pl.* **-mies**) the surgical excision of the vas deferens, or of a portion of it as a contraceptive measure.

vasoconstrictor /ˌveizoukənˈstriktə/ *adj.* **1.** serving to constrict blood vessels. *–n.* **2.** a nerve or drug that causes constriction of blood vessels. **–vasoconstriction**, *n.*

vasodilator /ˌveizoudaiˈleitə/ *adj.* **1.** serving to dilate or relax blood vessels. *–n.* **2.** a nerve or drug that causes dilation of blood vessels. **–vasodilation**, *n.*

vassal /ˈvæsəl/ *n.* (in the feudal system) a person holding lands by the obligation to render military service or its equivalent to a superior.

vast /vast/ *adj.* of very great extent or area; very extensive, or immense.

vat /væt/ *n.* a large container for liquids.

vaudeville /ˈvodəvil, ˈvodvil/ *n.* a theatrical piece of light or amusing character, interspersed with songs and dances.

vault¹ /vɒlt, vʊlt/ *n.* **1.** an arched space, chamber, or passage. **2.** a large safe for storing and protecting valuables.

vault² /vɒlt, vʊlt/ *v.i.* to leap or spring, as to or from a position or over something.

vaunt /vɒnt/ *v.t.* **1.** to speak boastfully of. *–n.* **2.** boastful utterance.

V-chip /ˈvi-tʃip/ *n.* a computerised device installed in a television set which responds to a signal accompanying a program identified as being violent, and which can be activated to prevent the showing of the program.

veal /vil/ *n.* the flesh of the calf as used for food.

vector /ˈvektə/ *n.* **1.** *Maths* a quantity which possesses both magnitude and direction. **2.** *Computers* the address of an entry in a memory which is conceptually organised into position-dependent entries of fixed length. **3.** *Biol.* an insect or other organism transmitting germs or other agents of disease.

veejay /ˈvidʒei/ *n.* → **VJ**.

veer /viə/ *v.i.* to turn or shift to another direction; change from one direction or course to another.

vegan /ˈvigən/ *n.* a strict vegetarian who does not eat or use any products of animal origin, including milk, eggs, leather, etc.

vegetable /'vɛdʒtəbəl/ n. **1.** any herbaceous plant whose fruits, seeds, roots, tubers, bulbs, stems, leaves, or flower parts are used as food. **2.** any member of the plant kingdom. **3.** *Colloq.* a person who, due to physical injury or mental deficiency, is entirely dependent on the agencies of others for subsistence.

vegetarian /vɛdʒə'tɛəriən/ n. someone who lives on vegetable food only.

vegetate /'vɛdʒəteɪt/ v.i. to live in an inactive, passive, or unthinking way.

vegetation /vɛdʒə'teɪʃən/ n. plants collectively; the plant life of a particular region considered as a whole.

vehement /'viəmənt/ adj. **1.** eager, impetuous, or impassioned. **2.** (of actions) marked by great energy, exertion, or unusual force.

vehicle /'viːkəl, 'viəkəl/ n. **1.** any receptacle, or means of transport, in which something is carried or conveyed, or travels. **2.** a medium by which ideas or effects are communicated. **–vehicular**, adj.

veil /veɪl/ n. **1.** a piece of material worn over the head and face, as that worn by some Muslim women to conceal the face. **2.** a piece of material worn over the head and sometimes the face as an adornment, or to protect the face. **3.** something that covers, screens, or conceals. –v.t. **4.** to cover or conceal with or as with a veil.

vein /veɪn/ n. **1.** one of the system of branching vessels or tubes conveying blood from various parts of the body to the heart. **2.** one of the strands or bundles of vascular tissue forming the principal framework of a leaf. **3.** any body or stratum of ore, coal, etc., clearly separated or defined. **4.** a strain or quality traceable in character or conduct, writing, etc.

velcro /'vɛlkroʊ/ n. (from trademark) a type of tape used as a fastening, comprising two strips of fabric, one with a dense arrangement of small nylon hooks and the other with a nylon pile, so that when the strips are pressed together one hooks into the other. Also, **Velcro**.

vellum /'vɛləm/ n. a sheet of calfskin prepared as parchment for writing or bookbinding.

velociraptor /və'lɒsəræptə/ n. a dinosaur capable of running at great speed.

velocity /və'lɒsəti/ n. (pl. **-ties**) **1.** rapidity of motion or operation; swiftness; quickness. **2.** *Physics* rate of motion, especially when the direction of motion is also specified.

velodrome /'vɛlədroʊm/ n. an arena with a banked track for cycle races.

velour /və'lʊə/ n. any of various fabrics with a fine, raised finish. Also, **velours**.

velvet /'vɛlvət/ n. **1.** a fabric with a thick, soft pile. **2.** something likened to the fabric velvet in softness, etc.

venal /'viːnəl/ adj. accessible to bribery; corruptly mercenary.

vend /vɛnd/ v.t. to dispose of by sale. **–vendor**, n.

vendetta /vɛn'dɛtə/ n. any prolonged or persistent quarrel, rivalry, etc.

veneer /və'nɪə/ n. **1.** a thin layer of wood or other material used for facing or overlaying wood. **2.** a superficially pleasing appearance or show.

venerable /'vɛnrəbəl, -nərəbəl/ adj. worthy of veneration or reverence, as on account of high character or office.

venerate /'vɛnəreɪt/ v.t. to regard with reverence, or revere. **–veneration**, n.

venereal disease /və'nɪəriəl/ n. any of those diseases which are transmitted by sexual intercourse with an infected person, especially syphilis and gonorrhoea.

venetian blind /vənɪʃən 'blaɪnd/ n. a window blind with overlapping horizontal slats that may be opened or closed.

vengeance /'vɛndʒəns/ n. the avenging of wrong, injury, or the like, or retributive punishment. **–vengeful**, adj.

venial /'viːniəl/ adj. eligible for forgiveness or pardon.

venison /'vɛnəsən/ n. the flesh of a deer or similar animal.

venom /'vɛnəm/ n. the poisonous fluid which some animals, as certain snakes, spiders, etc., secrete, and introduce into the bodies of their victims by biting, stinging, etc. **–venomous**, adj.

vent¹ /vɛnt/ n. an opening or aperture serving as an outlet for air, smoke, fumes, etc.

vent² /vɛnt/ v.t. to give free course or expression to (an emotion, passion, etc.).

ventilate /'vɛntəleɪt/ v.t. **1.** to provide (a room, mine, etc.) with fresh air. **2.** to submit (a question, etc.) to free examination and discussion. **–ventilation**, n.

ventral /'vɛntrəl/ adj. of or relating to the belly; abdominal.

ventricle /'vɛntrɪkəl/ n. *Anat.* **1.** any of various hollow organs or parts in an animal body. **2.** one of the two main cavities of the heart.

ventriloquism /vɛn'trɪləkwɪzəm/ n. the art or practice of speaking in such a manner that the voice appears to come from some other source, as a dummy. Also, **ventriloquy**. **–ventriloquist**, n.

venture /'vɛntʃə/ n. **1.** any undertaking or proceeding involving uncertainty as to the outcome. **2.** a business enterprise or proceeding in which loss is risked in the hope of profit. –v.i. **3.** to make a venture. **4.** (oft. fol. by on or upon or an infinitive) to take a risk; dare or presume.

venturous /'vɛntʃərəs/ adj. **1.** disposed to venture; bold; daring; adventurous. **2.** hazardous; risky.

venue /'vɛnju/ n. the scene of any action or event, as a hall for a concert, meeting, etc.

veracious /və'reɪʃəs/ adj. truthful. **–veracity**, n.

verandah /və'rændə/ n. an open or partly open portion of a house or other building, outside its principal rooms, but roofed usually by the main structure. Also, **veranda**.

verb /vɜb/ n. *Gram.* one of the major form classes, or parts of speech, comprising words which express the occurrence of an action, existence of a state, and the like.

verbal /'vɜbəl/ adj. **1.** of or relating to words. **2.** expressed in spoken words; oral rather than written. **3.** *Gram.* of, relating to, or derived from a verb.

verbalise /'vɜbəlaɪz/ v.t. to express (ideas, emotions, etc.) in words. Also, **verbalize**.

verbatim /vɜ'beɪtəm/ adv. word for word, or in exactly the same words.

verbiage /'vɜːbɪɪdʒ/ *n.* abundance of useless words, as in writing or speech; wordiness.

verbose /vɜː'bəʊs/ *adj.* expressed in, characterised by the use of, or using many or too many words; wordy.

verdant /'vɜːdnt/ *adj.* green with vegetation; covered with growing plants or grass.

verdict /'vɜːdɪkt/ *n.* **1.** *Law* the finding or answer of a jury given to the court concerning a matter submitted to their judgement. **2.** a judgement or decision.

verdure /'vɜːdʒuə/ *n.* greenness, especially of fresh, flourishing vegetation.

verge /vɜːdʒ/ *n.* **1.** the edge, rim, or margin of something. **2.** the limit or point beyond which something begins or occurs. *−v.i.* (**verged, verging**) **3.** to be on the verge or border, or touch at the border. **4.** (usu. fol. by *on* or *upon*) to come close to, approach, or border on some state or condition.

verger /'vɜːdʒə/ *n.* an official who takes care of the interior of a church and acts as attendant.

verify /'verəfaɪ/ *v.t.* (**-fied, -fying**) **1.** to prove (something) to be true, as by evidence or testimony; confirm or substantiate. **2.** to ascertain the truth or correctness, especially by examination or comparison. **–verification,** *n.*

veritable /'verɪtəbəl/ *adj.* being truly such; genuine or real.

verity /'verəti/ *n.* quality of being true, or in accordance with fact or reality.

verjuice /'vɜːdʒuːs/ *n.* an acidic liquid made from the sour juice of unripe grapes, etc., used especially in cooking.

vermiform /'vɜːmɪfɔːm/ *adj.* like a worm in form; long and slender.

vermiform appendix *n.* *Anat.* → **appendix** (def. 2).

vermilion /və'mɪljən/ *n.* brilliant scarlet red.

vermin /'vɜːmən/ *n.* (*pl.* **vermin**) (*construed as pl.*) troublesome, destructive, or disease-carrying animals collectively.

vermouth /'vɜːməθ, və'muːθ/ *n.* a white wine in which herbs, roots, barks, and other flavourings have been steeped.

vernacular /və'nækjələ/ *adj.* **1.** native or originating in the place of its occurrence or use, as language or words (often as opposed to *literary* or *learned* language). *−n.* **2.** the native speech or language of a place.

vernal /'vɜːnəl/ *adj.* of or relating to spring.

versatile /'vɜːsətaɪl/ *adj.* capable of or adapted for turning with ease from one to another of various tasks, subjects, etc.; many-sided in abilities. **–versatility,** *n.*

verse[1] /vɜːs/ *n.* **1.** (*in non-technical use*) a stanza or other subdivision of a metrical composition. **2.** one of the lines of a poem. **3.** a short division of a chapter in the Bible.

verse[2] /vɜːs/ *v.t.* *Sport* (*esp. in children's language*) to play against in a game or competition: *Who are we versing this week?*

versed /vɜːst/ *adj.* (fol. by *in*) experienced; practised; skilled.

version /'vɜːʒən/ *n.* **1.** a particular account of some matter, as from one person or source, as contrasted with some other account or accounts. **2.** a translation.

versus /'vɜːsəs/ *prep.* against (used especially in law to indicate an action brought by one party against another, and in sport to denote a contest between two teams or players). *Abbrev.:* v., vs.

vertebra /'vɜːtəbrə/ *n.* (*pl.* **-brae** /-briː/ *or* **-bras**) *Anat.* any of the bones or segments composing the spinal column.

vertebrate /'vɜːtəbreɪt, -brət/ *n.* **1.** a vertebrate animal. *−adj.* **2.** having vertebrae; having a backbone or spinal column.

vertex /'vɜːteks/ *n.* (*pl.* **-tices** /-təsiz/ *or* **-texes**) the highest point of something; the apex; the top; the summit.

vertical /'vɜːtɪkəl/ *adj.* **1.** being in a position or direction perpendicular to the plane of the horizon; upright. **2.** of or relating to the consolidation of businesses or industries that are closely related in the manufacture or sale of a certain commodity. *−n.* **3.** a vertical line, plane, or the like.

vertigo /'vɜːtɪgəʊ/ *n.* a disordered condition in which an individual, or whatever is around him or her, seems to be whirling about; dizziness.

verve /vɜːv/ *n.* enthusiasm or energy, as in literary or artistic work.

very /'veri/ *adv.* **1.** in a high degree, extremely, or exceedingly. *−adj.* **2.** precise or identical: *the very amount.* **3.** mere: *the very idea.* **4.** actual: *the very gun.*

vesicle /'vesɪkəl/ *n.* a little sac or cyst.

vessel /'vesəl/ *n.* **1.** a craft for travelling on water. **2.** a hollow or concave article, as a cup, bowl, pot, pitcher, vase, bottle, etc., for holding liquid or other contents. **3.** *Anat., Zool.* a tube or duct, as an artery, vein, or the like, containing or conveying blood or some other body fluid.

vest /vest/ *n.* **1.** a short, warm undergarment with sleeves, usually worn next to the skin under a shirt; a singlet **2.** a waistcoat. *−v.t.* **3.** to clothe, dress, or robe. **4.** (usu. fol. by *in*) to place or settle (something, especially property, rights, powers, etc.) in the possession or control of a person or persons. **5.** to invest or endow (a person, etc.) with something, especially with powers, functions, etc.

vestal /'vestl/ *adj.* virginal; chaste.

vestibule /'vestɪbjuːl/ *n.* a passage, hall, or room between the outer door and the interior parts of a house or building.

vestige /'vestɪdʒ/ *n.* a mark, trace, or visible evidence of something which is no longer present or in existence. **–vestigial,** *adj.*

vestment /'vestmənt/ *n.* an official or ceremonial robe.

vestry /'vestri/ *n.* (*pl.* **-tries**) a room in or a building attached to a church.

vet /vet/ *n.* **1.** a veterinary surgeon. *−v.t.* (**vetted, vetting**) **2.** to check the aptitude, character, etc., of (a person). **3.** to examine (a product, proposal, or the like) with a view to acceptance, rejection, or correction.

vetch /vetʃ/ *n.* any of various leguminous plants cultivated for forage and soil improvement.

veteran /'vetərən, 'vetrən/ *n.* **1.** someone who has seen long service in any occupation or office. *−adj.* **2.** experienced through long service or practice; having served for a long period; grown old in service.

veterinary science /'vetənri, 'vetərənri/, *Orig. US* /'vetrəneri/ *n.* that branch of medicine that concerns itself with the study, prevention, and treatment of animal diseases. Also, **veterinary medicine**.

veterinary surgeon n. someone who practises veterinary science or surgery. Also, **veterinarian**.

veto /'viːtəʊ/ n. (pl. **-tos** or **-toes**) **1.** the power or right of preventing action by a prohibition. *-v.t.* (**-toed, -toing**) **2.** to prevent (a proposal, legislative bill, etc.) being put into action by exercising the right of veto. **3.** to refuse to consent to.

vex /vɛks/ v.t. to irritate; annoy; provoke; make angry. **-vexatious**, adj.

VHS /viː eɪtʃ 'ɛs/ adj. (from trademark) relating to a unique format for coding and playing a videotape for a video cassette recorder.

via /'vaɪə/ prep. **1.** by way of; by a route that passes through. **2.** by means of.

viable /'vaɪəbəl/ adj. **1.** capable of living. **2.** practicable; workable.

viaduct /'vaɪədʌkt/ n. a bridge for carrying a road, railway, etc., over a valley, ravine, etc.

vial /'vaɪəl/ n. → **phial**.

vibe /vaɪb/ n. Colloq. a dominant quality or atmosphere: *a relaxed vibe*.

vibes /vaɪbz/ pl. n. Colloq. the quality, mood or atmosphere of a place or person.

vibrant /'vaɪbrənt/ adj. **1.** moving to and fro rapidly; vibrating. **2.** full of vigour; energetic; powerful; forceful.

vibrate /vaɪ'breɪt/ v.i. **1.** to move to and fro, as a pendulum; oscillate. **2.** to move to and fro or up and down quickly and repeatedly; quiver; tremble. **-vibratory**, adj. **-vibration**, n. **-vibrator**, n.

vibrato /və'brɑːtəʊ/ n. (pl. **-tos**) Music a pulsating effect produced in the singing voice or in an instrumental tone by rapid small oscillations in pitch about the given note.

vicar /'vɪkə/ n. a member of the clergy acting as priest of a parish.

vicarious /və'kɛəriəs, vaɪ-/ adj. performed, exercised, received, or suffered in place of another.

vice[1] /vaɪs/ n. **1.** an immoral or evil habit or practice; a grave moral fault. **2.** immoral conduct; indulgence in impure or evil practices.

vice[2] /vaɪs/ n. any of various devices used to hold an object firmly while work is being done upon it.

vice- a prefix denoting a substitute, deputy, or subordinate.

viceroy /'vaɪsrɔɪ/ n. a person appointed to rule a country or province as the deputy of the sovereign.

vice versa /vaɪs 'vɜːsə, vaɪs, vaɪsi/ adv. conversely; the order being changed (from that of a preceding statement).

vicinity /və'sɪnəti/ n. (pl. **-ties**) the region near or about a place.

vicious /'vɪʃəs/ adj. **1.** addicted to or characterised by vice or immorality; depraved; profligate. **2.** spiteful or malignant. **3.** unpleasantly severe.

vicissitude /və'sɪsətjud/ n. **1.** a change or variation, or something different, occurring in the course of something. **2.** (pl.) changes, variations, successive or alternating phases or conditions, etc., in the course of anything.

victim /'vɪktəm/ n. a sufferer from any destructive, injurious, or adverse action or agency.

victimise /'vɪktəmaɪz/ v.t. **1.** to make a victim of. **2.** to discipline or punish selectively, especially as a result of an industrial dispute. Also, **victimize**.

victory /'vɪktəri, -tri/ n. (pl. **-ries**) **1.** the ultimate and decisive superiority in a battle or any contest. **2.** any success or successful performance achieved over an adversary or opponent, opposition, difficulties, etc. **-victor**, n. **-victorious**, adj.

video /'vɪdiəʊ/ adj. **1.** relating to or employed in the transmission or reception of televised material as displayed on television screens or visual display units. **2.** of or relating to a video recording. **-n. 3.** a video recording. **4.** a video cassette. **5.** a video cassette recorder. *-v.t.* (**-eoed, -eoing**) **6.** to make a video recording of.

video camera n. a camera designed for filming on videotape. Also, **video-camera**.

video cassette n. a cassette enclosing a length of videotape for video recording or playing. Also, **videocassette**.

video cassette recorder n. a videotape recorder which allows for playing on or recording from a television set, the videotape being held in a video cassette. Abbrev.: VCR

video clip n. a short video recording, as one showing a performance of a popular song, a spectacular news event, etc. Also, **film clip**.

videophone /'vɪdiəʊfəʊn/ n. a telephone which allows visual, as well as verbal, communication.

video referee n. Sport a referee who adjudicates with the aid of video footage of the game.

videostreaming /'vɪdiəʊstriːmɪŋ/ n. the streaming of video data. See **streaming**.

videotape /'vɪdiəʊteɪp/ n. magnetic tape upon which a video signal is recorded, used for storing a television program or film.

video terminal n. a computer terminal in which information is displayed on a television screen.

vie /vaɪ/ v.i. to strive in competition or rivalry with another; to contend for superiority.

view /vjuː/ n. **1.** a seeing or beholding; an examination by the eye. **2.** range of sight or vision. **3.** a sight or prospect of some landscape, scene, etc. **4.** aim, intention, or purpose. **5.** a conception, notion, or idea of a thing; an opinion or theory. *-v.t.* **6.** to see or behold. **7.** to look at, survey, or inspect. **8.** to contemplate mentally; consider.

viewpoint /'vjuːpɔɪnt/ n. a point of view; an attitude of mind.

vigil /'vɪdʒəl/ n. a keeping awake for any purpose during the normal hours of sleep.

vigilant /'vɪdʒələnt/ adj. keenly attentive to detect danger; wary. **-vigilance**, n.

vigilante /vɪdʒə'lænti/ n. Chiefly US a member of an unauthorised body organised for the maintenance of order.

vigour /'vɪgə/ n. **1.** active strength or force, as of body or mind. **2.** healthy physical or mental energy or power. **3.** active or effective force. Also, **vigor**. **-vigorous**, adj.

vile /vaɪl/ adj. **1.** wretchedly bad. **2.** repulsive or disgusting, as to the senses or feelings;

despicably or revoltingly bad. **3.** of mean or low condition, as a person.

vilify /'vɪləfaɪ/ *v.t.* (**-fied**, **-fying**) to speak evil of; defame; traduce. **–vilification**, *n.*

villa /'vɪlə/ *n.* **1.** a country residence, usually of some size and pretensions, especially in a Mediterranean country. **2.** a small house, often one of a set of connected dwellings.

village /'vɪlɪdʒ/ *n.* a small assemblage of houses in a country district.

villain /'vɪlən/ *n.* a wicked person; scoundrel. **–villainous**, *adj.* **–villainy**, *n.*

vim /vɪm/ *n.* force; energy; vigour in action.

vinaigrette /vɪnə'grɛt/ *n.* a cold sauce of oil, vinegar, seasonings, and herbs.

vindicate /'vɪndəkeɪt/ *v.t.* **1.** to clear, as from a charge, imputation, suspicion, or the like. **2.** to uphold or justify by argument or evidence. **–vindicatory**, *adj.* **–vindication**, *n.*

vindictive /vɪn'dɪktɪv/ *adj.* disposed or inclined to revenge; revengeful.

vine /vaɪn/ *n.* **1.** a long, slender stem that trails or creeps on the ground or climbs by winding itself about a support or holding fast with tendrils or claspers. **2.** a plant bearing such stems.

vinegar /'vɪnɪgə, -nə-/ *n.* a sour, acidic liquid used as a condiment, preservative, etc.

vineyard /'vɪnjəd, 'vɪnjad/ *n.* a plantation of grapevines, for producing grapes for wine-making, etc.

vintage /'vɪntɪdʒ/ *n.* **1.** the wine from a particular harvest or crop. **2.** an exceptionally fine wine from the crop of a good year, designated and sold as the produce of that year. **3.** the season of gathering grapes, or of winemaking. *–adj.* **4.** of or relating to wine or winemaking. **5.** (of wines) designated and sold as the produce of a specified year. **6.** of high quality; exceptionally fine. **7.** old-fashioned; out of date.

vintner /'vɪntnə/ *n.* a dealer in wine; a wine merchant.

vinyl /'vaɪnəl/ *n. Chem.* a type of plastic made from a particular chemical group, used formerly in the making of gramophone records.

viol /'vaɪəl/ *n.* a musical instrument similar to the violin.

viola /vi'oʊlə/ *n.* a four-stringed musical instrument slightly larger than the violin.

violate /'vaɪəleɪt/ *v.t.* **1.** to break, infringe, or transgress (a law, rule, agreement, promise, instructions, etc.). **2.** to deal with or treat in a violent or irreverent way; desecrate or profane. **–violation**, *n.*

violent /'vaɪələnt/ *adj.* **1.** acting with or characterised by uncontrolled, strong, rough force. **2.** intense in force, effect, etc.; severe; extreme. **–violently**, *adv.* **–violence**, *n.*

violet /'vaɪələt/ *n.* **1.** a small plant with purple, blue, yellow, white, or variegated flowers. **2.** a bluish-purple colour.

violin /vaɪə'lɪn/ *n.* a bowed instrument held nearly horizontal by the player's arm, with the lower part supported against the collarbone or shoulder; a fiddle.

violoncello /vaɪələn'tʃɛloʊ/ *n.* (*pl.* **-los** *or* **-li** /-li/) → **cello**.

viper /'vaɪpə/ *n.* a venomous snake.

virago /və'ragoʊ/ *n.* (*pl.* **-goes** *or* **-gos**) a turbulent, violent, or ill-tempered, scolding woman; a shrew.

viral /'vaɪrəl/ *adj.* **1.** relating to or caused by a virus. **2.** increasing rapidly in numbers or effect in a way that is reminiscent of a virus. *–phr.* **3. go viral**, to be disseminated rapidly and widely as one person alerts another in an ever-widening circle, especially using the internet.

virgin /'vɜdʒən/ *n.* **1.** a person, especially a young woman, who has had no sexual intercourse. *–adj.* **2.** being a virgin. **3.** pure; unsullied; undefiled. **4.** untouched, untried, or unused. **–virginity**, *n.*

virginal[1] /'vɜdʒənəl/ *adj.* of, relating to, characteristic of, or befitting a virgin.

virginal[2] /'vɜdʒənəl/ *n.* a small harpsichord of rectangular shape.

virile /'vɪraɪl/ *adj.* **1.** of, relating to, or characteristic of a man, as opposed to a woman or a child; masculine or manly; natural to or befitting a man. **2.** having or exhibiting in a marked degree masculine strength, vigour, or forcefulness. **–virility**, *n.*

virology /vaɪ'rɒlədʒi/ *n.* the study of viruses and the diseases caused by them. **–virologist**, *n.*

virtual /'vɜtʃuəl/ *adj.* **1.** being such in power, force, or effect, although not actually or expressly such. **2.** *Computers* existing only as a computer representation, as opposed to physically: *a virtual bookshop.* **–virtually**, *adv.*

virtualise /'vɜtʃuəlaɪz/ *v.t.* to create in virtual reality rather than in the material world: *to virtualise a museum.* Also, **virtualize**.

virtual reality *n.* **1.** an artificial environment represented by a computer and intended to appear and feel real to the user, who, with the use of gloves, earphones and goggles connected to the computer, is able to interact with this environment as if it were physically real. **2.** any artificial environment represented by a computer.

virtual site *n.* a website which presents a virtual reality.

virtue /'vɜtʃu/ *n.* **1.** moral excellence or goodness. **2.** a particular moral excellence, as justice, prudence, etc. **3.** an excellence, merit, or good quality. *–phr.* **4. by** (or **in**) **virtue of**, by reason of.

virtuoso /vɜtʃu'oʊsoʊ, -'oʊzoʊ/ *n.* (*pl.* **-sos** *or* **-si** /-si, -zi/) someone who has special knowledge or skill in any field, as in music. **–virtuosity**, *n.*

virtuous /'vɜtʃuəs/ *adj.* morally excellent or good; conforming or conformed to moral laws.

virulent /'vɪrələnt/ *adj.* **1.** actively poisonous, malignant, or deadly. **2.** *Med.* highly infective; malignant or deadly.

virus /'vaɪrəs/ *n.* **1.** an infective agent smaller than a microscopic organism, inert outside a cell but able to reproduce within the host cell. **2.** any disease caused by a virus. **3.** a rogue program introduced into a computer network.

visa /'vizə/ *n.* an authority to enter a foreign country, usually for a temporary period, issued by the government of that country and usually stamped in a passport.

visage /'vɪzɪdʒ/ *n.* the face.

viscera /'vɪsərə/ *pl. n.* (*sing.* **viscus**) the soft interior organs in the cavities of the body, especially such of these as are confined to the abdomen.

viscid /'vɪsɪd/ *adj.* sticky, adhesive, or glutinous; of a glutinous consistency; viscous.

viscount /'vaɪkaʊnt/ *n.* a nobleman next below an earl or count and next above a baron. **–viscountess**, *fem. n.*

viscous /'vɪskəs/ *adj.* sticky, adhesive, or glutinous; of a glutinous character or consistency; thick. **–viscosity**, *n.*

visibility /vɪzə'bɪləti/ *n.* **1.** the state or fact of being visible; capability of being seen. **2.** *Meteorol.* visual range.

visible /'vɪzəbəl/ *adj.* capable of being seen; perceptible by the eye.

vision /'vɪʒən/ *n.* **1.** the act of seeing with the eye; the power, faculty, or sense of sight. **2.** the act or power of perceiving what is not actually present to the eye, whether by some supernatural endowment or by natural intellectual acuteness. **3.** a mental view or image, whether of supernatural origin or merely imaginative, of what is not actually present in place or time. **4.** something seen; an object of sight. **–v.t. 5.** to show, or to see, in or as in a vision.

visionary /'vɪʒənri/ *adj.* **1.** given to or characterised by radical, often unpractical ideas, views, or schemes. **2.** given to or concerned with seeing visions. **–n.** (*pl.* **-ries**) **3.** someone who sees visions. **4.** someone who is given to novel ideas or schemes which are not immediately practicable; an unpractical theorist or enthusiast.

vision-impaired /'vɪʒən-ɪmpɛəd/ *adj.* **1.** *Med.* deficient in sight, ranging from complete blindness to partial vision. **2.** of or relating to a person with partial vision (opposed to *blind*). **–visually-impaired**, *adj.*

visit /'vɪzət/ *v.t.* **1.** to go to see (a person, place, etc.) in the way of friendship, ceremony, duty, business, curiosity, or the like. **2.** (in general) to come or go to. **3.** to come upon or assail. **4.** *Internet* to access (a web site). **–n. 5.** an act of visiting. **–visitor**, *n.*

visitation /vɪzə'teɪʃən/ *n.* **1.** the act of visiting; a visit. **2.** a visiting or a visit for the purpose of making an official inspection or examination. **3.** an affliction or punishment from God.

visor /'vaɪzə/ *n.* **1.** the movable front parts of a helmet, covering the face, especially the uppermost part which protects the eyes. **2.** a small shield attached to the inside roof of a car, which may be swung down to protect the driver's eyes from glare or sunlight.

vista /'vɪstə/ *n.* a view or prospect.

visual /'vɪʒuəl/ *adj.* **1.** of or relating to sight. **2.** perceptible by the sight; visible.

visual display unit *n.* a computer terminal which displays information on a screen. Also, **visual display terminal, VDU.**

visualise /'vɪzjuəlaɪz/ *v.t.* to form a mental image of. Also, **visualize.**

vital /'vaɪtl/ *adj.* **1.** of or relating to life. **2.** having remarkable energy, enthusiasm, vivacity. **3.** necessary to life. **4.** necessary to the existence, continuance, or wellbeing of something; indispensable; essential. **5.** of critical importance.

vitality /vaɪ'tæləti/ *n.* exuberant physical vigour; energy; enthusiastic vivacity.

vitamin /'vaɪtəmən, 'vɪt-/ *n.* any of a group of food factors essential in small quantities to maintain life, but not themselves employing energy. The absence of any one of them results in a characteristic deficiency disease.

vitiate /'vɪʃieɪt/ *v.t.* **1.** to impair the quality of; make faulty; mar. **2.** to contaminate; corrupt; spoil. **3.** to make legally defective or invalid; invalidate.

viticulture /'vɪtikʌltʃə/ *n.* the culture or cultivation of the grapevine; grape-growing. **–viticulturist**, *n.*

vitreous /'vɪtriəs/ *adj.* of the nature of glass; resembling glass, as in transparency, brittleness, hardness, etc.; glassy.

vitri- a word element meaning 'glass'.

vitrify /'vɪtrəfaɪ/ *v.t.* (**-fied, -fying**) **1.** to convert or be converted into glass. **2.** to make or become vitreous.

vitriol /'vɪtriɒl/ *n.* **1.** sulphuric acid. **2.** something highly caustic, or severe in its effects, as criticism. **–vitriolic**, *adj.*

vituperate /və'tjupəreɪt, vaɪ-/ *v.t.* **1.** to find fault with abusively. **2.** to address abusive language to.

vivacious /və'veɪʃəs/ *adj.* lively, animated, or sprightly. **–vivacity**, *n.*

vivid /'vɪvəd/ *adj.* **1.** strikingly bright, as colour, light, objects, etc. **2.** lively or intense, as feelings, etc. **3.** clearly perceptible to the eye or mind.

vivify /'vɪvəfaɪ/ *v.t.* (**-fied, -fying**) to enliven; render lively or animated; brighten.

viviparous /və'vɪpərəs/ *adj. Zool.* bringing forth living young (rather than eggs), as most mammals and some reptiles and fishes.

vivisect /'vɪvəsɛkt, vɪvə'sɛkt/ *v.t.* to dissect the living body of. **–vivisection**, *n.*

vixen /'vɪksən/ *n.* a female fox.

viyella /vaɪ'ɛlə/ *n.* (*also upper case*) (*from trademark*) a soft fabric made of cotton and wool.

VJ /'vi dʒeɪ/ *n.* a presenter of music videos on television.

vlog /vlɒg/ *n.* a blog with video streaming. **–vlogging**, *n.* **–vlogger**, *n.*

vocabulary /voʊ'kæbjələri, və-/, *Orig. US* /-lɛri/ *n.* (*pl.* **-ries**) **1.** the stock of words used by a people, or by a particular class or person. **2.** a list or collection of the words of a language, book, author, branch of science, or the like, usually in alphabetical order and defined; a wordbook, glossary, dictionary, or lexicon.

vocal /'voʊkəl/ *adj.* **1.** of or relating to the voice; uttered with the voice; oral. **2.** rendered by or intended for singing, as music.

vocal cords *pl. n. Anat.* folds of mucous membrane projecting into the cavity of the larynx, the edges of which can be drawn tense and made to vibrate by the passage of air from the lungs, thus producing vocal sound.

vocalic /voʊ'kælɪk/ *adj.* of or relating to a vowel or vowels; vowel-like.

vocalise /'voʊkəlaɪz/ *v.t.* to make vocal; form into voice; utter or articulate; sing. Also, **vocalize.**

vocalist /'voʊkələst/ *n.* a singer.

vocation /voo'keɪʃən/ n. a particular occupation, business, or profession; a trade or calling. –**vocational**, adj.

vocative /'vɒkətɪv/ adj. Gram. relating to, or used in, addressing or calling (someone).

vociferous /və'sɪfərəs/ adj. crying out noisily; clamorous.

vodcasting /'vɒdkastɪŋ/ n. the online delivery of video on demand.

vodka /'vɒdkə/ n. an alcoholic drink of Russian origin.

vogue /voʊg/ n. the fashion, as at a particular time.

voice /vɔɪs/ n. **1.** the sound or sounds uttered through the mouth of living creatures, especially of human beings in speaking, shouting, singing, etc. **2.** such sounds considered with reference to their character or quality. **3.** expressed opinion or choice. **4.** the right to express an opinion or choice; vote; suffrage. **5.** Phonetics the sound produced by vibration of the vocal cords. **6.** Gram. **a.** (in some languages, as Latin) a group of categories of verb inflection denoting the relationship between the action expressed by the verb and the subject of the sentence (e.g., as acting or as acted upon). **b.** any one of such categories or constructions in a particular language, as the active and passive voices in Latin. –v.t. (**voiced**, **voicing**) **7.** to give voice, utterance, or expression to (an emotion, opinion, etc.); express; declare; proclaim.

voicemail /'vɔɪsmeɪl/ n. **1.** a system for recording messages over the telephone to be played back later. **2.** a message received on such a system.

voice messaging n. a system which records a spoken message for replay later, now often integrated in computer transfer of spoken information as well as data.

void /vɔɪd/ adj. **1.** Law without legal force or effect; not legally binding or enforceable. **2.** useless; ineffectual; vain. **3.** (fol. by of) completely empty; devoid; destitute. –n. **4.** an empty space. **5.** a place without the usual or desired occupant. **6.** emptiness; vacancy. –v.t. **7.** to make void or of no effect; invalidate; nullify. **8.** to empty or discharge the contents of; evacuate.

voile /vɔɪl/ n. a semitransparent dress fabric.

volatile /'vɒlətaɪl/ adj. **1.** evaporating rapidly; passing off readily in the form of vapour. **2.** light and changeable of mind; frivolous; flighty. **3.** relating to information in the memory bank of a computer which is lost when power is disconnected.

volcano /vɒl'keɪnoʊ/ an opening in the earth's crust through which molten rock (lava), steam, ashes, etc., are expelled from within, either continuously or at irregular intervals. –**volcanic**, adj.

volcanology /vɒlkə'nɒlədʒi/ n. the scientific study of volcanoes and volcanic phenomena. Also, **vulcanology**. –**volcanological**, adj. –**volcanologist**, n.

vole /voʊl/ n. a type of rodent.

volition /və'lɪʃən/ n. the act of willing; exercise of choice to determine action.

volley /'vɒli/ n. (pl. -**leys**) **1.** the discharge of a number of missiles or firearms simultaneously.

2. a burst or outpouring of many things at once or in quick succession. **3.** Tennis, etc. **a.** a return of the ball before it touches the ground. **b.** a succession of such returns. –v. (-**leyed**, -**leying**) –v.t. **4.** to discharge in or as in a volley. **5.** Tennis, Soccer, etc. to return, kick, etc., (the ball) before it strikes the ground. –v.i. **6.** to fly or be discharged together, as missiles. **7.** to move or proceed with great rapidity, as in a volley.

volleyball /'vɒlibɔl/ n. a game in which a large ball is struck from side to side over a high net with the hands or arms.

volt /voʊlt/ n. the derived SI unit of electric potential. Symbol: V –**voltage**, n.

voluble /'vɒljəbəl/ adj. characterised by a ready and continuous flow of words.

volume /'vɒljum/ n. **1.** a collection of written or printed sheets bound together and constituting a book. **2.** the size, measure, or amount of anything in three dimensions; the space occupied by a body or substance in cubic units; the SI unit of volume is the cubic metre (m^3). **3.** a mass or quantity, especially a large quantity, of anything. **4.** loudness or softness.

volumetric /vɒljə'mɛtrɪk/ adj. denoting, relating to, or depending upon measurement by volume. Also, **volumetrical**.

voluminous /və'lumənəs, -'lju-/ adj. of ample size, extent, or fullness, as garments, draperies, etc.

voluntary /'vɒlntri, -lantari/, Orig. US /-tɛri/ adj. **1.** done, made, brought about, undertaken, etc., of one's own accord or by free choice. **2.** Physiol. subject to or controlled by the will.

volunteer /vɒlən'tɪə/ n. **1.** someone who enters into any service of their own free will, or who offers himself or herself for any service or undertaking for no financial gain. –v.i. **2.** to offer oneself for some service or undertaking.

voluptuary /və'lʌptʃuəri/ n. (pl. -**aries**) one given up to luxurious or sensuous pleasures.

voluptuous /və'lʌptʃuəs/ adj. **1.** full of, characterised by, or ministering to pleasure or luxurious or sensual enjoyment. **2.** directed towards luxurious or sensual enjoyment. **3.** sensually pleasing or delightful. **4.** (of the female figure) full and shapely.

volute /və'ljut/ n. a spiral or twisted formation or object.

vomit /'vɒmət/ v.i. **1.** to eject the contents of the stomach by the mouth; spew; be sick. **2.** to be ejected or come out with force or violence. –v.t. **3.** to throw up or eject from the stomach through the mouth; spew. **4.** to cast out or eject as if in vomiting; to send out with force or copiously.

voodoo /'vudu/ n. a religion involving magic, sorcery and witchcraft, especially practised in certain parts of the Caribbean.

voracious /və'reɪʃəs/ adj. devouring or craving food in large quantities.

-vorous a word element meaning 'eating'.

vortex /'vɔtɛks/ n. (pl. -**texes** or -**tices** /-təsiz/) a whirling movement or mass of water, as a whirlpool.

votary /'voʊtari/ n. (pl. -**ries**) someone who is bound by a vow, especially one bound by vows to a religious life.

vote /vout/ *n.* **1.** a formal expression of will, wish, or choice in some matter, signified by voice, by ballot, etc. **2.** the right to such expression; suffrage. **3.** an expression of feeling, as approval, or the like. *–v.* (**voted, voting**) *–v.i.* **4.** to express or signify choice in a matter undergoing decision, as by a voice, ballot, or otherwise. *–v.t.* **5.** to enact, establish, or determine by vote; bring or put (*in, out, down,* etc.) by vote; grant by vote.

votive /'voutɪv/ *adj.* offered, given, dedicated, etc., in accordance with a vow.

vouch /vautʃ/ *v.i.* **1.** to answer (*for*) as being true, certain, reliable, justly asserted, etc. **2.** (fol. by *for*) to give one's own assurance, as surety or sponsor.

voucher /'vautʃə/ *n.* **1.** a document, receipt, stamp, or the like, which proves the truth of a claimed expenditure. **2.** a ticket used as a substitute for cash, as a gift voucher, luncheon voucher, etc.

vouchsafe /vautʃ'seɪf/ *v.t.* to grant or give, by favour, graciousness, or condescension.

vow /vau/ *n.* **1.** a solemn promise, pledge, or personal engagement. **2.** a solemn, religiously binding promise made to God or to any deity or saint, as to perform some act, make some offering or gift, or enter some service or condition. *–v.t.* **3.** to make a vow of; promise by a vow, as to God or a saint. **4.** to pledge oneself to do, make, give, observe, etc.; make a solemn threat or resolution of.

vowel /'vauəl/ *n. Phonetics* a voiced speech sound during the articulation of which air from the lungs is free to pass out through the middle of the mouth without causing undue friction.

voyage /'vɔɪdʒ/ *n.* **1.** a passage, or course of travel, by sea or water, especially to a distant place. *–v.i.* (**-aged, -aging**) **2.** to make or take a voyage; travel by sea or water.

voyeur /vɔɪ'ɜ, vwa'jɜ/ *n.* someone who attains sexual gratification by looking at sexual objects or situations. **–voyeurism,** *n.* **–voyeuristic,** *adj.*

vulcanology /vʌlkə'nɒlədʒi/ *n.* → **volcanology. –vulcanological,** *adj.* **–vulcanologist,** *n.*

vulgar /'vʌlgə/ *adj.* **1.** marked by ignorance of or want of good manners or taste, as actions, language, dress, display, etc. **2.** crude; coarse; unrefined. **3.** ostentatious; unsubtle. **4.** belonging to or constituting the common people of society. **5.** common or ordinary. **–vulgarity,** *n.*

vulnerable /'vʌlnrəbəl, -nərəbəl/ *adj.* **1.** susceptible to being wounded; liable to physical hurt. **2.** not protected against emotional hurt; highly sensitive. **–vulnerability,** *n.*

vulpine /'vʌlpaɪn/ *adj.* relating to, like, or characteristic of a fox.

vulture /'vʌltʃə/ *n.* any of various large, carrion-eating birds, those from Africa and Eurasia related to eagles, kites, hawks, falcons, etc., and those from America related to storks.

vulva /'vʌlvə, 'vulvə/ *n.* (*pl.* **-vae** /-vi/ *or* **-vas**) the external female genitalia.

vuvuzela /vuvə'zeɪlə/ *n.* a plastic horn (def. 3), up to one metre in length, which emits a loud buzzing sound.

vying /'vaɪɪŋ/ *adj.* that vies; competing.

W, w

W, w /'dʌbəlju/ *n.* the 23rd letter of the English alphabet.

wad /wɒd/ *n.* **1.** a small mass or lump of anything soft. **2.** a roll or bundle, especially of banknotes.

wadding /'wɒdɪŋ/ *n.* any fibrous or soft material for stuffing, padding, packing, etc.

waddle /'wɒdl/ *v.i.* to walk with short steps and swaying or rocking from side to side, as a duck.

waddy /'wɒdi/ *n.* (*pl.* **-dies**) an Aboriginal heavy wooden war club.

wade /weɪd/ *v.i.* to walk through any substance, as water, snow, sand, etc., that impedes free motion.

wafer /'weɪfə/ *n.* **1.** a thin, crisp cake or biscuit. **2.** any of various other thin, flat cakes, sheets, or the like.

waffle¹ /'wɒfəl/ *n.* a kind of batter cake.

waffle² /'wɒfəl/ *Colloq.* **1.** to speak or write vaguely, pointlessly, and at considerable length. *−n.* **2.** nonsense.

waft /wɒft/ *v.t.* **1.** to bear or carry through the air or over water. **2.** to bear or convey lightly as if in flight. *−v.i.* **3.** to float or be carried, especially through the air.

wag¹ /wæg/ *v.* (**wagged, wagging**) *−v.t.* **1.** to move from side to side, forwards and backwards, or up and down, especially rapidly and repeatedly. **2.** *Colloq.* to be absent from (school, etc.) without permission. *−v.i.* **3.** to be moved from side to side or one way and the other, especially rapidly and repeatedly, as the head or the tail. *−n.* **4.** the act of wagging.

wag² /wæg/ *n.* a humorous person; joker.

wage /weɪdʒ/ *n.* **1.** (*oft. pl.*) that which is paid for work or services, as by the day or week; hire; pay. **2.** *Econ.* (*pl.*) the share of the products of industry received by labour as distinct from the share going to capital. *−v.t.* (**waged, waging**) **3.** to carry on (a battle, war, conflict, etc.).

wager /'weɪdʒə/ *n.* **1.** something staked or hazarded on an uncertain event; a bet. *−v.t.* **2.** to hazard (something) on the issue of a contest or any uncertain event or matter; stake; bet.

waggle /'wægəl/ *v.t., v.i.* **1.** to wag with short, quick movements. *−n.* **2.** a waggling motion.

wagon /'wægən/ *n.* any of various kinds of four-wheeled vehicles, especially one designed for the transport of heavy loads, delivery, etc.

wagtail /'wægteɪl/ *n.* a small bird with a long, narrow tail which is habitually wagged up and down.

waif /weɪf/ *n.* a person without home or friends, especially a child.

wail /weɪl/ *v.i.* **1.** to utter a prolonged, inarticulate, mournful cry. *−n.* **2.** the act of wailing. **3.** a wailing cry, as of grief, pain, etc.

wainscot /'weɪnskət, -koʊt/ *n.* wooden panels serving to line the walls of a room, etc. *−***wainscoting**, *n.*

waist /weɪst/ *n.* the part of the human body between the ribs and the hips.

waistcoat /'weɪstkoʊt/ *n.* a close-fitting, sleeveless garment which reaches to the waist.

wait /weɪt/ *v.i.* **1.** (*oft. fol. by for, till,* or *until*) to stay or rest in expectation; remain in a state of quiescence or inaction, as until something expected happens. *−v.t.* **2.** to continue stationary or inactive in expectation of; await. *−n.* **3.** the act of waiting or awaiting; delay; halt. **4.** a period or interval of waiting. *−phr.* **5. wait on** (or **upon**), **a.** to perform the duties of an attendant or servant for. **b.** to supply the wants of (a person) at table.

waiter /'weɪtə/ *n.* a person, especially a man, who waits on tables, as in a restaurant, hotel, etc.

waitress /'weɪtrəs/ *n.* a woman who waits on tables, as in a restaurant, hotel, etc. *−***waitressing**, *n.*

waive /weɪv/ *v.t.* to forbear to insist on; relinquish; forgo.

waiver /'weɪvə/ *n.* an intentional relinquishment of some right, interest, or the like.

wake¹ /weɪk/ *v.* (**woke, woken, waking**) *−v.i.* **1.** (*oft. fol. by up*) to become roused from sleep; awake. *−v.t.* **2.** (*oft. fol. by up*) to rouse from sleep; awake. *−n.* **3.** a watching, or a watch kept, especially for some solemn or ceremonial purpose. **4.** a watch, especially at night, near the body of a dead person before burial, often accompanied by drinking and feasting.

wake² /weɪk/ *n.* the track left by a ship or other object moving in the water.

walk /wɔk/ *v.i.* **1.** to go or travel on foot at a moderate pace; to proceed by steps, or by advancing the feet in turn. *−v.t.* **2.** to proceed through, over, or upon by walking. **3.** to cause to walk; lead, drive, or ride at a walk, as an animal. *−n.* **4.** the act or course of walking, or going on foot. **5.** a spell of walking for exercise or pleasure. **6.** the gait or pace of a person or animal that walks. **7.** a department or branch of activity, or a particular line of work.

walkabout /'wɔkəbaʊt/ *n.* a period of wandering as a nomad, especially as undertaken by Aboriginal people.

walkie-talkie /wɔki-'tɔki/ *n.* a combined radio transmitter and receiver, light enough to be carried by one person, widely used by police, medical services, etc.

walking bus *n.* a group of schoolchildren who walk to each other's houses and then to school under the supervision of a parent at the front and tail of the group.

walkman /'wɔkmən/ *n.* (*from trademark*) a small portable transistor radio, cassette player, etc., with earphones. Also, **Walkman**.

walkout /'wɔkaʊt/ *n.* **1.** Also, **walk-off**. a strike by workers, especially one called suddenly. **2.** the act of leaving or boycotting a conference, meeting, etc., especially as an act of protest.

walkover /'wɔkoʊvə/ *n.* *Colloq.* an unopposed or easy victory.

wall /wɔl/ *n.* **1.** an upright structure of stone, brick, or similar material, serving for enclosure, division, support, protection, etc. **2.** anything which resembles or suggests a wall. *−v.t.* **3.** (*oft. fol. by in* or *off*) to enclose, shut off, divide, protect, etc., with or as with a wall.

wallaby /'wɒləbi/ n. (pl. **-bies** or, especially collectively, **-by**) any of several types of plant-eating marsupial found throughout Australia.

wallaroo /wɒlə'ru/ n. a stocky, coarse-haired kangaroo; euro.

wallet /'wɒlət/ n. a small, book-like folding case for carrying papers, paper money, etc., in the pocket.

wall-eyed /'wɒl-aɪd/ adj. having an eye or the eyes with little or no colour.

wallop /'wɒləp/ v.t. Colloq. to beat soundly; thrash.

wallow /'wɒloʊ/ v.i. to roll the body about, or lie, in water, snow, mud, dust, or the like, as for refreshment.

wallpaper /'wɒlpeɪpə/ n. 1. paper, commonly with printed decorative patterns in colour, for pasting on and covering the walls or ceilings of rooms, etc. 2. Computers a picture or design forming the background image on a computer screen.

walnut /'wɒlnʌt/ n. 1. an edible nut from a tree of temperate North America, south east Europe, and Asia. 2. the tree bearing this nut and also yielding valuable timber.

walrus /'wɒlrəs, 'wɒlrəs/ n. (pl. **-ruses** or, especially collectively, **-rus**) either of two large marine mammals of arctic seas, related to the seals, and having flippers, a pair of large tusks, and a thick, tough skin.

waltz /wɒls, wɒls/ n. 1. a dance in which couples move in a series of circles. –v.i. 2. to dance a waltz.

wan /wɒn/ adj. (**wanner, wannest**) of an unnatural or sickly pallor; pallid.

wand /wɒnd/ n. a slender stick or rod, especially one used by a conjurer, or supposedly by a magician or fairy to work magic.

wander /'wɒndə/ v.i. 1. to ramble without any certain course or object in view; roam. 2. to stray from a path, companions, etc.

wane /weɪn/ v.i. (**waned, waning**) 1. (of the moon) to decrease periodically in the extent of its illuminated portion after the full moon (opposed to wax). 2. to decline in power, importance, prosperity, etc. –n. 3. gradual decline in strength, intensity, power, etc.

wangle /'wæŋgəl/ v.t. Colloq. to bring about, accomplish, or obtain by contrivance, scheming, or often, indirect or insidious methods.

wank /wæŋk/ Colloq. (taboo) –v.i. 1. to masturbate. –n. 2. an act or instance of masturbation. 3. self-indulgent or egotistical behaviour. –**wanker**, n.

wannabe /'wɒnəbi/ n. Colloq. someone who aspires to be something or someone specified, but who is unlikely to be successful: a wannabe poet; a Madonna wannabe.

want /wɒnt/ v.t. 1. to feel a need or a desire for; wish for. 2. to be without or be deficient in. –v.i. 3. (oft. fol. by to) to wish; like; feel inclined to. 4. (sometimes fol. by for) to be deficient by the absence of some part or thing, or fall short. 5. to be in a state of destitution or poverty. 6. to be lacking or absent, as a part or thing necessary to completeness. –n. 7. something wanted or needed; a necessity.

wanton /'wɒntən/ adj. 1. done or behaving in an uncontrolled, selfish way. 2. uncontrolled with respect to sexual behaviour; lascivious; lewd.

WAP /wæp/ n. wireless application protocol; a standard set of protocols to enable wireless devices, such as mobile phones, to connect to the internet.

war /wɔ/ n. 1. a conflict carried on by force of arms, as between nations or states, or between parties within a state. 2. active hostility or contention; conflict; contest. –v.i. (**warred, warring**) 3. to make or carry on war; fight.

waratah /wɒrə'ta, 'wɒrətə/ n. a shrub or small tree with a dense globular head of red flowers.

warble /'wɔbəl/ v.i. to sing with trills, quavers, or melodic embellishments.

ward /wɔd/ n. 1. a division or district of a municipality, city or town, as for administrative or representative purposes. 2. a division of a hospital or the like, as for a particular class of patients. 3. each of the separate divisions of a prison. 4. Law a person, especially a minor, who has been legally placed under the care or control of a legal guardian. –v.t. 5. (usu. fol. by off) to avert, repel, or turn aside, as danger, an attack, assailant, etc.

-ward an adjectival and adverbial suffix indicating direction, as in onward, seaward, backward.

warden /'wɔdn/ n. 1. one charged with the care or custody of something; a keeper. 2. the head of certain colleges, schools, hospitals, youth hostels, etc.

warder[1] /'wɔdə/ n. → **prison officer**.

warder[2] /'wɔdə/ n. a truncheon or staff of office or authority, used in giving signals.

wardrobe /'wɔdroʊb/ n. 1. a stock of clothes or costumes, as of a person or of a theatrical company. 2. a piece of furniture for holding clothes, now usually a tall, upright, cupboard fitted with hooks, shelves, etc.

-wards an adverbial suffix indicating direction, as in onwards, seawards, backwards.

ware /wɛə/ n. (usu. pl.) articles of merchandise or manufacture, or goods.

warehouse /'wɛəhaʊs/ n. a storehouse for wares or goods.

warfare /'wɔfɛə/ n. 1. the act of waging war. 2. armed conflict.

warlock /'wɔlɒk/ n. someone who practises magic arts by the aid of the devil; a sorcerer or wizard.

warm /wɔm/ adj. 1. having or communicating a moderate degree of heat, as perceptible to the senses. 2. keeping or maintaining warmth. 3. (of colour, effects of colour, etc.) suggestive of warmth; inclining towards red or orange, as yellow (rather than towards green or blue). 4. characterised by or showing lively feelings, passions, emotions, sympathies, etc. 5. strongly attached, or intimate. –v.t. 6. (oft. fol. by up) to make warm; heat. 7. to excite ardour, enthusiasm, or animation in. 8. to inspire with kindly feeling; affect with lively pleasure. –v.i. 9. (oft. fol. by up) to become warm. –phr. 10. **warm up**, to prepare for a sporting event, musical or theatrical performance, etc. –**warmth**, n.

warm-blooded /'wɔm-blʌdəd/ adj. designating or relating to animals whose body temperature stays more or less the same regardless of the temperature of the surrounding medium.

warn /wɔn/ v.t. **1.** to give notice or intimation to (a person, etc.) of danger, impending evil, possible harm, or anything unfavourable. **2.** to admonish or exhort as to action or conduct. **3.** to give notice to (a person, etc.) to go, stay, or keep (away, off, etc.). **4.** to give authoritative or formal notice to, order, or summon. **-warning**, n.

warp /wɔp/ v.t. **1.** to bend or twist out of shape, especially from a straight or flat form. **2.** to distort from the truth, fact, true meaning, etc.; bias or pervert. -v.i. **3.** to become bent or twisted out of shape. **4.** to turn or change from the natural or proper course, state, etc. -n. **5.** a bend or twist in something, as in wood that has dried unevenly. **6.** a mental twist or bias. **7.** yarns placed lengthwise in the loom, across the weft or woof, and interlaced.

warrant /ˈwɔrənt/ n. **1.** authorisation, sanction, or justification. **2.** that which serves to give reliable or formal assurance of something; a guarantee. **3.** a writing or document certifying or authorising something, as a certificate, receipt, licence, or commission. -v.t. **4.** to give authority to; authorise. **5.** to afford warrant or sanction for, or justify. **6.** to give a formal assurance, or a guarantee or promise, to or for; guarantee.

warranty /ˈwɔrənti/ n. (pl. **-ties**) **1.** the act of warranting; warrant; assurance. **2.** Law an engagement, express or implied, in assurance of some particular in connection with a contract, as of sale.

warren /ˈwɔrən/ n. a place where rabbits breed or abound.

warrigal /ˈwɔrəgəl/ n. **1.** a dingo. **2.** a wild horse. **3.** an Aboriginal person living in the traditional manner. -adj. **4.** wild; untamed. Also, **warragul, warregal**.

warrior /ˈwɔriə/ n. someone engaged or experienced in warfare; soldier.

wart /wɔt/ n. **1.** a small, usually hard, abnormal elevation on the skin, caused by a virus. **2.** a small protuberance.

wary /ˈwɛəri/ adj. (**-rier, -riest**) watchful, or on one's guard, especially habitually; on the alert; cautious; careful. **-warily**, adv. **-wariness**, n.

was /wɔz/ v. first and third person singular past tense indicative of **be**.

wasabi /wəˈsabi/ n. a green paste with a hot, spicy taste, eaten with Japanese food.

wash /wɒʃ/ v.t. **1.** to apply water or some other liquid to for the purpose of cleansing; cleanse by dipping, rubbing, or scrubbing in water, etc. **2.** to flow over or against. -v.i. **3.** to wash oneself. **4.** Colloq. to stand being put to the proof; bear investigation. **5.** (oft. fol. by away) to be worn by the action of water, as a hill. -n. **6.** the act of washing with water or other liquid. **7.** a quantity of clothes, etc., washed, or to be washed, at one time. **8.** a liquid with which something is washed, wetted, coloured, overspread, etc. **9.** the flow, sweep, dash, or breaking of water. **10.** a broad, thin layer of colour applied by a continuous movement of the brush, as in watercolour painting.

washer /ˈwɒʃə/ n. **1.** a flat ring used to give tightness to a joint, to prevent leakage, and to

distribute pressure (as under the head of a bolt, under a nut, etc.). **2.** → **face washer**. **3.** Also, **washrag, washcloth**. a cloth used for washing dishes, etc.

wasn't /ˈwɒzənt/ v. contraction of was not.

wasp /wɒsp/ n. a stinging insect.

waspish /ˈwɒspɪʃ/ adj. quick to resent a trifling affront or injury.

wastage /ˈweɪstɪdʒ/ n. loss by use, wear, decay, wastefulness, etc.

waste /weɪst/ v. (**wasted, wasting**) -v.t. **1.** to consume, spend, or employ uselessly or without adequate return; squander. **2.** to fail to use, or let go to waste. **3.** to wear down or reduce, especially in health or strength. **4.** to destroy or devastate. -v.i. **5.** (oft. fol. by away) to become physically wasted. **6.** (oft. fol. by away) to diminish gradually, as wealth, power, etc. -n. **7.** useless consumption or expenditure, or use without adequate return. **8.** neglect, instead of use. **9.** gradual destruction or decay. **10.** a place in ruins. **11.** anything left over, as excess materials, etc. -adj. **12.** not used or in use. **13.** (of land, etc.) uninhabited and wild; desolate. **14.** left over or superfluous. **15.** Physiol. relating to material unused by or unusable to the organism.

wastewater /ˈweɪstwɔtə/ n. water that has been used in residences, businesses, factories, caravans, etc., containing waste such as faeces, chemicals, etc.

wastrel /ˈweɪstrəl/ n. a wasteful person; spendthrift.

watch /wɒtʃ/ v.i. **1.** to be on the lookout, look attentively, or be closely observant. **2.** (usu. fol. by for) to look or wait attentively and expectantly. -v.t. **3.** to keep under attentive view or observation, as in order to see or learn something; view attentively or with interest. **4.** to guard for protection or safekeeping. -n. **5.** close, constant observation for the purpose of seeking or discovering something. **6.** a lookout, as for something expected. **7.** vigilant guard, as for protection, restraint, etc. **8.** a small, portable timepiece.

watchful /ˈwɒtʃfəl/ adj. vigilant or alert; closely observant.

water /ˈwɔtə/ n. **1.** the liquid which in a more or less impure state constitutes rain, oceans, lakes, rivers, etc., and which in a pure state is a transparent, odourless, tasteless liquid, a compound of hydrogen and oxygen. **2.** (pl.) a body of water. **3.** any liquid or aqueous organic secretion. -v.t. **4.** to sprinkle, moisten, or drench with water. **5.** to supply (animals) with water for drinking. **6.** (oft. fol. by down) to dilute or adulterate with water. **7.** (fol. by down) to weaken. **8.** to produce a wavy lustrous pattern, marking, or finish on (fabrics, metals, etc.). -v.i. **9.** to discharge, fill with, or secrete water or liquid, as the eyes, or as the mouth at the sight or thought of tempting food. **-watery**, adj.

waterbed /ˈwɔtəbed/ n. a heavy durable plastic bag filled with water, used as a mattress often in a supporting wooden frame.

water bomb n. **1.** a balloon filled with water, used as a missile in play. **2.** a large amount of water or fire retardant dropped from an aircraft over a bushfire. Also, **waterbomb**.

water-bomb *v.t.* **1.** to throw a balloon filled with water at (someone) as in play. **2.** to fight (a bushfire) by means of water bombing. *–n.* **3.** → **water bomb**. Also, **waterbomb**.

water buffalo *n.* the largest species of buffalo, originally from India but now domesticated and widely used as a draught animal; feral in northern Australia. Also, **water ox**.

water chestnut *n.* an aquatic plant bearing an edible, nutlike fruit.

water closet *n.* a receptacle in which human excrement is flushed down a drain by water from a cistern; toilet. *Abbrev.*: WC

watercolour /'wɔtəkʌlə/ *n.* **1.** a pigment dispersed in water-soluble gum. **2.** the art or method of painting with such pigments. **3.** a painting or design executed by this method. Also, **watercolor**.

watercourse /'wɔtəkɔs/ *n.* **1.** a stream of water, as a river or brook. **2.** the bed of such a stream.

watercress /'wɔtəkrɛs/ *n.* a plant, usually growing in clear, running water, and bearing pungent leaves used in salads, etc.

waterfall /'wɔtəfɔl/ *n.* a steep fall or flow of water from a height; a cascade.

waterfront /'wɔtəfrʌnt/ *n.* **1.** land abutting on a body of water. **2.** (*collectively*) workers in industries using wharf facilities.

waterhole /'wɔtəhoʊl/ *n.* a natural hole or hollow in which water collects, as a spring in a desert, a cavity in the dried-up course of a river, etc.

waterlily /'wɔtəlili/ *n.* an aquatic plant having floating leaves and showy, often fragrant, flowers.

waterlog /'wɔtəlɒg/ *v.t.* (**-logged**, **-logging**) to soak or saturate with water.

watermark /'wɔtəmak/ *n.* **1.** a mark indicating the height to which water rises or has risen, as in a river, etc. **2.** a figure or design impressed in the fabric in the manufacture of paper and visible when the paper is held to the light.

watermelon /'wɔtəmɛlən/ *n.* a large melon with pink, juicy flesh.

water park *n.* a theme park which features water, with such attractions as water slides, wave pools, etc.

water police *n.* a civil force whose function is to police waterways.

water polo *n.* a water game played by two teams, each having seven swimmers, in which the object is to dribble or shoot the ball over the opposing team's goal line.

watershed /'wɔtəʃɛd/ *n.* the ridge or crest line dividing two drainage areas; divide.

waterside worker /'wɔtəsaɪd/ *n.* wharf labourer. Also, **watersider**.

waterski /'wɔtə,ski/ *n.* (*pl.* **-skis**) **1.** a type of ski used for gliding over water. *–v.i.* (**-ski'd** or **-skied** or **-skiing**) **2.** to glide over water on waterskis by grasping a rope towed by a speedboat.

watertable /'wɔtəteɪbəl/ *n.* in an aquifer, the upper limit of the portion of ground saturated with water.

watertight /'wɔtətaɪt/ *adj.* **1.** impervious to water. **2.** without fault; irrefutable; flawless.

waterway /'wɔtəweɪ/ *n.* a river, canal, or other body of water as a route or way of travel or transport.

watt /wɒt/ *n.* the derived SI unit of power, defined as one joule per second. *Symbol*: W

wattle /'wɒtl/ *n.* **1.** any of the very numerous Australian acacias, with spikes or globular heads of yellow or cream flowers. **2.** (*pl. or sing.*) rods or stakes interwoven with twigs or branches of trees, used for making fences, walls, roofs, etc. **3.** a fleshy lobe or appendage hanging down from the throat or chin, as of certain birds.

wattle and daub *n.* wattles (interwoven rods) plastered with mud or clay and used as a building material.

WAV /wæv/ *n.* a sound file format for computers, widely used to distribute sound over the internet.

wave /weɪv/ *n.* **1.** a disturbance of the surface of a liquid body, as the sea or a lake, in the form of a ridge or swell. **2.** a swell, surge, or rush, as of feeling, excitement, prosperity, etc. **3.** a widespread movement, feeling, opinion, tendency, etc. **4.** *Physics* a progressive vibrational disturbance propagated through a medium, as air, without corresponding progress or advance of the parts or particles themselves, as in the transmission of sound or electromagnetic energy. *–v.i.* **5.** to move loosely to and fro or up and down; flutter. **6.** to curve alternately in opposite directions; have an undulating form. *–v.t.* **7.** to cause to move loosely to and fro or up and down. **–wavy**, *adj.*

wavelength /'weɪvlɛŋθ/ *n.* *Physics* the length of each cycle of a wave (def. 4).

waver /'weɪvə/ *v.i.* **1.** to sway to and fro; flutter. **2.** to become unsteady or begin to fail or give way. **3.** to feel or show doubt or indecision, or vacillate.

wax¹ /wæks/ *n.* **1.** any of a group of solid, non-greasy, insoluble substances which have a low melting or softening point, especially mixtures of the higher hydrocarbons, as paraffin wax. **2.** a substance secreted by certain insects and plants. **3.** something suggesting wax as being readily moulded, worked upon, handled, managed, etc. *–v.t.* **4.** to rub, smear, stiffen, polish, etc., with wax; treat with wax.

wax² /wæks/ *v.i.* (**waxed**, **waxed** or, *Poetic*, **waxen**, **waxing**) **1.** to increase in extent, quantity, intensity, power, etc. **2.** (of the moon) to increase in the extent of its illuminated portion before the full moon (opposed to *wane*). **3.** to grow or become (as stated).

waxwork /'wækswɜk/ *n.* figures, ornaments, etc., made of wax, or one such figure.

way /weɪ/ *n.* **1.** manner, mode, or fashion. **2.** a course, plan, or means for attaining an end. **3.** respect or particular. **4.** direction. **5.** passage or progress on a course. **6.** a path or course leading from one place to another. **7.** (*oft. pl.*) a habit or custom. **8.** range of experience or notice. **9.** course of life, action, or experience. *–adv.* **10.** *Colloq.* extremely: *she's way cool; open till way late.* *–phr.* **11. by the way**, incidentally; in the course of one's remarks. **12. give way to, a.** to yield to. **b.** to lose control of (one's emotions, etc.). **13. in the way**, forming an obstruction or hindrance. **14. make one's way**, to proceed. **15. make**

way for, a. to allow to pass. **b.** to give up or retire in favour of. **16. under way,** in motion or moving along.

wayfarer /ˈweɪfeərə/ n. a traveller.

waylay /ˈweɪˈleɪ/ v.t. (**-laid, -laying**) to fall upon or assail from ambush, as in order to rob, seize, or slay.

-ways an adverbial suffix denoting position or direction, as in *sideways, lengthways.*

wayside /ˈweɪsaɪd/ n. the side of the way; the border or edge of the road or highway.

wayward /ˈweɪwəd/ adj. turned or turning away from what is right or proper; perverse.

WC /dʌbəlju ˈsi/ n. a toilet. Also, **wc.**

we /wi/ pron. the personal pronoun used by a speaker to refer to himself or herself along with at least one other person: *I'm ready. You're ready. We can go.*

weak /wik/ adj. **1.** liable to yield, break, or collapse under pressure or strain; fragile; frail; not strong. **2.** deficient in bodily strength or healthy vigour, as from age, sickness, etc.; feeble; infirm. **3.** lacking in force, potency, or efficacy. **4.** deficient in amount, volume, loudness, intensity, etc.; faint; slight. **5.** *Commerce* (of a market) characterised by falling prices.

weakling /ˈwiklɪŋ/ n. a weak or feeble creature (physically or morally).

weal /wil/ n. **1.** a small burning or itching swelling on the skin. **2.** a welt.

wealth /wɛlθ/ n. **1.** a great store of valuable possessions, property, or riches. **2.** a rich abundance or profusion of anything. **3.** *Econ.* **a.** all things having a value in money, in exchange, or in use. **b.** anything having utility and capable of being appropriated or exchanged. **—wealthy,** adj.

wean /win/ v.t. to accustom (a child or animal) to food other than its mother's milk.

weapon /ˈwɛpən/ n. any instrument for use in attack or defence in combat, fighting, or war, as a sword, rifle, cannon, etc.

weapon of mass destruction n. a biological, chemical or nuclear weapon capable of killing a great number of people. *Abbrev.:* WMD

wear /weə/ v. (**wore, worn, wearing**) —v.t. **1.** to carry or have on the body or about the person as a covering, equipment, ornament, or the like. **2.** to bear or have in the aspect or appearance. **3.** to impair, deteriorate, or consume gradually by use or any continued process. **4.** to make (a hole, channel, way, etc.) by such action. —v.i. **5.** (oft. fol. by *away, down, out,* or *off*) to undergo gradual impairment, diminution, reduction, etc., from wear, use, attrition, or other causes. **6.** to hold out or last under wear, use, or any continued strain. —n. **7.** gradual impairment, wasting, diminution, etc., as from use. —phr. **8. wear out, a.** to wear or use until no longer fit for use. **b.** to exhaust by continued use, strain, or any gradual process.

weariless /ˈwɪəriləs/ adj. unwearying.

wearisome /ˈwɪərisəm/ adj. tedious.

weary /ˈwɪəri/ adj. (**-rier, -riest**) **1.** exhausted physically or mentally by labour, exertion, strain, etc.; fatigued; tired. **2.** (oft. fol. by *of*) impatient or dissatisfied at excess or overlong continuance. —v.t., v.i. (**-ried, -rying**) **3.** to make or become weary; fatigue or tire. **4.** (oft. fol. by *of*) to make or grow impatient or dissatisfied at having too much of something.

weasel /ˈwizəl/ n. a small carnivore having a long, slender body, short legs and rounded ears, and feeding largely on small rodents.

weather /ˈwɛðə/ n. **1.** the state of the atmosphere with respect to wind, temperature, cloudiness, moisture, pressure, etc. —v.t. **2.** to bear up against and come safely through (a storm, danger, trouble, etc.). —v.i. **3.** to undergo change, as discolouration or disintegration, as the result of exposure to atmospheric conditions.

weatherboard /ˈwɛðəbɔd/ n. one of a series of thin boards nailed on an outside wall or a roof to form a protective covering.

weathervane /ˈwɛðəveɪn/ n. a vane for indicating the direction of the wind.

weave¹ /wiv/ v. (**wove or weaved, woven or weaved, weaving**) —v.t. **1.** to interlace (threads, yarns, strips, fibrous material, etc.) so as to form a fabric or texture. —v.i. **2.** to weave cloth, etc. —n. **3.** a manner of interlacing yarns.

weave² /wiv/ v. (**weaved or wove, weaving**) —v.t. **1.** to follow in a winding course; to move from side to side. —v.i. **2.** to move repeatedly from side to side.

web¹ /wɛb/ n. **1.** something formed as by weaving or interweaving. **2.** a thin silken fabric spun by spiders, and also by the larvae of some insects. **3.** a tangled intricate state of circumstances, events, etc. **4.** *Zool.* a membrane which connects the digits of some animals and birds.

web² /wɛb/ n. **the,** (*also upper case*) a large-scale, networked, hypertext information system available over the internet. Also, **World Wide Web.**

webbed /wɛbd/ adj. having the digits connected by a web, as the foot of a duck or a beaver.

web browser n. → **browser** (def. 2).

webcam /ˈwɛbkæm/ n. *Colloq.* a web camera. Also, **web cam.**

web camera n. a digital video camera linked to a computer for transmission of images over the internet. Also, *Colloq.,* **webcam.**

webcast /ˈwɛbkast/ v. (**-cast or -casted, -casting**) —v.i. **1.** to broadcast live or delayed transmissions on the internet. —v.t. **2.** to broadcast (a program, event, etc.) on the internet in such a way. —n. **3.** such a broadcast on the internet. —**webcaster,** n. —**webcasting,** n.

web crawler n. an internet search engine, originally designed to search keywords specified at URLs to locate required websites, but now capable of searching for other kinds of information, such as email addresses; robot.

webliography /wɛbliˈɒɡrəfi/ n. (pl. **-graphies**) a list of resources on a particular subject available on the internet.

web log n. → **blog.** Also, **weblog.**

webmaster /ˈwɛbmastə/ n. a person, usually a male, responsible for the development and maintenance of a web server or website.

web page n. *Internet* a document with a unique URL on the World Wide Web. Also, **webpage.**

web portal *n.* a website which offers information and sometimes direct links to other websites along with a range of services such as email, online shopping, etc. Also, **portal**, **portal site**.

web server *n. Internet* **1.** the software running at a website which sends out web pages in response to remote browsers. **2.** a computer which connects a user's computer to the World Wide Web on request. Also, **webserver**.

website /ˈwebsaɪt/ *n. Internet* a location on the World Wide Web where there is a set of resources, as text files, images, etc. Also, **web site**.

wed /wɛd/ *v.t.* (**wedded** *or* **wed**, **wedding**) **1.** to bind oneself to (a person) in marriage; take for husband or wife. **2.** to unite (a couple) or join (one person to another) in marriage or wedlock; marry.

we'd /wid/ contraction of *we had, we should* or *we would.*

wedding /ˈwɛdɪŋ/ *n.* the act or ceremony of marrying; marriage.

wedge /wɛdʒ/ *n.* **1.** a device consisting of a piece of hard material with two principle faces meeting in a sharply acute angle. **2.** a piece of anything of like shape. **3.** Also, **potato wedge.** a thick wedge of potato, seasoned and fried. **4.** something that serves to part, divide, etc. –*v.* (**wedged**, **wedging**) –*v.t.* **5.** to pack or fix tightly by driving in a wedge or wedges. **6.** to thrust, drive, or fix (in, between, etc.) like a wedge. –*v.i.* **7.** to force a way (in, etc.) like a wedge.

wedge politics *n.* the political strategy whereby one group seeks to weaken opposing groups by forcing them to divide over a particular issue rather than form an alliance.

wedgie /ˈwɛdʒi/ *n. Colloq.* the experience of having one's pants pulled up so sharply as to cause discomfort, usually done as a prank.

wedlock /ˈwɛdlɒk/ *n.* the state of marriage; matrimony.

wee¹ /wi/ *adj.* little; very small.

wee² /wi/ *Colloq.* –*n.* **1.** urine. –*v.i.* (**wee'd**, **wee'ing**) **2.** to urinate.

weed /wid/ *n.* **1.** a plant growing wild, especially in cultivated ground to the exclusion or injury of the desired crop. **2.** a thin or weakly person, especially one regarded as stupid or infantile. –*v.t.* **3.** to free from weeds or troublesome plants. **4.** to rid of what is undesirable or superfluous.

week /wik/ *n.* **1.** a period of seven successive days, commonly understood as beginning (unless otherwise specified or implied) with Sunday, followed by Monday, Tuesday, Wednesday, Thursday, Friday, and Saturday. **2.** the working days or working portion of the seven-day period. **3.** seven days after a specified day: *Tuesday week.*

weekend /ˈwikˈɛnd/ *n.* the end of the working week, especially the period from Friday night or Saturday to Monday, as a time for recreation.

weekly /ˈwikli/ *adj.* **1.** relating to a week, or to each week. **2.** done, happening, appearing, etc., once a week, or every week. –*adv.* **3.** once a week. **4.** by the week. –*n.* (*pl.* **-lies**) **5.** a periodical appearing once a week.

weep /wip/ *v.* (**wept**, **weeping**) –*v.i.* **1.** to shed tears, as from sorrow, unhappiness, or any overpowering emotion; cry. **2.** to exude water or liquid, as soil, rock, a plant stem, a sore, etc. –*v.t.* **3.** to shed (tears, etc.).

weevil /ˈwivəl/ *n.* a type of beetle destructive to nuts, grain, fruit, etc.

weft /wɛft/ *n.* **1.** *Textiles* woof or filling yarns which interlace with warp running from selvage to selvage. **2.** a woven piece.

weigh /weɪ/ *v.t.* **1.** to ascertain the weight of by means of a balance, scale, or other mechanical device. **2.** to bear (down) upon; weight, heaviness, oppression, etc. **3.** (sometimes fol. by *up*) to balance in the mind; consider carefully in order to reach an opinion, decision, or choice. **4.** to raise or lift (now chiefly in the phrase *to weigh anchor*). –*v.i.* **5.** to have weight or heaviness, often as specified.

weight /weɪt/ *n.* **1.** amount of heaviness; amount a thing weighs. **2.** a body of determinate mass, as of metal, for using on a balance or scale in weighing objects, substances, etc. **3.** any heavy mass or object, especially an object used because of its heaviness. **4.** importance, moment, consequence, or effective influence. –*v.t.* **5.** to add weight to; load with additional weight. –**weightless**, *adj.*

weightlifting /ˈweɪtlɪftɪŋ/ *n.* the sport of lifting barbells of specified weights, in competition or for exercise.

weighty /ˈweɪti/ *adj.* (**-tier, -tiest**) **1.** having considerable weight; heavy. **2.** of considerable importance; serious. –**weightily**, *adv.*

weir /wɪə/ *n.* a dam in a river or stream to stop and raise the water.

weird /wɪəd/ *adj.* **1.** involving or suggesting the supernatural; unearthly or uncanny. **2.** *Colloq.* startlingly or extraordinarily singular, odd, or queer.

welcome /ˈwɛlkəm/ *n.* **1.** a kindly greeting or reception. –*v.t.* (**-comed**, **-coming**) **2.** to greet the coming of (a person, etc.) with pleasure or kindly courtesy. –*adj.* **3.** gladly received.

welcome to country *n.* a welcoming speech, performance, etc., given by a representative or representatives of the traditional Indigenous custodians of the land on which a public event, meeting, etc., is taking place.

weld /wɛld/ *v.t.* to unite or fuse (pieces of metal, etc.), especially with the use of heat.

welfare /ˈwɛlfɛə/ *n.* the state of faring well; wellbeing.

welfare trap *n.* a situation in which the advantages of taking paid work and having an income is little more than the advantages received from social welfare, which can lead to the opinion that it is not worthwhile seeking employment. Also, **unemployment trap**.

well¹ /wɛl/ *adv.* (**better, best**) **1.** in a satisfactory, favourable, or advantageous manner; fortunately or happily. **2.** in a good or proper manner. **3.** thoroughly or soundly. **4.** easily; clearly. **5.** to a considerable extent or degree. –*adj.* (**better, best**) **6.** in good health, or sound in body and mind. **7.** satisfactory or good. –*phr.* **8. as well**, in addition. **9. as well as**, in addition to; no less than. **10. very well**, **a.** with certainty; undeniably. **b.** a phrase used to indicate consent, often with reluctance. **c.** (*ironic*) satisfactory; pleasing.

well² /wɛl/ *n.* **1.** a hole drilled into the earth, generally by boring, for the production of water, petroleum, natural gas, brine, or sulphur. **2.** a spring or natural source of water. *-v.i.* **3.** (oft. fol. by *up, out,* or *forth*) to rise, spring, or gush, as water, from the earth or some source.

we'll /wil/ contraction of *we will* or *we shall.*

wellbeing /'wɛlbiŋ/ *n.* good or satisfactory condition of existence; welfare.

well-done *adj.* (of meat) cooked thoroughly.

well-heeled /'wɛl-hild/ *adj. Colloq.* wealthy; prosperous.

wellington boot /'wɛlɪŋtən/ *n.* → **gumboot.**

well-known /'wɛl-noʊn/ *adj.* **1.** clearly or fully known. **2.** familiarly known, or familiar. **3.** generally or widely known.

well-mannered /'wɛl-mænəd/ *adj.* polite; courteous.

well-meaning /'wɛl-miniŋ/ *adj.* meaning or intending well.

well-off *adj.* in good or easy circumstances as to money or means; moderately rich.

well-read /'wɛl-rɛd/ *adj.* **1.** having read much. **2.** having an extensive and intelligent knowledge of books or literature.

well-spoken *adj.* **1.** having a cultured, refined accent. **2.** speaking well, fittingly, or pleasingly.

well-to-do *adj.* having a sufficiency of means for comfortable living; well-off or prosperous.

welsh /wɛlʃ/ *v.t., v.i. Colloq.* (sometimes fol. by *on*) to cheat by evading payment, especially of a gambling debt.

welt /wɛlt/ *n.* **1.** a ridge on the surface of the body, as from the stroke of a stick or whip. **2.** a strengthening or ornamental finish along a seam, the edge of a garment, etc.

welter /'wɛltə/ *n.* **1.** a rolling or tumbling about. **2.** commotion, turmoil, or chaos.

wen /wɛn/ *n.* a benign tumour of the skin, especially on the scalp.

wench /wɛntʃ/ *n.* **1.** a girl, or young woman. **2.** a rustic or working girl.

wend /wɛnd/ *v.t.* to direct or pursue (one's way, etc.).

went /wɛnt/ *v.* past tense of **go.**

wept /wɛpt/ *v.* past tense and past participle of **weep.**

were /wɜ/ *v.* past tense indicative plural of **be.**

we're /wɪə, wɜ, wɛə/ contraction of *we are.*

weren't /wɜnt/ contraction of *were not.*

werewolf /'wɛəwʊlf/ *n.* (*pl.* **-wolves** /-wʊlvz/) (in old superstition) a human being turned into a wolf.

west /wɛst/ *n.* **1.** a cardinal point of the compass (90° to the left of north) corresponding to the point where the sun is seen to set. **2.** (*usu. upper case*) **the,** the countries of Western Europe, North America, and other countries with a Western European background, such as Australia, especially as contrasted historically, culturally, or politically with other parts of the world. *-adj.* **3.** lying or proceeding towards the west. **4.** coming from the west. *-adv.* **5.** in the direction of the sunset; towards or in the

west. **6.** from the west (as of wind). **-westerly,** *adj., n.*

western /'wɛstən/ *adj.* **1.** lying towards or situated in the west. **2.** directed or proceeding towards the west. **3.** coming from the west, as a wind. **4.** (*usu. upper case*) having to to with the West. *-n.* **5.** (*usu. upper case*) a story or film about frontier life in the American west.

wet /wɛt/ *adj.* (**wetter, wettest**) **1.** covered or soaked, wholly or in part, with water or some other liquid. **2.** not yet dry; moist; damp. **3.** rainy; having a rainy climate. *-n.* **4.** that which makes wet, as water or other liquid; moisture. **5.** rain. *-v.t.* (**wet** or **wetted, wetting**) **6.** to make wet.

wet blanket *n.* a person or thing that has a discouraging or depressing effect.

wet cell *n.* an electric cell whose electrolyte is in liquid form and free to flow.

wether /'wɛðə/ *n.* a ram castrated when young.

wetlands /'wɛtlændz, 'wɛtləndz/ *pl. n.* an area in which the soil is frequently or permanently saturated with or under water, as a swamp, marsh, etc.

wet nurse *n.* a woman hired to breastfeed another's infant.

wet season *n.* the period of an annual cycle in the tropics when rainfall and humidity increases markedly, usually as a result of the change in the prevailing winds. Compare **dry season.**

wetsuit /'wɛtsut/ *n.* a tight-fitting rubber suit worn by divers, surfers, etc.

we've /wiv/, *unstressed* /wəv/ contraction of *we have.*

whack /wæk/ *v.t. Colloq.* to strike with a smart, resounding blow or blows.

whale¹ /weɪl/ *n. Zool.* any of numerous large cetaceans with fishlike bodies, modified foreflippers, and a horizontally flattened tail.

whale² /weɪl/ *v.t. Colloq.* **1.** (fol. by *into*) to throw oneself into something energetically. **2. a.** to beat up, bash. **b.** (fol. by *into*) to attack verbally, berate.

whalebone /'weɪlboʊn/ *n.* an elastic horny substance growing in place of teeth in the upper jaw of certain whales used in strips, especially in earlier times for stiffening corsets, etc.

wham /wæm/ *v.t.* (**whammed, whamming**) to hit forcefully, especially with a single loud noise.

wharf /wɔf/ *n.* (*pl.* **wharves** or **wharfs**) a structure built on the shore of, or projecting out into, a harbour, stream, etc., so that vessels may be moored alongside to load or unload or to lie at rest; a quay.

what /wɒt/ *pron.* **1.** an interrogative pronoun used when **a.** asking for something to be named or stated: *What is your name?; What did he do?* **b.** asking about the nature, character, class, origin, etc., of a thing or person: *What is that animal?* **c.** asking about the importance of something: *What is wealth without health?* **2.** a relative pronoun used to mean 'the thing that', or 'that which': *This is what he says; She didn't say what she wanted; I don't know what he meant; It doesn't matter what I do, I always seem to get it wrong; Say what you please. -adv.* **3.** to what extent or degree:

What does it matter?; *What do I care?* –*adj.*
4. which one: *What book are you reading?*
–*phr.* **5. what for?**, for what reason or purpose.

whatever /wɒt'evə/ *pron.* **1.** anything that: *Do whatever you like.*; *Just do whatever he does.*
2. no matter what: *Whatever you do, don't press the red button.* **3.** used to show that the thing under discussion is not important: *Red, yellow, blue, green, whatever – I like them all.*
4. a stronger form of the word *what* used when asking about something that has surprised you: *Whatever is the problem?* –*adj.* **5.** any...that: *whatever time I have.*

what's /wɒts/ contraction of *what is.*

wheat /wit/ *n.* the grain of a widely distributed cereal grass, used extensively in the form of flour.

wheedle /'widl/ *v.t.* to endeavour to influence (a person) by smooth, flattering, or beguiling words.

wheel /wil/ *n.* **1.** a circular frame or solid disc arranged to turn on an axis, as in vehicles, machinery, etc. **2.** any instrument, machine, apparatus, etc., shaped like this, or having such a frame or disc as an essential feature.
3. anything resembling or suggesting a wheel.
4. (*pl.*) moving, propelling, or animating agencies. **5.** (*pl.*) *Colloq.* a motor vehicle. **6.** a wheeling or circular movement. **7.** *Colloq.* a person of considerable importance or influence. –*v.t.* **8.** to cause to turn, rotate, or revolve, as on an axis. **9.** to move, roll, or convey on wheels, castors, etc. –*v.i.* **10.** to turn on or as on an axis or about a centre; rotate, revolve. **11.** to move in a circular or curving course. **12.** (oft. fol. by *about* or *round*) to turn or change in procedure or opinion. **13.** to roll along on, or as on, wheels; to travel along smoothly.

wheelbarrow /'wilbærou/ *n.* a barrow supported at one end by a wheel on which it is pushed along.

wheelchair /'wiltʃeə/ *n.* a chair mounted on large wheels, and used by invalids and those unable to walk.

wheeze /wiz/ *v.i.* to breathe with difficulty and with a whistling sound.

whelk /welk/ *n.* any of various large spiral-shelled marine gastropods.

whelp /welp/ *n.* the young of the dog, or of the wolf, bear, lion, tiger, seal, etc.

when /wen/ *adv.* **1.** at what time: *When are you coming?* –*conj.* **2.** at what time: *to know when to be silent.* **3.** at the time that: *When we were young, life was fun.* **4.** while on the contrary, or whereas: *You rush ahead, when you should think first.* –*pron.* **5.** what time: *Since when?*
6. which time: *They left on Monday, since when we have heard nothing.*

whenever /wen'evə/ *conj.* at whatever time; at any time when: *Come whenever you like.*

where /weə/ *adv.* **1.** a word used to ask **a.** in or at what place?: *Where is he?* **b.** in what position?: *Where do you want to stand?* **c.** to what place?: *Where are you going?* **d.** from what source?: *Where did you get this information?*
–*conj.* **2.** in or at what place, part, point, etc.: *Find where he is.* **3.** in or at the place, part, point, etc., in or at which: *It's where you left it.*

4. in or at which place; and there: *They came to the town, where they stayed overnight.*
–*pron.* **5.** what place: *From where?*

where- a word element meaning 'what' or 'which'.

whereabouts /'weərəbauts/, *interrogatively* /weərə'bauts/ *adv.* **1.** about where? where?
–*conj.* **2.** near or in what place. –*pl. n.*
3. (*sometimes construed as sing.*) the place where a person or thing is; the locality of a person or thing.

whereas /weər'æz/ *conj.* **1.** while on the contrary. **2.** it being the case that, or considering that (especially used in formal preambles).

whereby /weə'bai/ *conj.* by what or by which.

whereupon /weərə'pon/ *conj.* at or after which.

wherever /weər'evə/ *conj.* in, at, or to whatever place.

wherewithal /'weəwiðol, -θəl/ *n.* means or supplies for the purpose or need, especially money.

whet /wet/ *v.t.* (**whetted**, **whetting**) **1.** to sharpen (a knife, tool, etc.) by grinding or friction. **2.** to make keen or eager.

whether /'weðə/ *conj.* a word introducing the first of two or more alternatives, used in correlation with *or.*

whetstone /'wetstoun/ *n.* a stone for sharpening cutlery, etc., by friction.

whey /wei/ *n.* milk serum, separating as a watery liquid from the curd after coagulation, as in cheese-making.

which /witʃ/ *pron.* **1.** an interrogative pronoun used to ask what one (of a certain number): *Which of these do you want?* **2.** a relative pronoun used **a.** as the subject or object of a relative clause: *The house, which was deep in the bush, burnt down*; *What colour is the car which they stole?* **b.** to indicate what particular one or any one that: *She knows which she wants*; *Choose which you like.* **c.** to mean 'a thing that': *and, which is worse, they didn't pay.* –*adj.* **3.** what one (of a certain number mentioned or implied): *Which book do you want?*

whichever /witʃ'evə/ *pron.* **1.** any one (of those in question) that: *Take whichever you like.*
2. no matter which: *Whichever you choose, someone will be offended.* –*adj.* **3.** no matter which: *whichever book you like.*

whiff /wif/ *n.* **1.** a slight blast or puff of wind or air. **2.** a puff or waft of scent or smell.

while /wail/ *n.* **1.** a space of time. –*conj.*
Also, **whilst. 2.** during or in the time that.
3. throughout the time that, or as long as. **4.** at the same time that (implying opposition or contrast). –*v.t.* (**whiled**, **whiling**) **5.** (usu. fol. by *away*) to cause (time) to pass, especially in some easy or pleasant manner.

whim /wim/ *n.* an odd or fanciful notion; a freakish or capricious fancy or desire.

whimper /'wimpə/ *v.i.* **1.** to cry with low, plaintive, broken sounds, as a child, a dog, etc.
–*n.* **2.** a whimpering cry or sound.

whimsical /'wimzikəl/ *adj.* of an odd, quaint, or comical kind.

whimsy /'wimzi/ *n.* (*pl.* **-sies**) an odd or fanciful notion.

whine /wain/ *v.i.* (**whined**, **whining**) **1.** to utter a nasal, complaining cry or sound, as from uneasiness, discontent, peevishness, etc. −n. **2.** a whining utterance, sound, or tone.

whinge /wɪndʒ/ v.i. (**whinged, whingeing**) to complain; whine. **–whinger,** n.

whinny /'wɪni/ v.i. (**-nied, -nying**) (of a horse) to utter its characteristic cry; neigh.

whip /wɪp/ v. (**whipped, whipping**) −v.t. **1.** to strike with quick, repeated strokes of something slender and flexible; lash. **2.** to beat with a whip or the like, especially by way of punishment or chastisement; flog; thrash. **3.** (fol. by *away, out, up, into*, etc.) to move quickly and suddenly; pull, jerk, snatch, seize, put, etc., with a sudden movement. **4.** to beat (eggs, cream, etc.) to a froth with a whisk, fork, or other implement in order to incorporate air and produce expansion. −v.i. **5.** to move or go quickly and suddenly (*away, off, out, in*, etc.); dart; whisk. **6.** to beat or lash about, as a pennant in the wind. −n. **7.** an instrument to strike with, as in driving animals or in punishing, typically consisting of a lash or other flexible part with a more rigid handle. **8.** a party manager in a legislative body, who supplies information to members about the government business, secures their attendance for voting, supplies lists of members to serve on committees and keeps the leaders informed as to the trend of party opinion. −phr. **9. whip up, a.** to create quickly. **b.** to arouse to fury, intense excitement, etc.

whiplash /'wɪplæʃ/ n. an injury to the spine, usually in the cervical area, caused by sudden movement forwards or backwards, as in a motor accident.

whippet /'wɪpət/ n. a dog similar to a small greyhound.

whirl /wɜl/ v.i. **1.** to turn round, spin, or rotate rapidly. **2.** to move, travel, or be carried rapidly along on wheels or otherwise. −v.t. **3.** to cause to turn round, spin, or rotate rapidly. −n. **4.** the act of whirling; rapid rotation or gyration. **5.** a short drive, run, walk, or the like, or a spin. **6.** a rapid round of events, affairs, etc. **7.** a state marked by a dizzying succession or mingling of feelings, thoughts, etc.

whirlpool /'wɜlpul/ n. a whirling eddy or current, as in a river or the sea.

whirlwind /'wɜlwɪnd/ n. a mass of air rotating rapidly round and towards a more or less vertical axis.

whirr /wɜ/ v.i. (**whirred, whirring**) to go, fly, dart, revolve, or otherwise move quickly with a vibratory or buzzing sound.

whisk[1] /wɪsk/ v.t. **1.** to sweep (dust, crumbs, etc., or a surface) with a brush, or the like. **2.** to move with a rapid, sweeping stroke.

whisk[2] /wɪsk/ v.t. **1.** to whip (eggs, cream, etc.) to a froth with a whisk or beating implement. −n. **2.** a small bunch of grass, straw, hair, or the like, especially for use in brushing. **3.** an implement, in one form a bunch of loops of wire held together in a handle, for beating or whipping eggs, cream, etc.

whisker /'wɪskə/ n. **1.** (*pl.*) the beard generally. **2.** a single hair of the beard.

whisky /'wɪski/ n. a distilled spirit made from grain.

whisper /'wɪspə/ v.i. **1.** to speak with soft, low sounds, using the breath, lips, etc., without vibration of the vocal cords. **2.** (of trees, water, breezes, etc.) to make a soft, rustling sound. −v.t. **3.** to utter with soft, low sounds, using the breath, lips, etc. −n. **4.** the mode of utterance, or the voice, of someone who whispers. **5.** confidential information; rumour.

whist /wɪst/ n. a card game.

whistle /'wɪsəl/ v.i. **1.** to make a kind of clear musical sound, or a series of such sounds, by the forcible expulsion of the breath through a small orifice formed by contracting the lips, or through the teeth, together with the aid of the tongue. **2.** to make such a sound or series of sounds otherwise, as by blowing on a particular device. −n. **3.** an instrument for producing whistling sounds as by the breath, steam, etc., as a small wooden or tin tube or a small pipe. **4.** a sound produced by or as by whistling.

white /waɪt/ adj. **1.** of the colour of pure snow, reflecting all or nearly all the rays of sunlight. **2.** having a light skin; marked by comparatively slight pigmentation of the skin. **3.** pallid or pale, as from fear or other strong emotion, or pain or illness. **4.** (of wines) light-coloured or yellowish (opposed to *red*). **5.** (of coffee) with milk or cream. −n. **6.** a white colour. **7.** lightness of skin pigment. **8.** something white, or a white part of something. **9.** a pellucid viscous fluid which surrounds the yolk of an egg. **10.** the white part of the eyeball. −v.t. **11.** *Printing* (oft. fol. by *out*) to make white by leaving blank spaces. **12.** (fol. by *out*) to reduce the daylight visibility of, as a result of snow or fog.

white ant n. any of various species of wood-eating insects.

whitebait /'waɪtbeɪt/ n. (*pl.* **-bait**) any small delicate fish cooked without being cleaned.

white blindfold adj. of or relating to an interpretation of Australian history marked by Anglo-centrism and a disinclination to acknowledge past injustices, especially those committed against Indigenous Australians. Compare **black armband** (def. 2).

white blood cell n. → leukocyte.

whiteboard /'waɪtbɔd/ n. a board with a white plastic surface on which one writes with an erasable felt pens, used for teaching or presentations.

white-collar adj. belonging or relating to non-manual workers, as those in professional and clerical work.

white flag n. an all-white flag, used as a symbol of surrender, etc.

white gold n. any of several gold alloys possessing a white colour due to the presence of nickel or platinum.

whitegoods /'waɪtgʊdz/ pl. n. electrical goods as fridges, washing machines, etc., which have a white enamel surface.

white heat n. an intense heat at which a substance glows with white light.

white lie n. a lie uttered from polite, amiable, or pardonable motives.

white light n. light which contains all the wavelengths of the visible spectrum at approximately the same intensity.

white meat *n.* any light-coloured meat, as veal, the breast of chicken, etc. (distinguished from *red meat*).

white noise *n.* an electronically produced noise in which all frequencies are represented with equal energy in each equal range of frequencies.

white-out *n.* a thin white paint that is used to cover written mistakes on paper.

white paper *n.* an official report or policy proposal of a government on a specific subject.

whitewash /'waɪtwɒʃ/ *n.* **1.** a composition used for whitening walls, woodwork, etc. **2.** anything used to cover up defects, gloss over faults or errors, or give a specious semblance of respectability, honesty, etc., especially a dishonest official investigation.

white water *n.* any stretch of water in which the surface is broken, as in rapids or breaking waves, due to movement over a shallow bottom. –**whitewater**, *adj.*

whither /'wɪðə/ *adv. Archaic* to what place? where?

whiting /'waɪtɪŋ/ *n.* (*pl.* **-ting** or **-tings**) any of numerous species of estuarine and surf fishes, highly prized for sport and table.

whitlow /'wɪtloʊ/ *n.* an inflammation of the deeper tissues of a finger or toe.

whittle /'wɪtl/ *v.t.* **1.** to cut, trim, or shape (a stick, piece of wood, etc.) by taking off bits with a knife. **2.** (esp. fol. by *down*) to cut by way of reducing amount. –**whittler**, *n.*

whiz[1] /wɪz/ *v.i.* (**whizzed**, **whizzing**) to make a humming or hissing sound, as an object passing rapidly through the air.

whiz[2] /wɪz/ *n. Colloq.* a person who shows outstanding ability in a particular field or who is notable in some way; expert.

who /hu/ *pron.* **1.** an interrogative pronoun used when **a.** asking the question 'what person?': *Who told you so?* **b.** asking 'what?', as to the character, origin, position, importance, etc., of a person: *Who is the man in uniform?* **2.** a relative pronoun introducing an adjectival clause describing a person: *I know who did it*; *The woman who sold it to me has gone to lunch.*

who'd /hud/ contraction of *who would*.

whoever /hu'ɛvə/ *pron.* **1.** whatever person, or anyone that: *whoever wants it may have it.* **2.** *Colloq.* who ever? who?, used to give force to a question: *whoever is that?*

whole /hoʊl/ *adj.* **1.** comprising the full quantity, amount, extent, number, etc., without diminution or exception; entire, full, or total. **2.** undivided, or in one piece. **3.** uninjured, undamaged, or unbroken; sound; intact. **4.** being fully or entirely such. –*n.* **5.** the whole assemblage of parts or elements belonging to a thing; the entire quantity, account, extent, or number. **6.** a thing complete in itself, or comprising all its parts or elements. –**wholly**, *adv.*

wholehearted /'hoʊlhatəd/ *adj.* hearty; cordial; earnest; sincere.

wholemeal /'hoʊlmil/ *adj.* prepared with the complete wheat kernel, as flour or the bread baked with it.

whole number *n. Maths* an integer as 0, 1, 2, 3, 4, 5, etc.

wholesale /'hoʊlseɪl/ *n.* **1.** the sale of commodities in large quantities, as to retailers rather than to consumers directly (distinguished from *retail*). –*adj.* **2.** extensive and indiscriminate. –*adv.* **3.** in a wholesale way. –*v.t.*, *v.i.* **4.** to sell by wholesale. –**wholesaler**, *n.*

wholesome /'hoʊlsəm/ *adj.* **1.** conducive to moral or general wellbeing; salutary; beneficial. **2.** conducive to bodily health; healthful; salubrious.

wholistic /hoʊl'ɪstɪk/ *adj.* → **holistic**. –**wholism**, *n.*

who'll /hul/ contraction of *who will* or *who shall*.

whom /hum/ *pron.* **1.** the objective case of the interrogative pronoun **who**: *To whom did you speak?*; *Whom did you see?* **2.** the objective case of the relative pronoun **who**: *the woman whom I saw*; *the man to whom I gave the cheque.*

whoop /wup, hup/ *n.* **1.** a loud cry or shout, as one uttered by children or warriors. –*v.i.* **2.** to utter a loud cry or shout (originally the syllable *whoop*, or *hoop*), as a call, or in enthusiasm, excitement, frenzy, etc.

whooping cough /'hupɪŋ/ *n.* an infectious disease of the respiratory mucous membrane, especially of children.

whoops /wʊps/ *interj.* an exclamation of mild surprise, dismay, etc. Also, **whoops-a-daisy**.

whoosh /wʊʃ/ *n.* a loud rushing noise, as of water or air.

whopper /'wɒpə/ *n. Colloq.* **1.** something uncommonly large of its kind. **2.** a big lie.

whore /hɔ/ *n.* a female prostitute.

who're /'huə/ contraction of *who are*.

whorl /wɜl/ *n.* **1.** a circular arrangement of like parts, as leaves, flowers, etc., round a point on an axis. **2.** anything shaped like a coil.

who's /huz/ contraction of *who is* or *who has*.

whose /huz/ *pron.* **1.** the possessive case of the interrogative pronoun **who**: *Whose is this jacket?* **2.** the possessive case of the relative pronoun **who**: *the man whose dog I bought.* **3.** the possessive case of the relative pronoun **which**: *the house whose roof was replaced last week.* –*adj.* **4.** of, belonging or relating to whom: *Whose dog is this?*

who've /huv/ contraction of *who have*.

why /waɪ/ *adv.* **1.** for what? for what cause, reason, or purpose? –*conj.* **2.** for what cause or reason.

wick /wɪk/ *n.* a bundle or loose twist or braid of soft threads, or a woven strip or tube, as of cotton, which in a candle, lamp, oil stove, or the like serves to draw up the melted tallow or wax or the oil or other flammable liquid to be burned at its top end.

wicked /'wɪkəd/ *adj.* evil or morally bad in principle or practice; iniquitous; sinful.

wickerwork /'wɪkəwɜk/ *n.* work consisting of plaited or woven twigs.

wicket /'wɪkət/ *n.* **1.** a small door or gate, especially one beside, or forming part of, a larger one. **2.** *Cricket* **a.** either of the two frameworks, each consisting of three stumps and two bails in grooves across their tops, at which the bowler aims the ball. **b.** the area between the wickets, especially with reference to the state of the ground. **c.** the achievement of a player's dismissal by the fielding side.

wide /waɪd/ *adj.* **1.** having considerable or great extent from side to side; broad; not narrow. **2.** having a certain or specified extent from side to side. **3.** of great range or scope; embracing a great number or variety of subjects, cases, etc. **4.** open to the full or a great extent; expanded; distended. –*adv.* **5.** to a great, or relatively great, extent from side to side. **6.** to the full extent of opening. **7.** away from or to one side of a point, mark, purpose, or the like; aside; astray. –**width,** *n.*

wide area network *n.* a computer network which connects computers over a wide area. *Abbrev.*: WAN Compare **local area network**.

widespread /ˈwaɪdsprɛd/ *adj.* **1.** spread over or occupying a wide space. **2.** distributed over a wide region, or occurring in many places or among many persons or individuals. Also, **widespreading**.

widget /ˈwɪdʒət/ *n.* **1.** *Colloq.* (*humorous*) a mechanical device or gadget, the name of which you do not know or cannot think of. **2.** *Computers* a component of a graphical user interface that displays information that a user can interact with to change the information, such as a window or a text box.

widow /ˈwɪdoʊ/ *n.* a woman whose spouse has died and who has not married again.

widower /ˈwɪdoʊə/ *n.* a man who has lost his spouse by death and has not married again

wield /wild/ *v.t.* **1.** to exercise (power, authority, influence, etc.), as in ruling or dominating. **2.** to manage (a weapon, instrument, etc.) in use; handle or employ in action.

wife /waɪf/ *n.* (*pl.* **wives** /waɪvz/) a woman joined in marriage to another person.

wi-fi /ˈwaɪ-faɪ/ *n.* a communications networking standard which is used to create high-speed wireless local area networks.

wig /wɪg/ *n.* an artificial covering of hair for the head, worn to conceal baldness, for disguise, theatricals, etc., or formerly as an ordinary head covering.

wiggle /ˈwɪgəl/ *v.i.* **1.** to move or go with short, quick, irregular movements from side to side; wriggle. –*v.t.* **2.** to cause to wiggle; move quickly and irregularly from side to side. –*n.* **3.** a wavy line. –**wiggly,** *adj.*

wigwam /ˈwɪgwɒm/ *n.* a Native American hut made of poles with bark, mats or skins laid over them.

wiki /ˈwɪki/ *n.* a website in which the contents are contributed and edited by visitors to the site.

wild /waɪld/ *adj.* **1.** living in a state of nature, as animals that have not been tamed or domesticated. **2.** growing or produced without cultivation or the care of humans, as plants, flowers, fruit, honey, etc. **3.** of unrestrained violence, fury, intensity, etc.; violent; furious. **4.** unrestrained, untrammelled, or unbridled. **5.** extravagant or fantastic. **6.** disorderly or dishevelled. **7.** *Colloq.* intensely eager or enthusiastic. –*adv.* **8.** in a wild manner; wildly. –*n.* **9.** (*oft. pl.*) an uncultivated, uninhabited, or desolate region or tract; a waste; a wilderness; a desert.

wildcard /ˈwaɪldkad/ *n.* **1.** a playing card to which the holder may assign the value of any other card. **2.** *Computers* a non-alphanumeric character used especially in searches to represent

any character or set of characters. **3.** *Sport* a player or team allowed into a competition without having to compete in qualifying matches. **4.** *Colloq.* a person whose behaviour in a particular scenario or situation cannot be predicted. –*adj.* **5.** of or relating to a wildcard: *a wildcard search; a wildcard entry.* Also, **wild-card, wild card.**

wildcat strike /ˈwaɪldkæt/ *n.* a strike which has not been called or sanctioned by officials of a trade union; unofficial strike.

wildebeest /ˈwɪldəbist/ *n.* (*pl.* **-beests** or, *especially collectively,* **-beest**) any of several African antelopes characterised by an oxlike head, curved horns, and a long, flowing tail; gnu.

wilderness /ˈwɪldənəs/ *n.* a wild region, as of forest or desert; a waste; a tract of land inhabited only by wild animals.

wildlife /ˈwaɪldlaɪf/ *n.* animals living in their natural habitat.

wile /waɪl/ *n.* a trick, artifice, or stratagem.

wilful /ˈwɪlfəl/ *adj.* **1.** willed, voluntary, or intentional. **2.** self-willed or headstrong.

will¹ /wɪl/ *v.* (*aux.*) **1.** am (is, are, etc.) about or going to (in future constructions, denoting in the first person promise or determination, in the second and third persons mere futurity). **2.** am (is, are, etc.) disposed or willing to. **3.** am (is, are, etc.) determined or sure to (used emphatically).

will² /wɪl/ *n.* **1.** the faculty of conscious and especially of deliberate action. **2.** the power of choosing one's own actions. **3.** wish or desire. **4.** purpose or determination, often hearty determination. **5.** disposition (good or ill) towards another. **6.** *Law* a legal declaration of a person's wishes as to the disposition of his or her (real) property, etc., after death, usually in writing. –*v.t.* (**willed, willing**) **7.** to give by will or testament; to bequeath or devise. **8.** to influence by exerting willpower. **9.** to purpose, determine on, or elect, by act of will.

willing /ˈwɪlɪŋ/ *adj.* **1.** disposed or consenting (without being particularly desirous). **2.** cheerfully consenting or ready.

willow /ˈwɪloʊ/ *n.* a tree or shrub with tough, pliable twigs or branches which are used for wickerwork, etc.

willpower /ˈwɪlpaʊə/ *n.* control over one's impulses and actions.

willy-willy /ˈwɪli-wɪli/ *n.* a strong wind that moves around in circles, often collecting dust, waste matter, etc.

wilt /wɪlt/ *v.i.* to become limp and drooping, as a fading flower; wither.

wily /ˈwaɪli/ *adj.* (**-lier, -liest**) crafty.

wimp /wɪmp/ *n. Colloq.* a weak, timorous and ineffectual person. –**wimpish,** *adj.*

wimple /ˈwɪmpəl/ *n.* a woman's headcloth drawn in folds about the chin, as worn by some nuns.

win /wɪn/ *v.* (**won, winning**) –*v.i.* **1.** (sometimes fol. by *out*) to succeed by striving or effort. **2.** to gain the victory. **3.** to be placed first in a race or the like. –*v.t.* **4.** to get by effort, as through labour, competition, or conquest. **5.** to gain (a prize, fame, etc.). **6.** to be successful in (a game, battle, etc.). –*n.* **7.** an act of winning; a success; a victory. **-winner,** *n.*

wince /wɪns/ *v.i.* (**winced, wincing**) to shrink, as in pain or from a blow; start; flinch.

winch /wɪntʃ/ *n.* the crank or handle of a revolving machine.

wind[1] /wɪnd/ *n.* **1.** air in natural motion, as along the earth's surface. **2.** any stream of air, as that produced by a bellows, a fan, etc. **3.** a hint or intimation. **4.** gas generated in the stomach and bowels. *-v.t.* **5.** to expose to wind or air. **6.** to deprive momentarily of breath, as by a blow. **-windy,** *adj.*

wind[2] /waɪnd/ *v.* (**wound, winding**) *-v.i.* **1.** to change direction; bend; turn; take a frequently bending course; meander. **2.** to have a circular or spiral course or direction. **3.** to proceed circuitously or indirectly. **4.** to undergo winding, or winding up. *-v.t.* **5.** to encircle or wreathe, as with something twined, wrapped, or placed about. **6.** (oft. fol. by *up*) to roll or coil (thread, etc.) into a ball or on a spool or the like. **7.** to twine, fold, wrap, or place about something. **8.** (oft. fol. by *up*) to adjust (a mechanism, etc.) for operation by some turning or coiling process. **9.** to make (one's or its) way in a winding or frequently bending course. *-phr.* **10. wind up,** to terminate or conclude (affairs, a business, etc.).

windbreak /'wɪndbreɪk/ *n.* a growth of trees, a structure of boards, or the like, serving as a shelter from the wind.

windcheater /'wɪntʃitə/ *n.* (*from trademark*) a fleecy-lined garment for the upper part of the body designed to give protection against the wind.

wind energy *n.* energy derived from the wind, as by wind turbines in a wind farm.

windfall /'wɪndfɔl/ *n.* an unexpected piece of good fortune.

wind farm *n.* an array of wind turbines set up in a windy location to produce electricity.

wind generator *n.* → **wind turbine**.

wind instrument *n.* a musical instrument sounded by the player's breath or any current of air.

windlass /'wɪndləs/ *n.* a device for raising weights, etc.

windmill /'wɪndmɪl, 'wɪn-/ *n.* a mill or machine, as for grinding or pumping, operated by the wind, usually by the wind acting on a set of arms, vanes, sails, or slats attached to a horizontal axis so as to form a vertical revolving wheel.

window /'wɪndoʊ/ *n.* **1.** an opening in the wall or roof of a building, the cabin of a boat, etc., for the admission of air or light, or both, commonly fitted with a frame in which are set movable sashes containing panes of glass. **2.** anything likened to a window in appearance or function, as a transparent section in an envelope, displaying the address. **3.** a boxed-off section of a visual display unit screen in which secondary text or information is shown.

windpipe /'wɪndpaɪp, 'wɪn-/ *n.* the trachea of an air-breathing vertebrate.

windscreen /'wɪndskrin, 'wɪn-/ *n.* the sheet of glass which forms the front window of a motor vehicle.

windsock /'wɪndsɒk, 'wɪn-/ *n.* a wind-direction indicator, installed at airports and elsewhere, consisting of an elongated truncated cone of textile material, flown from a mast.

windsurfer /'wɪndsɜfə/ (*from trademark*) *n.* **1.** → **sailboard**. **2.** someone who sailboards.

wind turbine *n.* a modern windmill, usually with blades designed like aeroplane wings, which drives a generator to produce electricity when wind turns the blades.

wine /waɪn/ *n.* the fermented juice of the grape, in many varieties (red, white, sweet, dry, still, sparkling, etc.) used as a beverage and in cookery, religious rites, etc.

wing /wɪŋ/ *n.* **1.** either of the two appendages, of most birds and bats, which are adapted for flight. **2.** either of two corresponding parts in certain flightless birds, such as emus and penguins. **3.** (in insects) one of the thin, flat, movable extensions from the back of the thorax by means of which the insects fly. **4.** a similar structure with which gods, angels, demons, etc., are thought to fly. **5.** *Aeronautics* that portion of a main supporting surface confined to one side of an aeroplane. **6.** *Archit.* a part of a building projecting on one side of, or subordinate to, a central or main part. **7.** (*pl.*) the insignia or emblem worn by a qualified pilot. **8. a.** *Aust. Rules* either of the two centre-line positions on each side of the centre. **b.** *Hockey, Rugby Football, Soccer, etc.* either of the two areas of the pitch near the touchline and ahead of the halfway line, known as the left and right wings respectively, with reference to the direction of the opposing goal. **c.** a player in one of these positions. **9.** *Theatre* the platform or space on the right or left of the stage proper. *-v.t.* **10.** to equip with wings. **11.** to enable to fly, move rapidly, etc.; lend speed or celerity to. **12.** to wound or disable (a bird, etc.) in the wing. **13.** to wound (a person) in an arm or other non-vital part. *-v.i.* **14.** to travel on or as on wings; fly; soar.

wink /wɪŋk/ *v.i.* **1.** to close and open the eyes quickly. **2.** (oft. fol. by *at*) to close and open one eye quickly as a hint or signal or with some sly meaning. **3.** to shine with little flashes of light, or twinkle. *-v.t.* **4.** to close and open (the eyes or an eye) quickly; execute or give (a wink). *-n.* **5.** the act of winking. **6.** the time required for winking once; an instant or twinkling.

winning /'wɪnɪŋ/ *adj.* **1.** being the one that won: *the winning runner.* **2.** causing a win: *the winning goal.* **3.** attractive or charming: *a winning smile.*

winnow /'wɪnoʊ/ *v.t.* **1.** to free (grain, etc.) from chaff, refuse particles, etc., by means of wind or driven air. **2.** to subject to some process of separating or distinguishing; analyse critically; sift.

winsome /'wɪnsəm/ *adj.* engaging or charming; winning.

winter /'wɪntə/ *n.* **1.** the coldest season of the year. **2.** a period like winter, as the last or final period of life, a period of decline, decay, inertia, dreariness, or adversity. *-adj.* **3.** of, relating to, or characteristic of winter. **4.** suitable for wear or use in winter. **-wintry,** *adj.*

win-win *adj.* of or relating to a situation in which both parties to a dispute can achieve a satisfactory outcome.

wipe /waɪp/ *v.t.* **1.** to rub lightly with or on a cloth, towel, paper, the hand, etc., in order to clean or dry. **2.** (usu. fol. by *away, off, out*, etc.) to remove by rubbing with or on something. **3.** to destroy or eradicate, as from existence or memory. –*n.* **4.** the action of wiping. –*phr.* **5. wipe out**, to destroy completely.

wire /waɪə/ *n.* **1.** a piece of slender, flexible metal, ranging from a thickness that can be bent by the hand only with some difficulty down to a fine thread, and usually circular in section. **2.** a length of such material used as a conductor of electricity, usually insulated in a flex. **3.** to furnish with a wire or wires. **4.** to install an electric system of wiring, as for lighting, etc.

wired /waɪəd/ *adj.* **1.** tied or affixed with a wire or wires. **2.** *Colloq.* equipped with a (sometimes hidden) recording device, as a person or a room. **3.** *Colloq.* (of a person) stimulated or excited, especially excessively as result of taking stimulants. **4.** *Colloq.* having up-to-date knowledge or awareness, especially with regard to modern technology.

wireless /waɪələs/ *adj.* **1.** having no wire. **2.** of or relating to any of various devices which are operated with or set in action by electromagnetic waves. **3.** of or relating to telecommunications technology which is independent of telephone lines, cables, etc. –*n.* **4.** a radio.

wireless broadband *n.* a system of delivery for high-speed wireless internet access and data network access over a wide area.

wire tap *n.* a telephone tap. See **tap²** (def. 3). Also, **wiretap**.

wiry /waɪəri/ *adj.* **(-rier, -riest)** lean and sinewy.

wisdom /wɪzdəm/ *n.* the quality or state of being wise; knowledge of what is true or right coupled with just judgement as to action; sagacity, prudence, or common sense.

wise /waɪz/ *adj.* **1.** having the power of discerning and judging properly as to what is true or right. **2.** possessed of or characterised by scholarly knowledge or learning; learned; erudite. **3.** having knowledge or information as to facts, circumstances, etc.

-wise an adverbial suffix denoting: **1.** position or direction: *lengthwise; clockwise*. **2.** reference to something specified, as in *How are things going workwise?*

wish /wɪʃ/ *v.t.* **1.** to want; desire. –*v.i.* **2.** to have a desire, longing, or yearning. –*n.* **3.** a distinct mental inclination towards the doing, obtaining, attaining, etc., of something; a desire, felt or expressed. **4.** that which is wished.

wishbone /wɪʃboʊn/ *n.* the forked bone in front of the breastbone in most birds.

wishy-washy /wɪʃi-wɒʃi/ *adj.* lacking in substantial qualities; without strength or force; weak, feeble, or poor.

wisp /wɪsp/ *n.* **1.** a handful or small bundle of straw, hay, or the like. **2.** anything small or thin, as a shred, bundle, or slip of something, sometimes used as a brush or whisk.

wisteria /wɪs'tɪəriə, wəs-/ *n.* a climbing shrub with handsome purple flowers.

wistful /wɪstfəl/ *adj.* **1.** pensive or melancholy. **2.** showing longing tinged with melancholy; regretful; sad.

wit /wɪt/ *n.* **1.** keen perception and cleverly apt expression of connections between ideas which may arouse pleasure and especially amusement. **2.** a person endowed with or noted for such wit. **3.** (*pl.*) mental faculties, or senses.

witch /wɪtʃ/ *n.* a person, especially a woman, who professes or is supposed to practise magic. –**witchery,** *n.* –**witchcraft,** *n.*

witchetty grub /wɪtʃəti/ *n.* any of various large, white, edible, wood-boring grubs that are the larvae of certain Australian moths and beetles.

with /wɪð, wɪθ/ *prep.* **1.** in the company of: *I will go with you.* **2.** in some particular relation to: *to mix water with milk.* **3.** showing agreement or similarity: *in harmony with him.* **4.** *Colloq.* understanding the thinking of: *Are you with me?* **5.** in the same direction as: *with the flow of traffic.* **6.** by the use or means of: *Cut it with a knife.* **7.** at the same time as: *I rise with the dawn.* **8.** against: *fighting with each other for years.* **9.** in the care or keeping of: *Leave it with me.*

with- limited prefixal use of *with*, separative or opposing, as in *withdraw, withstand.*

-with a suffix indicating conjunction.

withdraw /wɪð'drɔ, wɪθ-/ *v.* **(-drew, -drawn, -drawing)** –*v.t.* **1.** to draw back or away; take back; remove. –*v.i.* **2.** to retire; retreat; go apart or away. **3.** to retract a statement or expression. –**withdrawal,** *n.*

wither /wɪðə/ *v.i.* **1.** to shrivel; fade; decay. –*v.t.* **2.** to make flaccid, shrunken, or dry, as from loss of moisture; cause to lose freshness, bloom, vigour, etc.

withers /wɪðəz/ *pl. n.* the highest part of a horse's or other animal's back, behind the neck.

withhold /wɪð'hoʊld, wɪθ-/ *v.t.* **(-held, -holding)** **1.** to hold back; restrain or check. **2.** to refrain from giving or granting. –**withholder,** *n.*

withholding tax *n.* that part of one's tax liability withheld by the employer, and paid directly to the government.

within /wɪð'ɪn, wɪθ-/ *adv.* **1.** in or into the interior or inner part, or inside. –*prep.* **2.** in or into the interior of or the parts or space enclosed by. **3.** at or to some amount or degree not exceeding.

without /wɪð'aʊt, wɪθ-/ *prep.* **1.** not with; with no; with absence, omission, or avoidance of; lacking (as opposed to *with*). **2.** beyond the compass, limits, range, or scope of (now used chiefly in opposition to *within*).

withstand /wɪð'stænd, wɪθ-/ *v.* **(-stood, -standing)** –*v.t.* **1.** to stand or hold out against; resist or oppose, especially successfully. –*v.i.* **2.** to stand in opposition.

witness /wɪtnəs/ *v.t.* **1.** to see or know by personal presence and perception. **2.** to be present at (an occurrence) as a formal witness or otherwise. –*n.* **3.** someone who, being present, personally sees or perceives a thing; a beholder, spectator, or eyewitness. **4.** a person or thing that affords evidence. **5.** someone who gives testimony, as in a court of law.

6. someone who signs a document in attestation of the genuineness of its execution.

witticism /'wɪtəsɪzəm/ *n.* a witty remark.

witty /'wɪti/ *adj.* (**-tier, -tiest**) possessing wit in speech or writing; amusingly clever in perception and expression.

wives /waɪvz/ *n.* plural of **wife**.

wizard /'wɪzəd/ *n.* someone who professes to practise magic; a magician or sorcerer. **–wizardry,** *n.*

wizened /'wɪzənd/ *adj.* dried-up; withered; shrivelled.

wobbegong /'wɒbigɒŋ/ *n.* a shark with a flattened body and mottled skin.

wobble /'wɒbəl/ *v.i.* **1.** to incline to one side and to the other alternately, as a wheel, top, or other rotating body, when not properly balanced. **2.** to move unsteadily from side to side.

woe /woʊ/ *n.* grievous distress, affliction, or trouble. **–woeful,** *adj.*

woebegone /'woʊbəgɒn/ *adj.* beset with woe; mournful or miserable; affected by woe, especially in appearance.

wog[1] /wɒg/ *n. Colloq. (derog.)* a person of Mediterranean extraction, or of similar complexion and appearance.

wog[2] /wɒg/ *n. Colloq.* **1.** a germ, especially one leading to a minor disease such as a cold or a stomach upset. **2.** such a cold, stomach upset, etc. **3.** a small insect.

wok /wɒk/ *n.* a large, shallow, metal pan used especially in Chinese cookery.

woke /woʊk/ *v.* past tense of **wake**[1].

woken /'woʊkən/ *v.* past participle of **wake**[1].

wolf /wʊlf/ *n.* (*pl.* **wolves** /wʊlvz/) **1.** a large, wild carnivorous mammal of the dog family, highly social and hunting in packs; occupying a variety of habitats in Eurasia and North America. **2.** *Colloq.* a man who is boldly flirtatious or amorous towards many women. **–v.t. 3.** *Colloq.* to eat ravenously.

wolves /wʊlvz/ *n.* plural of **wolf**.

woman /'wʊmən/ *n.* (*pl.* **women** /'wɪmən/) **1.** a female human being (distinguished from *man*). **2.** an adult female person (distinguished from *girl*).

womanise /'wʊmənaɪz/ *v.i.* (of a man) to have numerous casual affairs; philander. Also, **womanize.**

womb /wuːm/ *n.* the uterus of the human female and some of the higher mammalian quadrupeds.

wombat /'wɒmbæt/ *n.* a large, heavily-built burrowing marsupial with short legs and a rudimentary tail, found throughout Australia.

women /'wɪmən/ *n.* plural of **woman**.

women's business *n.* **1.** (in Aboriginal societies) matters, especially cultural traditions, which are the exclusive preserve of women, especially ceremonies which are only open to women. **2.** subjects which women may prefer to discuss with other women rather than with men, especially medical matters relating to women, bodily functions, etc. **3.** *Colloq. (humorous)* activities seen to be especially favoured or understood by women. Also, **secret women's business.**

women's liberation *n.* the movement which seeks to free women from sexist discrimination and make available to them the opportunity to play any role in society. Also, **women's lib.**

won /wʌn/ *v.* past tense and past participle of **win**.

wonder /'wʌndə/ *v.i.* **1.** to think or speculate curiously. **2.** (oft. fol. by *at*) to be affected with wonder; marvel. **–v.t. 3.** to be curious about; be curious to know (followed by a clause). **4.** to feel wonder at (now only followed by a clause as object). **–n. 5.** something strange and surprising; a cause of surprise, astonishment, or admiration. **6.** the emotion excited by what is strange and surprising; a feeling of surprised or puzzled interest, sometimes tinged with admiration.

wonderful /'wʌndəfəl/ *adj.* excellent; delightful; extremely good or fine.

wondrous /'wʌndrəs/ *adj.* wonderful.

wonky /'wɒŋki/ *adj.* (**-kier, -kiest**) *Colloq.* **1.** shaky; unsound. **2.** unwell; upset.

wont /woʊnt/ *adj.* **1.** accustomed; used: *he is wont to talk too much.* **–n. 2.** custom; habit; practice.

won't /woʊnt/ *v.* contraction of *will not*.

won ton /'wɒn tɒn/ *n.* a small ball of spicy pork wrapped in thin dough, usually boiled and served in soup in Chinese cooking. Also, **wonton.**

woo /wu/ *v.t.* **1.** to seek the favour, affection, or love of, especially with a view to marriage. **2.** to seek to win.

wood /wʊd/ *n.* **1.** the hard, fibrous substance composing most of the stem and branches of a tree or shrub, and lying beneath the bark. **2.** the trunks or main stems of trees as suitable for architectural and other purposes; timber or lumber. **3.** *Music* a wooden wind instrument. **4.** (oft. pl.) a large and thick collection of growing trees, usually less extensive than a forest. **5.** *Golf* a club with a wooden head. **6.** *Tennis, etc.* the frame part of a racquet, usually made of wood. **–adj. 7.** made of wood; wooden. **8.** used to cut, carve, or otherwise shape wood. **–v.t. 9.** to cover or plant with trees. **–woody,** *adj.*

woodchip /'wʊdtʃɪp/ *n.* **1.** (*pl.*) small pieces of wood, made by mechanically reducing trees to fragments for later industrial use. **–adj. 2.** of or relating to an industry, company, etc., which deals in woodchips. **–woodchipping,** *n.*

wooden /'wʊdn/ *adj.* **1.** consisting or made of wood. **2.** stiff, ungainly, or awkward. **3.** without spirit or animation.

woodpecker /'wʊdpekə/ *n.* a bird with a hard, chisel-like bill for boring into wood after insects.

woodpigeon /'wʊdpɪdʒən/ *n.* a large wild pigeon.

wood-turning /'wʊd-tɜnɪŋ/ *n.* the forming of wood articles upon a lathe.

woodwind /'wʊdwɪnd/ *n.* (sing., sometimes construed as pl.) the group of wind instruments which comprises the flutes, clarinets, oboes, and bassoons.

woodwork /'wʊdwɜk/ *n.* **1.** the interior wooden fittings of a house or the like. **2.** the art or craft of working in wood; carpentry.

woof[1] /wʊf/ *n.* yarns which travel from selvage to selvage in a loom, interlacing with the warp; weft.

woof[2] /wʊf/ *n.* the sound of a dog barking, especially deeply and loudly.

wool /wʊl/ n. **1.** a fibre produced from sheep's fleece or the like, that may be spun into yarn, or made into felt, upholstery materials, etc. **2.** any finely fibrous or filamentous matter suggestive of the wool of sheep.

wool clip n. the amount of wool yielded from the annual shearing season (by a station, district, etc.). Also, **clip**.

woollen /ˈwʊlən/ adj. made or consisting of wool.

woolly /ˈwʊli/ adj. (-lier, -liest) **1.** consisting of wool. **2.** resembling wool. **3.** not clear or firm, as thinking, expression, depiction, etc.; blurred, confused, or indistinct.

woolshed /ˈwʊlʃed/ n. a large shed for shearing and baling of wool.

woomera /ˈwʊmərə/ n. a type of throwing stick with a notch at one end for holding a dart or spear, thus giving increased leverage in throwing, traditionally used by Aboriginal people. Also, **womera**.

woozy /ˈwuzi/ adj. (-zier, -ziest) Colloq. **1.** muddled, or stupidly confused. **2.** out of sorts physically, as with dizziness, nausea, or the like.

word /wɜd/ n. **1.** a sound or a combination of sounds, or its written or printed representation, used in any language as the sign of a concept. **2.** a speech element which signifies; a term used to describe or refer. **3.** (pl.) contentious or angry speech; a quarrel. **4.** warrant, assurance, or promise. **5.** intelligence or tidings. **6.** Computers a unit of information, usually consisting of a number or of a group of alphanumeric characters, in the memory of a computer. –v.t. **7.** to express in words, or phrase; select words to express.

wordbreak /ˈwɜdbreɪk/ n. the point of division in a word which runs over from one line to the next.

word cloud n. a digital design produced by randomising selected words to form a pattern of text.

word processor n. a computer application designed for storing, editing and basic typesetting of text. –**word processing**, n.

word wrap n. Computers the automatic formatting of lines of text to fit into a computer screen.

wordy /ˈwɜdi/ adj. (-dier, -diest) characterised by or given to the use of many, or too many, words; verbose.

wore /wɔ/ v. past tense of **wear**.

work /wɜk/ n. **1.** exertion directed to produce or accomplish something; labour; toil. **2.** that on which exertion or labour is expended; something to be made or done; a task or undertaking. **3.** productive or operative activity. **4.** Physics the product of the force acting upon a body and the distance through which the point of application of force moves. The derived SI unit of work is the joule. **5.** employment; a job, especially that by which one earns a living. **6.** (pl. oft. construed as sing.) a place or establishment for carrying on some form of labour or industry. **7.** (pl.) Theology acts performed in obedience to the law of God, or righteous deeds. –v. (**worked** or, Archaic, **wrought**, **working**) –v.i. **8.** to do work, or labour; exert oneself (contrasted

with play). **9.** to be employed, as for one's livelihood. **10.** to be in operation, as a machine. **11.** to act or operate effectively. **12.** to get (round, loose, etc.), as if by continuous effort. **13.** to have an effect or influence, as on a person or on the mind or feelings. –v.t. **14.** to use or manage (an apparatus, contrivance, etc.) in operation. **15.** to operate (a mine, farm, etc.) for productive purposes. **16.** (fol. by in, off, out, or other completive words) to bring, put, get, render, etc., by work, effort, or action. **17.** to effect, accomplish, cause, or do. **18.** to make, fashion, or execute by work. **19.** to expend work on; manipulate or treat by labour. **20.** to arrange or contrive. **21.** (oft. fol. by up) to move, stir, or excite in feeling, etc. –phr. **22. work at**, to attempt to achieve or master (something) with application and energy. **23. work out, a.** to effect or achieve by labour. **b.** to solve (a problem) by a reasoning process. **c.** to cause to finish up, turn out, or culminate (satisfactorily, unless otherwise specified). **d.** to develop; elaborate. **e.** to undergo training or practice, especially intensively, as an athlete.

workable /ˈwɜkəbəl/ adj. practicable or feasible.

workaday /ˈwɜkədeɪ/ adj. humdrum.

worker /ˈwɜkə/ n. **1.** an employee, especially as contrasted with a manager or owner of a business. **2.** one employed in manual or industrial labour.

workers compensation n. payments by employers to employees as compensation for injuries incurred while engaged in the employers' business. Also, Colloq., **workers comp**.

workflow /ˈwɜkfloʊ/ n. the chain of events in a work process.

workforce /ˈwɜkfɔs/ n. the total of all those engaged in employment.

working class n. the class of people composed chiefly of manual workers and labourers; the proletariat.

working memory n. Computers a high-speed memory unit used to hold intermediate results during a calculation.

workload /ˈwɜkloʊd/ n. the amount of work done or to be done in a specified time.

workmanship /ˈwɜkmənʃɪp/ n. **1.** skill in working or execution. **2.** quality or mode of execution, as of a thing made.

work-out n. **1.** a trial match, race, etc. **2.** energetic physical exercise.

workplace /ˈwɜkpleɪs/ n. a place of employment.

workplace agreement n. a written formal agreement made between an employer and employees about pay and other employment conditions relating to a particular place of work.

work practice n. a procedure which is seen to be essential to the carrying out of a particular job.

workshop /ˈwɜkʃɒp/ n. **1.** a room or building in which work, especially mechanical work, is carried on (considered as smaller than a factory). **2.** a group meeting to exchange ideas and study techniques, skills, etc.: a theatre workshop. –v.t. (**workshopped**, **workshopping**) **3.** to revise (a theatre piece, television show, etc.) in collaboration with others, while reading or performing a provisional script.

workstation /'wɔksteɪʃən/ n. an area in an office which is assigned to a user of electronic equipment such as a computer terminal, etc. Also, **work station**.

work-to-rule n. → **go-slow**. Also, **work-to-regulation**.

world /wɜld/ n. **1.** the earth or globe. **2.** a particular section of the world's inhabitants. **3.** humankind; humanity. **4.** a particular class of humankind, with common interests, aims, etc. **5.** any sphere, realm, or domain, with all that pertains to it. **6.** the entire system of created things; the universe.

world-class adj. sufficiently good to be acceptable anywhere in the world. Also, **worldclass**.

worldly /'wɜldli/ adj. (**-lier, -liest**) **1.** experienced or knowledgeable about human affairs; sophisticated. **2.** earthly or mundane (as opposed to *heavenly, spiritual,* etc.). **3.** devoted to, directed towards, or connected with the affairs, interests, or pleasures of this world. **4.** secular (as opposed to *ecclesiastic, religious,* etc.). –adv. **5.** in a worldly manner. **–worldliness,** n.

world music n. the popular or folk music of different cultures and nationalities from around the world, outside the tradition of Western rock or pop music.

world-weary adj. weary of the world or of existence and its pleasures; blasé.

World Wide Web n. → **web²**. *Abbrev.:* www Also, **the Web**.

worm /wɜm/ n. **1.** Zool. a long, slender, soft-bodied invertebrate. **2.** something resembling or suggesting a worm in appearance, movement, etc. **3.** a grovelling, abject, or contemptible person. **4.** (pl.) any disease or disorder arising from the presence of parasitic worms in the intestines or other tissues. **5.** Computers a rogue program which, once it is loaded on a computer, replicates itself until it takes up all the available memory, bringing the whole system to a standstill. –v.i. **6.** to move or act like a worm; creep, crawl, or advance slowly or stealthily. –v.t. **7.** to make, cause, bring, etc., along by creeping or crawling, or by stealthy or devious advances.

worn /wɔn/ v. **1.** past participle of **wear**. –adj. **2.** impaired by wear or use. **3.** Also, **worn out**. wearied or exhausted. **–wornness,** n.

worrisome /'wʌrɪsəm, 'wɒrɪsəm/ adj. worrying, annoying, or disturbing; causing worry.

worry /'wʌri, 'wɒri/ v. (**-ried, -rying**) –v.i. **1.** to feel uneasy or anxious; fret; torment oneself with or suffer from disturbing thoughts. –v.t. **2.** to cause to feel uneasy or anxious; trouble; torment with annoyances, cares, anxieties, etc.; plague, pester, or bother. **3.** to harass by repeated biting, snapping, etc. –n. (pl. **-ries**) **4.** worried condition or feeling; uneasiness or anxiety. **5.** a cause of uneasiness or anxiety; a trouble.

worse /wɜs/ adj. **1.** bad or ill in a greater or higher degree; inferior in excellence, quality, or character. –n. **2.** that which is worse. –adv. **3.** in a more disagreeable, evil, wicked, severe, or disadvantageous manner. **4.** with more severity, intensity, etc.; in a greater degree. **5.** in a less effective manner.

worship /'wɜʃəp/ n. **1.** reverent honour and homage paid to God, a god, or a sacred personage, or to any object regarded as sacred. **2.** adoring reverence or regard. **3.** (with *your, his,* etc.) a title of honour used in addressing or mentioning certain magistrates and others of rank or station. –v.t. (**-shipped, -shipping**) **4.** to render religious reverence and homage to.

worst /wɜst/ adj. **1.** bad or ill in the greatest or highest degree. **2.** most faulty, unsatisfactory, or objectionable. –n. **3.** that which or someone who is worst or the worst part. –adv. **4.** in the most evil, wicked, or disadvantageous manner. **5.** with the most severity, intensity, etc.; in the greatest degree. **6.** in the least satisfactory, complete or effective manner.

worsted /'wʊstəd/ n. (cloth woven from) a type of woollen yarn.

wort /wɜt/ n. a plant; herb.

worth /wɜθ/ adj. **1.** good or important enough to justify (what is specified). **2.** having a value of, or equal in value to, as in money. –n. **3.** excellence of character or quality as commanding esteem. **4.** usefulness or importance, as to the world, to a person, or for a purpose. **5.** value, as in money. **6.** a quantity of something, of a specified value.

worthwhile /wɜθ'waɪl/ adj. such as to repay one's time, attention, interest, work, trouble, etc.

worthy /'wɜði/ adj. (**-thier, -thiest**) **1.** of adequate merit or character. **2.** (oft. fol. by *of*) deserving.

would /wʊd/, *weak forms* /wəd, d/ v. past tense of **will¹** used: **1.** specially in expressing a wish: *I would it were true.* **2.** often in place of *will,* to make a statement or question less direct or blunt.

would-be /'wʊd-bi/ adj. **1.** wishing or pretending to be. **2.** intended to be.

wouldn't /'wʊdənt/ v. contraction of *would not.*

wound¹ /wund/ n. **1.** an injury to an organism due to external violence or some mechanical agency rather than disease. –v.t. **2.** to inflict a wound upon; injure; hurt.

wound² /waʊnd/ v. past tense and past participle of **wind²**.

wove¹ /woʊv/ v. past tense and occasional past participle of **weave¹**.

wove² /woʊv/ v. a past tense and past participle of **weave²**.

woven /'woʊvən/ v. past participle of **weave¹**.

wow /waʊ/ interj. Colloq. (an exclamation of surprise, wonder, pleasure, dismay, etc.).

wow factor n. Colloq. a quality of a product, person, entertainment, etc., which excites instant admiration.

wowser /'waʊzə/ n. Colloq. a prudish teetotaller; a killjoy.

wraith /reɪθ/ n. a visible spirit.

wrangle /'ræŋgəl/ v.i. to argue or dispute, especially in a noisy or angry manner.

wrap /ræp/ v.t. (**wrapped** or **wrapt, wrapping**) **1.** (oft. fol. by *up*) to enclose, envelop, or muffle in something wound or folded about. **2.** to wind, fold, or bind (something) about as a covering. **3.** to surround, envelop or shroud. –n. **4.** something to be wrapped about the person, especially in addition to the usually indoor clothing, as a shawl, scarf, or mantle.

–phr. **5. wrap up,** *Colloq.* to conclude or settle.

wrapped /ræpt/ *adj. Colloq.* enthused (about).

wrasse /ræs/ *n.* (*pl.* **wrasse** or **wrasses**) any of various marine fishes, having thick, fleshy lips, powerful teeth, and usually a brilliant colour.

wrath /roθ/, *Orig. US* /ræθ/ *n.* strong, stern, or fierce anger; deeply resentful indignation; ire.

wreak /rik/ *v.t.* to inflict or execute (vengeance, etc.).

wreath /riθ/ *n.* (*pl.* **wreaths** /riðz/) something twisted or bent into a circular form; a circular band of flowers, foliage, or any ornamental work.

wreathe /rið/ *v.t.* **1.** to encircle or adorn with or as with a wreath or wreaths. **2.** to surround in curving or curling masses or form.

wreck /rɛk/ *n.* **1.** a vessel in a state of ruin from disaster at sea, on rocks, etc. **2.** the ruin or destruction of anything. *–v.t.* **3.** to cause the wreck of (a vessel), as in navigation; shipwreck. **4.** to cause the ruin or destruction of; spoil. **–wreckage,** *n.*

wren /rɛn/ *n.* a small bird with long legs and a long, almost upright tail.

wrench /rɛntʃ/ *v.t.* **1.** to twist suddenly and forcibly; pull, jerk, or force by a violent twist. *–n.* **2.** a wrenching movement; a sudden, violent twist. **3.** a sharp, distressing strain, as to the feelings, especially on parting or separation. **4.** a spanner.

wrest /rɛst/ *v.t.* **1.** to twist or turn; pull, jerk, or force by a violent twist. **2.** to take away by force.

wrestle /ˈrɛsəl/ *v.i.* **1.** to engage in wrestling. **2.** to contend, as in a struggle for mastery; grapple.

wrestling /ˈrɛslɪŋ/ *n.* an exercise or sport in which two persons struggle hand to hand, each striving to throw or force the other to the ground.

wretch /rɛtʃ/ *n.* a deplorably unfortunate or unhappy person.

wretched /ˈrɛtʃəd/ *adj.* very unfortunate in condition or circumstances; miserable; pitiable.

wrick /rɪk/ *v.t.* to wrench or strain.

wriggle /ˈrɪgl/ *v.i.* to twist to and fro, writhe, or squirm.

wring /rɪŋ/ *v.t.* (**wrung**) **1.** to twist forcibly, as something flexible. **2.** (oft. fol. by *out*) to twist and compress, or compress without twisting, in order to force out moisture. **3.** to clasp (one's hands) together, as in grief, etc.

wrinkle /ˈrɪŋkəl/ *n.* **1.** a ridge or furrow on a surface, due to contraction, folding, rumpling, or the like; corrugation; slight fold; crease. *–v.t.* **2.** to form a wrinkle or wrinkles in; corrugate; crease.

wrist /rɪst/ *n.* the part of the arm between the forearm and the hand.

writ /rɪt/ *n. Law* a formal order under seal, issued in the name of a sovereign, government, court, etc.

write /raɪt/ *v.* (**wrote, written, writing**) *–v.t.* **1.** to express or communicate in writing; give a written account of. **2.** to compose and produce in words or characters duly set down. **3.** to produce as author or composer. **4.** *Computers* to store (information) on a medium, such as magnetic tape or disk. *–v.i.* **5.** to trace or form characters, words, etc., with a pen, pencil, or other instrument or means, or as a pen or the like does. **6.** to be a writer, journalist, or author for one's living. **7.** to write a letter or letters, or communicate by letter. *–phr.* **8. write down,** *Commerce* to reduce the book value of. **9. write off,** to cancel, as an entry in an account, as by an offsetting entry. **10. write up,** *Accounting* to make an excessive valuation of (an asset). **–writer,** *n.*

write-off *n.* **1.** *Accounting* something written off from the books. **2.** *Colloq.* something irreparably damaged.

write-up *n.* a written description or account, as in a newspaper or magazine.

writhe /raɪð/ *v.i.* to twist the body about, or squirm, as in pain, violent effort, etc.

wrong /rɒŋ/ *adj.* **1.** not in accordance with what is morally right or good. **2.** deviating from truth or fact; erroneous. **3.** not correct in action, judgement, opinion, method, etc., as a person; in error. **4.** not suitable or appropriate. *–n.* **5.** that which is wrong, or not in accordance with morality, goodness, justice, truth, or the like; evil. **6.** an unjust act; injury. *–adv.* **7.** in a wrong manner; not rightly; awry or amiss. *–v.t.* **8.** to do wrong to; treat unfairly or unjustly; injure or harm. **9.** to impute evil to unjustly. **–wrongly,** *adv.*

wrongdoing /ˈrɒŋduɪŋ/ *n.* blameworthy action; evil behaviour.

wrong-foot *v.t.* **1.** (in various sports, as football, tennis, etc.) to trick (an opponent) into moving the wrong way. **2.** to catch unprepared: *to wrong-foot the opposition in the campaign.*

wrought /rɔt/ *v.* **1.** *Archaic* a past tense and past participle of **work.** *–adj.* **2.** fashioned or formed; resulting from or having been subjected to working or manufacturing. **3.** produced or shaped by beating with a hammer, etc., as iron or silver articles. **4.** ornamented or elaborated. **5.** not rough or crude.

wrung /rʌŋ/ *v.* past tense and past participle of **wring.**

wry /raɪ/ *adj.* (**wryer** or **wrier, wryest** or **wriest**) **1.** produced by the distortion of the facial features, usually to indicate dislike, dissatisfaction, or displeasure. **2.** ironically or bitterly amusing. **3.** abnormally bent or turned to one side; twisted or crooked. **4.** devious in course or purpose; misdirected. **5.** distorted or perverted, as in meaning.

wuss /wʊs/ *n. Colloq.* an overly timid or ineffectual person, especially a male; wimp.

WYSIWYG /ˈwɪziwɪg/ *n.* a computer system which displays text and images on screen exactly as it will appear in printed output. Also, **what-you-see-is-what-you-get.**

X, x

X, x /ɛks/ *n.* **1.** the 24th letter of the English alphabet. **2.** a term often used to designate a person, thing, agency, factor, or the like, whose true name is unknown or withheld.

xanthorrhoea /zænθəˈriə/ *n.* an Australian plant with a ring of spiky leaves at the base of a stocky trunk.

xeno- a word element meaning 'alien', 'strange', 'foreign'.

xenon /ˈzinɒn/ *n.* a heavy, colourless, chemically unreactive gaseous element. *Symbol:* Xe

xenophobia /zɛnəˈfoʊbiə/ *n.* fear or hatred of foreigners.

xero- a word element meaning 'dry'.

xerography /zɪəˈrɒgrəfi/ *n.* a method of photographic copying. **–xerograph**, *n.* **–xerographic**, *adj.*

xerox /ˈzɪərɒks/ *(from trademark)* **–***n.* **1.** a xerographic process. **2.** a copy obtained by this process. **–***v.t.*, *v.i.* **3.** to obtain copies (of) by this process.

X generation *n.* → **generation X**.

-xion variant of **-tion**.

XL /ɛks ˈɛl/ *adj.* (in clothing sizes) extra large.

Xmas /ˈɛksməs, ˈkrɪsməs/ *n.* Christmas.

XML /ɛks ɛm ˈɛl/ *n.* extensible markup language; a computer markup language designed especially for the creation of documents for the internet, comprising a simplified version of SGML which enables users to create customised tags for various types of data.

X-ray /ˈɛks-reɪ/ *n.* **1.** (*oft. pl.*) *Physics* electromagnetic radiation of shorter wavelength than light, which is able to penetrate solids, expose photographic plates, etc. **2.** a picture produced by the action of X-rays. **–***v.t.* **3.** to examine by means of X-rays.

xylo- a word element meaning 'wood'.

xylophone /ˈzaɪləfoʊn/ *n.* a musical instrument consisting of a graduated series of wooden bars, usually sounded by striking with small wooden hammers.

Y, y

Y, y /waɪ/ *n.* the 25th letter of the English alphabet.

-y¹ a suffix of adjectives meaning 'characterised by or inclined to' the substance or action of the word or stem to which the suffix is attached, as in *juicy, dreamy, chilly.* Also, **-ey**.

-y² a diminutive suffix, often affectionate, common in names, as in *Billy, pussy.* Also, **-ey, -ie**.

-y³ a suffix forming action nouns from verbs, as in *inquiry,* also found in other abstract nouns, as *carpentry, infamy.*

yabber /ˈjæbə/ *Colloq. –v.i.* **1.** to talk; converse. *–n.* **2.** talk; conversation.

yabby /ˈjæbi/ *n.* an Australian freshwater crayfish.

yacht /jɒt/ *n.* a sailing vessel used for private cruising, racing, or other like non-commercial purposes.

yahoo /ˈjahu, jaˈhu/ *n.* **1.** a rough, coarse, or uncouth person. *–v.i.* **2.** (fol. by *around*) to behave in a rough, uncouth manner. *–interj.* **3.** an exclamation expressing enthusiasm or delight.

yak¹ /jæk/ *n.* a long-haired, hollow-horned, wild ruminant.

yak² /jæk/ *v.i.* (**yakked, yakking**) to talk or chatter, especially pointlessly and continuously.

yakka /ˈjækə/ *n. Colloq.* work. Also, **yacker, yacka, yakker**.

yam /jæm/ *n.* the starchy, tuberous root of certain climbing vines.

yank /jæŋk/ *Colloq. –v.t., v.i.* **1.** to pull or move with a sudden jerking motion; tug sharply. *–n.* **2.** a jerk or tug.

yap /jæp/ *v.i.* (**yapped, yapping**) **1.** to yelp; bark snappishly. **2.** *Colloq.* to talk snappishly, noisily, or foolishly.

yard¹ /jad/ *n.* **1.** a unit of length in the imperial system, equal to about 91 centimetres. **2.** *Naut.* a long cylindrical spar slung crosswise to a mast and suspending a sail.

yard² /jad/ *n.* **1.** a piece of enclosed ground for use as a garden, for animals, or for some other purpose. **2.** an enclosure within which any work or business is carried on.

yardarm /ˈjadam/ *n.* either end of a yard of a square sail.

yardstick /ˈjadstɪk/ *n.* any standard of measurement.

yarmulke /ˈjamʊlkə/ *n.* a skullcap traditionally worn by Jewish males, especially in synagogue.

yarn /jan/ *n.* **1.** thread made by twisting fibres, as nylon, cotton or wool, and used for knitting and weaving. **2.** *Colloq.* a story or tale of adventure, especially a long one about incredible events. **3.** a talk, chat. *–v.i.* **4.** *Colloq.* to tell stories. **5.** to talk, chat.

yaw /jɔ/ *v.i.* **1.** to deviate temporarily from the straight course, as a ship. **2.** (of an aircraft, rocket, etc.) to have a motion about its vertical axis.

yawn /jɔn/ *v.i.* **1.** to open the mouth involuntarily with a prolonged, deep intake of breath,

as from drowsiness or weariness. **2.** to open wide like a mouth. *–n.* **3.** the act of yawning.

ye /ji/ *pron. Archaic* you (especially plural).

yea /jeɪ/ *interj.* yes.

yeah /jeə/ *adv. Colloq.* yes.

year /jɪə/ *n.* **1.** a period of 365 or 366 days, divided into 12 calendar months, based on the Gregorian calendar and now reckoned as beginning 1 January and ending 31 December (**calendar year**). **2.** a space of 12 calendar months reckoned from any point. **3.** the true period of the earth's revolution round the sun. **4.** a full round of the seasons. **5.** a level or grade in an academic program, usually indicating one full year's study. **6.** (*pl.*) age, especially of a person. **7.** (*pl.*) time, especially a long time.

yearling /ˈjɪəlɪŋ/ *n.* an animal one year old or in the second year of its age.

yearly /ˈjɪəli/ *adj.* **1.** relating to a year, or to each year. **2.** done, made, happening, appearing, coming, etc., once a year, or every year. *–adv.* **3.** once a year; annually. *–n.* (*pl.* **-lies**) **4.** a publication appearing once a year.

yearn /jɜn/ *v.i.* to have an earnest or strong desire; long.

yeast /jist/ *n.* a substance consisting of the aggregated cells of certain minute fungi, used to induce fermentation in the manufacture of alcoholic drink, especially beer, and as a leaven to make bread, light and spongy, and also used in medicine.

yell /jɛl/ *v.i.* **1.** to cry out with a strong, loud, clear sound. *–n.* **2.** a cry uttered by yelling.

yellow /ˈjɛloʊ/ *adj.* **1.** of a bright colour like that of butter, lemons, etc.; between green and orange in the spectrum. **2.** *Colloq.* cowardly; mean or contemptible. **3.** *Colloq.* (of newspapers, etc.) sensational, especially morbidly or offensively sensational. *–n.* **4.** a hue between green and orange in the spectrum.

yellowcake /ˈjɛloʊkeɪk/ *n.* uranium oxide in an unprocessed form, which has low radioactivity.

yellow card *n. Sport* a yellow card shown by the referee to a player who has committed a foul as an indication that the player has been cautioned. Compare **red card**.

yellow fever *n.* a dangerous, often fatal, infectious febrile disease.

yellow pages *pl. n.* (*sometimes construed as sing.*) (*from trademark*) a telephone directory listing businesses, professional people, organisations, etc.

yelp /jɛlp/ *v.i.* **1.** to give a quick, sharp, shrill cry, as dogs, foxes, etc. *–n.* **2.** a quick, sharp bark or cry.

yen /jɛn/ *n.* desire; longing.

yep /jɛp/ *interj. Colloq.* → **yes**.

yes /jɛs/ *interj.* **1.** (used to express affirmation or assent). *–n.* (*pl.* **yeses**) **2.** an affirmative reply.

yesterday /ˈjɛstədeɪ, -di/ *adv.* **1.** on the day preceding this day. *–n.* **2.** the day preceding this day.

yet /jɛt/ *adv.* **1.** at the present time. **2.** up to a particular time, or thus far. **3.** in the time still remaining, or before all is done. **4.** now or then as previously; still. **5.** in addition, or again. **6.** moreover. **7.** even or still (with comparatives). **8.** though the case be such;

nevertheless. *—conj.* **9.** and yet; but yet; nevertheless.

yew /juː/ *n.* an evergreen coniferous tree with thick, dark foliage.

Y generation *n.* → generation Y.

yield /jiːld/ *v.t.* **1.** to give forth or produce by a natural process or in return for cultivation. **2.** to produce or furnish as payment, profit, or interest. **3.** to give up, as to superior power or authority. *—v.i.* **4.** to give a return, as for labour expended; produce or bear. **5.** to give way to influence, entreaty, argument, or the like. **6.** the action of yielding or producing. **7.** that which is yielded. **8.** the quantity or amount yielded. **9.** *Stock Exchange* dividend return on investment outlay, usually expressed as a percentage.

yiros /ˈjɪərɒs/ *n.* a Greek dish consisting of slices of meat, usually cut from a vertical spit, rolled in pita bread with salad. Also, **yeeros**.

yobbo /ˈjɒboʊ/ *n. Colloq.* **1.** an unrefined, uncultured, slovenly young man. **2.** a hooligan or lout: *football yobbos.* Also, **yob**.

yodel /ˈjoʊdl/ *v.i.* (**-delled** *or, Chiefly US,* **-deled, -delling** *or, Chiefly US,* **-deling**) to sing with frequent changes from the natural voice to falsetto and back again.

yoga /ˈjoʊɡə/ *n.* any of various systems of discipline in the Hindu philosophical system concerned with achieving the union of the mind and body with the Universal Spirit, employing practices such as physical control of the body through the use of special movements or postures, etc.

yoghurt /ˈjoʊɡət, ˈjɒɡət/ *n.* a prepared food of custard-like consistency, sometimes sweetened or flavoured, made from milk that has been curdled by the action of enzymes or other cultures. Also, **yogurt, yoghourt**.

yogi /ˈjoʊɡi/ *n.* (*pl.* **-gis** /-ɡiz/) someone who practises yoga.

yoke /joʊk/ *n.* **1.** a contrivance for joining a pair of draught animals, especially oxen, for pulling a cart, etc. **2.** something resembling a yoke in form or use. **3.** a shaped piece in a garment from which the rest of the garment hangs. *—v.t.* **4.** to put a yoke on.

yokel /ˈjoʊkəl/ *n.* a country person or rustic.

yolk /joʊk/ *n.* the yellow and principal substance of an egg, as distinguished from the white.

yonder /ˈjɒndə/ *adj.* **1.** being the more distant, or farther. **2.** being in that place or over there, or being that or those over there. *—adv.* **3.** at, in, or to that place (specified or more or less distant); over there.

yonks /jɒŋks/ *n. Colloq.* a long time.

yore /jɔː/ *n.* time long past, now only in the phrase of yore.

you /juː/ *weak form* /jə/ *pron.* **1.** the personal pronoun used to refer to the person or people

spoken to. **2.** one; anyone; people in general: *It really makes you mad when you hear that kind of thing.*

you'd /juːd/ *weak form* /jəd/ contraction of *you had* or *you would.*

you'll /juːl/ *weak form* /jəl/ contraction of *you will* or *you shall.*

young /jʌŋ/ *adj.* **1.** being in the first or early stage of life, or growth; youthful; not old. **2.** of or relating to youth. **3.** not far advanced in years in comparison with another or others. *—n.* **4.** young offspring. **5.** young people collectively.

youngster /ˈjʌŋstə/ *n.* a young person.

your /jɔː/ *pron.* **1.** the possessive form of **you**, **ye**, used before a noun. **2.** (used to indicate all members of a particular group): *your typical suburban house.* Compare **yours**.

you're /jɔː/ contraction of *you are.*

yours /jɔːz/ *pron.* **1.** the possessive form of **you** used without a noun following: *That book is yours.* **2.** the person(s) or thing(s) belonging to you: *Yours is the plate on the left.*

yourself /jɔːˈsɛlf/ *pron.* (*pl.* **-selves**) **1.** a reflexive form of **you** (singular): *You've cut yourself.* **2.** a form of **you** (singular) used for emphasis: *You did it yourself.* **3.** your proper or normal self.

yourselves /jɔːˈsɛlvz, jəˈsɛlvz/ *pron.* **1.** the reflexive form of **you** (plural): *Have you both washed yourselves?* **2.** a form of **you** (plural) used for emphasis: *You've done it all yourselves.*

youth /juːθ/ *n.* **1.** (*pl.* **youths**) a young man: *a long-haired youth.* **2.** young people collectively: *The youth of this town need more facilities.* **3.** the condition of being young: *Youth would be an advantage in this job.* **4.** the time of being young: *He was a boxer in his youth.* **5.** the first or early period of anything. *—youthful, adj.*

you've /juːv/ contraction of *you have.*

yowl /jaʊl/ *v.i.* to utter a long distressful or dismal cry.

yo-yo /ˈjoʊ-joʊ/ *n.* (*pl.* **yo-yos**) (*from trademark*) a round toy with a groove round the edge, in which a string is wound by which it can be spun up and down. Also, **yoyo**.

yuck /jʌk/ *interj.* **1.** an expression of disgust. *—adj.* **2.** repulsive; disgusting. Also, **yuk**. *—yucky, yukky, adj.*

Yule /juːl/ *n.* Christmas, or the Christmas season.

yum cha /jʌm ˈtʃɑː/ *n.* a form of Chinese meal in which diners choose individual serves from selections arranged on trolleys.

yuppie /ˈjʌpi/ *n.* a young urban professional person, typified as having a good income and available cash to spend on luxury consumer goods. Also, **yuppy**.

Z, z

Z, z /zɛd/, *US* /ziː/ *n.* the 26th letter of the English alphabet.

zany /ˈzeɪmi/ *adj.* (**-nier**, **-niest**) **1.** extremely comical; clownish. **2.** slightly crazy; fantastic or ludicrous.

zeal /ziːl/ *n.* ardour for a person, cause, or object; eager desire or endeavour; enthusiastic diligence. **–zealous**, *adj.*

zealot /ˈzɛlət/ *n.* **1.** someone who displays zeal. **2.** someone carried away by excess of zeal. **3.** *Colloq.* a religious fanatic.

zebra /ˈzɛbrə/; *US*, *Brit. also* /ˈziːbrə/ *n.* a wild, horse-like animal, with regular black and white stripes over its entire body.

zebra crossing *n.* a crossing place on a road, marked with broad black and white stripes parallel to the kerb, and used by pedestrians.

zenith /ˈzɛnɪθ/ *n.* **1.** *Astron.* the point in the heavens vertically above any place or observer. **2.** any highest point or state; culmination. **–zenithal**, *adj.*

zephyr /ˈzɛfə/ *n.* a soft, mild breeze.

zeppelin /ˈzɛpəlɪn/ *n.* a large dirigible.

zero /ˈzɪəroʊ/ *n.* (*pl.* **-ros** *or* **-roes**) **1.** the figure or symbol 0, which stands for the absence of quantity. **2.** the origin of any kind of measurement; line or point from which all divisions of a scale (as a thermometer) are measured in either a positive or a negative direction. **3.** naught or nothing. **4.** the lowest point or degree. *–v.t.* (**-roed**, **-roing**) **5.** to adjust to a zero point. *–phr.* **6. zero in, a.** (fol. by *on*) to focus attention. **b.** (fol. by *on*) to arrive at a conclusion, etc., by a process of elimination.

zero tolerance *n.* the refusal to accept any criminal, antisocial, or other prohibited type of behaviour, usually manifested in very strict application of the law by police, etc. **–zero-tolerance**, *adj.*

zest /zɛst/ *n.* **1.** anything added to impart flavour or cause relish. **2.** an agreeable or piquant flavour imparted. **3.** piquancy, interest, or charm. *–v.t.* **4.** to give zest, relish, or piquancy to.

Z generation *n.* → **generation Z**.

zigzag /ˈzɪɡzæɡ/ *n.* a line, course, or progression characterised by sharp turns first to one side and then to the other.

zilch /zɪltʃ/ *n. Colloq.* nothing.

zinc /zɪŋk/ *n. Chem.* a bluish-white metallic element used in making alloys, and as a protective covering for roofs, etc. *Symbol:* Zn

zine /ziːn/ *n. Colloq.* a magazine, especially one about an alternative subculture, or one in electronic form published on the internet. Also, **zeen**, **'zine**.

zinnia /ˈzɪniə/ *n.* an annual plant with colourful flowers.

zip /zɪp/ **1.** Also, **zipper**, **zip-fastener**. a fastener consisting of an interlocking device set along two edges, which unites (or separates) them when an attached piece sliding between them is pulled, and used in place of buttons, hooks, etc. **2.** *Colloq.* energy or vim. *–v.i.* **3.** *Colloq.* to move with zip; hurry. **4.** to proceed with energy. *–v.* (**zipped**, **zipping**) *–v.t.* **5.** (fol. by *up*) to fasten with a zip. **6.** (**zipped**, **zipping**) *Computers* → **compress** (def. 2).

zip drive *n. Computers* a small portable disk drive used for backing up and archiving files.

zip file *n. Computers* a compressed version of a file. Also, (*in filenames*), **.zip**.

zircon /ˈzɜːkɒn/ *n.* a common mineral, transparent varieties of which are valued as a gem.

zit /zɪt/ *n. Colloq.* a pimple.

zither /ˈzɪðə/ *n.* a stringed musical instrument, played horizontally.

-zoa plural combining form naming zoological groups.

zodiac /ˈzoʊdiæk/ *n. Astron.* an imaginary belt of the heavens, containing twelve constellations and hence twelve divisions (called *signs*). **–zodiacal**, *adj.*

zombie /ˈzɒmbi/ *n.* **1.** a corpse supposedly brought to life by a supernatural force. **2.** (*derog.*) a person having no independent judgement, intelligence, etc. Also, **zombi**.

zone /zoʊn/ *n.* **1.** any continuous tract or area, which differs in some respect, or is distinguished for some purpose, from adjoining tracts or areas, or within which certain distinguishing circumstances exist or are established. **2.** an area or district under special restrictions or where certain conditions or circumstances prevail. *–v.t.* **3.** to divide into zones, according to existing characteristics, or for some purpose, use, etc. *–phr.* **4. in the zone**, *Colloq.* performing with effortless skill. **–zonal**, *adj.*

zoning /ˈzoʊnɪŋ/ *n.* the marking out of an area of land with respect to its use.

zoo /zuː/ *n.* a park or other large enclosure in which live animals are kept for public exhibition; a zoological garden.

zoo- a word element meaning 'living being'.

zoogamy /zoʊˈɒɡəmi/ *n.* sexual reproduction. **–zoogamous**, *adj.*

zooid /ˈzoʊɔɪd/ *n. Biol.* any organic body or cell which is capable of spontaneous movement and of an existence more or less apart from or independent of the parent organism.

zoological garden /zoʊəˈlɒdʒɪkəl/ *n.* (*oft. pl.*) a zoo.

zoology /zoʊˈɒlədʒi, zuˈ-/ *n.* **1.** the science that deals with animals or the animal kingdom. **2.** the animals existing in a particular region. **–zoologist**, *n.* **–zoological**, *adj.*

zoom /zuːm/ *v.i.* **1.** to make a continuous humming sound. **2.** to move with this speed. **3.** (of prices) to rise rapidly. **4.** *Film, TV, etc.* (oft. fol. by *in* or *out*) to use a lens which makes an object appear to approach or recede from the viewer.

zoophile /ˈzoʊəfaɪl/ *n.* someone who loves animals, especially someone who is opposed to vivisection or other such experimentation.

zot /zɒt/ *v.* (**zotted**, **zotting**) *Colloq.* *–v.i.* **1.** (usu. fol. by *off*) to depart quickly. *–v.t.* **2.** to knock, or kill.

zounds /zaʊndz, zʌndz/ *interj.* Archaic an emphatic exclamation, as of surprise, indignation, or anger.

zucchini /zəˈkiːni, zuˈ-/ *n.* (*pl.* **-ni** *or* **-nis**) a small vegetable marrow; courgette.

zygote /ˈzaɪɡoʊt, ˈzɪɡoʊt/ *n. Biol.* the cell produced by the union of two gametes. **–zygotic**, *adj.*

common abbreviations

A ampere
AA Alcoholics Anonymous
AAP Australian Associated Press
A'asia Australasia
AAT Australian Antarctic Territory; Administrative Appeals Tribunal
ABA Australian Broadcasting Authority
ABC Australian Broadcasting Corporation
ABN Australian Business Number
ABS Australian Bureau of Statistics
ac acre
AC alternating current
a/c account; air-conditioning
AC Companion of the Order of Australia
A/C account
ACA Australian Consumers' Association
ACCC Australian Competition and Consumer Commission
ACDST Australian Central Daylight Saving Time
ACN Australian Company Number
ACOSS Australian Council of Social Service
ACST Australian Central Standard Time
ACT Australian Capital Territory
ACTU Australian Council of Trade Unions
AD in the year of our Lord (Latin: *Anno Domini*)
ad lib. at pleasure; to the extent desired (Latin: *ad libitum*)
ad loc. at the place (Latin: *ad locum*)
Adm. Admiral
AEDST Australian Eastern Daylight Saving Time
AEST Australian Eastern Standard Time
AFC Australian Flying Corps; Australian Film Commission
AFI Australian Film Institute
AFL Australian Football League
AFP Australian Federal Police
aftn afternoon
AGM annual general meeting
a.h., AH after hours
AI artificial intelligence; artificial insemination; Amnesty International
AIATSIS Australian Institute of Aboriginal and Torres Strait Islander Studies
AIDC Australian Industry Development Corporation
AIF Australian Imperial Force
AIS Australian Institute of Sport
ALP Australian Labor Party
a.m. before noon (Latin: *ante meridiem*)
AM Member of the Order of Australia; (*Radio*) amplitude modulation
AMA Australian Medical Association
amt amount
ANC African National Congress
anon. anonymous
ANSTO Australian Nuclear Science and Technology Organisation
ANZAAS Australian and New Zealand Association for the Advancement of Science
ANZAC Australian and New Zealand Army Corps
ANZUS Australia, New Zealand and the United States (Security Treaty)

AO Officer of the Order of Australia
Ap., Apl, Apr. April
APEC Asia-Pacific Economic Cooperation (group)
approx. approximate; approximately
APRA Australasian Performing Right Association
ARA Australian Regular Army
arr. arranged; arrival; arrives; arrived
ASAP, a.s.a.p. as soon as possible
ASEAN Association of South-East Asian Nations
ASIC Australian Securities and Investments Commission
ASIO Australian Security Intelligence Organisation
ASIS Australian Secret Intelligence Service
Assn, assn association
assoc. associate; associated; association
asst assistant
ASX Australian Stock Exchange
atm standard atmosphere
at. no. atomic number
ATO Australian Taxation Office
attrib. attributed
at. wt atomic weight
AUD Australian dollar
Aug. August
Aus., Aust. Australia; Australian
Av., Ave Avenue
AV audio-visual
AWD all-wheel drive
AWL absent without leave
AWOL (*Chiefly US*) absent without leave
AWST Australian Western Standard Time

b. born; (*Cricket*) bowled; breadth; blend of; blended; bedroom; billion
BA building application; Bachelor of Arts
B & B bed and breakfast
B & W black and white
BAS Business Activity Statement
BBQ barbecue
BC Before Christ
bcc blind carbon copy; (in emails) blind courtesy copy
BCE Before the Common Era
b/d (*Accounting*) brought down
Bde Brigade
b/f (*Accounting*) brought forward
BH business hours
b.h.p. brake horsepower
bldg building
BLF Builders' Labourers Federation
Blvd, Boul. Boulevard
bps bits per second; bytes per second
BP Before Present (before 1950, in dating system used in geology, archaeology, etc.)
Brig. Brigadier
Brit. Britain; British
Bro. brother
Bros brothers
BSc Bachelor of Science
Btu British thermal unit
B/W black and white

c. cent; centigrade; century; (preceding dates) about (Latin: *circa*); (*Cricket*) caught
C Cape; Celsius; Centigrade; century; coulomb
C/– care of
ca about (Latin: *circa*)
cal. calibre; calorie
Cantab. of Cambridge (Latin: *Cantabrigiensis*)
Cap., Capt. Captain
CAT computerised axial tomography
CB citizen band (radio)
CBD Central Business District
cc cubic capacity; cubic centimetre(s); carbon copy; (in emails) courtesy copy
CCTV closed-circuit television
cd candela
c/d (*Accounting*) carried down
Cdr Commander
CDT Central Daylight Time
CE Common Era
cent. centigrade; central; century
CEO Chief Executive Officer
cert. certain; certificate; certified
cf. compare (Latin: *confer*)
c/f (*Accounting*) carried forward
CFC chlorofluorocarbon
CFO Chief Financial Officer
cg centigram
ch., chap. chapter
CIA (in the US) Central Intelligence Agency
CIB Criminal Investigation Branch; (in the UK) Criminal Investigation Bureau
C-in-C Commander-in-Chief
CID Criminal Investigation Department
circ. about (Latin: *circa*)
CIS Commonwealth of Independent States
cit. citation; cited (Latin: *citato*)
cl centilitre
CLC Central Land Council
cm centimetre
CM (metric) carat
CMF Citizen Military Forces
CMS content management system
CNG compressed natural gas
cnr corner
c/o care of
Co., Coy company
CO Commanding Officer
COB close of business
COD cash on delivery
C of E Church of England
Col. Colonel
Comm. Commonwealth
cont., contd continued
Corp. corporation; Corporal
CPA certified practising accountant; Communist Party of Australia
CPI Consumer Price Index
Cpl Corporal
CPO Chief Petty Officer
CPR cardiopulmonary resuscitation
CPU central processing unit
Cr Councillor
Cres. Crescent
c/s cycles per second
CSIRO Commonwealth Scientific and Industrial Research Organisation
CST Central Standard Time
cu. cubic
Cwlth, Cwth Commonwealth

CWA Country Women's Association
cwt hundredweight

d. daughter; density; diameter
DA development application
Dan. Danish
dB decibel
DC direct current; Double Certificated; (in the US) District of Columbia
Dec. December
dec. deceased
deg. degree
dep. departure; departs; departed; deposit
Dept, dept department
dip. diploma
Dip. Ed. Diploma of Education
DIY do-it-yourself
DMZ demilitarised zone
DNA deoxyribonucleic acid
DOB date of birth
DON Director of Nursing
DPP Director of Public Prosecutions
dpt department
Dr Doctor
Dr. Drive (in street names)
d.s.e. designated spouse equivalent
dup. duplicate
DST daylight saving time
DTV digital TV
DVI disaster victim identification
DX document exchange

E east; eastern
ea. each
EC European Community
ECG electrocardiogram; electrocardiograph
ECT electroconvulsive therapy
ed., edit. edited; edition; editor
EDT Eastern Daylight Time
EEG electroencephalogram; electroencephalograph
EEO Equal Employment Opportunity
EEZ Exclusive Economic Zone
EFL English as a foreign language
EFT electronic funds transfer
EFTPOS electronic funds transfer at point of sale
e.g. for example (Latin: *exempli gratia*)
EIA environmental impact assessment
EIS environmental impact statement
EMF, e.m.f. electromotive force
EMG electromyography
EN enrolled nurse
enc., encl. enclosed; enclosure
ENT (*Medicine*) ear, nose and throat
EPNS electroplated nickel silver
equiv. equivalent
ESL English as a second language
esp. especially
ESP extrasensory perception
Esq. Esquire
est. established; estimated
EST Eastern Standard Time
estab. established
ETA estimated time of arrival
et al. and others (Latin: *et alii*)
etc. and so on (Latin: *et cetera*)
ETD estimated time of departure
et seq. and that which follows (Latin: *et sequens*)
EU European Union
eV electronvolt

Exc. Excellency
excl. excluding; exclusive
exec. executive; executor
ex lib. from the library of (Latin: *ex libris*)

f. folio; following; franc; (*Music*) loud (Italian: *forte*)
f., fem. feminine, female
F Fahrenheit; farad
FAO Food and Agriculture Organisation
f.a.q. fair average quality
FAQ frequently asked question
FAS, f.a.s. free alongside ship
FBI (in the US) Federal Bureau of Investigation
FBT fringe benefits tax
Feb. February
ff folios; following; (*Music*) very loud (Italian: *fortissimo*)
FID financial institutions duty
fig. figure
figs figures
fl. flourished
fl dr fluid drachm
fl oz fluid ounce
Flt Lt Flight Lieutenant
FM (*Radio*) frequency modulation
FOB, f.o.b. free on board
FOI freedom of information
fol. folio; following
4WD four-wheel drive
Fr Father
Fr. Friday
freq. frequent; frequently
Fri., Frid. Friday
ft foot; feet
f.t. full-time
fur furlong
fwd forward
FYI for your information

g gram
G gigabyte; (*Film classification*) general viewing
gal. gallon
GATT General Agreement on Tariffs and Trade
GB gigabyte; Great Britain
Gdns Gardens
GDP Gross Domestic Product
gds goods
GE genetic engineering; genetically engineered
gen. general; genus; gender
Gen. (*Military*) General
G-G Governor-General
GHQ General Headquarters
GI glycaemic index
GM genetically-modified; General Manager
GMO genetically-modified organism
GMT Greenwich Mean Time
GNP Gross National Product
Gov. Governor
Govt, govt government
GP general practitioner
Gp Capt. Group Captain
GPO General Post Office
gr. wt gross weight
GST goods and services tax

h. height; hour
H henry
ha hectare
h.c.f. highest common factor

hcp handicap
hdqrs headquarters
h.f. high frequency
HFC hydrofluorocarbon; hydrogen fuel cell
HM Her (or His) Majesty
HMAS Her (or His) Majesty's Australian Ship
HO Head Office
Hon. honourable; honorary
hp horsepower
HQ headquarters
hr hour
HR human resources; House of Representatives
HRT hormone replacement therapy
HRH Her (or His) Royal Highness
HSC Higher School Certificate
Hts Heights
HTTP hypertext transfer protocol
hwy highway
Hz hertz

ibid. in the same place (Latin: *ibidem*)
i/c in charge; in command
IC integrated circuit
ICAC Independent Commission against Corruption
ICT information and communications technology
id. the same (Latin: *idem*)
ID identification
i.e. that is (Latin: *id est*)
illus. illustrated; illustration
ILO International Labour Organisation
IMF International Monetary Fund
imp. imperial; import
Imp. Emperor (Latin: *Imperator*); Empress (Latin: *Imperatrix*)
in inch
inc. included; including; inclusive; increase
Inc. Incorporated
inHg inch of mercury
in loc. cit. in the place cited (Latin: *in loco citato*)
Insp. Inspector
inst. in or of the present month
I/O input/output
IOU I owe you
IP intellectual property; internet protocol
IR industrial relations
IRC Industrial Relations Commission; internet relay chat
Is., is., isl Island; Isle
ISBN International Standard Book Number
ISD International Subscriber Dialling
ISP internet service provider
ISSN International Standard Serial Number
IT information technology
ital. italics
IU International Unit

J journal; joule; Judge; Justice
Jan., Ja. January
JBT Jervis Bay Territory
JI Jemaah Islamiah
Jn., Jun. June
jnr, jr junior
JP Justice of the Peace
Jul., Jl., Jy July

k kilometre; kilobyte
K thousand; kilometre; kilobyte; kelvin; king; Knight; (*Music*) Köchel
KB, Kb, kb kilobyte
kbps kilobits per second
kBps kilobytes per second
kbyte kilobyte
kg kilogram
kHz kilohertz
kJ kilojoule
KKK Ku Klux Klan
KL Kuala Lumpur
kL, kl kilolitre
km kilometre
km/h kilometres per hour
KO knockout
kPa kilopascal
k.p.h. kilometres per hour
Kt knight
kW kilowatt
kWh kilowatt hour

l litre
l. left; length
L learner (driver); litre; lambert; (*Electricity*) inductance; Lake
La lambert
LA Legislative Assembly; Los Angeles
LAC Leading Aircraftman
LAN local area network
lang. language
lat. latitude
lb pound
l.b.w. (*Cricket*) leg before wicket
l.c. lower case
LC Legislative Council
l.c.d. lowest common denominator
LCD liquid crystal display
l.c.m. lowest common multiple
LED light-emitting diode
l.h.s. left-hand side
Lib. Liberal (politics)
lic'd licensed
Lieut. Lieutenant
LNG liquefied natural gas
loc. cit. in the place cited (Latin: *loco citato*)
log. logarithm
long. longitude
lox liquid oxygen
LPG liquefied petroleum gas
LS Leading Seaman
l.s.d. pounds, shillings and pence (Latin: *librae, solidi, denarii*)
Lt Lieutenant
Lt-Col. Lieutenant-Colonel
Ltd Limited
Lt-Gen. Lieutenant-General
lx lux
l.y. light-year

m metre
m. male; masculine; married; mass; million; minute; month; noon (Latin: *meridiem*)
M (*Film classification*) mature
MA Master of Arts; (*Film classification*) mature accompanied
Maj. Major
Maj.-Gen. Major-General
Mar., Mch March
max. maximum
mb millibar

Mb megabit
MB megabyte
Mbps megabits per second
MBps megabytes per second
mbyte megabyte
MC Master of Ceremonies; Military Cross
MD Doctor of Medicine
MEAA Media, Entertainment and Arts Alliance
Messrs Gentlemen (French: *Messieurs*)
met. metropolitan
m.f. medium frequency
mfd manufactured
mfg manufacturing
MFN most favoured nation
mg milligram
Mgr, mgr Manager
MHA Member of the House of Assembly
MHR Member of the House of Representatives
MHz megahertz
MIA Murrumbidgee Irrigation Area
mill. million
min. minute; minimum
misc. miscellaneous
MKS metre-kilogram-second (system)
MJ megajoule
ML megalitre
ml, mL millilitre
MLA Member of the Legislative Assembly
MLC Member of the Legislative Council
mm millimetre
mo. month
MO mail order; money order; Medical Officer
mod. modern; moderate
Mon. Monday
MP Member of Parliament; Military Police
m.p.g. miles per gallon
m.p.h. miles per hour
m.p.s. miles per second
MRI magnetic resonance imaging
MS manuscript; multiple sclerosis
MSF Médecins sans Frontières
Msgr Monsignor
MSS manuscripts
Mt Mount; Mountain

n. born (Latin: *natus*)
N north; northern; newton
n/a, n.a. not applicable; not available
NASA (in the US) National Aeronautics and Space Administration
nat. national; native; natural
NATO North Atlantic Treaty Organisation
nav. navigation; navy; naval
NB note well (Latin: *nota bene*)
NDP Nuclear Disarmament Party
NE north-east; north-eastern
NFF National Farmers Federation
NGA National Gallery of Australia
NGO non-governmental organisation
NI Norfolk Island
NL no-liability company
NLC Northern Land Council
NLP natural language processing
NMA National Museum of Australia
no., No. number
nos, Nos numbers
Nov. November
NPA National Party of Australia
NSW New South Wales

NT Northern Territory; (*Bible*) New Testament
NTCE Northern Territory Certificate of Education
NW north-west; north-western
NZ New Zealand

O ohm
OA Order of Australia
obs. observation; observatory; obsolete
Oct. October
O/D overdraft; overdrawn; on demand
OECD Organisation for Economic Cooperation and Development
OHMS On Her (or His) Majesty's Service
o.n.o. or near(est) offer
op. cit. in the work cited (Latin: *opere citato*)
op. operation; opus
OPEC Organisation of Petroleum Exporting Countries
opp. opposite
opt. option
o.s. overseas
o/s out of stock
OS outsize; operating system; Ordinary Seaman
o/t overtime
OT (*Bible*) Old Testament
Oxon. of Oxford (Latin: *Oxoniensis*)
oz ounce

p. page; (*Music*) softly (Italian: *piano*)
P provisional (driver's licence)
p.a. yearly (Latin: *per annum*)
P & C Parents and Citizens Association
par., para. paragraph
PAYE pay-as-you-earn
PAYG pay-as-you-go
PBS Pharmaceutical Benefits Scheme
p.c. per cent
PC personal computer; politically correct
PCA patient-controlled analgesia
p.c.m. per calendar month
pd paid
p.d. per diem; potential difference
PDA personal digital assistant
PE physical education
Pen. Peninsula
perm. permanent
PET positron emission tomography
PG (*Film classification*) parental guidance recommended
pg. page
PhD Doctor of Philosophy
phys. ed. physical education
PI private investigator
Pk Park
pkt packet
Pl. Place (in street names)
pl., plur. plural
P/L Proprietary Limited
PLO Palestine Liberation Organisation
PLR public lending right
p.m. afternoon (Latin: *post meridiem*)
PM Prime Minister
PMG Postmaster-General
PNA Palestinian National Authority
PNG Papua New Guinea
PO postal order; Post Office; Petty Officer
POW prisoner of war
pp. pages; (*Music*) very softly (Italian: *pianissimo*)

PPS additional postscript (Latin: *post post scriptum*)
pr pair
PR public relations; permanent residence
pref. preference; preferred
prelim. preliminary
Pres. President
pro tem. for the time being (Latin: *pro tempore*)
Prof. Professor
prop. proprietor
prox. in or of the next or coming month (Latin: *proximo*)
PS postscript (Latin: *post scriptum*)
psi pounds per square inch
pt point; pint
p.t. part time
PT physical training
Pte Private
PTO, p.t.o. please turn over
Pty Proprietary
PVA polyvinyl acetate
PVC polyvinyl chloride
p.w., pw, p/w per week

Q Queen; Queensland
QC Queen's Counsel
Qd Queensland
QED which was to be proved (Latin: *quod erat demonstrandum*)
Qld Queensland
QM quartermaster
QMS quartermaster-sergeant
qr quarter
qto quarto
qtr quarter; quarterly
qual. qualified; quality
quot. quotation
q.v. which see (Latin: *quod vide*)

r. radius; right; (*Cricket*) runs
R (*Film classification*) restricted (to those aged 18 and over); roentgen; (*Electricity*) resistance
RA Royal Academy
RAAF Royal Australian Air Force
RAF Royal Air Force
RAN Royal Australian Navy
R & B rhythm and blues
RBA Reserve Bank of Australia
RBT random breath test
RC Red Cross; Roman Catholic; (*Film classification*) refused classification
Rd Road
RD rural delivery (used in addresses)
RDI recommended dietary intake
RDO rostered day off
Rear-Adm. Rear-Admiral
rec. receipt
recd received
ref. reference; referee
reg. registration; registered; regulation
Regt Regiment
rep. representative
retd retired
Rev., Revd Reverend
RFDS Royal Flying Doctor Service
r.h.s. right-hand side
RIP may he or she (or they) rest in peace (Latin: *requiescat in pace*)
rm room
RMB Roadside Mail Box

RN registered nurse; Royal Navy
RNA ribonucleic acid
r.p.m. revolutions per minute
r.p.s. revolutions per second
RSA Republic of South Africa
RSL Returned Services League
RSPCA Royal Society for the Prevention of Cruelty to Animals
RSVP please reply (French: *répondez s'il vous plaît*)
Rt Hon. Right Honourable
Rx prescription (Latin: *recipe*)

s. singular; second(s); south; southern
S south; southern; siemens
SA South Australia; South Africa; South America; Salvation Army
SACE South Australian Certificate of Education
s.a.e. stamped addressed envelope
SAS Special Air Service
Sat. Saturday
SBS Special Broadcasting Service
SC Senior Counsel
s/c self-contained
sci-fi, SF science fiction
SE south-east; south-eastern
SEATO South-East Asia Treaty Organisation
sec. second; secondary; secretary; section; secure
sect. section
sen., snr, sr senior
Sep., Sept. September
Sergt, Sgt Sergeant
s.g. specific gravity
shpt shipment
SI International System of Units (French: *Système International d'Unités*)
SM stipendiary magistrate
SMS short messaging service
snr, sr senior
Soc. Society
SOI Southern Oscillation Index
sp. gr. specific gravity
sp. special; species
spec. special
SPF sun protection factor
spp. species (pl.)
Sq. Square (in street names)
Sqn Ldr Squadron Leader
St Street; State; Saint; Strait
STD sexually transmitted disease; Subscriber Trunk Dialling
Sth south
Sthn southern
subj. subject
Sun., Sund. Sunday
SW south-west; south-western

t tonne
T tesla
TAB Totalisator Agency Board
TAFE Technical and Further Education
TAI International Atomic Time (French: *Temps Atomique International*)
Tas. Tasmania
TBA to be announced
TBC to be confirmed
tbs., tbsp. tablespoon
TCE Tasmanian Certificate of Education

TCP transmission control protocol
tech. technical; technology
TEE Tertiary Entrance Examination
tel. telephone
telecom. telecommunications
temp. temporary; temperature
TER Tertiary Entrance Rank
TES Tertiary Entrance Statement; Tertiary Entrance Score
TFN tax file number
Thu., Thurs. Thursday
TI Thursday Island
TM transcendental meditation
TNT trinitrotoluene
TO Technical Officer
TPV temporary protection visa
tr. translate; translated; translator
trad. traditional
trans. transcript; translated; translation; translator
tsp., t. teaspoon
Tues., Tue., Tu. Tuesday
TWI trade-weighted index

u atomic mass unit
U Union; United; University
u.c. upper case
UAE United Arab Emirates
UAI Universities Admissions Index
UAP United Australia Party
UHF, u.h.f. ultra high frequency
UHT ultra heat treated
UK United Kingdom
ult., ulto in or of the preceding month (Latin: *ultimo*)
UN United Nations
UNESCO United Nations Educational, Scientific and Cultural Organisation
UNICEF United Nations International Children's Emergency Fund
UPF ultraviolet protection factor
URL uniform resource locator
US United States
USA United States of America
USD US dollar
USSR Union of Soviet Socialist Republics
UT universal time
UTC universal time coordinated
UV ultraviolet

v. verb; verse; versus; volume; velocity
V volt
VAT value added tax
VC Victoria Cross; Vice-Chairman; Vice-Chancellor
VCE Victorian Certificate of Education
VET Vocational Education and Training
VG Valuer-General; Vicar-General
VHF, v.h.f. very high frequency
Vic. Victoria
vid. see (Latin: *vide*)
viz. namely (Latin: *videlicet*)
vol. volume
VP Vice-President
vs. versus; verse
vv. verses

w. week; weight; west; western; wide; width; with
W west; western; watt
WA Western Australia

WACE Western Australian Certificate of Education
WAN wide area network
WAP wireless application protocol
Wb weber
WC toilet (water closet)
wd word; would
WEA Workers' Educational Association
Wed. Wednesday
WEL Women's Electoral Lobby
Wg Cdr Wing Commander
WHO World Health Organisation
wk week; work
wkly weekly
wkt wicket
WO Warrant Officer
w.p.m. words per minute
WST Western Standard Time

wt weight
WTO World Trade Organisation
www World Wide Web

X Cross; (*Film classification*) restricted (to age 18 and over; contains sexually explicit material)

y. year
yd yard
YHA Youth Hostels Association
YMCA Young Men's Christian Association
yo, y/o year(s) old
yr year
yrs yours
YWCA Young Women's Christian Association

countries of the world

Country	People	Official/main language	Capital	Main unit of currency	Internet address suffix
Afghanistan	Afghan, Afghani	Pashto, Dari (Persian)	Kabul	afghani	af
Albania	Albanian	Albanian	Tirana	lek	al
Algeria	Algerian, Algerine	Arabic	Algiers	Algerian dinar	dz
Andorra	Andorran	Catalan, French, Spanish	Andorra la Vella	euro	ad
Angola	Angolan	Portuguese	Luanda	kwanza	ao
Antigua and Barbuda	Antiguan	English	St John's	East Caribbean dollar	ag
Argentina	Argentine, Argentinian	Spanish	Buenos Aires	Argentine peso	ar
Armenia	Armenian	Armenian	Yerevan	dram	am
Australia	Australian	English	Canberra	Australian dollar	au
Austria	Austrian	German	Vienna	euro	at
Azerbaijan	Azerbaijani	Azerbaijani	Baku	manat	az
Bahamas, the	Bahamian	English	Nassau	Bahamian dollar	bs
Bahrain	Bahraini	Arabic	Manama	Bahraini dinar	bh
Bangladesh	Bangladeshi	Bengali	Dhaka	taka	bd
Barbados	Barbadian	English	Bridgetown	Barbados dollar	bb
Belarus	Belarusian	Belarusian, Russian	Minsk	Belarusian rouble	by
Belgium	Belgian	Dutch, French, German	Brussels	euro	be
Belize	Belizean	English, Spanish, Carib, Maya	Belmopan	Belize dollar	bz
Benin	Beninese	French	Porto-Novo	CFA franc	bj
Bermuda	Bermudan	English	Hamilton	Bermuda dollar	bm

Country	Adjective	Language(s)	Capital	Currency	Code
Bhutan	Bhutanese	Dzongkha	Thimphu	ngultrum	bt
Bolivia	Bolivian	Spanish, Quechua, Aymará	Sucre, La Paz	boliviano	bo
Bosnia and Herzegovina	Bosnian	Bosnian, Serbian, Croatian	Sarajevo	convertible marka	ba
Botswana	Botswanan	Tswana, English	Gaborone	pula	bw
Brazil	Brazilian	Portuguese	Brasília	real	br
Brunei	Bruneian	Malay, English	Bandar Seri Begawan	Brunei dollar	bn
Bulgaria	Bulgarian	Bulgarian	Sofia	lev	bg
Burkina Faso	Burkinabe	French, Mossi	Ouagadougou	CFA franc	bf
Burma, see Myanmar					
Burundi	Burundian	French, Kirundi	Bujumbura	Burundi franc	bi
Cabo Verde	Cabo Verdean	Portuguese	Praia	Cabo Verde escudo	cv
Cambodia	Cambodian	Khmer, French	Phnom Penh	riel	kh
Cameroon	Cameroonian	French, English	Yaoundé	CFA franc	cm
Canada	Canadian	English, French	Ottawa	Canadian dollar	ca
Central African Republic	–	French, Sango	Bangui	CFA franc	cf
Chad	Chadian	French, Arabic	N'Djamena	CFA franc	td
Chile	Chilean	Spanish	Santiago	Chilean peso	cl
China	Chinese	Chinese (Mandarin)	Beijing	(renminbi) yuan	cn
Colombia	Colombian	Spanish	Bogotá	Colombian peso	co
Comoros	Comorian, Comoran	French, Arabic, Comorian	Moroni	Comorian franc	km
Congo, Democratic Republic of	Congolese	French	Kinshasa	Congolese franc	cd
Congo, Republic of	Congolese	French	Brazzaville	CFA franc	cg
Costa Rica	Costa Rican	Spanish	San José	Costa Rican colón	cr
Côte d'Ivoire (Ivory Coast)	Ivorian, Ivorian	French	Abidjan, Yamoussoukro	CFA franc	ci
Croatia	Croat, Croatian	Croatian	Zagreb	kuna	hr
Cuba	Cuban	Spanish	Havana	Cuban peso	cu
Cyprus	Cypriot	Greek, Turkish	Nicosia	euro	cy
Czech Republic	Czech	Czech	Prague	koruna	cz

Country	People	Official/main language	Capital	Main unit of currency	Internet address suffix
Denmark	Dane	Danish	Copenhagen	Danish krone	dk
Djibouti	Djiboutian	Arabic, French	Djibouti	Djibouti franc	dj
Dominica	Dominican	English	Roseau	East Caribbean dollar	do
Dominican Republic	Dominican	Spanish	Santo Domingo	Dominican peso	dm
East Timor, see Timor-Leste					
Ecuador	Ecuadorian	Spanish, Quechua	Quito	US dollar	ec
Egypt	Egyptian	Arabic	Cairo	Egyptian pound	eg
El Salvador	Salvadoran	Spanish	San Salvador	US dollar	sv
Equatorial Guinea	Equatorial Guinean, Equatoguinean	Spanish, French	Malabo	CFA franc	gq
Eritrea	Eritrean	Tigrinya	Asmara	nakfa	er
Estonia	Estonian	Estonian	Tallinn	euro	ee
Eswatini	Swazi	English, siSwati	Mbabane, Lobamba	lilangeni	sz
Ethiopia	Ethiopian	Amharic	Addis Ababa	birr	et
Fiji	Fijian	English, Fijian, Hindi	Suva	Fiji dollar	fj
Finland	Finn, Finlander, Finnish	Finnish, Swedish	Helsinki	euro	fi
France	French	French	Paris	euro	fr
Gabon	Gabonese	French, Fang	Libreville	CFA franc	ga
Gambia, The	Gambian	English	Banjul	dalasi	gm
Georgia	Georgian	Georgian	Tbilisi	lari	ge
Germany	German	German	Berlin	euro	de
Ghana	Ghanaian, Ghanian	English	Accra	cedi	gh
Greece	Greek	Greek	Athens	euro	gr
Grenada	Grenadian	English	St George's	East Caribbean dollar	gd
Guatemala	Guatemalan	Spanish	Guatemala City	quetzal	gt

Country	Nationality	Language(s)	Capital	Currency	Code
Guinea	Guinean	French	Conakry	Guinean franc	gn
Guinea-Bissau	Bissau-Guinean	Portuguese	Bissau	CFA franc	gw
Guyana	Guyanan	English	Georgetown	Guyanese dollar	gy
Haiti	Haitian	French, Haitian Creole	Port-au-Prince	gourde	ht
Honduras	Honduran	Spanish	Tegucigalpa	lempira	hn
Hungary	Hungarian	Hungarian	Budapest	forint	hu
Iceland	Icelandic	Icelandic	Reykjavik	krona	is
India	Indian	Hindi, English	New Delhi	Indian rupee	in
Indonesia	Indonesian	Bahasa Indonesia	Jakarta	rupiah	id
Iran	Iranian	Persian (Farsi)	Tehran	Iranian rial	ir
Iraq	Iraqi	Arabic, Kurdish	Baghdad	Iraqi dinar	iq
Ireland, Republic of	Irish	Irish (Gaelic), English	Dublin	euro	ie
Israel	Israeli	Hebrew, Arabic	Jerusalem	new shekel	il
Italy	Italian	Italian	Rome	euro	it
Jamaica	Jamaican	English	Kingston	Jamaican dollar	jm
Japan	Japanese	Japanese	Tokyo	yen	jp
Jordan	Jordanian	Arabic	Amman	Jordanian dinar	jo
Kazakhstan	Kazakh	Kazakh	Nursultan	tenge	kz
Kenya	Kenyan	Swahili, English	Nairobi	Kenyan shilling	ke
Kiribati	–	I-Kiribati, English	Tarawa	Australian dollar	ki
Korea, North	North Korean	Korean	Pyongyang	North Korean won	kp
Korea, South	South Korean	Korean	Seoul	South Korean won	kr
Kosovo	Kosovan	Albanian, Serbian	Pristina	euro	
Kuwait	Kuwaiti	Arabic	Kuwait City	Kuwaiti dinar	kw
Kyrgyzstan	Kyrgyz	Kyrgyz, Russian	Biskek	som	kg
Laos	Laotian	Lao	Vientiane	kip	la
Latvia	Latvian	Latvian	Riga	euro	lv
Lebanon	Lebanese	Arabic	Beirut	Lebanese pound	lb

Country	People	Official/main language	Capital	Main unit of currency	Internet address suffix
Lesotho	–	English, Sesotho	Maseru	loti	ls
Liberia	Liberian	English	Monrovia	Liberian dollar	lr
Libya	Libyan	Arabic	Tripoli	Libyan dinar	ly
Liechtenstein	Liechtensteiner	German (Alemannic)	Vaduz	Swiss franc	li
Lithuania	Lithuanian	Lithuanian	Vilnius	euro	lt
Luxembourg	Luxembourger	Luxembourgish, French, German	Luxembourg	euro	lu
Macedonia, *see* North Macedonia					
Madagascar	Madagascan	Malagasy, French	Antananarivo	ariary	mg
Malawi	Malawian	English, Chichewa	Lilongwe	Malawian kwacha	mw
Malaysia	Malaysian	Malay, English	Kuala Lumpur	ringgit	my
Maldives, the	Maldivian	Divehi	Malé	rufiyaa	mv
Mali	Malian	French	Bamako	CFA franc	ml
Malta	Maltese	Maltese, English	Valletta	euro	mt
Marshall Islands	Marshallese	Marshallese, English	Majuro	US dollar	mh
Mauritania	Mauritanian	Arabic, French	Nouakchott	ouguiya	mr
Mauritius	Mauritian	English, French Creole	Port Louis	Mauritian rupee	mu
Mexico	Mexican	Spanish	Mexico City	Mexican peso	mx
Micronesia, Federated States of	Micronesian	English	Palikir	US dollar	fm
Moldova	Moldovan	Romanian	Chişinău	Moldovan leu	md
Monaco	Monacan, Monegasque	French	Monaco	euro	mc
Mongolia	Mongolian	Khalkha Mongolian	Ulaanbaatar	tugrik	mn
Montenegro	Montenegrin	Montenegro Serbian	Cetinje, Podgorica	euro	
Morocco	Moroccan	Arabic	Rabat	Moroccan dirham	ma
Mozambique	Mozambican	Portuguese	Maputo	metical	mz
Myanmar	Myanmar	Myanmar (Burmese)	Nay Pyi Taw	kyat	mm

Namibia	Namibian	English	Windhoek	Namibian dollar	na
Nauru	Nauruan	Nauruan, English	–	Australian dollar	nr
Nepal	Nepalese, Nepali	Nepali	Kathmandu	Nepalese rupee	np
Netherlands, the	Dutch	Dutch	Amsterdam	euro	nl
New Zealand	New Zealander	English, Maori	Wellington	NZ dollar	nz
Nicaragua	Nicaraguan	Spanish	Managua	córdoba	ni
Niger	Nigerien	French	Niamey	CFA franc	ne
Nigeria	Nigerian	English	Abuja	naira	ng
North Macedonia	Macedonian	Macedonian, Albanian	Skopje	denar	mk
Norway	Norwegian	Norwegian	Oslo	Norwegian krone	no
Oman	Omani	Arabic	Muscat	rial Omani	om
Pakistan	Pakistani	Urdu, Punjabi	Islamabad	Pakistani rupee	pk
Palau	Palauan	Palauan, English	Ngerulmud	US dollar	pw
Panama	Panamanian	Spanish	Panama City	balboa	pa
Papua New Guinea	Papua New Guinean	Tok Pisin, Hiri Motu, English	Port Moresby	kina	pg
Paraguay	Paraguayan	Spanish, Guaraní	Asunción	guaraní	py
Peru	Peruvian	Spanish, Quechua, Aymara	Lima	nuevo sol	pe
Philippines, the	Filipino	Filipino, English	Manila	Philippine peso	ph
Poland	Pole, Polish	Polish	Warsaw	zloty	pl
Portugal	Portuguese	Portuguese	Lisbon	euro	pt
Qatar	Qatari	Arabic	Doha	Qatar riyal	qa
Romania	Romanian	Romanian	Bucharest	Romanian leu	ro
Russia	Russian	Russian	Moscow	rouble	ru
Rwanda	Rwandan	Kinyarwanda, French	Kigali	Rwandan franc	rw
Samoa	Samoan	Samoan, English	Apia	tala	ws
San Marino	San Marinese	Italian	San Marino	euro	sm
São Tomé and Principe	–	Portuguese	São Tomé	dobra	st
Saudi Arabia	Saudi Arabian, Saudi	Arabic	Riyadh	Saudi riyal	sa

Country	People	Official/main language	Capital	Main unit of currency	Internet address suffix
Senegal	Senegalese	French	Dakar	CFA franc	sn
Serbia	Serb, Serbian	Serbian	Belgrade	Serbian dinar	cs
Seychelles	–	Creole, English, French	Victoria	Seychelles rupee	sc
Sierra Leone	Sierra Leonean	English	Freetown	leone	sl
Singapore	Singaporean	Malay, Chinese, English, Tamil	Singapore	Singapore dollar	sg
Slovakia	Slovak, Slovakian	Slovak	Bratislava	euro	sk
Slovenia	Slovene, Slovenian	Slovene	Ljubljana	euro	si
Solomon Islands	Solomon Islander	English, Neo-Melanesian, Pidgin	Honiara	Solomon Islands dollar	sb
Somalia	Somali, Somalian	Somali, Arabic, English, Italian	Mogadishu	Somali shilling	so
South Africa	South African	English, Afrikaans, and 9 other official African languages	Pretoria, Cape Town, and Bloemfontein	rand	za
South Sudan	South Sudanese	Arabic, English	Juba	South Sudanese pound	ss
Spain	Spaniard, Spanish	Spanish	Madrid	euro	
Sri Lanka	Sri Lankan, Sinhalese	Sinhalese, Tamil, English	Colombo, Sri Jayawardenepura Kotte	Sri Lankan rupee	lk
St Kitts and Nevis	–	English	Basseterre	East Caribbean dollar	kn
St Lucia	St Lucian	English	Castries	East Caribbean dollar	lc
St Vincent and the Grenadines	–	English	Kingstown	East Caribbean dollar	vc
Sudan	Sudanese	Arabic, English	Khartoum	Sudanese pound	sd
Suriname	Surinamese	Dutch, English based creole	Paramaribo	Suriname dollar	sr
Swaziland, *see* Eswatini					
Sweden	Swede, Swedish	Swedish	Stockholm	krona	se
Switzerland	Swiss	German, French, Italian	Bern	Swiss franc	ch
Syria	Syrian	Arabic	Damascus	Syrian pound	sy
Tajikistan	Tajik	Tajik, Russian	Dushanbe	somoni	tj

Country	Adjective	Language(s)	Capital	Currency	Code
Tanzania	Tanzanian	Swahili, English	Dar es Salaam	Tanzanian shilling	tz
Thailand	Thai	Thai	Bangkok	baht	th
Timor-Leste	Timorese	Tetum, Portuguese	Dili	US dollar	tp
Togo	Togolese	French	Lomé	CFA franc	tg
Tonga	Tongan	Tongan, English	Nuku'alofa	pa'anga	to
Trinidad and Tobago	Trinidadian	English	Port of Spain	Trinidad and Tobago dollar	tt
Tunisia	Tunisian	Arabic, French	Tunis	Tunisian dinar	tn
Türkiye	Turk, Turkish	Turkish	Ankara	Turkish lira	tr
Turkmenistan	Turkmen	Turkmen	Ashgabat	Turkmen manat	tm
Tuvalu	Tuvaluan	Tuvaluan, English	Vaiaku (on Funafuti atoll)	Australian dollar, Tuvaluan dollar	tv
Uganda	Ugandan	English, Swahili	Kampala	Ugandan shilling	ug
Ukraine	Ukrainian	Ukrainian	Kiev	hryvnia	ua
United Arab Emirates	–	Arabic	Abu Dhabi	UAE dirham	ae
United Kingdom	Briton, British	English	London	pound sterling	uk
United States of America	American	English	Washington, DC	US dollar	
Uruguay	Uruguayan	Spanish	Montevideo	peso uruguayo	uy
Uzbekistan	Uzbek	Uzbek	Tashkent	sum	uz
Vanuatu	Ni-Vanuatu, Vanuatuan	Bislama, French, English	Port Vila	vatu	vu
Venezuela	Venezuelan	Spanish	Caracas	bolívar	ve
Vietnam	Vietnamese	Vietnamese	Hanoi	dông	vn
Yemen	Yemeni	Arabic	Sana'a	Yemeni rial	ye
Zambia	Zambian	English	Lusaka	Zambian kwacha	zm
Zimbabwe	Zimbabwean	English, and Bantu languages	Harare	Zimbabwean dollar	zw

roman numerals

NUMBER	ROMAN NUMERAL	NUMBER	ROMAN NUMERAL
1	I	43	XLIII
2	II	50	L
3	III	54	LIV
4	IV	60	LX
5	V	65	LXV
6	VI	70	LXX
7	VII	76	LXXVI
8	VIII	80	LXXX
9	IX	87	LXXXVII
10	X	90	XC
11	XI	98	XCVIII
12	XII	100	C
13	XIII	101	CI
14	XIV	115	CXV
15	XV	150	CL
16	XVI	200	CC
17	XVII	300	CCC
18	XVIII	400	CD
19	XIX	500	D
20	XX	600	DC
21	XXI	700	DCC
30	XXX	800	DCCC
32	XXXII	900	CM
40	XL	1000	M

Phonetic alphabet used in communication

A	Alpha	N	November
B	Bravo	O	Oscar
C	Charlie	P	Papa
D	Delta	Q	Quebec
E	Echo	R	Romeo
F	Foxtrot	S	Sierra
G	Golf	T	Tango
H	Hotel	U	Uniform
I	India	V	Victor
J	Juliet	W	Whisky
K	Kilo	X	X-ray
L	Lima	Y	Yankee
M	Mike	Z	Zulu